S0-BJL-058

WITHDRAWN

HANDBOOK OF PSYCHOLOGICAL AND EDUCATIONAL ASSESSMENT OF CHILDREN
Intelligence and Achievement

HANDBOOK OF PSYCHOLOGICAL AND EDUCATIONAL ASSESSMENT OF CHILDREN
Intelligence and Achievement

Edited by

Cecil R. Reynolds
Texas A&M University

Randy W. Kamphaus
University of Georgia

Foreword by George W. Hynd

CARL A. RUDISILL LIBRARY
LENOIR-RHYNE COLLEGE

THE GUILFORD PRESS
New York   London

BF
722
.H33
1990
V 1
150328
Nov.1990

© 1990 The Guilford Press
A Division of Guilford Publications, Inc.
72 Spring Street, New York, NY 10012

All rights reserved

No part of this book may be reproduced, stored in a retrieval system,
or transmitted, in any form or by any means, electronic, mechanical,
photocopying, microfilming, recording, or otherwise, without written
permission from the Publisher.

Printed in the United States of America

This book is printed on acid-free paper.

Last digit is print number: 9   8   7   6   5   4   3   2   1

Library of Congress Cataloging-in-Publication Data

Reynolds, Cecil R., 1952-
    Handbook of psychological and educational assessment of children:
Intelligence and achievement / Cecil R. Reynolds, Randy W. Kamphaus.
        p.   cm.
    Includes bibliographical references.
    ISBN 0-89862-391-X
    1. Psychological tests for children.   2. Achievement tests.
I. Kamphaus, Randy W.   II. Title.
BF722.R49   1990
155.4'028'7—dc20   89-38018
                                                                          CIP

Foreword

Sixty-three years ago, David Wechsler wrote a section on psychometric tests in his brother's book, *A Textbook of Clinical Neurology* (Wechsler, 1927). Even with the degree of scholarship one would expect of David Wechsler, it took only 12 pages of text to comprehensively treat this vital topic. To place this in context, consider for a moment that the front matter to this handbook consumes more space than David Wechsler required to discuss the entire clinical appraisal of mental ability.

There has obviously been a proliferation of research regarding the measurement of human ability, achievement, and personality within the last century and the rate of test publication and usage increases exponentially. The relative explosion of knowledge regarding the multifaceted nature of human abilities, achievement, and personality has led, most understandably, to new and uniquely different conceptualizations of not only what to test, but how to test it.

Assessment procedures, regardless of theoretical formulation or format, invariably reveal that children's development can be seen as a constellation of emerging capabilities manifested in a highly variable and dynamic fashion. By studying empirically how abilities emerge (i.e., determining the factors that comprise ability or personality, or those predictor variables that might best explain test performance in children), it becomes evident that the more we learn about factors associated with human diversity, the more we need to objectively assess their unique expression in children.

The need for this two-volume handbook should be clear then when viewed in this context. The prismatic nature of the emerging personality and associated facets of intellectual ability have been revealed to be so complex that specialization in child assessment has become more the norm than the exception. It is now unreasonable to expect that any one psychologist or educator could possibly have a comprehensive grasp of all of the various approaches to assessment with children. For this very reason, there is an urgent need for these volumes.

Each chapter in each volume is a concise treatise of a particular subject relevant to the assessment of children. The value in advancing such diverse yet well-organized contributions is that the editors have constructed a rich tapestry which not only reflects the major topics and issues relevant today, but highlights the lacunae in our present state of knowledge regarding the assessment of children. In this sense, the contents of these volumes serve as a conceptual landmark from which to judge not only the state of our current knowledge but to embark on new directions in research and clinical practice in assessing ability, achievement, personality, and behavior in children.

Perhaps most importantly, the editors have provided an exceptionally balanced handbook in which various assessment procedures have been given equal weight in terms of their representation. Projective assessment procedures, procedures to assess social skills, clinical interview techniques, behavioral assessment procedures, and so on have all been equally addressed in both volumes. This fact alone will insure that they will indeed become widely cited resources among those who assess children as part of their efforts to more fully understand how to assist children in attaining a healthy and productive life in our dynamic and rapidly evolving society.

This two-volume handbook approaches psychological and educational assessment in a very appropriate fashion in that it is comprehensive in its coverage of the many complexities encompassed in the measurement of ability, personality, and exceptionality in children. Without question, the contributors to these volumes represent the most

knowledgeable scholars in their respective fields of endeavor. The individual chapters have been organized in such a logical manner that the final products represent an achievement of singular importance in the last decade of this century.

GEORGE W. HYND
University of Georgia

Wechsler, I.S. (1927). *A textbook of clinical neurology.* Philadelphia: W.B. Saunders.

Preface

The general area of psychological testing and assessment continues to be, as it has been for several decades, the most prolific of research areas in psychology as is evident by its representation in psychological journals. Although always controversial, psychological testing has nevertheless grown in its application to include evaluation and treatment of children's disorders of development, learning, and behavior. Tests are being published at an increasing rate as well. The scholarly literature on psychological testing of children has grown significantly over the past 2 decades and is rapidly becoming unmanageable. More than 40 different scholarly, referrered journals exist in North America alone that publish articles on psychological and educational assessment of children, making the task of the professor, the student, and the practitioner seem an impossible one. Hence, periodic comprehensive reviews of this massive literature seem necessary although onerous. Such tasks require the work and the thoughts of many authors. In undertaking this task, we endeavored to devise a work suitable for the professor as a reference, the student as a text, and the practitioner as a sourcebook and guide. In order to do this effectively it seemed reasonable to separate the two major areas of assessment—intelligence and personality—into their own volumes. This has allowed us the space for in-depth coverage, while retaining cohesion of topic in each book. The two volumes can thus be used in tandem or as separate units depending on need.

Thus, our hope for this two-volume handbook was to develop a broad-based resource for those individuals who are charged with the assessment of children and adolescents. We also wanted to develop a comprehensive resource for researchers who are studying various aspects of children's assessment and psychodiagnostics, and to provide breadth and depth of coverage of the major domains of children's assessment in a single source. These include such diverse areas as academic achievement, intelligence, adaptive behavior, personality, and creativity assessment. Individual tests such as the WISC-R, the K-ABC, and the Rorschach are given their own treatments in addition to some general methods such as projective storytelling techniques. In each volume, the theoretical foundations and the measurement limitations of our approaches to these latent constructs are addressed.

In order to insure that the volumes are authoritative, we tried to identify and seek eminent scholars with a general command of assessment and a special expertise in research or practice in the area of their respective contributions. We think that we have been very successful in assembling such a group, which includes such luminaries as Wayne Holtzman, Alan Kaufman, David Lachar, Jeanne Chall, Paul Torrance, and June Tuma, just to name a few. The chapters purposely vary from an emphasis on specific applications in assessment to cutting-edge knowledge and critiques of research and statistical procedures. We hope that this will enhance the possibility of using this handbook as a graduate level text. Because of its breadth we think that this text could be useful for courses in intellectual and personality assessment, practica and internship course work, and courses on psychodiagnostics, psychopathology, and special education.

We are deeply indebted to a number of individuals for assisting us with this, at times, overwhelming project. First of all, we wish to thank the authors of the various chapters for their extraordinary talent and patience with this arduous effort. We wish them continued success in all of their professional activities. We also owe a great debt to Sharon Panulla, our editor at Guilford Publications. We greatly appreciate her faith in giving us the opportunity to produce this work, along with her patience and support throughout the lengthy developmental process. We have had the opportunity to work with a number of editors in the past, but clearly none with the combination of talent and personable demeanor of Sharon. We also thank publisher Seymour Weingarten of Guilford for his concurrence, as well as his early thoughts on the organization and development of the work. We are very appreciative of the efforts of our staff and students: Angela Bailey, Mary Cash, Jana Dresden, Alison Lorys-Vernon, and Jerry Slotkin for their organizational and clerical assistance. Without the support of administrators such as Mike Ash of Texas A&M University and Roy Martin and Joe Wisenbaker of the University of Georgia, this book also would not have been possible.

Finally, we wish to thank all of the researchers of the last century dating back to and including Sir Frances Galton and his modern-day counterpart, Arthur Jensen, for the great strides they have made in enhancing our ability to measure and consequently understand the nature of human behavior. To our common mentor, Alan S. Kaufman, we acknowledge a continuing debt for the superb model of scholarship that he continues to provide. However, it is to Julia and to Norma that we owe our greatest debts of gratitude. The strength they lend, the understanding they convey, and the support they give make our onerous schedules tolerable and enable us to be so much more than without them—thank you, again.

Contributors

ANN E. BOEHM, Ph.D., Department of Developmental and Educational Psychology, Teachers College, Columbia University, New York, New York

SUZANNE K. BURLEY, Ed.S., Center for Psychological Services and Abused Handicapped Children, Boys Town National Research Hospital, Omaha, Nebraska

CHRISTINE W. BURNS, Ph.D., Division of Professional Psychology, University of Northern Colorado, Greeley, Colorado

JEANNE S. CHALL, Ph.D., Graduate School of Education, Harvard University, Cambridge, Massachusetts

WARREN D. CROWN, Ph.D., Department of Education, Rutgers, The State University of New Jersey, New Brunswick, New Jersey

JACK A. CUMMINGS, Ph.D., Department of Counseling and Educational Psychology, Indiana University, Bloomington, Indiana

MARY E. CURTIS, Ph.D., Graduate School of Education, Harvard University, Cambridge, Massachusetts

RAYMOND S. DEAN, Ph.D., Neuropsychology Laboaratory, Ball State University, Muncie, Indiana; Department of Psychiatry, Indiana University School of Medicine, Indianapolis, Indiana

CATHERINE DeVINCENTIS, M.S., Department of Educational Psychology, University of Georgia, Athens, Georgia

THOMAS G. FETSCO, Ph.D., Center for Excellence in Education, Northern Arizona University, Flagstaff, Arizona

RICHARD A. FIGUEROA, Ph.D., Division of Education, University of California at Davis, Davis, California

ANTONIA A. FORSTER, Ph.D., Department of Medical Psychology, School of Medicine, Oregon Health Sciences University, Portland, Oregon

JOSEPH L. FRENCH, Ed.D, Division of Counseling and Educational Psychology, Pennsylvania State University, University Park, Pennsylvania

DOUGLAS FUCHS, Ph.D., Department of Special Education, George Peabody College, Vanderbilt University, Nashville, Tennessee

LYNN S. FUCHS, Ph.D., Department of Special Education, George Peabody College, Vanderbilt University, Nashville, Tennessee

JOSEPH J. GLUTTING, Ph.D., Department of Educational Studies, University of Delaware, Newark, Delaware

ERNEST T. GOETZ, Ph.D., Department of Educational Psychology, Texas A&M University, College Station, Texas

JOAN F. GOODMAN, Ed.D., Graduate School of Education, University of Pennsylvania, Philadelphia, Pennsylvania

JEFFREY W. GRAY, Ph.D., School of Nursing and Health Sciences, University of Evansville, Evansville, Indiana

MARTHA CROUTHERS GRINDLER, Ed.D., Department of Early Childhood Education and Reading, Georgia Southern College, Statesboro, Georgia

PATRICIA A. HAENSLY, Ph.D., Department of Educational Psychology, Texas A&M University, College Station, Texas

ROBERT L. HALE, Ph.D., Division of Counseling and Educational Psychology, Pennsylvania State University, University Park, Pennsylvania

ROBERT J. HALL, Ph.D., Department of Educational Psychology, Texas A&M University, College Station, Texas

RONALD K. HAMBLETON, Ph.D., School of Education, University of Massachusetts at Amherst, Amherst, Massachusetts

PATTI L. HARRISON, Ph.D., Area of Behavioral Studies, The University of Alabama, University, Alabama

MARI GRIFFITHS IRVIN, Ed.D., Department of Educational and Counseling Psychology, School of Education, University of the Pacific, Stockton, California

CRAIG JURGENSEN, Ed.D., School of Education, University of Massachusetts at Amherst, Amherst, Massachusetts

STEVEN M. KAISER, Ph.D., Utica Public Schools, Utica, New York

RANDY W. KAMPHAUS, Ph.D., Department of Educational Psychology, University of Georgia, Athens, Georgia

DAVID KAPLAN, Ph.D., Department of Educational Studies, University of Delaware, Newark, Delaware

ALAN S. KAUFMAN, Ph.D., Department of Educational Psychology and Research, The University of Alabama, University, Alabama

TIMOTHY Z. KEITH, Ph.D., College of Education and Department of Psychology, Virginia Polytechnic Institute and State University, Blacksburg, Virginia

SUZANNE LANE, Ph.D., Department of Psychology in Education, University of Pittsburgh, Pittsburgh, Pennsylvania

MARC LAQUERRE, Ph.D., M.Ed., Department of Counseling and Educational Psychology, Indiana University, Bloomington, Indiana

ALISON LORYS-VERNON, Ph.D., Department of Educational Psychology, University of Georgia, Athens, Georgia

JOSEPH D. MATARAZZO, Ph.D., Department of Medical Psychology, School of Medicine, Oregon Health Sciences University, Portland, Oregon

C. SUE McCULLOUGH, Ed.D., Department of Psychology and Philosophy, Texas Woman's University, Denton, Texas

PAUL A. McDERMOTT, Ph.D., Department of Psychology, University of Pennsylvania, Philadelphia, Pennsylvania

MONICA MORI, M.A., Department of Psychology, University of Western Ontario, London, Ontario, Canada

JACK A. NAGLIERI, Ph.D., Education Services and Research, Ohio State University, Columbus, Ohio

ANTHONY J. NITKO, Ph.D., Department of Psychology in Education, University of Pittsburgh, Pittsburgh, Pennsylvania

KATHLEEN D. PAGET, Ph.D., Department of Psychology, University of South Carolina, Columbia, South Carolina

PETER N. PREWETT, M.S., School Psychologist, Columbus Public Schools, Columbus, Ohio

CECIL R. REYNOLDS, Ph.D., Department of Educational Psychology, Texas A&M University, College Station, Texas

GARY J. ROBERTSON, Ph.D., Test Division, American Guidance Service, Circle Pines, Minnesota

JONATHAN SANDOVAL, Ph.D., Department of Education, University of California at Davis, Davis, California

JERRY SLOTKIN, M.A., Department of Educational Psychology, University of Georgia, Athens, Georgia

KRISTA J. STEWART, Ph.D., Department of Psychology, Tulane University, New Orleans, Louisiana

BEVERLY D. STRATTON, Ph.D., Department of Early Childhood Education and Reading, Georgia Southern College, Statesboro, Georgia

PATRICIA M. SULLIVAN, Ph.D., Center for Psychological Services and Abused Handicapped Children, Boys Town National Research Hospital, Omaha, Nebraska

E. PAUL TORRANCE, Ph.D., Department of Educational Psychology, University of Georgia, Athens, Georgia

RICHARD R. VALENCIA, Ph.D., Department of Speech Communication and Educational Psychology, The University of Texas at Austin, Austin, Texas

PHILLIP A. VERNON, Ph.D., Department of Psychology, University of Western Ontario, London, Ontario, Canada

Contents

PART III. ASSESSMENT OF ACADEMIC SKILL

19. Implications of Cognitive Psychology for Assessment of Academic Skill   477

Ernest T. Goetz, Robert J. Hall, and Thomas G. Fetsco

20. Assessment of Mathematics Ability   504

Warren D. Crown

21. Diagnostic Assessment of Reading   523

Beverly D. Stratton and Martha Crouthers Grindler

22. Diagnostic Achievement Testing in Reading   535

Jeanne S. Chall and Mary E. Curtis

23. Clinical Assessment of Children's Academic Achievement   552

Randy W. Kamphaus, Jerry Slotkin, and Catherine DeVincentis

PART IV. SPECIAL TOPICS IN MENTAL TESTING

Appropriate Application of Assessment Results   716
Summary   718
References   719

30. Computerized Assessment   723
    C. Sue McCullough

    A Brief History of Computerized Assessment   723
    Definitions and Background Information   724
    Issues in Computerized Assessment   737
    Future Trends in Computerized Assessment   742
    Summary and Conclusions   744
    References   744

PART V. ASSESSMENT OF SPECIAL POPULATIONS

I

GENERAL ISSUES

1

A History of the Development of Psychological and Educational Testing

JOSEPH L. FRENCH
ROBERT L. HALE
Pennsylvania State University

I f Adam and Eve were not the first evaluators of ability, personality, interest, and attitude, who were? Certainly assessment of human characteristics has been a part of life since the beginnings of recorded history. At least 2,000 years ago, the Chinese were using a system of civil service examinations (Bowman, 1989). Socrates advocated interweaving testing and teaching; his pupil Plato advocated selecting future leaders for training by identifying children who could detect deceit, learn quickly, and separate truth from superstition. As early as the 16th century A.D., a Mohammedan ruler is reported to have sought as potential leaders the "fairest, strongest, and most intelligent youth" (Sumption, 1941, p. 1). We do not know how he judged the fairest or most intelligent, but there must have been some criteria for ratings other than how many big rocks each candidate could lift.

The recognition that humans have individual differences in mental abilities can be traced back to the late 1700s. Freeman (1926) reports that in 1795 the first report of individual differences was published. One of the observers working at the Greenwich Astronomical Observatory, in England, was found to differ from his colleagues in estimating the time it took a star to travel across a section of the sky. Individual differences were neither understood nor tolerated, and the observer was fired. According to Free-

man, it was not until 1822 that astronomers understood that different people have different reaction times and took these individual differences into consideration when interpreting observational data. In 1859, Charles Darwin published *The Origin of Species*. In discussing the survival of the fittest, he spoke not about physical strength alone, but about a combination of human mental characteristics. Although there is ample evidence of interest in assessing personal attributes, formalized procedures for investigating these differences in human ability did not emerge in Europe or the United States until the middle to late 1800s. These early assessment procedures eventually led to the development of modern intelligence tests.

THE DEVELOPMENT OF INTELLIGENCE TESTS

Outside Influences

The Cross-Fertilization of European and American Ideas

It is literally impossible to discuss the history of the mental testing movement as it evolved in the United States without discussing the the European factors that provided the keystone for the movement. Like many early scientific pursuits, the roots of the testing movement in America began in Europe. The

3

more important of these European influences were the British civil service process; the establishment of Galton's anthropometric laboratory at the International Health Exhibition in 1884; the mathematical underpinnings of the statistical techniques of correlation by Karl Pearson; and Charles Spearman's interpretation that a correlation between two variables signifies the existence of a common factor. In addition, the Europeans focused on the precise measurement of various types of memory, reading, perceptual, and conceptual differences in the laboratories in Germany, and on the methods of measuring higher mental functions in France. All of these European developments were influential in directing the development of the mental testing movement in America.

The early European psychological laboratories were primarily interested in discovering *general* laws to account for human behavior. In the pursuit of these laws, it soon became apparent that individual differences in human ability necessarily had to be taken into account. The working partnerships that were established in these laboratories, as well as a fortuitous family relationship, substantially contributed to the investigative focus that eventually led to the development of the modern intelligence test. James McKeen Cattell (an American) and Wilhelm Wundt (the father of experimental psychology), working together in Germany, discovered the existence of individual differences in human sensation and perception that were important enough to differentiate between persons. The idea that individual differences were important topics of investigation may actually have been an American introduction into the German laboratory. According to Boring (1929), Cattell simply came to Wundt and said, "Herr Professor, you need an assistant, and I will be your assistant!" (p. 319). With these words, Cattell became Wundt's first assistant. Boring also remarks that Cattell was one of the first students in Wundt's laboratory to investigate problems in his own area of interest. Supposedly, Wundt was accustomed to assigning problems arbitrarily to his students. Wundt referred to the individual-difference problem as "*ganz Amerikanisch,*" and even in Boring's 1929 historical review of experimental psychology he remarks that this is indeed what "the problem has turned out

to be" (p. 319). The political reasons why American society was focused on individual differences are discussed later. However, this focus on individual differences, which in Germany was initially concerned with measuring differences in individuals' reaction times, directed this line of research down a path that emphasized the measurement of human physical attributes.

At the same time in England, Darwin, Wallace, Huxley, and Spencer were studying and formulating how physical characteristics were inherited. As Freeman (1926) notes, Sir Francis Galton (grandson of Erasmus Darwin and half-cousin to Charles Darwin) became interested in extending his cousin's work on the inheritance of physical attributes to the inheritance of mental abilities. To do this, Galton needed methods of measuring differences in mental abilities. He developed and presented some of these methods in his anthropometric laboratory. The measurement methodology developed by Galton focused primarily on the differences between people as manifested in physical or sensory tasks. The British philosophical doctrine of associationism was prevalent at the time, and according to Guilford (1973), Galton may have reasoned that since all that people know comes to them through their senses, the possessor of good senses must therefore have good intellect. Cattell, who had worked with Wundt as described above, was briefly a lecturer at Cambridge University. It was at Cambridge in 1888 that he was associated with Galton. The two men were drawn together by their similar views and interests in investigating individual differences. Shortly thereafter, Cattell moved back to the United States, where he became a professor of psychology at the University of Pennsylvania. In 1891 Cattell moved to Columbia, establishing a psychological laboratory there and remaining its head for the next 26 years until he was dismissed for his pacifistic views when the United States entered World War I in 1917 (Boring, 1929). This association among Cattell, Wundt, and Galton not only provided a link between the German and English psychological laboratories, but also provided for the transportation across the Atlantic of the European ideas mixed with the American interest in individual differences.

When Cattell took the position at Columbia University, he brought with him the European influences. His initial interest in individual differences, melded with Galton's interests in mental abilities, led to his publication of "Mental Tests and Measurements" in 1890. This paper was the first to propose that mental abilities could be tested and objectively measured. The paper was essentially an initial list of tests that purported to measure mental functioning; the tests consisted primarily of tasks involving physical acuity and/or differences in individual physical reaction times. As an example, one test measured how far apart two points must be placed on a person's skin to enable the person to differentiate the two points as distinctly separate. Another "mental test" was simply the measurement of a person's grip strength with a dynamometer. Cattell examined many college-age students at Columbia with his tests. Through his leadership, the American Psychological Association (APA) established a committee that in 1896 presented the membership with a list of recommended tests for measuring mental growth and ability in college students. According to Freeman (1926), these APA-recommended tests were simply extensions of the physical tests proposed by Cattell in 1890.

Most of the early American experimentation in mental functioning involved the measurement of these physical differences and attributes. Rarely was a test developed and given to people that did not primarily measure physical or sensory modalities. However, there were known problems with many of these tests, and a few divergent assessment techniques began to emerge. In 1891, Bolton developed and used a memory test that required children to remember arithmetic digits. While studying intellectual fatigue, Ebbinghaus invented the completion (fill-in-the-blank) test in 1897. In Europe, Binet was experimenting with some tasks unlike most of those he had been using. These new tasks required children to draw figures from memory that they had seen only for a brief period of time; to read and copy sentences; and to add numbers together. These were the first mental tasks that were not primarily measuring physical reactivity, and as such they were a break from the sensory tasks developed in the European labs.

Binet had more to do with the development of the tests than any one other individual. His

effect was due partly to the fact that he kept at the topic of the experimental measurement of individual differences from 1886, when he was only twenty-nine years old, until his death in 1911, twenty-five years later. He published in this period more than fifty articles that bear on the general subject. Moreover, the influence of Binet was enhanced by the course of discovery. Binet was seeking to measure the intellectual faculties, the complex mental processes, whereas Galton measured only simple capacities, hoping vainly that they might have some significance for the "intellect." Binet was right, Galton was wrong; presently the attention of the mental testers came to be centered almost entirely upon intelligence; and Binet is now one of the best known of psychologists. (Boring, 1929, p. 546)

Binet's efforts peaked in the development of the Binet–Simon Scale in 1905. The impetus for construction of this intelligence test was given by the Minister of Public Instruction in Paris in 1904. The minister appointed a committee, of which Binet was a member, to find a way to separate mentally retarded from normal children in the schools (Sattler, 1982). Originally, Binet's mental test results were to be used to determine how well children should achieve in school. Even with the emphasis on academics, the early Binet tasks were heavily influenced by physical measurement. Binet and Simon's 1905 scale consisted of 30 tests arranged in order of difficulty. The first of which required that a child follow with his or her eyes a lighted match. Henry H. Goddard, the director of research at the New Jersey Training School for Feeble-Minded Boys and Girls at Vineland, translated Binet's scale with the help of linguist Elizabeth Kite in 1911. According to Freeman (1926), this translation was very widely used in the United States until it was superseded by the more extensive revision made by Terman and his collaborators (Terman, 1916)—the Stanford Revision.

Kuhlmann was one of the first to produce a very useful American version of the Binet in 1912. Kuhlmann's 1922 revision, published by the Educational Test Bureau, was frequently used for decades, especially with those subjects below the educable level. Some attribute the eventually greater success of the Terman (1916) and Terman and Merrill (1937) versions of the Binet to the size and distribution of the publisher's sales force (i.e., the Houghton Mifflin book company with "travelers" throughout the states) and to Terman's longevity and productivity as an author of books and articles as well as tests. Even though the original Binet had been through translation, extention, revision, and adaptation to the experience of American children, the influence of the European laboratories (concentration on physical attributes) was still present in the protocol for the Stanford Revision. The following items were allotted space on the 1916 protocol where the information could be jotted down by the examiner: standing height, sitting height, weight, head circumference, right-hand grip strength, left-hand grip strength, and lung capacity.

Other technical and psychometric advances were being made in both the United States and Europe that continued the development of mental testing beyond Binet's efforts. William Stern was the first person to use the term "mental quotient." His mental quotient was calculated by simply dividing a child's mental age by his or her chronological age. Thus, a 12-year-old child whose mental age was 10 would have a mental quotient of .833. Terman thought that this method of measurement was substantially correct. Terman multiplied the mental quotient by 100, retained only the whole number, and called the result the "intelligence quotient" (IQ). Terman incorporated the concept of the intelligence quotient developed by Stern (1914) into the Stanford Revision (Terman, 1916).

The first point scale (instead of age scale) was developed by R. M. Yerkes, J. W. Bridges, and R. S. Hardwick (1915). When point scores for a child were compared to the average number of points of children the youngster's own age, the ratio was initially known as a "coefficient of intelligence." An average child would have a coefficient of 1.00, just as he or she would have an IQ of 100.

The Influence of the Correlation Coefficient

Another major influence on the direction of mental test development was the development of the correlation coefficient and Spearman's use of correlational techniques in the invention of factor analysis. Without this method of score comparison, mental tests might have remained basically sensory in nature. The investigation of relationships between the tests being proposed to measure mental functioning resulted in the progressive replacement of the physical–sensory tests by tests characterized as measuring higher cognitive processes.

Three men are usually given primary credit for the development of the ideas of correlation: Karl Pearson, Charles Spearman, and, again, Sir Francis Galton. Galton discovered the concept of regression when he was investigating the effects of heredity. In collecting the heights of parents and offspring and plotting scattergrams of fathers' heights versus sons' heights, Galton noted that the heights of sons whose fathers were either extremely short or tall tended to regress back toward the mean. "He spoke of this trend of the offspring 'falling back' toward the general mean as the law of 'filial regression' " (Games & Klare, 1967, p. 415). In 1896, Pearson developed the formula whereby correlations could be calculated without reference to regression lines; Pearson actually modified an earlier method developed by the French mathematician A. Bravais in 1846 (Boring, 1929). It is precisely because regression lines were discovered first that the Pearson product–moment correlation is symbolized by r instead of some other notation.

As noted previously, most of the early tests of intelligence involved "physical tests" (i.e., discrimination of two points on the skin) along with a sprinkling of tests that we might call "mental tests" by today's standards. The isolation of these "mental tests" in the development of tests of intelligence, with the concomitant elimination of the physical tests, was in large part due to the invention of the correlation coefficient. Early authors noted that the mental tests that measured higher cognitive functioning correlated with each other more highly, were more reliable, and correlated with estimated intelligence at higher levels. Of course, without the use of correlational techniques, none of these calculations and comparisons would have been possible. Two early studies that investigated the efficacy of the physical as opposed to the cognitive tests in measuring intelligence were Cyril Burt's (1909) article "Experimental Tests of General Intelligence" and Simpson's (1912) text Correlation of Mental Abilities. These publications led the way for the elimination of the sensory tests from the measurement of intelligence.

The fact that certain test scores correlated highly with others while certain other tests correlated only slightly with others led to the hypothesis of a central factor in intelligence. The higher-level cognitive tasks that, when evaluated, correlated with one another were retained in mental tests, while those sensory tests that previously had been thought to measure mental ability lost favor because of their inability to correlate with other tasks and were by and large dropped from intelligence tests. The idea that the resulting scores from higher-level cognitive tasks tended to correlate with one another was originally called "general intelligence" by Spearman (1904); later, he simply referred to this factor as g. General intelligence as a construct and as a guiding principle in developing intelligence tests has retained its power over the years. Obviously, if subtests correlate too highly with one another they share too much variance, and if included in new batteries do not appreciably add to the test's information. As examples of the power of g in the development of intelligence tests, two quotes from recently developed intelligence tests are illustrative.

Two new tests were tried out experimentally as possible additions to the WAIS-R [Wechsler Adult Intelligence Scale—Revised]. The first was a test of Level of Aspiration, which was studied as a possible means of broadening the coverage of the WAIS-R to include a measure of nonintellective ability. It had a number of interesting features, but seemed to require further research before it could be added as a regular member of the battery. The second test was a new measure of spatial ability; although this test also had a number of merits it was too highly correlated with Block Design to warrant inclusion in the revised scale. (Wechsler, 1981, p. 10)

If one is drawn to the conclusion that g is what makes the predictive wheels go around in most educational and vocational ability testing, one is then led to the question: What is the most effective strategy for measuring g? (Thorndike, Hagen, & Sattler, 1986, p. 5)

Of course, this reliance on the theory base behind g in the development of intelligence tests may have detracted from the actual measurement of intelligent behavior. In fact, general intelligence as an actual entity may

not exist. General intelligence may indeed only be a mathematical abstraction, and if its existence had not been reified quite early in the development of mental tests, the structure of current intelligence batteries might be quite different. The most persuasive argument against g has been set forth by Gould (1981). Interested readers are encouraged to read Gould's entire text. What immediately follows is our attempt to explain in a few paragraphs Gould's insights into the misinterpretation of the general intelligence factor.

Gould starts out by reiterating what every person with a modicum of statistical background can easily repeat—that correlations do not imply causation. He then states that not paying attention to this known fact is probably among the most serious of errors in human reasoning. He makes his case painfully clear with two quick examples. In the first example, he notes that if he measured people's arm length and their leg length and then calculated a correlation between these two variables, a positive and large correlation would probably be obtained. In this case, he even ventures that he could make a case for an underlying factor or cause for this correlation: "Arm and leg length are tightly correlated because they are both partial measures of an underlying biological phenomenon, namely growth itself" (p. 242). In the second example, he states that the same relationship could be found if he simply correlated his age with the price of gasoline during the years of 1971 to 1981. This large positive correlation between these two variables certainly does not imply that his age and the price of gasoline are measuring some underlying factor.

In studying mental tests, Spearman (1904) basically invented the procedures behind factor analysis in an attempt to explain what caused the correlations between mental tests. Spearman's statistical reasoning led to an idea that is identical to today's concepts behind the first principal component in factor analysis. The first principal component in components analysis is a linear combination of variables that accounts for the most variance possible in a set of data. Therefore, the first principal component is typically correlated with most variables in a data set. According to Gould, Spearman reified this component as an entity and tried to give it a causal interpretation. As another example of the futility of this exercise, Gould points out that a factor analysis for a 5×5 correlation matrix of his age, the population of Mexico, the price of Swiss cheese, his pet turtle's weight, and the average distance between galaxies during the past 10 years would yield a strong first principal component. The first principal component from that correlation matrix might even account for more variance in the variables than the first principal component derived from a typical correlation table calculated between mental tests. Even though it might explain more variance than g does in mental tests, it would have no enlightening physical or causal meaning whatever.

Gould (1981) marshals two other problems that detract from the interpretation of the first principal component as causal. The first is that both the hereditary view of intelligence (that people are born with a certain amount of g and therefore do about the same on mental tests, regardless of environmental factors) and a strictly environmental view of g (people do well on mental tests because they have socioeconomic advantages, have attended the right schools, live in the right communities, etc.) are entirely consistent with the general-intelligence interpretation of the first principal component. The second problem is that g can actually disappear, depending on whether the statistician rotates the derived factors or not.

The idea that the methodology used in doing the factor analysis can either find or eliminate g is best explained by using figures like those found in Gould. First, correlations can be easily depicted by variables drawn as unit vectors. Highly related variables have their vectors close together, and unrelated variables are drawn perpendicular to each

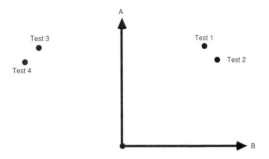

FIGURE 1.2. Unrotated factor solution.

other. Remember that statistics class where the instructor mentioned that unrelated variables are orthogonal (perpendicular) to each other? The cosines of the angles of these vectors represent the correlations. For example, the cosine of 90° is 0, the cosine of 0° is 1, and the cosine of 180° is –1. Figure 1.1 illustrates this graphical representation. Gould then presents a figure similar to Figure 1.2, which illustrates the intercorrelations between four tests. Tests 1 and 2 are highly correlated; Tests 3 and 4 are highly correlated; but the intercorrelations between either Tests 1 or 2 and Tests 3 or 4 are quite low. (To find the correlation between any two tests, simply find the angle between them and look up the cosine of that angle.) If one were to do a principal-components analysis, the first principal component would be placed at position A, where it would have moderate correlations with each of the variables. The second principal component would be independent of the first component (orthogonal or perpendicular to it) and therefore would be placed at position B. The first principal component would be interpreted as **g**. If, on the other hand, these components were rotated (see Figure 1.3),

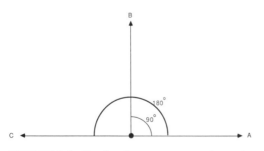

FIGURE 1.1. Graphical interpretation of correlations.

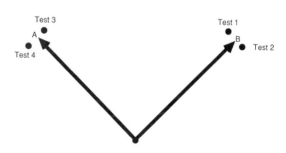

FIGURE 1.3. Rotated factor solution.

then instead of a factor correlated with all variables, we have two factors. The first, at position A, is highly correlated with Tests 3 and 4 and basically uncorrelated with Tests 1 and 2. The second component is highly correlated with Tests 1 and 2 and basically uncorrelated with Tests 3 and 4. Under this second situation (both factor solutions are equally defensible mathematically), one would not talk about g (it would not exist); instead, one would talk about intelligence as composed of primary mental abilities that are unrelated to one another.

Not everyone, of course, would agree with Gould's analysis. Judgment by persons who know the content of tests is essential in factor-analytic studies. Through correlational techniques, those items that measured physical more than mental ability were eliminated from early intelligence tests. Thorndike et al. (1986), in the introductory chapter to the *Technical Manual for the Stanford–Binet Intelligence Scale: Fourth Edition*, detail why they believe that g is not only an empirical fact but a viable psychological construct. They conclude the chapter by summarizing their feelings thus: "Still the general ability factor g, refuses to die. Like a phoenix, it keeps rising from its ashes and will no doubt continue to be an enduring part of our psychometric theory and psychometric practice" (p. 6).

The Influence of the U.S. Political Environment

As Marks (1976–1977) clearly points out, the decision to investigate individual differences or similarities is clearly arbitrary. One has to ask, "Why did it become so important to differentiate between people?" (Marks, 1976–1977, p. 3). One answer to this question is that in the United States the assessment of individual differences provided a way of organizing a society that by all accounts was very chaotic at the beginning of the 20th century. This was the beginning of the age of social reform, and mental testing was seen as a way to organize the provision of services that would be primarily dispensed through education.

With the election of Andrew Jackson in 1828, amid the loud cries of "Throw the rascals out," the spoils system had become firmly entrenched in American politics. During

the mid-1800s, each president was besieged by numerous persons crying for a position on the government payroll. In 1883, following the assassination of President James Garfield by a disappointed job seeker in 1881, Congress passed the Civil Service (Pendleton) Act to Regulate and Improve the Civil Services of the United States (U.S. Civil Service Commission [USCSC], 1884). The initial act covered only about 10% of the government positions, mostly clerical jobs in the Post Office and Treasury departments, but 80% of the jobs were covered by 1930 (Harvey, 1970). (Actually, President Ulysses S. Grant had appointed the first Civil Service Commission in the United States in 1872, which administered the first competitive examination. However, Congress, refusing to give up "patronage," did not appropriate funds, and the service was abandoned in 1875.)

The USCSC not only provided tests that were the forerunners of criterion-referenced achievement tests before the turn of the century, but they practiced "truth in testing" by providing specimen sets of items in reports, beginning with the second annual report of the service (USCSC, 1885). By 1939, a book including 10 practice examinations (with answers) provided potential examinees with the same kind of questions contained on the mental tests (Barse, 1939). "In the use of new examination methods (e.g. short answer and multiple choice) the Commission was, in many ways, well ahead of industry, the colleges and universities, and most of the few professional psychologists of the time and was to continue in the lead for many years" (Van Riper, 1958, p. 140).

The Pendleton Act had set the stage, and in the early 20th century, America was no longer going to tolerate the notion of robber barons building fortunes on the backs of children and immigrant labor. In 1901, Theodore Roosevelt succeeded William McKinley as president and greatly influenced the social reform movement. Roosevelt and the country took on two broad social aims. First, people were to be set free from the daily grind of work and poverty. Second, immigrants were to be set free from the liabilities of their status as foreigners through new social legislation and the resources provided through public education.

Marks (1976–1977) and Fass (1980) discuss 10 factors that were part of the American experience and directly influenced the testing movement: (1) massive immigration, with ethnic and racial diversity; (2) urbanization; (3) the growing influence of science; (4) the progressive educational movement; (5) World War I; (6) the supposed utility of the Army tests; (7) the putative empirical relation between race and IQ; (8) stricter school attendance laws: (9) the development of child labor legislation; and (10) the belief in a competitive, meritocratic society. All of these factors literally forced upon the schools a mandate to educate a population that was very heterogeneous. The impact of each of these 10 factors on the social fabric of America was enormous. Although we cannot discuss each factor in detail, here is an example of the first one: "Between 1901 and 1910 alone, nearly nine million people migrated to this country—more than the combined populations of the states of New York, Maryland, and New Hampshire in 1900" (Kownslar & Frizzle, 1967, pp. 600–601). Other evidence supporting the social reform nature of the age can be noted in the passing of the Keating–Owen Child Labor Act in 1916 and the fact that the last state to enact laws requiring child school attendance was Mississippi in 1918. This combination of political and social attitudes, child labor laws, and compulsory attendance laws assured that most youngsters would be in school. The task of turning these children into competent Americans then fell on the schools. To educate the diverse mass that constituted American society, the detection of individual differences in mental ability was thought to be necessary. Since the early development of the mental test by Binet clearly stemmed from an expressed need to differentiate between those French children who could be successful in traditional educational programs in France, a ready-made instrument was available. As noted earlier, Goddard, Kuhlmann, and Terman translated and revised Binet's test for use with American children in training and academic environs.

The Influence of School Organizational Practices

The primary organizational factor in the public schools has traditionally been chronological age and not mental age. The complete separation of children into "graded" classrooms, each with its own teacher, was reportedly accomplished first by John Philbrick, who reorganized the Quincy, Massachusetts grammar school in 1847 (Potter, 1967). The Ohio State Commissioner of Education reported that between 1854 and 1855, nearly 150 towns had converted to age-graded schools (Potter, 1967). Mental tests appeared to have potential in helping organize school systems within the age categories already adopted. With the additional structure offered by mental measures, the schools might better cope with their educational task. After all, mental tests were designed for exactly that purpose. They were used in World War I when over 1.7 million men were evaluated with the Army Alpha and Beta Tests (Fass, 1980). The publicly assumed success of these tests of mental abilities in the face of a national emergency helped contribute to their increased use in assessment areas outside of the military. The persons who worked directly on the Army tests (Robert Yerkes, Lewis Terman, Edward Thorndike, Henry Goddard, Arthur Sinton Otis, etc.) were responsible for the developments that led to the first group assessment techniques incorporated in the schools. The Otis Group Intelligence Scale and the National Intelligence Tests were introduced by the World Book Company in 1918.

Before proceeding, a review of what the early measures of intellectual functioning had been able to demonstrate is in order. First, on a limited basis, the tests were successful in differentiating between children who could be successful in schoolwork and those who could not (i.e., they could predict academic success). This is not to say that they could predict standardized achievement test results. The first standardized achievement battery to evaluate the academic areas of reading, spelling, sentence meaning, and vocabulary did not appear until 1920 in the first volume of the *Journal of Educational Research* (Pressey, 1920). However, the Stanford–Binet had been able to differentiate between pupils judged by their teachers to be adequately and inadequately achieving (Sattler, 1974). Second, the public believed that the tests had demonstrated on a very large scale that they could differentiate leadership ability in Army inductees. Third, and perhaps unfortunately most important, the Army report (Yerkes, 1921) brought to the public's attention the alleged differences in mental ability between blacks and whites, as well as between American-born inductees and inductees from Eastern Europe. Although these racial differences were based on inadequate statistical procedures and analyses, the racial interpretations given to the data ultimately captured the public's attention and increased the use of mental tests not only as a method of organizing schools, but as a method of categorizing persons in society at large. The interested reader is referred to Gould (1981) for a detailed review of the statistical inadequacies of these early studies.

Among the most unfortunate factors in the history of intellectual assessment and the testing movement were the well-documented prejudicial attitudes of Terman and Goddard. At this time, it is unnecessary to reiterate the racial slurs in their writings. Through the influence of these men and others, the original intent of Binet (to identify and assist children who were in need of special educational services) was frequently changed to one of rank-ordering children. Children who obtained very low scores on measures of intellectual development were often denied any opportunity for an educational experience. This denial of service only ended recently with the *PARC v. Commonwealth of Pennsylvania* decision in 1972. This legal decision became the basis for Public Law 94-142, the Education for All Handicapped Children Act (1975), which established the right of all children to an appropriate education. Because mentally retarded children could not be denied educational programs, the decision put an end to one of the major misuses of the IQ.

Item Development

One of the startling facts that quickly emerges when one explores the actual test questions is that the item types have changed very little since the initial physical tests were largely eliminated by the correlational studies. In *The Measurement of Intelligence*, Terman (1916) lists the tests as arranged by Binet in 1911 shortly before his death. Examples include the following: (1) At age 3, a child is supposed to point to nose, eyes, and mouth; (2) at age 6, copy a diamond; (3) at age 9, answer easy comprehension questions; (4) at age 12, compose one sentence given three words; and (5) at the adult level, give differences between pairs of abstract terms. These item types as well as many others listed by Terman should be quite familiar to current users of the Stanford–Binet Fourth Edition. Indeed, on page 1 of the Stanford–Binet manual, Thorndike et al. (1986) state, "The Fourth Edition resembles the 1960 Form L-M in that it covers the same age range, includes many of the same item types, and requires the examiner to establish for each examinee both a basal level and a ceiling level." Likewise, the interested observer can find many similarities in the present Wechsler intelligence scales and the 1939 Wechsler–Bellevue. Both authors and reviewers of the Stanford–Binet and Wechsler intelligence scales have pointed out that the test items are distinct from items typically found in academic achievement tests. For example, Sattler (1982) states, "In the last revision, the 1911 scale (Binet, 1911), further refinements were made, particularly in selecting tests that would measure intelligence rather than academic knowledge" (p. 99). However, both Wechsler and Binet employed empirical methods to find questions that differentiated between children who were successful and those who were unsuccessful in the public schools. "Binet's tests were given to mentally retarded children at the Salpêtrière and to mentally retarded and normal children in the primary schools of Paris" (Sattler, 1982 p. 99); tests that differentiated between these groups of children were included in the scale. Most of the original items that were incorporated in the original Wechsler Intelligence Scale for Children (WISC; Wechsler, 1949) were tried out by Miss Ventura Smith, a school psychologist working in the Westport, Connecticut school system. Again, items were chosen that differentiated between successful and unsuccessful children in academic environments. This emphasis on academics, along with the idea that the individual tests comprising the measure of intelligence needed to be correlated at least moderately with one another in order to support the *g* construct, probably reduced the pool of items that were considered as possible estimates of intelligence.

Intelligence Tests Today

Politically, intelligence tests are in dire straits. In November 1971, a group of black psychologists filed a class action suit claiming that intelligence tests were biased against black students and resulted in their being misdiagnosed and misplaced in special education classes in San Francisco (Larry P. v. Riles, 1979). In Chicago, a similar suit was filed (PASE v. Hannon, 1980). In the first case, Judge Peckham found that the intelligence tests were indeed biased, and a second ruling from the U.S. District Court for Northern California in September 1986 prohibits the use of intelligence tests with black children for any special education purposes. In Chicago, Judge Grady found that intelligence tests were *not* biased and permitted their use. The psychometric evidence concerning the alleged racial bias inherent in intelligence tests is summarized by Reynolds and Kaiser in Chapter 26 of this volume. Regardless of the psychometric evidence, intelligence tests are on trial, and current opinions dramatically differ. In the final analysis, the courts may decide where intelligence tests may be used.

However, as a pendulum swings, so does criticism of intelligence tests. Perhaps the first serious attack was launched by noted columnist Walter Lippman in the *New Republic* (Lippman, 1922) and by Terman's statistical consultant, Truman L. Kelley (1927). Lippman, Terman, and Yerkes exchanged arguments several times in the lay press, but the attack on tests only stymied the increasing use of tests for a short while. Such criticism has helped keep interpretation of scores more realistic.

JUDGMENTS ABOUT OTHER MENTAL ABILITIES

Early Focus on Physical Attributes

As industrial society and the U.S. economy flourished in the late 19th and early 20th centuries, many common men had opportunities for employment never known before. With geographic, economic, and social mobility came local autonomy, informal political and economic arrangements, increasingly radical labor unions, high rates of crime, corruption in government, and many other strains on society. Early in the 20th century, rapid growth and social unrest in the United States generated a "search for order" (Wiebe, 1967). As noted earlier in regard to the field of public education, psychological testing was also a part of the search for order with respect to adults in vocational and industrial settings. As the era developed, many thought that anyone willing to work could do any job well. However, the large number of bumbling clerks, confused telephone operators, and accident-prone drivers (even of horses) caused leaders to look for means of classifying people to achieve social efficiency and economic progress.

Efficiency experts introduced instruction and controls, but high rates of turnover and frequent accidents persisted as the Industrial Revolution continued. With only so much gained from the efficiency experts, attention turned from inanimate to animate raw materials. In 1918 Edward Thorndike caught the attention of influential leaders by saying, "Whatever exists at all exists in some amount," and that "to know it thoroughly involves knowing its quantity as well as its quality" (Thorndike, 1918, p. 16). Many agreed with Link, who believed that it would be "possible to select the right man for the right place" (1919, p. 293) and thereby to minimize industrial problems with man (and, later, woman) power. Unfortunately, early solutions included the use of graphology applied to completed application forms and character analyses based on brief interviews.

Increasingly, through the first third of this century, sales managers and marketing executives grasped at almost any straw to help them in hiring personnel and in helping those employees sell their products. Stereotypes played a major role in personnel selection. Norwegians, Greeks, and Russians were thought to be appropriate for most types of rough work, while French and Irish were thought to be more capable of tasks requiring enthusiasm and artistry. Poles and Lithuanians were thought to be good mill workers, and Italians and Swedes good at railroad construction. Karen Blackford's plan, popularized in *The Job, the Man, and the Boss* (Blackford & Newcomb, 1919), advised managers about whom to hire by character analysis; books such as *Character Analysis: How to Read People at Sight* (Bush & Waugh, 1923) and even 10 years later *Plus + Selling* (Fosbroke, 1933) instructed salespersons about approaching customers according to their physical appearance. In *Character Analysis*, Bush and Waugh described a nose that indicates "inclinations . . . toward the appetites [and that] shows plainly a commonplace mentality" (p. 62); a "money nose . . . [whose] owner will develop his trading instincts to the N-th degree, and if he entertains low-brow tastes, will have no other object in life but to acquire money, and that, no matter how" (p. 63); one nose that indicates "predominance of physical over mental strength," and "another nose suggestive of craftiness, treachery, cunning, and unwillingness to meet accepted conventional standards" (p. 64). Fosbroke provided artists' conceptions of various kinds of buyers and attributed buying styles to physical characteristics such as the "sincere buyer" with a narrow-high forehead (case 28); the "price motivated buyer" with a wide medium-high forehead (case 29); and, among others, the "tenacious buyer" with the angular jaw (case 32). Fosbroke described a person with a protruding forehead and light chin and jaw as a "slow-thinking yielding buyer" (case 33) and a person with the same chin and jaw but a slanting forehead as a "fast-thinking yielding buyer" (case 35).

Scientists were making some headway, but development of better instruments for assessing personality and interests than these stereotypical judgments about ethnicity, body type, and hair color took a long time. Personnel at the Carnegie Institute of Technology in Pittsburgh made major contributions to the advancement of scientific assessment. Carnegie, where about half the students were preparing for careers in industry, started a new Division of Applied Psychology that, among other tasks, was charged with developing tests for industry. Walter VanDyke Bingham came from Dartmouth in 1915 to head the organization, and soon had secured funding from nearly 30 firms to finance the work directed by Walter Dill Scott in the Bureau of Salesmanship Research (later known as the Bureau of Personnel Research) (Bingham, 1923a, 1923b).

Personality Tests

Objective Testing

Faced with an enormous number of interviews with military recruits to determine those who would be susceptible to wartime disorders, Robert Woodworth formalized oral questions often posed by psychiatrists about worry, daydreaming, enuresis, and so on into 116 short questions (Woodworth, 1918), which could be administered to groups of people who could read and check "yes" or "no." Even though the scores turned out to be influenced by the situation (i.e., scores for many soldiers changed markedly after the Armistice), the work served as a basis for the Thurstone Personality Scale, the Allport Ascendance–Submission Test, and others.

In 1921, Lewis Terman started one of the major longitudinal studies in the behavioral sciences with his studies of more than 1,000 school-age children with very high IQs. As part of that project, he used the Woodworth questionnaire and tests about moral judgment, overstatement, and honesty (Terman, 1925). In a test of honesty, children were asked to check those books on a list of 50 that they had read; 20 of the titles were fictitious. In another test, children were asked, not for an answer, but whether they could solve each of a series of problems. Later in the session they were given the problems to solve, the difference being the "overstatement" score.

Although Terman is best known for his tests of cognitive ability, he was quite interested in affective variables. One of his students, Robert G. Bernreuter (1933), developed, as part of his 1931 doctoral dissertation, an instrument called simply the Personality Inventory. He pooled items from tests by Thurstone, Allport, and others to measure four traits: neurotic tendency, introversion, dominance (others had sought to measure these first three), and self-sufficiency. "Personality inventory" became a generic term for such scales after Bernreuter's instrument became widely used in schools and industry through the 1930s and 1940s. The availability of four scores from the Personality Inventory and the face validity of the 125 items probably contributed to its widespread use, even though research indicated that the Neurotic and Introverted scores were correlated above .90 and that a better interpretation resulted from scores for Self-Confidence and Sociability. Use of the two latter scores followed a factor analysis by John Flannagan (1935). Flanagan's study preceded by more than 10 years factor-analytic studies by Cattell (1947), Guilford (1947), and Thurstone (1947), who used a more basic approach to trait identification (i.e., considering the intercorrelations between single items).

Another popular test of the time was the Humm–Wadsworth Temperament Scale (Humm & Wadsworth, 1935). It broke new ground with empirical keys based on the responses of groups of patients, criminals, and normals thought to have one of seven psychiatric classifications (e.g., paranoid, epileptoid, hysteroid, and normal). Wadsworth later claimed that the Humm–Wadsworth test could be used to identify those in the workforce who could enter "working relationships cooperatively" and to identify "chronic hotheads" before they were hired (Wadsworth, 1941, pp. 19, 59), even though answers to the questions in the inventory represented, at best, the client's perception of a situation. Such claims were of much interest to employers concerned with labor strife and employee turnover, which they deemed to be excessive.

The first criterion-keyed personality test to withstand both the tests of time and peer critiques was the Minnesota Multiphasic Personality Inventory (MMPI), which appeared in 1942. This self-report scale consisted of 495 items which were to be answered "true," "false," or "cannot say." The MMPI was designed for use in diagnosing abnormal personality patterns, but was soon used with college students and in employee selection situations, where it did not prove to be as helpful. With empirically based keys, the face validity of the items was disguised. Both the Humm–Wadsworth and the MMPI incorporate items and correction formulas to compensate for a client's tendency to give a favorable or unfavorable report.

Scott, Clothier, and Spriegel (1961) reported on the use of tests in the late 1950s by well-known companies. They found 80% to be using tests for selection; 78% using stenographic or clerical tests; 63% using intelligence tests; 45% using mechanical aptitude tests; 44% using personality or interest inventories; and about 33% of the companies using trade, dexterity, or performance tests of some kind. Even though the National Industrial Conference Board (1948), which surveyed a broader range of employers, did not find such widespread use, they found use of all tests to be rising markedly during the 1940s and 1950s. By the 1950s the Humm–Wadsworth Scale was dropping from use, but the MMPI was becoming very popular, and Bernreuter's Personality Inventory had sold over a million copies (Hathaway, 1964). A *Fortune* magazine survey published in 1954 (Whyte, 1954) indicated that most of the major corporations, such as General Electric, Sears, and Westinghouse, were using personality tests in screening applicants and selecting managers.

The inventories came under attack by such social critics as William Hollingworth Whyte in a 1954 *Fortune* article "The Fallacies of 'Personality' Testing," and later in *The Organization Man* (Whyte, 1956), and Martin Gross (1962) in *The Brain Watchers*. Such attacks led to congressional hearings and testimony by Civil Service Commissioner John W. Macy, Jr., to the effect that the personality tests of that era did not come close enough to meeting the technical standards of psychology to justify their use as selection methods (Macy, 1965b; see also Macy, 1965a). The popularity of personality tests in the schools faded, in part because few validity studies supported their use except with disturbed children, and in part because more general use violated the rights to privacy of those tested. The trend in the 1970s was toward a holistic approach in assessment centers, where psychologists used a number of approaches to identify personnel who would be likely to succeed in the company. In schools, assessment of personality was completed more by observing and interviewing children and interviewing their teachers and parents than by testing.

Emergence of Projective Testing

Projective testing arose in part from the problems with easily scored tests organized around particular traits, and in part from the desire for a test to yield insights into the structure of the whole personality. According to Frank (1939), who contributed the first major work on projectives, this approach to assessment is based both on Gestalt psychology, with its emphasis on the whole being more than the sum of its parts, and on psychoanalytic techniques of dream analysis. One indication of the difficulty in measuring projectively is found in the many different approaches and modifications of approaches that have been attempted. A curious discrepancy between research and practice has been illustrated over the years through the use of projective techniques. Projective tests remain popular in clinical use, despite their poor psychometric properties and thousands of articles in professional literature detailing problems with examiner and situation variables, norms, reliability, and validity. Instead of regarding projective techniques as tests, it is better to view them as clinical tools that are as valuable as the skills of the clinician who uses them. Their value lies in suggesting hypotheses about an individual for further investigation, rather than in producing a score from which a decision will be made (Anastasi, 1982).

One of the first approaches to projective personality appraisal, decades before the term "projective" was used, was by Galton and involved word associations. In 1879 Galton was working on his eighth list, one with 86 stimulus words all starting with the letter A (Forrest, 1974). An early list by Carl Jung (1910) provided stimulus words to represent "emotional complexes." Improving on the earlier work, Jung analyzed reaction time, content, and physically observable tension as well as the verbal responses. The list of Grace Kent and A. J. Rosanoff (1910), which avoided words likely to remind one of personal experiences, had objective scoring and norms and became popular in the United States. Sidney Pressey (1921), who spent more time working in the cognitive domain with achievement tests and teaching machines, produced a group-administered form. Pressey presented groups of words in a series. Subjects were asked to cross out one or more words in each series; when the words crossed out were tabulated, scores were obtained regarding things that the subject worried about, liked, found unpleasant, or was nervous about.

Pressey's work led Payne (1928) to introduce more freedom of response by presenting short phrases on a printed form and asking the subject to complete the sentences.

However, the sentence completion technique did not become popular until the 1940s, when the Psychological Corporation published the list developed by A. R. Rohde and Gertrude Hildreth (1940) and the technique was described by such well-known authors as Percival M. Symonds (1939) in the *Journal of Abnormal and Social Psychology*, Julian B. Rotter and B. Willerman (1947) in the *Journal of Consulting Psychology*, and others.

Binet and other early test authors used meaningless inkblots to investigate imagination and fantasy (Tulchin, 1940). But the man who made them work in personality assessment was Hermann Rorschach, a Swiss psychiatrist, who tried many variations of blots with hospital patients before settling on 10, which he published in 1921 with his monograph *Psychodiagnostik*. Rorschach developed a formal system of scoring that included determinants and location as well as content; his system was based on use of the plates with several patient groups and two normal groups of subjects. In the United States, Samuel J. Beck and Bruno Klopfer suggested more detailed scoring categories and helped the technique gain in popularity by their speeches and writings in the late 1930s.

It was not until 1935 that C. D. Morgan and H. A. Murray (1935) presented the Thematic Apperception Test (TAT), and then it came through a journal 8 years before it was published by the Harvard University Press (Murray, 1943). The test, stimulated by the work of Binet, Burt, and others who used pictures and stories about the pictures to study intellectual development, consists of 30 pictures (10 for men, 10 for women, and 10 for both). The pictures and procedures of the TAT, in contrast to the inkblot techniques, present more structured stimuli and require more complex and organized verbal responses. Subjects are asked to develop a story about each picture that describes the situation, events leading up to it, the outcome, and the thoughts and feelings of the people in the story; in other words, the person responding is asked to go beyond the information given by describing psychological states and by extending the story in time (forward or back). A number of other picture tests soon followed, such as Bellack and Bellak's (1952) pictures for children; Symond's

(1948) for adolescents; and Shneidman's (1948) Make-A-Picture Story Test, which allows subjects, chiefly schizophrenic patients, to work with 22 background pictures and 67 figures to be arranged on one of the backgrounds while telling a story.

Through the first half century of formal personality testing, psychologists have had a number of problems. In contrast with evaluators of ability and interest tests, personality evaluators need considerable training to deal with faking and malingering and the situational specificity of responses. Projective tests are less susceptible to faking than self-report inventories, but with projectives, subtle differences in phrasing and the behavior of the examiner can bring out different responses from the subject. Interpretation of responses to projective tests by many examiners "may reveal more about the theoretical orientation, favorite hypotheses, and personality idiosyncrasies of the examiner than it does about the examinee's personality dynamics" (Anastasi, 1982, p. 582). Improvements in interpretation have resulted from the efforts of Exner and Holtzman and are described in Chapters 7 and 8 of Volume 2 of the present work.

Interest Tests

Measurement of interests is one of the brighter topics in the history of testing. Reliability and validity studies over decades with the Strong Vocational Interest Blank (SVIB) and with Kuder's preference scales illustrate levels of quality that can be achieved in mental testing. Scores obtained on these classic instruments have remained relatively stable for 20 years in some studies and 30 years in others (Campbell, 1971).

Like many other aspects of vocational guidance, assessment of interest can be traced back to the Boston Vocational Bureau and Frank Parsons. Initially Parsons used interviews, questionnaires, and self-analysis in an eclectic approach to assess the aptitudes and interests of the youths with whom he worked. He believed that with "Light, Information, Inspiration, and Cooperation," boys could choose an appropriate occupation (Parsons, 1908, p. 92). A year later Parsons obtained the assistance of Hugo Munsterberg, an early president of APA from Harvard. With a background in anthropology,

Munsterberg helped bring science to psychology, and by publicizing the work of Parsons he helped attract others to constructing vocational tests (Munsterberg, 1910).

Although Parsons and Munsterberg talked about the interests of youths, E. L. Thorndike (1912) and T. L. Kelley (1914) were apparently the first formal investigators of interests. Thorndike initiated studies about the relationship of interest to abilities; with a questionnaire, Kelley asked about things "liked" and "not liked," which may have formed the basis for more profitable studies 5–10 years later at Carnegie Tech.

Among the group at Carnegie, Bruce Moore (1921) was the first to publish. He attempted to measure and distinguish between the mechanical and social interests of engineers. Others studied "successful" and "unsuccessful" salesmen. Much of the work at Carnegie, and elsewhere a short time later, was based on products from a seminar conducted by C. S. Yoakum. Under Yoakum, graduate students identified about 1,000 items that found their way into at least nine interest inventories in the next few years (Campbell, 1971), among them the SVIB in 1927. E. K. Strong, Jr., had worked at Carnegie with Moore on interest measurement and continued with this research for the rest of his life. Moore worked with the Westinghouse Electric Educational Department for a while, helping separate those who might do better in sales from those who would do better in engineering or management (Moore, 1921). In 1923 Strong moved to Stanford, where he continued to develop interest inventories, and Moore moved to Penn State, where he was soon head of the department of psychology and a distinguished leader in professional activities.

Building on a 1924 thesis by Karl Cowdery, Strong produced the SVIB in 1927 and the manual a year later. A full-time faculty member in the College of Business, Strong financed most of his research and the Vocational Interest Research Bureau at Stanford with profits from scoring the blanks. He had some financial help from the Carnegie Corporation and the Laura Spellman Fund in the 1930s, but much of the work fell to Strong, members of his family, and his assistant of many years, a Mrs. Nicholson. While puffing and chewing a cigar, he scored many blanks by keeping track of "likes" and "dislikes" with counters designed to aid golfers in keeping track of their scores. The first scoring machines were used with the SVIB in 1930, but automated scoring was not available until 1946.

Sales of the SVIB paralleled simplifications in scoring. Through the 1930s, about 40,000 booklets were printed each year. As interest in job placement rose, sales doubled in the late 1930s and early 1940s. After World War II, with many veterans seeking vocational help and with the development of automatic scoring, printing of blanks jumped to nearly 300,000 in 1947 and leveled off at about half that many per year for the next 20 years. With two to four people using each "reusable booklet," it was estimated that about 400,000 men a year were completing the SVIB annually (Campbell, 1971).

Today's Strong–Campbell Interest Inventory (SCII) is the current edition of the SVIB. High points in the long SVIB history include the following:

1927—First appearance of a 420-item SVIB for men, which was based on Strong's work at Carnegie and Cowdery's project and published by the Stanford University Press.
1933—Publication of the Women's SVIB with 410 items, of which 262 were in common with the Men's Form.
1938—Major revision of Men's Form and adoption of a modern profile.
1946—Women's Form revised with 400 items to equal Men's Form in revised length.
1966—Major revision of Men's Form with 399 items.
1969—Major revision of Women's Form with 398 items.
1974—Publication of the SCII (known as the SVIB-SCII), with the merging of the Men's and Women's Forms into a single booklet with 325 items and a theoretical framework from John Holland to guide organization and interpretation of scores.

When the second edition of the SVIB-SCII appeared (Campbell & Hansen, 1981), Campbell paid tribute to Strong in a preface as follows:

E. K. Strong, Jr., the original author of this inventory, was one of the most intense, dedicated, effective psychologists produced by America in the first half of the twentieth century. Over a 40-year span he developed—without benefit of modern funding or data processing machinery—one of the country's most widely used psychological inventories. His research instincts were remarkable, his persistence astonishing, and his insistence on producing a practical product of high quality all too rare among academic psychologists. (no page number)

The Kuder Interest Inventories (Kuder, 1934; Kuder, 1948) have been used almost as long as the Strong series. Strong approached the task of assessing interests by asking respondents to indicate whether they liked or disliked a wide variety of objects, activities, or types of persons commonly met in life, whereas Kuder asked respondents to indicate which of three items they would most and least like. Items on the Strong were empirically keyed to allow for comparisons of people in an occupation with people in general, whereas Kuder items were grouped on the basis of content validity for 10 broad interest areas. Kuder's tests (Kuder & Paulson, 1949, 1950) were more appropriate for high school students than Strong's, which were designed for college-age and older subjects. Some of Kuder's later work included criterion keying (Kuder, 1956). In more recent times, inventories based on the techniques perfected by Strong have been developed with items and keys for nonprofessional occupations.

Attitude Scales

Information about attitudes, beliefs, and opinions of people of all ages have been sought throughout recorded history; however, only in 1928, when Lewis Thurstone developed a technique for scaling items based on psychophysical methods, did measurement of such variables became effective. This psychometric advancement in item scaling paralleled the influence of the correlation coefficient in the development of cognitive tests. Before Thurstone's breakthrough, investigators relied on simple questionnaires. Most of the early scales lacked evidence of internal consistency and used arbitrary units of measurement.

Thurstone's (Thurstone & Chave, 1929) approach enabled the items to be arrayed on a continuous scale with a known distance between adjacent items. Each Thurstone scale consisted of items representing a full range of attitudes about a topic, from "highly favorable" to "highly unfavorable." Items were constructed by test authors and judged by other persons who were knowledgeable about the topic. Each item was judged by a panel of experts, who rated the location of the item (not their opinion) on a scale from 0 to 11, with 5.5 indicating a neutral statement. Item statistics involved an average based on the placement on the 11-point scale by the judges and a semi-interquartile range of the ratings for each item. Better scales had about 20 items with a rectilinear distribution of items filling the range of opinion, each with small variability. Respondents were to identify the one, two, or three items with which they agreed.

Alternate forms of Thurstone scales usually had coefficients of equivalence in the .80s, high enough that several measurements of the opinions of groups could be taken when this was desirable. Stability coefficients with months or years between measurement were moderate, not high.

A few years later, Rensis Likert (1932) developed a new technique for weighting responses, which eventually made "Likert-type scales" more popular for several reasons. Traditional Likert scales range in length from 18 to 200 items, with each statement being either definitely favorable or unfavorable about the object of concern. Judges are not used, so the content depends on the author's judgment. Each item is rated on a 5-point scale from "strongly agree" to "strongly disagree," with answers credited initially with equal intervals (e.g., 5, 4, 3, 2, or 1). While in development, the scale is administered to large groups of people, and biserial coefficients are computed to aid in the selection of items for the final scale. Responses to each item can be analyzed to determine the value of each point on the scale based on the distribution of responses from the sample. This technique is especially helpful when respondents tend to use less than the full range of points on the scale. Some investigators have used more than 5 points on a scale and have varied verbal descriptions of the points.

Later investigators (Edwards & Kenney, 1946, and others) found that Likert-type scales can be constructed in about half as much time as a Thurstone-type scale and that

Likert-type scales are more diagnostic because each person responds to each item. When the Likert approach is used with a Thurstone scale, investigators usually obtain higher reliability coefficients than when either strategy is used separately.

The Minnesota Teacher Attitude Inventory is an example of a published modified Likert-type scale. Many attitude scales are constructed for research and survey purposes, but few have been commercially published. Shaw and Wright (1967) produced in book form an extensive collection of attitude scales for a variety of purposes. An extensive collection is in the Educational Testing Service library.

Every decade or so, a new enthusiasm for the study of values develops, but in the first half of this century few tests that met the standards for more than experimental scales emerged. Basing their work on Spranger's *Types of Men* (1928), Allport, Vernon, and Lindzey (1931) copyrighted an early instrument that was used experimentally in a number of locations. Perhaps today its main value was the conceptualization of six basic interests or attitudes (Theoretical, Economic, Aesthetic, Social, Political, and Religious); these overlapped with both Holland's occupational themes, which were employed in interpretation of contemporary editions of the Strong-Campbell Interest Inventory occupational themes, and interest areas used by Kuder.

APPLICATION OF TESTS IN VARIOUS SETTINGS

Civil Service

Even before the Pendleton Act of 1883, examinations were used to select persons for employment in public service. For years they were known as "pass" (i.e., minimum-competence) exams, because examinees who passed were not rated according to score; instead, each person passing became eligible for employment. The key to employment was being admitted to the test by politicians, because the vast majority of those given the opportunity found it very easy to pass.

Some positions were more lucrative than others. Examinations for port authority customs inspectors, which officially paid only $2,000 per year, were sold for as much as $50,000 by some politicians (Hays & Kearney, 1982). Admission to examinations for other positions, such as those for which salary was the only source of income, may have been given to faithful voters in the politicians district. With passage of the Pendleton Act, examinees were ranked by score and applicants were selected for employment from the top down. By 1952, at least 85% of all "federal public servants" were admitted to service by some form of examination.

In contrast to the theoretical and scholarly essays used in the British competitive system, after which the Pendleton Act was modeled, exams in the United States were practical in character and emphasized job-related skills during the first 50 years. In 1936, the Brownlow Committee, appointed by President Franklin D. Roosevelt, expanded and decentralized the system in three important ways. Individual government agencies were authorized to administer the tests throughout the country; in the original system, tests were administered only in a few locations and only by the USCSC. Many of the tests became known as "continual open examinations" because they could be administered on short notice. The content was also expanded. Exams for college graduates were developed between 1934 and 1954, to assess general skills and capabilities needed by agency managers as opposed to the more specific practical knowledge needed in clerical and skilled positions. The most successful of these was the Junior Management Assistant Examination between 1948 and 1954.

In 1955, the Federal Service Entrance Examination (FSEE) was introduced to aid in the selection of generalists and to increase transfer opportunities by providing a single point of entry into civil service. For 20 years this exam served for appointment to midlevel positions. In 1974, the Professional and Administrative Career Examination (PACE) was introduced for applicants for a wide range of administrative/professional positions. However, in 10 years it was phased out in favor of a number of position-specific examinations, following widespread criticism about the difficulty members of minority groups had in attaining scores at the top of the PACE list (see Arvey, 1979).

Bureaus Using Tests in Schools

Associated with social concerns about child labor and the increased number of children entering and continuing in school in the early 1900s was the formation of research bureaus in the schools to monitor the progress of pupils and to evaluate the effectiveness of schools. In *Laggards in Our Schools* (1909), Leonard Ayres called attention to the problems of retention in grade. In that era, more than 15% failed first grade, and by eighth grade more than half of the pupils were behind expected age placement by 1 or more years. Many of those retained did not finish elementary school, to the dismay of many "efficiency experts" (and probably even more parents). Schools that had large numbers of failing students were thought to be economically inefficient and came under the scrutiny of persons conducting school surveys. Surveyors (e.g., known as researchers or members of the Committee on School Inquiry on organizational charts of school systems) were charged to keep educational records, to test children regarding pupil progress and promotion, and in many instances to develop homogeneous learning groups. There was competition among cities and states on many fronts, one of them being the educational attainment of the children and another being the cost of the educational programs (Chapman, 1927). A number of the Research Bureaus were formed to be agents of the board of education to evaluate the efficiency of the superintendent and his staff, instead of assisting the superintendent and his staff in making efficient plans for students. According to Chapman (1927), the "bureaus which were prominent in the school efficiency movement, (p. 53)" with their dates of organization, were as follows: Rochester, New York (1913); New York City (1913); Boston (1914); Kansas City, Missouri (1914); Detroit (1914); Chicago (1917); and Lincoln, Nebraska (1918). Defenbaugh (1923) provided descriptions of 19 such bureaus and listed the locations of 44 others: "Some type of 'research' is carried out in every wide awake school system" (Martens, 1934, p. 1).

Other types of research bureaus were formed to study children and to help with the placement of those who were not making normal progress. Chicago's Bureau of Child

Study was the first in 1899. Other early child study clinics, founded between 1907 and 1912, were located in Rochester, New York; New York City; Providence, Rhode Island; Oakland, California; Hibbing, Minnesota; Cincinnati; Grand Rapids, Michigan; Seattle; Philadelphia; Springfield, Massachusetts; New Orleans; and Milwaukee (Wallin, 1914). Such clinics usually involved psychologists in the individual study of a child, often in collaboration with a psychiatrist and a social worker, following the model of Healy and Bronner (1948) in Chicago or Witmer (1907) at the University of Pennsylvania.

Other "research bureaus" focused on testing associated with vocational training, guidance, and placement. In 1911 Helen Thompson Woolley established a psychological clinic in the Cincinnati public schools, the first such clinic in a vocational bureau (Veatch, 1978). In 1913 David Spence Hill initiated one of the earliest studies in the field of guidance through a Division of Educational Research with a gift of $800,000 from Isaac Delgado to establish a trade school in New Orleans. Other guidance-oriented research bureaus in the schools were started in Atlanta (1917); Providence, Rhode Island (1918); Reading, Massachusetts (1919); and Berkeley, California (1919) (Chapman, 1927).

Research bureaus were also developing in institutions for the mentally ill and/or retarded. Two were quite well known at the beginning of the century, and others followed their lead. The first was the Minnesota School for the Feeble-Minded and Colony for Epileptics at Faribault, where Dr. A. C. Rogers employed Dr. A. R. T. Wylie to devote half of his time in 1898 to research on emotion, instinct, memory, reaction time, and other factors with the mentally retarded. Wylie worked for about 3 years, but the laboratory was inactive for 9 years until 1910, when Frederick Kuhlmann was employed to organize a research bureau from which he would provide psychological evaluations of children and help schools organize classes for the feeble-minded. The second well-known research bureau of this type was established in Vineland, New Jersey. Working in the research bureau at Vineland with Henry Goddard was Edgar Doll, who in 1935 developed the first widely used adaptive behavior scale, the Vineland Social Maturity Scale. Establishing operations similar to

Goddard's research bureau were E. B. Huey at the Lincoln State School and Colony of Illinois in 1909; P. F. Lange at the Iowa Institution for Feeble-Minded Children at Glenwood in 1910; and J. E. W. Wallin as clinical psychologist at the New Jersey State Village for Epileptics at Skillman (Wallin, 1914). The test development activities in these settings by Goddard, Kuhlmann, and Doll were of major significance in the history of testing.

Independent Consulting Services

In 1919, Walter Dill Scott established the first independent psychological consulting service for industry. The Scott Company worked well with unions and focused on improving the efficiency of production; however, the company did not last long after Scott became president of Northwestern University in 1921. James McKeen Cattell, along with Edward L. Thorndike and Robert Woodworth, organized the Psychological Corporation in 1921. This company continues as a primary force in the development, publication, and distribution of tests for education, business, and industry. Then, as now, there was divided opinion in the scientific community, with Scott and Walter VanDyke Bingham championing tests of specific attributes and Robert Yerkes arguing for tests of more generalized ability.

Under President Cattell, the Psychological Corporation had an unusual organization, which he referred to as a "holding company" for the psychologists who were both stockholders and employees. Services of the corporation were publicized through press releases and reprints of newspaper stories about its activities. Fees were split evenly between the corporation and individuals performing the service, with each participating shareholder/psychologist agreeing to devote at least half of his or her payment to the research in which he or she was currently involved. In turn, the corporation paid little in dividends, but any excess of profit was earmarked to advance scientific research. With this organization, Cattell hoped to drive charlatans out of business, promote psychological research, expand the public's familiarity with psychology, and improve the social standing of psychologists. However, profits were few in the prosperous times of the early 1920s. Bingham was brought in as president in 1926 to administer a more conventional operation (Sokal, 1984). In 1976, the Psychological Corporation merged with the test development and sales unit of the World Book Company, which had been started in 1905. Now it is the oldest and largest commercial publisher of tests for psychological assessment, admissions, and credentialing, for use in business, education, industry, and government.

Collegiate Aptitude Testing

At the turn of the century, college enrollment began to increase dramatically. In 1870 there were only 500 secondary schools and about 80,000 students. By 1910 there were 10,000 secondary schools and 900,000 students, of whom only 10% were in private preparatory institutions. Yet it was from the private prep schools that prestigious colleges enrolled most of their students. In the 19th century, students were admitted to college on the basis of written examinations on the campus of their choice; as the pressure of numbers built, secondary schools were rated by professors, and admissions were accepted from those with high ratings. The College Entrance Examination Board (CEEB) was formed in 1899 to establish, administer, and evaluate examinations in subjects specified by about a dozen participating institutions, primarily Eastern colleges. CEEB tests were developed so that students would not need to take an examination at each college they were hoping to enter. Also, test scores were used to facilitate admission of (less affluent) students from the public schools. Each year, more colleges joined the CEEB. The pressures of preparing and evaluating essay tests increased greatly as the number of college applicants multiplied. Encouraged by the perceived success of aptitude testing in World War I for classifying inductees, the CEEB chose to experiment with a multiple-choice format in addition to essay questions beginning in 1926. Carl Brigham, a professor of psychology at Princeton, was charged with developing the Scholastic Aptitude Test (SAT), which attempted to measure "ability to learn" more than what students "had learned." By the late 1930s the SAT was preferred to the essay, but the writing portion was not dropped until 1942, when it was too

difficult to get examiners to central locations during World War II. Readers were again brought into use in the 1950s when the Advanced Placement Tests were introduced, but never again as part of the SAT.

In 1947, the testing functions of CEEB, the Carnegie Corporation, and the American Council on Education were merged to form the Educational Testing Service (ETS), a private, nonprofit corporation devoted to measurement and research in the field of education. Following the merger, ETS expanded its coverage to include professional schools, governmental agencies, and state educational agencies. As a nonprofit corporation, most of ETS's income is used for providing the educational testing and advisory services and to conducting the measurement research and development for which it was founded. In 1959 the American College Testing (ACT) program was established, also as a nonprofit corporation, to screen applicants for colleges not enrolled with CEEB and to select talented students for scholarship awards.

The early CEEB examinations were based on the curriculum content of secondary schools sending a number of students to the elite Eastern colleges. With the introduction of the SAT, the test content was extended beyond the rigid curriculum of the preparatory schools, and the multiple-choice format suggested a sex and race blindness associated with equitable selection. However, the subscribing colleges of the 1940s had curricula that were limited by today's practices. Between 1926 and 1941, interpretive scores were based on the characteristics of the group taking the test in a given year. Noting variations in the performance of groups taking the examination in different years and at certain times of the year, the CEEB decided to establish the 11,000 students who took the exam in 1941 as the permanent reference group (Anastasi, 1982; Angoff, 1962, 1971). As a result, contemporary interpretive scores from the SAT are based on the sample of persons taking the SAT in 1941 through the use of a chain of anchor items. In the meantime, the applicant pool has increased enormously, as have the kind, type, and number of institutions receiving scores of applicants. In the 1930s and 1940s, only a few (mostly male) students from certain secondary schools took the SAT, with a view toward enrolling in a relatively few Eastern (mostly private) colleges. Now, in some secondary schools, most students take the SAT in anticipation of enrolling in many types of colleges across the country. In 1980 about as many students (1.5 million) took the SAT as entered college that year. Although the purpose of the SAT and the range of persons taking it have expanded dramatically, the reference group for the norms has not. Use of norms based on the 1941 reference group is a major cause of demoralizing headlines each year about the sorry state of schooling in America as indicated by low SAT scores. Little or no attention is given in the popular press to the increasingly higher raw scores required for an IQ of 100 when the Stanford–Binet and Wechsler scales are renormed on representative samples of the population. (See Sattler, 1974, pp. 114 and 150–151.)

Angoff (1962) explained the use of one reference group by comparing measurement with the SAT to measurement with a yardstick. We do not know (or care) which king's foot was agreed upon as the ideal size for 12 inches, but a foot is a foot on every yardstick. And the mean and standard deviation of the students responding to the SAT in 1941 provide the basis for interpretation of the SAT today. If the same reasoning was used in determining IQs and other cognitive ability scores each time the test was revised and/or renormed, children of today would appear to be much smarter than portrayed by the media. (For a discussion of media bias in interpretation of intelligence tests, see Herrnstein, 1982.)

To help with the selection of college students for graduate work, the Miller Analogies Test was introduced in 1926 and the Graduate Record Examination in 1937. Many revisions later, these tests are still in use.

INFLUENTIAL STUDIES AND TALENT SEARCHES

Every few years a major study of the quality of education involves collection of data, primarily through the use of cognitive ability tests. Such data are usually interpreted with little regard for measurements in the past and are only part of the fuel for the fires of select groups issuing pronouncements about schooling. Advocates for change rarely point to the success of the past when encouraging investment in new strategies or techniques to move the system forward. Over the decades, several major studies of school achievement have been conducted.

The Carnegie Study

In 1928, the Carnegie Foundation started a study in Pennsylvania on a scale that had not been previously attempted. About 90% of the public school and about 50% of the private school seniors were tested, and those who went to Pennsylvania colleges were tested again in 1930 and 1932. In a report a few years later, Learned and Wood (1938) surprised many readers with such findings as these: (1) A large portion of the intellectually able did not go on to college; (2) students with the highest test scores in some colleges had scores below the lowest achievers in other colleges; and (3) grades in the various colleges were not functionally equivalent.

One of the Pennsylvania project investigators, Ben Wood, director of the Educational Records Bureau at Columbia University, used data from the project to encourage secondary schools and colleges to keep cumulative records for use in advising students and to provide accessible data for use when decisions were to be made. The American Council on Education adopted the record form he recommended in 1928. About 20% of the form was for information pertinent to the continuous development of students, other than that obtained from tests.

With the need to score so many tests from Pennsylvania, Ben Wood approached Thomas Watson at IBM about the possibilities of more efficient scoring and data processing. After many consultations, the IBM 805 was introduced in 1935 with a great reduction in the cost of scoring (Downey, 1965).

Eight-Year Study of the Progressive Education Association

Ralph Tyler directed the evaluation portion of the famous Eight-Year Study of the Progressive Education Association in 1933–1941. In this project, about 300 colleges were persuaded to admit students who graduated from about 30 public and private preparatory schools whose curriculum did not have the prescribed Carnegie units (which had been in place since 1909). The results (Smith, Tyler, and the Evaluation Staff, 1942) confirmed the need for more monitoring of student progress with standardized and other tests when the secondary schools were relieved of rigid curricular requirements. (These results are relevant to the arguments in the 1980s about the desirability of minimum-competence testing.)

New York Regents' Examinations

In the state of New York, Regents' examinations, introduced in 1865 and used since 1878, were (and still are) employed in part to determine eligibility for graduation from the secondary schools of the state. As such, the content of the academically oriented examinations was very closely related to the objectives of curriculum and instruction in the schools. As the schools enrolled more and more adolescents for whom college attendance was doubtful and as the colleges began experimenting with less rigid academic programs, a study was initiated to investigate not only the knowledge but also the work orientation and level of satisfaction of all youths who left the New York secondary schools in 1936–1937 before or after graduation. The results, published in several volumes, concluded, among other things, that the students needed much more guidance and that testing was very helpful (Gulick, 1938).

The Iowa Program

Also in the mid-1930s, E. F. Lindquist established a testing program for the state of Iowa. This program was self-supporting and not only enabled personnel under his direction to maintain an effective and comprehensive series of tests to measure achievement of school children in Iowa and throughout the nation, but also to develop a number of spinoffs. Following development of the Iowa Test of Basic Skills in 1935–1940 came the Iowa Test of Educational Development in 1942, which was designed to be given in the fall as a diagnostic test to aid teachers in planning for the year. Also from this center came achievement tests for the armed forces in World War II; the qualifying tests for the National Merit Scholarships in 1957; and the ACT program—a competitor,

especially in the Midwest and West, for ETS's SAT. The Merit Scholars had scholarships for use in the college of their choice provided by a large number of firms in the private sector as a very visible nongovernmental effort to help America catch up in the space race.

Three Recent Evaluation Programs

Three more recent large-scale testing programs are worthy of mention in a chapter on history. John C. Flanagan, with a long history of test development for military and commercial use, secured federal funding for a census of ability in the secondary schools to coincide with the traditional 1960 census. Russia's launching of Sputnik, which preceded launches by the U.S. space program, caused people in general and the Congress in particular to be concerned about the quality of American education. Flanagan's Project TALENT included use of a wide-ranging battery of specially constructed aptitude, achievement, interest, and temperament tests and inventories with a representative sample of about 400,000 students in 9th through 12th grades from more than 1,000 schools in 1960. The grand plan called for following up each cohort 1, 5, 10, 15, and 20 years after high school graduation (Flanagan, 1962). The Project TALENT tests were used as anchor tests to calibrate several tests used by the armed forces and the General Aptitude Test Battery. Several of the Project TALENT instruments resulted in commercially published inventories (e.g., the Planning Career Goals and other value and interest scales for career exploration).

"Personality tests" were not in public favor at the time. Outrage toward items such as "I like to sit in the bathtub and think" resulted in the burning of tests in Houston and elsewhere. As a result, Flanagan decided to use a "student activity blank" instead and not mention "personality" in the Project TALENT battery (Hoch, 1959).

Even more recently, in 1969 Ralph Tyler got back into the business of large-scale testing of the young people of America with the criterion referenced National Assessment of Educational Progress (NAEP), with large-scale federal funding. NAEP, an attempt was made to describe the knowledge, understanding, and skills acquired by the

American population at ages 9, 13, and 17, as well as by adults between 26 and 35. Instead of coming up with estimates of academic achievement, the investigators attempted to determine in each of several content areas: (1) what almost all persons know, (2) what typical or average persons know, and (3) what the most able people of that age level know. Today, assessment of reading, writing, and mathematical skills with NAEP tests is considered to be the report card on the nation's schools (Lapointe, 1984).

The Russians' success in space in the late 1950s is associated also with the National Defense Education Act (1958), which authorized large sums for, among other things, the education and training of many guidance counselors and testing programs in the schools. These funds helped produce thousands of school counselors and provided resources for tests to help them find and effectively guide the talented students of the nation into advanced educational programs that would benefit both the students and the welfare of the nation. By 1965 the program supported administration of 2,000,000 standardized tests in the public elementary schools and 7,000,000 in the secondary schools (U.S. Congress, 1967).

STANDARDS FOR TEST AUTHORS AND PUBLISHERS

The Mental Measurements Yearbooks

Forty-five years after Cattell's listing of the existing mental tests (Cattell, 1890), Oscar Krisen Buros picked up the task with publication of noncritical bibliographies of tests (Buros, 1935, 1936). These publications started Buros on more than 30 years of dedication to editing "yearbooks" and other volumes about existing psychological tests. His first paper of 44 pages included the tests of 1933 and 1934 and was published by the Rutgers University School of Education (Buros, 1935). In 1936, he added the tests he learned about in 1936 and doubled the size of the booklet. For 10 cents more (i.e., 60¢ instead of 50¢), one could get 58 additional pages that included a bibliography and a review or digest of measurement books and monographs (Buros, 1936). Critical reviews were introduced in 1938, and the title was

changed to *The Mental Measurements Yearbook*. However, sales and production complexities did not warrant yearly publication, so the "yearbooks" were preceded by numbers, with *The Fourth Mental Measurements Yearbook* being published in 1953 and *The Fifth . . .* in 1959. The yearbooks supplemented, but did not supplant, earlier volumes. Hence, users would need to look in more than one yearbook to locate and read evaluations of all of the commercially available educational, psychological, and vocational tests and measurements books published in English-speaking countries. *The Fifth . . . Yearbook* (Buros, 1959) contained listings of 957 tests, with more than half being reviewed by more than one authority. In addition, it included 485 reviews of books on measurements and closely related fields, along with 535 excerpts from book reviews from 81 journals.

As more recent yearbooks increased in size with the expanding inventory of tests, weight alone dictated publication of multiple volumes. More recently, electronic processing and communication have enabled Buros's dream of a "yearbook" to become reality. With the continuous updating of entries, today *The Mental Measurements Yearbook* might actually be called a "daybook."

Standards of Professional Associations

By 1951, committees on test standards appointed by the APA, the American Educational Research Association (AERA), and the National Council on Measurements Used in Education (NCMUE, later NCME) were appointed to prepare technical recommendations with regard to test standards. Initially, they intended to publish four separate manuals on ability, achievement, interest and personality, based on the work of different committees. However, the similarities found in early drafts suggested that the brochures would be more similar than different and that the differences would be very disturbing to consumers. It was resolved that APA would publish a volume on ability, interest, and personality, and that the AERA and NCME would publish one on achievement through the National Education Association (APA, Committee on Psychological Tests, 1955). Copies of letters from various committee members on file in the Library of Congress

Archives suggest that a number of strong personalities were present on the joint committee. To produce one volume (*Standards for Educational and Psychological Tests and Manuals;* APA, 1955) representing the various views and constituencies 10 years later required many deliberations, political compromises, and replacement of several committee members. Construct validity was only one of many topics about which consensus was difficult to obtain (Cronbach, 1954). But after final agreement on the content of one volume, an updated version has been prepared jointly by a committee representing the three organizations (APA, AERA, and NCME) about every 10 years. These are the standards (for the current version, see APA, 1986) to which each test should be compared before use.

USE OF TESTS TODAY

Today, testing in the United States is big business. Whereas in most countries educational testing is a function of the state, in this country more than 100 firms publish tests. Each year more than 20 million school students take standardized tests. Another 2–3 million students are evaluated or re-evaluated for special education services each year. About 2.5 million take the SAT or the ACT exam for college admission, and another 1.5 million tests are given to persons seeking entry to one of the professions or occupations regulated by state, local, or federal governments. Millions of others take tests administered by the U.S. Employment Service, the military services, and personnel offices in businesses and industries throughout the land.

With all of these tests being administered, scored, and interpreted, there has been concern expressed as to the amount of professional time involved in assessment. A current trend that is quite noticeable is the transferral of the actual test administration, and at times the test interpretation, to computing machinery. One need only look in the advertisement section of many professional journals to see the plethora of software products available that give tests, score them, and/or interpret assessment results. Professional opinions, as opposed to objective test results, are actually being used in some

software packages designed to yield classification decisions (McDermott & Watkins, 1985). We may hope that this "more objective" treatment of assessment information will benefit persons who have been evaluated. Certainly the APA (1986) has moved rapidly to promulgate guidelines to assure that these new assessment procedures meet both technical and ethical considerations.

REFERENCES

Allport, G. W., Vernon, P. E., & Lindzey, G. (1931). *Study of values: A scale for measuring the dominant interests in personality.* Boston: Houghton Mifflin.

American Psychological Association (APA). (1986). *Guidelines for computer-based tests and interpretations.* Washington, DC: Author.

American Psychological Association (APA). (1965). *Standards for educational and psychological tests and manuals.* Washington, DC: Author.

American Psychological Association (APA). (1985). *Standards for educational and psychological testing.* Washington, DC: Author.

American Psychological Association (APA), Committee on Psychological Tests. (1955, January 31). *Report to the Board of Directors, American Psychological Association.* Washington, DC: Author.

Anastasi, A. (1982). *Psychological testing* (5th ed.). New York: Macmillan.

Angoff, W. H. (1962). Scales with nonmeaningful origins and units of measurement. *Educational and Psychological Measurement, 22,* 27–34.

Angoff, W. H. (1971). *The College Board Admissions Testing Program: A technical report on research and development activities relating to the Scholastic Aptitude Test and achievement tests.* New York: College Entrance Examination Board.

Arvey, R. D. (1979). *Fairness in selecting employees.* Reading, MA: Addison-Wesley.

Ayres, L. P. (1909). *Laggards in our schools: A study of retardation and elimination in city school systems.* New York: Russell Sage Foundation.

Barse, W. J. (1939). *Mental tests for civil service examinations.* New York: Grosset & Dunlap.

Bellak, L., & Bellak, S. S. (1952). *Children's Apperception Test.* New York: CPS.

Bernreuter, R. G. (1933). The theory and construction of the Personality Inventory. *Journal of Social Psychology, 4,* 387–405.

Binet, A. (1911). Nouvelles recherches sur la mésure du niveau intellectuel chez les énfants d'école. *Année Psychologique, 17,* 145–201.

Binet, A., & Simon, T. (1905). Methodes nouvelles pour le diagnostic du niveau intellectuel des anormaux. *L' Année Psychologique, 11,* 191–244.

Bingham, W. V. (1923a). Psychology applied. *Scientific Monthly, 16,* 141–159.

Bingham, W. V. (1923b). Cooperative business research. *Annals of the American Academy of Political Science, 110,* 179–189.

Blackford, K. M. H., & Newcomb, A. (1919). *The job, the man, and the boss.* New York: Doubleday, Page.

Bolton, T. L. (1891). The growth of memory in school children. *American Journal of Psychology, 4,* 362–380.

Boring, E. G. (1929). *A history of experimental psychology.* New York: Appleton-Century.

Bowman, M. L. (1989). Testing individual differences in China. *American Psychologist, 44,* 576–578.

Buros, O. K. (1935). *Educational, psychological, and personality tests of 1933 and 1934* (Rutgers University Bulletin, Vol. 11, No. 11; Studies in Education No. 7). New Brunswick, NJ: School of Education, Rutgers University.

Buros, O. K. (1936). *Educational, psychological, and personality tests of 1936: Including a bibliography and book review digest of measurement books and monographs of 1933–1936* (Rutgers University Bulletin, Vol. 14, No. 2A; Studies in Education No. 11). New Brunswick, NJ: School of Education, Rutgers University.

Buros, O. K. (Ed.). (1959). *The fifth mental measurements yearbook.* Highland Park, NJ: Gryphon Press.

Burt, C. (1909). Experimental tests of general intelligence. *British Journal of Psychology, 3,* 94–177.

Bush, D. V., & Waugh, W. (1923). *Character analysis: How to read people at sight.* Chicago: Huron Press.

Campbell, D. P. (1971). *Handbook for the Strong Vocational Interest Blank.* Stanford, CA: Stanford University Press.

Campbell, D. P., & Hansen, J. C. (1981). *Manual for the SVIB-SCII: Strong–Campbell Interest Inventory* (3rd ed.). Stanford, CA: Stanford University Press.

Cattell, J. M. (1890). Mental tests and measurements. *Mind, 15,* 373–380.

Cattell, R. B. (1947). *The measurement of personality.* Yonkers, NY: World.

Chapman, H. B. (1927). *Organized research in education.* Columbus: Ohio State University Press.

Cronbach, L. J. (1954, October 25). Letter to David V. Tiedeman.

Darwin, C. (1859). *On the origin of species by means of natural selection, or the preservation of favoured races in the struggle for life.* London: John Murray.

Defenbaugh, W. S. (1923, January). *Research bureaus in city school systems* (City School Leaflet No. 5). Washington, DC: U.S. Department of the Interior, Bureau of Education.

Downey, M. T. (1965). *Ben D. Wood, educational reformer.* Princeton, NJ: Educational Testing Service.

Ebbinghaus, H. (1897). Ueber eine neue Methode zur Prüfung geistiger Fähigkeiten und ihre Anwendung bie Schulkindern. *Zeitschrift für Psychologie, 13,* 401–459.

Education for All Handicapped Children Act of 1975, P.L. 94-142, 20 U.S.C. § 1401 (1975).

Edwards, A. L., & Kenney, K. C. (1946). A comparison of the Thurstone and Likert techniques of attitude scale construction. *Journal of Applied Psychology, 30,* 72–83.

Fass, P. S. (1980). The IQ: A cultural and historical framework. *American Journal of Education, 88,* 431–458.

Flanagan, J. C. (1935). *Factor analysis in the study of personality.* Stanford, CA: Stanford University Press.

Flanagan, J. C. (1962). *A survey and follow-up of educational plans and decisions in relationship to aptitude patterns: Studies of the American high school.* Pittsburgh: U.S. Office of Education and the University of Pittsburgh.

Forrest, D. W. (1974). *Francis Galton: The life and work of a Victorian genius.* New York: Taplinger.

Fosbroke, G. E. (1933). *Plus + selling.* Minneapolis: Sales Engineering Institute.

Frank, L. K. (1939). Projective methods for the study of personality. *Journal of Psychology, 8,* 389–413.

Freeman, F. N. (1926). *Mental tests: Their history, principles and applications.* Boston: Houghton Mifflin.

Games, P. A., & Klare, G. R. (1967). *Elementary statistics data analysis for the behavioral sciences.* New York: McGraw-Hill.

Goddard, H. H. (1911). A revision of the Binet Scale. *Training School Bulletin, 8,* 56–62.

Gould, S. J. (1981). *The mismeasure of man.* New York: Norton.

Gross, M. L. (1962). *The brain watchers.* New York: Random House.

Guilford, J. P. (Ed.). (1947). *Printed classification tests* (AAF Aviation Psychology Program Research Report No. 5). Washington, DC: Government Printing Office.

Guilford, J. P. (1973). Theories of intelligence. In B. B. Wolman (Ed.), *Handbook of general psychology* (pp. 630–643). Englewood Cliffs, NJ: Prentice-Hall.

Guilford, J. P., & Lacey, J. I. (Eds.). (1947). *Printed classification tests* (AAF Aviation Psychology Program, Research Report No. 5). Washington, DC: U.S. Government Printing Office.

Gulick, L. H. (1938). *Education for American Life.* New York: McGraw-Hill.

Harvey, D. R. (1970). *The Civil Service Commission.* New York: Praeger.

Hathaway, S. R. (1964). MMPI: Professional use by professional people. *American Psychologist, 19,* 204–210.

Hays, S. W., & Kearney, R. C. (1982). Examinations in the public service. In D. H. Rosenbloom (Ed.), *Centenary issues of the Pendleton Act of 1883: The problematic legacy of civil service reform* (pp. 25–44). New York: Marcel Dekker.

Healy, W., & Bronner, A. F. (1948). The child guidance clinic: Birth and growth of an idea. In L. G. Lowery (Ed.), *Orthopsychiatry 1923–1948: Retrospect and prospect* (pp. 14–49). New York: American Orthopsychiatric Association.

Herrnstein, R. J. (1982, August). IQ testing and the media. *Atlantic Monthly,* pp. 68–74.

Hoch, E. L. (1959, October 22). Personal note to John Darley, American Psychological Association Executive Officer, following an AIR briefing at the Sheraton Park Hotel in Washington, DC.

Humm, D. G., & Wadsworth, G. W. (1935). The Humm–Wadsworth Temperament Scale. *American Journal of Psychiatry, 92,* 163–200.

Jung, C. G. (1910). The association method. *American Journal of Psychology, 21,* 219–269.

Keating–Owen Child Labor Act. (1916). An act to prevent interstate commerce in the products of child labor, and for other purposes (P.L. 64-249). *United States Statutes at Large, 39,* 675–676.

Kelley, T. L. (1914). *Educational guidance: An experimental study in the analysis and prediction of ability of high school pupils* (Contributions to Education No. 71). New York: Teachers College, Columbia University.

Kelley, T. L. (1927). *The interpretation of educational measurement*. Yonkers, NY: World.

Kent, G. H., & Rosanoff, A. J. (1910). A study of association in insanity. *American Journal of Insanity, 67,* 317–390.

Kownslar, A. O., & Frizzle, D. B. (1967). *Discovering American history*. New York: Holt, Rinehart & Winston.

Kuder, G. F. (1934). *Kuder Preference Record—Vocational*. Chicago: Science Research Associates.

Kuder, G. F. (1948). *Kuder Preference Record—Personal*. Chicago: Science Research Associates.

Kuder, G. F. (1956). *Kuder Preference Record—Occupational*. Chicago: Science Research Associates.

Kuder, G. F., & Paulson, B. B. (1949). *Discovering your real interests*. Chicago: Science Research Associates.

Kuder, G. F., & Paulson, B. B. (1950). *Exploring children's interests*. Chicago: Science Research Associates.

Kuhlmann, F. (1912). Binet–Simon's system for measuring the intelligence of children [Monograph supplement]. *Journal of Psycho-Asthenics, 1*(1), 76–92.

Kuhlmann, F. (1922). *Tests of mental development*. Minneapolis, MN: Educational Test Bureau.

Lapointe, A. E. (1984). The good news about American education. *Phi Delta Kappan, 65,* 663–666.

Larry P. v. Riles, No. C-71-2270 RFP (1979) & No. 80-4027 DC, No. CV 71-2270 (9th Cir. 1984).

Learned, W. S., & Wood, B. D. (1938). *The student and his knowledge: A report to the Carnegie Foundation on results of the high school and college examinations of 1928, 1930, and 1932*. New York: Carnegie Foundation for the Advancement of Teaching.

Likert, R. (1932). A technique for the measurement of attitudes. *Archiv für Psychologie 22*.

Link, H. C. (1919). *Employment psychology: The application of scientific methods to the selection, training and grading of employees*. New York: Macmillan.

Lippman, W. (1922, October 25). The mental age of Americans. *New Republic*, pp. 213–215.

Macy, J. W. (1965a). Psychological testing. *American Psychologist, 20,* 883–884.

Macy, J. W. (1965b). Testimony before the Senate Subcommittee on Constitutional Rights of the Committee on the Judiciary, June 7–10. *American Psychologist, 20,* 931–932.

Marks, R. (1976–1977). Providing for individual differences: A history of the intelligence testing movement in North America. *Interchange, 1,* 3–16.

Martens, E. H. (1934, January). *Organization of research bureaus in city school systems* (City School Leaflet No. 14). Washington, DC: Department of Interior, Bureau of Education.

McDermott, P. A., & Watkins, M. W. (1985). *Manual for McDermott Multidimensional Assessment of Children*. San Antonio, TX: Psychological Corporation/Harcourt Brace Jovanovich.

Moore, B. V. (1921). Personnel selection of graduate engineers: The differentiation of apprentice engineers for training as salesmen, designers, and executives of production. *Psychological Monographs, 30,* 1–84.

Morgan, C., & Murray, H. A. (1935). A method for investigating phantasies: The Thematic Apperception Test. *Archives of Neurological Psychiatry, 34,* 289–306.

Munsterberg, H. (1910). *American problems from the point of view of a psychologist*. New York: Moffat, Yard.

Murray, H. A. (1943). *Thematic Apperception Test*. Cambridge, MA: Harvard University Press.

National Defense Education Act of 1958, P.L. 85–864 (September 2, 1958).

National Industrial Conference Board (1948). Experience with employment tests. In *Studies in Personnel Policy No. 92*. New York: Author.

Parents in Action on Special Education (PASE) v. Joseph P. Hannon, No. 74C 3586 (N.D. Ill. 1980).

Parsons, F. (1908). *Choosing a vocation*. Boston: Houghton Mifflin.

Payne, A. F. (1928). *Sentence completions*. New York: New York Guidance Clinic.

Pennsylvania Association for Retarded Children (PARC) v. Commonwealth of Pennsylvania, 334 F. Supp. (1971) 343 F. Supp. 279 (E. D. PA 1972).

Potter, R. E. (1967). *The stream of American education*. New York: Van Nostrand Reinhold.

Pressey, S. L. (1920). Scale of Attainment No. 1: An examination of achievement in the second grade. *Journal of Educational Research, 1,* 572–581.

Pressey, S. L. (1921). A group scale for investigating the emotions. *Journal of Abnormal and Social Psychology, 16,* 55–64.

Rohde, A. R., & Hildreth, G. (1940). *Rohde–Hildreth Sentence Completion Blank*. New York: Psychological Corporation.

Rorschach, H. (1921). *Psychodiagnostik*. Bern: Bircher.

Rotter, J. B., & Willerman, B. (1947). The incomplete sentences test as a method of studying personality. *Journal of Consulting Psychology, 11,* 43–48.

Sattler, J. M. (1974). *Assessment of children's intelligence*. (rev. ed.). Philadelphia: W. B. Saunders.

Sattler, J. M. (1982). *Assessment of children's intelligence and special abilities* (2nd ed.). Boston: Allyn & Bacon.

Sheidman, E. S. (1948). *The Make a Picture Story Test*. New York: Psychological Corporation.

Scott, W. D., Clothier, R. C., & Spriegel, W. R. (1961). *Personnel management: Principles, practices, and a point of view* (6th ed.). New York: McGraw-Hill.

Shaw, M. E., & Wright, J. M. (1967). *Scales for the measurement of attitudes*. New York: McGraw-Hill.

Simpson, B. R. (1912). *Correlation of mental abilities*. New York: Teachers College, Columbia University.

Smith, E. R., Tyler, R. W., and the Evaluation Staff. (1942). *Appraising and recording student progress*. New York: Harper.

Sokal, M. M. (1984). James McKeen Cattell and American psychology in the 1920s. In J. Brozek (Ed.), *Explorations in the history of psychology in the United States* (pp. 273–323). Lewisburg, PA: Bucknell University Press.

Spearman, C. (1904). General intelligence objectively determined and measured. *American Journal of Psychology, 15,* 201–293.

Spranger, E. (1928). *Types of men* (P. J. W. Pigors, Trans.). Halle, Germany: Niemeyer.

Stern, W. (1914). *The psychological methods of testing intelligence*. Baltimore: Warwick & York.

Sumption, M. R. (1941). *Three hundred gifted children*. Yonkers, NY: World.

Symonds, P. M. (1939). Criteria for the selection of

pictures for the investigation of adolescent phantasies. *Journal of Abnormal and Social Psychology, 34,* 271–274.

Symonds, P. M. (1948). *Symonds Picture Story Test.* New York: Bureau of Publications, Teachers College, Columbia University.

Terman, L. M. (1916). *The measurement of intelligence.* Boston: Houghton Mifflin.

Terman, L. M. (1925). *Mental and physical traits of a thousand gifted children.* Stanford, CA: Stanford University Press.

Terman, L. M., & Merrill, M. (1937). *Measuring intelligence.* Boston: Houghton Mifflin.

Thorndike, E. L. (1912). The permanence of interests and their relation to abilities. *Popular Science Monthly, 18,* 449–456.

Thorndike, E. L. (1918). The nature, purposes, and general methods of measurements of educational products. In G. M. Whiffle (Ed.), *Seventeenth yearbook, Part II* (pp. 16–24). Bloomington, IL: National Society for the Study of Education.

Thorndike, R. L., Hagen, E. P., & Sattler, J. M. (1986). *Technical manual for the Stanford–Binet Intelligence Scale: Fourth Edition.* Chicago: Riverside.

Thurstone, L. L. (1947). *The dimensions of temperament* (Report No. 42, the Psychometric Laboratory). Chicago: University of Chicago Press.

Thurstone, L. L., & Chave, E. J. (1929). *The measurement of attitude.* Chicago: University of Chicago Press.

Tulchin, S. H. (1940). The preRorschach use of inkblot tests. *Rorschach Research Exchange, 4,* 1–7.

U.S. Civil Service Commission (USCSC). (1884). *First annual report.* Washington, DC: U.S. Government Printing Office.

U.S. Civil Service Commission (USCSC). (1885). *Second annual report.* Washington, DC: U.S. Government Printing Office.

U.S. Congress. (1967). *Notes and working papers concerning the administration of programs authorized under Title V of the National Defense Education Act,* *as amended* (Subcommittee on Education, Committee on Labor and Public Welfare, U.S. Senate, 90th Congress, 1st Session). Washington, DC: U.S. Government Printing Office.

Van Riper, P. P. (1958). *History of the United States Civil Service.* Evanston, IL: Row, Peterson.

Veatch, B. A. (1978). *Historical and demographic influences in the development of a situation specific model of school psychological services.* Unpublished doctoral dissertation, University of Cincinnati.

Wadsworth, G. W., Jr. (1941). The Humm–Wadsworth Temperament Scale at work. In *Studies in Personnel Policy No. 32.* New York: National Industrial Conference Board.

Wallin, J. E. W. (1914). *The mental health of the school child.* New Haven, CT: Yale University Press.

Wechsler, D. (1949). *Manual for the Wechsler Intelligence Scale for Children.* New York: Psychological Corporation.

Wechsler, D. (1981). *Manual for the Wechsler Adult Intelligence Scale—Revised.* New York: Psychological Corporation.

Whyte, W. H., Jr. (1954, September). The fallacies of "personality" testing. *Fortune,* 117–119, 204–208.

Whyte, W. H., Jr. (1956). *The organization man.* New York: Simon & Schuster.

Wiebe, R. (1967). *The search for order, 1877–1920.* New York: Hill & Wang.

Witmer, L. (1907). Clinical psychology. *Psychological Clinic, 1,* 1–9.

Woodworth, R. S. (1918). *Personal data sheet.* Chicago: Stoelting.

Yerkes, R. M. (1921). Psychological examining in the United States Army. In R. M. Yerkes (Ed.), *Memoirs of the National Academy of Sciences* (Vol. 15). Washington, DC: U.S. Government Printing Office.

Yerkes, R. M., Bridges, J. W., & Hardwick, R. S. (1915). *A point scale for measuring mental ability.* Baltimore: Warwick & York.

2

Measurement and Design Issues in Child Assessment Research

TIMOTHY Z. KEITH
Virginia Polytechnic Institute and State University

CECIL R. REYNOLDS
Texas A&M University

Both the content and the quality of published child assessment research are diverse. We conduct research on instruments varying from projective personality measures to intelligence tests to rating scales. And that research ranges from the simple correlation of one measure with another to sophisticated investigations of the relation between evoked cortical potentials and measured intelligence. Given the diversity in assessment research, it may seem fruitless to attempt to survey the body of research and come up with recommendations. Nevertheless, there do seem to be a number of problems common to much assessment research; each is discussed briefly below. (Much of this discussion is adapted from Keith, 1987.)

This chapter first focuses on needs in the design of assessment research, such as the need for consistency between research design and available theory. We then briefly skim over the normal basics of measurement research—reliability and validity—so that we can concentrate on several other topics in more depth. In particular, we discuss several complex research methods that are becoming increasingly common in assessment research (e.g., exploratory and confirmatory factor analysis; multiple regression analysis and path analysis), and we discuss one productive avenue of assessment research (test bias methods).

PROBLEMS AND NEEDS IN ASSESSMENT RESEARCH

Consistency with Theory

All too frequently, assessment research seems to pay little attention to relevant theory. Consider the following hypothetical, but realistic, examples.

1. Researchers administer several measures each of achievement and intelligence and then use multiple regression analysis to predict each measure from the others.
2. Researchers discover ethnic group differences in mean scores on a new test of intelligence (or achievement); they conclude that the test may be biased.

The common difficulty with these two studies is the unclear role of theory in the development of the research problem and interpretation of the results. In the first example, the researchers have essentially predicted everything from everything, a confusing process that quickly will become unmanageable. It is as if the researchers cannot decide which variable—achievement or intelligence—is the "cause" and which is the "effect." Yet a cursory glance at available theories of learning (e.g., Carroll, 1963; Walberg, 1981) suggests that intelligence should only be used to predict achievement, not the reverse.

The intelligence–achievement example may seem absurdly obvious, but what if the measures collected include adaptive behavior and achievement measures, instead? Should adaptive behavior be used to predict achievement (adaptive behavior as the "cause"), or vice versa? In this case, formal theory may provide little help in framing the research, but informal theory certainly can help; federal law and definitions of mental retardation *implicitly* assume that adaptive behavior should have some effect on learning or achievement (Oakland, 1983). It appears, then, that adaptive behavior should predict achievement, rather than the reverse; informal theory has helped guide the research.

These examples also illustrate some of the frustrations and problems in assessment research. Much of that research is nonexperimental in nature. There is no active manipulation of an independent variable, after which change in the dependent variable can be measured. Rather, each variable—achievement and intelligence or adaptive behavior—is measured, with the researchers deciding which is the independent variable (cause) and which is the dependent variable (effect). As noted elsewhere (e.g., Keith, 1988), theory is especially important for the valid analysis of nonexperimental research. The second example (test bias research) is almost atheoretical. Theories of intelligence and achievement consistently acknowledge the importance of home environment for the development of those skills. It is also well known that there are unfortunate differences in the environments of U.S. ethnic groups. If home environment affects these skills, and if there are differences in the home environments of different groups, then group intelligence or achievement differences should not be surprising. Indeed, this is one reason why the mean-score definition of test bias is almost universally rejected (cf. Salvia & Ysseldyke, 1988, p. 468).

Assessment research should also be consistent with—or at least consider—basic measurement theory (and statistical reality). Consider the following two examples.

1. A new intelligence test is administered to a group of students who were classified as gifted based, in part, on another commonly used intelligence scale. The new scale produces lower scores, on average, than did the previous measure.

2. An achievement test is administered to the same group, and its correlation with the intelligence test, although statistically significant, is of only moderate magnitude, and is considerably less than with normal samples.

Given these results (and they are to be expected), many readers and too many researchers would conclude that caution is warranted in using and interpreting the new intelligence scale; however, that conclusion might well be completely erroneous. (A quick perusal of validity research with the McCarthy Scales of Children's Abilities or the Kaufman Assessment Battery for Children [K-ABC] following their introduction would show that neither of these examples is unusual.) Such a conclusion is not warranted because similar results would be expected on purely statistical grounds. In the first example, we expect the group to score lower on the second test as a result of regression to the mean. Any group that is discrepant from the mean will probably score closer to the mean upon the administration of a second test. It matters little whether the same test is administered twice or whether two different tests are administered (although we would expect to see less change if one test were administered twice). Regression to the mean will occur; it is a statistical fact, and one that *must* be recognized in research of this type. The degree of change from one administration to the next depends primarily on the correlation between the two measures (which in turn depends on the reliability of measurement, the stability of the trait being measured, and the time lapse between measures; see Linn, 1980; Roberts, 1980) and the degree of discrepancy from the mean.

In the second example, we also expect a lower correlation between the two tests simply because of the reduction in variance resulting from using a selected group (e.g., gifted students). There is less variation (i.e., lower variance and standard deviation) in the selected group, and since the correlation between the two measures depends in part on the degree of variation, it too is lowered. Indeed, Linn (1983) has shown how a substantial positive correlation between two tests can become a large negative correlation simply as a result of preselection of a sample and restriction of range!

Researchers who conduct research with such discrepant groups must be aware when statistical phenomena, such as regression to the mean and restriction of range, are operating, and must take those phenomena into account when interpreting results.

Consistency with Practice

Assessment research should be more consistent with normal assessment practice. It is not unusual to see research in which a criterion such as achievement is predicted from a variety of other measures. For example, stepwise multiple regression analysis might be used to predict teacher ratings of achievement from the subtest scores of an intelligence test and an achievement test. In such an analysis, the first variable to enter the equation would probably be one of the achievement subtests, followed by whichever measure correlated well with the criterion, but was least redundant with the first-loading subtest; a nonverbal intelligence subtest would be a likely candidate. The ultimate result would be a hodgepodge of achievement and intelligence subtests predicting teacher ratings. Such research is often conducted to provide information about the validity of one of the instruments being used, but it is debatable whether the research as outlined provides that information.

The question addressed by this research is this: Which subsets of the two tests used can best predict teacher ratings of achievement? Unfortunately, this research bears little resemblance to normal practice, and therefore tells us little beyond the efficiency of group prediction. Few psychologists use bits and pieces of instruments in their assessment. School psychologists, for example, commonly administer standardized tests of intelligence and achievement to children who are referred for school problems, and then combine that information with observations, background information, and interview information before making a prediction about a child's future performance. If the goal in the present example is to learn something about the validity of the achievement test in this process, a better approach might be to use

hierarchical multiple regression analysis (discussed later) to determine whether the achievement measure improves the prediction of ratings above that accomplished by the intelligence measure alone. This approach is slightly more consistent with practice than is the initial stepwise approach. Even so, there are inconsistencies of which readers and researchers alike should be aware: The regression approach seeks to *reduce* redundancy among measures, whereas redundancy is often desired in actual assessment practice (Keith, 1987, p. 284). Nevertheless, other things being equal, when assessment research is consistent with normal practice, it will inform that practice more than when it is not. Phillips's (1982) "research-in-action" approach has much to offer academics and practitioners alike in this arena.

Hypothesis Testing

Another area of need in much assessment research is for the use of a hypothesis-testing approach. As an example, researchers might administer a new intelligence test to a sample of 50 children, along with commonly used measures of intelligence and achievement, in an effort to investigate the validity of the new scale. In a normal population, all of the correlations among these instruments would probably be significant, and all too often the researchers would conclude with some vague statements to the effect that the research supports the validity of the new scale.

A central problem with this type of research is that no real hypothesis is being tested. Simply reporting the significance of correlations does little to inform decisions about validity. Yet a very salient hypothesis *could* be tested: whether this new scale measures intelligence rather than simply academic achievement. Since correlations can be computed between the new scale and both an existing intelligence test and an existing achievement test, the researchers could easily compare the two correlations. If the intelligence–intelligence correlation were significantly higher than the intelligence–achievement correlation, the researchers would have better evidence of the validity of the new intelligence scale. Such research might be particularly salient when there is debate concerning what the new scale in fact measures; the Woodcock–Johnson cognitive scales are a good example (see Cummings & Moscato, 1984a, 1984b; Thompson & Brassard, 1984; for more information concerning hypothesis testing in correlational analysis, see Lindeman, Merenda, & Gold, 1980, pp. 49–54).

The problem of no testable hypothesis is not necessarily a function of the type of analysis being performed. Sophisticated factor analyses can suffer from the same faults. A joint factor analysis of the Wechsler Intelligence Scale for Children—Revised (WISC-R), the K-ABC, and the Wide Range Achievement Test (WRAT) would tell us little if interpreted in the usual fashion (i.e., performing the analysis and naming factors), because without a specific purpose it makes little sense to factor-analyze intelligence and achievement tests in combination. On the other hand, if we were testing whether the K-ABC achievement tests are better measures of achievement or intelligence, such an analysis might be very useful (cf. Keith & Novak, 1987).

It is easier to draw meaningful conclusions from research results when that research has tested specific hypotheses or research questions. And this seemingly obvious statement applies to assessment research just as it does to other types of research. For this reason, Landy (1986) has recently argued that the traditional validity "trinity"—content, concurrent, and construct validity—should be replaced with a general hypothesis-testing approach. We also argue for that approach, or, alternatively, for a research question approach (e.g., "What are we assessing?" and "Why are we assessing it?"; see Keith, 1987). In line with current psychometric thought that all validity is a subset of construct validity, using a carefully constructed research question approach may well lead to more, and more empirically validated, applications of tests as well.

RESEARCH METHODOLOGIES

The Basics of Assessment Research

Reliability

"Reliability of measurement" refers to the accuracy, reproducibility, or constancy of a device. If one gave the same test over and over (with no effects from the repeated testing), would the results be the same each time? To what degree would the results of the assessments differ? Although a variety of methods are used to estimate reliability, all methods attempt to address this essential question. The topic of reliability is well covered in most introductory assessment texts, and only a few salient points are made here.

If reliability can be considered constancy of measurement from a conceptual level, at a theoretical level it is defined as the square of the correlation of obtained scores with true scores (Kenny, 1979, Ch. 5; Kerlinger, 1986, Ch. 26). Of course we never know the true scores, so the best we can do is to *estimate* the reliability of a test. We do so through a variety of methods—correlating alternate forms of a test, or correlating odd with even items—but in each case we are attempting to estimate the same basic construct, the extent to which obtained scores correspond with true scores.

Each method of estimating reliability does so slightly differently, and, as a result, is also confounded with other information. Test–retest reliability estimation is a function both of the reliability of the test *and* of the stability of the construct being measured, for example, and these confounding factors should be considered when evaluating the adequacy of a reliability coefficient.

The need for reliable assessment devices is universal across types of measurement. It is just as important to establish the reliability of observational, curriculum-based, and personality assessments as it is to establish the reliability of normative achievement tests. Furthermore, although the methods of calculation of reliability may differ for different types of assessment, most still fit within the traditional triad (internal-consistency, test–retest, and alternate-forms reliability). The interobserver reliability estimated for behavioral assessments is conceptually similar to alternate-forms reliability with traditional assessments, for example.

Validity

All readers are no doubt familiar with the traditional categorizations of validity: content, criterion-related (including concurrent and predictive), and construct validity. Like reliability, these topics are well covered in most basic tests, and only a few points will be made here.

Readers of research are also undoubtedly aware of the considerable overlap among those categories, particularly the criterion and construct categories. Suppose a new test of intelligence is correlated with an existing measure. Should this be considered a test of concurrent criterion-related validity, with the old test considered a closely related criterion, or should this be considered a test of construct validity, with the old test accepted as a valid measure of that construct? In fact, the validity triad is simply a well-accepted categorization, similar to the levels-of-measurement categorization (nominal, ordinal, interval, ratio) that all beginning students of measurement are required to memorize. Both provide useful guidelines and structure and help in the initial understanding of the topic. Both are simply categorizations, and neither should be grasped too tightly; a rigid adherence to the categorizations can obscure important points. "The number of validity analyses available is limited only by the creativity and experience of the analyst. There are certainly more than three" (Landy, 1986, p. 1186). Landy further argues that validation research is best considered as hypothesis testing, with the primary hypothesis being "people who do well on test X will do well on activity Y" (p. 1186).

The traditional validity categorization should not be discarded; rather, those who read and conduct research should realize that the traditional categories are simply a subset of a more general approach. Another alternative is to approach validity research as answering research questions. Common questions that assessment research attempts to answer include the following: "What are we assessing?" "Are we assessing it well?" "Why are we assessing it?" and "What happens as a result of our assessments?" (Keith, 1987; see also Cronbach, 1971).

Variance Definitions of Reliability and Validity

Classical test theory's variance definitions of reliability and validity are useful for un-

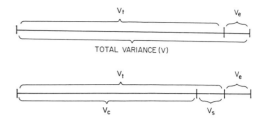

FIGURE 2.1. Variance definitions of reliability and validity. Variance in test scores may be due to true-score variation (V_t), or error variance (V_e). True-score variation may be further divided into common variance (V_c) and specific variance (V_s), as in the bottom half of the figure. Reliability is a function of V_t; validity is a function of V_c.

derstanding these two constructs and the relation between them. Briefly, a person's score on a test is a product of two things: that person's true (but unknown) score, and error. Similarly, the variance in a set of scores is a function of true-score variance (V_t) and error variance (V_e):

$$V = V_t + V_e$$

This relation is displayed pictorially in Figure 2.1. Using this definition, reliability is simply the proportion of true-score variance (V_t) to total variance (V). If a test is error-laden, it is unreliable. Conversely, if scores on a test are primarily the result of the test takers' *true* scores, the test is relatively reliable.

The true-score variance, a reflection of the reliability of the test, may also be subdivided. Suppose we administer several measures of reading comprehension. One measure requires children to read a passage and point to a picture that describes the passage read; the second requires the child to fill in a blank with a missing word; and the third requires the child to act out a sentence or passage (e.g., "Stick out your tongue"). Each method measures reading comprehension, and may do so very reliably. But each method also measures something else in addition to reading comprehension. In the first case, the child has to comprehend the passage, but also has to be able to recognize and interpret a picture depicting that passage; in the third measure, we are also requiring the child to be able to translate the passage into action. In other words, each method measures reading comprehension, but each also measures something *specific* to that measure, although both components may be measured reliably. Of course, the degree to which each test measures reading comprehension is the validity of that test. In Figure 2.1, we can further divide the V_t (reliability) into the variance each measure shares with the other (V_c, or common variance, in this example representing reading comprehension), and the variance that is specific to the test (V_s, representing pictorial understanding, etc.). As is the case with reliability, the validity of the test is simply the proportion of common variance to total variance (V_c/V). The relation of validity to reliability is clear using this definition: We may consider validity as simply a subset of reliability. This, then, is the reason for the rule learned (and often confused) by students of measurement: A test cannot be valid unless it is reliable (or "all valid tests are reliable; no unreliable tests may be valid; reliable tests may or may not be valid"; Salvia & Ysseldyke, 1988, p. 141). For a more complete discussion of these issues, see Kerlinger (1986, Chs. 26, 27), from which much of this discussion was borrowed (see also Guilford, 1954).

Factor Analysis

Factor analysis is becoming an increasingly common tool in assessment research. Fifteen years ago, it was unusual to see reports of factor analyses in the research literature, but now they are almost commonplace. The recent introduction of the K-ABC was greeted by a flurry of factor analyses (e.g., Kaufman & Kamphaus, 1984; Keith, 1985), and the latest version of the Stanford–Binet probably awaits a similar fate. The use of factor analysis to create composite variables (e.g., from several survey items) should also become commonplace (cf. Keith & Cool, 1990).

Factor analysis is useful because it can help answer the central question of validity—what it is that we are measuring. There are two primary types of factor analysis. Exploratory factor analysis is much more common, and most readers are probably acquainted with the technique. Still, confirmatory factor analysis (CFA), a newer and much more theory-

bound approach, promises to become an important tool in assessment research.

Exploratory Factor Analysis

Mathematically, exploratory factor analysis is nothing more than a reduction technique; it reduces many measures into few. It does so by grouping together those measures or scales that correlate highly with each other, and by grouping them separately from tests with which they do not correlate. Essentially, factor analysis is an efficient method of establishing convergent and discriminant validity.

Psychologically, we believe that factor analysis helps establish what it is those various scales measure, or the underlying "traits" or skills that result in the scores we get. The primary reason why two scales correlate highly is that they measure the same thing. And if those two scales do not correlate well with two other tests, a primary reason is that they measure something fundamentally different, especially if all four scales are measured using similar methods. Tests that measure something in common form a factor in a factor analysis; tests that measure something different form a separate factor.

An Informal Analysis. Table 2.1 shows a hypothetical correlation matrix for six tests, including three reading and three arithmetic tests. The correlations are made up, and are intended as for illustrations only; correlation matrices are never this neat. An inspection of the matrix shows that the three reading tests correlate highly with each other (in the .60–.75 range) and that the three arithmetic tests correlate highly with each other (.58–.81), but that the reading tests do not correlate well with the arithmetic tests (.01–.20). We have, in essence, two clusters of tests, one for reading and one for arithmetic, and this "eyeball factor analysis" can serve as the conceptual basis for understanding factor analysis. Factor analysis does something like this eyeball analysis, but efficiently and mathematically.

A Primer on How to Conduct a Factor Analysis. In practice, factor analysis is best conducted using computers, and there are

TABLE 2.1. Hypothetical Correlations among Six Reading and Mathematics Tests

Test	1	2	3	4	5	6
1. Reading Recognition	1.00					
2. Reading Comprehension 1	.64[a]	1.00				
3. Reading Comprehension 2	.60[a]	.75[a]	1.00			
4. Arithmetic Computation 1	.10	.05	.03	1.00		
5. Arithmetic Computation 2	.01	.13	.07	.81[b]	1.00	
6. Arithmetic Reasoning	.06	.16	.20	.63[b]	.58[b]	1.00

[a]The reading "factor."
[b]The arithmetic "factor."

many programs available to do a variety of types of factor analyses. The correlation matrix shown in Table 2.1 was used as the input for a factor analysis conducted using the Statistical Package for the Social Sciences (SPSS-X) subprogram Factor. A number of choices are required in using this or other such programs. The first choice is the type of analysis to be conducted. Here, we have used principal-factors analysis (PFA), probably the most common technique. The essential features of PFA may be illustrated by contrasting it with another common procedure, principal-components analysis (PCA). Although these two procedures often produce similar results, they are conceptually very different. PCA analyzes all the variance in the set of scores (or V from Figure 2.1), whereas PFA endeavors to analyze only the variance that is common among the measures (V_c in Figure 2.1). To accomplish these ends, PCA performs the analysis on the correlation matrix; PFA also begins with the correlation matrix, but substitutes an initial estimate of the common variance, squared multiple correlations (the square of the multiple correlation obtained when each measure in the factor analysis is predicted from all other measures) in the diagonal of the correlation matrix, rather than the 1.00s normally there. In other words, each measure in the PFA is predicted from all other measures, and the square of the multiple correlation coefficient is used as the initial estimate of the common variance, or communality. The square of the multiple correlation predicting reading recognition from Reading Comprehension 1 and 2, Arithmetic Computation 1 and 2, and Arithmetic Reasoning ($R^2 = .505$) would be inserted in place of 1.00 in the top left (row 1, column 1) of Table 2.1. These values are used as initial estimates, and the program then gradually improves these estimates through a series of iterations. Thus, articles discussing PFA will often note parenthetically "communalities estimated by squared multiple correlation," or "R^2s in the diagonal," and those using PCA will note "1.00s in the diagonal."

How many factors? Once a factor method has been chosen, the next choice required is the number of factors to be retained in the factor analysis. As noted above, the mathematical purpose of factor analysis is to reduce many things into a few, so some reduction is necessary. But how much reduction? There are no hard-and-fast rules, and therefore the process is a mixture of habit, subjectivity, and judgment. Probably the most common method is to retain factors with eigenvalues greater than 1.00. An eigenvalue may be thought of an indication of the size of (variance accounted for by) a factor, and these are computed as an initial step in the factor analysis. Factors with eigenvalues of less than 1.00 are generally considered trivial, and, in this approach, are not analyzed. For the data presented in Table 2.1, the first three eigenvalues are 2.61, 2.08, and 0.52; if we were using the eigenvalue criterion, we would retain only two factors in the factor analysis.

Another common technique for determining the number of factors to retain is the scree test (Cattell, 1966), in which the eigenvalues are plotted and a decision is made about how many factors to retain based on changes in the slope of the line drawn through the eigenvalues (for more information, see Cattell, 1966, or Kim & Mueller, 1978). It is also common for researchers to decide in advance, based on theory, how many factors to retain. In the present example, it would be perfectly reasonable to decide to retain only two factors, one representing reading and the other arithmetic. Finally, it is common to combine these

TABLE 2.2. Unrotated Factor Loadings of Six Reading and Mathematics Tests

Test	Factor 1	Factor 2
Reading Recognition	.49	.51
Reading Comprehension 1	.65	.61
Reading Comprehension 2	.61	.59
Arithmetic Computation 1	.70	−.62
Arithmetic Computation 2	.67	−.55
Arithmetic Reasoning	.59	−.35

Note. This factor analysis is based on the hypothetical correlation matrix shown in Table 2.1.

and other methods of deciding how many factors to retain, or to compare several approaches and use the one whose results make the most "psychological sense."

Factor rotation. The factor analyst also needs to choose a technique for rotating the factors, because the initial results of the factor analysis, without rotation, are often uninterpretable. Table 2.2 shows the initial results of a factor analysis of the six reading and arithmetic tests from the correlation matrix in Table 2.1. We used PFA (communalities estimated by squared multiple correlations), and retained two factors with eigenvalues greater than 1.00. The "factor loadings" are shown in Table 2.2, and they represent the correlations of each test with the two hypothetical factors. An examination of the factor loadings helps us name the factors, because it helps us understand the trait, skill, or characteristic measured by each factor. But the results shown in Table 2.2 do not provide much illumination; all of the tests load highly on the first factor, and there is a mixture of high positive and high negative loadings on the second factor.

Suppose, however, we plot the factor loadings shown in Table 2.2, using the two values for each test as points on X and Y axes, with the axes representing the two factors. This has been done in Figure 2.2. The X axis represents loadings for Factor 1, and the Y axis Factor 2. The point shown for Test 1 (Reading Recognition), then, represents a value of .49 on Factor 1 (X) and .51 on Factor 2 (Y). With this graphic representation of

factors, two clusters of tests again become evident. And since the placement of the axes is arbitrary, we are free, now that we have the points plotted, to *rotate* the axes to make the factors more interpretable. In the bottom of Figure 2.2, we have simply rotated the X and Y axes a few degrees clockwise—the old axes are shown as dotted lines, the new axes as solid lines. With this rotation, we see that one factor is primarily related to Tests 1, 2, and 3, and the other factor to Tests 4, 5, and 6. And with the rotated axes, the factor loadings also become more interpretable. With rotation, the reading tests (1–3) load highly on Factor 2 and the arithmetic tests (4–6) load highly on Factor 1 (the rotated factor loadings are shown in Table 2.3).

There are, of course, different methods available for rotation. The graphic method used in this example is one method, but it is difficult when the factors are not so clear-cut and when there are more than two factors. It is also too disconcertingly subjective for many researchers (although it is less subjective than presented here; cf. Carroll, 1985; Harman, 1976; Thurstone, 1947). Analytic methods are therefore more common. Orthogonal rotation techniques (e.g., varimax) are the most common, and simply specify that the factors are uncorrelated, or graphically, the factors are perpendicular (90° apart, as in Figure 2.2). Oblique rotations, allowing the factors to be correlated, are more common among British researchers (e.g., Eysenck, 1979).

Oblique rotations are probably more

TABLE 2.3. Rotated Factor Loadings for the Six Reading and Mathematics Tests

Test	Factor 1	Factor 2
Reading Recognition	.03	.71
Reading Comprehension 1	.08	.89
Reading Comprehension 2	.06	.85
Arithmetic Computation 1	.93	.00
Arithmetic Computation 2	.87	.03
Arithmetic Reasoning	.67	.13

Note. This factor analysis is based on the hypothetical correlation matrix shown in Table 2.1.

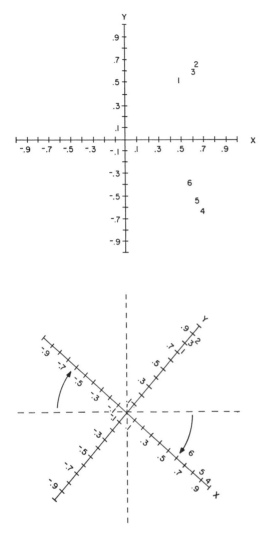

FIGURE 2.2. The unrotated factor solution of six hypothetical reading and arithmetic tests (top). In the bottom half of the figure, the reference axes are rotated 40° clockwise to allow easier interpretation of the factors.

theoretically defensible when we are analyzing such things as intelligence tests, because we know that the different components of intelligence (e.g., verbal and nonverbal intelligence) are correlated (because they both also measure general intelligence); however, orthogonal rotations are generally easier to interpret. They are also often more useful clinically, since they maximize the distinctions that can be made among theoretically related constructs. Nevertheless, in our experience, the two types of rotation often

yield similar results. Of course, if a *hierarchical* factor analysis is desired (a factor analysis of factors), then the rotation should be oblique, because the correlations among factors are what are used as the input for the second-order factor analysis. Indeed, it is generally recognized that *g*, or general intelligence, is best conceived as a higher-order factor resulting from oblique rotation of first- or higher-order factors (Carroll, 1985, pp. 52–53).

Interpretation. Choosing a factoring method, the number of factors, and the rotation method will produce a unique solution for a given set of data. And then comes the hard, but subjective and enjoyable, part: interpreting and naming the factors. Factors are named on the basis of the tests that load highly on them; based on what we know about the tests themselves (what they measure), we can infer something about the factors. If three tests that measure simultaneous mental processing load on the same factor, then that factor may well be a simultaneous factor. With our reading–arithmetic example, this is an easy process. We have three reading tests on one factor, and three math tests on another; Reading and Math Achievement are obvious names for the factors.

In practice, of course, things are never this easy. Tests generally measure a number of different skills. And the factors are never as clean as shown in this example; rather, some loadings on a factor may be large, others moderate, and still others small. The job of the factor analyst is to try to consider all the possible skills or abilities that the tests comprising a factor share in common, and contrast those to the skills shared by tests that do not load on the factor and tests that form different factors. Obviously, the process is subjective and inexact, and this is both a problem and an allure of factor analysis: It is not automatic; it requires skill and judgment. But as a result, different analysts from different orientations may come up with different names, and therefore interpretations, of different factors. For example, the third factor of the WISC-R has been variously interpreted as reflecting freedom from distractibility, short-term memory, or the ability to manipulate numbers mentally (Kaufman, 1979, Ch. 3), and the three factors of the K-ABC have been interpreted as reflecting simultaneous and sequential mental pro-

TABLE 2.4 Rotated Factor Structure of the WISC-R

Subtest	Factor 1	Factor 2	Factor 3
Information	.64*	.28	.36*
Similarities	.65*	.34	.27
Arithmetic	.37*	.22	.59*
Vocabulary	.78*	.25	.33
Comprehension	.65*	.31	.20
Digit Span	.18	.13	.60*
Picture Completion	.33	.56*	.12
Picture Arrangement	.34	.47*	.16
Block Design	.25	.71*	.32
Object Assembly	.23	.69*	.12
Coding	.16	.23	.37*
Mazes	.11	.48*	.21

Note. This analysis is based on the total intercorrelation matrix presented on page 47 of the WISC-R manual (Wechsler, 1974). Significant loadings (> .35) are marked with an asterisk.

cessing and achievement (e.g., Kaufman & Kamphaus, 1984; Kaufman & McLean, 1987) or as reflecting nonverbal reasoning, verbal memory, and verbal reasoning (e.g., Keith, 1985; Keith & Novak, 1987).

Exploratory Analysis of the WISC-R. Table 2.4 shows the results of an exploratory factor analysis of the WISC-R standardization data. The overall correlation matrix from page 47 of the WISC-R manual (Wechsler, 1974) was used as input for the factor analysis, which was PFA followed by varimax rotation.[1] We decided in advance to interpret the three-factor solution, based on earlier research with the WISC-R supporting such solutions (Gutkin & Reynolds, 1981; Kaufman, 1975).

The rotated first factor included significant loadings (defined here as ≥.35) by all of the Verbal tests except Digit Span, and high loadings by all of those except Arithmetic; the factor is obviously a verbal factor and is traditionally labeled Verbal Comprehension. Factor 2 included significant loadings by all of the Performance tests except Coding and

[1]We conducted our own analysis because we later contrast these results with a confirmatory analysis. However, the results reported here are very similar to those reported by Kaufman (1975) in his classic analysis of each age level of the WISC-R, and those reported by Gutkin and Reynolds (1981) in their analysis of factor structures for blacks and whites from the standardization data.

is usually labeled Perceptual Organization to reflect its nonverbal content.

The third factor nicely illustrates the difficulties in interpreting factor-analytic results. It included strong loadings by Digit Span and Arithmetic, and smaller, but significant, loadings by Coding and Information. This factor has traditionally been labeled Freedom from Distractibility, because it is assumed that in order to perform well on the three tests loading on it consistently (Digit Span, Arithmetic, and Coding), a child must be able to tune out distractions and concentrate. But the three tests also require short-term memory skills (and Information requires long-term memory) and the ability to manipulate numbers, so the names Memory or Quantitative are also reasonable (see Kaufman, 1979, for a discussion of this third factor).

This difficulty in interpreting the third factor illustrates the subjectivity of the technique. Different researchers, coming from different orientations, can interpret essentially the same factor structure as meaning different things (for an illustration, compare Jensen, 1984; Kaufman & Kamphaus, 1984; Kaufman & McLean, 1987; Keith, 1985; Keith & Novak, 1987). It is also a truism of factor analysis that one only gets out of the analysis what one puts into it. A nonverbal subtest will behave differently in a factor analysis if analyzed with nothing but verbal subtests than if analyzed with an assortment of verbal and nonverbal scales.

Factor analysis is a major method of establishing construct validity for new tests or scales. In particular, the factor analysis of new instruments in common with better-understood measures can lead to a better understanding of what these new scales measure (e.g., Kaufman & McLean, 1987; Keith & Novak, 1987). Finally, the use of factor analysis as a preliminary step in research will probably increase, and should lead to better measurement of constructs of interest. For example, initial factor analysis of survey items can help a researcher decide which items may be best combined to create a composite variable (cf. Keith & Cool, 1990).

Confirmatory Factor Analysis

Exploratory factor analysis has become fairly common in assessment research with children, but the use of CFA is just beginning.

For those who are disturbed by the subjectivity and looseness of exploratory analysis, CFA can be more reassuring. Unfortunately, it is also more difficult to perform, and can be abused just as exploratory analysis can be.

Differences between Confirmatory and Exploratory Analysis. In exploratory analysis, the researcher decides the technique, the criteria for choosing the number of factors, and the method of rotation. The results of the analysis are then subjectively compared to the expected results, often the actual or theoretical structure of the test being analyzed. In CFA, the researcher specifies in advance the number of factors, which tests load on those factors, and the relations among the factors (i.e., correlated or uncorrelated factors). Tests that are not expected to load on a factor are specified, in advance, as having loadings of 0 on that factor. The results of the analyses include statistics to describe the extent to which the factor structure specified in advance (called the "theoretical model") fits the data analyzed, and how the model might be modified to fit the data better. These fit statistics can be thought of as measures of the "correctness" of the model, and are derived by comparing the original correlation or covariance matrix with the matrix that would result if the model proposed were correct.

CFA also allows the testing of hierarchical factor models with any number of levels of factors (for examples, see Marsh & Hocevar, 1985). Furthermore, CFA tests all levels of the hierarchical analysis in combination. By contrast, for hierarchical exploratory analyses, one level of factors is commonly derived along with the correlations among those factors. The factor correlations are then factor-analyzed in a second step.

An Example: Confirmatory Analysis of the WISC-R. A simplified example will help illustrate CFA. Figure 2.3 is a pictorial representation of the generally accepted theoretical structure (although not the actual structure) of the WISC-R. The circles in the figure represent the "latent" or "unmeasured" variables (the factors), and the unenclosed variables represent the measured variables (the subtests for which scores are generated when the test is given). According to this model, the test first measures g, or

general intelligence. At the second level, there are three factors: a Verbal factor, a Nonverbal factor, and a third factor of unknown origin (these three factors are commonly labeled Verbal Comprehension, Perceptual Organization, and Freedom from Distractibility, respectively). At the third level are the 12 WISC-R subtests. Readers familiar with the WISC-R will recognize this theoretical structure as mirroring Kaufman's (1979) suggested order of interpretation of WISC-R results. The arrows in the model point from the factors to the tests, which may seem unusual at first glance. But this direction nicely illustrates an implicit assumption of factor analysis: The factors represent the constructs that underlie our measurement; they are what we are most interested in because they lead to or cause the scores we get on tests. The factors are reflections of properties of the individuals we are assessing—collections of skills and abilities, traits, or characteristics. These underlying abilities, often termed "latent traits," are what we are interested in assessing.

The overall correlation matrix reported in the WISC-R manual was used as input into the LISREL VI computer program (Jöreskog & Sörbom, 1984) to test the model shown in Figure 2.3. LISREL, which stands for *li*near *s*tructural *rel*ations, analyzes covariance structures, a technique that subsumes CFA. It is the most common method for performing confirmatory factor analysis, although others are available (e.g., EQS [Bentler, 1985], available as a part of BMDP).

Fit of the model. Figure 2.3 also shows some of the results of the analysis. The "goodness-of-fit" data are listed underneath the factor model, and they suggest that this strict factor model provides a relatively good fit to the standardization data. One measure of fit compares chi squared (χ^2) to the degrees of freedom; if the χ^2 is large in comparison to the degrees of freedom, the null hypothesis that the model fits the data is rejected. The probability, listed next, also involves a comparison of these two values, and may be thought of as the probability that the model is correct. Thus, unlike many other types of analyses, what is desired is a *low* χ^2 and a *high* ($\geq.05$) probability. However, both the probability and the χ^2 are dependent on sample size, with even good models being rejected with large samples such as this one (to illustrate, if we had specified an *n* of 200

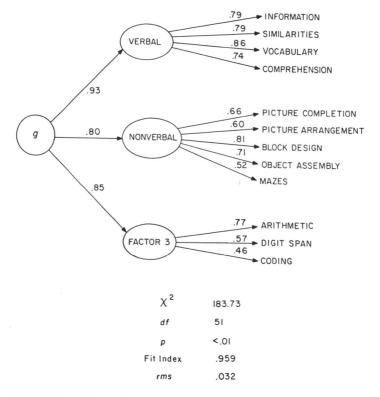

FIGURE 2.3. Hierarchical confirmatory factor structure of the WISC-R.

for these analyses rather than 1,100, the χ^2 would be 33.27, and $p > .50$). Therefore, χ^2 is *not* an appropriate test of significance when large samples are used, although it, along with the degrees of freedom, is very useful for comparing two competing, nested models (i.e., when one model is a subset of another; Bentler & Bonett, 1980).

The adjusted goodness-of-fit index ranges from 0 to 1, with a value of 1 suggesting a perfect fit (see Marsh, Balla, & McDonald, 1988, for a comparison of various fit indices). When a correlation matrix is used as input, the root mean square residual correlation (*rms*) is probably the easiest fit index to interpret. This statistic compares the original correlation matrix to the correlation matrix predicted by the model; the average of the differences between the two is the *rms*. Thus, the correlations predicted by the model shown in Figure 2.3 differ from the actual correlations by only .032, on the average. An *rms* below .10 is generally considered to suggest a good fit (Kerlinger, 1986, Ch. 36).

Taken together, these statistics suggest that the model provides an adequate fit to the data.[2]

Interpretation and respecification. Given this adequate fit, we can next turn to the factor loadings. All of those loadings are significant ($t > 2.0$), and all are substantial. Vocabulary had the strongest loading on Verbal, and Block Design had the strongest loading on Nonverbal. Interestingly, Arithmetic had the strongest loading on the third factor, followed by Digit Span, with a smaller loading by Coding. None of these results are surprising, and are in line with the earlier exploratory analyses. Of more interest are the second-order factor loadings. All three factors had high loadings on the g factor, with an especially high loading by the first-order

[2]We should note, however, that the second level of this model is just identified; that is, the number of correlations among first-order factors is equal to the number of paths from g to the first-order factors. Therefore, these fit statistics do not test the adequacy of this part of the model.

Verbal factor (.93). Interestingly, the third factor had the second strongest loading on this factor (.85)—a finding suggesting that, at least in the "pure" form analyzed here, this factor probably is more cognitive and less behavioral than the name "Freedom from Distractibility" suggests.

Other results reported by LISREL (e.g., modification indices and residuals) may provide hints about how the model proposed could be modified to fit the data better. For example, the residuals (a comparison of the predicted to the original correlation matrix) from this analysis suggest that the model shown here does not adequately account for the correlations between Picture Arrangement and many of the Verbal tests, nor for those between Coding and several of the Performance tests (for more information about model modification and CFA, see Glutting and Kaplan, Chapter 11, this volume). Again, this information can be useful in the modification of a model; however, all such modifications should also be theoretically defensible (MacCallum, 1986).

Uses of Confirmatory Factor Analysis. With its ability to test the adequacy of specific models, CFA can provide a much stronger test of the underlying structure of a scale than exploratory factor analysis, and can be especially useful for tests (such as the K-ABC and the Stanford–Binet Fourth Edition) that are based on a well-articulated underlying theory. CFA should therefore see increased use as a method to evaluate the correspondence between a test and the theory that has guided its construction (e.g., Keith, 1985; Keith, Cool, Novak, White, & Pottebaum, 1988; Strommen, 1988; Willson, Reynolds, Chatman, & Kaufman, 1985). CFA can also be used, and with greater power, to compare alternative theoretical structures for a test (e.g., Keith et al., 1988; Marsh & Hocevar, 1985).

CFA can provide a powerful test of the construct validity of a test, given the presence of a formal or informal theory underlying the scale and the fulfillment of the assumptions underlying the technique. But the technique can also help answer questions about the nature of the constructs that underlie our tests. By testing relations among the *factors* rather than the imperfect tests, CFA can move closer to the construct level,

essentially stripping away much of the error and unique variance that normally cloud our understanding (e.g., Keith, Fehrmann, Harrison, & Pottebaum, 1987).

Multiple Regression Analysis and Path Analysis

Multiple regression analysis has also become a common technique of analysis in child assessment research. Like ordinary correlation and regression, multiple regression allows us to estimate the extent to which a test is related to other measures of the same or related constructs. The difference between the two techniques is that in simple regression we are limited to two variables, whereas in multiple regression we can have multiple predictors of an outcome (and in multivariate multiple regression, multiple outcomes). In the traditional validity trinity, multiple regression can help establish criterion-related validity more powerfully, in many cases, than can simple regression. It is also a very general and flexible technique (most computer programs use multiple regression analysis to perform analysis of variance [ANOVA], for example). Unfortunately, this generality may make the technique confusing for the novice: It can be conducted in a variety of fashions, and when it is completed, a variety of statistics can be interpreted.

Multiple Regression: An Introductory Example

Let us assume that a researcher is interested in determining whether and to what extent children's eighth-grade achievement can be predicted from their second-grade intellectual ability and achievement scores. Table 2.5 shows a fictitious correlation matrix among second-grade intelligence (Ability),

TABLE 2.5. Fictitious Correlations among Second-Grade Intellectual Ability, Second-Grade Achievement (Ach-2), and Eighth-Grade Achievement (Ach-8)

Variable	1	2	3
1. Ability	1.00		
2. Ach-2	.70	1.00	
3. Ach-8	.62	.65	1.00

second-grade achievement (Ach-2), and eighth-grade achievement (Ach-8) for 200 children.

Using simple regression, our best method of predicting Ach-8 would be from Ach-2. But it also appears we could predict almost as successfully using Ability; perhaps we could predict even more accurately using both. This is exactly what multiple regression does: It predicts a criterion from the best linear combination of predictor variables. When multiple regression was used to predict Ach-8 from Ach-2 and Ability, the multiple correlation increased significantly, from .65 (simple r between Ach-8 and Ach-2) to .69 (multiple r, or R); the two variables together accounted for close to 50% of the variance in Ach-8 ($R^2 = .48$). Interestingly, if the two predictor variables, Ability and Ach-2, had been *less* highly correlated with each other, the two would have had a higher multiple correlation with Ach-8 (assuming that their correlations with Ach-8 remained constant).

A common question in this type of analysis is which variable is most important in the prediction of the criterion (here, Ach-8)? Unfortunately, the answer changes, depending on how the regression analysis is conducted and what is interpreted. If we used stepwise regression, a common approach, we would find that Ach-2 explained 42% of the variance in Ach-8, and that Ability explained only approximately 5% more variance (these do not sum to 48% because of errors from rounding); Ach-2 is clearly more important, according to this approach. On the other hand, we could reason that ability is theoretically prior to achievement, and that the Ability variable should therefore enter the regression equation first. Using this approach, we would find that Ability explained 38% of the variance in Ach-8 and that Ach-2 explained only 9% more; Ability seems more important, according to this approach. To confuse matters further, we could also interpret the beta (β) weights from this analysis rather than the R^2 (β's are standardized partial regression coefficients; they, or their unstandardized counterparts, b weights, could be used in actual prediction equations to predict an *individual's* Ach-8 from that person's Ability and Ach-2). Using this approach, we would find β's of .32 for Ability and .42 for Ach-2, suggesting that both are important in

predicting Ach-8, with Ach-2 slightly more important.

Prediction versus Explanation

Stepwise Regression. Stepwise regression is probably the most common multiple regression approach in assessment research, but methodologists generally discourage its use for all but a small portion of such research (e.g., Cohen & Cohen, 1983, Ch. 3; Pedhazur, 1982, Ch. 6). The reason for this condemnation, and also possibly the popularity of the approach, is that stepwise regression is an atheoretical approach.

In stepwise regression, the data, rather than the researcher, decide the order of entry of the variables in the regression equation (and we have already seen how order of entry can affect our conclusions). The variable that has the highest correlation with the criterion is the first to enter the regression equation. The multiple regression program then calculates the partial correlations between each of the remaining variables and the criterion (the partial correlation is the correlation of each variable with the criterion, *with the effects of the variable already in the equation removed*). The variable that can explain the most additional variance is entered next. The joint effects of these two variables are then removed from all of the other correlations, and the variable that can account for the next highest amount of variance is added. The process continues until some criterion for stopping is reached. Commonly, only a certain number of variables are allowed to enter the equation, or some value is set by which R^2 must increase before a variable is entered.

This may seem a perfectly reasonable approach: Let the data decide! And it is reasonable, if our interest is in prediction only. If our only interest were in the best prediction of Ach-8 in the example above, then Ach-2 would seem to offer the single best predictor from among the two variables we used in the equation (but remember that these data are fictitious).

In many cases, however, our intent is not simply prediction, but rather understanding. We may be interested in knowing which variables influence Ach-8, and how that influence works, or we may be interested in the extent to which Ach-2 affects Ach-8, after controlling for the important background variable of Ability. In either of these cases, we are concerned with more than prediction; we are interested in understanding or explaining Ach-8, and stepwise regression does not generally help in this regard.

There are a number of reasons why stepwise regression is not appropriate when we are interested in going beyond prediction, but the most important is that the technique does not generally encompass available theory or previous research. We do not have room to enumerate the reasons here, but multiple regression can produce very misleading results if not guided by theory, or at least by logic. Anything can be regressed against anything, but unless there is some logic for regressing one thing against another, the results are meaningless. Regression results are also very much dependent on the variables used in the analysis. Because the technique looks for *nonredundant* predictors, a variable can appear to be either a good or a poor predictor, based on the choice of the other predictor variables. If we want to interpret regression results as showing the effect or influence of one variable on another (an explanatory approach), then theory must guide both the selection on variables and their order of entry into the regression equation (for a more complete discussion of the need for theory, see Cohen & Cohen, 1983; Keith, 1988; or Pedhazur, 1982).

Hierarchical Regression. One approach that can incorporate theory, and that is therefore useful when explanation is desired, is hierarchical regression. This technique involves entering the variables, either one at a time or in groups, in a predetermined order; changes in R^2 are interpreted as reflections of the importance of each predictor variable. The technique thus has some similarities to stepwise regression, but the researcher, instead of the data, decides the order of entry of variables in the equation.

The order of entry of variables in multiple regression makes a great deal of difference in the variance they explain. The overlapping circles shown in Figure 2.4 illustrate why. In the figure, each circle represents the variance of a variable, and the overlap among the circles represents the variance they share

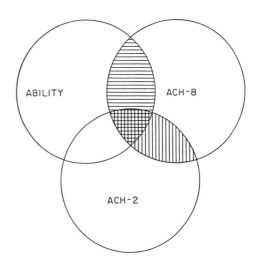

FIGURE 2.4. Unique and shared variance among second-grade intellectual ability (Ability), second-grade achievement (Ach-2), and eighth-grade achievement (Ach-8). The areas of overlap (common variance) are not drawn to scale.

(their covariance, or correlation). For the sake of consistency with the example above, we label these variables Ability, Ach-2, and Ach-8 (the overlap is not intended to be drawn to scale). Some of the variance in ability is shared with Ach-8, as depicted by the horizontally hatched overlap between the two variables. Some of the variance in Ach-2 is shared with Ach-8, as depicted by the vertically hatched area. Finally, some of the variance is shared among all three variables, as depicted by the double-hatched area of overlap; it is this area of overlap that makes the difference in R^2, depending on the order of entry of variables. Using this increase-in-R^2 approach, the first variable to enter the equation (Ability or Ach-2) would be attributed this variance, and the second, even though it is shared variance, would not be attributed any of the variance shared by all three variables. This treatment of shared variance is why the order of entry of variables in the regression equation can have such important effects on the conclusions we draw from the analyses.

Path Analysis

Another theory-based approach to regression is a technique known alternately as "path

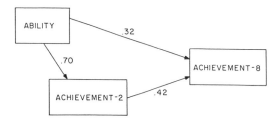

FIGURE 2.5. Path analysis of the effects of Ability and Ach-2 on Ach-8.

analysis," "causal modeling," or "structural equation modeling." In fact, path analysis incorporates a variety of techniques, including multiple regression, factor analysis, and LISREL (LISREL is most easily conceived as a combination of factor analysis and simple path analysis), but uses multiple regression in its simplest form and is a good method for illustrating and understanding multiple regression.

Path analysis begins with a theory displayed figurally as a path model. Essentially, a path model explicitly defines the researchers' theory of which variables affect which (or "cause" and "effect"), with decisions of causal ordering made on the basis of formal and informal theory, time precedence, previous research, and logic. Figure 2.5 shows a path model to explain Ach-8 as a function of Ability and Ach-2. An arrow or path is drawn from Ability to Ach-2, based on presumed time precedence and theory. Ability appears to be fairly stable from at least a preschool level (cf. Jensen, 1980, Ch. 7), and it therefore makes sense to place it before the achievement variables, which are primarily products of schooling. In addition, theories of school learning generally recognize ability or aptitude as an influence on learning or achievement (cf. Carroll, 1963; Walberg, 1981). Paths are drawn from Ability and Ach-2 to Ach-8 for similar reasons, and because second-grade achievement obviously occurs before eighth-grade achievement.

Given the viability of a number of assumptions (e.g., one-way causal flow) the paths may be estimated by the β weights from multiple regression; these are also inserted in Figure 2.5. The paths to Ach-8 were estimated by regressing it on Ability and Ach-2, and the path from Ability to Ach-2 was estimated by regressing Ach-2 on Ability. The paths are interpreted as the portion of a

standard deviation (SD) unit increase (or decrease in the case of negative paths) in the effect for each SD change in the cause. In other words, each SD increase in Ach-2 will increase Ach-8 by .42 SD.

Advantages of Path Analysis. One advantage of path analysis over other regression approaches is that it allows one to focus on indirect effects. In Figure 2.5, for example, Ability has a direct effect on Ach-8 ($\beta = .32$), but Ability also affects Ach-2, which in turn affects Ach-8; this indirect effect of ability on Ach-8 may be calculated by multiplying the two paths (.70 $\times$ .42 = .30).

Path analysis has other advantages as well. It requires an explicit, graphic statement of a researcher's theory of cause and effect, and its interpretation is straightforward; for this reason, path analysis avoids many of the ambiguities that can result from multiple regression. Because of these and other advantages, Keith (1988) has recommended it as the technique of choice when conducting explanatory analysis using nonexperimental data, and Cohen and Cohen go even further: "Although [path or causal analysis is] still new and in the process of rapid development, it seems clear to us that nonexperimental inference that is not consistent with its fundamental principles is simply invalid" (p. 14). The biggest danger in path analysis is that an important common cause (a variable that affects both the primary cause and effect of interest) may not be included in the model. But in a way, this too is an advantage of path analysis; this danger threatens *all* nonexperimental analyses in which the results are interpreted as one variable's effect or influence on another (see Keith, 1988). Because path analysis requires a graphic presentation of what affects what, it is often easier to spot a missing variable than with ordinary multiple regression.

More Complex Procedures. When the assumptions that underlie multiple regression (e.g., reliably measured variables, uncorrelated errors of measurement) are not met, other techniques besides multiple regression are used to estimate the paths. In its most powerful form, path analysis uses LISREL to perform joint CFA (the measurement model) and path analysis (the structural model). The measurement model cleanses the variables of their error to get closer to the construct level; the structural model estimates the effects of the *constructs* on each other. If multiple measures of the three variables shown in Figure 2.5 were available, a LISREL analysis would come closer to telling us the effect of "true" Ability on "true" Ach-8.[3]

We do not wish to oversell the power of LISREL. Although extremely powerful, LISREL has recently become faddish, and its ability to correct problems inherent in nonexperimental research has been exaggerated. The fit statistics of LISREL do not tell us when we have neglected to include an important common cause in our model, and (at least as outlined here) the technique does not tell us when we have drawn arrows in the wrong direction (another danger inherent in any nonexperimental research). The full LISREL model is complex and difficult to master. On the other hand, LISREL is very useful when there are questions concerning the reliability of variables in the model; when the same variable is measured more than once (in longitudinal models); when paths are drawn in two different directions (or when we wish to test for such reciprocal causation); and when several different models are being tested against one another. In the absence of such conditions, however, it makes little sense to add unnecessary complexity when less complex techniques (e.g., path analysis based on multiple regression) would serve just as well. LISREL should be reserved for a "relatively late stage of a research program when 'crucial' tests of complex hypotheses are needed" (Kerlinger, 1986, p. 614).

An Example Comparing Three Regression Approaches

Table 2.6 shows the correlations among the variables Ability, (academic) Motivation, (amount of academic) Coursework, and (aca-

TABLE 2.6. Correlations among Intellectual Ability, Academic Motivation, Academic Coursework, and Academic Achievement for 200 High School Students

Variable	1	2	3	4
1. Ability	1.00			
2. Motivation	.21	1.00		
3. Coursework	.50	.38	1.00	
4. Achievement	.74	.26	.62	1.00

Note. The data are from Keith & Cool (1990).

demic) Achievement for a sample of high school students (the correlations are taken from a larger matrix reported in Keith & Cool, 1990; the sample size was really more than 20,000, but for the purposes of illustration we have used a sample size of 200). Ability, Motivation, and Coursework are commonly recognized influences on learning (or achievement), and appear frequently in theories of school learning (e.g., Walberg, 1981); they are also commonly used as predictors of achievement. In our first analysis, we used stepwise multiple regression to predict Achievement from the other three variables. Ability was the first variable to enter the equation ($R^2 = .54$), followed by Coursework (change in $R^2 = .08$, $p < .01$); Motivation did not lead to a significant increase in the variance explained, and therefore did not enter the equation. Our best conclusion from these results would be that of the predictor variables used, Ability and Coursework are the best predictors of Achievement.

We could easily argue that the order of entry for the stepwise regression is wrong; available theory, research, and logic suggest that ability affects motivation, which in turn affects courses taken and achievement. The three variables were entered in that order in the second step of these analyses. Ability entered the equation first, with the same results, of course, as in the stepwise analysis. When Motivation entered the equation second, it did explain a small but significant amount of additional variance (change in $R^2 = .01$, $p < .05$); Coursework was entered last, and also significantly increased the variance explained (R^2 change $= .07$, $p < .01$). Our conclusion from this analysis would be that all three variables appear to affect Achievement.

[3]In fact, LISREL would be a good choice for estimating this model because it can allow for correlations between the unique variance (error and specific variance) of variables. If the same achievement test were given in second and eighth grades, some of the correlation between the two tests would be due to the correlation between true Ach-2 and true Ach-8, but some of the correlation would be the result of correlations between errors of measurement at the two times and between the specific variance of the test at the two times.

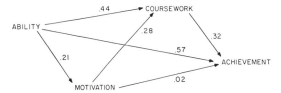

FIGURE 2.6. Effects of Ability, Motivation, and Coursework on Achievement in high school. The data are derived from Keith and Cool (1990).

TABLE 2.7. Direct, Indirect, and Total Effects of Ability, Motivation, and Coursework on Achievement in High School

Variable	Direct effects	Indirect effects	Total effects
Ability	.57*	.17*	.74*
Motivation	.02	.09*	.11*
Coursework	.32*	—	.32*

Note. The data are derived from Keith & Cool (1990).
* $p \leq .05$.

As the third step in this set of analyses, the variables were put into the path model shown in Figure 2.6. To solve for the path model, Ability, Motivation, and Coursework were regressed against Achievement, and the β weights were used as estimates of the paths to Achievement. Ability and Motivation were regressed on Coursework to estimate the paths to Coursework, and Ability was regressed on Motivation to estimate the path to Motivation from Ability. The results of the path analysis are also shown in Figure 2.6, and they may lead to a richer understanding of how the three variables of interest affect Achievement. All of the paths in the model are significant, with the exception of the path from Motivation to Achievement. These results, then, suggest that Motivation has no significant *direct* effect on Achievement, a considerably different conclusion from that reached using the hierarchical approach.

Motivation does appear, however, to have *indirect* effects on Achievement: Motivation affects Coursework ($\beta = .28$), which in turn affects Achievement ($\beta = .32$). Table 2.7 shows the direct (path), indirect, and total (direct + indirect) effect for each of the three variables on achievement; all of the *total* effects are significant. The path results, then, if fully interpreted, not only lead to conclusions similar to those suggested by the other theoretical approach, but also indicate how those effects may operate. It appears that Motivation affects Achievement primarily indirectly: Highly motivated students take more academic coursework, and that Coursework, in turn, increases Achievement.

This example may seem far removed from child assessment and assessment research. Assessment, however, provides the basis for intervention. Successful interventions need to be based on a solid research understanding of just what influences the characteristic we

are trying to change (e.g., achievement). It makes little difference if a variable is a good predictor of that characteristic; if it is not a meaningful *influence* on that characteristic, manipulating it will not produce the desired outcome. Theory and research are crucial to the design of interventions.

Use of Regression in Clinical Diagnosis and Classification Studies

One common use of multiple regression in assessment research is in classification or diagnostic studies. Researchers might use a technique based on multiple regression to see which subset of a larger set of tests could best predict which children are classified as mentally retarded and which as learning-disabled. Many such studies use a related technique, discriminant analysis, in which the criterion of interest is a nominal-level variable (e.g., different diagnostic categories—learning-disabled, mentally retarded, normal) rather than a continuous variable. The similarities between the two techniques are more important at this point than the differences, and both are commonly used in diagnostic studies.

Psychologists have long studied the ability of various tests and other diagnostic methods to differentiate one class of psychopathological disorders from another and to classify individuals correctly into one diagnostic group or another.

To their credit, researchers have recently brought sophisticated multivariate techniques to bear directly on the problem of diagnosis and classification of mental disorders; most such investigations involve regression analysis or related methods. In the quest to provide accurate diagnosis and a breadth of research findings, the typical study evaluates a large array of behaviors. For example, Rourke (1975), in discussing more than 20 years of research in differential diagnosis, reported that children seen in his laboratory and clinic are administered, on a routine basis, the WISC, the Peabody Picture Vocabulary Test, the Halstead Neuropsychological Test Battery for Children, an examination for sensory-perceptual disturbances, the Kløve–Mathews Motor Steadiness Battery, and a number of other tests for receptive and expressive language abilities" (p. 912). Multiple regression would seem an ideal technique for analyzing such data. But multiple regression and related methods are very powerful analytical tools that take advantage not only of fluctuations in performance, but also of any *chance* relations (i.e., correlated error variance) to maximize discriminability and thus determine group membership. Unfortunately, if a large set of variables is used along with a small group of subjects, those subjects can easily be grouped and classified purely on the basis of random or chance variation. The need for large numbers of subjects in such research is crucial.

In the study of clinical disorders, however, one is frequently limited to relatively small samples of convenience rather than larger random samples of design. Although most researchers acknowledge this difficulty, few realize the devastating effects that low subject-to-variable ratios (i.e., the number of variables approaching the number of subjects) have on the generalizability of studies of differential diagnosis. This is not to say that some excellent studies have not been completed. Studies of discriminability by Satz and his colleagues (e.g., Satz & Friel, 1974) use large numbers of variables but have considerable subject populations. Large-n studies of clinical populations are the exception rather than the rule. Willson and Reynolds (1982) have reviewed a number of studies of classification and assessed the effects of several statistical problems in the reported outcomes. The following discussions are taken largely from this work.

Shrinkage and Other Problems. Several considerations are important when predicting group membership (e.g., making a diagnosis) from a predictor set of variables (e.g., the clinical assessment). First, procedures that use samples from a target population always involve sampling error in the estimation of the relations being examined. This means that results are expected to fluctuate from sample to sample because of the random differences inherent in the samples. The usual measure of accuracy of prediction in multiple regression is the squared multiple correlation (R^2). When results of a particular sample are applied to a second sample, R^2 is expected to decrease, since correlation is a maximizing operation—R^2 is made as large as possible for the first sample because multiple regression capitalizes on chance variation in addition to true relations among variables. It is highly unlikely that the same fit of the data will occur in a second sample.

A second consideration occurs when the prediction uses a strategy for selecting a smaller number of variables from the larger predictor set (e.g., Purisch, Golden, & Hammeke, 1979). When a large number of predictors is available, stepwise procedures maximize the probability of selecting predictors that do not predict well in the population but, by chance, correlate highly with the outcome in the particular sample being used. We are only interested in the correlation of *true*-score variance among any set of variables, but because of chance fluctuation in data, error variances occasionally correlate. Multivariate methods, particularly stepwise techniques, take maximum advantage of these correlated error variances—correlations that cannot generalize beyond the sample.

The degree of decrease in R^2 from sample to population can be estimated. The most common estimate (Wherry, 1931; see also Lord & Novick, 1968, p. 286) is as follows:

$$\hat{R}^2 = 1 - (1 - R^2) \frac{(n-1)}{(n-K-1)} \quad \text{(Equation 1)}$$

Here, n is the number of observations, K the number of predictors, R^2 the observed squared multiple correlation between outcome and predictors, and $\hat{R}^2$ the estimate of the *population* squared multiple correlation (called the shrunken R^2). This formula may be applied to multiple regression analysis or discriminant analysis.

Cattin (1980) suggested that with a small n and a large K, another approximation should be used:

$$\hat{R}^2 = \frac{(n - K - 3)\, \rho^4 + \rho^4}{(n - 2K - 2)\, \rho^2 + K} \qquad \text{(Equation 2)}$$

where

$$\rho^2 = 1 - \frac{(n - 3)}{n - K - 1}(1 - R^2)\left[1 + \frac{2(1 - R^2)}{n - K - 1} + \frac{8(1 - R^2)^2}{(n - K + 1)(n - K + 3)}\right]$$

Although $\hat{R}^2$ is a biased estimate, the amount of bias is on the order of .01–.02 for $n = 60$ and $K = 50$.

Of special interest is the case where there are more predictors than people; for the equation above, $\hat{R}^2$ may become negative or greater than 1.00. Mathematically, with more predictors than observations of the outcome, there is no unique solution to a best prediction. In discriminant analysis, having more predictors than subjects will result in perfect classification *entirely at random!* This perfect prediction is a result of having more parameters to estimate than data points to use in the estimation, not because of some true relation between the predictors and groups. Since it is mathematically impossible to estimate all regression coefficients, there will be

$$\frac{K}{n} = \frac{K!}{n!\,(n - K!)} \qquad \text{(Equation 3)}$$

different solutions that would provide perfect classification in this case, but would not be expected to generalize to any other samples. Even when there are fewer predictors (e.g., test scores) than people, the $\hat{R}^2$ estimate will rapidly approach 0 as the number of predictors becomes a significant proportion of the number of subjects.

Multiple regression analysis and discriminant analysis have been discussed interchangeably to this point, and the two techniques are identical when there are only two groups; with more than two groups, discriminant analysis must be used (unless the groups form a continuous variable, such as severe, moderate, and mild mental retardation). In discriminant analysis, R can be calculated, and is useful in estimating shrinkage and in making comparisons across studies. The multiple correlation between predictor and between-group distance is first computed and is a canonical correlation (R_c; see Cooley & Lohnes, 1971, p. 170), but their squared sum (R_c^2) is the maximum possi-

ble R^2. R_c^2 may be useful as a liberal estimate of R^2 because, if it can be shown that R_c^2 is near 0, there is no need to estimate the study's R^2, which will produce an even smaller estimate of R^2.

Willson and Reynolds (1982) assessed the effects of sample size and the application of these regression-based procedures on the outcome of nine studies of diagnostic classification in a variety of clinical journals. The studies are listed in Table 2.8. Also listed are sample sizes used (n), total number of predictors used in stepwise procedures (K_T), number of predictors used in the final regression or discriminant equation (K_F), and the reported squared multiple correlation (R_F^2). In one case, R_F^2 was determined indirectly from a 2×2 classification table that was reported in the study.

Several other statistics are reported in Table 2.8 that represent estimated values of $\hat{R}^2$ and their significance via their associated F statistic. The statistic $\hat{R}_T^2$ represents the estimated R^2 shrunken by Equation 2 to account for all the predictors originally considered. $\hat{R}_T^2$ actually underestimates $\hat{R}^2$ to some degree. Its upper bound is given by $\hat{R}_F^2$, the shrunken estimate based on the number of predictors actually used in the final regression analysis. But $\hat{R}_F^2$, in turn, is an overestimate of the actual shrunken R^2.

Willson and Reynolds (1982) calculated a second set of statistics from the nine studies to estimate loss of classification power as a result of shrinkage. For reported R_F and for $\hat{R}_T^2$, the t statistic equivalent was computed according to this equation:

$$t = \left(\frac{R^2/K}{(1 - R^2)(n - K - 1)}\right)^{\frac{1}{2}} \qquad \text{(Equation 4)}$$

Although most studies had only two groups, in Selz and Reitan (1979) the t statistic was based on a reduction of three groups to two (normal vs. abnormal), which should have enhanced the diagnostic results. Then, an effect size was computed—

TABLE 2.8. Summaries of Prediction Studies from Three Special Population Journals

Study		Sample size	Total no. of predictors	No. of predictors used	R_F^2 (Reported)	$\hat{R}_T^2$	$\hat{R}_F^2$
Dean (1978)		120	14	4	.25*	.09	.21*
Selz & Reitan (1979)[a]		75	37	37	.57	.57	.57
Wallbrown, Vance, & Pritchard (1979)		200	8	3	.19*	.13	.17*
Purisch, Golden, & Hammeke (1979)	a.	100	282	40	1.00*	0^b	0^b
	b.	100	14	14	.88*	.84*	.84*
Taylor & Imivey (1980)	a.	30	16	5	.44*	.00	.26
	b.	30	3	1	.08	.00	.05
	c.	30	16	5	.30	.00	.10
	d.	30	3	1	.14*	.02	.12
	e.	30	16	2	.25*	.00	.22*
	f.	30	2	1	.11	.03	.09
Dunleavy, Hansen, & Baade (1981)		24	37	3	.82*	0^b	.79*
Fuller & Goh (1981)		80	22	12	.38*	.05	.19
Golden, Moses, Graber, & Berg (1981)	a.	60	11	2	.55*	.37*	.54*
	b.	120	11	2	.68*	.62*	.68*
Malloy & Webster (1981)[c]	a.	36	14	14	.57	.57	.57
	b.	36	14	14	$.94*^b$	$.94*^d$	.94*

Note. From "Methodological and Statistical Problems in Determining Membership in Clinical Populations" by V. L. Willson and C. R. Reynolds, 1982, *Clinical Neuropsychology, 4,* 134–138. Copyright 1982 by Robert Owens. Reprinted by permission.

[a] Trinomial classification table was reported; it was converted to a binomial (normal vs. brain-damaged or LD) and the tetrachoric correlation computed, which was squared to obtain R_F^2. Since it was based on a prediction equation from another study, no shrinkage was expected.

[b] An R^2 of 0.00 is expected in an overdetermined system in which there are more predictors than subjects. Perfect classification is always possible.

[c] Binomial classification was reported. The tetrachoric correlation was computed as in footnote a.

[d] The R^2 values were estimated from a misclassification rate of 20% with 36 subjects. While actual study was trinomial, the R^2 represents the equivalent for binomial classification for ease of computing.

*p < .05.

$$\epsilon = t \left(1/n_1 + 1/n_2\right)^{\frac{1}{2}} \qquad \text{(Equation 5)}$$

—as defined by Glass (1978). This statistic is the number of standard deviations separating the two groups. Finally, the percentile point under the normal curve for half the effect was presented. This is the point that minimizes misclassification, assuming equal cost for either false-positive or false-negative errors, and equal population base rates.

Effects on the Outcome of Diagnostic Research. Of the 17 R_F^2's obtainable from the

studies listed in Table 2.8, 12 were initially significant. After correcting for shrinkage, Willson and Reynolds (1982) reported that only four were significant as $\hat{R}_T^2$ and eight as $\hat{R}_F^2$ (see Table 2.9). Thus, half the results reported in these studies may be attributed to chance correlations. Under the most optimistic of circumstances, the upper limit of the $\hat{R}^2$ estimate shows a mean $\hat{R}_F^2$ of .37 versus a mean obtained R_F^2 value of .48 for all studies considered. The lower limit of the $\hat{R}^2$ estimate ($\hat{R}_T^2$) yields even more pessimistic results, demonstrating a mean value of only

TABLE 2.9. Expected Misclassifications from Nine Studies

Study	t-equivalent . . .		Estimated effect[a] size for two populations for . . .		Two-population % misclassification for . . .	
	$\hat{R}_F^2$	$\hat{R}_T^2$	$\hat{R}_F^2$	$\hat{R}_T^2$	$\hat{R}_F^2$	$\hat{R}_T^2$
Dean (1978)	2.76	.86	.50	.16	39%	47%
Purisch, Golden, & Hammeke (1979) a.	0	0	0	0	50%	50%
b.	6.17	6.27	1.25	1.25	27%	27%
Selz & Reitan (1979)[b]	1.15	1.15	.27	.27	45%	45%
Wallbrown, Vance, & Pritchard (1979)	3.12	1.89	.44	.27	41%	45%
Taylor & Imivey (1980) a.	1.69[c]	.00	.62	.00	38%	50%
b.	1.21[c]	.00	.44	.00	41%	50%
c.	.73[c]	.00	.27	.00	45%	50%
d.	1.95[c]	.42	.71	.15	36%	47%
e.	2.84[c]	.00	.73	.00	36%	50%
f.	1.76[c]	.65	.64	.24	37%	45%
Dunleavy, Hansen, & Baade (1981)	5.01	0	2.05	0	16%	50%
Fuller & Goh (1981)	1.14	.37	.25	.06	45%	49%
Golden, Moses, Graber, & Berg (1981) a.	5.78	1.61	1.49	.42	23%	42%
b.	11.15	4.00	2.04	.73	15%	36%
Malloy & Webster (1981)[b] a.	1.19	1.19	.40	.40	42%	42%
b.	5.04	5.04	1.68	1.68	20%	20%
Mean	3.11	1.38	.81	.33	35%	44%

Note. From "Methodological and Statistical Problems in Determining Membership in Clinical Populations" by V. L. Willson and C. R. Reynolds, 1982, *Clinical Neuropsychology*, *4*, 134–138. Copyright 1982 by Robert Owens. Reprinted by permission.
[a]effect $= t \sqrt{1/n_1 + 1/n_2}$; Glass (1978).
[b]No shrinkage occurred.
[c]Single-group statistics; effects were computed as if for two groups. Single-group results are smaller than reported here.

.25. Thus, when one is using powerful multivariate techniques, the chance variation that can *appear* to be reliable discrimination is rather considerable. The importance of large subject-to-variable ratios and proper cross-validation becomes immediately obvious in considering the results summarized here and in Tables 2.8 and 2.9.

It must be reiterated that the shrinkage occurs in research in which correlation-maximizing procedures have been used: stepwise multiple regression, stepwise discriminant analysis, and canonical correlation. The R^2 does not shrink in a fixed-variable study in which all variables are included and in which order is unimportant (balanced ANOVA design) or in which order is predetermined (path analysis or other theory-bound regression approaches). Diagnosis seeks to find the best empirical discriminators, but it is most prey to chance.

It should also be stressed that shrinkage and related problems with stepwise approaches are not only problems with diagnostic research; they apply to all uses of stepwise-regression-based techniques. Shrinkage would also occur in a stepwise analysis predicting achievement test scores from several other measures. Still, these problems are particularly salient for the diagnostic literature, with its common reliance on small samples. Furthermore, diagnostic research seems so applicable to everyday psychological practice; it is therefore particularly dangerous to neglect this very real and common danger in that research.

The Need for Cross-Validation. The estimation of a population or $\hat{R}^2$ and the expected misclassification rate are methods of correcting for the tendency of stepwise regression procedures to capitalize on chance variation. But the procedures only provide estimates of shrinkage, and are far from perfect. A better method of estimating shrinkage is through cross-validation, in which the regression weights and variance estimates from one sample are then tested on another sample.

Cross-validation requires two independent samples. Ideally, both samples are drawn independently from the same population, but often a single sample is split in half. In either case, the regression equation and statistics are computed for one sample (the screening sample), and then the equation is applied to the second sample (the validation or calibration sample) to predict scores on the outcome (or group membership, as appropriate). Those predicted scores are then correlated with the actual outcome scores, with the resulting squared correlation producing an excellent estimate of $\hat{R}^2$ (for more information, see Pedhazur, 1982, Ch. 6). Indeed, $\hat{R}^2$ as discussed above is really just a one-sample estimate of this correlation between predicted and actual scores. Unfortunately, in clinical samples the n is typically so small that splitting it is not a good idea. Two-sample cross-validation, in which two separate samples are drawn from the same population, is then the preferred approach.

Researchers should cross-validate prediction studies prior to publication. The Selz and Reitan (1979) research is an example where this procedure was followed, with quite credible results. We recognize that it is difficult to obtain subjects with rare disorders, but holding results until a second population is sampled would result in no real loss to our discipline. On the contrary, there would be a net gain, since only the cross-validated results would be published. The external validity of prediction studies would also be stronger.

Cross-validation is especially important for practicing clinicians. When actuarial rules for the diagnosis of psychological disorders appear in refereed professional journals, those in applied settings, especially those keeping closest to current developments in the field, may feel confident in applying such rules in the diagnosis and treatment of their clients. In the absence of proper cross-validation, however, diagnoses or classifications may be made on the basis of random relations—an unacceptable situation for all involved, but especially for the individuals under study.

Researchers need to be extremely cautious when subject-to-variable ratios are less than 10:1. When cross-validation is not possible and the results are important enough to be published without cross-validation (a rare occurrence, we hope), estimates of shrinkage in R^2 and the subsequent decrease in classification accuracy should be conveyed, and clear, appropriate cautions should be provided to the clinician.

TEST BIAS RESEARCH

As noted earlier in this chapter, many mistakenly accept research showing mean differences across ethnic or related groups in levels of performance on a psychological test as proof that the test is "biased" against one or more of these groups. Such simple comparisons err in assuming that demographically derived groups of individuals *cannot* differ on any psychological attribute, and hence that any differences revealed by a test mean the test is faulty. Groups, in fact, may or may not differ, and there is a cadre of research methods available to determine whether, when group differences are located, the differences are real ones requiring additional explanation, or artifacts resulting from a biased test. Tests can be examined for bias at the level of the total test or any of its subscales. Bias as a concept for study must first be defined, however.

The term "bias" carries many different connotations for the lay public and for professionals in any number of disciplines. To the legal mind, "bias" denotes illegal discriminatory practices, whereas to the lay mind it may conjure up notions of prejudicial attitudes. Much of the rancor in psychology and education regarding proper definitions of test bias results from the divergent uses of this term in general, but especially by professionals in the same and related academic fields. Contrary to more common or lay us-ages of the term, the term "bias" should be used in relation to educational and psychological tests in its widely recognized, distinct *statistical* sense. "Bias" denotes constant or systematic error, as opposed to chance or random error, in the estimation of some value; in test bias research, this constant or systematic error is usually the result of group membership or some other nominal variable, and occurs in the estimation of a score on a psychological or educational test.

Other uses of the term "bias" in research on the differential or cross-group validity of tests are unacceptable from a scientific perspective, for two primary reasons: (1) The imprecise nature of other uses of the term makes empirical investigation and rational inquiry exceedingly difficult; and (2) other uses of the term invoke moral and value systems that are the subject of intense, polemic, emotional debate without a mechanism for rational resolution. In this section, we note briefly the more common and promising methods for evaluating bias in assessment research. Methods for evaluating item bias are specifically not reviewed, and the interested reader is referred to Berk (1982) for an excellent review of item bias methodology. A review of the outcomes of bias research can be found in Chapter 26 by Reynolds and Kaiser in this same volume.

Research Methods for Detecting Bias

Internal Indices of Bias

Item bias studies evaluate the bias internal to the test at the level of the individual item, but deal principally with bias in test content (content validity). Construct validity across groups, on the other hand, is assessed primarily through internal analyses of tests taken as a whole. Bias exists in regard to construct validity of a test whenever that test can be shown to measure different hypothetical traits or constructs for one group than it does for another group, or to assess the same construct but with differing degrees of accuracy (Reynolds, 1982a).

Factor-Analytic Methods. One of the more popular and necessary empirical approaches to investigating construct validity is factor analysis (Anastasi, 1976; Cronbach, 1970). As noted earlier, factor analysis identifies clusters of test items or subtests that correlate highly with one another and less so with other subtests or items. Consistent factor-analytic results across populations provide strong evidence that whatever is being measured by an instrument is being measured in the same manner, and is in fact the same construct, within each group. If factor-analytic results are constant across groups, then one may have greater confidence that the individuals in each group perceive and interpret the test materials in a similar manner. The information derived from comparative factor analyses across populations is directly relevant to the use of educational and psychological tests in diagnosis and decision making.

Differences in factor structures. Two basic approaches, each with a number of variations, have been employed to compare factor-analytic results across populations. The first approach asks how similar the results are for each group; the second, less common, asks whether the factor-analytic results show a statistically significant difference between groups. The most sophisticated approach to the latter question has been the work of Jöreskog (1971), and builds upon the technique of CFA discussed earlier. Briefly, simultaneous factor analyses are performed for the groups of interest. To test for the equivalence of results across groups, parameters (e.g., factor loadings) are constrained to be equal across groups, with the resulting fit statistics (e.g., χ^2) providing evidence of the "correctness" of those constraints. For example, we could test the factor model shown in Figure 2.3 simultaneously for black and white students. If we wished to perform an extremely sensitive test of whether the WISC-R has an identical factor structure across groups, we could specify that all of the factor loadings should be identical for the two groups (this would be an unreasonable expectation, but is used for illustration). Less stringent tests could include fewer (or no) constraints across groups, and we could also test whether or not the two correlation matrices were equal. A full treatment of the method is certainly beyond the scope and intent of the present chapter. The computational procedure is quite complex, and the comparison of factors is very sensitive. As yet, little research has been reported in the bias literature using the multigroup confirmatory method (however, for an example not focusing on bias, see Marsh & Hocevar, 1985).

A related, but computationally simpler, method for determining the significance of the difference between individual factors for two groups, also employing the χ^2 test, has been presented by Jensen (1980). These methods may be used if one is interested in the significance of the difference between factor structures of a test for two or more groups.

Methods for determining the significance of the differences in the size and pattern of factor loadings between samples, while appropriate in certain circumstances, are not without difficulties. First, many of the fit statistics used to evaluate factor models, and especially χ^2, are dependent on sample size (Marsh et al., 1988); even good models may be rejected with large samples. For stable factor-analytic results, however, large sample sizes are needed, but those same large samples may lead to the rejection of a good model because of trivial differences between groups. Second, when practitioners are interpreting test scores across groups, the degree of *similarity* takes on greater importance; tests for statistically significant differences cannot, by themselves, answer questions of similarity. Nevertheless, both of these difficulties are resolvable, and we should expect to see bias-related factor analyses using these techniques.

Similarities in factor structures. There are a number of methods for determining factorial similarity across groups. These methods differ primarily along two lines: whether they allow estimates of shared variance between factors, and the various assumptions underlying their use. With large samples, various indices of factorial similarity typically produce consistent findings (Reynolds & Harding, 1983). With small samples, multiple methods of evaluation are necessary to guard against the overinterpretation of what may simply be sampling error.

The Pearson correlation can be used to examine directly the comparability of factor loadings on a single factor for two groups. The correlation coefficient between pairs of factor loadings for corresponding factors has been used in some previous work; however, in the comparison of factor loadings, assumptions of normality or linearity are likely to be violated. Transformation of the factor loadings using Fisher z-transformation prior to computing r helps to correct some of these flaws, but is not completely satisfactory. Other, more appropriate indices of factorial similarity exist and are no more difficult to calculate than the Pearson r in most cases.

One popular index of factorial similarity is the coefficient of congruence (r_c). It is similar to the Pearson r, and is based on the relation between pairs of factor loadings for corresponding factors. When one is determining the degree of similarity of two factors, an r_c value of .90 or higher is typically, although arbitrarily, taken to indicate equivalence of the factors in question or factorial invariance across groups (Cattell, 1978; Harman, 1976). The coefficient of congruence is given by the following equation:

$$r_c = \frac{\Sigma ab}{\sqrt{\Sigma a^2 \Sigma b^2}} \qquad \text{(Equation 6)}$$

where a represents the factor loading of a variable for one sample and b represents the factor loading of the same variable for the second sample on the same factor.

Cattell (1978) has described a useful nonparametric index for factor comparison, known as the salient variable similarity index (s). The calculation of s is straightforward, with one exception. In the determination of s, one first proceeds by classifying each variable by its factor loading as being salient or nonsalient and as being positive or negative, depending on the sign of the variable's loading. After reviewing several other options, Cattell (1978) recommended a cutoff value of .10 to indicate a variable with a salient loading. Although .10 is probably the best choice for item factor analyses (or with subscales, in the case of personality scales), this value is probably too liberal when examining subscales of cognitive batteries with high subtest reliabilities and a large general factor, especially given the sensitive nature of questions of potential bias. In the latter case, investigators should consider adopting more conservative values: between .15 and .25 for positive salience and between −.15 and −.25 for negative salience.

Many other methods of determining the similarity of factors exist, and a complete review of these techniques cannot be undertaken here. Configurative matching methods and the use of Cattell's coefficient of pattern similarity (r_p) are but two prominent examples. These and others are reviewed by Cattell (1978). The methods noted above, however, will be adequate for the vast majority of cases (especially if analyses are based on covariance matrices), and are certainly the most common procedures in the test bias literature. When one is using these indices of factorial similarity to evaluate overall results of an analysis, not only should individual factors be compared; the comparison of communalities, unique variances, and specific variances may also be appropriate, especially in the case of diagnostic psychological tests.

Comparing Internal-Consistency Estimates. The previously offered definition of bias in construct validity requires equivalency in the "accuracy" of measurement across groups for nonbiased assessment. Essentially, this means that any error due to domain sampling in the choice of items for the test must be constant across groups. The proper test of this condition is the comparison of internal-consistency reliability estimates (r_{xx}) or alternate-form correlations (r_{ab}) across groups; the two require different statistical procedures.

Internal consistency. Internal-consistency reliability estimates are such coefficients as Cronbach's alpha, Kuder–Richardson 20 (KR$_{20}$), KR$_{21}$, odd–even correlations with length corrections, or estimates derived through analysis of variance. Typically, the preferred estimate of r_{xx} is Cronbach's coefficient alpha or KR$_{20}$, a special case of alpha. Alpha has a variety of advantages; for example, it is the mean of all possible split-half correlations for a test and is also representative of the predicted correlation between true alternate forms of a test. Feldt (1969) has provided a technique that can be used to determine the significance of the difference between alpha or KR$_{20}$ reliabilities on a single test for two groups. Although originally devised as a test of the hypothesis that alpha or KR$_{20}$ is the same for two tests, the assumptions underlying Feldt's test are even more closely met by those of a single psychological or educational test and two independent samples (L. S. Feldt, personal communication, 1980). The test statistic is given by the ratio of 1 – alpha for the first group over 1 –

alpha for the second group, as shown in the following equation:

$$F = \frac{1 - \text{alpha}_1}{1 - \text{alpha}_2} \qquad \text{(Equation 7)}$$

where alpha$_1$ is the reliability coefficient of the test being studied for Group 1 and alpha$_2$ is the same reliability coefficient as calculated for Group 2. KR$_{20}$ reliabilities may be used in Equation 4 as well. The test statistic will be distributed as F with $n_1 - 1$ degrees of freedom in the numerator and $n_2 - 1$ degrees of freedom in the denominator. The expression 1 – alpha represents an error variance term, and the largest variance is always placed over the smallest variance.

Alternate forms. Comparison of correlations between alternate forms of a test across groups may be needed in cases where alpha or KR$_{20}$ is inappropriate or for some reason not available. With two samples, alternate-form correlations are calculated separately for each group, producing two independent correlations. The standard statistical test for the differences between independent correlations is then calculated (e.g., Lindeman et al., 1980, Ch. 2).

When a significant difference between alternate-form reliability estimates for two groups occurs, the investigator must consider several other factors before concluding that bias exists. The tests under consideration must be shown to be actual alternate forms for at least one of the two groups. Before two tests can be considered alternate forms, they must in fact be sampling items from the same domain. Other methodological problems that apply generally to the investigation of alternate-form reliability also will apply. Comparison of test–retest correlations across groups may also be of interest and can be conducted in the same matter. Whether a test–retest correlation is an appropriate measure of a test's reliability, however, should be carefully evaluated. Unless the trait the test is measuring is assumed to be stable, test–retest correlations speak more directly to the stability of the trait under consideration than to the accuracy of the measuring device.

Correlation of Age with Raw Scores. A potentially valuable technique for investigating the construct validity of aptitude or intelligence tests is the evaluation of the relation between raw scores and age. Virtually all theories of early cognitive development suggest that scores on tests of mental ability during childhood should increase with age. If a test is a valid measure of mental ability, then performance on the test—as measured by raw scores—should show a substantial correlation with age when data are compared across age levels. If a test is measuring some construct of mental ability in a uniform manner *across groups*, then the correlation of raw scores with chronological age should be constant across groups.

Kinship Correlations and Differences. Jensen (1980) has proposed that "the construct validity of a test in any two population groups is reinforced if the test scores show the same kinship correlations (or absolute differences) in both groups" (p. 427). The use of kinship correlation to test for bias is relatively complex and involves the much-debated calculation of heritability estimated across groups. Although this method of evaluating test bias is of little utility to the practitioner, it is a valid technique for investigating the construct validity of tests that are purported to be measures of *g*. An in-depth explanation of necessary methods can be found in Jensen (1980).

Multitrait–Multimethod Validation. One of the most convincing techniques for establishing the construct validity of a psychological test is through the use of a multitrait–multimethod validity matrix. This technique evaluates both the convergent and divergent validity of a test with multiple methods of assessment; that is, predictions regarding what will correlate with the test score are evaluated along with predictions regarding what the test *will not* correlate with (an equally important facet of validity), using multiple methods of assessment so that the observed relations are not artifacts of a common assessment method. Multiple methods are used to assess what we think are multiple traits. So, for example, we could use both test scores and teacher ratings (methods) to assess both reading and mathematics achievements (traits). The resulting correlation matrix would be the multitrait–multimethod matrix.

A square matrix can be produced that is amenable to evaluation through factor analysis. When one is evaluating bias, it is best to put the test reliabilities in the diagonal of the matrix. A multitrait–multimethod matrix would be calculated separately for each group under consideration. Each matrix could then be factor-analyzed and the results of the factor analysis could be compared using techniques described above. In the evaluation for bias, all methods or tests in the matrix, other than the specific test being evaluated, must be nonbiased—a potential drawback to the use of this technique. The procedure, however, when correctly carried out, has the greatest potential for the ultimate resolution of the question of bias.

External Indices of Bias

Defining bias with regard to the relation between a test score and some later level of performance on a criterion measure has produced considerable, and as yet unresolved, debate among scholars in the fields of measurement and assessment (e.g., see Reynolds, 1982b). Although the resulting debate has generated a number of selection models from which to examine bias, selection models focus on the *decision-making* system and not on the test itself. In fact, these selection models are all completely external to the issue of test bias, because each of the models deals solely with value systems and the statistical manipulations necessary to make the test scores conform to those values. In contrast, none of the various selection models of "bias" deals with constant error in the estimation of some criterion score (by an aptitude or other predictor test) as a function of group membership. But test bias deals directly with constant or systematic error in the estimation of some true value as a function of group membership. Within the context of *predictive* validity, bias is concerned with systematic error in the estimation of performance on some criterion measure (i.e., constant over- or underprediction).

Since the present section is concerned with statistical bias, and not the social or political justifications of any one particular selection model, a test is considered biased with respect to predictive validity when the inference drawn from the test score is not made with the smallest feasible *random* error or when there is *constant* error in an inference or prediction as a function of membership in a particular group (Reynolds, 1982a).

Evaluating Bias in Prediction. The evaluation of bias in prediction under this definition (the regression definition) is quite straightforward. With simple regressions, predictions take the form of $Y_i = aX_i + b$, where a is the regression coefficient and b is some constant. When this equation is graphed (forming a regression line), a represents the slope of the regression line and b the Y intercept. Since our definition of bias in predictive validity requires errors in prediction to be independent of group membership, the regression line formed for any pair of variables must be the same for each group for whom prediction is to be made. Whenever the slope or the intercept differs significantly across groups, there is bias in prediction if one attempts to use a regression equation based on the combined groups. When the regression equation for two (or more) groups are equivalent, prediction is the same for all groups. This condition is referred to as "homogeneity of regression across groups" (see Reynolds & Kaiser, Chapter 26, this volume, for illustration of these methods).

In actual clinical practice, regression equations are seldom generated for the prediction of future performance, although actuarial prediction is far more common in college admission and hiring decisions. Rather, some arbitrary (or perhaps statistically derived) cutoff score is determined, below which "failure" is predicted. For school performance, IQs two or more standard deviations below the test mean are used to infer possible retardation, and therefore a high probability of failure for the student in question. Essentially, these uses of test scores establish "mental" prediction equations that are assumed to be equivalent across race, sex, and other categories. Although these mental equations cannot readily be tested across groups, the actual form of criterion prediction can be compared across groups in several ways. Again, errors in prediction must be independent of group membership. If regression equations are equal, this condition is met. To test the hypotheses of simultaneous regression, slopes and intercepts must both be compared.

In the evaluation of slope and intercept

values, two basic techniques have been most often employed in the research literature. Gulliksen and Wilks (1950) and Kerlinger and Pedhazur (1973, Ch. 16) describe methods for separately testing regression coefficients and intercepts for significant differences across groups. But using separate, independent tests for these two values considerably increases the probability of a decision error and unnecessarily complicates the decision-making process. Potthoff (1966) has described a useful technique (also detailed in Reynolds, 1982b) that allows investigators simultaneously to test the equivalence of regression coefficients and intercepts across K independent groups with a single F ratio. If a significant F results, the researchers may then test the slopes and intercepts separately if they desire information concerning which value differs. When homogeneity of regression does not occur, three basic conditions can result: (1) Intercept constants differ; (2) regression coefficients (slopes) differ; or (3) slopes and intercepts both differ. Potthoff's approach seems clearly to be the best with one independent variable.

More than one independent variable. Potthoff (1966) has provided extensions of the above-described procedures that can be employed when more than a single test is being used to predict the criterion. The procedure is derived directly from the technique described above and will readily be deduced by the statistician. Others who wish to use this approach when more than one test is employed should consult Potthoff (1966).

Potthoff's (1966) extension has some slight difficulties in the estimation of exact probability levels that increase the possibility of a Type I error's being made by the investigator. Another method that may prove easier and more exact has been used by Reynolds (1980) and involves a direct examination of residual or error terms for each individual by group membership. In this procedure, a multiple-regression equation for the prediction of performance on the criterion variable is determined, using all independent variables with a single collapsed group of subjects. Using this equation based on the total sample, the investigator then predicts criterion scores and calculates a residual score ($\hat{Y}_i - Y_i$) for each individual. Standardized residual scores are then compared across groups using ANOVA to determine whether there are any mean differences in errors of prediction as a function of group membership. If there is no constant or systematic error in the prediction of the criterion variable for members of a particular group, the ANOVA will yield nonsignificant results and the *mean* residual for each group will approach 0. With multiple independent variables, the ANOVA approach has certain advantages, allowing for the examination of interactions and the direct evaluation of variances of each cell. Virtually any ANOVA design can be used with the standardized residuals, and effect sizes are readily determined (e.g., Winkler & Hays, 1975). The direct examination of residuals is also more readily interpretable to nonstatistical audiences.

More than one dependent variable. As Potthoff (1966) has noted, when more than one dependent or criterion variable is being predicted, the test in question may be a non-biased predictor of one variable but a biased predictor of another variable. Separate tests of bias can be conducted with regard to each dependent variable, with alpha levels adjusted for multiple comparisons (to control Type I error rates). This procedure is probably adequate when only two or three dependent measures are involved. A more exact, appropriate procedure would be a multivariate test for bias simultaneously across all dependent measures. Potthoff (1966, Sec. 7) presents the necessary formulas and matrices for carrying out the multivariate test for bias. A multivariate analogue of the procedure described in the preceding section of this chapter could also be used. With multiple independent and multiple dependent variables, comparisons of canonical analysis outcomes may prove useful, as might analyses using the full LISREL model (indeed, a multigroup LISREL analysis could be used to test bias with one or more independent or dependent variables, or both).

Testing for Equivalence of Validity Coefficients. The correlation between a test score and a criterion variable, whether measured concurrently or at a future time, is typically referred to as a "validity coefficient" (r_{xy}) and is a direct measure of the magnitude of the relation between two variables. Thus, another method for detecting bias in predictive (or concurrent) validity is the comparison of

validity coefficients across groups. The procedure described in an earlier section of this chapter for comparing alternate-form reliabilities may also be used to test the hypothesis that r_{xy} is the same for two groups.

Some researchers, in evaluating validity coefficients across groups, have compared each correlation to 0 and, if one correlation deviates significantly from 0 and the other does not, have concluded that bias exists. As Humphreys (1973) has explained so eloquently (and as we have suggested in the section on "Problems and Needs in Assessment Research"), the testing of each correlation for significance is incorrect. To determine whether two correlations are different, they must be compared directly with one another and not separately against hypothetical population values of 0. The many defects in the latter approach are amply explained in Humphreys (1973) and are not reiterated here. Other factors must be considered in comparing the correlations directly with one another, however, such as whether to make corrections for unreliability, restriction of range, and other study-specific elements, prior to making the actual comparisons. The particular questions involved, and whether the analyses are directed at questions of theory or those of practice, will influence the outcome of these deliberations.

A Path Model of Bias

The concept of bias, and especially predictive bias, may be explained using the concepts of path analysis and latent variables discussed earlier. Figure 2.7 shows a model in which an intelligence test (Ability) is the predictor of interest and Achievement is the criterion (the path models used here are adapted from Birnbaum, 1981, and Linn, 1984). Group Membership is the dichotomous bias variable, coded 0 for all those who are members of one group (e.g., the minority group) and 1 for all those who are members of another group (e.g., the majority). The unenclosed Ability variable represents measured Ability (the scores on an intelligence test), whereas the circled Ability variable represents *true* Ability (the latent variable or factor). The top half of the figure shows a no-bias model. Group Membership may affect true Ability (path *a*), but it only affects measured Ability

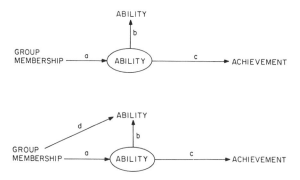

FIGURE 2.7. Path models of bias. The top model shows a condition of no bias; Group Membership may affect true Ability, but does not affect measured Ability except through true Ability. The bottom model depicts a condition in which the intelligence test is biased; group membership affects measured Ability directly. The model used here is adapted from Birnbaum (1981) and Linn (1984).

(and measured Achievement) through true Ability. The bottom half of the figure shows a model in which there is bias in the intelligence test. Group Membership affects true Ability (*a*), but it also affects measured Ability *independent* of true Ability (path *d*). To the extent that path *d* deviates from 0, the intelligence test is biased; the errors of measurement are related to Group Membership.

Given a model such as that displayed in the top of Figure 2.7 (the no-bias model), Birnbaum (1979, 1981) and Linn (1984) have illustrated a paradox that results from analyses of predictive bias. Assume that path *b* is less than 1 (i.e., the test is less than perfectly reliable); that path *a* is not equal to 0 (i.e., Group Membership affects true Ability); and that path *c* is not equal to 0 (Ability affects Achievement)—all plausible assumptions. Given these conditions, it can be shown that if Group 1 scores lower on the intelligence test than Group 2, then Group 1 will score lower on the achievement test than Group 2 members *of the same measured Ability*, but that Group 2 members will be higher in measured Ability than Group 1 members *of the same measured Achievement*. The first part of this paradox would seem to suggest bias in the intelligence test against Group 1, and the second half against Group 2, but the paradox occurs in the absence of any bias. Furthermore, the second half of this paradox (Group 2 members are higher in measured Ability than Group 1 members of the same measured Achievement) is equivalent to the common finding of intelligence tests' over-

predicting the performance of minority group members on the criterion (see Reynolds & Kaiser, Chapter 26, this volume). That common finding may therefore not suggest any reverse bias, but rather may simply be a consequence of imperfect measurement.[4]

The models shown in Figure 2.7 are probably unreasonable, however, because they suggest that Group Membership can affect Achievement *only* through true Ability. But suppose that Group 2 completed more academic coursework in high school than Group 1; the Coursework variable would not affect Ability, but would affect Achievement (see Figure 2.6). If we adhered to the models shown in Figure 2.7, that Coursework effect would show up as a path from Group Membership directly to Achievement, and would be taken as evidence of bias. The model shown in Figure 2.8 allows that Group Membership may affect true Ability (*a*) or true Achievement, either directly (*b*) or indirectly through Ability (*a* × *c*). This modified model would allow for Group Membership's affecting Achievement in ways other than through Ability (e.g., through

---

[4]For more detail, see Birnbaum (1979, 1981) or Linn (1984). Birnbaum originally demonstrated this paradox (Birnbaum's paradox) in a discussion of gender differences in university salaries; Linn (1984) adapted Birnbaum's models to a discussion of selection bias. These models can also be used to calculate ranges of permissible correlations between group membership and achievement (or other criteria) if the intelligence test (or other predictor) is unbiased.

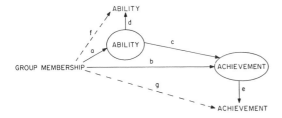

FIGURE 2.8. A more complete path model of bias.

Coursework), but paths from Group Membership to *measured* Ability (*f*) or Achievement (*g*) that are not equal to 0 would be evidence of bias.

SUMMARY

Assessments of children must be grounded in research if those assessments are to be valid. We have focused here on a diversity of issues in assessment research. We have presented several complex research methodologies (multiple-regression analysis and factor analysis) that are becoming more widely used. Our emphasis has been on providing a basic understanding of those methods, focusing more often on conceptual rather than statistical understanding. We have also discussed both the promises and problems of those methods. We have focused on a research area—test bias—that has generated intense controversy, but that has also been extremely productive. This avenue of research illustrates well how multiple methods and procedures can be used to focus on the same research question. Finally, we have briefly covered several basic points about reliability and validity that we believe are often overlooked or that are important for understanding these all-important topics. Our assumption, in all of these presentations, has been that these are topics with which consumers of research (and those who conduct research) will need to be increasingly familiar.

We re-emphasize the problems and needs that seem to be too common in assessment research: Our research needs more consistency with theory and practice, and our research should more often involve the testing of hypotheses. Still, there is much excellent assessment research being conducted, which can form an excellent basis for practice. In order to use that research as a guide for assessment, however, practitioners will need to evaluate that research—to separate the wheat from the chaff. We hope the topics presented here will help in that evaluation.

Acknowledgments. Portions of this chapter were written while Keith was Senior Research Fellow, Office of Educational Research and Improvement (OERI), U.S. Dpartment of Education; the opinions expressed are our own and do not represent the official position of OERI.

Portions of this chapter are adapted from the following sources:

"Assessment Research: An Assessment and Recommended Interventions" by T. Z. Keith, 1987, *School Psychology Review, 16*, 276–289. Copyright 1987 by *School Psychology Review*. Adapted by permission.

Foundations of Behavioral Research (3rd ed.) by F. N. Kerlinger, 1986, New York: Holt, Rinehart & Winston. Copyright 1986 by CBS College Publishing.

Testing Models of School Learning: Effects of Quality of Instruction, Motivation, Academic Coursework, and Homework on Academic Achievement by T. Z. Keith and V. A. Cool, 1990, manuscript submitted for publication. Adapted by permission of the authors.

"Methodological and Statistical Problems in Determining Membership in Clinical Populations" by V. L. Willson and C. R. Reynolds, 1982, *Clinical Neuropsychology, 4*, 134–138. Copyright 1982 by Robert Owens. Adapted by permission.

REFERENCES

Anastasi, A. (1976). *Psychological testing* (4th ed.) New York: Macmillan.
Bentler, P. M. (1985). *Theory and implementation of EQS: A structural equations program*. Los Angeles: BMDP Statistical Software.
Bentler, P. M., & Bonett, D. G. (1980). Significance tests and goodness of fit in the analysis of covariance structures. *Psychological Bulletin, 88*, 588–606.
Berk, R. A. (Ed.). (1982). *Handbook of methods for detecting test bias*. Baltimore: Johns Hopkins University Press.

Birnbaum, M. H. (1979). Procedures for the detection and correction of salary inequities. In T. H. Pezzullo & B. E. Brittingham (Eds.), *Salary equity* (pp. 121–144). Lexington, MA: Lexington Books.

Birnbaum, M. H. (1981). Reply to McLaughlin: Proper path models for theoretical partialling. *American Psychologist, 36,* 1193–1195.

Carroll, J. B. (1963). A model for school learning. *Teachers College Record,* 723–733.

Carroll, J. B. (1985). Exploratory factor analysis: A tutorial. In D. K. Detterman (Ed.), *Current topics in human intelligence: Vol. 1. Research methodology* (pp. 25–58). Norwood, NJ: Ablex.

Cattell, R. B. (1966). The scree test for the number of factors. *Multivariate Behavioral Research, 1,* 245–276.

Cattell, R. B. (1978). *The scientific use of factor analysis in behavioral and life sciences.* New York: Plenum.

Cattin, P. (1980). Note on the estimation of the squared cross-validated multiple correlation of a regression model. *Psychological Bulletin, 87,* 63–65.

Cohen, J., & Cohen, P. (1983). *Applied multiple regression/correlation analysis for the behavioral sciences* (2nd ed.). Hillsdale, NJ: Erlbaum.

Cooley, W. W., & Lohnes, P. R. (1971). *Multivariate data analysis.* New York: Wiley.

Cronbach, L. J. (1970). *Essentials of psychological testing* (3rd ed.). New York: Harper & Row.

Cronbach, L. J. (1971). Test validation. In R. L. Thorndike (Ed.), *Educational measurement* (2nd ed., pp. 444–507). Washington, DC: American Council on Education.

Cummings, J. A., & Moscato, E. M. (1984a). Research on the Woodcock–Johnson Psycho-Educational Battery: Implications for practice and future investigations. *School Psychology Review, 13,* 33–40.

Cummings, J. A., & Moscato, E. M. (1984b). Reply to Thompson & Brassard. *School Psychology Review, 13,* 45–48.

Dean, R. S. (1978). Distinguishing learning-disabled and emotionally disturbed children on the WISC-R. *Journal of Consulting and Clinical Psychology, 46,* 381–382.

Dunleavy, R. W., Hansen, J. L., & Baade, L. E. (1981). Discriminating powers of Halstead Battery tests in assessment of 9 to 14 year old severely asthmatic children. *Clinical Neuropsychology, 3,* 9–12.

Eysenck, H. J. (1979). *The structure and measurement of intelligence.* New York: Springer-Verlag.

Feldt, L. S. (1969). A test of the hypothesis that Cronbach's alpha or Kuder–Richardson coefficient twenty is the same for two tests. *Psychometrika, 34,* 363–373.

Fuller, G. B., & Goh, D. S. (1981). Intelligence, achievement, and visual–motor performance among learning disabled and emotionally impaired children. *Psychology in the Schools, 18,* 262–268.

Glass, G. V. (1978). Integrating findings: The meta-analysis of research. In L. Shulman (Ed.), *Review of research in education* (Vol. 5, pp. 351–379). Washington, DC: Educational Research Association.

Golden, C. J., Moses, J. A., Graber, B., & Berg, R. (1981). Objective clinical rules for interpreting the Luria–Nebraska Neuropsychological Battery: Derivation, effectiveness, and validation. *Journal of Consulting and Clinical Psychology, 49,* 616–618.

Guilford, J. P. (1954). *Psychometric methods* (2nd ed.). New York: McGraw-Hill.

Gulliksen, H., & Wilks, S. S. (1950). Regression tests for several samples. *Psychometrika, 15,* 91–114.

Gutkin, T. B., & Reynolds, C. R. (1981). Factorial similarity of the WISC-R for white and black children from the standardization sample. *Journal of Educational Psychology, 73,* 227–231.

Harman, H. (1976). *Modern factor analysis* (2nd ed.) Chicago: University of Chicago Press.

Humphreys, L. G. (1973). Statistical definitions of test validity for minority groups. *Journal of Applied Psychology, 58,* 1–4.

Jensen, A. R. (1980). *Bias in mental testing.* New York: Free Press.

Jensen, A. R. (1984). The black–white difference on the K-ABC: Implications for future tests. *Journal of Special Education, 18,* 377–408.

Jöreskog, K. G. (1971). Simultaneous factor analysis in several populations. *Psychometrika, 36,* 409–426.

Jöreskog, K. G., & Sörbom, D. (1984). *LISREL VI: Analysis of linear structural relationships by the method of maximum likelihood: User's guide.* Mooresville, IN: Scientific Software.

Kaufman, A. S. (1975). Factor analysis of the WISC-R at 11 age levels between $6\frac{1}{2}$ and $16\frac{1}{2}$ years. *Journal of Consulting and Clinical Psychology, 43,* 135–147.

Kaufman, A. S. (1979). *Intelligent testing with the WISC-R.* New York: Wiley–Interscience.

Kaufman, A. S., & Kamphaus, R. W. (1984). Factor analysis of the Kaufman Assessment Battery for Children (K-ABC) for ages $2\frac{1}{2}$ through $12\frac{1}{2}$ years. *Journal of Educational Psychology, 76,* 623–637.

Kaufman, A. S., & McLean, J. E. (1987). Joint factor analysis of the K-ABC and WISC-R with normal children. *Journal of School Psychology, 25,* 105–118.

Keith, T. Z. (1985). Questioning the K-ABC: What *does* it measure? *School Psychology Review, 14,* 9–20.

Keith, T. Z. (1987). Assessment research: An assessment and recommended interventions. *School Psychology Review, 16,* 276–289.

Keith, T. Z. (1988). Path analysis: An introduction for school psychologists. *School Psychology Review, 17,* 343–362.

Keith, T. Z., & Cool, V. A. (1990). *Testing models of school learning: Effects of quality of instruction, motivation, academic coursework, and homework on academic achievement.* Manuscript submitted for publication.

Keith, T. Z., Cool, V. A., Novak, C. G., White, L. J., & Pottebaum, S. M. (1988). Confirmatory factor analysis of the Stanford–Binet Fourth Edition: Testing the theory–test match. *Journal of School Psychology, 26.*

Keith, T. Z., Fehrmann, P. G., Harrison, P. L., & Pottebaum, S. M. (1987). The relation between adaptive behavior and intelligence: Testing alternative explanations. *Journal of School Psychology, 25,* 32–43.

Keith, T. Z., & Novak, C. G. (1987). Joint factor structure of the WISC-R and K-ABC for referred school children. *Journal of Psychoeducational Assessment, 4,* 3470–386.

Kenny, D. A. (1979). *Correlation and causality.* New York: Wiley.

Kerlinger, F. N. (1986). *Foundations of behavioral research* (3rd ed.). New York: Holt, Rinehart & Winston.

Kerlinger, F. N., & Pedhazur, E. J. (1973). *Multiple regression in behavioral research.* New York: Holt, Rinehart & Winston.

Kim, J. O., & Mueller, C. W. (1978). *Factor analysis: Statistical methods and practical issues*. Beverly Hills, CA: Sage.

Landy, F. J. (1986). Stamp collecting versus science: Validation as hypothesis testing. *American Psychologist, 41*, 1183–1192.

Lindeman, R. H., Merenda, P. F., & Gold, R. Z. (1980). *Introduction to bivariate and multivariate analysis*. Glenview, IL: Scott, Foresman.

Linn, R. L. (1980). Discussion: Regression toward the mean and the interval between test administrations. In G. Echternacht (Ed.), *New directions for testing and measurement: Vol. 8. Measurement aspects of Title I evaluations* (pp. 83–89). San Francisco: Jossey-Bass.

Linn, R. L. (1983). Pearson selection formulas: Implications for studies of predictive bias and estimates of educational effects in selected samples. *Journal of Educational Measurement, 20*, 1–14.

Linn, R. L. (1984). Selection bias: Multiple meanings. *Journal of Educational Measurement, 21*, 33–47.

Lord, F. M., & Novick, M. R. (1968). *Statistical theories of mental tests*. Reading, MA: Addison-Wesley.

MacCallum, R. (1986). Specification searches in covariance structure modeling. *Psychological Bulletin, 100*, 107–120.

Marsh, H. W., Balla, J. R., & McDonald, R. P. (1988). Goodness-of-fit indexes in confirmatory factor analysis: The effect of sample size. *Psychological Bulletin, 103*, 391–410.

Marsh, H. W., & Hocevar, D. (1985). Application of confirmatory factor analysis to the study of self-concept: First- and higher-order factor models and their invariance across groups. *Psychological Bulletin, 97*, 562–582.

Oakland, T. (1983). Joint use of adaptive behavior and IQ to predict achievement. *Journal of Consulting and Clinical Psychology, 51*, 198–201.

Pedhazur, E. J. (1982). *Multiple regression in behavioral research: Prediction and explanation* (2nd ed.). New York: Holt, Rinehart & Winston.

Phillips, B. N. (1982). Reading and evaluating research in school psychology. In C. R. Reynolds & T. B. Gutkin (Eds.), *The handbook of school psychology* (pp. 24–47). New York: Wiley.

Potthoff, R. F. (1966). *Statistical aspects of the problem of bias in psychological tests* (Institute of Statistics Mimeo Series No. 479). Chapel Hill: University of North Carolina, Department of Statistics.

Purisch, A. D., Golden, C. J., & Hammeke, T. A. (1979). Discrimination of schizophrenic and brain-injured patients by a standardized version of Luria's neuropsychological tests. *Clinical Neuropsychology, 1*, 53–59.

Reynolds, C. R. (1980). An examination for bias in preschool battery across race and sex. *Journal of Educational Measurement, 17*, 137–146.

Reynolds, C. R. (1982a). The problem of bias in psychological assessment. In C. R. Reynolds, & T. B. Gutkin (Eds.), *The handbook of school psychology* (pp. 178–208). New York: Wiley.

Reynolds, C. R. (1982b). Methods for detecting construct and predictive bias. In R. A. Berk (Ed.), *Handbook of methods for detecting test bias* (pp. 192–227). Baltimore: John Hopkins University Press.

Reynolds, C. R., & Harding, R. D. (1983). Outcome in two large sample studies of factorial similarity under six methods of comparison. *Educational and Psychological Measurement, 43*, 723–278.

Roberts, A. O. H. (1980). Regression toward the mean and the regression-effect bias. In G. Echternacht (Ed.), *New directions for testing and measurement: Vol. 8. Measurement aspects of Title I evaluations* (pp. 59–82). San Francisco: Jossey-Bass.

Rourke, B. P. (1975). Brain–behavior relationships in children with learning disabilities: A research program. *American Psychologist, 30*, 911–920.

Salvia, J., & Ysseldyke, J. E. (1988). *Assessment in special and remedial education* (4th ed.). Boston: Houghton Mifflin.

Satz, P., & Friel, J. (1974). Some predictive antecedents of specific disability: A preliminary two year follow-up. *Journal of Learning Disabilities, 7*, 437–444.

Selz, M., & Reitan, R. M. (1979). Rules for neuropsychological diagnosis: Classification of brain functions in older children. *Journal of Consulting and Clinical Psychology, 47*, 358–264.

Strommen, E. F. (1988). Confirmatory factor analysis of the Kaufman Assessment Battery for Children (K-ABC): A reevaluation. *Journal of School Psychology, 26*, 13–23.

Taylor, R. K., & Imivey, J. K. (1980). Diagnostic use of the WISC-R and McCarthy Scales: A regression analysis approach to learning disabilities. *Psychology in the Schools, 17*, 327–330.

Thompson, P. L., & Brassard, M. R. (1984). Cummings and Moscato soft on Woodcock–Johnson. *School Psychology Review, 13*, 41–44.

Thurstone, L. L. (1947). *Multiple factor analysis*. Chicago: University of Chicago Press.

Walberg, H. J. (1981). A psychological theory of education productivity. In F. H. Farley & N. Gordon (Eds.), *Psychology and education* (pp. 36–77). Berkeley, CA: McCutchan.

Wallbrown, F. H., Vance, H., & Pritchard, K. K. (1979). Discriminating between attitudes expressed by normal and disabled readers. *Psychology in the Schools, 4*, 472–477.

Wechsler, D. (1974). *Manual for the Wechsler Intelligence Scale for Children—Revised*. New York: Psychological Corporation.

Wherry, R. J., Sr. (1931). A new formula for predicting the shrinkage of the coefficient for multiple correlation. *Annals of Mathematical Statistics, 2*, 440–457.

Willson, V. L., & Reynolds, C. R. (1982). Methodological and statistical problems in determining membership in clinical populations. *Clinical Neuropsychology, 4*, 134–138.

Willson, V. L., Reynolds, C. R., Chatman, S., & Kaufman, A. S. (1985). Confirmatory analysis of simultaneous, sequential and achievement factors on the K-ABC at 11 age levels $2\frac{1}{2}$ to $12\frac{1}{2}$. *Journal of School Psychology, 23*, 261–269.

Winkler, R. L., & Hays, W. L. (1975). *Statistics: Probability, inference, and decision*. New York: Holt, Rinehart & Winston.

3

A Practical Model for Test Development

GARY J. ROBERTSON
American Guidance Service

The publication of educational and psychological tests is a highly specialized, little-known part of the educational publishing industry. A major portion of the revenue realized from the sale of testing materials within the United States is accounted for by only a dozen or so companies. "Test development," as the term is used in this chapter, refers to the process of constructing standardized, objective tests for sale by commercial publishing firms. Excluded here are college admissions testing and other professional licensure and certification examinations. The context within which the various phases of test development are described and from which examples are drawn is entrepreneurial, even though many of the test development activities apply to the construction of any test, regardless of the setting.

A primary requisite for successful test development is a highly trained, experienced staff. The most responsible research and development positions in publishing firms are held by persons with doctoral-level training in measurement. Expertise is needed in such academic areas as statistics, psychometrics, research methodology, and (depending upon the types of tests published) administration and interpretation of specialized psychological tests and diagnostic devices. Skilled editorial and clerical personnel are also needed to complete the many and varied tasks undertaken in test development. Although computers have done much to lighten the work load during the past 25

years or so, test development is still a labor-intensive activity. Teamwork is required of many highly specialized, trained individuals if test development is to occur effectively.

The material presented in this chapter is based on the following major steps of test development:

1. Preliminary ideas.
2. Evaluate proposal (approval/reject).
3. Make formal arrangements (sign contract if publication is approved).
4. Prepare test specifications.
5. Write items.
6. Conduct item tryout.
   a. Prepare tryout sample specifications.
   b. Prepare participants.
   c. Prepare tryout materials.
   d. Administer tryout items.
   e. Analyze tryout data.
7. Assemble final test form(s).
8. Conduct national standardization.
   a. Prepare standardization sample specifications.
   b. Obtain participants.
   c. Prepare standardization materials.
   d. Administer tests.
   e. Analyze data.
   f. Develop norms tables.
9. Prepare final materials.
   a. Establish publication schedule.
   b. Write manual.
   c. Prepare test books and answer forms.

d. Manufacture/produce/print materials.
10. Prepare marketing plan.
   a. Initiate direct mail promotion.
   b. Initiate space advertising.
   c. Train sales staff.
   d. Attend professional meetings and conventions.
11. Publish.

These steps summarize the process used to develop tests that are commercially available to diverse sources, such as school districts, psychological clinics, individual practitioners, industrial concerns, and government agencies. It is assumed, moreover, that tests are developed by recognized professionals who are not employed by test publishers. There is, however, no reason why test publications cannot be produced "in house" as long as the requisite expertise is present in the publisher's staff.

Although there are not and cannot be rigidly prescribed standards for test construction that are imposed uniformly upon all test publishers, both professional organizations and market forces definitely exert an influence that motivates test publishers to produce publications that meet accepted technical standards. For example, the American Educational Research Association (AERA), the American Psychological Association (APA), and the National Council on Measurement in Education (NCME) have produced various editions of a joint volume of technical standards; these date from 1954, and the most recent version is the *Standards for Educational and Psychological Testing* (AERA, APA, & NCME, 1985). These volumes have exerted a very positive influence on the development of commercially produced tests. The current *Standards* volume represents a consensus among professionals in the three organizations mentioned concerning appropriate testing practices within a broad, general context, while still leaving room for needed diversity in individual applications.

The sections that follow adhere generally to the steps in test development listed above. Activities proceed in sequence from preliminary steps in the test development process through item tryout, standardization and norms development, and finally publication.

PRELIMINARY STEPS

All test publications begin with an idea or concept, which is refined until the essential characteristics are clear enough to permit the publisher to evaluate both the theoretical or pedagogical soundness and the financial feasibility of the proposed publication. Ideas for test publications often come from individuals outside the publisher's staff, who become authors if their publication ideas are accepted and eventually published. As previously stated, ideas may also come from within a publisher's test development staff. The extent to which test publishers rely on outside authors as opposed to the internal professional staff varies considerably. This section discusses the development and refinement of publication ideas, the evaluation of proposed publications, and formal arrangements for publication.

Development and Refinement of Publication Ideas

Ideas for test publications come from a variety of sources. Scholars such as university faculty members who are conducting various types of research constitute the main group of individuals outside a publisher's staff who submit publication proposals. Graduate students and teachers who may have designed a single measurement device for a specific area of inquiry or a specific assessment need constitute another significant group of individuals contacting publishers with new publication ideas. All of these proposals are intended to meet perceived areas of need where available instrumentation is either of poor quality or entirely lacking. Publication ideas often evolve from within a publisher's staff because both developmental and marketing staff members have the relevant product knowledge and market awareness to develop sound publication ideas. Publishers are now beginning to use more sophisticated market research methods to identify market needs and opportunities.

Test publication submissions range from one-paragraph descriptions supplied in short letters of inquiry to complete publication proposals with extensive documentation. An entire doctoral dissertation or report of a research study is frequently received to substantiate a proposal. Because there is wide

TABLE 3.1. American Guidance Service's Publication Proposal Submission Requirements

The publisher requests that as much of the following information as is available be submitted with the publication proposal:

  I. Statement of the purpose and rationale for the test
 II. Description of the test
     a. Measurement properties
     b. Age/grade range
     c. Structure/subtests
     d. Administration time
     e. Method of administration
     f. Type of scoring/time
III. Components
     a. Nonconsumable items
     b. Consumable items
 IV. Primary markets
     a. Users
     b. Qualifications needed for administration and interpretation
     c. Types of users
  V. Competition
     a. Availability of similar tests
     b. Need for new test
     c. Advantages over competitors
 VI. Research summary
     a. Pilot studies
     b. Special research studies
     c. Additional research planned
VII. Review
     a. Results of expert review
     b. Results of submission to other publishers
VIII. Author credentials (vita)

Note. Reprinted by permission of American Guidance Service, Inc.

variability in the nature and extent of documentation submitted, publishers have developed guidelines for the type of information that should be submitted with a publication idea. An example of the type of information needed to evaluate a submission is shown in Table 3.1, which is routinely sent by American Guidance Service to all persons who make inquiries about publication of their material. Although all of the information listed in Table 3.1 may not be available, it represents an ideal that, if met, would provide most of the details needed for a thorough evaluation of a publication idea.

Frequently, the product that emerges as the final publication is rather different from the idea originally proposed. This occurs as a result of the process of refinement that takes places once the publisher contributes additional ideas or market-related data that help to reshape or better define a publication. Most major test publications represent a blending of ideas and expertise from the original author and the test publisher's professional development and marketing staffs. The nature of test publishing at present is such that the expertise, judgment, and experience of a variety of professional staff members are needed to launch a successful publication. The decision to publish is probably the most important decision a publisher makes, because the results of such decisions are what determine the professional reputation and financial success of a publishing firm. A key to the right publishing decisions lies in the procedures used to evaluate and screen publication submissions.

Evaluation of Proposed Publications

A first step in evaluating a proposed publication is to ascertain the extent to which it fits with a particular publisher's general publication goals. Test publishers do, to some extent, specialize in the types of publications they develop and market. A publisher specializing in personality and clinical tests, for example, would probably not be interested in publishing a new type of group-administered diagnostic reading test. This specialization among test publishers has occurred for both historical and economic reasons. It means, however, that different publishers fit into different niches of the testing materials market, and hence have developed the specialization and expertise necessary to reach their particular market segment efficiently.

Because resources are limited, test publishers must select publishing opportunities from among those available. This may be done either informally or in a more formal, structured way. Selection criteria typically include some measure of the proposed publication's theoretical soundness, as well as the extent to which it meets a market need. An attempt to gauge profitability may also be required before management reaches a final decision. A formal, systematic approach to evaluation increases the likelihood of selecting good publications that will, in turn, benefit the publisher both professionally and financially.

The procedure used by American Guidance Service is illustrated by the outline shown in Table 3.2. Each new submission or idea is evaluated using the Proposed New Product Rating System shown in the table. This system looks at both intangible and tangible (financial) factors. Intangible factors include ratings for various aspects of product integrity, marketability, research and development capability, and production capability. Ratings are assigned to each of several subfactors, and a total weighted composite score on a scale ranging from 10 to 100 is computed. In addition, the publication must meet a certain return on investment or other prescribed financial criteria. Publications whose composite rating and financial return index meet specified criteria are then placed on the publisher's list of approved publication proposals. Available resources dictate when work will begin on a particular publication submission. Experience with a particular evaluation system produces the criteria used to define acceptability. The publication rating system shown in Table 3.2 was developed from one originated by O'Meara (1961) which he applied to the evaluation of consumer products.

Some publishers place the final publishing decisions in the hands of executive staff members who comprise a publications advisory board. Such groups typically have editorial and marketing executives who pass judgment on proposed publications. A variety of approaches is possible. One publisher may use only an executive advisory board; another may choose ratings or a combination of formal ratings and group evaluation. Publishers must first routinize the screening process so that consistent methods are applied to all new publication submissions. Only a systematic approach to publications evaluation will result in generating dependable data useful to publishers in selecting successful publications.

Formal Arrangements for Publication

After a proposed publication has been evaluated by a publisher, a formal decision to accept or reject the proposal is made. If the

TABLE 3.2. Factors and Subfactors Comprising American Guidance Service's Proposed New Product Rating System

I. Product integrity
  a. Theoretical soundness
  b. Ease of use
  c. Originality
  d. Authorial credentials
  e. Proof of effectiveness
  f. Product longevity
II. Marketability
  a. Size of market
  b. Market needs/wants
  c. Nature of competition
  d. Importance of consumables/services
  e. Prime/value relationship
  f. Relation to present customer/promotion mix
  g. Effects on sales of present products
  h. Order fulfillment demands
III. Research and development capability
  a. Staff knowledge
  b. Staff experience
  c. Outside consultation required
  d. Managerial complexity
  e. Magnitude of project
  f. Time needed for development
  g. Access to outside resources
  h. Authorial compatibility
IV. Production capability
  a. Staff knowledge/experience
  b. Inventory complexity
  c. Assembly requirements
  d. Existing vendor capability
  e. Outside design requirements

Note. Reprinted by permission of American Guidance Service, Inc.

proposal is rejected, then the prospective author can, if desired, submit it to another publisher. If the proposal is accepted, then a contract is written to specify the responsibilities of author and publisher. A contract is typically a work-for-hire agreement that contains the terms and conditions to which both parties are expected to adhere during the time period covered by the contract. A contract usually covers such items as royalty rates, sharing of development costs, advances to authors, and revisions. In addition, some publishers include a time and task schedule for the entire development cycle. Due dates for critical items in the development schedule may also be added. Such a schedule seems to offer a number of obvious advantages, as well as to provide a time schedule to guide development of the publication. Contracts are usually written to cover one edition of a test; however, multiple-edition contracts also exist. Authorized rights to revisions may be specified, but a new contract is usually needed to cover all aspects of a revision.

As soon as a contract has been signed by both author and publisher, formal work on the publication commences. The master project budget developed during the financial analysis stage is used as a guide to financial planning and control. Once the preliminary steps of submission, evaluation, and contractual arrangements are concluded, content specifications and item development begin. The following section addresses these next steps.

CONTENT DEVELOPMENT

Once a decision to publish has been made and a formal agreement between the author and publisher has been executed, content development begins. In some cases, content may have already been developed by the time a publication contract is signed.

A first step in the development of content is the creation of a set of test specifications to guide the preparation of the test items. Such specifications, often termed a "blueprint," establish the basic content structure to guide item development. Once the scope of the content to be sampled by the test has been defined, test items can then be written. When an acceptable number of items have been prepared, critiqued, revised, and edited, they are subsequently administered in a tryout edition for the purpose of obtaining statistical data that permit the determination of item quality. The final step in content development is the use of item analysis data to aid in the assembly of the final form(s) of the test. This section discusses a variety of issues pertaining to the various facets of content development.

Preparing Specifications for an Achievement Test

Achievement tests are nearly always designed to assess student learning in a specific curricular area or course of study. For teacher-made tests, a single textbook or curriculum guide will often suffice as the source for content specification. In the case of achievement tests developed for state or national use, the specification of test content is complicated by the diversity of curriculum content across school districts, states, and geographic regions. In any given curricular area, the multiplicity of textbooks and courses of study is truly staggering. Attempting to distill common elements from these diverse sources is the task of the developer of a broad achievement test designed for state or national consumption.

In addition to content, a second requirement for an effective test blueprint is the specification of appropriate so-called "process objectives." In cognitive learning, certain mental processes are frequently called upon as a student engages in various aspects of learning content. Such mental processes as recalling, recognizing, defining, identifying, applying, analyzing, synthesizing, evaluating, generalizing, and predicting are examples of common process objectives (Thorndike & Hagen, 1977). These terms all attempt to describe overt, objectively verifiable behaviors that should occur if "learning" is really taking place in an instructional program. In a sense, these objectively verifiable behaviors become the means for assessing the degree to which learning is actually occurring in a specific curriculum.

An important influence on both education and test construction that deserves mention in connection with the specification of process objectives is Bloom's *Taxonomy of Educational Objectives*, particularly *Handbook I: Cognitive Domain* (Bloom, 1956). The six major categories of the cognitive domain, according to Bloom, are Knowledge, Comprehension, Application, Analysis, Synthesis, and Evaluation. The structure of knowledge that Bloom envisioned is hierarchical in nature, with the most basic requirement being the recall or recognition of certain facts (Knowledge). Knowledge was seen as a basic requirement necessary for the application of Comprehension, Application, Analysis, Synthesis, and Evaluation (see Tinkelman, 1971, for a more complete discussion). At least one important effect of Bloom's work was that it made teachers and test developers aware of the desirability of including the so-called "higher" mental processes both in education and in the assessment of educational outcomes. Not surprisingly, Bloom's work revealed that much of education dealt only with recall and recognition of facts and information, with the result that the processes of Analysis, Application, Synthesis, and Evaluation generally received less emphasis than was deemed desirable.

An example of a part of the content and process structure (behavioral objectives) for the KeyMath—Revised: A Diagnostic Inventory of Essential Mathematics (KeyMath-R; Connolly, 1988) is shown in Table 3.3. The KeyMath-R is a norm-referenced, individually administered assessment of basic mathematical skills designed for kindergarten through eighth grade. The content structure of KeyMath-R is pyramidal in nature, starting with three broad content groupings comprised of 13 strands; these are, in turn, comprised of 43 content domains, each of which has 6 items, for a total of 258 items in the complete test. The nature of the mathematics content is such that the exact specification of the elements of content (areas, strands, and domains) is precise and orderly. These content relationships were determined from a survey of a broad sampling of mathematics instructional materials and curricula, as well as a polling of nationally recognized mathematics curriculum experts (Connolly, 1988). The behavioral objectives for the items within a content domain illustrate the fusing of content and process as these relate to the establishment of criteria (behavioral objectives) for determining acquisition of a particular skill. Thus, the KeyMath-R example illustrates the manner in which the test specifications are prepared for a nationally standardized mathematics test.

Writing Items for an Achievement Test

Once the set of test specifications, or blueprint, has been prepared, item writing can begin. Items of good quality are essential if a test is to perform its intended purpose well. Skill in developing good achievement test items is something that takes considerable effort and practice, as well as supervision by an experienced item writer. This is particularly true of so-called "objective" items such

as multiple-choice or true–false. Several writers have provided excellent, extensive guidelines for writing good objective test items (see, e.g., Ebel, 1972; Mehrens & Lehman, 1984; Thorndike & Hagen, 1977; and Wesman, 1971). Despite the existence of a number of compilations of rules for writing effective test items, item writing is still an art that requires good general writing skills, creativity, and a knowledge of the rules for writing effective items. Irrespective of the skill of the item writer, all test items must be subjected to rigorous editorial scrutiny before actual tryout with the target population of examinees.

Preparing Specifications for an Ability Test

Unlike achievement tests, aptitude or ability tests are not based upon a specified curriculum or course of study; they are tied much more closely to the test developer's theoretical notions about the important constituents or indicators of the particular trait for which a test is being constructed. If, for example, a psychologist is constructing an intelligence test, the types of items used and the test format will depend to some extent on the psychologist's theoretical orientation; a test reflecting an adherence to g, or general intelligence, would be quite different from one reflecting, say, an adherence to a multiple-factor point of view. Irrespective of the theoretical orientation underlying the conceptualization of an ability test, it is not unusual for additional refining and reshaping to occur after data from item tryout or standardization become available. Factor-analytic procedures, as well as correlation/regression analyses of various sorts, are the methodological tools frequently used to help define and structure ability tests. Standard item analysis is, of course, important to insure item quality.

Writing Items for an Ability Test

Taxonomies of the types of items used in ability tests have been devised by both French (1951) and Guilford (1967), using somewhat different approaches. French (1951) surveyed available factor-analytic studies, inventoried the results and published a Kit of Tests for Reference Factors,

TABLE 3.3. Partial Content Structure for KeyMath—Revised: A Diagnostic Inventory of Essential Mathematics

Content area	Content strand (subtest)	Domains	Item objectives[a]
Basic Concepts (66 items; 11 domains)	Numeration (24 times)	A. Numbers 0–9 B. Numbers 0–99 C. Numbers 0–999 D. Multidigit numbers	The student can . . . A-1 count objects (1–5 in a set) A-2 form a set . . . A-3 read one-digit numerals (0–9) A-4 order a set . . . A-5 count objects (1–9) in a set A-6 name the ordinal position
	Rational Numbers (18 items)	A. Fractions B. Decimals C. Percents	B-1 determine decimal tenths B-2 determine decimal hundredths B-3 give the next number in a sequence of decimal values B-4 Express decimal hundredths as a fraction B-5 order a set of decimal values from smallest to largest B-6 identify which decimal value in a set is closest to a given common fraction
	Geometry (24 times)	A. Spatial/attribute relations B. Two-dimensional-shapes C. Coordinate . . . geometry D. Three-dimensional shapes	

Operations (90 items; 15 domains)

Addition (18 items)
A. Models and basic facts
B. Algorithm to add
C. Adding rational numbers

Subtraction (18 items)
A. Models and basic facts
B. Algorithm to subtract
C. Subtracting rational numbers

Multiplication (18 items)
A. Models and basic facts
B. Algorithm to multiply
C. Multiplying rational numbers

A-1 determine the total . . . .
A-2 determine the total . . . .
A-3 identify the multiplication
A-4 complete multiplication
A-5 complete multiplication fact . . . .
A-6 complete multiplication facts

Division (18 items)
A. Models and basic facts
B. Algorithms to multiply
C. Dividing rational numbers

Mental Computation (18 items)
A. Computation chains
B. Whole numbers . . . .
C. Rational numbers . . . .

(continued)

TABLE 3.3. (*continued*)

Content area	Content strand (subtest)	Domains	Item objectives[a]
Applications (102 items; 17 domains)	Measurement (24 items)	A. Comparisons . . . . B. Using non-standard units . . . C. Using standard units—length D. Using standard units—weight	
	Time and Money (24 items)	A. Identifying passage of time B. Using clocks C. Monetary amounts . . . . D. Monetary amounts . . .	A-1 identify a season of the year A-2 sequence a set of events in chronological order A-3 identify yesterday, today, and tomorrow A-4 read a monthly calendar to identify date of a given day A-5 read a monthly calendar to identify the date at the end of a given interval A-6 read a date presented in short form
	Estimation (18 items)	A. Whole and rational numbers B. Measurement C. Computation	
	Interpreting Data (18 items)	A. Charts B. Graphs C. Probability statistics	
	Problem Solving (18 items)	A. Solving routine problems B. Understanding non-routine problems C. Solving non-routine problems	

Note. Adapted from *KeyMath—Revised: A Diagnostic Inventory of Essential Mathematics* by A. J. Connolly, 1988, Circle Pines, MN: American Guidance Service. Copyright 1988 by American Guidance Service, Inc. Adapted by permission.

[a]Each domain contains six item objectives; only selected item objectives are shown as examples.

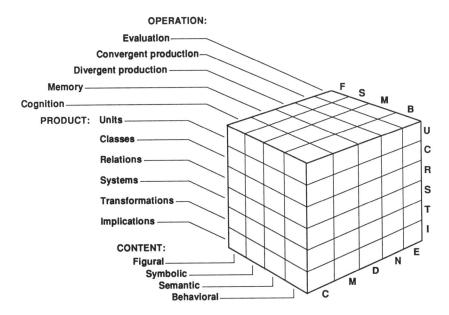

FIGURE 3.1.   Structure-of-intellect model (SIM). From *The Nature of Human Intelligence* by J. P. Guilford, 1967, New York: McGraw-Hill. Copyright 1967 by McGraw-Hill. Reprinted by permission.

which contained recommended tests for the factors identified. Guilford and his colleagues conducted numerous factor-analytic studies as part of a large-scale aptitude research project, in an attempt to confirm the dimensions of Guilford's (1967) structure-of-intellect model (SIM), shown in Figure 3.1.

The SIM, as shown, is a three-dimensional model defined by "content," "operations," and "products." Each of the 120 cells is defined by a unique combination of the content–operation–product dimensions of the model. Guilford's research has resulted in a highly splintered and somewhat controversial view of human abilities, leaving a number of the cells still unconfirmed.

A survey of commonly used ability tests has resulted in the catalogue of the most frequently used types of items shown in Table. 3.4. Items are classified by the three content dimensions frequently encountered in such tests—verbal, symbolic, and figural. Analogies, for example, are commonly found in all three content formats. Verbal and figural analogies are commonly used in tests of general ability; analogies in symbolic form that employ letters or numerals, though less frequently encountered, are sometimes used. In no sense are the types of items given in Table 3.4 intended to be an exhaustive

inventory. Space limitations preclude giving illustrations of the various types of items; readers unfamiliar with them may wish to consult Thorndike (1982), who provides illustrations for many.

One of the primary requisites for constructing good ability items seems to be ingenuity, particularly in devising figural items and in creating good foils, or misleads. There are no extensive guidelines for preparing ability items, as there are for achievement test items; definition is provided by the trait or characteristic being assessed, applicable statistical methodology, and the judgment and ingenuity of the test developer.

Two Additional Considerations in Item Development

Two additional considerations in item preparation to be addressed here are the number of items to be prepared and the item review process. First, there is almost always a question about the number of items that need to be written for tryout; unfortunately, there is no simple or pat answer to this question. Factors that should be considered are (1) the age or grade range covered by the test; (2) number of forms/length of test; (3) skill of the item writer; (4) novelty of the item type; and

TABLE 3.4. Types of Items Commonly Used in Ability Tests

Item type	Verbal/semantic (words/sentences)	Symbolic (letters/numerals)	Figural/pictorial (geometric/abstract)
Analogies	×	×	×
Classification	×	×	×
Series completion	×	×	×
Matrices	×	×	×
Synonym/antonym	×		
Sentence completion	×		
Reasoning problems	×	×	
Disarranged stimuli	×	×	
Synthesis	×	×	×
Immediate/delayed recall	×	×	×
Visualization: two dimensions			×
Visualization: three dimensions			×

(5) cost of the enterprise. All of these factors must be weighed carefully in any final decision pertaining to the number of items needed. Cost factors definitely permeate the entire development process and need to be considered at an early stage. A heavy reliance on expensive illustrations or artwork is not advisable if funds for such work are restricted or unavailable. If figure analogy items, for example, are being written for ages 8–18, more items will obviously be required than for a test that spans only two or three age levels. Other things being equal, inexperienced items writers will need to produce more items to meet the target number than will experienced item writers. As a general rule-of-thumb to allow for attrition, it is recommended that 25%–50% more items than are needed should be prepared. All of the factors stated previously will influence the final decision.

A second consideration is that of the process of editorial and content review of items prior to tryout. In the case of achievement tests, content review is recommended as a check for inaccuracies and ambiguities unforeseen by the item writer. Ability items need scrutiny in regard to the plausibility or implausibility of misleads. All items will benefit from a thorough editorial review to check for mechanical errors or omissions. Item tryout costs can be substantially reduced if flawed or poor-quality items are located in the content and editorial review stages prior to tryout. Such items can then either be discarded or revised to correct problems spotted by reviewers. Review of items by ethnic or minority group members, if needed, should be undertaken at this review stage prior to tryout.

Item Tryout

After item writing, review, and editing have been completed, the items are ready for administration to the sample of individuals designated for tryout. The dimensions of the item tryout program will be determined by the following considerations: (1) availability of funds for tryout; (2) age or grade span for which data are needed; (3) size of the tryout sample; and (4) logistical details, such as time required, time of year, and various administrative details. Each of these dimensions of the tryout program is discussed below.

Availability of Funds for Tryout

The scope of the tryout program is dictated by the funds available from the publisher. To some extent, the characteristics of a particular test determine the amount that will be spent on tryout; however, the availability of research and development funds from the publisher can certainly influence test de-

TABLE 3.5. Item Tryout Budget for a General Achievement Battery

Type of expenditure	Explanation	Budgeted amount (in dollars)	Percentage of total budget
Inducements	Materials for participating schools	500	1.1
Clerical services	Payments to hourly clerical worker	6,500	14.4
Item writing	Preparation of additional items	1,000	2.2
Testing	Examiner payments for test adminis- tration (to 1,000 students)	26,000	57.8
Consulting	Payments to subject-matter experts	4,500	10.0
Shipping	Shipment of tryout materials to coor- dinators	1,000	2.2
Printing and binding	Preparation of tryout materials	2,000	4.4
Travel	Travel to authorial meeting	2,500	5.6
Miscellaneous	Uncategorized expenditures	1,000	2.2
	Project total	45,000	99.9

velopment plans. A significant portion of the cost is dictated by the type of test. For individually administered tests, examiners must be paid for each examinee located and tested. For comprehensive test batteries, this fee can be as much as $15–$25 per examinee.

Table 3.5 shows the tryout budget for an individually administered general achievement battery. For each expense category, the percentage it represents of the total tryout budget is also shown. This budget was based upon a plan to test 1,000 students in 1st through 12th grades.

Age or Grade Span

Serious consideration and careful planning must be given to the age or grade span for the tryout program. It is essential that items be tried out at the age or grade levels where they are intended to be used. Items should, as a rule, be tried out at enough age or grade levels to obtain sufficient data to permit decisions about the item to be made. Items for which some tryout data are already available can be targeted to the functional age or grade level more easily than can untried items. In the case of group tests, items may be repeated at adjacent test levels in order to obtain a broader spectrum of item performance data. For individual tests, the tailored testing format typically permits item data to be obtained across all functional age or grade levels.

Size of the Tryout Sample

The size of the group used for item analysis depends on both theoretical and practical considerations. Obviously, enough individuals must be tested to permit reasonably stable estimates of basic item statistics. Although no single number can be given, authorities agree that stable estimates of classical item difficulty and discrimination indices are possible with tryout sample sizes of about 200–500 individuals (Henrysson, 1971; Thorndike, 1982). As a general rule, the tryout sample should adequately represent the final target population of test takers. Thus, the item tryout sample should match the final target population on relevant demographic variables, insofar as this is possible. This ideal can frequently only be approximated in actual practice. For some group achievement and ability tests, it is necessary to include diverse types of schools from all major geographic regions, even at the item tryout stage, in order to meet local school district requirements for representation in test research programs. Such requirements are often conditions of the sale of materials after publication. If ethnic subgroups are needed for special item bias studies, care must be taken to oversample from these groups to meet the minimum sample size requirements given above.

Practical Details

A number of practical details must be considered in planning and executing item analysis programs. Care must be taken to avoid overtaxing examinees by trying out too many items. If group tests are administered within a specified time limit, too many items per time unit will result in too many omissions of items at the end of the test, with the result that adequate item statistics will be unavailable. A good rule to follow is that of preparing multiple test forms whose length will permit about 90% of the examinees to finish all items within the allotted time period. Multiple forms of individual tests are also advisable when the testing period will last more than 1 to $1\frac{1}{2}$ hours, depending on the age of the examinees.

Another administrative detail that merits careful consideration is the time of year for which item analysis data are obtained. If the final test forms are intended for fall testing, then it is important that the item analysis program take place in the fall. This is particularly true of achievement tests, where differential growth rates in school subjects occur during the school year. Finally, it is important that directions, answer sheets or record forms, and other elements of the testing program be clearly prepared and well organized so that testing will occur smoothly under relatively uniform conditions.

Item Analysis

"Item analysis" refers to the statistical analysis of examinees' responses to test items. Various methodological procedures have been developed in an attempt to differentiate among items in terms of their quality or desirability for use in a particular test. "Classical" item analysis procedures are defined as standard item statistics used over the past 60 years, such as item difficulty (e.g., percentage of examinees passing) and item discrimination. "Item response theory" (IRT), also known as "item–test regression," has evolved over the last 25 years and includes various latent-trait models useful in the calibration of individual test items. Both

types of item analysis procedures are discussed here.

Classical Item Analysis

In classical item analysis, individuals similar to those for whom the test is ultimately intended are identified and tested with the tryout items. For each item tried out, standard item analysis statistics, such as percentage passing, item–total test correlation, and (for multiple-choice items) the percentage choosing each distractor, are determined. There are two types of applications of classical item analysis: (1) within-group applications and (2) between-group applications.

Within-group applications are item analyses based on a single reference group. The group may, for example, consist of college-bound high school seniors, students enrolled in beginning French, or students studying mechanical drafting. Whatever the nature of the group, there is typically an interest in the performance of that group. Acceptance or rejection of tryout items is usually based on statistics computed for that single reference group. There is no interest in the performance of the items in multiple reference groups.

Between-group applications are item analyses based on multiple reference groups. Such information is important for studying item functioning across several age or grade groups. Multiple reference groups may, for example, be successive age or grade groups. In broad-gauge tests of ability and achievement, items must function satisfactorily—not merely in a single group, but in all such groups where an item is to be used. For example, in a test of intelligence, items must show an increase in percentage of examinees passing from age to age in order to be retained for inclusion in the final test. These analytical methods are, in reality, based on a form of item regression on age, where the slope of the line depicting percentage passing by age is of central importance in deciding on the item status. This particular application of classical item analysis was used by Terman and Merrill (1937) in their revision of the *Stanford–Binet Intelligence Scale*. From percentage-passing curves for each item, the age where 50% of the individuals pass the item is determined. An "item age" thus becomes available for each item and can be used as a way to position items over a relatively broad span of ages.

Item Response Theory

The relatively widespread availability of high-speed computers has stimulated significant advances in IRT. IRT applications are also known as "item calibration," "latent-trait analysis," and "item characteristic curve theory." Essentially, IRT is a type of item–test score regression that permits single test items to be calibrated or referenced against the underlying, or latent, trait measured by a test (Lord, 1980). These capabilities have at least two advantages. First, test items can be referenced to the ability scale for the underlying trait; thus, it becomes possible to express item difficulty and ability on the trait assessed by the item in common terms. This capability is highly desirable from a test construction standpoint and is not easily accomplished with classical item analysis methods. Second, because IRT is essentially a type of regression procedure, item parameters remain invariant across groups of varying abilities (Lord, 1980). Unlike classical item analysis, in which item parameters change as the group upon which they are based changes, IRT frees estimates of item parameters from the ability level of the group on which the estimates were obtained. The benefits to be realized in test construction from both advantages mentioned constitute persuasive arguments for the use of IRT methods.

In summary, both classical and IRT methods provide valuable information about the functional utility of individual test items. The choice of methodology depends upon what sort of information is needed and the nature of the trait measured by the items. There can be little doubt that IRT approaches offer several advantages, although more research is still needed to document IRT application fully.

STANDARDIZATION

"Standardization" is the process employed to introduce objectivity and uniformity into test administration, scoring, and interpretation. If the test results are to be meaningful, then different examiners must have the same carefully worked-out instructions for administering and scoring in order to insure that the test data are gathered under uniform, standard conditions. Normative interpretation of performance on a test is possible only if these conditions are met (Anastasi, 1982).

This section considers the various facets of test standardization: assembly of the final test, including directions for administering and scoring; the standardization of individually administered tests; the standardization of group-administered tests; norms development; and auxiliary studies.

Assembly of Final Test Form(s)

Item analysis yields the information necessary to select the items for the final standardization edition of a test. Essentially, the pool of tryout items is sorted into such classifications as "rejects," "salvageable with additional work," and "acceptable." A work plan is developed that logically begins with the "acceptable" items, allocates these to one or more test forms, and then draws as required from items that are "salvageable with additional work." If more items are required to meet the test blueprint than are available in the "acceptable" and "salvageable . . ." categories of the item tryout pool, additional items will have to be prepared and tried out before development of the final test forms is completed. In order to avoid losing time and increasing development costs, it is recommended that a sufficient surplus of items be tried out to allow for such attrition (see above, for a more complete discussion).

If multiple test forms are being developed, then items will need to be allocated from the tryout pool so that the forms are as nearly identical as possible in content coverage, item difficulty, and item intercorrelations. Careful balancing of test forms using the item statistics mentioned will help insure that the final test forms meet the statistical requirements for parallel test forms—for example, that they have equal means, equal variances, and equal intercorrelations (Gulliksen, 1950). In actual practice, the matching of test forms on these statistics is seldom if ever perfect, so that this represents an ideal to be approximated as closely as possible.

After the standardization test forms are developed, several types of auxiliary materials must be prepared for the standardization program. Included among these are the directions for administering the test, answer sheets or record forms, and various other record blanks and directions needed to select the standardization sample and complete the testing program. For some individually administered tests, special manipulatives must be designed and manufactured.

It is essential that the directions for administering the test receive careful scrutiny before they are finalized. Thorough editing of all test directions is recommended before standardization, because the directions need to be in final form before normative data are gathered. Answer sheets must be developed for group-administered tests; record forms need to be designed for individually administered tests. These answer forms need not be in final form for publication, but it is essential that they be functional and easily used by both students and examiners. If test items use the completion or free-response format, as is frequently done in individual tests, then directions for evaluating the responses or recording the examinees' responses must be developed. If responses are merely recorded, then it becomes possible to evaluate them later, after responses obtained in the standardization program are analyzed.

Selecting the Standardization Sample

Selection of the test standardization sample begins with a carefully prepared plan for obtaining the individuals who will be tested. The elements necessary for such a plan are discussed below, followed by separate sections devoted to standardization sampling plans for group administered and individually administered tests.

Planning the Norming Program

A careful plan for obtaining the standardization sample is required, because the test results obtained from the norm group are typically generalized to an entire national population referenced by age or grade. Thus, it becomes essential that the norm group constitute a representative sample from the national population it represents. If such representation is to occur in the sample, then

procedures must be spelled out from the start to insure that the norming sample is systematically and meticulously identified and tested. Control is sought over as many relevant factors as possible, in order to minimize the likelihood of introducing bias into the selection of the norming sample.

Every norming program is, in reality, a compromise between what is desirable from a strictly scientific perspective and what is practically feasible from the standpoint of the financial resources available. The goal of all norming efforts should be to obtain the best standardization sample possible within the financial limitations of the project. A systematic, well-articulated sampling specification plan is the key to obtaining a standardization sample that is both scientifically defensible and practically obtainable.

Sampling specifications must carefully delineate the various population reference groups that must be sampled. For educational and psychological tests, the two most common national reference groups are age and grade; however, in some instances local norms groups of various sorts may be the appropriate reference groups of interest. The specifications for obtaining national and local norms groups will, of necessity, differ considerably. The former usually require more complex, multistage sampling methods; the latter require simpler, less elaborate designs for obtaining norming samples. A well-prepared plan or design is essential in either case.

In addition to the reference group, the standardization sampling plan must specify the extent to which such demographic factors as socioeconomic level, gender, geographic region, urban–rural residence, and race or ethnic group are to influence the selection of the sample. If the standardization sample is to represent a national population, then the success in representing that population will be judged by comparing the sample's demographic statistics with those of the national reference population of interest. Obviously, it is essential to work out sampling procedures in advance, so that the demographic statistics for the standardization sample compare as favorably as is practically feasible with those of the national reference population.

A careful plan must specify in detail the method to be used to obtain the sample. Although norms samples at one time were largely samples of convenience, their quality has improved dramatically over the past 25 years or so. The introduction of probability sampling techniques by test publishers has substantially increased the precision of their test norms. Although probability sampling methods are desirable because they permit estimation of the amount of error present in the norms (Angoff, 1971), they present an ideal that can at best be only approximated in actual practice. This fact is illustrated by comparing the methods used to obtain norms samples for group-administered and individually administered tests. Although both types of tests usually share the same goal of securing a norms sample representative of broad national age or grade reference groups, differences in test format together with their associated costs necessitate the use of different sampling procedures for the two types of tests. Procedures for each type of test are discussed separately in the next two sections.

Group Test Samples

An important characteristic of group tests for norms sample selection is their lower administrative cost per examinee when compared with individual tests. The very fact that individuals can be tested in naturally occurring units such as grades or classes has an important bearing on the type of norming program that is practically and economically feasible. When schools or classes are used as the units to define the sample, then it becomes possible to use a type of probability sampling known technically as "multi-stage stratified random cluster sampling." This class of sampling methods has certain distinct advantages: (1) The process of selecting the elements of the sample is automatic and is not left up to idiosyncratic judgment or mere availability; (2) each element in the sample has a known probability of being selected; and (3) the known selection probabilities can be used to develop weights to correct for over- or underrepresentation within the sample when the norms are developed (Angoff, 1971).

Because schools and classes are naturally occurring units, or "clusters," an individual student is included in the norm sample as a direct result of this or her class's and/or school's having been selected by the sampling procedure used. Although the goal may, for example, be to estimate the performance of all U.S. fourth-grade pupils on a reading test, it is not practically feasible to list all fourth-grade pupils in the United States and then draw a random sample from such a list. Instead, multistage sampling methods are used; these begin with a known, manageable listing, such as school districts. For efficiency, the school districts may be grouped in different ways (e.g., by size, socioeconomic status, geographic region, etc.). Once these subunits, or "strata," are formed, it does become possible to sample randomly within the strata. Thus, one proceeds via systematic sampling methods to schools, classes, and finally to individual students within selected classes. These students then become participants in the norming program.

The use of a multistage cluster sampling method, in conjunction with the decreased cost per student associated with group tests, results in much larger group test standardization samples than are employed for individually administered tests. Although size per se is not a guarantee of precision of the norms, well-designed group test standardization programs in which 10,000–20,000 students per grade or age group are tested permit more precise estimates of population performance than do individual test standardization efforts based on only a fraction of those numbers of individuals.

The use of sophisticated probability sampling methods never permits an entirely precise estimate of the norms, however, because some school districts and/or schools refuse to participate. Thus, despite attempts at randomized selection procedures, all norming programs consist of voluntary participants. The rate of acceptance of participation permits an estimation of the extent to which the ideal probability sampling model was realized in a particular norming effort.

Individual Test Samples

The need to test each participant in the norming sample individually precludes the use of probability sampling methods with individually administered tests. A procedure known as "quota sampling" is typically used in the selection of individual test standardization samples. For this procedure, a quota of examinees is assigned to each testing center participating in the norming program. It then becomes the responsibility of the test center supervisor to locate each person specified in the quota. The judgment of the supervisor is, in effect, the determining factor in deciding which individuals meet the criteria used to define the quota. Even if multistage sampling procedures similar to those used for group tests were feasible for individual tests, the quota sample is, in the final analysis, a voluntary sample: Examinees of school age can only be tested with parental consent, and norming at the adult ages is totally dependent upon volunteers. Thus, it is not possible to specify the precision of the norms for individual tests that use quota sampling methods to designate norming samples (Angoff, 1971).

There are several ways in which errors present in sample selection can be minimized. American Guidance Service, which has conducted extensive norming studies for several individually administered tests during the past few years, uses a variation of the quota sampling procedure in which individuals to be tested are selected randomly by computer from pools of available examinees. Although this method is not a probability sampling procedure, it minimizes the influence of subjective judgment, which is always present when the test center supervisor must locate examinees of a certain age, gender, ethnic group, urban or rural residence, and socioeconomic status. Experience has shown that substantial error is introduced in particular when local personnel must classify individuals in terms of socioeconomic status. Coding of demographic characteristics is accomplished by trained employees under the supervision of the publisher. This procedure also saves considerable time, because each test center supervisor is told whom to test instead of being asked to locate individuals who meet specified demographic characteristics. This procedure also enables alternate examinees to be easily identified, should some of the primary test subjects be unavailable on the day of the test. Although this procedure requires more lead time before testing so that available examinees can be located and entered into a central computerized data bank, the increased accuracy and efficiency in conducting the actual testing program more than compensate for the extra step in identifying potential examinees.

As a general rule of thumb, individually administered tests employ a minimum of 100 examinees per grade or year of age. Compared with group tests, which typically test several thousand individuals per grade or year of age, individual tests are handicapped by their small standardization samples. To generalize from a sample of 100 children aged 10 to the entire population of U.S. 10-year-olds is, even with careful sample selection, risky at best. Small samples are typically selected by proportionate allocation across test centers; recent census data are used as the basis for such allocations. For example, the specification for one examinee might be as follows:

Geographic Region: Northwestern United States
Age: Between 10 years, 0 months and 10 years, 5 months
Ethnic group: Black
Parental Education: High school graduate
Gender: Male
Type of community: Large city

Such allocation procedures insure that the census demographic characteristics are reflected in the norming sample. There is no way, however, to determine mathematically the amount of sampling error present.

Finally, the standardization of any test, group or individual, is a complicated, expensive undertaking that depends upon the cooperation of countless individuals, particularly examiners and examinees. Despite the most extensive, detailed plans, there will always be unforeseen circumstances to complicate what is already a complex procedure. One can only hope that the compromises inevitably required do not seriously impair the quality of the normative data, and that the sound judgment and good will of all persons participating in the norming program will bring the project to a successful completion.

Auxiliary Studies

Special studies must often be undertaken concurrently with the standardization program to provide data needed to support a test. For example, test–retest reliability studies with the same or an alternate test form are frequently needed. Other possible purposes for special studies include equating of old and new editions, equating forms or levels of a test, and correlating test results with external criteria (e.g., results of other standardized tests, course grades, and supervisors' ratings).

Examinees tested in these studies may either be selected from the regular standardization sample or obtained from supplementary sources. Criteria used to select these special study participants are usually less rigorous than those imposed on standardization sample participants. There is really no need to impose rigorous selection criteria on these studies unless there is a special reason to study certain properties of the test (e.g., validity with certain types of individuals). For most classical equating studies it is desirable to test a wide range of ability, in order to estimate equivalence at various points of the score scale with reasonable precision. For reliability studies, it is desirable to estimate reliability with individuals comparable in ability to those in the norming sample. Care should be taken to insure that there is not undue restriction in range of ability in the sample used to study reliability. The *Standards for Educational and Psychological Testing* (AERA, APA, & NCME,1985) serves as a general guide to the types of additional data required at the time of test publication.

Development of Test Norms

As soon as the standardization testing has been completed, statistical analyses of the data gathered can begin. It is essential that the statistical analyses by carefully planned with reference to the types of norms required. Much time, effort, and expense can be spared by a comprehensive analysis of the data needed and the preparation of a well-articulated plan for norms development *before* any statistics are produced. The steps required to develop norms usually fall into the following general pattern: (1) data editing and checking, (2) data entry and scoring, (3) statistical analysis, (4) development of norms tables, and (5) supplementary studies. Each of these operations is discussed below.

Data Editing and Checking

Inspection, editing, and checking of the completed answer forms are especially important for individually administered tests that do not employ machine-scannable documents

for recording examinee responses. Data recorded on the answer forms may need to be coded by hand before they can be entered into the computer. For example, such demographic data as age/date of birth, grade, and other information may be given special numerical codes before data entry. The coding scheme must be carefully worked out to insure that all of the data needed for any part of the analysis are captured and coded at this time.

Response forms for individually administered tests may need to be checked to make certain that each individual tested meets the requirements originally established for the quota of examinees assigned to a particular test center. Also, the response forms may need to be inspected to insure that basal and ceiling rules, if required, were properly followed and that test administration generally seems to have been satisfactory. Occassionally, test item responses may need to be hand-scored or coded as correct–incorrect before computer entry can occur. In most cases, this first manual inspection by clerical personnel is done quickly and is designed to identify any gross anomalies that need attention before additional processing occurs.

For group tests where responses have been recorded on machine-scannable test booklets or answer sheets, little manual inspection is required, because most checks can be performed by the computer if the data have been coded in preassigned grids on the booklets or answer sheets. In most cases, answer sheets for group tests have only to be batch-coded using a scannable document known as a "header sheet," and assembled for transport to the electronic equipment used to scan or "read" the marks coded on the sheets.

Data Entry and Scoring

If answer forms cannot be scanned by machine, the response recorded for each test item must be keypunched or entered onto magnetic computer tape before computer analysis can begin. Once the response record has been recorded on computer tape, raw scores can be produced by comparing the examinee's responses with the key programmed into the computer. As soon as raw scores are obtained and recorded on magnetic tape, subsequent statistical analyses can be undertaken.

Machine-scannable answer sheets are designed to be scanned or "read" by high-speed electronic machines capable of processing several thousand sheets per hour of operation. These machines use either reflected or transmitted light to produce a record of answer sheet marks on computer tape. Once these marks are recorded on computer tape, scoring can occur; raw scores can be derived and recorded for further computer analysis.

Statistical Analysis

As soon as raw scores are available, statistical analyses of various types may be conducted with the data base. Such analyses often begin with basic information for each subtest, such as raw-score frequency distributions, cumulative percentages, means, and standard deviations. These data provide the basic descriptive information about how the test has performed in the standardization program. Such data are usually obtained for subgroups of interest, such as each age or grade group tested. For multiscore tests, subtest intercorrelations may be important at this point and are usually generated as a part of the basic summary statistics. Demographic counts are often prepared along with the basic summary statistics.

Other types of analyses that are sometimes performed subsequent to the basic analyses include population subgroup analyses, item analyses, composite and total test score analyses, and factor analyses, to mention the more common types. When the norms tables become available, raw scores for the norms sample are usually converted to derived scores, so that several analyses may be obtained using the normative scores instead of raw scores. The foregoing types of data analysis procedures are all essential pre-

requisites to the development of norms tables.

Development of Norms Tables

Development of norms tables refers to the process of preparing the tables of derived scores used to interpret performance on a test. Such tables form a major part of the test manual and must be offered at the time a norm-referenced test is released for general use.

Anastasi (1982) has offered a useful classification scheme for the most common types of derived scores. As summarized in Table 3.6, norms are of two basic types: developmental and within-group. Developmental norms locate an individual along a span or continuum of development. Age and grade equivalents are the most common examples of developmental norms. Both scales offer rather limited information, because they match an individual's performance to the typical or average performance of a particular age or grade group. For example, an age equivalent (mental age) of 5 years, 6 months on an intelligence test means that the individual's score corresponds to the typical or average score for children aged 5 years, 6 months. A similar interpretation referenced to school grades can be offered for grade equivalents. Because developmental norms are tenuous from a psychometric perspective and cannot be manipulated easily from a statistical standpoint, within-group norms are generally preferred for test interpretation.

Within-group norms reference an individual's performance to a single reference group of interest. Age and grade are two of the most common reference groups, but

TABLE 3.6. Classification of Some Common Norm-Referenced Scores

Type of comparison	Norm-referenced scores	Frame of reference
Developmental	Grade equivalents Age equivalents	Multiple grade groups Multiple age groups
Within-group	Percentile ranks Standard scores Stanines T-scores	Single age groups Single grade groups Single reference groups of any sort

Note. Adapted from *Psychological Testing* (5th edition) by A. Anastasi, 1982, New York: Macmillan. Copyright 1982 by Macmillan. Adapted by permission.

many others can be used. As shown in Table 3.6, there are several types of within-group normative scores to choose from, depending upon the type of test and the interpretation to be made. Within-group norms can be applicable to any reference group of interest. Thus, standard scores can be prepared for age groups, for grade groups, for job applicants, for licensure candidates, and so on.

Within-group norms yield more precise, psychometrically sound information than do developmental norms, because it becomes possible to place an individual more precisely in a reference group of particular interest. Percentile ranks, for example, show the rank of an individual in a typical group of 100 persons; standard scores convey information about the extent to which an individual's test performance deviates from the mean of a particular age or grade group as expressed in standard deviation units. Thus, it becomes possible to describe a person's performance with more precision than is true of age and grade equivalents. It should be pointed out that Table 3.6 is merely suggestive of the more common types of within-group norms and is certainly not an exhaustive listing.

In the comparison of group and individual test standardization procedures made above, one major difference cited is that of sample size. This difference has a direct bearing on the ease of norms development. With their larger sample sizes, group test results are usually more stable across grade or age reference groups than are those for individual tests. Norms are much more stable and amenable to statistical treatment if they can be derived from a sample of 10,000–20,000 individuals per age or grade, for example, than for samples of 100 persons of a given age or grade. A procedure to compensate for small sample sizes has been proposed by Angoff and Robertson (1987) and has been used successfully in several norming programs for individual tests.

The development of norms tables is both an art and a science. In the past, much of the work needed to develop norms tables was done by graphic methods, which required plotting data points and smoothing the curves by eye. Thus, norms development was time-consuming and costly. Recently, computer programs that do the plotting, curve fitting, and smoothing have shown promise as tools to streamline norms development. These will undoubtedly receive even greater use as advances in computer technology occur.

Norms tables appearing in a test manual are the result of many complex, interrelated steps. These require that the norms developer have (1) a thorough knowledge of statistics and the ability to work with data; and (2) the skill to create norms that compensate and adjust as needed for anomalies present in the data, while at the same time preserving the fundamental integrity of the data base.

If a collection of test items has been calibrated by using one of the common IRT models (see "Item Response Theory," above), and if the underlying latent-trait scale has been normed on a suitable reference group, it becomes possible to use the same norms with new items or test forms as long as such new items or test forms are calibrated to the original set of items. This application of IRT has implications for norming item banks, because it permits the generation of norms for a large number of different test forms constructed from an item bank. The only requirement, as stated, is that all items in the bank be "chained" or linked together on a common item difficulty scale.

Supplementary Studies

Reliability information and, to some extent, validity data constitute separate data sets that must be developed concurrently with the norms tables. Plans must be made to collect, analyze, and develop the types of supporting data that are needed for a particular test. In some situations, equating of test forms and/or levels must also be completed before the actual norms development process can be undertaken. This is especially true of multilevel test batteries administered across a wide span of grades. Space does not permit detailed coverage of the methodology used to conduct reliability, validity, and equating studies and to analyze the results. Excellent discussions are available in Angoff (1971) and Thorndike (1982).

PUBLICATION

As soon as the standardization program and norms development are completed, final publication plans can be made. It is not always possible, especially for individually administered tests, to gauge the duration of the standardization program exactly; therefore, once that activity has been completed, more precise scheduling is possible. Additional activities leading toward final publication are as follows: establishing the publication schedule, producing publication components, developing the publication marketing plan, doing postpublication research, and evaluating the entire publication process. Each of these topics is discussed below.

Establishing the Publication Schedule

The development of the final publication really occurs in two rather distinct phases. The first is the component development period, during which final manuscript copy for each component is created. The second is the production process, which begins with manuscript copy and terminates with printed and bound typeset materials ready for publication. Of these two phases of activity, the manuscript development phase usually cannot be scheduled as precisely as the final production phase.

Although the final publication schedule is typically set after standardization and norms development are completed, the schedule will need to be reviewed carefully; revised dates, as required, must be established after the final manuscript development phase is completed. Unforeseen delays in the preparation of final manuscript copy for publication components are not uncommon.

An effective publication schedule must, first of all, be realistic. Establishing impossible due dates for the various facets of the final publication development process creates frustration and disillusionment in everyone, and can create serious staff morale problems. Because marketing activities depend substantially on establishing a firm publication date, any delays can have an adverse impact on marketing activities planned to launch a new publication.

A second requisite for an effective publication schedule is that it is established jointly in a cooperative effort by those staff members who must adhere to it. Those persons who must actually do the day-to-day work are best informed and qualified to establish time requirements for various activities to be un-

dertaken during final publication. A schedule imposed from above by management is almost always doomed to failure if it does not reflect the knowledge and experience of staff members and if their endorsement is not secured before the schedule is set.

An example of a publication schedule is shown in Table 3.7 for a hypothetical instrument, the ABC Reading Skills Test. Although this schedule was developed for illustrative purposes only, it is based on my own experience in developing similar schedules for actual test publications. Table 3.7 shows the completion dates for the various development tasks expressed in weeks prior to publication. For example, norms development is scheduled for completion 78 weeks prior to publication. Note that at this stage in the development process, each component must be scheduled separately; the publication date is really dependent upon the amount of time required to complete the test manual, the most complex component to be developed and published. Note also that all steps from typesetting through receipt of final print materials by the warehouse are production steps, whereas all prior steps are under the direction of the research and development staff. In this example, the various editing steps for the manual require 21 weeks to complete. This may seem excessive, but experience has proved otherwise, particularly for manuals similar in length to the one shown here. It is assumed also in this example that the test booklet has been used in practically its final form during the standardization process and needs only minor changes for publication. Development of the answer sheet is begun at about the same time as manuscript development for the manual, mainly because design details are needed to write certain sections of the manual describing the test and giving directions for administering and scoring.

Producing Publication Components

Producing test components is a highly complex, demanding task that requires specialized training in various technologies used in publishing. Production personnel typically begin with an edited manuscript and, through various processes, supervise the transformation of that manuscript into printed copy. The "manuscript" is often re-

TABLE 3.7. Final Publication Schedule for the ABC Reading Skills Test

Component	Activity	Completion time in weeks[a]
Manual (150 pages)	Norms development	P − 78
	Manuscript development; Chapters 1 and 2: General Background administration, scoring	P − 72
	Manuscript development; Chapters 3, 4, and 5: Technical and interpretive material	P − 52
	Editing steps	P − 51 to P − 30
	Final edit, Chapters 1–5	P − 29
	Typesetting (galley proofs), Chapters 1–5	P − 25
	Proofreading, Chapters 1–5	P − 23
	Keylining, Chapters 1–5	P − 15
	Silver proofs, Chapters 1–5	P − 11
	Printing	P − 7
	Binding	P − 1
	Warehouse	P
Answer sheet (2 sides)	Basic layout, design	P − 74
	Typesetting	P − 26
	Final proof	P − 14
	Printing/packaging	P − 8
	Warehouse	P
Test booklet (24 pages)	Design cover/pages	P − 44
	Final edit of items and directions	P − 36
	Typesetting (galley proofs)	P − 29
	Proofreading	P − 25
	Keylining	P − 17
	Silver proofs	P − 12
	Printing	P − 8
	Binding	P − 2
	Warehouse	P

[a]Completion time is in terms of weeks before publication; P − 78, for example, means 78 weeks prior to publication.

corded on a computer disk, and hence may not be literally a paper manuscript. Typesetting is now done by computer, sometimes by the publisher and sometimes by out-of-house typesetters. Editors are now able to edit some material on cathode ray tube (CRT) devices; this edited material can then be transferred to automated typesetting equipment, thus bypassing paper or "hard" copy. Computer interfaces now make it possible to develop norms on one computer and then transfer the norms tables to the computer used for typesetting. Thus, computerization has eliminated the intermediate, time-consuming step of transferring all norms data to paper before typesetting can occur.

Manuals become more complex as the number of statistical tables and figures increases. Careful checking is required at the keyline stage (the point where final typeset proofs are pasted on boards prior to photographing to make the printing plates) to make certain that tables and figures are correctly placed. Special expertise is needed to design answer sheets and record forms. If machine-scorable forms are required, then care must be taken to design the forms according to the requirements of the scanner used. The design and manufacture of manipulatives for individually administered tests also require considerable ingenuity and skill on the part of editorial and production personnel.

Developing the Publication Marketing Plan

As a publication approaches its final stages, a marketing plan is implemented. Two types of activities are commonly undertaken for test products: direct mail promotion and space advertising. If a publisher has a sales force, these individuals will receive training in order to sell the new product to the appropriate clientele. Attending professional meetings is another way to advertise new products. These aspects of product marketing are discussed briefly below.

Direct Mail Promotion

Direct mail promotion relies on attractive, informative brochures sent to prospective test purchasers by mail to convey product information. Mailing lists are available at a reasonable cost from commercial sources, so it becomes easy to reach potential purchasers as long as a mailing list is available. The publisher's catalog is also a major source of product information disseminated by direct mail.

Space Advertising

Space advertisements in journals, newsletters, convention programs, and professional magazines are also a commonly used source of new test product information. Care must be taken in preparing space ads to depict a publication honestly and correctly. This is especially difficult with small advertisements.

Field Sales Staff

The publisher's sales staff may engage in direct product sales to individuals by visiting school districts and by appearing at professional meetings and conventions (see below). The larger test publishers have sales personnel carefully selected and trained to present their products.

Professional Meetings and Conventions

Attendance at professional meetings and conventions provides a cost-effective means for publishers to reach a number of individuals.

Also, the fact that most meetings focus on a special market segment means that publishers can target particular products for maximum exposure.

Doing Postpublication Research

For some publications, it is necessary to collect data following publication. Such data are usually needed to furnish evidence of validity. This is especially true for new tests that lack extensive validation. Postpublication research requires careful planning and attention if it is to meet the needs of a particular publication. Periodic updates to the manual or more extensive revisions to the manual may be required. It is important that new data be disseminated as widely as possible.

Evaluating the Entire Publication Process

All publications seem to have their so-called "ups and downs." Some activities proceed smoothly according to plan; others may be more difficult than anticipated, thus requiring more time and incurring higher costs. All publications should be evaluated after their completion in an attempt to identify both successes and problems. Such an evaluation is not designed to fix blame or reprimand development personnel, but rather to develop an awareness of problems and how to solve them in the next publication to be undertaken. It is important that staff members understand the purpose of such analyses and approach them in a positive way.

CONCLUSION

The purpose of this chapter on test development has been to give readers a brief survey of the way in which commercial test publishers develop standardized tests. Although the actual procedures may vary to some extent among publishers, the material presented in this chapter represents the basic process adhered to by most commercial test publishers. Unfortunately, some topics, of necessity, have been omitted or have only been touched upon briefly. Readers who desire additional information on any of the topics presented should consult the references because most of these sources contain extensive information on a variety of topics likely to be of interest to test developers and users.

REFERENCES

American Educational Research Association (AERA), American Psychological Association (APA), & National Council on Measurement in Education (NCME). (1985). *Standards for educational and psychological testing*. Washington, DC: American Psychological Association.

Anastasi, A. (1982). *Psychological testing* (5th ed.). New York: Macmillan.

Angoff, W. H. (1971). Scales, norms, and equivalent scores. In R. L. Thorndike (Ed.), *Educational Measurement* (2nd ed., pp. 508–600). Washington, DC: American Council on Education.

Angoff, W. H., & Robertson, G. J. (1987). A procedure for standardizing individually administered tests, normed by age or grade level. *Applied Psychological Measurement, 11*(1), 33–46.

Bloom, B. M. (Ed.). (1956). *Taxonomy of educational objectives: Handbook I. Cognitive domain*. New York: McKay.

Connolly, A. J. (1988). *KeyMath—Revised: A diagnostic inventory of essential mathematics*. Circle Pines, MN: American Guidance Service.

Ebel, R. L. (1972). *Essentials of educational measurement*. Englewood Cliffs, NJ: Prentice-Hall.

French, J. W. (1951). The description of aptitude and achievement tests in terms of rotated factors. *Psychometric Monographs* (No. 5).

Guilford, J. P. (1967). *The nature of human intelligence*. New York: McGraw-Hill.

Gulliksen, H. (1950). *Theory of mental tests*. New York: Wiley.

Henrysson, S. (1971). Gathering, analyzing, and using data on test items. In R. L. Thorndike (Ed.), *Educational measurement* (2nd ed., pp. 130–159). Washington, DC: American Council on Education.

Lord, F. M. (1980). *Applications of item response theory to practical testing problems*. Hillsdale, NJ: Erlbaum.

Mehrens, W., & Lehman, I. (1984). *Measurement and evaluation in education and psychology*. New York: Holt, Rinehart & Winston.

O'Meara, J. T., Jr. (1961, January–February). Selecting profitable products. *Harvard Business Review*, pp. 83–89.

Terman, L. M., & Merrill, M. M. (1937). *Measuring intelligence*. Boston: Houghton Mifflin.

Thorndike, R. L. (1982). *Applied Psychometrics*. New York: Wiley.

Thorndike, R. L., & Hagen, E. P. (1977). *Measurement and evaluation in psychology and education* (4th ed.). New York: Wiley.

Tinkelman, S. N. (1971). Planning the objective test. In R. L. Thorndike (Ed.), *Educational measurement* (2nd ed., pp. 46–80). Washington, DC: American Council on Education.

Wesman, A. G. (1971). Writing the test item. In R. L. Thorndike (Ed.), *Educational measurement* (2nd ed., pp. 81–129). Washington, DC: American Council on Education.

4

Legal and Ethical Issues in the Assessment of Children

JONATHAN SANDOVAL
University of California at Davis

MARI GRIFFITHS IRVIN
University of the Pacific

> *Before I built a wall I'd ask to know*
> *What I was walling in or walling out,*
> *And to whom I was like to give offense.*
>
> FROST (1939, p. 47)

T here is nothing illegal about a test. The right to construct and publish a test is guaranteed under the First Amendment of the U.S. Constitution, which protects freedom of speech. However, *using* a test may bring about situations that jeopardize three important rights held by individuals: the right to equal protection, the right to due process, and the right to privacy. Most of the legal issues in testing are a result of legislation, regulation, or litigation directed at securing these rights when tests are used to make decisions about individuals. To the extent that tests become walls or barriers keeping people in or out of programs, they may give offense and stimulate legal challenges.

The first two individual rights—that is, to equal protection and due process—are set forth by the Fourteenth Amendment of the U.S. Constitution. This amendment reads in part, "No state shall . . . deprive any person of life, liberty, or property without due process of law, nor deny any person within its jurisdiction, the equal protection of the laws." The equal protection clause of the amendment has been interpreted to mean that with respect to governmental actions (which includes actions by school personnel), an individual should enjoy the same rights and receive the same benefits or burdens as all other citizens, unless it may be shown that there is a valid reason to withhold those rights or to single out an individual or a class of individuals for differential treatment.[1]

[1] In *San Antonio Independent School District v. Rodriguez* (1973), the U. S. Supreme Court ruled that education is not a fundamental right for purposes of equal protection analysis. This ruling weakened the constitutional basis for challenging testing procedures. Bersoff (1979) points out that federal statutes extending equal protection guarantees to the educational domain have become the more usual basis for litigation. Another Supreme Court case, *Plyler v. Doe* (1982), suggests that the right to education is protected by the equal protection clause. Under *state* constitutions (e.g., California's) however, education *is* a fundamental right, and any procedure affecting access to education is subject to strict scrutiny. Any classification that affects access to education should receive heightened attention.

When a test is used (even in part, along with other information) to assign a different treatment, such as special education, or to promote or assign an individual to a different job classification, then the use of the test must be strongly justified and the test must be shown to be valid for the purposes for which it is used. Thus, test use that results in minorities' disproportionately receiving benefits or not receiving them creates a situation where it is a possibility that the equal protection principle is being violated, unless it can be shown that the differential representation is a valid and reasonable outcome.

Due process rights, which are also protected by the Fifth Amendment, may be divided into two categories: procedural due process and substantive due process (Reutter, 1985). "Procedural due process" means that an individual has the right to protest and be heard prior to any action taken with respect to him or her. As a result, individuals must be informed before any procedure may be instituted that potentially deprives them of protected interests in liberty or property, and have a right to examine and comment on any evidence used to justify the deprivation. In addition, individuals have a right to a fair and impartial hearing prior to the action. In the case of a psychological or educational assessment, individuals (or their parents) must be informed of testing and of the results of any test that may be used to make a change in educational or other placement, and must have access to an unbiased hearing.

"Substantive due process" means that individuals may not have rights and privileges arbitrarily or unreasonably removed from them, and that the government cannot act capriciously or unfairly in dealing with individuals. Once again, if a test is used to make a decision that denies rights and privileges, it must be valid and fair. Substantive due process rights and equal protection rights are related because they both protect citizens from arbitrary and discriminatory treatment.

There is no mention of the right of privacy in the U.S. Constitution. The right to privacy is, however, inherent in several provisions of the Bill of Rights, and the U.S. Supreme Court has consistently ruled in favor of protecting the privacy of individuals. There are limits, however (see *Bowers v. Hardwick*, 1986). Justice Douglas, announcing the decision in *Griswold v. Connecticut* (1965), suggested that there exist within the Bill of Rights guarantees creating zones of privacy: the First Amendment, protecting the rights of association (friends); the Third Amendment, prohibiting the intrusion of the government in quartering soldiers without the consent of the property's owner (home); the Fourth Amendment, protecting against unreasonable search and seizure (home and possessions); and the Fifth Amendment, protecting an individual against self-incrimination (attitudes, opinions, and beliefs). Privacy is also considered to be one aspect of liberty protected by the due process clause of the Fourteenth Amendment, according to Justice Brennan (*Carey v. Population Services International*, (1977). Other scholars (e.g., Kemerer & Deutsch, 1979) point to privacy as an unmentioned individual right that the government cannot remove, according to the Ninth Amendment. Substantive due process is also linked to the protection of privacy. With the passing of time, the courts have begun to protect the right to privacy, and legislative action has created privacy rights in various spheres. (The advent of computer data bases has stimulated numerous new problems.) Increasingly, an individual has the right to choose whether, when, and how behaviors, attitudes, beliefs, and opinions are to be shared with others. The control of revealing test results, as one example of private data, rests with the individual under the right to privacy.

SPECIFIC ISSUES RELATED TO EQUAL PROTECTION

Whether or not a test is valid and reliable for members of particular groups becomes an issue of equal protection when the use of that test results in the denial of rights and benefits to individuals belonging to that group. The key sign of a violation of these rights is that a disproportionate number of group members are either receiving or being denied access to a program or benefit.

The Civil Rights Act of 1964 was a major landmark in the securing of constitutional rights by various minority groups. Its titles, particularly Title IV, spelled out that individuals cannot be discriminated against or deprived of the equal protection of the law on the basis of race or color in educational institutions. It specified that racially discriminatory impact—that is, events resulting in smaller percentages of minority group members' receiving benefits than would be expected by their numbers in the population—may signal an illegal practice. Although originally directed at the practice of racial segregation at the school site level, a number of complaints related to other educational practices were brought to court, charging a violation of this statute.

Language Minorities

Legal challenges and related legislative provisions have resulted in the generally accepted principle that children whose primary language is other than English should be tested in their first or predominant language. The first major court case questioning educational practice relevant to language minority children was *Lau v. Nichols* (1974), where the U.S. Supreme Court held that English instruction for Chinese-speaking children amounted to depriving these children of the benefits of education. The important court cases generalizing this principle to the testing of non-English-speaking children were *Diana v. State Board of Education* (1970), *Covarrubias v. San Diego Unified School District* (1971), and *Guadalupe Organization Inc. v. Tempe Elementary School District No. 3* (1972). These cases were brought on behalf of Hispanic children who had been placed in special education classrooms for the educable mentally retarded (EMR), in districts where the results of tests administered in English were used in making the decision. Hispanic children were overrepresented in such classrooms. All of these cases were settled out of court with an agreement that children be tested only in their primary language. It was further agreed that a fair and proper assessment of a non-English-speaking child for special education would begin with a determination of the child's primary language prior to using that language for assessment. A proper assessment would include the evaluation of adaptive behavior and the use of nonverbal tests and materials. The defendants further agreed to re-evaluate the children previously classified as mentally retarded, to reintegrate into

regular classrooms all misclassified children, and to monitor the proportion of the minorities placed in special classes. It was agreed that any disproportionate numbers of Hispanic children in special education would be explained and justified in keeping with equal protection principles. It was reaffirmed in the settlements that IQ tests should not be the primary or only basis for making this diagnosis. In addition, procedural due process rights to prior notice, informed consent, and open, impartial hearings in the parent's language were reasserted (Prasse, 1984). The provisions of these settlements soon found their way in to law within the Education for All Handicapped Children Act of 1975 (Public Law 94-142), which requires testing in the child's "native" language.

Ethnic Minorities

The landmark event signaling a change in the civil rights of minorities was the famous case of *Brown v. Board of Education* (1954), in which the U.S. Supreme Court ruled that segregated schools and unequal educational opportunities for black children were not constitutionally permissible. In the decade following that decision, schools resisted the mandate, and some districts used intelligence and achievement tests to maintain a segregated school system. An early case addressing this practice was *Stell v. Savannah–Chapham County Board of Education* (1965). Fifth Circuit Judge Griffin Bell, writing for the court, stated that individual students could be assigned to different schools on the basis of intelligence or achievement if the program was uniformly administered and race was not a factor in making the assignment (Bersoff, 1979). Since race was established to be a factor in the procedure under adjudication, the court ruled for the plaintiffs.

By far the most influential case securing equal opportunity for black students was *Hobson v. Hanson* (1967). In this case, the District of Columbia was challenged for using standardized group tests to place children into academic tracks. The case was begun by the discovery of a disproportionate number of black children in the lower tracks. One of the tracks, labeled the "special academic" track, was equivalent to EMR classrooms in other parts of the country. Although the criteria for being placed in one of the tracks included teacher and counselor evaluations, estimates of grades, school history, and physical condition, testing was determined to be one of the most important factors in an assignment. When disproportional impact is discovered, as in this case, it is important for the court to determine whether or not the classification has a rational, valid basis. The court ruled against the school district, and found that the tracking system was indefensible because students were placed in the tracks on the basis of traits that were not relevant. The court decided that the standardized *group* aptitude tests were inappropriate (i.e., not valid) because the tests were standardized on white middle-class children and could not be appropriately generalized to black children. This notion of standardization became the first legal definition of test bias or lack of validity. In the decision, the court particularly disapproved of the inflexibility of the tracking system and its stigmatizing effect on black children. Because placement in a lower track was perceived to be harmful, the issue of equal educational opportunity was identified. In addition, the judge criticized the practice of using ability tests as the sole basis (or a major factor) for deciding on placement.

Prasse (1984) points out two ironies in Judge Skelly Wright's decision. First, Wright ruled that because the tests did not assess "innate ability," they could not form the basis of a tracking system; a system based on measures of innate ability presumably might be legal. Few psychologists believe that measures of innate ability exist. Second, because *individual* tests had been used to identify misplacement, many psychologists believed that the decision supported their use. In later cases, this fact would not prove to be important. (In the *Larry P*. case, discussed in the next section, the plaintiffs also used individual test results to indicate that the children were misplaced.)

Another important case brought under Title VII of the Civil Rights Act of 1964, but under the section forbidding discriminatory practices in employment, was *Griggs v. Duke Power Co*. (1971). Although this litigation did not have to do with children, it established a precedent regarding a number of principles related to achievement testing. In this suit, a group of black employees chal-lenged the use of intelligence tests as one device to determine job categories (e.g., coal shoveler) and promotion in a power plant. In ruling in favor of the plaintiffs, the U.S. Supreme Court noted that even though there was no explicit intent to discriminate, the number of blacks holding low-paying jobs and the disproportionate infrequency of promotions to supervisor earned by blacks indicated unfairness; moreover, any requirement for promotion must show a clear and manifest relationship to job success. The burden of proof—here, of demonstrating test validity by correlating test results to job performance—was placed on the employers (or users of tests). If a test could not be shown to have demonstrated concurrent validity with respect to relevant performance, its use was illegal. In this instance, of course, IQ tests could not be shown to correlate very highly with physical performance, and the defendants lost. This case was particularly important because *tests* were directly implicated in illegal practice for the first time. A similar case brought 4 years later, *Albemarle Paper Co. v. Moody* (1975), resulted in the same judgment. In this opinion, however, the U.S. Supreme Court explicitly noted the American Psychological Association's (APA's) test standards as appropriate to follow in planning studies to determine the job-related validity of employment tests.

Another case a year later, *Washington v. Davis* (1976), *upheld* the use of ability tests for screening applicants for police training in Washington, D.C. Although black applicants failed the test in disproportionately high numbers, the test was determined by the court to have content validity and to predict grades in the police academy. As an equal protection case it was important, because the Supreme Court rejected the notion that disproportional impact alone was enough to signal an illegal practice, but ruled that the plaintiffs must prove intent to discriminate instead of intent to predict accurately. A second case concerning selection in a police department, *Guardians Association of New York City v. Civil Service Commission* (1981), resulted in the U.S. Supreme Court's concluding that content-oriented validation methods were appropriate for establishing the validity of certain kinds of tests. However, the court acknowledged that construct validity is perhaps more appropriate than content validity for abstract abilities (e.g., intelligence) (Bersoff, 1981).

Ethnic Minority Bias and Individual Intelligence Tests

The major cases in which the use of intelligence tests with children has received judicial attention are *Larry P. v. Riles* (1979) and *PASE v. Hannon* (1980). Both have been the subjects of numerous articles (e.g., Bersoff, 1979, 1981, 1982; Condras, 1980; Lambert, 1981; Prasse & Reschly, 1986; Reschly, 1981; Sattler, 1981, 1982) and an excellent comprehensive book (Elliott, 1987). Both of these cases were settled in federal district courts but were not reviewed by the U.S. Supreme Court. In each case, attorneys for the plaintiffs, who were black children assigned to EMR classes, sought to lay the blame for disproportionate black assignment to such classes on the intelligence tests used by school psychologists in the process in determining eligibility. The two cases were decided differently, however, with Judge Robert Peckham ruling in *Larry P.* that IQ tests should not be used with black children, and Judge John Grady ruling in favor of the defense in PASE and vindicating the use of standardized IQ tests. Elliott (1987) outlines a number of differences in context and in lines of argument and evidence between the two cases that led, in all likelihood, to the conflicting decisions. Differences in context included differences in the political climates and demography of the two cities involved (San Francisco in *Larry P.* and Chicago in *PASE*), differences in judicial temperament, and differences in the amount of legal representation on both sides. Difference in argument and evidence, according to Elliott, included the fact that "the cases in *PASE* were briefer, and the two sides less intransigently unaccomodating, than in *Larry P.* There were not the same extended discussions of stigma and self-concept, or of mainstreaming and its effects, or of the inadequacies of EMR education" (1987, p. 197). In addition, the defense was able to learn from the materials produced by the *Larry P.* trial to stress four arguments: "the socioeconomic (SES) basis of black deficit; the relevance of tests for school, even though both tests and schools might be in some sense biased; internal evidence against test bias; and the appropriateness of a narrow definition of intelligence" (Elliott, 1987, p. 197). Of most relevance for assessment, the *Larry P.* trial focused on several issues in test bias: the historical background of test development (i.e., the "racist" attitudes of the early pioneers of the American testing movement); the inclusion of black children in the standardization sample (important because of Hobson); the selection of items for the tests (items were selected to minimize sex differences, but no such parallel effort directed at race differences); the failure to tap the "black experience pool" in developing items; and, most importantly, the internal and external validity of tests (Elliott, 1987). Judge Peckham was persuaded by the plaintiffs that the tests had not been validated for the specific purpose of selecting children from each minority group who are unable to profit from instruction in regular classes with remedial instruction. He accepted as relevant only studies correlating black children's test scores with classroom grades. He also accepted the plaintiffs' arguments on other validity issues, rather than evidence from the defendant's witnesses, particularly evidence on internal validity (similarity of item performance between races) (Bersoff, 1979).

The *PASE* case differed, in that Judge Grady did not accept that a difference in performance on IQ measures automatically indicated test bias (Elliott, 1987). For the first time, a judge requested information on item performance by the two races. When little was forthcoming, he proceeded to perform an "armchair" analysis of the items and used this rational approach as the main justification for his decision. Test validity for the different groups, in this instance, was defined as internal validity and differential item response. This type of evidence, item performance on achievement and ability tests, will continue to be important in the future.

The cases are still active, in the sense that the state has had to continue reporting on the representation of black children in special education. Because of continued overrepresentation, Judge Peckham has issued a new ruling. In the fall of 1986, he extended the ban against using IQ tests to the testing of black children for *any* special education purpose within the public schools and indicated that no records on IQ test results could be kept by the schools. Black parents could not even be asked to permit IQ testing.

Two principles seem to have emerged from these court cases and have been explicitly codified in P.L. 94-142 and in Section 504 of the Rehabilitation Act of 1973: Namely, tests must be validated for the specific purpose for which they are used, and should not be discriminatory. The process of determining whether a test is biased is a long and controversial one (Flaughter, 1978; Reynolds & Kaiser, Chapter 26, this volume). Neither the law nor the courts have indicated what level of validity must obtain before a test may be used and considered nondiscriminatory. Bersoff, writing about *Larry P.*, has stated:

> [T]est publishers and users must now produce data showing that tests have validity for each discrete group for which they will be used. Standardization samples that include minority groups but do not yield separate norms for each race will not be judged valid. I.Q. scores will have to be correlated with relevant measures, not simply scores derived from other standardized ability tests. One wishes that the court had gone further and guided examiners as to the level of validity—that is, the coefficient of correlation—required to make a test acceptable or how much disparity between minority and white correlations would be tolerated before a test was considered discriminatory. (Bersoff, 1979, p. 96)

The validity of a test can seldom be established with a single correlation, however, and correlations can be misleading when a criterion is inappropriate. Validity would seem to be best thought of as a judgment about a test made on the basis of the preponderance of empirical evidence. Furthermore, this judgment probably should be made by professionals, not by the courts. In other domains, the court has left educational decisions to professionals.

Issues related to grouping and placement practices have also been tested in *Marshall v. Georgia* (1984). In this case, the plaintiffs representing black school children alleged that the students were improperly assigned to achievement groups in regular education, overrepresented in EMR classrooms, and underrepresented in special education classrooms for the learning-disabled (LD). The case has parallels to *Hobson* and to *Larry P.* that have been thoroughly explored by Reschly, Kicklighter, and McKee (1988a,

1988b, 1988c). In this case, as well as in a similar Florida case, *S-1 v. Turlington* (1986), IQ tests were not the central issue (Reschly et al., 1988c). The emphasis in these trials was on illustrating that children's placements were legitimately related to educational needs. The court ruled in *Marshall* that overrepresentation was not discriminatory; in *S-1*, the case was dismissed. Both decisions upheld the notion of multidisciplinary assessment, and granted that professionals should have reasonable latitude in selecting and using individual tests.

Other Testing Cases

Achievement tests, either locally produced or nationally standardized, have been used with increasing frequency to verify student's competency, typically for high school graduation but also for promotion at lower grade levels (Lerner, 1981). Although this practice has been viewed with some skepticism by psychologists (e.g., Glass & Ellwein, 1986), indications are that it will continue for some time.

In practice, use of these competency tests has had a disproportionate impact on minorities, and suits have resulted (DeMers & Bersoff, 1985). It is noteworthy that similar competency tests have been developed for teachers, and these tests have also been challenged in the courts (e.g., *United States v. Chesterfield County School District*, 1973).

The most prominent case involving competency tests for graduation has been *Debra P. v. Turlington* (1983). In this case, the Florida State Department of Education had to demonstrate that its functional literacy examination, used to establish eligibility for a high school diploma, was a fair test of what was actually taught in the schools. The plaintiffs, noting a disparate impact on black students, challenged this requirement; they lost, because the defendants presented a convincing validation study. Tests of achievement and other curriculum-based measures seem to be much easier to defend against legal challenge than do aptitude or ability tests (Galagan, 1985). It remains to be seen how defensible school readiness tests and minimum-competency tests used for school promotion might be, inasmuch as there have been no notable challenges to these procedures (Smith & Jenkins, 1980).

Recently, a case involving a suit brought by Golden Rule Insurance Company against Educational Testing Service (ETS) and the Illinois Department of Insurance over the use of the Multistate Insurance Licensing Examination has moved, for better or worse, to specify one criterion of test bias and to suggest how much of a difference in item performance between groups may be permissible (see Anrig, 1987). This case, like PASE, has gone beyond the examination of group differences in the test scores to define bias and has looked to item performance. The Golden Rule settlement, in addition to calling for the disclosure of results after tests have been administered, also requires that item statistics be calculated separately for minority test takers and that these item statistics be used to construct new tests. The new tests would be developed so that there is no more than a 15% disparity in the pass rate of majority and minority test takers, and so that the pass rate is greater than 40%. This procedure of using test items on which black and white performance is most similar has become the focus for draft legislation in New York and elsewhere, inasmuch as it has been advocated as a means to correct for racial bias by the National Center for Fair and Open Testing. The president of ETS (Anrig, 1987) has since repudiated the settlement, arguing that "The procedure ignores the possibility that differences in performance may validly reflect real differences in knowledge or skill. . . . The National Council on Measurement in Education has written that such general use [of the procedure] would undermine the construct validity of tests and might even worsen group differences" (p. 3). Anrig reports that ETS has begun using other statistical procedures (the Mantel–Haenszel method) that match individuals in terms of relevant knowledge and skill before comparing their item performance. APA's Committee on Psychological Costs and Assessment has also criticized the Golden Rule procedure (Denton, 1987).

In spite of the phrase's appearance in a number of court decisions and in its occurrence in a number of laws, exactly what it means for a test to be "valid for the purpose for which it is used" has not yet been specified. Since standards change, however, perhaps the most reasonable approach would be to require that a test meet the standards set forth by professional organizations. In fact, some recent legislation in New York has proposed just this, and the courts have begun to reference the Standards for Educational and Psychological Testing (APA, 1985) as a reasonable authoritative standard on which to judge evidence and base decisions on validity issues (Lerner, 1978).

Cases Mandating Assessment

In a somewhat ironic turn of events, some cases have been settled that seemingly mandate the use of tests by psychologists. In an early case, Frederick L. v. Thomas (1976), the plaintiffs, LD children in Philadelphia, charged that they were being denied equal protection rights to education because they had not been screened and identified as handicapped and thus eligible for special classes (Tillery & Carfioli, 1986). The court ruled that the school district should develop an identification process presumably based on screening and individual testing, since the court pointed out that parent and teacher referral was not adequate. The court left the details of the plan to the district and its professionals, however, and did not require tests per se.

Another related New York case, Lora v. Board of Education of City of New York (1978), involved black and Hispanic emotionally disturbed children who claimed that the overuse of culturally biased tests led to disproportionate placement in special day schools (Wood, Johnson, & Jenkins, 1986). The court chose to focus on the failure to follow acceptable practice in the use of tests (such as the assessment of minorities by nonminorities and the failure to perform annual reviews), rather than on the adequacy of the tests themselves. As a result, the ruling was to require a more comprehensive evaluation procedure to be put in place that involved more use of psychologists and tests. A related case, Luke S. v. Nix (1981), led to similar reforms in Louisiana (Taylor, Tucker, & Galagan, 1986).

ISSUES RELATED TO PROCEDURAL DUE PROCESS

In order for an individual to protest and be heard about any test-based decision that has been made about him or her, the individual must be informed about the test. To make an effective protest, the individual should have access to the information that has been generated by the test and the validity of that information. Procedural safeguards for parents have been set up by law (P.L. 94-142) and the courts (Buss, 1975); these include the right (1) to be notified of procedures in advance, (2) to submit evidence, (3) to cross-examine witnesses, (4) to be represented by a lawyer, (5) to have a case decided by an independent and impartial hearing officer, (6) to examine all school records, (7) to receive a state-provided independent psychological examination, and (8) to appeal. How far a tested administrator must go in providing test information has been the subject of several legislative mandates and court cases. In the achievement domain, test critics have worked for full disclosure of test items and correct answers under the banner of "truth in testing." A landmark law passed in New York in 1979 (a similar but less stringent law was passed in California in the same year) requires testing companies to release general statistics about the test to the public; to identify the test items used in assessment; and, for individual examinees upon request, to provide the individual's answers and the keyed correct answers. The rationale is that an examinee may then challenge any of the answers and should have the right to protest effectively any test score. This legislation at present only applies to tests used for admissions purposes, but the practice has been established and may be expanded to other kinds of tests.

The *Golden Rule* case, cited above, has been one of several that have explored whether or not the test taker or his or her guardians may examine test protocols and individual test responses. The courts generally have held that the individual's right to protest holds priority over the copyrights of test publishers and/or the privacy rights of the examiner.

The most important guarator of the right to inspect and correct educational records is the Family Educational Rights and Privacy Act of 1974 (P.L. 93-380), commonly known as "the Buckley Amendment." This law gives parents (or individuals over the age of 18) the right to inspect, review, and amend all educational records pertaining to their children

(or themselves). Similar provisions have been incorporated into P.L. 94-142. For the purposes of this discussion, the most important issue springing from these two pieces of legislation is whether or not test protocols and/or individual item responses must be revealed to parents. In the past, if a psychologist were to grant access to protocols, he or she might violate professional ethics related to safeguarding psychological tests (to be discussed later). Recently, however, ethical standards are being modified to permit disclosure. The Buckley Amendment does not require a psychologist's private notes—that is, notes that are not shown to anyone and are in the sole possession of the psychologist—to be revealed. But records that are used in the provision of treatment to the student (such as special education) may be reviewed by an appropriate professional of the student's choice. Since psychologists' reports and often the protocols are shown to others in the schools (the multidisciplinary team of P.L. 94-142), and constitute the basis of treatment decisions, presumably they must be revealed. The question of whether they may be directly revealed to parents still remains. In *Detroit Edison v. NLRB* (1979), the U.S. Supreme Court did indicate in a case related to testing that the federal statutory obligation to reveal information takes precedence over the ethical standards of a private group (in this case, the APA). The court in *Lora* indicated that the failure to provide unspecified clinical records to parents would be a violation of due process rights. Spitzzeri (1987) reports an Illinois case, somewhat clouded by the fact that the plaintiff's mother held a doctorate in counseling psychology, in which the parents won the right to inspect the specific Rorschach responses elicited from their daughter. The principal rationale for the decision was that the test protocol was created to evaluate the child and that it must be available for review to protect due process rights. New issues may be raised in the future with the use of computerized testing (Burke & Normand, 1987). If a computerized output is used, must it be revealed? Probably so (Walker & Myrick, 1985).

APA's Division of School Psychology has adopted the position that parents should be given the right to inspect protocols under appropriate professional supervision, but should not be given photocopies of completed protocols or permitted to copy extended portions of protocols word for word (Martin, 1986).

ISSUES RELATED TO PRIVACY

Both the test giver and the test taker have rights of privacy, although, as we have seen above, the test giver's rights may be secondary. The most sweeping laws that have addressed this issue are P.L. 94-142, the Buckley Amendment, and the Hatch Amendment (i.e., Sections 439(a) and (b) of the General Education Provisions Act, P.L. 90-247), all of which require that parent permission be secured before any kind of testing takes place or before any release of information is given to a third party. The Hatch Amendment requires permission for psychological testing if the primary purpose is to reveal information concerning "mental and psychological problems potentially embarrassing to the student or his [sic] family" [Section 439(b)(2)], among other sorts of information, and thus is rather broad in impact.

Test responses may be considered to be privileged information given to a psychologist by a client, and to that extent may be protected from the disclosure to other parties, given that a psychologist has such privileges of confidentiality. It is clear that parents must give permission before any testing can take place; once the testing has occurred, however, it is not as clear to what extent the information that has been developed during the process of testing must be reported back. Although the information is privileged in most states, psychologists are bound to report indications of child abuse or indications that children constitute a danger to themselves or others (i.e., are suicidal of homicidal). To the degree that the test may reveal such tendencies or situations, a psychologist may be bound to break this confidence (e.g., *Phillis P. v. Clairmont Unified School District*, 1986, involving a school psychologist.

DeMers and Bersoff (1985) have pointed out that informed consent has three elements: knowledge, voluntariness, and competence. To give consent, an individual must understand what will be done, why it will be done, and how it will be done. Furthermore, the consent must not be obtained under any duress, and the individual must be legally competent. Obviously, informed consent

means that psychologists must work hard to explain their procedures in language that parents can understand (Pryzwansky & Bersoff, 1978).

An issue that has not been adequately determined, either legally, religiously, psychologically, or otherwise, is the age at which a child is capable of giving consent for testing or any psychological procedure (Grisso & Vierling, 1978; Melton, Koocher, & Saks, 1983). The age of 18 is most often cited in legislation (e.g., the Buckley Amendment), but if one were to keep in the spirit of the law, one might give children the option to consent whenever they individually seem able to rationally understand the request.

ISSUES RELATED TO MALPRACTICE

What constitutes malpractice with respect to psychological testing? A tort occurs when a professional acts negligently in the provision of services and harm has resulted to the client. Negligence may be an act of omission, such as failure to include an appropriate test in a battery, or in an act of commission, such as using an inappropriate test. Not performing up to standard could occur in any of a number of areas, such as explaining the testing procedure to the client or representatives inadequately, selecting testing materials that are not appropriate, administering the test incorrectly, selecting a faulty computer scoring/interpreting system, or interpreting test data incorrectly (Walker & Myrick, 1985).

Besides negligence, another tortious act is defamation (i.e., libel or slander). In one case, a psychologist was sued, unsuccessfully, for reporting that a child was a "high-grade moron" (McDermott, 1972). However, reporting test results that may be perceived as defamatory (or injurious to reputation of individual) is not illegal if the results are transmitted to a professional or another person with a legitimate interest in the child (McDermott, 1972).

Torts actions in the courts are generally decided on the basis of whether or not other competent professionals would have made the same decisions or would have reached the same conclusions as the person under question. (Other defenses against negligence and defamation are used first, of course—

e.g., establishing that an injury did not occur.) Once again, professional standards become important in determining whether or not a professional has been acting correctly and whether or not the harm done to the client would have been avoided by most other professionals. A consideration of legal issues soon turns into a consideration of ethics.

RELATIONSHIP OF LAW AND ETHICS

There is often overlap in conceptual understanding when "law" and "ethics" are discussed. Both are related to values identifying that which is "the good." "Values" generally are reflections of strong feeling that can be supported by rational justification. More critically, they imply preferences that specify a course of action (Kieffer, 1979). "Ethics" refers to judgments of value or judgments of obligation. The focus of ethics is on what ought to be in contrast to what is (Steininger, Newell, & Garcia, 1984). Ethical reasoning, then, is the process by which the individual resolves conflicts in values and makes decisions for what ought to be done.

"Laws" may be defined as values or ethical judgments that have societal sanction. When a value or ethical judgment is elevated to the status of law, a given individual's rejection of that value or judgment does not excuse the person from societal responsibility under the law. By contrast, a professional "code of ethics" reflects values and ethical judgments that individuals voluntarily assume when they join the particular professional group. In some states, however, the professional standard of practice embodied in such ethical principles is accepted as the minimal legal standard of practice. When this is the case, violation of a professional ethical standard affects the individual's ability to function professionally, whether or not the person is a member of the professional organization (Pinckney, 1986).

PROFESSIONAL ETHICAL STANDARDS

The ethical task in regard to assessment is to identify that which is valued without sanction of law, and, if necessary, to resolve conflicts in values so that professional behavior may be enacted in the effort to attain the ideal of what "ought" to be done. It will be recognized that "what is" is often not "what should be." Ethical behavior represents the self-conscious attempt of the individual to reach the ideal behaviorally.

The major national professional psychological associations, APA and the National Association of School Psychologists (NASP), have developed standards for professional conduct that are binding on their members (APA, 1981a; NASP, 1985). Each association has also developed guidelines for the delivery of services by school psychologists (APA, 1981b; NASP, 1985). Each of these documents contains sections relative to assessment goals and activities. In addition, standards for educational and psychological testing have been developed jointly by three national professional organizations: the American Educational Research Association (AERA), APA, and the National Council on Measurement in Education (NCME) (APA, 1985). Each of these five documents has been revised in recent years, and future revisions are anticipated as knowledge and profesional practice values change.

"Ethical Principles of Psychologists" (APA, 1981a) is the most recent version of the standards of conduct affecting members of APA. The preamble of the document identifies the values of importance to professional psychologists:

Psychologists respect the dignity and worth of the individual and strive for the preservation and protection of fundamental human rights. They are committed to increasing knowledge of human behavior and of people's understanding of themselves and others and to the utilization of such knowledge for the promotion of human welfare. While pursuing these objectives, they make every effort to protect the welfare of those who seek their services and of the research participants that may be the object of study. They use their skills only for purposes consistent with these values and do not knowingly permit their misuse by others. While demanding for themselves freedom of inquiry and communication, psychologists accept the responsibility this freedom requires: competence, objectivity in the application of skills, and concern for the best interest of clients, colleagues, students, research participants, and society. In the pursuit of these ideals, psychologists subscribe to principles in the following area: 1. Responsibility, 2. Competence, 3. Moral and Legal Standards, 4.

Public Statements, 5. Confidentiality, 6. Welfare of the Consumer, 7. Professional Relationships, 8. Assessment Techniques, 9. Research With Human Participants, and 10. Care and Use of Animals. (APA, 1981a, p. 633)

Members of NASP are subject to ethical standards approved for implementation in 1984. The introduction to "Principles for Professional Ethics," which constitutes part of the NASP's (1985) *Professional Conduct Manual*, states that the most basic ethical principle is "the responsibility to perform only those services for which that person has acquired a recognized level of competency" (NASP, 1985, p. 2). Particular reference is made to "the uncertainties associated with delivery of psychological services in a situation where rights of the student, the parent, the school and society may conflict" (NASP, 1985, p. 2). In contrast to the APA's "Ethical Principles of Psychologists," the NASP statement is particularly sensitive to the fact that school psychologists are employees who must function within an organizational setting where the primary mission is not that of providing psychological services.

"Specialty Guidelines for the Delivery of Services by School Psychologists" (APA, 1981b) and "Standards for the Provision of School Psychological Services" (also part of the *Professional Conduct Manual;* see NASP, 1985), are documents acknowledging that state statutes, not professional psychological associations, govern the services provided by school psychologists. It is recognized that these guidelines are "advisory" to the governing organizations; nonetheless, specific guidelines are set forth for the provision of school psychological services, including assessment activities. It is expected that members of the individual psychological associations will work to implement their particular guidelines in the school districts of their employment. Although there are some differences in the specificity contained within the guidelines, there is much commonality in the values stressed as critical for the delivery of adequate school psychological services.

Standards for Educational and Psychological Testing (APA, 1985), prepared by a joint committee comprised of members of APA, AERA, and NCME, provides the greatest degree of specificity regarding the comprehensive nature of the assessment effort.

The focus is exclusively on "tests" (which are defined broadly enough to encompass a variety of assessment techniques and methodologies). The language in this document is much more operational than that in the APA and NASP statements of ethical principles; thus, much more specific direction is given to the user of the document. Both primary and secondary standards are given. "Primary standards are those that should be met by all tests before their operational use and in all test uses, unless a sound professional reason is available to show why it is not necessary, or technically feasible, to do so in a particular case. . . . Secondary standards are desirable as goals but are likely to be beyond reasonable expectation in many situations" (APA, 1985, pp. 2–3).

SPECIFIC ETHICAL ISSUES IN REGARD TO ASSESSMENT OF CHILDREN

A review of the statements of values contained in these professional standards of conduct leads to the identification of some specific ethical issues in regard to assessment in general and the assessment of children in particular.

Test Construction

Psychologists are expected to use scientific procedures and observe organizational standards in the development of assessment techniques (APA, 1981a). The *Standards for Educational and Psychological Testing* volume (APA, 1985) is the most comprehensive statement of ethical practice regarding testing. Included in this manual are specific standards for all aspects of test construction. In addition, commentary is provided that facilitates the reader's understanding of the intent of the standard.

Test Publication

Technical manuals and user's guides should be provided to prospective test users at the time a test is published or released. These manuals should contain all relevant information needed by the test giver, whose responsibility is to determine whether the test is reliable and valid for the purpose intended in any given situation. Promotional material about a given test should be accurate, not intended to mislead, and supported by the research base of the instrument. If test misuse can be anticipated, the test manual should provide specific cautions about such possible misuse (APA, 1985).

Test Usage

Assessment techniques should be employed for the purpose of "maximizing student achievement and educational success" (NASP, 1985, p. 17). Attention is to be given to maximizing the client's "opportunities to be successful in the general culture, while respecting the student's ethnic background" (NASP, 1985, p. 17). Interpretation of assessment results is to be based on empirically validated research (NASP, 1985). Care is to be taken that assessment results and interpretations are not misused by others (APA, 1981a).

Assessment procedures and test selection should be made with attention to validity and reliability for the purpose intended (APA, 1981a, 1985; NASP, 1985). The psychologist is to have autonomous decision-making responsibility in the selection of assessment techniques for any given evaluation, and differences in age, sex, socioeconomic status, and ethnic backgrounds are to be taken into account in the assessment provided (NASP, 1985). Obsolete measures are not to be used (APA, 1981a).

Ysseldyke and Algozzine (1982) indicated that 200 million standardized tests are administered to 44 million students annually. Unfortunately, it is probable that technically inadequate instruments—tests deficient in validity or reliability or with poorly developed norms—are used in many of these test administrations. With reference to the tests most commonly administered to children for special education purposes, evidence was not provided by the publishers of many of these instruments to support their claims for validity, reliability, or standardization (Ysseldyke & Algozzine, 1982).

Validity for Testing Purpose

Cole (1981) raised another issue in the choice of assessment tools. She distinguished between questions of technical validity of a given test and the question of whether a test should be used, even if it is valid. She quoted Messick (1975, p. 962) in her discussion of this distinction:

> First, is the test any good as a measure of the characteristic it is interpreted to assess? Second, should the test be used for the proposed purpose? The first question is a technical and scientific one and may be answered by appraising evidence bearing on the test's psychometric properties, especially construct validity. The second question is an ethical one, and its answer requires an evaluation of the potential consequences of testing in terms of social values.

Cole continued her argument about the limits of validity by citing an example that goes beyond the argument in the *Larry P.* case in the presentation of testing as an activity with social policy implications:

> As members of a scientific community, testing scholars clearly value scientific evidence on whether a test is accurate for some intended inference. For example, an intelligence test might accurately (validly) identify mentally retarded children. However, if a test is accurate (valid), validity theory does *not* say whether the use of the test, or the whole system in which the test use is embedded, will produce a social good or a social evil. Thus, the use of a valid intelligence test to identify mentally retarded children for assignment to a special educational intervention does not ensure that the special intervention will provide the education the children need. (Cole, 1981, p. 1068)

In this regard, the standards for the provision of school psychological services published by NASP (1985) state that assessment techniques should be used that increase the probability of effective interventions and follow-up.

Nonbiased Assessment

The documents setting forth ethical principles for both APA (1981a) and NASP (1985) mention the responsibility of psychologists to insure that appropriate instruments and methodologies are used in the assessment of clients. However, the *Standards for Educational and Psychological Testing* (APA, 1985) are the most explicit in regard to nonbiased assessment. These standards include not only those related to the assessment of persons from racial/ethnic minority groups and of lower socioeconomic status; specific attention is also called to the particular needs of persons in linguistic minority groups and persons who have handicapping conditions. Clients are to be tested in their dominant language or an alternative communication system, as required; modifications of the conditions under which the test is administered should be considered for handicapped persons. Yet there remain many unanswered, even unresearched questions about the effect of such nonstandardized accomodations upon the ability to use such test data. Does the test still measure that which was intended by the test developer (i.e., has the validity of the instrument been altered)? Because the ethical standards do not provide case-specific answers to many of the questions that will confront the ethically sensitive psychologist regarding the use of a given instrument in a specific situation, caution is advised when tests are administered to persons whose particular linguistic or handicapping condition is not represented in the standardized sample.

Although the various standards provide cautions to the practicing psychologist about the need to use instruments in assessment that are culture-fair, Ysseldyke and Algozzine (1982) reviewed the literature and concluded that there is little agreement among the experts as to the definition of a "fair test." They went on to cite Peterson and Novick's (1976) belief that some of the models are in themselves internally contradictory. Yet even if a "fair" test is found for each testing situation, test abuse may still occur when the test results are used in the decision-making process.

Decision Making

In most instances, testing is done to gather data that are needed to make a decision about the child. Thus, the choice of assessment instruments should be based at least in part on the type of decision that needs to be made (Ysseldyke & Algozzine, 1982). Depending on the age of the client, the client or parent/guardian should be "informed of all essential information considered and its relevancy to decision-making" (NASP, 1985, p. 18).

When the assessment data are obtained through means other than empirically standardized tests—methods that include interview and behavioral observation techniques—special cautions are warranted. Such techniques should yield

> multiple hypotheses regarding the behavior of the subject . . . with each hypothesis modifiable on the basis of further information. . . . When one of these measures is so used, interpretations are judged by its total contribution to the clinical understanding of an individual rather than by the validity of each hypothesis. (APA, 1985, p. 45)

There are also multiple postassessment decision-making variables. Some of these variables reside in the decision makers themselves. For example, who are the decision makers? How do they see their responsibility? What personal meanings do they assign to the decision-making process? Do they understand the assessment results? What process of decision making will be used? In this regard, the NASP principles specify that a multidisciplinary team including "a fully trained and certified school psychologist" (NASP, 1985, p. 17) is to be involved in program decision making that utilizes assessment results.

Additional variables may interact with the assessment results and affect decision-making outcomes. Examples of such specific variables are the client's physical attractiveness, appropriateness of nontesting behavior, gender, socioeconomic status, and reason for referral (Ysseldyke & Algozzine, 1982).

Informed Consent

DeMers (1986) has defined informed consent as "the receipt of specific permission to do something following a complete explanation of the nature, purpose, and potential risks involved" (p. 45).

Clearly, both law and professional ethical guidelines specify that in most instances, assessment should not take place without the informed consent of the client (APA, 1981a), or the client's parent/guardian if the client has not reached the age of majority (NASP, 1985). But the guidelines regarding informed consent contain some ambiguity. The NASP standard for professional practices urges the psychologist to serve as advocates of pupils'/

clients' rights and welfare: "Course of action takes into account the rights of the student, rights of the parent, the responsibilities of the school personnel, and the expanding self-independence and mature status of the student" (NASP, 1985, p. 4). Principle 5 of the APA "Ethical Principles of Psychologists" states: "When working with minors or other persons who are unable to give voluntary, informed consent, psychologists take special care to protect these persons' best interests" (APA, 1981a, p. 636). With both of these statements as guidelines, what action is the psychologist to take when the parent gives consent for the assessment and the "mature" child does not wish the assessment to take place? Although it appears to be assumed in professional practice that parents/guardians "always" act with the best interest of their children at heart, it is realistic to assume that such is not always the case.

It is important to distinguish between "informed consent" and the "right to know." Although the "right to know" issue most frequently is within the context of the receipt of assessment results, there are situations when the law does not require consent for testing (e.g., statewide and schoolwide testing programs; participation by the school in certain types of research studies). Yet even in these situations, the clients themselves and their parents/guardians have the right to know about the testing activity (APA, 1985). The same standards that provide clarification about this type of testing state that children even as young as 2 or 3 should receive an "understandable" explanation of the reasons for testing. Clearly, such explanations require particular thought and skill on the part of the psychologist.

Invasion of Privacy

As with informed consent, the implicit assumption in law and ethical codes is that parents are to serve as their children's agents in the actualization of the children's right to privacy. Psychologists might well consider the possibility that the parents' right to determine when and under what circumstances consent is provided, and their legal right to obtain information about their children, may in reality violate the children's right to privacy. In a similar manner, obtaining information from a child even when parental consent

is given may violate the privacy rights of the parent or guardian.

Exposure of Self to Others

The assessment process may be considered a "probe" that results in the exposure of self to others and hence represents a threat to the invasion of privacy. When assessment is warranted by the need for information to be used in decision making, "how much" assessment information is needed may be a matter of professional judgment. A good rule of thumb may be that only the information actually needed for good decision making should be obtained in response to the referral concern or the presenting problem. This guideline, if practiced conscientiously, may result in considerably less "testing" per se. A corollary outcome might be the freeing up of some psychological service time—a scarce resource in most professional settings.

Self-Confrontation

The assessment process may result in a type of self-confrontation experience for the client—an experience that may be of positive or negative value to the client. Because it is difficult to predict how clients will experience themselves in such circumstances, it may be necessary for the psychologist to consider either possibility in any given situation. The degree of feedback to a child about the testing results should be considered in this light. To what degree should the "right to know" be tempered by the psychologist's judgment of the ability of the minor client to profit from the assessment experience? Of ethical importance is that the client may have provided "informed consent" without a full understanding of the impact of the process upon the self; hence an unknown "risk" may result, even when every attempt has been made to inform the client's parent/guardian fully before obtaining consent for assessment.

Confidentiality

Parents/guardians have the legal right to obtain information about the results of assessments of their minor children. Except under specific circumstances, such as suspected child abuse or the voluntary waiver of parental rights, they similarly have the right to determine to whom and under what conditions these results are disseminated to others. Yet "school psychologists consider the pupils/clients to be their primary responsibility and [they are] to act as advocates of their rights and welfare" (NASP, 1985, p. 4). Again, in relation to the confidentiality issue as well as to other matters regarding a multiple-client system, the psychologist needs to be sensitive to the possibility of ethical violation of the rights of children when the legal rights of parents are upheld. The NASP "Principles for Professional Ethics" speaks to the process to be used in the eventuality of such conflict:

> School psychologists in public and private practice have the responsibility of adhering to federal, state and local laws and ordinances governing their practice. If such laws are in conflict with existing ethical guidelines, school psychologists proceed toward resolution of such conflict through positive, respected and legal channels. (NASP, 1985, p. 4)

Even when parent–child conflict of interest is not an issue, it is good practice for the psychologist to advise the minor child of the rights of certain other persons to the results of assessment efforts. A case can be made for doing this at an early stage in the development of the assessment relationship between child and psychologist, as a corollary to the informed consent process.

The psychologist also has the responsibility to insure that assessment records, including technological data management material, are maintained in a manner to insure confidentiality (APA, 1981b, 1985; NASP, 1985). The provision of confidentiality in assessment records may also extend to the systematic review and possible destruction of information that is not longer appropriate, as these ethical standards also attend to this issue. Again, even when the psychologist is an employee with limited input to the policy development of the organization, the psychologist has the responsibility to seek resolution of matters that invoke professional ethical conflict (NASP, 1985).

Reporting of Results

Much of the material previously presented and discussed relates to the reporting of assessment results. Obviously, the reporting of results should be done in a manner that respects

> the right of clients to have full explanations of the nature and purpose of the techniques in language the clients can understand, unless an explicit exception to this right has been agreed upon in advance. When explanations are to be provided by others, psychologists establish procedures for ensuring the adequacy of these explanations. . . . In reporting assessment results, psychologists indicate any reservations that exist regarding validity or reliability because of the circumstances of the assessment or the inappropriateness of the norms for the person tested. (APA, 1981a, p. 637)

Technological assistance obtained in the scoring, analysis, report writing, or interpretation of test data is to be obtained only if the psychologist assumes full responsibility for the use of such aid (NASP, 1985).

Competence of Examiner

A multidisciplinary team is to be used in the assessment process (NASP, 1985), but only persons professionally trained are to use assessment techniques (APA, 1981a, 1985; NASP, 1985). If the assessment need is outside the scope of the psychologist's training, the psychologist is to refer the client to another professional who is competent to provide the needed service. Care is to be taken to inform all involved parties of the change and the reason for the change (APA, 1981b; NASP, 1985). The various ethical standards also require that the professional psychologist keep current in the use of professional skills, including those involved in assessment.

Allocation of Limited Resources

As in bioethical cases involving medically related decision making (Kieffer, 1979), psychological assessment services most frequently involve the allocation of limited organizational resources. Agencies such as schools generally do not have an abundance of psychological services staff; thus, the time of the psychologist represents financial expenditure. Within this framework, the use of alternative assessment services, such as those mandated by court order in California for black students (Landers, 1986; Remage, 1987), almost always involves a longer process of assessment. Not only are the issues of the validity and reliability of such measures an ethical problem, but an additional problem is presented for the ethically sensitive participants in this process: Given the demand for the services of psychologists, is the use of this additional time justified? If one is to use a utilitarian ethical standard to evaluate the consequences of a given assessment situation, is the "greater good" achieved by the use of time-consuming alternative assessment practices? More basically, what is the "good" in question? Should the movement away from traditional intellectual assessment in California continue, the scope of this ethical concern is likely to become broader.

BEYOND CODES OF ETHICS

Although the professional guidelines for assessment appear explicit, full and careful reading of the documents reveals that more than factual determinations must be made in many instances if the psychologist is to function ethically. In the various codes and standards, the psychologist is directed to respect certain values in relation to professional practice, but no process is prescribed to aid the psychologist in the operationalization of this value system. For example, what is the psychologist to do if membership in multiple professional organizations results in a situation in which one code of ethics appears to be in conflict with another about a specific course of action? Such would appear to be the case in relation to the use of projective techniques for the psychologist who holds membership in both APA and NASP. In other words, in order to resolve some conflicts in values that affect professional practice, the psychologist must sometimes make judgments that go beyond the guidance provided by codes of ethics.

Furthermore, the attentive reader of codes of ethics will discover that certain statements in such documents appear to rely on utilitarian ethical theory: The "right" course of action in a given situation is that which results when more "good" results from the action than "evil." Other statements in the same codes of ethics appear to be deontological or principle-directed: The rightness of a given action is independent of the consequence that results from the action. In a given real-life moral dilemma, the psychologist committed to acting ethically may choose different courses of action, depending upon whether principle alone or anticipated consequences from the action determine the "ought" in the situation. Thus, the choice of different behaviors may result in different consequences; yet each choice may be the "right" choice, given the ethical theory underlying the behavior selected.

The limitations involved in relying on codes of ethics alone to provide ethical direction should not result in cynicism on the part of the psychologist who is committed to acting ethically. Rather, it should be recognized that a primary function of codes of ethics is to sensitize the individual to the ethical dimensions of providing psychological services. The next step is to develop the analytical skills necessary to engage in ethical reasoning or problem solving.

This process needs to be begun with an acknowledgment that some decisions that have ethical dimensions are made unknowingly. Because of the psychologist's own internalization of values developed through the early socialization and educational processes, as well as those acquired through professional education, the psychologist may often be unaware that such "decisions" have been made or how they are made. Thus, self-conscious and deliberate processing and identification of personal and professional values are prerequisites to the development of ethical reasoning skills.

The ethical reasoning process in the professional work place has received increasing attention in recent years. The teaching of applied ethics in universities and professional schools has had a cross-disciplinary emphasis (Hastings Center Institute, 1980), but formal training in ethical decision making has not had widespread emphasis in clinical and school psychology graduate training programs (Nagle, 1987; Tymchuk et al., 1982).

Ethics education for psychologists has become a topic of professional concern (Carroll, Scheider, & Wesley, 1985; Eberlein,. 1987; Handelsman, 1986; Nagle, 1987; Steininger et al., 1984; Tannebaum, Greene, & Glickman, 1989). Problem-solving methodologies have been developed that allow for systematic and case-specific consideration of alterna-

CARL A. RUDISILL LIBRARY
LENOIR-RHYNE COLLEGE

tive courses of action in the working through of ethical dilemmas (Keith-Spiegel & Koocher, 1985; Kitchener, 1984; Tymchuk, 1986). Eberlein (1987) pointed out that ethical codes are limited to statements of consensus—of what has been professionally validated by the majority of psychologists regarding certain values. The development of problem-solving and decision-making skills will enable psychologists to function more in the present tense as they encounter ethical questions in practice.

Increasingly, it is recognized that practicing psychologists have the responsibility to go beyond ethical codes in resolving the complex ethical dilemmas that appear to be increasingly common in their professional experience. Ultimately, the psychologist has an even greater responsibility, as Eberlein (1987) reminded his readers by quoting from the newly developed Canadian Psychological Association (CPA) ethical code: "Assumption of responsibility for the consequences of the action taken, including correction of negative consequences, if any, or re-engaging in the decision-making process if the ethical issue is not resolved" (CPA, Committee on Ethics, 1986, p. 6E). For those psychologists who find themselves enmeshed in the "natural environments" of school and family as they attempt to work through the issues involving the assessment of children, this guideline to professional practice is particularly challenging.

REFERENCES

Albemarle Paper Co. v. Moody, 422 U.S. 405 (1975).

American Psychological Association (APA). (1981a). Ethical principles of psychologists. *American Psychologist, 36*, 633–628.

American Psychological Association (APA). (1981b). Specialty guidelines for the delivery of services by school psychologists. *American Psychologist, 36*, 670–681.

American Psychological Association (APA). (1985). *Standards for educational and psychological testing*. Washington, DC: Author.

Anrig, G. R., (1987, January). *Golden Rule*: Second thoughts. *APA Monitor*, pp. 1–3.

Bersoff, D. N. (1979). Regarding psychologists testily: Legal regulation of psychological assessment in the public schools. *Maryland Law Review, 39*, 27–120.

Bersoff, D. N. (1981). Testing and the law. *American Psychologist, 36*, 1047–1056.

Bersoff, D. N. (1982). The legal regulation of school psychology. In C. R. Reynolds & T. B. Gutkin (Eds.), *The handbook of school psychology* (pp. 1043–1074). New York: Wiley.

Bowers v. Hardwick, 106 S.Ct. 2841 (1986).

Brown v. Board of Education, 347 U.S. 483 (1954).

Burke, M. J., & Normand, J. (1987). Computerized psychological testing: Overview and critique. *Professional Psychology: Research and Practice, 18*, 42–51.

Buss, W. (1975). What proceedural due process means to a school psychologist: A dialogue. *Journal of School Psychology, 13*, 298–310.

Canadian Psychological Association (CPA), Committee on Ethics. (1986, January). Code of ethics. *Highlights*, pp. 6E–12E.

Carey v. Population Services International Inc., 431 U.S. 678 (1977).

Carroll, M. A., Scheider, H. G., & Wesley, G. R. (1985). *Ethics in the practice of psychology*. Englewood Cliffs, NJ: Prentice-Hall.

Civil Rights Act of 1964, §701 et seq., 701(b) as amended, 42 U.S.C.A. §§2000 et seq., 2000e(b); U.S.C.A. Const. Amend. 14.

Cole, N. (1981). Bias in testing. *American Psychologist, 36*, 1067–1077.

Condras, J. (1980). Personal reflections on the *Larry P.* trial and its aftermath. *School Psychology Review, 9*, 154–158.

Covarrubias v. San Diego Unified School District, Civ. No. 70-394-S (S.D. Cal. filed Feb. 1971) (settled by consent decree, July 31, 1972).

Debra P. v. Turlington, 564 F. Supp. 177 (1983).

DeMers, S. T. (1986). Legal and ethical issues in child and adolescent personality assessment. In H. Knoff (Ed.), *The assessment of child and adolescent personality* (pp. 35–55). New York: Guilford Press.

DeMers, S.T., & Bersoff, D. (1985). Legal issues in school psychological practice. In J. R. Bergan (Ed.), *School psychology in contemporary society: An introduction* (pp. 319–339). Columbus, OH: Charles E. Merrill.

Denton, L. (1987, September). Testing panel weighs science, social factors. *APA Monitor*, p. 39.

Detroit Edison v. NLRB, 440 U.S. 301 (1979).

Diana v. State Board of Education, C.A. No. C-70-37 (N.D. Cal. July 1970) (settled by consent decree).

Eberlein, L. (1987). Introducing ethics to beginning psychologists: A problem-solving approach. *Professional Psychology: Research and Practice, 18*, 353–359.

Education For All Handicapped Children Act of 1975, P.L. 94-142, 20 U.S.C. §1401 (1975).

Elliott, R. (1987). *Litigating intelligence*. Dover, MA: Auburn House.

Family Educational Rights & Privacy Act of 1974, P.L. 93-380, 20 U.S.C. §§1232g (1974).

Fisher, K. (1987, September). Revision intended to clarify principles. *APA Monitor*, p. 19

Flaughter, R. L. (1978). The many definitions of test bias. *American Psychologist, 33*, 671–679.

Frederick L. v. Thomas, 419 F. Supp. 960 (E.D. Pa. 1976).

Frost, R. (1939). Mending wall. In *Collected poems of Robert Frost* (pp. 47–48). New York: Halcyon House.

Galagan, J. E. (1985). Psychoeducational testing: Turn out the lights, the party's over. *Exceptional Children, 52*, 288–299.

General Education Provisions Act (GEPA), P.L. 90-247, 20 U.S.C. 1232h (as amended, 1975).

Glass, G. U., & Ellwein, M. C. (1986, December).

Reform by raising test standards: Evaluation comment, Los Angeles: UCLA Center for the Study of Evaluation.

Griggs v. Duke Power Co., 401 U.S. 424 (1971).

Grisso, T., & Vierling, L. (1978). Minors' consent to treatment: A developmental perspective. *Professional Psychology, 9*, 412–427.

Griswold v. Connecticut, 381 U.S. 479 (1965).

Guadalupe Organization Inc. v. Tempe Elementary School District No. 3, 587 F.2d 1022 (9th Cir. 1972).

Guardians Association of New York City v. Civil Service Commission, 630 F.2d 79 (2d Cir. 1980), cert. denied, 49 U.S.L.W. 3932 (June 15, 1981).

Handelsman, M. M. (1986). Problems with ethics training by "osmosis." *Professional Psychology: Research and Practice, 17*, 371–372.

Hastings Center Institute of Society, Ethics, and the Life Sciences. (1980). *The teaching of ethics in higher education*. Hastings-on-Hudson, NY: Author.

Hobson v. Hanson, 269 F. Supp. 401 (D.C. 1967).

Kieffer, G. H. (1979). *Bioethics: A textbook of issues*. Reading, MA: Addison-Wesley.

Keith-Spiegel, P., & Koocher, G. P. (1985). *Ethics in psychology: Professional standards and cases*. New York: Random House.

Kemerer, F. R., & Deutsch, K. L. (1979). *Constitutional rights and student life*. St. Paul, MN: West.

Kitchener, K. S. (1984). Intuition, critical evaluation, and ethical principles: The foundation for ethical decisions in counseling psychology. *The Counseling Psychologist, 12*, 43–55.

Lambert, N. (1981). Psychological evidence in *Larry P. v. Wilson Riles:* An evaluation by a witness for the defense. *American Psychologist, 36*, 937–952.

Landers, S. (1986, December). Judge reiterates I.Q. test ban. *APA Monitor*, p. 12.

Larry P. v. Riles, 343 F. Supp. 1306 (N.D. Cal. 1972) (order granting preliminary injunction), aff'd, 502 F.2d 963 (9th Cir. 1974), 495 F. Supp. 926 (N.D. Cal. 1979) (decision on merits), aff'd, No. 80-427 (9th Cir. Jan. 23, 1984), No. C-71-2270 RFP (Sept. 25, 1986) (order modifying judgment).

Lau v. Nichols, 414 U.S. 563 (1974).

Lerner, B. (1978). The Supreme Court and the APA, AERA, NCME test standards: Past references and future possibilities. *American Psychologist, 33*, 915–919.

Lerner, B. (1981). The minimum competency testing movement: Social, scientific and legal implications. *American Psychologist, 36*, 1057–1066.

Lora v. Board of Education of City of New York, 456 F. Supp. 1211, 1227 (E.D.N.Y. 1978).

Luke S. v. Nix, Civil Action No. 81-1331 (E.D. La. 1981).

Marshall v. Georgia, No. CV 482-233 (S.D. Ga. 1984).

McDermott, P. (1972). Law, liability, and the school psychologist: Malpractice and liability. *Journal of School Psychology, 10*, 397–407.

Martin, R. P. (1986, February). Ethics column. *The School Psychologist*, pp. 1, 7.

Melton, G. B., Koocher, G. P., & Saks, M. J. (Eds.). (1983). *Children's competence to consent*. New York: Plenum Press.

Messick, S. (1975). The standard problem: Meaning and values in measurement and evaluation. *American Psychologist, 30*, 955–966.

Nagle, R. J. (1987). Ethics training in school psychology. *Professional School Psychology, 2*, 163–171.

National Association of School Psychologists (NASP). (1985). *Professional conduct manual*. Washington, DC: Author.

PASE v. Hannon, 506 F. Supp. 831 (N.D. Ill. 1980).

Petersen, N. S., & Novick, M. R. (1976). An evaluation of some models for culture-fair selection. *Journal of Educational Measurement, 13*, 3–29.

Phillis P. v. Clairmont Unified School District, 183 Cal. App. 3rd 1193 (1986).

Pinckney, N. T. (1986). *Law and ethics in counseling and psychotherapy: Case problems*. (Available from the author at P.O. Box 7148, Sacramento, CA 95826-0848)

Plyler v. Doe, 457 U.S. 202, 102 S.Ct. 2382 (1982).

Prasse, D. P. (1984). School psychology and the law. In J. E. Ysseldyke (Ed.) *School psychology: The state of the art* (pp. 245–278). Minneapolis: National School Psychology Inservice Training Network, University of Minnesota.

Prasse, D. P., & Reschly, D. J. (1986). *Larry P.:* A case of segregation, testing, or program efficacy? *Exceptional Children, 52*, 333–346.

Pryzwansky, W., & Bersoff, D. (1978). Parental consent for psychological evaluations: Legal, ethical and practical considerations. *Journal of School Psychology, 16*, 274–281.

Ramage, J. (1987, September). *Larry P.* decision continues impact. *NASP Communique*, pp. 1, 16.

Rehabilitation Act of 1973, Section 504, 29 U.S.C. §794. (1973).

Reschly, D. J. (1981). Psychological testing in educational classification and placement. *American Psychologist, 36*, 1094–1102.

Reschly, D. J., Kicklighter, R., & McKee, P. (1988a). Recent placement litigation, Part I: Regular education grouping: Comparison of *Marshall* (1984, 1985) and *Hobson* (1967, 1969). *School Psychology Review, 17*, 9–21.

Reschly, D. J., Kicklighter, R., & McKee, P, (1988b). Recent placement litigation, Part II: Minority EMR overrepresentation: Comparison of *Larry P.* (1979, 1984, 1986) with *Marshall* (1984, 1985) and *S-1* (1986). *School Psychology Review, 17*, 22–38.

Reschly, D. J., Kicklighter, R., & McKee, P. (1988c). Recent placement litigation, Part III: Analysis of differences in *Larry P., Marshall,* and *S-1* and implications for future practices. *School Psychology Review, 17*, 39–50.

Reutter, E. E. (1985). *The law of public education* (3rd ed.). Mineola, NY: Foundation Press.

S-1 v. Turlington, No. 79-8020-Civ-CA QPB (S.D. Fla. June 15, 1979) (order granting preliminary injunction), aff'd, 635 F.2d 342 (5th Cir. 1981).

San Antonio Independent School District v. Rodriguez, 411 U.S. 1, 28 (1973).

Sattler, J. R. (1981). Intelligence tests on trial: An interview with judges Robert F. Peckham and John F. Grady. *Journal of School Psychology, 19*, 359–369.

Sattler, J. R. (1982). The psychologist in court: Personal reflections of one expert witness in the case of *Larry P. et al. v. Wilson Riles, et al. School Psychology Review, 11*, 306–318.

Smith, J. D., & Jenkins, D. S. (1980). Minimum competency testing and handicapped students. *Exceptional Children, 46*, 440–443.

Spitzzeri, A. A. (1987, January). Court upholds releasing raw test data. *NASP Communique*, p. 5.

Steininger, M., Newell, J. D., & Garcia, L. T. (1984). *Ethical issues in psychology*. Homewood, IL: Dorsey Press.

Stell v. Savannah–Chapman County Board of Education, 255 F. Supp. 83 (S.D. Ga. 1965).

Tannenbaum, S. I., Greene, V. J., & Glickman, A. S. (1989). The ethical reasoning process in an organizational consulting situation. *Professional Psychology: Research and Practice, 20,* 229–235.

Taylor, J. M., Tucker, J. A., & Galagan, J. E. (1986). The *Luke S.* class action suit: A lesson in system change. *Exceptional Children, 52,* 376–382.

Tillery, W. L., & Carfioli, J. C. (1986). *Frederick L.:* A review of the litigation in context. *Exceptional Children, 52,* 367–375.

Tymchuk, A. J. (1986). Guidelines for ethical decision making. *Canadian Psychology, 27,* 36–43.

Tymchuk, A. J., Drapkin, R., Major-Kingsley, S., Ackerman, A. B., Coffman, E. W., & Baum, M. S. (1982). Ethical decision making and psychologists' attitudes toward training in ethics. *Professional Psychology, 13,* 412–421.

United States v. Chesterfield County School District, 484 F. 2d 70 (4th Cir. 1973).

Walker, N. W., & Myrick, C. C. (1985). Ethical considerations in the use of computers in psychological testing and assessment. *Journal of School Psychology, 23,* 51–57.

Washington v. Davis, 426 U.S. 229 (1976).

Wood, F. H., Johnson, J. L., & Jenkins, J. R. (1986). The *Lora* case: Nonbiased referral, assessment, and placement procedures. *Exceptional Children, 52,* 323–331.

Ysseldyke, J. E., & Algozzine, B. (1982). *Critical issues in special and remedial education*. Boston, MA: Houghton Mifflin.

5

Professional Standards and Practice in Child Assessment

KRISTA J. STEWART
Tulane University

CECIL R. REYNOLDS
Texas A&M University

ALISON LORYS-VERNON
University of Georgia

T he profession of psychology, as represented by its professional associations, has developed standards to address a broad range of services offered and developed by its practitioners. This is a natural outgrowth of the maturation of an area of practice into a profession. Practitioners of a profession become accountable to the profession. One of the key characteristics of a profession is the relationship among the profession, its members, and the public. Professions are essentially self-regulating, and members, although ultimately always accountable to individuals and their organizational clients, are first accountable to the profession. The profession, in turn, is held accountable directly to society. Professions of all types traditionally develop and promulgate standards of practice, in order to inform service providers, consumers, and regulatory bodies about acceptable practice and behavior by practitioners of a discipline. Licensing laws in most states closely follow model statutes developed by professional associations.

Ethical principles are among the first standards to be devised by most professions and describe the behavior expected by members of the profession. Ethics serve another role as well, in defining the special responsibilities that members of a profession have to one another and to the society (typically the public at large through its elected officials) that has granted them the rights and privileges inherent to the practice of their profession (Reynolds, Gutkin, Elliott, & Witt, 1984). Of the many professional standards documents developed by psychology, of specific interest here are standards that relate to and have implications for the psychological and educational practice of child assessment.

Two professional organizations in particular have outlined standards for practice in the delivery of psychological services to children and adolescents: the American Psychological Association (APA) and the National Association of School Psychologists (NASP). Each of these organizations has developed documents that outline standards for practice in assessment (as well as other areas of service delivery). Some APA divisions have developed standards for special forms of testing and assessment (e.g., see APA, Division of

Industrial–Organizational Psychology, 1980), but these do not concern us here. The recently published document *Guidelines for Computer-Based Tests and Interpretations* (APA, 1986) is relevant to our purposes and is treated elsewhere in this volume (see McCullough, Chapter 30), but is also reviewed here. Many of the pre-existing standards related to test use and interpretation also apply directly to computerized test administration, scoring, and interpretation.

APA has developed several documents that work together to address high-quality assessment practices. "General Guidelines for Providers of Psychological Services" (APA, 1987) replaces the earlier *Standards for Providers of Psychological Services* (APA, 1977). The 1987 guidelines were derived from yet another document, "Ethical Principles of Psychologists" (APA, 1981a), with the intent of giving specific content to the profession's concept of ethical practice. The guidelines are aspirational in intent, encouraging continual improvement in the quality of practice and service. Four sets of specialty guidelines have also been developed, the one most relevant to child assessment practices being "Specialty Guidelines for the Delivery of Services by School Psychologists" (APA, 1981b). These four sets of specialty guidelines were derived from the 1977 standards, and are intended to be consistent with them; the 1987 guidelines, however, take precedence where questions of interpretation emerge.

The APA Board of Professional Affairs has the responsibility for overseeing these standards and guidelines and is constantly monitoring the documents and their effectiveness, always with an eye toward revision. Revisions of these documents are anticipated to occur relatively frequently. The documents address issues of practice and service delivery, and provide a standard for self-regulation of the profession, with the goals of promoting the welfare and best interests of psychologists and their clients.

Two additional APA documents specifically address issues of test use in all circumstances by psychologists. The volume *Standards for Educational and Psychological Testing* (APA, 1985) was produced by APA in conjunction with the American Educational Research Association (AERA) and the National Council on Measurement in Education (NCME). These standards, often referred to in abbreviated form as the "joint technical standards" (JTS), were formulated with the intent of being consistent with APA's ethical principles (1981b) and generic standards (1977). *Guidelines for Computer-Based Tests and Interpretations* (APA, 1986) was published by APA to set standards for those developing and offering computer-based administration, scoring, and interpretation of psychological tests.

Parallel documents regarding ethics and standards of practice have been developed by NASP. These include the *Principles for Professional Ethics* (NASP, 1985a) and *Standards for the Provision of School Psychological Services*, second edition (NASP, 1985b). During preparation of the NASP standards, a number of relevant NASP documents were reviewed, including the earlier *Standards for the Provision of School Psychological Services* (NASP, 1978), *Standards for Field Placement and Training Programs* (NASP, 1983), and the *Resolution on Non-Biased Assessment* (NASP, 1976), as well as APA's "Specialty Guidelines for the Delivery of Services by School Psychologists" (1981b). The stated objective of the NASP standards is "to inform policy and decision makers of the major characteristics of comprehensive school psychological services" (1985b, p. 14), and to serve as a model of "good practice" for service units that are developing but currently do not meet every standard. Within the context of the NASP standards, the issue of assessment is specifically addressed.

Readers who are interested in the exact wording of these documents are referred to the respective documents. The purpose of this chapter is to draw out points from these documents and others (e.g., the rules and regulations set forth by such laws as the Education for All Handicapped Children Act of 1975, P.L. 94-142) that have specific implications for child assessment practices, and to describe how some of these issues have been or might be addressed by the profession through position, theory, and research. The first section takes a broad look at psychological and psychoeducational assessment services that are provided to children and examines some of the issues to be considered in determination of high-quality practice. Next, standards for tests used in assessment are considered. Other issues to be discussed include use of computers in assessment, confidentiality of data, contractual service, the physical testing environment, and finally training and accountability. Based on these discussions, suggestions for needed research are made.

PSYCHOLOGICAL AND PSYCHOEDUCATIONAL ASSESSMENT SERVICES

What constitutes high-quality as opposed to inadequate or even inappropriate psychological and psychoeducational assessment services? Three issues come to mind: the use of multifactor assessment; the relationship between assessment and intervention; and the issue of validity in all contexts.

The idea of using multiple instruments and gathering information across multiple settings and multiple raters is one that is widely accepted. Reynolds and Brown (1984) note that multiple abilities should be assessed in order to insure a nonbiased assessment. These two authors emphasize the idea that psychologists need to consider multiple data sources before arriving at any conclusion concerning an individual. The data should be accurately derived, using the most reliable instruments available that are appropriate for that individual. The primary disadvantage in using the multifactor method is that selection of data sources and tests may be difficult (Kazdin, 1980). When one is evaluating handicapped children for agencies that receive federal funds, the regulations governing P.L. 94-142 take precedence and require specifically that multiple abilities be assessed.

Selection of given measures should be dictated by theoretical considerations, the nature of the referral question, and sometimes practical limitations. Self-report and behavior rating scales tend to be much more convenient than face-to-face assessment measures, but do not always yield relevant data. Timelines and efficient use of professionals' time must also be considered. Nonetheless, the use of multifactor assessment gives a clearer picture of the complex, multifaceted nature of behavior, cognition, and psycholog-

ical functioning that arises with every referral question. Ecological models seem particularly promising in this regard (Reynolds et al., 1984).

Current assessment procedures emphasize the inextricable link between assessment and intervention (Nagle, 1983). A key question in referral is often differential diagnosis. Differential diagnosis is important to the choice of intervention procedures with children, just as it is with adults. However, we must recognize that the ability to diagnose disorders often exceeds the ability to treat them in nearly all of the clinical sciences. Sometimes differential diagnosis will not lead to differential treatment plans, for example, in the case of many children diagnosed as learning-disabled in the public schools. The reasons for difficulties in developing differential treatment plans are complex (see Hayes & Jenkins, 1986; Reynolds, 1988), and are largely unrelated to the degree of ability to design effective treatments, which has led some authors (e.g., Ysseldyke & Mirkin, 1982) to argue against diagnosis and classification at all, and some even posit that diagnosis may be unethical if it does not lead to improved treatment (e.g., Reschly & Gresham, 1989).

These are extreme positions and are not recognized by professional standards, nor do they seem to follow the logic of the scientific basis of the practices of psychology. Accurate diagnosis is required to identify disorders before research on effective treatment can be conducted. If we cannot reliably recognize a disorder, it is far more difficult to develop appropriate treatment strategies. It is often the pressure of new or more accurate diagnostic techniques that lead to the development of new treatments.

In addition, many disorders of childhood do have specific treatments that are dependent upon accurate diagnosis, and psychologists are in an excellent position to make treatment recommendations in such cases. To diagnose disorders of childhood without a clear eye toward treatment is surely unacceptable practice. Diagnosis should be more than classification as well. Diagnosis provides a detailed description and not just a label; the more that is known about a child's circumstances, the better the treatment plans that can be derived.

STANDARDS FOR TESTS USED
IN ASSESSMENT

In order to understand the various standards for assessment measures, it is necessary to have a grasp of several basic testing issues— validity, reliability, and nonbiased assessment. Our discussion of these concepts is brief, but should provide a guide to understanding information about these issues in test manuals and evaluating specific tests used in child assessment. Individuals who are interested in a more detailed discussion of these concepts are referred to the JTS (APA, 1985), from which the majority of this material is drawn, as well as other educational and psychological testing sources. The APA's (1987) general guidelines, and the NASP's (1985b) standards, do not specifically discuss these issues.

General Testing Issues

"Validity," the degree to which a test achieves the purposes for which it is designed, is the most important consideration in test evaluation. According to the JTS (APA, 1985), the concept refers to the appropriateness, meaningfulness, and usefulness of the specific inferences made from test scores. It should be noted that the *inferences* are what are validated; the test itself is not validated. A *test* is thus never "valid" or "invalid," but interpretations of performance or responses to a test certainly possess the quality of validity. Validity even in this regard is seldom an all-or-none phenomenon, but exists on a continuum. How much "validity" is necessary before an interpretation can be accepted? This is an often-asked question without a specific answer. The best answer seems to be that an interpretation is valid if it improves our ability to make predictions about behavior, circumstances, or outcomes above the level of predictions we would achieve without the test. In this sense, a test can be treated much as an expert witness in court is treated. Under the liberal interpretation of the federal rules of evidence, one may testify as an expert if the testimony would improve the judge's (or jury's) understanding of a problem in the case. A test's validity can be viewed in the same way: If it helps the clinician's understanding of the case, it is valid for use. However, a test, like an expert,

may not be the best choice, for other tests may have greater validity (as well as credibility), and the most efficacious choice is usually the best. There are three traditional types of validity: content, criterion-related, and construct validity. Many have argued (e.g., Cronbach, 1970) that all aspects of validity are merely subtypes of construct validity, but we note them separately here, as has been the tradition.

"Content validity" refers to the extent to which the items on a test constitute a representative sample of the domain of items the test is intended to measure (Berk, 1986). As stated in the JTS (APA, 1985), the methods for evaluating content validity often rely on expert judgments to assess the relationship between parts of the test and the defined domain. However, certain logical and empirical procedures can also be employed, such as systematic observation of behaviors that represent variables in the domain. The use of expert judges as part of the validation procedure is most common in the evaluation of achievement or content area tests and in personality assessment.

Content validity should be a central concern during the test development phase. Anastasi (1982) notes that the discussion of content validity in the manual of an educational achievement test should include a description of the procedures followed in insuring the appropriateness and representativeness of the test. This description should be as precise as possible, to assure test users that the test development process was as thorough as possible. However, Anastasi goes on to note that as important as content validity is for achievement tests, content validation may be misleading and *inappropriate* for aptitude and personality tests. She believes that the content of aptitude and personality tests reveals the hypotheses with which the test constructor has worked in choosing a type of content for measuring a specified trait. The hypotheses need to be empirically confirmed. The basis for this idea is that the same test may be measuring different functions in different individuals, because there is so much interindividual variation in responses to items on these type of tests. Since these tests are also widely used in child assessment practices, it is important to consider this argument.

"Criterion-related validity" refers to the

extent to which test performance is related to some criterion measure of performance (Berk, 1986). The JTS volume (APA, 1985) distinguishes two research designs widely used in attempts to establish criterion-related validity: "predictive" and "concurrent" studies.

A predictive study yields information regarding the accuracy with which test data predict furture performance. This type of validation study is used most commonly in selecting and classifying personnel in business. Concurrent studies are used in the same manner, but obtain prediction and criterion information simultaneously. This type of study is used when it is impractical to extend data gathering over time. Tests are administered to subjects from whom prior criterion data have been gathered. Anastasi (1982) notes that concurrent validity is the most appropriate type for certain uses of psychological tests, mainly when the tests are used in the diagnosis of existing status. In such situations, the distinction between the use of predictive and concurrent validation is based on the objectives of testing.

"Construct validity" refers to the extent to which the test may be said to measure a theoretical construct or trait (Anastasi, 1982). Herein lies the claim that all validity is construct validity, since all we have to work with in psychology and education are theoretical constructs regarding latent traits. Intelligence is a good example. It is one of the most frequently assessed functions in psychology, yet its existence can only be inferred from observation and behaviors. It cannot truly be seen, touched, or felt. Constructs are developed to organize consistencies in observed responses into a framework that specifies the meaining of the construct, distinguishes it from other constructs, and indicates how measures of the construct should relate to other variables (APA, 1985). Sociability, anxiety, and spatial ability are examples of other constructs. Construct validity has been said to be the most general type of validity. Sources of evidence for the construct validity of a test include experts' judgments that test content is related to the construct; correlation of the tests with other tests and variables that sample the same construct; and analysis of the internal consistency of the test.

The concept of validity in child assessment

practices is an important one. Validation reports in test manuals should address the three principal components described above. If such a description is not considered by the test user to be adequate, another measure should be chosen and used.

The next basic testing concept, "reliability," refers to the consistency of scores obtained by the same individual on the same instrument on different occasions, or with different sets of equivalent items, or under variable examining conditions (Anastasi, 1982). Reliability of a test may also be said to refer to the degree to which test scores are free from error of measurement (APA, 1985). There are two types of measurement errors: "systematic" and "unsystematic." The larger the amount of unsystematic error (also called "random" error), the lower the reliability of the test. The generalizability of the test is also diminished. Unsystematic error can be introduced by varied conditions of administration, children's motivation, level of fatigue, and prior practice with items.

On the other hand, systematic errors of measurement either deflate or inflate test scores, but in a constant manner. Therefore, the reliability of the test is not affected adversely, although there may be a detrimental effect on the validity of the test. Examples of variables that produce systematic errors are reaction time, test-taking skills, and social desirability.

The process of identifying the major sources of measurement errors, the size of the errors resulting from these sources, the degree of reliability that can be expected between pairs of scores in certain situations, and the generalizability of the test is an integral part of test evaluation (APA, 1985). This evaluation process should take place during the test development and publication process. The types of decisions anticipated by test developers that will be based on test scores (i.e., the way a test will be used and interpreted) must be taken into consideration when estimating reliability.

For example, the same test may be administered twice, and the percentage of change in the scores may be of interest. However, more commonly, indices of reliability are expressed as correlation coefficients. The question of test use and future interpretation is important in the determination of which reliability coefficient will be calculated, such as the coefficient of stability versus the coefficient of equivalence. Each is calculated using a slightly different statistical formula. As noted regarding the validation process, the process of estimating reliability should also be described in the test manual.

The establishment of reliability and the validation process lead to a third general testing issue, the issue of nonbiased assessment. Techniques and instruments should be used that have established reliability and validity for the purposes and populations for which they are intended (NASP, 1985b). There is still considerable debate regarding nonbiased assessment, basically centering around what constitutes a nonbiased assessment. The JTS (APA, 1985), the APA's (1987) general guidelines, and the NASP's (1985b) standards all address the issue. Entire books have been written on bias, and therefore the following should be considered a skeletal discussion pertaining to the above-cited documents. However, as Reynolds and Brown (1984) report, "test bias" and "test misuse" are often confused. "Bias" denotes constant or systematic error in the estimation of a test score as a function of some nominal variable such as gender or ethnic group. The "misuse" of tests means an inappropriate or invalid application of a test.

The JTS volume (APA, 1985) deals with the issue of nonbiased assessment in two major sctions under "Standards for Particular Application," as well as more generally throughout the publication. The first section outlines the standards to be used in testing linguistic minorities; the second section outlines the standards to be used in testing people with handicapping conditions. Both sections extend the reliability and validity discussions presented earlier. Limitations of interpretations of test scores are emphasized, particularly when linguistic, cultural, or handicapping variables are not considered.

The APA's (1987) general guidelines indirectly present the idea of nonbiased assessment practices in the section "General Guidelines for Programs." According to the APA guidelines, the composition and programs of a psychological service unit should strive to be responsive to the needs of the people and setting served. Psychological services should be adapted to any linguistic, experiential, attitudinal, and socioeconomic characteristics of the population being served. Inherent in this adaptation is the use of nonbiased assessment techniques.

In the NASP (1985b) standards, nonbiased assessment and program planning are specifically addressed. Assessment procedure should maximize the student's opportunities to be successful. However, the student's ethnic background is not to be ignored in the process. The communications are to be held in the client's primary language. The standards (NASP, 1985b) further state that all assessment information should be interpreted in the context of the student's sociocultural background and functional setting.

The general issues of validity, reliability, and nonbiased assessment are necessary concepts to be taken into account in child assessment practices. Definition of these concepts and standards for assessment measures are presented in the three major documents considered here.

LEGAL REGULATION OF TESTING

Considerable case law and legislation now regulate the psychological testing of children. Legal regulation of testing is growing as special interest groups push many issues that were once solely in the province of the profession of psychology into the public arena. The case law includes such cases as *Guadalupe Organization Inc. v. Tempe Elementary School District No. 3* (1972), where clear misuse of tests was evident. Some legislative efforts, such as the so-called state of New York "truth-in-testing" laws, have less noble goals.

P.L. 94-142 (the Education for All Handicapped Children Act of 1975) authorized the regulation of testing of handicapped children for placement in special education program. Subsequent regulations for the implementation of this law (Rules and Regulations Implementing Education for All Handicapped Children Act of 1975, 1977) contained extensive commentary on how testing was to be conducted. Some of these provisions were taken from the *Guadalupe* decision, and others from professional standards and commentary received from individuals as well as professional organizations when the regulations were being drafted. These requirements are consistent with current professional standards promulgated by APA and NASP, although they do tend to be more specific than professional standards documents. The requirements are also consistent with good sound practice and are neither burdensome upon the evaluator nor cumbersome to implement. With the legal challenges to testing practices that abound in this era, it behooves practitioners to follow the requirements of P.L. 94-142 in any setting, clinical or educational; doing this and adhering carefully to the JTS not only should protect one from careless or ill-informed assessment practices, but should produce solid evaluation results that provide the maximum benefit to the client.

USE OF COMPUTERS IN ASSESSMENT

The rapid expansion of computer technology has resulted in many and varied applications of this technology to psychological and educational assessment. In turn, concerns regarding standards of practice have emerged regarding the use of computers in assessment. Although the more general standards for tests apply to computerized tests as well, the nature of computerized testing creates some special concerns. Computers have been used in three general ways in the assessment process (see Hartman, 1986; and McCullough, 1985; see also McCullough, Chapter 30, this volume). First, some tests are actually administered, scored, and/or interpreted using a computer. In child assessment, examples of areas that might be assessed using computer-administered tests include reading and math achievement, personality, and reaction time. Second, computers are used to generate reports. The most extreme use is that of employing the computer to generate an integrated written report from raw data—a task that can be performed by a clerical assistant without psychological knowledge or expertise. Progressively less extreme features that allow for more customization of reports include (1) standardized text with insertion of customized information; (2) routinely used blocks of texts with supplemental information; and (3) starter text files that provide a general framework for the report. Third, computers

are used for data management purposes, including storage of assessment results (e.g., to facilitate record keeping or to allow research on outcomes of local practice).

Although the "Specialty Guidelines for the Delivery of Services by School Psychologists" (APA, 1981b) and the "General Guidelines for Providers of Psychological Services" (APA, 1987) address the issue of validity of computer-generated interpretations, the primary document outlining standards for use of computers in assessment is *Guidelines for Computer-Based Tests and Interpretations* (APA, 1986). These guidelines are intentionally slanted toward personality assessment because of the numerous tests that have been adapted for computer presentation (most notably the Minnesota Multiphasic Personality Inventory [MMPI]), as well as those developed specifically for computer presentation, such as the Millon Clinical Multiaxial Inventory (MCMI). Under current professional standards, psychologists or others who use computerized tests have a variety of specific responsibilities: "They should be aware of the method used in generating the test scores and interpretation and be sufficiently familiar with the test in order to be able to evaluate its applicability to the purpose for which it will be used" (APA, 1986, p. 8). In turn, test developers are responsible for describing how interpretive statements are derived from the scores and the extent to which interpretive statements are based on clinical opinion versus quantitative research. (Having come from a computer often gives test interpretations an unwarranted facade of credibility or authority.)

Test users are to limit their use of computerized testing techniques to those with which they are familiar and that they are able to use in a competent manner. Clinicians not competent to use a test without benefit of computer-generated scoring or interpretations should not feel competent to use a test just because computer-generated reports or other assistance may be available. Such accoutrements are designed to aid in developing more efficient and superior interpretive styles, and are no substitute for a competent clinician. Computer-generated interpretive reports are to be used only in conjunction with professional judgment and always require review by a qualified professional. Also, the test user is responsible for communicating test results to the test taker in an understandable manner, indicating any limitations of the test results and report. Of particular importance is that the user should be familiar with any limitations in the validity of the computer-based tests, keeping in mind the fact that the generalizability of validity from a conventional to a computer-administered form of a test cannot be assumed unless the equivalence of the two forms has been established. The test developer should provide the test user with information on consistency or classifications resulting from the use of the computer-based test. As Plake (1988) has so aptly noted, some so-called "creative" applications of computers to testing are merely more complex means of accomplishing a task that can be done better without the computer. Having a test administered, scored, or interpreted by a computer is not always an improvement, and *caveat emptor* continues to be the order of the day.

In his discussion of critical issues in the use of computer-based test interpretations (CBTIs), Mitchell (1986) cited three major concerns:

(a) the secrecy often surrounding the algorithms and decision rules that govern the inferential narrative statements that make up a CBTI report, (b) the conspicuous lack of validation of most of the CBTI systems, and (c) the magnitude of the problems inherent in any effort to provide adequate validity evidence for such systems. (p. 546)

He noted that those individuals reviewing CBTI systems for *The Ninth Mental Measurements Yearbook* repeatedly cited the fact that test publishers had neither provided enough information to evaluate the decision rules used for generating the test interpretations, nor described the research and/or clinical experience on which those decisions were based. Mitchell implied that this practice is inconsistent with scientific values. Addressing the issue of computer-generated narratives, Mitchell noted that the real problem is "nobody really knows how to do it" (p. 547). Hartman (1986) has also written an excellent critique of clinical use of microcomputers that covers issues similar to those addressed by Mitchell.

Jacob and Brantley (1987) have reported the results of a survey of school psychologists, conducted to explore legal and ethical problems associated with computer applications in school psychology. Of those surveyed, 37% were using computers for data storage, 35% for test scoring or verification of scores, 33% for test interpretation, and 32% for report writing. Respondents reported the occurrence of legal–ethical problems in their service area as follows: 19% reported illegal copying of software, 14% reported use of test scoring and interpretation software without full evaluation by the user, and 12% reported misuse of interpretation programs by unsophisticated users. In addition, 65% reported anticipating problems associated with computer-based test scoring and interpretation, and 62% anticipated problems associated with computerized record keeping. In response to the concerns about possible misuse of computers by school psychologists, Jacob and Brantley (1987) formulated a set of "suggestions for best practice." The "suggestions" are consistent with the APA (1986) guidelines, but, for the interested reader, provide more specific suggestions regarding standards of practice in use of computers in testing children in educational environments.

Although computers have added a new dimension to the assessment process, it is not one that is free of problems. The situation is one in which the standards of practice have not been able to keep pace with the technology. Psychologists who use computers in the process of child assessment need to be mindful of the possible shortcomings and pitfalls in so doing.

CONFIDENTIALITY IN ASSESSMENT

The issue of confidentiality is one that is addressed in each of the sets of professional standards described to this point. Confidentiality is a particularly relevant issue in assessment, because the direct product of assessment is a set of records that typically includes (at a minimum) the test protocols, records of observation, the examiner's notes, and a written report documenting the test results. The records are to be kept confidential as required by federal law in the

Family Educational Rights and Privacy Act (1976), more commonly referred to as the Buckley Amendment (P.L. 93-380). The Buckley Amendment gives parents access to their child's educational records, enables them to challenge records they feel might be inaccurate, and requires their written consent before the written records can be given to a third party.

Table 5.1 indicates the portions of the various standards documents that address confidentiality, as well as other issues to be discussed later in the chapter. The subsequent discussion here focuses on the major points that serve to define high-quality practice in assessment as it relates to confidentiality.

Broadly stated, psychologists are expected to establish and maintain a system that will protect the confidentiality of their clients' records. More specifically, psychologists have the responsibility for maintaining confidentiality of all information about children, from whatever source derived (e.g., themselves or supervisees). If the psychologists are directed otherwise—for example, by court order—then they should "seek a resolution that is both ethically and legally appropriate; for example, psychologists might request 'in camera' (judge's chambers) hearings when they are requested by the court to produce records" (APA, 1987, p. 20). Also, all persons supervised by psychologists—for example, students or nonprofessionals (e.g., secretaries)—are to be trained regarding confidentiality of records (and, in the case of nonprofessionals, are expected to maintain confidentiality as a condition of their employment).

Prior to assessment, written "informed consent" must be obtained from a client's parent or, if he or she is over 18 years of age, from the client. Users of assessment services are to be informed in advance of any limits to confidentiality. For example, the parent is informed regarding who will have access to the information and how requests for test results will be handled if the information is to be sent to individuals not normally having access. When a parent or client waives the right to confidentiality, the psychologist discusses the implications of doing so and assists the user in limiting disclosure to only necessary information. However, the ultimate decision concerning release of information is that of the user. If a parent does give written

TABLE 5.1. Index to Selected APA and NASP Guidelines and Standards Related to Specific Ethical and Practice Concerns

	APA (1987)	APA (1981b)	NASP (1985b)
Accountability	3	3	4.7
Training		1.6	4.4
Continuing professional development		1.5	4.6
Contractual services			3.4
Environment	2.4	4	4.3.2.4
Confidentiality	2.37	2.3.5	3.6
Nonbiased assessment			3.5

permission to release information about a child, then that material is clearly marked as "confidential."

The use of confidentiality becomes quite complex when psychological testing relates to a judicial proceeding. In this case, the parent and the minor may forfeit some or all rights to confidentiality. A juvenile undergoing court-ordered or voluntary psychological evaluations (when a psychologically based defense is being raised) does not have the right to confidentiality in the assessment. Results of the evaluation will be available not only to the child's or adolescent's attorney, but to the officers of the court as well. This is also true of adults. In the case of a minor, the minor and the parent or legal guardian should be informed of the limits placed on the patient–psychologist relationship before the assessment begins. Under most circumstances, the same will be true of custody evaluations.

The clinician must be careful, however. Not all federal or state jurisdictions follow precisely the same rules governing confidentiality, and any practitioner who does juvenile forensic psychological work in particular would be well advised to consult the practices of the courts in the local jurisdiction. To complicate matters further, some parts of a forensic evaluation may remain confidential. In some cases, only those parts of the evaluation that are related to the referral question need be revealed, and incriminating information revealed by the juvenile that is unrelated to the referral question may remain confidential. Because of the significant variations across jurisdictions, competent, informed practice in forensic assessment demands knowledge of local judicial policies.

In the "General Guidelines for Providers of Psychological Services" (APA, 1987), the issue of parental examination of psychological records in school setting is specifically addressed in detail; this issue was not included in the earlier APA standards documents. The APA guidelines note that the parent has the legal right to examine such psychological records, but emphasize the preferability of his or her doing so in the presence of a psychologist who can explain assessment results in a way that is meaningful and useful to the parent. In addition, this document states that when a family moves from one school system to another, the parents have the legal right to examine records from the former school in the new school setting. This right insures that the parents are not put at a disadvantage, should they decide to challenge any decision made by the school about their child. The guidelines, however, go on to describe specifically the condition under which such information should be passed on to the parents: "Disclosure of such psychological information in the records from a former school is conducted under secure conditions; such records have to be transmitted to the new school to a psychologist under whose supervision the records may be examined" (APA, 1987, p. 722).

The specific records that are available to parents are unclear in present federal legislation. Record forms and specific answers given by a child have been the topics of considerable controversy. Bersoff (1982) argued that such information is readily available to parents under the Buckley Amendment and P.L. 94-142. In a recent case in Texas, the state attorney general's office refused to defend a case wherein a school psychologist refused to give a parent access to responses to a sentence completion test, and advised the school district to allow the parent access to the test protocol. Test publishers counter that such record forms are confidential, secure material, and that security and integrity of the test protocols are conditions of sale. The psychologist is placed in a particularly precarious position when revealing answers may be damaging to the ongoing therapeutic process. As yet, no definitive answer to this question is available. Interested readers may wish to consult Bersoff (1982), Melton, Petrila, Poythress, and Slobogin (1987), and Reynolds et al. (1984).

Confidentiality of records is one issue of importance in terms of best assessment practice. Another related issue that emerges in assessment, however, is that of privileged, confidential communication. According to Prasse (1979),

> The doctrine of privileged communication prevents, where expressly stated by state statute, certain professionals from sharing information about their clients gathered within the context of the professional relationship. . . . it is a privilege granted to the client of the professional (psychologist), not to the profession. (p. 3)

Confidentiality of communication, on the other hand, is embodied in ethical and professional standards, not state statutes, and is a promise made by the psychologist to the client to keep communication confidential unless there is legal cause to do otherwise.

Whether a psychologist's services are covered under privileged communication at all will depend upon the laws of a particular state. If not, the psychologist may be forced by parents via legal channels to break a promise of confidentiality given to the child (Panteleno, 1983). Thus, in states where privileged communication is not upheld by the law, psychologists must consider it their professional responsibility to inform children of the limits of confidentiality regarding any information given to the psychologist during the course of an evaluation. At present, 26 states grant minors the right to privileged communication with psychologists.

CONTRACTUAL SERVICES

One manner in which assessment services in schools have been delivered is on a contractual basis. Use of contractual testing services has been particularly common in locations in which few psychologists are available or in areas where student-to-psychologist ratios are high. Although use of contractual services has made services possible for these children who might otherwise not receive any, concerns and even objections to this form of service have been raised by psychologists familiar with contracting practices in schools (Doyle, 1984; Ochroch & Hines, 1984). Because of such concerns, the issue of contractual services is specifically addressed in the NASP standards (NASP, 1985b, Section 3.4). NASP does not endorse the use of contractual services (Professional Standards and Employment Relations Committee, 1985). Nonetheless, because some school systems do obtain services on a contractual basis, standards were developed to give guidance to this practice.

Concerns about contractual testing have centered around several issues. One concern is that school administrators may perceive contracting for service as a less costly alternative to employing a full-time psychologist. In Ballston Spa Central School District in New York, the school psychologist, Bert Friedman, was fired because of the district's intent to contract for services that previously had been performed by Friedman (*In re Friedman*, 1980). Despite the fact that in this case the school district was ordered to reinstate Friedman in his position as school psychologist, such cases are bound to make other psychologists apprehensive about contractual service.

Another concern with contractual testing is that the evaluations may be of inferior quality if those doing the evaluations are poorly trained. It was, in fact, the early proliferation of "Binet testers" that led to the initiation of certification of school psychologists as a means of preventing inadequately trained persons from engaging in psychological evaluations (Cornell, 1941). Contractual evaluations, however, may also be of poor quality if contractual testers, even though well qualified, do not feel accountable to the system doing the contracting. Other concerns are that contracting may interfere with the child's right to privacy; that contractors may actually hire other workers or assistants to do the work; that employment as a contractor may limit the psychologist's advocacy role; and that contracting may interfere with the due process rights of children if it is used as a way to prevent data from being entered in school records (Doyle, 1984; Ochroch & Hines, 1984).

According to the NASP standards, contractual services "should encompass the same comprehensive continuum of services provided by regularly employed school psy-chologists" (1985b, p. 17), rather than serving as a means to decrease the services provided by the employing agency. Contractual services, if used, should augment the full range of services to be provided rather than supplanting them. In addition, those providing contractual services should be familiar with the instructional resources of the employing agency, in order to insure that the services recommended for children are not limited by lack of familiarity with those services. Also, services should be "provided in a manner which protects the due process rights of students and their parents" (NASP, 1985b, p. 17). Those providing contractual services should have appropriate credentials and are expected to deliver services in a manner consistent with the ethics and standards of the profession. To be considered an acceptable form of service, contractual service must to conform to these prescribed standards.

Stewart-Lester (1982) has described a service delivery model that incorporates contracting for testing services as one component of the model. In this model, the school district's regular school psychologists "employ" one or two outside evaluators who are certified school psychologists. The two psychologists essentially work as a team on each contracted case, with the contracted psychologist doing the major portion of the psychoeducational testing and the regular psychologist doing observations, meeting with parents and teachers, and doing follow-up on the case. The contracted psychologist works directly under the regular psychologist's supervision, and all evaluation reports are cosigned by the regular psychologist, who is ultimately responsible for the evaluation.

Some of the potential benefits of this model include the following: greater flexibility in how the regular psychologists in the the school district spend their time; a reduction in lag time for provision of services; a means for double-checking the scoring and interpretation of test results, thus yielding increased accuracy of the results; and the opportunity for the school's regular psychologist to discuss the child with an outside professional who is able to provide a second opinion in the case.

The potential for abuse when contractual assessment services are used is clear.

Nonetheless, contractual testing is not inherently a poor-quality service. If, in fact, contractual assessment services are included as part of a school district's service plan, great care must be taken to insure that all relevant professional standards are addressed. In addition, however, data need to be gathered systematically from a national sample of school districts currently using contractual services, in order to facilitate more meaningful and accurate conclusions about the appropriateness of using contract testing.

PHYSICAL TESTING ENVIRONMENTS

One standard of importance to high-quality assessment, although not as commonly discussed as others, is that concerning the environmental conditions in which the assessment occurs. In high-quality assessment, giving consideration to the assessment environment is important, whether formal standardized testing procedures are being used directly with the child or the assessment of environment is a separate component of an ecological evaluation.

Environment as a Factor in Standardized Assessment

Attention is first given here to the assessment environment during formal testing of a child. The various standards documents all give attention to this issue. The JTS volume (APA, 1985), in Section 15, prescribes that the testing environment should be one of reasonable comfort and with minimal distraction. In addition, it notes that any modification in standard administration procedures (and presumably also testing conditions) should be noted, with appropriate cautions regarding possible effects on validity. In the APA (1987) guidelines, the section on "Environment" (2.4) states that "Providers of psychological services promote the development of a physical, organizational, and social environment in the service setting that facilitates optimal human functioning" (p. 718). The "Illustrative Statement" of this standard gives emphasis to insuring the comfort and privacy of the service user, and also emphasizes

observation of federal, state, and local requirements for safety, health, and sanitation. Guideline 4 of the specialty guidelines for school psychologists (APA, 1981b), the standard in this document that addresses environment and one that is interpreted with greater specificity, emphasizes maximizing children's privacy; for example, "they should have the opportunity to leave their classroom inconspicuously and should be free from interruptions when meeting with the psychologist" (p. 679).

These standards bring to light a number of questions that should be addressed when children are being tested. Is the child able to leave the classroom without having attention drawn to him or her? Calling a child over the intercom system, or even having the teacher single out a child in front of the class to go with the psychologist, is a situation the psychologist must guard against. Is the testing room private, comfortable, quiet, and free from interruptions? Book rooms, cafeterias, stairwells, and hallways, where testing is often done in schools, typically do not meet these standards. Is attention given to health, safety, and sanitation standards? Using soiled test materials or having a sick examiner test a child are examples of lack of attention to these standards.

Manuals for standardized tests often include a statement describing the specific conditions appropriate for administering the test. For example, Wechsler (1974), in the manual for the Wechsler Intelligence Scale for Children—Revised (WISC-R), indicates that the test should be administered in a room with good ventilation and lighting that is free from noise and interruptions; ideally, the room should be a familiar one. The furniture should be comfortable and of appropriate size for the child; the table top should be smooth and below the child's line of vision. Anastasi (1982) has emphasized the importance of realizing the extent to which testing conditions may influence test scores, noting that even minor aspects may appreciably alter performance. According to Anastasi, when administering standardized tests, examiners should follow standardized procedures to the minutest detail; should record unusual conditions, however minor; and, when interpreting test results, should take testing conditions into account.

Environment as a Component of Ecological Evaluation

Assessment of the environment may also be considered a separate but integral component of the assessment process. According to the NASP (1985) guidelines (Section 4.3.2.4), "When conducting psychological and psychoeducational assessment, school psychologists have explicit regard for the content and setting in which their assessments take place and will be used" (p. 19). Reynolds et al. (1984) propose that assessment of the environment is of major importance in reaching accurate diagnostic/prognostic conclusions. They note, nonetheless, that environmental assessment per se typically takes a low priority. They cite several possible reasons to account for this phenomenon: Most assessment texts devote little if any attention to evaluation of the environment; parents, teachers, and principals may resist environmental assessment because it raises the possibility that they might be implicated in the child's problem; accepted and comprehensive theories on which to base environmental assessment are lacking; and when they do use it, psychologists have tended to employ environmental assessment in program evaluation rather than evaluation of individual students. They propose that many of the advances in environmental assessment as employed in program evaluation could be translated for use in assessing environments of individual students.

TRAINING

According to the APA's general guidelines (APA, 1987) and the specialty guidelines for school psychologists (APA, 1981b), psychologists should limit their practice to their demonstrated areas of competence as defined by their verifiable education, training, and experiences (1981b, Section 1.6). This guideline is based on the ethical obligation of psychologists to maintain high standards of competence, continue their education, and provide services only for which they are qualified (Principles 2, 2c; APA, 1981a). Similarly, according to the NASP standards, "practice is restricted to those areas in which the school psychologists has received formal training and supervised experience" (1985b, p. 20). In addition, the NASP standards indicate that all school psychologists should actively participate in activities to enhance and build their professional skills, in order to insure provision of quality services. The implication of these professional standards is that psychologists should not engage in particular assessment activities unless they have received appropriate training (1) during their graduate work or (2) through subsequent continuing professional development activities.

The expectation is that in order to offer high-quality services, psychologists should keep abreast of new developments in assessment and seek training in these procedures. Hynd and Schakel (1981) reported that at least 19 states had implemented continuing education requirements for renewal of certification as a psychologist, and an additional 8 states were considering proposals for such criteria.

A Review of Training and Continuing Education Surveys

Several surveys relating to training in assessment have examined skills learned during graduate school and/or those learned thereafter. Based on their survey results, Oakland and Zimmerman (1986) reported that in school psychology programs, individual mental testing is typically taught in a one-semester 3-hour graduate course; the primary focus is typically on four topics (administration, scoring, interpreting, and reporting) and three tests (the WISC-R, the Wechsler Adult Intelligence Scale—Revised, and the Stanford–Binet Intelligence Scale).

In another survey, Stewart, Duhe, and Shelley (1985) gathered survey data from 151 school psychology training programs and from a national sample of 121 school psychology practitioners to assess the adequacy of training to consult with teachers regarding academic problems. As part of this survey, directors of training programs were asked whether or not their programs provided training in certain academic assessment techniques. In turn, the practitioners (the majority [i.e., 67%] of whom had more than 5 years of work experience) were asked whether or not they had received training in those same techniques when they were in their training programs, as well as whether or not they were currently using the techniques in their practice. Results from the survey are presented in Table 5.2.

The results suggest that newer tests, such as the Test of Written Language and the Woodcock–Johnson Psycho-Educational Battery, were being taught by many pro-

grams at the time of the survey, but that psychologists may not have been trained on those tests when they were in school. Clearly, the psychologists were using some methods in which they were not orginially trained and were not using some tests in which they had been trained—a result that would be expected if psychologists were continually upgrading their assessment skills.

TABLE 5.2. Tests Taught by Trainers of Psychologists versus Tests Learned and Used by Practitioners

Tests	Trainers taught	Practitioners	
		Learned	Used
Reading assessments			
Doren Diagnostic Test	11%	7%	2%
Durrell Analysis of Reading Difficulties	52%	44%	11%
Gates–McKillop–Horowitz Reading Diagnostic Test	36%	16%	4%
Gilmore Oral Reading Test	41%	32%	14%
Gray Oral Reading Test	59%	52%	18%
Miscue Analysis	20%	11%	4%
Peabody Individual Achievement Test	93%	70%	67%
Spache Diagnostic Reading Test	47%	33%	24%
Stanford Diagnostic Reading Test	36%	18%	9%
Wide Range Achievement Test	88%	87%	77%
Woodcock Reading Mastery Tests	66%	46%	63%
Woodcock–Johnson Psycho-Educational Battery	69%	18%	40%
Informal assessment measures	67%	39%	56%
Curriculum-based assessment measures	35%	13%	26%
Other	15%	9%	16%
Mathematics assessments			
KeyMath Diagnostic Arithmetic Test	84%	68%	73%
Peabody Individual Achievement Test	90%	71%	65%
Stanford Diagnostic Arithmetic Test	25%	12%	8%
Wide Range Achievement Test	90%	88%	78%
Woodcock–Johnson Psycho-Educational Battery	77%	25%	44%
Informal assessment measures	49%	35%	51%
Curriculum-based assessment measures	30%	14%	27%
Written language assessments			
Test of Written Language	59%	17%	46%
Informal assessment measures	77%	57%	59%
Other	13%	6%	19%

Note. From *School Psychologists as Academic Consultants: Is Training Adequate for Practice?* by K. J. Stewart, D. A. Duhe, and M. A. Shelley, 1985, April, paper presented at the meeting of the National Association of School Psychologists, Las Vegas. Reprinted by permission of the authors.

When asked the source(s) of their skills for doing academic consultation (a question intended to reflect training in consultation as well as academic assessment skills), 20% of the psychologists reported that they relied primarily on skills learned in their training programs; 36% on skills obtained through continuing education; 10% on techniques suggested by recent research; 49% on self-developed techniques; and 19% on "other" sources. These results indicate that some of these psychologists were acquiring additional training through formal continuing education activities. On the other hand, almost half of the respondents indicated that they had relied upon "self-developed techniques," a term that was not defined in the survey. The vagueness of such an approach at least raises the question of adequacy of training. "Other" was typically defined by the respondent as "experience" or "learning from another educator" (e.g., a reading specialist).

Anderson, Cancelli, and Kratochwill (1984) also reported the results of a survey of a national sample of school psychologists regarding assessment practices. Of particular interest to them were practices in social–emotional assessment. Some of their findings are of particular relevance to the present discussion. The majority of respondents in their study indicated that graduate school was where they had first learned various techniques to assess social–emotional functioning: objective tests, 83%; projective tests, 88%; and behavioral techniques, 56%. In Anderson et al.'s sample, 37% of the respondents identified their current orientation as behavioral or cognitive–behavioral; at the same time, however, 44% reported not having learned behavioral assessment techniques in graduate school. In addition, 70% of the respondents indicated that they would increase their use of behavioral assessment strategies if there were more published instruments, more normative standards available, and standardized procedures that could be used in specific settings. Over 53% of the respondents reported receiving and reading journals that provided them with exposure to behavioral assessment information, whereas 23% reported having little exposure to behavioral assessment information. These findings suggest that these psychologists, many of whom were not trained in behavioral

assessment in their graduate programs, were interested in increasing their use of behavioral assessment techniques. Although at least some of the respondents might have obtained information on behavioral assessment techniques in journals they read, whether or not doing so is adequate for reaching a competent skill level needs to be evaluated.

Barona, Boyd, Guerra, Hernandez, and McNamara (1986) surveyed a sample of members of the Division of School Psychology (Division 16) of APA to evaluate continuing education preferences and needs. The area of assessment was found to be a preferred topic in all three regions evaluated. Strongest interest was expressed in review and update of instruments and techniques and in personality assessment. When respondents were asked to indicate the topics they thought would be most needed by Division 16 members in the next 3 years, intervention and assessment were the most frequently identified.

Defining High-Quality Continuing Education

Another issue of concern, which has been addressed by Hynd and Schakel (1981), is how to define acceptable continuing education. From their survey on continuing education requirements, they found that the most common requirement for recertification was 6 hours of academic coursework within a period of 5 years. Other states, however, have adopted various other options, including requiring an accumulation of so many continuing education "clock hours" of contact within a given time period. The question raised by Hynd and Schakel, though, is whether mere attendance at college courses, workshops, or conventions is sufficient to insure that skills have been updated. Other studies that have been reported here suggest that some psychologists are attempting to upgrade their assessment skills in ways that may be even less effective than formal courses or workshops. In this time of rapidly increasing technology and information, the importance of keeping abreast of advances cannot be underestimated or ignored if high-quality practice is to be insured. The question of optimal methods for upgrading assessment skills and knowledge is a matter that needs to be explored.

ACCOUNTABILITY

A psychologist's degree of "accountability" has to do with the extent to which he or she is answerable for services rendered. Accountability has various components and can be evaluated at various levels. Numerous aspects of accountability are discussed in the professional standards documents (see Table 5.1), and applications of those standards as they relate particularly to child assessment are discussed here.

Promotion of Human Welfare

In the specialty guidelines for school psychologists (APA, 1981b) and the general guidelines (APA, 1987), the first component of accountability that is addressed and one that is considered primary is the "promotion of human welfare." More specifically, psychologists are expected to interact with users of their services in a manner that is considerate, effective, economical, and humane, always taking steps to protect confidentiality, and being ever mindful of their accountability to sanctioners of their services as well as to the general public. In addition, they are not to withhold services from any group in a way that results in class discrimination. Psychologists can, however, limit their services to specific categories of clients (e.g., infants, elementary school children, exceptional children) if, at the time of employment, they state their wish to do so. They should keep in mind that their employers will assign them their duties; however, it is the right and responsibility of a psychologist to "withhold an assessment procedure when not validly applicable" (APA, 1981b, p. 678).

In the process of delivering assessment services, many of these accountability issues are likely to be raised. For example, disputes can emerge when users or sanctioners of services require or prohibit certain assessment procedures, and the consequence may be that services are not consistent with standards of professional practice (see Stewart, 1986, for a detailed discussion of this issue). Two cases in point have appeared in the school psychology literature. Muriel Forrest (*Forrest v. Ambach*, 1980) was prohibited by her Westchester County, New York school district from engaging in several activities, including conducting full evaluations and writing comprehensive reports discussing the results of these evaluations. When she attempted to defend the rights of the parents and handicapped children she was serving, she lost her job. Although the courts upheld Forrest's right to speak out and to be guided by the standards of her profession, they did not order that she be reinstated in her job (Stewart, 1986).

In the San Francisco Unified School District (SFUSD), in the aftermath of the *Larry P. v. Riles* (1979) case, the use of standardized intelligence tests for any purpose was banned by administrative directive (Carpignano, 1987). This directive went beyond the actual decision in the case, which prohibited the use of IQ tests with black students being considered for placement in classrooms for the educable mentally retarded. The psychologists in SFUSD were expected by the school administration to assess cognitive ability and diagnose various handicapping conditions using evaluation methods (e.g., Feuerstein's Learning Potential Assessment Device and "professional judgment") that were supposed to be less discriminatory, but that in reality would be inconsistent with standards of the profession. Carpignano (1987) has described several examples of cases in which a psychologist's not being allowed to use reliable, validated, standardized intelligence tests was detrimental to a child. The Office of Civil Rights eventually intervened in this case, preventing the continued use of Feuerstein's approach because of its lack of validity evidence.

As the *Forrest* and *Larry P.* cases suggest, the issue of accountability to employers regarding assessment practices can be a complicated one. In the case of such disputes, psychologists must keep in mind their primary responsibility of promoting human welfare and must be prepared to work to uphold this standard.

Evaluation of Services

Another aspect of accountability—one that is addressed in all three sets of standards and that has important implications for childhood assessment—has to do with evaluation of services. To demonstrate accountability, psychologists must keep systemtic records of their services and develop a plan by which they can evaluate whether or not they have met their service goals. Services can be evaluated in terms of effectiveness, efficiency, continuity, availability, accessibility, and adequacy. According to Zins (1985), some accountability data may be quantitative and some may be qualitative.

In discussing the gathering of accountability data, Zins (1985) notes that several dimensions should be considered: the consumers who are the recipient of the services; the types of services; and the way in which effectiveness is measured. Here, the service of concern is assessment. According to Zins, each consumer group (e.g., children, parents, teachers, administrators) that a psychologist serves may be a potential source of acountability data, or data may be gathered from colleagues through peer review. Effectiveness of assessment services can be measured by gathering data of three types: "enumerative," "process," and "outcome."

Enumerative data can be recorded to assess aspects such as number of evaluations completed, time between referral and evaluation and between evaluation and placement decision making, and time required to complete an assessment. Assessment is an area of services that is particularly amenable to being evaluated through enumerative data. However, although enumerative data give information about quantitative aspects of service such as efficiency, they tell little about the more qualitative aspects of assessment.

Process data are used to evaluate the more qualitative aspects of the service (Zins, 1985). One type of process data ia attitudinal information from those receiving services, which usually is gathered with the aid of surveys or rating scales. For example, parents or teachers may be asked to rate the helpfulness of reports of assessment results or the accessibility and availability of assessment services. Process in assessment, however, may be evaluated even more directly by examination of the assessment process itself. To do so, psychologists may periodically have a colleague assess the adequacy

and accuracy of their test administration skills. Instruments that have been developed for evaluating the accuracy of WISC-R administration (Fantuzzo, Sisemore, & Spardlin, 1983; Stewart, 1987), for example, can be used in process evaluation.

The third type of accountability data, outcome or product data, can only be obtained on assessment when it is conceptualized as a part of the assessment–intervention process. As noted earlier, in assessment, interest is not in the outcome of the assessment per se but rather in continuity—that is, the outcome of the intervention that the assessment is used to formulate. Thus, outcome data, although clearly important to evaluating assessment, can only be used to do so indirectly.

Responsiveness to Consumer Concerns

The final aspect of accountability that is addressed in the standards is responsiveness to consumer concerns regarding services. Humes (1974) found that consumers were more interested in outcomes, whereas school psychologists were more process-oriented. Although consumers' concerns and rights clearly need to be taken into consideration when making decision about services, consumers may have to be educated about the role assessment plays in the assessment–intervention process to aid them in giving meaningful input.

CONCLUSION

Standards of practice—and, indeed, "standard practice"—are constantly evolving. There is much to be learned, and competent as well as ethical practice requires adherence to the ever-changing body of professional standards. However, professional standards and ethics are in large part what make all of us professionals and our discipline accepted as a profession with a right to a protected practice. As arduous as it may seem at times, learning the details of these standards and ethical principles and implementing them in practice are necessary to the welfare of clients, individual practitioners, and the profession.

REFERENCES

Aiken, L. R. (1985). *Psychological testing and assessment* (5th ed.). Boston: Allyn & Bacon.

American Psychological Association (APA). (1977). *Standards for providers of psychological services*. Washington, DC: Author.

American Psychological Association (APA). (1981a). Ethical principles of psychologists. *American Psychologist, 36*, 633–638.

American Psychological Association (APA). (1981b). Specialty guidelines for the delivery of services by school psychologists. *American Psychologist, 36*, 670–681.

American Psychological Association (APA). (1985). *Standards for educational and psychological testing*. Washington, DC: Author.

American Psychological Association (APA). (1986). *Guidelines for computer-based tests and interpretation*. Washington, DC: Author.

American Psychological Association (APA). (1987). General guidelines for providers of psychological services. *American Psychologist, 42*, 712–723.

American Psychological Association (APA), Division of Industrial–Organizational Psychology. (1980). *Principles for the validation and use of personnel selection procedures* (2nd ed.). Berkeley, CA: Author.

Anastasi, A. (1982). *Psychological testing* (5th ed.). New York: Macmillan.

Anderson, T. K., Cancelli, A. A., & Kratochwill, T. R. (1984). Self-reported assessment practices of school psychologists: Implications for training and practice. *Journal of School Psychology, 22*, 17–29.

Barona, A., Boyd, L. A., Guerra, N. S., Hernandez, A. E., & McNamara, J. F. (1986). *Continuing education needs and preferences of school psychologists: Findings from a national survey of APA Division 16 members*. Unpublished manuscript.

Berk, R. R. (1986). Minimum competency testing: Stature and potential. In B. S. Plake & J. C. Witt (Eds.), *The future of testing* (pp. 89–144). Lincoln, NE: University of Nebraska Press.

Bersoff, D. (1982). The legal regulation of school psychology. In C. R. Reynolds & T. B. Gutkin (Eds.), *The handbook of school psychology*. New York: Wiley.

Carpignano, J. (1987, April). Problems in the practice of responsible school psychology. *The School Psychologist*, pp. 1–4.

Cornell, E. (1941). The certification of specialized groups: School psychologists. *Journal of Consulting Psychology, 5*, 62–65.

Cronbach, L. J. (1970). *Essentials of psychological testing* (3rd ed.). New York: McGraw-Hill.

Doyle, K. M. (1984, August). [Letter to the editor]. *The School Psychologist*, pp. 2–3.

Education for All Handicapped Children Act of 1975, P.L. 94-142, 20 U.S.C. § 1401 (1975).

Family Educational Rights and Privacy Act, P.L. 93-380 (1976).

Fantuzzo, J. W., Sisemore, T. A., & Spardlin, W. H. (1983). A competence model for teaching skills in the administration of intelligence tests. *Professional Psychology, 14*, 224–231.

Forrest v. Ambach, No. 7715-80 (N.Y. Sup. Ct. Dec. 11, 1980).

Guadalupe Organization Inc. v. Tempe Elementary School District No. 3, 587 F. 2d 1022 (9th Cir. 1972).

Hartman, D. E. (1986). Artificial intelligence or artificial psychologist? Conceptual issues in clinical microcomputer use. *Professional Psychology: Research and Practice, 17*, 528–534.

Hayes, M. C., & Jenkins, J. R. (1986). Reading instruction in special education resource rooms. *American Educational Research Journal, 23*, 161–190.

Humes, C. W., II. (1974). School psychologist accountability via PPBS. *Journal of School Psychology, 12*, 40–45.

Hynd, G. W., & Schakel, J. A. (1981). Continuing education and school psychology: A review of state requirements. *Psychology in the Schools, 18*, 303–308.

Re Bert Friedman, No. 10236 (State of N.Y., State Education Department, City of Albany, April 2, 1980).

Jacob, S., & Brantley, J. C. (1987). Ethical–legal problems with computer use and suggestions for best practices: A national survey. *School Psychology Review, 16*, 69–77.

Kazdin, A. E. (1980). *Research design in clinical psychology*. New York: Harper & Row.

Larry P. v. Riles, 495 F. Supp. 926 (N.D. Cal. 1979).

McCullough, C. S. (1985). Best practice in computer applications. In A. Thomas & J. Grimes (Eds.), *Best practice in school psychology* (pp. 301–310). Kent, OH: National Association of School Psychologists.

Melton, G. B., Petrila, J., Poythress, N. G., & Slobogin, C. (1987). *Psychological evaluations for the courts: A handbook for mental health professionals and lawyers*. New York: Guilford Press.

Mitchell, J. V., Jr. (1986). Measurement in the larger context: Critical current issues. *Professional Psychology: Research and Practice, 17*, 544–550.

Nagle, R. J. (1983). Psychoeducational assessment: Cognitive domain. In G. W. Hynd (Ed.), *The school psychologist* (pp. 169–194). Syracuse, NY: Syracuse University Press.

National Association of School Psychologists (NASP). (1976). *Resolution on non-biased assessment*. Kent, OH: Author.

National Association of School Psychologists (NASP). (1978). *Standards for the provision of school psychological services*. Kent, OH: Author.

National Association of School Psychologists (NASP). (1983). *Standards for field placement and training programs*. Kent, OH: Author.

National Association of School Psychologists (NASP). (1985a). *Principles for professional ethics*. Kent, OH: Author.

National Association of School Psychologists (NASP). (1985b). *Standards for the provision of school psychological services* (2nd ed.). Kent, OH: Author.

Oakland, T. D., & Zimmerman, S. A. (1986). The course on individual mental assessment: A national survey of course instructors. *Professional School Psychology, 1*, 51–59.

Ochroch, R., & Hines, L. (1984, August). [Letter to the editor]. *The School Psychologist*, pp. 3–4.

Pantaleno, A. P. (1983). Parents as primary clients of the school psychologist, or why it is we are here? *Journal of School Psychology, 21*, 107–113.

Plake, B. S. (1988). *Creative computer-based testing of achievement: Psychometric boom or bust*. Invited address to the annual meeting of the American Psychological Association, Atlanta.

Prasse, D. (1979, March). Privileged confidential communication: Who is protected? *NASP Communique*, pp. 3–5.

Professional Standards and Employment Relations Committee. (1985, August). Contractual services: Questions and answers about the NASP standards. *NASP Communique*, p. 4.

Reschly, D., & Gresham, F. (1989). Neuropsychological diagnosis of learning disorders: A leap of faith. In C. R. Reynolds & E. Fletcher-Janzen (Eds.), *Handbook of clinical child neuropsychology* (pp. 503–509). New York: Plenum.

Reynolds, C. R. (1988). Putting the individual into the aptitude by treatment interaction. *Exceptional Children, 54*, 324–331.

Reynolds, C. R., & Brown, R. T. (1984). Bias in testing: Introduction to the issues. In C. R. Reynolds & R. T. Brown (Eds.), *Perspectives on bias in mental testing* (pp. 1–40). New York: Plenum.

Reynolds, C. R., Gutkin, T. B., Elliott, S. N., & Witt, J. C. (1984). *School psychology: Essentials of theory and practice*. New York: Wiley.

Rules and Regulations Implementing Education for All Handicapped Children Act of 1975, P.L. 94-142, 42 Fed. Reg. 42474 (1977).

Stewart, K. J. (1986). Disentangling the complexities of clientage. In S. N. Elliott & J. C. Witt (Eds.), *The delivery of psychological services in schools: Concepts, processes, and issues* (pp. 81–107). Hillsdale, NJ: Erlbaum.

Stewart, K. J. (1987). Assessment of technical aspects of WISC-R administration. *Psychology in the Schools, 24*, 221–228.

Stewart, K. J., Duhe, D. A., & Shelley, M. A. (1985, April). *School psychologists as academic consultants: Is training adequate for practice?* Paper presented at the meeting of the National Association of School Psychologists, Las Vegas.

Stewart-Lester, K. J. (1982). Increased consultation opportunities for school psychologists: A service delivery model. *Psychology in the Schools, 19*, 86–91.

Wechsler, D. (1974). *Manual for the Wechsler Intelligence Scale for Children—Revised*. New York: Psychological Corporation.

Ysseldyke, J. E., & Mirkin, P. (1982). The use of assessment information to plan instructional intervention: A review of research. In C. R. Reynolds & T. B. Gutkin (Eds.), *The handbook of school psychology* (pp. 395–409). New York: Wiley.

Zins, J. (1985). Best practices in accountability. In A. Thomas & J. Grimes (Eds.), *Best practices in school psychology* (pp. 493–503). Kent, OH: National Association of School Psychologists.

II

ASSESSMENT OF INTELLIGENCE, LEARNING STYLES, AND LEARNING STRATEGIES

6

Assessment of Children's Intelligence with the Wechsler Intelligence Scale for Children—Revised (WISC-R)

CECIL R. REYNOLDS
Texas A&M University

ALAN S. KAUFMAN
The University of Alabama

The evaluation of individuals' intellectual integrity and level of intellectual functioning has been the métier, and in many cases the *raison d'être* of employment, of psychologists in applied settings since the earliest attempts to apply the special methods of psychology to the human condition. Though the role of psychologists has expanded considerably since World War II, assessment of intelligence remains an integral component of this role, whether in private practice or in the public sector. The uses of intelligence tests are many and quite varied—ranging from predicting future academic levels, to distinguishing organic from psychiatric syndromes, to evaluating personality. Intelligence tests are among the most frequently administered of all tests by clinical psychologists (Korchin, 1976); school psychologists, who spend more than 60% of their time engaged in testing activities (Hughes, 1979), administer intelligence batteries more frequently than any other category of tests (Goh, Teslow, & Fuller, 1981). Despite the controversy over their use, the commercial development and publication of intelligence tests have increased significantly in recent years (Reynolds & Elliott, 1982). Even though psychologists are increasingly engaging in activities that are far removed from assessing intelligence, it seems clear that the clinical evaluation of mental functioning will remain an important aspect of school and clinical psychology for some time.

This volume contains special chapters on the major scales of intelligence designed for use with children and adolescents, in addition to chapters on conceptual approaches to assessment. No series of intelligence tests has yet equaled the success in research and practice of the Wechsler scales. The Wechsler Intelligence Scale for Children (WISC), first published in 1949 and revised as the WISC-R in 1974, has had unprecedented success in the testing and evaluation of children aged 6 years, 0 months to 16 years, 11 months. This chapter reviews the literature on the WISC-R, with an eye toward research most relevant to practice. Since the original publication of the WISC, there have been more than 1,100 articles published in the scholarly literature, and most of these pertain to the WISC-R. Hence, many views and data are not presented herein; only what we consider essential and practical works are reviewed.

We begin with a brief review of Wechsler's contribution to the field of intelligence testing and then move to a presentation of the philosophy of "intelligent testing." We then go directly into the WISC-R literature, to which the remainder of the chapter is devoted.

DAVID WECHSLER'S CONTRIBUTION TO INTELLECTUAL EVALUATION

The study of intelligence and its measurement traces its roots to physicians, educators, and psychologists who were deeply involved with populations at the extremes of the intellectual continuum. Esquirol (1828, 1838) and Seguin (1866/1907) were committed to the study of mentally retarded individuals, and Galton (1833, 1869) was fascinated by the mental abilities of geniuses. The separate contributions of these pioneers have been profoundly felt in the field of intelligence testing; however, it was the innovative research of Binet (1903), who focused on the mental abilities of typical or average children at each age, that has had the longest-lasting and most direct effect on individual intelligence testing as we know it today.

The tremendous success of the Binet–Simon scales (Binet & Simon, 1905), particularly the Terman revisions in the United States (Terman, 1916; Terman & Childs, 1912; Terman & Merrill, 1937, 1973), led to a 40-year domination of the intelligence testing literature and practice by the Stanford–Binet Intelligence Scale. In the 1930s and 1940s, however, there was some discontent with only being able to obtain an overall or summary score from the Binet scale. Yet the Binet was so entrenched that it led David Wechsler's publisher to reject his first attempts at developing an intelligence test with the admonition that one simply could not compete with the Binet scales. Wechsler persisted in his own concepts and efforts, and produced the biggest challenge to the Stanford–Binet monopoly when, in 1939, he published the Wechsler–Bellevue Scale (Wechsler, 1939). Present-day instruments that trace their heritage to Form I and Form II of the Wechsler–Bellevue are the WISC-R, the Wechsler Preschool and Primary Scale of Intelligence (WPPSI; Wechsler, 1967), and the

Wechsler Adult Intelligence Scale—Revised (WAIS-R; Wechsler, 1981). All Wechsler scales include 10–12 separate subtests, with about half included on a Verbal scale and half on a Performance scale. Three IQs are yielded—a Verbal IQ (VIQ), a Performance IQ (PIQ), and a Full Scale IQ (FSIQ). The yielding of a global IQ, despite the separate subtests and scales, is consistent with Wechsler's (1958) notion about the existence of the construct of global intelligence. He stated:

[T]he groupings of subtests into Verbal . . . and Performance . . ., while intending to emphasize a dichotomy, as regards possible types of ability called for by the individual tests, does not imply that these are the only abilities involved in the tests. Nor does it presume that there are different kinds of intelligence, e.g., verbal, manipulative, etc. It merely implies that these are different ways in which intelligence may manifest itself. The subtests are different measures of intelligence, not measures of different kinds of intelligence, and the dichotomy into Verbal and Performance areas is only one of several ways in which the tests could be grouped. (p. 64)

Wechsler was thus basically accepting the Terman–Binet definition of intelligence as a global entity, but he used a different methodology to measure it. Instead of employing a plethora of brief tasks organized by age level, so that any individual would get an arbitrary sampling of these tasks based on his or her age and ability level, Wechsler limited his scale to a smaller number of reliable tasks, predetermining that all people would be administered all tasks. He selected nonverbal tests, which are conspicuously absent at most age levels of the Stanford–Binet, to constitute fully half of his intelligence scale.

Wechsler followed four procedures before selecting 11 subtests for his original 1939 Wechsler–Bellevue Scale: (1) careful analysis of all existing standardized tests regarding functions measured and reliability; (2) empirical assessment of each test's validity claims; (3) subjective judgment of each test's clinical values; and (4) tryout data collected over a 2-year period on individuals with "known" levels of intelligence (Wechsler, 1958, p. 63). By limiting his tests to those already in existence, Wechsler selected the best measurement tools available in the mid-1930s; in actuality, all his tasks were developed not later than the early 1920s.

Many Wechsler tasks were taken directly from the work of Binet and the Americans who adapted the Binet scales from 1900 to 1915. These include several direct analogues (i.e., Comprehension, Similarities, Vocabulary, Digit Span, and Picture Completion), and some that are closely similar to Binet tasks (e.g., Arithmetic [Making Change] and Object Assembly [Patience Pictures]). Besides Binet's work, other sources of Wechsler subtests were the Army examinations developed during World War I. Extremely similar versions of Wechsler Information, Arithmetic, and Comprehension subtests appeared in Army Picture Examination Alpha; close analogues of Mazes, Digit Symbol (Coding), and Picture Completion appeared in Army Group Examination Beta; and the direct ancestors of Object Assembly, Digit Symbol (Coding), Mazes, Picture Arrangement, and Picture Completion comprised half of the Army Individual Performance Scale Examination (Yoakum & Yerkes, 1920). Although a cousin of Wechsler's Block Design subtests appeared on the Army Individual Test (Cube Construction), Wechsler's task follows directly from the test originated by Kohs (1923).

Thus, forms of all the subtests in the WISC-R and WAIS-R were developed and used at least 70 years ago. They were constructed without benefit of a theoretical model, at a time when diverse and comprehensive theories of learning, cognition, and intelligence had not yet been developed. Since the 1920s, impressive theories and research investigations have emerged from separate disciplines, such as cognition, learning, child development, and neuropsychology; many of these theories and studies relate directly to the measurement of intelligence. The work of Piaget, Cattell, Horn, Guilford, Gagne, Luria, Bruner, Sperry, Hebb, and many others has been blatantly ignored by the publishers of individual tests of intelligence. The tradition, as well as the tasks, of Alfred Binet and World War I psychologists are alive and well in all popular present-day individual-assessment tools for measuring the intelligence of adults, as well as of preschool, elementary school, and high school students.

These assertions are not intended to diminish the genius of Alfred Binet and David Wechsler. Binet was a man of vision and a true innovator and pioneer. Wechsler, whose death in May 1981 was a deep loss to psychology, had the clinical insight to provide verbal and nonverbal scales and the empirical sophistication to select and standardize tasks with exceptional psychometric properties. Many others had developed primarily verbal versions (the Binet adaptations) of performance scales (Cornell & Coxe, 1934; Pintner & Patterson, 1925), but Wechsler was the one who realized just how clinically valuable a verbal–nonverbal comparison would be for all individuals if it could be derived from well-standardized scales.

Binet and Wechsler were both courageous. Binet had the courage to speak out strongly against the sensory–motor view of intelligence that had attained almost worldwide acceptance. Wechsler was bold enough to challenge the Stanford–Binet monopoly in the United States; to many psychologists, a Binet age scale was synonymous with "intelligence test." Both men ultimately triumphed.

Binet's victory, with assistance from Terman, led to supremacy in the United States for about half a century. Wechsler settled for second place for many years. However, when the Stanford–binet failed to respond to a changing environment, Wechsler did indeed try harder. The two forms of the Wechsler–Bellevue were replaced by improved models known as the WISC and WAIS. As these scales became outmoded, they were replaced by the WPPSI, WISC-R, and WAIS-R—test batteries with better and more representative norms, updated content, and greatly improved psychometric properties. Further refinements are underway in the upcoming publication of the WPPSI-R and the current development work that is leading to WISC-3.

With the increasing stress on the psychoeducational assessment of learning disabilities in the 1960s, and on neuropsychological evaluation in the 1970s, the VIQ–PIQ discrepancies and the subtest profiles yielded by Wechsler's scales were waiting and ready to overtake the one-score Binet. The WISC and WISC-R have been used widely with exceptional populations, and this value has been documented in hundreds of research investigations. Even now, the Stanford–Binet Fourth Edition (Thorndike, Hagen, &

Sattler, 1986; see Glutting & Kaplan, Chapter 11, this volume) has failed to supplant the WISC-R. Its only serious rival at this point seems to be the Kaufman Assessment Battery for Children (K = ABC, Kaufman & Kaufman, 1983; see Kamphaus & Kaufman, Chapter 10, this volume).

A PHILOSOPHY OF INTELLIGENT TESTING

Conventional intelligence tests and even the entire concept of intelligence testing are perennially the focus of considerable controversy and strong emotions. The past decade has seen intelligence tests placed on trial in the federal courts (*Larry P. v. Riles*, 1979; *Marshall v. Georgia*, 1984; *PASE v. Hannon*, 1980), state legislatures (e.g., New York's "truth-in-testing" legislation), the lay press, and open scholarly forums (Reynolds & Brown, 1984; Sattler, Hilliard, Lambert, Albee, & Jensen, 1981). At one extreme of the issues are those such as Albee (Sattler et al., 1981), Hilliard (Hilliard, 1979, 1984; Sattler et al. 1981), and Williams (see Reynolds & Brown, 1984), who contend that IQ tests are inherently unacceptable measurement devices with no real utility; at the other extreme are such well-known figures as Herrnstein (1973) and Jensen (1980), who believe that the immense value of intelligence tests is by now clearly self-evident. Although the critics of testing demand a moratorium on their use with children, psychologists are often forced to adhere to rigid administrative rules that require the use of precise obtained IQs when making placement or diagnostic decisions, with no consideration for measurement error, the influence of behavioral variables on performance, or appropriate sensitivity to children's cultural or linguistic heritage.

A middle ground is sorely needed. Tests need to be preserved, along with their rich clinical heritage and their prominent place in the neurological, psychological, and educational literature. At the same time, the proponents of tests need to be less defensive and more open to rational criticisms of the current popular instruments. Knowledge of the weaknesses as well as the strengths of individually administered intelligence tests can serve two functions: (1) improving examiners' ability to interpret profiles of any given instrument; and (2) enabling them to select pertinent supplementary tests and subtests to secure a thorough assessment of the intellectual abilities of any child, adolescent, or adult referred for evaluation. The quality of individual mental assessment is no longer simply a question to be answered in terms of an instrument's empirical or psychometric characteristics. High reliability and validity coefficients, a meaningful factor structure, and normative data obtained from stratified random samples do not insure that an intelligence test is valuable for all or even most assessment purposes. The skills and training of the psychologists engaged in using intelligence tests will certainly interact with the utility of intelligence testing beyond the level of simple actuarial prediction of academic performance.

Indeed, with low-IQ children, the primary role of the intelligent tester is to use the test results to develop a means of intervention that will "beat" the prediction made by global IQs. A plethora of research during this century has amply demonstrated that very-low-IQ children show concomitantly low levels of academic attainment. The purpose of administering an intelligence test to a low-IQ child, then, is at least twofold: (1) to determine that the child is indeed at high risk for academic failure, and (2) to articulate a set of learning circumstances that defeat the prediction (see Reynolds & Clark, 1985, for special application of this approach to very-low-IQ children). For individuals with average or high IQs, the specific tasks of the intelligent tester may change, but the philosophy remains the same. When evaluating a learning-disabled (LD) child, for example, the task is primarily one of fulfilling the prediction made by the global IQs. Most LD children exhibit average or better general intelligence, but have a history of academic performance significantly below what would be predicted from their intelligence test performance. The intelligent tester then takes on the responsibility of preventing the child from becoming an outlier in the prediction; that is, he or she must design a set of environmental conditions that will cause the child to achieve and learn at the level predicted by the intelligence test.

When an examiner is engaged in intelligent testing, the child or adult becomes the primary focus of the evaluation, and the tests fade into the background as only a vehicle to understanding. The test setting becomes completely examinee-oriented. Interpretation and communication of test results in the context of the individual's particular background, referral behaviors, and approach to performance on diverse tasks constitute the crux of competent evaluation. Global test scores are de-emphasized; flexibility, a broad base of knowledge in psychology, and insight on the part of the psychologist are demanded; and the intelligence test becomes a dynamic helping agent, not an instrument for labeling, placement in dead-end programs, or disillusionment of eager, caring teachers and parents. Intelligent testing through individualization becomes the key to accomplishment and is antithetical to the development of computerized or depersonalized form reporting for individually administered cognitive tests, such as espoused by Alcorn and Nicholson (1975) and Vitelli and Goldblatt (1979). (See reviews by Reynolds, 1980a, 1980b.) For the intelligent tester, it is imperative to be sensitive and socially aware, and to be clearly aware that intelligence and cognition do not comprise the total human being (see also Reynolds, 1987, 1988).

Intelligent testing urges the use of contemporary measures of intelligence as necessary to achieve a true understanding of the individual's intellectual functioning. The approach to test interpretation adopted under this philosophy has been likened to that of a psychological "detective" (Kaufman, 1979a) and requires a melding of clinical skill, mastery of psychometrics and measurement, and extensive knowledge of differential psychology, especially those aspects related to theories of cognitive development and intelligence. A far more extensive treatment of this approach to test interpretations appears in the book *Intelligent Testing with the WISC-R* (Kaufman, 1979a). Discussion of applications of this philosophy to preschool children may be found in Kamphaus and Reynolds (1987), Kaufman and Kaufman (1977), and Reynolds and Clark (1982).

Clinical skills with children are obviously important to the intelligent tester in building rapport and maintaining the proper ambience during the actual testing setting. Although adhering to standardized procedures and obtaining valid scores are quite important, the child must remain the lodestar of the evaluation. Critical to the dynamic understanding of the child's performance is close, insightful observation and recording of behavior during the testing period. Fully half the important information gathered during the administration of an intelligence test comes from observing behavior under a set of standard conditions. Behavior at various points in the course of the assessment will often dictate the proper interpretation of test scores. Many inidividuals earn IQs of 100, but each in a different manner, with infinite nuances of behavior interacting directly with a person's test performance.

Knowledge and skill in psychometrics and measurement are requisite to intelligent testing. The clinical evaluation of test performance must be directed by careful analyses of the statistical properties of the test scores, the internal psychometric characteristics of the test, and the data regarding its relationship to external factors. As one example, difference scores have long had inherent interest for psychologists, especially between subparts of an intelligence scale. Difference scores are unreliable, and small discrepancies between levels of performance may be attributed best to measurement error. If large enough, however, difference scores can provide valuable information regarding the choice of an appropriate remedial or therapeutic program. The psychometric characteristics of the tests in question dictate the size of the differences needed for statistical confidence in their reflecting real rather than chance fluctuations. Interpretation of subscale differences rests with data on the relationship of the test scores to other factors, and with theories on intelligence; however, it must first be established that the differences are real and not based on error.

One major limitation of most contemporary intelligence tests is their lack of foundation in theories of intelligence, whether these theories are based on research in neuropsychology, cognitive information processing, factor analysis, learning theory, or other domains. Nevertheless, many profiles obtained by children and adults on intelligence tests are interpretable from diverse theoretical perspectives, and can frequently be shown to display a close fit to one or another theoretical approach to intelligence. Theories then become useful in developing a full understanding of the individual. Competing theories of intelligence literally abound (e.g., see Reynolds, 1981b; Vernon, 1979, 1981; White, 1979; and Wolman, 1985). Well-grounded, empirically evaluated models of intellectual functioning enable the examiner to reach a broader understanding of the examinee and to make specific predictions regarding behavior outside of the testing situation itself. These will not always be correct; however, the intelligent tester has an excellent chance of making sense out of the predictable individual variations in behavior, cognitive skills, and academic performance by invoking the nomothetic framework provided by theory. The alternative often is to be stymied or forced to rely on trial and error or anecdotal, illusionary relationships when each new set of profile fluctuations is encountered. Theories, even speculative ones, are more efficient guides to developing hypotheses for understanding and treating problems than are purely clinical impressions or armchair speculations.

Through the elements of clinical skill, psychometric sophistication, and a broad use of knowledge of theories of individual differences emerges intelligent testing. None of these elements is sufficient; yet, when properly implemented, they engage in a synergistic interaction to produce the greatest possible understanding. Obviously, all these factors cannot be presented here and occur only as the product of extensive training. The remaining portions of this chapter are devoted to providing the psychometric groundwork for intelligent testing. Though the focus is on the WISC-R in particular and the Wechsler scales in general, the conceptual nature of the methods described is applicable to most standardized tests, including intellectual, neuropsychological (Reynolds, 1982a), and personality scales.

The literature regarding the validity of the major intelligence scales, as well as the construct of intelligence itself, has become quite massive over the years. Sattler (1982) has provided a most thorough review of this plethora of evidence. Though one can debate the nature of the construct of intelligence and defend many different viewpoints, the data from intelligence tests are, outside of achievement tests, the best available predictors of academic achievement. Measures of general intelligence also are very good predictors of success in most job training and vocational training programs, though prediction of actual job performance is more difficult. Intelligence test scores predict a variety of other criteria as well. General intellectual level consistently has been shown to be one of the best predictors of success in psychotherapy, and premorbid IQ is the best available predictor of rehabilitative success of patients with acute brain trauma and a number of neurological diseases (Reynolds, 1981b). The diagnostic use of IQ tests is also quite formidable in such categories as mental retardation and intellectual giftedness (though we do not recommend making any diagnostic statements about any individual on the basis of any single psychological test). Validity has, for the most part, been demonstrated across a host of demographic variables as well (e.g., see Jensen, 1980; Reynolds, 1982b; and Reynolds & Kaiser, Chapter 26, this volume).

Though intelligence is omnipresent in our daily activities and influences much of what we do and are able to accomplish, intelligence is not omnipotent. Forgetting this rather simple distinction—"omnipresent, not omnipotent"—has resulted in many abuses of intelligence tests. Such abuses can be avoided if we have an adequate understanding of validity and of the limitations of intelligence as a construct.

SCREENING WITH INTELLIGENCE TESTS

Comprehensive evaluation of intellectual functioning, though highly desirable and recommended when questions of cognitive function arise, realistically is time-consuming, expensive, and not always necessary. Hence, a variety of brief measures of intelligence have been developed over the years. When one decides to use a brief measure of intelligence, one must recognize and accept a considerable loss of clinical information and much material potentially relevant to diagnosis and treatment. Before we turn to a discussion of screening methods, it is useful to review the purpose of screening and to evaluate the use of screening techniques.

More detailed discussions of the issues to follow can be found in several sources (Kaufman, 1979a; Kaufman & Kaufman, 1977; Reynolds, 1979, 1981d; Stangler, Huber, & Routh, 1980).

Purposes of Screening and Use of Screening Techniques

Although nearly all individuals with intellectual disorders will ultimately be identified during their public school careers, it is during the early years that corrective, habilitative efforts have the greatest probability of eventual success. In addition, parents, teachers, and pediatricians, though good sources of referral, cannot be expected to identify all mentally handicapped children; consequently, numerous brief screening measures of intelligence have been developed. In the course of comprehensive psychological assessments of children or adults, a brief screening measure of intelligence will sometimes be sufficient to meet the clinician's need for information. With young children, brief screening measures are more likely to be used to evaluate large numbers of children in a short time period. In this instance, screening has as its direct goal identifying children who are most likely to develop learning, behavior, or other problems that can interfere with appropriate social, emotional, or academic development.

Screening is conducted on a probability basis and reduces the cost of identifying handicapped children by selecting out (or screening out) those children most likely to have problems. A screening test is not a criterion measure. No matter how badly a child performs on a screening test, it does not necessarily mean that the child is handicapped. In fact, a good screening process has a built-in pathological bias. Because it is usually considered less tolerable to miss locating a handicapped child (a false-negative error) than to recommend comprehensive evaluation of a nonhandicapped child (a false-positive error), whenever a screening test is "in doubt" about a child, it should identify the child as potentially handicapped. This can be accomplished most directly by setting cutting scores to identify the largest number of children that can receive comprehensive evaluations.

Each child identified as potentially handicapped through a screening test (or other process) can then be referred for a thorough individual evaluation intended to result in (1) determining that the child has been incorrectly identified and is not in need of therapeutic intervention, special assistance, or placement in a special education program; or (2) confirming and more accurately appraising the child's specific difficulties. The latter appraisal is multifaceted and involves determination of an appropriate classification and delineation of an individual educational program or plan of therapy that capitalizes on the child's assets, limits the effects of his or her liabilities, and makes treatment as palatable and successful as possible. Even in the comprehensive individual assessment, however, one must remember that tests are nothing more than methods for obtaining quantifiable samples of behavior.

Screening tests, as a rule, provide very limited, restrictive samples of behavior and are all but useless with respect to diagnostic decision making and the development of instructional plans. Screening tests are usually less reliable measures of a child's skills, since they are designed to detect areas of deficit or handicap; hence, they typically do not allow for the identification of a child's strengths. From a legal standpoint, the vast majority of screening tests do not meet the requirements of P.L. 94-142 for use in educational placement. The results of a screening test cannot substitute for the comprehensive information of an individual assessment, and screening information certainly cannot be allowed to override the results of the individual assessment of the referred pupil. However, when used appropriately, screening tests can enhance, economically, a clinician's or school district's ability to identify and to serve the handicapped. When used in an attempt to circumvent, stunt, or substitute for a comprehensive individual evaluation, screening tests can lead to major errors in the identification–programming process and provide a great disservice to the teachers, parents, and other individuals involved. Not all intellectual screening tests are group-administered. Some of the best screening tests are individually administered, although individual administration does not elevate the status of a screening measure within the total evaluation process.

Individual Screening of Intellectual Function

The use of individually administered screening tests need not be an extremely expensive or time-consuming enterprise. Individual screening instruments are available that are valid, reliable, and informative, and require only 20–30 minutes for administration. Of these, the most reasonable methods seem to be carefully developed short forms of the major individually administered intelligence tests, and the use of such forms is the procedure most strongly recommended here. These short forms are typically at least as reliable as other brief tests, have more validity information available, are more familiar to educational and psychological personnel, and are traditionally better normed than nearly all other brief tests of intelligence. Short forms of the major scales have an added advantage in that, if an individual is noted to be at risk on the screening measure, the remainder of the scale can be administered without a duplication of effort. The development of short forms of the Wechsler scales has been a popular topic in the psychometric literature for some time and several short forms of the WISC-R have been proposed. Of these, the most useful appears to be the one proposed by Kaufman (1976d).

Previously, short forms typically have been developed on purely empirical grounds, without regard to rational and psychological bases for the inclusion of specific subtests. Although empirical development is necessary, it seems insufficient as the sole method of choosing subtests for a short form. Kaufman's (1976d) four-test short form of the WISC-R was developed on the basis of empirical and rational psychological characteristics of the various subtests; data gleaned from the large national standardization sample of the test were used, with careful delineation of the short form's psychometric properties.

In choosing subtests for the short form, Kaufman determined that two Verbal and two Performance tests would be included and that each dyad should be truly representative of its respective scale. For the Verbal dyad, the Arithmetic and Vocabulary sub-

tests were chosen. For the 10 possible dyads, the range of correlations with IQ was .88–.93; thus any combination was about equally empirically adequate. The Arithmetic–Vocabulary combination was chosen because (1) the tests rap diverse mental skills; (2) the verbal–numerical combination is known to be an excellent predictor of school or academic attainment; (3) Vocabulary is the best single measure of g, or general intelligence, on the WISC-R; and (4) the inclusion of Arithmetic insures that the Freedom from Distractibility factor (see later discussion of factor analysis of the WISC-R) is represented.

For the 10 possible Performance scale dyads, the range of correlations with PIQ was again quite restrictive, though smaller on the average than the Verbal scale dyad–VIQ correlations. Kaufman (1976d) selected the Picture Arrangement–Block Design dyad to represent the Performance scale. It had the largest correlation with the PIQ (.89) and has considerable intuitive and rational appeal: Block Design is the best measure of g among the nonverbal scales and is the most reliable of all Performance scale tests. Block Design and Picture Arrangement measure diverse sets of mental skills, and Picture Arrangement is more complex than the remaining Performance tasks, in addition to being one of the most clinically interesting of all Wechsler tasks. Once chosen from results with the "even" age groups of the standardization sample, both dyads were cross-validated using the "odd" age groups.

Using a method of linear equating described by Tellegen and Briggs (1967), Kaufman (1976d) generated conversion equations for the estimation of FSIQ from short-form scores at each age level. Since the equations were all so similar, a single equation determined from the intercorrelation matrix of all 11 age groups was used to convert short-form scores to estimate FSIQs. The equation is applicable to the entire age range of the WISC-R and is as follows:

$$\text{Estimated WISC-R FSIQ} = 1.64 X_{SF} + 34.1$$

where X_{SF} is the sum of the child's *scaled* scores on the four component subtests. Though this formula is easy to use, Kaufman (1976d, Table 3, p. 185) also provides a conversion table for estimating FSIQs based on this equation.

The psychometric characteristics of the Kaufman WISC-R short form are admirable, given its brevity. The split-half reliability ranges from .89 to .93 across the age range, while short-term test–retest reliability estimates range from .83. to .91. At every age, the short form correlates above .90 with the FSIQ. At the appropriate age levels, the WISC-R short-form IQs correlate .80 with the WPPSI and .89 with the WAIS. The short-form estimates of WISC-R FSIQs, on the average, are within 3 points of the FSIQ obtained from administration of the total scale (Kaufman, 1976d). The standard error of estimate of the short-form estimated FSIQs is about 5 points.

Short forms of other individual intelligence tests have also been developed, but are not described in detail here. For adults, Reynolds, Willson, and Clark (1983) have recently developed a short form of the WAIS-R (Wechsler, 1981). For young children, short forms of the WPPSI (Kaufman, 1972) and the McCarthy Scales of Children's Abilities (Kaufman, 1977) are the most important and appropriate individual screening methods (see Reynolds & Clark, 1982, for a discussion of various proposed short forms of these scales). When choosing or developing short forms of existing or new intelligence tests, psychologists would probably be best served by adhering to the blend of psychological, clinical, and psychometric considerations proposed by Kaufman (1972, 1976d, 1977).

OBSERVING TEST BEHAVIOR

Clinical skills with children are obviously important to the intelligent tester for building rapport and maintaining the proper ambience during the actual testing setting. Although adhering to standardized procedures and obtaining valid scores are quite important, the child must remain the lodestar of the evaluation. Critical to the dynamic understanding of the child's performance are close, insightful observation and recording of behavior during the testing period. As noted earlier, fully half or more of the important information to be gathered during the administration of an intelligence test comes from observing behavior under a set of standard conditions. Behavior at various points in the course of the assessment will often dictate the proper interpretation of test scores, and can offer information on a child's characteristic approach to problem solving, reactions to frustrations or successes, or cognitive style. Again as noted earlier, many individuals earn IQs of 100; however, each does so in a different manner, with infinite nuances of behavior interacting directly with a person's test performance. Table 6.1 provides a sampling of behaviors that will frequently be of interest in the context of an individual assessment in general, but particularly when one is assessing intelligence and special abilities. It will be important, particularly to the generalizability of any inferences made on the basis of the child's behavior during the testing, to observe the child's behavior in other settings (e.g., in the waiting room, on the playground, and at day care or in a formal classroom setting). It is best to make such observations prior to formal testing, to lessen the impact of the observation on the behavior of interest. Intelligence and achievement tests themselves can be evaluated from the perspective of applied behavior analysis (e.g., see Sattler, 1982, Ch. 18, for a brief review), though such is not the featured approach here.

Concomitantly, intelligent testing requires the communication of results in a meaningful manner that is child-oriented, and not simply a test-by-test recital of results. Though results are often communicated orally to some staff members, the most universal means is through the psychological report. The key to the intelligent tester's report is that it is written about a child, not about a test or series of tests. Further discussions of this can be found in Kamphaus and Reynolds (1987), Kaufman and Reynolds (1984), and Shellenberger (1982).

TRADITIONAL NORMATIVE APPROACHES TO TEST INTERPRETATION

The first line of attack in test interpretation is the evaluation of the individual's performance relative to the performance of an appropriate reference group. In the vast majority of cases, this group consists of the individuals' age peers. For the Wechsler

TABLE 6.1. Examples of Observations and Behaviors That May Be Useful in the Context of Intellectual and Academic Assessment

1. Appearance. Size, height, and weight; facial and other physical characteristics; grooming and general cleanliness; clothing style (appropriateness for age).

2. Language Development. Articulation, syntax, language patterns, use of standard English, dialects, or slang.

3. Responses to Test Materials and Setting.
   a. *General Activity Level*. Evidence of tension, anxiety, or restlessness, such as nail biting, foot wiggling, fidgeting, excessive talking, blocks in talking, intermittent stutters, voice tremors.
   b. *Attention Span*. Resistance to extraneous stimuli, general distractibility, ability to focus behavior, remaining on task, and sustaining purposive acts.
   c. *Cooperation or Resistance*. Rapport, personal relationship with psychologist, attempts to cooperate, refusal of specific tasks, interest in the various tasks, attempts to perform at a high level of proficiency, motivation.
   d. *Cognitive and Problem-Solving Styles*. Impulsive, quick to respond, contemplates solutions, employs trial and error, develops systematic plan, checks answers, disregards obviously incorrect responses.
   e. *Reactions to Failure, Challenges, and Success*. Continues to work as long as time limits allow, gives up at first hint of difficulty, frequently asks for assistance or special directions, failure on one task reduces interest in following tasks, difficulty heightens interest, seeks challenges, becomes aggressive when meeting failure, withdraws, becomes dependent.
   f. *Attitudes toward Self*. Displays confidence, a superior attitude, frequently says "I can't," seems defeatist, seeks examiner's approval, responds positively to praise and encouragement, sulks, makes disparaging remarks about self or about test materials.

Note. This list is suggestive, not exhaustive, and refers to both behaviors and inferences drawn from those behaviors. Typically, both levels of information are important and should be provided.

scales, the three global IQs are first examined and compared to the mean level of performance of the standardization sample. Since the Wechsler IQs are standardized within separate age levels and assume an essentially normal distribution, the normative evaluation of performance is relatively simple and straightforward. Given the constant mean (100) and standard deviation (15) of the VIQ, PIQ, and FSIQ, the relative standing of the individual with regard to age peers is readily revealed from tables in the test manual or a table of the normal curve. However, Wechsler grouped tasks into these three IQ scales on a purely intuitive basis; before direct interpretations of the scales can be made, evidence for the reality of their existence must be examined. Such evidence comes most directly from factor analysis.

Factor Analysis of the Wechsler Scales

One of the most frequent avenues of research with the Wechsler scales has been factor analysis. A striking consistency of results has occurred across a number of ages and populations, and this has implications for test interpretation. Some major differences occur

across the three Wechsler scales (WPPSI, WISC-R, WAIS-R) that are important to note as well.

Three consistent and pervasive factors emerged for each of the 11 age groups in the WISC-R standardization sample, regardless of whether orthogonal or oblique rotational procedures were employed: Verbal Comprehension, Perceptual Organization, and Freedom from Distractibility (Kaufman, 1975). Each of the 12 WISC-R subtests was found to have a primary loading on one and only one of these factors, as shown below:

1. Verbal Comprehension
   Information
   Similarities
   Vocabulary
   Comprehension
2. Perceptual Organization
   Picture Completion
   Picture Arrangement
   Block Design
   Object Assembly
   Mazes
3. Freedom from Distractibility
   Arithmetic
   Digit Span
   Coding

The first two factors bear an obvious relationship to the Verbal and Performance scales, respectively. The third factor was labeled "Freedom from Distractibility" to follow the historical precedent established by Cohen (1959) for other Wechsler batteries; in addition, research with hyperactive children has shown that drug therapy leads to decreased distractibility and improved memory and arithmetic skills (Wender, 1971).

Tables 6.2 through 6.4 show the median varimax loadings obtained for the 11 age groups between $6\frac{1}{2}$ and $16\frac{1}{2}$ years in the normative sample, along with results from a series of replications with various normal and clinical groups. Note that Information had a substantial loading on the third factor for the standardization sample (median = .41). However, this relationship was not obtained for two oblique rotations of the WISC-R factors, so it was concluded that the Freedom from Distractibility factor was composed only of Arithmetic, Digit Span, and Coding. The conclusion has been given additional support from the results of factor analyses of supplementary populations. A Freedom from Distractibility dimension emerged for mentally retarded children and adolescents (Van Hagen & Kaufman, 1975), for adolescent psychiatric patients (DeHorn & Klinge, 1978), for normal groups of Anglos and Chicanos (Reschly, 1978), for blacks (Gutkin & Reynolds, 1981), and for children referred to school or clinical psychologists for suspected learning and/or behavioral disorders (Lombard & Reidel, 1978; Stedman, Lawlis, Cortner, & Achterberg, 1978; Swerdlik & Schweitzer, 1978). As indicated in Table 6.3, the median loadings for these samples on the Freedom from Distractibility factor were above .40 for Arithmetic, Digit Span, and Coding, but only .30 for Information. Thus the existence of the WISC-R Freedom from Distractibility factor, as well as its composition, has been cross-validated for an impressive variety of normal and clinical groups.

Even more striking than the cross-validation evidence for the third factor is the evidence for the first two factors. Verbal Comprehension and Perceptual Organization dimensions have emerged for every sample whose WISC-R subtest scores have been subjected to factor analysis, including two groups that did not produce a Freedom from Distractibility factor (the black and Native American Papagos subjects investigated by Reschly, 1978). Furthermore, when hierarchical factor solutions have been applied to WISC-R data, clear verbal and perceptual dimensions are yielded even after the extraction of a large general intelligence (g) factor (Vance & Wallbrown, 1978; Wallbrown, Blaha, Wallbrown, & Engin, 1975). Tables 6.2 and 6.3 present the median varimax loadings for 13 samples on the Verbal Comprehension and Perceptual Organization factors. The median loadings for these cross-validation samples on the nonverbal dimension are quite close to the medians for the standardization sample on the Perceptual Organization factor. The Verbal Comprehension factors for the standardization sample and the supplementary populations are also close in composition. The main difference concerns the Arithmetic and Digit Span subtests. For the standardization sample, these tasks were far more closely associated with the third than the first factor; for the cross-validation groups, they loaded almost equally on the Verbal Comprehension and Freedom from Distractibility dimensions. Examination of data for the separate supplementary populations revealed that the approximately equal loadings by Arithmetic and Digit Span on the first and third factors characterized the normal as well as the clinical samples.

One important inference to be drawn from the various factor analyses is that the empirical results support the construct validity of the WISC-R. The Verbal Comprehension factor reflects the construct purported to be measured by Wechsler to be measured by the Verbal scale. Four Verbal subtests have very high loadings on this factor, and although Arithmetic is a distant fifth, it is clearly associated with the Verbal Comprehension dimension. The fact that Digit Span was the sixth best measure of Verbal Comprehension for the cross-validation samples (but not for the standardization groups) offers tentative support for its placement by Wechsler on the Verbal scale. Equally good evidence is provided by factor analysis for the construct validity of the Performance scale. The pattern of loadings on the Perceptual Organization factor suggests that this dimension corresponds to a unitary ability underlying the Performance scale. Only Coding, among the six nonverbal subtests, is given no empirical

TABLE 6.2. Factor Loadings on the Verbal Comprehension Factor for a Variety of Normal and Clinical Samples

WISC-R subtest	(1)	(2)	(3)	(4)	(5)	(6)	(7)	(8)	(9)	(10)	(11)	(12)	(13)	(14)	Median
Verbal															
Information	63	63	72	66	70	73	82	59	84	71	76	69	73	70	71
Similarities	64	59	66	67	59	67	75	69	77	69	68	70	66	67	67
Arithmetic	37	43	65	40	42	41	44	43	66	48	39	43	62	24	43
Vocabulary	72	74	76	67	74	57	82	81	82	70	76	82	82	78	76
Comprehension	64	64	74	61	71	53	65	77	82	55	56	72	64	68	64
Digit Span	18	35	46	33	31	46	23	28	38	14	—	—	44	19	33
Performance															
Picture Completion	35	20	36	32	22	16	30	31	16	24	28	29	37	18	29
Picture arrangement	33	20	39	17	23	46	38	30	48	18	23	25	41	33	30
Block Design	27	17	23	20	14	27	37	32	23	22	31	20	33	26	23
Object Assembly	21	07	09	14	09	04	20	20	23	28	10	25	20	19	20
Coding	15	12	35	14	21	26	27	20	07	14	21	11	38	39	20
Mazes	12	18	30	06	16	10	—	08	—	—	—	—	23	—	14

Note. Decimal points are omitted. Loadings of .35 and above are italicized. The groups are as follows:

(1) Standardization sample, ages $6\frac{1}{2}$–$16\frac{1}{2}$ ($n = 2,200$). 85% white, 15% nonwhite; median varimax loadings for 11 age groups are shown in table. Source: Kaufman (1975).
(2) Anglos, grades 1–9 ($n = 252$). Source: Reschly (1978).
(3) Blacks, grades 1–9 ($n = 235$). Source: Reschly (1978).
(4) Chicanos, grades 1–9 ($n = 223$). Source: Reschly (1978).
(5) Native American Papagos, grades 1–9 ($n = 240$). Source: Reschly (1978).
(6) Mentally retarded sample ages 6–$16\frac{1}{2}$ ($n = 80$), mean WISC-R IQ = 50.6, 82% white, 18% nonwhite. Source: Van Hagen and Kaufman (1975).
(7) Adolescent psychiatric sample, ages $10\frac{1}{2}$–16 ($n = 100$), 68% white, 32% nonwhite. Source: DeHorn and Klinge (1978).
(8) Sample of children referred because of concerns about intellectual ability, ages 7–16 ($n = 164$), mean WISC-R IQ = 85.9, 63% white, 24% black, 13% Latino. Source: Swerdlik and Schweitzer (1978).
(9) Sample of children referred for learning and/or behavior problems, ages 6–13 ($n = 106$), 90% Spanish surname, 8% white, 2% black. Source: Stedman, Lawlis, Cortner, and Achterberg (1978).
(10) Sample of Chicano children referred for school-related problems, mean age = $10\frac{1}{2}$ ($n = 142$). Source: Gutkin and Reynolds (1980).
(11) Sample of Anglo children referred for learning difficulties, mean age = 11 ($n = 109$). Source: Dean (1979).
(12) Sample of learning-disabled children, mean age = $10\frac{1}{2}$ ($n = 275$). Source: Schooler, Beebe, and Koepke (1978).
(13) Sample of low-SES children from the WISC-R standardization sample ($n = 782$). Source: Carlson, Reynolds, and Gutkin (1983).
(14) Sample of emotionally disturbed children ($n = 60$). Source: Reynolds and Struer (1982).

TABLE 6.3. Factor Loadings on the Perceptual Organization Factor for a Variety of Normal and Clinical Samples

WISC-R subtest	(1)	(2)	(3)	(4)	(5)	(6)	(7)	(8)	(9)	(10)	(11)	(12)	(13)	(14)	Median
Verbal															
Information	25	32	32	20	26	12	29	33	10	13	09	11	29	25	25
Similarities	34	26	30	15	34	08	45	22	23	33	39	30	34	19	30
Arithmetic	20	26	37	13	37	16	40	39	13	31	-23	37	27	24	27
Vocabulary	24	23	19	26	14	27	31	23	30	27	22	23	26	16	24
Comprehension	30	22	16	20	13	48	38	25	18	33	-12	15	34	19	22
Digit Span	12	02	32	14	36	06	10	26	23	22	—	—	19	17	19
Performance															
Picture Completion	*57*	*49*	*44*	*52*	*54*	*83*	*68*	*59*	*83*	*56*	*66*	*47*	*59*	*68*	*57*
Picture Arrangement	*41*	*53*	*47*	*38*	*43*	*41*	*58*	*52*	*31*	*72*	*59*	*56*	*44*	*49*	*47*
Block Design	*66*	*60*	*66*	*59*	*68*	*62*	*71*	*70*	*75*	*64*	*73*	*70*	*74*	*72*	*68*
Object Assembly	*65*	*59*	*57*	*58*	*56*	*70*	*76*	*76*	*68*	*51*	*69*	*80*	*73*	*77*	*68*
Coding	20	16	27	16	25	45	30	44	05	37	29	43	19	32	27
Mazes	*47*	*42*	*47*	*47*	*56*	*67*	—	*55*	—	—	—	—	*52*	—	*50*

Note. Decimal points are omitted. Loadings of .35 and above are italicized. The groups are as follows:
(1) Standardization sample, ages $6\frac{1}{2}$–$16\frac{1}{2}$ (n = 2,200). 85% white, 15% nonwhite; median varimax loadings for 11 age groups are shown in table. Source: Kaufman (1975).
(2) Anglos, grades 1–9 (n = 252). Source: Reschly (1978).
(3) Blacks, grades 1–9 (n = 235). Source: Reschly (1978).
(4) Chicanos, grades 1–9 (n = 223). Source: Reschly (1978).
(5) Native American Papagos, grades 1–9 (n = 240). Source: Reschly (1978).
(6) Mentally retarded sample ages 6–$16\frac{1}{2}$ (n = 80), mean WISC-R IQ = 50.6, 82% white, 18% nonwhite. Source: Van Hagen and Kaufman (1975).
(7) Adolescent psychiatric sample, ages $10\frac{1}{2}$–16 (n = 100). 68% white, 32% nonwhite. Source: DeHorn and Klinge (1978).
(8) Sample of children referred because of concerns about intellectual ability, ages 7–16 (n = 164), mean WISC-R IQ = 85.9, 63% white, 24% black, 13% Latino. Source: Swerdlik and Schweitzer (1978).
(9) Sample of children referred for learning and/or behavior problems, ages 6–13 (n = 106), 90% Spanish surname, 8% white, 2% black. Source: Stedman, Lawlis, Cortner, and Achterberg (1978).
(10) Sample of Chicano children referred for school-related problems, mean age = $10\frac{1}{2}$ (n = 142). Source: Gutkin and Reynolds (1980).
(11) Sample of Anglo children referred for learning difficulties, mean age = 11 (n = 109). Source: Dean (1979).
(12) Sample of learning-disabled children, mean age = $10\frac{1}{2}$ (n = 275). Source: Schooler, Beebe, and Koepke (1978).
(13) Sample of low-SES children from the WISC-R standardization sample (n = 782). Source: Carlson, Reynolds, and Gutkin (1983).
(14) Sample of emotionally disturbed children (n = 60). Source: Reynolds and Struer (1982).

139

TABLE 6.4. Factor Loadings for the Freedom from Distractibility Factor for a Variety of Normal and Clinical Samples

WISC-R subtest	(1)	(2)	(4)	(6)	(7)	(8)	(9)	(11)	(13)	(14)	Median
Verbal											
Information	41	26	33	24	14	38	16	−19	42	14	26
Similarities	28	26	22	23	22	27	04	−26	28	17	23
Arithmetic	58	45	45	54	49	49	40	52	58	81	49
Vocabulary	33	12	30	02	17	17	03	20	33	21	17
Comprehension	24	21	06	12	45	16	09	21	26	28	21
Digit Span	56	40	31	29	37	65	42	—	56	53	41
Performance											
Picture Completion	11	09	12	12	−01	19	01	27	13	35	12
Picture Arrangement	12	00	39	45	12	43	21	−17	24	42	21
Block Design	28	22	16	05	23	17	04	47	30	22	22
Object Assembly	12	18	09	09	13	12	36	24	11	07	12
Coding	42	40	37	43	57	19	94	44	38	28	42
Mazes	22	10	20	24	—	22	—	—	23	—	22

Note. Decimal points are omitted. Loadings of .35 and above are italicized. Groups 3 and 5 are omitted from this table because a Freedom from Distractibility factor did not emerge for those two samples. Hence, the loadings shown in Tables 6.2 and 6.3 reflect dta obtained not from Reschly's (1978) two-factor solutions for blacks and Native-American Papagos, but from his three-factor solutions for whites and Chicanos. Groups 10 and 12 are also omitted from this table because Gutkin and Reynolds (1980) only identified two meaningful factors, and Schooler, Beebe, and Koepke (1978) did not even investigate three-factor solutions. The groups are as follows:

(1) Standardization sample, ages $6\frac{1}{2}$–$16\frac{1}{2}$ (n = 2,200). 85% white, 15% nonwhite; median varimax loadings for 11 age groups are shown in table. Source: Kaufman (1975).

(2) Anglos, grades 1–9 (n = 252). Source: Reschly (1978).

(4) Chicanos, grades 1–9 (n = 223). Source: Reschly (1978).

(6) Mentally retarded sample ages 6–$16\frac{1}{2}$ (n = 80), mean WISC-R IQ = 50.6, 82% white, 18% nonwhite. Source: Van Hagen and Kaufman (1975).

(7) Adolescent psychiatric sample, ages $10\frac{1}{2}$–16 (n = 100), 68% white, 32% nonwhite. Source: DeHorn and Klinge (1978).

(8) Sample of children referred because of concerns about intellectual ability, ages 7–16 (n = 164), mean WISC-R IQ = 85.9, 63% white, 24% black, 13% Latino. Source: Swerdlik and Schweitzer (1978).

(9) Sample of children referred for learning and/or behavior problems, ages 6– 13 (n = 106), 90% Spanish surname, 8% white, 2% black. Source: Stedman, Lawlis, Cortner, and Achterberg (1978).

(11) Sample of Anglo children referred for learning difficulties, mean age = 11 (n = 109). Source: Dean (1979).

(13) Sample of low-SES children from the WISC-R standardization sample (n = 782). Source: Carlson, Reynolds, and Gutkin (1983).

(14) Sample of emotionally disturbed children (n = 60). Source: Reynolds and Struer (1982).

support for its inclusion on the Performance scale.

Review of the WISC-R factor-analytic literature has thus shown that three factors are typically isolated—two that are related closely to Wechsler's Verbal–Performance dichotomy, and a third that may correspond to a behavioral attribute. These factors are remarkably similar in composition from age to age and across sex (Reynolds & Gutkin, 1980) throughout the entire range serviced by the WISC-R, and also from group to group, whether normal or exceptional populations are tested. The three factors have been isolated for Spanish-speaking as well as English-speaking children (Gutkin & Reynolds, 1980; Reschly, 1978; Stedman et al., 1978). Furthermore, the factors do not fragment and split into highly specific factors when four or five are rotated (Kaufman, 1975).

The robust nature of the various WISC-R factors is important for clinicians to understand, because of the implications of these data for competent interpretation of the WISC-R. More so than profiles on the old WISC, children's WISC-R profiles should be attacked by featuring the Verbal and Performance scales, and subserving fluctuations in the pattern of subtest scores. The large, omnipresent Verbal Comprehension and Perceptual Organization factors suggest that the VIQ and PIQ correspond to real, unitary dimensions of ability in children. As such, profile interpretation should begin by focusing on these global verbal and nonverbal skill areas. This suggestion seems simple enough, but a great many methods of interpretation focus on the individuality of the 10–12 subtests, as if the WISC-R were a mixed bag of about a dozen separate and diverse skills, each assessing a finite aspect of a child's intellect (see Reynolds, 1980b, for a brief critique). Even a table such as the one appearing in the WISC-R manual (Wechsler, 1974, Table 12), which presents the differences between pairs of scaled scores required for statistical significance, can impel examiners to focus off target. The pairwise comparison technique places a stress on the subtests (taken two at a time), rather than on the two major scales; furthermore, this procedure offers clinicians a series of statements about a child's strong and weak abilities, but fails to provide a succinct overview or integration of his or her skills. The so-called "paired-comparison" method of subtest interpretation is statistically unsound.

Later we present logical and statistical methods for the very necessary look beyond the IQ scales, but intelligent test interpretation begins by first viewing overall performance on g (as estimated by the FSIQ) and the Verbal and Performance scales. The third factor will also need to be examined for many children. Gutkin (1979c) provides a formula for estimating a deviation IQ with a mean of 100 and standard deviation of 15 for the Freedom from Distractibility factor.

The third WISC-R factor, which may be a measure of attention/distractibility, anxiety, symbolic ability, sequential processing, or memory, is a particularly intriguing one. Its pervasiveness and robustness on the WISC-R are not matched in factor analyses of other Wechsler batteries. Recent factor-analytic studies of the WAIS-R show a large general factor, accompanied by strong Verbal Comprehension and Perceptual Organization factors; these correspond to the FSIQ, VIQ, and PIQ, respectively (Gutkin, Reynolds, & Galvin, 1984). When WAIS-R Freedom from Distractibility factors do appear for the various adult age groups, they are much smaller in magnitude than their WISC-R counterparts; indeed, for some groups, the WAIS-R Freedom from Distractibility dimensions have such small eigenvalues that they are of questionable significance (Naglieri & Kaufman, 1982). Numerous studies of the preschool version of the Wechsler, the WPPSI, have repeatedly located only a large general factor and the two corresponding to the a priori determined IQ scales (e.g., Carlson & Reynolds, 1981; Kaufman & Hollenbeck, 1974). Since the publication of the K-ABC, several studies have reported on factor analyses of the WISC-R subtests taken simultaneously with the K-ABC subtests. Results of these analyses shed additional light on the interpretation of both scales, but are particularly relevant to the third WISC-R factor and its understanding.

Conjoint Factor Analysis of the WISC-R and the K-ABC

Normal Children

Kaufman and McLean (1987) recently completed a study with 212 normal children tested on the WISC-R and the K-ABC in a counterbalanced fashion. Intuitively, there appears to be some correspondence between the three subscales of the K-ABC and the three factorially derived scales of the WISC-R (the so-named Verbal Comprehension, Perceptual Organization, and Freedom from Distractibility factors). Kaufman and McLean's work provides an opportunity to evaluate these and related hypotheses with a reasonably sized sample of normal children.

Three factors emerged in the joint analysis of the K-ABC and the WISC-R. A strong g factor also emerged whose four highest-loading variables were two WISC-R subtests (Information, .80; Comprehension, .76) and two K-ABC subtests (Reading/Understanding, .80; Riddles, .76). Both scales, then, contributed strongly to the g factor present in the combined analysis. The three factors extracted and rotated to approximate simple structure represent, with great accuracy, the hypothesized match-up between the K-ABC and the WISC-R scales. The complete results are shown in Table 6.5.

As can be seen, the first rotated factor was a combination of the WISC-R Verbal Comprehension factor and the K-ABC Achievement scale. This is in line with arguments that the WISC-R Verbal scale is aligned with acquired factual knowledge and is subsequently more related to achievement than to intelligence. The traditionalist, however, may interpret this finding as evidence that the K-ABC Achievement scale is heavily laden with tests of verbal reasoning skill (cf. Kamphaus & Reynolds, 1984). The presence of subtests such as Riddles argues for the latter interpretation, but the large loading of Reading/Understanding supports the former equally well.

The second and third factors in Table 6.5 seem far more straightforward. The second factor to emerge was a blending of the K-ABC Simultaneous Processing scale subtests and the WISC-R Performance scale subtests, with the possible exception of Coding, which had the smallest loadings of these subtests. However, in the joint analysis, Coding loaded poorly on all factors. A close correspondence is clear, not only intuitively but empirically, between the K-ABC Simultaneous Processing scale and the WISC-R Performance scale.

The third factor shown in Table 6.5 was a combination of the K-ABC Sequential Processing scale subtests with Arithmetic and Digit Span, the key components of the WISC-R Freedom from Distractibility factor, Coding also loaded at .30 on this factor, not a large loading but certainly respectable. Is this then just a memory factor, as has been suggested by some (e.g., Jensen, 1974; Keith & Dunbar, 1984)? The presence of Arithmetic (WISC-R) and Coding seems to preclude such a rigid interpretation. The large loading by Hand Movements is anathema to a "verbal memory" interpretation, as is the Coding loading. Even the K-ABC Arithmetic subtest, with its heavily visual presentation, loaded .30 on this factor. We think that the evidence points to an interpretation of this factor as sequential processing for most children. However, for some children, this will be primarily a memory factor: With a very poor short-term memory, a child just cannot perform adequately on these tasks. For some children, this may be a distractibility factor: A child who cannot pay adequate attention will be unable to get the stimuli into short-term store. Anxiety may be another culprit. Only full analysis of behavior and the resulting profile can provide definite answers. Memory and attentional skills are necessary but insufficient for performance on these subtests; where they are present even at minimal levels, sequential processing is probably the most salient variable of assessment with these tasks. When they are not present in adequate amounts, it should be readily discernible from the child's behavior and other features of the profile (e.g., low scores on Spatial Memory, Information, or Faces and Places).

Naglieri and Jensen (1987) also conducted a joint factor analysis of the K-ABC and the WISC-R subtests for a sample of 172 normal children. Their sample contained 86 whites and 86 blacks. These authors used a different, more esoteric procedure—the Schnid–Leiman orthogonalized hierarchical factor analysis. This procedure extracts the strongest factor present and reduces the correlation matrix, removing the variance attributable to this factor, and then goes back into the now residualized matrix and repeats this process until the desired number of factors has been extracted.

Using this methodology, Naglieri and Jensen (1987) identified three factors, which

TABLE 6.5. Three-Factor Solution of Two Joint Analyses of the K-ABC and WISC-R for Normal Children

Subtest	Unrotated factor		Factor 1: Achievement/Verbal		Factor II: Simultaneous/ Perceptual		Factor III: Sequential/Distractibility	
	Study 1	Study 2	Study 1	Study 2	Study 1	Study 2	Study 1	Study 2
K-ABC								
Sequential Processing								
3. Hand Movements	.47	.42	.15	−.02	.25	.08	.50	.34
5. Number Recall	.47	.34	.20	−.04	−.05	−.08	.75	.56
7. Word Order	.49	.38	.28	−.10	.03	.01	.56	.55
Simultaneous Processing								
4. Gestalt Closure	.18	.36	.04	−.11	.34	.31	−.05	−.18
6. Triangles	.68	.55	.28	−.06	.62	.46	.34	.07
8. Matrix Analogies	.63	.58	.33	.12	.44	.25	.36	.13
9. Spatial Memory	.44	.41	.12	−.16	.42	.44	.30	.08
10. Photo Series	.64	.40	.34	.02	.46	.31	.34	.00
Achievement								
12. Faces and Places	.70	.55	.70	.57	.22	.00	.16	.18
13. Arithmetic	.74	.57	.59	.28	.27	−.03	.38	.28
14. Riddles	.76	.67	.72	.47	.37	.12	.12	−.08
15. Reading/Decoding	.67	.57	.57	.45	.16	−.11	.37	.16
16. Reading/Understanding	.80	.59	.73	.47	.25	−.03	.31	.04
WISC-R								
Verbal								
Information	.80	.60	.77	.55	.27	−.01	.23	−.08
Similarities	.71	.62	.75	.43	.21	.08	.12	−.02
Arithmetic	.72	.50	.44	.20	.36	.00	.47	.27
Vocabulary	.73	.64	.78	.60	.07	−.02	.25	−.10
Comprehension	.76	.58	.73	.45	.25	.01	.23	.00
Digit Span	.51	.42	.19	−.08	.12	−.02	.66	.62
Performance								
Picture Completion	.52	.48	.35	.06	.48	.38	.05	−.08
Picture Arrangement	.43	.42	.20	.04	.54	−.31	.02	−.03
Block Design	.62	.66	.25	.08	.64	.44	.24	.06
Object Assembly	.53	.47	.17	−.04	.71	.48	.10	−.08
Coding	.34	.25	.06	−.15	.31	−.28	.30	.10
Percent of common factor variance	.77	NR	.47	NR	.28	NR	.25	NR
Percent of total factor variance	.38	NR	.23	NR	.14	NR	.13	NR

Note. Study 1 data from Kaufman and McLean (1987), using a three-factor varimax solution. Study 2 data from Naglieri and Jensen (1987), using a three-factor Schmid–Leiman hierarchical orthogonolized solution. NR, not reported.

143

they labeled Verbal, Spatial, and Memory Span. Despite these labels, the differences in methodology, and the different sample, the factors are remarkably similar to those of Kaufman and McLean (1987). The more distinctive nature of the differences within the Naglieri and Jensen factors is a result of the hierarchical procedures employed, which force a greater separation of the factors extracted. The labeling of the third Naglieri and Jensen factor as Memory Span is consistent with Jensen's Level I–Level II theory of intelligence, but is inconsistent in several regards with the specific results of this study. Spatial Memory, which should be a rote memory task in Jensen's model, did not load beyond .11 on the so-called Memory Span factor for whites, blacks, or the combined samples. Arithmetic, which can hardly be viewed as having strong short-term memory components on the K-ABC and certainly is not rote recall after about age 8 or 9, loaded about equally well on the Verbal and Memory Span factors. Essentially, the results of Naglieri and Jensen are consistent with those of Kaufman and McLean.

Naglieri and Jensen also evaluated the g factor of the two batteries and reached several important conclusions. The first, which is the precursor to acceptance of the second, is that the g factors extracted with their sample for each scale are virtually identical to the g factor from each scale's respective standardization data. Combining the two batteries does not detract from the g factor. The second, and more clinically and theoretically important, conclusion is that the general factor in both batteries represents essentially the same g.

When viewed in context, these results have some important clinical implications for the use of the WISC-R and the K-ABC. The most prominent are as follows:

1. There is much congruence between the various constructs assessed by the K-ABC and WISC-R. What, specifically, the two scales are measuring may vary for individual children, but for most there seems to be a distinction among sequential processing, simultaneous processing, and achievement.

2. For certain classes of children, verbal reasoning may be more salient than pure achievement as an interpretation of the WISC-R Verbal scale and of Expressive Vocabulary, Faces and Places, Riddles, and Arithmetic from the K-ABC.

3. The WISC-R Verbal scale may best be interpreted as a measure of achievement or acquired knowledge for many children, consistent with the loadings of these subtests with the K-ABC Achievement scale subtests.

4. For certain classes of children, memory, anxiety, or distractibility may be more salient explanations than sequential processing in analyzing K-ABC and WISC-R performance, and such an option should be recognized and entertained when pertinent behavioral observations and other profile characteristics are in evidence.

5. The K-ABC and the WISC-R seem to be measuring the same g, which also seems to be heavily contaminated with achievement.

6. The K-ABC and WISC-R subtests that are intuitively related to each other do have substantial, but far from perfect, intercorrelations. Kaufman and McLean (1987) found the following pairs to have substantial correlations: Faces and Places (K-ABC) and Information (WISC-R), Riddles (K-ABC) and Vocabulary (WISC-R), and to a lesser extent Triangles (K-ABC) and Block Design (WISC-R). In contrast, examiners should not expect similar levels of performance for a child on Photo Series (K-ABC) and Picture Arrangement (WISC-R), as they share only a modest relationship.

For certain classes of exceptional children, modification of these recommended views may be required. Two joint factor analyses of the WISC-R and the K-ABC for exceptional children have some utility in this regard, as discussed in the next section.

Exceptional Samples

Keith, Hood, Eberhart, and Pottebaum (1985) recently competed a joint factor analysis of the subtests of the WISC-R and K-ABC for a sample of 568 children referred for evaluation or "relevant re-evaluation." Contrary to results with normal children, Keith et al. found four factors with eigenvalues greater than 1.00 for their referred children. The additional factor was defined by the two K-ABC reading subtests, Reading/Decoding and Reading/Understanding. Information and both Arithmetic subtests had significant loadings on this factor (in the .30s), but the two readings subtests loaded with such magnitude (.78 and .77) that they are clearly the most salient and definitional variables on this factor. The remaining factors are highly consistent with the three-factor solution of Kaufman and McLean (1987) with normal children. The full set of factor loadings is displayed in Table 6.6.

Kaufman and McLean (1986) also conducted a joint factor analysis of the K-ABC and the WISC-R for 198 LD children. They found three-factor and four-factor solutions to be equally defensible, and subsequently reported both solutions. Their three-factor solution yielded dimensions readily identifiable as mergers of the WISC-R Verbal and K-ABC Achievement scales (Factor I), the WISC-R Perceptual Organization factor and K-ABC Simultaneous Processing scale (Factor II), and the WISC-R Freedom from Distractibility factor and K-ABC Sequential Processing scale (Factor III). These factors are essentially indistinguishable from those reported by Kaufman and McLean (1987) for normal children.

For the 198 LD children of Kaufman and McLean's (1986) study, the four-factor solution is more interesting and, we think, also equally justified. The scree plot suggests four factors as most appropriate to us, and the fourth factor barely misses on the eigenvalue criterion as well. Eigenvalues of the first four factors were 8.03, 2.07, 1.42, and 0.99. The first three factors were essentially the same as in the three-factor solution, except that the Achievement/Verbal factor split with the two K-ABC reading subtests, forming a fourth. For Kaufman and McLean's LD children, the fourth factor was even more distinctly defined by Reading/Decoding (which loaded .93) and Reading/Understanding (which loaded .74) than in the Keith et al. (1985) analyses with their more heterogeneous sample.

The other principal difference between the two studies lay in the larger loadings of the two Arithmetic subtests, Faces and Places, and Information, making the Achievement/Verbal factor more generally achievement-oriented, although the two latter subtests are certainly related to time spent reading and to comprehension skills. However, it is important to note that all results of Kaufman and McLean (1986) and of Keith et al. (1985) are far more similar than different. Calculation of coefficients of congruence between matching factors in Table 6.6 yields values in excess of .90 in all cases—values large enough to indicate that the factors are invariant across the two studies (see Reynolds & Kaiser, Chapter 26, this volume).

The distinctions in the joint factor analyses of the WISC-R and the K-ABC for exceptional versus normal samples are theoretically and clinically important. When the two scales are considered singly, the differences do not emerge; yet in both studies a fourth factor was clearly warranted, denoting a somewhat different organization of skills among academically troubled children. The consistency of these results across the two studies reflects an important robustness in the findings as well, and points toward the need for additional investigation.

When one is evaluating children with educational problems, these results also indicate the need to view the reading subtests of the K-ABC as distinct from the other Achievement subtests. Kaufman and McLean (1986) argue similarly when they encourage K-ABC users to fragment the Achievement scale when assessing learning disabled children.

In addition, these studies support the inclusion of Hand Movements on the K-ABC Sequential Processing scale. Whereas for normal children Hand Movement tends to become more simultaneous at the school-age level, for these two exceptional samples (and in conjunction with the WISC-R) it comes across more clearly as a sequential task, although it retains a significant secondary loading on the Simultaneous Processing scale. A processing approach to the interpretation of WISC-R subtests may be justifiable for normal and exceptional samples, in addition to the content-based interpretive schema typically taught for use with the Wechsler scale.

Normative Evaluation of IQs

Once IQs have been derived, some judgment of the individual's level of intellectual functioning relative to same-age peers is appropriate. Probably the most readily understandable approach is through the reporting of a percentile rank with a descriptive classification. Wechsler IQs are essentially normally distributed, and tables of percentile

TABLE 6.6. Varimax-Rotated Four-Factor Solutions for Two Joint Analyses of the K-ABC and WISC-R for Samples of Exceptional Children

Subtest	Unrotated g factor [a]	Factor I: Achievement/Verbal		Factor II: Simultaneous/Perceptual		Factor III: Sequential/Distractibility		Factor IV: Reading	
		Study 1 [b]	Study 2 [c]	Study 1	Study 2	Study 1	Study 2	Study 1	Study 2
K-ABC									
Sequential Processing									
3. Hand Movements	.48	.14	.19	.34	.23	.44	.48	.16	.10
5. Number Recall	.41	.17	.11	.09	.03	.75	.80	.13	.04
7. Word Order	.51	.24	.20	.22	.12	.65	.67	.11	.13
Simultaneous Processing									
4. Gestalt Closure	.38	.37	.04	.49	.56	−.02	−.02	.00	−.07
6. Triangles	.68	.22	.21	.70	.62	.09	.30	.12	.17
8. Matrix Analogies	.54	.24	.28	.45	.50	.26	.12	.20	.08
9. Spatial Memory	.53	.08	.06	.63	.59	.25	.28	.10	.05
10. Photo Series	.58	.28	.22	.67	.54	.25	.27	.09	.04
Achievement									
12. Faces and Places	.59	.68	.44	.22	.20	.16	.17	.20	.38
13. Arithmetic	.75	.42	.44	.48	.34	.36	.31	.33	.44
14. Riddles	.78	.73	.69	.33	.31	.20	.17	.19	.33
15. Reading/Decoding	.43	.33	.09	.13	.00	.26	.10	.78	.93
16. Reading/Understanding	.59	.43	.38	.12	.07	.18	.14	.77	.74
WISC-R									
Verbal									
Information	.71	.63	.57	.31	.22	.22	.18	.34	.47
Similarities	.66	.61	.69	.28	.19	.28	.26	.29	.15
Arithmetic	.59	.28	.22	.42	.32	.42	.32	.33	.38
Vocabulary	.67	.76	.75	.22	.18	.25	.16	.26	.18
Comprehension	.58	.66	.75	.32	.22	.24	.05	.10	.04
Digit Span	.47	.19	.06	.14	.17	.71	.67	.13	.15
Performance									
Picture Completion	.48	.39	.21	.54	.57	.15	.04	.00	.02
Picture Arrangement	.57	.38	.33	.58	.50	.22	.11	.04	.09
Block Design	.72	.24	.23	.76	.75	.13	.23	.15	.12
Object Assembly	.53	.22	.13	.69	.78	.10	−.03	.06	.01
Coding	.35	−.01	.05	.38	.42	.22	−.07	.25	.10

Note. Study 1 data from Keith, Hood, Eberhart, and Pottebaum (1985) and T. Z. Keith (personal communication, March 16, 1986). Study 2 data from Kaufman and McLean (1986).

[a] Reported for Study 2 only.

[b] 568 children constituting a heterogeneous referral sample.

[c] 198 learning-disabled children.

146

ranks, expressing the percentage of the population scoring above and below a given score, are available in a variety of sources, including Reynolds (1981a), Sattler (1982), and many measurement texts. When one is reporting IQ, it is helpful to give a descriptive classification in addition to the percentile rank. Wechsler (1974) and others (such as Kaufman & Kaufman, 1977) present various descriptive classification schemes.

The terminology of certain systems can be offensive, and care must be taken in choosing certain descriptors. The term "mentally defective" for the description of Wechsler or Binet IQs below 70, though perhaps accurate, seems unduly harsh. On the other hand, accuracy is an important concern. For these reasons, a system for descriptive classification of IQ level adapted from Kaufman and Kaufman (1977) is presented in Table 6.7 (it was originally adapted by these authors from Wechsler, 1974).

When reporting IQs, percentile ranks, and descriptive classifications of performance level, it is important to make some statement regarding measurement error. Even though the three Wechsler scales have FSIQs with reliability coefficients in the middle .90s, considerable error can still be present for individuals. From the reliability estimates, a very practical statistic known as the standard error of measurement (*SEM*) can be derived; this permits the establishment of an confidence interval around the reported IQ. Though it varies somewhat from scale to scale, the *SEM* of the Wechsler FSIQs is about 3 IQ points. Since the *SEM* is normally distributed around the true score of the individual, we can band the obtained score to represent any given level of confidence desired, simply by multiplying the *SEM* by the necessary value of z from a table of the normal curve. For example, 1 *SEM* will capture about 68% of a child's scores and 2 *SEM*s about 96%. We feel that the 85%–90% level of confidence is appropriate for most clinical purposes for the Wechsler scales; this requires banding the reported FSIQ about 5 points on each side. The primary purpose of such reporting is to highlight the concept of error, guarding against overinterpretation and rigidity in the use of cutoff scores.

Normative evaluation of levels of performance is crucial to intelligent testing. Performance on IQ tests is related to various factors, the most important for children being school attainment. The IQ test makes a good prediction of the child's future level of academic performance, and can help to explain current levels of academic performance. (Predictive studies with IQ tests may be found in Kamphaus and Reynolds, 1987; Lutey, 1977; and Sattler, 1982.) Important information is gleaned for adults as well, including predictions of success in certain jobs, response to various psychotherapies, and the probability of recovery from neurological insult. However, although it is crucial, normative interpretation is insufficient for intelligent testing. Much more information lies beyond comparisons of individuals to their peers. Intraindividual differences can be important in altering the predictions made by the IQs, for these predictions assume no major changes occurring in the environment. One must look past the IQs to generate hypotheses for intervention.

TABLE 6.7 Descriptive Classification Corresponding to Various Levels of IQ on the Weschler Scales

IQ range	Percentile ranks	Descriptive classification
130 and above	98 and above	Very superior
120 to 129	91 to 97	Superior
110 to 119	75 to 90	High average
90 to 109	25 to 73	Average
80 to 89	9 to 23	Low average
70 to 79	3 to 8	Borderline
69 and below	2 and below	Cognitively deficient

Note. Compiled from Kaufman and Kaufman (1977) and Wechsler (1974).

IPSATIVE EVALUATION OF TEST PERFORMANCE

Normative assessment of performance of the Wechsler scales proceeds from the assumptions that g is primarily the determinant of the FSIQ; that verbal comprehension ability is the primary determinant of scores on the Verbal scale; that perceptual organization ability is the determinant of scores on the Performance scale; and, where applicable, that some unitary trait or ability underlies performance on the Freedom from Distractibility factor. A corollary assumption is that fluctuations in a child's profile are due to chance or error. Fortunately, statistics and formulas are available to permit clinicians to test these important assumptions. When the assumptions cannot be refuted by the simple empirical procedures, then examiners should not ordinarily go beyond a normative interpretation of the Wechsler profile. However, when fluctuations between scales and among subtest scores are statistically significant, causing the examiners to reject some or all of the assumptions, then ipsative (intraindividual) evaluation takes over and the clinical "detective work" predominates.

Verbal–Performance IQ Differences

During ipsative assessment of scores, the individual's own mean level of performance becomes the "normative standard" against which scores are held for comparison. The first step in the process is to examine the VIQ and PIQ to determine whether use of the FSIQ is justifiable. To do this, the examiner first compares the VIQ with the PIQ to find the difference between these scores. For the WISC-R, a difference in these two scores of 12 points is statistically significant at p ≤ .05 and 15 points at $p \leq .01$; for the WAIS-R, the comparable values are 10 and 13, respectively; and for the WPPSI, the corresponding values are closer to 11 and 14.

What does it mean if these scores differ significantly? First, it renders the FSIQ inadequate as a summary statistic representing the general level of ability for the individual. It means that the levels of performance on the Verbal and Performance scales are different to the extent that we can be reasonably confident that the differences are real, not due to chance or the error inherent in all tests that are less than perfectly reliable. It also, by inference, tells us that this individual does not think, reason, or express himself or herself at an equivalent level through the verbal modality of language as when using more concrete, nonverbal methods. The existence of the differences does not, however, tells us why it is there.

Many explanations of VIQ–PIQ differences are possible. Factor analysis is a group data-analytic procedure; as noted earlier, this technique provides strong support for interpretation of distinct Verbal and Perfor-

mance scales, but it does not explain why an individual child or adult might score substantially higher on one scale than the other. Kaufman (1979a) has offered various potential explanations for VIQ–PIQ differences on the WISC-R, which in most instances are equally applicable to the WPPSI and the WAIS-R. Kaufman suggests that VIQ–PIQ differences for individuals may reflect (1) sensory deficits, (2) differences in verbal and nonverbal intelligence, (3) differences in fluid and crystallized intelligence, (4) psycholinguistic deficiencies, (5) bilingualism, (6) effects of a specific dialect, (7) problems in motor coordination, (8) reactions to time pressures on the Performance scale, (9) differences in field dependence–independence, (10) differences on Guilford's operation of evaluation, or (11) the influence of socioeconomic status (SES). Proper interpretation of VIQ–PIQ discrepancies requires close observation of children or adults while they perform the various tasks making up the Wechsler scales, in addition to a comprehensive understanding of contemporary theories of intelligence. Once the best explanation of a child's reliable Verbal–Performance difference has been found, this explanation will almost invariably have something to contribute to the development of appropriate teaching methods for the child that will reflect strengths in the individual's methods and preferences for learning, as well as to a choice of therapeutic interventions. For adults, VIQ–PIQ differences can assist in localization of neurological trauma, as well as in the evaluation of differences in learning. Attempts have been made to link Verbal–Performance differences to personality characteristics and such factors as obsessive–compulsive tendencies (e.g., see Blatt & Allison, 1981), but as yet no satisfactory data-based support for these interpretations is available.

Another factor to consider in evaluating the meaning of VIQ–PIQ differences is the frequency of occurrence of a difference score of a given magnitude. For a difference to have diagnostic significance, it should be relatively infrequent in the normal population. Large discrepancies between the VIQ and PIQ have commonly been associated with a variety of abnormalities, such as neurological impairment (Holroyd & Wright, 1965). However, these clinical assumptions have usually been made in the absence of hard data on normal individuals. How can inferences be made relating interscale of intrascale scatter on a Wechsler battery to abnormalities, without first considering normal VIQ–PIQ discrepancies? The concept of base rates must be imposed.

Wechsler (1974) reports the magnitude of VIQ–PIQ differences required for statistical significance at various levels. About 9 points are required for significance at $p < .15$; about 12 points are needed for $p < .05$; and about 15 points are necessary for $p < .01$. These values reflect the degree to which the VIQ and PIQ must differ for the discrepancies to be meaningful, as opposed to being due merely to chance error, and are based on the reliability coefficients of the respective IQs. The probabilities translate into the amount of confidence one should have that a VIQ–PIQ discrepancy stands for a true difference in the individual's verbal and nonverbal intelligence. However, even though statistical significance provides important information for determining whether a child has "real" differences in the abilities underlying the Verbal and Performance scales, the significance or meaningfulness of the discrepancy does not translate to the frequency of occurrence of a given Verbal–Performance difference. Yet it is the frequency of occurrence among a normal population that is most pertinent for understanding abnormal conditions.

In a study of the WISC-R standardization sample, the average child aged $6\frac{1}{2}$ to $16\frac{1}{2}$ had a VIQ–PIQ discrepancy, regardless of direction, equal to 9.7 points ($SD = 7.6$) (Kaufman, 1976c). The mean discrepancy was approximately the same for each of the 11 age groups; similarly, discrepancies were unrelated to sex and race. In contrast, a trend was noted with regard to SES. The mean discrepancy was nearly 11 points for children of professional parents, decreasing steadily to a mean of about 9 points for children of unskilled workers. For all youngsters in the normative sample, one out of two normal children had a significant VIQ–PIQ difference at the 85% level of confidence (9 or more points); one out of three had a significant discrepancy at the 95% level of confidence (12+ points); and one out of four had a significant discrepancy at the 99% level of confidence (15+ points). Thus 25% of normal school-age children have a VIQ–PIQ differ-

ence of a magnitude that Wechsler (1974, p. 34) claims "is important and calls for further investigation."

The VIQ–PIQ discrepancies for the WISC-R surprise many clinicians, even though analogous data have been available for years on the original WISC (Seashore, 1951) and the original WAIS (Matarazzo, 1972). If earlier studies have been ignored to some extent by clinicians and researchers, it is essential for the WISC-R data to be internalized by test users—particularly in view of the current controversy over labeling, and legal definitions of various exceptionalities. Results for the WISC-R and WAIS have been replicated for the WPPSI (Reynolds & Gutkin, 1981c).

Kaufman (1979a) has provided a table summarizing the distribution of VIQ–PIQ differences on the WISC-R, which is reproduced here as Table 6.8. Table 6.8 shows the magnitude of Verbal–Performance discrepancies occurring at different frequencies within the normal population. These values provide an index of "unusualness" or "abnormality" of various discrepancies. When one considers the rightmost column of Table 6.8, it is evident that discrepancies of 15 or more points occur less than 25% of the time among normal children; discrepancies of 19 points occur less than 15% of the time; discrepancies of 30 points occur less than 2% of the time; and so on. These values enable examiners to evaluate every significant ($p < .01$) VIQ–PIQ discrepancy they observe, and to determine whether the differences in the child's verbal and nonverbal abilities is unusual or abnormal. They are, therefore, worthy of considerable attention. Separate norms are presented in Table 6.8 for five different SES categories, because, as noted above, VIQ–PIQ discrepancies were found to be a function of SES, with larger differences associated with the higher occupational groups. Clinicians have the option of using the base rates for the total group or the rates for the separate parental occupation categories, based on their personal preferences. Similarly, they may choose any degree of abnormality that makes sense for a given purpose. When an examiner is merely attempting to describe in a case report whether a child's Verbal–Performance discrepancy is rare or typical, a criterion such as "less than 15%" seems adequate. However, when the examiner is intending to base a diagnosis of

TABLE 6.8. Percentage of Normal Children Obtaining WISC-R Verbal–Performance (V-P) Discrepancies of a Given Magnitude or Greater, by Parental Occupation

Size of V-P discrepancy (regardless of direction)	Parental occupation					Total sample
	Professional and technical	Managerial, clerical, sales	Skilled workers	Semiskilled workers	Unskilled workers	
9	52	48	48	46	43	48
10	48	44	43	41	37	43
11	43	40	39	36	34	39
12	40	35	34	31	29	34
13	36	33	31	28	26	31
14	32	29	29	25	24	28
15	29	25	26	21	22	24
16	26	22	22	19	19	22
17	24	19	18	15	16	18
18	20	16	16	14	15	16
19	16	15	13	12	14	14
20	13	13	12	10	13	12
21	11	11	8	9	10	10
22	10	9	7	7	9	8
23	8	8	6	6	8	7
24	7	7	5	5	6	6
25	6	6	4	4	5	5
26	5	5	3	3	4	4
27	4	4	2	2	3	3
28–30	3	3	1	1	2	2
31–33	2	2	<1	<1	1	1
34+	1	1	<1	<1	<1	<1

Note. From *Intelligent Testing with the WISC-R* by A. S. Kaufman, 1979, New York: Wiley-Interscience. Copyright 1979 by Wiley-Interscience. Reprinted by permission.

an exceptionality partly on the degree of interscale scatter, then a more conservative criterion, such as "less than 5%" or "less than 2%," should be employed.

Although tables of these values for the WAIS (Matarazzo, 1972) and the WPPSI (Reynolds & Gutkin, 1981c) are available, Kaufman's (1979a) WISC-R table corresponds almost exactly to the distributions of difference scores for the other scales. Comparable data for the WAIS-R are available elsewhere in this volume (see Chapter 7), but the WAIS-R distributions closely resemble the WISC-R distributions.

The focus in this section on the abnormality of profile fluctuations is not intended to minimize the importance of statistically significant differences in a person's abilities. VIQ–PIQ discrepancies that are large enough to be significant are quite valuable, even if they are not large enough to be termed "rare." These significant differences indicate real discrepancies in individuals' abilities, and therefore provide valuable input for making educational and other prac-

tical recommendations. The key distinction here is between diagnosis and treatment. When differences are both significant and rare, they may be used as one piece of evidence in formulating diagnostic hypotheses, and they are likely to be translatable to remedial action. However, differences that are significant but not unusual in their occurrence have only remedial implications; a diagnosis of an abnormality should not be based, even partly, on deviations that occur with reasonable frequency among normal individuals unless such deviations form part of a carefully delineated syndrome.

Fluctuations in Performance on Subtests

The next line of attack for interpreting the Wechsler scales requires the examiner to evaluate the child's performance on each subtest of the Verbal and Performance scales. First, the subtest must deviate from the mean of all subtests on the same scale by a statistically significant amount; second, the subtests must have at least adequate "specificity" (reliable unique variance). Both conditions must be met prior to interpretation of a child's performance on any single subtest.

To determine whether a child's performance on any subtest deviates significantly from the mean of all subtests, the Verbal and Performance scales should be considered separately. To use the Verbal scale as an example, the child's mean scaled score on the Verbal scale should be calculated and then substracted from each subtest scaled score. Exact values are available in Sattler (1982) for determining whether a subtest's deviation is statistically significant; however, the values are all quite close to 3 scaled-score points for the WISC-R Verbal scale and 4 points for the Performance scale. These are the recommended values for determining whether a difference is real or is the result of measurement error on other uncontrolled, random factors. Thus any subtests deviating from the means of all subtests by the designated number of points (or more) on the Verbal scale should be considered candidates for individual interpretation that may reflect significant strengths or weaknesses in the child's ability spectrum. This procedure is then repeated for the Performance scale.

Once it has been ascertained that a significant discrepancy exists, one must evaluate the amount of specific variance (or subtest specificity) that the subtest possesses and judge whether or not it is adequate to support interpreting the subtest independently of the g factor. "Subtest specificity" refers to the amount of variance in a score that is both reliable and unique to that subtest—that is, not shared or held in common with other subtests of the same scale. Subtest specificity is reliable variance minus either the multiple correlation of all other subtests with the subtest or the communality estimate from factor analysis. Kaufman (1979a) has calculated the specific variances of the WISC-R subtests and classified each as possessing ample, adequate, or inadequate specificity. Table 6.9 summarizes this classification. It can be seen in the table that adequate specificity exists to allow the interpretation of most of the WISC-R subtests at most ages. However, some significant fluctuations do occur, and Table 6.9 should be a useful guide. The classification in Table 6.9 are based on the

TABLE 6.9. Classification of WISC-R Subtests According to Relative Proportion of Subtests' Specific Variance

Ample	Adequate	Inadequate
Information	Vocabulary	Similarities (ages $9\frac{1}{2}$–$16\frac{1}{2}$)
Similarities (ages $6\frac{1}{2}$–$8\frac{1}{2}$)	Comprehension	Object Assembly
Arithmetic	Picture completion (ages $9\frac{1}{2}$–$16\frac{1}{2}$)	
Digit Span		
Picture Completion (ages $6\frac{1}{2}$–$8\frac{1}{2}$)		
Picture Arrangement		
Block Design		
Coding		
Mazes		

Note. The data are from Kaufman (1979).

following criteria: For ample specificity, the subtests must display specific variance of at least 25%, and specific variance must exceed error variance; for adequate specificity, subtests must show 15%–24% specific variance, and specific variance must be greater than error variance; for inadequate specificity, subtests fall below 15% specific variance and typically show error variance in excess of specific variance.

Once a subtest has been identified as deviating significantly from the mean and as having at least adequate specificity, one still must determine just what interpretation is appropriate for this finding. Behavioral observations taken during the testing may strongly influence this interpretation. It is also necessary to know just what is measured by the subtest(s) in question. This can be determined through a content analysis of the mental operations necessary to perform the tasks called for by the subtests and by reviewing the primary correlates of the subtests in the research literature. Kaufman (1979a), Lutey (1977), and Sattler (1982) are excellent sources of information on the skills tapped by the various subtests, but the examiner must meld this information with his or her own observations of the child's performance. It is also preferable to look for trends in abilities across multiple subtests, instead of becoming too excited about a single subtest that deviates from the child's mean subtest score. It is always appropriate to apply logic, intuition, and good common sense to test interpretation, along with one's statistical and psychometric expertise. For individual assessment, neither intuition nor psychometric expertise is adequate by itself, especially when one is atempting to devise appropriate instructional programs for a special-needs learner or to gain significant insights into the cognitive structure and function of the individual.

Just as with VIQ–PIQ discrepancies, it is also useful to examine the range of subtest scatter. Both the range of subtests scores obtained by an individual and the number of subtests deviating from the mean of the subtests are of interest. It is frequently quite surprising to clinicians to learn of the results of such investigations with normal children, since the notion of scatter has long been associated with a variety of abnormal conditions. Kaufman (1976b) has reported on the degree of subtest scatter characterizing the 2,200 normal children of the WISC-R standardization sample.

For each normal child aged 6½ to 16½ years, scaled scores on the 10 regular subtests were rank-ordered from high to low. Then the lowest score was subtracted from the higher score, yielding a scaled-score range for each youngster. Whereas the informally obtained estimates of these ranges from clinicians with years of experience tended to cluster around 3–4 points, the actual ranges determined by computer for the standardization group averaged an astonishing 7 points ($SD = 2$) (Kaufman, 1976b). Furthermore, a mean scaled-score range on the FSIQ of 7 ± 2 characterized each of the 11 age groups, males and females, blacks and whites, and children from each of five parental occupation categories.

In practical terms, a scaled-score range of 7 means that the average child's subtest scores ranged from about 6 to 13 or 7 to 14. Since normality is often defined as ± 1 SD from the mean, even a scaled-score range as large as 9 points (7 ± 2) can be considered normal. Thus a range of scaled scores from 3 to 12, from 6 to 15, or from 8 to 17 can legitimately be termed "normal" when empirical guidelines are used. One has to wonder how many

times ranges such as these have been interpreted as indicative of marked scatter, and how many times youngsters have been assigned a label such as "LD," at least in part because of the so-called scatter in their WISC-R profiles.

Table 6.10 provides a summary of the results of Kaufman's (1976b) analysis of scaled-score ranges for this group of children, and should serve as a guide to interpreting the range of subtests performance for individual children. To use Table 6.10, the examiner should compute the child's ranges on the Verbal scale, the Performance scale, and the Full Scale; subtract the child's lowest scaled score from his or her highest scaled score for each of the three scales; and then enter these values into the pertinent columns in Table 6.10 to determine whether the child's intrascale scatter is rare or fairly typical. For example, let us suppose that only the 10 regular subtests are administered, and a girl obtains a Verbal scaled-score range of 5, a Performance range of 10, and a Full Scale range of 11. Her Verbal scaled-score range of 5 reflects normal variability, because a range of 7 is required to occur less than 15% of the time in the normal population. However, her Performance range of 10 and her Full Scale range of 11 are both reasonably rare, each occurring less than 10% at the time. As with VIQ–PIQ discrepancies, clinicians may select any degree of abnormality that makes sense to them, and they would probably be wise to adapt the specific level to the circumstances surrounding the evaluation and the purposes for which the test scores are intended.

Kaufman (1976b) has also provided results from an analysis of the WISC-R standardization data with regard to the number of subtests deviating significantly from the mean of all subtests on the same scale. More than half the children showed at least one subtest deviating significantly from the scale mean; nearly one-fourth showed at least three significant deviations from the mean of all subtests. These findings are not unique to the WISC-R. Reynolds and Gutkin (1981c) reported values nearly identical to those published by Kaufman (1976b) for scaled-score range and number of deviant subtests for the WPPSI sample of children aged from 4 to 6½. Comparable data for the WAIS-R are not yet available. However, clinicians would certain-

TABLE 6.10. Degree of Abnormality of an Index of Subtest Scatter (Scaled-Score Range)

Frequency of occur-rence in normal population	Size of scaled-score range					
	Verbal scale		Performance scale		Full scale	
	5 subtest	6 subtest	5 subtest	6 subtest	10 subtest	12 subtest
<15%	7	8	9	9	10	11
<10%	8	9	10	10	11	12
<5%	9	10	11	11	12	13
<2%	10	11	12	13	13	14
<1%	11	12	13	13	14	14

Note. Scaled-score range equals a child's highest scaled score minus his or her lowest scaled score. The data are from Kaufman (1976b).

ly not be far afield if they applied the WISC-R data on scatter, summarized in Table 6.10, directly to WAIS-R profiles. When doing so, they should eliminate Digit Span from the computations for the Full Scale score, since this subtest is optional on the WISC-R.

The fact that it is normal for children to evidence peaks and valleys in their ability spectra has vital implications for assessment. Clinicians and researchers who deal with exceptional populations should routinely consult the baseline data for the standardization sample in order to interpret the profiles of the children they test. No diagnosis of an exceptionality should be based in any way on Wechsler scatter, unless the degree of interscale or intrascale scatter in a child's profile is shown, by empirical comparison, to be rare within the normal population. Furthermore, no clinical sample should be claimed to exhibit considerable scatter unless there is empirical evidence to show that the indices of scatter, VIQ–PIQ discrepancy, scaled-score ranges, and so on for the clinical group are significantly greater than the indices for normal children.

Results of studies with the WISC-R standardization sample have challenged the stereotype that normal children have "flat" profiles. Now it is time to investigate empirically the stereotypes pertaining to the considerable scatter that supposedly characterizes the Wechsler profiles of individuals with emotional, neurological, and school-related disorders. Fortunately, a number of these studies have been conducted; the interesting results of these investigations are reviewed in the next section.

Subtest scatter and the specific fluctua-tions occurring for individuals should also be evaluated from the standpoint of theory. Neuropsychological, componential, cognitive, factor, and psychometric models of intelligence all have contributions to make to intelligent test interpretation. Although space limitations do not permit us to review such models and their application to intelligence testing, discussions may be found in Kamphaus and Reynolds (1987, especially Ch. 7), Kaufman (1979a), Reynolds (1981b), and White (1979). Kaufman (1979a), in particular, provides a thorough discussion of the theoretical underpinning and meaning of the trait or ability underlying the third WISC-R factor (Freedom from Distractibility).

THE WECHSLER SCALES AND ASSESSMENT OF LEARNING DISABILITIES

The Wechsler scales have always held an affinity for researchers and practitioners concerned with LD populations or with those variously referred to as having minimal brain damage, minimal brain dysfunction, dyslexia, or other neurologically based learning disorders. The WISC and now the WISC-R have been especially intriguing to these workers as the instruments of choice in evaluating LD children.

The aims of this section are to examine the use of the WISC-R for LD assessment, and to chart some appropriate pathways for future avenues of study. Three main areas are covered: (1) factor analysis of the WISC-R, as related to LD populations; (2) recategorization of the WISC-R subtests scores according to Bannatyne's (1971, 1974) system, an approach that has apparently produced a characteristic group profile for LD samples; and (3) evaluations of scatter in WISC-R profiles for LD youngsters, since they are frequently stereotyped as having much interscale and intrascale variability.

Learning Disabilities and Factor Analysis of the WISC-R

As we have noted, every study conducted to date has supported the construct validity of the Verbal and Performance scales. Robust Verbal Comprehension and Perceptual Organization factors have emerged for children across a host of demographic characteristics, and for a variety of exceptional populations: clinic-referred (Lombard & Riedel, 1978; Swerdlik & Schweitzer, 1978), mentally retarded (Schooler, Beebe, & Koepke, 1978; Van Hagen & Kaufman, 1975), gifted (Karnes & Brown, 1980), LD (Blaha & Vance, 1979; Peterson & Hart, 1979; Schooler et al., 1978), and emotionally or behaviorally disordered (DeHorn & Klinge, 1978; Finch et al., 1979; Peterson & Hart, 1979; Reynolds & Struer, 1981).

Some investigators did not investigate three-factor solutions (e.g., Schooler et al., 1978), but most researcher have explored the third factor and have typically found a dimension labeled "Freedom from Distractibility." This factor, not hypothesized by Wechsler in his dichotomous treatment of the WISC-R subtests, usually has significant loadings by at least two of the following three tasks: Arithmetic, Digit Span, and Coding. Occasionally other subtests join in, such as Picture Arrangement (Swerdlik & Schweitzer, 1978; Van Hagen & Kaufman, 1975), Picture Completion (Karnes & Brown, 1980), or Block Design (Dean, 1979; Peterson & Hart, 1979), but the overwhelming consistency from sample to sample is clearly limited to the Arithmetic–Digit Span–Coding triad.

Relevance to Assessment of Learning Disabilities

The emergence of solid Verbal Comprehension and Perceptual Organization factors for LD groups would seem to bode well for the meaningful interpretation of the VIQ and PIQ and the differences between them. For most groups, this generalization tends to be true, but there is a mitigating circumstance for LD children: the consistent findings of the so-called "ACID" profile—low scores in Arithmetic, Coding, Information, and Digit Span—for diverse groups of this exceptional population. Rankings of the 10 regularly administered WISC-R subtests are given in Table 6.11 for seven examples of LD children. Digit Span, the last member of the ACID profile, is not always administered, though we feel it should be. Relatively low scores on Information and Arithmetic (both directly related to school achievement) will often distort the meaning of the IQ, and a weakness on Coding will likewise render the IQ an inefficient estimate of nonverbal intelligence. Despite the factor-analytic construct validity support for Wechsler's VIQ–PIQ dichotomy, there is thus reason to doubt the practical value of the simple VIQ–PIQ discrepancy for LD or potentially LD children. Since three-quarters of the ACID profile (ACD) corresponds precisely to the Freedom from Distractibility factor, it is evident that the third factor may hold the key to competent LD assessment.

Avenues for Future Research

We now understand the factor structure of the WISC-R and do not need to know more about the slight differences in the two or three factors for various or exceptional groups. Small differences in factorial composition from sample to sample cannot be attributed to ethnic membership or type of exceptionality; they are just as likely to be due to an irrelevant, uncontrolled variable or, most likely of all, to the chance fluctuations that are known to characterize matrices.

Future research in this area should focus on what the factors mean in either a theoretical or a clinical sense. Does the Verbal Comprehension factor measure so-called general intelligence, or is it more closely aligned to school achievement or to Guilford's semantic-content dimension? Does Perceptual Organization reflect conventional nonverbal intelligence, fluid ability from the Cattell–Horn approach, Spatial ability from Bannatyne's regrouping (see below), the cognitive style of field independence, or simultaneous processing? Does Freedom from Distractibility assess what its label claims, or is the third

TABLE 6.11. **Rank Ordering of Subtest Means for a Variety of Learning-Disabled Populations**

WISC-R subtest	Anderson, Kaufman, & Kaufman (1976) (n = 41)	Smith, Coleman, Dokecki, & Davis (1977) High IQ (n = 132)	Smith, Coleman, Dokecki, & Davis (1977) Low IQ (n = 76)	Vance, Gaynor, & Coleman (1976) (n = 58)	Zingale & Smith (1978) High SES (n = 30)	Zingale & Smith (1978) Med. SES (n = 56)	Zingale & Smith (1978) Low SES (n = 36)	Consensus rankings
Object Assembly	3	1	1	1	1	1	1	1
Picture Completion	1	2	2	2	2	2	2	2
Picture Arrangement	4	3	4	5.5	3	3	3	3
Block Design	5	4	3	7	4	4	4	4
Comprehension	2	5	5	3	5	7	5	5
Similarities	10	6	6.5	5.5	7	5	6	6
Vocabulary	8.5	7	6.5	4	6	6	9	7
Coding	6	8	9	9	8	8	7	8
Arithmetic	7	9	8	10	9	10	8	9
Information	8.5	10	10	8	10	9	10	10
Mean Verbal IQ	82	90	76	91	90	87	82	
Mean Performance IQ	89	100	80	91	98	96	90	
Mean Full Scale IQ	84	93	76	91	93	90	84	

Note. The subtests are rank-ordered from easiest (highest mean, rank = 1) to hardest (lowest mean, rank = 10) for each learning-disabled population. Subtests are listed from easiest to hardest, based on consensus rankings for the seven samples. The table as a whole is from "The Impact of WISC-R Research for School Psychologists" by A. S. Kaufman, 1982, in C. R. Reynolds and T. B. Gutkin (Eds.), *The Handbook of School Psychology.* New York: Wiley. Copyright 1982 by John Wiley and Sons. Reprinted by permission.

factor more closely related to successive processing, Guilford's symbolic operations, memory, automatic processing, stimulus trace (Baumeister & Bartlett, 1962), attention–concentration, anxiety, or Bannatyne's Sequencing ability? We have answered this question partially in our preceding section on conjoint factor analyses of the WISC-R and the K-ABC. The third factor in these studies looks much like a sequential processing factor; however, the strength of the individual testing method and the philosophy of intelligent testing defy such a simple interpretation. Factor analysis is based on aggregated data reduced to the least common denominator. For all children, but especially LD children, it is important to make individualized interpretations of performance on this factor; these should be supported by careful observation, clinical insight, and patterns of performance on other subtests of the WISC-R.

Bannatyne's Recategorizations

The preceding discussion of WISC-R factor analyses and LD populations leads directly to the topic of recategorizing Wechsler's subtests into Bannatyne's four categories: Conceptual (Similarities, Vocabulary, Comprehension), Spatial (Picture Completion, Block Design, Object Assembly), Sequencing (Arithmetic, Digit Span, Coding), and Acquired Knowledge (Information, Arithmetic, Vocabulary). The relationship to the factor-analytic section is twofold. First, the three WISC-R factors could easily be labeled totally in accordance with the Bannatyne model—namely, Conceptual (Verbal Comprehension), Spatial (Perceptual Organization), and Sequencing (Freedom from Distractibility). Second, the characteristic LD profile of low scores on the ACID subtests make much more sense when interpreted from Bannatyne's four-category approach than from Wechsler's two-scale system.

Pertinent Research Findings

A seemingly characteristic Wechsler profile of Spatial > Conceptual > Sequencing has been found for groups of reading-disabled (Rugel, 1979) and LD (Clarizio & Bernard, 1981; Smith, Coleman, Dokecki, & Davis, 1977) children. However, the consistency of this finding, which has almost come to be accepted as fact, has been challenged on several grounds by other investigations. Some studies simply have not produced the expected relationships among the three Bannatyne categories for LD samples (Thompson, 1981) or failed to find significant differences among the group means (Vance & Singer, 1979). Other investigations have shown different Bannatyne patterns when another variable is introduced in addition to the presence of LD: Mexican-American LD children showed a Spatial > Sequential > Conceptual pattern (Gutkin, 1979a), and LD youngsters with superior intelligence displayed a Conceptual > Spatial > Sequential pattern (Schiff, Kaufman, & Kaufman, 1981).

Furthermore, despite mean differences in Bannatyne categories for groups, the proportions of individuals in the group displaying the characteristic pattern has generally been quite small. Gutkin's (1979a) Caucasian sample of 53 LD children had substantial differences in the group means for Spatial (25.85), Conceptual (21.47), and Sequential (19.66) abilities; however, only 30% of the individuals in this group displayed the predicted pattern, a value that dropped to a mere 2% when statistical criteria ($p < .05$) were imposed on the comparisons. Similarly, fewer than half of 60 Israeli LD children displayed the predicted pattern, despite striking differences in the mean scores on the Spatial (27.48), Conceptual (23.33), and Sequential (18.88) categories (Raviv, Margolith, Raviv, & Sade, 1981).

Of equal concern to the negative findings cited above is the emergence of Spatial > Conceptual > Sequential group patterns for exceptionalities other than LD. Groups such as juvenile delinquents, emotionally handicapped children, and even nonimpaired referrals displayed the identical Bannatyne patterning and could not be differentiated significantly from LD children on the basis of the latter group's so-called "characteristic pattern" (Clarizio & Bernard, 1981; Groff & Hubble, 1981; Henry & Wittman, 1981; Thompson, 1981).

Relevance to Assessment of Learning Disabilities

The findings above virtually speak for themselves regarding LD diagnosis. What was once considered an optimistic, exciting approach for the diagnosis of LD has ground to a halt. It is reasonable to conclude that differential diagnosis of LD will not be aided by application of knowledge about the so-called characteristic Bannatyne pattern. One should not conclude, however, that Bannatyne's recategorizations are irrelevant to LD assessment; that would be far from the truth. Although the groupings do not facilitate differential diagnosis, they still provide a convincing framework for understanding the LD child's assets and deficits. As indicated earlier, the VIQ–PIQ dichotomy is not sufficient for understanding the fluctuations that characterize the profiles of LD samples. The four-category system espoused by Bannatyne still succeeds in making more sense out of many WISC-R profiles, especially of LD children, than does a simple VIQ–PIQ split or even the three-way factor-analytic division. The more that WISC-R profiles can be systematized and understood, the easier it is to translate test results to educational action. Brief discussions and statistics for applying Bannatyne's recategorization to the performance of individual children on the WISC-R can be found in Reynolds (1981c) and Reynolds and Gutkin (1981b).

Another potentially valuable categorization scheme has been proposed by Witkin, Dyk, Faterson, Goodenough, and Karp (1974): Verbal Comprehension (Information, Vocabulary, Comprehension), Analytic–Field Approach (Object Assembly, Picture Completion, Block Design), and Attention–Concentration (Arithmetic, Digit Span, Coding). The first category is a variant of the Verbal Comprehension factor and of Bannatyne's Conceptual triad. The latter two categories are identical in composition to Bannatyne's Spatial and Sequencing groups, respectively, but are assigned quite different interpretations by Witkin et al. Stevenson (1979) applied this approach to a group of 55 LD children and found a depressed score in Attention–Concentration, agreeing with the bulk of Bannatyne LD research. The interpretations stemming from the grouping by Witkin et al. are important and worthy of consideration when one is analyzing the profile of any LD child. However, Bannatyne's four-category approach is still superior to Witkin et al.'s for LD assessment, because (1) Information is included in Witkin et al.'s Verbal Comprehension grouping; (2) LD children typically score low on the Information subtest; and (3) Bannatyne offers an Acquired Knowledge grouping, of extreme value for interpreting LD profiles.

Avenues for Future Research

It is surely time to stop looking at Bannatyne scores on the Conceptual, Spatial, and Sequencing categories for heterogeneous groups of LD children. This approach seems to have no future for differential diagnosis, and no longer will be contributing new knowledge to the field. However, the results of Schiff et al. (1981) with superior-IQ LD children suggest that it is possible to find a profile that characterizes not only a group, but also substantial proportions of individuals within the group. Perhaps the key variable is to investigate LD populations that are defined rather homogeneously.

A second line of needed research is to explore the utility of Bannatyne's Acquired Knowledge category, frequently forgotten in WISC-R studies. Logically, LD youngsters of average intelligence should perform relatively poorly in the achievement-oriented WISC-R subtests, and this has been borne out in the studies that have used all four Bannatyne categories (Smith et al., 1977; Thompson, 1981; Vance & Singer, 1979). Longitudinal investigations of a potential decline in the Acquired Knowledge scores (and, hence, in the IQs) of LD children would be of special value; any such decline would imply that the VIQ becomes a less valid estimate of verbal intelligence as LD children go from the primary grades to high school. Indeed, there is certainly a question of whether the VIQ is valid for any LD child who performs poorly on the Acquired Knowledge subtests, regardless of age. That, too, is an important and researchable issue.

The final avenue of research in this area, and undoubtedly the most important, is that of determining the theoretical and clinical meaning of strengths and weaknesses exhibited by LD children in the Bannatyne categories—which brings us full circle to the suggested line of research in the area of factor analysis. Once again, the recommendation is to conduct construct validity investigations of the abilities, traits, processes, or behaviors underlying each Bannatyne category.

Whether an LD child's elevated scores in the Picture Completion–Block Design–Object Assembly triad, for example, reflect good Spatial ability, Perceptual Organization, simultaneous processing, or Analytic–Field Approach is a question that can be answered by well-designed research studies.

Scatter

The stereotypes that LD children have WISC-R profiles replete with subtest scatter, and that they exhibit large VIQ–PIQ differences, still persist in many assessment circles, despite the findings presented earlier. For years, these notions were accepted as clinical axioms; now a body of research has accumulated to challenge these stereotypes.

Pertinent Research Findings

As we have noted, normal children have substantial VIQ–PIQ discrepancies, averaging about 10 points (regardless of direction), and it is not unusual for normal youngsters to have differences of 15 or more points. Similarly, considerable subtest scatter characterizes the profiles of normal youngsters.

A number of studies have now been published comparing the VIQ–PIQ discrepancies and subtest scatter of LD and other exceptional groups to the basal levels found in the normal population. Table 6.12 summarizes these studies. The VIQ–PIQ discrepancies for LD children have tended to be significantly (but not overwhelmingly) larger than normal values, although some studies have shown no differences at all (Stevenson, 1979; Thompson, 1980). A similar finding has emerged for subtest scatter. For the 436 LD children listed in Table 6.12 (spread across seven studies, and excluding the group with superior IQ), the mean scaled-score range for the 10 regular WISC-R subtests equals 7.8. This value is not consequentially larger than the 7.0 for normal children. Interestingly, Naglieri's (1979) LD sample had significantly more subtest scatter than the normative population, but *not* more than a local control group. In fact, Naglieri's normal control group had the fourth highest index of subtest scatter among all groups listed in Table 6.12.

The findings with the conventional WISC-R reported in Table 6.12 have received some cross-cultural validation. Using a Hebrew translation of the WISC-R, Raviv et al. (1981) compared the scatter for a group of 60 Israeli LD children with that for a sample of 60 matched controls. The mean VIQ–PIQ discrepancy of 11.6 for the LD sample did not differ significantly from the mean of 10.8 for the normals. Although the mean scatter index of 7.5 for the LDs was significantly greater than the value of 6.8 for the controls, the magnitude of the difference is of little practical consequence.

Only Schiff et al.'s (1981) group of LD children with superior IQs showed an impressively high VIQ–PIQ discrepancy and subtest scatter index, suggesting that certain homogeneously defined exceptional samples may have characteristic amounts of inter- and intrascale variability of potential diagnostic value. Otherwise, conventional LD, emotionally disturbed, juvenile delinquent, mentally retarded, and clinic-referred populations tend to be close to "normal" in their fluctuations.

Relevance to Assessment of Learning Disabilities

Contrary to existing stereotypes about LD children, they do not seem to be characterized by abnormal scatter in their WISC-R profiles. The small differences between LD and normal scatter observed in previous investigations may, in fact, represent a selection bias stemming from the stereotypes; that is, other things being equal, children with apparent WISC-R scatter are more likely to be labeled as LD than those with flatter profiles. The data presented in Table 6.12 strongly imply that the magnitude of VIQ–PIQ discrepancy and the size of scaled-score range are not likely to be very useful in the diagnosis of LD or in its differential diagnosis. Nevertheless, significant strengths or weaknesses in a WISC-R profile are potentially valuable, even when the overall scatter is within normal limits, when clinicians are planning educational inventions for LD youngsters.

Avenues for Future Research

Plenty of handicapped samples have been analyzed for WISC-R scatter, and the results clearly imply that future research along this line will contribute only minimally to knowl-

TABLE 6.12. WISC-R VIQ–PIQ Discrepancies and Subtest Scatter Indices for a Variety of Samples

Source	n	Description of sample	Mean VIQ–PIQ discrepancy (regardless of sign)	Mean scaled-score range (high minus low scaled score— 10 subtests)
Kaufman (1976a, 1976b)	2,200	Normal standardization sample	9.7	7.0
Anderson, Kaufman, & Kaufman (1976)	41	Learning-disabled	12.5	7.5
Gutkin (1979b)	51	Learning-disabled	11.9	7.7
Naglieri (1979)	20	Learning-disabled	13.6	8.5
Stevenson (1979)	55	Learning-disabled	10.1	7.2
Tabachnick (1979)	105	Learning-disabled	—	7.6
Thompson (1980)	64	Learning-disabled	10.0	7.6
Ryckman (1981)	100	Learning-disabled	—	8.2
Schiff, Kaufman, & Kaufman (1981)	30	Learning-disabled (superior IQ)	18.6	9.3
Gutkin (1979b)	23	Minimally brain-injured	11.8	7.3
Weiner and Kaufman (1979)	46	Referrals for learning and/ or behavior problems	9.2	7.3
Stritchart and Love (1979)	40	Referrals for learning dis- abilities	9.8	7.3
Moore and Wielan (1981)	434	Referrals for reading problems	11.2	—
Naglieri (1979)	20	Mentally retarded	9.6	6.6
Thompson (1980)	14	Mentally retarded	7.6	5.9
Gutkin (1979b)	10	Mentally retarded	8.5	6.0
Gutkin (1979b)	17	Emotionally disturbed	12.9	7.8
Thompson (1980)	51	Psychological or behavioral disorder	8.4	7.2
Ollendick (1979)	121	Juvenile delinquents	—	7.3
Naglieri (1979)	20	Normal control group	12.6	8.0

edge in this area. Perhaps very homogeneously defined groups, such as Schiff et al.'s (1981) sample with superior IQs, should continue to be examined to determine the diagnostic utility of scatter indices; heterogeneous or loosely defined samples, however, should be left alone. A more fruitful line of research may be to reverse the procedure—that is, to identify samples of children with abnormally large VIQ–PIQ discrepancies and/or scaled-score ranges, and to examine the characteristics of these empirically defined samples. What proportion of these children with unusual profiles are brain-injured, LD, emotionally disturbed, language-disordered, normal, and so forth? By working "backward," we should be able to determine whether much WISC-R profile variability

is indeed diagnostic of LD, and whether this information contributes significantly to differential diagnosis.

Whenever researchers do evaluate samples of known exceptional children, future studies should meet two additional criteria besides a homogeneous definition of the disorder in question: (1) The experimental group should be large in size (preferably at least 200), to reduce errors inherent in sampling procedures; and (2) a local control group of normal individuals, similar to the experimental group in background variables but necessarily smaller in size, should be tested to provide an additional pertinent comparison. Naglieri's (1979) study shows the advisability of using a local control group in addition to the standardization sample for effective evaluation of abnormal profile variability.

Conclusions

Research since the WISC-R's arrival in 1974, and especially since 1979, has added greatly to our understanding of the role of the WISC-R in LD assessment. We know that the factor structure is rather stable for a variety of normal and exceptional samples, including children with LD and children referred for possible LD, and that the three-factor solution corresponds reasonably well to the group profile of children with LD. Research with Bannatyne's recategorization has shown that this four-category approach seems to fit LD data even better than the three-factor approach, and certainly better than the simple two-scale approach advocated by Wechsler. Unfortunately, the initial optimism regarding the diagnostic utility of the Bannatyne regrouping has been rebuffed by a stream of studies that mitigate against its use for differential diagnosis.

Finally, we have learned that normal children do not have flat WISC-R profiles, and that virtually all exceptional samples do not possess the stereotypical high VIQ–PIQ discrepancies or large amounts of intersubtest variability. Like the Bannatyne categories, the use of scatter indices for diagnosis is suspect.

Although the implications of the research results may leave researchers and clinicians alike feeling depressed and pessimistic, there is also reason for hope. The studies have taught us about LD and have broken some persistent and long-enduring axioms. If assessment procedures can be improved substantially by the bulk of knowledge gained from the studies reviewed here, then that improvement represents an important advance in the field. Also, the recategorizations have permitted and encouraged the application of psychological theory to WISC-R interpretation. By departing from a simplistic VIQ–PIQ dichotomy, the regroupings have fostered analysis in terms of simultaneous and sequential processing from the neuropsychological and cognitive literature, analytic–field approach from the literature on cognitive style, and so forth. This application of theory fosters a deeper and more meaningful understanding of the WISC-R profile, leading to a more process-oriented treatment of LD children's strengths and weaknesses. If future researchers succeed in uncovering the construct underlying each LD child's test profile, then the translation of these processes, traits, or abilities into educational intervention becomes a logical outcome of the investigations.

ESTIMATING PREMORBID LEVELS OF INTELLECTUAL FUNCTIONING

In the neuropsychological assessment of children and adults with head injury or other sudden neurological trauma, premorbid intellectual status may prove to be an important consideration. Frequently, premorbid levels of functioning are estimated clinically from the history, parental background, and teacher reports of academic functioning. Attempts to use "hold" versus "don't hold" marker subtests from the Wechsler scales have been made in an effort to place such estimation on a more empirical, and thereby less subjective, footing. These methods frequently prove to be inaccurate (see Lezak, 1976; Matarazzo, 1972), leaving the clinician with few alternatives other than subjective (clinical) impressions.

Recently, more objective methods based on regression modeling from demographic data have been proposed. Wilson et al. (1978) have provided formulas for estimating the premorbid IQs of adults on the WAIS, given knowledge of their age, race, sex, educational level, and occupational status; this work has been replicated for the WAIS-R (Barona, Reynolds, & Chastain, 1984).

Following up on the Wilson et al. (1978) approach with adults, Reynolds and Gutkin (1979) generated regression equations for predicting the premorbid intellectual status of children using demographic variables, with the WISC-R standardization sample providing the data source. For adults, age and number of years in education were good estimators in the multiple regression; however, for children, the method of standardization eliminated the use of these two variables. The relevant and available demographic variables for children were as follows: SES (as determined by parent's occupation), race, sex, geographic region, and urban versus rural residence. All five variables were found to contribute significantly to estimation of the WISC-R VIQ and FSIQ; geographic region dropped out of the equation for the PIQ.

The actual regression equations and standard errors of estimation obtained were as follows:

Estimated VIQ = 127.85 − 3.7 (SES) − 8.86 (race) − 2.40 (sex) − 0.68 (region) − 1.16 (residence)

Standard error of estimate for VIQ = 13.47

Estimated PIQ = 121.08 − 9.18 (race) − 2.80 (SES) − 1.07 (residence) − 0.64 (sex)

Standard error of estimate for PIQ = 13.07

Estimated FSIQ = 126.9 − 3.65 (SES) − 9.72 (race) − 1.79 (sex) − 1.20 (residence) − 0.41 (region)

Standard error of estimate for FSIQ = 13.50

For each equation, demographic variables take the following values (descriptions for making these classifications are available in Wechsler, 1974):

Sex: male = 1, female = 2
Race: white = 1, black = 2, other = 3
SES (based on father's occupational group): upper = 1, upper middle = 2, lower middle = 4, lower = 5
Region: Northeast = 1, North Central = 2, South = 3, West = 4
Residence: urban = 1, rural = 2

These equations essentially provide a short cut to developing tables to display the mean IQs of groups of children with the same demographic characteristics. Their use in clinical diagnosis and decision making remains to be adequately tested. The multiple R's obtained for the children were not large, ranging from .37 to .44. However, this method has certain advantages over clinical estimation. The regression equations provide a standardized quantitative procedure for estimating premorbid IQs, and the necessary data are typically easily and readily available to the clinician and can quickly be evaluated. Reynolds and Gutkin (1979) provide an example of how this technique might be applied, and discuss its limitations and further research needs in more detail. Though much remains to be done, regression modeling to estimate premorbid levels of function appears to be superior to other purely clinically derived estimates.

CONCLUSION

As this chapter goes to press, much is known about the Wechsler scales, and most of this is about the WISC-R. As much as we know, however, much, much more remains to be learned. The revision of the WPPSI (the WPPSI-R) is imminent and should be published about the same time as this work, and WISC-3, the working name of the WISC-R revision, is well underway. In addition, the introduction of the K-ABC, the fact that several other innovative intelligence tests are now in development, and the tremendous gains in our understanding of brain–behavior relationships all make this a difficult but exciting time to be in research and in practice in this field. It is difficult because there is so much to be learned; it is also exciting because there is so much to be learned, and so much of it is new, promising, and innovative.

Acknowledgments. Portions of this chapter are adapted from the following sources:

"Clinical Evaluation of Intellectual Function" by A. S. Kaufman and C. R. Reynolds, 1983, in I. Weiner (Ed.), *Clinical Methods in Psychology*, New York: Wiley-Interscience. Copyright 1983 by John Wiley and Sons. Adapted by permission.

"The Impact of WISC-R Research for School Psychologists" by A. S. Kaufman, 1982, in C. R. Reynolds and T. B. Gutkin (Eds.), *The Handbook of School Psychology*, New York: Wiley. Copyright 1982 by John Wiley and Sons. Adapted by permission.

"Assessing Intelligence and Academic Achievement" by A. S. Kaufman and C. R. Reynolds, 1984, in T. Ollendick and M. Hersen (Eds.), *Child Behavioral Assessment: Principles and Procedures*, New York: Pergamon Press. Copyright 1984 by Pergamon Press, Inc. Adapted by permission.

"Clinical Assessment of Children's Intelligence with the Wechsler Scales" by C. R. Reynolds and A. S. Kaufman, 1985, in B. B. Wolman (Ed.), *Handbook of Intelligence*,

New York: Wiley-Interscience. Copyright 1985 by John Wiley and Sons. Adapted by permission.

REFERENCES

Alcorn, C. L., & Nicholson, C. L. (1975, April). *A technique for programming interpretation and educational recommendations based on the WISC-R.* Paper presented at the annual meeting of the National Association of School Psychologists, Atlanta.

Anderson, M., Kaufman, A. S., & Kaufman, N. L. (1976). Use of the WISC-R with a learning disabled population: Some diagnostic implications. *Psychology in the Schools, 13,* 381–386.

Bannatyne, A. (1971). *Language, reading, and learning disabilities.* Springfield, IL: Charles C Thomas.

Bannatyne, A. (1974). Diagnosis: A note on recategorization on the WISC scale scores. *Journal of Learning Disabilities, 1,* 272–274.

Barona, A., Reynolds, C. R., & Chastain, R. A. (1984). Premorbid index of intelligence for the WAIS-R. *Journal of Consulting and Clinical Psychology 52,* 885–887.

Baumeister, A. A., & Bartlett, C. J. (1962). A comparison of the factor structure of normals and retardates on the WISC. *American Journal of Mental Deficiency, 66,* 641–646.

Berger, M. (1970). The third revision of the Stanford–Binet (Form L-M): Some methodological limitations and their practical implications. *Bulletin of the British Psychological Society, 23,* 17–26.

Binet, A. (1903). *L'Étude experimentale de l'intelligence.* Paris: Schleicher.

Binet, A., & Henri, V. (1896). La psychologie individuelle. *L'Année Psychologique, 2,* 411–465.

Binet, A., & Simon, T. (1905). Methodes nouvelles pour le diagnostic du niveau intellectuel des anormaux. *L'Année Psychologique, 11,* 191–244.

Blaha, J., & Vance, H. (1979). The hierarchical factor structure of the WISC-R for learning disabled children. *Learning Disabilities Quarterly, 2,* 71–75.

Blatt, S. J., & Allison, J. (1981). The intelligence test in personality assessment. In A. Rabin (Ed.), *Assessment with projective techniques: A concise introduction.* New York: Springer-Verlag.

Bogen, J. E., DeZure, R., Tenhoutne, N., & Marsh, J. (1972). The other side of the brain: IV. The A/P ratio. *Bulletin of the Los Angeles Neurological Society, 37,* 49–61.

Carlson, L. C., & Reynolds, C. R. (1981). Factor structure and specific variance of the WPPSI subtests at six age levels. *Psychology in the Schools, 18,* 48–54.

Carlson, L. C., Reynolds, C. R., & Gutkin, T. B. (1983). Comparative structure of the WISC-R for upper and lower SES groups. *Journal of School Psychology, 21,* 319–326.

Clarizio, H., & Bernard, R. (1981). Recategorized WISC-R scores of learning disabled children and differential diagnosis. *Psychology in the Schools, 18,* 5–12.

Cohen, J. (1952). A factor-analytically based rationale for the Wechsler Bellevue. *Journal of Consulting Psychology, 16,* 272–277.

Cohen, J. (1959). The factorial structure of the WISC at ages 7-6, 10-6, and 13-6. *Journal of Consulting Psychology, 23,* 285–299.

Cornell, E. L., & Coxe, W. W. (1934). *A performance ability scale: Examination manual.* New York: World.

Dean, R. S. (1979, September). *WISC-R factor structure for Anglo and Hispanic children.* Paper presented at the meeting of the American Psychological Association, New York.

DeHorn, A., & Klinge, V. (1978). Correlations and factor analysis of the WISC-R and the Peabody Picture Vocabulary Test for an adolescent psychiatric sample. *Journal of Consulting and Clinical Psychology, 46,* 1160–1161.

Esquirol, J. E. D. (1828). Observation pour servir a l'histoire de l'idiotie. *Les Maladies Mentales.*

Esquirol, J. E. D. (1838). *Des maladies mentales considerées sous les rapports medical, hygienique, et medico-legal* (2 vols.). Paris: Baillière.

Finch, A. J., Kendall, P. C., Spirito, A., Entin, A., Montgomery, L. E., & Schwartz, D. J. (1979). Short form and factor-analytic studies of the WISC-R with behavior problem children. *Journal of Abnormal Child Psychology, 7,* 337–344.

Galton, F. (1833). *Inquiries into human faculty and its development.* London: Macmillan.

Galton, F. (1869). *Hereditary genius: An inquiry into its laws and consequences.* London: Macmillan.

Goh, D. S., Teslow, C. J., & Fuller, G. B. (1981). The practice of psychological assessment among school psychologists. *Professional Psychology, 12,* 696–706.

Groff, M., & Hubble, L. (1981). Recategorized WISC-R scores of juvenile delinquents. *Journal of Learning Disabilities, 14,* 515–516.

Gutkin, T. B. (1979a). Bannatyne patterns of Caucasian and Mexican-American learning disabled children. *Psychology in the Schools, 16,* 178–183.

Gutkin, T. B. (1979b). WISC-R scatter indices: Useful information for differential diagnosis? *Journal of School Psychology, 17,* 368–371.

Gutkin, T. B. (1979c). The WISC-R Verbal Comprehension, Perceptual Organization, and Freedom from Distractibility deviation quotients: Data for practitioners. *Psychology in the Schools, 16,* 356–360.

Gutkin, T. B., & Reynolds, C. R. (1980). Factorial similarity of the WISC-R for Anglos and Chicanos referred for psychological services. *Journal of School Psychology, 18,* 34–39.

Gutkin, T. B., & Reynolds, C. R. (1981). Factorial similarity of the WISC-R for white and black children from the standardization sample. *Journal of Educational Psychology, 73,* 227–231.

Gutkin, T. B., Reynolds, C. R., & Galvin, G. A. (1984). Factor analysis of the Wechsler Adult Intelligence Scale—Revised (WAIS-R): an examination of the standardization sample. *Journal of School Psychology, 22,* 83–93.

Henry, S. A., & Wittman, R. D. (1981). Diagnostic implications of Bannatyne's recategorized WISC-R scores for identifying learning disabled children. *Journal of Learning Disabilities, 14,* 517–520.

Herrnstein, R. (1973). *IQ in the meritocracy.* Boston: Little, Brown.

Hilliard, A. G. (1979). Standardization and cultural bias as impediments to the scientific study and validation of "intelligence." *Journal of Research and Development in Education, 12,* 47–58.

Hilliard, A. G. (1984). IQ testing as the emperor's new clothes: A critique of Jensen's *Bias in mental testing*. In C. R. Reynolds & R. T. Brown (Eds.), *Perspectives on bias in mental testing*. New York: Plenum.

Holroyd, J., & Wright, F. (1965). Neurological implications of WISC Verbal–Performance discrepancies in a psychiatric setting. *Journal of Consulting Psychology, 29*, 206–212.

Hughes, J. (1979). Consistency of administrators' and psychologists' actual and ideal perceptions of school psychologists' activities. *Psychology in the Schools, 16*, 234–239.

Jensen, A. R. (1974). How biased are culture-loaded tests? *Genetic Psychology Monographs, 90*, 185–224.

Jensen, A. R. (1979). g: Outmoded theory or unconquered frontier? *Creative Science and Technology, 2*, 16–29.

Jensen, A. R. (1980). *Bias in mental testing*. New York: Free Press.

Kamphaus, R. W., & Reynolds, C. R. (1984). Development and structure of the Kaufman Assessment Battery for Children. *Journal of Special Education, 18*, 213–228.

Kamphaus, R. W., & Reynolds, C. R. (1987). *Clinical and research applications of the K-ABC*. Circle Pines, MN: American Guidance Service.

Karnes, F. A., & Brown, K. E. (1980). Factor analysis of the WISC-R for the gifted. *Journal of Educational Psychology, 72*, 197–199.

Kaufman, A. S. (1972). A short form of the Wechsler Preschool and Primary Scale of Intelligence. *Journal of Consulting and Clinical Psychology, 39*, 361–369.

Kaufman, A. S. (1975). Factor analysis of the WISC-R at 11 age levels between $6\frac{1}{2}$ and $16\frac{1}{2}$ years. *Journal of Consulting and Clinical Psychology, 43*, 135–147.

Kaufman, A. S. (1976a). Do normal children have "flat" ability profiles? *Psychology in the Schools, 13*, 284–285.

Kaufman, A. S. (1976b). A new approach to the interpretations of test scatter on the WISC-R. *Journal of Learning Disabilities, 9*, 160–168.

Kaufman, A. S. (1976c). Verbal–Performance IQ discrepancies on the WISC-R. *Journal of Consulting and Clinical Psychology, 9*, 160–168.

Kaufman, A. S. (1976d). A four-test short form of the WISC-R. *Contemporary Educational Psychology, 1*, 180–196.

Kaufman, A. S. (1977). A McCarthy short form for rapid screening of preschool, kindergarten, and first-grade children. *Contemporary Educational Psychology, 2*, 149–157.

Kaufman, A. S. (1979). *Intelligent testing with the WISC-R*. New York: Wiley-Interscience.

Kaufman, A. S. (1982). The impact of WISC-R research for school psychologists. In C. R. Reynolds & T. B. Gutkin (Eds.), *The handbook of school psychology*. New York: Wiley.

Kaufman, A. S., & Hollenbeck, G. P. (1974). Comparative structure of the WPPSI for blacks and whites. *Journal of Clinical Psychology, 30*, 316–319.

Kaufman, A. S., & Kaufman, N. L. (1977). *Clinical evaluation of young children with the McCarthy Scales*. New York: Grune & Stratton.

Kaufman, A. S., & Kaufman, N. L. (1983). *Kaufman Assessment Battery for Children*. Circle Pines, MN: American Guidance Services.

Kaufman, A. S., & McLean, J. E. (1986). K-ABC/WISC-R factor analysis for a learning disabled population. *Journal of Learning Disabilities, 19*, 145–153.

Kaufman, A. S., & McLean, J. E. (1987). Joint factor analysis of the K-ABC and WISC-R with normal children. *Journal of School Psychology, 25*, 105–118.

Kaufman, A. S., & Reynolds, C. R. (1983). Clinical evaluation of intellectual function. In I. Weiner (Ed.), *Clinical methods in psychology* (2nd ed.). New York: Wiley-Interscience.

Kaufman, A. S., & Reynolds, C. R. (1984). Assessing intelligence and academic achievement. In T. Ollendick & M. Hersen (Eds.), *Child Behavioral assessment: Principles and procedures*. New York: Pergamon Press.

Keith, T. Z., & Dunbar, S. B. (1984). Hierarchical factor analysis of the K-ABC: Testing alternate models. *Journal of Special Education, 18*, 367–375.

Keith, T. Z., Hood, C., Eberhart, S., & Pottebaum, S. M. (1985, April). *Factor structure of the K-ABC for referred school children*. Paper presented at the meeting of the National Association of School Psychologists, Las Vegas, NV.

Kohs, S. C. (1923). *Intelligence measurement*. New York: Macmillan.

Korchin, S. J. (1976). *Modern clinical psychology*. New York: Basic Books.

Larry P. v. Riles, 495 F. Supp. 926 (N.D. Cal. 1979).

Lezak, M. (1976). *Neuropsychological assessment*. New York: Oxford University Press.

Lombard, T. J., & Riedel, R. G. (1978). An analysis of the factor structure of the WISC-R and the effect of color on the Coding subtests. *Psychology in the Schools, 15*, 176–179.

Lutey, C. (1977). *Individual intelligence testing: A manual and sourcebook* (2nd ed.). Greeley, CO: Author.

Marshall v. Georgia, No. CV 482-233 (S.D. Ga. 1984).

Matarazzo, J. D. (1972). *Wechsler's measurement and appraisal of adult intelligence* (5th ed.). Baltimore: Williams & Wilkins.

Moore, D. W., & Wielan, O. P. (1981). WISC-R scatter indices of children referred for reading diagnosis. *Journal of Learning Disabilities, 14*, 416–418.

Naglieri, J. A. (1979). *A comparison of McCarthy GCI and WISC-R IQ scores for educable mentally retarded, learning disabled and normal children*. Unpublished doctoral dissertation, University of Georgia.

Naglieri, J. A., & Jensen, A. R. (1987). Comparison of black–white differences on the WISC-R and the K-ABC: Spearman's hypothesis. *Intelligence, 11*, 21–43.

Naglieri, J. A., & Kaufman, A. S. (1982, August). *Determining the number of WAIS-R factors using several methods*. Paper presented at the annual meeting of the American Psychological Association, Washington, DC.

Ollendick, T. H. (1979). Discrepancies between Verbal and Performance IQs and subtest scatter on the WISC-R for juvenile delinquents. *Psychological Reports, 45*, 563–568.

PASE v. Hannon, 506 F. Supp. 831 (N.D. Ill. 1980).

Peterson, C. R., & Hart, D. H. (1979). Factor structure of the WISC-R for a clinic-referred population and specific subgroups. *Journal of Consulting and Clinical Psychology, 47*, 643–645.

Pintner, R., & Patterson, D. G. (1925). *A scale of performance tests*. New York: Appleton.

Raviv, A., Margolith, M., Raviv, A., & Sade, E. (1981). The cognitive pattern of Israeli learning disabled children as reflected in the Hebrew version of the WISC-R. *Journal of Learning Disabilities, 14*, 411–415.

Reschly, D. J. (1978). WISC-R factor structures among Anglos, Blacks, Chicanos, and Native-American Papagos. *Journal of Consulting and Clinical Psychology, 46*, 417–422.

Reynolds, C. R. (1979). Should we screen preschoolers? *Contemporary Educational Psychology, 4*, 175–181.

Reynolds, C. R. (1980a). Two commercial interpretive systems for the WISC-R. *School Psychology Review, 9*, 385–386.

Reynolds, C. R. (1980b). Review of the TARDOR Interpretive Scoring System for the WISC-R. *Measurement and Evaluation in Guidance, 14*, 46–48.

Reynolds, C. R. (1981a). The fallacy of "two years below grade level for age" as a diagnostic criterion for reading disorders. *Journal of School Psychology, 19*, 350–358.

Reynolds, C. R. (1981b). The neuropsychological basis of intelligence. In G. Hynd & J. Obrzut (Eds.), *Neuropsychological assessment and the school-aged child: Issues and procedures*. New York: Grune & Stratton.

Reynolds, C. R. (1981c). A note on determining significant descrepancies among category scores on Bannatyne's regrouping of WISC-R subtests. *Journal of Learning Disabilities, 14*, 468–469.

Reynolds, C. R. (1981d). Screening tests: Problems and promises. In N. Lambert (Ed.), *Special education assessment matrix*. Monterey, CA: CTB/McGraw-Hill.

Reynolds, C. R. (1982a). Determining statistically reliable strengths and weaknesses in the performance of single individuals on the Luria–Nebraska Neuropsychological Battery. *Journal of Consulting and Clinical Psychology, 50*, 525–529.

Reynolds, C. R. (1982b). The problem of bias in psychological assessment. In C. R. Reynolds & T. B. Gutkin (Eds.), *The handbook of school psychology*. New York: Wiley.

Reynolds, C. R. (1987). Intelligent testing. In C. R. Reynolds & L. Mann (Eds.), *Encyclopedia of special education*. New York: Wiley-Interscience.

Reynolds, C. R. (1988). Intelligence and intelligence testing. In R. Gorton, G. Schenider, & J. Fisher (Eds.), *Encyclopedia of school administration and supervision*. New York: Oryx Press.

Reynolds, C. R., & Brown, R. T. (Eds.). (1984). *Perspectives on bias in mental testing*. New York: Plenum.

Reynolds, C. R., & Clark, J. H. (1982). Cognitive assessment of the preschool child. In K. Pager & B. Bracken (Eds.), *Psychoeducational assessment of preschool and primary aged children*. New York: Grune & Stratton.

Reynolds, C. R., & Clark, J. H. (1985). Profile analysis of standardized intelligence test performance of very low functioning individuals. *Journal of School Psychology, 23*, 277–283.

Reynolds, C. R., & Elliott, S. N. (1982, March). *Trends in test development and test publishing*. Paper presented at the annual meeting of the National Council on Measurement in Education, New York.

Reynolds, C. R., & Gutkin, T. B. (1979). Predicting the premorbid intellectual status of children using demographic data. *Clinical Neuropsychology, 1*, 36–38.

Reynolds, C. R., & Gutkin, T. B. (1980). Stability of the WISC-R factor structure across sex at two age levels. *Journal of Clinical Psychology, 36*, 775–777.

Reynolds, C. R., & Gutkin, T. B. (1981b). Statistics for the interpretation of Bannatyne recategorizations of WPPSI subtests. *Journal of Learning Disabilities, 14*, 464–467.

Reynolds, C. R., & Gutkin, T. B. (1981c). Test scatter on the WPPSI: Normative analyses of the standardization sample. *Journal of Learning Disabilities, 14*, 460–464.

Reynolds, C. R., & Kaufman, A. S. (1985). Clinical assessment of children's intelligence with the Wechsler scales. In B. B. Wolman (Ed.), *Handbook of intelligence* (pp. 601–662). New York: Wiley-Interscience.

Reynolds, C. R., & Struer, J. (1981, April). *Factor structure of the WISC-R for emotionally disturbed children*. Paper presented at the annual meeting of the National Association of School Psychologists, Houston.

Reynolds, C. R., & Struer, J. (1982). Comparative structure of the WISC-R for emotionally disturbed and normal children. *The Southern Psychologist, 1*, 27–35.

Reynolds, C. R., Willson, V. L., & Clark, P. L. (1983). A WAIS-R short form for clinical screening. *Clinical Neuropsychology, 5*, 111–116.

Rugel, R. P. (1979). WISC subtest scores of disabled readers: A review with respect to Bannatyne's recategorization. *Journal of Learning Disabilities, 7*, 48–55.

Sattler, J. M. (1982). *Assessment of children's intelligence and special abilities* (2nd ed.). Boston: Allyn & Bacon.

Sattler, J. M., Hilliard, A., Lambert, N., Albee, G., & Jensen, A. (1981, August). *Intelligence tests on trial: Larry P. and PASE*. Symposium presented at the annual meeting of the American Psychological Association, Los Angeles.

Schiff, M. M., Kaufman, A. S., & Kaufman, N. L. (1981). Scatter analysis of WISC-R profiles for learning disabled children with superior intelligence. *Journal of Learning Disabilities, 14*, 426–430.

Schooler, D. L., Beebe, M. C., & Koepke, T. (1978). Factor analysis of WISC-R scores for children identified as learning disabled, educable mentally impaired, and emotionally impaired. *Psychology in the Schools, 15*, 478–485.

Seashore, H. G. (1951). Differences between Verbal and Performance IQs on the WISC. *Journal of Consulting Psychology, 15*, 62–67.

Seguin, E. (1907). *Idiocy: Its treatment by the physiological method*. New York: Bureau of Publications, Teachers College, Columbia University. (Original work published 1866)

Shellenberger, S. (1982). Presentation and interpretation of psychological data in educational settings. In C. R. Reynolds & T. B. Gutkin (Eds.), *The handbook of school psychology*. New York: Wiley.

Smith, M. D., Coleman, J. M., Dokecki, P. R., & Davis, E. E. (1977). Recategorized WISC-R scores of learning disabled children. *Journal of Learning Disabilities, 10*, 437–443.

Stangler, S. R., Huber, C. J., & Routh, D. K. (1980). *Screening growth and development of preschool children*. New York: McGraw-Hill.

Stedman, J. M., Lawlis, G. F., Cortner, R. H., & Achterberg, G. (1978). Relationship between WISC-R factors, Wide-Range Achievement Test scores, and visual–motor maturation in children referred for psychological evaluation. *Journal of Consulting and Clinical Psychology, 46,* 869–872.

Stevenson, L. P. (1979, April). *WISC-R analysis for diagnosis and educational intervention of LD children.* Paper presented at the meeting of the Council for Exceptional Children, Dallas.

Strichart, S. S., & Love, E. (1979). WISC-R performance of children referred to a university center for learning disabilities. *Psychology in the Schools, 16,* 183–188.

Swerdlik, M. E., & Schweitzer, J. (1978). A comparison of factor structures of the WISC and WISC-R. *Psychology in the Schools, 16,* 166–172.

Tabachnick, B. G. (1979). Test scatter on the WISC-R. *Journal of Learning Disabilities, 12,* 626–628.

Tellegen, A., & Briggs, P. F. (1967). Old wine in new skins: Grouping Wechsler subtests into new scales. *Journal of Consulting Psychology, 31,* 499–506.

Terman, L. M. (1916). *The measurement of intelligence.* Boston: Houghton Mifflin.

Terman, L. M., & Childs, H. G. (1912). A tentative revision and extension of the Binet–Simon Measuring Scale of Intelligence. *Journal of Educational Psychology, 3,* 61–74, 133–143, 198–208, 277–289.

Terman, L. M., & Merrill, M. A. (1937). *Measuring intelligence.* Boston: Houghton Mifflin.

Terman, L. M., & Merrill, M. A. (1973). *Stanford–Binet Intelligence Scale: 1972 norms edition.* Boston: Houghton Mifflin.

Thompson, R. J. (1980). The diagnostic utility of WISC-R measures with children referred to a developmental evaluation center. *Journal of Consulting and Clinical Psychology, 48,* 440–447.

Thompson, R. J. (1981). The diagnostic utility of Bannatyne's recategorized WISC-R scores with children referred to a developmental evaluation center. *Psychology in the Schools, 18,* 43–47.

Thorndike, R. L., Hagen, E. P., & Sattler, J. M. (1986). *Stanford–Binet Intelligence Scale: Fourth Edition.* Chicago: Riverside.

Vance, H. B., Gaynor, P., & Coleman, D. (1976). Analysis of cognitive abilities for learning disabled children. *Psychology in the Schools, 13,* 477–483.

Vance, H. B., & Singer, M. G. (1979). Recategorization of the WISC-R subtest scaled scores for learning disabled children. *Journal of Learning Disabilities, 12,* 487–491.

Vance, H. B., & Wallbrown, F. H. (1978). The structure of intelligence for black children: A hierarchical approach. *Psychological Record, 28,* 31–39.

Van Hagen, J., & Kaufman, A. S. (1975). Factor analysis of the WISC-R for a group of mentally retarded children and adolescents. *Journal of Consulting and Clinical Psychology, 43,* 661–667.

Vernon, P. A. (1979). *Intelligence: Heredity and environment.* San Francisco: W. H. Freeman.

Vernon, P. A. (1981). *Speed of information processing and general intelligence.* Unpublished doctoral dissertation, University of California at Berkeley.

Vitelli, R., & Goldblatt, R. (1979). *The TARDOR interpretive scoring system for the WISC-R.* Manchester, CT: TARDOR.

Wallbrown, F., Blaha, J., Wallbrown, J., & Engin, A. (1975). The hierarchical factor structure of the Wechsler Intelligence Scale for Children—Revised. *Journal of Psychology, 89,* 223–235.

Wechsler, D. (1939). *Measurement of adult intelligence.* Baltimore: Williams & Wilkins.

Wechsler, D. (1958). *Measurement and appraisal of adult intelligence* (4th ed.). Baltimore: Williams & Wilkins.

Wechsler, D. (1967). *Manual for the Wechsler Preschool and Primary Scale of Intelligence (WPPSI).* New York: Psychological Corporation.

Wechsler, D. (1974). *Manual for the Wechsler Intelligence Scale for Children—Revised (WISC-R).* New York: Psychological Corporation.

Wechsler, D. (1981). *Manual for the Wechsler Adult Intelligence Scale—Revised (WAIS-R).* New York: Psychological Corporation.

Weiner, S. G., & Kaufman, A. S. (1979). WISC-R vs. WISC for black children suspected of learning or behavioral disorders. *Journal of Learning Disabilities, 12,* 100–105.

Wender, P. H. (1971). *Minimal brain dysfunction in children.* New York: Wiley-Interscience.

White, W. (Ed.). (1979). Intelligence [Special issue]. *Journal of Research and Development in Education, 12*(1).

Wilson, R. S., Rosenbaum, G., Brown, G., Rourke, D., Whitman, D., & Grisell, J. (1978). An index of premorbid intelligence. *Journal of Consulting and Clinical Psychology, 46,* 1554–1555.

Witkin, H. A., Dyk, R. B., Faterson, H. G., Goodenough, D. R., & Karp, S. A. (1974). *Psychological differentiation.* Potomac, MD: Erlbaum.

Wolman, B. B. (Ed.). (1985). *Handbook of intelligence.* New York: Wiley-Interscience.

Yoakum, C. S., & Yerkes, R. M. (1920). *Army mental tests.* New York: Henry Holt.

Zingale, S. A., & Smith, M. D. (1978). WISC-R patterns for learning disabled children at three SES levels. *Psychology in the Schools, 15,* 199–204.

7

Assessing the Intelligence of Adolescents with the Wechsler Adult Intelligence Scale—Revised (WAIS-R)

ANTONIA A. FORSTER
JOSEPH D. MATARAZZO
Oregon Health Sciences University

B ecause one of childhood's major tasks is the maturing of cognitive skills, intelligence testing is considered an essential part of the psychological assessment of children (Reynolds & Kaufman, 1985). The need for valid assessment of children's intelligence has, if possible, increased in importance with the advent of Public Law 94-142 and the need to make specific recommendations concerning the cognitive skills of learning-disabled and other children with special needs. In fulfilling that responsibility, child psychologists typically make use of the Wechsler Intelligence Scale for Children—Revised (WISC-R). Child psychologists also occasionally make use of the Wechsler Adult Intelligence Scale—Revised (WAIS-R), however. It is the aim of this chapter to discuss issues that child psychologists may face in their use of the WAIS-R with adolescents aged 16–19. Space does not permit a comprehensive discussion of the administration and interpretation of the WAIS-R, and this chapter attempts to cover only material that is of particular importance in using the WAIS-R with adolescents. The following topics are included: information concerning the standardization and psychometric properties of the WAIS-R; relationship between WAIS-R and WISC-R scores; deciding

when to use the WAIS-R and when to use the WISC-R; differences in WAIS-R and WISC-R administration; discussion of test results with adolescents and their families; and two illustrative case examples of the use of the WAIS-R with adolescents.

STANDARDIZATION OF THE WAIS-R WITH ADOLESCENTS

The WAIS-R (Wechsler, 1981) is normed for nine age groups, including two adolescent groups (16–17 and 18–19); thus, the age range for the WISC-R (Wechsler, 1974) overlaps with that of the WAIS-R for 1 year (16 years, 0 months through 16 years, 11 months). The norming samples for both instruments were identical in size at this age (n = 200). Both instruments were standardized against 1970 census data, using the same stratification sampling plan for six variables (age, sex, race, geographic region, occupation, and urban–rural residence). For the WAIS-R, education was added as a seventh variable. Individuals with disabling emotional problems and individuals institutionalized because of cognitive impairments were excluded from both standardization samples.

  To stratify the WAIS-R sample according

166

to occupation, six categories were used for the seven adult age groups (ages 20–74). Five of these categories represented persons in the labor force, from professionals to laborers. The sixth category represented individuals not in the labor force, such as homemakers, full-time students, retired persons, and disabled persons. For the two WAIS-R adolescent groups, which were stratified according to the occupation of the head of the subject's household, the sixth category was not used. Thus, the standardization sample did not include children of parents who were unemployed.

In the standardization of the WISC-R, children's scaled scores were derived from raw scores separately for each age group, and then transformed to IQ equivalents using one table (Wechsler, 1974). Deriving scaled subtest scores yields a comparison with the subject's age peers. Thus, the mean scaled subtest score within each age group is 10. In the standardization of the WAIS-R, on the other hand, scaled subtest and IQ scores were derived from the raw scores of a "reference group" composed of the 500 subjects aged 20 to 34. Therefore, the transformation of raw scores to scaled scores on the test answer sheet yields a comparison with the reference group of 500, and not with the subject's age peers. There are separate tables for calculating the IQ for each WAIS-R age group; this is not the case with the WISC-R. Thus, the WAIS-R IQ scores, and not the WAIS-R scaled scores, yield comparisons with same-age peers (although a separate reference of WAIS-R norms is provided for the examiner who desires this latter comparison).

Because the total number of items answered correctly on each of the Wechsler subtests increases through the late 20s and early 30s, the mean scaled scores of the two younger WAIS-R adolescent groups are understandably lower than those of the 20- to 34-year-old reference groups for the subtests in both the Verbal and the Performance scales (see Table 7.1). In interpreting WAIS-R scaled scores for adolescents, therefore, it is important to remember that (unlike WISC-R scaled scores for adolescents), scaled scores obtained from the WAIS-R test protocol are comparisons with the scaled scores of the 20- to 34-year-old reference group, and not with the scaled scores of the 16- to 19-year-old adolescent group. To interpret a WAIS-R adolescent profile accurately (against same-age peers), it is necessary to select age-scaled scores using Table 21 in the WAIS-R manual (Wechsler, 1981, Appendix D, p. 142). Plotting such supplemental age-scaled scores is helpful in determining accurately which test scores are above or below average within the individual's own age group.

Furthermore, in inspecting a profile for "spikes" across subtests (significant intraindividual strengths and weaknesses), which may affect whether a subject is judged to have deficits or strengths in a given area, age-scaled scores are important because individual subtest scores are differentially affected. Apparently, the cognitive skills measured by the Wechsler scales and subtests change at different rates as individuals pass from adolescence to adulthood. Thus there is a greater mean difference (on the order of 10 points) between the WAIS-R Verbal scores of the 16- to 19-year-olds and the 20- to 34-year-olds than between the Performance scores (which are on the order of

TABLE 7.1. Comparison of Adolescent and Reference Group Scaled Scores

| | | Sum of scaled scores | | | | | |
| | | Verbal scale | | Performance scale | | Full Scale | |
Age group	n	Mean	SD	Mean	SD	Mean	SD
Adolescent groups							
16–17	200	50.72	12.52	47.37	9.49	98.10	20.47
18–19	200	51.72	12.66	46.92	10.09	98.65	20.99
Reference groups							
20–24	200	58.62	13.61	51.14	10.27	109.76	22.09
25–34	300	61.42	15.26	49.89	11.63	111.31	25.27

Note. The data are from Wechsler (1981, Table 7, p. 26).

only 3 points) of these groups (see Table 7.1). At the subtest level, a 16-year-old receiving a WAIS-R *raw* score of 14 on Arithmetic receives a WAIS-R *scaled* score of 11 when compared to the 20- to 34-year-old reference groups, but receives a corresponding WAIS-R *age-scaled* score of 14. A raw WAIS-R Vocabulary score of 34 for a 16-year-old yields a WAIS-R scaled score of 7, but a corresponding WAIS-R age-scaled score of 10. For Arithmetic and Vocabulary scores, then, comparing an adolescent's WAIS-R scores to those of same-age peers instead of to those of the 20- to 34-year-old reference groups yields significantly different results regarding their interpretation. In contrast, a raw score on Digit Symbol of 60 for a 16-year-old yields identical WAIS-R scaled and age-scaled scores of 10. It is evident that for most purposes, when one is using the WAIS-R with adolescents, inter- or intraindividual comparisons of test scores should be based on age-scaled scores.

WAIS-R VERSUS WISC-R FACTOR STRUCTURES IN ADOLESCENT AGE GROUPS

As also reported by Matarazzo (1972) for each of Wechsler's prior scales, Reynolds and Kaufman (1985) concluded that the three-factor solution typically reported in factor-analytic studies of the WISC-R (see Table 7.2) is a robust finding discernible in each age group of the standardization sample (Kaufman, 1975) and in all but two cross-validation samples, in normal or exceptional and English- or Spanish-speaking subjects. The domains of the first and second factors (Verbal Comprehension and Perceptual Organization) have been interpreted to represent broad areas of cognitive skill by all reviewers of this literature. The domain of the third

factor, however, is less easily specified, as subtests subsumed by the third-factor scores are generally accorded several interpretations, including so-called behavioral hypotheses (attention/distractibility, anxiety) as described by Matarazzo (1972), and Leckliter, Matarazzo, and Silverstein (1986), and cognitive hypotheses (symbolic ability, sequential processing, memory) as described by Kaufman (1979), and Hill, Reddon, and Jackson (1985).

The same three-factor structure has often been hypothesized for the WAIS-R, but the third factor may not be as pervasive or as robust as it is in studies using the WISC-R (Reynolds & Kaufman, 1985). Indeed, two-factor solutions have been offered for some samples (Leckliter et al., 1986). Consistent with the interpretation earlier offered by Matarazzo (1972), Leckliter et al. (1986), after reviewing all the factor-analytic studies on the WAIS-R to date, conclude that "the factor solution that one selects as providing the 'best' fit to the data is highly dependent upon one's theoretical biases and clinical purposes" (p. 341), and that the three-factor solution provides the richest source of clinical hypotheses for use in individual evaluations or in research with special populations. From their review of the same literature, Reddon et al. (1985) offer a similar conclusion.

Germane to the purposes of the present chapter, two studies have examined the factor structure of the WAIS-R in the standardization sample separately for each of the nine age groups (Glass, 1982; Parker, 1983). For the 18- to 19-year-old group, Parker's (1983) results revealed that the two tests having their highest loading on the third factor were not those shown in Table 7.2 but were Picture Completion and Picture Arrangement, with Object Assembly a close third. In this particular sample of 18- to 19-

TABLE 7.2. Factorial Structure of the WISC-R and the WAIS-R across All Age Groups

Verbal Comprehension	Perceptual Organization	Freedom from Distractibility
Information	Picture Completion	Arithmetic
Similarities	Picture Arrangement	Digit Span
Vocabulary	Block Design	Digit Symbol
Comprehension	Object Assembly	

year-olds, then, the familiar "Freedom from Distractibility" factors did not emerge. According to Leckliter et al.'s (1986) reasoning, however, as well as suggestions for interpretation from Leckliter et al. (1986) and Reynolds and Kaufman (1985), the third factor might continue to be used by clinicians to explain individual adolescent WAIS-R profiles, in cases where the profile pattern and other test data warrant such an interpretation (e.g., as reflecting the effects of distractibility due to anxiety in one individual, or lowered attention and concentration as a result of brain injury in another, etc.).

As Reynolds and Kaufman (1985) caution for the WISC-R, the prevalence of two- and three-factor reported solutions should lead the clinician to interpret intrascale or intrafactor scatter only when interpretation of the Full Scale IQ (FSIQ), Verbal IQ (VIQ), and Performance IQ (PIQ), or of the factor scores, does not explain a profile satisfactorily. The arguments for conservatism in interpreting "scatter" apply equally to WISC-R and to WAIS-R profiles, and are not discussed here. The reader is referred to Kaufman (1979), Leckliter et al. (1986), Matarazzo (1972), Matarazzo, Daniel, Prifitera, and Herman (1988), Matarazzo and Prifitera (1989), and Reynolds and Kaufman (1985) for reviews and commentary of these issues.

WAIS-R AND WISC-R IQ SCORES

As was the case with the WAIS–WISC overlapping scores, and later with WAIS–WISC-R scores, the relationship between WAIS-R and WISC-R scores has been the focus of some concern. The 1955 WAIS yielded FSIQ scores substantially higher than FSIQ scores from the WISC-R (Wechsler, 1974; Zimmerman, Covin, & Woo-Sam, 1986). Wechsler (1981) administered the 1974 WISC-R and the 1981 WAIS-R in counterbalanced order with an intervening interval of 1–6 weeks to eighty 16-year-olds, and reported nearly identical mean FSIQ scores for the two instruments (Wechsler, 1981, p. 48). The mean FSIQ scores (101.0, WAIS-R; 101.9, WISC-R) and the standard deviations (13.8, WAIS-R; 14.5, WISC-R) reported for these same eighty 16-year-olds indicate that the distribution of scores in Wechsler's sample of 16-

year-olds resembles that in the WISC-R and WAIS-R standardization samples as a whole.

Other investigators have examined the relationship between WISC-R and WAIS-R IQ scores in samples of individuals whose level of cognitive functioning falls below the average range. The similarity of scores on the two instruments has particular importance among persons with borderline or lower scores, because placement decisions are often based on FSIQ scores. Thus, Sattler, Polifka, Polifka, and Hilsen (1984) reported that in a sample of 30 special education children who took the WISC-R and, 4 years later, the WAIS-R, VIQs, PIQs, and FSIQs on the two instruments were not significantly different. In a similar study by Zimmerman et al. (1986), however, WAIS-R FSIQs significantly exceeded WISC-R FSIQs obtained 3 years earlier by 3–5 points in two samples with mean FSIQs approximately 5 points lower than those of Sattler et al.'s (1984) sample. Finally, for residentially placed adolescents with FSIQs in the retarded range, the WAIS-R has been reported to yield FSIQs that are 11 points higher, on the average, than WISC-R FSIQs (Rubin, Goldman, & Rosenfeld, 1985). The conflicting findings from these three studies require further study and clarification.

For example, in many settings, children receiving special services based on their FSIQ scores are routinely retested every 3 years. Adolescents obtaining substantially higher WAIS-R scores than their former WISC-R scores are in some cases no longer eligible to receive special services. If the higher WAIS-R FSIQ scores are due to a lack of equivalence between WAIS-R and WISC-R scores, and not to genuine gains in cognitive functioning or to regression effects, individuals may lose needed services to which they are entitled. In their study dealing with this issue, Zimmerman et al. (1986) report that in their sample, large differences between the two sets of scores occurred primarily in individuals whose FSIQs were below 70. This phenomenon helps to explain the discrepant results of studies examining this question. If there is truly a lack of equivalence between WAIS-R and WISC-R scores, it remains to be explained why scores of individuals with FSIQs in the mildly retarded range should be differentially affected. In order to rule out regression effects, genuine gains in cognitive functioning, and other competing explanations, it would be helpful to inspect the individual test–retest scores of members of the standardization samples of the WISC-R and the WAIS-R, in comparison with the scores of those individuals in this age range taking both the WISC-R and the WAIS-R. Zimmerman et al. (1986) note that the discrepancy between WISC-R and WAIS-R IQ scores for these groups is smaller than that reported between WISC-R and WAIS IQ scores. To what extent individuals who would have fallen in the retarded range on the WISC-R actually have lost services because of higher WAIS-R IQ scores is not clear (Zimmerman et al., 1986).

It is worth noting that for adolescents the WAIS-R and the WISC-R are similar on another dimension: They produce nearly identical test–retest gains (approximately $3\frac{1}{2}$ points for the VIQ, 9 points for the PIQ, and 7 points for the FSIQ) after several weeks. Another respect in which the WISC-R and the WAIS-R are similar for the adolescent age groups is the pattern of correlations between subtest scores and FSIQ scores (see Table 7.3). There are several exceptions, however. As shown in Table 7.3, the correlations between Arithmetic scaled score and VIQ score for the WAIS-R (r's = .71, .69) are somewhat higher than the corresponding correlation for the WISC-R (r = .57). Similarly, the correlations between Digit Symbol score and PIQ (r's = .41, .50) are somewhat higher than that between Coding B and PIQ (r = .31). With these two exceptions, test scores have approximately similar relationships to their respective scales in both instruments.

As noted above, the potential importance for the clinician of the comparabilities between WISC-R and WAIS-R IQ scores, test–retest gains, and the pattern of intercorrelations arises in testing adolescents to whom the WISC-R has previously been administered. All other things being equal, sample *mean* (but not necessarily individual) WAIS-R scores should match WISC-R scores almost as closely as one would expect two sets of WAIS-R scores to match, in *groups* having mean FSIQs above the retarded range. The same is not necessarily true when dealing with the *individual* youngster. Thus, a caveat concerning just how closely one should expect two sets of scores for a given *individual* to match has been offered by Matarazzo and Herman (1984), based on the WAIS-R standardization data. Analyzing test–retest gains, they found out, in addition to a large number who showed a gain, a surprisingly large number of individuals in the standardization sample actually showed losses in their scores on retest 5–7 weeks later. Namely, 20.2% had lower VIQ scores on retest, 8.4% had lower PIQ scores, and

TABLE 7.3. Correlations of Test Scores with FSIQ Scores for WISC-R and WAIS-R Adolescent Groups

	Verbal score			Performance score		
	WISC-R	WAIS-R		WISC-R	WAIS-R	
Test	16½	16–17	18–19	16	16–17	18–19
Information	.74	.80	.80	.57	.57	.56
Digit Span	.49	.50	.51	.58	.50	.43
Vocabulary	.82	.84	.84	.41	.67	.60
Arithmetic	.57	.71	.69	.61	.58	.63
Comprehension	.69	.73	.72	.55	.62	.58
Similarities	.70	.75	.74	.31	.59	.58
Picture Completion	.53	.53	.49	.53	.57	.53
Picture Arrangement	.37	.45	.50	.41	.38	.46
Block Design	.55	.59	.52	.70	.66	.60
Object Assembly	.43	.40	.45	.63	.47	.57
Digit Symbol Coding B	.46	.54	.55	.31	.41	.50

Note. The data are from Wechsler (1974, Table 14, p. 46) and Wechsler (1981, Table 15, pp. 37–38).

6.7% had lower FSIQ scores. Furthermore, although the *mean* gains were +3.3 (VIQ), +8.4 (PIQ), and +6.2 (FSIQ), the size of the individual gains and losses noted for a not inconsequential number of subjects was substantial, ranging from −12 to +28.

It is clear that, even over a 5–7 week interval, substantial test–retest change in IQ scores for a given examinee may occur with relative frequency. Because these changes occurred in the WAIS-R (and WISC-R) standardization samples, which excluded individuals with known brain injury, severe emotional or behavioral disturbance, or other conditions that presumably might introduce greater-than-normal variability in the IQ scores, it is obvious that large test–retest changes can occur in such presumably "healthy" community-living individuals, and may therefore have a benign explanation (e.g., the other-than-perfect psychometric properties of such tests, as detailed by Matarazzo and Prifitera [1989]).

The meaning of these issues to the clinician is that care is required in interpreting test–retest "gains" or "losses" of any magnitude. The clinician who examines an adolescent previously tested with the WISC-R and who finds significantly discrepant results may be assured that, *on the average*, individuals are expected to achieve similar WISC-R and WAIS-R scores. Although true for the group mean, however, this clearly does not hold for an individual subject, inasmuch as a not inconsequential number of presumably healthy individuals retested with the same instrument a few weeks later achieve a score that differs substantially from their initial score (Matarazzo & Herman, 1985). Therefore, before assuming, for example, that a decrement is the result of cognitive dysfunction caused by brain injury, emotional disturbance, or the like, as emphasized by Matarazzo and Prifitera (1989) for the WAIS-R, the examiner would be wise to search for clear substantiating evidence in the clinical history, in other test results, in other testing sessions, and in objective neuroradiological, neurological, and related findings that also suggests impairment relative to previous testing or the individual's previous level of social, educational, or occupational functioning. In addition to the other-than-perfect psychometric properties of the WISC-R and WAIS-R, substantial decrements could be due to transient anxiety, a headache, a poor night's rest, or other factors. Similarly, substantial test–retest gains are not necessarily the result of successful remediation or recovery from an injury; and a lack of change in scores should not be assumed, without additional evidence, to mean that remediation or recovery has failed.

VERBAL–PERFORMANCE DIFFERENCES

Knowing when and how to interpret differences between an individual's Verbal and Performance scores is a necessary part of the effective use of the Wechsler scales. The size of such discrepancies needed for statistical (psychometric) significance is approximately the same for 16- to 19-year-old adolescents, whether the WAIS-R or the WISC-R is used. As reported by Wechsler (1981, p. 36), at the .05 level of probability, the mean VIQ–PIQ discrepancy for 16- to 17-year-olds on the WAIS-R is 12.04, and for 18- to 19-year-olds it is 10.97; for 16-year-olds on the WISC-R, it is 11.41 (Wechsler, 1974, p. 35). Nevertheless, the point has been made (Grossman, Herman, & Matarazzo, 1985; Kaufman, 1979; Matarazzo & Herman, 1984, 1985) that the size of VIQ–PIQ differences needed for "psychometrically oriented" statistical significance is not all that the clinician needs to consider in deciding how best to interpret "clinically" a given VIQ–PIQ discrepancy.

Traditionally, the logic of interpreting VIQ-PIQ differences has been assumed to be that individuals without significant cognitive dysfunction should have approximately equal Verbal and Performance scores. Statistically significant discrepancies between these two major types of abilities therefore presumably require an explanation, because they are statistically rare in a "normal" population. R. G. Matarazzo, Wiens, Matarazzo, and Manaugh (1973), Kaufman (1979), and Matarazzo and Herman (1984) have shown that statistically significant discrepancies are not rare, however, in a normal population. Thus, for the WAIS-R, although a VIQ–PIQ difference of only 9.7 points across the nine age groups is needed for statistical significance (i.e., to conclude that the VIQ–PIQ difference is *psychometrically* "real" for this person and not based on sampling error) at the .05 level

TABLE 7.4. Cumulative Percentages of Individuals in Standardization Samples Obtaining WAIS-R and WISC-R VIQ–PIQ Differences of Various Magnitudes

Size of actually observed VIQ–PIQ difference (regardless of sign)	WAIS-R	WISC-R
10 or greater	37.8	43
13 or greater	24.3	31
16 or greater	15.5	22
22 or greater	5.8	8

Note. The data are from Kaufman (1979, p. 26) and Matarazzo and Herman (1984, p. 363).

(Wechsler, 1981, p. 35), such a difference of 10 or more points *actually occurred* in 38% of the standardization sample (Matarazzo & Herman, 1984). Such large VIQ–PIQ differences are observed even more frequently in children than in adults. For the presumably healthy adults and children in the respective standardization samples, Table 7.4 presents a comparison for four discrepancy sizes of WAIS-R versus WISC-R VIQ–PIQ differences. As Kaufman (1979, p. 25) states, although statistically (i.e., psychometrically) different from zero, such differences "cannot be considered 'abnormal' by any reasonable statistical standard." (The reader should consult Matarazzo & Herman, 1985, and Reynolds & Kaufman, 1985, for a fuller discussion of the ways in which psychometric, statistical VIQ–PIQ discrepancies differ from clinically relevant VIQ–PIQ discrepancies.)

The fact that statistically significant VIQ–PIQ discrepancies are not rare in the normal population does not, unfortunately, remove the burden of attempted explanation from the shoulders of the clinician. As with large test–retest losses, the error to be avoided is an inference of neurological dysfunction on the basis of these test data alone (Kaufman, 1979; Matarazzo, 1972; Matarazzo & Herman, 1985). Many explanations of VIQ–PIQ discrepancies are possible, and no conclusions should be drawn without supporting evidence from the clinical history, other test data, and observation.

Some factors underlying VIQ–PIQ differences occur with greater frequency among adolescents referred for psychological evaluation than among adult referrals. For ex-

ample, adolescents with conduct disorders are frequently referred for evaluation, and may have higher PIQ than VIQ scores (see Matarazzo, 1972, pp. 436–439). Adolescents with severe learning disabilities may be referred, usually not for the first time, and may (or may not) have large VIQ–PIQ discrepancies in either direction. A fuller discussion of the process of forming and testing hypotheses concerning VIQ–PIQ discrepancies is beyond the scope of this chapter, but is included in Matarazzo (1972, Chs. 13, 14, and 15), Kaufman (1979), Matarazzo and Herman (1985), and Matarazo and Prifitera (1989).

WHETHER TO USE THE WAIS-R OR THE WISC-R

Wechsler notes that either the WAIS-R or the WISC-R may be used with 16-year-olds. The examiner's choice of instruments will depend on several factors. Sattler (1982) suggests that, all other things being equal, in choosing between the WAIS-R and the WISC-R, the examiner should choose the instrument that has the smaller standard error of measurement at the age level in question. Nevertheless, comparing the standard errors of measurement of the subtest scaled scores and of the VIQ, FSIQ, and PIQ for the WISC-R and the WAIS-R (Wechsler, 1974, p. 30; Wechsler, 1981, p. 33), we find that although these statistics do seem to give the WAIS-R a slight edge, the two instruments do not differ greatly on this measure. As Sattler (1982) also suggests, if all other things are equal, the examiner would do well to use the test with which he or she is more familiar, especially since the familiarity of the examiner with the test may affect the size of the error on any given individual administration.

There are, however, other considerations that may help the examiner in deciding which instrument to use with a particular teenager. Some youngsters with exceptional academic difficulties may be repeatedly tested. As discussed above, for adolescents with FSIQs in the retarded range, in appropriate instances involving P.L. 94-142, it may be advisable to use the WISC-R because of the tendency for the WAIS-R to yield higher FSIQ scores than the WISC-R in this population, if testing continues to be required. Sattler (1982) also recommends the use of the WISC-R rather than the WAIS-R with 16-year-olds whose cognitive abilities are suspected to be significantly below average, because they will complete more test items in obtaining the same scaled score on the WISC-R than on the WAIS-R. Consequently, Sattler argues, their abilities will be more thoroughly sampled with the WISC-R than with the WAIS-R. If retesting will take place in a relatively short period of time (perhaps in the case of retesting following an acute brain dysfunction), Sattler (1982) recommends the use of both tests, one for the initial administration and one for retesting.

ADMINISTRATION OF THE WAIS-R

The content and organization of the WAIS-R are substantially identical to those of the WISC-R. Therefore, for an examiner familiar with the WISC-R, administering the WAIS-R should pose no special problems. Care is needed, however, because there are some differences that should be noted (see Table 7.5).

Another kind of consideration concerning the administration of the WAIS-R to adolescents is their motivation to do their best. With teenagers, rebelliousness and oppositionality often are central features of the reasons for referral. Perhaps more frequently than any other groups, adolescents arrive to be evaluated against their will. Whether referred by their parents, their schools, or their juvenile court officers, such adolescents pose a problem for the clinician. Although no methods are foolproof, experience suggests some guideposts for clinicians.

If there is any reason to suspect a rift in parent–teenager relations, it often is good for the adolescent's self-esteem to interview and examine such an adolescent alone before meeting with the parent(s). A sullen adolescent is likely to see the clinician as an agent of

TABLE 7.5. Differences in WAIS-R and WISC-R Administration

| Test | Administration | |
	WISC-R	WAIS-R
Information	Give help if subject fails item 1.	Give no help.
Picture Completion	After cards 1 and 2, may help a total of three times (see manual).	After cards 1 and 2, may help only once.
Digit Span	No differences.	
Picture Arrangement	Demonstrate item 1. Correct errors in items 1–4. Time bonuses for correct completion.	Do not demonstrate unless subject fails item 1. Give no further help. No time bonuses.
Vocabulary	Slight wording differences.	
Block Design	Administration depends on age of subject.	All subjects construct item 1 from examiner model, not from card.
Arithmetic	Slight wording differences. No time bonuses.	Time bonuses.
Object Assembly	Demonstrate with sample item. Tell subject what objects 1 and 2 will be when completed. For incorrect solutions, use weighted scores (see manual).	No sample item. Do *not* tell subject what objects will be. No weighted scores.
Comprehension	No differences.	
Digit Symbol/Coding B	Slight wording differences.	
Similarities	Give help on items 1, 2, 5, 6.	Give help on item 1 only.

Note. Because of the nature of these differences, the examiner is advised to follow the manual closely during administration; relying on one's memory can easily lead to invalid scaled scores.

the tyrannical parent or other authority figure; meeting with the youngster first may help to convey that the clinician's point of view is independent and supportive to all parties and will be based on input from all parties to the conflict or issue.

Describing the limits of confidentiality at the outset is helpful; clinical experience suggests that adolescents appreciate knowing exactly what will and what will not be communicated to their parents, *before* they decide what to tell the clinician. (It is, of course, important to share with parents this same guideline.) Parents usually know how their children will feel about being examined; it is often helpful to ask them about this when the appointment is made. At examination, if it is anticipated that a particular youngster has no desire to participate in the evaluation, an opening statement to this effect from the clinician may disarm and enlist cooperation: "If you're anything like other kids your age, you'd just as soon not be here." Such a candid discussion of the purpose of the evaluation before any testing takes place may help to take an adolescent off the defensive.

Occasionally, however, even clinicians who are relatively easily liked by most teenagers, and who skillfully blend empathy and humor in their approach, may fail completely in gaining the trust of some adolescents. In such instances, careful observation of behaviors during testing that communicate such distrust is especially important. In addition, examination with the Minnesota Multiphasic Personality Inventory (MMPI) may be helpful in suggesting that an individual may have a defensive or uncooperative attitude, which could jeopardize the validity of test results. Reports from other sources, especially school records, can help determine the likelihood that an individual is trying to do his or her best during assessment by the psychologist.

PRESENTING WAIS-R RESULTS TO ADOLESCENTS AND THEIR PARENTS

The clinician trusts that the results of a psychological evaluation will be put to good use. The effect of an assessment depends in part on the way in which the results are conveyed, and to whom. The importance of an accurate and comprehensive written report has been discussed in detail (e.g., Kaufman, 1979; Sattler, 1982). The verbal presentation of results to the adolescent (and parents) immediately following an evaluation can have equal importance in determining whether or not the recommendations made will be followed, especially because occasionally (and as necessary) the report itself may be technical and therefore incomprehensible or intimidating to many people. Such considerations are especially relevant when examining adolescents. Clinical experience suggests that referred adolescents frequently feel that no one understands their point of view or takes them seriously. Furthermore, a written report will be even less accessible to the average adolescent than it is to the average parent. For these reasons, it is beneficial to give adolescents a face-to-face opportunity to discuss assessment results.

One way of presenting results is to meet separately (albeit later conjointly as required) with the teenager and with the parents or other referring agent. This arrangement conveys procedurally that the adolescent is not merely the object of inquiry, but is an important agent in resolving whatever problems are at issue. It also promotes the active participation of the adolescent, who otherwise may let the parents do the talking. And although the actual wording of the results conveyed to all parties may be the same, the wording best suited to making the content understandable and acceptable may, for example, have to differ considerably for a punctilious, well-dressed attorney and his underachieving, sullen son.

As with any other individual (see Matarazzo, 1972, pp. 18–23), it is on the whole better to present results to an adolescent in a constructive light rather than in negative terms. Thus, a boy who achieves an FSIQ of 100 may be told that he did well and has the cognitive ability to complete high school and go beyond, should he wish. It may be helpful to gifted underachievers to be told their scores in terms of percentiles, which have more intuitive meaning for most people than FSIQs, in a context that also includes the observation that they appear to be "late bloomers."

CLINICAL APPLICATIONS OF THE WAIS-R WITH ADOLESCENTS

There are several issues central to assessment that may occur with greater frequency among adolescents than among adults, and two cases are presented here to exemplify the usefulness of the WAIS-R in addressing these issues. Needless to add, many of the reasons why the WAIS-R is useful with adolescents are the same as the reasons why one of the Wechsler scales is useful with any individual: Namely, the multiple quantitative indices (FSIQ, VIQ, PIQ, factor scores, scaled scores) are indispensable to many clinicians in formulating and checking hypotheses about an individual's cognitive functioning. In addition, the wealth of clinical information discerned from the observation of the individual's performance during the examination often provides personal and behavioral data that are not as readily available through other assessment modes. The case studies that follow have been chosen to illustrate these broad uses among adolescent subjects. All names used are pseudonyms, and information that might identify the subjects has been withheld or modified appropriately. For the interested reader, Lindemann and Matarazzo (in press) present case histories using the WAIS-R with adults.

Case Study 1: Mike D.

Child psychologists specializing in assessment will often be asked to see children who have had multiple psychological evauations. A child with severe learning difficulties, especially if they are accompanied by behavior problems, poses a challenging, frustrating, and often painful problem for his or her parents and for the school system. The purposes of a psychological evaluation in such instances are to identify and describe (for the adolescent as well as the others) problem areas, and to recommend intervention strategies to remediate the problems. In instances where the interventions suggested are unsuccessful in remediating the perceived problems, closure is not yet achieved, and further evaluations are carried out in the hope that such a professional's achieving a better understanding of the teenager will lead to successful remediation. In cases where repeated evaluations have occurred because of unmet expectations (on the part of either the parents or the school), it is important for the clinician to address this latter issue as part of the evaluation process.

Mike D. (age 16 years, 11 months) was referred for a psychological evaluation because of continued poor school achievement and his parents' disagreement with the school over the best education program for Mike in his remaining $1\frac{1}{2}$ years of high school. Mike's clinical history revealed that he was the product of a 36-week pregnancy and birth complicated by abruptio placenta, with probable intrauterine anoxia. Physical and gross motor development were above average, but Mike had numerous illnesses during his first 5 years (e.g., otitis media, bronchitis, pneumonia), and the onset of speech was delayed (e.g., naming objects at 3 years, phrases at 4 years), with poor articulation. At age 6, Mike was described by school personnel as hyperactive and as having learning difficulties, which his mother attributed to his behavior problems.

At the time of psychological assessment, Mike had already been evaluated by a psychologist at least six times (in addition to at least four school assessments); these included two complete neuropsychological examinations with the Halstead–Reitan Neuropsychological Test Battery, and one trip across the country to a center for the evaluation of dyslexics. The reasons for the multiple evaluations were Mike's severe learning problems and his upper-middle class parents' difficulty in accepting his condition. As is so poignantly observed in most such families, Mr. and Mrs. D. seemed to have considerable emotional investment in having Mike described as learning-disabled rather than as mentally retarded. It was as though they felt that if the correct diagnosis were made and proper instructional methods used, Mike would be able to improve upon his current academic skills. They were inclined to blame the school for Mike's difficulties, and were reluctant to approve the special education program that the school had recently recommended. In fact, their disappointment and dissatisfaction with the school's past efforts had resulted in their taking the school to court.

At the time of examination, Mr. and Mrs. D. reported to the psychologist that the school wanted to give Mike "survival skills only," and that they felt Mike continued to need individual tutoring (which had been provided by the school in the past), instead of the small classroom situation that the school now felt was appropriate. They stated that Mike had lately become very self-conscious about himself and his learning difficulties, that his self-confidence was very low, and that he seemed to have "given up" on learning to read. They described Mike as well adjusted socially and as one of the most popular boys in his high school; they said he participated in varsity wrestling, was on the football team, and had many friends who were in the regular classrooms. Mike's parents reported that his friends spent a lot of time at his house.

Mr. and Mrs. D. also added that away from school, "people don't suspect Mike is slow." They cited his ability at sports and his normal adolescent interests (i.e., friends, girls, music). They felt strongly that because of Mike's good gross motor skills and because of his many ordinary interests, the diagnosis of mental retardation was inappropriate.

A detailed interview with Mr. and Mrs. D. concerning adaptive behavior skills revealed that, in some respects, Mike functioned like an average 17-year-old boy. Of the several areas in which Mike's adaptive functioning needed improvement, some were characteristic of adolescents. For example, Mike did not always put his clothes away or do his own laundry. Nevertheless, he frequently prepared simple meals for himself and regularly performed a number of household chores. Areas in which Mike's skills were deficient for his age were those requiring numerical or reading ability. Specifically, Mike did not tell time accurately, did not read for enjoyment, and had trouble making change.

Because the Halstead–Reitan had been administered to Mike during two previous evaluations with consistent results, it was omitted on this occasion. Previous evaluations had, of course, included the WISC-R, but the WAIS-R had never been administered to Mike. From the history, it was anticipated that the important assessment issues in this case quite likely were not quantitative indices of Mike's intellectual deficits, but, rather, his parents' acceptance of his in-

tellectual limits. If Mike were to benefit from the remainder of high school, it would be necessary for his parents and the school to agree on a program for him and to support him in completing it. It was felt that the reason for his parents' insistence on repeated psychological evaluations of Mike, which he found to be stressful, was the lack of resolution of these issues. It was decided to administer the WAIS-R, to incorporate these findings with those of the previous Halstead–Reitan and related findings, and then to have an extensive discussion with Mr. and Mrs. D. to help them to achieve some closure concerning Mike's needs and abilities.

The results of the current WAIS-R findings are presented in Table 7.6, along with the results of the two previous administrations of the WISC-R. It may be seen that, in Mike's case, the results of the three administrations were remarkably consistent, over a span of 6 years, across three examiners and two different instruments. There was relatively little subtest scatter among Mike's subtest scores across all three administrations—a pattern that is often seen in individuals who are normal (adaptive) in most respects but who score in measurable intelligence in the bottom 3% of the population (Matarazzo & Prifitera, 1989), as well as in individuals with demonstrable brain injury early in life. Although Mike was in 10th grade, the results of achievement testing (as seen at the bottom of Table 7.6) indicated that Mike was currently functioning at the second- or third-grade level in all basic skills, consistent with his Wechsler scores. Thus, these 1987 WAIS-R and Peabody findings indicate that in spite of intensive remediation, with one-on-one tutoring during a considerable number of years of his schooling, Mike's academic skills, even at nearly 17 years of age, still remained at the level of a student in the primary grades.

Mike's attitude toward taking the test was understandably resistive. His parents reported that he had commented, "I know I'm stupid. Why do I have to take more tests?" Yet he was highly motivated and persistent. He struggled with each item, spending the full allotment of time on most Performance items, and doing his best to give responses to Verbal items. His responses to some Verbal items requiring extended answers gave the examiner the impression of even greater im-

TABLE 7.6. Case Study 1: Mike D.

	Wechsler scales		
Scale/test	1981 WISC-R	1983 WISC-R	1987 WAIS-R[a]
VIQ	79	75	76
PIQ	75	70	69
FSIQ	76	71	72
Information	6	6	6
Similarities	8	7	5
Arithmetic	5	6	5
Vocabulary	6	4	5
Comprehension	8	7	7
Digit Span	—	—	7
Picture Completion	7	5	4
Picture Arrangement	4	7	5
Block Design	8	6	5
Object Assembly	8	2	6
Coding B/Digit Symbol	5	7	5

Achievement testing: Peabody Individual Achievement Test (1987 evaluation)		
Test	Grade equivalent	Percentile
Arithmetic	2.9	1
Reading Recognition	3.0	1
Reading Comprehension	2.6	1
Spelling	2.4	1
General Information	4.6	3

[a]Age-scaled scores (ages 16–17) are presented.

poverishment of Verbal skills than was suggested by his relatively low VIQ of 76. For example, his thinking was concrete, as is common among persons who score at the low end of measurable intelligence. For example, in response to "What does this saying mean? 'Strike while the iron is hot,' " he replied, "When it's hot, you can bend it better." The logic of some items was apparently too complex for him. For example, he responded to the question "Why does the state require people to get a license before they get married?" by saying, "If they don't want to get married, they just throw away the license."

Because of this family's history of repeated prior psychological evaluations and dissatisfaction with school programs, an important part of the evaluation was the discussion of the results summarized in Table 7.6 first with Mike and then with Mr. and Mrs. D. With hopefully the requisite blend of

objectivity and compassion, it was explained to him and them that Mike had now taken the adult version of the Wechsler intelligence tests, and because the scores of all three administrations of the Wechsler were very consistent, it would not be necessary to retest Mike again soon. The psychologist shared with Mr. and Mrs. D. that they were correct in thinking that Mike did not fit the category of mental retardation, because previous neuropsychological testing showed him to have important abilities in the average range (especially tactual, spatial, and sensory–perceptual abilities). It was also explained to them that the meaning of Mike's low scores on the WAIS-R, combined with his failure (as mirrored in the Peabody) to learn to read beyond a second- or third-grade level, was that Mike was deficient in the conceptual and visual–perceptual skills needed to master reading and other basic academic tasks with any degree of proficiency. It was suggested to them that they were correct in continuing to be concerned for Mike, and the basis of their anxiety was discussed. It became clear to the psychologist/consultant that as Mike got older, his parents were becoming more and more concerned about his future and the problems he would face in leading an independent life. Namely, the reason for their concern over his reading skill was that they viewed reading as an integral part of independent living, and feared that if Mike could not read or do basic arithmetic, he would remain dependent on them. An opportunity was provided for them to express their grief over Mike's deficits, during which they were able to acknowledge that he would probably never be a proficient reader.

Once the problem of Mike's living independently was thus identified, it became possible to consider other means of helping him toward this goal. First, Mike's relative strength in the area of adaptive intelligence skills was identified and elaborated upon. Then Mr. and Mrs. D. were encouraged to adopt a creative, problem-solving approach to helping Mike. For example, it was suggested that, given his social success to date, survival skills would be relatively easy to acquire and more productive for him in the long run than a basic reading program. They had mentioned that a few of his deficits did interfere with his social functioning; for example, he was unable to write down his name and phone number for friends, and had trouble telling time. As examples of how to approach this kind of problem, it was suggested that they obtain cards for Mike with his name and address printed on them, and that they buy him a digital watch. Fortunately, these solutions were accepted by Mr. and Mrs. D., once they had been helped to accept the fact that Mike would probably not easily be able to learn to write his name and address legibly. As had been done privately with Mike, vocational issues were also discussed with Mr. and Mrs. D.; community resources were identified; and suggestions were offered concerning possible summer jobs for Mike.

It was discussed with Mike and Mr. and Mrs. D. that his great strengths were his social success to date, and his motivation and willingness to persevere in spite of overwhelming obstacles. It was emphasized that avoiding repeated failures would be important for Mike, so that he could sustain his motivation to succeed, and avoid becoming discouraged and pessimistic about himself. An important element of this meeting with Mike and his parents was the suggestion that they telephone or return to see the psychologist as often as questions occurred.

The recommendations shared with Mike and his parents were also discussed thoroughly with the school, and suggestions were made as to how the school and the parents could get along better in the future. In a happy follow-up 1 year later, the school reported that Mike's special education program had been set up as suggested, and that his parents seemed pleased with his progress and were no longer hostile to school personnel.

Case Study 2: Donald O.

Donald O. (age 16 years, 8 months) was referred by a psychologist for a comprehensive assessment because of the progressive deterioration of his academic performance and his behavior at home and in school during the preceding 2 years. At the time of the consultation, Donald was receiving F's in all of his subjects in the 10th grade. Donald lived with his mother and stepfather; his parents had been divorced for 10 years, and his mother had been married to Mr. O. for about 9 years. Donald continued to have regular contact with his biological father, and no problems were reported in that relationship. Shortly before the deterioration in Donald's behavior, Donald's older brother had suddenly moved out of the home to get married.

His stepfather, Mr. O., reported that in school Donald did not pay attention, did not do his work, and had been skipping classes. At home, he said, Donald spent much time alone in his bedroom. He was no longer helping with household chores and "had to be told everything," according to Mr. O. In addition to Donald's lack of responsibility and cooperation, Mr. O. was also concerned about recent antisocial behavior. It was suspected that Donald had taken money from family members. On several occasions, he had taken family cars and damaged them with reckless abuse, in spite of restrictions having been placed on his driving privileges.

Mr. O., a conscientious and caring parent, described the means he and Donald's mother had used to attempt to help Donald change his behavior. All their efforts had failed, and they had begun to feel that Donald was willfully and purposefully trying to thwart them. The turmoil caused by Donald's behavior and their efforts to discipline him was causing problems within their marriage.

Donald admitted to the consulting psychologist that he had several times taken family cars, knowing he did not have permission. He said he felt unable to control himself during his joy rides, "like I'm not really doing it, like in a dream, and everthing gets quiet." In spite of evidence to the contrary, he insisted that he obeyed all traffic laws. He reported weekend alcohol use, but denied using other drugs.

When questioned further, Donald said that at times during the past several months when he was home alone, he had heard "conversations going on in the other rooms." He said that he could not hear what the voices were saying. He also described when he was alone at home hearing friends "say things which I hear in my mind"; he said he looked to see whether they were there because it sounded as if they were right behind him, but they were not. He reported feelings of unreality, describing his activities at times as "like in a dream." Donald commented that he felt he had a serious problem of "not caring," and that this apathetic attitude was the consequence of something that he had lost in the sixth grade. When asked to explain this feeling, he remarked that his entire sixth-grade year was a blank in his memory. He described himself as being depressed, sad, and lonely. When queried, he was unable to articulate any course of action that could improve his mental status, except being allowed to retain his driver's license.

Donald described studying as difficult because his "thoughts get mixed up." He stated that it was hard to think clearly because he became confused with thoughts about what he was going to do or had done, and was unable to put these thoughts aside in order to concentrate on the academic or other task at hand.

Donald's interpersonal behavior during the examination was distant and unresponsive. Long latencies characterized his verbal interaction style with different examiners throughout the clinical interview and structured testing. For example, on the Comprehension subtest of the WAIS-R, when asked, "Why does the state require people to get a license before they get married?" he was silent for 23 seconds before responding, "It has to do with taxes." Similar long silences preceded several other items on that subtest. However, he appeared motivated to do as well as possible on the tests administered. The test results are presented in Table 7.7.

As is shown, there was a 28-point discrepancy between Donald's VIQ (80) and PIQ (108) scores—a difference seen in fewer than 2% of the standardization population. A VIQ–PIQ difference of this magnitude, rare in otherwise healthy individuals, needs examination and interpretation in every instance in which it is observed. As examples, such a relatively poor VIQ is seen in individuals who are learning-impaired, in individuals who are recent immigrants, and in some youngsters whose parents have had little formal education. Such a relatively low VIQ is also seen in some forms of brain disorders and, although relatively less frequently, in other forms of psychopathology needing clarification. For subtests within both the Verbal and Performance scales, Donald's performance was consistent: All of his Verbal test scores were below the average range, and all of his Performance test scores were average or above. Some of Donald's responses to Verbal items illustrated the concrete thinking that is seen in such verbally or conceptually deficient youngsters, or that may also be present in thought-disordered individuals. For example, on the WAIS-R Similarities subtest, to the question "How are an orange and a banana alike?" Donald responded, "They have skin." In response to the question "How are a dog and a lion alike?" Donald replied, "They growl."

The results on the Wide Range Achievement Test—Revised, second edition (WRAT-R[2]) indicated that Donald's school achievement was substantially below grade level, although consistent with his VIQ, and suggested that his poor grades reflected a lack of learning and not merely truancy or failure to complete assignments. Furthermore, given Donald's history of average grades 2 years previously, these low WRAT-R[2] scores confirmed that his performance had deteriorated during that period.

TABLE 7.7. Case Study 2: Donald O.

WAIS-R	
Scale/test	Score
VIQ	80 (9th percentile)
PIQ	108 (70th percentile)
FSIQ	91 (26th–28th percentile)
Information	6
Digit Span	7
Vocabulary	7
Arithmetic	5
Comprehension	7
Picture Completion	12
Picture Arrangement	10
Block Design	15
Object Assembly	11
Digit Symbol	9

Achievement testing: WRAT-R[2]			
Test	Standard score	Age percentile	
Reading	84	14th	
Spelling	79	8th	Trails B: 88th percentile
Arithmetic	94	34th	Trails B: 88th percentile

Other tests

Rey Complex Figure Test
  Copy: 88th percentile Disorganized execution
  Recall: 55th percentile
MMPI
  Welsh code: 87 24'93-610/5:F/LK:

His performance on the Rey Complex Figure Test was consistent with his relatively good proficiency on the Performance tests of the WAIS-R in suggesting that Donald had no dysfunction of visual–spatial construction memory. Consistent with elements of his clinical history, however, his mode of executing this complex figure appeared disorganized. From both the examination findings and the clinical and medical history, there was little reason to believe that Donald had a brain disorder. For instance, although Trails A or B tend to be difficult tasks for many individuals with brain injuries, Donald's performance was above average on these tasks.

Donald's responses on the MMPI (abnormally elevated scores on Scales 8, 7, 2, and 4) revealed an individual reporting considerable psychological distress over problems perceived as beyond his own coping abilities. Difficulty with logic, concentration, and judgment, and feelings of tension and alienation, are common characteristics of individuals with a profile similar to his. MMPI subscale profile analysis reveals that such individuals complain of autonomous thought processes and mental dullness. Instead of maintaining meaningful relationships with others, they tend to be introspective, ruminative, and overideational. Relationships with family members are disrupted, and often family discord is the cause of anger and alienation.

The sudden onset in adolescence of Donald's deterioration, and his WAIS-R and

WRAT-R[2] results, ruled out diagnostic possibilities such as pervasive developmental disorder or borderline mental retardation; they pointed instead to disordered thinking. Donald's history of school truancy, alcohol use, stealing, and other infractions indicated a conduct disorder. Donald's report during the clinical interview of confusion and auditory hallucinations, his lack of insight, his long response latencies, and the objective test results suggested that the beginning stages of a thought disorder may have been superimposed on or were themselves responsible for the conduct problems. This possibility had important implications for treatment. Although no prior measures of intellectual functioning were in his records, Donald's history of average school achievement 2 years prior to this evaluation suggested that his present VIQ score and WRAT-R[2] scores might represent a deterioration in his verbal and academic abilities as a result of confusion and concentration difficulties. Whether or not there had been such postulated deterioration, the currently obtained WAIS-R results made it clear that Donald's ability to complete regular high school work would pose a problem. Even the use of strategies such as the employment of behavioral management to increase his school attendance and to encourage him to complete his homework would not necessarily enable him to bring up his grades. Although Mr. and Mrs. O. had been painfully aware of Donald's conduct-disordered behaviors, they had been less sensitive to his disordered thought processes, possibly because of his withdrawal from family interactions. The implications of his disordered thinking were discussed with the family, and ways of managing or eliminating stressors were suggested to Donald and to his parents by the psychologist as being necessary to improve Donald's stability. Ongoing individual psychotherapy was recommended for him, with the possibility of a concurrent referral at some future date to a psychiatrist or family physician who could treat Donald with medication. At follow-up, although Donald's school performance had not improved, he was no longer engaging in antisocial behaviors such as theft and reckless driving. Apparently, his parents' realization of the basis of his conduct had enabled them to view him with greater understanding instead of anger, and family relationships had improved, lessening the stress within the family system.

Acknowledgments. The case of Donald O. was brought to our attention by John R. Crossen, PhD, and Arthur N. Wiens, PhD, who kindly offered it for inclusion in the present chapter.

REFERENCES

Glass, A. (1982, August 27). *Factor structure of the WAIS-R*. Paper presented at the 90th Annual Convention of the American Psychological Assocation, Washington, D.C.

Grossman, F. M., Herman, D. C., & Matarazzo, J. D. (1985). Statistically inferred vs. empirically observed VIQ–PIQ differences in the WAIS-R. *Journal of Clinical Psychology, 41,* 268–272.

Hill, T. D., Reddon, J. R., & Jackson, D. N. (1985). The factor structure of the Wechsler scales: A brief review. *Clinical Psychology Review, 5,* 287–306.

Kaufman, A. S. (1975). Factor analysis of the WISC-R at 11 age levels between $6\frac{1}{2}$ and $16\frac{1}{2}$ years. *Journal of Consulting and Clinical Psychology, 43,* 135–147.

Kaufman, A. S. (1979). *Intelligent testing with the WISC-R.* New York: Wiley.

Leckliter, I. N., Matarazzo, J. D., & Silverstein, A. B. (1986). A literature review of factor analytic studies of the WAIS-R. *Journal of Clinical Psychology, 42,* 332–342.

Lindemann, J. C., & Matarazzo, J. D. (in press). Intellectual assessment of adults. In G. Goldstein & M. Hersen (Eds.), *Handbook of psychological assessment.* New York: Pergamon Press.

Matarazzo, J. D. (1972). *Wechsler's measurement and appraisal of adult intelligence* (5th ed.) Baltimore: Waverly Press.

Matarazzo, J. D., Daniel, M. H., Prifitera, A., & Herman, D. (1988). Inter-subtest scatter in the WAIS-R standardization sample. *Journal of Clinical Psychology, 44,* 940–950.

Matarazzo, J. D., & Herman, D. O. (1984). Base rate data for the WAIS-R: Test–retest stability and VIQ–PIQ differences. *Journal of Clinical Neuropsychology, 6,* 351–366.

Matarazzo, J. D., & Herman, D. O. (1985). Clinical uses of the WAIS-R: Base rates of differences between VIQ and PIQ in the WAIS-R standardization sample. In B. B. Wolman (Ed.), *Handbook of intelligence: Theories, measurements, and applications* (pp. 899–932). New York: Wiley.

Matarazzo, J. D., & Prifitera (1989). Subtests scatter and premorbid intelligence: Lessons from the WAIS-R standardization sample. *Psychological Assessment: A Journal of Consulting and Clinical Psychology, 1,* 186–191.

Matarazzo, R. G., Wiens, A. N., Matarazzo, J. D., & Manaugh, T. S. (1973). Test–retest reliability of the WAIS in a normal population. *Journal of Clinical Psychology, 29,* 194–197.

Parker, K. (1983). Factor analysis of the WAIS-R at nine age levels between 16 and 74 years. *Journal of Consulting and Clinical Psychology, 51,* 302–308.

Reynolds, C. R., & Kaufman, A. S. (1985). Clinical assessment of children's intelligence with the Wechsler scales. In B. B. Wolman (Ed.), *Handbook of intelligence: Theories, measurements, and applications* (pp. 601–661). New York: Wiley.

Rubin, H. H., Goldman, J. J., & Rosenfeld, J. G. (1985). A comparison of WISC-R and WAIS-R IQ's in a mentally retarded residential population. *Psychology in the Schools, 22,* 392–397.

Sattler, J. M. (1982). *Assessment of children's intelligence and special abilities* (2nd ed.). Boston: Allyn & Bacon.

Sattler, J. M., Polifka, J. C., Polifka, S., & Hilsen, D. E. (1984). A longitudinal study of the WISC-R and WAIS-R with special education students. *Psychology in the Schools, 21,* 294–295.

Wechsler, D. (1974). *Manual for the Weschler Intelligence Scale for Children—Revised.* New York: Psychological Corporation.

Wechsler, D. (1981). *Manual for the Wechsler Adult Intelligence Scale—Revised.* New York: Psychological Corporation.

Zimmerman, I. L., Covin, T. M., & Woo-Sam, J. M. (1986). A longitudinal comparison of the WISC-R and WAIS-R. *Psychology in the Schools, 23,* 148–151.

8

Infant Intelligence: Do We, Can We, Should We Assess It?

JOAN F. GOODMAN
University of Pennsylvania

If the successful prediction of adolescent and adult intelligence from early childhood scores is one of the great accomplishments of applied psychology, then the failure to predict intelligence from infancy to early childhood ranks as one of its greatest failures. For over 50 years, articles on infant assessment regularly begin by affirming Nancy Bayley's initial observation (1933), reiterated in 1949, 1955, and 1970, that findings from infant assessments "have been repeated sufficiently often so that it is now well-established that test scores earned in the first year or two have relatively little predictive validity (in contrast to tests at school age or later), although they may have high validity as measures of the children's cognitive abilities at the time" (1970, p. 1174).

Despite the pre-eminence of the author and her test, investigators have refused to lie low, and clinicians keep testing infants. Acceptance of the null hypothesis does not come easily to psychologists. Three primary arguments have been raised against Bayley's pessimism: (1) Current infant tests may be poor predictors in general, but are good for particular populations (Honzik, 1976; Kopp & McCall, 1982; McCall, 1979); (2) the use of batteries or risk inventories, of which the intelligence test is merely one ingredient, will give better predictions than intelligence tests alone (Parmelee, Kopp, & Sigman, 1976); (3) the design of better tests directed to those cognitive capacities that are con-

tinuous across the developmental period (Lewis & Sullivan, 1985), to replace the early tests composed largely of sensory–motor items, will belie Bayley's pessimism. Very few investigators consider infant tests inherently incapable of prediction. The most articulate exception is Robert McCall (1976, 1979, 1981a; McCall, Eichorn, & Hogarty, 1977; McCall, Hogarty, & Hurlburt, 1972), who maintains that years of empirical study have proven that no matter how much we refine items to make them psychometrically pure or target them at the infant's underlying information processes, we will continue to fail at prediction. The infant is not father to the man (or mother to the woman). Development goes through significant transformations. The destiny of an individual's intelligence simply will never yield its secrets to psychological investigation in the first year or so of life.

The professionals who daily make decisions about the care of infants are betting that McCall is wrong, and, in any case, rely on the tests for judgments as to current status. The neonatologist needs to have, and share with parents, informed views on the future of a 1,500-gram baby. And many, many people—from policy planners and legislators to health care deliverers and educators—have a vital stake in predicting the future of the infant saved by the neonatologist. Tests are widely used in early intervention programs as entrance requirements, for program planning, and for evaluation (Ramey, Bryant, & Suarez, 1985). A significant rise in scores serves as a marker of a successful intervention. In hospitals and well-baby clinics all over the country, babies are administered tests on the assumption that the scores give meaningful diagnostic data. Should a moratorium be declared on this testing? Is it sufficient that the tests provide a glimpse of present but not future functioning?

In this chapter, after a review of the basic tests, each of the following issues is addressed: What kinds of predictions can be made from infant testing? What happens to the predictions when more variables are included? Why the mixed predictive record? Is there a value to infant tests even if prediction is poor? Are there better methods on the horizon that promise to do an improved job? Can we expect to improve predictors from infant tests? What are some future directions we need to consider?

THE INSTRUMENTS

There are a number of excellent recent reviews on the history and current status of infant intelligence tests (Brooks & Weinraub, 1976; Honzik, 1976; Lewis & Sullivan, 1985; Thomas, 1970; Yang, 1979). The following overview has used these sources except where otherwise noted. For a full discussion of general tests designed to give an overall assessment, specific tests designed to measure single areas such as sensory–motor or language functioning, and screening tests, the reader should consult the sources listed at the end of the chapter under "Recommended Readings." The review here is limited to the primary general instruments.

All authorities acknowledge Arnold Gesell to be the grandfather of infant testing. His Developmental Schedules, which trace motor, language, adaptive (what would pass for cognitive today), and personal–social behavior, were developed in the 1920's and have not been fundamentally altered since, though they were revised and updated by Knobloch and Pasamanick in 1974. The schedules have provided a reservoir of items for other commonly used infant tests. Lewis and Sullivan (1985) illustrate, by comparing items from 11 different infant tests spanning over 50 years (Kuhlman–Binet, 1922; Mer-

rill–Palmer, 1926; Iowa Tests for Young Children, 1936; Minnesota Pre-School Scale, 1932; Kuhlman Tests of Mental Development, 1939; Gesell Developmental Schedules, 1939; Cattell, 1940; Griffiths, 1945–1970; Bayley, 1969; Uzgiris–Hunt, 1976; Denver Developmental Screening Test, 1976), the high degree of commonality in items for infants from 1 to 36 months of age.

Gesell's views were highly maturational (Ball, 1977; Gesell, 1940, Gesell & Ilg, 1943; Honzik, 1976; Lewis & Sullivan, 1985). Although he acknowledged the role of family, school, and environment in shaping the child's intelligence, his focus was on tracing the general ontogenetic development of the child as it unfolds according to the laws of biology. The role of acculturation, as he saw it, is to respond sensitively to the innate but highly individualized unfolding process. Environmental features "support, inflect, and modify, but do not generate the progressions of development" (1933, p. 211). In a reply to the environmentalists, Gesell elaborated on his view of maturation:

The environment furnishes the foil and the milieu for the manifestations of development, but these manifestations come from inner compulsion and are primarily organized by inherent inner mechanics and by an intrinsic physiology of development. The very plasticity of growth requires that there be limited and regulatory mechanisms. Growth is a process so intricate and so sensitive that there must be powerful stabilizing factors, intrinsic rather than extrinsic, which preserve the balance of the total pattern and the direction of the growth trend. Maturation is, in a sense, a name for this regulatory mechanism. . . . The phenomena of maturation suggests [sic] the stabilizing and inexpungable factors which safeguard the basic patterns of growth . . . against extreme conditioning, whether favorable or unfavorable. (Gesell, 1973, pp. 17–18)

It is ironic that although the Gesell Developmental Schedules have been the feeder source for subsequent intelligence tests used to delineate individual differences, Gesell himself denied that they were measures of intellectual functioning, for he believed there was no metric that could adequately calibrate mental changes. Furthermore, given an integrated organismic orientation, Gesell thought it scientifically impossible to isolate and measure intelligence. He preferred that his schedules be used as clinical guides rather than as the basis for a point score system.

What Gesell called "mental growth" was quite different from modern views of intelligence. The aim of Gesell's genetic psychology was to describe, through close observation, structural changes (morphogenesis) in development (Gesell, 1933; Gesell & Thompson, 1938). Behavior, growth, and the mind were not conceptually separated, as the following passage indicates:

> Behavior may well be the culminating and integrated expression of the growth of the individual. If this behavior is regarded as an index of the mind or the psyche of the individual it falls within the scope of genetic psychology. . . . Growth is a more or less a unitary complex. A complete scientific account of growth would bring all the aspects into coordination and define the conditions as well as evidences of mental growth. The nontechnical term "mental growth" denotes the whole series of behavior changes which characterize the life history of the individual. (Gesell, 1928, p. 4)

Gesell's observations of the existence of interindividual differences were of less moment to his scheme than tracing the evolutionary growth of infancy in general and noting the patterned variations produced by intraindividual discrepancies (Gesell, 1946). He minimized cross-child comparisons, stating that his "age norms are not set up as standards" (Gesell & Ilg, 1943, p. 2). He advised those who would interpret deviations from the norms to respect but not to judge variability in attainments. In the last analysis, he declared that "the child himself is the norm" (Gesell & Ilg, 1943, p. 72). His quote from John Kendrick Bangs brings the point home:

> I met a little Elfman, once
> Down where the lilies blow.
> I asked him why he was so small
> And why he did not grow.
>
> He slightly frowned, and with his eyes
> He looked me through and through.
> "I'm quite as big for me," he said,
> "As you are big for you."
>
> (GESELL & ILG, 1943, P. 72)

Despite Gesell's disclaimers, the Developmental Schedules have been used to assess intelligence. As psychometric instruments, their standardization is considered inadequate by the reviewers (Brooks & Weinraub, 1976; Lewis & Sullivan, 1985; Werner, 1965; Yang, 1979). For infants between 4 weeks and 2 years of age, Gesell presented 19 different sets of normative age expectations. To cover this range, there were only 107 infants in the longitudinal sample, with approximately 35 seen at each observation from 4 to 56 weeks (not all children were seen each time). Families were primarily of middle-class background from the New Haven, Connecticut area. No adequate reliability or validity has been reported, with the exception of a study by Knobloch and Pasamanick (1967), who found a correlation of .70 between scores on the Gesell scales administered to infants before 1 year of age and scores 7 years later with the Stanford–Binet; the sample ($n = 123$) was a heterogeneous one of normal and clinical children. Despite these limitations, the test continues to have a strong attraction, especially for medical personnel (Werner, 1965).

Psyche Cattell believed that the Gesell Developmental Schedules could become a genuine test of intelligence, if converted into a downward extension of the well-established Stanford–Binet test for children aged 2 through 30 months. For an excellent appraisal of the Cattell Infant Intelligence Scale (Cattell, 1940) the interested reader should consult Hooper, Conner, and Umansky (1986), as well as the other general reviews cited earlier. Cattell followed the Binet format by organizing items at age intervals, initially monthly and then more widely spaced. A traditional IQ could then be derived (mental age/chronological age × 100). In selecting items, Cattell sifted through the Developmental Schedules, eliminating those she considered excessively motoric, personal–social, or family-influenced. The items were field-tested. Those that could not be administered easily or did not show a consistent pattern of increased passes with increased chronological age were eliminated. The resulting instrument, therefore, reflected Gesell's picture of "mental growth" modified by Cattell's subjective understanding of those behaviors that more purely reflect inborn intellectual ability. Although Cattell believed that with the proper precautions her test could be used for diagnosis, she was well aware of the possibility that scores may be unstable over time. For this reason, she cautioned examiners not to report test results to parents (Cattell, 1940)—a reminder of how practices, if not tests, have radically changed!

Like that for the Gesell, the standardization sample for the Cattell (n = 274) was limited to middle-class children; parents had to pay $50.00 for enrollment in the project. The psychometric properties of the test are weak, though better than those of the Gesell. Cattell limited her reliability reporting to split-half (which was high). The adequacy of test–retest stability, especially at the younger ages, is questionable. The Cattell does not correlate well with the Stanford–Binet; this is unfortunate, given the assumption that it is a downward extension and the fact that Binet items are included on the test. However, it does correlate highly with the early Bayley administered concurrently (r = .97). Evidence for predictive validity is mixed and does not justify consumer confidence in diagnostic judgments that project the future (Hooper et al., 1986).

Another ambitious attempt, this time in England, to develop a test of infant intelligence was that of Ruth Griffiths, who in 1951 published the Griffiths Mental Development Scale for Testing Babies from Birth to Two Years. She, too, borrowed heavily from Gesell in a search for behaviors that would tap innate abilities. In addition to the general reviews listed earlier, the reader should consult Hindley (1960, 1965) for opinion on and research with the Griffiths. In the tradition of Gesell, Griffiths selected a wide variety of developmental parameters to test, but, departing from him, she equated the results with general intelligence (Griffiths, 1954). Like the Cattell and Binet, the Griffiths is an age scale with three items per week in the first year and two items per week in the second, so that a mental age and IQ can be derived. The author has grouped items into five broad subscales: Locomotor, Personal–Social, Hearing and Speech, Eye and Hand, and Performance. The test is more heavily loaded with speech items than other baby tests, and also relies on parental report (as does the Gesell) for a number of items.

The Griffiths was standardized on a sample of 571 children from day nurseries and welfare clinics in a borough of London. Here again, no effort was made to secure either a representative or a random sample. Griffiths

did not report split-half reliability, but claimed test–retest correlations averaging .87 over an average interval of 30 weeks. Hindley (1960) was unable to replicate this achievement. He obtained correlations ranging from .46 to .58 over four separate test intervals in the first 18 months. He also found the mean score to be unstable at different age levels for the same sample of children. Although Hindley and others are disappointed in the poor predictive validity of the Griffiths, Honzik (1976) points out that Griffiths, like Cattell, did not anticipate permanence; rather, her objective was the detection of deficits. A clinical test, she asserted, "should enable the examiner to distinguish readily and certainly between different groups of children, the normal and the handicapped, the deaf and the defective, the emotionally disturbed and inhibited and the permanently mentally disabled" (Griffiths, 1954, p. 35).

The most popular (Lewis & Fox, 1986) and psychometrically sophisticated (Anastasi, 1976) infant instruments to date are the Bayley Scales of Infant Development (Bayley, 1969). These scales, which originated in the California First Year Mental Scale of 1933 (covering actually the first 18 months), are the product of over 40 years of work by Nancy Bayley. They are divided into a Mental Scale, a Motor Scale, and an Infant Behavior Record. Although reviewers often describe the Bayley Mental Scale as "sensory–motor," it is designed to measure memory, learning, problem solving, early communication, classification, and generalization as well. By the time the 1969 scales were complete, Bayley had long known that they would not be predictive of later mental ability scores. Through her longitudinal appraisal of children (the Berkeley Growth Study), she had come to the conclusion that development is unstable in the first 2 years of life: Abilities important at 1 month are, in short order, lost or subsumed by other skills. She found no evidence for a general trait of intelligence either in factor analyses or single test scores. Rather than positing a general factor of intelligence, Bayley concluded that there are multiple functions going through qualitative transformations with age, with no necessary correlation existing between earlier and later periods of maturity. Her perceptions of mental transformations were consistent with

Piaget's stage theory. Bayley saw no possibility of tracing development lines or psychometric factors consistently from infancy to childhood (Bayley, 1933, 1949, 1955; Bayley & Shaefer, 1964). She states in the manual (Bayley, 1969) that the test's primary value is to establish the current comparative status of a child, thereby identifying mental and motor retardation. With a subset of children thus isolated, clinicians can select those in need of early corrective measures and look for underlying causes of the developmental problem. The two important questions raised by Cattell, Griffiths, and Bayley—whether a test lacking predictive utility can be helpful in detecting the deviant population or can serve as a criterion for the instigation of interventions—are discussed later.

The test was standardized on 1,262 children from 2 to 30 months of age, selected to be representative of the U.S. population. Unlike the prior infant tests, the Bayley has norms based on standard deviations rather than ratios. Split-half reliabilities for the Mental Scale range from .81 to .93; percentage of agreement on 90 babies who were given a version highly similar to the 1969 scales was 89.4%, and test–retest agreement is reported at .76.

DISCUSSION OF THE GENERAL TESTS

The authors of the general intelligence tests for infants operated under two unfortunate but self-imposed constraints: first, a close adherence to the exhaustive observational work of Gesell in selecting items for their own tests; and, second, a commitment to age-graded scaling. As previously stated, Gesell disavowed any intention of measuring intelligence per se, preferring to look more broadly at growth. The items measuring intelligence were not distinguished from those in other developmental realms. He filmed children's behavior and then, from a vast quantity of observational material, arbitrarily selected particular areas to include (Ball, 1977) without ever adequately justifying the selections or groupings. He did not explain why, for instance, banging a spoon, looking for a fallen object, reacting to a mirror image, looking under a cup for a hidden block, and building a tower with cubes (all items that

reappear in other tests explicitly designed to measure intelligence) are valued as important indices of maturation, harbingers of things to come, rather than as trivial and random bits of behavior lacking long-term adaptive value. Though one could, and investigators did, impose theoretical structures on what is being measured at different ages (McCall et al., 1977), Gesell himself did not make clear why looking at an object is more important than looking at the administrator's face, why pushing a cup to the floor is less valuable than lifting it, or what the relationships are among the items and real-life adaptation.

Gesell's successors, committed to a narrower conceptualization of mental development in the construction of their tests, made choices from his large collection of behaviors that were guided by intuition and practicality. They, too, never adequately justified item selection. Their winnowing (and additions) were determined by administrative considerations and goodness of age fit. When they discovered through longitudinal studies—and each of the investigators discussed above followed at least a group of infants over time—that in an important respect the tests were not working (i.e., children's scores were unstable over time), each author determined that the instability proved intelligence to be irregular or discontinuous over the early lifespan. Despite the atheoretical and unsystematic manner in which the items had been selected, the evidence did not provoke them to ask whether they had chosen poorly, whether the tests themselves might be at fault. Even more surprisingly, despite their findings of unstable scores, they believed that the tests could be used for assessing current function and pathology.

From today's distance, one wonders why the one fundamental criterion for item selection was goodness of fit with evolving age. Apparently no effort was made to predefine the nature of intelligence and then to select items that most adequately fit the construct(s), regardless of how smoothly they paralleled age changes. Theories of mental growth were generated by, rather than generating, item development. As one commentator put it, criticizing the effort to derive developmental progressions from Gesell and Bayley data:

[T]he way to go about testing for the manifestation of intellectual structures is, first, to conceptualize the structures, and then to find tasks which might best reflect their operation. Reading out structures from a heterogeneous selection of tasks seems to me to be a slippery enterprise. (Uzgiris, 1977, pp. 100–101)

Given that no adequate theory was available for the early developers of infant tests (and still is not), one questions retrospectively why there was not more effort to consider features of adult or childhood intelligence and then proceed downward, instead of always observing intellectual growth epigenetically. To some extent this was, of course, done. Each test, for example, emphasizes language reception and expression from its earliest manifestations. Still it was an ad hoc enterprise, and such variables as attention, curiosity, exploration, memory, and effort were measured sporadically rather than systematically. The fact that a few current studies have found the infant tests better predictors of psychomotor than of general abilities (Rose, McClure, & Roe, 1983; Siegel, 1983; Ulvund, 1984) raises further doubt as to the accuracy of the item content as a measure of intelligence.

Only recently have test authors moved from item selection by age grading to the calibration of items by difficulty levels. This method of test construction, called the "latent–trait model" (see Elliott, 1983, Bashaw, 1982, for helpful discussions), aims at establishing scales that are homogeneous in content (items differ only in difficulty), sample-free, and of equal intervals. That is, as with height and weight, an individual's score is calculated on a metric established independently of sample (age, class, sex) considerations. It removes the distortions that come from forcing a developmental dimension onto an equal-interval age scale. Existing tests are like a growth scale in which the average child's height is assumed to increase by the same number of inches each year. The new methodology allows the test constructor to trace a developmental function as it progresses in unequal increments over age and establishes a child's position on the dimension without concern for maximization of individual differences or equivalency of annual increments.

In sum, tests were developed from a cor-

pus of items designed to track infant development, but not specifically intelligence. When scores achieved by infants failed to predict future intelligence test results, the authors concluded that the problem was the instability of infant intelligence, not the selection of items. Little effort was made to develop items that might reflect a theory of intelligence rather than merely change with age. The major attraction of the newer tests of visual attention, to be discussed in a later section, is their derivation from theories of intelligence. Notwithstanding predictive failures, Cattell, Griffiths, and Bayley claimed that the performance of an infant at any particular age indicated his or her current intelligence and that deviations from the expected norms yielded useful diagnostic information. As we shall see, in this last regard they may well have been right—a surprising outcome, given the questionable reasoning and patchwork item assemblage.

PREDICTIONS

General Findings

The conventional wisdom is that the correlation between infant and childhood tests, while positive and often statistically significant, is unimpressive (Escalona & Moriarty, 1961; Fagan & Singer, 1983; Honzik, 1976; Kopp & McCall, 1982; Lewis & Fox, 1986; Lewis & Sullivan, 1985; McCall, 1976, 1979, 1981a; McCall et al., 1972; Stott & Ball, 1965; Thomas, 1970). Tests administered to normal infants between 1 and 30 months of age correlate from .01 to .59 with childhood tests at ages 3–8 (Hozik, 1976; Lewis & Sullivan, 1985; McCall, 1979; McCall et al., 1972). Although the early correlations may have been depressed because they were established with small populations weighted toward the upper end of the social and economic continuum (e.g., the Berkeley Growth Study, the Fels Research Institute longitudinal study), larger populations with much greater numbers of lower-class children (Broman, Nichols, & Kennedy, 1975) have not altered the generalization. Nor have item clusters or groupings of easy and hard items succeeded any better than single scores in isolating long-term strengths and weaknesses (Hunt & Bayley, 1971). As might be ex-

TABLE 8.1. Median Correlations between Infant
and Childhood Tests for Normals

Age of initial infant test (months)	Age of childhood test (years)		
	3–4	5–7	8–18
1–6	.21	.09	.06
7–12	.32	.20	.25
13–18	.50	.34	.32
19–30	.59	.39	.49

Note. From *The Handbook of Infant Development* (p. 712) by R. B. McCall, 1979, New York: Wiley. Copyright 1979 by John Wiley. Adapted by permission.

pected, correlations increase positively with age and negatively with elapsed time between tests. McCall (1976) sums up the research:

Generally speaking, there is essentially no correlation between performance during the first six months of life with IQ score after age 5; the correlations are predominantly in the 0.20s for assessments made between 7 and 18 months of life when one is predicting IQ at 5–18 years; and it is not until 19–30 months that the infant test predicts later IQ in the range of 0.40–0.55. (p. 101)

Table 8.1 adapted from McCall (1979), illustrates McCall's conclusions through a summary of multiple prediction studies of infant intelligence.

This view, however, is not universally held, and some studies have produced divergent findings. Wilson (1983), who through his extensive investigations of twin development has emerged as a strong defender of the early stability of intelligence, reports the following correlations with IQ scores for children aged 3 through 7: .32 to .40 for children tested at age 1; .47 to .60 for children tested at 18 months; .54 to .74 for children tested at 24 months; and .60 to .78 for children tested at 30 months. Ramey, Campbell, and Nicholson (1973) reported correlations of .71 and .90 between 3-year Stanford–Binet scores and Bayley (MDI) at 9–12 months and 13–16 months, respectively. These are impressive correlations—they compare favorably to those found by Bayley (1949) of .60 between age 5 and adulthood, and to those found by

McCall, Appelbaum, and Hogary (1973) of .80 for children tested between 7 and 18. High correlations were also reported by Knobloch and Pasamanick (1967). In a mixed group of normal and abnormal infants, correlations between the Gesell administered before age 1 and the Stanford–Binet at ages 6–8 were .48 for those with IQs above 80 and .68 for those with IQs below 80. These correlations are similar to those of Werner, Honzik, and Smith (1968) in their longitudinal study of the children of Kauai, though the infant tests were administered somewhat later. For the total group of children, correlations between the 20-month Cattell and intelligence tests at age 10 were .41 to .49. For the children with IQs below 80, the correlation was .71.

The literature hints at, but by no means proves, the intriguing possibility that correlations are stronger earlier for girls than for boys (see McCall et al., 1972, and Honzik, 1976, for summaries). Although many studies either report no differences or fail to investigate the issue, earlier stabilization of scores for girls has been found across tests and ages (see Cohen & Parmelee, 1983, and Sigman, Cohen, & Forsythe, 1981, for correlations on the Gesell from infant risk factors to 9- and 24-month tests; Hindley, 1960, for correlations on the Griffiths between 3 and 18 months; Rosenblith, 1979, for correlations between the Graham–Rosenblith neonatal test and testing at age 4; and Thomas, 1970, for correlations on the Brunet–Lezine from 12, 24, and 30 months to 3 and 4 years). One of the sharpest discrepancies in the sexes has been reported by McCall et al. (1972) from the Fels longitudinal data. Correlations between the Gesell given at 12, 18, and 24 months with the Stanford–Binet given at 6 years were as follows: for girls, .51, .43 and .65; for boys, .22, .28 and .39. Another remarkably high correlation for girls only was reported by Cameron, Livson, and Bayley (1967). The authors developed a scoring system based on age of first passing an item, gathered from the data of children in the Berkeley Growth Study who had been tested monthly until 15 months old. Correlations between the infant cluster (heavily weighted with language items) and verbal intelligence scores from 6 to 26 years of age ranged from the .20s to .76. In a prospective study of high-risk infants, Sigman and Parmelee

(1979) assessed the validity of 16 infant diagnostic measures in predicting 2-year-olds' Bayley and Gesell scores. The multiple-regression coefficients for boys (R^2) were .22 and .27 (r's = .47 and .52); for girls they were .71 and .74 (r's = .84 and .86). Not only do girls show more personal consistency than boys, but their scores in early life also correlate more highly with their parents' (Bayley & Shaefer, 1964; Hindley, 1960; Kagan & Moss, 1959).

Socioeconomic Status and Combined Predictors

Any infant test that claims value must overcome the hurdle of socioeconomic status (SES). Sameroff, Seifer, Barocas, Zax, and Greenspan (1987) found generally that SES explained only 20% of the variance. However, in their own longitudinal study, the correlation between SES and a 4-year intelligence test was .59. McCall et al. (1972) put the correlation between SES and IQ at $1\frac{1}{2}$ to 4 years of age at .60. Broman et al. (1975), reporting on the large Collaborative Perinatal Project (n = 26,760), found a multiple correlation of .42 between SES plus mother's IQ and 4-year intelligence tests.

There is widespread agreement that for both normal infants and children at risk because of prematurity, family characteristics, though uncorrelated to infant tests, are much better predictors of childhood IQ than the infant measures. With high-risk groups, they also outpredict complex risk inventories that take into account a host of medical conditions surrounding birth (Aylward, Gustafson, Verhulst, & Colliver, 1987; Bee et al., 1982; Broman et al., 1975; Finkelstein & Ramey, 1980; Ireton, Thwing, & Gravem, 1970; McCall et al., 1972; Rubin & Balow, 1979; Sameroff, 1979; Sameroff et al., 1987; Siegel, 1982, 1983; Werner et al., 1968; Willerman, Broman, & Fiedler, 1970). The greater predictive success of SES over infant tests, while true across all classes and children, may be heightened for poorer and more at-risk infants (Bee et al., 1982; Werner, Bierman, & French, 1971; Willerman et al., 1970).

As disillusionment with infant tests has grown, investigators have attempted to enhance prediction by combining social–environmental, medical, and developmental data in various ways. Sameroff et al. (1987), for example, correlating SES and 10 other environmental variables (e.g., parental mental health, parent perspective on child rearing, family support, stressful life events) with 4-year-old IQ, obtained a multiple R^2 of .51 (r = .71). Finkelstein and Ramey (1980), using information available from birth certificates (race, mother's education, age of mother, number of previous live births that subsequently died, birth order, legitimacy of birth, month prenatal care began, and birth weight), registered a multiple R of .56 with Peabody first-grade score.

Surprisingly, risk indicators (e.g., obstetrical history and complications, delivery and postnatal complications, polygraph at birth and 3 months, and newborn neurological indicators) have not been of much value in predicting childhood IQ in populations of children at risk, because of very low birth weight—<2,500 grams or even, in some studies, <2,000 or 1,500 (Capute, Goldstein, & Taub, 1981; Cohen & Parmelee, 1983; Cohen, Sigman, Parmelee, & Beckwith, 1982; Sigman & Parmelee, 1979). After the few children with obvious and severe deficits are omitted from the samples, mean IQs of premature infants, initially in the border-line–normal range, become average by school age (Kitchen, Ford, Rickards, Lissenden, & Ryan, 1987; Vohr & Garcia Coll, 1985; Wilson, 1985), though the excessive instances of learning disabilities found at school age despite normal IQ appear to be a residual impact of early insult (see Cohen, 1986, for an excellent summary; Hunt, 1981; Kitchen et al., 1980; Klein, Hack, Gallagher, & Fanaroff, 1985; Taub, Goldstein, & Capute, 1977). Perinatal risk factors do not, therefore, usually add anything substantial to regression analyses. Looking at the determinants of childhood Wechsler Intelligence Scale for Children—Revised (WISC-R) scores, Capute et al. (1981) found no impact from a set of variables related to premature status; when these were combined with mother's IQ, however, the multiple R rose to .67, and when social class and ethnicity were added, it rose to .72.

What happens when infant tests are combined with social and perinatal variables? For normal children, McCall et al. (1972) found that these tests added nothing to the predictions from SES during the first year. Tests given at 18 months, while still less potent than SES, do raise the multiple R over that obtained from SES data alone, and tests administered at 24 months actually shift the balance, adding more to the multiple R than SES. In tests predicting from 24 months to 6 years and using both data sets, the multiple R for boys is .51 and for girls .77. In a mixed sample of normal and abnormal children, Werner et al. (1968) combined 20-month Cattell scores, SES, parent education, pediatric appraisal at 20 months, and perinatal stress scores for a multiple R of .50 with Primary Mental Abilities (Thurstone & Thurstone, 1954) at 10 years. The same picture described the premature population. Infant tests did not appreciably increase the multiple correlation of .51 to 5-year-old McCarthy scores once perinatal, reproductive, and SES variables were accounted for in Siegel's (1982, 1983) study of low-birth-weight children. SES eventually prevailed for this group as well as for normal infants.

Particularly interesting is the tendency of SES, a surrogate for genetic as well as environmental determinants, to overwhelm the influence of even extreme prematurity. In studies of at-risk children, it has been shown repeatedly that high SES serves to mask or correct initial deficits, whereas lower SES compounds them. Therefore, IQ differences by SES are greater for children who at birth were premature rather than healthy. For example, Werner et al. (1968) reported that on a 20-month Cattell given to their sample of infants from Kauai, the IQ differences between children with and without perinatal stress for high-SES families was 5–7 points, whereas in low-SES families the difference was 19–37 points. Wilson (1985) described prematurity as having a short-lived suppressor effect on intelligence; in his twin studies, it no longer had an independent impart after 6 years, but was replaced by parent education and family SES. Whereas at 6 months of age infants who weighed below 1,750 grams at birth were 19 points below nonpremature infants, there was little difference between those of high and low SES. At 6 years the high-SES premature infants had recovered fully as a group, with a mean IQ of 101.1, while the low-SES "premies" had a mean IQ of 86.5. The amplification of deficiency by low SES and the muting of it by high SES have been reported by others (Cohen et al., 1982; Drillien, 1964; Escalona, 1984; Knob-

loch & Pasamanick, 1967; Sameroff, 1975; Willerman et al., 1970). This influence, then, obscures predictions from infant assessments. Overall, there is recovery from prematurity, but the upward climb is not uniform. Children who initially perform poorly are more likely to improve if they come from high-SES families; those without these environmental/genetic benefits are more likely to remain behind, and some who start out with average scores will decrease in levels. In the individual case, of course, prediction is poor.

To sum up, prediction from the major infant assessment instruments has not been strikingly successful in general. For normal and at-risk infants until age 2, these tests tell little of future ability—much less than SES or parent IQ. At about age 2, combining both is sometimes fruitful. Further multiplication of variables (e.g., subdividing SES or adding to it perinatal stress and child assessment scores) helps a little more. But the multiple scores explain no more than 50% of the variance, and only a few studies achieve even that. Before giving up on the predictive utility of infant tests, however, we need to review their record with handicapped populations.

Abnormal Infants

The last bastion of predictive optimism is the repeated finding that infant tests are good at identifying abnormal function in early life (for reviews of this literature, see Brooks & Weinraub, 1976; Fagan & Singer, 1983; Honzik, 1976; Kopp & McCall, 1982; Lewis & Sullivan, 1985; McCall, 1979; McCall et al., 1972). The studies that support this generalization, however, are open to a number of methodological objections. Children are seen at oddly spaced intervals; subject attrition over time is substantial, with unclear selection procedures for re-evaluation; different tests are employed within the same study; the heterogeneity of the samples inflates the standard deviation (often not reported), a factor that alone might explain the better predictions; children tend to be seen at shorter retest intervals and tracked more briefly than in the longitudinal studies of normal children; sample sizes are often very small; outcomes vary as a function of diagnosis; and the research is usually carried out retrospectively from clinical records.

These drawbacks prompt Fagan and Singer (1983) to conclude:

> [G]reat variability in predictive validity among differing groups of abnormal infants tested at 1 year of age or less does not provide much support for faith in the long term stability of the low scoring infant. In fact, studies which fuel this faith are primarily of much older infants and are not necessarily generalizable to the first year of life. (p. 35)

Summarizing multiple studies, the authors conclude that the mean correlation between infant tests given in the first year of life and again at age 4–5 is .18 for "at-risk" (including here clinical–handicapped) children compared to .16 for normal children, and that the correlation between infant tests and tests at age 6 and above for the "at-risk" group is .21 compared to .10 for normals—a very small difference.

This issue is extremely important. I would argue that if the tests successfully identify handicaps that are not otherwise obvious in early life, they are worthwhile, notwithstanding their failure to describe the development of normal children. Conversely, if they are not diagnostically useful with suspect populations, success with normals is of little clinical moment. If Fagan and Singer are correct, then clinics all through the country are doing a disservice to families by regularly using tests as a major component in the diagnosis of suspect infants. That these tests may have concurrent (as opposed to predictive) validity is not, as I argue below, sufficent justification.

My own appraisal of the clinical findings of abnormal children, however, is more optimistic, as Table 8.2 shows. In assembling the material, I selected only those studies in which most of the children had developmental quotients below 80. I also omitted studies of Down syndrome infants for two reasons. First, one does not need a development test to establish the diagnosis; second, it is well known that for most Down syndrome children IQ declines with age—not necessarily at a uniform rate—so that correlations naturally would be depressed. (For a similar table that does include studies of children with Down syndrome, see Kopp & McCall, 1982.) Liberties were taken where necessary to fit findings into the table as con-

TABLE 8.2. Correlations between Infant and Children Tests for the Handicapped

Age of initial infant test (years)	Age of childhood test (years)					
	1	2	3	4	5–7	8+
<1	.72[a] .65[d]	.76[i] .60[d]	.74[c]	—	.68[b] .26[d] .52[l]	—
1	—	.80[a] .82[d]	.80[a] .77[i]	.63[a]	.52[d] .82[d] .71[l] .73[l]	.71[h]
2	—	.94[a]	.80[k]	.92[a] .97[g] .90[i] .85[k]	.89[a] .76[d] .76[e] .79[l]	—
3	—	—	—	.81[k]	.88[e] .88[i] .87[f] .90[k]	—
4	—	—	—	—	.95[e] .95[i] .67[j] .88[k]	—

[a]Erickson (1968), n = 12–40   [b]Knobloch & Pasamanick (1967), n = 28;   [c]Knobloch & Pasamanick (1960, n = 48;   [d]Fishman & Palkes (1974), n = 15–21;   [e]Fishler, Graliker, & Koch (1964–65), n = 30 (congenital cerebral anomalies);   [f]Nielsen (1971), n = 5–17;   [g]VanderVeer & Schweid (1974), n = 23;   [h]Werner, Honzik, & Smith (1968), n = 36;   [i]Goodman & Cameron (1978), n = 27–52;   [j]Vig, Kamner, & Jedrysek (1987), n = 38;   [k]Field, Fox, & Radcliffe (1987), n = 31–70;   [l]Largo, Graf, Kundu, Hunziker, & Molinari (in press), n = 50–59.

structed. For example, when a test was given to infants up to 18 months of age, I included it under the 1-year category; when a span of years was given for a re-evaluation, I took the midpoint. I only reported correlations for n's > 12.

There are indeed significant difficulties with the data. The pool of studies is subject to most of the criticisms mentioned above. Populations are poorly described, and subject attrition is very great. Test–retest intervals are short, sometimes a year or even less. Important data, such as SES, are usually omitted. Nonetheless, correlations are high and repeated across studies: Almost all the correlations are over .50 even for tests separated by 3–5 years. Usually, for tests given at age 1 or older, they are in the .70s to .90s. To make the comparison between tests of handicapped and normal infants clearer, Table 8.3 juxtaposes Bayley's (1949) findings (which

TABLE 8.3. Correlations between Infant and
Children Tests for the Normal (Bayley, 1949) and
Handicapped (Table 8.2 Data) Samples

Age of initial infant test (years)	Age of childhood test (years)					
	1	2	3	4	5–7	8+
<1	.52	.23	.10	−.16	−.07	−.06
	(.69)	(.68)	(.74)	(—)	(.49)	(—)
1		.60	.45	.27	.20	.19
		(.81)	(.79)	(.63)	(.70)	(.71)
2			.80	.49	.50	.37
			(.91)	(.91)	(80)	(—)
3				.72	.70	.58
				(.81)	(.88)	(—)
4					.82	.71
					(.86)	(—)

Note. Numbers not in parentheses are from Bayley (1949);
numbers within parentheses refer to mean handicapped
scores from Table 8.2.

closely resemble those of Table 8.1) with the
averages on handicapped children from
Table 8.2. The differences are particularly
striking in the first 2 years. In general, the
likelihood that young children once diagnosed as retarded will remain so is 75%–
80% (Goodman & Cameron, 1978; Hallowell,
1941; Hohman & Freedheim, 1959; Illingworth & Birch, 1959; Jewell & Wursten,
1952; Knobloch & Pasamanick, 1960; Kogan,
1957; Nielsen, 1971; VanderVeer & Schweid,
1974).

At the very least, the literature gives some
support to clinicians who find infant tests
important in diagnostic evaluations of referred populations. The results should not be
discounted entirely because of imperfect
methods. Nor should they be dismissed on
grounds of superfluousness (i.e., that it is
easy to pick out handicapped children even
without tests). It is still true that most delayed children do not have explanatory
medical diagnoses. They are distinguished
from the normal population in early life only
by functional levels (Goodman & Cameron,
1978). And even where there is an established medical diagnosis, it alone, with
the exception of Down syndrome, gives poor
prognostic information (Goodman, 1977;
Goodman, Cecil, & Barker, 1984). We need

good evaluation instruments. Findings to
date should encourage more and better prospective research with referred infant populations—research of the same quality as the
classic longitudinal studies of normal children.

Why the greater stability of scores among
low-functioning children? Could it be just a
psychometric artifact? Looking retrospectively at 100 children who at 4 years of age
had IQs of 140 or more, Willerman and Fiedler (1974) found that their scores at 8 months
did not differ from those of the total Collaborative Perinatal Project population. Hallowell (1941) reported that scores were twice
as sensitive for low-functioning as for high-
functioning children, and Drillien (1964)
noted that it was the preschool high scorers
who demonstrated the biggest discrepancy at
a 3- to 4-year follow-up.

Nothing like this happens at the lower extreme of the spectrum. With a large retarded
sample, we (Goodman & Cameron, 1978)
found that IQs under 50 were more stable
than those within the 51–80 range (see also
Dubose, 1977; Hohman & Freedheim, 1959;
Klapper & Birch, 1967; Knobloch & Pasamanick, 1963; McCall, 1979). It appears that the
higher up one goes on the intelligence scales,
from bottom to top, the poorer test–retest
correlations are. A partial explanation for less
stability in higher scores, suggested by
Robert McCall (personal communication,
November 1987), is that items at the upper
end of the scale are worth more mental
months than corresponding items at the bottom of the scale. This is true on the Bayley
starting at 18 months of age.

If it is not the construction of the test, what
else might be producing these results? The
argument that the dull get stuck, fail to go
through normal cognitive stages, and so separate themselves from those making expect-
able progress is not an adequate response, for
if it were true, it would predict a decreasing
score with age. This does not occur outside of
institutions (Goodman, 1977; Goodman &
Cameron, 1978; Klapper & Birch, 1967).
Even within the retarded range, children at
the lowest levels (those with IQs below 50),
though more stable than others, do not manifest declining scores over time (Field, Fox,
& Radcliffe, 1987; Hohman & Freedheim,
1959; Goodman & Cameron, 1978). Because
scores in the retarded show categorical as

well as rank-order stability, the picture of them as imperviously unchanging is probably wrong. It is more likely that experience, stage transitions, genetically determined abilities, and personality factors have a regular, albeit slowed-down, impact on their intelligence.

A possible explanation (and it is admittedly unsatisfactory) for the higher correlations in delayed and retarded samples is simply that normal infants show limited variability. There is so little distinction among them that very small (and behaviorally insignificant) departures from the mean produce sharp drops or gains in scaled scores. These shifts, which fluctuate during the early years, are unimportant noise in the developmental process, but receive exaggerated play in the standard scores. The retarded, with somewhat larger discrepancies, get established at the low end of the spectrum and stay there.

Bayley scores (see Table 8.4) nicely illustrate the tightness of early development. A 12-month-old performing one standard deviation below the Bayley mean (an MDI of 84) will have the same raw score as an average 11-month-old (ratio IQ of 92); an infant of the same age performing one standard deviation above the mean (MDI of 116) will have the raw score of a 13½-month-old. Thus two-thirds of 1-year-olds fall within a span of just over 2 months. To continue, a 12-month-old performing two standard deviations below the mean (MDI of 68) will score as an average 9-month-old (ratio IQ of 75), and one per-

forming three standard deviations below the mean (MDI of 52) will score as an average 8-month-old (ratio IQ of 67). The same relative relationships, only slightly modified, hold at age 2. The plummeting of MDI scores below ratio equivalents reflects the homogeneity of normal infant development. By contrast, a 6-year-old performing two standard deviations below the Stanford–Binet (Form L-M) mean (IQ of 68) will have the score of an average 4-year-old (ratio IQ of 67), and one performing three standard deviations below the mean (IQ of 52) will have the score of an average child aged 3 years, 2 months (ratio IQ of 53). These standard deviation IQs are almost identical to ratio IQs, not lower, as with the 1- and 2-year-old Bayley ratio IQs. Both proportionately and absolutely, then, variability in mental age increases with chronological age, so that performance at half or three-fourths of chronological age represents a greater deficit in younger than in older children. Development in early life, at least as reflected on infant tests, is in such close synchrony with chronological age that small differences in an age cohort make for large differences in standard scores.

Finally, the explanation for higher IQ correlations with lower IQ level may lie not in psychometrics or in the nature of normal children, but in the mental development of the retarded themselves. Could it be that though the delayed children make progress at some regular fraction of their mental age (see Goodman & Cameron, 1978), going

TABLE 8.4. Test Scores as Illustrative of Limited Infant Variability

Chronological age	Mental age	MOI (Bayley); deviation IQ (Stanford–Binet)	Ratio IQ
		Bayley Scales	
12 months	11 months	84	92
12 months	13.5 months	116	113
12 months	9 months	68	75
12 months	8 months	52	67
12 months	21 months	84	88
24 months	27 months	116	113
24 months	17 months	68	71
24 months	15 months	52	63
		Stanford–Binet (1972)	
6 years	4 years	68	67
6 years	3 years, 2 months	52	53

through the same developmental sequences as normal children, they are nonetheless less susceptible to environmental influences? When achievement does not come easily but is labored and long, there may be less sensitivity to subtleties in the environment, to both favorable and unfavorable opportunites. Along these lines, Claire Kopp has suggested (personal communication, September 1987) that there is an inflexibility in the behavior of retarded children, reflected in failure to use caregivers as resources, failure to shift strategies when a situation demands it, and difficulties in modifying activities in response to environmental changes. Interestingly, evolutionary theorists have identified flexibility—"What wasps lack and human beings possess in unparalleled abundance"—as the "hallmark of humanity" (Gould, 1987, pp. 62, 64), the trait that best differentiates smaller- from larger-brained animals. The poor synchrony between child and environment may be intrinsic to retardation or may be due to inappropriate demands and stimulation. The greater insulation of the slow child is both a protection against adversity and a limitation on expansion.

This position has some empirical support. Krakow and Kopp (1983) found that although from a macrocosmic perspective young retarded children follow normal developmental stages, upon close observation they tend to monitor and apprise their environment less, play more repetitively, and are more often unoccupied than normal children matched for mental age. The distinguishing feature between retarded and normal children, Berg and Sternberg (1985) speculate, is that because of deficiencies either in motivation or in the processing of information, the former are less drawn to novelty. In studies with the Lock Box, an instrument designed to measure mental organization in preschoolers, I found that retarded children displayed poorer search strategies and greater aimlessness than children of the same mental age when confronted with the task of opening 10 locked doors and playing with the toys within (Goodman, 1981). These traits—clearly unconducive to learning spurts—may be responsible for the even developmental pace. In a very interesting essay, Fisher (1959) noted that generally tests predict nonadaptive behavior more accurately than adaptive

behavior. The reason, he speculated, is that the injured organism loses the capacity for variable, substitutive, compensatory behaviors. It may be that the retarded, too, have less natural developmental elasticity.

Before leaving this topic, I want to make it clear that just because the retarded tend to maintain a relatively constant developmental progression, this does not mean that concerted remedial efforts will be ineffective. The literature on early intervention reports enough successes to leave this an open question. As in all behavior, substantial environmental alteration is likely to bring about changes in the phenotype. The greater behavioral stability of the retarded suggests only that their condition may be especially resistant to change and may require more determined corrective efforts.

THE VALUE OF TESTS WITHOUT PREDICTION

No one wants to give up on the tests. Many authorities believe that infant instruments, even though powerless as predictors, are valuable as measures of present functioning—detailing an infant's strengths and weakness, as well as guiding and evaluating intervention (Cohen, Parmelee, Beckwith, & Sigman, 1986; Cross & Johnston, 1977; Goldberg, 1983; McCall, 1979; Ramey, Campbell, & Wasik, 1982; Sheehan & Gallagher, 1984). Thus, they say, just as we are glad to know an infant's weight even though we recognize its instability, so we should be interested also in the results of infant intelligence tests (McCall, 1979). If we are to accept this argument, one of two positions must be correct: Items on the tests are independently important, analogous to overweight and underweight, or they are symptomatic of underlying cognitive abilities, analogous to body temperature. Thus far, I do not find substantiation for either. What is the concern provoked by not playing with containers? That a child has no aptitude or interest in placing round pegs in round holes cannot matter in itself, yet foolishly we often work with children to remediate these apparent deficiencies. Our investment in training children to perform ephemeral skills because we have a built-in expectation of continuity is at best wasteful and possibly pernicious. The infant tests, with the exception of the Gesell, were designed to predict future outcome. To defend them as important descriptors of present function is, in my judgment, an unsatisfactory rationalization.

There are other tests that do serve useful short-term purposes. A prime example is the Brazelton Neonatal Behavioral Assessment Scale (Brazelton, 1984; see also Als, Tronick, Lester, & Brazelton, 1979; Sameroff, 1978), which probes how an infant organizes responses to a variety of environmental and internal assaults. It examines the conditions under which the baby seeks stimulation, the self-comforting devices used by the infant in various circumstances, and the nature and effectiveness of the infant's coping skills. The test is targeted at helping parents better understand the particular interactive patterns of their infant, so that parental care can be more sensitively individualized. Although the test can be a screen for neurological dysfunction, this is not its primary orientation. That it has little predictive validity is irrelevant if it produces better parent–child interactions.

Another instrument of potential value even without predictive validity is the Uzgiris–Hunt Scale, designed to measure where an infant falls on an ordinal sequence of Piagetian stages. The items here are not meant to be stand-ins for other, more general abilities, but direct indicators of whether a child understands means–ends relationships, causality, object permanence, imitation, and so on. If one accepts this theory, each stage is dependent upon its predecessor, and the overall sequence expresses (rather than acts as a surrogate for) intelligence. The deficits disclosed by this test are obstacles to further growth and *ought* to be remediated.

Generally, to be useful without predictive validity, a test must have other good justifications. It could include items— overweight, for instance—that one would want to change even in the short term for aesthetic, health, or cultural reasons. It could enlighten families about nonobvious qualities that will make it easier to handle their infants (as the Brazelton ostensibly does). Accomplishment of the items could be pivotal to higher accomplishments (as in the Uzgiris– Hunt Scale or in the usual relationship between crawling and walking). The rate of progress in nonessential skills, insignificant in themselves, may be a precursor of later success. (This, in fact, was the unfulfilled expectation of the infant tests.) Finally, the test could be tapping essential components of intelligence that are called upon throughout the life span (as in the visual discrimination tests discussed below).

The omnibus infant tests we have been discussing do not meet any of these criteria. They are characterized by rather random "accretions of increasingly complex behavioral units" (Yang, 1979, p. 178). The units are not conceptually linked to later childhood and adult intelligence (either as proxies or as essential capacities), to stage theory, to coping with infants, or to culturally valued behaviors. That they sometimes are useful predictors for the subpopulation of low-functioning children is gratifying but not adequately understood. I have reviewed explanations based on psychometrics, the distribution of infant abilities, and the nature of the retarded. It is also possible that for this group the tests have incidentally tapped skills linked to the future (perhaps in the language items or through background capacities of attention and persistence that are part of all test performance). In the absence of predictive validity, beyond the important function of diagnosing the disabled, it is difficult to see in what respects the traditional infant tests are useful.

VISUAL HABITUATION: A BETTER MOUSETRAP?

Researchers who believe that intelligence is continuous across the lifespan argue that infant tests should focus on information processing rather than sensory–motor achievements. From the work of Fantz, who demonstrated the preference of infants for patterned stimuli, a paradigm has emerged for measuring visual recognition memory or habituation. The theory maintains that characteristics of infant perception—attention, encoding, comparative analysis, retention, and retrieval—represent the beginning of information processing. Babies just a few months of age focus on and recall visual stimuli. As the stimulus becomes familiar, however, there is a decrement in attention. This phenomenon, known as "habituation," dissipates when a novel stimulus is presented; attention then recovers. The smarter the child, the more quickly the stimulus is coded, an accurate trace formed, and a distinction made between the familiar and the novel. Therefore, speed of habituation or response decrement and recovery to novelty can be used as measures of cognitive functioning. (For reviews of this literature, see Berg & Sternberg, 1985; Bornstein & Sigman, 1986; Fagan & Singer, 1983.)

In addition to the familiar–novel paradigm, researchers have explored the ability of infants to distinguish configurational from merely elemental differences—the beginning of concept formation (Caron, Caron, & Glass, 1983); to recognize similar and different objects when presented across modalities—for example, touch or taste and then vision (Rose, 1981; Rose & Wallace, 1985b); and to discriminate auditory stimuli (O'Connor, Cohen, & Parmelee, 1984). Related to the visual novelty experiments are tasks measuring exploration and mastery behavior (Messer et al., 1986; Vietze, McCarthy, McQuiston, MacTurk, & Yarrow, 1983).

The procedures and stimuli used in visual habituation testing are various. A typical procedure is to show the baby two identical stimuli (often faces) for a given period of time and then to present a novel stimulus together with the familiar one (paired comparison). A preference for novelty is indicated if the child spends more than 50% (chance) of the time looking at the novel target. The child's visual fixation is determined by the reflection of the target on the cornea, viewed through a peephole situated between the two targets. The number and frequency of familiar–novel pairings, and age of administration, vary among researchers. Another procedure is to display the same stimulus for a fixed number of trials or until a criterion of habituation is reached, then to present the novel target and measure decrement of fixation over habituation trials or amount of fixation under the recovery condition. Many methodological options are still in dispute. Is it preferable to measure habituation or recovery? Should a trial last for a fixed amount of time or until fixation stops? What is an adequate criterion for cessation of fixation? Should the measure of fixation be first, longest, total, average, or number of fixations? Should ratio or difference scores be used? Should recovery be measured as the difference between last habituation and novelty trial, or should decline over multiple presentations be considered? Is a 50% cutoff high enough to indicate novelty preference? (See Fagan & McGrath, 1981; Lewis & Brooks-Gunn, 1981; McCall, 1981b; Rose, Slater, & Perry, 1986, for good reviews of the measurement problems.) Given infants' short attention span, it is not surprising that research in this area has been plagued by poor reliability, reported by Fagan and Singer (1983) to be .42 and by Bornstein and Sigman (1986) (aggregating five studies) to be .44.

Predictions from infant recognition memory to early childhood assessments of cognitive functioning are fairly consistent for both normal and at-risk samples. Table 8.5 presents findings from recent studies for testing done in the first year of life, generally between 5 and 7 months. Fagan and Singer (1983) found a range of correlations from .33 to .66, and Fagan (1984a) reports an average correlation of .45. In a meta-analysis of 8 decrement and 11 recovery studies, Bornstein and Sigman (1986) report a correlation of .42, which explains only 18% of the variance in childhood scores. Adding parent education and birth order has produced a

TABLE 8.5. Correlations between Infant and Children Tests of Recognition Memory

Age of initial infant test (years)	Age of childhood test (years)			
	2	3	4	5–7
<1	.53[b]	.66[b]	.37[c]	56[b]
	.40[d]	.49[e]	.55[f]	57[c]
	.52[d]	.42[g]	.45[h]	56[f]
	.42[i]	.35[j]	.41[i]	42[g]
	.42[k]	.38[l]		46[i]
		.44[l]		60[m]
1	.46[n]	.47[n]	—	.57[n]

[a]Infants under 1 year of age are generally tested at 5–7 months; [b]Rose & Wallace (1985a), n = 13–35, high-risk; [c]Fagan & McGrath (1981), n's = 54 and 39, normal; [d]Lewis & Brooks-Gunn (1981), n's = 57 and 22, normal (visual attention to an article); [e]Fagan (1988), n = 128, high-risk; [f]Bornstein & Sigman (1986), high-risk, meta-analysis; [g]Fagan (1984b), n = 36, normal; [h]Rose, Slater, & Perry (1986), n = 16, normal; [i]Bornstein & Sigman (1986), normal, meta-analysis; [j]Yarrow et al. (1975), n = 39, normal (manipulation of novel object); [k]Caron, Caron, & Glass (1983), n = 64, normal (Binet correlations selected from other measures; [l]Fagan (1982), n's = 16 and 52, normal; [m]O'Connor, Cohen, & Parmelee (1984), n = 28, high-risk (auditory rather than visual habituation recovery experiment; [n]Rose & Wallace (1985b), n = 19–33, high-risk (cross-modal and intramodal measures averaged).

multiple R of .65 (Fagan, 1984b), though others have found no increase in correlations with the addition of SES data (Fagan & McGrath, 1981; O'Connor et al, 1984).

Supporting concurrent validity of the recognition memory tasks are findings that there is improvement with scores over age; that full-term babies usually do better than preterm ones; that those suspected to be abnormal and clearly abnormal do more poorly than normals; and that high scores are associated with advanced sensory–motor development, play, exploration, problem solving, and other measures of satiation (Bornstein & Sigman, 1986; Cohen, 1981; Fagan, 1985; Lewis, 1969; Miranda & Hack, 1979; Rose & Wallace, 1985a). There have even been reports that higher SES (Cohen, 1981; Lewis, 1969; Rose, 1981), intelligent parents (Fagan, 1985), and stimulating mothers (Bornstein, 1985; Lewis, 1969) are associated with better performance. In a curious twist, several authors report that the infant recognition tests given at about 6 months of age do better than the Bayley administered at the same age in predicting performance on later Bayley tests (Berg & Sternberg, 1985; Lewis & Brooks-Gunn, 1981; Rose & Wallace, 1985a). Once again, there is a hint that correlations from infancy are higher for girls than boys (Caron et al., Glass, 1983; Fagan & McGrath, 1981; Messer et al, 1986).

How promising are these findings? Clearly, the predictions are stronger over the first year than those we have seen in Tables 8.1 and 8.3 for normal children on the traditional tests. Increasing the reliability and finding the best combination of measurements will probably improve the predictive validity. How well the new devices will succeed in diagnosing the handicapped is not yet clear. Fagan (1988; see also Fagan & Montie, 1988) has begun investigating diagnostic questions. In a study of 27 high-risk infants given both the Bayley and a visual recognition test at 3–7 months and an intelligence test at 3 years, he found that the visual novelty task had a sensitivity (ability to predict retardation) of 91%, compared to the Bayley's 45% and a specificity (ability to predict normality) of 81% as against the Bayley's 38%. Prediction of mild and moderate retardation was as accurate as prediction of more severe disability. The fact that these results are from a high-risk but not a clinically referred popula-

tion gives them enhanced credibility. Still, the findings are less strong than those of the largely clinical studies reported in Table 8.2 for the handicapped on traditional tests. Furthermore, they have not exceeded the SES–child correlation of at least .50 and the parent–child correlation of approximately .50 (McCall et al., 1973) for the nonhandicapped.

Correlations aside, can it be said that these tests, unlike their predecessors, are tapping individual differences in fundamental information-processing skills identical to those used in later life? A surprising finding throws doubt on this claim. When Fagan (1984b) gave recognition memory tests along with the Peabody Picture Vocabulary Test to children who as infants had received the visual novelty test, he found high correlations between the two childhood tests and between the infant test and the Peabody, but lower correlations between the early and later recognition tests (see also Fagan, 1984c, and Mundy, Seibert, Hogan, & Fagan, 1983). Now if correlations between the infant test and both childhood tests were strong, it could be argued persuasively that the infant tests measured a pervasive skill, or g. Strong correlations between the two visual discrimination tasks alone would have been convincing evidence for continuity in a particular cognitive process such as visual memory, but the reversal of expectation—better predictions from infant visual recognition to the Peabody than to childhood visual recognition—means that if continuity exists, it is of an underlying ability that peculiarly affects infant visual discrimination and childhood language.

Fagan believes that the common dimensions between infant novelty tests and the Peabody are capacities to retain and retrieve mental representations of an object, and to generalize the invariant features so that prototypes are formed. (See Bornstein & Sigman, 1986, for a similar viewpoint.) One can see how forming mental representations might pay off on the Peabody, but why would the same abilities not also help on the childhood visual recognition task (which, like the infant version, tested ability to differentiate a novel from a familiar stimulus)? In addition, forming prototypes, clearly essential for a picture vocabulary test, was not part of the predictor task, which demanded identity recognition. If one retreats to general mental features such as speed (Fagan 1984a, has claimed that his test measures speed of knowledge acquisition; see also Rose et al., 1986), motivation, or attention to explain the common variance, it is not at all apparent why the Peabody rather than the visual recognition test is the beneficiary.

The findings can be reconciled if the Peabody and infant recognition tests tap a common mental process that childhood recognition tests do not. A drive for mastery or environmental vigilance might promote success in the infant novelty tests and continue to operate during the early years, enabling the child to build up a good sight vocabulary; yet it may be irrelevant to the later recognition test, which the child sees as trifling and unrelated to current learning. It is the job of infants to make and remember visual discriminations; it is the job of young children to learn language, with visual memory becoming of declining importance and increasingly automatic. Along these lines, Fagan (personal communication, August 1987) speculates that perhaps the childhood recognition test is less conceptually demanding than either the infant recognition test or the Peabody. Until we have more predictors and criteria, it will remain unclear just what the visual recognition tasks are measuring and how much reliance can be placed on them.

WHITHER INFANT TESTS?

The yield to be expected from infant tests is tied to conceptions of infant development. Those who adhere to the infant-as-miniature-adult theory will seek measures that tap the same elements in the infant and child. Those adhering to the infant-as-separate-species theory will give up on the tests, at least for predictive purposes. Let us look a bit further at these views, with the assumption that the predictive criteria for infant tests—childhood intelligence tests—are valuable measures of a general learning aptitude.

An important initial distinction is often drawn between stability of individual progress and developmental stages or functions (see McCall, 1979; McCall et al., 1977). Individual growth curves may be variable, but developmental sequences may be continuous. Alternatively, it is possible that children progress at a steady rate, preserving individual differences, despite the quali-

tatively unrelated stages through which they pass. Another distinction made is between manifest behavior and underlying dimensions. Here, too, the same surface behavior may have different sources, or different behaviors may have the same sources. Developmental processes, surface behavior, and individual differences in progression rates must all be considered in a conceptualization of infant assessment.

In Figure 8.1, I have illustrated the possible combinations assuming, oversimply for diagrammatic purposes, that the variables are dichotomous: continuous or discontinuous developmental functions, same or different behavior, stable or unstable rates of progression. The truth is undoubtedly more complex, with some skills continuous, some discontinuous, some a mixture, and so on. Fagan has consistently claimed that the predictive validity of his test supports a continuity view of development; the same underlying information processes, he believes, are measured by infant recognition memory tests and childhood Peabody scores (see Fagan, 1984a, 1985; Fagan & Montie, 1988). This puts him in Box 2 of Figure 8.1 (continuous function, different behavior). Strong correlations between infant and childhood tests presumably fall into Box 1 (continuous function, same behavior), where I have placed the example of attention. Questioning behavior, in Box 3, illustrates underlying discontinuity in the same behavior. Early questioning is more likely to be a bid for attention than later questioning, which is more information-seeking in nature. In Box 4 are several discontinuous functions expressed by different behaviors—for example, childhood behaviors that may have no infant precursors, such as symbol manipulation; infant behaviors that have no sequelae, such as sensory–motor accomplishments (e.g., walking); and ordinal stages, which, though dependent on prior accomplishments, mark significant departures.

Because of these complexities, it is very difficult to know what we have when we have it. For example, a Fagan finding of high correlations between infant and childhood recognition tasks would suggest Box 1 (continuous function, same behavior), unless different processes mediate the same behavior at different ages, in which case it would fit Box 3 (discontinuous processes, same behavior). The actual Fagan finding of strong correlations between two different behaviors is most easily attributed to Box 2 (continuous function, different behavior), but could fall into Box 4 (discontinuous function, different behavior). Given the constant rate of progression, the processes mediating the accomplishments are probably, but not necessarily, the same. On the right side of Figure 8.1, I have suggested that a child's rate of progress is more likely to be stable when a continuous function is manifested by the same behavior and more likely to be unstable when different skills emerge at different ages independently of one another. But this is speculation without empirical support. Until we have better-elaborated and better-validated constructs pertaining to developmental functions, the question of what is being measured will remain unanswered. Even with this knowledge, there are reasons—the extreme immaturity of infants, the restricted variability among them, and the interactional influences of genes with the social environment over time—to doubt that infant tests will ever differentiate well among children destined to be low-normal to superior.

We are likely to forget, in our admiration of the accomplishments of infants, just how undeveloped they are. Humans in contrast to other mammals, are highly neotenous (Gould, 1977); that is, they preserve infantile features over a long period. Our developmental rates are the slowest in the animal kingdom. Gould points out that if humans were born at the same state of development as other mammals, we would not be born until 21 months of gestation. Birth comes sooner because our heads, still growing at fetal rates, could not pass through the birth canal at a later age. The result is that the human infant has achieved only 23% of his or her final cranial capacity at birth, and, 3 years later, only 70%. By contrast, chimpanzees have reached 40.5% at birth and 70% by 1 year (Gould, 1977; Prechtl, 1984). In that sense, "the 1-year-old monkey is about twice as intelligent as the 1-year-old human being" (Harlow & Mears, 1979, p. 3; see also Scarr-Salapatek, 1976). The prolonged immaturity and dependency of humans insure that we are learning rather than instinctual animals, highly flexible and adaptable. I conclude from these evolutionary facts

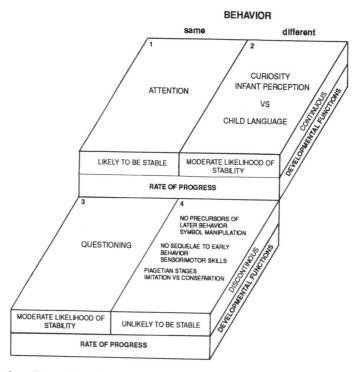

FIGURE 8.1. The effect of developmental functions and individual rate of progress on behavioral variability.

that whether or not mental development is continuous, not much occurs in the early months of life. Furthermore, the large percentage of the central nervous system that is uncommitted in early life leaves room for the strong imprint of the environment on the phenotype (Wilson, 1983).

The narrow range of variability is another infant feature working against the early detection of individual differences. That physical as well as mental growth displays the same limited range suggests this finding is not just due to poor measures. The average 1-year-old boy, for example, is 29.7 inches tall, with a standard deviation of 1.1 inches. By the time his height has doubled at age 13, the standard deviation has tripled. The same fanning out occurs with weight (Krogman, 1972). As a result, the correlations between adult height and height at various ages for males and females, respectively, are as follows: birth, .25 and .29; age 1, .65 and .70; and age 2, .79 and .74 (Tanner, Healy, Lockhart, MacKenzie, & Whitehouse, 1956). Correlations between birth and age 5 for height and weight—roughly .50—are similar to those reported in the visual recognition research (Dine et al., 1979). Here too, Fisher's (1959) argument that it is easier to predict deviancy has merit: Obesity during the preschool years is more predictive of adult status than is low or average weight (Garn & LaVelle, 1985).

Early behavioral homogeneity is probably due to evolutionary processes that have determined "creods," or developmental paths, uniformly applicable to all members of the species. These species-specific growth patterns, subject to long and strong natural selection, are the basic sensory–motor adaptive schema insuring survival. Higher-order genetic variability, apparent later in life, remains well hidden behind these early creods. Because of their antiquity and importance to survival, the behaviors are strongly canalized or resilient. That is, they are well buffered against permanent alteration and tend to correct themselves when deflections occur (Kopp & McCall, 1982; McCall, 1979, 1981a; Scarr-Salapatek, 1976; Wilson, 1979, 1983). The return to stability explains why even premature infants with serious neurological signs end up in the normal range. Wilson (1985) has found that in identical twin pairs where one twin is markedly premature (birth

weight < 1,750 grams), initial test score differences soon dissipate, so that by age 6 "the common genotype was able to reach through the inequalities of prenatal growth and bring both twins to a common level" (pp. 802–803). Recovery of high-risk infants also has been documented by Aylward et al. (1987), Escalona (1984), Kitchen et al. (1987), Siegel (1983), Sigman (1982), and Vohr and Garcia Coll (1985).

The primitive sensory–motor behaviors give way to higher forms of intelligence, McCall and Wilson believe, beginning at about 18 months or 2 years; this parallels a growth spurt in the association areas of the brain from 45% of the adult surface at age 1 to 70% at age 2 (Wilson, 1979). This is the time when infant tests begin to be predictive. McCall and colleagues have likened the epigenetic passage to a scoop. At first infants pass along the narrow and deep handle of the scoop; the steep side banks protect against the influence of environmental winds and push the children back on course if minor deviations occur. Then the scoop broadens and the sides flatten; there is increased disparity among individuals and more susceptibility to external influences.

From an infant state of limited behavior and limited variability, in which interindividual differences are small and unimportant, children grow more complex and diverse. The complexity and diversity are fueled by biology, society, and their interaction. Although it is obvious that environmental influences are cumulative, it is sometimes forgotten that gene-controlled biochemical processes are released all during an individual's lifespan and that timing is variable across individuals (McClearn, 1981). The increased cognitive complexity that accompanies maturity permits more differentiated responses by a child to the more complex circumstances he or she meets. Thus, although all 1-year-olds may be equally insensitive to the amount of cultural enrichment provided by parents and so show similar developmental levels, the child with favorable opportunities will gradually pull ahead of the less advantaged one. The changes, animal research suggests, are likely to be structural and biochemical as well as behavioral (Gottlieb, 1976; Rosenzweig, 1981; Rosenzweig & Bennett, 1978). Cumulative spiraling effects continue to enlarge differences among children, as Sameroff (1975) has convincingly pointed out, particularly when favorable gene potential encounters positive environmental influences and vice versa.

To summarize, what we seem to have in the infant are strong recuperative powers and a good deal of plasticity because of the immature nervous system, combined with a fairly uniform, highly buffered set of behavioral progressions. That is, limited variability along a deeply canalized course coexists with uncommitted higher-level potential. Gradually, behavior comes to reflect genes programmed for release later in life and continuing environmental influences; hence, with age, children with low-SES/low-IQ parents show declining scores, and those with high-SES/high-IQ parents show rising scores. The behaviors common to the species make all infants, except the truly abnormal, look alike; plasticity (or environmental responsiveness) and age-linked gene action make children look different, but not until the age of 18 months to 2 years. This is bad news for early prediction, but good news for interventionists.

CONCLUSIONS

We have come full circle. More than 50 years ago, Gesell doubted that mental development could be isolated and tabulated. His successors—Cattell, Griffiths, Bayley—tried nonetheless, but failed to develop tests that were predictively useful for the general or at-risk populations. Infant tests do not as yet predict childhood intelligence better than parent SES does, though a multiple R that includes infant scores and risk inventories is sometimes superior to social variables alone. The better predictions for children with scores under 80, though encouraging, are based on sufficiently poor data that some skepticism about the value of infant tests, especially in the first year of life, must be maintained. To those who argue that infant tests are valuable as indicators of present functional levels or as sources for planning interventions, my response is that, without predictive power, an atheoretical test containing items of no intrinsic importance (such as the Gesell and its derivatives) provides no worthwhile information.

Some critics of the old tests believe that continuity in mental development is displayed through information-processing skills, which are critical over the lifespan, rather than sensory–motor skills, which plateau early and are discontinuous with later abilities. Current measures in this genre evaluate infant visual recognition memory and response to novelty. Fagan, the most prominent investigator, reports correlations with childhood intelligence that sometimes match but do not surpass those with SES. It is too early to know whether the new procedures will be useful, and, if so, with what populations. Thus far, it is also unclear just what processes are being evaluated at which ages. The relationship between manifest behavior and underlying developmental functions over time is sufficiently complex, and admits of so many possible combinations, that even with good predictions what actually is being measured may well remain obscure. This will be a problem if we look to the tests for prescriptions. It just may be that infant testing with powerful long-term predictive validity will have to await an improved grasp of mental development and the construction of theory-based tests that are clear and direct measures of the identified dimensions. However, whether an adequate reading can be taken in the first year of life is open to doubt; certainly this will not happen soon.

The infant is extraordinarily unformed at birth and enjoys exceedingly rapid development during the first year of life. Most of this early growth has to do with behaviors common to the species that show little variation among individuals; such variation as does appear is apt to be temporary and of little future importance. Major brain areas responsible for the higher intellectual processes do not reach maturity for several years. Thus, though there may be epigenetic continuities with a partial blueprint of the future hidden within the infant, the existing behavioral repertoire prevents useful judgments. It is only after 18 months or so that genes responsible for higher-order intelligence and social influences begin to make their permanent imprint on the child.

But do we need good infant tests in the first year of life? For research purposes, it is of course desirable to understand the nature of growth as early and completely as possible. From a clinical standpoint, however, the identification of those who will be normal or better in later life is of questionable value. We need to be concerned with even a small risk of false positives—risks that are unavoidable, since, as we have reviewed, many babies perform poorly in the early months of life but then improve spontaneously. Screening tests to date have erred most heavily in erroneous diagnosis of deficits (Brooks-Gunn & Lewis, 1983; Byrne, Backman, & Smith, 1986; Frankenburg, Goldstein, & Camp, 1971; Kenny, Hebel, Sexton, & Fox, 1987). The terrible heartache and misdirected interventions resulting from iatrogenic errors cannot lightly be dismissed.

On the other hand, accurate identification of the true positives in early life—the clear ambition of Fagan's efforts (Fagan, 1988; Fagan & Montie, 1988)—should have considerable value. Early detection, in theory, allows for proper targeting of early intervention. As Fagan and associates point out, it also gives information on the sequelae of various prenatal experiences without contamination of strong environmental influences, and enables us to track changes for high-risk populations, thereby affording greater understanding of medical, genetic, and social factors.

The plasticity of the infant—a plasticity that gradually diminishes with age—puts a premium on early identification. Intervention programs that start early appear to be more effective than those starting later, but "early" in this work usually means under 3 years of age (Fowler, 1983; for other recent reviews see Lerner, 1984; MacDonald, 1986; Sigman, 1982). Children adopted before age 2 also score higher than those adopted after age 2, but selective sampling may explain the finding (MacDonald, 1986). How early is sufficient? Brain immaturity and deep behavioral canalization caution against expecting very early responsiveness to external stimulation in the first year or so. It is a difficult area of study. In the literature, "early" is usually not separated from duration, intensity, or content. Quite possibly, assuming the existence of sensitive periods, age and outcome depend on the particular behavior targeted. For example, it may be wiser to encourage exploration or curiosity rather than language in an infant. Research matching readiness to specific interventions has yet to be done. To date, we just do not know generally whether intervention is more profitable with a child

under 1 year of age than over 1 year, and, if so, in what areas.

Given all the uncertainties regarding best age of intervention, what we need are better, not necessarily earlier, tests. We may hope that the next generation of instruments will consist of items that are direct, not surrogate, measures of essential skills. Results should then give solid concurrent as well as predictive information.

Meanwhile, the practitioner should keep in mind that though existing instruments are flawed, their success in identifying the retarded is no small contribution. Furthermore, it is probable that in the individual case, when a careful evaluation is conducted that combines tests, judgments from a careful developmental history, and a trained clinical eye, the yield is greatly increased. Following children at regular intervals and observing them across settings will undoubtedly add further to improvement in understanding both current and future function. For the present, the message from the research is to use caution and multiple measures, particularly when assessing an infant or toddler above the retarded range.

RECOMMENDED READINGS

For additional information on general, specialized, and screening tests, the following sources are suggested:

Cross, L., & Johnston, S. (1977). A bibliography of assessment instruments. In L. Cross & K. Goin (Eds.), *Identifying handicapped children: A guide to case-finding, diagnosis, assessment and evaluation* (pp. 63–109). New York: Walker.

Johnson, H. W. (1979). *Preschool test descriptions: Text matrix and correlated test descriptors*. Springfield, IL: Charles C Thomas.

Johnson, O. G. (Ed.). (1984). *Tests and measurement in child development: Handbooks* (Vols. 1 & 2). San Francisco: Jossey-Bass.

Lichtenstein, R., & Ireton, H. (1984). *Preschool screening: Identifying young children with developmental and educational problems*. New York: Grune & Stratton.

Paget, K. D., & Bracken, B. A. (Eds.). (1983). *The psychoeducational assessment of preschool children*. New York: Grune & Stratton.

Peterson, N. L., & Meier, J. H. (1987). Assessment and evaluation processes. In N. L. Peterson (Ed.), *Early intervention for handicapped and at-risk children* (pp. 275–326). Denver: Love.

Southworth, L. E., Burr, R. L., & Cox, A. E. (1980). *Screening and evaluating the young child*. Springfield, IL: Charles C Thomas.

Ulrey, G., & Rogers, S. J. (1982). *Psychological assessment of handicapped infants and young children*. New York: Grune & Stratton.

REFERENCES

Als, H., Tronick, E., Lester, B. M., & Brazelton, T. B. (1979). Specific neonatal measures: The Brazelton Neonatal Behavioral Assessment Scale. In J. D. Osofsky (Ed.), *Handbook of infant development* (pp. 185–216). New York: Wiley.

Anastasi, A. (1976). *Psychological testing* (4th ed.). New York: Macmillan.

Aylward, G. P., Gustafson, N., Verhulst, S. J., & Colliver, J. A. (1987). Consistency in the diagnosis of cognitive, motor, and neurologic function over the first three years. *Journal of Pediatric Psychology, 12,* 77–98.

Ball, R. S. (1977). The Gesell Developmental Schedules: Arnold Gesell (1880–1961). *Journal of Abnormal Child Psychology, 5,* 233–239.

Bashaw, W. L. (1982). Educational testing applications of the Rasch model. In C. R. Reynolds & T. B. Gutkin (Eds.), *The handbook of school psychology* (380–392). New York: Wiley.

Bayley, N. (1933). Mental growth during the first three years. *Genetic Psychology Monographs, 14*(1).

Bayley, N. (1949). Consistency and variability in the growth of intelligence from birth to eighteen years. *Journal of Genetic Psychology, 75,* 165–196.

Bayley, N. (1955). On the growth of intelligence. *American Psychologist, 10,* 805–818.

Bayley, N. (1969). *Bayley Scales of Infant Development.* New York: Psychological Corporation.

Bayley, N. (1970). Development of mental abilities. In P. H. Mussen (Ed.), *Carmichael's manual of child psychology* (Vol. 1, 3rd ed., pp. 1163–1209). New York: Wiley.

Bayley, N., & Shaefer, E. S. (1964). Correlates of maternal and child behaviors with the development of mental ability: Data from the Berkeley Growth Study. *Monographs of the Society for Research in Child Development, 29* (6, Whole No. 97).

Bee, H. L., Barnard, K. E., Eyres, S. J., Gray, C. A., Hammond, M. A., Spietz, A. L., Snyder, C., & Clark, B. (1982). Prediction of IQ and language skill from perinatal status, child performance, family characteristics, and mother–infant interaction. *Child Development, 53,* 1134–1156.

Berg, C. A., & Sternberg, R. J. (1985). Response to novelty: Continuity versus discontinuity in the developmental course of intelligence. In H. W. Reese (Ed.), *Advances in child development and behavior* (Vol. 19, pp. 1–47). New York: Academic Press.

Bornstein, M. H. (1985). Habituation of attention as a measure of visual information processing in human infants: Summary, systematization, and synthesis. In G. Gottlieb & N. A. Krasnegor (Eds.), *Measurement of audition and vision in the first year of postnatal life: A methodological overview* (pp. 253–300). Norwood, NJ: Ablex.

Bornstein, M. H., & Sigman, M. D. (1986). Continuity in mental development from infancy. *Child Development, 57,* 251–274.

Brazelton, T. B. (1984). *Neonatal Behavioral Assessment Scale* (2nd ed.) (*Clinics in Developmental Medicine* No. 88). London: Spastics International Medical.

Broman, S. H., Nichols, P. L., & Kennedy, W. A. (1975). *Preschool IQ: Prenatal and early developmental correlates.* New York: Wiley.

Brooks-Gunn, J., & Lewis, M. (1983). Screening and diagnosing handicapped infants. *Topics in Early Childhood Special Education, 3,* 14–28.

Brooks, J., & Weinraub, M. (1976). A history of infant intelligence testing. In M. Lewis (Ed.), *Origins of intelligence: Infancy and early childhood* (pp. 19–58). New York: Plenum Press.

Byrne, J. M., Backman, J. E., & Smith, I. M. (1986). Developmental assessment: The clinical use and validity of parental report. *Journal of Pediatric Psychology, 11,* 549–559.

Cameron, J., Livson, N., & Bayley, N. (1967). Infant vocalizations and their relationship to mature intelligence. *Science, 157,* 331–333.

Capute, D. V., Goldstein, K. M., & Taub, H. B. (1981). Neonatal compromise and later psychological development: A 10-year longitudinal study. In S. L. Friedman & M. Sigman (Eds.), *Preterm birth and psychological development* (pp. 353–386). New York: Academic Press.

Caron, A. J., Caron, R. F., & Glass, P. (1983). Responsiveness to relational information as a measure of cognitive functioning in nonsuspect infants. In T. Field & A. Sostek (Eds.), *Infants born at risk: Psychological, perceptual, and cognitive processes* (pp. 181–209). New York: Grune & Stratton.

Cattell, P. (1940). *The measurement of intelligence of infants and young children.* Lancaster, PA: Science Press.

Cohen, L. (1981). Examination of habituation as a measure of aberrant infant development. In. S. L. Friedman & M. Sigman (Eds.), *Preterm birth and psychological development* (pp. 241–253). New York: Academic Press.

Cohen, S. E. (1986). The low-birthweight infant and learning disabilities. In M. Lewis (Ed.), *Learning disabilities and prenatal risk* (pp. 153–193). Urbana: University of Illinois Press.

Cohen, S. E., & Parmelee, A. H. (1983). Prediction of 5 year Stanford–Binet scores in preterm infants. *Child Development, 54,* 1242–1253.

Cohen, S. E., Parmelee, A. H., Beckwith, L., & Sigman, M. (1986). Cognitive development in preterm infants: Birth to 8 years. *Journal of Developmental and Behavioral Pediatrics, 7,* 102–110.

Cohen, S. E., Sigman, M., Parmelee, A. H., & Beckwith, L. (1982). Perinatal risk and developmental outcome in preterm infants. *Seminars in Perinatology, 6,* 334–339.

Cross, L., & Johnston, S. (1977). A bibliography of assessment instruments. In L. Cross (Ed.), *Identifying handicapped children: A guide to case-finding, screening, diagnosis, assessment and evaluation* (pp. 63–109). New York: Walker.

Dine, M. S., Gartside, P. S., Glueck, C. J., Rheines, L., Greene, G., & Khoury, P. (1979). Where do the heaviest children come from? A propective study of white children from birth to 5 years of age. *Pediatrics, 63,* 1–7.

Drillien, C. M. (1964). *The growth and development of the prematurely born infant.* Baltimore: Williams & Wilkins.

Dubose, R. F. (1977). Predictive value of infant intelligence scales with multiply handicapped children. *American Journal of Mental Deficiency, 81,* 388–390.

Elliott, C. D. (1983). *British Ability Scales: Manual 1.*

Introductory handbook. Windsor, England: National Foundation for Educational Research/Nelson.

Erickson, M. (1968). The predictive validity of the Cattell Infant Intelligence Scale for young mentally retarded children. *American Journal of Mental Deficiency, 72*, 728–733.

Escalona, S. K. (1984). Social and other environmental influences on the cognitive and personality development of low birthweight infants. *American Journal of Mental Deficiency, 88*, 508–512.

Escalona, S. K., & Moriarty, A. (1961). Prediction of school-age intelligence from infant tests. *Child Development, 32*, 597–605.

Fagan, J. F., III (1984a). The intelligent infant: Theoretical implications. *Intelligence, 8*, 1–9.

Fagan, J. F., III (1984b). The relationship of novelty preferences during infancy to later intelligence and later recognition memory. *Intelligence, 8*, 339–346.

Fagan, J. F., III (1984c). Recognition memory and intelligence. *Intelligence, 8*, 31–36.

Fagan, J. F., III (1985). A new look at infant intelligence. In D. K. Determan (Ed.), *Current topics in human intelligence: Vol. 1. Research methodology* (pp. 223–246). Norwood, NJ: Ablex.

Fagan, J. F., III (1988). Screening infants for later mental retardation: From theory to practice. In P. Vietze & H. Vaughan (Eds.), *Early identification of infants with developmental disabilities* (pp. 252–265). New York: Grune & Stratton.

Fagan, J. F., III, & McGrath, S. K. (1981). Infant recognition memory and later intelligence. *Intelligence, 5*, 121–130.

Fagan, J. F., III, & Montie, J. E. (1988). The behavioral assessment of cognitive well-being in the infant. In. J. Kavanagh (Ed.), *Understanding mental retardation: Research accomplishments and new frontiers* (pp. 207–221). Baltimore: Paul H. Brookes.

Fagan, J. F., III, & Singer, L. T. (1983). Infant recognition memory as a measure of intelligence. In L. P. Lipsett (Ed.), *Advances in infant research* (Vol. 2, pp. 31–78). Norwood, NJ: Ablex.

Field, M., Fox, N., & Radcliffe, J. (1987). *Later IQs of delayed pre-schoolers*. Unpublished manuscript.

Finkelstein, N., & Ramey, C. T. (1980). Information from birth certificates as a risk index for educational handicap. *American Journal of Mental Deficiency, 84*, 546–552.

Fisher, J. (1959). The twisted pear and the prediction of behavior. *Journal of Consulting Psychology, 23*, 400–405.

Fishler, K., Graliker, B. U., & Koch, R. (1964–65). The predictability of intelligence with Gesell Developmental Scales in mentally retarded infants and young children. *American Journal of Mental Deficiency, 69*, 515–525.

Fishman, M., & Palkes, H. (1974). The validity of psychometric testing in children with congenital malformations of the central nervous system. *Developmental Medicine and Child Neurology, 16*, 180–185.

Fowler, W. (1983). *Potentials of childhood: Vol. 1. A historical view of early experience*. Lexington, MA: Lexington Books.

Frankenburg, W. K., Goldstein, A. D., & Camp, B. W. (1971). The revised Denver Developmental Screening Test: Its accuracy as a screening instrument. *Journal of Pediatrics, 79*, 988–995.

Garn, S. M., & LaVelle, M. (1985). Two-decade follow-up of fatness in early childhood. *American Journal of Diseases of Childhood, 139*, 181–185.

Gesell, A. (1928). *Infancy and human growth*. New York: Macmillan.

Gesell, A. (1933). Maturation and the patterning of behavior. In C. Murchison (Ed.), *A handbook of child psychology* (2nd ed. pp. 209–235). Worcester, MA: Clark University Press.

Gesell, A. (1940). *The first five years of life*. New York: Harper.

Gesell, A. (1946). The ontogenesis of infant behavior. In L. Carmichael (Ed.), *Manual of child psychology* (pp. 295–331). New York: Wiley.

Gesell, A. (1973). Maturation and infant behavior pattern. In S. G. Sapir & A. C. Nitzburg (Eds.), *Children with learning problems: Readings in a developmental–interaction approach* (pp. 9–18). New York: Brunner/Mazel.

Gesell, A., & Ilg, F. L. (1943). *Infant and child in the culture of today*. New York: Harper & Row.

Gesell, A., & Thompson, H. (1938). *The psychology of early growth*. New York: Macmillan.

Goldberg, S. (1983). *Born too soon*. San Francisco: W. H. Freeman.

Goodman, J. F. (1977). Medical diagnosis and intelligence levels in young mentally retarded children. *Journal of Mental Deficiency Research, 21*, 205–211.

Goodman, J. F. (1981). The Lock Box: A measure of psychomotor competence and organized behavior in retarded and normal preschoolers. *Journal of Consulting and Clinical Psychology, 49*, 369–378.

Goodman, J. F., & Cameron, J. (1978). The meaning of IQ constancy in young retarded children. *Journal of Genetic Psychology, 132*, 109–111.

Goodman, J. F., Cecil, H. S., & Barker, W. F. (1984). Early intervention with the handicapped: Promising findings. *Developmental Medicine and Child Neurology, 26*, 47–55.

Gottlieb, G. (1976). The roles of experience in the development of behavior and the nervous system. In G. Gottlieb (Ed.), *Neural and behavioral specificity: Vol. 3. Studies on the development of behavior and the nervous system* (pp. 25–54). New York: Academic Press.

Gould, S. J. (1977). *Ontogeny and phylogeny*. Cambridge, MA: Belknap Press.

Gould, S. J. (1987). *An urchin in the storm*. New York: Norton.

Griffiths, R. (1951). *The Griffiths Mental Development Scale for Testing Babies from Birth to Two Years*. London: Child Development Research Centre.

Griffiths, R. (1954). *The abilities of babies: A study in mental measurement*. New York: McGraw-Hill.

Hallowell, D. K. (1941). Validity of mental tests for young children. *Journal of Genetic Psychology, 58*, 265–288.

Harlow, H. F., & Mears, C. (1979). *The human model: Primate perspectives*. New York: Wiley.

Hindley, C. B. (1960). The Griffiths Scale of Infant Development: Scores and predictions from 3 to 18 months. *Journal of Child Psychology and Psychiatry, 1*, 99–112.

Hindley, C. B. (1965). Stability and change in abilities up to five years: Group trends. *Journal of Child Psychology and Psychiatry, 6*, 85–99.

Hohman, L. B., & Freedheim, O. K. (1959). A study of

IQ retest evaluations on 370 cerebral palsied children. *American Journal of Physical Medicine, 38*, 180–187.

Honzik, M. P. (1976). Value and limitations of infant tests: An overview. In M. Lewis (Ed.), *Origins of intelligence* (pp. 59–95). New York: Plenum.

Hooper, S. R., Conner, R. E., & Umansky, W. (1986). The Cattell Infant Intelligence Scale: A review of the literature. *Developmental Review, 6*, 146–164.

Hunt, J. V. (1981). Predicting intellectual disorders in childhood for pre-term infants with birthweights below 1501 grams. In S. L. Friedman & M. Sigman (Eds.), *Preterm birth and psychological development* (pp. 329–352). New York: Academic Press.

Hunt, J. V., & Bayley, N. (1971). Explorations into patterns of mental development and prediction from the Bayley Scales of Infant Development. In J. P. Hill (Ed.), *Minnesota Symposia on Child Psychology* (Vol. 5, pp. 52–71). Minneapolis: University of Minnesota Press.

Illingworth, R. S., & Birch, L. B. (1959). The diagnosis of mental retardation in infancy: A follow-up study. *Archives of Disease in Childhood, 34*, 269-273.

Ireton, H., Thwing, E., & Gravem, H. (1970). Infant mental development and neurological status, family socioeconomic status, and intelligence at age four. *Child Development, 41*, 937–946.

Jewell, B. T., & Wursten, H. (1952). Observations on the psychological testing of cerebral palsied children. *American Journal of Mental Deficiency, 56*, 630–637.

Kagan, J., & Moss, H. A. (1959) Parental correlates of children's IQ and height: A cross-validation of the Berkeley Growth Study results. *Child Development, 30*, 325–332.

Kenny, T. J., Hebel, J. R., Sexton, M. J., & Fox, N. L. (1987). Developmental screening using parent report. *Journal of Developmental and Behavioral Pediatrics, 8*, 8–11.

Kitchen, W. H., Ford, G. W., Rickards, A. L., Lissenden, J. V., & Ryan, M. M. (1987). Children of birthweight <1000 grams: Changing outcome between ages 2 and 5. *Journal of Pediatrics, 110*, 283–288.

Kitchen, W. H., Ryan, M. M., Rickards, A. L., McDougall, A. B., Billson, F. A., Keir, E. H., & Nailor, F. D. (1980). A longitudinal study of very low-birthweight infants: IV. An overview of performance at eight years of age. *Developmental Medicine and Child Neurology, 22*, 172–188.

Klapper, Z. S., & Birch, H. G. (1967). A fourteen-year follow-up of cerebral palsy: Intellectual change and stability. *American Journal of Orthopsychiatry, 37*, 540–547.

Klein, N., Hack, M., Gallagher, J., & Fanaroff, A. (1985). Preschool performance of children with normal intelligence who were very low-birth-weight infants. *Pediatrics, 75*, 531–537.

Knobloch, H., & Pasamanick, B. (1960). An evaluation of the consistency and predictive value of the 40 week Gesell developmental schedule. In C. Shagass & B. Pasamanick (Eds.), *Child development and child psychiatry* (Psychiatric Research Reports No. 13, pp. 10–41). Washington, DC: American Psychiatric Association.

Knobloch, H., & Pasamanick, B. (1963). Predicting intellectual potential in infancy. *American Journal of Diseases of Children, 106*, 43–51.

Knobloch, H., & Pasamanick, B. (1967). Prediction from the assessment of neuromotor and intellectual status

in infancy. In J. Zubin & G. A. Jervis (Eds.), *Psychopathology of mental development* (pp. 387–400). New York: Grune & Stratton.

Knobloch, H., & Pasamanick, B. (1974). *Gesell and Amatruda's developmental diagnosis* (3rd ed.) New York: Harper & Row.

Kogan, K. (1957). Repeated psychometric evaluations of preschool children with cerebral palsy. *Pediatrics, 19*, 619–622.

Kopp, C. B., & McCall, R. B. (1982). Predicting later mental performance for normal, at-risk, and handicapped infants. In P. B. Baltes & O. G. Brim (Eds.), *Life-span development and behavior* (Vol. 4, pp. 33–61). New York: Academic Press.

Krakow, J. B., & Kopp, C. B. (1983). The effects of developmental delay on sustained attention in young children. *Child Development, 54*, 1143–1155.

Krogman, W. M. (1972). *Child growth*. Ann Arbor: University of Michigan Press.

Largo, R. H., Graf, S., Kundu, S., Hunziker, U., & Molinari, L. (in press). Predicting developmental outcome at school age from infant tests in normal, at risk and retarded children. *Developmental Medicine and Child Neurology*.

Lerner, R. M. (1984). *On the nature of human plasticity*. Cambridge, England: Cambridge University Press.

Lewis, M. (1969). A developmental study of information processing within the first three years of life: Response decrement to a redundant signal. *Monographs of the Society for Research in Child Development, 34*(9).

Lewis, M., & Brooks-Gunn, J. (1981). Visual attention at three months as a predictor of cognitive functioning at two years of age. *Intelligence, 5*, 131–140.

Lewis, M., & Fox, N. A. (1986). Infant assessment: Challenges for the future. In M. Lewis (Ed.), *Learning disabilities and prenatal risk* (pp. 307–331). Urbana: University of Illinois Press.

Lewis, M., & Sullivan, M. W. (1985). Infant intelligence and its assessment. In B. B. Wolman (Ed.), *Handbook of intelligence: Theories, measurements, and application* (pp. 505–599). New York: Wiley.

MacDonald, K. (1986). Early experience, relative plasticity, and cognitive development. *Journal of Applied Developmental Psychology, 7*, 101–124.

McCall, R. B. (1976). Toward an epigenetic conception of mental development in the first three years of life. In M. Lewis (Ed.), *Origins of intelligence: Infancy and early childhood* (pp. 97–122). New York: Plenum.

McCall, R. B. (1979). The development of intellectual functioning in infancy and the prediction of later IQ. In S. D. Osofsky (Ed.), *The handbook of infant development* (pp. 707–741). New York: Wiley.

McCall, R. B. (1981a). Nature–nurture and the two realms of development: A proposed integration with respect to mental development. *Child Development, 52*, 1–12.

McCall, R. B. (1981b). Early predictors of later IQ: The search continues. *Intelligence, 5*, 141–147.

McCall, R. B., Appelbaum, M. I., & Hogarty, P. S. (1973). Developmental changes in mental performance. *Monographs of the Society for Research in Child Development, 38*(3).

McCall, R. B., Eichorn, D. H., & Hogarty, P. S. (1977). Transitions in early mental development. *Monographs of the Society for Research in Child Development, 42*(3).

McCall, R. B., Hogarty, P. S., & Hurlburth, N. (1972).

Transitions in infant sensory–motor development and the prediction of childhood IQ. *American Psychologist, 27,* 728–748.

McClearn, G. E. (1981). Evolution and genetic variability. In E. S. Gollin (Ed.), *Developmental plasticity: Behavioral and biological aspects of variations in development* (pp. 3–31). New York: Academic Press.

Messer, D. J., McCarthy, M. E., McQuiston, S., Mac-Turk, R. H., Yarrow, L. J., & Vietze, P. M. (1986). Relation between mastery behavior in infancy and competition in early childhood. *Developmental Psychology, 22,* 366–372.

Miranda, S. B., & Hack, M. (1979). The predictive value of neonatal visual–perceptual behaviors. In T. M. Field (Ed.), *Infants born at risk: Behavior and development* (pp. 69–90). New York: Spectrum.

Mundy, P. C., Seibert, J. M., Hogan, A. E., & Fagan, J. F., III. (1983). Novelty responding and behavioral development in young developmentally delayed children. *Intelligence, 7,* 163–174.

Nielsen, H. H. (1971). Psychological appraisal of children with cerebral palsy: A survey of 128 re-assessed cases. *Developmental Medicine and Child Neurology, 13,* 707–720.

O'Connor, M. J., Cohen, S., & Parmelee, A. H. (1984). Infant auditory discrimination in preterm and full-term infants as a predictor of 5-year intelligence. *Developmental Psychology, 20,* 159–165.

Parmelee, A. H., Kopp, C. B., & Sigman, M. (1976). Selection of developmental assessment techniques for infants at risk. *Merrill–Palmer Quarterly, 22,* 177–199.

Prechtl, H. F. R. (1984). Continuity and change in early neural development. In H. F. R. Prechtl (Ed.), *Continuity of neural functions from prenatal to postnatal life* (pp. 1–15). London: Spastics International Medical.

Ramey, C. T., Bryant, D. A., & Suarez, T. M. (1985). Preschool compensatory education and the modification of intelligence: A critical review. In D. K. Detterman (Ed.), *Current topics in human intelligence: Research methodology* (pp. 247–296). Norwood, NJ: Ablex.

Ramey, C. T., Campbell, F. A., & Nicholson, J. E. (1973). The predictive power of the Bayley Scales of Infant Development and the Stanford–Binet Intelligence Test in a relatively constant environment. *Child Development, 44,* 790–795.

Ramey, C. T., Campbell, F. A., & Wasik, B. H. (1982). Use of standardized tests to evaluate early childhood special education programs. *Topics in Early Childhood Special Education, 1,* 51–60.

Roe, K. W., McClure, A., & Roe, A. (1983). Infant Gesell scores versus cognitive skills at age 12 years. *Journal of Genetic Psychology, 142,* 143–147.

Rose, S. A. (1981). Lags in the cognitive competence of prematurely born infants. In S. L. Friedman & M. Sigman (Eds.), *Preterm birth and psychological development* (pp. 255–269). New York: Academic Press.

Rose, D. H., Slater, A., & Perry, H. (1986). Prediction of childhood intelligence from habituation in early infancy. *Intelligence, 10,* 251–263.

Rose, S. A., & Wallace, I. F. (1985a). Visual recognition memory: A predictor of later cognitive functioning in preterms. *Child Development, 56,* 843–852.

Rose, S. A., & Wallace, I. F. (1985b). Cross-modal and intra-modal transfer as predictors of mental development in full-term and pre-term infants. *Developmental Psychology, 21,* 949–962.

Rosenblith, J. F. (1979). The Graham/Rosenblith behavioral examination for newborns: Prognostic value and procedural issues. In J. D. Osofsky (Ed.), *Handbook of infant development* (pp. 216–249). New York: Wiley.

Rosenzweig, M. R. (1981). Neural bases of intelligence and training. *Journal of Special Education, 15,* 105–123.

Rosenzweig, M. R., & Bennett, E. L. (1978). Experiential influences on brain anatomy and brain chemistry in rodents. In G. Gottlieb (Ed.), *Studies on the development of behavior and the nervous system* (Vol. 4, pp. 289–335). New York: Academic Press.

Rubin, R., & Balow, B. (1979). Measures of infant development and socioeconomic status as predictors of later intelligence and school achievement. *Developmental Psychology, 15,* 225–227.

Sameroff, A. J. (1975). Early influences on development: Fact or fancy? *Merrill–Palmer Quarterly, 21,* 267–294.

Sameroff, A. J. (Ed.). (1978). Organization and stability of newborn behavior: A commentary on the Brazelton Neonatal Behavioral Assessment Scale. *Monographs of the Society for Research in Child Development, 43* (5–6).

Sameroff, A. J. (1979). The etiology of cognitive competence: A systems perspective. In R. B. Kearsley & I. E. Sigel (Eds.), *Infants at risk: Assessment of cognitive functioning* (pp. 115–151). Hillsdale, NJ: Erlbaum.

Sameroff, A. J., Seifer, R., Barocas, R., Zax, M., & Greenspan, S. (1987). Intelligence quotient scores of 4-year-old children: Social–environmental risk factors. *Pediatrics, 79,* 343–350.

Scarr-Salapatek, S. (1976). An evolutionary perspective on infant intelligence: Species patterns and individual variations. In M. Lewis (Ed.), *Origins of intelligence: Infancy and early childhood* (pp. 165–197). New York: Plenum Press.

Sheehan, R., & Gallagher, R. J. (1984). Assessment of infants. In M. J. Hanson (Ed.), *Atypical infant development* (pp. 81–106). Baltimore: University Park Press.

Siegel, L. S. (1982). Reproductive, perinatal and environmental variables as predictors of development of preterm (<1501 grams) and fullterm children at 5 years. *Seminars in Perinatology, 6,* 274–279.

Siegel, L. S. (1983). The prediction of possible learning disabilities in preterm and full-term children. In T. Field & A. Sostek (Eds.), *Infants born at risk: Physiological, perceptual and cognitive processes* (pp. 295–315). New York: Grune & Stratton.

Sigman, M. (1982). Plasticity in development: Implications for intervention. In L. A. Bond & J. M. Joffe (Eds.), *Facilitating infant and early childhood development* (pp. 98–116). Hanover, NH: University Press of New England.

Signman, M., Cohen, S. E., & Forsythe, A. B. (1981). The relation of early infant measures to later development. In S. L. Friedman & M. Sigman (Eds.), *Preterm birth and psychological development* (pp. 313–327). New York: Academic Press.

Sigman, M., & Parmelee, A. H. (1979). Longitudinal evaluation of the preterm infant. In J. M. Field, A. M. Sostek, S. Goldberg, & H. H. Shuman (Eds.), *Infants* born at risk: Behavior and development (pp. 193–217). New York: Spectrum.

Stott, L. H., & Ball, R. S. (1965). Infant and preschool mental tests: Review and evaluation. Monographs of the Society for Research in Child Development, 30(30.

Tanner, J. M., Healy, M. J. R., Lockhart, R. D., Mac-Kenzie, J. D., & Whitehouse, R. H. (1956). Aberdeen Growth Study: I. The prediction of adult body measurements from measurements taken each year from birth to five years. Archives of Diseases of Childhood, 31, 372–381.

Taub, H. B., Goldstein, K. M., & Capute, D. V. (1977). Indices of neonatal prematurity as discriminators of development in middle childhood. Child Development, 48, 797–805.

Thomas, H. (1970). Psychological assessment instruments for use with human infants. Merrill–Palmer Quarterly, 16, 179–224.

Thurstone, L., & Thurstone, T. (1954). SRR Primary Mental Abilities (Elementary Form) (Revised Edition). Chicago: Science Research Associates.

Ulvund, S. E. (1984). Predictive validity of assessments of early cognitive competence in light of some current issues in developmental psychology. Human Development, 27, 76–83.

Uzgiris, I. C. (1977). Commentary. In R. B. McCall, D. H. Eichorn, & P. S. Hogarty (Eds.), Transitions in early mental development (pp. 95–102). Monographs of the Society for Research in Child Development, 42(3).

VanderVeer, B., & Schweid, E. (1974). Infant assessment: Stability of mental functioning in young retarded children. American Journal of Mental Deficiency, 79, 1–4.

Vietze, P. M., McCarthy, M., McQuiston, S., MacTurk, R., & Yarrow, L. J. (1983). Attention and exploratory behavior in infants with Down's syndrome. In T. Field & A. Sostek (Eds.), Infants born at risk: Physiological, perceptual and cognitive processes (pp. 251–268). New York: Grune & Stratton.

Vig, S., Kaminer, R. K., & Jedrysek, E. (1987). A later look at borderline and mildly retarded preschoolers. Developmental and Behavioral Pediatrics, 8, 12–17.

Vohr, B. R., & Garcia Coll, C. T. (1985). Neurodevelopmental and school performance of very low-birthweight infants: A seven-year longitudinal study. Pediatrics, 76, 345–350.

Werner, E. E. (1965). Review of Gesell Developmental Schedules. In O. K. Buros (Ed.), The sixth mental measurement yearbook (p. 522). Lincoln: University of Nebraska Press.

Werner, E. E., Bierman, J. M., French, F. E. (1971). The children of Kauai: A longitudinal study from the prenatal period to age ten. Honolulu: University of Hawaii Press.

Werner, E. E., Honzik, M. P., & Smith, R. S. (1968). Prediction of intelligence and achievement at 10 years from 20 months pediatric and psychologic examinations. Child Development, 39, 1063–1075.

Willerman, L., Broman, S. H., & Fiedler, M. (1970). Infant development, preschool IQ and social class. Child Development, 41, 69–77.

Willerman, L., & Fielder, M. F. (1974). Infant performance and intellectual precocity. Child Development, 45, 483–486.

Wilson, R. S. (1979). Synchronies in mental development: An epigenetic perspective. In S. Chess & A. Thomas (Eds.), Annual progress in child psychiatry and child development (pp. 144–167). New York: Brunner/Mazel.

Wilson, R. S. (1983). The Louisville Twin Study: Developmental synchronies in behavior. Child Development, 54, 298–316.

Wilson, R. S. (1985). Risk and resilience in early mental development. Developmental Psychology, 21, 795–805.

Yang, R. K. (1979). Early infant assessment: An overview. In J. D. Osofsky (Ed.), Handbook of infant development (pp. 165–184). New York: Wiley.

Yarrow, L. J., Klein, R. P., Lomanaco, S., & Morgan, G. A. (1975). Cognitive and motivational development in early childhood. In B. X. Friedlander, G. M. Sterritt, & G. E. Kirk (Eds.), Exceptional Infant (Vol. 3, pp. 491–502). New York: Brunner/Mazel.

9

Clinical Assessment of Young Children with the McCarthy Scales of Children's Abilities

RICHARD R. VALENCIA
The University of Texas at Austin

S ince the first comprehensive, integrated review of the McCarthy Scales of Children's Abilities (MSCA; McCarthy, 1972) by Kaufman (1982), research on this cognitive–motor test has expanded immensely. In his review, Kaufman referred to 61 studies published in scholarly journals and 11 doctoral dissertations. Since then, I have identified 68 new MSCA-related journal articles (a 112% increase) and 44 new dissertations (a 300% increase). In addition, there is evidence that the MSCA is used with regularity among some practitioners (Krohn, 1980) and has become one of the major tests for assessing the abilities of children (Sattler, 1982).

The primary goal of this chapter is to integrate the available body of research literature on the MSCA. As the chapter title indicates, the focus is on information that practitioners in the clinical setting should find useful in their assessment of young children. Because of the burgeoning of publications on the MSCA, the present coverage is selective rather than exhaustive. Emphasis is placed on those studies published since Kaufman's (1982) excellent review—in short, this is an update. I strive to address some of the unanswered issues Kaufman proposed for future study. Furthermore, in an attempt to control for the quality of reviewed literature, the focus here is on studies that have been subjected to peer review (i.e., journal arti-

cles). On occasion, however, reference is made to unpublished material (e.g., doctoral dissertations). (Incidentally, I have identified over 50 dissertations in which the MSCA has been examined or utilized; for a list of these dissertations, please contact me.)

In the present review, the organizational structure closely follows the format presented by Kaufman (1982) in his review. This procedure allows for a more efficient update of Kaufman's coverage of nearly a decade of research on the MSCA. For the reader who is relatively unfamiliar with the MSCA, I begin by providing a brief overview (i.e., standardization, composition, strengths, limitations). Following this, the chapter reviews four substantive areas: (1) reliability, stability, and validity; (2) early screening for learning problems; (3) clinical utility for exceptional populations; and (4) assessment of domestic ethnic minorities (also briefly covered are a number of cross-cultural studies from outside the United States). A summary and conclusions section closes the chapter.

OVERVIEW OF THE MSCA

Standardization

The MSCA, also known as the "McCarthy Scales" and the "McCarthy" (the preferred term for this review), has been favorably reviewed regarding its standardization, particularly the care taken in the comprehensive nature of the sampling (e.g., Nagle, 1979). In accordance with 1970 U.S. census data, the McCarthy was standardized on a nationwide sample stratified by age, sex, father's occupation, ethnicity, geographic region, and (informally) urban versus rural residence. The sample included 1,032 boys and girls equally divided among 10 age intervals between $2\frac{1}{2}$ and $8\frac{1}{2}$ years, the specific age range for which the McCarthy was designed. Of the total standardization group, the white and ethnic minority samples constituted 83.5% and 16.4%, respectively; these proportions were almost identical to the white and ethnic minority percentages in the 1970 U.S. population. Comprising the ethnic minority sample were 170 Asian-American, black, Philipino-American, Native American, Puerto Rican, and Mexican American children. Black children ($n = 154$) comprised 91% of the total minority sample. Only children who "could speak and understand English" were eligible for testing (McCarthy, 1972, p. 16).

Composition of the Scales

The McCarthy, an individually administered test, is comprised of 18 subtests that are grouped into six scales (see Table 9.1). (For a comprehensive overview of the McCarthy Scales and what they measure, see Kaufman and Kaufman, 1977a.) The Verbal, Perceptual–Performance, and Quantitative scales are content-oriented (respectively, they employ words; tangible, "game-like" materials; and number/numerical digits). On the other hand, the Memory and Motor scales are process-oriented; the former measures short-term memory, and the latter assesses gross and fine motor coordination. The sixth scale is the General Cognitive Index (GCI). It is an estimate of the child's global intellectual functioning and is formed by additively combining performance on the Verbal, Perceptual–Performance, and Quantitative Scales, which do not overlap in content. Despite the deliberate avoidance of the term "IQ" by Dorothea McCarthy in the formulation of the MSCA (i.e., her argument about misconceptions and unfortunate connotations of "IQ"), the GCI is considered a measure of intelligence and an IQ analogue.

Based on rational and empirical evidence, Kaufman and Kaufman (1977a) argue that the GCI is an index of intellectual functioning, and that it may be utilized interchangeably with the IQ. The mean and standard deviation for the GCI are 100 and 16, respectively. For the other five scales, the mean is set at 50, and the standard deviation is 10.

Strengths

Kaufman and Kaufman (1977a) have identified several strengths of the McCarthy. These include (1) consideration of the young child's needs and interests; (2) incorporation of aspects of developmental theory; and (3) value in psychoeducational diagnosis. Each of these strengths is briefly described here.

Because of their shorter attention spans, tendency to become distracted and bored, and greater probability of demonstrating variability in performance, preschool and kindergarten children are often difficult to test. In the development of the instrument, Dorothea McCarthy had these problems in mind. As a whole, the McCarthy contains many features that attempt to address the difficulties in testing young children. These characteristics include familiar objects (e.g., Block Building), colorful material (e.g., Pictorial Memory), manipulatives (e.g., Tapping Sequence), and game-like equipment (e.g., Arm Coordination, which contains Ball Bouncing, Beanbag Catch Game, and Beanbag Target Game).

Aside from the attractive tasks involving toy-like objects, Kaufman and Kaufman (1977a) also note the equally important rapport-establishing feature of subtest sequence. The McCarthy begins with two manipulative, imitative tasks (Block Building and Puzzle Solving); progresses to colorful pictures requiring the child to respond verbally for the first time (Pictorial Memory); and moves next to more difficult conceptual tasks (Word Knowledge and Number Questions). About halfway through the McCarthy (a time when fatigue is likely to set in), there is a built-in break in which the three gross motor tests are administered. Following this, the administration of the Draw-A-Design and Draw-A-Child subtests helps to calm the child from the motor activity expended during the gross motor tests and helps to prepare him or her for the attentional and cognitive

TABLE 9.1. Composition of the McCarthy Scales and Abilities Measured

Subtest[a]	Scale	Abilities measured[b]
1. Block Building	P, GCI	Visual–motor coordination; spatial relations
2. Puzzle Solving	P, GCI	Visual perception; nonverbal reasoning; visual–motor coordination; spatial relations
3. Pictorial Memory	V, GCI, Mem	Short–term memory (auditory and visual); early language development; attention
4. Word Knowledge	V, GCI	Verbal concept formation; early language development; verbal expression (Part II)
5. Number Questions	Q, GCI	Numerical reasoning; computational skills; number facts and concepts; concentration; verbal comprehension
6. Tapping Sequence	P, GCI, Mem	Short-term memory (primarily visual); visual–motor coordination; attention
7. Verbal Memory	V, GCI, Mem	Short-term memory (auditory); verbal comprehension; attention; concentration (Part I); verbal expression (Part II)
8. Right–Left Orientation[c]	P, GCI	Spatial relations; verbal concept formation; nonverbal reasoning; directionality
9. Leg Coordination	Mot	Gross motor coordination; balance
10. Arm Coordination	Mot	Gross motor coordination; precision of movement
11. Imitative Action	Mot	Gross motor coordination; fine motor coordination
12. Draw-A-Design	P, GCI, Mot	Fine motor coordination
13. Draw-A-Child	P, GCI, Mot	Fine motor coordination
14. Numerical Memory	Q, GCI, Mem	Short-term memory (auditory); attention; reversibility (Part II)
15. Verbal Fluency	V, GCI	Verbal concept formation; logical classification; creativity (divergent thinking); verbal expression
16. Counting and Sorting	Q, GCI	Rote counting; number concepts; numerical reasoning
17. Opposite Analogies	V, GCI	Verbal concept formation; early language development; verbal reasoning
18. Conceptual Grouping	P, GCI	Logical classification; nonverbal reasoning; verbal concept formation

Note. V, Verbal scale; PP, Perceptual–Performance scale; Q, Quantitative scale; GCI, General Cognitive Index; Mem, Memory scale; Mot, Motor scale.

[a]Subtests are listed in order of administration.

[b]As discussed by Kaufman and Kaufman (1977a).

[c]Administered only to children 5 years of age and above.

demands of the Numerical Memory and Verbal Fluency subtests. Toward the end of the McCarthy administration—a time when the effects of fatigue are most likely to occur—two of three subtests (Counting and Sorting, and Conceptual Grouping) utilize colorful manipulative cubes. In addition, the three subtests only require a maximum of one word per item for the child's vocalizing of answers.

Kaufman and Kaufman (1977a) point out that in addition to the attractiveness of materials and a carefully structured subtest se-

quence, the McCarthy also contains other aspects that help to optimize the test performance of young children. For example, (1) extra trials are provided, at times, for children who give incorrect responses the first time (e.g., Block Building); and (2) there are many multipoint items. Thus, children are rewarded for approximately correct responses (e.g., Word Knowledge; Part II: Oral Vocabulary).

In summary, the McCarthy is a very well-conceived test to meet the needs and interests of young children. Materials, sequencing, and scoring are such that the McCarthy is an excellent test for establishing and maintaining rapport, building confidence, making the testing experience enjoyable, and keeping children engaged—all features that help to optimize performance for children, who typically show considerable variability in testing situations. (There is some suggestive empirical evidence that the McCarthy does measure relatively stable performance in young children. These findings on test–retest stability are discussed in the "Reliability, Stability, and Validity" section). On a final note, there is some empirical evidence that the McCarthy is an excellent instrument for establishing and maintaining the interest of children. Krohn (1980), in a survey of over 100 practitioners who had administered the McCarthy in their work, asked the respondents to evaluate the instrument in comparison with three other major cognitive tests: the Stanford–Binet (Terman & Merrill, 1973), the Wechsler Preschool and Primary Scale of Intelligence (WPPSI; Wechsler, 1967), and the Wechsler Intelligence Scale for Children—Revised (WISC-R; Wechsler, 1974). There were 10 categorical ratings. On the evaluation item concerned with "interest of child," the McCarthy received the highest ranking (significantly) of the four tests.

The second area of strength discussed by Kaufman and Kaufman (1977a) involves the incorporation of developmental theory into the McCarthy. Although the content and scale groupings were primarily derived from Dorothea McCarthy's vast teaching, clinical, and training experience in testing and developmental psychology (McCarthy, 1972, p. 2), developmental theory is clearly present. Kaufman and Kaufman refer to the influence of Piaget and Gesell. Regarding Piaget, most of the cognitive tasks (e.g., Conceptual Grouping; Counting and Sorting) reflect many of the abilities seen in the preoperational and concrete operational child (e.g., organizing and labeling the environment; applying basic concepts; demonstrating knowledge of spatial objects). The inclusion of gross motor tasks and the drawing tests is in accordance with Gesell's theorizing and practical work in child development, clinical diagnosis, and school readiness measures. Suffice it to say that

although the McCarthy was largely developed with intuitive and functional considerations in mind (and some factor analyses), prominent developmental theory has indeed shaped it.

A third major strength of the McCarthy, according to Kaufman and Kaufman (1977a), is its value as a psychoeducational diagnostic tool. Kaufman and Kaufman describe a number of advantages the McCarthy has over conventional tests (e.g., the Stanford–Binet). Examples of these strengths are: (1) applicability to the assessment of children with learning disabilities; (2) inclusion of the Motor scale, the drawing tests, and assessment of laterality; (3) good short-term memory tasks and other school-related tasks that are predictive of early schooling performance and lend themselves to educational interpretation and remediation; and (4) applicability of the McCarthy for the distractible or emotionally labile child. Taken together, the advantages described here can best be summarized in this way: The McCarthy is a multiscore instrument that provides broad exposure to cognitive, perceptual, and motor functioning, thus reducing the number of separate tests a clinician may need for psychoeducational diagnosis and intervention to be effective. In the section on "Clinical Utility for Exceptional Populations," I return to the subject of the value of the McCarthy in psychoeducational diagnosis and examine, in light of the available literature, Kaufman and Kaufman's contentions of diagnostic strengths.

Weaknesses

Several limitations of the McCarthy are discussed by Kaufman and Kaufman (1977a). These areas of concern are (1) administrative issues, (2) the lack of items dealing with social comprehension and judgment, (3) problems in the testing of school-age children, and (4) difficulties with scale interpretation.

It is interesting to note that Kaufman and Kaufman's discussion of administrative limitations (i.e., considerable effort required to learn to administer and score the McCarthy properly; considerable amount of clerical work by the examiner to transform raw scores to index scores (i.e., standard scores) on the six scales; much examiner skill and experience involved) are consistent with criticisms raised by some reviewers (e.g., Davis, 1974). In addition, in the previously mentioned opinion-based survey research on the McCarthy, Krohn (1980) found that clinicians rated the McCarthy lowest, or next to the lowest, in the administrative-type categories (e.g., "ease in scoring," "ease in manipulation of materials," "time required to administer"). This finding needs to be qualified, however, as Krohn notes that administrative criticisms of the McCarthy decreased as clinician familiarity (measured by frequency of administrations) increased. Thus, it is likely that administrative criticisms of the McCarthy are confounded with examiner familiarity (i.e., experience testing with the McCarthy)—an apparent, solvable problem. Those practitioners who wish to gain some highly valuable tips on administration and scoring problems of the McCarthy's 18 subtests are referred to the excellent treatment of this topic in Kaufman and Kaufman's (1977a) *Clinical Evaluation of Young Children with the McCarthy Scales*.

The McCarthy is devoid of items measuring social comprehension and judgment. Although it is not explicitly stated, the reason why such tasks were excluded during the McCarthy's development was that Dorothea McCarthy was trying to avoid the alleged negative impact of culture-loaded items on ethnic minority group performance (McCarthy, 1972). Kaufman and Kaufman (1977a) argue, however, that the absence of "social intelligence" tasks (e.g., common-sense judgment; ability to evaluate problem situations that are relatively familiar) do not permit the clinician to gain a full picture of any child's functioning. To rectify this, Kaufman and Kaufman suggest the administration of supplementary sociocultural tasks (e.g., the WPPSI or WISC-R Information and Comprehension subtests). This may be a sound suggestion, but would the administration of such culture-bound questions penalize minority children? Although the evidence is quite meager, there is some research indicating that it would not. For example, Shellenberger and Lachterman (1979) found that bilingual Puerto Rican children (aged 5–8½ years) scored no lower on the highly culture-loaded WPPSI and WISC-R Information and Comprehension subtests than they did on the less culture-loaded McCarthy Verbal scale (although both McCarthy Verbal scale

and Wechsler subtest mean performance was quite depressed; this was probably related to some lack of facility in English).

A third, and perhaps the major, weakness of the McCarthy pertains to problems in testing school-age children (i.e., above 6½ years of age). It is a bit ironic, as Kaufman and Kaufman (1977a) point out, that the same features that make the McCarthy a very good instrument for younger children (e.g., test sequence, item examples) are not necessary for most older children and fail to contribute to the overall effective measurement of their abilities. Pertinent to the testing of older children are the previously discussed problems of lack of social intelligence items, lack of verbal reasoning tasks, few items tapping abstract problem solving, lack of a sufficient ceiling on many of the subtests, and an absence of continuity in testing (as the McCarthy stops abruptly at age 8½ years). Notwithstanding some exceptions (e.g., testing of suspected mentally retarded children who would benefit from the rapport-related characteristics of the McCarthy), Kaufman and Kaufman (1977a) recommend that "the McCarthy should usually not be the featured ability test in a battery for older children. . . . the examiner may prefer to give a WISC-R or Stanford–Binet to children above 6½ years of age, and use some McCarthy tasks for supplementary assessment" (p. 17). This recommendation against preferential use of the McCarthy for children older than 6 or 6½ years is also underscored in Kaufman's later (1982) integrated review of nearly a decade of research on the McCarthy.

The final cluster of McCarthy limitations discussed by Kaufman and Kaufman (1977a) consists of problems related to scale interpretations. These interpretive difficulties pertain to (1) low internal-consistency reliability of several of the indices; (2) overlap in content of several scales; (3) limited range of GCIs and scale indices when testing extremely retarded or highly gifted children; (4) inadequate floor when testing 2½ year olds; and (5) the issue of subtests that are spoiled or cannot be administered (the McCarthy has no alternative subtests, as does the WPPSI, in the event of spoilage). After discussing each of these problems, Kaufman and Kaufman offer helpful, corrective suggestions to address such interpretive difficulties. For example, in the case of limitations pertaining to reliability and scale overlap, Kaufman and Kaufman devote an entire chapter to describing reasonable proposals for interpreting a child's index profile. Another example of a proposed solution is concerned with the issue of test spoilage. A full chapter is presented that discusses, in detail, a very useful technique for prorating spoiled or unadministered subtests. The proposed method, which can be used for normal and exceptional populations (e.g., the blind, the deaf), is more complex than the techniques offered by the Stanford–Binet or Wechsler tests, but it appears objective and psychometrically appropriate. The Kaufman and Kaufman prorating technique also has some possibile utility in the area of nonbiased assessment of minority populations (see Valencia & Rankin, 1985).

RELIABILITY, STABILITY, AND VALIDITY

In this section I discuss the psychometric properties of the McCarthy, a subject of great importance to clinicians. The main purpose of this section is to provide researchers with an updated overview of psychometric research on the McCarthy. The focus here is on empirical studies completed since the Kaufman (1982) McCarthy review. Investigations of reliability, test–retest stability, and validity are examined (construct, concurrent, and predictive validity; studies of content validity are discussed in the section on "Ethnic Minority Assessment"). Several tables are presented for ease of reporting. Those studies discussed in Kaufman (1982) and the newer investigations (i.e., post-Kaufman [1982] studies) are identified in the tables.

Reliability

Based on the internal-consistency reliability estimates provided by McCarthy (1972) from the normative groups, previous reviewers have commented on the very good reliability of the McCarthy (e.g., Kaufman & Kaufman, 1977b; Nagle, 1979; Sattler, 1978).

In addition to the reliability estimates described by McCarthy (1972), four other reliability studies exist (Laosa, 1984; Mishra & Powers, 1984; Shellenberger, 1982; Valen-

cia & Rankin, 1983). It is quite interesting that in each of these latter reliability investigations (all with normal children), Hispanic children comprised the main population of study. The reliability coefficients of the six scales of the McCarthy for all of the studies listed above are shown in Table 9.2.

An appropriate place to begin discussion of the McCarthy's reliability is with the data presented by McCarthy (1972) for the standardization sample. Overall, the McCarthy demonstrates reliability coefficients that are quite high (if $.80\ r_{xx}$ is used as an arbitrary criterion for acceptability), suggesting accuracy that ranges in general from reasonably good to excellent. Importantly, the global estimate of intellectual functioning—the GCI—has very high reliability (mean r_{xx} of .93 for the total normative group). This GCI reliability of .93 compares quite favorably with that of other prominent intelligence tests. For example, based on the standardization sample, the overall average reliability for the Full Scale IQ (FSIQ) for the WPPSI is .96 (Wechsler, 1967). For the 10 standardization age groups, the GCI reliability coefficients range from a low of .90 ($6\frac{1}{2}$ years) to a high of .96 ($3\frac{1}{2}$ years). The average standard error of measurement *(SEM)* is 4.1 for the GCI for the 10 normative groups.

Overall, the reliability estimates derived from the standardization sample for the other scales are satisfactory. The average coefficients range from .79 (Memory, Motor) to .88 (Verbal). As Kaufman and Kaufman (1977a) point out, some of the reliabilities at certain age levels have unacceptable levels (i.e., they are below the criterion of .80 and above for satisfactory reliability). Of the 60 reliability coefficients presented by McCarthy (1972) for the 10 age groups in the normative sample, 15 (25%) are below .80 (3 in Perceptual–Performance, 3 in Quantitative, 5 in Memory, and 4 in Motor). Particularly troublesome is the Motor scale. The only reliability coefficients less than .70 are seen in the Motor scale at ages $6\frac{1}{2}$ and $8\frac{1}{2}$ (it is important to note that for the $7\frac{1}{2}$-year-old group, the reliability is .75). McCarthy (1972) suggests that lower reliabilities for older children are observed in the Motor scale because the Motor tasks were designed primarily for younger children. It is of interest that two of the three reliability coefficients below .80 in the Perceptual–Performance scale are at the

TABLE 9.2. Investigations of Reliability (r_{xx}) of the McCarthy Scales

Author(s)	Sample	n	Age range (in years and months)	r_{xx} V	PP	Q	GCI	Mem	Mot
*McCarthy (1972)[a]	Standardization	1,032	2 years, 6 months to 8 years, 6 months	.88	.84	.81	.93	.79	.79
*Shellenberger (1982)	Puerto Rican[b]	100	5 years, 10 months to 8 years, 7 months	.79	.84	—	.94	.63	.64
Valencia & Rankin (1983)	Mexican-American English-speaking	154 }	4 years, 3 months to 5 years, 9 months	—	—	—	.86	—	—
	Spanish-speaking	176 }		—	—	—	.82	—	—
Laosa (1984)	Mexican-American[c]	79	2 years, 3 months to 2 years, 10 months	.94	.73	.82	—	.94	.60
	White	87	2 years, 3 months to 2 years, 6 months	.93	.84	.79	—	.92	.77
Mishra & Powers (1984)	Mexican-American[d]	58	5 years, 6 months to 8 years, 6 months	.89	.87	.84	—	.84	.84

Note. Studies discussed and referenced in Kaufman (1982) are marked with an asterisk. V, Verbal scale; PP, Perceptual–Performance scale; Q, Quantitative scale; GCI, General Cognitive Index; Mem, Memory scale; Mot, Motor scale. Dashes under the r_{xx} columns indicate unavailable data.

[a] Reliability coefficients are weighted means (computed by me) for the 10 age groups from the normative sample.

[b] Spanish-speaking sample.

[c] Mexican-American children were administered the McCarthy in their preferred language—English, Spanish, or mixed. Reliability coefficients are for the aggregated sample.

[d] English-speaking sample.

215

older age levels (i.e., $6\frac{1}{2}$ and $8\frac{1}{2}$ years). This is not surprising in the context of the lower reliabilities for older children seen in the Motor scale, as the intercorrelation between the Perceptual–Performance and Motor scales is relatively high ($r = .70$) for the standardization group (McCarthy, 1972, p. 39).

Concerning the problem of questionable reliability of *some* scales for *some* age levels, Kaufman and Kaufman (1977a) offer a helpful technique for clinicians who wish to interpret a child's index profile. Basically, the strategy takes into account the reliability of each scale. Kaufman and Kaufman state that clinicians who adhere to their suggested technique "will avoid overinterpretation of *any* Scale Index—whether it is one that merits cautious treatment, or one that is extremely reliable" (p. 20).

The remaining reliability investigations of the McCarthy are informative (see Table 9.2). Since these studies deal primarily with minority populations, discussion is deferred until the section on "Ethnic Minority Assessment." It is useful, however, to state a few pertinent points at this time. First, the overall picture that emerges from these reliability studies is impressive, in that the findings generally reflect the analyses provided by McCarthy (1972) with the standardization sample—in short, some confirming evidence of patterns. Note, for example, the reliability of .94 for the GCI in Shellenberger (1982). The reliability coefficients of .86 and .82 for the GCI reported in Valencia and Rankin (1983) are lower than reported in other studies, but they are still satisfactory. The observed reliabilities in Valencia and Rankin (1983) are probably lower because of a conservative technique used to estimate reliability (see that study for a discussion). Second, the reliability coefficients reported by Laosa (1984) are particularly informative, in that the sample included $2\frac{1}{2}$-year-old children (an age group usually underinvestigated in McCarthy research). The observed reliabilities are generally of high magnitudes (except Verbal for Mexican American children and Motor for both groups). Third, the lower reliabilities in the Motor scale seen in Shellenberger (1982) and Laosa (1984) are suggestive of the lower reliability estimates reported for the Motor scale by McCarthy (1972). The .84 reliability for the Motor scale

seen in Mishra and Powers (1984), however, is higher than that observed in Shellenberger and Laosa. It is probable that differences in reliability estimates in the Motor scale (and other scales) in the three latter studies are related to variations in sampling (e.g., age, language status).

In conclusion, the available research on the McCarthy suggests very good, acceptable reliability (particularly good accuracy is seen in the GCI and Verbal scale). The results of the previous studies demonstrate that the McCarthy, notwithstanding some problematic areas, is internally consistent and provides quite accurate indicators of children's abilities. As McCarthy (1972) and Nagle (1979) point out, this is especially impressive in light of the appreciable variation typically observed in test behaviors of young children.

Stability

As Jensen (1980) notes, there is some confusion in the measurement community between reliability and stability. "Reliability" refers to the degree to which items are intracorrelated and estimated on a particular test at a particular point in time. "Stability" refers to test score consistency over time (i.e., an observed correlation between scores derived from the same test administered to the same subjects on two occasions over time). Jensen argues that the property of test stability should not be confused with reliability, and that the outmoded term "test–retest reliability" should be avoided when one is really referring to stability. In this section, I use the term "stability" as defined above.

As is the case with reliability, the stability of a particular instrument is also very important (particularly in tests that are geared for the assessment of young children, whom as we previously underscored, are characterized by fluctuation in test performance). A test should be stable, and the stability index of the test should be available for clinicians to examine. How stable is the McCarthy?

In addition to the stability investigation by McCarthy (1972) using the standardization sample, there are seven other studies of the McCarthy's stability. The available investigations are listed in Table 9.3. These studies include relatively short and long test–retest intervals, various ethnic groups, and normal and mentally retarded samples. A

TABLE 9.3. Investigations of Stability (r_{12}) of the McCarthy Scales

Author(s)	Sample	n	Age range (in years and months)[a]	Test–retest interval (M)	r_{12}					
					V	PP	Q	GCI	Mem	Mot
*McCarthy (1972)[b]	Standardization White "Nonwhite"	104 } 21 }	3 years, 0 months to 8 years, 6 months	1 month	.85	.79	.88	.90	.81	.74
*Davis & Slettedahl (1976)	Mixed ethnicity[c]	43	5 years, 7 months to 6 years, 7 months[d]	12.3 months	.76	.62	.75	.85	.73	.33
*Davis (n.d.)	Mixed ethnicity[c]	20	5 years, 7 months to 8 years, 4 months	2.0 years (approx.)	.76	.84	.77	.85	.40	.65
*Bryant & Roffe (1978)[e]	NA	38	5 years, 6 months to 5 years, 11 months	24 days	.76	.85	.83	.88	—	.76
*Lake (1979)	African[f]	21	NA	8.5 days (approx.)	—	—	—	.86	—	—
*Ernhart & Landa (1980)	Black	27	4 years, 6 months to 8 years, 5 months	4.0 years	.29	.45	.47	.53	.43	.76
*Brooks (1981)	Black (retarded)	20	5 years, 7 months to 6 years, 4 months	1 month	.76	.69	.74	.86	.85	.77
Valencia (1983a, 1985)[e,g]	Mexican-American English-speaking Spanish-speaking	42 } 42 }	3 years, 11 months to 7 years, 4 months	11.3 months	.90 .89	.91 .85	.92 .88	.86 .79	.86 .91	— —

Note. Studies discussed and referenced in Kaufman (1982) are marked with an asterisk. V, Verbal scale; PP, Perceptual–Performance scale; Q, Quantitative scale; GCI, General Cognitive Index; Mem, Memory scale; Mot, Motor scale. Dashes indicate unavailable data. NA, not available.

[a]Minimum and maximum cover test–retest interval.

[b]Stability coefficients are weighted means for three age groups, computed using Fisher's r-to-z transformation.

[c]Sample included white and Mexican-American children; r_{12} values are for aggregated sample.

[d]Based on mean ages at test and retest.

[e]Stability coefficients corrected for range restriction.

[f]Children were from Zimbabwe/Rhodesia; Shona translation of McCarthy used.

[g]Valencia (1985) is a computational erratum to Valencia (1983a).

217

particularly striking finding is the consistently high stability of the GCI across the eight studies, with the exception of Ernhart and Landa's (1980) 4-year test–retest investigation; it is not surprising to observe such low stability coefficients in that study, as the magnitude of the coefficient is a function of the time span between measurements (see Jensen, 1980). If one were also to exclude the Spanish-speaking group (Valencia, 1983a, 1985) from the analysis (see "Ethnic Minority Assessment" section for a discussion of the rationale for my colleagues' and my inclusion of Spanish-speaking children in McCarthy psychometric research), the GCI stability coefficients for the remaining seven studies range from .85 to .90. Considering the diverse nature of these investigations, this is an impressive comment on the stability of the GCI. Next, I turn to a brief discussion of several of the stability studies.

McCarthy (1972), using composite raw scores, retested three different age groups ($3-3\frac{1}{2}$, $5-5\frac{1}{2}$, and $7\frac{1}{2}-8\frac{1}{2}$ years) from the normative sample. The time lapse was about 1 month. Generally speaking, the estimates of stability presented in Table 9.3 (weighted means for the three age groups) reflect a high degree of stability. The 18 stability coefficients (six scales × three age groups) reported by McCarthy range from .69 to .91, with two-thirds of the coefficients above .80. The lowest coefficient was .69 for the Motor scale at the $7\frac{1}{2}-8\frac{1}{2}$ age level.

The Davis and Slettedahl (1976) and Davis (n.d.) studies are interesting in two ways. First, after 1- and even 2-year test–retest intervals, the GCI and the Verbal and Quantitative scales remained relatively stable for the samples studied. Second, the Motor scale indicated the lowest stability, giving some credence to McCarthy's (1972) findings. Bryant and Roffe (1978) retested 38 boys and girls on the McCarthy after a mean interval of about 3 weeks. Although the ethnicity of the children tested was not specified, it is assumed they were white. The observed stability coefficient for the GCI was .88, and the study, in general, supported the findings reported by McCarthy.

The investigations by Brooks (1981) and Valencia (1983a, 1985) are informative, as they provide McCarthy stability data on blacks and Mexican American samples, respectively. In addition, the Brooks study is the only available inquiry into the stability of the McCarthy for a mentally retarded sample. These investigations are discussed later in "Ethnic Minority Assessment." Suffice it to say, however, that these two studies provide evidence for the stability of the McCarthy for the groups investigated.

Overall, the stability coefficients observed in Table 9.3 uphold the conclusions drawn by McCarthy (1972) and the various subsequent investigators that the McCarthy is a relatively stable testing instrument. Thus, clinicians can have some sense of confidence that the McCarthy measures children's abilities with relative accuracy over time.

Construct Validity

In the McCarthy review by Kaufman (1982), four construct validity studies were discussed (see Table 9.4). Since that review, seven additional studies have been identified. As seen in Table 9.4, these 11 investigations, taken together, are quite diverse in the populations studied (standardization, normal, and referred; white, black, Mexican American, and cross-cultural; male and female).

It is well beyond the scope of this chapter to discuss in any detail the complexities and findings of factor-analytic research on the McCarthy. For more in-depth discussion, the reader is referred to Kaufman (1982) for an informative summary of positive and negative findings of earlier factor-analytic results on the McCarthy (with normal children). The reader should also see Kaufman and Kaufman (1977a) for a thorough, readable discussion of the McCarthy's construct validity in light of three aspects: (1) Guilford's (1967) Structure-of-Intellect Model; (2) factor-analytic findings; and (3) developmental trends. Furthermore, Stucky (1984) provides a very good tabular summary of seven construct validity studies on the McCarthy (i.e., sample information; factor-analytic procedures; factor composition and interpretation). I provide here only a brief discussion of the most salient points culled from the available research on construct validity of the McCarthy.

1. Although it is frequently mentioned that Dorothea McCarthy developed the McCarthy primarily through intuitive and functional considerations (e.g., Teeter, 1984), factor-analytic research (i.e., Kaufman

& Hollenbeck, 1973) did aid McCarthy in her predominantly "armchair" approach to selecting the scales. In addition, subsequent earlier factor-analytic studies (Kaufman, 1975; Kaufman & DiCuio, 1975) isolated factors corresponding closely to the scales of the McCarthy, providing empirical evidence and general support for McCarthy's choice and organization of the McCarthy subtests (Nagle, 1979). In short, the earlier work offers good evidence for construct validity of the McCarthy.

2. Table 9.4 reports an apparent inconsistency. In some studies, a General Cognitive factor has emerged (e.g., Kaufman & Hollenbeck, 1973; Keith & Bolen, 1980); in others, it has not emerged (e.g., Kaufman & DiCuio, 1975; Teeter, 1984); and in still others it has both emerged and not emerged (e.g., Kaufman, 1975). Clinicians, however, should not be alarmed. As noted by Naglieri, Kaufman, and Harrison (1981), the failure of a General Cognitive factor to emerge from factor analysis need not be taken as no support for the existence of the factor. The point made by Naglieri et al. is that in principal factor analyses, global factors typically fail to emerge (e.g., Cohen's [1959] analysis of the Wechsler). Support for the Wechsler FSIQ, however, is often provided by second-order analysis or by scrutinizing loadings on the large unrotated first factor (as done in Naglieri et al. 1981, for the McCarthy).

3. Cross-validation and construct validity of the factor structure derived from Kaufman's (1975) factor analyses of the McCarthy standardization group are available with normal populations (e.g., Mishra, 1981; Teeter, 1984; Trueman, Lynch, & Branthwaite, 1984). One exception, however, is Watkins and Wiebe (1980), who investigated (via regression analysis) the construct validity of the McCarthy with 240 white preschoolers. The authors concluded that the GCI appears to be the only valid interpretable scale of the McCarthy, and that diagnostic use of the other scales should not be practiced. The Watkins and Wiebe investigation should be interpreted with extreme caution, however, as Branthwaite and Trueman (1985) criticize the study on grounds of the data base (i.e., inappropriate calculations of raw scores) and data analysis (i.e., problems in the regression procedures).

4. A most striking and interesting feature of the construct validity research on the McCarthy is the nearly complete absence of an identifiable Quantitative factor, particularly for normal children younger than 5 years of age or referred children who score about 1 standard deviation below the norm on the GCI. This pattern is seen in the standardization data (Kaufman & Hollenbeck, 1973; Kaufman, 1975), cross-validation studies (Teeter, 1984), studies of ethnic minority groups (Kaufman & DiCuio, 1975; Mishra, 1981), cross-cultural investivations (British; Trueman et al., 1984), referred populations (Keith & Bolen, 1980; Naglieri et al., 1981), and studies of sex differences (Purvis & Bolen, 1984). This major, consistent finding has led some researchers to conclude, quite appropriately, that the Quantitative index should probably be ignored for children with GCIs below 84 (1 standard deviation below the norm) or for children whose chronological age is less than 5 years (Naglieri et al., 1981). Certainly, this is a valuable recommendation for practitioners.

5. There are data suggesting that the McCarthy also has good construct validity for referred populations (Keith & Bolen, 1980; Naglieri et al., 1981). In brief, these two studies taken together provide some construct validity support for the GCI and the Verbal, Perceptual–Performance, and Motor scales, as well as limited support for the Memory scale (Kaufman, 1982). Some caution, nevertheless, should be used in interpreting these two investigations. Possible interpretative and generalizability problems may be related to (a) the wide range of schooling problems (e.g., educable mental retardation, learning disabilities, behavior problems); (b) level of intellectual functioning (mean GCIs were 88.1 and 61.6 in Naglieri et al. 1981, and Keith & Bolen, 1980, respectively; and (c) ethnicity (which may have had a confounding effect, in that blacks and whites were aggregated for the analyses).

6. Although there are some differences in how factors emerged and loaded (e.g., an extra factor for the black sample as compared to the white sample in Kaufman & DiCuio, 1975; variations in loading levels across the factors for Mexican Americans and whites in Mishra, 1981), there is suggestive evidence that the McCarthy possesses similar construct validity for blacks and whites (Kaufman

TABLE 9.4. Investigations of Construct Validity of the McCarthy Scales

Author(s)	Sample	n	Age range (in years and months)	Factors								
				V	Mot	GC	Mem	PP	D	SM	R	Q
*Kaufman & Hollenbeck (1973)	Standardization (partial)	99	3 years, 0 months to 3 years, 6 months	X	X	X	X	X				
		132	5 years, 0 months to 5 years, 6 months		X	X	X					X
		142	7 years, 0 months to 7 years, 6 months	X	X	X	X	X				
*Kaufman (1975)	Standardization	102	2 years, 6 months	X	X	X	X					
		204	3 years, 0 months to 3 years, 6 months	X	X	X	X	X	X			
		206	4 years, 0 months to 4 years, 6 months	X	X	X	X	X	X	X		
		206	5 years, 0 months to 5 years, 6 months	X[a]	X	X[a]	X	X	X			
		314	6 years, 6 months to 8 years, 6 months	X[a]	X	X[a]	X	X			X	X
*Kaufman & DiCuio (1975)	Standardization (partial)											
	Black	124 }	3 years, 0 months to 7 years, 6 months	X	X			X				
	White	688 }		X	X			X				
*Keith & Bolen (1980)[b]	Mixed ethnicity[c] (school problems)	300	6 years, 0 months to 8 years, 6 months	X	X	X	X					
Wiebe & Watkins (1980)	White (total)	200 }	2 years, 6 months to 5 years, 0 months	X[d]		X						
	Male	100 }		X[d]		X	X[g]	X[e]				
	Female	100 }		X[f]	X	X						

Study	Group	n	Age range						
Mishra (1981)	Mexican-American White	126 } 186 }	5 years, 6 months to 7 years, 6 months	X X	X X			X X	
*Naglieri, Kaufman, & Harrison (1981)	Mixed ethnicity[h] (low GCIs)	77	6 years, 0 months to 8 years, 6 months	X	X		X	X	
Purvis & Bolen (1984)[i]	Mixed ethnicity[j] (referred) Males Females	301 } 177 }	6 years, 0 months to 8 years, 6 months	X X	X		X	X	X
Stucky (1984)	Mexican (standardization)	575	2 years, 6 months to 8 years, 6 months	(see text, "Ethnic Minority Assessment")					X[m]
Teeter (1984)	Mixed ethnicity[k] (M GCI = 115)	105	4 years, 11 months to 6 years, 7 months	X[e]	X		X	X	
Trueman, Lynch, & Braithwaite (1984)	British	89	4 years, 3 months (M)	X[n]	X	X	X	X	

Note. Studies discussed and referenced in Kaufman (1982) are marked with an asterisk. V, Verbal; Mot, Motor; GC, General Cognitive; Mem, Memory; PP, Perceptual–Performance; D, Drawing; SM, Semantic Memory; R, Reasoning; Q, Quantitative. The table is adapted from *A Factorial Study of the McCarthy Scales: A Cross-Cultural Comparison* by P. E. Stucky (1984), unpublished doctoral dissertation, George Peabody College for Teachers, Vanderbilt University. Adapted by permission of the author.

[a] Actual label was General Cognitive.
[b] A fourth factor, labeled Visual Performance, was identified; it accounted for 9% of the variance and was considered by authors to have little psychological meaning.
[c] Blacks (n = 159) and whites (n = 141).
[d] Labeled Abstract Verbal Reasoning.
[e] Labeled Nonverbal Cognition.
[f] Labeled Motor Imitation.
[g] Labeled Remote Verbal Reasoning.
[h] Blacks (n = 42) and whites (n = 35).
[i] Four other factors identified, but authors commented only on those deemed meaningful.
[j] Blacks (n = 169) and whites (n = 132.)
[k] "Majority of children were White"; others unspecified.
[l] Labeled Verbal Comprehension.
[m] Labeled Quantitative Reasoning.

& DiCuio, 1975) and Mexican Americans and whites (Mishra, 1981). One other study (Brooks, 1981) investigated the construct validity of the McCarthy in a black, educable mentally retarded sample; according to Brooks, however, the factor analysis was invalid because of an unacceptable ratio of subjects to variables. Further discussion of Kaufman and DiCuio (1975) and Mishra (1981) can be found in the "Ethnic Minority Assessment" section.

7. Two studies exist that have investigated the factor structure of the McCarthy for males and females. Yet it is difficult to get a good sense of whether construct validity is similar or varies across sex. Purvis and Bolen (1984), whose sample was an ethnically mixed, referred group, identified three psychologically meaningful factors for males (Verbal, Perceptual–Performance, Motor) and three for females (General Cognitive, Verbal, Memory). The authors' major conclusion was that the results indicate a high degree of similarity between the two groups' first two factors and the General Cognitive/Verbal factors identified in the standardization analysis by Kaufman (1975). Purvis and Bolen's investigation is informative; however, the study's generalizations need to be made with caution, given that the sample was a referred group, the analyses were done by aggregating black and white children, and the mean GCI of the boys was higher ($M = 83.9$) than that of the girls ($M = 78.8$).

Wiebe and Watkins (1980), studying 200 white, normal preschoolers, concluded that the major sex differences in factor structure were related to "verbal versus nonverbal parameters" and that "should one or more of the MSCA scales be sex-specific, as indicated in these data, individual diagnosis based upon a profile of MSCA score relationships should be based upon separate norms" (p. 161). This is a difficult conclusion to accept, in light of other factor-analytic studies on the McCarthy. Stucky (1984) observes that in the Wiebe and Watkins study, their factor matrices indicate large differences among factor-analytic techniques (an exception to what is seen in other McCarthy factor-analytic research). Furthermore, Stucky (1984), commenting on Wiebe and Watkins (1980), notes, "Indeed, their findings present a confusing pattern of loadings, and some of their

factor interpretations differ substantially from those in other studies" (p. 15).

In his integrated review of McCarthy research a number of years ago, Kaufman (1982) concluded that there is outstanding empirical support for the construct validity of the GCI and of the Verbal, Motor, and Perceptual–Performance scales (less so for the Memory scale, and clearly less so for the Quantitative). The newer research on the McCarthy's construct validity offers, in general, affirming evidence for Kaufman's earlier conclusion. It is recommended, nevertheless, that further research be pursued on the construct validity of the McCarthy, particularly of populations with known or suspected exceptionalities.

Concurrent Validity

On the subject of concurrent validity, Kaufman (1982) wisely comments:

> The most important type of validity for an intelligence test that aspires to join the elite corps of instruments on the practitioner's shelf is the degree to which the global score yielded by the new test agrees with the global scores produced by the existing monopoly. (p. 122)

It is this relation between the McCarthy and prominent intelligence tests (and others) that is examined next. In particular, I investigate the nagging issue of GCI–IQ discrepancies (e..g., Lidz & Ballester, 1986) for exceptional groups.

Of the various psychometric studies on the McCarthy (e.g., reliability, construct validity), it is the category of concurrent validity that proportionally dominates in the number of investigations. Because of this large data base on McCarthy concurrent validity research, and the problem of limited space, the tabular reporting of these studies is greatly modified. As seen in Table 9.5, the sample information provided is quite abbreviated, and studies are clustered by criterion measure and footnoted by relevant sample characteristics. Table 9.5 reveals that the concurrent validity of the McCarthy (i.e., the GCI) has been comprehensively investigated (52 studies, 2,078 subjects, and 11 different criterion tests). Validity data are available for normal samples, known or suspected exceptional samples (e.g., learning-disabled),

TABLE 9.5. Coefficients of Correlation and Mean Differences between the McCarthy GCI and IQs of Various Intelligence Tests

Test	Author(s)[a]	n	Difference[b] in means (GCI–IQ)	r[c]
S-B[d]	Bickett, Reuter, & Stanin (1984)[e,f]: 0, .69; *Bracken (1983)[g]: −10, .30; Brooks (1981)[e,h]: −4, .65; *Davis (1975): 0, .91; *Davis & Rowland (1974)[f,i]: −2, .77; *Davis & Walker (1976)[f]: +1, .82; *Gerken, Hancock, & Wade (1978)[f]: −10, .90; *Harrison & Wiebe (1977): +3, .45; Kasper (1973)[j]: −5, .66; *Krohn & Traxler (1979)[f]: −3, .82; *Levinson & Zino (1979a)[f]: +4, .90; *Levinson & Zino (1979a, 1979b)[e,f]: −20, .76; Lidz & Ballester (1985)[e,f,k,l]: −4, .73; *Loxley & Gerken (1980): −5, .85; *McCarthy (1972)[j]: −5, .81; *Naglieri & Harrison (1979)[e,f]: −18, .60		*Total*	
		578	−4	.77
			Normal	
		392	−2	.81
			EMR	
		84	−8	.68
			LD	
		29	−4	NA
			Speech-impaired	
		15	−6	NA
			Gifted	
		32	−10	.30
WISC	DeBoer, Kaufman, & McCarthy (1974)[k]: −16, .53; *Harrison & Wiebe (1977): 0, .74		*Total*	
		96	−6	.68
			Normal	
		63	0	.74
			LD	
		33	−16	.53
WISC-R	*Arinoldo (1982)[f]: −7, .82; *Davis & Walker (1977)[f]: −2, .75; Goh (1976)[k]: −4, .90; *Goh & Youngquist (1979)[k]: −10, .69; Hynd, Quackenbush, Kramer, Conner, & Weed (1980)[m]: −2, .85; Ivimey & Taylor (1980): −5, .87; Ivimey & Taylor (1980)[k]: −5, .40; *Knack (1978); −8, .90; *Knack (1978)[e]: 0, .75; *Knack (1978)[k]: −8, .66; *Naglieri (1980)[f]: −1, .51; *Naglieri (1980a)[f,k]: −5, .67 *Naglieri (1980a)[e,f]: −7, .82; Reilly, Drudge, Rosen, Loew, & Fischer (1985): +3, .89		*Total*	
		377	−4	.78
			Normal	
		206	−3	.82
			EMR	
		53	−4	.80
			LD	
		136	−7	.71
WPPSI	*Arinoldo (1982)[f]: −1, .72; Brooks (1981)[e,h]: −1, .73; *Knack (1978): −8, .80; *Knack (1978)[e]: −8, .72; *Knack (1978)[k]: −5, .64; *McCarthy (1972): −2, .71; *Phillips, Pasewark, & Tindall (1978): −7, .74; *Schmits & Beckenbaugh (1979): −7, .86; Valencia & Rothwell (1984)[n]: −1, .77		*Total*	
		247	−4	.75
			Normal	
		184	−4	.76
			EMR	
		48	−3	.73
			LD	
		15	−5	.64
K-ABC	Kaufman & Kaufman (1983b, Study 6)[f]: +1, .60; Kaufman & Kaufman (1983b, Study 22)[f]: −5, .68; Kaufman & Kaufman (1983b, Study 31)[f]: −1, .55; Lyon & Smith (1986)[o]: 0, .59; Naglieri (1985): −1, .55; Zucker (1985); NA, .55; Zucker (1985)[o]: NA, .74		*Total*	
		304	−1	.61
			Normal	
		203	−2[p]	.59
			At-risk	
		101	0[p]	.64

(continued)

TABLE 9.5. (*continued*)

Test	Author(s)[a]	n	Difference[b] in means (GCI–IQ)	r[c]
PPVT	*DeBoer et al. (1974)[k]: −17, .43; Ferrari (1980)[q]: +7, .84; *Goh (1976)[k]: −12, .74; *Taylor (1979): +1, .47		*Total*	
		120	−8	.57
			Normal	
		41	+1	.47
			LD	
		71	−15	.59
			Autistic	
		8	+7	.84
PPVT-R	Bracken & Prasse (1983)[f,o]: −3, .66[r]; Gullo & McLoughlin (1982): +10, .59; Naglieri (1981): 0, .78		*Total*	
		91	+2	.68
			Normal	
		56	+5	.69
			At-risk	
		35	−3	.66
SIT	Bondy, Sheslow, Norcross, & Constantino (1982)[f]: −14, .81; Bondy, Constantino, Norcross, & Sheslow (1984)[e,f]: −27, NA; Bondy et al. (1984)[e,g]: −14, NA		*Total*	
		68	−16	NA
			Normal	
		44	−14	.81
			EMR	
		10	−27	NA
			Gifted	
		14	−14	NA
CMMS	*Phillips et al. (1978)		*Normal*	
		60	−5[s]	.71
DTLA	*Wiebe & Harrison (1978)		*Normal*	
		111	−3[t]	.82
WC	Reilly et al. (1985)		*Normal*	
		26	0	.83

Note. Studies discussed and referenced in Kaufman (1982) are marked with an asterisk. NA, not available. Unless indicated by superscript (e, g, k, n, or q), all samples are or are assumed to be normal. Tests: S-B, Stanford–Binet; WISC, Wechsler Intelligence Scale for Children; WISC-R, Wechsler Intelligence Test for Children—Revised; WPPSI, Wechsler Preschool and Primary Scale of Intelligence; K-ABC, Kaufman Assessment Battery for Children; PPVT, Peabody Picture Vocabulary Test; PPVT-R, Peabody Picture Vocabulary Test—Revised; SIT, Slosson Intelligence Test; CMMS, Columbia Mental Maturity Scale; DTLA, Detroit Tests of Learning Aptitude; WC, Woodcock–Johnson Tests of Cognitive Ability. Other abbreviations: EMR, educable mentally retarded; LD, learning-disabled.

[a]First numeral following author and year is the mean GCI–IQ difference. Second numeral (decimal fraction) is the correlation coefficient between GCI and IQ.

[b]GCI minus IQ. Mean differences are weighted and rounded to nearest whole number.

[c]Weighted mean coefficients of correlation were computed using Fisher's *r*-to-*z* transformation.

[d]1972 Stanford–Binet.

[e]EMR sample.

[f]Sample includes mixed ethnic groups. Data are aggregated.

[g]Gifted sample.

[h]Black sample.

[i]S-B IQ reported as the median.

and ethnic minority samples. Before the concurrent validity of the McCarthy is discussed on an instrument-by-instrument basis, here are two major generalizations culled from the 52 investigations:

1. Correlations between the GCI and IQ range from a low of .57 (Peabody Picture Vocabulary Test [PPVT] to a high of .83 (Woodcock–Johnson Tests of Cognitive Ability [WC]). The mean correlation coefficient (weighted calculation of the various "Total" r's) between the McCarthy GCI and the various IQs is .74, indicating a substantial relation; thus there is strong evidence for concurrent validity.

2. With the exception of the GCI–IQ comparisons on the revised PPVT (PPVT-R), the GCI consistently underestimates IQ. This underestimation ranges from –1 point (Kaufman Assessment Battery for Children [K-ABC] to –8 points (PPVT). The mean GCI-IQ difference (weighted calculation of the various "Total" differences in means is 3.5 points. As Kaufman (1982) notes, the overall superiority of several points in favor of IQ seems minor and of little clinical consequence, given the strong correlation between the GCI and conventional IQ tests. It is recommended, however, that clinicians be aware that the GCI tends to underestimate IQ. More discussion on the underestimation issue is presented later in the section on "Clinical Utility for Exceptional Populations."

Relation of GCI to Stanford–Binet IQ

Since the review by Kaufman (1982), several additional investigations (Bickett, Reuter, & Stancin, 1984; Brooks, 1981; Kasper, 1973; Lidz & Balister, 1986) have been identified in which the McCarthy has been compared to the Stanford–Binet. Among the 16 studies listed in Table 9.5, it is evident that for the aggregated samples ($n = 578$), the GCI and Stanford–Binet IQ correlate substantially ($r = .77$). An even higher correlation is seen with normal samples (mean $r = .81$; $n = 392$). On the other hand, the GCI–IQ correlation is lower ($r = .68$) for the educable mentally retarded samples. Mean GCI-IQ discrepancies range from –2 points (normal samples) to –10 points (gifted sample).

Relation of GCI to Wechsler IQs

From Table 9.5, it is evident that the relation between the GCI and the FSIQs of the various Wechsler tests has been examined for a diversity of normal and exceptional samples. As is the case with GCI–IQ correlations for the Stanford–Binet, the relationships between the GCI and the Wechsler IQs are acceptably high. For the aggregated samples, the GCI correlates .68 with WISC FSIQ, .78 with WISC-R FSIQ, and .75 with WPPSI FSIQ. If the nine WISC-R studies ($n = 397$ subjects) are used as a referent point, the GCI–FSIQ correlation of .78 is nearly identical to the GCI–IQ correlation for the Stanford–Binet. Likewise, the GCI–FSIQ discrepancy of 4 points is identical to that between the GCI and the Stanford–Binet IQ.

Relation of GCI to K-ABC Mental Processing Composite

There are six correlational investigations involving the McCarthy and the relatively new K-ABC (Kaufman & Kaufman, 1983a). In

---

[j]Kasper (1973) and McCarthy (1972) reported means based on 1960 S-B norms. Kaufman and Kaufman (1977b) recomputed McCarthy's (1972) S-B means, using the 1972 S-B norms, and I did likewise for Kasper's (1973) reported means, using Davis and Rowland (1974) as a guide.

[k]Sample was LD or included children with learning disabilities.

[l]Sample included speech-impaired children.

[m]Navajo sample.

[n]Mexican American sample.

[o]At-risk sample.

[p]Mean differences not available for Zucker (1985).

[q]Autistic sample.

[r]Weighted mean for r's on Form L and M.

[s]Mean score on CMMS is the Age Deviation Score.

[t]Mental age computed for both the McCarthy and DTLA; unit difference is in months.

these studies, the GCI was correlated with the Mental Processing Composite (MPC) of the K-ABC. The MPC is intended as the measure of global intelligence in the K-ABC. For the aggregated samples ($n = 304$ subjects), the weighted mean correlation coefficient is .61. The lower r of .61 for GCI–MPC relations (as compared to the higher r's for relations between the GCI and the Stanford–Binet and Wechsler IQs is not unexpected in view of the reduced verbal and quantitative content in the K-ABC. Finally, it is interesting to note that the mean GCI–MPC difference for the aggregated samples in Table 9.5 is only 1 point, indicating that for all of the intelligence tests listed, the GCI–MPC discrepancy is the smallest.

Relation of GCI to Peabody IQ

Several studies have been done that correlate the McCarthy GCI with the PPVT (Dunn, 1959) and the PPVT-R (Dunn & Dunn, 1981). Although there is debate about whether the PPVT and PPVT-R should be considered intelligence tests (see Bracken & Prasse, 1983), the Peabody tests—which report an IQ—are typically viewed as measures of verbal intelligence (Salvia & Ysseldyke, 1985). For the studies of the GCI and the PPVT or PPVT-R listed in Table 9.5, the observed concurrent validity coefficients are of moderate magnitudes (.47 to .69) for the various samples. As Bracken and Prasse (1983) observe, despite the moderate strength of the correlations, the McCarthy and Peabody tests suggest that somewhat different skills are measured (i.e., wide range for the former and limited range for the latter). Also, note that with respect to the mean discrepancies between the GCI and Peabody IQ, the results are conflicting: In some studies the GCI overestimates IQ (e.g., Ferrari, 1980; Gullo & McLoughlin, 1982), and in other studies the GCI underestimates IQ (e.g., Goh, 1976). Taken together, the available concurrent validity research on the McCarthy and the Peabody strongly suggests that the two instruments should not be used interchangeably (see Gullo & McLoughlin, 1982).

Relationship of GCI to IQs of Other Intelligence Tests

Table 9.5 lists five studies in which the GCI has been correlated with IQs of other cognitive tests, including the Slosson Intelligence Test (SIT; Slosson, 1960), the Columbia Mental Maturity Scale (CMMS; Burgenmeister, Blum, & Lorge, 1972), the Detroit Tests of Learning Aptitude (DTLA; Baker & Leland, 1967), and the WC (Woodcock, 1978). The observed correlations for these studies are of substantial magnitudes, and the mean discrepancies between the GCI and the measures of intelligence of the various tests are slight. The exception is the difference between the GCI and the SIT IQ; the latter greatly overestimates intelligence, compared to the McCarthy. Caution is recommended when using the SIT with normal and exceptional young children (see Bondy, Constantino, Norcross, & Sheslow, 1984; Bondy, Sheslow, Norcross, & Constantino, 1982).

Relation of GCI to Other Measures

The McCarthy GCI has been correlated with several other instruments whose contents are of a language nature (e.g., Illinois Test of Psycholinguistic Abilities; Kirk, McCarthy, & Kirk, 1968) of or a visual–motor nature (Developmental Test of Visual–Motor Integration; Beery, 1967). Because of space limitations, discussion of these investigations is not possible. Interested clinicians and researchers should consult Kaufman (1982) for a brief review of this research.

In conclusion, it is evident that the relation between the McCarthy GCI and intelligence, as measured by a number of cognitive instruments, has been examined widely. The reported substantial correlations demonstrate strong evidence for the concurrent validity of the McCarthy. Also, to underscore a point made earlier, the slight underestimation of IQ by the GCI appears of little significance, given the strong relation between the GCI and IQ. Yet it is recommended that clinicians be aware of this underestimation.

Predictive Validity

Since the advent of psychoeducational assessment, a major aspect of the clinician's work when administering cognitive tests to children is to use such data for making predictions about future school performance, particularly academic achievement as measured by standardized tests. Thus, it is important for the clinician to have information about, and trust in, intelligence measures used as statistical predictors of school achievement. How does the McCarthy fare in this commonplace assessment concern? Because of space restrictions, I discuss only the highlights of the existing research. The discussion centers largely on predictive validity in general; "at-risk" investigations are covered in the following section, "Early Screening for Learning Problems."

In his review of research on the McCarthy, Kaufman (1982) concluded that the McCarthy was a significant predictor of school achievement for a variety of samples. Research on the McCarthy's predictive validity since the Kaufman review gives further credence to the conclusion that the McCarthy significantly predicts achievement. What follows is a list of predictive validity studies and a brief discussion of salient findings (studies with asterisks refers to investigations referenced in Kaufman, 1982): Blachman (1981); Ernhart and Landa (1980); Funk, Sturner, and Green (1986); Harrison (1981)*; Harrison and Naglieri (1981)*; Ivimey and Taylor (1980); Johnson and McGowan (1984); Kaufman (1973)*; Lake (1979)*; Long (1976)*; Lorton (1976)*; Loxley and Gerken (1980)*; Massoth (1985); Massoth and Levenson (1982); Naglieri (1980b*, 1985); Naglieri and Harrison (1982)*; Reilly, Drudge, Rosen, Loew, and Fischer (1985); Schodlatz (1978)*; Shellenberger (1977*, 1982); Simons and Goh (1982)*; Strom, Hathaway, and Slaughter (1981); Sturner, Funk, & Green (1984); Taylor and Ivimey (1980a*, 1980b*); Teeter (1983); Valencia (1982, 1984).

Several observations and conclusions can be drawn from this data base of over two dozen studies of the McCarthy's predictive validity:

1. A variety of standardized achievement tests have been used as criterion variables. These include individually administered tests, such as the Peabody Individual Achievement Test (PIAT; see Naglieri, 1985; Naglieri & Harrison, 1982) and the Wide Range Achievement Test (Naglieri, 1980; Reilly et al., 1985), and group-administered instruments, such as the Comprehensive Tests of Basic Skills (CTBS; see Valencia, 1982, 1984) and the Metropolitan Achievement Tests (MAT; see Harrison, 1981; Kaufman 1973). These studies, and others,

have included children spanning the preschool through third-grade levels.

2. An analysis of the observed correlations between the McCarthy GCI and the various norm-referenced individual- and group-administered achievement tests indicates the following: (a) The r's range from .15 (learning-disabled sample in Ivimey and Taylor, 1980) to .79 (normal sample in Naglieri, 1985); (b) there are a few r's in each of the .10s, .20s, .30s, .40s and .50s, but approximately two-thirds of the r's are in the .60s and .70s; and (c) in studies that have examined the comparison of major intelligence tests (i.e., McCarthy, WISC-R, WC, WPPSI, Stanford–Binet) as predictors of academic achievement (e.g., Johnson & McGowan, 1984; Kaufman, 1973; Reilly et al., 1985), the McCarthy (GCI) correlated at least as well or as well as the other established tests (i.e., they did not differ significantly in predictive power).

3. In addition to the strength of the McCarthy in predicting academic achievement as measured by formal standardized tests, there is evidence that the McCarthy significantly predicts school functioning and children's behavior as indexed by less conventional means. For example, Simons and Goh (1982) and Sturner et al. (1984) found the McCarthy to be a good predictor of children's school achievement (e.g., reading, mathematics), as measured by teachers' ratings. Significant correlations have also been observed between the McCarthy and mothers' attitudes toward child rearing (Strom et al., 1981) and between the McCarthy and teachers' perceptions of children's classroom behavior (Johnson & McGowan, 1985). Finally, there is suggestive research that the McCarthy (GCI, Verbal scale index, and Memory scale index) significantly predicts school grades. Massoth (1985), in a 5-year follow-up study of a normal sample initially tested in kindergarten, reported that the McCarthy GCI correlated .55 with course grade average in sixth grade. On the other hand, Johnson and McGowan (1984)— who compared the predictive power of the McCarthy, the WISC-R, and the Stanford–Binet—found that only the Stanford–Binet predicted grades significantly. The results of the McCarthy–grades aspect of this study should be interpreted with caution, as the children were administered the three intelligence tests at three different times

(spanning 4–6 years), and the number of children involved from test to test varied.

In conclusion, based on a substantial body of psychometric research, there is ample evidence that the McCarthy correlates significantly with school achievement. Furthermore, the McCarthy fares well—comparatively speaking—in that the observed correlations are of similar magnitude to those observed for other major cognitive tests (i.e., typically in the .60s to .70s range). Notwithstanding the importance of the established predictive validity of the McCarthy, a more useful question for the clinician is this: "How effective is the McCarthy for the screening of potential learning problems of school children?" It is this concern to which the chapter turns next.

EARLY SCREENING FOR LEARNING PROBLEMS

Since the passage of Public Law 94-142 (see Rules and Regulations Implementing Education for All Handicapped Children Act of 1975, 1977), there has been an increased interest in the screening of young children who may be "at risk" regarding normal development in the school setting. In general, developmental screening—which should be brief, inexpensive, and accurate—attempts to identify children who require further evaluation because of the possible presence of a learning condition that might limit their potential for growth (Meisels, Wiske, & Tivnan, 1984). Clinicians must confront the problem of finding screening instruments that are practical to use, effective in their results, and technically adequate. The purpose of the present section is to discuss how well the McCarthy fares in this important concern faced by practitioners of assessment.

Since Kaufman's (1982) review of research on the McCarthy, there has been a sharp rise in the number of investigations dealing with the utility of the McCarthy as a screening instrument for identification of children with possible learning problems. This body of research is examined here in three ways. First, I discuss a number of studies in which the complete McCarthy has been investigated as a screening tool. Second, the effectiveness of three McCarthy short forms is examined.

Third, I discuss those studies that have investigated the two McCarthy drawing subtests as screening instruments.

The Complete McCarthy as a Screening Tool

In his review of research on the McCarthy, Kaufman (1982) identified only one study (Schodlatz, 1978) that attempted to explore the complete McCarthy as a screening test to identify "at-risk" children. By now, a number of new studies have in some form or another attempted to address the issue of McCarthy screening (Bondy et al., 1982; Funk et al., 1986; Katz, 1978; Meisels et al., 1984; Prasse, Siewart & Ellison, 1983; Sturner et al., 1984; Weiss, 1977). Some of the major findings of this research are discussed here.

The two studies by Sturner and associates (Funk et al., 1986; Sturner et al., 1984) are particularly informative to clinicians with regard to the McCarthy's utility as a screening test. These investigations provide significant contributions in that they were well designed, used a variety of criteria outcomes to measure school success–failure, and were longitudinal. The Sturner et al. (1984) sample contained 74 ethnically mixed kindergarten children (stratified from an initial sample of 382 children who underwent a routine screening program). Data on the 74 children included McCarthy performance and scores on three criteria variables: concurrent standardized reading and mathematics achievement, teacher ratings of ability to learn, and kindergarten school failure. One major finding involved prevalence of academic difficulties as per GCI performance. That is, when all three outcome criteria were considered jointly, the following "at-risk" rates were observed: 100% of the children who scored below 68 on the GCI also had low scores on at least one of the criteria, whereas 53% of the children scoring in the GCI range of 68–83 and 12% of those scoring above 83 had academic problems. Especially revealing was the relationship between McCarthy performance and failure of kindergarten. The failure rates for the low-GCI group (<68), intermediate-GCI group (68–83), and normal-GCI group (>83) were 52%, 26%, and 5%, respectively.

The investigation by Funk et al. (1986), an extension of a sort to Sturner et al. (1984), included 129 children who were administered the McCarthy prior to school entry. In turn, criteria data (i.e., standardized achievement scores, retention, and special education outcomes) were collected in kindergarten, first grade, and second grade. Following the design used in Sturner et al. (1984), Funk et al. (1986) divided the sample into low-GCI, intermediate-GCI (borderline), and normal-GCI groups. Of particular interest to the clinician who works with the McCarthy are the percentages of children in each GCI group who subsequently did poorly in school. Funk et al. found these outcomes:

> [O]f those children in the Low GCI group, 60% had poor school outcomes by kindergarten, 74% by first grade, and 94% by second grade. A similar, though less extreme, pattern was observed for the children in the Borderline group: 40%, 78%, and 74% were classified as having poor school outcomes by kindergarten, first, and second grades, respectively. These two groups were quite distinct from the Normal group, where only 6% had poor outcomes by kindergarten, 15% by first grade, and 29% by second grade. (pp. 186–187)

An important feature of the study by Funk et al. (1986) is that the results were replicated through the first grade, using a second cohort.

One study is available that investigated the relation between McCarthy performance and neurological functioning of children born "at risk" (Prasse et al., 1983). The sample included 232 children (mean age of 4.3 years) who were part of a longitudinal perinatal study involving children born "at risk" (e.g., birth complications associated with prematurity; asphyxia; pneumonia). In brief, there were two major findings. First, although the "at-risk" children's mean performance on the GCI and the Verbal, Perceptual–Performance, Quantitative, and Memory scales closely approximated the means and standard deviations of the standardization group, the mean Motor scale performance (42.92) was substantially lower. The authors observed that this result supports previous findings that specific neurological impairment may not be revealed in overall cognitive functioning, but that assessment of motor abilities may be more salient in assessing "at-risk" preschool children. Second, it was found that scores from three

neurological measures (one administered when the children were approximately 6 and 15 months old, and two administered at age 4 years) correlated significantly with McCarthy performance (particularly the Motor scale).

Other studies provide some support for the utility of the McCarthy as a screening instrument. Katz (1978) observed that the Perceptual–Performance scale was the best predictor of kindergarten children's problems with school learning (as judged by teacher ratings and an observation instrument). Bondy et al. (1982) found that preschool teachers' estimates of children's overall intellectual functioning correlated significantly ($r = .74$) with the GCI. Meisels et al. (1984), whose sample contained 102 children aged 4 and 5 who were being screened for learning problems, reported that the McCarthy GCI correlated significantly ($r = .72$) with the Early Screening Inventory (Meisels & Wiske, 1983), a sound screening tool.

In summary, the available evidence suggests that the complete McCarthy does have utility as a screening instrument. The studies by Funk et al. (1986) and Sturner et al. (1984) are especially revealing as to the McCarthy's efficacy in the early identification of children who are likely to experience academic difficulties.

The McCarthy Short Forms as Screening Tools

A very real problem clinicians face in the intellectual screening of young children (i.e., preschool, kindergarten, first grade) is the administrative time factor. For purposes of mass screening, conventional cognitive tests, such as the McCarthy and the WPPSI, are impractical because they require about an hour of testing per child. This issue of time is not a new concern. As I have noted elsewhere (Valencia, 1984), abbreviated tests developed from established intelligence instruments have been present since the 1937 Stanford–Binet. The current interest, however, in these shortened versions— commonly referred to as "short forms"—has been revitalized by legislation emphasizing the need to detect potential learning difficulties in young children. Given this need, the development of short forms that are reliable and valid, and can be administered in a short period of time (i.e., 20–25 minutes), would be valuable for the school psychologist.

In the case of the McCarthy, three short forms exist (Kaufman, 1977; Psychological Corporation, 1978; Taylor, Slocumb, & O'Neill, 1979). In his review of the McCarthy, Kaufman (1982) claims that available research on the three McCarthy short forms indicates that the Kaufman (1977) version may hold the most promise as an effective screening instrument. In contrast, the McCarthy Screening Test (MST; Psychological Corporation, 1978) has been criticized for having poor reliability and stability, and for being a weak predictor in terms of identifying children with learning problems referred by their teacher (Kaufman, 1982). The third McCarthy short form, developed by Taylor et al. (1979), has been adversely reviewed as a viable short form because its development was based on data from a very small and nonrepresentative sample; it used an inappropriate regression analysis; and it contains subsets that are not representative of the different scales of the McCarthy (Kaufman, 1982; also, see Dennehy, 1981, and Grimm, 1983, for critiques). Here, Kaufman's (1982) positive claims for his short form, as well as criticisms of the MST and the Taylor et al. short form, are re-examined in light of some new evidence. First, studies are reviewed that have investigated the psychometric properties of the three short forms. Second, I examine several studies that have researched the utility of the McCarthy short forms in the actual screening of children.

Psychometric Properties

The McCarthy short form developed by Kaufman (1977)—henceforth referred to as the "Kaufman SF"—consists of these six subtests: Puzzle Solving, Word Knowledge, Numerical Memory, Verbal Fluency, Counting and Sorting, and Conceptual Grouping. Two subtests from each of the three cognitive scales (Verbal, Quantitative, Perceptual–Performance) are represented. Kaufman used both empirical and rational considerations to select the six subtests. The McCarthy standardization sample of 1,032 children formed the data base for the SF's construction. Raw scores from the six subtests are summed and then placed into

regression equations (for each quarter year from $2\frac{1}{2}$ to $8\frac{1}{2}$) to predict an estimated GCI (see Kaufman, 1977, and Kaufman & Kaufman, 1977a, for a fuller discussion of how the Kaufman SF was developed).

A number of psychometric investigations of the Kaufman SF exist. There are several concurrent validity studies with diverse samples, in which the estimated GCI has been correlated with the full-form GCI (Dennehy, 1981; Kaufman, 1977; Valencia, 1984; Valencia & Rankin, 1983). These investigations have shown that the correlations between the estimated and full-form GCI ranged from .79 to .96 (with the vast percentage of the r's in the low .90s), thus providing strong support for the concurrent validity of the Kaufman SF. The Kaufman SF has also been found to correlate significantly with other established intelligence tests. Kaufman (1977) found the SF to correlate .78 with the Stanford–Binet and .74 with the WPPSI. Regarding reliability, quite respectable estimates of .74 (Valencia & Rankin, 1983) and .88 (Kaufman, 1977) have been reported, indicating that the Kaufman SF is relatively accurate.

Finally, a number of studies exist in which the Kaufman SF GCI has been examined to see how well it predicts academic achievement (Grimm, 1983; Harrison & Naglieri, 1981; Kaufman, 1977; Long, 1976; Nagle & Gepford, 1978; Naglieri & Harrison, 1982; Valencia, 1984). These investigations have reported moderate to high correlation coefficients ranging from .44 to .76 across several different established individually and group-administered tests. The general conclusion we can draw from these predictive validity studies is that the Kaufman SF GCI correlates significantly with academic achievement.

The MST (Psychological Corporation, 1978) is comprised of six subtests, which purportedly reflect a proportional representation of the five scales of the McCarthy: Right–Left Orientation, Draw-A-Design, Numerical Memory (Parts 1 and 2), Verbal Memory (Part 1), Leg Coordination, and Conceptual Grouping. Designed for children aged 4–6 years, the MST does not yield a total score. Rather, the test user arbitrarily decides on two criteria for identifying children who may be "at risk": that is, (1) scoring below one of three cutoff points (10th, 20th, or 30th percentile); and (2) "failure" of one, two, or three subtests.

Some research has investigated the psychometric properties of the MST. Vance, Blixt, and Kitson (1982) examined the factor structure of the MST using 555 kindergarten children and the MST standardization sample ($n = 516$). Depending on the age level, the authors found either one- or two-factor solutions. In the one-factor solution (for ages $4\frac{1}{2}$ and $5\frac{1}{2}$ from the standardization group, and $5\frac{1}{2}$ from the authors' sample), the factor was labeled General Cognitive. In the two-factor solution (for ages 4, 5, and $6\frac{1}{2}$ from the standardization group), Factor 1 was labeled Verbal, and Factor 2 (which barely met criterion) was termed Motor–Perceptual. Vance et al. concluded that the findings provide support that the MST measures parts of the same attributes (cognitive and sensory–motor functioning) in different degrees. As the authors note, the results and conclusions should be generalized with caution, given that factor-analytic research is quite dependent upon the nature of the sample and the factor analysis used.

Evidence of test–retest stability of the MST is limited and unimpressive. The stability coefficients reported in the MST manual for the six subtests range from .32 (Right–Left Orientation) to .69 (Numerical Memory); these are unacceptable magnitudes by conventional psychometric standards. In fact, such data prompted this caution in the MST manual: *"The reliability values of the MST are not high enough to warrant making fine distinctions within a group"* (Psychological Corporation, 1978, p. 9, italics in original). Umansky, Paget, and Cohen (1981) also investigated the stability of the MST. From an original sample of 975 kindergarten children, 276 were identified to be "at risk." In turn, these children were retested, on the average, $1\frac{1}{2}$ months later. After corrections for restricted range, the stability coefficients ranged from .30 to .83. Umansky et al. noted: "Despite higher correlations for the study sample, they do not appear to be high enough or consistent enough across subtests to deny the manual's *caveat*" (1981, p. 652). The authors concluded that the MST is not stable enough to be used by itself to identify children who may have learning problems.

Prediction of academic achievement with the MST has been investigated in several studies (Grimm, 1983; Gullo, Clements, & Robertson, 1984; Harrison & Naglieri, 1981; Naglieri & Harrison, 1982). Gullo et al., using 88 kindergarten children, correlated MST performance with the Metropolitan Readiness Test (MRT; Nurss & McGauvran, 1974) at the end of kindergarten and with the Scott, Foresman Achievement Test (SFAT; Wick & Smith, 1981) administered at the end of first grade. Correlations between the MST total score and five subtest scores of the MRT ranged from .51 to .66, and r's between the MST and three subtest scores of the SFAT ranged from .41 to .57. Although all the observed r's were statistically significant, Gullo et al. concluded that the magnitudes were not high enough for a satisfactory decision to be made regarding "at risk" classification.

Grimm (1983) compared the predictive validity of five screening tests (including the Kaufman SF and the MST) in a sample of 88 nonreferred kindergarteners. The criterion measure was the MRT. Grimm examined all nine possible combinations of cutoffs for identifying "at-risk" children on the MST. Biserial correlations for the nine comparisons ranged from .26 to .81; seven of nine MST–MRT correlations were *below* the observed .61 predictive validity coefficient between the Kaufman SF and the MRT. Also, the MST resulted in a higher percentage of false positives than the Kaufman SF (i.e., 0%–45% for the MST and 11%–23% for the Kaufman SF).

In a study similar to Grimm's (1983) investigation, Harrison and Naglieri (1981) correlated the MST and the Kaufman SF with the MAT (Prescott, Balow, Hogan, & Farr, 1978) in a sample of 53 normal first-graders. It was found that the Kaufman SF correlated .71 with the MAT, and that the correlations between the nine cutoff scores of the MST and the MAT ranged from .43 to .78. The Kaufman SF was a stronger predictor than eight of the nine MST criteria, with three of the eight correlations being significantly higher.

Naglieri and Harrison (1982), in another predictive validity study, found the Kaufman SF and the MST to correlate .55 and .54, respectively, with the PIAT in a sample of 39 nonreferred children in kindergarten through third grade. The finding of nonsignificance for Kaufman SF–PIAT and MST–

PIAT correlations contrasts with the Harrison and Naglieri (1981) study, in which the Kaufman SF was the superior predictor. Naglieri and Harrison (1982) suggest that the discrepancy between the two studies may be related to the loss of precision resulting from the dichotomous scoring system of the MST ("at risk–not at risk").

In a concurrent validity study utilizing 39 kindergarteners, Vance, Kitson, and Singer (1983) correlated the six subtests of the MST with the PPVT-R, and found low to moderate correlations from .13 to .47. As Grimm (1983) admonishes, the Vance et al. (1983) study should be interpreted with caution, in that the correlational analyses were computed using dissimilar metrics (i.e., PPVT-R standard scores, MST raw scores); thus, age was uncontrolled.

In a final study of the MST, Umansky and Cohen (1980) administered the instrument to 819 white and 152 minority (78% Hispanic) kindergarten boys and girls. The authors observed that there were significant race and sex differences on the MST, and concluded that the claims by Kaufman and DiCuio (1975) and Kaufman and Kaufman (1973a, 1973b) that the subtests in question were free of sex and race bias could not be supported. In a critical response, Kaufman (1981) legitimately raised a number of reasoning errors and methodological flaws in the Umansky and Cohen study.

The third McCarthy short form (Taylor et al., 1979), hereafter referred to as the "Taylor et al. SF," was developed using a forward stepwise regression program from data on 50 kindergarten children. The six subtests include the three subtests from the entire Quantitative scale (Number Questions, Numerical Memory, Counting and Sorting), two from the Verbal scale (Pictorial Memory, Verbal Fluency), and one from the Perceptual–Performance scale (Tapping Sequence). The Taylor et al. SF is designed only for children between the ages of $5\frac{1}{2}$ and $6\frac{3}{4}$, and does not provide standardized regression weights for each of the six subtests.

Some positive findings for the psychometric properties of the Taylor et al. SF have been observed. Taylor et al. reported an r of .96 between McCarthy GCI and performance of the six subtests. Taylor and Ivimey (1980b) found the Taylor et al. SF to correlate significantly (.63) with the PIAT when ad-

ministered 1 year later to 23 of the original 50 children in Taylor et al. (1979). Despite these findings, the Taylor et al. SF has been sharply criticized, as noted earlier, as a serious nominee for a screening tool. This is discussed in more detail later.

Utility in Actual Screening

Certainly, synthesizing available psychometric research on the McCarthy short forms provides helpful information. For practitioners, however, the real concern is the proverbial "proof of the pudding." That is, how effective are the McCarthy short forms in actual screening situations that seek to identify children with potential learning problems? Here, I briefly review several studies that have attempted to address this concern (Dennehy, 1981; Flanagan, 1984; Harrison & Naglieri, 1981; Umansky et al., 1981).

Dennehy's (1981) study sought to determine the concurrent validity between the McCarthy full-form GCI and the Kaufman SF GCI, as well as between the full-form GCI and the Taylor et al. SF GCI. The author estimated GCI in the Taylor et al. SF by standardizing scores of the six subtests and forming an equally weighted composite score. To enable a comparison between the two short forms, the same standardized weighting method was used in estimating GCI from the Kaufman SF. The sample included 41 primary-grade children from Victoria, Australia; 23 of the 41 had been referred by their teachers as children with suspected learning problems. Although there was little difference between the full-form GCI and the Kaufman SF GCI ($r = .84$) or between the full-form GCI and the Taylor et al. SF GCI ($r = .81$), Dennehy concluded that because of major problems in the development of the Taylor et al. SF (e.g., small size of sample used in the regression analysis), the Kaufman SF appeared more useful to the practitioner.

The dissertation study by Flanagan (1984)—which utilized discriminant function, correlational, and classificational analyses—investigated the comparative validity of the Kaufman SF and the MST. Eighty preschool children underwent extensive screening and were subsequently placed into a criterion group of children ($n = 40$) who were identified as having learning or developmental difficulties ("handicapped") or a control group ($n = 40$) determined to be developing normally ("not handicapped"). Although in the discriminant-function analysis the Kaufman SF was able to classify more cases correctly (73.75%) than was the MST (68.75%), it was observed that the MST surpassed the Kaufman SF on most of the analyses (e.g., was more consistently accurate). Yet, during the course of the study, Flanagan noted major difficulties with the normative procedures utilized in the MST development. This led him to conclude: "The current study suggests that the MST may produce more frequent accurate identifications, but there seemed to be internal construction difficultues with this scale. Therefore, the [Kaufman SF] would be the instrument of choice with a middle class, preschool population" (p. 78).

In a study discussed earlier, Harrison and Naglieri (1981) compared the effectiveness of the Kaufman SF and the MST in predicting MAT performance in a group of normal first-graders. Scores below the 10th percentile on the Basic Battery of the MAT were defined as failure. The major results were as follows: (1) In four of nine comparisons, the MST criteria yielded a significantly larger number of false negatives than did the Kaufman SF; (2) one of the MST criteria showed a significantly larger number of false positives than did the Kaufman SF; (3) the Kaufman SF yielded a significantly larger number of false positives than three of the nine MST criteria.

In their test–retest stability study of the MST, Umansky et al. (1981) administered the MST to an original pool of 971 kindergarten children. On this first screening, 300 children were identified as "at risk"; 276 were rescreened. Also, teachers were requested to refer children they suspected of having learning problems. Umansky et al., commenting on the MST's effectiveness in identifying children who are likely to demonstrate learning problems, state

The results . . . are quite distressing. . . . Forty-nine percent of the cases who were classified "At Risk" on the first screening were "Not At Risk" on the retest, yet teachers referred 42% of the original "At Risk" group. In other words, teachers referred a large percentage of those children who had been missing using the MST alone. (1981, p. 652)

Umansky et al. also note the astonishing finding that the MST missed about one-half of the children referred by teachers for a possible learning disability. Likewise, the MST did not identify large percentages of other types of referrals (i.e., 73% of children with speech and language problems; 44% of mentally retarded children; 69% of children with behavior disorders; 29% of children with multiple problems).

Taken together, the available research on the three McCarthy short forms clearly points to the Kaufman SF as the instrument of choice, and thus I endorse it as a useful screening tool. Both psychometric and "hands-on" studies speak to its effectiveness as a screening tool. On the other hand, for reasons stated previously, the Taylor et al. (1979) SF can be easily dismissed as a viable candidate. Research on the MST, though containing some positive findings (e.g., Flanagan, 1984), has typically yielded unimpressive results regarding its psychometric properties and its clinical utility. In addition, Kaufman (1982) has criticized the test publishers' choice of subtests on the MST (e.g., Right–Left Orientation can only be administered to half the target group; sex bias has been noted on two subtests).

McCarthy Drawing Subtests

As Kaufman and Kaufman (1977a) point out, numerous studies have been undertaken that have shown design-copying and human figure-drawing tests to be positively correlated with school readiness and academic achievement (e.g., Ilg & Ames, 1972; Kaufman & Kaufman, 1972; Koppitz, 1975). Reynolds (1978a) observes, however, that the established drawing tasks (e.g., Bender–Gestalt Test; Koppitz, 1963) have been designed for adults and older children. Thus, if drawing tests could be administered easily to young children in a group setting, could be scored quickly, and had sound psychometric properties, such instruments would be highly beneficial to the practitioner.

There has been some research suggesting that the two McCarthy drawing subtests, Draw-A-Design and Draw-A-Child, could be used as a valid and reliable *group* instrument to screen *young* children (i.e., target population of 4–6 years) for early identification of learning problems. This is an attractive observation, in that the McCarthy is well respected for its excellent standardization. Reynolds (1978a) administered the McCarthy Draw-A-Design and Draw-A-Child subtests to 83 children from kindergarten to second grade. In addition to group testing, a randomly selected subsample ($n = 30$) from the 83 children was individually administered the two tests, so that equivalence of scores from group to individual administration could be investigated. The Draw-A-Design and Draw-A-Child scores correlated .86 and .83, respectively, for the two testing settings. Reynolds (1978a) also reported test–retest stability correlations for both tests in the middle .80s (7- to 10-day interval). Finally, Reynolds found significant correlations between the two drawing tests and tests of academic achievement (zero-order correlations of .31 to .50). Moore and Burns (1977) also found, in a preschool sample, that the Draw-A-Design subtest correlated significantly with a developmental screening inventory ($r = .75$) and the PPVT ($r = .67$).

In the Reynolds (1978a) study, the administration time of the drawing subtests ranged from 20 to 24 minutes, and scoring for the two subtests was done in 3–5 minutes by properly trained personnel. With regard to scoring the drawing subtests, Reynolds (1978b) raised a good point: "The utility of these tests in preschool screening would be enhanced if teachers could be trained to score the two drawing tests accurately" (p. 538). To investigate this contention, Reynolds (1978b) provided a 2-hour training session on scoring for 20 kindergarten teachers, who administered the drawing subtests to 322 children. A doctoral-level school psychologist rescored, blindly, all tests. The teacher-psychologist interscorer reliability for Draw-A-Design and Draw-A-Child were .76 and .87, respectively. Reynolds noted that since the interscore reliability failed to reach a minimally adequate value of .90, extreme caution is in order when interpreting Draw-A-Design and Draw-A-Child performance scored by teachers. He also advised that whenever possible, psychologists should score the two drawing subtests.

In an extension of Reynolds (1978b), Reynolds (1979) questioned whether the poor interscorer reliability seen in the former study was largely due to lack of training of the teachers or perhaps to a defect in the scoring procedure for the drawing subtests. Addressing this, Reynolds (1979) had two trained psychologists score 50 protocols. The observed interscorer reliability coefficients were .93 and .96 for Draw-A-Design and Draw-A-Child, respectively. These acceptably high correlations provided further evidence for the use of the drawing subtests in the screening of young children.

In a related study, Sattler and Squire (1982) sought to examine possible scoring difficulties of the McCarthy drawing subtests (likewise the McCarthy Oral Vocabulary, Part II of the Word Knowledge subtest; however, results of this are not pertinent to the present discussion). Twelve graduate students in psychology served as scorers. Sattler and Squire reported intraclass correlations of .81 for Draw-A-Child and .22 for Draw-A-Design. They contended that the McCarthy scoring procedure (compared to the Koppitz procedure for the Bender–Gestalt) probably led to ambiguities among scorer judgments. This conclusion should be tempered, however, because of a possible shortcoming of the study (one that the authors acknowledge): The graduate students, though they had some experience administering established individual intelligence tests (e.g., six WISC-R, four WPPSIs) and Bender–Gestalt Tests, had *not* administered any McCarthy tests.

In another study investigating the scoring of the McCarthy drawing tests, Piersel and Santos (1982) compared the Goodenough–Harris system (Harris, 1963) and the McCarthy procedure for scoring the Draw-A-Child. The subjects were 60 white and Mexican American kindergarteners. A school psychologist and a doctoral student in school psychology scored—in a counterbalanced design—all the Draw-A-Child protocols using the two scoring systems. The authors reported acceptable interscorer reliability for the McCarthy (.93) and the Goodenough–Harris (.91) systems, and an intrascorer correlation of .87 between the two systems for one scorer and .89 for the other scorer. It was also reported that an inspection of the Goodenough–Harris scoring categories showed that a maximum of 20 of 73 possible categories were used, whereas all 10 categories of the McCarthy system were used. Piersel and Santos concluded that given the high interscorer and intrascorer reliabilities, and because the Goodenough–Harris system is more complex and time-consuming, the McCarthy scoring system appears preferable.

It used to be the case that clinicians who attempted to use the McCarthy drawing subtests in their evaluation of children were faced with the problem of being unable to interpret the scores because these subtests did not have scaled scores. This issue has been rectified recently by Reynolds (1985), who developed standard-score tables for the Draw-A-Design and Draw-A-Child. Using the raw-score means and standard deviations on the drawing subtests for the standardization sample, Reynolds computed simple linear transformations for each raw-score point. The new distribution was scaled to a mean of 100 and a standard deviation of 15 at quarter-year intervals from $4\frac{1}{2}$ to $8\frac{1}{2}$ years. For practitioners who use or plan to use the two drawing subtests, the scaled scores developed by Reynolds (1985) should prove valuable in facilitating their clinical application.

In conclusion, the McCarthy drawing subtests have been shown to be reliable and valid when administered in a group setting. Second, it has been suggested that the scoring system of the McCarthy drawing subtests is preferable over those of other drawing tests. Third, the Draw-A-Design and Draw-A-Child are the best normed of all drawing tests, and there are now standard score tables available for clinical use. With these factors in mind, and in the context of screening, I agree with Kaufman's (1982) strong recommendation that the following combination would serve as a viable screening instrument: "the Kaufman short form administered individually by a qualified examiner *in conjunction with* the two drawing subtests administered in a group format" (p. 145, italics in original). Finally, for special considerations and helpful hints on administering and scoring the drawing subtests, the reader should consult Kaufman and Kaufman (1977a).

CLINICAL UTILITY FOR EXCEPTIONAL POPULATIONS

In this section, I attempt to shed some light on that significant clinical question—"How effective is the McCarthy in discriminating between normal and exceptional pop-ulations?" A particular concern here is to probe an unsettled issue: Given the persistent finding of a discrepancy between McCarthy GCI and IQ, how meaningful are such discrepancies in diagnosing learning disabilities and other exceptionalities? Here, "exceptional children" are defined as children whose performance deviates, either above or below the norm, to such an extent that special education is required (Heward & Orlansky, 1984). Regarding the psychometric properties of the McCarthy for exceptional groups, I only touch here upon pertinent investigations, as such studies have been introduced in the earlier section on "Reliability, Stability, and Validity."

For the reader's aid, clusters of exceptionalities are presented next with a listing of their respective investigations (studies with asterisks refer to investigations referenced in Kaufman, 1982). Following this list are brief discussions of salient findings and interpretations.

Learning disabilities: Bracken (1981)*; De-Boer, Kaufman, and McCarthy (1974)*; Goh (1976)*; Goh and Simons (1980)*; Goh and Youngquist (1979)*; Ivimey (1979); Ivimey and Taylor (1980); Kaufman (1972); Kaufman and Kaufman (1974); Keith and Bolen (1980)*; Klein (1982); Knack (1978)*; Lidz and Ballester (1986); Naglieri (1980a*, 1980b*, 1982); Naglieri et al. (1981)*; Simons and Goh (1982)*; Taylor and Ivimey (1980a)*.

Mental retardation: Bickett et al. (1984); Bondy et al. (1984); Brooks (1981); Harrison, Kaufman, and Naglieri (1980)*; Harrison and Naglieri (1978)*; Keith and Bolen (1980)*; Knack (1978)*; Levinson and Zino (1979a, 1979b)*; Lidz and Ballester (1986); Naglieri, (1980a*, 1980b*, 1982); Naglieri and Harrison (1979)*; Naglieri et al. (1981)*.

Reading problems: Healy (1981); Johnson and Wollersheim (1976)*; Nagel, Paget, and Mulkey (1980)*; Weiss (1977)*.

Hearing impairment: Christie (1982); Weiner (1980).

Visual impairment: Christie (1982).

Orthopedic impairment: Christie (1982).

Autism: Ferrari (1980).

Multiple categories: Vulpe (1983).

Health and related issues: Atkinson (1981); Bauman (1980); Conrad (1980); De Varona

Thompson (1980); Friedrich, Einbender, and Luecke (1983); Jacob (1981); Kinder (1982); Perino and Ernhart (1974).
Giftedness: Bondy et al. (1984); Bracken (1983)*; Harrison & Naglieri (1978)*.

Learning Disabilities

In his review of research on the McCarthy with learning-disabled populations, Kaufman (1982) presented four major conclusions. I briefly summarize each conclusion and then attempt to offer further understanding on the issue by integrating newer findings.

GCI–IQ Discrepancy

Kaufman (1982) noted that the earlier studies (DeBoer et al., 1974; Kaufman & Kaufman, 1974) reporting a difference of about one standard deviation between GCI and IQ were subsequently called into question for methodological flaws (see Bracken, 1981; Kaufman & Kaufman, 1977b). Later research on the GCI–IQ discrepancy issue has found the discrepancy to be considerably less than first observed. Table 9.5 in the present chapter shows that for comparisons between GCI and WISC-R FSIQ with learning-disabled groups (Goh, 1976; Goh & Youngquist, 1979; Ivimey & Taylor, 1980; Knack, 1980; Naglieri, 1980a), the weighted mean difference is 7 points. (The discrepancy between the GCI and the WISC FSIQ [DeBoer et al., 1974] is not discussed here because of methodological problems [see Bracken, 1981]). Between the GCI and the WPPSI FSIQ, Knack (1978) reported a mean difference of 5 points. Finally, in the only study available in which a comparison was made between the GCI and the Stanford–Binet IQ, Lidz and Ballester (1986) found a mean discrepancy of only 4 points with 29 learning-disabled preschool children.

Taken together, the aggregated weighted mean difference—based on the above-described seven studies and 180 learning-disabled children—between the GCI and the various IQs is 6.4 points. Regarding GCI–IQ discrepancies for *normal* children ($n = 845$), the findings from 24 studies in Table 9.5 reveal a difference of 2.8 points (i.e., for GCI and Stanford–Binet IQ, WISC-R FSIQ, and WPPSI FSIQ comparisons). It is noteworthy that this discrepancy figure is almost iden-

tical to the figure of 2.5 points that Kaufman (1982) reported in his review ($n = 676$ children; $n = 19$ studies). One can argue, as does Kaufman (1982), that given the consistently observed GCI–IQ discrepancy of about 6 points for learning-disabled populations and the typically observed GCI–IQ difference of about 3 points for normal children, the discrepancies for learning-disabled children do not appear to be dramatic. Naglieri (1980a) concludes, however, that "On an individual basis, an index which underestimates intellectual ability by about 5 points can be quite important" (p. 594).

In the final analysis, is it then legitimate for a clinician to use the GCI as an estimate of intellectual functioning of a child who is referred for a possible learning disability? Based on the available research, I agree with Kaufman (1982), who answers "yes" to this question. For reasons discussed in this chapter and elsewhere (Kaufman & Kaufman, 1977a), the McCarthy has many strong features that demonstrate it to be a viable instrument for assessing the abilities of young children, and thus it should not be categorically dismissed as a useful clinical tool for assessing learning-disabled children. Two caveats, nevertheless, are in order: First, because normal children typically exhibit a GCI–IQ discrepancy of a few points, clinicians should always keep this in mind (Kaufman, 1982). Second, the research findings on the GCI–IQ discrepancy issue underscore the need for flexibility in interpretation of clinical data and in classification. Thus, the GCI, like the IQ, should not be used rigidly (Naglieri, 1980a).

Characteristic Profiles

Do learning-disabled children, as a group, tend to have discernible patterns of strengths and weaknesses on the five separate McCarthy scales? To address this question, Kaufman (1982) integrated the results of six studies (DeBoer et al., 1974; Goh, 1976; Goh & Simons, 1980; Goh & Youngquist, 1979; Kaufman & Kaufman, 1974; Knack, 1978), and offered two major conclusions. First, on the GCI, the weighted mean for the aggregated sample ($n = 194$ children) in these studies was 78.9 (range = 66.2 to 86.9), demonstrating convincingly that the index of global functioning for most learning-disabled children falls below the average range. Second, the overall weighted mean scores for the five scales, in descending order, were as follows: 39.5 (Perceptual–Performance), 39.5 (Verbal), 37.6 (Quantitative), 37.3 (Memory), and 36.1 (Motor), indicating a fairly narrow range (3.4 points). Thus, as Kaufman noted, the observed intrascale fluctuations across the studies revealed no consistent weaknesses or strengths. It needs to be emphasized, nevertheless, that although group profiles are important, they fail to inform us about particular individuals within the group. Clinicians need to approach each child's profile as a separate interpretive challenge (Kaufman & Kaufman, 1977a; see this reference for useful suggestions in interpreting and communicating the profile of the McCarthy scale indices).

Discrimination between Learning-Disabled and Normal Children

Kaufman (1982) reviewed five studies in which investigators sought to examine the effectiveness of the McCarthy in discriminating between learning-disabled and non-learning-disabled groups (DeBoer et al., 1974; Goh & Simons, 1980; Kaufman & Kaufman, 1974; Knack, 1978; Taylor & Ivimey, 1980a). Two major conclusions were drawn. First, in two studies (Knack, 1978; Taylor & Ivimey, 1980a) that compared the McCarthy's discriminating ability to that of WISC-R, the McCarthy performed quite well. Second, when results of the five studies are taken as a whole, "the McCarthy Scales and subtests are quite effective in discriminating between learning disabled and nonlearning disabled groups, but the best variables for making these discriminations are unpredictable" (Kaufman, 1982, p. 156). In that no new research on this topic has been published since Kaufman's (1982) review, his conclusions are current.

Scatter

It is of great diagnostic interest for clinicians to ask: "On the McCarthy, do learning-disabled children exhibit more scatter (intratest variability) than do normal children?" Investigations by Goh and Simons (1980), Knack (1978), and Naglieri (1980a) have led

Kaufman (1982) to conclude: "Overall, there is only limited evidence of scatter in the McCarthy Indexes of learning disabled children" (p. 157). Furthermore, when speaking of the McCarthy and the WISC-R, Kaufman (1982) noted that, in general, research on both tests appears to dispute the stereotype of marked scatter in the test profiles of children with learning disabilities.

Mental Retardation

It is ironic that although mental retardation is the third most prevalent category in special education (about 18%, third only to learning disabilities and speech impairments; Hallahan & Kauffman, 1986), it has been a relatively neglected topic in McCarthy research. Furthermore, the research that does exist has identified two major problems, which raise some concerns about the validity and utility of the McCarthy in assessing the cognitive abilities of mentally retarded children. These issues are the GCI–IQ discrepancy and the McCarthy scale interpretation for very-low-functioning children.

GCI–IQ Discrepancy

Indeed, there have been consistent findings with mentally retarded populations that when the McCarthy GCI is compared to IQ performance on conventional tests, the GCI is typically lower than IQ. The magnitude of the discrepancy, however, appears to be confounded by the intelligence test used, the level of intellectual functioning of the particular sample, and an interaction of these two aspects.

With regard to the issue of the intelligence test used, Levinson and Zino (1979a, 1979b) and Naglieri and Harrison (1979) found Stanford–Binet IQ to be greater than GCI by 20 and 18 points, respectively, with mildly mentally retarded children. (In the present discussion, "mild mental retardation" refers to IQ ranges from about 50–55 to approximately 70; "moderate mental retardation" refers to IQ ranges from 35–40 to 50–55. See Hallahan & Kauffman, 1986.) In both studies, the mean IQ was 64. Also, in both investigations, the GCI composite raw score was so low for many subjects that it was not possible to tabulate GCIs. Thus, extrapolated GCIs were assigned using a table developed by Harrison and Naglieri (1978).

Bickett et al. (1984), using a sample of 11 moderately retarded children (mean IQ = 50.46 on Stanford–Binet), found IQ to average more than 17 points higher than GCIs (the mean GCI was established at 28, using the tables of extrapolation constructed by Harrison and Naglieri, 1978). On the other hand, in another study comparing discrepancies between the GCI and the Stanford–Binet IQ, Lidz and Ballester (1986) found only a 6.8-point difference (GCI < IQ) for 14 preschool mildly mentally retarded and pseudo-mentally retarded children (subjects were of low socioeconomic status [SES], ethnically mixed, and primarily black). The aggregated mean IQ performance on the Stanford–Binet for the two retarded groups was 70.9—a higher level of functioning than those seen in the mentally retarded samples studied by Levinson and Zino (1979a, 1979b), Naglieri and Harrison (1979), and Bickett et al. (1984). Finally, Brooks (1981) administered the McCarthy and Stanford–Binet to 33 low-SES black, educable mentally retarded students (ie., mildly retarded; mean IQ = 70). The observed GCI-IQ discrepancy of about 4 points is the lowest difference reported in the literature.

Investigations of mentally retarded children that have examined the GCI-IQ discrepancy issue with the Wechsler scales (i.e., WPPSI and WISC-R) have typically reported considerably smaller test differences (GCI < FSIQ) than those seen in the comparisons of the GCI and the Stanford–Binet IQ. In studies of the McCarthy and the WPPSI, Knack (1978) and Brooks (1981) reported GCI–FSIQ discrepancies of 8 points and 1.4 points, respectively. The mean FSIQ scores of the samples in Knack ($M = 64$) and Brooks ($M = 66$) were slightly different, possibly indicating that a slight relation exists between level of IQ perfomance on the criterion measure (WPPSI) and the magnitude of the GCI–IQ discrepancy; that is, as performance on IQ increases, GCI–IQ discrepancy decreases. This is a similar pattern to that found in the studies of the GCI and the Stanford–Binet IQ. In comparisons of the GCI and the WISC-R FSIQ, Knack (1978) and Naglieri (1980a) found discrepancies of 0 points and 8 points, respectively.

In conclusion, it appears that the issue of GCI–IQ discrepancy is more complicated than meets the eye. That is, the magnitude of the difference appears to be related to whether observed discrepancies are noted between the GCI and the Stanford–Binet IQ or the Wechsler FSIQ, with the former discrepancies being much larger than the latter. Furthermore (as pointed out above), as the intellectual functioning of mentally retarded children increases (particularly on the Stanford–Binet), the GCI–IQ discrepancy tends to decrease. This observation is somewhat substantiated by comparing the studies by Levinson and Zino (1979a), Naglieri (1980a), and Bickett et al. (1984) with those by Lidz and Ballester (1986) and Brooks (1981).

What are the implications of this finding for clinicians? The suggestion of several studies is that in the assessment of preschool children who are functioning in the middle to upper mildly retarded range (as determined by IQ performance), the GCI may be relatively interchangeable with the Stanford–Binet (see Brooks, 1981; Lidz & Ballester, 1986), the WPPSI (see Brooks, 1981), and the WISC-R (see Knack, 1978). This is an important point, in that approximately 80%–85% of identified mentally retarded children are classified in the mild (i.e., educable) category (Heward & Orlansky, 1984). Caution, however, is advised: On a case-by-case basis, some children who are being assessed for possible educable mentally retarded classification are likely to score much lower on the McCarthy GCI than on the Stanford–Binet or Wechsler scales. Furthermore, given the critical importance of cognitive assessment in identifying mildly retarded children, it is best for the clinician to be conservative in judgment. Thus, I recommend that if the McCarthy is used as an instrument in the assessment of suspected educable mental retardation, it should be utilized as a collaborative test (preferably with the WPPSI or WISC-R) and not as the sole cognitive instrument.

Scale Interpretation

A frequently cited criticism of the McCarthy is that the GCI is of limited use with very-low-functioning mentally retarded children because of its inadequate floor (Kaufman & Kaufman, 1977a; Levinson & Zino, 1979b). As Kaufman and Kaufman (1977a) note, the clinician may prefer the McCarthy as an assessment tool for moderately mentally retarded children, because it contains many items of appropriate difficulty and it is oriented to young children. Problems may arise, nevertheless, when the clinician tests children for whom the McCarthy does not contain ample "bottom," forcing the clinician to assign a GCI of "below 50" and a scale index of "below 22" on all five scales. Clearly, in situations like this, the clinician is unable to discriminate among children and is unable to discern individual children's strengths and weaknesses. Two strategies have been proposed to deal with these issues: extrapolated GCI values (Harrison & Naglieri, 1978) and "Scale Age" (i.e., mental age) equivalents (Kaufman & Kaufman, 1977a).

Harrison and Naglieri (1978) have developed conversion tables that take composite raw scores and provide extrapolated GCIs below 50 (and above 150 for potentially gifted children). As the authors note, since extrapolated values are not based on normative data, some precision is lost. Yet the extrapolated GCIs can be of use to the practitioner who wishes to have some rough cognitive data discriminating *among* low-functioning children, rather than just a "below 50" designation. Furthermore, until a great deal more research has been completed on the use of the McCarthy as an assessment tool with mentally retarded children, Harrison and Naglieri's extrapolated tables should be used only for research purposes and not for individual diagnosis (Kaufman, 1982).

Kaufman and Kaufman (1977a) have developed tables to estimate a child's "Scale Age," which is "equivalent to a mental age, but has the advantage of being derived from the standardization data (rather than estimated from a formula)" (p. 110). The Scale Age tables provide equivalents for the General Cognitive Age and the five scale indices. Kaufman and Kaufman (1977a) note that despite the problems attached to age norms (e.g., they are less psychometrically precise than standard scores), Scale Ages may frequently assist the clinician in highlighting a low-functioning retarded child's important strengths and weaknesses.

In a study that utilized the Scale Age procedure, Bickett et al. (1984) sought to compare the performance of a sample of 21 moderately retarded children (IQs from 36 to 51)

on the McCarthy, the Stanford–Binet, and the Minnesota Child Development Inventory (MCDI; Ireton & Thwing, 1974). The main purpose of the study was to compare the children's mental age for the GCI and five scale indices (based on the Kaufman & Kaufman, 1977a, Scale Age tables) with the Stanford–Binet mental age and the MCDI developmental age. Bickett et al. found significant correlations among the ages derived from the three instruments. Also, there were no significant mean differences among the mean McCarthy mental age (GCI = 41.4), the Stanford–Binet mental age (41.8), and the developmental age (45.1). The authors concluded:

> The results suggest that the MSCA MA [mental age] Scores provided by Kaufman and Kaufman (1977) are valid estimates of the abilities of moderately mentally retarded children. . . . Therefore, for children already classified and known to be functioning developmentally in the $2\frac{1}{2}$ to $8\frac{1}{2}$ year age range, MSCA MAs may have some utility for description of abilities and estimation of strengths and weaknesses. (1984, p. 311)

Bickett et al. do underscore, however, that despite their positive findings, the utility of McCarthy GCI mental age scores for educational classification purposes with moderately retarded children must be called into question, given the inherent problem of mental age scores (see Thorndike & Hagen, 1977).

In summary, although McCarthy research with mentally retarded children has been quite meager, one is still able to get a sense of the McCarthy's clinical utility. Based on the limited evidence, the McCarthy may have some collaborative usefulness in assessing mentally retarded children functioning in the upper educable mentally retarded range. Also, for lower-functioning retarded children, the McCarthy's extrapolated GCI and Scale Age scores may be helpful in discerning very approximate rankings among children and in identifying strengths and weaknesses of individual children, but they appear to have little value in classification.

Reading Problems

Kaufman (1982) reviewed three studies in which the McCarthy performance of children with reading problems was examined (Johnson & Wollersheim, 1976; Nagle et al., 1980; Weiss, 1977). The consensus of these investigations was that the McCarthy does have some effectiveness in distinguishing between below-average and average readers. To avoid unnecessary reiteration here of Kaufman's review, the reader is directed to that summary for details.

One "new" study has been identified. Healy (1981) attempted to investigate hyperlexia, a rare disorder in which children who are clearly delayed in language and cognitive development begin suddenly to recognize words at quite an early age. Upon development, however, the children fail to achieve written material comprehension in any manner one might predict for their precocity in word-calling abilities. To study this phenomenon, Healy gathered test and background data on 12 hyperlexic children aged 5–11 years (11 boys and 1 girl). In addition to the McCarthy, a number of cognitive, linguistic, and reading tests/tasks were administered. Healy reported depressed McCarthy GCI performance, with scores ranging from 47 to 91. Language disabilities were also observed, as measured by considerably low language quotients. Furthermore, it is of interest that autistic-type behaviors were reported in 10 or 12 children, and in 10 of 12 families, a close paternal relative had some type of language-learning disability typical of dyslexia.

Much more McCarthy research in the area of reading problems needs to be done. Particularly insightful would be investigations of children with diagnosed reading disabilities.

Hearing Impairment

Although Kaufman and Kaufman (1977a) offer administrative and interpretive advice for testing hearing-impaired children with the McCarthy, extremely little empirical research has been done investigating the clinical utility of the instrument with this exceptional population.

Christie's (1982) dissertation compared the McCarthy and the Batelle Developmental Inventory (BDI; Guidubaldi, 1980) for use in assessing three groups of handicapped children (children with hearing, visual, and orthpedic impairments). The BDI assesses developmental progress across five areas

(e.g., cognition, personal–social, and psychomotor), and it relies on parent and teacher report, child observations, and individual testing of the child.

The basic design of Christie's study involved correlating the McCarthy and the BDI with "traditional" intelligence or developmental tests (i.e., "IQ"). With regard to the hearing-impaired sample ($n = 12$; 3- to 4-year-olds; majority profoundly deaf; normal intelligence), Christie found a higher correlation between the BDI Developmental Quotient (DQ) and IQ ($r = .54$) than the GCI–IQ correlation ($r = .27$) and concluded that the McCarthy is inappropriate for use with hearing-impaired children (although there was no significant difference between the r's).

Christie's (1982) blanket conclusion about the inappropriateness of the McCarthy does not appear totally defensible. First, the higher correlation between the BDI DQ and IQ is not surprising, given that of the three *different* criterion intelligence tests administered, 9 of 12 children were given the Leiter International Performance Scale (LIPS; Leiter, 1969), a performance test. Second, an inspection of the mean performance of the children on the McCarthy reveals a mean Perceptual–Performance scale score of 48.9 (1 point away from the standardization mean of 50), indicating that this scale index may have value in assessing young, profoundly to severely hearing-impaired children. The low mean GCI of 70.6 was severely depressed by a very low mean score of 25.6 on the Verbal scale index and by the low mean score of 36.5 on the Quantitative scale index. Christie's discussion of this issue is informative, in that she reminds us that of the 17 subtests administered, 6 have a totally oral presentation. Certainly, this would present testing problems for seriously hearing-impaired 3- to 4-year-olds who are in the formative stages of communicative development. In addition, Christie raises serious issues about the usefulness of the Kaufman and Kaufman (1977a) prorating system.

In another dissertation, Weiner (1980) has provided indirect support for the usefulness of the McCarthy with hearing-impaired children. Her intent was not to investigate the McCarthy's utility per se, but rather to compare the cognitive and language skills of two groups of deaf children receiving instruction in two different communication methods (total communication vs. auditory/oral). The subjects were 43 profoundly and prelingually deaf children (5–7 years of age; at least average intelligence). The McCarthy, which served as the dependent variable (i.e., the basis of cognitive comparison between the two groups), was administered to the children using their accustomed communication mode. Since the purpose of the study was to compare cognitive performance of the two instructional groups, not to compare the children's performance with the McCarthy's norms, Weiner only reported raw scores. Thus, discussion of the children's McCarthy performance relative to standardization data is not possible.

Several informative points and implications, however, arose from the study. First, Weiner found it necessary for administrative reasons to make some modifications in the language of the directions and test items (i.e., reduction of length and complexity of language used). Weiner has provided, in an appendix, the altered directions and items for 15 of the 18 subtests. Clinicians who need to test profoundly deaf children on the McCarthy should find these administrative alterations useful. Second, the overall superiority of the total-communication group over the auditory/oral group (on all scales except Perceptual–Performance and Motor) may have been "attributed to the reduction in ambiguity of language afforded by the use of manual signs" (p. 76). That is, for the total-communication group, no confusion of phonemically similar words occurred. On the other hand, the auditory/oral group demonstrated consistent patterns of word confusion, which had a negative effect on responses. This response pattern was very likely related to the fact that in the English language, only about 30% of sounds can be detected through speech reading alone. Exacerbating this, about 50% of English words have some other word or words homophonous to them (i.e, they sound different, but they look alike on the lips; Heward & Orlansky, 1984). These difficulties lend support to the argument that speech reading can create problems during assessment. Clinicians need to be aware of this when administering the McCarthy to the hearing-impaired. A third point raised by Weiner is that the types of verbal tasks in general were too difficult for the expected level of comprehension of the children (e.g.,

some vocabulary tasks, retelling a story). Thus, the range of verbal tasks in the McCarthy may not be broad enough for measuring the actual abilities of the population studied.

Visual Impairment

In the previously described study by Christie (1982), 12 legally blind children (4 totally blind) were administered the McCarthy and the BDI. Mean "IQ" was based on aggregated scores from five different intelligence tests (all children were in the normal and above normal range of intelligence). The correlation between BDI DQ and IQ ($r = .58$) was significantly different from the GCI–IQ correlation ($r = .05$). Based on this, Christie concluded the McCarthy to be inappropriate for assessing visually impaired preschool children.

Once again, and reasons similar to those presented earlier, this conclusion is shaky. The moderate correlation for the DQ–IQ comparison and the near-zero correlation for the GCI–IQ comparison were not unexpected, as it appears that of the 12 intelligence test scores, the majority were derived from tests specially modified for assessing the blind. Therefore, one could predict a higher correlation between the BDI and the intelligence measures. Contrary to Christie's conclusion, there does appear to be evidence that the McCarthy was effective in assessing the blind children. An inspection of the mean performance on the scales of the McCarthy indicated that the children performed in the normal range (GCI = 104.7; Quantitative = 55.1), and, on two scales, about a standard deviation above the normative mean (Verbal = 59.3; Memory = 58.3). The only below-average performance was on the Perceptual–Performance scale (39.0). This was not surprising, in that tasks on this scale require visual perception and visual–motor coordination.

Orthopedic Impairment

Christie (1982) also assessed 11 preschool children who had a wide range of orthopedic impairments (cerebral palsy, spina bifida, muscular dystrophy, amputation, lower-extremity paralysis). The mean IQs were 104 and 109 for the 3-year-olds and 4-year-olds, respectively.

Christie found the GCI–IQ *r* of .83 to be higher (but not significantly so) than the BDI DQ–IQ *r* of .67, leading her to conclude that the McCarthy appears to be appropriate for the assessment of orthopedically impaired preschoolers. The high correlation between the GCI and IQ scores, by the way, makes considerable sense, because in 10 of 11 of the intelligence test administrations, the Stanford–Binet and the WPPSI (instruments known to correlate highly with the McCarthy) were used. Further support for this effectiveness of the McCarthy in assessing children of this population comes from an analyisis of the mean performance on the McCarthy. The 11 children's performance on the scales, which was consistently in the normal range, showed these means: GCI (98.4), Verbal (51.9), Perceptual–Performance (44.9), Quantitative (49.6), and Memory (52.4).

Christie shared some observations about the children's physical responses that might be informative for clinicians. She stated that for some children with lower-extremity difficulties, certain motor subtests had to be omitted. Also, 5 of 11 children who had upper-extremity problems had enough control to be able to respond to all McCarthy subtests, including Block Building, Puzzle Solving, Tapping Sequence, Draw-A-Design, and Draw-A-Child. Finally, except for the omission of some motor subtests for some children, the administration of the McCarthy essentially followed the standard procedure for normal children.

Autism

Aside from the previously described McCarthy study by Healy (1981), who tangentially reported autistic-type behaviors in hyperlexic children, only one other study exists in which the McCarthy was administered to autistic children. Ferrari (1980), in a concurrent validity investigation, administered the PPVT and the McCarthy to eight children (5–9 years of age, *M* = 7½ years; six boys, two girls) who had met all the criteria for autism. The PPVT IQ and the GCI were 46.86 and 53.75, respectively (*r* = .84). For some children, extrapolated GCIs were obtained following the procedure by Harrison and Naglieri (1978).

Ferrari offered two conclusions. First, the PPVT significantly underestimated the autistic children's abilities when compared to the McCarthy, thus indicating that the PPVT IQ and GCI are not interchangeable. Second, generalizations from this study should be guarded, as the children were low-functioning, and therefore the results may not be applicable to less regressed autistic children.

It is important to note, as Ferrari does, that at one time it was widely believed that autistic children were of normal intelligence and their typically low IQ scores largely reflected their "untestability." Recent research, however, indicates that a large percentage of autistic children are intellectually retarded (e.g., DeMyer et al., 1974). Thus, if this is kept in mind, the McCarthy may hold some promise in assessing the cognitive abilities of autistic children.

Multiple Categories

Vulpe (1983) hypothesized in her dissertation: "Measures of intelligence of many young, handicapped children are biased when testing procedures require verbal information processing" (p. 4). To test this hypothesis, Vulpe administered the McCarthy and the LIPS (Leiter, 1969), an intelligence test that has been recommended for assessing language- and sensory-handicapped children (Sattler, 1982; Swanson & Watson, 1982). The subjects were 102 children (aged 2–10 years; blacks and whites) with a broad range of handicapping conditions (i.e., Down syndrome, cerebral palsy, "other health impairments," "noncategorical," educable and trainable mentally retarded, learning-disabled, emotionally disturbed).

Vulpe's major finding was that in about two-thirds of the cases, the LIPS IQ was greater than the McCarthy GCI (about a 23-point difference); this, she claimed, gave some support to her hypothesis. Overall, the mean difference for the 102 children was about 9 points (mean IQ about 86; mean GCI about 75). Such results are not necessarily unexpected, given the verbal loading of the McCarthy and the nonverbal nature of the LIPS.

Any conclusions and generalizations drawn from this study, however, should be interpreted with caution. First, the aggregated nature of the handicapping conditions does not lend itself to meaningful generalizations for particular exceptional populations. Second, ethnicity may be a confounding variable, as black and white children's performances were aggregated. Third, the manner in which some children were initially classified is suspect. For example, one child who was diagnosed as trainable mentally retarded had an IQ of 105 on the LIPS and a GCI of 67 on the McCarthy. Furthermore, several children who were diagnosed as educable mentally retarded had IQs and GCIs that did not correspond to conventional cutoffs. For example, one such child had a LIPS IQ of 114 and a GCI of 94. Fourth, determining bias in testing by simply comparing mean differences between groups is considered by many in the measurement community to be an untenable technique (e.g., Jensen, 1980; Reynolds, 1982). Notwithstanding these possible limitations, Vulpe's concluding point, when speaking of the LIPS and the GCI, is well taken: "[B]oth testing methods are needed to obtain a balanced view of a child's intellectual potential and information processing pattern" (1983, p. 90).

Health and Related Issues

The McCarthy's effectiveness has also been investigated in distinguishing various health and related conditions. These areas have included congenital heart disease (Atkinson, 1981); maternal drug addiction (Bauman, 1980); lead poisoning (Conrad, 1980; Perino & Ernhart, 1974); maternal toxemia (De Varona Thompson, 1980); physical abuse (Friedrich et al., 1983); oxygen therapy and blood gas analysis (Kinder, 1982); and prematurity (Jacob, 1981). Taken together, these various studies consistently indicate that the McCarthy is relatively effective in distinguishing between abnormal and normal health conditions. Since these investigations are quite lengthy (i.e., the vast majority are doctoral dissertations), the reader is referred to the actual sources for details.

Giftedness

The topics of gifted children's performance on the McCarthy and the McCarthy's clinical usefulness in identifying such children continue to be neglected by researchers. One informative study, nevertheless, is that by Bracken (1983), who administered the Stanford–Binet and the McCarthy to 32 white preschool and primary-age children (mean age about $4\frac{1}{2}$ years). An r of .30 was observed between IQ and GCI, as well as a 10-point GCI–IQ discrepancy (mean IQ = 129.53; mean GCI = 119.94). Except for the Motor scale (M = 52.66), the children performed consistently about 0.7 to 1.0 standard deviation above the normative means on the other scales.

The implication of underidentification of gifted children raised by Bracken has potential clinical value. That is, if a Stanford–Binet IQ cutoff of 120 had been used, all 32 children would have been identified as gifted, whereas only 11 (34%) of the 32 would have been selected on the basis of the GCIs. Bracken suggests two hypotheses to explain why the McCarthy, relative to the Stanford–Binet tended to underestimate the children's performance. First, the Standard–Binet is a more heavily loaded verbal test than the McCarthy. Thus, gifted children—who have well-developed verbal abilities (e.g., Sattler, 1982)—may not have the opportunity to express these skills as well on the McCarthy as they do on the Stanford–Binet. Second, the McCarthy is troubled by an insufficient ceiling for young bright children (Kaufman & Kaufman, 1977a; see Naglieri & Harrison, 1978, for extrapolated GCIs above 150).

In the only other study investigating the McCarthy with gifted children, Bondy et al. (1984) administered the SIT and the McCarthy to 14 preschool children (13 white, 1 black; mean age $4\frac{3}{4}$ years). The GCI–IQ mean discrepancy was about 14 points (mean IQ = 148.6; mean GCI = 135.0). The considerably higher SIT IQ was in line with previous research with normal children (e.g., Ritter, Duffy, & Fishman, 1973), indicating that the SIT provides spurious estimates of children's intelligence.

Clearly, much more research in this area is needed, particularly investigations designed to see whether Bracken's (1983) findings with the Stanford–Binet can be replicated. Also, concurrent validity research is encouraged with other criterion measures (e.g., WISC-R, WPPSI) and with diverse populations (e.g., minority children).

In summary, the available research on the clinical utility of the McCarthy with exceptional populations has grown over the years. Although there are very limited amounts of research on some exceptionalities, and mixed findings accompanied with cautions in other categories, the existing research taken as a whole points to a general conclusion that the McCarthy has value in clinical applications with exceptional groups.

ETHNIC MINORITY ASSESSMENT

The number of minority-related studies on the McCarthy has increased about 200% since Kaufman's (1982) review (from $n = 12$ to $n = 36$), with investigations of Mexican American children accounting for about 71% of the increase ($n = 17$ to 24). Because of the historical controversy surrounding the use of standardized intelligence tests in the assessment of minority children, recent reforms in nondiscriminatory assessment, and dramatic increases in minority populations, it is important to examine the utility of instruments such as the McCarthy for minority children (Valencia, 1983). The present section analyzes the available research on the McCarthy in which black, Mexican American, Puerto Rican, and Native American children have served as subjects. Two primary themes guide this review: (1) McCarthy performance of minority children compared to the normative data and/or compared to the performance of white children; and (2) psychometric findings.

Black Children

Table 9.6 lists 15 studies in which the McCarthy, in whole or part, was administered to black children. These investigations include psychometric studies, comparisons of black–white McCarthy performance, and studies in which the McCarthy's inclusion was secondary to the research question under investigation (e.g., Curry, 1980). I now turn to a brief discussion of salient findings.

Comparative Findings

Despite the large number of studies listed in Table 9.6, there is meager information available as to how black children perform on the McCarthy, compared to the normative sample or compared to white children in independent studies. Excluding those studies of exceptional black children (i.e., Brooks, 1981; Ernhart & Landa, 1980; Ernhart, Landa, & Callahan, 1980; Perino & Ernhart, 1974), only three comparative black–white studies have been identified with normal children (Arinoldo, 1981; Kaufman & Kaufman, 1973a; Long, 1976).

The investigation by Kaufman and Kaufman (1973a) is the most informative, because the data source was the standardization sample. Comparisons were made between 148 matched pairs of black and white children, with these three age groupings: $2\frac{1}{2}$–$3\frac{1}{2}$, 4–$5\frac{1}{2}$, and $6\frac{1}{2}$–$8\frac{1}{2}$ years. The weighted mean GCIs (aggregated age groups) for the black and white samples were 93.6 and 98.8, respectively. This aggregated comparison is misleading, however, because ethnic mean differences appeared to be confounded by age. That is, Kaufman and Kaufman reported a 5.9-point GCI ethnic difference (nonsignificant) at $2\frac{1}{2}$–$3\frac{1}{2}$ years, a 1.5-point difference (nonsignificant) at 4–$5\frac{1}{2}$ years, and a 9.5-point difference (significant) at $6\frac{1}{2}$–$8\frac{1}{2}$ years. All mean differences favored whites.

On the other five scales of the McCarthy, it was reported that blacks and whites did not differ significantly on mean performance, although the white sample scored significantly higher by about 0.5 standard deviation on all scales (except Motor) at ages $6\frac{1}{2}$–$8\frac{1}{2}$. The slightest mean differences between ethnic groups were seen at ages 4–$5\frac{1}{2}$ with differences ranging between 0 and 1.1 points (except for Motor, in which Blacks performed significantly higher than whites). Finally, for 51 comparisons made at the subtest level, Kaufman and Kaufman reported only 10 significant differences (8 favoring whites, 2 favoring blacks).

Arinoldo's (1981) cross-validation study of Kaufman and Kaufman (1973a) also reported a striking age interaction on McCarthy performance. The subjects—matched on pertinent variables (e.g., sex, parents' occupation)—were 20 black and white children aged 4–$5\frac{1}{2}$, and 20 black and white children aged 7–$8\frac{1}{2}$. The mean GCI difference between blacks ($M = 90.5$) and whites ($M = 94.3$) at ages 4–$5\frac{1}{2}$ was only 3.8 points, whereas the mean difference at ages 7–$8\frac{1}{2}$ was 15.5 points (black $M = 86.1$; white $M = 101.6$). In a related study, Long (1976) administered the McCarthy to 111 white children and 40 black

TABLE 9.6. McCarthy Investigations with Black Samples

Type of study/author(s)	n	Age range (in years and months)	Comments
Construct validity			
*Kaufman & DiCuio (1975)	124	3 years, 0 months to 7 years, 6 months	
*Reynolds (1980)	146	4 years, 6 months to 6 years, 6 months	DAD and DAC subtests only
Concurrent validity			
Brooks (1981)	20	5 years, 7 months to 6 years, 4 months	EMR sample; criterion tests were Stanford–Binet, WPPSI
Predictive validity			
Blachman (1981)	68	Preschool; first grade	
Ernhart, Landa, & Callahan (1980)	68	Approx. 4 years, 6 months to 9 years, 5 months	Sample recruited from screening program for lead poisoning
*Long (1976)	40	Preschool	
Stability			
Brooks (1981)	20	5 years, 7 months to 6 years, 4 months	EMR sample
*Ernhart & Landa (1980)	68	Approx. 4 years, 6 months to 10 years, 0 months	Sample recruited from screening program for lead poisoning
Ernhart et al. (1980)	68	Approx. 4 years, 6 months to 9 years, 5 months	Same as above
Black–white differences			
*Arinoldo (1981)	20	Approx. 4 years, 0 months to 8 years, 6 months	Age major variable
Averitt (1981)	NA	Preschool	Four variables (e.g., sex, SES)
*Kaufman & Kaufman (1973a)	148	2 years, 6 months to 8 years, 6 months	Age major variable
*Kaufman & Kaufman (1975)	154	2 years, 6 months to 8 years, 6 months	SES major variable
*Long (1976)	40	Preschool	Preschool experience, sex major variables
*Reynolds, McBride & Gibson (1981)	148	2 years, 6 months to 8 years, 6 months	Hemisphericity major variable
Other			
Curry (1980)	72	4 years, 1 month to 5 years, 1 month	Curricular intervention
Lewis (1979)	40	5 and 7-year-olds	Dialect major variable
*Perino & Ernhart (1974)	80	3 years, 0 months to 5 years, 11 months	Relation of lead levels to McCarthy performance

Note. Studies discussed and referenced in Kaufman (1982) are marked with an asterisk. NA, not available; DAD, Draw-A-Design; DAC, Draw-A-Child; EMR, educable mentally retarded; WPPSI, Wechsler Preschool and Primary Scale of Intelligence; SES, socioeconomic status.

children prior to first-grade entrance. Long reported a significant difference of 6 points on GCI performance (black M = 95; white M = 101.2). This observed difference may have been confounded because SES was not controlled.

The available research on the comparative McCarthy performance of black children leads to several conclusions that clinicians may find informative. First, based on aggregated data (n = 188) from Arinoldo (1981), Kaufman and Kaufman (1973a), and Long (1976), the weighted mean GCI for black children is 93.4. This finding of about 0.5 standard deviation below the McCarthy standardization mean of 100 is impressively less than the consistent mean difference of about one standard deviation (aggregated analysis) between blacks and whites observed on other intelligence tests over many decades (e.g., Jensen, 1980; Shuey, 1966). Second, based on the findings by Arinoldo (1981) and Kaufman and Kaufman (1973a), it appears that the slightest mean differences between black and white children are observed at the "target" age populations of the McCarthy—preschool and kindergarten. Kaufman and Kaufman (1973a, 1977a) conclude that since these mean differences are quite small, the McCarthy may be "color-blind" in assessing young black children. It should be kept in mind, however, that minimal or no mean differences in cognitive performance between white and minority children do not *a priori* indicate the absence of possible test bias (e.g., Reynolds, 1982). Third, clinicians should be aware that the pervasive positive correlation between SES and intellectual functioning seen in the general literature has also been observed with black children in regard to the McCarthy (Kaufman & Kaufman, 1975).

Psychometric Findings

It is of considerable interest to note that although the issue of bias in intellectual assessment of black children has been at the center of controversy in the measurement, judicial, and legislative communities (Henderson & Valencia, 1985), extremely little psychometric research has been done on the McCarthy with blacks. A scrutiny of Table 9.6 underscores the distressing absence of such research. That is, not a *single* study exists that has investigated the concurrent validity and stability with normal black children. Furthermore, not a *single* study exists on the reliability and content validity of the McCarthy with normal *or* exceptional black children. Finally, except for one investigation (Kaufman & DiCuio, 1975), no study exists that has attempted to address the possibility of test bias in the McCarthy by *simultaneously* examining black and white children. This is a significant area of underinvestigation, since the issue of test bias (e.g., possible differential predictive validity) implies the comparison of two or more groups (Jensen, 1980).

Despite the paucity of psychometric research on the McCarthy with black children, what does the available research tell us? Regarding construct validity, Kaufman and DiCuio (1975) performed separate factor analyses of the McCarthy for groups of black ($n = 124$) and white ($n = 688$) children from the standardization sample. The results indicated "highly similar" factor structures for

blacks and whites, suggesting construct validity for both groups (see Table 9.4 of the present chapter for the factors that emerged).

Brooks (1981), who investigated the concurrent validity of the McCarthy with 20 black, educable mentally retarded children (see Table 9.5), found moderate validity coefficients with the Stanford–Binet ($r = .65$) and the WPPSI ($r = .73$). Also, Brooks reported acceptably high stability coefficients for the GCI ($r_{12} = .86$) and Memory scale ($r_{12} = .85$) (see Table 9.3).

In another stability study, Ernhart and Landa's (1980) subjects were 80 black children recruited as preschoolers from a screening program for lead poisoning. The observed stability coefficients for the primary sample ($n = 27$) were considerably lower (see Table 9.3) than permitted by conventional standards. The low coefficients were very likely related to the long interval between first and second testing (M = about 4 years).

Regarding predictive validity, Blachman (1981) administered the McCarthy to 68 kindergarten and first-grade black children attending inner-city schools. It was reported that the McCarthy GCI and the Quantitative and Memory scales were significant predictors of reading achievement. Ernhart et al. (1980) also attempted to investigate the McCarthy's predictive validity. Of 80 black children recruited from a screening program for lead poisoning when they were preschoolers, 68 children were administered reading achievement tests about 5 years later. The predictive validity coefficients for the various scales of the McCarthy were as follows: .52 (GCI), .33 (Verbal), .49 (Perceptual–Performance), .35 (Quantitative), .13 (Memory), and .29 (Motor). Although the correlations were significant (except for the Memory scale), they are not of impressive magnitudes. A possible factor related to the low correlations was that the reading scores were based on 10 *different* tests, thus inviting the possibilities of different standards and variability across norming populations.

Mexican American Children

In his integrated review of the McCarthy, Kaufman's (1982) discussion of research with Mexican American children referred only to work in progress, as no studies had yet been published. An observation of Table 9.7,

TABLE 9.7. McCarthy Investigations with Mexican-American Samples

Type of study/author(s)	n	Age range (in years and months)	Comments
Construct validity			
Mishra (1981)	126	Approx. 5 years, 6 months to 7 years, 6 months	Also included white sample (n = 186)
Reliability			
Laosa (1984)	79	2 years, 3 months to 2 years, 10 months	Also included white sample (n = 87)
Mishra & Powers (1984)	58	5 years, 6 months to 8 years, 6 months	Also included white sample (n = 56)
Valencia & Rankin (1983)	154	4 years, 3 months to 5 years, 9 months	Also included Spanish-speaking sample (n = 176); also examined Kaufman SF
Concurrent validity			
Laosa (1982)	187	Approx. 3 years, 6 months to 4 years, 0 months	Criterion was Preschool Inventory
Sattler & Altes (1984) Sattler (1978)	11	3 years, 7 months to 5 years, 5 months	Perceptual–Performance scale only criterion was PPVT-R; also included Spanish-speaking sample (n = 20)
Valencia & Rothwell (1984)	39	4 years, 5 months to 5 years, 6 months	Criterion was WPPSI
Predictive validity			
Johnson & McGowan (1984)	27–31	Approx. 4-year-olds	
Valencia (1982)	31	6 years, 11 months to 8 years, 6 months	
Valencia (1984)	31	6 years, 11 months to 8 years, 7 months	Also included Spanish-speaking sample (n = 43); predictor was Kaufman SF
Stability			
Valencia (1983a, 1985)	42	5 years, 1 month to 6 years, 4 months	Also included Spanish-speaking sample (n = 42)
Content validity			
Murray & Mishra (1983a)	59	Approx. 5 years, 6 months to 8 years, 6 months	Verbal scale only; also included white sample (n = 59)
Murray & Mishra (1983b)	NA	NA	Face validity study
Valencia & Rankin (1985)	142	Approx. 4 years, 7 months (M)	Also included Spanish-speaking sample (n = 162)
Valencia (1983b)	60	3 years, 5 months to 5 years, 7 months	Examination of Head Start children's entry-level abilities; also included Spanish-speaking sample (n = 55)
Valencia, Henderson, & Rankin (1981)	71	2 years, 9 months to 5 years, 9 months	Examination of numerous sociocultural and familial correlates of cognitive performance; also included Spanish-speaking sample (n = 119)
Valencia, Henderson, & Rankin (1985)	52	3 years, 2 months to 5 years, 11 months	Same focus as Valencia et al. (1981), but also included a home environmental independent variable; also included Spanish-speaking sample (n = 88)

Note. NA, not applicable; SF, short form; PPVT-R, Peabody Picture Vocabulary Test—Revised; WPPSI, Wechsler Preschool and Primary Scale of Intelligence.

however, demonstrates that a great deal of research activity has occurred over the last several years. The 17 investigations listed in the table include an interesting variety of subjects and research concerns. Given this data base, I first inquire how well Mexican American children have performed on the McCarthy, compared to normative data; second, I synthesize the available research on psychometric studies.

Comparative Findings

Elsewhere (Valencia, 1988), I have presented an integrated, detailed review of available research on the McCarthy with Mexican American children, covering comparative performance and psychometric findings. This section describes the review's major conclusions.

Five studies exist in which the mean McCarthy performance of English-speaking Mexican American children has been reported. The subjects (all normal) included a span of grade levels: preschool (Johnson & McGowan, 1984; Valencia, 1983b; Valencia & Rankin, 1985), kindergarten (Valencia, 1983a, 1985) and second grade (Valencia, 1982). The recent review (Valencia, 1988) provides these findings:

1. Based on the weighted mean of the aggregated samples for the five studies ($n = 307$ children), the mean GCI of 99.9 was *identical* (when rounded) to the McCarthy standardization mean of 100. This is an impressive score, in that the children in the five studies were from low-SES families and differed culturally from the white children who comprised 84% of the McCarthy standardization sample (I estimate that Mexican American children comprised less than 1% of the standardization group).

2. The weighted means on the other scales for the 307 children were *at or above* the normative mean of 50: Perceptual–Performance ($M = 53.2$), Quantitative ($M = 51.3$), and Memory ($M = 49.6$). The exception, though, was performance on the Verbal scale ($M = 47.1$), which was about 0.3 standard deviation below the normative mean. Elsewhere (Valencia, 1982), I have hypothesized that the slightly depressed Verbal scale performance of these Mexican American children may have been related to variability in their linguistic backgrounds. Although the children were determined to be fluent in English as assessed by direct and indirect measures, it is likely that some of the children varied in English abilities and/or were reared in Spanish-speaking or bilingual families. That is, it is conceivable that some of the children may have lacked broad exposure to English in their formative years of language development or during the time of McCarthy testing. The clinical implication of this finding regarding the Verbal scale is that "school psychologists should be aware of the potential problems when administering the MSCA to Mexican American children even though they are considered to be fluent in English" (Valencia, 1982, p. 1277).

3. Very little information is available on the performance of Mexican American children on the Motor scale. In my colleagues' and my research, this scale was not administered because of time restrictions. Data are available, however, from Johnson and McGowan (1984). The mean Motor scale performance for 32 children aged 4 was 50.2. This is not an unexpected finding, in that it has been consistently documented that Mexican American children perform well within the normal range on perceptual–motor tests (Valencia, 1977).

4. In the five investigations described above, slight to considerable restricted variability on all scales was observed. I have noted (Valencia, 1988) that the weighted mean standard deviations for the scales for the aggregated sample ($n = 307$) were as follows: GCI (13.6), Verbal (9.3), Perceptual–Performance (8.6), Quantitative (9.5), and Memory (9.2). Since it is well known that restricted variability can depress correlation coefficients, researchers should be aware of this when undertaking validity research with Mexican American children. In some cases, it may be advisable to correct statistically for range restriction (e.g., see Valencia & Rothwell, 1984).

5. The recent review of McCarthy research with Mexican American children (Valencia, 1988) also includes a synthesis of studies in which Spanish-speaking Mexican American children served as subjects along with their English-speaking peers (Valencia, 1983a, 1983b, 1984, 1985; Valencia & Rankin, 1983, 1985). A careful Spanish translation of the standard McCarthy (Valencia & Cruz,

THE MCCARTHY SCALES OF CHILDREN'S ABILITIES

1981) was used in these studies. The Spanish version was initially intended to serve strictly as a research instrument in our (Valencia & Cruz, 1981) study of Mexican American mothers' perceptions of their children's intellectual abilities. Subsequently, the Spanish version's psychometric properties became focal points of study (e.g., Valencia, 1983a, 1985). (Some possible assessment implications of the Spanish version are discussed later.) Furthermore, the Spanish translation of the McCarthy has proven useful as the dependent variable in studies investigating sociocultural factors, familial factors, and home intellectual environment as salient predictors of Mexican American children's performance (Valencia, Henderson, & Rankin, 1981, 1985).

What do we know about the relative performance of Spanish-speaking Mexican American children on the Spanish McCarthy version? The review (Valencia, 1988) summarizes these pertinent findings (Valencia, 1982, 1983a, 1983b, 1985); Valencia & Rankin, 1985): First, based on an aggregated weighted mean analysis (n = 302 children; preschool, kindergarten, second grade), the Spanish-speaking children's mean GCI of 92.7 was about 0.5 standard deviation lower than the McCarthy norm. Second, the mean performances on the Verbal (M = 41.8), Quantitative (M = 46.4), and memory (M = 44.3) scales were about 0.8, 0.3, and 0.6 standard deviation below the norms, respectively. Third, as expected, the mean score on the much less verbal Perceptual–Performance scale (M = 52.3) was near the standardization mean of 50. Fourth, on all scales, including the GCI, variability was restricted.

Psychometric Findings

An informative body of studies has examined the psychometric properties of the McCarthy with Mexican American children (see Table 9.7). This research has produced a nice variety of studies and a solid base of psychometric knowledge from which to expand further research. Here is a summary of major points of the recent review (Valencia, 1988):

1. Mishra (1981) has provided the only construct validity of the McCarthy with Mexican American children. In his study, Mishra reported three similar factors for Mexican American and white children (See Table 9.4). He concluded that the McCarthy had construct validity for both ethnic groups; yet he admonished that the results should be interpreted with caution because of ethnic group differences in the loading patterns of the different scales.

2. Several studies exist in which the McCarthy's reliability has been investigated with a wide age range of Mexican American children (Laosa, 1984; Mishra & Powers, 1984; Valencia & Rankin, 1983; see Table 9.2). Overall, the observed reliability coefficients were of acceptable magnitudes (.73 to .94). Evidence of reliability for the Kaufman SF with Mexican American children also exists (Valencia & Rankin, 1983).

3. Valencia and Rothwell (1985) provided some evidence of the concurrent validity of the McCarthy with Mexican American preschool children (see Table 9.5). The correlation between the GCI and WPPSI FSIQ was .77. The majority of the correlations were in the high .70s and low .80s.

4. The stability of the McCarthy with Mexican American children has been investigated (Valencia, 1983a, 1985; see Table 9.3). Over a 1-year test–retest period, an acceptably high stability coefficient of .86 was observed for the GCI. The r's for the other scales ranged from .86 to .92. A GCI stability coefficient of .79 was also reported for a sample of Spanish-speaking children.

5. Support for the McCarthy's predictive validity has been provided (Valencia, 1982). Significant correlations were observed between the various scales of the McCarthy and the reading and mathematics subtests of the CTBS (CTB/McGraw-Hill, 1974). The salient findings were as follows: (a) A correlation of .75 was reported between the GCI and Total Reading; (b) the McCarthy appeared to be a stronger predictor of reading than of mathematics scores; and (c) the McCarthy Verbal scale was a significant but moderate predictor of reading achievement (r = .43), a finding similar to that reported in Shellenberger (1982) with Puerto Rican children.

Another study (Valencia, 1984) investigated the predictive validity of the Kaufman SF for English-speaking and Spanish-speaking children. The criterion was the CTBS. The major finding was that the actual

GCI and estimated GCI predicted academic achievement about equally well, and there were no significant differences in r's between the two language groups.

6. The content validity of the McCarthy has been examined in several studies (Mishra & Powers, 1984; Murray & Mishra, 1983a, 1983b; Valencia & Rankin, 1985). Mishra and Powers included white and Mexican American children). The biased items were those tapping comprehension of complex numerical and verbal knowledge. The authors concluded that the negligible amount of bias in content validity suggested the McCarthy to be equally appropriate for both ethnic groups.

Murray and Mishra's (1983a) item bias study was restricted to the 46 items comprising the Verbal scale. Of the total items, only three revealed systematic cultural bias (bias against the Mexican American sample).

Our content validity study (Valencia & Rankin, 1985) included English- and Spanish-speaking preschool children. The method of bias detection was the item–group (partial) correlation technique, in which the correlation between the test item and language group membership is computed, with the contribution of the general ability score (GCI) partialed out. In short, GCI was controlled. Of the 157 McCarthy items investigated, 23 (14.7%) were noted to be biased: 6 were biased against the English-speaking sample and 17 against the Spanish-speaking group. The pattern of bias for the English-speaking children was not discernible. On the other hand, of the 17 items baised against the Spanish-speaking group, 12 (71%) clustered in two subtests (Verbal Memory I and Numerical Memory I). These two subtests tap serial-order short-term memory. We hypothesized that because the words and numerals in the Spanish list contained considerably more syllables, and because the phonemes in Spanish were more acoustically similar, the Spanish-speaking children tended to have an information overload on short-term memory. These hypotheses were grounded in empirical evidence from human short-term memory research. The findings are discussed in light of translated tests, particularly the issue of item equivalence.

In summary, an analysis of the existing research on the McCarthy with Mexican American English-speaking children led to this conclusion: "Based on the available evidence, it appears justified to recommend it as an instrument in the psychoeducational assessment of these children. It is admonished, however, that performance on the Verbal Scale be interpreted with extreme caution" (Valencia, 1988, p. 100). It is also noted that "In light of the very limited choice of alternative assessment instruments school psychologists have in testing Spanish-speaking Mexican American children, it appears that the administration of the MSCA Perceptual–Performance subtests may be of some use" (Valencia, 1988, p. 100).

Puerto Rican Children

In my summary of studies with Mexican American children (Valencia, 1988), available research on the McCarthy with Puerto Rican children is also reviewed. Here are key points from the review:

1. Mean performance data on the McCarthy are limited to one study. In Shellenberger and Lachterman (1979), the mean performance of 30 English-speaking Puerto Rican children (aged 5–8½ years) was near the standardization mean on the Perceptual–Performance scale ($M = 47.3$) and the Motor scale ($M = 49.7$). On the other hand, mean performance on the Quantitative and Memory scales and the GCI was approximately 1 standard deviation below the norm. The mean performance of the children on the Verbal scale was about 1.3 standard deviations below the standardization mean. I have argued (Valencia, 1988) that the very low performance of the children on the Verbal scale ($M = 36.6$), and likewise the GCI ($M = 82.5$), was probably related to the subjects' language status. Although Shellenberger and Lachterman conducted a "screening interview" to insure the children's facility in English, it appears nevertheless that a sizable number of children spoke only limited English. Thus, any interpretations and generalizations of Shellenberger and Lachterman's reporting of mean McCarthy performance of Puerto Rican children should be made with extreme care.

2. Several studies exist that have attempted to examine the psychometric properties of the McCarthy with Puerto Rican children (see Table 9.8). Shellenberger

TABLE 9.8. McCarthy Investigations with Puerto Rican and Native American Samples

Type of study/author	n	Age range (in years and months)	Comments
		Puerto Rican	
Reliability *Shellenberger (1982)	100	5 years, 10 months to 8 years, 4 months	Sample was Spanish-speaking
Concurrent validity *Shellenberger & Lachterman (1979)	30	Approx. 5 years, 0 months to 8 years, 6 months	Criterion tests were two WISC-R, WPPSI subtests
Predictive validity *Shellenberger (1982)	100	5 years, 10 months to 8 years, 4 months	Sample was Spanish-speaking
		Native American	
Concurrent validity Hynd, Quackenbush, Kramer, Conner, & Weed (1980)	44	7 years, 3 months (M)	Criterion was WISC-R

Note. Studies discussed and referenced in Kaufman (1982) are marked with an asterisk. WISC-R, Wechsler Intelligence Scale for Children—Revised; WPPSI, Wechsler Preschool and Primary Scale of Intelligence.

(1982) administered the "Spanish McCarthy" to 100 first- and second-grade Puerto Rican children. The reliability coefficients were as follows: GCI (.94), Verbal (.79), Perceptual–Performance (.84), Memory (.63), and Motor (.64)—generally adequate values. The study by Shellenberger (1982) also investigated the McCarthy's predictive validity. The Spanish version of the Stanford Early School Achievement Test (Harcourt Brace Jovanovich, 1974) served as the criterion test. It was reported that the GCI correlated strongly with Total Achievement (.77). The other scales of the McCarthy correlated .50 to .73 with Total Achievement, with the majority of the r's in the .50s. The Perceptual–Performance and Quantitative scales were especially good predictors. A major finding by Shellenberger was that the Verbal scale was *not* the best predictor of achievement (a finding similar to that reported in Valencia, 1982, with Mexican American children). This was contrary to a large body of research that has commonly reported verbal ability as the strongest predictor of school achievement (Kaufman, 1982).

Shellenberger and Lachterman's (1979) concurrent validity study involved the administration of the McCarthy and the verbally loaded Information and Comprehension subtests of the WISC-R to 30 Puerto Rican children. All tests were administered in English. McCarthy scores and WISC-R combination scores (Information and Comprehension) were correlated, and the resultant coefficients were as follows: GCI (.68), Verbal (.67), Perceptual–Performance (.49), Quantitative (.61), Memory (.67), and Motor (.35). The authors concluded that the more verbal a McCarthy scale is, the more highly correlated is that scale with the two WISC-R subtests.

Native American Children

As noted on Table 9.8, only one McCarthy study exists that has included Native American children. In a concurrent validity study, Hynd, Quackenbush, Kramer, Connor, and Weed (1980) administered the McCarthy and the WISC-R to 44 primary-grade, full Navajo children. Navajo was the children's primary language. The observed r between the GCI and the FSIQ was .85. All other McCarthy and WISC-R correlations were also significant, and ranged from .37 to .88.

Regarding mean performance data, the children's GCI was a very low 75.9, about 1.5 standard deviations below the standardization mean. Similarly low means were also observed for the Verbal ($M = 28.3$), Quantitative ($M = 39.4$), and Memory ($M = 33.7$) Scales, as well as for the WISC-R Verbal IQ ($M - 64.1$) and FSIQ ($M - 77.9$). As might be expected, the children's mean performance was within the normal range on the McCarthy Perceptual–Performance ($M = 53.4$) and Motor ($M = 55.0$) scales, as well as on the WISC-R Performance IQ ($M = 95.4$). Hynd et al. concluded that given the low mean performances, the McCarthy GCI and the Verbal, Quantitative, and Memory scales were "culturally biased" against the children. This conclusion is unwarranted for two reasons. First, it is an untenable assumption that mean differences between standardization norms and minority children's performance connotes *a priori* bias (Reynolds, 1982). Second, it is inappropriate to administer a test such as the McCarthy to children whose primary language is not English.

Other Groups

There are a number of studies in which the McCarthy has been investigated with cultural/national groups outside the United States. Because space does not permit discussion of these, only a brief descriptive note is provided for each study.

Lynch and associates (Lynch, Mitchell, Vincent, Trueman, & MacDonald, 1982; Trueman et al., Branthwaite, 1984) have provided research on normative data and factor analyses of the McCarthy with English preschoolers. Tierney, Smith, Axworthy, and Ratcliffe (1984) have studied the McCarthy for sex and handedness effects in Scottish 5-year-olds.

The previously presented section on "Early Screening for Learning Problems" has discussed the study by Dennehy (1981), who investigated two McCarthy short forms with Australian children.

Two McCarthy investigations with African children also exist (Ashem & Janes, 1978; Lake, 1979). Lake (1979) examined the stability of the McCarthy with preschool children in Zimbabwe-Rhodesia; a Shona translation of the McCarthy was used (see Table 9.3 for further information in sample, design, and finding). In the study by Ashem and Janes (1978), a translated Yoruban version of the McCarthy proved useful in investigating the relation between undernutrition and cognitive development in Nigerian children.

The dissertation study by Stucky (1984) sought to examine the factor structure of a Mexican version of the McCarthy. Stucky reports that confirmatory factor analysis did not support the organization of the McCarthy into the five scales, nor did the analysis "support the plausibility of the factor structure empirically derived in the U.S. as valid for the Mexican data" (p. 92).

Berdjis-Pirnia's (1983) dissertation investigation, an exception to the present section in that it was conducted in the United States, translated and adapted the McCarthy for Iranian children aged 5–7½. Half of the sample was tested in English, and approximately half was tested in Farsi. Acceptably high reliability and validity coefficients were reported.

CONCLUSIONS

The last decade and a half have produced a great deal of research activity on the McCarthy, including over 125 journal articles and 50 dissertations. The integrated review of this research provided in this chapter permits four major conclusions:

1. Numerous psychometric research investigations attest to the reliability and validity of the McCarthy. Clinicians can have a good sense of confidence in the test's psychometric properties. As I have underscored, however, clinicians should be aware of the typically small GCI underestimation of IQ for normal populations.

2. The available research evidence suggests strongly that the complete McCarthy has clinical efficacy in the early identification of children who are likely to experience later academic difficulties. Furthermore, a solid body of research points to the Kaufman SF version of the McCarthy—as well as to the two McCarthy drawing subtests—as effective screening tools.

3. McCarthy research with exceptional populations has gradually increased over the years. Although the quantity of research with some exceptionalities is limited, and there are mixed findings in some categories, a safe generalization can be made that the McCarthy has value in clinical applications with exceptional children.

4. Existing McCarthy research with ethnic minority children is certainly encouraging, though there are some gross areas of underinvestigation (e.g., very limited psychometric investigations with black children; virtual absence of research with Native

American children). One particular bright spot, however, is the research base suggesting the McCarthy's utility in assessing English-speaking Mexican American children.

Taken together, 15 years of research on the McCarthy informs us that this instrument—notwithstanding some weaknesses—has earned a reputation as one of the best multi-score batteries for the psychoeducational assessment of young children. To this effect, I wish to echo Kaufman's (1982) major clinical recommendation that of all existing instruments, the McCarthy is the test to be preferred. Succinctly put, "the literature on the McCarthy, coupled with the limited choice of alternative assessment techniques, can easily be evaluated as supporting the administration of the McCarthy to *preschool* children (aged 3 to 6 or 6½) in most psychoeducational evaluations" (1982, p. 164, italics in original).

REFERENCES

Arinoldo, C. G. (1981). Black–white differences in the General Cognitive Index of the McCarthy Scales and in the Full Scale IQs of Wechsler's scales. *Journal of Clinical Psychology, 37,* 630–637.

Arinoldo, C. G. (1982). Concurrent validity of McCarthy's Scales. *Perceptual and Motor Skills, 54,* 1343–1346.

Ashem, B., & Janes, M. D. (1978). Deleterious effects of chronic under-nutrition on cognitive abilities. *Journal of Child Psychology and Psychiatry, 19,* 23–31.

Atkinson, B. L. (1981). *Cognitive sequelae of congenital heart disease.* Unpublished doctoral dissertation, University of Houston.

Averitt, C. H. (1981). *The interrelationships between several sociocultural variables and cognitive sex differences in preschool children.* Unpublished doctoral dissertation, North Carolina State University, Raleigh.

Baker, H. J., & Leland, B. (1967). *Detroit Tests of Learning Aptitude.* Indianapolis: Bobbs-Merrill.

Bauman, P. S. (1980). *A controlled study of drug-addicted mother's parenting and their children's development.* Unpublished doctoral dissertation, California School of Professional Psychology.

Beery, K. E. (1967). *Developmental Test of Visual–Motor Integration: Administration and Scoring Manual.* Chicago: Follett Educational.

Berdjis-Pirnia, N. (1983). *Application of the McCarthy Scales of Children's Abilities on Iranian children in relation to years of residence in public schools in the United States.* Unpublished doctoral dissertation, University of Southern California.

Bickett, L., Reuter, J., & Stancin, T. (1984). The use of the McCarthy Scales of Children's Abilities to assess moderately mentally retarded children. *Psychology in the Schools, 21,* 305–312.

Blachman, B. A. (1981). *The relationship of selected language measures and the McCarthy Scales to kindergarten and first-grade reading achievement.* Unpublished doctoral dissertation, University of Connecticut.

Bondy, A. S., Constantino, R., Norcross, J. C., & Sheslow, D. (1984). Comparison of Slosson and McCarthy Scales for exceptional preschool children. *Perceptual and Motor Skills, 59,* 657–658.

Bondy, A. S., Sheslow, D., Norcross, J. C., & Constantino, R. (1982). Comparison of Slosson and McCarthy Scales for minority pre-school children. *Perceptual and Motor Skills, 54,* 356–358.

Bracken, B. A. (1981). McCarthy Scales as a learning disability diagnostic aid: A closer look. *Journal of Learning Disabilities, 14,* 128–130.

Bracken, B. A. (1983). Comparison of the performance of gifted children on the McCarthy Scales of Children's Abilities and the Stanford–Binet Intelligence Scale. *Journal for the Education of the Gifted, 6,* 289–293.

Bracken, B. A., & Prasse, D. P. (1983). Concurrent validity of the PPVT-R for "at risk" preschool children. *Psychology in the Schools, 20,* 13–15.

Branthwaite, A., & Trueman, M. (1985). Ambiguities in Watkins and Wiebe's regression analysis of the McCarthy Scales of Children's Abilities. *Educational and Psychological Measurement, 45,* 425–428.

Brooks, R. S. (1981). *An investigation of the validity and the reliability of the McCarthy Scales of Children's Abilities using kindergarten-aged mentally retarded children.* Unpublished doctoral dissertation, Georgia State University.

Bryant, C. K., & Roffe, M. W. (1978). A reliability study of the McCarthy Scales of Children's Abilities. *Journal of Clinical Psychology, 34,* 401–406.

Burgenmeister, B., Blum, L., & Lorge, I. (1972). *Columbia Mental Maturity Scale.* New York: Harcourt Brace Jovanovich.

Christie, A. E. (1982). *A comparison of the McCarthy Scales of Children's Abilities and the Battelle Developmental Inventory for use with handicapped preschool children.* Unpublished doctoral dissertation, Kent State University.

Cohen, J. (1959). The factorial structure of the WISC at ages 7-6, 10-6, 13-6. *Journal of Consulting Psychology, 23,* 285–299.

Conrad, M. K. (1980). *An examination of the environmental and psychological correlates of lead poisoning in young children.* Unpublished doctoral dissertation, University of Wisconsin-Milwaukee.

CTB/McGraw-Hill. (1974). *Comprehensive Tests of Basic Skills, Level C, Form S: Examiner's Manual and Technical Bulletin No. 1.* Monterey, CA: Author.

Curry, E. S. (1980). *The retention of specific language skills, acquired through a short-term, intensive, teacher-directed program, among economically disadvantaged preschoolers.* Unpublished doctoral dissertation, University of Maryland.

Davis, E. E. (n.d.). *Suggestive data concerning the stability of the McCarthy Scales.* (ERIC Document Reproduction Service No. ED144 968)

Davis, E. E. (1974). Review of the McCarthy Scales of Children's Abilities. *Measurement and Evaluation in Guidance, 6,* 250–251.

Davis, E. E. (1975). Concurrent validity of the McCarthy Scales of Children's Abilities. *Measurement and Evaluation in Guidance, 8,* 101–104.

Davis, E. E., & Rowland, T. (1974). A replacement for the venerable Stanford–Binet? *Journal of Clinical Psychology, 30,* 517–521.

Davis, E. E., & Slettedahl, R. W. (1976). Stability of the McCarthy Scales over a one-year period. *Journal of Clinical Psychology, 32,* 798–800.

Davis, E. E., & Walker, C. (1976). Validity of the McCarthy Scales for Southwestern rural children. *Perceptual and Motor Skills, 42,* 563–567.

Davis, E. E., & Walker, C. (1977). McCarthy Scales and WISC-R. *Perceptual and Motor Skills, 44,* 966.

DeBoer, D. L., Kaufman, A. S., & McCarthy, D. (Chairs). (1974, April). *The use of the McCarthy Scales in identification, assessment, and deficit remediation of preschool and primary age children.* Symposium presented at the meeting of the Council for Exceptional Children, New York.

DeMeyer, M. K., Barton, S., Alpern, G. D., Kimberlin, J. A., Yang, E., & Steele, R. (1974). The measured intelligence of autistic children. *Journal of Autism and Childhood Schizophrenia, 4,* 42–60.

Dennehy, S. E. (1981). Two short forms of the McCarthy Scales of Children's Abilities applied to a sample of Victorian children. *Australian Psychologist, 16,* 93–100.

De Varona Thompson, M. (1980). *Maternal toxemia and low estriol levels: Implications for the infant's later development.* Unpublished doctoral dissertation, University of North Carolina at Chapel Hill.

Dunn, L. M. (1959). *Peabody Picture Vocabulary Test: Manual of directions and norms.* Circle Pines, MN: American Guidance Service.

Dunn, L. M., & Dunn, L. M. (1981). *Peabody Picture Vocabulary Test—Revised.* Circle Pines, MN: American Guidance Service.

Ernhart, C. B., & Landa, B. (1980). "Cumulative deficit," a longitudinal analysis of scores on McCarthy Scales. *Psychological Reports, 47,* 283–286.

Ernhart, C. B., Landa, B., & Callahan, R. (1980). The McCarthy Scales: Predictive validity and stability scores for urban black children. *Educational and Psychological Measurement, 40,* 1183–1188.

Ferrari, M. (1980). Comparisons of the Peabody Picture Vocabulary Test and the McCarthy Scales of Children's Abilities with a sample of autistic children. *Psychology in the Schools, 17,* 466–469.

Flanagan, D. M. (1984). *Comparative validity of two short forms of the McCarthy Scales of Children's Abilities for preschool screening: Discriminant, correlation and classificational analyses.* Unpublished doctoral dissertation, Temple University.

Friedrich, W. N., Einbender, A. J., & Leucke, W. J. (1983). Cognitive and behavioral characteristics of physically abused children. *Journal of Consulting and Clinical Psychology, 51,* 313–314.

Funk, S. G., Sturner, R. A., & Green, J. A. (1986). Preschool prediction of early school performance: Relationship of McCarthy Scales of Children's Abilities prior to school entry to achievement in kindergarten, first, and second grades. *Journal of School Psychology, 24,* 181–194.

Gerken, K. C., Hancock, K. A., & Wade, T. H. (1978). A comparison of the Stanford–Binet Intelligence Scale and the McCarthy Scales of Children's Abilities with preschool children. *Psychology in the Schools, 15,* 468–472.

Goh, D. S. (1976). *A psychometric evaluation of the McCarthy Scales of Children's Abilities.* Paper presented at the meeting of the Michigan Association of School Psychologists, Boyne Point, MI.

Goh, D. S., & Simons, M. R. (1980). Comparison of learning disabled and general education children on the McCarthy Scales of Children's Abilities. *Psychology in the Schools, 17,* 429–436.

Goh, D. S., & Youngquist, J. (1979). A comparison of the McCarthy Scales of Children's Abilities and the WISC-R. *Journal of Learning Disabilities, 12,* 344–348.

Grimm, L. L. (1983). *A comparison of the predictive validity of five kindergarten screening instruments.* Unpublished doctoral dissertation, Northern Arizona University.

Guidubaldi, J. (1980). *Manual for the Batelle Developmental Inventory: Norming edition.* New York: Walker.

Guilford, J. P. (1967). *The nature of human intelligence.* New York: McGraw-Hill.

Gullo, D. F., Clements, D. H., & Robertson, L. (1984). Prediction of academic achievement with the McCarthy Screening Test and Metropolitan Readiness Test. *Psychology in the Schools, 21,* 264–269.

Gullo, D. F., & McLoughlin, C. S. (1982). Comparison of scores for normal preschool children on Peabody Picture Vocabulary Test—Revised and McCarthy Scales of Children's Abilities. *Psychological Reports, 51,* 623–626.

Hallahan, D. P., & Kauffman, J. M. (1986). *Exceptional children: Introduction to special education* (3rd ed.). Englewood Cliffs, NJ: Prentice-Hall.

Harcourt Brace Jovanovich. (1974). *Stanford Early School Achievement Test, Level I and II: Specific directions for administering Puerto Rican Spanish edition.* New York: Author.

Harris, D. B. (1963). *Children's drawings as measures of intellectual maturity.* New York: Harcourt, Brace & World.

Harrison, K. A., & Wiebe, M. J. (1977). Correlational study of McCarthy, WISC, and Stanford–Binet Scales. *Perceptual and Motor Skills, 44,* 63–68.

Harrison, P. L. (1981). Mercer's Adaptive Behavior Inventory, the McCarthy Scales, and dental development as predictors of first-grade achievement. *Journal of Educational Psychology, 73,* 78–82.

Harrison, P. L., Kaufman, A. S., & Naglieri, J. A. (1980). Subtest patterns and recategorized groupings of the McCarthy Scales of EMR children. *American Journal of Mental Deficiency, 85,* 129–134.

Harrison, P. L., & Naglieri, J. A. (1978). Extrapolated General Cognitive Indexes on the McCarthy Scales for gifted and mentally retarded children. *Psychological Reports, 43,* 1291–1296.

Harrison, P. L., & Naglieri, J. A. (1981). Comparison of the predictive validities of two McCarthy short forms. *Psychology in the Schools, 18,* 389–393.

Healy, J. M. (1981). *A study of hyperlexia.* Unpublished doctoral dissertation, Case Western Reserve University.

Henderson, R. W., & Valencia, R. R. (1985). Nondiscriminatory school psychological services: Beyond non-biased assessment. In J. R. Bergan (Ed.), *School psychology in contemporary society* (pp. 340–377). Columbus, OH: Charles E. Merrill.

Heward, W. L., & Orlansky, M. D. (1984). *Exceptional*

children: An introductory survey of special education (2nd ed.). Columbus, OH: Charles E. Merrill.

Hynd, G. W., Quackenbush, R., Kramer, R., Conner, R., & Weed, N. (1980). Concurrent validity of the McCarthy Scales of Children's Abilities with Native American primary grade children. *Measurement and Evaluation in Guidance, 13,* 29–34.

Ilg, F. L., & Ames, L. B. (1972). *School readiness* (rev. ed.). New York: Harper & Row.

Ireton, H., & Thwing, E. (1974). *Minnesota Child Development Inventory.* Minneapolis: Behavior Science Systems.

Ivimey, J. K. (1979). *Differential performance of L.D. and Non L.D. grade 2 students on the WISC-R, McCarthy Scales of Children's Abilities and WRAT.* Unpublished doctoral dissertation, Boston University School of Education.

Ivimey, J. K., & Taylor, R. L. (1980). Differential performance of learning disabled and non-learning disabled children on the McCarthy Scales, WISC-R, and WRAT. *Journal of Clinical Psychology, 36,* 960–963.

Jacob, S. (1981). *Cognitive, perceptual, and personal–social development of prematurely and maturely born preschoolers.* Unpublished doctoral dissertation, Michigan State University.

Jensen, A. R. (1980). *Bias in mental testing.* New York: Free Press.

Johnson, D. L., & McGowan, R. J. (1984). Comparison of three intelligence tests as predictors of academic achievement and classroom behaviors of Mexican-American children. *Journal of Psychoeducational Assessment, 2,* 345–352.

Johnson, D. A., & Wollersheim, J. P. (1976). A comparison of the test performance of average and below average readers on the McCarthy Scales of Children's Abilities. *Journal of Reading Behavior, 8,* 397–403.

Kasper, J. F. (1973). *Comparison of the McCarthy's Scale [sic] of Children's Abilities and the Stanford–Binet Intelligence Scale.* Unpublished master's thesis, University of Wyoming.

Katz, D. R. (1978). *Validity of the McCarthy Scales of Children's Abilities for screening prekindergarten children "at risk."* Unpublished doctoral dissertation, Harvard University.

Kaufman, A. S. (1973). Comparison of the WPPSI, Stanford–Binet, and McCarthy Scales as predictors of first-grade achievement. *Perceptual and Motor Skills, 36,* 67–73.

Kaufman, A. S. (1975). Factor structure of the McCarthy Scales at five age levels between $2\frac{1}{2}$ and $8\frac{1}{2}$. *Educational and Psychological Measurement, 35,* 641–656.

Kaufman, A. S. (1977). A McCarthy short form for rapid screening of preschool, kindergarten, and first-grade children. *Contemporary Educational Psychology, 2,* 149–157.

Kaufman, A. S. (1982). An integrated review of almost a decade of research on the McCarthy Scales. In T. R. Kratochwill (Ed.), *Advances in school psychology* (Vol. 2, pp. 119–169). Hillsdale, NJ: Erlbaum.

Kaufman, A. S., & DiCuio, R. F. (1975). Separate factor analysis of the McCarthy Scales for groups of black and white children. *Journal of School Psychology, 13,* 10–17.

Kaufman, A. S., & Hollenbeck, G. P. (1973). Factor analysis of the standardization edition of the McCarthy Scales. *Journal of Clinical Psychology, 29,* 358–362.

Kaufman, A. S., & Kaufman, N. L. (1972). Tests built from Piaget's and Gesell's tasks as predictors of first grade achievement. *Child Development, 43,* 521–535.

Kaufman, A. S., & Kaufman, N. L. (1973a). Black–white differences at ages $2\frac{1}{2}$–$8\frac{1}{2}$ on the McCarthy Scales of Children's Abilities. *Journal of School Psychology, 11,* 196–206.

Kaufman, A. S., & Kaufman, N. L. (1973b). Sex differences on the McCarthy Scales of Children's Abilities. *Journal of Clinical Psychology, 29,* 362–365.

Kaufman, A. S., & Kaufman, N. L. (1975). Social-class differences on the McCarthy Scales for black and white children. *Perceptual and Motor Skills, 41,* 205–206.

Kaufman, A. S., & Kaufman, N. L. (1977a). *Clinical evaluation of young children with the McCarthy Scales.* New York: Grune & Stratton.

Kaufman, A. S., & Kaufman, N. L. (1977b). Research on the McCarthy Scales and its implications for assessment. *Journal of Learning Disabilities, 10,* 30–37.

Kaufman, A. S., & Kaufman, N. L. (1983a). *Kaufman Assessment Battery for Children.* Circle Pines, MN: American Guidance Service.

Kaufman, A. S., & Kaufman, N. L. (1983b). *Interpretive manual for the Kaufman Assessment Battery for Children.* Circle Pines, MN: American Guidance Service.

Kaufman, N. L. (1972). Evaluation of the McCarthy Scales of Children's Abilities for use with children having minimal brain dysfunction. *Proceedings of the 80th Annual Convention of the American Psychological Association, 7,* 555–556.

Kaufman, N. L. (1981). A critical comment on Umansky and Cohen's (1980) "Race and sex differences on the McCarthy Screening Test." *Psychology in the Schools, 18,* 369–371.

Kaufmam, N. L., & Kaufman, A. S. (1974). Comparison of normal and minimally brain dysfunctioned children on the McCarthy Scales of Children's Abilities. *Journal of Clinical Psychology, 30,* 69–72.

Keith, T. Z., & Bolen, L. M. (1980). Factor structure of the McCarthy Scales for children experiencing problems in school. *Psychology in the Schools, 17,* 320–326.

Kinder, D. R. (1982). *The relationship between oxygen therapy, blood gas analysis factors, and later learning ability in high risk infants.* Unpublished doctoral dissertation, Indiana State University.

Kirk, S., McCarthy, J., & Kirk, W. (1968). *Illinois Test of Psycholinguistic Abilities.* Champaign: University of Illinois Press.

Klein, B. (1982). *The diagnostic use of geometric form-copying tests: An investigation of normal kindergarten and learning disabled children's error production.* Unpublished doctoral dissertation, University of Western Ontario.

Knack, T. M. (1978). *Assessment of learning disabilities in young children with the McCarthy Scales.* Unpublished doctoral dissertation, University of Michigan.

Koppitz, E. M. (1963). *The Bender–Gestalt Test for Young Children.* New York: Grune & Stratton.

Koppitz, E. M. (1975). *The Bender–Gestalt Test for Young Children: Vol. 2. Research and application, 1963–1973.* New York: Grune & Stratton.

Krohn, E. J. (1980). *Use and evaluation of the McCarthy Scales of Children's Abilities.* Unpublished doctoral dissertation, St. Louis University.

Krohn, E. J., & Traxler, A. J. (1979). Relationship of the McCarthy Scales of Children's Abilities to other measures of preschool cognitive, motor, and perceptual development. *Perceptual and Motor Skills, 49,* 783–790.

Lake, V. (1979). *The Early Learning Centre, St. Mary's: Annual report on research activities from April 1978–April 1979.* Zimbabwe (Rhodesia).

Laosa, L. M. (1982). Psychometric characteristics of Chicano and non-Hispanic White children's performance on the Preschool Inventory. *Journal of Applied Developmental Psychology, 3,* 217–245.

Laosa, L. M. (1984). Ethnic, socioeconomic, and home language influences upon early performance on measures of abilities. *Journal of Educational Psychology, 76,* 1178–1198.

Leiter, R. (1969). *Examiners manual for the Leiter International Performance Scale.* Chicago: Stoelting.

Levenson, R. L., & Zino, T. C. (1979a). Assessment of cognitive deficiency with the McCarthy Scales and Stanford–Binet: A correlational analysis. *Perceptual and Motor Skills, 48,* 291–295.

Levenson, R. L., & Zino, T. C. (1979b). Using McCarthy Scales Extrapolated General Cognitive Indexes below 50: Some words of caution. *Psychological Reports, 45,* 350.

Lewis, R. J. (1979). *The influence of dialect, age, and race on the McCarthy Scales of Children's Abilities.* Unpublished doctoral dissertation, University of Georgia.

Lidz, C. S., & Ballester, L. E. (1986). Diagnostic implications of McCarthy Scale General Cognitive Index/Binet IQ discrepancies of low-socioeconomic-status preschool children. *Journal of School Psychology, 4,* 381–384.

Long, M. L. (1976). *The influence of sex, race, and type of preschool experience on scores on the McCarthy Scales of Children's Abilities.* Unpublished doctoral dissertation, University of Georgia.

Lorton, E. F. (1976). *Prediction of academic achievement with the First Grade Screening Test and the McCarthy Scales of Children's Abilities.* Unpublished doctoral dissertation, Texas Woman's University.

Loxley, L., & Gerken, K. C. (1980). The predictive validity of the McCarthy Scales vs. Stanford–Binet. *National Association of School Psychologists Convention Proceedings,* 149–151.

Lynch, A., Mitchell, L. B., Vincent, E. M., Trueman, M., & MacDonald, L. (1982). The McCarthy Scales of Children's Abilities: A normative study of English 4-year-olds. *British Journal of Educational Psychology, 52,* 133–143.

Lyon, M. A., & Smith, D. K. (1986). A comparison of at-risk preschool children's performance on the K-ABC, McCarthy Scales, and the Stanford–Binet. *Journal of Psychoeducational Assessment, 4,* 35–43.

Massoth, N. A. (1985). The McCarthy Scales of Children's Abilities as a predictor of achievement: A five year follow-up. *Psychology in the Schools, 22,* 10–13.

Massoth, N. A., & Levenson, R. L. (1982). The McCarthy Scales of Children's Abilities as a predictor of reading readiness and reading achievement. *Psychology in the Schools, 19,* 293–296.

McCarthy, D. (1972). *Manual for the McCarthy Scales of Children's Abilities.* New York: Psychological Corporation.

Meisels, S. J., & Wiske, M. S. (1983). *The Early Screening Inventory.* New York: Teachers College Press.

Meisels, S. J., Wiske, M. S., & Tivnan, T. (1984). Predicting school performance with the Early Screening Inventory. *Psychology in the Schools, 21,* 25–33.

Mishra, S. P. (1981). Factor analysis of the McCarthy Scales for groups of white and Mexican-American children. *Journal of School Psychology, 19,* 178–182.

Mishra, S. P., & Powers, S. (1984, April). The McCarthy Scales and evidence of item bias for Hispanic children. Paper presented at the meeting of the American Educational Research Association, New Orleans.

Moore, C. L., & Burns, W. J. (1977). Brief screening for developmentally delayed preschoolers. *Perceptual and Motor Skills, 45,* 1169–1170.

Murray, A. M., & Mishra, S. P. (1983a). Interactive effects of item content and ethnic group membership on performance on the McCarthy Scales. *Journal of School Psychology, 21,* 263–270.

Murray, A. M., & Mishra, S. P. (1983b). Judgments of item bias in the McCarthy Scales of Children's Abilities. *Hispanic Journal of Behavioral Sciences, 5,* 325–336.

Nagle, R. J. (1979). The McCarthy Scales of Children's Abilities: Research implications for the assessment of young children. *School Psychology Review, 8,* 319–326.

Nagle, R. J., & Gepford, J. D. (1978). *A validation study of the short-form McCarthy Scales of Children's Abilities.* Unpublished manuscript, University of South Carolina.

Nagle, R. J., Paget, K. D., & Mulkey, M. S. (1980). Comparison of good and poor readers on the McCarthy Scales. *National Association of School Psychologists Convention Proceedings,* 138–140.

Naglieri, J. A. (1980a). Comparison of McCarthy General Cognitive Index and WISC-R IQ for educable mentally retarded, learning disabled, and normal children. *Psychological Reports, 47,* 591–596.

Naglieri, J. A. (1980b). McCarthy and WISC-R correlations with WRAT achievement scores. *Perceptual and Motor Skills, 51,* 392–394.

Naglieri, J. A. (1981). Concurrent validity of the revised Peabody Picture Vocabulary Test. *Psychology in the Schools, 19,* 286–288.

Naglieri, J. A. (1982). Interpreting WISC-R and McCarthy scatter: A caution. *Contemporary Educational Psychology, 7,* 90–94.

Naglieri, J. A. (1985). Normal children's performance on the McCarthy Scales, Kaufman Assessment Battery, and Peabody Individual Achievement Test. *Journal of Psychoeducational Assessment, 3,* 123–129.

Naglieri, J. A., & Harrison, P. L. (1979). Comparison of McCarthy General Cognitive Indexes and Stanford–Binet IQs for educable mentally retarded children. *Perceptual and Motor Skills, 48,* 1251–1254.

Naglieri, J. A., & Harrison, P. L. (1982). McCarthy Scales, McCarthy Screening Test, and Kaufman's McCarthy short form correlations with the Peabody Individual Achievement Test. *Psychology in the Schools, 19,* 149–155.

Naglieri, J. A., Kaufman, A. S., & Harrison, P. L. (1981). Factor structure of the McCarthy Scales for school age children with low GCIs. *Journal of School Psychology, 19,* 226–232.

Nurss, J. R., & McGauvran, M. E. (1974). *Metropolitan Readiness Tests (Level II, Form P).* New York: Harcourt Brace Jovanovich.

Perino, J., & Ernhart, C. B. (1974). The relation of subclinical lead level to cognitive and sensorimotor impairment in black preschoolers. *Journal of Learning Disabilities, 7,* 616–620.

Piersel, W. C., & Santos, L. (1982). Comparison of McCarthy and Goodenough–Harris scoring systems for kindergarten children's human figure drawings. *Perceptual and Motor Skills, 55,* 633–634.

Phillips, B. L., Pasewark, R. A., & Tindall, R. C. (1978). Relationship among McCarthy Scales of Children's Abilities, WPPSI, and Columbia Mental Maturity Scale. *Psychology in the Schools, 15,* 352–356.

Prasse, D. P., Siewert, J. C., & Ellison, P. H. (1983). McCarthy performance and neurological functioning in children born "at risk." *Journal of Psychoeducational Assessment, 1,* 273–283.

Prescott, G. A., Balow, I. H., Hogan, T. P., & Farr, R. C. (1978). *Metropolitan Achievement Tests.* New York: Psychological Corporation.

Psychological Corporation. (1978). *The McCarthy Screening Test.* New York: Author.

Purvis, M. A., & Bolen, L. M. (1984). Factor structure of the McCarthy Scales for males and females. *Journal of Clinical Psychology, 40,* 108–114.

Reilly, T. P., Drudge, O. W., Rosen, J. C., Loew, D. E., & Fischer, M. (1985). Concurrent and predictive validity of the WISC-R, McCarthy Scales, Woodcock–Johnson, and academic achievement. *Psychology in the Schools, 22,* 380–382.

Reynolds, C. R. (1978a). The McCarthy drawing tests as a group instrument. *Contemporary Educational Psychology, 3,* 169–174.

Reynolds, C. R. (1978b). Teacher–psychologist interscorer reliability of the McCarthy drawing tests. *Perceptual and Motor Skills, 47,* 538.

Reynolds, C. R. (1979). Objectivity of scoring for the McCarthy drawing tests. *Psychology in the Schools, 16,* 3.

Reynolds, C. R. (1980). Differential construct validity of a preschool battery for blacks, whites, males and females. *Journal of School Psychology, 18,* 112–125.

Reynolds, C. R. (1982). The problem of bias in psychological assessment. In C. R. Reynolds & T. B. Gutkin (Eds.), *The handbook of school psychology* (pp. 178–208). New York: Wiley.

Reynolds, C. R. (1985). Standard score tables for the McCarthy drawing tests. *Psychology in the Schools, 22,* 117–121.

Reynolds, C. R., McBride, R. D., & Gibson, L. J. (1981). Black–white IQ discrepancies may be related to differences in hemisphericity. *Contemporary Educational Psychology, 6,* 180–184.

Ritter, D., Duffy, J., & Fishman, R. (1973). Comparability of Slosson and S-B estimate of intelligence. *Journal of School Psychology, 11,* 224–226.

Rules and Regulations Implementing Education for All Handicapped Children Act of 1975, P.L. 94-142, 42 Fed. Reg. 42474 (1977).

Salvia, J., & Ysseldyke, J. E. (1985). *Assessment in special and remedial education* (3rd ed.). Boston: Houghton Mifflin.

Sattler, J. M. (1978). Review of the McCarthy Scales of Children's Abilities. In O. K. Buros (Ed.), *The eighth mental measurements yearbook* (Vol. 1, pp. 311–313). Highland Park, NJ: Gryphon Press.

Sattler, J. M. (1982). *Assessment of children's intelligence and special abilities* (2nd ed.). Boston: Allyn & Bacon.

Sattler, J. M., & Altes, L. M. (1984). Performance of bilingual and monolingual Hispanic children on the Peabody Picture Vocabulary Test—Revised and the McCarthy Perceptual–Performance Scale. *Psychology in the Schools, 21,* 313–316.

Sattler, J. M., & Squire, L. S. (1982). Scoring difficulty of the McCarthy Scales of Children's Abilities. *School Psychology Review, 11,* 83–88.

Schmits, D. W., & Beckenbaugh, L. A. (1979). Comparison of the WPPSI and McCarthy scores in a preschool population. *National Association of School Psychologists Convention Proceedings, 126.*

Schodlatz, D. R. (1978). *The validity of the McCarthy Scales of Children's Abilities for screening prekindergarten children "at risk."* Unpublished doctoral dissertation, Harvard University.

Shellenberger, S. (1977). *A cross-cultural investigation of the validity of the Spanish version of the McCarthy Scales of Children's Abilities for Puerto Rican children.* Unpublished doctoral dissertation, University of Georgia.

Shellenberger, S. (1982). Assessment of Puerto Rican children: A cross-cultural study with the Spanish McCarthy Scales of Children's Abilities. *Bilingual Review, 9,* 109–119.

Shellenberger, S., & Lachterman, T. (1979). Cognitive and motor functioning on the McCarthy Scales by Spanish-speaking children. *Perceptual and Motor Skills, 49,* 863–866.

Shuey, A. M. (1966). *The testing of Negro intelligence* (2nd ed.). New York: Social Science Press.

Simons, M. R., & Goh, D. S. (1982). Relationships between McCarthy Scales of Children's Abilities and teachers' ratings of school achievement. *Perceptual and Motor Skills, 54,* 1159–1162.

Slosson, R. L. (1960). *Slosson Intelligence Test for Children and Adults.* East Aurora, NY: Slosson Educational Publications.

Strom, R., Hathaway, C., & Slaughter, H. (1981). The correlation of maternal attitudes and preschool children's performance on the McCarthy Scales of Children's Abilities. *Journal of Instructional Psychology, 8,* 139–145.

Stuckey, P. E. (1984). *A factorial study of the Mexican McCarthy Scales: A cross-cultural comparison.* Unpublished doctoral dissertation, George Peabody College for Teachers, Vanderbilt University.

Sturner, R. A., Funk, S. G., & Green, J. A. (1984). Predicting kindergarten school performance using the McCarthy Scales of Children's Abilities. *Journal of Pediatric Psychology, 9,* 495–503.

Swanson, H. L., & Watson, B. L. (1982). *Educational and psychological assessment of exceptional children.* St. Louis: C. V. Mosby.

Taylor, R. L. (1979). Comparison of the McCarthy Scales of Children's Abilities and the Peabody Picture Vocabulary Test. *Psychological Reports, 45,* 196–198.

Taylor, R. L., & Ivimey, J. K. (1980a). Diagnostic use of the WISC-R and McCarthy Scales: A regression analysis approach to learning disabilities. *Psychology in the Schools, 17,* 327–330.

Taylor, R. L., & Ivimey, J. K. (1980b). Predicting academic achievement: Preliminary analysis of the McCarthy Scales. *Psychological Reports, 46,* 1232.

Taylor, R. L., Slocumb, P. R., & O'Neill, J. (1979). A short form of the McCarthy Scales of Children's Abilities: Methodological and clinical applications. *Psychology in the Schools, 16,* 347–350.

Teeter, P. A. (1983). The relationship between measures of cognitive–intellectual and neuropsychological abilities for young children. *Clinical Neuropsychology, 5,* 151–158.

Teeter, P. A. (1984). Cross validation of the factor structure of the McCarthy Scales for kindergarten children. *Psychology in the Schools, 21,* 158–164.

Terman, L. M., & Merrill, M. A. (1973). *Stanford–Binet Intelligence Scale: 1972 norms edition.* Boston: Houghton Mifflin.

Thorndike, R. L., & Hagen, E. P. (1977). *Measurement and evaluation in psychology and education* (4th ed.). New York: Wiley.

Tierney, I., Smith, L., Axworthy, D., & Ratcliffe, S. G. (1984). The McCarthy Scales of Children's Abilities: Sex and handedness effects in 128 Scottish five-year-olds. *British Journal of Educational Psychology, 54,* 101–105.

Trueman, M., Lynch, A., & Branthwaite, A. (1984). A factor analytic study of the McCarthy Scales of Children's Abilities. *British Journal of Educational Psychology, 54,* 331–335.

Umansky, W., & Cohen, L. R. (1980). Race and sex differences on the McCarthy Screening Test. *Psychology in the Schools, 17,* 400–404.

Umansky, W., Paget, K. D., & Cohen, L. R. (1981). The test–retest reliability of the McCarthy Screening Test. *Journal of Clinical Psychology, 37,* 650–654.

Valencia, R. R. (1977). *Comparison of perceptual–motor performance, non-verbal intelligence, and the relationship between perceptual–motor performance and non-verbal intelligence in Anglo and Chicano, low socioeconomic status third-grade boys.* Unpublished doctoral dissertation, University of California at Santa Barbara.

Valencia, R. R. (1982). Predicting academic achievement of Mexican American children: A preliminary analysis of the McCarthy Scales. *Educational and Psychological Measurement, 42,* 1269–1278.

Valencia, R. R. (1983a). Stability of the McCarthy Scales of Children's Abilities over a one-year period for Mexican-American children. *Psychology in the Schools, 20,* 29–34.

Valencia, R.R. (1983b). *An examination of the skills of entry level Mexican American Head Start children.* Unpublished manuscript.

Valencia, R. R. (1984). The McCarthy Scales and Kaufman's McCarthy short form correlations with the Comprehensive Test of Basic Skills. *Psychology in the Schools, 21,* 141–147.

Valencia, R. R. (1985). Erratum to "Stability of the McCarthy Scales of Children's Abilities over a one-year period for Mexican-American children." *Psychology in the Schools, 22,* 231.

Valencia, R. R. (1988). The McCarthy Scales and Hispanic children: A review of psychometric research. *Hispanic Journal of Behavioral Sciences, 10,* 81–104.

Valencia, R. R., & Cruz, J. (1981). *Mexican American mothers' estimations of their preschool children's cognitive performance* (Report No. 90-C-1777). Washington, DC: Administration for Children, Youth and Families, Office of Human Development Services, U.S. Department of Health and Human Services.

Valencia, R. R., Henderson, R. W., & Rankin, R. J. (1981). Relationship of family constellation and schooling to intellectual performance of Mexican American children. *Journal of Educational Psychology, 73,* 524–532.

Valencia, R. R., Henderson, R. W., & Rankin, R. J. (1985). Family status, family constellation, and home environmental variables as predictors of cognitive performance of Mexican American children. *Journal of Educational Psychology, 77,* 323–331.

Valencia, R. R., & Rankin, R. J. (1983). Concurrent validity and reliability of the Kaufman version of the McCarthy Scales for a sample of Mexican-American children. *Educational and Psychological Measurement, 43,* 915–925.

Valencia, R. R., & Rankin, R. J. (1985). Evidence of content bias on the McCarthy Scales with Mexican American children: Implication for test translation and nonbiased assessment. *Journal of Educational Psychology, 77,* 197–207.

Valencia, R. R., & Rothwell, J. G. (1985). Concurrent validity of the WPPSI with Mexican-American preschool children. *Educational and Psychological Measurement, 44,* 955–961.

Vance, B., Blixt, S., & Kitson, D. L. (1982). Factor structure of the McCarthy Screening Test. *Psychology in the Schools, 19,* 33–38.

Vance, B., Kitson, D. L., & Singer, M. (1983). Comparison of the Peabody Picture Vocabulary Test—Revised and the McCarthy Screening Test. *Psychology in the Schools, 20,* 21–24.

Vulpe, S. G. (1983). *Language disability and measures of intelligence in handicapped children: A comparison of the McCarthy Scales of Children's Abilities and the Leiter International Performance Scale.* Unpublished doctoral dissertation, College of William and Mary.

Watkins, E. O., & Wiebe, M. J. (1980). Construct validity of the McCarthy Scales of Children's Abilities: Regression analysis with preschool children. *Educational and Psychological Measurement, 40,* 1173–1182.

Wechsler, D. (1967). *Manual for the Wechsler Preschool and Primary Scale of Intelligence.* New York: Psychological Corporation.

Wechsler, D. (1974). *Manual for the Wechsler Intelligence Scale for Children—Revised.* New York: Psychological Corporation.

Weiner, H. I. (1980). *A comparison of the performance of two groups of young deaf children on tasks of cognitive and language skills as measured by the McCarthy Scales of Children's Abilities.* Unpublished doctoral dissertation, Boston College.

Weiss, L. I. (1977). *The utility of the McCarthy Scales of Children's Abilities in the identification of potentially reading disabled kindergarten children and its application to the maturational lag hypothesis.* Unpublished doctoral dissertation, University of Southern Mississippi.

Wick, J. W., & Smith, J. K. (1981). *Scott, Foresman Achievement Series.* Glenview, IL: Scott, Foresman.

Wiebe, M. J., & Harrison, K. A. (1978). Relationships of the McCarthy Scales of Children's Abilities and the Detroit Tests of Learning Aptitude. *Perceptual and Motor Skills, 46,* 355–359.

Wiebe, M. J., & Watkins, E. O. (1980). Factor analysis of the McCarthy Scales of Children's Abilities on preschool children. *Journal of School Psychology, 18,* 155–162.

Woodcock, R. (1978). *Development and standardization of the Woodcock–Johnson Psycho-Educational Battery.* Boston: Teaching Resources.

Zucker, S. (1985, April). *MSCA K-ABC with high risk preschoolers.* Paper presented at the meeting of the National Association of School Psychologists, Las Vegas.

10

Clinical Assessment Practice with the Kaufman Assessment Battery for Children (K-ABC)

RANDY W. KAMPHAUS
University of Georgia

ALAN S. KAUFMAN
PATTI L. HARRISON
The University of Alabama

The Kaufman Assessment Battery for Children (K-ABC; Kaufman & Kaufman, 1983) has been the subject of scores of research investigations, and is being used with increasing frequency in schools and clinics. In a nationwide survey of school psychologists conducted in 1987 by Obringer (1988), respondents were asked to rank the following instruments in order of their usage: Wechsler's scales, the K-ABC, and both the old and new Stanford–Binets. The Wechsler scales earned a mean rank of 2.69, followed closely by the K-ABC with a mean of 2.55; then came the old Stanford–Binet (1.98) and the Stanford-Binet, Fourth Edition (1.26). The K-ABC has been the subject of controversy within the psychological profession, as attested by the strongly "pro" and "con" articles written for a special issue of the *Journal of Special Education* devoted to the K-ABC (Miller & Reynolds, 1984), and its clinical and research applications have been expounded in a recent text by Kamphaus and Reynolds (1987).

That the K-ABC has many features to recommend it for clinical assessment is clear from its theoretical foundation, psychometric qualities, administration procedures, and task selection. The intelligence or Mental Processing scales are derived from an aggregate of theories of neuropsychological processing, depending heavily on the cerebral specialization work of Sperry and the neurological research of Luria. The separate processing scales focus on the *process* used to solve a problem (linear/analytic/*sequential*, akin to left-hemisphere thinking, vs. Gestalt/holistic/*simultaneous*, or right-hemisphere processing); most other tests, such as the Wechsler Intelligence Scale for Children—Revised (WISC-R), attend more to the *content* of the items (verbal or figural). Attending to the process, or the "how" of problem solving, cues into the kind of action-oriented approach that facilitates either remedial or therapeutic clinical intervention.

The K-ABC Mental Processing scales are primarily nonverbal. This reflects a deliberate decision by the test authors to enhance fair assessment of minority group members, bilingual children, individuals with speech or language difficulties, and learning-disabled youngsters, all of whom may fail verbal, fact-oriented items because of their low *achievement*, not low intelligence. The verbal and factual items are

259

included on the K-ABC, but on separate Achievement scales, to facilitate assessment of learning disabilities as well as a fairer estimate of minority intellectual functioning.

Psychometrically, the K-ABC has been praised by Anastasi (1988) as "an innovative, cognitive assessment battery whose development meets high standards of technical quality" (pp. 269–270). A strong empirical foundation is necessary for any test to realize its clinical potential. The K-ABC has other features that make it useful clinically—for example, the inclusion of "teaching items" to help insure that each child understands task demands; a varying set of tasks based on the child's developmental level; several novel subtests and others with a strong research basis; and the use of photographs for several tasks to provide realistic stimuli for evoking clinical responses.

Negative aspects of the K-ABC include a limited "floor" on several subtests for very young and retarded children; insufficient "ceiling" to challenge gifted youngsters above the age of 10; the question of whether "ability" and "achievement" can be neatly divided into separate components; and the question of whether the Mental Processing scales truly measure the intended processes, or some other set of skills such as semantic memory and nonverbal reasoning (Keith & Dunbar, 1984). In this chapter, we attempt to integrate the diverse features of the K-ABC as we discuss the test's applicability for meeting clinical assessment needs for the following populations: the mentally retarded, the learning-disabled, the intellectually gifted, the emotionally disturbed, the hearing-impaired, the brain-injured, and "at-risk" preschoolers. Next are sections considering the use of the test for educational remediation and the use of K-ABC short forms for screening of exceptional children. Finally, two case reports are included to help integrate and illustrate the points raised in this chapter, and to show how the WISC-R and K-ABC can be interpreted in tandem to produce powerful hypotheses about a child's functioning.

MENTALLY RETARDED CHILDREN

If nothing else, an intelligence test must be able to differentiate mentally retarded from nonretarded children; it was the need for the accurate diagnosis of mental retardation that led to the development of intelligence tests such as the Binet scales (Binet & Simon, 1905). The K-ABC should yield scores at or near the second percentile rank (standard score $\cong 70$) for groups of children who are referred for suspected mental retardation or have already been identified as mentally retarded. Unfortunately, data on referred populations are not yet available, and data for previously identified retarded children are available, but tainted by confounding variables.

K-ABC data for samples of previously identified (usually with the WISC-R) mentally retarded children are shown in Table 10.1. Note that the mean Mental Processing Composite (MPC) for the samples ranges from the middle 60s to about 70. Although these means are acceptable and indicate the K-ABC's utility for mentally retarded children, they are likely to be abnormally high because of confounding variables such as regression effects and selection bias. For example, every experienced psychologist knows that when mentally retarded children are re-evaluated, some are declassified; that is, they obtain an IQ score considerably higher than 70. (Adaptive behavior must also be taken into account in classification of mental retardation, of course.) This is expected, since scores from repeated testings regress toward the mean due to lack of perfect reliability. Since the WISC-R does not correlate perfectly with itself in a re-evaluation, re-evaluation scores will usually be higher than initial evaluation scores, or move toward the mean. This regression effect is exacerbated when a new test such as the K-ABC is given to a group of children already classified as mentally retarded using the WISC-R. The K-ABC correlates less (about .70) with the WISC-R than the WISC-R correlates with itself. Hence, whenever a psychologist uses a test other than the original placement test, more regression effect is likely; mean scores, such as those in Table 10.1, are probably higher than those that would be obtained during an initial evaluation.

This regression effect is even further enhanced by selection bias, which is discussed later in the context of assessment of the gifted and talented. In light of the confounding variables, the K-ABC findings regarding the

TABLE 10.1. K-ABC Global Scale and Subtest Standard Score Means for Samples of Mentally Retarded Children

	Sample			
Scale of subtest	Naglieri, 1985b (n = 33)	Nelson, Obrzut, & Cummings, 1984 (n = 30)	Naglieri, 1985a (n = 37)	Obrzut, Nelson, & Obrzut, in press (n = 29)
Global scales				
Sequential Processing	77.9	72.4	67.2	72.4
Simultaneous Processing	81.9	72.8	67.7	72.8
Mental Processing Composite	77.8	69.7	65.1	69.7
Achievement	69.7	58.3	64.0	58.3
Mental processing subtests				
3. Hand Movements	6.9	—	—	7.2
4. Gestalt Closure	8.2	—	—	6.6
5. Number Recall	6.0	—	—	4.0
6. Triangles	7.1	—	—	5.2
7. Word Order	6.1	—	—	4.9
8. Matrix Analogies	6.4	—	—	7.0
9. Spatial Memory	7.0	—	—	5.2
10. Photo Series	7.4	—	—	4.5
Achievement subtests				
12. Faces and Places	78.9	—	—	65.9
13. Arithmetic	75.2	—	—	66.0
14. Riddles	78.5	—	—	70.7
15. Reading/Decoding	70.8	—	—	64.6
16. Reading/Understanding	68.0	—	—	62.6

Note. From *Clinical and research applications of the K-ABC* (p. 71) by R. W. Kamphaus and C. R. Reynolds, 1987, Circle Pines, MN: American Guidance Service. Copyright 1987 by American Guidance Service. Reprinted by permission.

overall intelligence of mentally retarded children are reasonable and support its use for the diagnosis of mental retardation.

The K-ABC was standardized with a sample that overlapped the standardization sample of the Vineland Adaptive Behavior Scales (Sparrow, Balla, & Cicchetti, 1984). The overlap was large enough and the characteristics of the standardization samples of both instruments were similar enough for their normative base to be considered comparable. Thus, direct comparisons can be made between the K-ABC and the Vineland—a useful comparison for the classification of mental retardation. The Vineland manuals supply tables indicating differences between K-ABC and Vineland scores that are required for statistical significance.

On the other hand, the K-ABC has some practical limitations that examiners must consider in using the test to diagnose mental retardation. First is the issue of subtest floor. Kamphaus and Reynolds (1987) note that the K-ABC lacks easy items for some low-functioning children. In other words, a 5-

year-old mentally retarded child may obtain too many raw scores of 0. This lack of floor is less likely to occur for an 8-year-old child. Second, the K-ABC composite score norms usually do not go below a standard score of 55, making the K-ABC less useful for the diagnosis of moderate or severe levels of retardation. Tests such as the Stanford–Binet Fourth Edition may be better suited for the purpose, since its composite score norms often go down as low as a standard score of 36. However, a test should never be selected primarily because scores have been extrapolated to very low or high levels. The new Stanford–Binet, for example, has questionable norms (Reynolds, 1987); its scale structure has dubious construct validity support (Reynolds, Kamphaus, & Rosenthal, 1988); and its stability has been challenged for preschool children (Bauer & Smith, 1988). In comparison to the K-ABC's stability for preschool children, the new Stanford–Binet did poorly over a 1-year interval for 28 children aged about 4–6 years: The K-ABC MPC produced a test–retest coefficient of

.93, whereas the Stanford–Binet Test Composite yielded a value of .20 (Bauer & Smith, 1988).

Although the K-ABC appears appropriate for the diagnosis of mild retardation, there are some cautions for examiners to keep in mind. The K-ABC may not yield scores low enough to diagnose moderate levels of mental retardation. In addition, the K-ABC may yield too many raw scores of 0 for younger mentally retarded children. The examiner who keeps these cautions in clear focus will find the K-ABC appropriate and useful for the diagnosis of mild retardation with many referral cases.

LEARNING-DISABLED CHILDREN

Mean K-ABC global scale and subtest scores for a number of samples of learning-disabled (LD) children are shown in Table 10.2. An interesting trend appears in these data. In four of the five studies, a profile in which Simultaneous Processing scores were greater than Sequential Processing scores emerged at the global scale level. In these four studies, the average differences between the two scales ranged from 6 to 8 standard-score points. (In the fifth study, the Sequential Processing and Simultaneous Processing mean standard scores were almost identical.) Whether this trend toward different global scale scores is of practical utility is unknown because of the limited research at this time; however, because of its consistency, it cannot be ignored. The trend of Simultaneous Processing > Sequential Processing for LD children is reminiscent of the mild trend of Performance > Verbal for the WISC-R (Kavale & Forness, 1984).

Another pattern of note is that in four of the five studies, the average MPC was greater than the average Achievement scale score. (Note that Klanderman, Perney, & Kroes-

TABLE 10.2. K-ABC Global Scale and Subtest Standard Score Means for Samples of Learning-Disabled Children

	Sample				
Scale of subtest	Naglieri, 1985a ($n = 34$)	Klanderman, 1985 ($n = 44$)	Smith, Lyon, Hunter, & Boyd, 1986 ($n = 32$)	Hooper & Hynd, 1985 ($n = 87$)	Fourqurean, 1987 ($n = 42$)
Global scales					
Sequential Processing	92.1	92.7	90.0	86.7	80.5
Simultaneous Processing	99.6	92.3	98.1	92.9	87.7
Mental Processing Composite	96.1	—	94.2	89.0	82.9
Achievement	86.2	87.8	89.8	89.5	67.7
Mental processing subtests					
3. Hand movements	8.6	—	—	7.5	6.8
4. Gestalt Closure	11.4	—	—	9.4	9.1
5. Number Recall	8.7	—	—	8.4	7.2
6. Triangles	9.9	—	—	9.6	7.6
7. Word Order	9.1	—	—	7.7	6.5
8. Matrix Analogies	8.5	—	—	7.7	8.2
9. Spatial Memory	9.9	—	—	9.3	8.5
10. Photo Series	10.5	—	—	9.8	7.5
Achievement subtests					
12. Faces and Places	91.6	—	—	89.3	72.8
13. Arithmetic	90.4	—	—	88.9	77.7
14. Riddles	96.9	—	—	96.0	74.0
15. Reading/Decoding	81.2	—	—	87.5	72.2
16. Reading/Understanding	80.8	—	—	93.1	66.4

Note. From *Clinical and research applications of the K-ABC* (p.70) by R. W. Kamphaus and C. R. Reynolds, 1987, Circle Pines, MN: American Guidance Service. Copyright 1987 by American Guidance Service. Reprinted by permission.

chell, 1985, did not present data on the MPC, but the MPC most certainly would be about 92, as opposed to about 88 for the Achievement standard score.) In only one study were the MPC and Achievement standard scores similar (89.0 and 89.5, respectively).

This pattern of MPC > Achievement is strongly reinforced by the results of the study by Fourqurean (1987) for a sample of Latino LD children. This group was also documented as having limited proficiency in English. With this group, it appears that the Achievement scale is adversely affected not only by problems with achievement, but also by cultural and/or linguistic differences. In addition, it is noteworthy that in this investigation the authors of the K-ABC met their goal of designing a test that to some extent was able to circumvent linguistic or cultural differences in order to assess intelligence. The mean WISC-R Verbal IQ of 68.1 for these children, for example, was almost identical to their mean Achievement scale score on the K-ABC of 67.7. As a result, the MPC for this sample was considerably higher (82.9) than the Full Scale IQ (76.7). The K-ABC, because it has a separate Achievement scale, may indeed be valuable in those cases where a clinician is presented with the challenge of trying to differentiate among intellectual and cultural or linguistic influences on learning.

The data on LD children's performance on the K-ABC subtests are so limited that any gereralizations are tentative at this time. In fact, a number of additional studies using the K-ABC with LD children will have to be conducted in order to demonstrate the viability of even global scale profile analysis.

A few preliminary conclusions regarding the use of the K-ABC with LD children do seem to be in order. In general, these children's performance on the K-ABC is typically below the population mean. In addition, they are most likely to have their lowest scores on the Sequential Processing and Achievement global scales of the K-ABC.

A study from the Stanford–Binet Fourth Edition technical manual (Thorndike, Hagen, & Sattler, 1986) reinforces these findings. In this study, involving 30 students, the K-ABC MPC and Stanford–Binet Composite means were below average: 94.2 and 92.5, respectively. Furthermore, there was

again a mild Simultaneous Processing (97.5) > Sequential Processing (91.9) pattern. Further replications of these findings will support the use of the Sequential and Simultaneous Processing scales to make differential diagnoses for LD and normal children.

The relationship of the K-ABC to neuropsychological measures for samples of public school LD children has also been studied. Two studies (Leark, Snyder, Grove, & Golden, 1983; Snyder, Leark, Golden, Grove, & Allison, 1983) have compared the K-ABC to the Luria–Nebraska Neuropsychological Battery—Children's Revision. In the first study (Snyder et al., 1983), the Luria–Nebraska scales were used as predictors of K-ABC composite scores for 46 children aged 8 to $12\frac{1}{2}$ who were referred for evaluation for a variety of types of suspected LD. The resulting multiple-regression analysis yielded very predictable results. For example, the best predictor of the K-ABC MPC and Sequential Processing, Simultaneous Processing, and Nonverbal scales was the Intelligence scale of the Luria–Nebraska. The best predictor of the K-ABC Achievement scale composite was the Arithmetic scale of the Luria–Nebraska.

In a second and very similar investigation, Leark et al. (1982) tested 65 LD children with both the K-ABC and the Luria–Nebraska. The obtained intercorrelations were again highly plausible, in that the Intelligence scale of the Luria–Nebraska had among the highest correlations with the K-ABC composite scores. The high correlates of the K-ABC Achievement scale included the Perceptive and Expressive Language, Reading, Arithmetic, and Memory scales of the Luria–Nebraska. There was also some evidence that the K-ABC composite scores may be sensitive indices of brain dysfunction, because of the fact that the Pathognomic Signs scale of the Luria–Nebraska was significantly related (correlations ranging from .47 to .65) to *all* of the K-ABC composite scores.

Although the K-ABC correlates in a predictable fashion with the Luria–Nebraska, some less predictable nuances were found in a factor-analytic investigation of the K-ABC for a sample of 198 public school children identified as LD (Kaufman & McLean, 1986). In this unusual opportunity to factor-analyze the data for a large sample of LD children, a factor structure emerged that showed a strong correspondence between K-ABC scales and WISC-R factors: K-ABC Achievement subtests loaded on the same factor as WISC-R Verbal tasks; K-ABC Simultaneous Processing and WISC-R Performance subtests formed a second factor; and K-ABC Sequential Processing and WISC-R Freedom from Distractibility subtests loaded together on a third factor.

Objective and clinical methods for determining the number of factors to rotate suggested that either three or four factors might be interpreted as meaningful. When four factors were rotated, a separate dyad composed of the two K-ABC reading subtests constituted the fourth factor. Considering that the group was composed of LD children, many of whom were identified because their reading ability did *not* correlate with their intelligence, the splitting off of the two reading tasks was an expected outcome. This type of split did *not* occur for a sample of 212 normal children tested on both instruments (Kaufman & McLean, 1987). Which interpretation of the factors is correct—the K-ABC labels or the WISC-R labels? The four-factor solution for the LD sample suggests that the Wechsler labels might be more appropriate. The Verbal/Achievement dimension, for example, was defined primarily by verbal conceptual and reasoning tasks (WISC-R Vocabulary and Comprehension). In contrast, the three-factor solutions for both the normals and the LDs seemed to favor a K-ABC approach to factor definition. For the LD group, the Verbal/Achievement factor was defined mostly by factual and school-oriented subtests (WISC-R Information; K-ABC Reading/Understanding and Riddles). The most sensible approach is to realize that there is no one answer to the question, but that test interpretation depends on understanding a test's constructs for each individual. The K-ABC can be interpreted from a Wechsler approach, and the WISC-R can be evaluated from the vantage point of the K-ABC Sequential-Simultaneous model. This type of integration is evident in the case reports that appear at the end of the chapter.

One practical limitation of the K-ABC in LD diagnosis is the lack of several needed academic measures on the K-ABC Achievement scale. In order to assess all possible areas of learning disability, the K-ABC Achievement scale must be supplemented with measures of written spelling, mathematics calculation, and so on. It should be noted, however, that the K-ABC Achievement scale, although limited, does provide more measures of academic functioning than most other intelligence test batteries.

INTELLECTUALLY GIFTED CHILDREN

Global scale profiles for the gifted are difficult to discern from the results for the four samples of gifted children shown in Table 10.3. Two samples, for example, show a Simultaneous Processing > Sequential Processing pattern; one shows just the opposite pattern; and the fourth shows no meaningful difference between Sequential Processing and Simultaneous Processing means. This diversity probably results from the many differences in the goals and selection criteria of programs for the gifted.

Some trends are identifiable at the subtest level. Gestalt Closure is one of the worst subtests for gifted children. Apparently, to some extent, the higher the general intelligence (g) loading of the subtest, the more likely it is that gifted samples will score higher. Triangles and Matrix Analogies are among the best subtests for these children.

What is most striking, however, in the findings for samples of gifted children is the fact that the K-ABC MPC is consistently lower than the Stanford–Binet and Wechsler IQs for these children. In the Naglieri and Anderson (1985) study, for example, the K-ABC mean was 126.3, and the WISC-R mean was 134.3. Similar results occurred in other studies. In the McCallum, Karnes, and Edwards (1984) study, the mean Stanford–Binet IQ (1972 edition) was about 16.19 points higher than the mean K-ABC MPC. In the Barry (1983) study, the difference between the Stanford–Binet and K-ABC was about 6.8 points.

A number of factors may be involved in explaining this phenomenon, but two seem to loom largest: selection bias and different norming samples. Both the Naglieri and Anderson (1985) and the McCallum et al. (1984) gifted samples were preselected as gifted by individually administered tests such as the 1972 Stanford–Binet and the WISC-R. In

TABLE 10.3. K-ABC Global Scale and Subtest Standard Score Means for Samples of Gifted Children

	Sample			
Scale of subtest	Meslor & Curtiss, 1985 (n = 40)	Barry, 1983 (n = 50)	McCallum, Karnes, & Edwards, 1984 (n = 41)	Naglieri & Anderson, 1985 (n = 38)
Global scales				
Sequential Processing	116.7	129.0	114.8	122.4
Simultaneous Processing	122.2	123.3	118.2	122.8
Mental Processing Composite	123.1	130.5	119.2	126.3
Achievement	122.3	126.5	120.2	124.4
Mental Processing subtests				
3. Hand Movements	11.7	13.2	11.9	—
4. Gestalt Closure	12.0	11.9	11.6	—
5. Number Recall	12.8	15.7	13.2	—
6. Triangles	13.6	13.7	12.9	—
7. Word Order	13.4	14.4	11.8	—
8. Matrix Analogies	14.1	14.3	13.7	—
9. Spatial Memory	13.0	13.3	12.6	—
10. Photo Series	12.9	13.1	12.1	—
Achievement subtests				
12. Faces and Places	115.9	118.8	116.9	—
13. Arithmetic	118.5	122.2	116.2	—
14. Riddles	123.4	126.2	116.9	—
15. Reading/Decoding	119.1	119.4	118.3	—
16. Reading/Understanding	115.8	122.6	116.2	—

Note. From *Clinical and research applications of the K-ABC* (p.72) by R. W. Kamphaus and C. R. Reynolds, 1987, Circle Pines, MN: American Guidance Service. Copyright 1987 by American Guidance Service. Reprinted by permission.

other words, individuals with relatively low scores on these tests were not allowed to participate in these studies; this biased the outcome. Linn (1983) and others (Kaufman, 1972) have written about this problem extensively, and these results exemplify the failure to correct for regression effects when using preselected samples. As can be seen from Figure 10.1, this bias makes it virtually impossible to compare means in validity studies of this nature, because it artificially inflates the mean of the selection test (in this case, the WISC-R and the Stanford–Binet).

Figure 10.1 illustrates the problem by showing the scatter plot of the relationship (r = .61) between the Stanford–Binet and the K-ABC. Note that if the sample is preselected based on a cutoff score of 130 (as seen by the horizontal line), a number of low scores will be removed from the sample. This seems to eliminate low scores on the selection test (1972 Stanford–Binet; quadrants 3 and 4). As a result, the K-ABC mean is deflated and the 1972 Stanford–Binet mean is inflated. We can get a rough estimate of the magnitude of this problem by computing the amount of regression toward the mean, given the correlation between the K-ABC MPC and the 1972 Stanford–Binet IQ. The correlation between these two measures, as shown in Table 4.21 on page 117 of the K-ABC interpretive manual (Kaufman & Kaufman, 1983), was .61.

Using the mean Stanford–Binet IQ of 130.94 for the previously identified gifted sample tested by McCallum et al. (1984), and applying the procedure described by Hopkins and Glass (1978) based on the correlation between the two tests, we can obtain a predicted K-ABC MPC of 118.87. The MPC actually obtained for this sample, as shown in Table 10.3, was 119.24. Hence, the K-ABC mean MPC can be fairly accurately predicted if we know the mean Stanford–Binet IQ and the correlation between the two tests.

Another reason why the K-ABC mean is lower in these studies is that the K-ABC yields lower scores when compared to tests

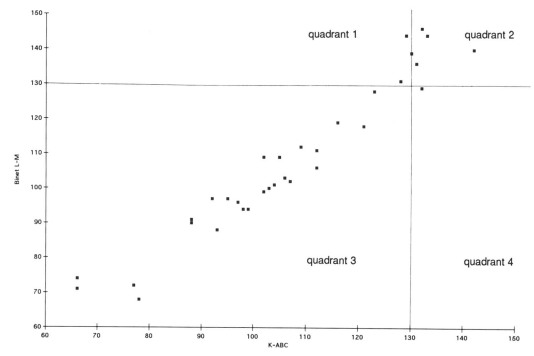

FIGURE 10.1. An illustration of selection bias where the Stanford–Binet is the selection test and the K-ABC is the new test under investigation. From *Clinical and Research applications of the K-ABC* (p. 73) by R. W. Kamphaus and C. R. Reynolds, 1987, Circle Pines, MN: American Guidance Service. Copyright 1987 by American Guidance Service. Reprinted by permission.

with substantially older standardization samples. It should be noted that for the Barry (1983) study shown in Table 10.3, the problem of selection bias was avoided by testing a referred sample of gifted children as opposed to an identified (preselected) sample of gifted children. As a result, the children who scored below 130 on the Stanford–Binet remained in the sample.

Even with this referral sample, however, the mean K-ABC MPC was still about 6.8 standard-score points lower than the mean Stanford–Binet IQ. Based on the data cited earlier, we think that it is reasonable to expect the K-ABC mean to be about 2–4 standard-score points lower than the 1972 Stanford–Binet mean. This still leaves a 2- to 4-point difference in standard scores between the K-ABC and Stanford–Binet unaccounted for, even when selection bias is controlled. Perhaps this remaining small difference between the K-ABC and the WISC-R or Stanford–Binet for gifted students is due to a lack of "top" in the K-ABC. The samples for the four studies cited in

Table 10.3 were all children near the upper end of the K-ABC age range. Naglieri and Anderson (1985), using a sample with a mean age of about 11 years, 6 months, found considerable problems with a lack of difficulty on the K-ABC. They noted that perfect subtest scores were obtained 14 times on the WISC-R but 67 times on the K-ABC. This is probably to be expected, since the K-ABC age range goes only to $12\frac{1}{2}$. Examiners should probably use the same logic that they do when selecting other intelligence tests, and always keep the K-ABC age range and the referral questions clearly in mind. In effect, examiners are as likely to experience problems with a lack of difficulty for gifted children on the K-ABC at age 12 as on the WISC-R at age 15.

Another possible explanation for the remaining difference between the 1972 Stanford–Binet and the K-ABC for gifted children is that the 1972 Stanford–Binet may tend to give high estimates of intelligence for academically precocious children. Two pieces of data suggest this. First, one study

(Zins & Barnett, 1984) shows an extremely high correlation (.86) between the 1972 Stanford–Binet and the K-ABC Achievement scale. Second, a study from the Stanford-Binet Fourth Edition technical manual (Thorndike et al., 1986) indicates that the 1972 Stanford–Binet produces much higher scores (mean IQ = 135.3) than the 1986 Fourth Edition (mean IQ = 121.8). It may be that the 1972 Stanford–Binet shares too much overlap with measures of academic achievement.

EMOTIONALLY DISTURBED CHILDREN

In a recent study, Pommer (1986) administered the K-ABC and the WISC-R to a group of 59 seriously emotionally disturbed children. Individual subtest scores were not reported, but a clear difference was found between the Simultaneous Processing (mean = 82.52) and Sequential Processing (mean = 89.52) scales. This trend did not emerge for the group of behavior-disordered children cited in the K-ABC interpretive manual (Kaufman & Kaufman, 1983).

There are, however, several differences between the Pommer (1986) study and the one cited in the manual. It is interesting that the children in the Pommer study generally scored lower than the group cited in the K-ABC interpretive manual. Also, the majority of the children in the Pommer study were black. Data from Table 4.35 on page 151 of the K-ABC interpretive manual (Kaufman & Kaufman, 1983) indicate that blacks tend to perform better on the Sequential Processing scale. Hence, the data from the Pommer study could be interpreted in several ways.

The results of the Pommer study fortunately have been replicated in recent investigations. Hickman and Stark (1987) identified two groups of third- and fourth-graders as impulsive (n = 27) versus nonimpulsive (n = 18), using latency scores from the Matching Familiar Figures Test (Kagan & Salkind, 1965). They found that whereas normal children differed from impulsive children by only 5 points on the Sequential Processing scale, they scored, on average, 11 points higher than the impulsive children on the Simultaneous Processing scale. Overall, impulsive children scored lower than normal

children on all of the K-ABC global scales, with Simultaneous Processing showing the most pronounced deficit.

A group of autistic children has also shown a trend in favor of Simultaneous Processing (Freeman, Lucas, Forness, & Ritvo, 1985). This study involved 21 children aged 6 through 12 years. Although this sample obtained a 4-point advantage on the Sequential Processing scale (Simultaneous Processing mean = 98.2, Sequential Processing mean = 101.9), they performed relatively poorly on the Achievement scale (mean = 92.8).

These three early investigations indicate that perhaps many behaviorally or emotionally disturbed children tested with the K-ABC can attend to the brief stimuli on the Sequential Processing scale but have problems sustaining attention and concentration on the more involved Simultaneous Processing scale items. In any case, this important finding requires replication.

HEARING-IMPAIRED CHILDREN

At least three studies have evaluated the utility of the K-ABC Nonverbal scale with severely hearing-impaired children (Ham, 1985; Porter & Kirby, 1986; Ulissi, Brice, & Gibbons, 1985). All of these studies found that hearing-impaired children, even residential populations, scored in the average range when a pantomimed administration of the K-ABC Nonverbal scale was used (see Table 10.4). The mean Nonverbal scale standard score for the Porter and Kirby (1986) sample was 98.8; for the Ham (1985) sample, 96.5; and for the Ulissi et al. (1985) sample, 100.7. Although the samples for these studies were relatively small, the trend is clear: Hearing-impaired children have relatively normal intelligence as assessed by the K-ABC Nonverbal scale.

The Porter and Kirby (1986) study also tested the utility of pantomimed versus sign language administrations of the K-ABC Nonverbal scale. The means for the pantomimed and sign language administration groups were 98.8 and 96.8, respectively. For this relatively small sample, this difference was not statistically significant. These results argue for using the K-ABC Nonverbal scale as it was originally designed, in pantomime.

TABLE 10.4. K-ABC Global Scale and Subtest Standard Score Means for Samples of Hearing-Impaired Children

Scale of subtest	Sample		
	Ullssi, Brice, & Gibbons, 1985 (n = 50)	Ham, 1985 (n = 17)	Porter & Kirby 1986 (n = 25)[a]
Global scales			
Sequential Processing	87.9	—	—
Simultaneous Processing	101.2	—	—
Mental Processing Composite	95.3	—	—
Nonverbal	100.7	96.5	98.8
Subtests			
3. Hand Movements	10.3	8.2	10.6
4. Gestalt Closure	10.7	—	—
5. Number Recall	7.1	—	—
6. Triangles	10.3	10.7	11.0
7. World Order	6.5	—	—
8. Matrix Analogies	10.2	11.0	9.3
9. Spatial Memory	9.3	9.1	9.1
10. Photo Series	10.1	8.6	9.4
12. Faces and Places	—	11.8	—

Note. From *Clinical and research applications of the K-ABC* (p. 75) by R. W. Kamphaus and C. R. Reynolds, 1987, Circle Pines, MN: American Guidance Service. Copyright 1987 by American Guidance Service. Reprinted by permission.
[a]These data are for the group in this study that received pantomimed as opposed to American Sign Language instructions.

BRAIN-INJURED CHILDREN

There are a few investigations of the use of the K-ABC with brain-injured children. Morris and Bigler (1985) investigated the relationship of the K-ABC and WISC-R to hemispheric functioning for 79 brain-injured children seen at a neurology clinic. These children had received intensive neurological evaluations, including computed axial tomography (CAT) scans, electroencephalograms (EEGs), and neuropsychological evaluations with the Halstead–Reitan. Based on the neuropsychological test results, composite scores were computed for right- and left-hemisphere functioning, and these scores were correlated with Verbal and Performance scores from the WISC-R and Sequential and Simultaneous Processing scores from the K-ABC. The main conclusion from this study was that the K-ABC Sequential and Simultaneous Processing scales were more highly related to right-hemisphere (Simultaneous Processing) and left-hemisphere (Sequential Processing) functioning than the Wechsler scales. The authors concluded further that the main reason for this finding was that the WISC-R was not able to diagnose right-hemisphere dysfunction at a significant level.

Similar findings resulted in a smaller scale investigation of 27 brain-injured children by Shapiro and Dotan (1985). These investigators also used EEGs, CAT scans, and other measures to norm groups of children with focal right- and left-hemisphere damage. These authors corroborated the results of Morris and Bigler (1985) by finding a K-ABC Sequential Processing < Simultaneous Processing pattern for the majority of children with left-hemisphere findings, and a Simultaneous Processing < Sequential Processing pattern for the majority of children with right-hemisphere findings. The predicted patterns were even more accurate for right-handed boys. In direct contrast, the relationship of the WISC-R Verbal and Performance scales to hemispheric functioning was unclear. Shapiro and Dotan (1985) concluded that, as compared to K-ABC, the lack of relationship between WISC-R Verbal–Performance differences and neurological findings may reflect lack of homogeneity of function in those scales.

These results for brain-injured children

are encouraging, in that the K-ABC's Sequential–Simultaneous Processing dichotomy may have an intuitive relationship to left- and right-hemisphere cognitive functions as defined by the split-brain research tradition. There is, however, a great need for research that will clarify this relationship, since moderator variables (such as gender and handedness) may confound the findings for an individual child. Even though there is some relationship between the K-ABC and localization of function, this does not make the K-ABC particularly useful for localizing damage. Medical procedures such as magnetic resonance imaging (MRI) will fill the need. The K-ABC may, on the other hand, be useful for identifying analytic or holistic processing dysfunction.

AT-RISK PRESCHOOLERS

Several studies have evaluated the use of the K-ABC in the assessment of high-risk preschoolers. Lyon and Smith (1986) compared the performance of at-risk ($n = 44$) and normal ($n = 49$) preschoolers ranging in age from 45 to 70 months. In all cases, the mean K-ABC global scales were significantly lower for the high-risk than for the normal preschoolers. The mean K-ABC Sequential and Simultaneous Processing, MPC, and Achievement standard scores for the high-risk group ranged from 89.3 to 92.5, consistently below average.

In a concurrent validity study, Smith and Lyon (1987) administered the K-ABC and the McCarthy Scales of Children's Abilities to groups of repeating ($n = 13$) and nonrepeating preschoolers ($n = 27$). The K-ABC and McCarthy Scales both discriminated between the group recommended for retention in a preschool program and the group recommended for advancement to kindergarten. The mean MPC for the repeaters was 76.2 and for the nonrepeaters was 91.4. Similarly, other K-ABC global scales were lower for the repeaters (Sequential Processing mean = 80.3, Simultaneous Processing mean = 77.5, Achievement mean = 80.5) than for the nonrepeaters (Sequential Processing mean = 91.3, Simultaneous Processing mean = 93.4, Achievement mean = 94.7).

Ricciardi and Voelker (1987) essentially cross-validated the findings of Smith and Lyon (1987) by testing four groups of preschoolers with the K-ABC: normal ($n = 15$), language-impaired ($n = 14$), behavior problems ($n = 17$), and language-impaired plus behavior problems ($n = 13$). Again, the K-ABC clearly discriminated between the normal and handicapped samples. The normal group had a mean MPC of 104.0, while the means for the remaining groups were as follows: language-impaired, 83.1; behavior problems, 95.3; and language-impaired plus behavior problems, 77.0.

As Kamphaus and Kaufman (in press) note, a number of characteristics of the K-ABC make it attractive for use with preschoolers. These include its relative brevity, attractive materials, simple examiner instructions, theoretical model, and sample and teaching items. On the other hand, the K-ABC has some weaknesses when used with preschoolers, including ceiling (too many perfect raw scores) and floor (too many raw scores of 0) effects, a lack of assessment of expressive language, and a lack of manipulatives. Kamphaus and Kaufman (in press) suggest that because of these various contingencies regarding the use of the K-ABC with preschoolers, examiners should simply use the K-ABC on a trial basis to determine its worthiness for use in a particular setting.

EDUCATIONAL REMEDIATION RESEARCH

One of the goals in developing the K-ABC was to produce a test that is helpful in the educational remediation process (Kaufman & Kaufman, 1983). The question of whether or not the K-ABC remedial model is effective is still not answered. There are simply no large-scale, well-controlled studies available on this topic. Unfortunately, it does not appear likely that research on this issue will become available in the near future.

Some pilot data presented in the K-ABC interpretive manual (Kaufman & Kaufman, 1983) suggest that the K-ABC may be useful for designing educational interventions. In direct contrast, a study by Ayres, Cooley, and Severson (1988) suggests that the K-ABC will not be useful for treatment planning. Both of these pieces of research have methodological weaknesses. The jury is out on this issue, and, as a result, the individual clinician has only clinical acumen to guide his or her practice.

K-ABC SHORT FORMS

Applegate and Kaufman (1988) developed short forms of the K-ABC, which may be useful when only general measures of mental processing and achievement that can be administered in relatively brief amounts of time are needed. Examples of uses of short forms include preschool screening for identification of "at-risk" or potentially gifted children, research, and certain clinical or educational circumstances. Although the administration of a short form can never replace the multiple scores and clinical evaluations obtained from administration of a complete battery, short forms of the K-ABC demonstrate excellent psychometric properties and offer useful estimates of functioning.

Extensive analysis of the reliability and validity of various combinations of subtests led to the selection of the following short forms for ages 4 through $12\frac{1}{2}$ years. (Short forms were not developed for younger children because the K-ABC is already relatively brief for these ages.)

Mental processing Dyad: Triangles, Word Order
Mental Processing Triad: Triangles, Word Order, Matrix Analogies
Mental Processing Tetrad: Hand Movements, Triangles, Word Order, Matrix Analogies
Achievement Dyad: Riddles, Reading/ Decoding

Mean reliability coefficients for the short forms are excellent, ranging from .88 to .93. Although the corrected validity coefficient between the Mental Processing Dyad and the complete K-ABC is a marginal .80, the remaining short forms demonstrate excellent validity, with corrected coefficients of .86 for the Mental Processing Triad, .88 for the Mental Processing Tetrad, and .93 for the Achievement Dyad. Applegate and Kaufman (1988) recommend using either the Mental Processing Triad or Tetrad along with the Achievement Dyad whenever a short form of the K-ABC is needed. Applegate and Kauf-

man (1988) provide equations for computing *Estimated* MPC and Achievement standard scores ($X = 100$, $SD = 15$), based on the sum of subtest scaled or standard scores (X_c). The word "*Estimated*" should be used whenever scores from short forms are reported.

ILLUSTRATIVE CASE REPORTS

The two case reports that follow are of actual cases tested by qualified examiners. In both instances, the children—an LD girl almost 7 years of age and a gifted 7-year-old boy— were administered both the K-ABC and WISC-R. Ordinarily, one would choose one test battery or the other, although occasionally giving both tests is warranted. In this instance, we have deliberately selected children who were tested on both instruments to illustrate how the tasks on both tests can be integrated to form stronger hypotheses, and to enable Wechsler-oriented clinicians to get more of an understanding of how a K-ABC profile can facilitate competent assessment.

Cassie

Background and Testing Behavior

Cassie, an LD girl aged 6 years, 11 months, was referred for a complete psychological evaluation by the special education coordinator of her school. She had received speech pathology services during kindergarten. Cassie had reportedly had a febrile seizure at the age of 10 months, which lasted for several hours, and she had been administered phenobarbital for seizure control until she was 3 years old.

In first grade, Cassie was having significant difficulty, especially with organization and orientation. She reportedly was unable to find things in her desk because of extreme lack of order; her things were often on the floor. Cassie also reportedly could not be allowed out of the classroom alone, because she would get lost. She was far behind her classmates in all academic subjects.

Involving Cassie appropriately in testing required considerable energy on the part of the examiner, as she appeared to have her own agenda. She attempted to use test materials inappropriately by scrambling and spinning picture cards, building block towers, and naming things block patterns brought to mind. Cassie was virtually in constant motion, compulsively adjusting and readjusting her chair. At one point during testing, she announced, "Can't. My brain is on something else." And, indeed, it seemed to be. Some of Cassie's inappropriate activity appeared to be an avoidance technique she used when tasks became difficult.

Though Cassie was very self-distracting, she did not appear to be distracted when a room next door became unusually noisy. Her reactions to difficult items ranged from a very realistic "Beats me," to whining, "I don't kn-o-o-w." She wanted the examiner to help her with some items she was unable to do, saying such things as "Show me. I have to know." Cassie displayed much difficulty in copying designs using pencil and paper. With her attempt on the first design, she became extremely frustrated; she scratched it out, flipped the paper over, and did all of her designs on the opposite side of the paper, literally piling some of them on top of one another.

Test Results and Interpretation

On measures of intellectual ability, Cassie's scores were similar (see Table 10.5). She obtained a WISC-R Full Scale IQ of 91 ± 6. The chances were 95 out of 100 that her true Full Scale IQ would fall in the range 85–97, placing her at the 27th percentile of children her age. Cassie's K-ABC MPC score of 101 ± 7 indicated a 95-out-of-100 chance that her true MPC would fall in the range of 94–108, placing her at the 53rd percentile of children her age. Intellectually, then, Cassie showed average ability. She was better able to process information simultaneously—that is, to integrate a number of stimuli at one point in time in order to solve a problem (K-ABC Simultaneous Processing 111 ± 8)—than to

TABLE 10.5. Test Results for Cassie

Scale/subests/other	Cassie's score
Bender–Gestalt Test for Young Children (Koppitz scoring)	
Error score	9 ($SD = 0.51$)
Developmental age equivalent	5 years, 9 months to 5 years, 11 months
Emotional indicators	5

K-ABC

Global scales	
Sequential Processing	87 ± 9^a
Simultaneous Processing	111 ± 8^b
MPC	101 ± 7^c
Achievement	89 ± 6
Achievement subtests (standard scores)	
Mean	91
Faces and Places	95 ± 13
Arithmetic	76 ± 11^d
Riddles	114 ± 11^e
Reading/Decoding	77 ± 5^d
Mental Processing subtests (scaled scores)	
Mean	10
Sequential Processing subtests (scaled scores)	
Hand Movements	6^d
Number Recall	9
Word Order	9
Simultaneous Processing subtests (scaled scores)	
Gestalt Closure	16^e
Triangles	11
Matrix Analogies	13^e
Spatial Memory	9
Photo Series	9

WISC-R

Global scales	
Verbal IQ	100^f
Performance IQ	85^g
Full Scale IQ	91 ± 6^f
Verbal subtests (scaled scores)	
Information	10
Similarities	13^e
Arithmetic	7
Vocabulary	9
Comprehension	11
Performance subtests (scaled scores)	
Picture Completion	11^e
Picture Arrangement	6
Block Design	11^e
Object Assembly	8
Coding	3^d

[a]Sequential Processing < Simultaneous Processing ($p < .01$).
[b]Simultaneous Processing > Achievement ($p < .01$).
[c]MPC > Achievement ($p < .05$).
[d]Area of weakness.
[e]Area of strength.
[f]Average.
[g]Below average.

solve problems in a step-by-step manner (K-ABC Sequential Processing 87 ± 9). Cassie was also better able to express her mental ability verbally (WISC-R Verbal Comprehension factor—63rd percentile) than nonverbally (WISC-R Perceptual Organization factor—37th percentile), though this difference was not significant. Cassie's Bender–Gestalt designs (30th percentile) indicated average visual–motor integration and nonverbal intelligence, commensurate with the WISC-R Perceptual Organization factor. The WISC-R third factor, the so-called Freedom from Distractibility factor (5th percentile), is a measure of sequencing ability, and Cassie's performance on this factor supported the K-ABC evidence of significantly weaker Sequential than Simultaneous Processing. Attention and concentration are also necessary for success on the K-ABC Sequential Processing scale and the WISC-R Freedom from Distractibility factor. Cassie's self-distracting behaviors undoubtedly influenced these scores; however, Cassie's also doing poorly on a sequencing task requiring her to arrange picture cards in the correct order to tell a story (9th percentile) suggested that she did have sequencing deficits as well as deficits in attention and concentration.

Cassie earned a K-ABC Achievement standard score of 89 ± 6. She performed better than 24% of the children her age on this scale, and the chances were 95 out of 100 that the range 83–95 would include her true Achievement standard score. Cassie earned average to above-average scores on those Achievement tasks measuring acquired factual knowledge, such as being able to identify familiar faces and places (37th percentile) and to simultaneously integrate several verbal concepts to solve riddles (82nd percentile). Her strength in solving riddles was also a reflection of her strong Simultaneous Processing ability and of her well-developed Verbal Comprehension. She functioned at well below average level on those reading (6th percentile) and arithmetic (5th percentile) tasks heavily dependent on applied, school-related skills.

Cassie's strength in Simultaneous Processing was evident in her functioning at the upper extreme level (98th percentile) on the purest measure of this type of processing, requiring her mentally "filling in the gaps" in inkblot drawings and supplying verbal labels for the drawings. Her strength (63rd percentile) in identifying parts missing from pictures called upon her strong Simultaneous Processing also. Cassie functioned at the average to above-average level on reasoning tasks, both verbal and nonverbal, commonsense and abstract. She showed strengths in both verbal (84th percentile) and nonverbal (63rd percentile) abstract thinking, as demonstrated by her ability to state the categories to which unlike things belong and her ability to analyze and construct abstract designs with blocks. Cassie also displayed strength in nonverbal analogical thinking (84th percentile). Cassie's most serious intellectual deficit appeared to be her planning ability (1st percentile), measured by her finding her way out of mazes. Cassie was unable to find her way out of the two simple mazes that were presented to her. This, together with her getting lost when she left her classroom, was evidence of her significant difficulty with orientation.

Cassie's use of more than the one page of paper for her Bender–Gestalt designs was unusual; according to Koppitz (1975), this occurs almost exclusively on the protocols of emotionally disturbed children with neurological impairment. She completed the Bender–Gestalt with other emotional indicators of impulsiveness, anxiety, acting out, and lack of interest and attention, as seen with children who are preoccupied with problems or who are trying to avoid doing what they are told to do. Cassie's avoidance behaviors have been discussed earlier.

Summary and Recommendations

At this time, Cassie was functioning intellectually in the average range, with a WISC-R Full Scale IQ of 91 ± 6 and a K-ABC MPC of 101 ± 7. She expressed her intelligence better verbally than nonverbally and was better at simultaneous intellectual processing than at sequencing information and processing it in a step-by-step fashion. Cassie had average to above-average reasoning abilities. She had significant difficulty with attention and concentration and with orientation. She was achieving well below her mental ability and well below her current grade level in reading and arithmetic.

Cassie's history, behaviors, and test results suggested neurological impairment. Emotional factors were probably also contributing to her poor classroom performance and to her academic deficits in reading and arithmetic. Referral to the clinical psychologist for psychological evaluation was recommended. Referral to a specialist in LD for further educational diagnostic testing was also recommended, to determine the most effective means of capitalizing on her strengths in simultaneous processing to help remediate her deficiencies in reading and arithmetic. Numerous valuable and specific remedial suggestions appear in the K-ABC interpretation manual (Kaufman & Kaufman, 1983, Ch. 7). At last report, Cassie was evaluated by the speech pathologist to determine her speech therapy needs.

Jesse

Background and Test Behavior

Jesse, a gifted boy aged 7 years, 1 month, was referred for a psychological assessment by his father. He was reportedly not making a good adjustment to the first grade of school, and this evaluation was requested to clarify his intellectual and emotional status. Jesse was an attractive, lively, normally developed youngster who was eager to participate in the testing procedures. He enjoyed the intellectual challenge presented by many of the tests, and responded well to encouragement and positive reinforcement. He showed a healthy curiosity throughout the testing. His home environment was warm and supportive, and one in which intellectual achievement was valued.

Test Results and Interpretation

On the WISC-R, Jesse was functioning at the "very superior" range of intelligence, with a Verbal IQ of 137, Performance IQ of 133, and Full Scale IQ of 140. This placed him above the 99th percentile of the sample population in his age range. The specific subtest scores and subtest percentiles he obtained are shown in Table 10.6.

Although Jesse showed superb overall intellectual organization, the fact of his very high IQ should not distract from the fact that there were also areas of relative weaknesses in his profile. These had to do with tasks requiring the maintenance of a sequence of

symbols and rapid eye–hand coordination. His performance on these tasks was still above average, but not in the range of his performance on such functions as concept formation (Similarities) or constructional tasks (Object Assembly). An example of his difficulty with maintaining a sequence of symbols was seen in his attempts to repeat a series of numbers in either the right order or the reverse order of presentation; he often responded by scrambling them.

To enable the examiner to study this phenomenon in more detail, Jesse was administered the K-ABC, with particular attention to the Sequential versus Simultaneous Processing scales. Here again, Jesse performed superbly, obtaining an MPC of 149, which placed him above the 99.9th national percentile rank. As expected, he showed a statistically significant difference between his "low" Sequential Processing, with a score 126, and his high Simultaneous Processing, with a score of 156. The difference was significant at the .01 level, and the 30 points separating the two methods of processing had clear educational implications that are explored later. His level of Achievement on the K-ABC was "very superior" and consistent, ranging from the 98th to the 99.8th percentile levels (see Table 10.6).

On the Wide Range Achievement Test— Revised (WRAT-R), Jesse's scores were not as spectacular as those on the previously described batteries (see Table 10.6), although again we are talking only in relative terms; he was consistently above his present grade level placement. Part of the reason for this discrepancy lay in the fact that this test measures specific application and integration of classroom-learned material rather than more general functions.

One of the problems with Jesse's spelling derived from the same difficulty that has been discussed previously: He was following a sequential approach (phonics) to spelling, when he would do better learning words as wholes. His misspelled words were often more or less phonetically correct but missing letters; or, as in "drees," he doubled the letter at the wrong point in the sequence. Given the fact that he was only in first grade, not much probably needed to be done about these spelling problems at present; however, given his weakness in Sequential Processing and his strength in Simultaneous Processing

TABLE 10.6. Test Scores for Jesse

Scale/subtests/other	Jesse's score	Percentile
WISC-R		
Global scales		
Verbal IQ	137	99
Performance IQ	133	99
Full Scale IQ	140	99.62
Verbal subtests (scaled scores)		
Information	14	91
Similarities	17	99
Arithmetic	15	95
Vocabulary	16	98
Comprehension	17	99
Digit Span	13	84[a]
Performance subtests (scaled scores)		
Picture Completion	16	98
Picture Arrangement	14	91
Block Design	15	95
Object Assembly	18	99
Coding	11	63[a]
K-ABC		
Global scales		
Sequential Processing	126	96
Simultaneous Processing	156	above 96
MPC	149	99.9
Achievement	146	99.9
Achievement subtests (standard scores)		
Faces and Places	134	99
Arithmetic	143	99.8
Riddles	130	98
Reading/Decoding	131	98
Reading/ Understanding	144	99.8
WRAT-R		
Reading (standard score	121	92[b]
Spelling (standard score)	108	70[a,c]
Arithmetic (standard score)	126	96[d]

[a]Area of relative weakness.
[b]Grade equivalent: End of third.
[c]Grade equivalent: End of second.
[d]Grade equivalent: Beginning of third.

on the K-ABC Jesse's learning would be greatly accelerated if the simultaneous approach were followed for the time being, leading to the goal of his eventually mastering both forms of cognitive processing.

Summary and Recommendations

Jesse was a superendowed child who was experiencing minor adjustment problems in the first grade of school. He came from a stable family environment and had a background of resources to permit him to actualize his potentials. It was strongly recommended that he should be in classes for the gifted, should be permitted to advance through the grades at his own pace, and above all should be challenged to excel in his work. His assessment revealed a significant discrepancy between sequential and simultaneous approaches to learning, and for the time being it was advised that the simultaneous approach should be favored over the sequential one.

Jesse was unlikely to encounter any cognitive difficulties in absorbing and integrating school material. Emphasis, therefore, should be on character development, on the learning of discipline, and on experiencing the joys of achieving competence through hard work.

There were no vocational limits to be placed on him because of intelligence. This should be kept in mind later on in allowing him to know and to experience as much as possible about the different professions and what they entail.

Acknowledgments. We thank Dr. Fernando Melendez and Ruth Oliver for permission to use their case reports in this chapter. All names and identifying information have been changed in the case reports.

REFERENCES

Anastasi, A. (1988). *Psychological testing* (6th ed.). New York: Macmillan.

Applegate, B., & Kaufman, A. S. (1988). *Short form estimation of K-ABC Sequential and Simultaneous Processing for research and screening purposes.* Manuscript submitted for publication.

Ayres, R. R., Cooley, E. J., & Severson, H. H. (1988). Educational translation of the Kaufman Assessment Battery for Children: A construct validity study. *School Psychology Review, 17,* 113–124.

Barry, B. J. (1983). *Validity study of the Kaufman Assessment Battery for Children compared to the Stanford–Binet, Form L-M, in the identification of gifted nine- and ten-year-olds*. Unpublished master's thesis, National College of Education, Chicago.

Bauer, J. J., & Smith, D. K. (1988, April). *Stability of the K-ABC and S-B: 4 with preschool children*. Paper presented at the meeting of the National Association of School Psychologists, Chicago.

Binet, A., & Simon, T. (1905). Méthodes nouvelles pour le diagnostic du niveau intellectuel des anormaux. *L'Année Psychologique, 11*, 191–244.

Fourqurean, J. M. (1987). A K-ABC and WISC-R comparison for Latino learning-disabled children of limited English proficiency. *Journal of School Psychology, 25*, 15–21.

Freeman, B. J., Lucas, J. C., Forness, S. R., & Ritvo, E. R. (1985). Cognitive processing of high-functioning autistic children: Comparing the K-ABC and the WISC-R. *Journal of Psychoeducational Assessment, 3*, 357–362.

Ham, S. J. (1985). *A validity study of recent intelligence tests on a deaf population*. (Available from the author, School Psychologist, North Dakota School for the Deaf, Devils Lake, ND 58301)

Hickman, J. A., & Stark, K. D. (1987, April). *Relationship between cognitive impulsivity and information processing abilities in children: Implications for training programs*. Paper presented at the meeting of the National Association of School Psychologists, New Orleans.

Hooper, J. R., & Hynd, G. W. (1985). Differential diagnosis of subtypes of developmental dyslexia with the Kaufman Assessment Battery for Children (K-ABC). *Journal of Clinical Child Psychology, 14*, 145–152.

Hopkins, K. D., & Glass, G. V. (1978). *Basic statistics for the behavioral sciences*. Englewood Cliffs, NJ: Prentice-Hall.

Kagan, J., & Salkind, N. J. (1965). *Matching Familiar Figures Test*. (Available from J. Kagan, Harvard University, 33 Kirkland Street, 1510 William James Hall, Cambridge, MA 02138)

Kamphaus, R. W., & Kaufman, A. S. (in press). Applications of the K-ABC with preschoolers. In B. Bracken (Ed.), *Assessment of preschool children*. Boston: Allyn & Bacon.

Kamphaus, R. W., & Reynolds, C. R. (1987). *Clinical and research applications of the K-ABC*. Circle Pines, MN: American Guidance Service.

Kaufman, A. S. (1972, May). *Restriction of range: Questions and answers* (Test Service Bulletin No. 59). New York: Psychological Corporation.

Kaufman, A. S., & Kaufman, N. L. (1983). *Interpretive manual for the Kaufman Assessment Battery for Children*. Circle Pines, MN: American Guidance Service.

Kaufman, A. S., & McLean, J. E. (1986). K-ABC/WISC-R factor analysis for a learning disabled population. *Journal of Learning Disabilities, 19*, 145–153.

Kaufman, A. S., & McLean, J. E. (1987). Joint factor analysis of the K-ABC and WISC-R with normal children. *Journal of School Psychology, 25*, 105–118.

Kavale, K. A., & Forness, S. R. (1984). A meta-analysis of the validity of Wechsler scale profiles and recategorizations: Patterns or parodies. *Learning Disability Quarterly, 7*, 136–156.

Keith, T. Z., & Dunbar, S. B. (1984). Hierarchical factor analysis of the K-ABC: Testing alternate models. *Journal of Special Education, 18*, 367–375.

Klanderman, J. W., Perney, J., & Kroeschell, Z. B. (1985, April). *Comparisons of the K-ABC and WISC-R for LD children*. Paper presented at the meeting of the National Association of School Psychologists, Las Vegas, NV.

Koppitz, E. M. (1975). *The Bender–Gestalt Test for Young Children: Vol. 2. Research and application, 1963–1973*. New York: Grune & Stratton.

Leark, R. A., Snyder, T., Grove, T., & Golden, C. J. (1983, August). *Comparison of the K-ABC to standardized neuropsychological batteries: Preliminary results*. Paper presented at the meeting of the American Psychological Association, Anaheim, CA.

Linn, R. L. (1983). Pearson selection formulas: Implications for studies of predictive bias and estimates of educational effects in selected samples. *Journal of Educational Measurement, 20*, 1–15.

Lyon, M. A., & Smith, D. K. (1986). A comparison of at-risk preschool children's performance on the K-ABC, McCarthy Scales, and Stanford–Binet. *Journal of Psychoeducational Assessment, 4*, 35–43.

McCallum, R. S., Karnes, F. A., & Edwards, R. P. (1984). The test of choice for assessment of gifted children: A comparison of the K-ABC, WISC-R, and Stanford–Binet. *Journal of Psychoeducational Assessment, 21*, 57–63.

Mealor, D. J., & Curtiss, D. J. (1985, April). *Comparative analysis of the K-ABC and WISC-R for selected minority students*. Paper presented at the meeting of the National Association of School Psychologists, Las Vegas, NV.

Miller, T. L. & Reynolds, C. R. (1984). The K-ABC [Special Issue]. *Journal of Special Education, 18*.

Morris, J. M., & Bigler, E. (1985, January). *An investigation of the Kaufman Assessment Battery for Children (K-ABC) with neurologically impaired children*. Paper presented at the meeting of the International Neuropsychological Society, San Diego, CA.

Naglieri, J. A. (1985a). Use of the WISC-R and K-ABC with learning disabled, borderline, mentally retarded, and normal children. *Psychology in the Schools, 22*, 133–141.

Naglieri, J. A. (1985b). Assessment of mentally retarded children with the Kaufman Assessment Battery for Children. *American Journal of Mental Deficiency, 89*, 367–371.

Naglieri, J. A., & Anderson, D. F. (1985). Comparison of the WISC-R and K-ABC with gifted students. *Journal of Psychoeducational Assessment, 3*, 175–179.

Nelson, R. B., Obrzut, A., & Cummings, J. (1984). Construct and predictive validity of the K-ABC with EMR children. Available from R. Brett Nelson, Weld County School District #6, Greeley, CO 80631.

Obringer, S. J. (1988, November). *A survey of perceptions by school psychologists of the Stanford-Binet IV*. Paper presented at the meeting of the Mid-South Educational Research Association, Louisville, KY.

Obrzut, A., Nelson, R. B., & Obrzut, J. E. (in press). Construct validity of the K-ABC with mildly mentally retarded students. *American Journal of Mental Deficiency*.

Pommer, L. T. (1986). Seriously emotionally disturbed children's performance on the Kaufman Assessment

Battery for Children: A concurrent validity study. *Journal of Psychoeducational Assessment, 4,* 155–162.

Porter, L. J., & Kirby, E. A. (1986). Effects of two instructional sets on the validity of the Kaufman Assessment Battery for Children—Nonverbal Scale with a group of severely hearing impaired children. *Psychology in the Schools, 23,* 1–6.

Reynolds, C. R. (1987). Playing IQ roulette with the Stanford–Binet, 4th edition. *Measurement and Evaluation in Counseling and Development, 20,* 139–141.

Reynolds, C. R., Kamphaus, R. W., & Rosenthal, B. (1988). Factor analysis of the Stanford–Binet Fourth Edition for ages 2 years through 23 years. *Movement and Evaluation in Counseling and Development, 21,* 52–63.

Ricciardi, P. W. R., & Volker, S. L. (1987, August). *Measuring congitive skills of language impaired preschoolers with the K-ABC.* Paper presented at the annual meeting of the American Psychological Association, New York, NY.

Shapiro, E. G., & Dotan, N. (1985, October). *Neurological findings and the Kaufman Assessment Battery for Children.* Paper presented at the meeting of the National Association of Neuropsychologists, Philadelphia.

Smith, D. K., & Lyon, M. A. (1987). *K-ABC/McCarthy performance for repeating and nonrepeating preschoolers.* Paper presented at the annual meeting of the National Association of School Psychologists, New Orleans. (ERIC Document Reproduction Service No. ED 280889)

Smith, D. K., Lyon, M. A., Hunter, E., & Boyd, R. (1986, April). *Relationships between the K-ABC and WISC-R for students referred for severe learning disabilities.* Paper presented at the meeting of the National Association of School Psychologists, Hollywood, FL.

Snyder, T. J., Leark, R. A., Golden, C. J., Grove, T., & Allison, R. (1983, March). *Correlations of the K-ABC, WISC-R, and Luria–Nebraska Children's Battery for exceptional children.* Paper presented at the meeting of the National Association of School Psychologists, Detroit.

Sparrow, S. S., Balla, D. A., & Cicchetti, D. V. (1984). *Vineland Adaptive Behavior Scales.* Circle Pines, MN: American Guidance Service.

Thorndike, R. L., Hagen, E. P., & Sattler, J. M. (1986). *Technical manual for the Stanford–Binet Intelligence Scale: Fourth Edition.* Chicago: Riverside.

Ulissi, S. M., Brice, P. J., & Gibbons, S. (1985, April). *The use of the Kaufman Assessment Battery for Children with the hearing impaired.* Paper presented at the meeting of the National Association of School Psychologists, Las Vegas, NV.

Zins, J. E., & Barnett, D. W. (1984). A validity study of the K-ABC, the WISC-R, and the Stanford–Binet with nonreferred children. *Journal of School Psychology, 22,* 369–371.

11

Stanford–Binet Intelligence Scale, Fourth Edition: Making the Case for Reasonable Interpretations

JOSEPH J. GLUTTING
DAVID KAPLAN
University of Delaware

The Stanford–Binet Intelligence Scale; Fourth Edition (SB4; Thorndike, Hagen, & Sattler, 1986a) is the most recent edition in a line of instruments whose origin dates to the beginning of this century (viz., Binet & Simon, 1905). The revision attempts to revitalize the Stanford–Binet through the twofold strategy of maintaining links with previous editions of the scale and simultaneously incorporating more recent developments found in other popular tests of intelligence. Continuity with earlier editions has been enhanced by retaining as much item content as possible from the Stanford–Binet Intelligence Scale, Form L-M (SB-LM; Thorndike, 1973). SB4 also respects tradition by covering approximately the same age range as SB-LM (age 2 to adult); it incorporates familiar basal and ceiling levels during testing; and it provides an overall score that appraises general cognitive functioning.

Despite these similarities, SB4 is substantially different from its predecessors. Gone is the traditional age scale format. In its place are 15 subtests whose age-corrected scaled scores make it possible to interpret profile elevations and profile depressions. Four "area" scores, derived from theoretically based subtest groupings, are also new. These reformulations add to interpretative possibilities, and they reflect an attempt to broaden coverage of cognitive ability over that offered by SB-LM. Flexibility in interpretation is further supported by recalibration of the Composite (overall IQ) for performances based on specific "abbreviated batteries," as well as for *any* combination of subtests psychologists wish to regroup.

This chapter familiarizes readers with the structure and content of SB4. It also evaluates selected aspects of the test's psychometric and technical properties. Related to these goals, the chapter attempts to sensitize psychologists to factors pertinent to the administration of SB4 and to the interpretation of its test scores.

The accolades and criticisms to follow should be placed in context. The highest professional standards were applied throughout the development of SB4. Prior to publication, the authors and publisher dedicated over 8 years to development and 2 years to extensive data analyses of the final product.

It therefore should come as no surprise that unique and praiseworthy features are identified. Similarly, no test is without faults, and this thought should serve as a referent when discussion turns to the limitations of SB4.

The first section of this chapter outlines the theoretical model underlying SB4. We turn then to a general description of the structure of SB4 and issues related to its test materials, administration, and scaling. Thereafter, we discuss the strengths and weaknesses associated with SB4's standardization, its reliability and validity, and factors related to the interpretation of its test scores.

THEORETICAL FOUNDATION

Perhaps the most fundamental change incorporated into SB4 is the expansion of its theoretical model. Figure 11.1 shows that SB4 has three levels, which serve both traditional and new Binet functions. At its apex is the Composite, or estimate of general ability, traditionally associated with Binet scales. The second level is new to SB4. It proposes three group factors: Crystallized Abilities, Fluid-Analytic Abilities, and Short-Term Memory. The first two dimensions originate from the Cattell–Horn theory of intelligence

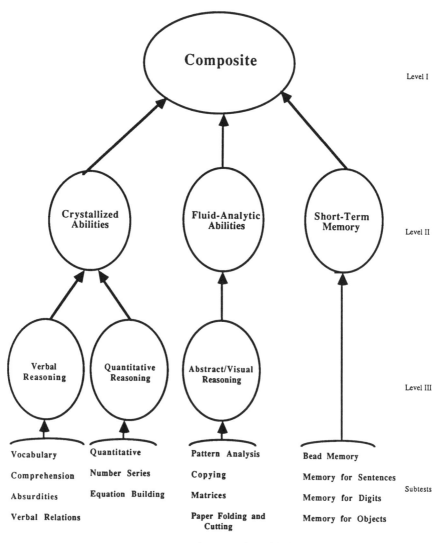

FIGURE 11.1. Theoretical model for SB4.

(Cattell, 1940; Horn, 1968; Horn & Cattell, 1966). The additional component, Short-Term Memory, is not contained in the Cattell–Horn theory. Its inclusion reflects the way in which psychologists used previous editions of the Binet and, to some extent, factor-analytic work with other intelligence tests (Thorndike, Hagen, & Sattler, 1986b, 1986c). Likewise, "[empirical] relationships between short-term memory and long-term memory and between memory and more complex learning and problem solving justify the inclusion of short-term memory in the cognitive-abilities model" (Thorndike et al., 1986c, p. 4).

The third level illustrates another difference between the SB4 and earlier editions of the scale. Here, factors are identified in terms of three facets of reasoning: Verbal Reasoning, Quantitative Reasoning, and Abstract/Visual Reasoning. These components resemble the third level of Vernon's (1950) hierarchical model of intelligence, wherein well-known Verbal–Educational and Practical–Mechanical factors are subdivided to obtain even more homogeneous estimates of ability. Vernon, for example, splits the Verbal–Educational factor into the scholastic content of verbal fluency, numerical operations, and so on. SB4 follows this orientation by incorporating dimensions for the assessment of Verbal Reasoning and Quantitative Reasoning. Similarly, SB4's Abstract/Visual Reasoning dimension parallels the Practical–Mechanical component of the Vernon model.

The three group factors at the third level (Verbal Reasoning, Quantitative Reasoning, Abstract/Visual Reasoning), plus the Short-Term Memory factor at the second level, form the four "area" scores derived by SB4. The Abstract/Visual Reasoning score at the third level corresponds to the Fluid-Analytic Abilities dimension at the second level. No area score is readily available for the third dimension at the second level, Crystallized Abilities; nevertheless, scores for this broad-band factor can be secured by collapsing results across the remaining two of the four areas (Verbal Reasoning and Quantitative Reasoning).

Prominent in the SB4 model is the unification of multiple theories of intelligence. Such synthesis is not unique to SB4. The Kaufman Assessment Battery for Children (K-ABC; Kaufman & Kaufman, 1983) also accounts for test performance through interrelationships among theories (i.e., the Luria–Das and Cattell–Horn theories of ability). In addition, both tests share the praiseworthy quality of using explicit theoretical frameworks as guides for item development and for the alignment of subtests within modeled hierarchies.

TEST STRUCTURE

Subtest Names and Content

SB4's subtests retain some reliable variance that is distinct from the score variation captured by area scores or the Composite. This knowledge has been used to identify the "unique abilities" evaluated by SB4's subtests. Profile analysis is a sanctioned method for explicating an examinee's strengths and weaknesses on these abilities (see Delaney & Hopkins, 1987; Sattler, 1988a). Therefore, inasmuch as SB4 supports comparisons among subtest scores, it is worthwhile to understand the identity and composition of these measures.

Descriptions of the 15 SB4 subtests are provided below, according to the area each occupies in the scale.

Verbal Reasoning

Vocabulary. Examinees supply word definitions. The first 15 items tap receptive word knowledge, and items 16 through 46 evaluate oral vocabulary.

Comprehension. Items 1 through 6 require the receptive identification of body parts. Items 7 through 42 elicit verbal responses associated with practical problem solving and social information.

Absurdities. This subtest presents situations that are essentially false or contrary to common sense. Examinees point to the inaccurate picture among three alternatives (items 1 through 4), or they verbalize the absurdity in a single picture (items 5 through 32).

Verbal Relations. Examinees state how three words, out of a four-word set, are similar. The fourth word in each item is always different from the three words preceding it.

Quantitative Reasoning

Quantitative. Examinees are required to count, add, seriate, or complete other numerical operations.

Number Series. A row of four or more numbers is presented, and the task is to identify the principle underlying a series of four or more numbers and to apply that principle to generate the next two numbers in the series (e.g., 1, 3, 7, 15, _, _).

Equation Building. Examinees resequence numerals and mathematical signs into a correct solution (e.g., 15, 12, 2, 25, =, +, −).

Abstract/Visual Reasoning

Pattern Analysis. Items 1 through 6 require examinees to complete formboards. Items 7 through 42 involve the replication of visual patterns through block manipulations.

Copying. Examinees either reproduce block models (items 1 through 12) or draw geometric designs (items 13 through 28).

Matrices. Each item presents a matrix of figures in which one element is missing. The task is to identify the correct element among multiple-choice alternatives.

Paper Folding and Cutting. Figures are presented in which a piece of paper has been folded and cut. Examinees chose among alternatives that show how the paper might look if it were unfolded.

Short-Term Memory

Bead Memory. Examinees recall the identity of one or two beads exposed briefly (items 1 through 10), or they reproduce bead models in a precise sequence (items 11 through 42).

Memory for Sentences. Examinees are required to repeat each word in a sentence in the exact order of presentation.

Memory for Digits. Examinees repeat digits either in the sequence they are presented, or in reverse order.

Memory for Objects. Pictures of objects are viewed briefly. Examinees then identify the objects in correct order from a larger array.

Content Similarity with Other IQ Tests

SB4 items appear representative of the item content found in intelligence tests (see Jen-

sen, 1980, for a detailed analysis of item types common among IQ tests). Given that this is the case, one might reasonably expect to find content overlap between SB4 subtests and subtests from other major tests of intelligence. Besides being of theoretical interest, this knowledge would have practical advantages whenever there is a need to compare results across instruments.

Visual inspection reveals that six SB4 subtests share core content with the Wechsler Intelligence Scale for Children—Revised (WISC-R; Wechsler, 1974). For example, both SB4 Vocabulary and WISC-R Vocabulary assess word knowledge. SB4 Comprehension and WISC-R Comprehension summate breadth of knowledge of social and interpersonal situations, and visual–perceptual abilities evaluated by SB4 Pattern Analysis generally apply to WISC-R Block Design. Likewise, content from the SB4 Quantitative subtest is reflected by most items in WISC-R Arithmetic, and SB4 Memory for Digits demonstrates a strong link with content in WISC-R Digit Span. Finally, reasoning via analogies in SB4 Verbal Relations is shared by WISC-R Similarities.

Resemblances in subtest content are also apparent between SB4 and the K-ABC. The four most striking parallels occur between (1) SB4 Pattern Analysis and K-ABC Triangles, (2) SB4 Matrices and K-ABC Matrix Analogies, (3) SB4 Memory for Digits and K-ABC Number Recall, and (4) SB4 Memory for Objects and K-ABC Word Order.

MATERIALS

Three manuals accompany SB4: the *Guide for Administering and Scoring* (Thorndike et al., 1986b), the *Technical Manual* (Thorndike et al., 1986c), and the supplementary *Examiner's Handbook* (Delaney & Hopkins, 1987). All three manuals are well written and informative. Chapters pertinent to test administration are especially well organized in the *Examiner's Handbook*. Consequently, psychologists new to SB4 are encouraged to read these sections of the handbook prior to reviewing the *Guide for Administering and Scoring.*

SB4 materials are attractive, well packaged, and suitable to the age groups for which they are applied. One exception, however, is the Bead Memory subtest. Directions for Bead Memory caution psychologists to "BE SURE THAT EXAMINEES DO NOT PLAY WITH THE BEADS. THERE IS A DANGER THAT YOUNG EXAMINEES MAY TRY TO PUT THE BEADS IN THEIR MOUTHS" (Thorndike et al., 1986b, p. 23; bold face in original). This caution is insufficient for the danger presented. Two of the four bead types fit easily in a "choke tube"—an apparatus used to determine whether objects are sufficiently small that young children will gag or suffocate on them. Psychologists, therefore, should *never* allow young children to play with these objects.

The problem of small test pieces extends beyond SB4. A number of tests administered to young children, including the Bayley Scales of Infant Development (Bayley, 1969), contain item pieces so small they are dangerous. Of course, test publishers could argue that it is the responsibility of psychologists to exercise due caution with test materials. Such a position, however, ignores the likelihood that the publisher will be named in any lawsuit stemming from accidents with test materials. (This statement is especially true whenever one considers the financial resources of test publishers versus that of the typical psychologist.) Thus, in addition to being a financial concern, it is in the best interest of *children* that test materials be safe.[1]

Publishers are increasingly adding color to test stimuli. Rich colors enhance the attractiveness of test stimuli, and they have the positive effect of making test materials more child-oriented. Color thereby helps to maintain children's interest during testing, and it augments the probability of obtaining valid test scores. However, a drawback occurs when color serves as an unintended distractor. Such a situation can arise when assessments are conducted with examinees who are color-blind. For these individuals, color represents an additional source of score variance that can reduce test validity.

Two examples are presented where color may alter SB4 item difficulties. Item 1 of the Vocabulary subtest shows a red car on a brown background. This color combination makes it more difficult for some color-blind individuals to distinguish the important foreground stimulus (car) from its background. Another example can be seen in the formboard items in Pattern Analysis. The red puzzle pieces and green background make the formboard more difficult for examinees with red–green color blindness.

I. Dvorine, author of the Dvorine Color Vision Test (Dvorine, 1958), indicates that color-blind individuals are most likely to experience difficulty when confronted by the following color combinations: red–brown, green–orange, red–grey, blue–purple, and red–green (personal communication, February 20, 1986). Fortunately, the problems associated with color stimuli can be corrected by simply *not* pairing these colors within test items. By adopting such changes, test publishers will be able to continue offering the benefits of color stimuli and simultaneously reduce the visual discrimination problems of examinees who are color-blind.

ADMINISTRATION

SB4 uses "adaptive testing" to economize on administration time. This format offers the added benefit of decreasing frustration, because examinees are exposed only to those test items most appropriate to their ability level. Assessments begin by using the Vocabulary subtest as a "routing" measure. Performance on the Vocabulary subtest, in conjunction with an examinee's chronological age, is used to determine the appropriate entry level for succeeding subtests. Entry levels are arranged hierarchically by item pairs (labeled "A" through "Q" on the test protocol). Basal and ceiling rules are then applied within subtests. A basal level is established when all items are passed at two consecutive levels. A ceiling is reached, and testing advances to the next subtest, when three failures (out of four possible failures) take place across adjacent levels.

SB4 is to be credited for its efficient testing format and for directions that are quite readable and straightforward. In contrast to SB-LM, testing has been simplified by incorporating most of the directions, stimuli,

---

[1]Some psychologists have expressed concern regarding SB4's de-emphasis of toy-like materials or "manipulatives." Although manipulatives are useful for obtaining clinically rich data (e.g., children's capabilities for creative play), this information is peripheral to scorable responses. The common purpose of intelligence tests is to obtain scorable estimates of ability. For this reason, we find no problem with SB4's emphasis of scorable responses at the expense of peripheral information offered by manipulatives.

and scoring criteria onto easel kits. The use of sample items further facilitates administration by familiarizing examinees with directions and item formats in advance of actual testing. In addition, SB4 is a power test—only one subtest requires mandatory time limits (Pattern Analysis). Consequently, from another angle, doing away with the need for accurate time keeping has made SB4's administration more convenient.

Administration times *appear* reasonable. On average, testing takes between 30 and 40 minutes for preschool-age-children; 60 minutes for children between the ages of 6 and 11; and between 70 and 90 minutes for those at higher age levels. It is important to note that the *Technical Manual* (Thorndike et al., 1986c) does not offer administration times by age level. Delaney and Hopkins (1987) provide administration times by entry level (A through M or higher), and we used this information to approximate testing times by age. Nevertheless, these values may underestimate actual testing times. Sattler (1988a, 1988b) reports that the full battery is much too long to complete in most circumstances, and he indicates that it may take 2 hours to administer the entire test to an adolescent.

Preschoolers vary in their knowledge of basic concepts (e.g., "top," "behind," "same as"). As a result, basic concepts in test directions may hinder preschool children's understanding of what is expected of them. Kaufman (1978) examined this issue by comparing the number of basic concepts in the Boehm Test of Basic Concepts (BTBC; Boehm, 1971) to those found in the directions for several preschool-level ability tests, including the following: SM-LM; the McCarthy Scales of Children's Abilities (MSCA; McCarthy, 1972); and the Wechsler Preschool and Primary Scale of Intelligence (WPPSI; Wechsler, 1967). Results revealed that scores from SB-LM (5 basic concepts) were less susceptible to this influence than scores from the MSCA (7 basic concepts) or WPPSI (14 basic concepts).

We compared directions in SB4 to basic concepts in the BTBC.[2] In particular, directions were analyzed for the eight SB4 subtests routinely administered to preschoolers. Our findings show that SB4 assumes young children know eight BTBC basic concepts. Although this represents an increase over the number found for SB-LM, it compared favorably to the number of basic concepts in the MSCA, and it is fewer than that found for the WPPSI. Thus, SB4 directions are as likely to be understood by preschoolers as those contained in other IQ tests.

SCALING

Raw SB4 scores are converted to standard age scores (SASs). SASs for the four areas and the Composite are synonymous with deviation IQs ($M = 100$, $SD = 16$). The measurement unit for the Composite maintains the Binet tradition of using deviation units set at 16. Subtest SASs are normalized standard scores with $M = 50$ and $SD = 8$. This metric is highly unusual. We find no compelling reasoning for this choice, and we share Cronbach's (1987) criticism of SB4 that there is no advantage for choosing these units over conventional *T*-scores.

Percentile ranks are available for subtests, area scores, and the Composite. Although SB4 is no longer an age scale, age equivalents are supplied for the 15 subtests. Moreover, a conversion table is produced for professionals who wish to interpret area scores and the Composite in a metric identical to the Wechsler series ($M = 100$, $SD = 15$).

An advantage of Binet scales lies in their extended floors for detecting moderate to severe retardation. Psychologists, no doubt, will be disappointed that this benefit is generally unavailable for young children on SB4. Table 11.1 presents minimum overall ability scores for preschoolers on SB-LM, SB4, WPPSI, and the K-ABC. Column 2 indicates that SB-LM is fully capable of diagnosing mild intellectual retardation by age 3, and moderate retardation by age 3 years, 6 months. In contrast, column 3 reveals that for all practical purposes, SB4's Composite is unable to diagnose mild intellectual deficits prior to age 4, and it shows no capacity for detecting moderate retardation until age 5.

Tests such as the WPPSI and the K-ABC have been criticized for being insensitive to preschoolers who perform at the lower end of

---

[2]Although the BTBC was replaced recently by the Boehm Test of Basic Concepts—Revised (Boehm, 1986), the original BTBC was used so that current results would be comparable to those reported by Kaufman (1978).

TABLE 11.1. Preschoolers' Minimum Overall Ability Scores on SB-LM, SB4, WPPSI, and K-ABC

Age in years and months	SB-LM	SB4[a]	WPPSI	K-ABC
2 years, 0 months	87[b,c]	94[b,c]	—	—
2 years, 6 months	69[c]	87[b,c]	—	79[b,c]
3 years, 0 months	57[c]	73[b,c]	—	70[b,c]
3 years, 6 months	47	66[c]	—	60[c]
4 years, 0 months	40	55[c]	55[c]	60[c]
4 years, 6 months	31	50	49	54
5 years, 0 months	27	44	45	58[c]
5 years, 6 months	24	41	45	55[c]

Note. $M = 100$, $SD = 16$ for SB-LM and SB4. $M = 100$, $SD = 15$ for WPPSI and K-ABC.

[a]SB4 Composites are based on the assumption that a valid score (i.e., raw score ≥ 1) is obtained on each subtest appropriate for administration at a given age level and ability level.

[b]Principal indicator is insensitive to performances more than two standard deviations below the test mean.

[c]Principal indicator is insensitive to performances more than three standard deviations below the test mean.

the ability continuum (Bracken, 1985; Olridge & Allison, 1968; Sattler, 1988a). Column 5 in Table 11.1 shows that SB4 is somewhat more precise in this regard than the K-ABC. However, column 4 also reveals that SB4 is no more sensitive than the WPPSI. Thus, results from these comparisons, in combination with existing views on the limitations of the WPPSI and the K-ABC, make it reasonable to conclude that SB4 provides an insufficient floor for young children. These findings are especially disappointing, since SB-LM was the only IQ test capable of diagnosing mental retardation with preschoolers between the ages of 2 years, 6 months (the upper age range of the Bayley Scales) and 4 years, 0 months.

Problems are compounded for younger preschoolers by the fact that area scores evidence even higher floors than the Composite. By way of example, the lowest SAS for Quantitative Reasoning is 72 between the ages of 2 years, 0 months and 4 years, 6 months. This score is above the retarded range, and the median SAS is 87 for children between these ages. Apparent here is that it is impossible for younger preschoolers to show deficient or abnormal functioning in Quantitative Reasoning. Even more disturb-

ing, by virture of its truncated floor, is the high probability that a "pattern" of strength in Quantitative Reasoning will emerge for any such preschooler whose Composite is in the retarded range. Thus, these findings cast further doubt upon the efficiency of SB4 with young children.

Floor limitations dissipate by the age of kindergarten entry. That is to say, SB4's Composite is able to identify both mild and moderate intellectual regardation at the age of 5 years, 0 months. Similarly, shortcomings noted for the Quantitative Reasoning area are resolved essentially by the age of 4 years, 6 months.

Table 11.2 illustrates SB4's facility to uncover functioning at the upper extreme. By virtue of standard scores 3 or more standard deviations above the test mean, SB4 discriminations talent as adequately as SB-LM at all age levels, and it accentuates slightly higher ceilings at ages 16 and above (columns 2 and 3). The Composite also compares favorably to optimal performance on Wechsler scales and the K-ABC (columns 4 and 5). Consequently, it seems fair to surmise that SB has substantial merit when its goal is to discover examinees who are gifted.

STANDARDIZATION

Two interrelated issues must be considered in regard to the representativeness of SB4s norms. The first is the loss of randomness that resulted from the need to obtain examinee's cooperation. The second is the weighting of test scores to compensate for discrepancies between the designated sampling plan for socioeconomic status (SES) and SES levels in the obtained sample.

Prior to elaborating these issues, we must first consider the methods used to standardize SB4. The test was normed on 5,013 individuals arranged into 17 age groups (2 years, 0 months through 23 years, 11 months). Quota sampling was employed to approximate the U.S. population in terms of geographic region, community size, race, gender, and SES. Unfortunately, lower-SES examinees were underrepresented in the sample (10.6% vs. 29.2% of the U.S. population) and higher-SES examinees were overrepresented (43.1% vs. 19.0%, respectively).

TABLE 11.2. Maximum Overall Ability Scores for
Select Age Groups on SB4, SB-LM, Wechsler
Scales, and K-ABC

Age in years and months	SB4[a]	SB-LM	Wechsler scale[b]	K-ABC
2 years, 0 months	164	162	—	—
4 years, 0 months	164	160	155	160
6 years, 0 months	164	159	160	160
8 years, 0 months	164	164	160	160
10 years, 0 months	164	160	160	160
12 years, 0 months	164	164	160	155
14 years, 0 months	158	154	160	—
16 years, 0 months	152	138	158	—
18 years, 0 months	149	136	150	—
20 years, 0 months	149	—	150	—

Note. $M = 100$, $SD = 16$ for SB4 and SB-LM. $M = 100$, $SD = 15$ for all Wechsler scales and K-ABC.

[a]For any given age level, SB4 Composites are based on the maximum number of subtests specified in Appendix F of the *Guide for Administering and Scoring* (Thorndike et al., 1986b).

[b]The WPPSI Full Scale IQ (FSIQ) is the principal Wechsler indicator at age 4 years, 0 months; the WISC-R FSIQ is used at ages 6 years, 0 months through 16 years, 0 months; and the WAIS-R FSIQ is used at ages 18 years, 0 months and 20 years, 0 months.

Sample disproportions on SES have been attributed to the necessity of obtaining examinees' consent for testing and to the fact that "parents of higher SES tended to return [permission] forms more frequently than those of lower SES" (Thorndike et al., 1986, p. 24). Once these misproportions had occurred, the SES variables of occupation and education were weighted so that examinees' scores would conform to their correct percentages in the U.S. population. That is, "each child from an advantaged background was counted as only a fraction of a case (as little as 0.28), while each child from a less advantaged background was counted as more than one case" (Thorndike et al., 1986c, p. 24).

Nonrandomness and General Referents

One popular view holds that the strength of an IQ test is dependent upon the degree to which its sample represents the general population. Accordingly, "stratified random sampling" is a relatively efficient method for

obtaining such a representation. Many practitioners, as well as notable measurement specialists (e.g., Hopkins & Hodge, 1984), assume that individually administered IQ tests are normed on stratified random samples. This, however, is never the case. Test developers must request examinees' cooperation. The net effect is a loss of randomness, because people who volunteer are rarely like those who do not (Jaeger, 1984).

The common alternative to stratified random sampling is to select examinees purposively through "quota sampling." The shortcoming of quota sampling is that its selections are likely to be biased, unless of course cooperation rates are high and uniform across strata (Hansen, Hurwitz, & Madow, 1953; Kish, 1965; Thorndike, 1982). In the case of SB4, no information is provided for overall cooperation rates. Nonetheless, systematic sampling bias is suggested by the differential cooperation of lower- and higher-SES groups.

It would be simplistic to discredit SB4 for sampling problems. The quota sampling in SB4, as well as the differential rates of cooperation, are common to *all* individually administered IQ tests. Therefore, before condemning SB4 for sampling bias, psychologists should take note that we will have to generalize this recommendation to other favored instruments, including the K-ABC and WISC-R.

Nonrandomness and Other Referents

An alternative perspective is that it is not necessary for IQ tests to reference the general population. There are other legitimate referents to which test scores can be compared. Instruments such as SB4 are most often administered to two groups—namely, examinees who truly volunteer to be tested and examinees with suspected handicaps. Consequently, it is essential that IQ tests accurately reflect the capabilities of these two groups.

Examinees who willingly consent to testing (the self-referred, those who may be gifted, segments of the special education population) do not necessarily differ from the "volunteer" subjects in standardization samples. Thus, for this group, IQ test norms should be appropriate.

The second group is more problematic.

The handicapped are administered IQ tests for special purposes (e.g., assignment to special education categories, mandatory re-evaluations). As such, the majority of these individuals cannot be truly regarded as volunteers. Clearly linked to this phenomenon is the need to consider the handicapped *systematically*—if not directly in test norms, then through special studies.

One proposal for test development is to sample the handicapped in proportion to their presence in the general population. Integral to any such attempt is the notion that prevalence rates are known for the various exceptionality subtypes. Drawbacks quickly become evident for conditions such as learning disabilities, for which there is no uniformly accepted rate of occurrence in the general population and for which diagnostic rates continue to escalate (see Ysseldyke & Stevens, 1986). The dilemma in such instances becomes this: "What is the appropriate percentage of the learning-disabled to include in standardization samples?"

More unsettling are problems that arise when prevalences are known. A prevalence of 3% is the standard endorsed for mental retardation (American Psychiatric Association, 1987; Grossman, 1983). Yet it would be improper to systematically target retarded individuals as 3% of a test's sample. Probability theory dictates that a percentage of the *nonhandicapped* in the sample will also be retarded. When the retarded and the nonhandicapped are merged, retarded individuals will be overrepresented. As contradictory as it may appear, this overrepresentation increases the likelihood that test norms will be diagnostically insensitive to the retarded. That is, the overrepresentation of low-scoring (retarded) examinees will affect the conversion of raw scores to normalized standard scores. Thereafter, a *lower* raw score will be needed to obtain an IQ in the retarded range (i.e., an IQ < 70) than if retarded examinees had not been in the sample. The diagnostic result is that test norms will fail to qualify higher-functioning retarded individuals for needed services.

Enhancing Diagnostic Utility

Evident from the discussion above is that proportional sampling of the handicapped is likely to create as many problems as it solves.

A more practical response is to systematically oversample the handicapped, but not necessarily to include them in test norms. Instead, special studies should be conducted to determine how the test behaves. Confirmatory factor analysis, for example could identify whether test dimensions are similar for the handicapped and nonhandicapped. Comparisons based on item response theory (IRT) would verify whether item difficulties are identical among exceptional and nonexceptional groups. IRT would also uncover whether item calibrations are sufficient for the maximum differentiation of low-scoring and high-scoring exceptionalities. Moreover, slope comparisons (and not bivariate correlations) would supply information relevant to whether test scores predict equally for the handicapped and nonhandicapped. Finally, univariate and multivariate contrasts would shed light on whether all possible test scores (e.g., overall IQs, factor scores, subtest scores) differ between the general sample and the various exceptionality subtypes (the retarded, the learning-disabled, etc.).

By these standards, SB4 is less than fully adequate. This finding is dismaying, since sufficient data were gathered during SB4's development to complete nearly all of the analyses identified above. SB4 is to be commended for verifying that its Composite and area scores (but not necessarily subtest scores) differ between normal and exceptional samples. Nevertheless, no attempt was made to determine whether SB4's items are unbiased for the handicapped, or that its test dimensions are similar for individuals functioning normally and exceptionally. Likewise, although criterion-related validity is reported for the handicapped, quantitative comparisons were not conducted for the relative accuracy of predictions between the handicapped and nonhandicapped.

It would only be fair to point out that no IQ test has met these standards at the time of its publication. However, the issue is not whether SB4 should be excused because it is less deficient than other ability tests. Rather, the issue is why IQ tests are marketed without adequate evidence that they reflect the aptitudes of the handicapped. We, as professionals responsible for the welfare of clients, must demand this information at the time of a test's publication. Otherwise, we must accept the fact that we are willing to apply tests whose diagnostic capabilities are unknown.

Elimination versus Weighting

There is often "slippage" between a test's sampling plan and the testing as executed (Thorndike, 1982). Two methods can bring a sample back into alignment with its sampling plan. The first option is to randomly *eliminate* examinees from oversampled strata (e.g., discard the scores of some high-SES examinees). The second option is to *weight* scores from each stratum to their correct percentage of the population. Whereas both methods have their benefits, neither can fully compensate for a loss of randomness in the sampling process (R. M. Jaeger, personal communication, May 24, 1988).

Until SB4, norms for individually administered IQ tests were aligned by eliminating examinees from oversampled strata. The benefit of elimination is that there is no redundancy in subject-generated variance (i.e., examinees are not counted as more, or less, than one case). Moreover, the practice is tidy. "Final" samples often align well with the population, in part, because test manuals provide little discussion of discarded cases. Therefore, had SB4 used elimination, it would have been easy to marvel at how well the sample approximated the general population on race, sex, SES, and so on.

One advantage of weighting is that it accounts for all scores in the sample. Relatedly, it produces estimates of higher reliability than does elimination. A potential flaw is that weighted estimates are not based entirely on actual cases. Examinees in underrepresented strata are counted *more than once* by multiplying the original sample variance upward to the desired population estimate. Thus, the sample variance becomes redundant with itself, and the process is dependent upon the assumption that examinees in the sample are representative of the *entire* population— including those individuals who, for whatever reason, were not sampled.

There is no guarantee that the scores of examinees already in the sample are similar to the scores of potential examinees who were not tested. However, this assumption becomes more plausible when the obtained sample has large numbers of examinees in each stratum who are representative of that particular population segment. SB4's standardization sample is quite large ($n = 5,013$), and its strata are probably of sufficient subject size for weighting. Moreover, weighting is an accepted procedure for standardizing group tests. Consequently, from this perspective, the weighting of test scores in SB4 appears as reasonable as the weighting used to norm group tests.

RELIABILITY

By and large, SB4's reliabilities are quite good. Internal consistency for the Composite is excellent, with Kuder–Richardson 20 coefficients ranging from .95 to .99 across age levels. Reliabilities for area scores are also substantial. Internal consistency for two-, three-, and four-subtest groupings vary from .86 to .97 for Verbal Reasoning (median $r = $ .95). Coefficients for Abstract/Visual Reasoning range from .85 to .97 and show a median of .95. Similarly, estimates for Quantitative Reasoning vary from .80 to .97 (median $r - $ .94), and internal consistency for Short-Term Memory ranges from .86 to .95 (median $r = $ .86).

Subtest internal consistencies are lower, as would be expected from their shorter test lengths. Nonetheless, with the exception of one subtest, median coefficients are reasonably high (range $= .83$ to .94 across age groups). The exceptional subtest (Memory for Objects) is located in the Short-Term Memory area, and it produces coefficients of marginal reliability (median $r = .73$). The subtest with the second lowest reliability is also in the Short-Term Memory area (Memory for Digits; median $r = .83$). As a result, psychologists should be alert that subtest scores from the Short-Term Memory area are likely to be less precise than subtest scores from other areas in SB4.

Standard errors of measurement (*SEM*s), and "confidence bands" derived from *SEM*s, are the reliability issues most likely to affect everyday practice. Confidence bands produce information relevant to the fallibility of test scores. In this regard, confidence bands help to clarify the relative verity and utility of test scores in decision making (Glutting, McDermott, & Stanley, 1987).

Memory for Objects provides the least precise scores in SB4 (i.e., the largest confidence bands). Its *SEM* shows a median of 4.15 points across age groups. The subtest with the second largest *SEM* is Memory for Digits (median = 3.25). However, the *SEM*s of these two subtests (and for all other more reliable subtests) are within reasonable limits. Also, as might be expected, greater score precision is found when interpretations are based on the four area scores. Median *SEM*s for Verbal Reasoning, Abstract/Visual Reasoning, Quantitative Reasoning, and Short-Term Memory are as follows: 3.9, 3.6, 3.8, and 4.8, respectively. Finally, the most precise score in SB4 is the Composite (median *SEM* = 2.3).

The *Technical Manual* (Thorndike et al., 1986c) calculates score stability for samples of preschoolers (5-year-olds) and children attending elementary school (8-year-olds). Preschoolers' test–retest coefficients are reasonable for the Composite ($r = .91$) and for area scores (range = .71 to .78). Less stability is evident for individual subtests, and, in particular, for Bead Memory ($r = .56$). The pattern of test–retest coefficients of elementary school children is similar to that found for preschoolers. Appreciable stability is present for the Composite ($r = .90$) and for the areas of Verbal Reasoning, Abstract/Visual Reasoning, and Short-Term Memory (r's = .87, .67, and .81, respectively). However, somewhat lower stability is found for the Quantitative Reasoning area ($r = .51$).

Preschoolers' Composites will, on average, increase approximately 8.2 points from test to retest administrations. Similarly, Composites are likely to increase by 6.4 points for elementary school children who are tested twice across short intervals. SB4 offers no stability data for examinees of junior high or high school age, or for young adults. Therefore, it is impossible to approximate the score increases that might be expected of these age groups.

VALIDITY

An impressive amount of validity information has been gathered in support of SB4. In particular, investigations have addressed developmental changes of raw scores by age; quantitative analyses of item fairness across gender and ethnic groups; correlations with other IQ tests, using samples of both normal and exceptional examinees; correlations with achievement tests; score differences between the standardization sample and special groups (gifted, learning-disabled, retarded); and the factorial integrity of SB4's test dimensions.

Table 11.3 presents concurrent correlations between SB4 and other IQ tests administered to normal samples. This compilation was obtained from studies reported in the *Technical Manual* (Thorndike et al., 1986c), as well as from studies conducted by independent investigators. Results show substantial associations between SB4's Composite and overall scores on SB-LM, all Wechsler scales, the K-ABC, and the Peabody Picture Vocabulary Test—Revised (PPVT-R). Indeed, the consistency and magnitude of these relationships speak very well for the Composite's construct validity.

We know by way of Spearman's (1923) principle of the "indifference of the indicator" that the specific item content in intelligence tests is quite unimportant to the evaluation of general ability (or g). The truly important phenomenon for g is that IQ tests measure inductive and deductive reasoning. Thus, correlations between one IQ test and IQ tests with dissimilar content can help evaluate the extent to which the first test measures g. Squaring and then averaging the correlations in Table 11.3 reveal that, at a minimum, 63.7% of the Composite's variance is accounted for by g. As such, the data suggest that the Composite provides reasonably trustworthy estimates of general intelligence.

Of applied interest are score differences that can be expected between SB4 and other IQ tests. Column 7 in Table 11.3 (labeled "IQ difference") shows that the Composite *averages* 2.9 points lower than the IQs from other intelligence tests. Individual comparisons are more risky because of the smaller number of studies between SB4 and any one test. With this caveat in mind, psychologists might expect SB4 to produce IQs that are about 2 points lower than those from SB-LM; 5 points lower than those from the WISC-R; 3 points lower than those from the Wechsler Adult Intelligence Scale—Revised (WAIS-R), 3 points lower than those from the WPPSI; 3 points lower than those from the PPVT-R; and nearly identical to those from the K-ABC.

TABLE 11.3. Score Characteristics and Correlations of SB4 with Other IQ Tests Administered to Normal Samples

Study	n	Mean age in years	Mean SB4 composite	Name of other IQ test	Mean IQ on other test	IQ difference	Correlation
Hartwig, Sapp, & Clayton (1987)	30	11.3	113.1	SB-LM	114.4	−1.3	.72
Thorndike, Hagen, & Sattler (1986c, Study 1)	139	6.9	105.8	SB-LM	108.1	−2.3	.81
Rothlisberg (1987)	32	7.8	105.5	WISC-R	112.5	−7.0	.77
Thorndike et al. (1986c, Study 2)	205	9.4	102.4	WISC-R	105.2	−2.8	.83
Carvajal, Gerber, Hewes, & Weaver (1987)	32	18.0	100.9	WAIS-R	103.5	−2.6	.91
Thorndike et al. (1986c, Study 4)	47	19.4	98.7	WAIS-R	102.2	−3.5	.91
Thorndike et al. (1986c, Study 5)	175	7.0	112.7	K-ABC	112.3	0.4	.89
Thorndike et al. (1986c, Study 3)	75	5.5	105.3	WPPSI	110.3	−5.0	.80
Carvajal, Hardy, Smith, & Weaver (1988)	20	5.5	114.4	WPPSI	115.6	−1.2	.59
Carvajal, Gerber, & Smith (1987)	32	18.9	102.1	PPVT-R	105.3	−3.2	.69

The most controversial aspect of SB4 concerns the interpretability of its area scores. That is, do the capabilities evaluated by SB4 actually conform to the four-factor model of intelligence that has been advanced for the test? This question of construct validity is open to empirical verification, and it is one that can be usually answered through factor analysis.

To date, exploratory factor analyses have been performed for SB4 using principal-components analyses (Reynolds, Kamphaus, & Rosenthal, 1987; Sattler, 1988a) and principal-factor analysis (Reynolds et al., 1987). Likewise, confirmatory factor analyses have been conducted using LISREL (Hoffman, Carleton, Bishop-Marbury, & Goodwin, 1988; Keith, Cool, Novak, & White, 1988) and a "variant" of confirmatory factor analysis (Thorndike et al., 1986c, p. 52). The common element in all this is that no single study has fully substantiated the existence of *four* area

factors. It therefore stands to reason that psychologists should refrain from interpreting area scores until more evidence is offered in their behalf.

Particularly disconcerting is the tendency by the authors of SB4 to disagree on the number of interpretable factors. Thorndike, for example, in light of his own factor-analytic results, offers no explanation for why the four-factor model should be applied to examinees younger than age 12. He "confirms" only two factors between ages 2 and 6 (Verbal, Abstract /Visual). His analyses then support a three-factor model between ages 7 and 11 (Verbal, Abstract/Visual, Memory). Most importantly, the proposed four-factor model does not emerge until ages 12 through 23.

Sattler (1988a), on the other hand, totally eschews the SB4 model. He proposes a two-factor solution between ages 2 and 6 (Verbal Comprehension, Nonverbal Reasoning/Visualization) and a three-factor solution at ages 7 through 23 (Verbal Comprehension, Nonverbal Reasoning/Visualization, Memory). Conspicuously absent in Sattler's findings is a dimension for Quantitative Reasoning, and at no age level does he recommend the interpretation of all four area scores.

Psychologists will be tempted to make "area" interpretations, even though there is little justification for this practice. Indeed, Hopkins (1988) appears to believe that SB4's four area scores should be interpreted and that practitioners need not "become emotionally involved in the 'great debate' regarding the theoretical structure of intelligence as determined by the factor analytic method" (p. 41). Hopkins's position is incorrect, because it implies clinical necessity should supersede that which can be supported empirically. However, the need to generate hypotheses about an examinee is *never* sufficient grounds for the interpretation of a test score. This is especially true in the case of SB4's four area scores, since claims for their construct validity have yet to be substantiated.

It should be kept in mind that current inabilities to support a four-factor model may not necessarily represent a failure of SB4 per se. Rather, the difficulty may lie in the sensitivity of factor analysis to data-related issues in SB4. This is particularly true when confirmatory factor analysis is applied. The relationship between confirmatory factor analysis and SB4 is explored in Appendix 11.1 of this chapter for those who wish to obtain a fuller understanding of these issues.

SCORE INTERPRETATION

Intelligence tests can be time-consuming to administer. The authors of SB4 recognize the service demands placed on psychologists, and in response, they offer four short forms that result in a substantial savings of testing time: the six-subtest General Purpose Battery; the four-subtest Quick Screening Battery; the four- to six-subtest Battery for the Assessment of Students for Gifted Programs; and the six-subtest Battery for Students Having Problems Learning in School. Short forms with four or fewer subtests are intended for screening purposes, but batteries composed of at least six subtests can be used

for placement decisions (Thorndike et al., 1986c, p. 50). This latter possibility makes it essential that test scores from six-subtest abbreviated batteries be psychometrically equivalent to those from the full test.

Split-half reliabilities for two-, and four-, and six-subtest short forms are fairly constant and appreciable for examinees of different ages. Correlations between Composites from short forms and the complete battery are also acceptable. However, virtually no information is available for differences between estimated Composites and area scores from abbreviated batteries and actual scores on the full test. Psychologists therefore are left wondering about the diagnostic consequences of accepting estimated test scores from abbreviated batteries.

This situation could be rectified. For instance, estimated Composites for examinees in the standardization sample could be subtracted from their actual Composites on the full test. These errors of estimation (i.e., difference scores) would then be averaged within age level. Final calculations would subsequently produce age-level data relevant to the accuracy of short-form Composites in comparison to those from the full test.

SB4 is further remiss in not supplying correlations between abbreviated batteries and *external* criteria. It cannot be readily assumed, for example, that the criterion validity of Composites from the full test will hold for Composites from short forms. The external validity of a short form may be quite low (e.g., $r = .07$), even when the short form correlates .90 with the full test and the full test correlates .50 with an external criterion (Levy, 1968; McCormick, 1956).

Norms tables in SB4 make it possible to calculate Composites from practically *any* combination of subtests. Thus, practitioners can develop their own short forms by "picking and choosing" among favorite subtests.

No matter how the particular combination is chosen, problems are likely to arise for short forms if the *administration sequence* of the subtests is disturbed.[3] Assume, for example, that a psychologist elects to administer a short form consisting of subtests 1, 3, 4,

---

[3]The abbreviated batteries discussed earlier do not suffer from this problem, because they are composed of subtests 1 through 6 in SB4's administration sequence.

5, 6, and 13. The psychologist in such an instance is operating under the belief that norms for the 13th subtest (Paper Folding and Cutting) will remain constant, irrespective of the fact this subtest now occupies the 6th position in the new battery. Thus, the validity of the procedure is critically dependent on the assumption that norms and examinees' performance are independent of a subtest's location in the battery.

The assumption of such independence is certainly suspect. It overlooks the possibility that any decrease in testing time may lessen an examinee's frustration and improve test scores on the shorter battery. Likewise, this assumption does not allow for any differences in the fatigue of the psychologist or examinee, or the fact that the full test offers more opportunities to gain experience in understanding test directions and familiarity with test materials. In other words, independence assumptions compel the psychologist to posit that any practice or learning that takes place on one subtest will have no carryover to subsequent subtests. This last set of restrictions is particularly unlikely for measures that require examinees to manipulate objects (i.e., noverbal/performance subtests). Finally, even if these assumptions are satisfied, the psychologist must consider whether the external validity of the shorter battery is the same as that of the full test. Consequently, it would be wise for psychologists to administer SB4 in its entirety and to refrain from "picking and choosing" subtests they wish to administer and interpret.

RECOMMENDATIONS

The findings that emerge from this chapter can be summarized in six recommendations. We caution in offering these guidelines that an increasing empirical literature is emerging for SB4. Naturally, as these data accumulate, the recommendations presented below will need revision.

1. Earlier, we have argued IQ tests should not be marketed without adequate evidence that they reflect the aptitudes of the handicapped. Our position remains constant. It follows, however, that we cannot reasonably hold SB4 to standards that have never been imposed on any IQ tests at the time of their publication. Therefore, inasmuch as SB4 meets many if not most standards for high technical quality, its use is recommended.

2. SB4 should not be administered to preschoolers suspected of functioning in the retarded range. The test shows minimum capacity for detecting moderate to severe retardation at these age levels. Moreover, the WPPSI generally supports floors equal to or slightly lower than those of SB4.

3. SB4 provides a sufficient ceiling for the identification of examinees who may be gifted at any age. The recency of its norms and its extended age range also increase the likelihood that SB4 will become a favored instrument for the assessment of giftedness.

4. Reasonable construct validity is present for the Composite, and this is the score psychologists should interpret.

5. SB4 is predicated on a factor-analytic model of intelligence. Thus, the failure of factor analysis to reproduce hypothesized dimensions leads us to advise psychologists to refrain from interpreting SB4's four area scores. We have also advanced the position that current inabilities to identify a four-factor model may not necessarily represent a failure of SB4 per se. In addition, we have identified methodologies that show promise for confirming the SB4 model (see Appendix 11.1). Nevertheless, until these procedures are applied and empirical evidence supports four underlying factors, psychologists would do well to avoid comparing or interpreting these scores.

6. We believe we have amply demonstrated the hazards psychologists face in constructing their own SB4 short forms. Preference, therefore, should be given to administering the test in its entirety.

CONCLUSION

At the beginning of this chapter, we have stated that no test is without its faults or its virtues. Perhaps SB4's greatest limitation is that it tries too hard to offer "everything" psychologists want in an IQ test. Nevertheless, SB4's potential for meeting the avowed purposes of IQ tests is great, and, as is far too rare in the field of test development, the positive features of this instrument outweigh its limitations.

APPENDIX 11.1. BRIEF REVIEW OF CONFIRMATORY FACTOR ANALYSIS

Whereas exploratory factor analysis (EFA) has been available since the time of Spearman, confirmatory factor analysis (CFA) is a relatively new tool. The development of CFA can be traced back to Anderson and Rubin (1956), and to the extension of this work by Jöreskog (1969). CFA, like EFA, is designed to explain interrelationships among a set of variables in terms of a smaller number of parameters. That is, if p is the number of subtest scores, then there are $p^* = p(p + 1)/2$ nonredundant elements in the sample covariance matrix, S. If these elements can be accounted for by a smaller set of parameters, say $m < p^*$, then a "structure" has been imposed on the covariance matrix. Since the metric of scores is constant in IQ tests, the correlation matrix R can be used instead of the covariance matrix, and the number of nonredundant elements becomes $p(p - 1)/2$.

The parameters of interest in CFA are the same as those in EFA—namely, factor loadings, factor correlations, and error variances. Where CFA and EFA diverge is that CFA forces an *a priori* placement of *fixed* elements based on the theoretical model. "Fixed" elements in CFA are usually set at 0, reflecting the belief that certain subtests do not load on a particular factor. "Free" elements are those that are to be estimated and interpreted according to the hypothetical model proposed by an investigator. For example, the Vocabulary subtest in SB4 is hypothesized to load on the Verbal Reasoning factor, but not on the Quantitative Reasoning factor (see Figure 11.1). Thus, in the factor-loading matrix, the loading of the Vocabulary subtest on the Verbal Reasoning factor would be a free parameter to be estimated, while its loading on the Quantitative factor would be fixed to 0.

A number of computer programs exist for estimating free parameters in CFA. Common programs are LISREL (Jöreskog & Sörbom, 1984), EQS (Bentler, 1985), and more recently LISCOMP (Muthen, 1987). These programs produce a variety of estimation algorithms. Most common among these is "maximum likelihood" (ML). Although the details of ML are beyond the scope of this chapter, it is important to note that this is the method used by Hoffman et al. (1988) and Keith et al. (1988) in their CFAs of SB4.

As stated above, the pattern of fixed and free parameters is specified by investigators according to their beliefs about the structure of the test. The fact that the number of estimated parameters is usually smaller than the number of elements in S (i.e., subtests) allows for a direct test of the hypothesis implied by the model. More specifically, LISREL computes a covariance matrix on the basis of the estimation of the parameters in the model, Σ. The match between Σ and S is evaluated via a chi-square test of fit. If the obtained chi-square is statistically significant, the null hypothesis that the subtests fit the proposed model is rejected in favor of the alternative that there is no underlying factor structure. Conversely, if the obtained chi-square value is nonsignificant, then the null hypothesis is not rejected, and one can be fairly confident that the subtests fit the proposed model.

Robustness of Chi-Square

As indicated already, the test statistic formed from comparing Σ to S is distributed as chi-square with degrees of freedom equal to $p^* - m$. It would be useful to examine how the restrictive set of assumptions underlying the chi-square distribution break down in the application of CFA to SB4. We briefly discuss three of these possibilities: non-normality due to floor and ceiling effects, missing data, and sample size.

Chi-Square and Non-Normality

The number and combination of subtests administered in SB4 vary, according to an examinee's age and suspected ability level. The lack of subtest continuity across age levels is understandable, because particular item types are either too easy or too difficult for certain age groups. However, this discontinuity also creates the possibility of floor effects at the earliest ages a subtest is administered and ceiling effects at the latest ages. Such floor and ceiling effects can, in turn, make the data for SB4 non-normal (i.e., skewed and/or kurtotic).

A number of articles in the psychometric literature suggest that the assumption of multivariate normality is crucial for the appropriate use of ML to estimate parameters in CFA, and to obtain "well-behaved" chi-square tests. Browne (1984), for example, examined the effect of skewness and kurtosis values (2.0 and 6.0, respectively) on the results of ML analyses with continuous variables. Results showed that ML chi-square tests were too high, indicating that models would often be rejected inappropriately. A similar result emerged for categorical (Likert) variables in a study by Muthen and Kaplan (1985). These results serve notice that caution must be exercised when assessing the fit of ML-estimated CFA models where the univariate skewness exceeds an absolute value of 2.0.

Skewness values for SB4's subtests rival those in the Browne (1984) and Muthen and Kaplan (1985) studies. For example, the skewness value for the Bead Memory subtest is 1.76 for 3-year-olds in the standardization sample. It seems likely, therefore, that CFAs using ML algorithms may reject the SB4 model inappropriately.

It should be pointed out that new methodologies are available for the factor analysis of non-normal variables. In particular, the asymptotic-distribution-free (ADF) method of Browne (1984) and the categorical variable method (CVM) of Muthen (1984), both of which are available in LISCOMP, show some promise. Their application to applied situations is currently constrained, however, by the number of variables considered. A problem with more than 20 variables would exceed the capacity of LISCOMP to conduct ADF estimations. The 15 subtests in SB4 are clearly under this limit. The true "difficulty" is that ADF and CVM require the scores of each examinee in a sample, and the test's publisher has refused to release this data.

Missing Data

Researchers often do not have complete data on all variables of interest. In the context of SB4, this problem arises as a result of examinees' not taking all 15 subtests in the battery. The net effect is that when the entire sample is analyzed through CFA, the elements of S are based on subtests whose numbers systematically vary from one age to the next.

A number of ad hoc methods have been devised to handle missing data. The two most popular are listwise deletion and pairwise deletion. In listwise deletion, only those examinees who have complete data are retained for analysis. This method has the drawback of possibly eliminating a large number of examinees, thereby reducing efficiency. Also, if those who omit responses are not a random sample of the population as a whole, then

one can expect some distortion in chi-square and bias in the parameter estimates.

In pairwise deletion, S is constructed on the basis of differing sample sizes. Again, the major drawback is that those who have omitted responses may not be a random sample from the population as a whole. S may also not be positive definite—a condition required for conducting CFA (see Tatsuoka, 1988, for a discussion of positive definiteness). The lack of positive definiteness found by Thorndike in his analysis of SB4 may be due to the problem of a pairwise-constructed S. New procedures currently exist, however, for the correct estimation of CFA models when data are not missing completely at random. For example, full quasi-likelihood estimation, developed by Muthen, Kaplan, and Hollis (1987), may show some promise for confirming the SB4 model.

Sample Size and Power

The most common reason offered for the rejection of a CFA model is that the sample size, n, is too large. This reason is cited because the chi-square test statistic is a monotonically increasing function of n. The problem here is that there is no agreed-upon value of what constitutes a large sample (Saris, den Ronden, & Satorra, 1985). Furthermore, sample size interacts with other characteristics of the model to inflate chi-square. Consequently, when the issue is testing the hypothesis implied by the model with a fixed sample size and fixed level of statistical significance, discussion naturally turns to the assessment of power.

Relatively simple methods exist for determining power in CFA (e.g., see Saris & Stronkhorst, 1984, p. 202). It is recommended that power be studied before the conclusion is drawn that a lack of SB4 model fit is due to sample size. If the power is high for only trivial deviations from the model, it may be due to large sample sizes (assuming normality and no missing data). However, the lack of fit may also be due to large and substantively important errors in the model, to which chi-square is sensitive.

Methods of Model Modification

It may seem fair to infer a poor model fit when the data-related problems discussed above are not present, or if alternative methods of estimation are applied and the chi-square statistic remains significant. However, in such instances, it still is possible to improve the fit of the model by relaxing constraints imposed by the *a priori* specifications in the model. In the case of SB4, this means that the pattern of fixed and free loadings that define its four factors might be too restrictive, indicating that a relaxation of constraints be attempted.

Two common methods of CFA model modification are inspection of residuals and the "modification index" (MI; Jöreskog & Sörbom, 1984). Residuals are formed by subtracting Σ from S. Large residuals indicate regions of the model (i.e., subtest loadings on a factor) that are inconsistent with the data. In some cases, an inspection of residuals is sufficient to tell the investigator which part(s) of the model to relax for a better fit. Keith et al. (1984) utilized this method in their CFA of SB4. The difficulty with this procedure is that there is no agreement as to what constitutes a large residual value.

A more statistically motivated method is the MI (also referred to as the "Lagrange multiplier" in EQS; Bentler, 1985). For each fixed parameter in the matrix of the factor analysis, there is an associated MI giving the expected drop in the value of chi-square if that parameter is relaxed. The principal advantage of MI is that it provides the investigator with an indication of which parameter constraints are contributing to the lack of fit. A disadvantage is that a particularly large MI may not be associated with a *substantively* meaningful parameter. That is, once the parameter is relaxed, its estimated value may be of only trivial theoretical importance (Kaplan, 1988). This deficiency can be overcome by calculating the expected value of the parameter when it is freed (Saris, Satorra, & Sorbom, 1987). In this way, an investigator can choose modifications that yield important substantive changes, rather than solely reducing the value of chi-square. Also, the number of modifications will probably be reduced, thereby decreasing the probability of finding a well-fitting model by chance (Kaplan, 1989). Finally, if most substantively important modifications have been made, and chi-square continues to be large, it may be a matter of too much power because of a large sample. Again, other data-related explanations will have to be ruled out.

In sum, the first conclusion that can be drawn for SB4 is that its factor structure is far from clear. Second, it is quite evident that attempts to uncover interpretable SB4 factors will, at the very

least, be difficult. Finally, the possibility exists that the nature of SB4's data may ultimately preclude the discovery of substantively meaningful dimensions for this test.

Acknowledgments. We gratefully acknowledge the helpful comments offered by George Bear, Joan Goodman, Linda Gottfredson, Timothy Keith, Mary Kelly, Tom Oakland, Aurelio Prifitera, Jeff Slinde, and Robert Thorndike on an earlier draft of this chapter.

REFERENCES

American Psychiatric Association. (1987). *Diagnostic and statistical manual of mental disorders* (3rd ed., rev.). Washington, DC: Author.

Anderson, T. W., & Rubin, H. (1956). Statistical inference in factor analysis. In J. Neyman (Ed.). *Proceedings of the Third Berkeley Symposium on Mathematical Statistics and Probability* (Vol. 1, pp. 111–150). Berkeley: University of California Press.

Bayley, N. (1969). *Bayley Scales of Infant Development: Birth to two years*. New York: Psychological Corporation.

Bentler, P. M. (1985). *Theory and implementation of EQS, a structural equation program*. Los Angeles: BMDP Statistical Software.

Binet, A., & Simon, T. (1905). Méthodes nouvelles pour le diagnostic du niveau intellectual des anormaux. *L'Année Psychologique, 11*, 191–244.

Boehm, A. E. (1971). *Boehm Test of Basic Concepts: Manual*. New York: Psychological Corporation.

Boehm, A. E. (1986). *Boehm Test of Basic Concepts— Revised: Manual*. San Antonio, TX: Psychological Corporation.

Bracken, B. A. (1985). A critical review of the Kaufman Assessment Battery for Children (K-ABC). *School Psychology Review, 14*, 21–36.

Browne, M. W. (1984). Asymptotically distribution-free methods for the analysis of covariance structures. *British Journal Mathematical and Statistical Psychology, 37*, 62–63.

Carvajal, H., Gerber, J., Hewes, P., & Weaver, K. A. (1987). Correlations between scores on Stanford–Binet IV and Wechsler Adult Intelligence Scale—Revised. *Psychological Reports, 61*, 83–86.

Carvajal, H., Gerber, J., & Smith, P. D. (1987). Relationship between scores of young adults on Stanford–Binet IV and Peabody Picture Vocabulary Test—Revised. *Perceptual and Motor Skills, 65*, 721–722.

Carvajal, H., Hardy, K., Smith, K., & Weaver, K. (1988). Relationships between scores on Stanford–Binet IV and Wechsler Preschool and Primary Scale of Intelligence. *Psychology in the Schools, 25*, 129–131.

Cattell, R. B. (1940). A culture-free intelligence test, I. *Journal of Educational Psychology, 31*, 161–179.

Cronbach, L. J. (1987). [Review of *The Stanford Binet Intelligence Scale: Fourth Edition*]. (Report No. 1007-310 from on-line document service). Lincoln: Buros Institute of Mental Measurements, University of Nebraska.

Delaney, E. A., & Hopkins, T. F. (1987). *Examiner's handbook: An expanded guide for Fourth Edition users*. Chicago: Riverside.

Dvorine, I. (1958). *Dvorine Color Vision Test*. New York: Psychological Corporation.

Glutting, J. J., McDermott, P. A., & Stanley, J. C. (1987). Resolving differences among methods of establishing confidence limits. *Educational and Psychological Measurement, 47*, 607–614.

Grossman, H. J. (Ed.). (1983). *Classification in mental retardation*. Washington, DC: American Association on Mental Deficiency.

Hansen, M H., Hurwitz, W. N., & Madow, W. G. (1953). *Sample survey methods and theory*. New York: Wiley.

Hartwig, S. S., Sapp, G. L., & Clayton, G. A. (1987). Comparison of the Stanford–Binet Intelligence Scale: Form L-M and the Stanford Binet Intelligence Scale Fourth Edition. *Psychological Reports, 60*, 1215–1218.

Hoffman, R., Carleton, R., Bishop-Marbury, A., Goodwin, G. (1988, April). *Exploratory and extended confirmatory analyses of the common factor structure of the new Binet intelligence test: A re-evaluation of hypothesized structures*. Paper presented at the annual meeting of the National Association of School Psychologists, Chicago.

Hopkins, K. D., & Hodge, S. E. (1984). Testing the test: Review of the Kaufman Assessment Battery (K-ABC) for Children. *Journal of Counseling and Development, 63*, 105–107.

Hopkins, T. F. (1988). Commentary: The Fourth Edition of the Stanford Binet: Alfred Binet would be proud . . . *Measurement and Evaluation in Counseling and Development, 21*, 40–41.

Horn, J. L. (1968). Organization of abilities and the development of intelligence. *Psychological Review, 79*, 242–259.

Horn, J. L., & Cattell, R. B. (1966). Refinement and test of the theory of fluid and crystallized intelligence. *Journal of Educational Psychology, 57*, 253–270.

Jaeger, R. M. (1984). *Sampling in education and the social sciences*. New York: Longman.

Jensen, A. R. (1980). *Bias in mental testing*. New York: Free Press.

Jöreskog, K. G. (1969). A general approach to confirmatory maximum likelihood factor analysis. *Psychometrika, 34*, 183–202.

Jöreskog, K. G., & Sörbom, D. (1984). *LISREL VI: Analysis of linear structural relationships by maximum likelihood and squares methods*. Mooresville, IN: Scientific Software.

Kaplan, D. (1988, April). *Modification of structural equation models: Application of the expected parameter change statistic*. Paper presented at the meeting of the American Educational Research Association, New Orleans.

Kaplan, D. (1989). The problem of error rate inflation in covariance structure models. *Educational and Psychological Measurement, 49*, 333–337.

Kaufman, A. S. (1978). The importance of basic concepts in the individual assessment of preschool children. *Journal of School Psychology, 16*, 207–211.

Kaufman, A. S., & Kaufman, N. L. (1983). *K-ABC: Kaufman Assessment Battery for Children*. Circle Pines, MN: American Guidance Service.

Keith, T. Z., Cool, V. A., Novak, C. G., & White, L. J. (1988, April). *Hierarchical confirmatory factor analysis of the Stanford–Binet Fourth Edition: Testing the theory—test match*. Paper presented at the annual meeting of the American Educational Research Association, New Orleans.

Kish, L. (1965). *Survey sampling*. New York: Wiley.

Levy, P. (1968). Short-form tests: A methodological review. *Psychological Bulletin, 69*, 410–416.

McCarthy, D. A. (1972). *Manual for the McCarthy Scale of Children's Abilities*. New York: Psychological Corporation.

McCormick, R. L. (1956). A criticism of studies comparing item-weighting methods. *Journal of Applied Psychology, 40*, 343–344.

Muthen, B. (1984). A general structure equation model with dichotomous ordered categorical, and continuous latent variable indicators. *Psychometrika, 49*, 115–132.

Muthen, B. (1987). *LISCOMP: Analysis of linear structural equations using a comprehensive measurement model*. Mooresville, IN: Scientific Software.

Muthen, B., & Kaplan, D. (1985). A comparison of some methodologies for the factor analysis of non-normal Likert variables. *British Journal of Mathematical and Statistical Psychology, 38*, 171–189.

Muthen, B., Kaplan, D., & Hollis, M. (1987). On structural equation modeling with data that are not missing completely at random. *Psychometrika, 52*, 431–462.

Olridge, O. A., & Allison, E. E. (1968). [Review of *Wechsler Preschool and Primary Scale of Intelligence (WPPSI)*]. *Journal of Educational Measurement, 5*, 347–348.

Reynolds, C. R., Kamphaus, R. W., & Rosenthal, B. L. (1987, August). *Factor analysis of the Stanford–Binet Fourth Edition for ages 2 through 23 years*. Paper presented at the annual convention of the American Psychological Association, New York.

Rothlisberg, B. A. (1987). Comparing the Stanford–Binet: Fourth Edition to the WISC-R: A concurrent validity study. *Journal of School Psychology, 25*, 722–723.

Saris, W. E., den Ronden, J., Satorra, A. (1985). Testing structural equation models. In P. F. Cuttance & J. R. Ecob (Eds.), *Structural modeling*. Cambridge, England, Cambridge University Press.

Saris, W. E., Satorra, A., & Sörbom, D. (1987). The detection and correction of specification errors in structural equation models. In C. C. Clogg (Ed.), *Sociological methodology* (pp. 105–129). San Francisco: Jossey-Bass.

Saris, W. E., & Stronkhorst, H. (1984). *Causal modeling in nonexperimental research*. Amsterdam: Sociometric Research Foundation.

Sattler, J. M. (1988a). *Assessment of children* (3rd ed.). San Diego, CA: Author.

Sattler, J. M. (1988b, June). [An interview with Jerome Sattler by E. Bard]. *NASP Communique*, p. 4.

Spearman, C. (1923). *The nature of intelligence and the principles of cognition*. London: MacMillan.

Tatsuoka, M. M. (1988). *Multivariate analysis: Techniques educational and psychological research* (2nd ed.). New York: Macmillan.

Thorndike, R. L. (1973). *Stanford–Binet Intelligence Scale: Form L-M, 1972 norms tables*. Boston: Houghton Mifflin.

Thorndike, R. L. (1982). *Applied psychometrics*. Boston: Houghton Mifflin.

Thorndike, R. L., Hagen, E. P., & Sattler, J. M. (1986a). *Stanford–Binet Intelligence Scale: Fourth Edition*. Chicago: Riverside.

Thorndike, R. L., Hagen, E. P., & Sattler, J. M. (1986b). *The Stanford–Binet Intelligence Scale: Fourth Edition: Guide for administering and scoring* (2nd printing). Chicago: Riverside.

Thorndike, R. L., Hagen, E. P., & Sattler, J. M. (1986c). *Technical manual. Stanford–Binet Intelligence Scale: Fourth Edition*. Chicago: Riverside.

Vernon, P. E. (1950). *The structure of human abilities*. London: Methuen.

Wechsler, D. (1967). *Manual for the Wechsler Preschool and Primary Scale of Intelligence*. New York: Psychological Corporation.

Wechsler, D. (1974). *Wechsler Intelligence Scale for Children—Revised*. New York: Psychological Corporation.

Ysseldyke, J. E., & Stevens, L. J. (1986). Specific learning deficits: The learning disabled. In R. T. Brown & C. R. Reynolds (Eds.), *Psychological perspectives on childhood exceptionality: A handbook* (pp. 391–422). New York: Wiley.

12

Principles and Problems in Learning Potential

JOSEPH J. GLUTTING
University of Delaware

PAUL A. McDERMOTT
University of Pennsylvania

Intelligence test scores have long been recognized as the best independent predictors of children's future academic performance. However, litigious child advocacy is forcing psychologists to seek alternatives to the IQ test. A case in point is the most recent ruling in *Larry P. v. Riles*. In September 1986, Judge Robert Peckham banned schools in the state of California from using intelligence tests in the assessment of black children referred for special education services. Although the court order focuses exclusively on the use of IQ tests with black children, individual school districts such as the San Francisco Unified School District and the Los Angeles city schools have extended the prohibition to all children.

Legal challenges aside, the IQ test has been found wanting when confronting questions about how to avert the academic failure it forecasts. More specifically, traditional IQ tests have not met the challenge of providing effective aptitude–treatment interactions (ATIs) for evaluating how children best learn, or for determining how a particular child's style of learning is different from the styles manifested by other children (Conger, Conger, Farrell, & Ward, 1979; Kavale & Forness, 1984; Kramer, Henning-Stout, &

Schellenberg, 1987). Integral to ATI models is the assumption that mediating perceptual, cognitive, or metacognitive processes underlie academic performance. These models then advance the theory that the integrity of such processes is fundamental to successful achievement. The goal of ATI models is to differentiate the processing strengths and weaknesses of children and then to intervene accordingly. In the past, interventions in the ATI model included programs based on assessments of children's perceptual modality and psycholinguistic processing. Despite the limited success of these programs (Arter & Jenkins, 1977; Hammill & Larsen, 1974; Ysseldyke & Mirkin, 1982), the lure of ATIs remains appealing. Transactional inquiry suggests either that aptitude is more causal of achievement than achievement is causal of aptitude (Crano, Denny, & Campbell, 1972), or that aptitude and achievement interact reciprocally across time to influence subsequent achievement (Snow & Yalow, 1982).

The ATI model has gained new popularity with the recent introduction of dynamic assessment procedures designed to measure children's "learning potential" (LP; Budoff, 1975b; Feuerstein, Rand, & Hoffman, 1979). The "test–teach–retest" sequence of LP assessments represents a significant departure from the evaluation formats found in traditional IQ tests. This chapter is devoted to the nontraditional methodology of LP assessments. Two clinically based systems for evaluating LP are presented and distinguished from evaluation strategies that incorporate practice or coaching. The chapter turns then to the presentation of methodological concerns. The capability of dynamic methodology to diagnose potential in aberrant learners is evaluated through the presentation of factors likely to affect its reliability and validity. Thereafter, the practical merit of LP is placed in context by reviewing the empirical literature on dynamic assessments.

LEARNING POTENTIAL METHODOLOGY

Theoretical Underpinning

LP represents a synthesis of a family or class of developmental theories. The most comprehensive exposition of LP is presented by Reuven Feuerstein. The origins of LP, however, can be traced to works by Jean Piaget, Alexander Luria, and Lev Vygotsky. Feuerstein and his associates in Israel (Feuerstein, Rand, & Hoffman, 1979) conceptualize intelligence as a rule-learning process that is primarily induced by the quality and form of children's interactions with the environment. The most interesting and perhaps the most profound environmental interactions are referred to as "mediated learning experiences." In mediated learning, a knowledgeable adult guides children to solve problems that are beyond their manifest capabilities. Mediated learning modifies the cognitive repertoire of children and stimulates increasingly complex levels of manifest functioning.

Traditional IQ tests emphasize the assessment of manifest functioning, and therefore do little to advance our understanding of the cognitive processes responsible for children's IQs. LP, by contrast, attempts to measure cognitive processes directly through training-based assessments. Feuerstein, Rand, and Hoffman (1979) maintain that traditional IQ tests underestimate the extent to which children are modifiable. This shortcoming is par-

ticularly evident with children diagnosed as mildly retarded and with children outside the dominant culture (e.g., blacks, Hispanics, and Native Americans in the United States and immigrants of low socioeconomic status [SES] in Israel). Thus, for example, the manifest functioning of two 15-year-old children may show that they are able to independently solve tasks up to the degree of difficulty expected for 10-year-olds. When the two are provided with a mediated learning experience, it may turn out that the first child can solve problems normally associated with the expectations for 11-year-olds, but that the second child shows capabilities associated with 15-year-olds. Two conclusions can be drawn from this example. First, children demonstrate a capability to change relative to their initial level of functioning. Second, children vary considerably in the degree to which they are modifiable.

The cognitive modification evident from a single exposure to mediated learning is not expected to endure. Nevertheless, such phenomena are interpreted by LP advocates as evidence of the potential for permanent change. Feuerstein takes the additional step of asserting that the only suitable method for facilitating permanent cognitive change is through intense instruction, in the curriculum known as "Instrumental Enrichment" (Feuerstein, Rand, Hoffman, & Miller, 1980).

Feuerstein's Assessment System

Feuerstein, Rand, and Hoffman (1979) developed the Learning Potential Assessment Device (LPAD) to fulfill the substantive goal of assessing cognitive modifiability. Evaluative strategies in the LPAD are clearly more complex than the assessment procedures found in traditional IQ tests. The essence of LPAD assessments is to identify and locate specific cognitive deficiencies and then to evaluate, by intrachild comparisons, responses to instruction in general cognitive principles. Proponents maintain that a comprehensive LPAD battery is currently unattainable because the domain of possible cognitive deficiencies is diverse. Rather, a selection of tests is offered in the LPAD. From this selection, examiners choose instruments on the basis of children's personal competencies and learning characteristics.

Whereas Feuerstein frequently refers to the "test–teach–retest" paradigm, closer examination reveals that the LPAD has rarely been applied in this manner. More commonly, a "teach–test" format is employed, in which children are presented problems similar to the ones found in traditional IQ tests. The items may be verbal or nonverbal. If failure occurs, the examiner produces increasingly explicit mediated learning experiences until the correct solution is obtained. The examiner then notes the *amount* and *type* of assistance required to answer the question. On subsequent items, the process is repeated, and thereafter a posttest is administered to assess transference.

The teach–test format is illustrative of the LPAD Representational Stencil Design Test, the Organization of Dots Test, and the Numerical Progressions Test. Alternatively, a "within–test" format appears in the Raven Progressive Matrices–LPAD Variations Test (Raven-LPAD). Mediated learning experiences are applied throughout the Raven-LPAD administration. Neither a pretest nor a posttest is required, but on occasion, researchers have preceded and followed the dynamic measure with standard administrations of the Raven Progressive Matrices (RPM; Raven, 1958). Even more complex methodologies are found in the Plateaux Test and the Test of Verbal Abstractions. Continuous mediated assessment is implemented in the Plateaux Test until a criterion of three or more errorless performances is achieved. The Test of Verbal Abstraction, on the other hand, incorporates a branching assessment format, in which item presentations are tailored to children's correct and incorrect responses.

Budoff's System

Milton Budoff's (1968, 1969, 1975a) LP methodology is composed of three distinct phases: pretesting, teaching, and posttesting. A fluid-analytic reasoning task, such as the RPM or the Kohs Block Designs Test (KBD; Kohs, 1923), most commonly serves as the pretest. Although the pretest is traditional, its emphasis on fluid-analytic reasoning diminishes the verbal bias found in traditional IQ tests (Budoff, 1970). Assessments are conducted either individually or in groups, and no prompts or elaborated instructions are provided during the pretest. Nonverbal items similar in content to the pretest, and mediated instruction in adaptive problem solving, are used during the training phase (e.g., developing appropriate problem definitions, engaging in comparative behavior, controlling first-choice impulses). Transference of problem-solving principles is then evaluated on the posttest. Posttesting uses the same instrument and administration procedure found in the pretest.

Three LP scores are derived. "Pretest" scores represent traditional measures of nonverbal functioning. "Gain" and "posttest" (retest) scores evaluate potential. Gain scores are obtained by simple subtraction of the pretest score from the posttest score. Gain scores are dynamic; they represent the capacity to profit from instruction in cognitive principles. Posttest scores are summative indices that contain both traditional and nontraditional estimates of ability. As a result, posttest scores are postulated to be more predictive of children's true potential than the traditional IQ.

LP validity is an extraordinarily difficult question. The essence of the validity problem stems from the LP goal of attempting to defeat the very predictions made by traditional IQ tests. Traditional instruments such as the Wechsler Intelligence Scale for Children—Revised (WISC-R; Wechsler, 1974) become valid, in part, by providing stable forecasts of future scholastic performance. LP assessments, by contrast, attempt to decrease predictive validity by modifying retarded performers to subsequently higher levels of functioning. Nevertheless, it is possible to examine LP validity by predicting from the theory of cognitive modifiability how dynamic "status" groups should perform on subsequent academic and learning tasks.

Dynamic LP status groups can be formed, for example, with respect to children's traditional IQs and the amount of modifiability they demonstrate under LP assessments. Budoff (1975a) uses test–teach–retest scores to group children into three discrete categories. "High scorers" are predominantly white, middle-class children who score high on the pretest and show little gain on the posttest. "Gainers" tend to be children who are unfamiliar with the demands of testing.

These children score low on the pretest and obtain substantially higher posttest scores following mediated instruction. Test training is seen as helping gainers narrow differences between their native problem-solving abilities and the lower performance they demonstrate on traditional IQ tests. More often than not, gainers come from homes of low SES where English may or may not be the dominant language (Budoff, 1975b). As a result, LP evaluations are hypothesized to be superior to traditional IQ tests in diagnosing the capabilities of children from low-SES and culturally different backgrounds. "Nongainers" do less well than high scorers and gainers on both the pretest and posttest. These children have marked difficulty in profiting from the instruction presented during LP assessments, and they are seen as having lower capabilities (Budoff, 1967, 1969).

Practice and Coaching

Nontraditional methodologies, other than dynamic assessment, have been attempted to assure test takers an equal opportunity for success. "Practice" and "coaching" are the most extensively researched methods for enhancing the performance of low-scoring, naive test takers. Practice involves administering either an identical or an alternative form of the test prior to or subsequent to the first test administration. Coaching involves the presentation of demonstration problems, extensive drill, or combinations of the two between test and retest. From trends observed in summaries of the relevant literature (Hopkins & Stanley, 1981; Jensen, 1980), as well as endeavors that have applied the statistical methods of meta-analysis (DerSimonian & Laird, 1983; Kulik, Kulik, & Bangert, 1984; Scruggs, White, & Bennion, 1986), several generalizations can be made with regard to the effects of practice and coaching on test scores:

1. Practice and coaching effects are greatest for individuals with limited educational backgrounds.
2. Practice and coaching effects are greater on retesting with an *identical* test than with an alternate form of the test.
3. Assessments that provide extensive practice or coaching are more effective in raising scores than are brief treatments.

4. Practice and coaching result in larger score increases on nonverbal tests than on verbal tests.
5. The average gain for practice is approximately 5 IQ points. (All tests are made comparable by equating the standard deviation to 15, the typical standard deviation of IQ tests.)
6. The average gain for coaching is approximately 9 IQ points.
7. Contrary to the premise that such nontraditional testing would help close the "artificial" gap between the test-naive and the test-wise, ability-level comparisons show that individuals of higher ability tend to gain more than individuals of lower ability.

The prevailing LP view holds that several types of cognitive deficiencies are responsible for learning problems. Children with cognitive deficiencies show marked inabilities to simultaneously integrate two sources of information, compare relationships among events, and the like. As indicated previously, LP assessments focus on uncovering these deficiencies, and they proceed to induce short-term improvements through the direct teaching of broadly applicable cognitive skills. Coaching, by contrast, retains more of the qualities of traditional IQ tests. Its instruction is limited to drill and demonstrations in working out sample problems. There is little to no discussion of generalizable cognitive skills in the coaching literature. Therefore, for those advancing the LP perspective, it becomes very important that score effects from LP assessments be distinguishable from score effects attributable to coaching or practice. Furthermore, notwithstanding whether LP assessments produce distinctly *higher* posttest scores for children with learning difficulties, the ultimate question is whether LP assessments are more *valid* than traditional IQ, practice, or coaching assessments.

METHODOLOGICAL CONCERNS

Today, LP methodology can be divided conveniently into three major categories, although the three are not always distinct in their application.

The teach–test format represents the principal assessment methodology in the LPAD. However, the comparative advantages of teach–test assessments over traditional IQ assessments are not compelling. Teach–test methodology is unable to rule out even the most elementary rival explanations for the observed performance. That is, it is impossible to determine empirically whether test performance subsequent to the experimental inducement of mediated learning is due to the treatment or to a host of problems, not the least of which is IQ. This flaw compelled Campbell and Stanley (1963) to observe that teach–test methodology has "such a total absence of control as to be of almost no scientific value" (p. 6).

Within–test assessment is the second most prevalent methodology in the LPAD. Psychologists recognize the importance of rigorous adherence to prescribed procedures of test administration. Departures from the standard delivery of directions serve to reduce test reliability, and they affect the quality of test score interpretations. Instead of providing reliable summative indices, within-test evaluations are dependent on formative behavioral observations collected throughout the administration of mediated learning experiences. Therefore, the efficacy of such structured behavior samples must be substantiated by providing a sufficiently articulated system for the standard delivery of its treatment. This means that "directions to a test taker that are intended to produce a particular behavior sample (often called a 'prompt') should be standardized, just as the directions are standardized for any other test" (American Psychological Association, 1985, Standard 3.23, p. 30). Although the LPAD contains directions for administration, its format hardly approximates the step-by-step directions familiar to users of standardized intelligence tests. Not only is improvisation in teaching permissible; creative latitude in the administration of mediated learning experiences is presented as a *strength* of the LPAD. A clear drawback of this procedure is the possibility that some children will receive noticeably more or less help than others as a consequence of how examiners deliver the mediated learning experiences. Furthermore, teaching prompts on early test items can result in autonomous changes in the difficulty level of subsequent items. Such alterations in the measuring instrument are referred to as "instrument decay" (Campbell & Stanley, 1963, p. 9) and represent a second substantive threat to the validity of performance interpretations.

In an effort to approximate some appreciable level of reliability and validity, Budoff and Friedman (1964) introduced test–teach–retest methodology to the evaluation of LP. In comparison to teach–test and within-test assessments, this methodology represents a considerable procedural advancement in efforts to assess LP. The discussion and literature review to follow are limited to attempts to assess LP through test–teach–retest methodology. Teach–test and within-test techniques are not analyzed further, because the procedures are so nebulous and lacking in reliability as to render attempts at microanalysis futile.

The concepts of reliability and validity are familiar to all behavioral and social scientists. Such concepts are applied whenever one considers the requirements of data collection. It should not be surprising, therefore, that analogues of reliability and validity can be extended to analyze the facility of test–teach–retest methodology to diagnose potential in aberrant learners. Specifically, the test–teach–retest sequence is evaluated here in light of the reliability of LP gain scores, the propriety of LP critical values, the consistency of diagnoses of LP status, the prevalence and comprehensiveness of LP classifications, and the comparative verity of LP status. The first methodological concern is discussed directly. The other concerns are addressed in empirical inquiries regarding the expected score increases children exhibit when they are tested twice with the same instrument.

Reliability of Gain Scores

Gain scores have received considerable psychometric scrutiny because they have been employed, on occasion, to judge the efficacy of educational and psychological treatments. Three factors are likely to affect the integrity of gain scores: (1) the reliability of the pretest, (2) the reliability of the posttest, and (3) the correlation of the pretest with the posttest. Psychometric theorists (e.g., Cronbach & Furby, 1970; Linn & Slinde, 1977; Stanley, 1971) have used this knowledge to show that gain scores possess many undesirable characteristics. One problem is that gain scores tend to be more unreliable than the pretest and posttest used to calculate the gain. A second problem is that the amount of measurement error in gain scores is as large as or larger than the measurement error in the pretest and posttest. Third, as the correlation between pretest and posttest increases, the reliability of the gain score decreases.

The psychometric deficiencies of gain scores present several paradoxes in the valid estimation of LP. For example, if examiners wish to obtain reliable LP gain scores, they must select an instrument with highly *inconsistent* items (i.e., a test with low internal-consistency reliability). Similarly, reliable LP gain scores are found when an *unstable* instrument is used to judge children's modifiability (i.e., a test with low test–retest reliability). Traditional IQ tests such as the RPM and KBD are most commonly employed as the LP pretest and posttest. These instruments show substantial internal-consistency reliability and substantial test–retest reliability. The consequence of such high instrument reliability is that the reliability of the LP gain score deteriorates and its subsequent *validity* becomes suspect. This situation arises because classical test score theory shows that validity is incapable of exceeding the square root of reliability (for a detailed analysis, see Allen & Yen, 1979, p. 75). Thus, the LP gain score becomes unreliable as a consequence of high instrument reliability, and inasmuch as reliability affects validity, LP diagnoses based on unreliable gain scores are most likely to be invalid. (See Appendix 12.1 for further discussion of these problems.)

Propriety of Learning Potential Critical Values

To date, the most well established system for the identification of high scorers, gainers, and nongainers is found in Budoff's (1975a) LP procedure for the RPM. A "critical value," obtained by multiplying the pretest's raw-score mean by 0.9, is used to diagnose LP status. The critical value was developed from age group norms for the RPM. The RPM normative sample was obtained in California by Arthur Jensen, and children received a single administration of the test. As

a consequence of standard scores' being unavailable for the U.S. norm group, Budoff elected to multiply the RPM's raw-score mean by 0.9 to approximate an IQ of 90 (M. Budoff, personal communication, March 5, 1987).

It is improper to diagnose LP status from a single critical value. To understand this, one must consider the decision rules in Budoff's (1975a) system. First, a look-up table is consulted to locate the raw-score critical value for a particular age group. Second, the critical value is compared to children's pretest and posttest scores. High scorers are children whose pretest raw scores equal or exceed the critical value. Gainers are children whose pretest raw scores fall below the critical value and whose posttest raw scores equal or exceed the critical value. Both the pretest and posttest raw scores of nongainers fail to equal or exceed the critical value.

A drawback inherent in Budoff's nosology is that *the critical value fails to control for raw-score increases on the posttest*. Whenever a population is given a test twice, raw scores on the second administration will, on average, increase. The consequences of this phenomenon for the diagnosis of LP status becomes apparent when posttest score increases are examined on an ability measure that was administered twice to a nationally representative sample. The Animal House (AH) subtest in the Wechsler Preschool and Primary Scale of Intelligence (WPPSI; Wechsler, 1967) was given twice to 1,193 of the 1,200 children who took part in the test's standardization. The first column in Table 12.1 presents select frequencies of AH raw-score difference values from the WPPSI standardization sample. Difference values were calculated by subtracting AH first administration raw scores from retest raw scores. The bottom of the first column shows a mean posttest increase of 6.0. This value represents the natural improvement children experience as a consequence of taking the subtest twice. The posttest increase is not attributable to any appreciable modification of cognitive functioning, because no mediated learning experience intervened between the test and retest administrations. Rather, the increase establishes the groundwork for demonstrating that children more easily exceed the LP critical value on subsequent test administrations, and are classified

TABLE 12.1. Animal House (AH) Test–Retest Difference Scores

Raw score		Scaled score	
Difference[a]	Cumulative percentage	Difference[b]	Cumulative percentage
−41[c]	0.1	−9	0.2
−32	0.2	−7	0.4
−22	0.3	−6	0.9
−18	0.6	−5	2.0
−12	1.7	−4	4.4
−6	6.3	−3	10.2
−1	16.5	−2	23.8
0	25.9	−1	41.1
1	27.3	0	62.7
6	62.4	1	77.5
12	79.7	2	88.8
18	90.4	3	94.2
24	96.5	4	97.2
30	98.7	5	98.6
35	99.6	6	99.2
39	99.7	7	99.8
43[d]	100.0	8	100.0
$M = 6.0$, $SD = 9.1$		$M = -0.01$, $SD = 2.2$	

[a]Select raw-score difference values are presented. Difference values are based on AH retest raw scores minus AH raw scores from the WPPSI standardization sample ($n = 1,193$).

[b]Scaled-score difference values are inclusive. Difference values are based on AH retest scaled scores minus AH scaled scores from the WPPSI standardization sample.

[c]Lower raw-score limit.

[d]Upper raw-score limit.

as gainers, simply as a result of taking the same test twice.

A case example may clarify why LP status is affected by retest score increases. Consider the circumstance wherein a 60-month-old child is administered the AH subtest twice. The child's pretest raw score (28) falls below the 0.9 critical value for her age group, 32 (see Table 12.2, column 3). The child therefore fails to qualify for the high-scorer group. On retesting, her raw score increases by 6 points—the natural or typical score improvement found on second AH administrations. The child's posttest score (34) now exceeds the critical value (32), and she is classified as a "gainer."

The gainer classification, however, is problematic because the child has shown *no true growth* on the posttest, but merely the unremarkable raw-score elevation expected on

the second administration of the AH subtest. The error becomes more apparent when the critical value is properly adjusted to account for natural raw-score increases on the posttest. The adjusted posttest critical value for children in this age group is 41. When the adjusted raw-score critical value is compared to the obtained posttest score of 34, the child not only fails to qualify for the gainer group, but is properly classified as a nongainer.

Some advocates of dynamic assessment have attempted to overcome the difficulties of raw scores (and their corresponding critical values) by converting pretest–posttest scores to standard scores. Unfortunately, this methodology also suffers from psychometric problems. Scaling inconsistencies become manifest whenever posttest standard scores are based on norms from a *single* test administration. Assume, for example, that a 78-month-old child is identified as a gainer. Her raw score on the AH pretest is 48. This value converts to an IQ of 85, which is below the standard-score critical value of 90. On the LP posttest, the child receives a raw score of 49. Table 12.2 (bottom row, columns 3 and 4)

TABLE 12.2. AH Critical Values for High-Scorer, Gainer, and Nongainer Status Groups

Age in months	Raw-score mean	LP critical value		
		Raw score[a]	Test IQ[b]	Adjusted retest IQ
47–49	17	15	95	90
50–52	20	18	100	90
53–55	27	24	100	90
56–58	30	27	95	90
59–61	36	32	95	90
62–64	40	36	95	90
65–67	44	40	95	90
68–70	47	42	95	85
71–73	50	45	95	85
74–76	52	47	90	80
77–79	54	49	90	75

[a]Mean raw scores converted to 0.9 values in accord with the procedure used by M. Budoff (1975a) in *Learning Potential Test Using Raven Progressive Matrices* (circulated research report from the Research Institute for Educational Problems). Table values are rounded to the nearest whole number.

[b]WPPSI AH scaled scores converted to IQs for convenient presentation. Scaled-score conversions are based on the WPPSI standardization sample (Wechsler, 1967), where the population $M = 10$ and $SD = 3$.

shows that the posttest raw score is trans-formed to an IQ of 90 when the conversion is based on norms from a single administration of the subtest. The posttest IQ of 90 equals the standard-score critical value (90), and the child is identified as a "gainer." However, this classification is improper because it fails to consider that retest norms invariably differ from norms based on a single test administration. Column 5 ("Adjusted retest IQ") shows the posttest IQ conversion when the AH retest norms are applied. In the current case, the child's actual posttest IQ is 75.

As contradictory as it may appear, the example demonstrates that under the popular LP methodology, it is possible for a child's performance to *deteriorate* from a pretest IQ of 85 to a posttest IQ of 75, but for the child still to be diagnosed as a gainer! The example also makes it clear that retest norms and corresponding critical values are essential to control for natural performance improvements on the LP posttest.

It is not necessary that retest norms be developed for the full complement of subjects in a test's standardization sample. Rather, retest norms could be approximated from parameters developed from a *representative* subset of subjects exposed to test and retest administrations. This possibility exists because the size of the group on which norms are established is much less important than the degree to which the group is representative of the relevant population (Hopkins & Stanley, 1981). However, the full practical impact of this requirement is accentuated when one realizes that the test–retest reliability samples of IQ tests rarely correspond to the total population with respect to race, age, parental occupation level, and so on. Consequently, psychologists would be well advised to refrain from LP assessments in their practice until test–retest norms are obtained for a representative sample.[1]

---

[1]Researchers do not have to operate under these constraints. Analysis of covariance and hierarchical regression can control score characteristics that result from repeat test administrations. However, the propriety of such adjustments is reduced in LP research when range restrictions are imposed on the covariate by explicit selection of homogeneous samples on the basis of IQ (e.g., low, average, or high LP pretest scores). For a more detailed analysis of this concern, see text discussion on the effects of explicit selection in the "Literature Review" section.

Diagnostic Consistency of Learning Potential Status

Another concern is the diagnostic consistency of LP critical values based on 0.9 of the raw-score mean. Budoff's (1975a) use of U.S. norms for the RPM is laudable. However, multiplying each raw-score mean by 0.9 does not commensurately reduce the critical value to an IQ of 90 *across* age groups. Table 12.2 uses AH data to provide raw-score critical values based on Budoff's (1975a) LP procedure. Pretest raw-score critical values are displayed in column 3 under the subheading "LP critical value." Column 4 ("Test IQ") is most important because it shows IQs corresponding to the raw-score critical values. In the first row of the column, for the ages of 47–49 months, 0.9 of the raw-score mean corresponds to an IQ of 95. Rather than the desired IQ of 90, children in this age group actually must obtain an IQ of 95 to qualify as high scorers on the pretest. Between the ages of 50 and 52 months, the raw-score critical value converts to an IQ of 100. Thus, no scaled-score reduction occurs in the older age group, and children must obtain an even higher pretest IQ for placement in the high-scorer group.

The comparisons of age groups answer questions regarding the diagnostic reliability of LP status. Generally speaking, older children are more likely to be classified as high scorers than younger children. Clearly linked to this phenomenon is the conclusion that the differential diagnosis of LP status is unreliable across age groups. Therefore, inasmuch as an erratic delivery system has dubious consequences for the validity of a diagnostic methodology, the ultimate effect of LP status on the lives of children becomes suspect.

Prevalence of Learning Potential Diagnoses

In light of the demonstrated deficiencies of LP methodology, a logical question is this: Do diagnoses of LP status adversely affect child welfare? Table 12.3 presents prevalence rates for diagnoses of LP status when Budoff's (1975a) raw-score critical values are applied to the AH data (column A) and when test and *retest* standard-score critical values are applied (column B). The results show that Budoff's methodology proportionately un-

TABLE 12.3. Prevalence of LP Classifications Using Raw-Score and Standard-Score Critical Values

Group[a]	A. Raw-score critical value		B. Standard-score critical value		Prevalence[b]
	Number	Percentage	Number	Percentage	
High scorer	761	63.8	941	78.9	B > A**
Nongainer	190	15.9	145	12.2	A > B*
Gainer	242	20.3	107	9.0	A > B**

[a]Groupings are based on AH test–retest scores from the WPPSI standardization sample ($n = 1,193$).

[b]Identification of significant prevalence trends is based on tests of the standard error or proportional differences corrected for simultaneous statistical contrasts by the Bonferroni method, where observed frequencies equal the number of children in an LP status category.

*$p < .05$.

**$p < .0001$.

deridentifies high scorers ($p < .0001$) and proportionately overidentifies gainers and nongainers ($p < .05$ for both groups). Closer inspection reveals that Budoff's system identifies gainers twice as often as do diagnostic decision rules that control statistical artifacts better (20.3% vs. 9.0%, respectively). These findings indicate that, at their very best, gainer diagnoses will be incorrect over 50% of the time. The ethics of LP assessments must be questioned when, in over half the cases, the initial optimism raised by diagnoses of gainer status is destined to change to disappointment when children fail to manifest prophesied potential. Thus, it follows that LP information convolutes decision making, and that it is likely to result in diagnoses that are unstable and invalid.

Comprehensiveness of Learning Potential Criterion Groups

Existing LP systems focus exlusively on exceptional functioning. Budoff's (1975a) methodology, for instance, attempts to differentiate among children with low IQs (gainers, nongainers), but no accounting is offered for discrepancies among children with IQs in the average range or above (high scorers). Similarly, although an interest is expressed in learning disabilities, Feuerstein, Rand, and Hoffman (1979) direct attention to variations among children with low IQs (e.g., the "educable mentally retarded," "culturally different," etc.). LP assessments miss relevant child variation when their primary focus is the test performance of children of low IQs.

Learning difficulties extend beyond the lower IQ extreme. A relevant enterprise would be the identification of "gainers" with average or above-average IQs. For example, children outside the dominant culture who obtain traditional IQs in the high-average range (e.g., an IQ of 115) are denied access to gifted programs. Dynamic assessments, by contrast, might elevate performances sufficiently (e.g., a posttest IQ of 130) so that more minority children would become eligible for gifted programs. Alternatively, unique child requirements are unfulfilled by overlooking individuals with average or high traditional IQs who show subsequent LP posttest *decrements*. For example, column 3 in Table 12.1 presents the difference-score frequency distribution of AH test–retest scaled scores. Interestingly, column 4 shows that 41% of the preschool children in the United States experience a *relative score decrement* on the posttest. Likewise, column 2 shows that 16% of the children demonstrate an *absolute* (raw-score) *loss*.

With the exception of two studies (Glutting & McDermott, 1987, Williams, 1980), children who experience either relative or absolute posttest losses have not been discussed in the LP literature, and their performance is not accounted for by nosologies of LP status. To be suitably comprehensive, a classification system must cover all relevant aspects of child functioning in the domain of interest (for a more thorough exposition of this issue, see McDermott & Watkins, 1985). LP methodology obscures meaningful differences when average and high-IQ children are

TABLE 12.4. Prevalence of Nine-Group LP Nosology

LP classification	AH IQ	Percentage	Prevalence[b]
Gainer	A. High	0.8	
	B. Average	5.3	B > A**
	C. Low	5.1	C > A,*** C > B***
Nongainer	D. High	14.3	
	E. Average	48.4	E > D,* E > F*
	F. Low	15.8	
Loser	G. High	4.9	G > H,*** G > I***
	H. Average	5.1	H > I**
	I. Low	0.3	
	Cumulative percentage =	100.0	

[a]Groupings are based on AH test–retest scaled scores from the WPPSI standardization sample ($n = 1,193$).

[b]Identification of significant prevalence trends is based on tests of the standard error or proportional differences corrected by the Bonferroni method for the number of simultaneous statistical contrasts within an LP status group. Observed frequencies in a comparison equal the number of children at a given IQ level who obtained a particular classification (gainer, nongainer, loser). Population frequencies are based on expected proportions of occurrence for any given IQ level (68% for the average-IQ group; 16% each for high- and low-IQ groups).

*$p < .01$.

**$p < .001$.

***$p < .0001$.

lumped together as "high scorers" and their posttest results are ignored.

To address this issue, a more comprehensive, two-stage system for rendering LP diagnoses was developed and applied to the AH data. The system uses the more refined procedure of assigning classifications according to children's traditional pretest IQ (low, average, high) and relative posttest gain (gain, no gain, loss). Table 12.4 displays the resulting nine-group nosology. Children were placed in the low-IQ group when their pretest scaled scores were equal to or less than 7 (a score one standard deviation below the subtest's mean, 10). High-IQ children obtained pretest scaled scores equal to or greater than 13, and children were placed in the average-IQ group when their scaled scores exceeded 7 but were less than 13. The standard deviation of the AH scaled-score differences (2.2; see Table 12.1) was used to place children in three "dynamic" classifications. "Gainers" obtained scaled-score differences of +3 or more. "Nongainers" obtained differences between +2 and –2, and a newly identified group, labeled "losers," obtained scaled-score differences of –3 or less.

The results show that 10.3% of the children qualified for classification as LP losers. The results also demonstrate that posttest improvements and *decrements* extended be-

yond children who performed poorly on the pretest: All three IQ levels showed posttest performance changes. These findings indicate that Budoff's (1975a) LP nosology is unable to account for meaningful child variation (e.g., LP losers) and that it does not operate throughout the entire ability range. It therefore becomes apparent that the dominant LP nosology fails to satisfy standards for comprehensiveness.

Although the nine-group classification system is an improvement over previous LP nosologies, it is improper. Like Budoff's (1975a) system, it fails to consider the unreliability of gain scores. Nonetheless, the nine-group system is useful for highlighting another deficiency of LP classifications. Row C in Table 12.4 shows that low-IQ children *gained* disproportionately on the AH posttest. Conversely, children with high pretest IQs *lost* disproportionately on the posttest (row G). As in previous AH examples, performance changes on the posttest were not due to modified cognition, because no mediated learning experience was administered between the pretest and posttest. Rather, the overrepresentations illustrate the failure of LP nosologies to account for "*regression to the mean due to errors of measurement*" (Stanley, 1971, p. 376; italics in original).

An individual's posttest score will generally lie closer to a test's mean than his or her pretest score. The more extreme the pretest score, the greater the regression. Thus, higher proportions of low-IQ children will be identified as gainers during LP assessments simply as a consequence of ubiquitous posttest regression, rather than because of any genuine modification of cognitive structures.

Comparative Verity of Learning Potential Status

A principal advantage proposed for LP assessments is that they capture capabilities not assessed by traditional IQ tests. Thus far, attention has been focused primarily on the development of LP status groups and the study of decision rules governing such formations. However, once the constituent LP groups have been formed, it is possible to investigate the extent to which such groupings are explainable in terms of IQ. If a substantial percentage of the differences among ability groups are accounted for by IQ, the relative impact of the LP status groups becomes questionable, and it can be reasonably argued that LP assessments and traditional IQ tests measure essentially identical phenomena.

Six direct multiple-discriminant analyses, one for each age group in the WPPSI standardization sample, were conducted to explore whether high scorers, gainers, and nongainers could be differentiated solely on the basis of IQ. LP status was determined in accordance with the diagnostic rules put forth in Budoff's (1975a) classification system. AH pretest scores served as the traditional IQs. Results showed that the three LP groups could be differentiated (median Wilks's $\lambda = .242$, median $F = 302.7$, $df 1 = 12$, median $p < .0001$). However, statistically significant findings sometimes lead to practically meaningless results; the omega-square multi statistic (Sachideva, 1973) was calculated to determine the variance between the LP groups that are related to IQ. Approximately 75% of the actual differences among the high-scorer, gainer, and nongainer categories was accounted for by the traditional IQ ($\omega^2_{multi} = .752$).

Since each child's original membership in an LP status group was already known, classification analyses were conducted to dis-

TABLE 12.5. Hits and Misses for LP Status Group Classifications Based on Traditional IQ

Actual group[a]	Predicted group		
	High scorer	Gainer	Nongainer
High scorer	696	65	0
Gainer	0	177	65
Nongainer	0	59	131
Total	696	301	196

Note. Hits = 1,004, or 84.16%.

[a]Groupings are based on AH test–retest scores from the WPPSI standardization sample ($n = 1,193$).

cover the ability of traditional IQs to place children back into their original LP groupings. Table 12.5 shows the hits and misses rendered by the classification analyses. The overall hit rate of of 84.16% correct classifications was 69% above chance (1,004 hits out of 1,193 possible correct classifications). However, the greatest concern lies with the hit rate for the gainer group, because such children are most likely to be diagnosed as having greater potential than would be inferred from their results on a traditional IQ test. A classification accuracy of 73.14% was found for the gainer group—a hit rate 32.5% above chance.

The classification results serve to clarify findings from the prior discriminant analyses. Although a mediated learning experience did not intervene between the AH test and retest administrations, the results strongly suggest that knowledge of children's traditional IQs is sufficient for the competent identification of LP status. The most straightforward interpretation is that LP assessments provide little to no diagnostic information beyond that supplied by traditional IQ tests. Moreover, these findings have implications for LP research. It is well established that children with higher IQs demonstrate better academic performance and adjustment than children with lower IQs. Therefore, it is not surprising that motivational, academic, and behavioral differences have been found between LP gainers and nongainers; after all, the greater percentage of variation between these groups can be attributed to differences in traditional IQs.

LITERATURE REVIEW

Abundant research exists describing the benefits of LP assessments. For example, LP scores have been reported to be more predictive of teacher-rated achievement than traditional IQs (Babad & Budoff, 1974; Budoff & Hamilton, 1976; Hamilton & Budoff, 1974). Gainers from special education classes have been said to learn more than nongainers from special education classes, and as much as peers from regular classes (Budoff, 1968; Budoff & Corman, 1976; Budoff, Meskin, & Harrison, 1971). Demographic characteristics have indicated that although LP and Stanford–Binet scores equally predicted the achievement of white first-graders, LP scores were superior predictors for black children (Sewell, 1979). LP posttest scores of school-age and adult samples also have been found to be less closely related to race and SES than are traditional IQs (Budoff & Corman, 1974). Finally, personality correlates have indicated that gainers possess higher frustration tolerances, more conceptual flexibility, and more positive self-concepts and realistic career goals than do nongainers (Budoff, 1968; Budoff & Gottlieb, 1976; Budoff & Pagell, 1968; Folman & Budoff, 1971; Harrison, Singer, Budoff, & Folman, 1972; Pines & Budoff, 1970).

The LP research has not been reviewed within the context of methodological issues presented earlier. The major objective of this section is to summarize research evidence relating to LP assessments and to redress the balance of findings by analyzing information relevant to the methodological efficacy of LP assessments. The major question addressed here is this: How do methodological concerns affect outcomes presented in the LP literature?

Locating Studies

Using such terms as "coaching," "practice," "test–teach–test," "learning potential," "dynamic assessment," and the names of well-known investigators in the field (e.g., Budoff, Feuerstein), we used several procedures to find as many empirical studies of LP as possible. First, we made computer searches of the PsychINFO data base and manual searches of library data bases, including *Psycholog-ical Abstracts* and *Dissertation Abstracts International*. Primary sources identified in this way were examined for other references to appropriate sources. Our search was not limited to published investigations or dissertations; technical reports were included whenever applicable. Master's theses were excluded from the search.

The major criterion for including a study was that a central concern of the investigation was LP. We further restricted our analysis to studies where test–teach–restest treatments were employed. Studies conducted through teach–test or within-test assessments were not analyzed. The search produced 52 empirical investigations. The number was further reduced to 46 studies by collapsing results from duplicate investigations (e.g., dissertations or technical reports subsequently published in books or refereed journals). These investigations represent the body of the empirical literature examining LP up through the summer of 1987. Interestingly, 13 of the 46 investigations (26.2%) failed to support the relative efficacy of LP assessments.

Appendix 12.2 to this chapter presents distinguishing characteristics of the available research. Here, we summarize the contents of the appendix, although the reader is advised to review Appendix 12.2 itself to obtain an understanding of unique features associated with any given study.

Target Samples and Definition of Learning Potential Status

Concerning target samples, the median sample size was 60 (ranging from 16 to 1,560), with approximately 15 % of studies involving preschool-age children, 47% involving elementary school children, and 37% involving high schoolers and adults. The majority of studies (63.0%) focused exclusively on *exceptional* individuals, such as the retarded, the learning-disabled, and the physically handicapped, whereas 17.4% contrasted exceptional with normal groups. The remaining 19.6% were composed of undifferentiated samples (mixtures of the exceptional, normal, etc.). Earlier in this chapter, we have shown that by focusing on the test performance of children with low IQs, LP assessments miss relevant child variation. This finding, in conjunction with the clear research concentration on exceptional samples, would suggest some limitations to the generality of LP findings for the greater population of learners.

Over 80% of the research applied the RPM, the KBD, or the Series Learning Potential Test (SLPT) as the LP instrument. The remaining studies used subtests or modified administrations of currently existing IQ instruments (e.g., the Triangles subtest of the Kaufman Assessment Battery for Children; the Geometric Design subtest of the WPPSI; the Representational Stencil Design Test of the LPAD). The instruments were used to identify LP status groups for half of the cited studies, with 57.1% of those studies identifying gainers and nongainers, 28.5% adding a high-scorer group, and only one study formally recognizing a loser group.

As discussed previously, such status groups are defined by critical values. The more well-established strategy is Budoff's (1975a) LP procedure for the RPM, whereby a pretest raw-score mean is multiplied by 0.9 to obtain the critical value. However, little consistency is found in critical-value methodology; for example, in studies employing the KBD, one study used a 1-point gain, another used a 2-point gain, five used a 4-point gain, and still another used a 5-point gain. Ten studies employing the KBD or other instruments defined LP status by an arbitrary decision process wherein the sample was partitioned on the basis of mean gain (e.g., subjects below the mean gain value were considered nongainers, and those at or above were considered gainers). Variation in critical values ultimately renders the differential diagnosis of LP status incompatible across studies. Therefore, in this respect, it seems fair to surmise that the results and attendant implications of LP research generally cannot be viewed as uniformly meaningful.

Delivery of Treatments

Inconsistency seems to have been manifested as well in how experimental treatments were delivered. Given the long-recognized influence of treatment duration in research on human learning, it is troubling to note that treatment duration remained unspecified for nearly one-third of cited LP studies. And duration was found to range anywhere from 15 minutes to 25 hours (M = 105.9 minutes,

SD = 291.1 minutes, median = 45 minutes), with little attention given to rationale for preferring one length of duration over others. The problem is compounded by the fact that, apart from actual duration of treatment, the time interval between pretest and posttest assessments varied from as little as 2 to 4 hours to as much as 116 days, with one-quarter of the investigations giving no report of interval.

Use of Raw Scores and Alternative Procedures

Investigators' preference for raw scores is obvious. Nearly 90% of the studies turned to raw scores (as opposed to norm-based standard scores) as the basis for decisions about status group identification, critical values, gains, and the magnitude of results. In comparison to standard scores, raw score at the extremes of performance distributions (very low or very high) tend to disproportionately magnify performance changes between pretest and posttest. Thus, score changes ordinarily attributed to measurement error (mean regression, practice) mask themselves as meaningful improvement. (As further examples, see discussions above on the diagnostic consistency of LP status and how raw scores affect the propriety of LP critical values.)

Most recently, Budoff has recommended that *residualized* gain scores be calculated to offset the attendant limitations of simple (raw) gain scores: "This residualized score represents the child's responsiveness to training, and, by extension to the classroom, it is hypothesized to indicate the student's amenability to instruction, given suitable school experiences" (Budoff, 1987, p. 60). Fortunately, such methodology is not yet prevalent in LP research. Cronbach and Furby (1970) demonstrate the arbitrariness of this and other adjustments of gain scores, and conclude that "there appears to be no need to use measures of change [i.e., gain scores] and no virtue in using them" (p. 78).

To understand alternative procedures, one must first consider that residualized gain scores are found by regressing the LP posttest (Y) on the pretest to obtain a predicted posttest score (Y'). The residualized gain (RG) is subsequently obtained by *subtracting* the predicted posttest score from the obtained posttest score as follows: $RG = Y - Y'$. In cases where only pretest and posttest scores are available, Cronbach and Furby (1970) recommend use of the adjusted posttest score (Y'). The superiority of predicted posttest scores over residualized gain scores is related to avoiding the subtraction of Y' from Y.[2] Although predicted posttest scores are clearly superior to simple and residualized gain scores, it is inappropriate to correlate any of the three measures with external criteria (e.g., scholastic achievement, personality variables). That is, in studies where an external criterion is present, Cronbach and Furby recommend that *obtained* posttest scores (Y) be regressed simultaneously on *both* the pretest and the criterion to obtain a new performance estimate, $\hat{Y}$. Of course, however, children's $\hat{Y}$ scores will differ generally from their Y' scores, and $\hat{Y}$ will change systematically from criterion to criterion in response to difference in intercorrelations of the pretest, posttest, and criterion.

Methodological Problems

Appendix 12.3 to this chapter presents an account and evaluation of the cited LP research on selected methodological criteria. Considering the utility aspects of the LP critical value, the studies do no fare well. The usefulness of LP status is dubious because there is no consistency across studies. That is, an individual construed as a gainer in one study would be a nongainer in another, and so forth. Moreover, every investigation except one has ignored the existence of individuals whose performance deteriorates as a function of LP treatment (i.e., LP losers). Such individuals, by definition, must be present whenever comparisons are conducted throughout the entire ability range. Possible reasons for this shortcoming include concentration on samples of low-functioning individuals and floor effects on LP instruments. In the first instance, regression toward the mean makes it unlikely that posttest scores will deteriorate beyond the unusually low pretest scores; in the second,

instrument deficiencies render the posttest insensitive to performance deteriorations.

Interestingly, investigators noted for the initial design and application of LP assessment devices have later acknowledged that specific instruments are deficient for assessing claims of the LP paradigm. Corman and Budoff (1973), for example, conclude that

> because of the ceiling on Series Test (SLPT) scores, and because of the relationship of Series scores to race and social class, the Series Test appears to be a less useful measure of learning potential than either the Kohs Block Designs or Raven Progressive Matrices. (p. 14)

More unsettling, however, is the compilation of studies showing floor or ceiling effects on LP instruments. Fewer than half of the cited studies applied content learning material sufficiently simple (or complex) to be sensitive to actual improvements or individual differences in performance.

Another factor affecting outcomes is the interaction of LP assessments and ability level. Fully 56% of reviewed investigations failed to compare the performance of exceptional subjects to that of normals. This finding is especially intriguing in light of research on test practice and coaching, in which individuals of higher ability have gained more than individuals of lower ability. When contrasts among both higher- and lower-IQ exceptional individuals are considered, as well as contrasts between normal and exceptional subjects, over 83% of those studies demonstrated that higher-functioning subjects profited more from LP assessments than lower-functioning subjects. Such results are contrary to expectations from the LP hypothesis. In comparison to higher-IQ subjects, subjects with lower IQs appeared *relatively* worse off on the LP posttest than they were initially on the traditional LP pretest. Moreover, these findings concur with the AH analyses presented earlier in this chapter and suggest that IQ is the principal determinant of the gains that subjects display in LP assessments.

Perhaps as important as any question to the validity of LP assessments is the validity question itself. We have emphasized the idea that the novel testing formats in LP assessments must serve to increase criterion validity. Meaning is ascribed to IQ test scores and

[2]This description is accurate in a conditional sense, and readers should see Cronbach and Furby (1970) for further clarification.

LP scores on the basis of their capacity to facilitate norm-referenced comparisons among ranks in a distribution. Criterion validity for LP scores is improved over that for scores on IQ tests only when performance rankings are reordered in such a way that the new ranks reduce a tendency for criterion performance to be underestimated or overestimated for lower- and higher-ability children. However, test ranks remain unchanged and criterion validity unimproved when LP assessments uniformly increase the test scores of *all* children. Furthermore, just as the validity of an IQ test may be diminished for the case of the inexperienced or culturally different, so too is validity diminished when LP assessments alter performance rankings without appreciating estimation in the criterion domain for which they were intended (Anastasi, 1981; Gulliksen, 1950). Thus, application of LP assessments is justified only when the resultant scores are redistributed in a way that increases external validity.

Essential to any type of comparative research is the use of control or no-treatment conditions. LP assessments have been advanced as viable alternatives to coaching and test practice by virtue of their presumed alteration of cognitive structures through mediated instruction. However, empirical contrasts of the efficacy of unique LP learning experiences have been limited to less than 33% of the research. Similarly, although most studies examined LP validity on external criteria, fewer than 60% of these investigations examined relationships between LP assessments and achievement. When both elements are considered simultaneously, only four studies addressed the most fundamental issue of whether LP assessments are more *valid* predictors of achievement (Bailey, 1979, 1981; Glutting & McDermott, 1987; McDaniel, 1983; Platt, 1977). More importantly, results across these studies were equivocal in supporting the LP hypothesis. It therefore would seem appropriate to infer that LP assessments are no more valid in predicting academic achievement than are assessments incorporating practice or coaching elements.

Particularly disconcerting is the tendency to place subjects into homogeneous IQ groups and to ask thereafter whether IQ or nontraditional LP scores are better predictors of criterion performance. For example, several studies demonstrated that for select IQ levels (e.g., subnormal, average), nontraditional LP posttest scores provided better criteria predictions than did traditional IQ test scores (Babad & Budoff, 1974, Study 2; Bardsley, 1980; Budoff & Hamilton, 1976; Burns, Vye, Bransford, Delclos, & Ogan, 1987; Hamilton, 1972; Hamilton & Budoff, 1974; Hausman, 1973; Platt, 1977). However, without appropriate statistical corrections, such comparisons are methodologically improper. Placing subjects into homogeneous IQ groups attenuates the range of IQ test scores (relative to LP posttest scores) associated with the achievement criteria. This process is formally referred to as "explicit selection" on IQ. Gulliksen (1950, p. 146) demonstrates that whenever a test is used to assign subjects to homogeneous blocks (such as with traditional IQ tests in LP studies), it is relatively easy to try out another test (e.g., the LP posttest) and discover that the other test correlates more highly with a criterion. No LP investigation has statistically corrected for explicit selection on IQ. Thus, at best, reported findings of higher criterion validity for LP scores are misleading.

Serious confounding occurs when status groups presumably distinguished from one another by their potential to profit from mediated instruction are reduced to a lesser number of categories. Several researchers merged high scorers and gainers into one category when too few of either group were found in their studies (Bertumen, 1978; Budoff, 1967, 1968; Budoff & Gottlieb, 1976; Platt, 1977; Wolf, 1985). Thereafter, the performance of the newly formed group was compared to that of nongainers on criteria of interest. Such comparisons make it impossible to determine whether criteria differences were due to traditional IQ (the *high scorers* in the collapsed group) or to the ability to profit from mediated instruction (the *gainers* in the collapsed group).

Contrasting the criterion performance of status groups is a popular strategy in LP research. Occasionally, investigators have taken the added step of covarying IQ in an attempt to assure that criterion differences among status groups were independent of traditional ability estimates. The purpose of analyses of covariance is to remove from the dependent variable that variance predictable by knowledge of the linear relationship between the covariate and dependent variable (Keppel, 1973). Covariance is a legitimate enterprise when the covariate correlates highly with a *dependent* variable and information contained in the covariate is obtained *separately* from the blocking variable.

Discriminant analyses presented earlier in this chapter have shown that IQ accounts for a substantial percentage of variation separating the LP status groups of high scorers, gainers, and nongainers (75%). Likewise, inasmuch as the status group of high scorers is diagnosed solely in terms of traditional IQ (i.e., a high pretest score), an appreciable amount of variation among LP groupings must be attributable to IQ. The high correlation between IQ and LP status represents a violation of assumptions underlying the analysis of covariance, inasmuch as the covariate (IQ) and blocking variable (LP status) are not obtained independently. Therefore, whenever LP status is the blocking variable in a contrast, a substantial percentage of criterion heterogeneity will be due to IQ. Covarying IQ *subsequent* to forming LP status groups will not remove this variation.

As a final note, brief consideration is extended to the intervention component of LP. Instrumental Enrichment (IE) is the course of study that Feuerstein et al. (1980) developed for permanently integrating and extendng the cognitive skills of deficient learners. Naturally, LP assessments function to identify unique constellations of cognitive deficiencies; these thereby serve as the targets of instruction.

The number of empirical studies devoted to IE is impressive (Comfort, 1984; Feuerstein et al., 1980; Feuerstein, Rand, Hoffman, Hoffman, & Miller, 1979; Haywood & Arbitman-Smith, 1981; Katz & Buchholz, 1984; Rand, Mintzker, Miller, Hoffman, & Friedlender, 1981; Rand, Tannenbaum, & Feuerstein, 1979; Sewell, Winikur, Berlinghof, Berkowitz, & Miner, 1984). Nevertheless, this number can be reduced to six by collapsing results from duplicate investigations, four of which were conducted in the United States and two in Israel. More importantly, existing studies on the efficacy of IE have yet to identify methodology that would be reasonably commensurate with what is acceptable in other areas of educational research. Conspicuously absent is the very basis for tailoring instruction to individual needs. Only one of the six studies used LP assessments to guide treatments. Moreover, that single study (Katz & Buchholz, 1984) used case-study methodology—no group study incorporated learning assessments.

Other methodological trends are evident in IE research. In particular, despite claims to provide effective ATIs, ability-level contrasts are not considered. One study was exceptional in this respect (Comfort, 1984). Here, however, higher-functioning children profited more from IE than lower-functioning children. Thus, inasmuch as no evidence was given for the alteration of performance rankings, one cannot regard IE an effective ATI treatment. Finally, in every study, the attention devoted to delivery of IE exceeded that accorded to control conditions, thereby opening the research to the classic threat of halo effects.

CONCLUSION

It stands to reason that there can be little promise for any area of inquiry lacking reasonable support. LP Methodology and the prevailing trends of existing research are discouraging and raise suspicions about the overall integrity of LP assessments. Moreover, grave concerns emerge when one considers the vast time and energy that highly trained professionals (such as school psychologists) might devote to LP assessments, the accuracy of which is dubious at best and the ultimate effects of which on the lives of children are unknown.

Throughout this century, position statements have been developed expounding the benefits of popular educational and psychological treatments, but those benefits have been diminished or refuted when held up to the rigor of empirical scrutiny. If school psychologists and other child specialists seriously intend to evaluate the cognitive processes of LP, they ultimately must shift attention from preoccupations with popular practices to the production of methodologically sound research. Otherwise, LP, like its popular predecessors, is destined to be another promise unfulfilled.

APPENDIX 12.1. FURTHER CONSIDERATION OF THE RELIABILITY OF GAIN SCORES

The relationships revealed in the "Reliability of Gain Scores" section suggest a dismal situation, because generally whatever a test developer does to increase the reliability of a test will also increase the intercorrelation for repeated administrations of the test. However, it can be argued that the situation may not be hopeless. The principal way to increase the reliability of a test is to lengthen it, using items of similar content and process. The impact of increased test reliability *and intercorrelation* can be estimated for gain scores, using the following variant of the Spearman–Brown prophecy formula:

$$r_{DD} = \frac{\dfrac{KP}{1 + KP - P} - \dfrac{KC}{1 + KC - C}}{1 - \dfrac{KC}{1 + KC - C}}$$

where:

P = the mean reliability of the pretest and posttest
C = the intercorrelation of the pretest and posttest
K = the factor by which the test is lengthened

This equation appears to be analytically intractable, so some values that are theoretically possible have been compared. For example, if the initial mean reliablity for the LP measure is .50 and the initial correlation is 1.00, lengthening the LP pretest and posttest by a factor of 2.5 is predicted to increase the reliability of the gain score from .444 to .635. Thus, the situation is not as gloomy as it seems at first.

The presentation above makes evident that it is *theoretically* possible to obtain satisfactory reliabilities for LP gain scores. However, it is questionable whether, in actual practice, some values in the example above are realistic. Consider an applied example. The Kohs Block Design (KBD) test is a popular instrument used to assess LP. Norms for the KBD are dated (Kohs, 1923), but modified versions of this measure are found in the popular Wechsler series. In particular, the Block Design (BD) subtest of the WISC-R is a widely recognized measure of nonverbal functioning, and most researchers would accept its use as a measure of LP.

Consider again the formula above for the reliability of a difference score, where:

P = the mean reliability of the pretest and posttest. Wechsler (1974) reports in the WISC-R manual that the mean split-half reliability of the BD subtest equals .85 for the standardization sample. Therefore, let P = .85.
C = the intercorrelation of the pretest and posttest. The intercorrelation of the BD subtest with itself is obtained quite easily. Wechsler (1974) reports the 1-month stability coefficient for BD as .81. Therefore, let C = .81. Please note that inasmuch as the 1-month interval between first and second BD administrations is likely to be longer than the interval typically reported between LP pretest–posttest administrations ($M \approx 7$ days), we can assume that this coefficient is likely to be conservative (i.e., we should underestimate the 1-week intercorrelation between the pretest and posttest).
K = the factor by which the test is lengthened.

When values are substituted, the reliability of the LP gain score remains undesirable even when the pretest and posttest are both lengthened by a factor of 5 ($r_{DD} = .244$).

An additional problem is present, irrespective of whether it is possible to develop new items whose quality is similar to those in the original BD instrument (a common criticism of assumptions underlying the Spearman–Brown prophecy formula). This problem relates to increasing the subtest's length by a multiple of 5. This value of K was not chosen at random. Rather, the multiple of 5 matches the number of subtests in the Performance scale of the WISC-R, and inasmuch as it would be necessary to give the BD subtest twice during an LP assessment, the actual increase in administration time is approximated by a factor of 10 (i.e., $5 \times 2 = 10$). At this point, the LP assessment approximates the administration time necessary for the WISC-R. (There are 10 subtests in the standard WISC-R battery.) Furthermore, since "teaching" would have to intervene between the BD pretest and posttest, the LP assessment now takes much longer to administer than the *entire* WISC-R! Yet, even in this instance, the reliability of the gain score remains dismal (i.e., $r_{DD} = .244$).

Study	Age[a]	Sample/n[b]	Sample type	Treatment	LP instrument and duration of treatment	LP metric employed in study	LP status groups identified	Results
Babad (1977)	7 to 15	58	Educable mentally retarded (EMR)	Compared criterion differences between "high"- and "low" LP EMR subjects on the Test of General Ability (TOGA), the Wide Range Achievement Test (WRAT), and teacher ratings of pleasantness, cooperation, and academic potential 8 months after the LP assessment.	Series Learning Potential Test (SLPT); 45 minutes of training; unspecified interval between pretest and posttest.	Pretest post-test, and gain raw scores (RS), partial correlation (PC)	High- and low-LP subjects; method: sample-specific splits based on post test score	When the LP pretest scores or LP pretest scores and age were controlled for, results showed that high-LP subjects obtained higher TOGA Reasoning IQs than low-LP subjects. However, no high versus low group differences were reported for the three other criteria (TOGA Verbal IQ, WRAT, teacher ratings).
Babad & Bashi (1977)	7 to 11	952	High and low socioeconomic status (SES)	Compared LP posttest score increases of high-SES and low-SES subjects in second, fourth, and sixth grades.	SLPT; one training session of unspecified duration; 3 to 5 days between pretest and posttest.	Pretest, post-test, and gain RS	Not applicable (NA)	Second- and fourth-grade subjects of low SES showed larger gains on the LP posttest than high-SES subjects (12 RS points vs. 9.2 points, respectively). No statistical tests were applied to the differences. Sixth-graders were not compared because the scores of high-SES subjects showed a ceiling on the LP posttest.
Babad & Budaoff (1974, Study 1)	8 years, 0 months to 10 years, 11 months	126	Average, dull-average, sub-normal	Compared LP posttest score increases of average, dull-average, and subnormal subjects.	SLPT; 30 to 45 minutes of training; 3 days between pretest and posttest.	Gain RS	NA	Both subnormal and dull-average subjects showed larger gains on the LP posttest than average subjects.

(continued)

313

APPENDIX 12.2. (*continued*)

Study	Age[a]	Sample/n[b]	Sample type	Treatment	LP instrument and duration of treatment	LP metric employed in study	LP status groups identified	Results
Babad & Budaoff (1974, Study 2)	8	207	Average, dull-average, sub-normal	Compared concurrent validity of LP scores vs. TOGA IQs in estimating teacher-rated achievement for average, dull-average, and sub-normal subjects.	SLPT; 30 to 45 minutes of training; 3 days between pretest and posttest.	Pretest and posttest RS	NA	The LP posttest was superior to IQ in predicting the teacher-rated achievement of subnormal and dull-average subjects.
Bailey (1979, 1981)	5 to 6	124	General sample, including exceptional children	Compared 4-month predictive validity of an LP assessment, an assessment involving coaching, and traditional IQs from the Stanford–Binet (SB) with results for a general sample. Criteria included a curriculum-based achievement measure, teacher ratings of academic risk, items from a behavior rating scale, and scores from the Boehm Test of Basic Concepts.	Raven Progressive Matrices (RPM); 15 minutes of training; 6 days between pretest and posttest.	Gain and posttest RS	NA	Coaching scores were better predictors of performance on the four criteria than nontraditional LP posttest scores. However, neither procedure predicted criterion performance as well as traditional IQs from the SB. In addition, traditional LP pretest scores predicted end-of-year academic risk as well as nontraditional LP posttest scores.

Bardsley (1980)	7 years, 11 months to 10 years, 11 months	33	Learning disabled (LD)	Examined whether LP methodology would increase posttest scores for LD subjects. Also compared the validity of LP scores vs. Wechsler Intelligence Scale for Children—Revised (WISC-R) IQs in estimating achievement on the KeyMath Diagnostic Arithmetic Test, Woodcock Reading Mastery Tests, WRAT, and Systems Fore Language test.	RPM; 30 to 45 minutes of training; 7 days between pretest and posttest.	Pretest, posttest and gain RS	NA	Significant pretest-to-posttest gains were found. Traditional WISC-R IQs predicted performance on the verbally loaded academic tasks (reading and language), whereas the nontraditional LP posttest and gain scores did not do so. Furthermore, although the LP pretest and posttest predicted mathematics achievement and WISC-R IQs did not, the traditional LP pretest was a better predictor of mathematics achievement than the nontraditional LP posttest.
Bergman (1980)	12 years, 9 months to 19 years, 6 months	60	Normal, EMR	Normals and EMR subjects were administered LP assessments. However, statistical analyses were limited to comparisons between mean scores of EMR gainers (G) and nongainers (NG) on the RPM, a paired-associate learning task (PA), PA with mediated instruction, a word recall task, a digit span test, word recall clustered into meaningful word categories, a word recall clustering "index," and a picture-word game.	Kohs Block Designs (KBD); one training session of unspecified duration; 2 days between pretest and posttest.	RS gain, residualized gain (RG)	Gainers (G) and nongainers (CNG); method: sample-specific splits	No differences were found between G and NG on seven of the eight external criteria.

(continued)

315

APPENDIX 12.2. (*continued*)

Study	Age[a]	Sample/n[b]	Sample type	Treatment	LP instrument and duration of treatment	LP metric employed in study	LP status groups identified	Results
Bertumen (1978)	7 to 10	40	General sample of first- and second-grade Filipinos	Compared the efficacy of LP assessments and test practice in increasing the posttest scores of Filipino second-graders. Three external criteria were also administered.	RPM; 60 minutes of training; approximately 3 to 5 days between pretest and posttest.	Pretest and posttest RS	NA	LP assessments and test practice failed to increase posttest scores significantly. Differences on the external criteria were not compared by condition.
Budoff (1967)	17 to 23	36	Retardates in institutional setting	Examined whether LP methodology would increase posttest scores for retardates in an institutional setting. Also compared mean scores of G and NG on the RPM, SB, PA, and problem-solving and learning tasks.	KBD; one training session of unspecified duration; 7 days between pretest and posttest.	Pretest RS, posttest RS weighted for speed of solution	G, NG; method: 4-point RS increase	G obtained significantly higher scores on the WISC Performance IQ (PIQ). RPM, PA, and problem-solving criteria. No difference was found between G and NG on the WISC Verbal IQ (VIQ), and SB.
Budoff (1968)	16 years, 6 months to 23	76	Retardates in institutional setting	Extended Budoff (1967) study by pooling subjects from the original study and a replication sample. Compared mean scores of G and NG on the RPM, SB, WISC- Wechsler Adult Intelligence Scale (WAIS), and a problem-solving task.	KBD; one training session of unspecified duration; 7 days between pretest and posttest.	Gain and posttest RS	G, NG; method: 4-point RS increase	G obtained significantly higher scores than NG on the WISC PIQ, RPM, and problem-solving criteria.
Budoff & Corman (1974)	8 to 40	627	EMR	Compared whether nontraditional LP posttest scores vs. traditional WISC, SB, and LP pretest scores were related to the demographic and family background characteristics of EMR subjects.	KBD; one training session of unspecified duration; 7 days between pretest and posttest.	Pretest and posttest RS, PC	NA	The traditional WISC VIQ, the SB, and the LP pretest correlated significantly with race and SES. The nontraditional LP posttest, on the other hand, showed little to no association with the demographic variables. Results therefore support the cultural fairness of LP assessments.

Study	Age	N	Population	Description	RPM/Training		Results
Budoff & Corman (1976)	6 to 14	533	Normal, EMR	Four factor scores were developed for the RPM, which served as the LP pretest and posttest. The efficacy of LP assessments vs. practice in increasing posttest factor scores was compared for both EMR and normal subjects.	RPM; number and duration of the training session(s) was not specified; 2 weeks or less between pretest and posttest.	Pretest and posttest RS converted to factor scores	NA	Repeated-measures analysis of variance (ANOVA) showed that LP assessments resulted in higher posttest scores than test practice on one of the four RPM factors. Although EMR subjects in the LP condition obtained significantly higher posttest scores than EMR subjects in the practice condition, LP assessments were ineffective in narrowing the gap between normal and retarded subjects. A three-way interaction showed no differential effects between normal and EMR subjects in the LP condition on any of the four RPM factors.
Budoff, Corman, & Gimon (1974)	6 years, 7 months to 13 years, 8 months	54	Spanish-dominant Puerto Ricans	Compared nontraditional LP posttest vs. traditional WISC PIQ, WISC Vocabulary subtest, Semantic Test of Intelligence, and RPM pretest scores in predicting domain-referenced achievement on a 26-lesson electricity curriculum. The criterion was divided into subtests requiring verbal versus nonverbal and symbolic versus concrete responses.	RPM; 45 minutes of training; approximately 2 days between pretest and posttest.	Pretest and posttest RS	NA	Stepwise multiple-regression analyses showed that the LP posttest predicted performance on the minimally verbal and symbolic criterion of electrical knowledge. By contrast, the three traditional IQs did not predict performance on any of the four achievement criteria.

(continued)

317

APPENDIX 12.2. (*continued*)

Study	Age[a]	Sample/n[b]	Sample type	Treatment	LP instrument and duration of treatment	LP metric employed in study	LP status groups identified	Results
Budoff & Friedman (1964)	16 years, 6 months to 19	32	Retardates in institutional setting	Compared the efficacy of LP assessments, coaching, and test practice in increasing the posttest scores of institutionalized retardates 1 day and 1 month after training.	KBD; one training session of unspecified duration; 7 days between pretest and posttest.	Posttest RS and posttest RS weighted for speed of solution	NA	Subjects in the LP condition obtained significantly higher posttest scores 1 day and 1 month following training than subjects in the coaching and practice conditons.
Budoff, Gimon, & Corman (1974)	6 years, 2 months to 14 years, 10 months	188	Spanish-dominant Puerto Ricans	Compared nontraditional LP posttest vs. traditional WISC PIQ and WISC Vocabulary subtest in predicting six achievement criteria (verbal, nonverbal, and numeric measures administered in English and Spanish).	RPM and SLPT; 45 minutes of training on RPM, duration of training on SLPT of unspecified duration; approximately 2 days between pretest and posttest.	Posttest RS	NA	Numeric and nonverbal achievement in both Spanish and English were significantly related to posttraining scores on the SLPT and WISC PIQ. The nontraditional SLPT predicted achievement better than WISC Vocabulary subtest scores. Interestingly, the authors note that "one difficulty of the Series Test (SLPT) is that children older than 9 years of age tend to attain a *de facto* ceiling, which accounts for the lower average gain displayed by intermediate grade children" (p. 11).

Study	Age	N	Subjects	Description	Dependent measure	Groups; method	Results
Budoff & Gottlieb (1976)	7 years, 9 months to 14	31	EMR	Special education G and NG from self-contained and mainstream placements were compared on multiple achievement, motivational, cognitive style, and behavioral criteria. The criteria were obtained up to three times during one school year.	Gain RS	RPM; 60 minutes of training; approximately 3 days between pretest and posttest.	G, NG; method: Budoff's RPM procedure	Combining results across the three times the criteria were administered showed that G showed higher reading and mathematics scores on the Metropolitan Achievement Test (MAT), better cognitive styles on the Matching Familiar Figures Test, and better motivation (this held true only for mainstreamed G). No difference was found between G and NG on the behavior rating scales.
Budoff & Meskin (1970); Budoff, Meskin, & Harrison (1971)	12 to 14	91	Normal, EMR	Identified LP high scorers (HS), G, & NG among low-achieving normal and EMR subjects. Normal subjects and half of the EMR subjects were taught a 26-lesson curriculum on electricity. The dependent variable was a domain-referenced test on electricity administered before and after the intervention.	Gain RS	KBD; the duration of the training session and the interval between pretest and posttest were not specified.	Normal and EMR, HS, G, and NG; method: sample-specific splits	Although normal subjects obtained higher scores than EMR subjects on the electricity posttest, multivariate analysis of variance (MANOVA) results showed that both normal and EMR HS performed better than their respective G counterparts, who in turn outperformed the NG in their respective groups.
Budoff & Pagell (1966)	12 to 17	40	Normal, EMR	EMR G and NG, mental age (MA) controls, and chronological age (CA) controls were compared on repetitive tasks designed to assess cognitive rigidity and conceptual flexibility.	Gain RS	KBD; the duration of the training session and the interval between pretest and posttest were not specified.	G, NG; method: 4-point RS increase	G demonstrated less rigidity and greater conceptual flexibility than NG or MA controls. Normal subjects of the same CA as EMR subjects outperformed both the G and NG groups on the two tasks.

(continued)

APPENDIX 12.2. (*continued*)

Study	Age[a]	Sample/n^b	Sample type	Treatment	LP instrument and duration of treatment	LP metric employed in study	LP status groups identified	Results
Burns (1984, 1987)	4 to 6	60	EMR and subjects with IQs less than 90	Compared mean score effects of exposure to LP assessments using mediated learning experiences, assessments using nontraditional "graduate prompts," and test practice on an independent set of test items and a tranference task (Animal House subtest [AH] of the Wechsler Preschool and Primary Scale of Intelligence [WPPSI]).	Stencil designs adapted from the Stencil Design Test-1 (SDT-1) of the Arthur Point Scale of Performance Tests; 23 minutes of training; 1 day between pretest and posttest.	None; compared group differences on external criteria	NA	Subjects receiving LP assessments obtained significantly higher scores on the independent test items than subjects receiving mediated prompts, who in turn outperformed subjects receiving test practice. Subjects in the LP and mediated-prompt conditions obtained higher scores on the transfer task than subjects in the practice condition, but no difference was found on the transfer task between subjects in the LP condition and subjects in the mediated-prompt condition.

Study	Age	Population	N	Description	Test/Training	Scoring	Method	Results
Burns, Vye, Bransford, Delclos, & Ogan (1987)	5 years, 6 months	EMR	44	Correlated scores from LP assessments using nontraditional "graduated prompts," and test practice on select subtests of the McCarthy's Abilities (MSCA). Also compared criterion differences between "high"- and "low"-LP subjects on an animal stencil task, the WPPSI AH subtest, and a shape construction task.	SDT-1; one training session of unspecified duration; pretest and posttest were administered on the same day.	Posttest RS	High- and low-LP subjects; method: three items out of four possible correct items	Although the MSCA Perceptual–Performance scale showed a significant correlation with the LP posttest ($r = .48$), LP performance generally was independent of traditional IQs from the MSCA. High-LP subjects obtained significantly higher scores than low-LP subjects on the animal stencils and AH criteria, but not on the construction task. Results indicated that LP assessments are relatively independent of performance on traditional IQ tests and that LP assessments offer information not provided by traditional IQ tests.
Corman & Budoff (1973)	6 to 9	General sample, including exceptional children	1,560	Multiple reliability and validity studies were presented for the SLPT. Data were gathered in 79 classrooms across five communities in Connecticut.	SLPT; 30 to 45 minutes of training; unspecified interval between pretest & posttest.	Pretest, posttest and gain RS	NA	SLPT scores were positively related to IQ, achievement, and race. Middle-class and white subjects showed larger gains on the SLPT than lower-class and minority subjects. The authors conclude that "because of the ceiling on Series Test (SLPT) scores, and because of the relationship of Series scores to race and social class, the Series Test appears to be a less useful measure of learning potential than either the Kohs Block Designs or Raven Progressive Matrices" (p. 14).

(continued)

321

322

APPENDIX 12.2. (*continued*)

Study	Age[a]	Sample/n[b]	Sample type	Treatment	LP instrument and duration of treatment	LP metric employed in study	LP status groups identified	Results
Delclos (1984)	11 years, 1 month to 14 years, 7 months	26	EMR, LD	Identified G and NG; thereafter, total scores and the specific types of errors made on a modified version of the Representational Stencil Design Test (RSDT) were compared between groups. Traditional IQs served as covariates in the study.	Representational Stencil Design Test (RSDT); one training session of unspecified duration; the interval between pretest and posttest was not specified.	Pretest, posttest and gain RS, and PC	HS, G, & NG; method: mean gain obtained from a pilot study	When traditional IQs were controlled for, results showed that G obtained significantly higher LP posttest scores than NG. G also made fewer errors than NG when performance on "solid" stencils was examined, and they were also less likely to order the stencil cutouts incorrectly. The results indicated a direct correspondence between the cognitive principles taught in the LP assessment and what was learned by successful subjects.
Folman & Budoff (1971)	13 years, 7 months	80	Normal, EMR	Identified HS, G, & NG among EMR and low-achieving subjects. Thereafter, the groups were compared with respect to their current vocational status and future vocational aspirations.	SLPT; one training session of unspecified duration; 7 days between pretest and posttest.	Pretest, posttest and gain RS	HS, G, & NG; method: 4-point RS increase	Results showed few differences in vocational development between EMR and normal subjects. However, within the EMR group, greater proportions of HS and G held after-school jobs and had more realistic vocational aspirations than NG. In addition, HS had more realistic vocational aspirations than G.

Study	Age	N	Sample	Description	Instrument/Method	Data	Groups/Method	Results
Glutting & McDermott (1987)	5 years, 0 months to 6 years, 2 months	408	General sample, including exceptional children	Compared the efficacy of LP assessments; coaching, and test practice in increasing the posttest scores of kindergarten subjects. Also compared the mean scores of low-, average-, and high-IQ G, NG, and losers on two standardized (MAT) and two teacher-rated criteria of reading and mathematics achievement.	Geometric Design (GD) subtest of the WPPSI; 60 minutes of training; 4 days between pretest and posttest.	Pretest and posttest scaled scores, scaled-score gain, PC	Nine groups; method: initial IQ and sample-specific gain	When pretest scores were controlled for, results showed that LP assessments were no more effective in elevating test scores than coaching or test practice. Of greater importance, however, was that no differences were found among the nine LP status groups on either the standardized or teacher-rated criteria of academic achievement.
Glutting, McDermott, & Burnett (1987)	5 years, 0 months to 5 years, 11 months	115	General sample, including exceptional children	Compared the predictive increment of the nontraditional LP posttest, above the traditional LP pretest, in predicting two standardized (MAT) and two teacher-rated criteria of reading and mathematics achievement.	GD; 60 minutes of training; 4 days between pretest and posttest.	Pretest and posttest scaled scores, and PC	NA	Hierarchical-regression results showed that the predictive efficacy of the nontraditional LP posttest, above the prediction provided by the traditional LP pretest, was negligible across the four achievement criteria (mean change in $R^2 = .0021$).

(continued)

APPENDIX 12.2. (*continued*)

Study	Age[a]	Sample/n[b]	Sample type	Treatment	LP instrument and duration of treatment	LP metric employed in study	LP status groups identified	Results
Guller Wertz, Sewell, & Manni (1985)	10 years, 11 months	63	EMR	Compared the effectiveness of the Estimated Learning Potential (ELP; a score in the System of Multicultural Pluralistic Assessment [SOMPA]) and traditional WISC-R IQs in predicting the performance of EMR subjects on an LP assessment.	RPM; the duration of the training session and the interval between pretest and posttest were not specified.	Posttest RS	G, NG; method: Budoff's RPM procedure	Results showed that traditional IQs from the WISC-R correlated more highly with the nontraditional LP criterion than the nontraditional ELPS from the SOMPA. However, of the 21 G or HS identified, all had ELPs higher than the EMR cutoff of 70. Results showed that those children likely to be declassified on the basis of their ELPs were likely to demonstrate greater capability during the LP assessment than the level suggested by their traditional IQs.
Hamilton (1972); Budoff & Hamilton (1976)	12 to 22	38	Moderately and severely retarded	Compared mean scores of institutionalized retarded G and NG on the Leiter International Performance Scale, Peabody Picture Vocabulary Test (PPVT), SB, and RPM. Also compared the facility of traditional IQs vs. nontraditional LP scores in predicting ratings of adaptive behavior and the ability to retain information.	KBD; 30 minutes of training; 7 days between pretest and posttest.	Posttest and gain RS	G, NG; method: 2-point RS increase	G obtained significantly higher scores than NG on the Leiter, PPVT, SB, and RPM. Nontraditional LP posttest scores also correlated more highly with ratings of adaptive behavior and the ability to retain information than traditional IQs from the SB and PPVT.

Study	Age	N	Subjects	Description	Procedure	Design	Measures	Results
Hamilton (1972); Hamilton & Budoff (1974)	12 to 22	40	Moderately and severely retarded	Compared the efficacy of LP assessments and test practice in increasing the posttest scores of moderately and severely retarded subjects. Traditional IQs and multiple criteria were administered and correlated with performance on the LP measure.	KBD; 30 minutes of training; 7 days between pretest and posttest.	Pretest, posttest and gain RS and PC	G, NG; method: 1-point RS increase	Subjects receiving LP assessments obtained significantly higher posttest scores than subjects in the test practice condition. When LP pretest scores were controlled for, results showed that the nontraditional LP posttest was minimally related to traditional IQs from the PPVT, but was related to visual-memory scores on the Knox Cube Test. A supplementary finding showed a significant correlation between LP status and teachers' ratings of classroom gain status.
Harrison & Budoff (1972)	13 to 15	151	EMR	LP scores (pretest, gain, posttest) obtained 1 day and 1 month after training and the LP status of EMR subjects were correlated to personality factors. Criteria were the 11-, 29-, and 38-factor solutions from combined factor analyses of the Laurelton Self-Concept Scale and Bialer–Cromwell Locus of Control Scale for Children.	KBD; the duration of the training session and the interval between pretest and posttest were not specified.	Pretest, posttest and gain RS	HS, G, NG; method: not specified	LP performance correlated positively with adjustment and friendliness. Children assessed as having the highest potential during LP assessments were reported to have fewer emotional and social handicaps than other subjects in the study.
Harrison, Singer, Budoff, & Folman (1972)	12 years, 6 months to 16 years, 3 months	32	EMR	The aspirations of EMR G and NG were compared on verbal and nonverbal tasks following the experimental manipulation of task success and task failure.	KBD; one training session of unspecified duration; 7 days between pretest and posttest.	Pretest, posttest and gain RS	G, NG; method: 4-point RS increase	NG set goals that were not in accord with their previous task performances, whereas G were more realistic in their goal-setting decisions.

(continued)

APPENDIX 12.2. (*continued*)

Study	Age[a]	Sample/n[b]	Sample type	Treatment	LP instrument and duration of treatment	LP metric employed in study	LP status groups identified	Results
Hausman (1973)	8 years, 6 months to 11 years, 6 months	45	EMR Mexican-American	Compared the effectiveness of two LP instruments (KBD, RPM) and two traditional IQ tests (Primary Mental Abilities, WISC) in predicting mathematics achievement on the MAT.	KBD, RPM; one training session of unspecified duration; 1 day between pretest and posttest.	Posttest and gain RS converted to standard scores based on sample data	G, NG; method: 4-point RS increase	Results showed that both LP instruments predicted performance on the MAT mathematics criterion. Comparing the two LP instruments indicated that the RPM was a better predictor than the KBD. The findings served to question the use of traditional IQ tests alone as estimates of intellectual potential.
Huberty & Koller (1984)	12 to 15	68	Normal, hearing-impaired	High- and low-achieving hearing-impaired subjects and high- and low-achieving subjects with normal hearing were administered either LP assessments or assessments incorporating test practice. The LP and practice instrument was the RSDT. In addition, some subjects were told which of the many RSDT stencils were necessary to solve items during posttesting (input condition).	RSDT; 30 minutes of training; unspecified interval between pretest and posttest.	Pretest and posttest RS	NA	Repeated-measures ANOVAS showed that regardless of hearing ability, low-achieving subjects in the LP condition performed as well on the posttest as high achievers in the test practice condition. Input was a powerful factor. When input was given, deaf and hearing subjects performed equally well. The results demonstrated that deaf subjects can think as abstractly as their hearing counterparts when factors such as mediated instruction and inputs are equated.

Study	Age	N	Purpose	Task/Procedure	Scores	Method	Results
Koehler (1977)	6 years, 7 months to 10 years, 7 months	60	Hearing-impaired	Compared the efficacy of LP assessments and test practice in increasing the posttest scores of hearing-impaired subjects. Further consideration was directed to correlating posttest scores by condition on the Leiter, and comparing agreement between LP status and teachers' ratings of classroom gain status.	RPM; 30 to 45 minutes of training, 3 to 4 days between pretest and posttest.	Pretest and posttest standard scores	HS, G, NG; method: Budoff's RPM procedure (critical value = IQ of 100)	LP assessments and practice did not significantly increase posttest scores. For subjects in the LP condition, nontraditional posttest scores did not correlate appreciably with IQs from the Leiter. In addition, although the agreement between LP status and teacher ratings of classroom gain status was 87%, the observed agreement did not exceed the agreement rate that would be expected by chance.
Lidz, Winfrey, Starobin, & Ballester (1987)	4 years, 3 months	24	Subjects in a specialized preschool program	Compared nontraditional LP posttest vs. traditional IQs in predicting achievement on the Cooperative Preschool Inventory.	Triangles subtest of the Kaufman Assessment Battery for Children (K-ABC); 60 minutes of training; 7 days between pretest and posttest.	Posttest RS, PC	NA	Although the traditional IQ showed a significant correlation with the achievement criterion, the nontraditional LP posttest failed to do so. Similarly, when LP pretest scores were controlled for, the nontraditional LP posttest failed to correlate with the achievement criterion.
McDaniel (1983)	10 years to 14 years, 11 months	70	EMR	Compared the efficacy of LP assessments vs. test practice in increasing the posttest scores of EMR subjects. Also compared group differences on the Mathematics subtest of the Stanford Achievement Test and the Columbia Test of Mental Maturity (CTTM).	RPM; 25 hours of training; 4 weeks between pretest and posttest.	Posttest RS, PC controlling for WISC-R IQs	NA	When WISC-R IQs were controlled for, results showed that subjects in the LP condition obtained significantly higher LP posttest scores and Stanford Mathmetics scores than subjects in the practice condition. No group differences were found on the CTTM criterion.

(continued)

327

APPENDIX 12.2. (*continued*)

Study	Age[a]	Sample/n[b]	Sample type	Treatment	LP instrument and duration of treatment	LP metric employed in study	LP status groups identified	Results
Pines & Budoff (1970)	10 years, 7 months to 16 years, 7 months	27	EMR	EMR subjects in special classes were diagnosed as HS, G, and NG. Thereafter, responses to hypothetically frustrating situations were compared among the three groups.	KBD; the duration of the training session and the interval between pretest and posttest were not specified.	Pretest, post-test, and gain RS	HS, G, NG; method: not specified	HS and G responded more positively to frustration than NG. When asked to compare their capabilities to the capabilities of classmates, HS and G reported that they were equal to, or more able than, their peers. Conversely, NG perceived themselves as less able than their peers.
Platt (1977)	6 to 10	40	LD	Compared the efficacy of LP assessments and test practice in increasing the posttest scores of LD subjects. Further consideration was directed to comparing the relationship of LP scores to Reading and Mathematics achievement on the WRAT, traditional IQs on the Slosson Intelligence Test (SIT), and minutes to acquire a skill (MPS).	RPM; one training session of unspecified duration; 30 days between pretest and posttest.	Pretest, post-test, and gain RS	HS, G, NG; method: sample-specific splits	Subjects in the LP condition obtained significantly higher posttest scores than subjects in the test practice condition. Bivariate correlation. Bivariate correlations and a stepwise multiple-regression analysis showed that posttest scores for the 40 subjects in the study were essentially unrelated to performance on the WRAT, SIT, and MPS. Likewise, a multiple-discriminant analysis showed that the WRAT, SIT, and MPS were unable to differentiate among the LP status groups. The results demonstrated the cultur-

al fairness of LP assessments and suggested that LP assessments are useful for teaching LD subjects how to solve problems.

Popoff-Walker (1980, 1982)

7 to 11

60

Normal, EMR

Compared the efficacy of traditional LP pretest scores, IQ, and nontraditional assessments from the Adaptive Behavior Inventory for Children (ABIC) in predicting performance on the nontraditional LP posttest. Also compared the efficacy of LP assessments and test practice in increasing the posttest scores of normal and retarded subjects.

RPM; 90 minutes of training; 8 days between pretest and posttest.

Pretest, posttest RS, RG, and PC

NA

The traditional LP pretest was the best predictor of the nontraditional LP posttest. When the pretest score was controlled for, IQ was highly predictive, with SES and the nontraditional ABIC contributing only negligibly. An informal examination showed that EMR subjects in the LP condition made larger posttest gains than EMR subjects in the practice condition. However, rather than offsetting the initial score differences between normal and retarded subjects, ability-level comparisons showed that normal subjects in the LP condition exhibited posttest gains four times larger than the posttest gains of EMR subjects in the LP condition (6.57 and 1.57 RS points, respectively). Therefore, the results stand in contrast to expectations from the LP hypothesis. In comparison to normal

(continued)

Study	Age[a]	Sample/n[b]	Sample type	Treatment	LP instrument and duration of treatment	LP metric employed in study	LP status groups identified	Results
								subjects, the EMR subjects appeared relatively *worse off* on the LP posttest than they were initially on the traditional LP pretest.
Regan, Platt, & Banks (1974)	19 to 21	16	LD	Compared the efficacy of LP assessments and test practice in increasing the posttest scores of LD subjects. Also compared mean group differences on the Spelling subtest of the Peabody Individual Achievemen Test (PIAT) 1 day and 1 month following training.	KBD; one training session of unspecified duration; the interval between pretest and posttest was not specified.	Pretest, posttest, and gain RS	HS, G, NG; method: not specified	No significant score modifications were found on either the LP posttest or the PIAT Spelling task. A reason cited for the findings was that improvement on the posttest was made difficult by the large proportion of subjects who scored at a high level on the LP pretest.
San Miguel (1977)	Adult, age not specified	64	EMR	Compared the efficacy of LP assessments and test practice in increasing the posttest scores of mentally retarded adults who lived in residential centers and worked in sheltered workshops. Also compared the relationship of LP status and traditional WAIS IQs in predicting vocational competence and adjustment.	KBD; one training session of unspecified duration; 8 days between pretest and posttest	Pretest, posttest, and gain RS	G, NG; method: 5-point RS increase	Repeated-measures ANOVA showed that subjects in the LP condition obtained significantly higher posttest scores than subjects in the test practice condition. Neither the traditional IQ test nor LP status predicted vocational competence or adjustment.
Sewell (1974); Sewell & Severson (1974)	5 years, 10 months to 7 years, 5 months	72	General sample, including exceptional children	Compared the efficacy of traditional IQs, nontraditional LP scores, diagnostic teaching, and PA learning in predicting the Arithmetic and Word Reading subtests of the Stanford Achievement Test. Tradi-	RPM; 30 minutes of training; 1 day before pretest and posttest.	Pretest, posttest, and gain RS	NA	Factor analyses showed that traditional WISC IQs and nontraditional LP scores were highly interrelated. In general, traditional WISC IQs predicted achievement as well as the three LP

Study	Age	N	Sample	Procedure	Measures	Results
				from the administration of seven WISC subtests.		posttest). PA learning related very little to achievement, and diagnostic teaching was a better predictor of achievement than either IQs or LP scores.
Sewell (1979)	6 to 7	70	General sample, including exceptional children	Replicated and extended the Sewell & Severson (1974) study by comparing the efficacy of traditional SB IQs, traditional LP pretest scores, and nontraditional LP posttest scores in predicting the achievement of black and white subjects. Achievement criteria were the Reading, Language, and Total Battery scores from the California Achievement Test (CAT).	RPM; 30 minutes of training; 1 day between pretest and posttest.	NA	Stepwise multiple-regression analyses showed that the nontraditional LP posttest was the best predictor of achievement for both white and blacks. Although traditional IQs from SB enhanced estimation on the CAT Total Battery criterion for whites, they failed to do so for blacks. The nontraditional LP posttest was the only variable that contributed significantly to the multiple correlation for blacks. Consequently, the results indicated that the nontraditional LP posttest was a better predictor of achievement for blacks than IQs from the SB.
Taylor (1983)	8 years, 0 months to 8 years, 11 months	126	Project Follow Through children	Compared the LP performance of subjects who participated in Project Follow Through vs. those of matched control subjects who did not participate in the program.	RPM; 30 minutes of training; 6 to 7 days between pretest and posttest.	Posttest and gain RS, RG	No significant differences were found between the Follow Through and non-Follow Through groups on either the traditional LP pretest or the nontraditional LP posttest. Likewise, no group differences were found on either the LP RS or RG scores.

(continued)

APPENDIX 12.2. (*continued*)

Study	Age[a]	Sample/n[b]	Sample type	Treatment	LP instrument and duration of treatment	LP metric employed in study	LP status groups identified	Results
Thomas, Hoopes, & Lidz (1987)	Preschool, age not specified	60	Head Start children	Compared the efficacy of LP assessments vs. coaching in increasing the posttest scores of Head Start children referred for special education services. Also compared mean differences among high-, medium-, and low-LP gainers on the California Preschool Social Competency Scale (CPSCS).	K-ABC Traingles; 60 minutes of training; 7 days between pretest and posttest.	Gain RS, PC	High- to low-LP subjects; method: not specified	When LP pretest scores were controlled for, subjects in the LP condition obtained significantly higher posttest scores than subjects in the coaching condition. Comparisons conducted within the LP condition showed that subjects with higher gain scores were better adjusted on the CPSCS than subjects with medium and low gain scores.
Williams (1980)	3 to 13	53	Normal, orthopedically handicapped (OH)	Examined whether LP methodology would increase the posttest scores of OH subjects residing in a state institution and OH subjects in local school programs. A third group was composed of normal subjects attending first and second grade. Two criteria were also administered: the CMMS and teacher ratings of the ability to learn a new task.	Modified RPM (KBD given to subjects with low RPM scores); one training session of unspecified duration; 9 to 116 days between pretest and posttest.	Pretest, posttest, and gain RS, and error score	NA	Significant posttest gains were found for normal subjects and OH subjects attending local school programs, but not for the institutionalized OH subjects. Similarly, the non-traditional LP posttest correlated significantly with the CMMS for normal subjects and OH subjects attending local school programs, but not for the institutionalized OH subjects. On the other hand, the LP posttest correlated significantly with the teacher-rated criterion only for

Study	N	Sample	Description	Measure	Scores	Results
						the institutionalized OH subjects. Results indicated that LP assessments are feasible for OH subjects attending local school programs. However, they may be of little use for assessments conducted with institutionalized OH subjects.
Wolf (1985)	31	LD	LD subjects were administered LP assessments and were classified as HS, G, and NG. Thereafter, subjects were given 20 minutes of tutoring for 11 days. Tutoring emphasized the use of a strategy sequence for solving mathematics word problems. The dependent variable was a composite score from a series of domain-referenced mathematics worksheets.	RPM; 60 minutes of training; unspecified interval between pretest and posttest.	Pretest, posttest, and gain RS	HS, G, NG; method: Budoff's RPM procedure (critical value = 50th percentile)	The small number of gainers from the LP assessment ($n = 4$) resulted in G and HS being collapsed into one group. Preliminary analyses revealed that the traditional IQs of the two remaining groups differed significantly. Score improvements during the 11-day intervention showed that tutoring was effective in elevating mathematics performance. Nevertheless, when group differences in WISC IQs were controlled for, no difference was found between higher-LP subjects (high HS, G) & lower-LP subjects (NG) on the mathematics criterion.

[a]Ages in years for studies reporting grade levels only are based on the assumption that most first-graders are 6 years old, most

[b]Sample size is based on the sample employed for the LP analyses and disregards analyses based on other sample subsets.

APPENDIX 12.3. REVIEW AND ANALYSIS OF CITED LEARNING POTENTIAL RESEARCH

Study	Utility of LP critical value in diagnosing LP status	Floor or ceiling effect[a] on LP tests	Interaction of ability and LP assessment	Control group (practice or coaching)	Examined LP validity on external criteria	Examined LP validity on achievement criteria	Comments
Babad (1977)	?	?	−	−	+	+	On the majority of criteria (three out of four), results were *contrary* to the LP hypothesis: High-LP-status subjects either performed no better or slightly worse than subjects of low status.
Babad & Bashi (1977)		+	+	−	−	−	
Babad & Budoff (1974, Study 1)		+	+	+	−	−	
Babad & Budoff (1974, Study 2)		+	+	−	+	+	Results indicate that for average and subnormal subjects, the nontraditional LP measure was a better predictor of achievement than was IQ. However, the placement of subjects into homogeneous IQ groups (average, dull-average, subnormal) attenuated the range of IQ test scores (relative to LP scores) associated with the achievement criteria. The direct placement of subjects into homogeneous IQ groups is referred to as "explicit selection." Gulliksen (1950, p. 146) demonstrated that whenever a test is used to explicitly assign subjects into groups (such as with the traditional IQ test in this study), it is relatively easy to try out another test (e.g., an LP measure) and discover that the other test correlates more highly with a criterion. Therefore, the higher criterion validity reported for LP scores is misleading as a consequence of explicit selection on the IQ test. Not surprisingly, when the negative effects of explicit selection were removed (see Babad & Budoff, 1974, Table 2), results for the total sample showed that traditional IQs provided slightly *better* predictions than the nontraditional LP measure (r's = .56 and .54, respectively). Furthermore, inasmuch as the LP assessment requires more time to complete than the traditional IQ test, results from this study show that IQ actually was the more *practical* predictor of achievement.

Study						
Bailey (1979, 1981)	+	+	+	+	+	Subjects under the coaching condition received more practice (10 sessions) than subjects in the LP condition received mediated learning experiences (1 session). Thus, the duration of treatment across conditions was largely inequitable.
Bardsley (1980)	+	?	−	+	+	The nontraditional LP posttest correlated more highly with the mathematics criterion than did IQs from the Wechsler Intelligence Scale for Children–Revised (WISC-R). The meaningfulness of this higher correlation for the nontraditional LP posttest is unclear, given that the learning-disabled (LD) subjects were identified, in part, on the basis of their IQ test scores. Thus, explicit selection becomes a validity threat. (For a more detailed analysis of this concern, see text and comments above for Babad & Budoff, 1974, Study 2.)
Bergman (1980)	?	?	−	+	−	No differences were found between LP gainers and nongainers on seven of the eight external criteria. Furthermore, despite a possible ceiling for normal subjects on the LP measure, their pretest–posttest gain was comparable to that of the educable mentally retarded (EMR) gainers (12.6 to 14.8 and 4.1 to 6.9 raw-score points, respectively; maximum Kohs Block Designs [KBD] score = 16).
Bertumen (1978)	?	?	+	−	−	The validity of the LP assessment condition over the test practice condition was not compared on the external criteria. Rather, scores from both conditions were pooled and thereafter correlated with the criteria. Hence, it is impossible to determine whether obtained validity coefficients were due to practice elements, LP elements, or a combination thereof.

(continued)

335

APPENDIX 12.3. (*continued*)

Study	Utility of LP critical value in diagnosing LP status	Floor or ceiling effect[a] on LP tests	Interaction of ability and LP assessment	Control group (practice or coaching)	Examined LP validity on external criteria	Examined LP validity on achievement criteria	Comments
Budoff (1967)	?	?	−	−	+	−	High scorers and gainers were collapsed into one group. The performance of that group was compared to that of nongainers on several external criteria. This comparison, however, makes it impossible to determine whether criteria differences were due to traditional IQ (the *high scorers* in the collapsed group) or to the ability to profit from mediated instruction (the *gainers* in the collapsed group).
Budoff (1968)	?	?	−	−	+	−	As in the Budoff (1967) study, high scorers and gainers were combined in a single group, and the group's performance was compared to that of nongainers on several external criteria. Once again, the merger of high scorers and gainers makes it impossible to tell whether improvement on the criteria for the merged group was as a function of IQ or of better LP. Moreover, empirical support was present for the inference that criteria differences were, in fact, due to traditional IQ: The merged group had significantly higher traditional (pretest) IQs than the nongainer group, $t(43) = 2.4$, $p < .05$.
Budoff & Corman (1974)	?	?	−	−	+	−	When the unique contribution of the LP pretest was considered, the partial correlation of the nontraditional LP posttest averaged .0275 on the WISC, Standord-Binet (SB), and Raven Progressive Matrices (RPM) criteria. Therefore, the relative contribution of the nontraditional LP posttest was merely 2.75% greater than that provided by the traditional LP pretest.
Budoff & Corman (1976)	?	?	+	+	−	−	

Study						Description
Budoff, Corman, & Gimon (1974)	+	+	−	+	+	Although stepwise multiple-regression analyses showed that nontraditional LP posttest scores were related (and traditional WISC Performance IQs [PIQs] were not) to the nonverbal-symbolic criterion for academic achievement, neither the nontraditional LP posttest nor WISC PIQ predicted performance on the three other criteria. In addition, although the WISC Full Scale IQ (FSIQ) and Verbal IQ (VIQ) were obtained for the subjects, neither was used as a predictor. It therefore appears unresolved as to whether nontraditional LP or traditional WISC IQs are the better predictors of achievement.
Budoff & Friedman (1964)	−	−	+	−	?	EMR subjects with higher traditional IQs showed larger gains on the nontraditional LP posttest than did EMR subjects with lower IQs (approximately 3.25 vs. 2.5 raw-score points, respectively). Similar findings were reported for the second posttest obtained 1 month after training. Such results are contrary to expectations from the LP hypothesis. In comparison to higher-IQ subjects, subjects with lower IQs appeared *relatively* worse off on the LP posttest than they were initially on the traditional LP pretest. Also, the findings concur with the Animal House (AH) analyses presented earlier in this chapter and suggest the IQ is the principal determinant of the gain subjects display in LP assessments.
Budoff, Gimon, & Corman (1974)	+	+	−	+	−	The authors report that the Series Learning Potential Test (SLPT) may not be useful with children older than 9 years of age because of *de facto* score ceilings. The results indicated that the LP posttest was a better predictor of achievement than the WISC Vocabulary subtest. However, entries in Table 3 of this study indicate that the WISC PIQ may be an equally good or better predictor.

(continued)

337

APPENDIX 12.3. (*continued*)

Study	Utility of LP critical value in diagnosing LP status	Floor or ceiling effect[a] on LP tests	Interaction of ability and LP assessment	Control group (practice or coaching)	Examined LP validity on external criteria	Examined LP validity on achievement criteria	Comments
Budoff & Gottlieb (1976)	?	?	–	–	+	+	Reported differences between LP gainers and nongainers on academic, motivational, and cognitive style criteria may be misleading. It appears that high scorers and gainers were merged into one group and that criterion contrasts were made between the merged group and nongainers. (For a more detailed analysis of this concern, see comments above for Budoff, 1967 and 1968.)
Budoff & Meskin (1970); Budoff, Meskin, & Harrison (1971)	?	?	+	–	+	+	Multivariate analysis of variance (MANOVA) results showed that both normal and EMR high scorers obtained higher achievement scores than did their counterpart gainers, who in turn out performed nongainers in their respective groups. The MANOVA retained cells of unequal size, and some cells with minimum or inadequate membership (four cells contained only two subjects and one contained one subject). For samples of unequal size, violations of equal variance dispersion can have a marked effect on tests of statistical significance. The impact of violations on reported significance levels can be either positive or negative. For example, based on a cursory test for significance of variance heterogeneity on one of the four major dependent variables employed by investigators (simple circuits), we found that the variance dispersion was inequitable, $F_{max}(12.4) = 58.54$, $p < .05$. It therefore appears that results from this study are uninterpretable.
Budoff & Pagell (1966)	?	?	+	–	+	–	On the two external criteria employed, normal subjects outperformed EMR gainers and nongainers.
Burns (1984, 1987)	?	?	–	+	+	–	

Study						Notes
Burns, Vye, Bransford, Delclos, & Ogan (1987)	?	−	−	+	−	The nontraditional LP posttest showed little to no association with traditional IQs from the McCarthy Perceptual–Performance scale. This could be due to explicit selection on the IQ test. (For a more detailed analysis of this concern, see text and comments above for Babad & Budoff, 1974, Study 2.) However, other results give support to the LP hypothesis.
Corman & Budoff (1973)	?	+	+	+	+	Based on data from the multiple reliability and validity studies presented here, the authors conclude that "because of the ceiling on Series Test (SLTP) scores, and because of the relationship of Series scores to race and social class, the Series Test appears to be a less useful measure of learning potential than either the Kohs Block Designs or Raven Progressive Matrices" (p. 14).
Delclos (1984)	?	−	−	−	−	Nongainers made more errors than gainers on "solid" stencil items in the LP measure (Representational Stencil Design Test [RSDT]), and were more likely to order stencil cutouts incorrectly. However, these cannot be regarded as remarkable phenomena, inasmuch as nongainers had to make a larger number of errors on the *total* test simply to qualify as nongainers. Thus, it would have been useful to determine whether nongainers and gainers erred differently on particular item types *after* group difference in mean performance were controlled and considered. This might have been accomplished by ascertaining whether the rank order of item difficulties differed significantly across gainers and nongainers.
Folman & Budoff (1971)	?	?	+	+	−	
Glutting & McDermott (1987)	+	+	+	+	+	When pretest scores were considered, results indicated that LP assessments were not more effective in elevating test scores than coaching or test practice. Moreover, no differences were discovered among the nine LP status groups for either standardized or teacher-rated achievement criteria.

(continued)

APPENDIX 12.3. (*continued*)

Study	Utility of LP critical value in diagnosing LP status	Floor or ceiling effect[a] on LP tests	Interaction of ability and LP assessment	Control group (practice or coaching)	Examined LP validity on external criteria	Examined LP validity on achievement criteria	Comments
Glutting, McDermott, & Burnett (1987)		+	+	–	+	+	Hierarchical-regression results showed that the predictive efficiency of the nontraditional LP posttest (relative to that afforded by the traditional LP pretest) was negligible across four criteria of academic achievement.
Guller Wurtz, Sewell & Manni (1985)	?	+	–	–	+	+	EMR gainers and high scorers were more likely to obtain Estimated Learning Potentials (ELPs; a score in the System of Multicultural Pluralistic Assessment) above the EMR cutoff of 70. The results also showed, however, that traditional IQs from the WISC-R correlated more highly with the LP posttest criterion than did nontraditional ELP scores. In addition, rather than reducing mean-score "bias" between whites and blacks, it was apparent that white EMR subjects made larger gains than black EMR subjects (6.2 vs. 5.6 raw-score points, respectively). Thus, contrary to the LP hypothesis, results indicate that more white than black EMR subjects would be declassified during LP assessments.
Hamilton (1972); Budoff & Hamilton (1976)	?	–	–	–	+	–	Higher criteria correlations are reported for non-traditional LP scores over traditional IQs. The meaningfulness of this result is unclear, given the explicit selection of subjects on the basis of IQ. (For a more detailed analysis of this concern, see text and comments above for Babad & Budoff 1974, Study 2.)

Study							Description
Hamilton (1972); Hamilton & Budoff (1974)	?	−	−	−	+	+	−	Higher criterion correlations are reported for nontraditional LP scores than traditional IQs. However, explicit selection of subjects on IQ reduces the interpretability of results. (For a more detailed analysis of this concern, see text and comments above for Babad & Budoff, 1974, Study 2.) Notwithstanding this problem, subjects having higher traditional IQs showed larger gains on the LP posttest. Thus, contrary to what would be expected from the LP hypothesis, lower-IQ subjects were relatively worse off on the LP posttest than they were initially on the traditional LP pretest. This finding concurs with the AH analyses presented earlier in this chapter and suggests that IQ is a principal determinant of the gain subjects show in LP assessments.
Harrison & Budoff (1972)	?	−	−	−	+	+	−	LP scores and LP status were correlated with personality dimensions derived from 11-, 29-, and 38-factor solutions for the Laurelton Self-Concept Scale and Bialer–Cromwell Locus of Control Scale for Children. A total of 312 predictor–criterion correlations were possible, given the four LP predictors (LP pretest, posttest, gain score, and LP status) and 78 criteria (11-, 29-, and 38-factor solutions). In such an instance, approximately 16 statistically significant associations could be expected by chance. Findings show that 18 correlations were statistically significant. Thus, most of the significant correlations could be chance results, and it is very difficult to separate out the chance effects from real associations.
Harrison, Singer, Budoff, & Folman (1972)	?	−	−	−	+	+	−	EMR gainers and nongainers differed in IQ. Although the IQ difference was not statistically significant, the trend was in this direction ($p < .07$). Thus, observed differences in goal setting between gainers and nongainers may have been due to IQ.

(continued)

APPENDIX 12.3. (*continued*)

Study	Utility of LP critical value in diagnosing LP status	Floor or ceiling effect[a] on LP tests	Interaction of ability and LP assessment	Control group (practice or coaching)	Examined LP validity on external criteria	Examined LP validity on achievement criteria	Comments
Hausman (1973)	?	?	–	–	+	+	Higher criteria correlations are reported for nontraditional LP posttest scores relative to traditional IQ posttest scores. The meaningfulness of this finding is misleading as a consequence of explicit selection of subjects on IQ. (For a more detailed analysis of this concern, see Babad & Budoff, 1974, Study 2.) Moreover, when the effects of IQ were considered, the two *combined* LP posttests (RPM, KBD) incremented criterion estimation only minimally (less than 10%).
Huberty & Koller (1984)	?	+	+	+	–	–	
Koehler (1977)	?	+	?	+	+	–	
Lidz, Winfrey, Starobin, & Ballester (1987)	?	?	?	–	+	+	Higher criteria correlations are reported for IQ test scores over nontraditional LP posttest scores. Findings might have been even more favorable for the traditional IQ test if subjects had not been selected, in part, on IQ. (For a more detailed analysis of this concern, see text and comments above for Babad & Budoff, 1974, Study 2.)
McDaniel (1983)		+	–	+	+	+	
Pines & Budoff (1970)	?	?	–	–	+	–	
Platt (1977)	?	+	?	+	+	+	Criterion validity of the traditional IQ test was not compared directly to that of the nontraditional LP posttest. Rather, posttest scores from the LP and test practice conditions were pooled, and thereafter correlated with the external criteria. Hence, the observed superiority of the posttest in predicting criteria is confounded by whether findings are attributable to practice elements, LP

elements, or combinations thereof. The interpretation of these higher criteria correlations may be misleading for another reason: Explicit selection occurred when the LD subjects were identified, in part, according to their IQ results. (For a more detailed analysis of this concern, see text and comments above for Babad and Budoff, 1974, Study 2.)

Rather than offsetting initial score differences between normal and retarded subjects, ability-level comparisons showed that normal subjects in the LP condition exhibited posttest gains four times larger than those of counterpart EMR subjects (6.57 vs. 1.57 raw-score points, respectively). These results stand in contrast to expectations from the LP hypothesis. In comparison to normal subjects, the EMR subjects appeared relatively worse off on the LP posttest than they were initially on the traditional LP pretest. Furthermore, the findings concur with the AH analyses presented earlier in this chapter and suggest that IQ is the principal determinant of the gain subjects show in LP assessments.

Equally low criteria correlations are reported for the IQ test and LP posttest. Results might have been more favorable for the IQ test if subjects had not been selected on IQ. (For a more detailed analysis of this concern, see text and comments above for Babad & Budoff, 1974, Study 2.)

Study						
Popoff-Walker (1980, 1982)	+	+	+	+	−	
Regan, Platt, & Banks (1974)	−	?	−	+	?	
San Miguel (1977)	+	−	+	+	−	
Sewell (1974); Sewell & Severson (1974)	+	+	−	+	+	
Sewell (1979)	+	+	−	+	+	

(continued)

APPENDIX 12.3. (continued)

Study	Utility of LP critical value in diagnosing LP status	Floor or ceiling effect[a] on LP tests	Interaction of ability and LP assessment	Control group (practice or coaching)	Examined LP validity on external criteria	Examined LP validity on achievement criteria	Comments
Taylor (1983)		+	?	−	−	−	No significant LP pretest or posttest differences were found between subjects who participated in Project Follow Through and matched control subjects who did not participate in the intervention program.
Thomas, Hoopes, & Lidz (1987)	?	−	−	+	+	−	When LP pretest scores were considered, subjects in the LP condition obtained significantly higher posttest scores than subjects in the coaching condition. Comparisons on the adaptive behavior criterion were limited to contrasts within the LP condition (high vs. medium vs. low LP gainers). Criterion contrasts were not conducted between the LP and coaching conditions.
Williams (1980)		+	+	−	+	−	Normal subjects gained more on the nontraditional LP posttest than orthopedically handicapped (OH) subjects attending local school programs, who in turn outperformed institutionalized OH subjects. Although IQs were not reported for normal subjects, OH subjects attending local school programs had higher IQs than institutionalized OH subjects (68.5 vs. 35.6, respectively). It therefore appears that higher-IQ subjects made larger gains on the LP posttest than subjects with lower IQs. Thus, relative to their pretest standings, lower-IQ subjects were relatively worse off on the nontraditional LP posttest. This finding concurs with the AH analyses presented earlier in this chapter and suggests that IQ is the principal determinant of the gain subjects show in LP assessments.
Wolf (1985)	?	?	−	−	+	+	Higher-LP subjects (high scorers, gainers) performed no better than lower-LP subjects (nongainers) on the domain-referenced mathematics criterion when group differences in IQ were considered.

Note. A minus sign indicates a definite weakenss; a plus sign indicates that the validity concern was addressed sufficiently; a question mark indicates a potential source of concern; and a blank indicates that the factor was not relevant.

[a]Question marks have been given whenever the information in a given study was insufficient for a clear determination of a floor orceiling effect. Examples of such an occurrence include studies where means and standard deviations were not provided for the LP pretest and LP posttest.

Acknowledgments. We gratefully acknowledge the helpful comments offered by Andrew R. Baggaley, Thomas Oakland, Herman H. Spitz, and Julian C. Stanley on an earlier draft of this chapter.

REFERENCES

Allen, M. J., & Yen, W. M. (1979). *Introduction to measurement theory*. Monterey, CA: Brooks/Cole.

American Psychological Association. (1985). *Standards for educational and psychological testing*. Washington, DC: Author.

Anastasi, A. (1981). Coaching, test sophistication, and developed abilities. *American Psychologist, 36,* 1086–1092.

Arter, J. A., & Jenkins, J. R. (1977). Examining the benefits prevalence of modality considerations in special education. *Journal of Special Education, 11,* 281–298.

Babad, E. Y. (1977). Pygmalion in reverse. *Journal of Special Education, 11,* 81–90.

Babad, E. Y., & Bashi, J. (1977). Age and coaching effects on the reasoning performance of disadvantaged and advantaged Israeli children. *Journal of Social Psychology, 103,* 169–176.

Babad, E. Y., & Budoff, M. (1974). Sensitivity and validity of learning-potential measurement in three levels of ability. *Journal of Educational Psychology, 66,* 439–447.

Bailey, D. B. (1979). A comparison of non-biased screening procedures to identify high-risk kindergarten children (Doctoral dissertation, University of Washington, 1979). *Dissertation Abstracts International, 40,* 3226A.

Bailey, D. B. (1981). Investigation of learning measures as screening procedures with kindergartners. *Psychology in the Schools, 18,* 489–495.

Bardsley, J. R. (1980). An exploration of learning potential assessment with learning disabled students (Doctoral dissertation, University of Oregon, 1979). *Dissertation Abstracts International, 40,* 6226A.

Bergman, M. M. (1980). The ability to learn in mentally retarded persons: An exploration of learning potential and intellectual potential (Doctoral dissertation, Temple University, 1980). *Dissertation Abstracts International, 41,* 1902A.

Bertumen, D. C. (1978). An investigation of the applicability of the Raven learning potential assessment procedure to first and second grade Filipino children and its relationship to other nonverbal measures (Doctoral dissertation, University of Kansas, 1977). *Dissertation Abstracts International, 38,* 7266A–7267A.

Budoff, M. (1967). Learning potential among institutionalized young adult retardates. *American Journal of Mental Deficiency, 72,* 404–411.

Budoff, M. (1968). Learning potential as a supplementary assessment procedure. In J. Helmuth (Ed.), *Learning disorders* (Vol. 3, pp. 295–343). Seattle, WA: Special Child.

Budoff, M. (1969). Learning potential: A supplemental procedure for assessing the ability to reason. *Seminars in Psychiatry, 1,* 278–290.

Budoff, M. (1970). Learning potential: Assessing ability to reason in the educable mentally retarded. *Acta Paedopsychiatrica, 37,* 293–309.

Budoff, M. (1972). Providing special education without special classes. *Journal of School Psychology, 10,* 199–205.

Budoff, M. (1975a). *Learning Potential Test Using Raven Progressive Matrices*. (Available from Research Institute for Educational Problems, 29 Ware Street, Cambridge, MA 02139)

Budoff, M. (1975b). Measuring learning potential: An alternative to the traditional intelligence test. In G. R. Gredler (Ed.), *Ethical and legal factors in the practice of school psychology: Proceedings of the First Annual Conference in School Psychology* (pp. 75–89). Philadelphia: Temple University Press.

Budoff, M. (1987). The validity of learning postential assessment. In C. S. Lidz (Ed.), *Dynamic assessment: An interactional approach to evaluating learning potential* (pp. 52–81). New York: Guilford Press.

Budoff, M., & Corman, L. (1974). Demographic and psychometric factors related to improved performance on the Kohs learning-potential procedure. *American Journal of Mental Deficiency, 78,* 578–585.

Budoff, M., & Corman, L. (1976). Effectivness of a learning potential procedure in improving problem-solving skills of retarded and nonretarded children. *American Journal of Mental Deficiency, 81,* 260–264.

Budoff, M., Corman, L., & Gimon, A. (1974). *An educational test of learning potential assessment with Spanish-speaking youth*. (Available from Research Institute for Learning Problems, 29 Ware Street, Cambridge, MA 02139)

Budoff, M., & Friedman, M. (1964). "Learning potential" as an assessment approach to the adolescent mentally retarded. *Journal of Consulting Psychology, 28,* 434–439.

Budoff, M., Gimon, A., & Corman, L. (1974). *Learning potential measurement with Spanish-speaking youth as an alternative to IQ tests: A first report*. (Available from Research Institute for Learning Problems, 29 Ware Street, Cambridge, MA 02139)

Budoff, M., & Gottlieb, J. (1976). Special-class EMR children mainstreamed: A study of an aptitude (learning potential) × treatment interaction. *American Journal of Mental Deficiency, 81,* 1–11.

Budoff, M., & Hamilton, J. L. (1976). Optimizing test performance of moderately and severely mentally retarded adolescents and adults. *American Journal of Mental Deficiency, 81,* 49–57.

Budoff, M., & Meskin, J. (1970). *An educational test of the learning potential hypothesis with adolescent mentally retarded special class children*. (Available from Research Institute for Educational Problems, 29 Ware Street, Cambridge, MA 02139)

Budoff, M., Meskin, J., & Harrison, R. H. (1971). Educational test of the learning-potential hypothesis. *American Journal of Mental Deficiency, 76,* 159–169.

Budoff, M., & Pagell, W. (1968). Learning potential and rigidity in the adolescent retarded. *Journal of Abnormal Psychology, 73,* 479–486.

Burns, M. S. (1984). Comparison of "graduated prompt" and "mediational" dynamic assessment and static assessment with young children (Doctoral dissertation, George Peabody College for Teachers, Vanderbilt University, 1983). *Dissertation Abstracts International, 45,* 4409A.

Burns, M. S. (1987). *Instruction in "graduated prompt" and "mediational" dynamic assessment with young children*. Manuscript submitted for publication.

Burns, M. S., Vye, N. J., Bransford, J. D., Delclos, V. R., & Ogan, T. A. (1987). *Alernative assessments of handicapped children: A series of technical reports and working papers* (Report No. 8). Nashville, TN: John F. Kennedy Center for Research on Education and Human Development, Vanderbilt University.

Campbell, D. T., & Stanley, J. C. (1963). *Experimental and quasi-experimental designs for research*. Boston: Houghton Mifflin.

Comfort, M. (1984). *The effects of a thinking skills curriculum on learning ability and achievement of second grade students*. Unpublished doctoral dissertation, Oklahoma State University.

Conger, A. J., Conger, J. C., Farrell, A. D., & Ward, D. (1979). What can the WISC-R measure? *Applied Psychological Measurement, 3,* 421–436.

Cook, T. D., & Campbell, D. T. (1979). *Quasi-experimentation: Design and analysis issues for field settings*. Boston: Houghton Mifflin.

Corman, L., & Budoff, M. (1973). *The Series Test as a measure of learning potential*. (Available from Research Institute for Learning Problems, 29 Ware Street, Cambridge, MA 02139)

Crano, W. D., Denny, D. A., & Campbell, D. T. (1972). Does intelligence cause achievement? A cross-lagged panel analysis. *Journal of Educational Psychology, 63,* 258–275.

Cronbach, L. J., & Furby, L. (1970). How should we measure "change"—or should we? *Psychological Bulletin, 74,* 68–80.

Delclos, V. R. (1984). Differential error analysis in the group administration of the representational stencil design test. (Doctoral dissertation, George Peabody College for Teachers, Vanderbilt University). *Dissertation Abstracts International, 44,* 3188B–3189B.

DerSimonian, R., & Laird, N. M. (1983). Evaluating effects of coaching on SAT scores: A meta-analysis. *Harvard Educational Review, 53,* 1–15.

Feuerstein, R., Rand, Y., & Hoffman, M. B. (1979). *The dynamic assessment of retarded performers: The Learning Potential Assessment Device, theory, instruments, and techniques*. Baltimore: University Park Press.

Feuerstein, R., Rand, Y., Hoffman, M., Hoffman, M., & Miller, R. (1979). Cognitive modifiability in retarded adolescents: Effects of instrumental enrichment. *American Journal of Mental Deficiency, 83,* 539–550.

Feuerstein, R., Rand, Y., Hoffman, M. B., & Miller, R. (1980). *Instrumental Enrichment: An intervention program for cognitive modifiability*. Baltimore: University Park Press.

Folman, R., & Budoff, M. (1971). Learning potential and vocational aspirations of retarded adolescents. *Exceptional Children, 38,* 121–130.

Glutting, J. J., & McDermott, P. A. (1987). *Misguided learning evaluations: Comparative utility of learning potential assessments vs. test practice* (Tech. Rep.). Newark: University of Delaware, Department of Educational Studies.

Glutting, J. J., McDermott, P. A., & Burnett, T. R. (1987). *Comparative function of three nontraditional assessment procedures in predicting achievement* (Tech. Rep.). Newark: University of Delaware, Department of Educational Studies.

Guller Wurtz, R., Sewell, T., & Manni, J. L. (1985). The relationship of estimated learning potential to performance on a learning task and achievement. *Psychology in the Schools, 22,* 293–302.

Gulliksen, H. (1950). *Theory of mental tests*. New York: Wiley.

Hamilton, J. L. (1972). *Application of the learning potential paradigm to severely mentally retarded adolescents*. Unpublished doctoral dissertation, University of Missouri.

Hamilton, J. L., & Budoff, M. (1974). Learning potential among the moderately and severely mentally retarded. *Mental Retardation, 12,* 33–36.

Hammill, D. D., & Larsen, S. C. (1974). The effectiveness of psycholinguistic training. *Exceptional Children, 41,* 5–14.

Harrison, R. H., & Budoff, M. (1972). Demographic, historical, and ability correlates of the Laurelton Self-Concept Scale in an EMR sample. *American Journal of Mental Deficiency, 76,* 460–480.

Harrison, R. H., Singer, J., Budoff, M., & Folman, R. (1972). Level of aspiration as a function of the learning-potential status in the educable mentally retarded. *Psychological Reports, 30,* 47–57.

Hausman, R. M. (1973). Efficacy of three learning potential assessment procedures with Mexican-American educable mentally retarded children (Doctoral dissertation, George Peabody College for Teachers, Vanderbilt University, 1972). *Dissertation Abstracts International, 33,* 3438A.

Haywood, H. C., & Arbitman-Smith, R. (1981). Modification of cognitive functions in slow-learning adolescents. In P. Mittler (Ed.), *Frontiers of knowledge in mental retardation: Vol. 1. Social, educational, and behavioral aspects* (pp. 129–140). New York: Holt, Rinehart & Winston.

Hopkins, K. D., & Stanley, J. C. (1981). *Educational and psychological measurement and evaluation* (6th ed.). Englewood Cliffs, NJ: Prentice-Hall.

Huberty, T. J., & Koller, J. R. (1984). A test of the learning potential hypothesis with hearing and deaf students. *Journal of Educational Research, 78,* 22–28.

Jensen, A. R. (1980). *Bias in mental testing*. New York: Free Press.

Katz, M. A., & Buchholz, E. S. (1984). Use of the LPAD for cognitive enrichment of a deaf child. *School Psychology Review, 13,* 99–106.

Kavale, K. A., & Forness, S. R. (1984). A meta-analysis of the validity of Wechsler scale profiles and recategorizations: Patterns or parodies? *Learning Disability Quarterly, 7,* 136–156.

Keppel, G. (1973). *Design and analysis: A researcher's handbook*. Englewood Cliff, NJ: Prentice-Hall.

Koehler, L. J. (1978). Learning-potential assessment of a hearing-impaired population (Doctoral dissertation, University of Kansas, 1977). *Dissertation Abstracts International, 38,* 7271A.

Kohs, S. C. (1923). *Intelligence measurement*. New York: Macmillan.

Kramer, J. J., Henning-Stout, M., & Schellenberg, R. P. (1987). The variability of scatter analysis on the WISC-R and SBIS: Examining a vestige. *Journal of Psychoeducational Assessment, 5,* 37–47.

Kulik, J. A., Kulik, C. C., & Bangert, R. L. (1984). Effects of practice on aptitude and achievement test scores. *American Educational Research Journal*, *21*, 435–477.

Larry P. v. Riles, No. C-71-2270 (N.D. Cal. 1986).

Lidz, C. S., Winfrey, A., Starobin, H. S., & Ballester, L. E. (1987). *The Preschool Learning Potential Assessment Device: A concurrent and predictive validity study*. Manuscript submitted for publication.

Linn, R. L., & Slinde, J. A. (1977). The determination of the significance of change between pre- and posttesting periods. *Review of Educational Research*, *47*, 121–150.

McDaniel, A. (1983). Learning potential assessment in educable mentally retarded students (Doctoral dissertation, Georgia State University, 1982). *Dissertation Abstracts International*, *43*, 3272A.

McDermott, P. A., & Watkins, M. W. (1985). *Microcomputer systems manual for McDermott Multidimensional Assessment of Children*. New York: Psychological Corporation.

Pines, A., & Budoff, M. (1970). *Studies in personality correlates of learning potential status in adolescent EMRs: Reactions to frustration and self–peer evaluation*. (Available from Research Institute for Educational Problems, 29 Ware Street, Cambridge, MA 02139)

Platt, J. S. (1977). The effect of the modified Raven Progressive Matrices learning potential coaching procedure on Raven's post-test scores and their correlation value with predictive variables of learning disabilities (Doctoral dissertation, University of Kansas, 1976). *Dissertation Abstracts International*, *38*, 731A–732A.

Popoff-Walker, L. E. (1980). The relationship between IQ, SES, adaptive behavior, and performance on a measure of learning potential (Doctoral dissertation, Fordham University, 1980. *Dissertation Abstracts International*, *40*, 5797A–5798A.

Popoff-Walker, L. E. (1982). IQ, SES, adaptive behavior, and performance on a learning potential measure. *Journal of School Psychology*, *20*, 222–231.

Rand, Y., Mintzker, Y., Miller, R., Hoffman, M. B., & Friedlender, Y. (1981). The Instrumental Enrichment program: Immediate and long-term effects. In P. Mittler (Ed.), *Frontiers of knowledge in mental retardation: Vol. 1. Social, educational, and behavioral aspects* (pp. 141–152). New York: Holt, Rinehart & Winston.

Rand, Y., Tannenbaum, A. J., & Feuerstein, R. (1979). Effects of instrumental enrichment on the psychoeducational development of low-functioning adolescents. *Journal of Educational Psychology*, *71*, 751–763.

Raven, J. C. (1958). *Standard Progressive Matrices, sets A, B, C, D, and E*. London: H. K. Lewis.

Regan, M., Platt, J. S., & Brook, M. W. (1974). *The screening and transfer of the learning potential coaching approach for an adult learning disabled population*. Unpublished manuscript, University of Kansas.

Sachideva, D. (1973). Estimating strength of relationship in multivariate analysis of variance. *Educational and Psychological Measurement*, *33*, 627–631.

San Miguel, C. L. (1977). Learning potential approaches to the mentally retarded (Doctoral dissertation, University of Houston, 1976). *Dissertation Abstracts International*, *31*, 378B–379B.

Scruggs, T. E., White, K. R., & Bennion, K. (1986). Teaching test-taking skills to elementary-grade students: A meta-analysis. *Elementary School Journal*, *87*,69–82.

Sewell, T. E. (1974). Learning potential and intelligence as cognitive predictors of achievement in first grade black children (Doctoral dissertation, University of Wisconsin, 1973). *Dissertation Abstracts International*, *34*, 5730A.

Sewell, t. E. (1979). Intelligence and learning tasks as predictors of scholastic achievement in black and white first-grade children. *Journal of School Psychology*, *17*, 325–332.

Sewell, T. E., & Severson, R. A. (1974). Learning ability and intelligence as cognitive predictors of achievement in first-grade black children. *Journal of Educational Psychology*, *66*, 948–955.

Sewell, T. E., Winikur, D., Berlinghof, M., Berkowitz, G., & Miner, M. (1984). *Cognitive modifiability of retarded performers: The effects of intervention on cognitive and academic performance*. Paper presented at the meeting of the National Association of School Psychologists, Philadelphia.

Snow, R. E., & Yalow, E. (1982). Education and intelligence. In R. J. Sternberg (Ed.), *Handbook of human intelligence* (pp. 493–585). London: Cambridge University Press.

Stanley, J. C. (1971). Reliability. In R. L. Thorndike (Ed.), *Educational measurement* (2nd ed., pp. 356–442). Washington, DC: American Council on Education.

Taylor, R. M. (1983). Evaluation of direct instruction follow through using a learning potential assessment instrument (Doctoral dissertation, University of Oregon, 1982). *Dissertation Abstracts International*, *43*, 2917A–2917A.

Thomas, C. M., Hoopes, J. L., & Lidz, C. S. (1987). *The effects of mediation on the performance of disadvantaged preschool children on two cognitive tasks*. Manuscript submitted for publication.

Wechsler, D. (1967). *Manual for the Wechsler Preschool and Primary Scale of Intelligence*. New York: Psychological Corporation.

Wechsler, D. (1974). *Manual for the Wechsler Intelligence Scale for Children—Revised*. New York: Psychological Corporation.

Williams, P. B. (1980). Learning potential assessment of the orthopedically impaired (Doctoral dissertation, University of Oregon, 1980). *Dissertation Abstracts International*, *41*, 2073A.

Wolf, R. K. (1985). Learning potential and its relationship to success on a math problem-solving strategy with junior high learning disabled adolescents (Doctoral dissertation, University of Kansas, 1984). *Dissertation Abstracts International*, *45*, 2490A.

Ysseldyke, J. E., & Mirkin, P. K. (1982). The use of assessment information to plan instructional interventions: A review of the research. In C. R. Reynolds & T. B. Gutkin (Eds.), *The handbook of school psychology* (pp. 395–409). New York: Wiley.

13

Nonverbal Intelligence Measures: A Selected Review of Instruments and Their Use

JACK A. NAGLIERI
Ohio State University

PETER N. PREWETT
Columbus Public Schools

Measures of nonverbal ability, which typically consist of nonverbal and verbal materials that do not require spoken or written language (Sattler, 1982), have long been used to evaluate the intellectual status of children and adults. For example, children's drawings of the human figure have been used to evaluate developmental status since the late 1800s, when Cooke and Ricci published findings that described the changes in these drawings over the course of development (Harris, 1963). Shortly thereafter, the use of human figure drawings to estimate development became a widely used method, essentially because of the work of Goodenough (1926). Other early nonverbal measures were the Porteus Maze Test (Porteus, 1959), the Arthur Point Scale of Performance Tests (Arthur, 1947), and the Wechsler Performance scale (Wechsler, 1939). Although these measures differed from the human figure drawing tests in their content and task requirements, especially since some used manipulatives and/or materials that involved pictorial items, all of these measures employed a nonverbal medium to investigate intellectual functioning. The distinctions among these and the other nonverbal measures presented in this chapter are

important to consider; this is done in the context of a definition of terms.

"Nonverbal intelligence tests" are those that are designed to measure a theoretical construct called "nonverbal intelligence." The Wechsler Intelligence Scale for Children—Revised (WISC-R) Performance scale (Wechsler, 1974) and the Raven Progressive Matrices (Raven, 1947a, 1947b) can both be considered measures of nonverbal intelligence. They measure this construct, however, through tasks that differ in two important ways. The WISC-R measures nonverbal intelligence through tasks that are called "performance measures" because they usually (with the exception of Picture Completion) require the subject to physically perform some action (e.g., manipulate blocks), although Performance subtests are not intended to measure physical dexterity. In contrast, progressive matrices tests such as those developed by Raven and more recently by Naglieri (1985a, 1985b) require no physical response and rely solely on the subject's ability to solve a problem when it is presented in a figural or pictorial format. In this case, all items are presented through the use of an illustration of one kind or another.

The WISC-R and matrices tests also differ

in the breadth of types of tasks used to measure the construct. Whereas in the Matrix Analogies Tests and Raven's Matrices all items are matrices, the WISC-R includes figural, design construction, copying, puzzle assembly, and pictorial sequencing items. Although both types of tests are designed to measure the same construct, nonverbal intelligence, they do so by different means. It is this breadth of subtest types, as opposed to the similarity in scope, that distinguishes the two types of tests and illustrates the variety of approaches to the measurement of nonverbal ability.

Nonverbal test items vary considerably from test to test, despite the similarities in task presentation and response requirements (i.e., both nonverbal tasks with minimal language involvement). For example, some nonverbal items require the subject to build a diagram with blocks to match a model (e.g., WISC-R Block Design), copy a geometric design (e.g., Copying on the Stanford–Binet), assemble a puzzle (Puzzle Solving on the McCarthy Scales of Children's Abilities), solve a progressive matrix (Matrix Analogies Tests), and draw a picture of a human figure (McCarthy's Draw-A-Child, the Goodenough–Harris Draw-A-Person, Naglieri's Draw A Person). These tasks differ in the extent of motor involvement, degree of structure of the task, nature of the nonverbal content (abstract or concrete), and imposition of time limits and bonus credits for rapid completion. Despite the differences among the various nonverbal measures, they are devised so that the directions for administration are generally minimal (or should be), and no reading or other language variable should influence the individual's score. The overriding similarity of these tests is their use of a nonverbal medium to measure ability.

The assumption behind nonverbal intelligence tests is that tests can be conceptualized and distinguished on the basis of their content. This assertion has recently come under criticism from those who advocate a processing as opposed to a content perspective. For example, Das, Kirby, and Jarman (1979), Naglieri (1989), and Naglieri and Das (1988) have stated and provided evidence that the content of a task is less critical than the process involved in solving a task. This approach to the conceptualization of tasks on the basis of their processing require-

ments is a relatively new one (Sternberg, 1984), which postdates the development and use of most nonverbal tests. Despite the differences in perspectives regarding the classification of tasks on the basis of content as opposed to process, nonverbal measures have been used and will continue to be used in various situations.

USES OF NONVERBAL TESTS

Nonverbal tests have been used in at least two ways—as a portion of a larger intelligence test or individually, usually as part of a test battery, or as a screening device (Naglieri, 1985b). Nonverbal tests exist in all the major ability measures, including the WISC-R (Wechsler, 1974), the McCarthy Scales of Children's Abilities (McCarthy, 1972), the Stanford-Binet (Thorndike, Hagen, & Sattler, 1986), and the Kaufman Assessment Battery for Children (K-ABC; Kaufman & Kaufman, 1983). In all these cases, the nonverbal tasks yield a standard score identified as nonverbal in one way or another (usually, such scales are labeled "Performance") and contribute to a composite score intended to be an overall measure of ability. Inasmuch as these tests are typically employed in a variety of situations during psychological evaluations, nonverbal tests have been extensively used and have played a significant role in the determination of intellectual status.

When nonverbal scales are administered within the context of a larger test, they typically are used to obtain a comprehensive assessment of intelligence. In some instances, however, the nonverbal tests are singled out for emphasis according to the needs of the examinee. When an examinee has limited language skills because of bilingualism, a language deficit, or auditory difficulties, or is simply unwilling to interact verbally, greater emphasis on the nonverbal sections of these tests may be appropriate.

The nonverbal portion of a major intelligence test may be considered a better indication of the child's general intellectual ability when it circumvents the difficulty of the child. That is, if a child is bilingual and has limited knowledge of the English language, we would expect low scores on the WISC-R Verbal scale, while the Performance scale would be less affected. This was borne out in a study conducted by Naglieri (1984), who found that normal Native American Navajo students earned a mean Verbal IQ of 75 and Performance IQ of 103. In this case, the Performance IQ scores were less influenced by the intervening variable of limited English-language proficiency and can thus be considered better indicators of these students' intellectual levels. In these situations, the Verbal IQ is best viewed as a reflection of English-language proficiency, not verbal intelligence (Naglieri, 1982). Similarly, the Verbal and Performance IQ scores of a child with an expressive language disorder would be interpreted as a measure of the extent of language deficiency and nonverbal intellectual level, respectively.

The nonverbal scales included in the various major intelligence tests are also subject to the influences of extraneous variables. Perhaps the most important of these intervening variables are physical dexterity and, to a lesser extent, comprehension of oral directions. It is well known that the WISC-R Performance subtests have motoric components (Kaufman, 1979); this is best illustrated by the Coding subtest, which requires rapid writing of symbols paired with numbers. Although the test is not intended to be a measure of physical dexterity, a child with a significant motor problem, such as cerebral palsy, will probably perform more slowly and thereby earn a lower score on this and other subtests with a substantial motoric requirement. In these cases, the nonverbal score is influenced by the intervening variable of motor difficulty, and a nonmotor nonverbal measure is appropriate.

Nonmotor nonverbal tests are typically those that use a figural format and provide multiple-choice options. They should be used when a performance test is deemed inappropriate and motor facility is considered an intervening variable. One advantage of tests such as Raven's Progressive Matrices (Raven, 1947a, 1947b) or the Matrix Analogies Test—Expanded Form (Naglieri, 1985b) is that they do not require physical actions on the part of the respondent. Moreover, there are fewer numbers of possible intervening variables for these matrix tests than for the WISC-R, for example, because of their limited variation in format. This is an advantage because the reduction in the influence of extraneous variables makes the measures more efficient. For this reason, nonverbal matrices tests are appropriate for use with individuals with language and hearing limitations (since the directions are so brief), as well as for those with physical handicaps.

Nonverbal intelligence tests are especially useful when screening children who are illiterate or semiliterate; children who are educationally disadvantaged or socially diverse; and children who are bilingual or have limited language skills. In these contexts, nonverbal tests may uncover potentially capable individuals who might not otherwise be identified by parents and teachers (Jensen, 1980). Naglieri (1985b) suggests that brief measures such as matrices and human figure drawing tests are ideal for this purpose because they are easily and quickly administered.

Nonverbal tests have been considered useful for assessing the abilities of minority students, because they are viewed as nonbiased and less culturally loaded than language tests. This assertion, however, is not supported by the literature for black children (Anastasi, 1982, p. 345), because nonlanguage tests may be as culturally loaded as language tests. The Performance and Verbal scales on the WISC-R, for instance, have been found to be equally difficult for low-socioeconomic-status black children (Anastasi, 1982). This finding was recently supported by Naglieri (1986), who found that a sample of 76 normal black students earned similar WISC-R Verbal (92) and Performance (94) mean scores. For bilingual students such as Native American Navajos and Hispanics, however, a different finding emerges. These groups consistently score higher on nonverbal than on verbal measures (Naglieri, 1984; Sattler, 1982). Since the reason for this disparity (limited English-language skills) is obvious, nonverbal measures offer a means of measuring at least nonverbal intelligence for these individuals, and therefore are valuable in these instances.

In order to provide the reader with a review of the relevant attributes of various nonverbal tests, the remainder of this chapter focuses on the psychometric, standardization, reliability, and validity issues of selected nonverbal measures. Our intent is not to review every nonverbal measure in existence, but to review those that have been widely used in the situations described above and to provide information that is likely to be of interest to the reader. Although major intelligence tests such as the WISC-R, the McCarthy Scales of Children's Abilities, the K-ABC, and the Stanford–Binet Fourth Edition all contain nonverbal scales, these measures are not included here, as information about these tests has been provided elsewhere (see, e.g., Anastasi, 1982; Kaufman, 1979; Kaufman & Kaufman, 1977; and Sattler, 1988; see also Chapters 6, 9, 10, and 11 of this volume). The tests that are reviewed are presented in order of their publication dates.

THE HISKEY–NEBRASKA TEST OF LEARNING APTITUDE

Description

The Hiskey–Nebraska Test of Learning Aptitude (HNTLA) was developed as an individually administered test to use when estimating the cognitive abilities of young deaf individuals (Hiskey, 1966). To achieve this goal, the HNTLA was standardized on deaf children (with pantomimed instructions), as well as on hearing children (with spoken instructions), between the ages of 3 and 16. The test contains 12 subtests, 5 of which are administered to children between the ages of 3 and 10, 3 to all age groups, and 4 to children aged 11 and above (unless mental retardation is suspected). These subtests measure a variety of skills and are described below. According to the test author, the test can be administered in 45–50 minutes after the examiner gains experience with the materials.

Bead Patterns (ages 3–10). This subtest is divided into three sections: Stringing Beads, Copying Bead Patterns, and Memory for Bead Patterns. Stringing beads is administered to children below the age of 5 and requires them to string as many beads as possible within a 1-minute time period. Copying Bead Patterns requires the child to string beads in the same order as the model completed by the examiner. Memory for Bead Patterns is similar to Copying Bead Patterns, except that now the child must complete the bead patterns from memory.

Memory for Color (ages 3–10). On this subtest, the examiner presents plastic strips of various colors to the child and then shields them from view. The child then picks from his or her own set the colored strips that are the same color as the ones previously presented. Each item is scored on accuracy of color selection, regardless of order.

Picture Identification (ages 3–10). This subtest consists of seven stimulus cards that contain five pictures each, and 22 individual pictures. The child's task is to place under each picture on a stimulus card the picture that matches it from the individual pictures. The child's score is the total number of correct selections.

Picture Association (ages 3–10). This subtest consists of 14 stimulus cards that contain two pictures each, and 56 individual pictures. The child's task is to determine the conceptual or perceptual relationship between the two stimulus pictures on each card and then to pick the picture that goes best with them.

Paper Folding (ages 3–10). This subtest requires the child to fold 6-inch squares of paper in the same pattern in which another piece of paper has been folded by the examiner. The score is the number of patterns correctly completed by the child.

Visual Attention Span (all ages). This subtest is similar to the Memory for Color subtest, except that pictures are used instead of color strips. An item is passed if the child chooses the correct pictures from memory, and a bonus point is given if the child picks the pictures in the correct sequence.

Block Patterns (all ages). This subtest requires the subject to use 1-inch wooden blocks to reproduce block patterns pictured on cards. Although the patterns must be reproduced exactly to be scored as correct, rotations are not penalized. There is a 3-minute time limit on each item, and bonus points are given for quicker performance.

Completion of Drawings (all ages). This subtest consists of 28 drawings, each of which has some part missing. After determining what is missing, the subject draws in the missing part with a pencil. The score is the number of drawings correctly completed.

Memory for Digits (ages 11 and above unless mental retardation is suspected). This subtest is an upward extension of the Memory for Colors subtest. On this task, the examiner visually presents a series of numbers and then shields them; the subject then reproduces the series from memory using plastic numbers. The subject receives 1 point if the correct numbers are remembered and 2 points if they are remembered in the correct order.

Puzzle Blocks (ages 11 and above unless mental retardation is suspected). This subtest requires the subject to assemble seven red cubes that have been cut into pieces. Bonus points are earned for constructing the cubes with the correct colors showing and for quickness.

Picture Analogies (ages 11 and above unless mental retardation is suspected). On this subject, the subject is presented with two sets of pictures. The first set contains three drawings of which the first two are related in some way. After determining how the pictures are related, the subject looks at the third drawing and then chooses from five drawings in the second set of pictures the one that is related to it in the same way the first two drawings are. The subject's score is the total number correct.

Spatial Reasoning (ages 11 and above unless mental retardation is suspected). This subtest is made up of 10 plates of drawings, each of which contains a complete geometric design followed by four groups of geometric figures. The subject's task is to pick the group of figures that could be put together to form the original design. The subject's score is the total number correct.

Norms

According to the manual (Hiskey, 1966), the HNTLA was standardized on 1,079 deaf and 1,074 hearing children ranging in age from 2 years, 6 months to 17 years, 5 months. Although the samples were drawn from "10 widely separated states extending from New York to Utah to Florida" (Hiskey, 1966, p. 9), the manual does not provide specific geographic data, such as what other states were involved, the percentage of the sample that was obtained from each state, and the percentage of students from urban and rural areas. Most of the deaf children attended schools for the deaf, and all children who fell within the appropriate age ranges at these schools were usually tested. The author states that the 3-year-old group of deaf children was limited and that ratings at the up-

per age ranges were based on extrapolations. The hearing sample was selected on the basis of parental occupation, using the 1960 U.S. census data as a guideline. The selection of minority groups was not systematic, and the examiners were told to "test children on a random basis in regard to race" (Hiskey, 1966, p. 10). The breakdown of the sample by sex is also not addressed by the manual.

Scores

The HNTLA manual provides tables for converting a child's earned raw scores on the 12 subtests to mental ages ("learning ages" when using deaf norms). The author felt that the mental or learning age is the most appropriate score for comparing a child's performance with the performance of the norm group, because "it is more widely known and better understood than percentiles or standard scores" (Hiskey, 1966, p. 16). The subject's age rating for the entire test is the midpoint (median) between the lowest and highest mental or learning age earned on the individual subtests. The median age rating can be converted by use of a table to a deviation IQ (DIQ) with a mean of 100 and standard deviation of 16 when the hearing norms are used. When the deaf norms are used, the median age rating can be converted to a learning quotient (LQ) by using the formula $LQ = LA \div CA \times 100$ (where LA is learning age and CA is chronological age). The author repeatedly cautions that the learning age obtained for deaf children should not be compared to the mental age rating obtained for hearing children.

Uses

The primary purpose for the development of the HNTLA, as noted earlier, was to meet the need for an individually administered intelligence test designed for and standardized on deaf children (Hiskey, 1966). This is the most common use for the test, and Levine (1974) found it to be the third most frequently used intelligence test with deaf children (behind the WISC and the Leiter). Since the test does not require a verbal response, the HNTLA is also useful when working with children with language deficits (see Richman, 1980; Richman & Kitchell, 1981) or whose primary language is not English (see Shutt & Hannon, 1974).

Validity

The manual reports correlation coefficients between the HNTLA, for hearing children, and the WISC (.82) and Stanford–Binet, Form L-M (.86 for ages 3–10 and .78 for ages 11–17) as evidence for concurrent validity (Hiskey, 1966). Other studies have looked at the concurrent validity of the HNTLA with hearing-impaired children. Comparing the HNTLA and the WISC-R Performance scores for a sample of 59 hearing-impaired children, Hirshoren, Hurley, and Hunt (1977) found a correlation of .89. Watson, Sullivan, Moeller, and Jensen (1982) found the HNTLA to correlate .45 with a measure of language skills (Test of Language Development) when both were administered to 25 deaf children aged 6–10 years.

The predictive validity of the HNTLA has also been studied by comparing the test with measures of academic achievement. Giangreco (1966) compared the scores of 225 students (aged 7–17) at the Iowa School for the Deaf on the HNTLA and the Stanford Achievement Test, the Metropolitan Achievement Test, the Gates Reading Test, and a Teacher Rating Scale for 2nd through 12th grades. The results found the HNTLA to correlate significantly with achievement at all grade levels except for the 5th. The highest correlations were with the math computation and the reasoning measures, while the lowest were with the tests of reading skill. Hurley, Hirshoren, Hunt, and Kavale (1979), however, concluded that the HNTLA, when compared to the Stanford Achievement Test, was not a good predictor of academic achievement with black ($n = 23$) and white ($n = 36$) deaf children.

The factor structure of the HNTLA was investigated by Bolton (1978), who found that the organization of subtest abilities was different for 3- to 10-year-old deaf and hearing children. The Memory for Colors and Block Patterns subtests, in particular, were found to measure different abilities in younger deaf and hearing children.

Reliability

Evidence for the reliability of the HNTLA is provided by the split-half coefficients using the Spearman–Brown formula provided in the manual (Hiskey, 1966). The coefficients for the deaf children were .947 for the 3- to 10-year-old group and .918 for the 11- to 17-year-old group. Similarly, the internal-consistency coefficients for the hearing children were .933 for the 3- to 10-year-old group and .904 for the 11- to 17-year-old group. Although the test–retest reliability of the HNTLA was not addressed in the manual, Watson (1983) found these reliability coefficients to be .79 after a 1-year, .85 after a 3-year, and .62 after a 5-year interval for 41 hearing-impaired children and adolescents. Other reliability information, such as standard errors of measurement (SEMs) and subtest reliability, is not available.

Summary and Comments

The major appeal of the HNTLA is that it is the only multisubtest ability test to be specifically designed for and standardized on a deaf population. Since the test was standardized using pantomimed instructions, the test can be administered to deaf students without breaking standardization procedures, as is often necessary when administering tests such as the Performance scale of the WISC-R to this population. Although this characteristic of the HNTLA may make it potentially useful when an estimate of the cognitive abilities of deaf children is needed, the paucity of research data addressing its statistical qualities is a major drawback. Although the author states that "the best evidence of the validity of a test is to be found in its successful use over a period of years" (Hiskey, 1966, p. 12), this criterion does not answer the central questions regarding a test's validity— whether or not the test measures the constructs it purports to measure, and how effectively it measures these areas (see Anastasi, 1982). The inadequate description of the standardization sample in the manual, and its datedness, are also indicators that the test scores should be interpreted with caution.

THE COLUMBIA MENTAL MATURITY SCALE

Description

The Coumbia Mental Maturity Scale (CMMS; Burgemeister, Blum, & Lorge, 1972) is a 92-item, individually administered test designed to estimate the general reasoning ability of children aged 3 years 6 months through 9 years 11 months (Burgemeister et al., 1972). The 92 items, which consist of 6-by 9-inch cards with three to five drawings on each, are divided among eight overlapping levels. Each child is administered three training items and the appropriate level, determined by the child's chronological age, which contains between 51 and 65 items. The child may also be administered an additional level, either below or above the starting level, depending on the raw score earned.

The cards are presented one at a time, and the child is instructed to look at all of the drawings and to point to the one that does not belong with the others. The lower-level items require the child to discriminate on the bases of color, size, or form; the upper levels require the child to make judgments based on relatively more subtle or abstract differences.

The child taking the test is assumed to have had the opportunity to become familiar with the objects depicted on the cards. Although the test is untimed, the usual administration time is between 15 and 20 minutes.

Scoring

The CMMS manual (Burgemeister et al., 1972) provides tables for converting the child's earned raw score into four other derived scores: "age deviation score" (ADS), percentile rank, stanine, and "maturity index" (MI).

The principal score for comparing the child's performance with the performance of the norm group is the ADS. The ADS is a standard score, ranging in value from 50 to 150, with a mean of 100 and a standard deviation of 16. The manual provides ADSs for each 1-month interval for ages 3 years, 6 months to 4 years, 5 months; for each 2-month interval for ages 4 years, 6 months to 7 years, 11 months; and for each 3-month interval for ages 8 years, 0 months to 9 years, 11 months.) The child's ADS is obtained by choosing the appropriate table, based on the child's chronological age, raw score, and the level administered. The manual provides confidence intervals at the 68% level (±5 points for ages 3 years, 6 months to 5 years, 6 months and ±6 points for ages 6 years, 0 months to 9 years, 6 months), but additional .10, .05, and .01 levels would have been helpful. A table is provided

for converting ADSs to percentile ranks and stanines.

A new derived score for the 1972 edition of the CMMS is the MI. This score is similar to mental age equivalents used on previous additions of the CMMS, in that it is "a means of expressing a child's performance in terms of the performance level of successive age groups" (Burgemeister et al., 1972, p. 27). The authors consider the MI an improvement over the previous system for two reasons. First, the 6-month age groups used by each of the 13 MIs may avoid some of the extrapolation problems encountered when the 1-month intervals of mental age equivalents are used. That is, each MI represents the performance of a group that was actually tested during standardization. The second change follows from the first. Because MIs are only reported for groups that were included in the standardization sample, extrapolations for younger and older "mental ages" are not included. Although these changes correct the extrapolation problems of mental age equivalents, the other drawbacks of using developmental scores remain (see Salvia & Ysseldyke, 1981).

To determine a child's MI, a table that converts the child's raw score on a particular level of the test is used. The child's MI is designated by a number (1–9) and a letter (U or L). The number indicates the year group, and the letter indicates either the lower (L) or the upper (U) 6 months of the year that the child's performance falls into. For example, 4L includes ages 4 years, 0 months to 4 years, 5 months, and 4U includes ages 4 years, 6 months to 4 years, 11 months.

Uses

Because the CMMS does not require a verbal response and requires only minimal motor response, the test authors feel that the CMMS is appropriate for use with children who have cerebral palsy, brain damage, mental retardation, visual handicaps, speech impairment, or hearing loss (Burgemeister et al., 1972). Although the authors consider the test useful with visually handicapped students, the test should not be used with students whose visual handicaps prevent them from making an accurate visual inspection of the drawings.

The authors also consider the CMMS

appropriate for use with non-English-speaking children, since the test does not require the testee to use language or to be able to read. The manual provides directions in Spanish, and the authors suggest that an interpreter administer the test to children who speak other languages. The CMMS may be useful when testing certain culturally deprived children. The authors state that the pictures used in the test should be familiar to virtually all American children, since most children have been exposed to television since birth. They warn, however, that the test may not be appropriate with children "from another country or from an extremely isolated background" (p. 8).

Standardization

The CMMS standardization sample consisted of 2,600 children (1,300 boys and 1,300 girls) who were divided into thirteen 6-month age groups ranging from 3 years, 6 months to 9 years, 11 months, with 200 children in each group. The children included in the sample were selected on the basis of geographic region, race, sex, and parental occupation. The sample was generally representative of the U.S. population (1960 census), although large communities (population > 100,000) were overrepresented and smaller communities (population < 2,500) were underrepresented.

Validity

The CMMS manual reports correlation coefficients between the CMMS and the Stanford Achievement Test, as well as two intelligence tests. Correlations with the Stanford Achievement Test ranged from .31 to .61, with a median of .57 for all Primary Battery I subtests (first grade) and a median correlation of .47 for all Primary Battery II subtests (second grade). The CMMS was found to correlate .67 with the Stanford–Binet Form L-M with a sample consisting of 52 preschoolers and first-graders. In a study using two samples of students from the same school system in Virginia, the CMMS correlated .62 ($n = 90$) and .69 ($n = 263$) with the Otis–Lennon Mental Ability Test. An independent study that compared the scores earned by 45 educable mentally retarded children on the CMMS and the Stanford–

Binet Form L-M found the two to yield similar mean scores and to correlate .74 (Ritter, Duffey, & Fischman, 1974). Another study, using a sample of 60 kindergarten students, found the CMMS to yield a somewhat higher score than the General Cognitive Index of the McCarthy Scales of Children's Abilities, although the two correlated .71 (Phillips, Pasewark, & Tindall, 1978).

Reliability

Evidence for the CMMS's reliability is provided by the split-half and test–retest reliability coefficients reported in the manual. Split-half reliabilities were corrected by using the Spearman–Brown prophecy formula. The coefficients were excellent and ranged from a low of .85 for level H to a high of .91 for level C, with .90 being the median coefficient for all levels combined. *SEMs* were calculated from the split-half reliabilities for each level and are reported in the manual. The test–retest reliability, as reported by the manual, is also excellent and consistent across ages. The test–retest reliability coefficients for three age groups were .86 for 4 years, 0 months to 4 years, 11 months; .84 for 5 years, 6 months to 6 years, 11 months; and .85 for 7 years, 6 months to 8 years, 5 months. The median test–retest coefficient was .85, and the average increase in ADS over the 7- to 10-day period was 4.6 points. These figures are consistent with the results of another study, which found the test–retest reliability of the CMMS to be .85 over a 7-day period for a group of 36 preschool children (Pascale, 1973). Similarly, Riviere (1973), in a study with institutionalized mentally retarded children, found the test–retest reliability of the CMMS over a 9-month period to be .93 for the younger children and .87 for the older children.

Summary

The CMMS's adequate standardization sample, excellent statistical qualities, and ease of administration support the use of the test as a screening instrument for normal as well as handicapped children (Kaufman, 1978; Pascale, 1973; Riviere, 1973). It should be pointed out, however, that the 1970 standardization data, which were based on the 1960 census information, are outdated.

Although dated tests often yield scores that are relatively higher than those of recently normed tests (Flynn, 1987), this effect has not been empirically studied with the CMMS. Users should be aware of this possible effect when using the CMMS to screen children for potential learning problems.

Although the CMMS was designed to estimate the general reasoning ability of children, other reviewers feel that the factors assessed by the test are limited to discrimination and classification (Egeland, 1978; Salvia & Ysseldyke, 1981). Because of the narrow band of abilities assessed by the instrument, CMMS test results should not be overgeneralized and should never be used as the sole indicators of a child's cognitive ability.

THE LEITER INTERNATIONAL PERFORMANCE SCALE

Description

The Leiter International Performance Scale (LIPS; Leiter, 1979) is a 54-item nonverbal intelligence test that was last revised in 1948. This last date of revision is obvious in the datedness of some of the pictures on the blocks. In general, the requirements of the test items are perceptual in nature below the age of 5 and conceptual thereafter (Johnston, 1982). The perceptual items include matching geometric patterns and colors and completing block designs, whereas the conceptual items require reasoning and higher-level problem-solving ability.

The LIPS is a relatively bulky and cumbersome test containing three trays of test materials. The test materials consist of numerous square wooden blocks with either a shape, a design, a color, or a picture of each of them. Each test item has its own blocks (four to eight) and a paper strip with a corresponding number of stimuli. Each stimulus is related in some way to one of the blocks. The paper strip is placed on a wooden frame containing eight notches so that each stimulus is aligned with a notch. The object is to match each block with the correct stimulus by placing the blocks into the corresponding notches on the frame.

According to the manual, the test should be administered with as little conversation as possible (Leiter, 1979). The directions can be pantomimed, and verbal cues are kept to a minimum (Leiter, 1979).

The items are divided into age groups ranging from II to XVIII. There are four test items at each age level except for level XVIII, which has six. The age levels progress at 1-year intervals from II to X (3 months' credit for each correct answer) and at 2-year intervals from X to XVIII (6 months' credit for each correct answer). Testing is begun with the items that are 2 year levels below the subject's estimated mental age and is continued until all tests items at 2 consecutive year levels are failed (Leiter, 1979). All items are untimed except for the block design tasks at the X, XII, and XVI year levels. The total administration time varies but is usually between 30 and 90 minutes.

Scoring

The subject's answer to each problem is recorded as right or wrong on a 5- by 8-inch protocol. The subject's total raw score is used to calculate a mental age in much the same way as on the Stanford–Binet Intelligence Scale, Form L-M. The mental age is then converted to a ratio IQ by use of a table found in the manual. Because Leiter found that the LIPS yielded scores that were about 5 IQ points and about 6 months of mental age too low, he developed procedures whereby 5 points are added to the IQ score and the mental age is adjusted (Leiter, 1979). These adjusted scores are then reported as the obtained scores. Although Leiter did not address interpretation of the LIPS in the test manual, Levine, Allen, Alker, and Fitzgibbon (1974) have constructed a clinical profile based on eight categories related to problem solving approaches: concrete matching; symbolic transformation; quantitative discriminations; spatial imagery; genus matching; progression discriminations; immediate recall; and speed.

Uses

Since the LIPS does not require verbal directions or responses and requires only minimal fine motor skills, it is sometimes used in the assessment of individuals who, for one reason or another, exhibit barriers to effective communication or have difficulty executing fine motor movements. The test is used, therefore, with normal subjects who are non-English-speaking or culturally disadvantaged, and with subjects with handicapping conditions such as severe/profound mental retardation, hearing impairments, expressive and/or receptive language disabilities, autism, or cerebral palsy.

Standardization

Information about the standardization procedures and sample is not adequately presented in the manual.

Validity

Several studies have compared the LIPS with the Stanford–Binet Intelligence Scale and the WISC. In a review of 13 of these studies, Ratcliffe and Ratcliffe (1979) found the median correlation between the LIPS and the Stanford–Binet Intelligence Scale to be .77. Eight of these studies compared the LIPS with the 1937 and the 1960 editions of the Stanford–Binet. When their results were combined, Ratcliffe and Ratcliffe found that the LIPS yielded IQ scores an average of 6.4 points lower than the Stanford–Binet's. In contrast, Reeve, French, and Hunter (1983) found this difference to be only 1 point, with a sample consisting of kindergarten students, when the LIPS was compared with the 1972 version of the Stanford–Binet.

In their reviews of studies comparing the LIPS with the WISC, Ratcliffe and Ratcliffe also concluded that the LIPS yields lower scores when compared with the WISC Full Scale and Performance scores. Their conclusion is misleading, however, since, as Matey (1982) points out, the average LIPS IQ was actually 0.07 points higher than the average WISC Full Scale IQ and was only 0.12 points lower than the WISC Performance IQ. Even this apparent similarity is misleading because of the different standard deviations of the two tests (LIPS $SD = 16$; WISC $SD = 15$). If the obtained Leiter IQ scores are adjusted to standard scores with standard deviations of 15, which would allow direct comparisons with the WISC IQ scores, the average LIPS IQ score is 2.32 points higher than the WISC Full Scale IQ and 1.71 points higher than the WISC Performance IQ.

On the other hand, Bonham (1974) found the LIPS IQ to average 17 points lower than the WISC IQ in a population of deaf children, and Ratcliffe and Ratcliffe (1980) found the LIPS IQ to be significantly lower than the WISC-R IQ in a sample of educationally handicapped children. In contrast, Shah and Holmes (1985) found the LIPS to yield scores that were significantly higher than WISC-R IQ scores when both were administered to autistic children. It appears, then, that the LIPS may yield IQ scores similar in magnitude to those of the Wechsler tests and the Stanford–Binet, although with some populations and under some circumstances it may yield significantly lower or higher scores.

Reliability

Similar to the results of the validity studies, the test–retest reliability coefficients found for the LIPS also vary. In a study with preschool deaf children, Mira (1962) found the test–retest reliability to be only .36 over an 18-month period. In contrast, Weiner (1971) found reliability coefficients of .64 after a 6-month and .63 after a 2-year test–retest interval, with a sample of preschool language-disordered children. Additional studies are needed to determine the long-term stability of the LIPS. Internal reliability coefficients are reported to be high and the resulting *SEM* for the total LIPS is 3.3 (Anastasi, 1982).

Summary

The datedness and the lack of adequate technical information available for the LIPS are major drawbacks in the use of this test. In view of the availability of more current and statistically sound tests, it is difficult to imagine an instance where the LIPS would be recommended as an instrument to estimate the cognitive functioning of a child.

RAVEN'S PROGRESSIVE MATRICES

Description

The two more widely used versions of Raven's Progressive Matrices are the Standard and Coloured versions. The Coloured

Progressive Matrices (Raven, 1947a) contain 35 items, and the Standard Progressive Matrices (Raven, 1947b) contain 60 items. Both versions include early items, where a portion of a diagram is excluded and the task is to determine which of several options best fits in the location, and later items of 2 × 2 or 3 × 3 matrices. As is the case for the Matrix Analogies Tests (Naglieri, 1985a, 1985b), these matrices are constructed so that a logical relationship exists between the horizontal and vertical dimensions of the item, and the individual's task is to uncover these relationships to determine which option best fits the missing location in the matrix.

Standardization

The Standard and Coloured Progressive Matrices were recently administered in a group of local norms development projects using American samples, and the result of this process is presented in a research supplement called *A Compendium of North American Normative and Validity Studies* (Raven, 1986). This "compendium" is a collection of approximately 10 local norms tables and a table described as providing norms for the United States of America (Raven, 1986, p. 15). The manual is completely devoid of the kinds of information typically provided about a normative sample; for example, a description of the total number of individuals used to develop the "detailed norms of the United States of America" (Tables RS3SPM6 for the Standard and RS3CPM3 for the Coloured Matrices) is not provided in the manual. This makes the determination of the degree to which these "norms" are consistent with the population characteristics of the United States impossible. In addition, the local norms were collected using sampling procedures that "vary widely as a result of local constraints and the support available" (Raven, 1986, p. 8), making interpretation very tentative.

Test Materials

The Standard and Coloured Progressive Matrices items are divided into sets of items, but the 1986 manual does not provide part scores for these groups of items.

Scoring

Raw scores on the Standard and Coloured Progressive Matrices can be converted to percentile ranks for individuals aged 6½ to 16½ years. These percentiles can then be converted to standard scores, using conversion tables provided in many standard texts for this purpose. However, this method of conversion, especially at the upper and lower extremes, is not always easy, since percentile ranks may coincide with several standard scores.

Uses

The nature of the Standard and Coloured Progressive Matrices appears to make the tests appropriate for those who exhibit either verbal or motoric barriers to effective communication, and for those with handicapping conditions such as hearing impairments, expressive and/or receptive language disabilities, or cerebral palsy. According to Sattler (1982), the test is useful when measuring the nonverbal ability of culturally diverse individuals because the items are relatively less culturally loaded than verbal tests.

Validity

Raven (1986) provides recent results of several validity investigations conducted during the collection of data in the United States. Although the paucity of information about these results limits the interpretation of the data, some useful information is available. According to Raven (1986), the Standard Progressive Matrices' raw scores correlated .76 with the California Achievement Test, and significant correlations with the Metropolitan Achievement Test are also provided. Similarly, the author reports correlations of .69 and .61 between the Standard and Coloured Progressive Matrices, and the WISC Full Scale, respectively, for Mexican-American students. Similar coefficients are reported for Anglo samples.

Reliability

Internal reliability coefficients for the Standard and Coloured Progressive Matrices are not provided in the 1986 manual. According to Sattler (1982), however, the tests have adequate test–retest reliability. Although Raven (1986) does provide confidence bands for three percentile scores (5th, 50th, and 95th percentiles) from "approximate Standard Errors of Measurement" (p. 85), no internal reliability data are presented.

Summary

There are several problems with the 1986 norms for the Raven's Progressive Matrices that are critical to the use of the test. First, there is a lack of adequate technical information about the nature of the normative sample. For example, the degree to which the normative sample is similar to the U.S. population is not provided, and the sample has not been adequately described. Reliability evidence based on the U.S. sample is also not provided. Local normative tables are provided, but there is considerable variation in how these data were collected, making the results tentative at best. Although validity data for the tests in relation to achievement and the WISC are provided, little information (such as means and standard deviations) is provided to permit one to evaluate these findings adequately. Given that other tests with known psychometric qualities and representative U.S. norms are available, neither the Raven's Standard nor Coloured Progressive Matrices can be recommended as the instrument of choice to examine nonverbal cognitive functioning.

THE TEST OF NONVERBAL INTELLIGENCE

Description

The Test of Nonverbal Intelligence (TONI) is a 50-item individual- or group-administered test designed to be a "language free measure of cognitive ability" with a "reduced cultural loading," which can be used with subjects that are "linguistically handicapped or deprived" (Brown, Sherbenou, & Johnsen, 1982, p. 2). According to the authors, the primary ability assessed by the TONI is problem solving. This area was chosen because "it seemed to be a general component of intelligent behavior as opposed to a subskill"

and because "problem solving lends itself readily to the abstract content and the nonverbal testing format" used in the TONI (Brown et al., 1982, p. 12).

The problems on the TONI require the subject to determine how various figures are related by choosing from four or six response alternatives the one that best goes with three or more stimulus drawings. The figures used on the TONI are somewhat crude black-and-white line drawings of geometric and abstract figures. The relationship among the figures making up each item is a function of one or more of five rules:

1. Simple Matching—identify the figure that is identical to the stimulus drawings.
2. Analogies—identify the design that best completes the analogy.
3. Classification—identify from sets of figures the one of which the stimulus figure would be a member.
4. Intersections—identify the design that would be formed when parts of figures in the rows and columns are joined.
5. Progressions—identify the figure that would result if the serial change in the stimulus set continued (Brown et al., 1982).

To keep the test language-free, the instructions are pantomimed by the examiner, and the testee indicates item responses by pointing. Testing is begun by administering six training items. After administration of the practice items, the actual test items are given, with the starting point being determined by the age of the subject. The basal rule is five consecutive correct answers, and testing is stopped when the subject misses three out of five items. The test comes in equivalent A and B forms, with the A version having relatively more difficult problems and thus a higher ceiling. The TONI can be used with subjects ranging in age from 5 years, 0 months to 85 years, 11 months; although untimed, it usually takes about 15 minutes to administer.

Norms

The TONI standardization sample consisted of 1,929 subjects (47% male, 53% female) ranging in age from 5 years, 0 months to 85 years, 11 months. With the 1980 U.S. census data as guidelines, the sample was stratified on race, sex, ethnicity, grade (school-age sample), parental educational/occupational attainment (school-age sample), current educational/occupational attainment (adult sample), and geographic region. Subjects suspected of impaired intellectual ability were excluded from the standardization sample. Forms A and B were administered to 98% of the standardization sample in immediate succession, with the order of the tests being random. The cumulative frequencies of raw scores were divided into 6-month age intervals for the 5- to 18-year-olds, 1-year age intervals for the 19- to 24-year-olds, and 5-year age intervals for the rest of the sample in order to derive the standard scores (TONI quotient).

Scores

The TONI manual provides tables for converting the subject's earned raw score to a TONI quotient and percentile rank. The TONI quotient is a standard score with a mean of 100 and standard deviation of 15. A table of SEMs for the different age groups is also provided in the manual (Brown et al., 1982).

Uses

Since the TONI is administered nonverbally and does not require a verbal response, it may be useful with children and adults with speech and/or hearing handicaps. Similarly, the TONI's nonverbal format also makes it useful when testing bilingual or non-English-speaking subjects. On the other hand, its minimal motor requirements may make it useful with subjects with physical handicaps such as cerebral palsy. One of the TONI's strong points, however, is that it is one of the few nonverbal tests to include norms for adult populations.

Validity

The TONI manual provides evidence of concurrent and construct validity by comparing it to other achievement and ability tests. Although the results appear impressive, they are not very useful, because they were derived from extremely small samples. It is well known that small sample sizes adversely affect the generalizability and reliability of a study's results (see Borg & Gall, 1979). For example, the manual reports one study that found the Full Scale of the WISC-R to correlate .95 with Form A and .94 with Form B of the TONI. However, this conclusion was based on the test results of only 11 learning-disabled students (mean age 9 years, 5 months). In contrast, Haddad (1987), using a sample of 66 learning-disabled students (mean age 9 years, 5 months), found Form A of the TONI to correlate .34 with the Verbal IQ and .44 with the Performance and Full Scale IQ scores of the WISC-R. Similarly, other studies reported in the manual that compared the TONI and the WISC-R for special education students used another sample of only 16 learning-disabled students and a sample of only 10 educable mentally retarded students. The manual does not report validity studies with adults.

Reliability

The TONI manual provides evidence of internal consistency using coefficient alpha and Kuder–Richardson Formula 21. For samples of 100 in each of four age groups (6–7, 13–14, 35–40, and 60–65), the coefficient alpha ranged from .78 (6–7 age group) to .92 (35–40 age group). The coefficient alpha for the entire sample of 400 subjects was .96 for both Forms A and B. The Kuder–Richardson coefficients were below .80 for the 5- and 6-year-olds, but were .80 and .90 for the rest of the age groups.

The SEMs for both TONI forms at the different age levels are also provided in the manual. The confidence-interval at the 68% level ranged from ±9 for the 5-year-olds to ±5 for ages 15 and above. The confidence interval at the more useful .05 and .01 confidence levels are not provided. The alternate-forms reliabilities ranged from .78 (for the group aged 8 years, 6 months to 10 years, 11 months) to .95 (for the group aged 50 years, 0 months to 85 years, 11 months). Test–retest reliability is not addressed in the manual. Although similar reliability coefficients are reported for special education students, these coefficients were derived from limited sample sizes and should be interpreted with caution.

Summary and Comments

The TONI's good standardization sample, wide age range, and ease of administration may make it a test to consider when an estimate of the cognitive abilities of normal as well as language- and/or hearing-impaired subjects is needed. Its minimal response requirements may also make it appropriate for use with subjects with physical handicaps. The two equivalent forms of the TONI may make it useful when pre- and posttesting is needed, and should also reduce the problems associated with administering the same test repeatedly to the same person (as is often done over the school years to special education students). However, the lack of adequate empirical data concerning its statistical qualities and the generally unappealing black-and-white stimuli make it less attractive. Although the manual reports evidence for validity and reliability, the data were generally derived from extremely small sample sizes, which limits the results' generalizability. This indicates that TONI scores should be used with caution, especially with special education students, until research with larger and more representative samples is available. Since the TONI was designed to assess a single type of ability, problem solving, it should not be used as a sole indicator of a subject's general intellectual abilities. It should be used, therefore, to complement rather than to replace more comprehensive tests.

THE MATRIX ANALOGIES TEST— EXPANDED FORM

Description

Naglieri recently published two forms of a nonverbal ability test using figural matrices, the Matrix Analogies Test—Short Form (MAT-SF; Naglieri, 1985a) and the Matrix Analogies Test—Expanded Form (MAT-EF; Naglieri, 1985b). The MAT-SF (Naglieri, 1985a) is comprised of 34 multiple-choice (five or six options) items, which use abstract designs of the standard progressive matrix type, printed two per page (in black, white, blue, and yellow). The MAT-EF (Naglieri, 1985b) is comprised of 64 items (34 items from the MAT-SF and an additional 30) using

the same types of matrices; however, these are printed one per page (in black, white, blue, and yellow).

The MAT-SF is intended to be used as a group-administered screening test, and the MAT-EF was designed for individual use. Since the latter test is more likely to be of interest to the readers of this volume, the MAT-EF is emphasized. Information about the MAT-SF is provided where it has bearing on the MAT-EF.

Standardization

The MAT-EF Form was standardized using a total sample of 5,718 American students between the ages of 5 and 17 years, stratified according to age, sex, race, geographic region, community size, and socioeconomic status. The test was normed via a system of equating the scores of 1,250 students who were individually administered the entire 64-item test with those of 4,468 students who were administered the MAT-SF. The MAT-SF was standardized on a sample of 4,468 American students between the ages of 5 and 17 years, also stratified according to age, sex, race, geographic region, community size, and socioeconomic status. According to Naglieri (1985b), the standardization sample used to norm the MAT-EF closely matches the characteristics of the U.S. population according to the 1980 census data.

Test Materials

The MAT-EF items are divided into four item groups on the basis of the method required to solve each of the four kinds of matrices. These are Pattern Completion (requiring the individual to choose the option that accurately completes the pattern); Reasoning by Analogy (requiring the examinee to see how the change or changes in one figure relates to the analogous change or changes in another); Serial Reasoning (requiring the individual to discover the order in which items appear throughout the matrix); and Spatial Visualization (requiring the individual to imagine how a figure will look when two or more designs are combined). See Naglieri (1985b, pp. 5–6 for a more thorough description of these groups of items, and Ch. 5 of the same volume for information on their interpretation. Although there is a maximum time limit of 12 minutes per item group (intended to place a maximum limit on testing time), the total administration time usually takes 20 (± 5) minutes.

Scoring

The MAT-EF raw scores are converted to standard scores with a mean of 100 and standard deviation of 15 (as well as age equivalents and percentiles), for easy comparison to other measures such as the WISC-R. (Raw scores on the MAT-SF can be converted to percentiles, stanines, and age equivalent scores.) These standard scores are obtained from conversion tables organized into quarter-year intervals for 5- to 10-year-olds, half-year intervals for 11- and 12-year-olds, and full-year intervals for 13- to 16-year-olds. Standard scores for item groups, with a mean of 10 and standard deviation of 3, are provided. Confidence intervals for the MAT-EF Total Test and item groups are also included in the manual.

Uses

Since the MAT-EF has minimal verbal directions, requires only minimal verbal responses or a pointing response, and requires essentially no fine motor skills, it is appropriate for use with individuals who, for one reason or another, exhibit verbal or motoric barriers to effective communication. The test may therefore be used with normal subjects who are non-English-speaking or culturally disadvantaged, and with subjects with handicapping conditions such as mental retardation, hearing impairments, expressive and/or receptive language disabilities, or cerebral palsy. According to Naglieri (1985b), the MAT-EF is especially useful for measuring the nonverbal ability of culturally diverse individuals, as well as of linguistically and culturally diverse gifted students. In the manual for the MAT-EF, Naglieri (1985b) provides evidence that both the short and expanded forms yield similar scores for matched samples of American blacks and whites and for males and females, and that they are also useful for assessment of Native American children's nonverbal intellectual ability. In addition, Naglieri and Bardos (1987a) have reported that Greek and American, as

well as Canadian and American (Naglieri & Bardos, 1988), children earned similar mean scores on the MAT-SF. These results suggest that the test yields similar scores for a variety of individuals.

Validity

The validity of the MAT-EF has been examined in several studies, in both the test's manual and the literature. Naglieri (1985b) reports significant correlations with the WISC-R Performance IQ for samples of normal ($r = .41$), hearing-impaired ($r = .68$), and Native American ($r = .43$) students. Similarly, significant correlations with Raven's Coloured Progressive Matrices are reported for samples of normal ($r = .71$) and Native American ($r = .64$) students in first through fifth grades. Finally, Naglieri (1985b) reports significant correlations between the MAT-SF and reading (median $r = .52$) and math (median $r = .58$) for a sample of 3,022 students in 4th through 12th grades, as well as significant correlations between the MAT-SF and Stanford Achievement Test Reading and Spelling scores for hearing-impaired children. Stutzman (1986) has reported the MAT-EF to correlate significantly with the Wide Range Achievement Test (WRAT) Reading subtest (.45) and the Stanford Reading subtests (Literal Comprehension .42 and Inferential Comprehension .34). Similarly, Naglieri and Bardos (1989) reported that the MAT-EF correlated significantly with the WRAT-R Reading (.60), Spelling (.60), and Arithmetic (.64) subtests for a sample of 39 normal students. Finally, Lillis (1987) found significant correlations between the MAT-EF and the Differential Ability Scales' (Elliott, 1986) measures of nonverbal functioning (.87) and achievement (.36).

Results of investigations of the WISC-R and the MAT-EF suggest that the WISC-R Performance IQ is likely to be approximately 10 points higher for normal, referred, and gifted samples (Anderson, 1987; Naglieri, 1985b; Naglieri & Bardos, 1987b; Naglieri & Wisnewski, 1987). The lower MAT-EF mean scores have been interpreted as an expected and appropriate finding, due to softening of norms, when a new test is compared to an old one (Flynn, 1987; Naglieri, 1985b). In order to provide a means of comparing the MAT-EF and WISC-R Performance IQ scores obtained for an individual child, Naglieri and Wisnewski (1987) provide the differences needed for significance (12 and 16 points at the .05 and .01 levels, respectively) when the inflation of Performance IQ scores is corrected.

Reliability

Naglieri (1985b) provides evidence that the MAT-EF has excellent internal reliability. The median Cronbach alpha for the Total Test score is .93 (range = .88 to .95), and the item groups' internal-consistency coefficients (medians) are as follows: Pattern Completion, .76; Reasoning by Analogy, .77; Serial Reasoning, .85; Spatial Visualization, .87. A test–retest reliability of .77 for the MAT-EF Total Test has been reported by Naglieri (1985b) over a 1-month interval. Naglieri (1986) also reports a test–retest reliability coefficient of .78 for the MAT-SF over a similar period, and Wisnewski, Rodeheffer, and Genshaft (1988) report a 1-week test–retest reliability coefficient of .90 for the MAT-EF with a sample of 35 referred children. These results indicate that the MAT-EF has excellent reliability.

Summary

The MAT-EF measures nonverbal ability through the use of figural matrices. It has been normed on a large, nationally representative sample of individuals in the United States; its use as a measure of nonverbal ability is supported by investigations that have found high internal reliability and evidence of validity. This test, like other matrices tests, measures a relatively narrow band of ability (since the content is exclusively figural matrices) and is useful with certain populations, since there are fewer extraneous variables (e.g., motor or speed) to influence the score.

THE DRAW A PERSON: A QUANTITATIVE SCORING SYSTEM

Description

The Draw A Person: A Quantitative Scoring System (DAP; Naglieri, 1988) is a recently published system of scoring human figure drawings to obtain an estimate of ability. The same 64 items are used to rate the drawings of a man, a woman, and the self according to the number of body parts drawn, the extent to which these are elaborated, and the degree to which the body parts are drawn in the proper proportions and connected in the correct manner. The system has been devised to be easy to use; to provide a way of rating the drawings using modern scoring criteria (e.g., to reduce the influences of current styles of dress and hair); and to yield an objective and reliable system of evaluation.

Standardization

The DAP was normed on a sample of 2,622 individuals aged 5 through 17 years who were representative of the 1980 U.S. census data according to age, sex, race, geographic region, ethnic group, socioeconomic status, and community size. Naglieri (1988) reports that the characteristics of the DAP normative sample closely approximate those of the U.S. population, according to the 1980 census reports, on these stratification variables.

Test Materials

The DAP test materials consists of a Student Response Form, an Examiner Record Form, and the actual scoring system. The Student Response Form is intended to provide a permanent record of the individual's production and to be appropriate for group or individual administration of the test. The Examiner Record Form contains a page for the recording of all demographic data, raw scores, derived scores, and other relevant information. The remaining pages contain directions for administration of each drawing (man, woman, and self); places for recording and tabulation of item scores; and space for examiner comments for each drawing. The 64 items that comprise the scoring system are included in the DAP manual and a two-page scoring chart, and are organized so that the drawings can be quickly and easily scored. For example, items are organized according to four principles: (1) presence of the body part, (2) detail of the body part, (3) proportion of the body part, and (4) bonus credit. Subjectivity is reduced by making the rules for scoring concise and clear. Also included in the DAP manual is a self-training program to help examiners learn to use the scoring system. Upon completion of such training, examiners typically spend less than 5 minutes per drawing in applying the 64 items. There is a time limit of 5 minutes per drawing making the total administration time no more than 15 minutes.

Scores

The DAP yields raw scores ranging from 0 to 64 for each of the three drawings. The raw scores for the man, woman, and self drawings are combined to form a DAP Total Test, and all of these scores are converted to standard scores with a mean of 100 and standard deviation of 15. These scores can also be used to obtain percentile ranks and age equivalents. Confidence intervals for the individual drawing and Total Test standard scores are provided, as are the differences needed for significance when comparing the standard scores earned on each of the drawings.

Uses

According to the author, the DAP is intended to be used as a part of a larger group of tests or for screening purposes. Since the test is nonverbal and easy to administer, the influences of verbal skills, primary language, fine motor coordination, cultural diversity, and language disabilities are reduced. The DAP is therefore useful as a nonverbal measure for exceptional populations because of the nonverbal and nonacademic content and ease of administration. Since the test does not require a verbal response, its usefulness for language-impaired individuals and those simply unwilling to interact verbally is clear. Similarly, because the DAP system credits a child for inclusion of body parts, with minimal (or no) requirement that the drawing be precisely produced, individuals with motor coordination problems such as those resulting from cerebral palsy are not unduly penalized. In addition, its value as a culturally reduced test is suggested by research (Naglieri & Bardos, 1987; Bardos, Softas, & Petrogiannis, 1989) showing that Greek and American, and Canadian and American, children earned similar mean scores on the test.

Validity

Naglieri (1988) reports that the DAP raw scores evidence significant developmental changes over age, a basic aspect of validity (Anastasi, 1982). Evidence of concurrent validity is given by a study (Naglieri, 1988) that found a high correlation (r's ranging from .75 to .84) between this scoring system and the Goodenough–Harris system (Harris, 1963) for a sample of 90 students. Naglieri (1988) also reports similar findings in an additional study involving 100 children aged 9, drawn from the DAP standardization sample (r's with the Goodenough–Harris system ranged from .79 to .87). Further evidence of the DAP's concurrent validity was reported by Smith (1987), who found that the DAP and Goodenough–Harris standard scores correlated .87 for 40 normal, .85 for 40 reading-disabled, and .92 for 40 developmentally handicapped students in fourth and fifth grades.

Research examining the extent to which the DAP correlates with other measures is reported by Naglieri (1988). Significant correlations with the MAT-SF (Naglieri, 1985b) and achievement in reading and math for a sample of 594 students in kindergarten through third grade are also provided. In addition, Naglieri (1988) reports that results of investigations into the differences in standard scores obtained by matched black and white samples (total $n = 500$) and Hispanic and non-Hispanic (total $n = 148$) students from the standardization sample were nonsignificant, providing support for use of the DAP. Similarly, male–female ($n = 1,596$) comparisons by age from 5 to 17 years indicated that the DAP standard scores do not substantially differ by sex.

Examination of the differences between mean scores obtained using the DAP and Goodenough–Harris systems reported by Naglieri (1988) indicate that for students of elementary school age, the DAP yields mean scores about 10 points lower than those for the Goodenough–Harris system. At the middle school ages, however, the difference is about 5 points, with the DAP mean scores higher than those for the Goodenough–Harris system (Naglieri, 1988). Similarly, Smith (1987) found that the DAP yielded slightly higher mean scores than the Goodenough–Harris for fourth- and fifth-grade normal (3 points higher), reading-disabled (6 points higher), and developmentally handicapped (5 points higher) students. These results support some researchers' contention that the Goodenough–Harris norms are about 10 points too hard, but also indicate that further research into these differences is needed.

Reliability

The DAP internal reliability coefficients reported by Naglieri (1988), using the standardization sample data, range from .83 to .89 (median = .86) for the Total Test and .56 to .78 (median = .70) for the man, woman, and self drawings separately. Test–retest reliability coefficients obtained for a sample of 112 students in first through seventh grades ranged from .60 to .89, with a mean of .74, for the DAP Total Test. Gottling (1985) found the interrater reliability of the scoring system to be quite good and reported coefficients of .95 and .93 for subjects in first through third grades (n = 45) and fifth through seventh grades (n = 44), respectively. Similarly high intrarater reliabilities of .97 and .95, respectively, for the same two groups of subjects were reported by Gottling (1985).

Summary

The DAP has features that make it attractive as a nonverbal measure. Perhaps the most important aspects of the system are the Total Test score (and the relatively high reliability it provides), easy scoring rules, and modern standardization. Initial research indicates that the system is sufficiently reliable and valid for use as described by the author.

CONCLUSION

Our intent in this chapter has been to provide an examination of some nonverbal measures of ability that may have utility in the assessment of school-age individuals. Although these tests may be used with normal individuals, they offer particular advantages in the assessment of persons with hearing impairments, physical limitations,

limited knowledge of the English language, or language/communication disorders, as well as those who for whatever reason are unwilling to interact verbally. The tests reviewed include some that have usefulness and others that, because of technical problems, provide little advantage to the practitioner. Psychologists who must decide which of these tests to use should examine the information provided here, as well as all other relevant information, in making their selection. In addition to the technical aspects of these tests, practitioners will need to consider the defensibility of their choice, given the close scrutiny that ability measures have recently received (Elliott, 1987).

POSTSCRIPT

Before ending this chapter on nonverbal ability tests, we feel the need to provide an evaluation of the concept of nonverbal ability, given how it is assessed in the tests described here and in other measures. Our goal is to critically re-examine the concept in light of current views of what intelligence testing should be, and to provide a recommendation for what a good nonverbal measure of intelligence should include so that practitioners will be able to critically examine future measures. In our discussion, we do not limit ourselves to the tests reviewed here, but include the major intelligence tests such as the Wechsler scales.

Nonverbal Intelligence Revisited

In the introduction of this chapter, we have stated that despite the differences in the various nonverbal measures, the overriding similarity of these tests is in the use of a nonverbal medium to measure ability; we have also stated that the assumption behind these nonverbal intelligence tests is that tests can be conceptualized and distinguished on the basis of their content. It is this content-based perspective that we would like to return to and expand upon.

Conceptualizing and constructing measures of intellectual functioning on the basis of the content (e.g., verbal or nonverbal) of the tasks involved have received much criticism in recent years, especially from those who advocate a cognitive processing perspective. Researchers such as Das et al. (1979), Naglieri (1989), Naglieri and Das (1988), Kaufman and Kaufman (1983), Sternberg (1984), and many others have stated and provided evidence that the content of a task is less critical than the process involved to solve a task. This concept of process-based versus content-based measures has been recently advocated by Kaufman and Kaufman (1983) in their test, the K-ABC.

The K-ABC is organized into two processing scales, one intended to measure simultaneous and one intended to measure sequential processes. The Simultaneous and Sequential Processing scales are combined to form a Mental Processing Composite, and a combination of some of the subtests from each scale yields a Nonverbal scale. The Simultaneous and Sequential Processing scales are process-based, in that the tasks included in each scale are conceptualized according to the intellectual process required to solve the task, rather than on the basis of the content of the items. Simultaneous Processing tasks are those that are "spatial, analogic, or organizational in nature . . . [where] the input has to be integrated and synthesized simultaneously to produce the appropriate solution" (Kaufman & Kaufman, 1983, p. 30). Sequential Processing tasks involve solution of a "problem which must be solved by arranging the input in sequential or serial order . . . [where] each idea is linearly and temporally related to the preceding one" (Kaufman & Kaufman, 1983, p. 30). The addition of a Nonverbal scale in the K-ABC gives us the opportunity to examine one way in which a process and content approach to test construction may be combined.

The K-ABC Nonverbal scale is comprised of from three to five selected subtests, depending on the age of the person tested. Although it would be desirable to have an equal number of subtests from each of the scales, the K-ABC Nonverbal scale never contains more than one test from the Sequential Processing scale. In addition, the one Sequential Processing subtest included at all ages (Hand Movements) has evidenced strong loadings on the Simultaneous Processing factor (Kaufman & Kamphaus, 1984), indicating that the Sequential Processing component of the Nonverbal scale is virtually nonexistent for school-age individuals. Thus,

the K-ABC Nonverbal scale is essentially the same as the K-ABC Simultaneous Processing scale.

The K-ABC Nonverbal scale, like the Simultaneous Processing scale, is comprised of tasks that are closely related to the WISC-R Performance scale (Naglieri & Jensen, 1987) and can be viewed as nonverbal spatial measures. Similarly, tests such as the Matrix Analogies Tests (Naglieri, 1985a, 1985b) and Raven's Progressive Matrices (Raven, 1947a, 1947b) are also nonverbal measures with heavy emphasis on spatial tasks. The result is, therefore, that so-called nonverbal tests actually could be better described as those involving nonverbal spatial or nonverbal spatial tasks with performance components. Why is this important?

Nonverbal ability scales within tests, such as the K-ABC Nonverbal scale, the WISC-R Performance scale, the McCarthy Scales of Children's Abilities (McCarthy, 1972) Perceptual–Performance scale, and the Stanford–Binet (Thorndike et al., 1986) Abstract/Visual Reasoning scale, need to be viewed as tests that measure a narrow scope of intellectual functioning. Even though the scales contain a greater variety of tasks (e.g., abstract and concrete content) than the more specific measures, such as those only involving matrices or human figure drawing, all of these nonverbal tests are limited in terms of their processing requirements. That is, a thorough nonverbal measure of ability should include more than tasks that can be described as involving simultaneous processing.

Blueprint for a Nonverbal Ability Measure

If one accepts that a process approach to understanding and conceptualization of human cognitive functioning is desirable, as has been suggested and is clearly a trend in the field of intellectual assessment (Kaufman & Kaufman, 1983; Naglieri, 1989; Naglieri & Das, 1987, 1988), then nonverbal measures should also be more broadly based than is currently the case. In addition, such a test should provide for measurement of all aspects of a theory upon which it might be built. To provide an illustration of how this could be accomplished, we propose that a nonverbal measure of cognitive processing should be based upon a theory of cognitive processing that has been shown to have merit.

To illustrate how a nonverbal measure of ability could be constructed, we use the "planning–attention–simultaneous–successive" (PASS) model following from Luria (1966, 1973, 1980), as initially operationalized by Das, Kirby, and Jarman (1975, 1979) and recently examined by Naglieri and Das (1987, 1988) as a base. Through the use of this perspective, we hope to demonstrate the possibility of and need for a thorough assessment of cognitive functioning using nonverbal content. Since the theoretical model has been described in detail (see the references cited above), only a brief summary is presented here.

Luria divided the processes involved in cognitive functioning into three functional units. Luria's first functional unit is responsible for maintaining attention and a proper state of arousal or cortical tone. This functional unit is important to competent cognitive functioning, because maintaining an appropriate level of arousal is vital for effective performance. Attention, which is specifically directed arousal, may require consistent activity over an extended period of time or specific signal detection. Although "attention" is a broad term, and one with many facets (e.g., selective and sustained attention; Davies, Jones, & Taylor, 1984), it has an obvious place in assessment of cognitive functioning. Attention is also important for the proper processing of information and for making effective plans of action (Das, 1984b). The first functional unit of attention works in conjunction with the planning and information-coding units to obtain effective responding.

Luria's second functional unit entails information coding, which is responsible for the acquisition, storage, and retrieval of knowledge through simultaneous and successive processes. Simultaneous processing involves the integration of stimuli into groups (where each element of the task is related to every other), and successive processing involves the integration of stimuli into a specific linear series (where each element is related only to the next). Simultaneous and successive processes can be applied to tasks of various modalities (auditory, visual, kinesthetic) involving different types of stim-uli (verbal or nonverbal), and may take place during direct perception, during retention of information (memory), and at conceptual levels (Das et al., 1979; Naglieri & Das, 1987, 1988).

Finally, Luria's third functional unit, planning, provides the individual with a mechanism for regulation and verification of activity; generation of plans of action; inspection and regulation of the actions so that the aims of the plans may be attained; and the development of new plans if necessary. This component entails the aptitude for asking new questions, solving problems, and self-monitoring, which Das (1984) suggests as the most complex forms of human behavior. Adequacy of processing in this unit, as well as the second functional unit, requires a proper state of cortical tone and direction of attention, illustrating the interrelatedness of the units.

Using the PASS processing model as a theoretical base, a thorough nonverbal measure of intellectual functioning should include measurement of each process. Following from the reports of Naglieri and Das (1987, 1988) and Naglieri, Prewett, and Bardos (1989), several nonverbal tests could be chosen. First, as a measure of nonverbal planning processes, Naglieri and Das's (1987, 1988) tasks called Visual Search, Trails, and Matching Numbers are all appropriate. These tasks all require the individual to develop a plan of action or develop a strategy to solve various kinds of problems. The first task would involve only a pointing response, whereas the other two would require some facility with a pencil, although a minimal amount. Nonverbal assessment of planning processes would, therefore, be a relatively easy thing to achieve.

Operationalization of the second functional unit using nonverbal tasks would involve selection of tests such as Matrices and Figure Recognition to assess simultaneous processes; successive processes could be assessed by tests such as Successive Ordering and Hand Movements (Naglieri & Das, 1987, 1988). (Note that this Hand Movements test differs from that used in the K-ABC.) Finally, attentional processes could be measured using nonverbal variations on the Stroop test (Stroop, 1935) and experimental tasks like those used by Posner and Boies (1971).

Current tests used as measures of nonverbal ability clearly involve simultaneous processing. The K-ABC Simultaneous Processing, WISC-R Performance, and McCarthy Perceptual–Performance scales have all been shown to be highly related (Naglieri, 1985c; Naglieri & Jensen, 1987) and the validity of these measures as simultaneous processing tasks has been suggested through the correlations of these scales or some of their subtests with simultaneous marker tasks (Naglieri, 1989). When one measures nonverbal ability using these tests, therefore, they all involve simultaneous processing, despite their variety. Thus, the use of these nonverbal tests or scales is providing an estimate of ability that is considerably limited in its scope of cognitive competence.

The major advantage of the development of a measure of cognitive functioning based on the PASS theory described here would be that a more thorough measure of intellectual functioning could result. Considering that Naglieri and Das (1987) found that planning correlated as well as information coding with math and reading achievement for normal students, the addition of planning measures to simultaneous, successive, and attentional ones could provide a better understanding of cognitive functioning. A nonverbal ability measure, like a general ability measure, should be broad-based, so that a greater understanding of each individual assessed is made possible. When a nonverbal measure such as this one is available, a more complete evaluation of the cognitive processing components of individuals with hearing impairment, physical limitations, limited knowledge of the English language, and language/communication disorders, as well as those of normal persons, may be possible.

REFERENCES

Anastasi, A. (1982). *Psychological testing* (5th ed.). New York: Macmillan.

Anderson, K. M. (1987). *Concurrent validity of the Matrix Analogies Test—Expanded Form, PPVT-R, and WISC-R for children identified as gifted*. Unpublished master's thesis, Ohio State University.

Arthur, G. A. (1947). *Point Scale of Performance Tests: Form II* (rev.). New York: Psychological Corporation.

Bardos, A. N., Softas, B. C., R. Petrogiannis, K. (1989). Comparison of the Goodenough–Harris and Naglieri's Draw-A-Person Scoring Systems for Greek children. *School Psychology International, 10,* 205–209.

Bolton, B. (1978). Differential ability structure in deaf and hearing children. *Applied Psychological Measurement, 2,* 147–149.

Bonham, S. J. (1974). Predicting achievement for deaf children. *Psychological Service Center Journal, 14,* 35–44.

Borg, W. R., & Gall, M. D. (1979). *Educational research* (3rd ed.). New York: Longman.

Brown, L., Sherbenou, R. J., & Johnsen, S. K. (1982). *Test of Nonverbal Intelligence*. Austin, TX: Pro-Ed.

Burgemeister, B. B., Blum, L. A., & Lorge, I. (1972). *Columbia Mental Maturity Scale* (3rd ed.). New York: Harcourt Brace Jovanovich.

Das, J. P. (1984). Aspects of planning. In J. R. Kirby (Ed.), *Cognitive strategies and educational performance*. New York: Academic Press.

Das, J. P., Kirby, J. R., & Jarman, R. F. (1975). Simultaneous and successive synthesis: An alternative model. *Psychological Bulletin, 82,* 87–103.

Das, J. P., Kirby, J. R., & Jarman, R. F. (1979). *Simultaneous and successive cognitive processes*. New York: Academic Press.

Das, J. P., & Naglieri, J. A. (1988). *Das–Naglieri Cognitive Assessment System Experimental Test Battery*. New York: Psychological Corporation.

Davies, D. R., Jones, D. M., & Taylor, A. (1984). Selective- and sustained-attention tasks: Individual and group differences. In R. Parasuraman & D. R. Davies (Eds.), *Varieties of attention* (pp. 395–448). New York: Academic Press.

Egeland, B. R. (1978). Review of Columbia Mental Maturity Scale. In O. K. Buros (Ed.), *The eighth mental measurements yearbook* (pp. 298–299). Highland Park, NJ: Gryphon Press.

Elliott, C. D. (1986). *Differential Ability Scales Standardization Edition*. New York: Psychological Corporation.

Elliott, R. (1987). *Litigating intelligence*. Dover, MA: Auburn House.

Flynn, J. R. (1987). Massive IQ gains in 14 nations: What IQ test really measure. *Psychological Bulletin, 101,* 171–191.

Giangreco, C. J. (1966). The Hiskey–Nebraska Test of Learning Aptitude (Revised) compared to several achievement tests. *American Annals of the Deaf, 111,* 566–577.

Goodenough, F. L. (1926). *Measurement of intelligence by drawings*. New York: Harcourt, Brace & World.

Gottling, S. (1985). *Comparison of the reliability of the Goodenough–Harris Draw-A-Man Test with the Naglieri Draw A Person: A Quantitative Scoring System*. Unpublished master's thesis, Ohio State University.

Haddad, F. A. (1987). Concurrent validity of the Test of Nonverbal Intelligence with learning disabled children. *Psychology in the Schools, 23,* 361–364.

Harris, D. B. (1963). *Children's drawings as measures of intellectual maturity*. New York: Harcourt Brace Jovanovich.

Hirshoren, A., Hurley, O. L., & Hunt, J. T. (1977). The WISC-R and Hiskey–Nebraska Test with Deaf children. *American Annals of the deaf, 122,* 392–394.

Hiskey, M. S. (1966). *Hiskey–Nebraska Test of Learning Aptitude: Manual*. Lincoln, NE: Union College Press.

Hurley, O. L., Hirshoren, A., Hunt, J. T., & Kavale, K. (1979). Predictive ability of two mental ability tests with black deaf children. *Journal of Negro Education, 48,* 14–19.

Jensen, A. R. (1980). *Bias in mental testing.* New York: Free Press.

Johnston, J. R. (1982). Interpreting the Leiter I.Q.: Performance profiles of young normal and language disordered children. *Journal of Speech and Hearing Research, 25,* 291–296.

Kaufman, A. S. (1978). Review of Columbia Mental Maturity Scale. In O. K. Buros (Ed.), *The eighth mental measurements yearbook* (pp. 299–301). Highland Park, NJ: Gryphon Press.

Kaufman, A. S. (1979). *Intelligent testing with the WISC-R.* New York: Wiley.

Kaufman, A. S., & Kamphaus, R. W. (1984). Factor analysis of the Kaufman Assessment Battery for Children (K-ABC) for ages 2½ through 12½. *Journal of Educational Psychology, 76,* 623–637.

Kaufman, A. S., & Kaufman, N. L. (1977). *Clinical evaluation of young children with the McCarthy Scales.* New York: Grune & Stratton.

Kaufman, A. S., & Kaufman, N. L. (1983). *Kaufman Assessment Battery for Children.* Circle Pines, MN: American Guidance Service.

Leiter, R. G. (1979). *Leiter International Performance Scale: Instruction manual.* Chicago: Stoelting.

Levine, E. S. (1974). Psychological tests and practices with the deaf: A survey of the state of the art. *The Volta Review, 76,* 298–319.

Levine, M. N., Allen, R. M., Alker, L. N., & Fitzgibbon, W. (1974). Clinical profile for the Leiter International Performance Scale. *Psychological Service Center Journal, 14,* 45–50.

Lillis, W. T. (1987). *Correlations of the Differential Ability Scales with the Matrix Analogies Test and the Draw A Person: A Quantitative Scoring System.* Unpublished master's thesis, Ohio State University.

Luria, A. R. (1966). *Human brain and psychological processes.* New York: Harper & Row.

Luria, A. R. (1973). *The working brain: An introduction to neuropsychology.* New York: Basic Books.

Luria, A. R. (1980). *Higher cortical functions in man* (2nd ed.). New York: Basic Books.

Matey, C. (1982). Leiter International Performance Scale. In D. J. Keyser & R. L. Sweetland (Eds.), *Test Critiques* (pp. 411–420). Kansas City: Test Corporation.

McCarthy, D. (1972). *McCarthy Scales of Children's Abilities.* New York: Psychological Corporation.

Mira, M. (1962). The use of the Arthur Adaptation of the Leiter International Performance Scale and the Nebraska Test of Learning Aptitude with preschool deaf children. *American Annals of the Deaf, 107,* 224–228.

Naglieri, J. A. (1982). Does the WISC-R measure verbal intelligence for nonEnglish speaking children? *Psychology in the Schools, 19,* 478–479.

Naglieri, J. A. (1984). Concurrent and predictive validity of the Kaufman Assessment Battery for Children with a Navajo sample. *Journal of School Psychology, 22,* 373–380.

Naglieri, J. A. (1985a). *Matrix Analogies Test—Short Form.* New York: Psychological Corporation.

Naglieri, J. A. (1985b). *Matrix Analogies Test—Expanded Form.* New York: Psychological Corporation.

Naglieri, J. A. (1985c). Normal children's performance on the McCarthy Scales, Kaufman Assessment Battery, and Peabody Individual Achievement Test. *Journal of Psychoeducational Assessment, 3,* 123–129.

Naglieri, J. A. (1986). WISC-R and K-ABC comparison for matched samples of black and white children. *Journal of School Psychology, 24,* 81–88.

Naglieri, J. A. (1988). *Draw A Person: A Quantitative Scoring System.* New York: Psychological Corporation.

Naglieri, J. A. (1989). A cognitive processing theory for the measurement of intelligence. *Educational Psychologist, 24,* 185–206.

Naglieri, J. A., & Bardos, A. N. (1987). *Draw A Person and Matrix Analogies Tests' cross cultural validity.* Paper presented at the annual meeting of the National Association of School Psychologists, New Orleans.

Naglieri, J. A., & Bardos, A. N. (1988). Canadian children's performance on the Matrix Analogies Test. *School Psychology International, 9,* 309–313.

Naglieri, J. A., & Bardos, A. N. (1989). *Use of the WISC-R, PPVT-R, MAT-EF, WRAT-R and PIAT with normal children.* Manuscript submitted for publication.

Naglieri, J. A., & Das, J. P. (1987). Construct and criterion related validity of planning, simultaneous and successive cognitive processing tasks. *Journal of Psychoeducational Assessment, 5,* 353–363.

Naglieri, J. A., & Das, J. P. (1988). Planning –arousal–simultaneous–successive (PASS): A model for assessment. *Journal of School Psychology, 26,* 35–48.

Naglieri, J. A., & Jensen, A. R. (1987). Comparison of Black–White differences on the WISC-R and the K-ABC: Spearman's hypothesis. *Intelligence, 11,* 21–43.

Naglieri, J. A., Prewett, P. N., & Bardos, A. N. (1989). An exploratory study of planning, attention, simultaneous and successive cognitive processes. *Journal of School Psychology, 27,* 347–364.

Naglieri, J. A., & Wisnewski, J. J. (1987). Clinical use of the WISC-R, MAT-EF, and PPVT-R. *Journal of Psychoeducational Assessment, 6,* 390–395.

Pascale, P. J. (1973). Validity concerns of preschool testing. *Educational and Psychological Measurement, 33,* 977–978.

Phillips, B. L., Pasewark, R. A., & Tindall, R. C. (1978). Relationship among McCarthy Scales of Children's Abilities, WPPSI, and Columbia Mental Maturity Scale. *Psychology on the Schools, 15,* 352–356.

Porteus, S. D. (1959). *The Maze Test and clinical psychology.* Palo Alto, CA: Pacific Books.

Posner, M. I., & Boies, S. J. (1971). Components of attention. *Psychological Review, 78,* 391–408.

Ratcliffe, K. J., & Ratcliffe, M. W. (1979). The Leiter scales: A review of validity findings. *American Annals of the Deaf, 124,* 38–45.

Ratcliffe, M. W., & Ratcliffe, K. J. (1980). A comparison of the Wechsler Intelligence Scale for Children—Revised and Leiter International Performance Scale for a group of educationally handicapped adolescents. *Journal of Clinical Psychology, 36,* 310–312.

Raven, J. C. (1947a). *Standard Progressive Matrices.* London: H. K. Lewis.

Raven, J. C. (1947b). *Coloured Progressive Matrices.* London: H. K. Lewis.

Raven, J. C. (1986). *A compendium of North American normative and validity studies.* New York: Psychological Corporation.

Reeve, R. R. French, J. L., & Hunter, M. (1983). A validation of the Leiter International Performance Scale with kindergarten children. *Journal of Clinical Psychology, 51,* 458–459.

Richman, L. C. (1980). Cognitive patterns and learning

disabilities in cleft palate children with verbal deficits. *Journal of Speech and Hearing Research, 23,* 447–456.

Richman, L. C., & Kitchell, M. M. (1981). Hyperlexia as a variant of developmental language disorder. *Brain and Language, 12,* 203–212.

Ritter, D., Duffey, J., & Fischman, R. (1974). Comparability of Columbia Mental Maturity Scale and Stanford–Binet, Form L-M, estimates of intelligence. *Psychological Reports, 34,* 174.

Riviere, M. S. (1973). The use of the Columbia Mental Maturity Scale with institutionalized mentally retarded children. *Educational and Psychological Measurement, 33,* 993–995.

Salvia, J., & Ysseldyke, J. E. (1981). *Assessment in special and remedial education* (2nd ed.). Boston: Houghton Mifflin.

Sattler, J. M. (1982). *Assessment of children's intelligence and special abilities.* Boston: Allyn & Bacon.

Sattler, J. M. (1988). *Assessment of children.* San Diego: Author.

Shah, A., & Holmes, N. (1985). The use of the Leiter International Performance Scale with autistic children. *Journal of Autism and Developmental Disabilities, 15,* 195–203.

Shutt, D. L., & Hannon, T. A. (1974). The validity of the HNTLA for evaluation of the abilities of bilingual children. *Educational and Psychological Measurement, 34,* 429–432.

Smith, J. M. (1987). *Construct and criterion-related validity of the Draw A Person: A Quantitative Scoring System for normal, reading disabled, and developmentally handicapped children.* Unpublished master's thesis, Ohio State University.

Sternberg, R. J. (1984). Toward a triarchic theory of human intelligence. *Behavioral and Brain Sciences, 7,* 269–287.

Stroop, J. R. (1935). The basis of Ligon's theory. *American Journal of Psychology, 47,* 499–504.

Stutzman, R. L. (1986). *A cross validation study of Das's simultaneous–successive–planning model.* Unpublished doctoral dissertation, Ohio State University.

Thorndike, R. L., Hagen, E. P., & Sattler, J. M. (1986). *Stanford–Binet Intelligence Scale: Fourth Edition.* Chicago; Riverside.

Watson, B. U. (1983). Test–retest stability of the Hiskey–Nebraska Test of Learning Aptitude in a sample of hearing-impaired children and adolescents. *Journal of Speech and Hearing Disorders, 48,* 145–149.

Watson, B. U., Sullivan, P. M., Moeller, M. P., & Jensen, J. K. (1982). Nonverbal intelligence and English language ability in deaf children. *Journal of Speech and Hearing Disorders, 47,* 199–204.

Wechsler, D. (1939). *The measurement of adult intelligence.* Baltimore: Williams & Wilkins.

Wechsler, D. (1974). *Manual for the Wechsler Intelligence Scale for Children—Revised.* New York: Psychological Corporation.

Weiner, P. S. (1971). Stability and validity of two measures of intelligence used with children whose language development is delayed. *Journal of Speech and Hearing Research, 14,* 254–261.

Wisnewski, J. J., Rodeheffer, D., & Genshaft, J. L. (1988). Test–retest reliability of the Matrix Analogies Test–Expanded Form. *Perceptual and Motor Skills, 67,* 319–322.

14

Traditional Approaches to Neuropsychological Assessment

RAYMOND S. DEAN
Ball State University
Indiana University School of Medicine

JEFFREY W. GRAY
University of Evansville

Neuropsychology is the study of the neurological bases of behavior. The field evolved through the interaction of psychology and other neurosciences (Reitan, 1955). Although a number of 19th-century attempts were made to link complex psychological functions to specific areas of the brain, our present knowledge base owes more to the past 40 years than to any other time in history (Dean, 1985, 1986a). Indeed, the present clinical sensitivity to neurological issues stems in large part from recent research that has linked behavior to specific autonomical features of the brain (Dean, 1985). Neuropsychological assessment is a clinical attempt to define an individual's brain functioning with objective measures of human behavior.

Using the methods of psychology, neuropsychological assessment samples behavior known to depend on the integrity of the central nervous system (Boll, 1981; Dean, 1985). The specific tests used are based on clinical research in which cognitive, sensory–motor, and emotional functioning have been shown to correlate with localized brain damage recognized during radiological imagery, during surgery, or at autopsy. Historically, neuropsychological assessment grew out of a need to clarify pathophysiology conditions in clinical situations where evidence of brain

dysfunction is inconsistent. In addition to differential diagnosis, these assessment procedures offer a theoretical framework in which both neurological and behavioral information is integrated into a comprehensive view of the individual's level of functioning (Dean, 1983b; Reitan, 1966). Clearly, although a neurologist or radiologist may be able to document and localize brain lesions, it is rarely possible to make specific predictions about behavioral outcomes in a patient's premorbid environment (Dean, 1982; Reitan, 1974). As such, neuropsychological assessment provides information that is useful in diagnosis, treatment, aftercare planning, and follow-up.

Neuropsychological assessment, as noted above, grew out of a need in a clinical setting. Indeed, the medical community's concern for the behavioral effects of brain damage and need for a source of noninvasive diagnostic information were salient influences in the development of specific assessment procedures (Reitan, 1976). The administration of experimental and standardized psychological measures to patients with documented structural brain lesions, in the post-World War II years, gave rise to a data base that allowed the investigation of the sensitivity of these measures to localized cortical damage

(Boll, 1981; Dean, 1985; Golden, 1978; Goldstein, 1942; Halstead, 1947; Hartlage, 1982). This data base, when combined with the emphasis of the 1930s, nurtured a quantitative approach that has characterized neuropsychological assessment in North America (Dean, 1985, 1986a; Goldstein, 1979; Lezak, 1976; Reitan, 1974).

From this viewpoint, a theory of the brain function matters less than the documented utility of an assessment procedure in predicting and localizing brain damage. With such an actuarial approach, specific measures are employed on the basis of data favoring their ability to localize and predict neuropathology in patients with documented neuropathology (see Dean, 1985, for a review). Although early attempts were made to localize functions to microstructures of the brain (Broca, 1861/1960; Jackson, 1874/1932; Wernicke, 1874), such attempts are seen as naive in light of our present knowledge of cerebral functioning (Dean, 1985). Indeed, the magnitude, site, and chronicity of a brain lesion all interact with the patient's developmental history and individual differences in brain structure and chemistry to such an extent that highly specific localization is a quixotic pursuit (Reitan, 1955, 1958; Russell, Neuringer, & Goldstein, 1970; Sperry, Gazzaniga, & Bogen, 1969). Thus, inflexible relationships between function and brain structure have been reconsidered (see Gibson, 1962). However, a quantitative approach that focuses upon differential diagnosis of dysfunction through an understanding of brain–behavior correlates remains the taproot of neuropsychological assessment in North America (Boll, 1981; Dean, 1982; Smith, 1975; Wedding, 1983). Specifically, neuropsychological assessment relies upon a knowledge of brain–behavior relationships in conjunction with normative standards and critical-value cutting scores (Dean, 1986a; Struss & Trites, 1977; Wedding, 1983; Wheeler, Burke, & Reitan, 1963; Wheeler & Reitan, 1963).

Although our present data base does not encourage a notion of static localization of functions (Boll, 1972; Crockett, Clark, & Klonoff, 1981), the validity of "organicity" as a diagnostic entity is also questionable (Dean, 1982; Reitan, 1955; Matthews, Shaw, & Kløve, 1966). The notion of "organicity" grew out of early theories that the effects of

brain damage are similar, regardless of location (e.g., Goldstein, 1942; Hunt, 1943).

From this perspective, behavioral changes are the result of an interaction between the severity and extent of the damage and the subject's premorbid personality (Goldstein, 1942; Tymchuk, 1974). Since Goldstein's (1942) early arguments, numerous researchers have attempted to isolate behavioral and psychogenic markers of this classical "organic syndrome" (see Meier, 1963). Although this search for a unitary organic syndrome continues for some, it has been given up by the field at large (see Dean, 1982, for a review). Clearly, a wealth of data favors the discrete localization of cortical functions. It seems a curious discrepancy between research and clinical practice in psychology that the search for a single measure of organicity (e.g., Bender–Gestalt) continues (Tymchuk, 1974). In addition to clear evidence favoring localization, the notion of "organicity" is at odds with evidence showing that the time since damage, patient's age at onset, and the length of time between damage and assessment are important factors in the behavioral expression of neuropathology (Meier, 1963; Parsons & Prigatano, 1978; Reitan, 1974).

HISTORICAL ELEMENTS

For well over a century, attempts have been made to relate specific functions to anatomical areas of the brain (Broca, 1861/1960; Jackson, 1874/1932). Summarizing his observations of brain-damaged patients, Jackson (1874/1932) argued that "in most people the left side of the brain is the leading side—the side of the so-called will, and the right side of the brain is the automatic side" (p. 141). Such a conclusion was consistent with Broca's (1861/1960) hypothesis that most aspects of speech are served by the left hemisphere of the brain. Renewed experimental interest over the past 40 years, consistent with advances in technology, has further refined our appreciation of hemispheric specialization.

From research of the recent past, it seems clear that for most people, the right hemisphere of the brain is closely associated with the processing of visual–spatial representations of the environment. In contrast, the left hemisphere is responsible for the complex linguistic, serial functions necessary for the decoding of language (see Dean, 1986b, for a review). Typically, the differences attributable to hemispheric functioning seem more closely related to the mode in which information is processed than to the stimuli or modality of presentation (Sperry et al., 1969). Importantly for the present context, these hemispheric differences are the bases for inferences during neuropsychological assessment (Reitan, 1974). For example, in a patient presenting with gross linguistic problems and a history of normal language functioning, one would hypothesize a left-hemisphere dysfunction (Reitan, 1960).

It should be clear at this point that our present corpus of knowledge of hemispheric specialization has evolved from inferential methods (see Dean, 1986b). In the main, these data involve the study of behavioral deficits that accompany localized lesions. Clearly, it should be recognized that the correlational nature of this research interferes with attempts to link structure and function (Willson & Reynolds, 1982). With this caveat in mind, neuropsychology in North America could be characterized by its attempt to link structure and function almost completely on the basis of empirical methods (Luria & Majovski, 1977; Wedding, 1983). Such methods stand in contrast to the qualitative, theoretical approach represented by Luria (1963, 1966, 1970, 1973). Trained as a physician in the Soviet Union, Luria rejected the structural orientation and its goal of direct cerebral localization in favor of a theory of functional systems, which he argued to be the foundation of all coordinated processes (Luria, 1973). The problem with this system relates to its subjective nature in the interpretation of assessment and an inability to validate procedures in any public way (Dean, 1982).

In contrast to Luria's system, the structural approach that has characterized neuropsychology in the West requires little theory for its use (Luria & Majovski, 1977). Thus, inferences from scores on neuropsychological measures are based on strict empirical findings. For example, Reitan (1955) showed that damage to the left hemisphere of the brain corresponded to deficits in Verbal IQ scores on the Wechsler Adult Intelligence Scale (WAIS) (see Matarazzo, 1972). Conversely, deficiencies in nonverbal intelligence were related to right-hemisphere lesions in adults.

Thus, differences in verbal versus nonverbal behavior exhibited on the WAIS have come to hold implications for hemispheric functioning (Matarazzo, 1972). The fact that such conclusions have not held with children makes it clear that generalizations established with adults cannot be applied to children without empirical confirmation (Benton, 1974; Reed & Reitan, 1969).

These findings with IQ scores point to the fact that intelligence tests are but an aggregate of neuropsychological measures. The selection of subtests has most often been based upon the tests' social utility. From this point of view, it becomes clear that the neuropsychological assessment is comprehensive, in that functions with and without social importance are examined. Thus, most intelligence batteries are atheoretical, in that the choice of individual tests is based on their perceived social value and their utility as predictors of behaviors such as school performance (Dean, 1986b).

It should be recognized that the radical quantitative approach taken in the choice of neuropsychological tests in the West, while increasing prediction, has often eluded interpretation (Dean, 1983b). To take a familiar example, the choice of subtests comprising the Wechsler scales was based on quantitative grounds and Wechsler's (1958) broad notion of ability aggregates. Clearly, the Wechsler batteries have been shown to offer one of the best single predictors of extratest behaviors (see Dean, 1982). However, the interpretation of subtest scores for individuals and groups has been one of the most researched and yet controversial topics in psychological assessment (see Kaufman, 1979). This is less of an indictment of the quantitative approach than a sign of the primitive status of our knowledge of brain–behavior relationships.

A notable exception to the paradigm above in the construction of intelligence tests is the Kaufman Assessment Battery for Children (K-ABC; Kaufman & Kaufman, 1983). It is a wide-band cognitive battery constructed around a functional theory of the brain. Unlike the atheoretical approach taken in the development of cognitive measures such as the Wechsler scales, the Mental Processing scales of the K-ABC were designed to conform to the sequential–simultaneous processing dichotomy articulated by Luria (1966) and operationalized by Das (e.g., 1973). Although this dichotomy is not without controversy, Kaufman and Kaufman (1983) present a good deal of factor-analytic evidence for a sequential–simultaneous dimension. The K-ABC, because of its theoretical base, also makes a useful distinction between mental processing and the more socially related elements of academic achievement. Because the K-ABC relies less on social experience for scales of cognitive efficiency, Kaufman and Kaufman (1983) argue that the battery has less social bias than measures such as the Wechsler Intelligence Scale for Children—Revised (WISC-R).

FUNCTIONS ASSESSED

As mentional above, traditional neuropsychological assessment approaches in North America have evolved with a distinct quantitative emphasis (Anthony, Heaton, & Lehman, 1980). Consistent with a classical psychometric view, specific tests and procedures have been assembled more because of their psychometric adequacy than because of their relationship to any functional theory of the brain (see Dean, 1982). The adequacy of most measures has been evaluated in terms of their ability to predict neurological disorders when unambiguous diagnoses exist (e.g., Reitan, 1974). Historically, this has allowed the continuous estimation of the utility of neuropsychological procedures while establishing their credibility within the medical setting (Crockett et al., 1981; Reitan, 1966). Within this framework, the neuropsychological examination represents the most comprehensive approach to the understanding of the individual's psychological functioning (Boll, 1981; Dean, 1985). This comprehensiveness is evident in most traditional batteries (Golden, Hammeke, & Purisch, 1978; Reitan, 1964, 1969; Smith, 1975).

Most batteries involve measures of language, cognitive, sensory–motor, and emotional functioning (Boll, 1981; Dean, 1982; Reitan, 1974; Reitan & Davison, 1974). The specific tests used may vary with the psychologist, but the neuropsychological functions most consistently examined in the course of assessment are listed in Table 14.1. It should be recognized that the attempt to assess a particular function while excluding all others is often an impossible pursuit (Dean, Schwartz, & Smith, 1981). This is the case because neurological dysfunction is rarely isolated to one specific function (e.g., Luria, 1966), and because higher-order functions (e.g., memory) rely upon normal lower-level functions (e.g., receptive language) (Dean, 1983b). From this point of view, low-level performance on a measure of memory is but one necessary precondition for inferring memory dysfunction. Indeed, memory functioning includes attention, receptive features, and the registration of elements to be recalled (e.g., Barbizet, 1970; Crovitz, 1979; Hebb, 1949; Watson & Benton, 1976). Thus, assessing individual functions to the exclusion of all others is often impossible. For this reason, and for other psychometric considerations, the wide-band approach offered by a battery is most often the examination of choice (Seretny, Dean, Gray, & Hartlage, 1986). Although many of the assessment procedures used as part of the neuropsychological examination are the same as those routinely administered by the psychologist in general practice, the interpretation of the results may differ drastically (Dean, 1982).

APPROACHES TO INTERPRETATION

The interpretation of neuropsychological examination has relied upon four inferential techniques (Reitan, 1974). Although these methods are used individually, they are most often used in some combination when considering an individual's test results. The first and most basic consideration concerns the patient's "level of performance" on individual measures. When normative standards are used, "cutoff scores" indicative of either aberrant or normal functioning are compared with the subject's results. Low levels of performance are suggestive of impairment; however, they are rarely sufficient in themselves for inferring cortical dysfunction (Baron, 1978; Dean, 1985). Although levels of performance are problematic with both adults and children, Reed, Reitan, and Kløve (1965) have shown a greater number of false-positive and false-negative results when using level-of-performance inferences with children than with adults. This seems to be the case because of the relatively greater in-

TABLE 14.1. Functions Evaluated in Neuropsychological Assessment

I. Cognitive functions
A. General ability
B. Verbal functions
  1. Language
    a. Receptive
    b. Expressive
    c. Fund of knowledge
  2. Abstract reasoning
    a. Concept formation
    b. Symbolic manipulation
  3. Memory/learning
    a. Registration of information
    b. Immediate (short-term) memory
    c. Long-term (intermediate) memory
    d. Memory for remote events
    e. Acquisition rate
  4. Integrative functions
    a. Visual–verbal
    b. Auditory–verbal
    c. Motor–verbal
  5. Numerical ability
    a. Receptive
    b. Expressive
    c. Knowledge base
C. Nonverbal functions
  1. Perceptual organization
    a. Receptive
    b. Expressive
  2. Abstract reasoning
    a. Concept formation
    b. Spatial manipulation
  3. Memory
    a. Registration of information
    b. Immediate (short-term) memory
    c. Long-term (intermediate) memory
    d. Memory for remote events
    e. Rate of acquisition
  4. Integrative functions
    a. Visual–motor
    b. Auditory–motor
    c. Tactile–motor
  5. Construction
II. Perception
A. Visual
  1. Acuity
  2. Ocular dominance
  3. Fields of vision
B. Auditory
  1. Acuity
  2. Discrimination
    a. Verbal
    b. Nonverbal
  3. Lateralization of ability

C. Tactile–kinesthetic
  1. Acuity
  2. Discrimination
  3. Lateralization of ability
III. Motor functions
A. Strength
B. Speed of performance
C. Perceptual–motor speed
D. Coordination
E. Dexterity
F. Lateral preference
IV. Emotional/control functions
A. Attention
B. Concentration
C. Frustration tolerance
D. Interpersonal/social skills
E. Flexibility
F. Emotional functioning
G. Personality

fluence of environmental and developmental factors on cortical impairment for children than for adults. Boll (1974) has argued that these same factors may contribute to less reliable neuropsychological conclusions with young children than with adults.

Research concerning the cerebral lateralization of left- and right-hemisphere abilities (e.g., Boll, 1972; Reitan, 1974) has established that intentional activities are served by the contralateral hemisphere; this allows one to make inferences concerning hemispheric functioning when motor and sensory functioning is compared for the left and right sides of the body. Knowledge of the lateralization of cerebral functions also permits an inference of a left–right localization of damage (Dean, 1986b). For example, an adult with right-hemisphere focal lesions is *likely* to present with sensory and motor deficits on the left side of his or her body, and to exhibit poorer performance on nonverbal than on verbal tasks (Boll, 1972).

More familiar in medicine than in psychology, a third method of inference involves the consideration of pathogenic signs. This approach considers constellations of behaviors that hold significance as indicators of neuropathology (see Chelune, Heaton, Lehman, & Robinson, 1979; Satz, Fennell, & Reilly, 1970). Pathogenic signs rely upon symptoms that would rarely be displayed in a patient without the presence of neurological dysfunction. The presence of a positive sign is far more informative than the lack of one. In other words, a pathognomonic sign very rarely occurs without pathology, but the lack of a sign is not indicative of normality.

Pattern analysis is an integration of the level-of-performance, lateralization, and pathogenic-sign approaches. This method involves the consideration of psychometric and behavioral data that result from the neuropsychological examination. In this case, the patient's relative areas of strengths and weaknesses are compared with patterns for groups of patients with known neuropathology. This method reduces subjectivity in interpretation while emphasizing the diagnosis and localization of dysfunction with both adults and children (Anthony et al., 1980; Selz & Reitan, 1979). Although the method one uses to isolate test patterns has received considerable debate, a statistical actuarial approach has been shown to be superior to clinical methods (e.g., Goldstein, 1979; Knights, 1973; Wedding, 1983).

ASSESSING CHILDREN

Our understanding of children's neuropsychological functioning is more primitive than our knowledge of the functioning of adults (Benton, 1974; Dean, 1982; Reitan, 1974). Correspondingly, neuropsychological assessment of children is a relatively recent pursuit that has grown out of our success in defining brain–behavior relationships with adults (Benton, 1974; Boll, 1981). The reasons for this state of affairs include the greater numbers of adult referrals with documented lesions and the opportunity to validate assessment procedures during surgery and autopsy (Dean, 1985).

The interpretation of children's performances on neuropsychological measures is further complicated by a number of factors that do not play a prominent role with adults (Boll, 1974). Clearly, the results of a child's neuropsychological examination must be interpreted in light of the child's developmental stage at the time of onset (Boll, 1974), premorbid developmental history (Benton, 1974), perinatal history (Gray, Dean, Rattan, & Bechtel, 1988), acuteness of the disorder (Dean, 1985), and environmental history (Benton, 1974). These factors can be responsible for very different assessment results for

similar lesions in mature and developing nervous systems (e.g., Ernhart, Graham, Eichman, Marshall, & Thurston, 1963). In addition, patterns of recovery differ for adults and children (e.g., Klonoff, Low, & Clark, 1977).

Klonoff and his associates (Klonoff et al., 1977; Klonoff & Robinson, 1967; Klonoff & Thompson, 1969) have offered data suggesting that the type of brain damage most frequently occurring in childhood is responsible in part for adult–child differences in assessment. Epidemiological estimates indicate that brain damage resulting from "falls" is some three times more prevalent in children than in adults (Klonoff et al., 1977). Thus, not only are closed head injuries more prevalent with children than with adults, but they also occur in developing brains—a fact that further obscures comparisons.

In general, differential diagnosis of neurological disorders with children remains a more complex undertaking than that with adults (Dean, 1985). Similar to findings for adults, a good deal of research indicates that neuropsychological batteries are sensitive to brain dysfunction with children (Boll, 1972; Dean, 1982; Golden, 1981; Hartlage, 1982; Klonoff & Low, 1974; Reed et al., 1965; Reitan, 1971; Reitan & Heineman, 1968). However, Reed et al. (1965) and Boll (1974), using extensive neuropsychological batteries, offer data indicating that patterns of deficits for adults and children who have sustained head injuries are very different. In general, brain damage in children seems to have more global effects than those found in adults with similar lesions. Children are more likely to exhibit a general impairment of those cognitive abilities that are resistant to impairment with adults (Ernhart et al., 1963; Reed, et al., 1965). Using the Halstead Neurological Test Battery for Children (see below), Reitan (1974) reported scores on the WISC to be more salient predictors of brain damage in children (6–8 years) than similar measures for adults. It would seem that well-practiced skills are more resistant to cerebral insult in adults than has been found in children (Dean, 1985). So, too, the effects of neuropathology in childhood are more profound than those of pathology in later years (e.g., Reitan, 1974). From our present data base, it would appear that the earlier the insult occurs, the more generalized the resulting effect on neuropsychological measures is (Boll, 1972; Fitzhugh & Fitzhugh, 1965; Reed & Fitzhugh, 1966; Reitan, 1974). Although real problems exist in translating adult neuropsychological research to children, attempts at direct applications of these data continue (Boll, 1974).

A related problem in the neuropsychological assessment of children is the relative lack of data regarding normal development trends for children on tests of neuropsychological functioning. Such data would give us a much clearer picture of the development of cortically related behaviors and the amount of normal variability that can be expected. Crockett, Klonoff, and Bjerring (1969) emphasized the importance of such development changes with data showing that increasing neuropsychological complexity occurs with age on some 32 neuropsychological measures. Whether these findings represent invariant developmental trends or fluctuations between development levels remains unclear.

In sum, for numerous reasons, while consistent behavioral patterns have been shown to predict specific adult cortical disorders, the assumption that these same test patterns reflect underlying cortical dysfunctions in children is untenable (Dean, 1985, 1986). This problem is underscored for children with learning disorders. Indeed, for over a century, attempts have been made to explain children's classroom learning problems in terms of neurological aberrations. Although early overzealous attempts to explain *all* children's learning problems in terms of neurological disorders have been rejected by most researchers, problems remain in the differential diagnosis of children's learning disorders.

THE HALSTEAD–REITAN NEUROPSYCHOLOGICAL TEST BATTERIES

Consistent with the quantitative approach that has characterized neuropsychological assessment in North America, such assessment has involved the development of test batteries (see Dean, 1982, for a review). The goal in each case has been the prediction of neurological disorders while offering a comprehensive view of the patient's individual functions (Golden et al., 1978; Reitan, 1969;

Smith, 1975). Although numerous batteries have been offered, the Halstead–Reitan Neuropsychological Test Battery (HRNTB; Reitan, 1969) remains the most widely used and researched measure in North America (Seretny et al., 1986). The battery itself was originally developed by Halstead (1947) to operationalize his theory of biological intelligence. However, its present configuration owes more to the efforts of Ralph Reitan (1955). Halstead's (1947) original collection of some 27 measures was reduced by Reitan (1955) to the 10 that would best discriminate between normals and patients with unambiguous neuropathology. To achieve this consolidation, Reitan used a radical quantitative approach in which individual measures were included only after substantial evidence was obtained for the incremental validity of those measures in the differential diagnosis of various forms of brain damage (Reitan, 1974). Clearly, this approach served to increase the sensitivity of the battery to cortical dysfunction. On balance, however, such procedures would seem to have compromised the utility of the HRNTB in assessing individual functions (e.g., abstract reasoning).

The HRNTB was originally developed for use with adults (Reitan, 1955). However, based on research in which the battery was administered to successively younger children, a downward revision was developed that was appropriate with children aged 9–14 years (Reitan, 1969). This version is referred to as the Halstead Neuropsychological Test Battery for Children (HNTB-C), and, aside from changes in the number and organization of the items, it remains the same as the adult version. Other necessary alterations have included the use of age-appropriate allied measures (e.g., the WAIS was replaced with the WISC).

Basically, both the HRNTB and the HNTB-C include tests proported to measure elements of language, perception, sensation, abstract thought, sensory–motor integration, lack of perception, and dexterity. Table 14.2 offers a précis of the individual measures included in the batteries and of measures seen as allied tests. It should be kept in mind that the measurement of individual functions to the exclusion of all others is not possible. As alluded to above, conclusions of impaired nonverbal reasoning, for example, must be deferred without evidence of intact memory.

TABLE 14.2. Texts Included in the Halstead–Reitan Neuropsychological Batteries, and Adjunct Measures

Name	Origin	Format	Technical information	Explicit constructs assessed	Implicit constructs assessed	Forms	Scores
			Tests included in the batteries				
Category Test	Halstead (1947)	Semiautomated visual presentation of slides with underlying concept. Feedback provided as to correctness after depression of one of four levers. Controlled learning experience.	Reitan (1955); Klove (1974)	Concept formation, abstraction, integration	Visual acuity, attention, concentration	Adult—208 slides 9–14—168 slides 5–9—80 slides	Total errors
Tactual Performance Test	Sequin–Goddard Form Board; Halstead (1947)	Shapes placed in form board without aid of vision (dominant, nondominant both hands). Recall of shapes and location of board.	Reitan (1974); Boll (1974)	Tactual discrimination, manual dexterity, kinesthesis, incidental memory, spatial memory	Kinesthesis, tactual–motor integration	Adult—10 shapes 9–14—6 shapes 5–9—6 shapes	1. Time 2. Memory 3. Location
Speech–Sounds Perception	Halstead (1947)	Select paralog presented auditorially from alternatives, total of 60 items.	Reitan (1974); Klove (1974)	Verbal auditory discrimination, auditory–visual integration, phonetic skills	Auditory acuity, language, attention	Adult—4 alternatives 9–14—3 alternatives	Total errors
Rhythm Test	Seashore Tests of Musical Talent	Identification to 30 pairs of rhythmic beats as being "same" or "different."	Reitan (1955)	Nonverbal auditory discrimination, auditory perception	Attention, concentration	—	Total errors
Trail Making	Army Individual Test; Adjutant General's Office (1944)	A. Connect 25 (15) numbered circles in numerical order. B. Connect 25 (15) numbered or lettered circles, alternating between numerical and alphabetical order (i.e., 1-A-2-B . . .).	Reitan (1955, 1974); Boll (1974)	A. Motor speed, visual scanning. B. Visual–motor integration of alphabetical and numerical systems	Visual acuity, attention, concentration	Adult—25 circles 9–15—15 circles	Separate time, A and B

378

Adjunct measures[a]

Test	Reference	Measure	Reference	Function	Distractibility	Items/Norms	Scoring
Finger Oscillation Test	Halstead (1947)	Measure of number of taps in 10 seconds with index finger for each hand. Dominant, nondominant scores = means of five trials for each hand.		Motor speed, dexterity	Distractibility, concentration	Same	Mean taps each hand
Adjunct measures[a]							
Reitan–Indiana Aphasia Screening Test	Halstead & Wepman (1952); Reitan (1969)	32 items requiring naming, spelling, reading, writing, math, calculations, enunciating, identifying body parts, performing pantomiming actions, performing actions drawing shapes, and identifying directions.	Reitan (1969); Kløve (1974); Dean (1982)	Wide-band language and nonverbal functions	Education, occupation, concentration	Adult—32 items 9-15—32 items 5-9—22 items	By item; total error score
Reitan–Kløve Sensory Perceptual Examinations	Reitan (1969)	Accuracy of unilateral and bilateral simultaneous tactile, auditory, and visual imperception; finger localization from tactile stimulation without vision; tactile number perception on fingertips; tactile recognition of shapes without vision.	Reitan (1969); Kløve (1974)	Lateralized sensory perseption (visual, auditory, and tactile)	distractibility	—	Errors (left vs. right side of body)
Strength of Grip Test (Hand Dynamometer)	Reitan (1955)	Measure of strength of grip; alternating measures for preferred and nonpreferred hands.	Reitan (1955)	Motor strength	—	—	Left- and right-hand scores.

[a]In addition to these, the age-appropriate Wechsler intelligence scale, the Minnesota Multiphasic Personality Inventory, the Lateral Dominance Examination, the Wide Range Achievement Test, and the Wechsler Memory Scale are often incorporated.

This is true because recall of information is prerequisite to abstract reasoning.

From Table 14.2, it is clear that the majority of the measures comprising the two batteries were developed for other purposes. In each case, tests were adapted and interpretations expanded to neuropsychological functions (Reitan, 1969). Dean (1985) has described, and this table reflects, constructs implicit to performance on these measures. Although functions such as sensory acuity, attention, concentration, and distractibility play a role in most psychological tests, these abilities are crucial in making inferences about cerebral functions.

The sensitivity of the HRNTB and HRNB-C to cerebral dysfunction has been investigated continuously since their development (see Dean, 1985, for a review). Most early studies of the "validity" of the HRNTB and HRNB-C have come from investigations using a "clinical blind" technique (Dean, 1982). This approach involves the administration and interpretation of the batteries without knowledge of the subject's history or diagnosis (Reitan, 1974). Inferences made on the basis of test results are then compared with independent information from radiological, surgical, and/or autopsy. This methodology is not without problems, in that it is difficult to isolate the utility of the batteries from the clinical acumen of the interpreter (Dean, 1985). Since these early efforts, numerous, more rigorous empirical (mechanical/actuarial) approaches to the study of the batteries have been made (e.g., Finkelstein, 1976).

The Halstead Impairment Index does provide some aid in interpretation. This summary measure reflects the proportion of the most impairment-sensitive tests of the batteries on which the individual patient has scored in the impaired range (Kiernan & Matthews, 1979). Although it is of little value in outlining a patient's strengths in terms of individual functions, in adults this index is the most sensitive indicator of brain damage (Reitan, 1959).

Validation studies with the HRNTB have, in the main, indicated its sensitivity to cortical dysfunction with adults (see Boll, 1981; Dean, 1982; Reitan, 1974). In general, group studies with the battery have shown it to discriminate normal controls from neurological patients with considerable accuracy (84%–98%; see Boll, 1981). A number of investigators have offered convincing data favoring better localization of brain damage with the HRNTB for acute lesions than for more chronic neuropathology (Reed & Reitan, 1963; Reitan, 1955). When chronic schizophrenics are excluded from consideration, a number of researchers have also shown the HRNTB to distinguish between patients with specific organic pathology and those with psychiatric disorders (see Heaton & Crowley, 1981).

Similar to the findings with adults, research indicates that the HNTB-C is sensitive to childhood neurological dysfunction (Boll, 1974; Klonoff & Low, 1974; Reed et al., 1965; Reitan, 1971; Reitan & Heineman, 1968). However, these efforts to examine the HNTB-C with children constitute a more recent line of research (Dean, 1985). This state of affairs results from the fact that there are greater numbers of adult referrals with discretely localized lesions than of child referrals. It is also true that adult neurological disorders, as opposed to those seen in children, are more likely to provide the opportunity to validate assessment techniques during surgery and autopsies (Dean, 1982; Reitan, 1974). As mentioned previously, a number of moderator variables exist that influence children's neuropsychological functioning.

Unlike the findings with adults, brain-damaged children are often found to be in the impaired range on most measures (e.g., Boll, 1974; Reitan, 1974). In fact, neuropsychological assessment of children with brain damage is more likely to uncover global impairment of functions than is assessment of adults who sustain similar structural damage (Ernhart et al., 1963; Reed & Reitan, 1969; Reed et al., 1965; Reitan, 1974). This general depression of cognitive functioning may well be the result of less firmly established or "overlearned" skills (see Dean, 1982). Generally, older children (over 11 years of age) with neurological dysfunction display a greater discrepancy from normals on higher-level language and motor functions than do younger children. The fact that children in general show greater variability on psychometric measures than adults must also be considered when reviewing the research in this area (Dean, 1986). Indeed, Reed and Reitan (1969) offered data showing that fewer lateralized effects result from brain damage in children than in adults. Although the findings of impaired performance on the HNTB-C for brain-damaged children seem robust, differential diagnosis of the location of dysfunction with children is a far more tenuous procedure with children than with adults (e.g., Boll, 1981).

As pointed out earlier, the Halstead Impairment Index is the most sensitive indicator of brain damage for adults (Reitan, 1969). Interestingly, this is not true for children. A number of studies have shown the Full Scale IQ score offered by the WISC to be a more salient predictor than the Halstead Index of brain damage in children (e.g., Reitan, 1974). One reason for this may be that overlearned material (which is most often sampled in the Wechsler scales) may be more resistant to neurological damage in adults because of more pathways to the same information. Differences between children and adults may be also related, in part, to developmental changes in functional lateralization in childhood (Dean, 1982).

EMOTIONAL DISTURBANCE

Dean (1986c) has argued in favor of considering the combination of neurological and emotional factors in the interpretation of children's neuropsychological assessment results. The relationship between emotional disturbance and neurological dysfunction in children is a complex one. A number of researchers have reported emotional disturbance to occur with significantly greater frequency in children who have suffered brain damage than in normals (e.g., Shaffer, 1974). From another point of view, neuropsychological impairment occurs significantly more frequently in emotionally disturbed children without obvious neurological abnormality than in samples of normal children (Reed & Reitan, 1963). Although neurologically impaired children may well react to a perceived loss of function in an emotional fashion (Dean, 1982), it is also plausible that the onset of emotional symptoms is concomitant with damage to specific structures of the brain (Shaffer, 1974). The truth, of course, will probably be most clearly understood on a continuum involving etiological and environmental factors.

Recent estimates suggest that some 60% of child psychiatric patients have some form of neuropsychological impairment on the HNTB-C (e.g., Tramontana, Sherrets, & Golden, 1980). Although generalizations are difficult, the most severe deficits seem to occur on tasks requiring complex cognitive–perceptual manipulation, followed closely by sensory–motor deficits. These findings are consistent, of course, with other data suggesting that children with psychiatric disorders and normal neurological findings are likely to present with neuropsychological evidence of cerebral dysfunction (Rutter, 1977).

The extent of neuropsychological impairment occurring in child psychiatric patients would seem to be related to the chronicity of their disorders. Indeed, a number of studies have shown a higher probability of neuropsychological dysfunction when a psychiatric disorder has been present for more than 2 years (Tramontana et al., 1980). This relationship between neuropsychological impairment and psychiatric chronicity has been reported with schizophrenics (e.g., Klonoff, Fibiger, & Hutton, 1970; Wehler & Hoffman, 1978). Although any statement regarding causation must be approached with care, neuropsychological impairment in a psychiatric patient increases the probability that the patient has a more static disorder with a less-than-encouraging prognosis (Dean, 1985).

In light of the fact that children with neurological dysfunction must cope with an environment in which few opportunities exist for success, concomitant emotional disturbance is not surprising. Such children present a unique challenge in assessment, in that it is often difficult or impossible to consider neuropsychological impairment apart from a child's emotional response to failure (Dean & Rattan, 1987). It is not clear whether brain-damaged children are also predisposed to emotional disorders or whether academic difficulties stress these children's coping mechanisms. The truth may be found in a subtle interaction.

It is apparent that neuropsychological assessment of the child cannot be approached without an appreciation of both emotional and cognitive factors. Meaningful assessment must consider the interaction of both emotional and more traditional neuropsychological factors (Dean, 1983). Dean (1983) showed that a combination of neurological and emotional factors in what amounted to a systematic desensitization procedure was more effective in treating children's learning deficits than a cognitive-only approach. Interestingly, although this approach was shown to be effective in teaching cognitive skills, it produced little change in children's measured neuropsychological functioning. Behavioral problems in the classroom were also reported, concomitant with gains in academic achievement.

PERINATAL COMPLICATIONS

With medical advances have come improved survival rates for infants following complications during the perinatal period. However, the improved survival rates have resulted in a larger number of children with neuropsychological impairment (Gray et al., 1988). Indeed, children who have experienced perinatal complications are more likely than children with no such complications to manifest cerebral palsy, mental retardation, and seizure disorders (see Freeman, 1985, for a review). In addition, a considerable data base exists to suggest that perinatal difficulties increase the probability of less pervasive neuropsychological disorders, such as developmental delays and attentional, speech, and learning disorders (see Gray et al., 1988).

Data concerning the perinatal period of life are important in the interpretation of a child's neuropsychological examination. Indeed, as perinatal complications increase, so does the likelihood that impairment found during assessment may represent a longstanding disorder. Although numerous methods exist for identifying children at risk from perinatal problems, few offer the clinician an economical method of identifying early problems.

Apgar assessments are routinely performed in most delivery rooms. Although low Apgar scores are clearly related to neonatal mortality (e.g., Apgar & James, 1962), they are less than significant in predicting childhood neuropsychological impairment (Nelson & Ellenberg, 1981). Another method involves a retrospective review of the child's medical chart for the birth. However, the medical chart may be inaccessible; thus this method, while important, may be of limited

utility to the clinician in our highly mobile society.

Information concerning the perinatal period has most often been collected as part of an unstructured maternal interview. However, this approach has been shown to offer less reliability than is necessary in the clinical setting (e.g., Robbins, 1963). Problems here relate to errors of omission, as well as selective memory and confabulation (e.g., Rutt & Offord, 1971). Recognizing these problems in a self-report methodology, we (Gray, Dean, & Rattan, 1986) showed that reliability in the collection of such information could be enhanced with a highly structured measure. Using a 47-item measure that asked for information pertaining to pregnancy, birth, and the first month of life, we (Gray et al., 1988) found that mothers were able to report information reliably when several response alternatives were provided. In addition, the mothers' reports were in high agreement with the same information gleaned from the hospital chart.

It is clear that complications during the perinatal period place the infant at risk of later neuropsychological impairment. However, it is important to note that there does not seem to be a one-to-one relationship between perinatal complications and neurological dysfunction. One clear mediating factor is the environment in which the high-risk child is raised. Indeed, it seems to be the case that high-risk infants born to middle-class families are less likely to experience long-term neuropsychological sequelae (see Gray et al., 1986).

LEARNING DISORDERS

For somewhat more than a century, attempts have been made to explain children's classroom learning problems in terms of neurological aberrations. Indeed, classroom learning disorders represent some 30% of pediatric neurological referrals (Dean, 1985). Although for some of these children a clear neurological disorder exists, for many the etiology is complicated by other factors (Dean, 1986c). However, as a diagnostic tool, a neuropsychological assessment has shown to be useful both in delineating cognitive processing deficits and in ruling out a more frank neurological disorder (Dean, 1983a). In fact, we (D'Amato, Gray, & Dean, 1988) have shown that the HNTB-C offers a good deal of unique information in understanding the learning-disabled, over and above that provided by the traditional psychological assessment. In this study, it was shown that some 90% of variability of the HNTB-C was nonredundant with the WISC-R. The overlap in information that did occur could be attributed to "general" cognitive reasoning in each measure.

Difficulties in the diagnosis of learning disabilities continue to exist. This problem in diagnosis is quite clearly related to the tenuousness of a single syndrome that would represent the full spectrum of learning disorders. The utility of any syndrome lies in the ability to identify children displaying common behaviors, or children with a similar etiology, or children who are best treated with a single approach. Difficulties arise, however, because the range of learning disabilities offers few common elements.

The question of a single syndrome versus multiple syndromes in learning disabilities is considered by Vellutino, Smith, Steger and Kaman (1975) and by Satz and colleagues (Fletcher & Satz, 1979). Vellutino et al. (1975) have argued in favor of a unitary understanding of reading disabilities, based upon a similar underlying linguistic deficit. They suggest that since problems in discrimination of letters or words are not due to visual acuity difficulties, reading errors may more appropriately be attributed to phonological, semantic, and syntactic deficits. Clearly, a linguistic as opposed to a perceptual deficit hypothesis would seem to best fit the data offered by Vellutino and his associates (Vellutino, et al., 1975; Vellutino, Steger, Moyer, Harding, & Niles, 1977).

In contrast, Satz and his colleagues (Satz, Taylor, Friel, & Fletcher, 1978) offer evidence for subtypes of reading disorders that interact with developmental changes. Using a longitudinal approach, Satz and his group have shown that younger children (aged 5–8) with reading problems are more likely to present with sensory–motor and perceptual deficits, as shown in errors of copying and recognition of letters and words. However, after age 8, children with reading disorders are likely to display deficits in more higher-order linguistic skills, as expressed in lower verbal comprehension. Consistent with

Satz's multiple-subtype paradigm of reading disabilities, numerous diagnoses have been applied to children with these disorders, such as "hyperkinetic syndrome," "developmental clumsiness," "perceptual–motor handicap," "congenital aphasia," and others (Benton, 1974; Gubbay, Ellis, Walton, & Court, 1965; Stewart, Pitts, Craig, & Dierof, 1966).

The enactment of federal legislation (the Education for All Handicapped Children Act of 1975, P.L. 94-142) has offered some direction for diagnosing learning disabilities, in that the criteria used by public schools in the United States are more uniform. In keeping with this law, the learning-disabled child is seen as exhibiting a severe perceptual, integrative, or expressive deficit that adversely affects the ability to learn. Such disorders are seen in impaired processes or skills (e.g., listening, thinking, talking, reading, writing, spelling, or arithmetic). This federal legislation excludes learning problems that are the result of other handicapping conditions (e.g., visual, hearing, motoric handicaps, mental retardation, emotional disturbance, and the like) from the category of learning disabilities. In sum, a learning disability is seen to require a severe discrepancy between ability (intelligence) and achievement in the academic areas of reading (recognition and comprehension), expressive language, and/or mathematics. Normal or near-normal ability has often been defined on intelligence tests (e.g., the WISC-R) as an IQ score of 90 or above on either the Verbal or the Performance scales (Clements, 1966). Although problems clearly exist with the approach, this ability–achievement discrepancy is usually operationalized as achievement 2 or more academic years below what would be expected by grade placement.

Over the past two decades, a number of attempts have been made to identify specific learning disorder subtypes using neuropsychological batteries (e.g., Denckla, 1972; Doehring & Hoshko, 1977; Fisk & Rourke, 1979; Morris, Blashfield, & Satz, 1981). These studies have, in the main, included psychomotor, visual–perceptual, and expressive language measures, along with tests of integrative functions (e.g., abstract reasoning and problem-solving strategies). The goal of such subtyping efforts is the formation of homogeneous groups, and with it the isolation of diagnostic markers, enhanced matching of rehabilitation approaches, and more meaningful study of the etiological factors for individual disorders.

As mentioned above, both longitudinal (Satz et al., 1978; Spreen & Haaf, 1986) and cross-sectional (Fisk & Rourke, 1979) investigations have shown age-related changes in skill deficits for learning-disabled children. In one early study, Satz et al. (1978) conducted a follow-up of kindergarten children when they had reached the sixth grade and found that younger children with learning disabilities were likely to present with process impairments involving problems in sensory–motor and cross-modal integration. In contrast, older children with learning problems had difficulty in conceptual–linguistic skills. In a recent longitudinal study, Spreen and Haaf (1986) did neuropsychological assessments of children at a mean age of 10 years and again some 14 years later. Their findings were somewhat similar to Satz et al.'s, in that the subtypes at 10 years of age involved problems of visual–perceptual, articulation–graphomotor, and linguistic functioning. When the subjects were examined at some 24 years of age, however, only the visual–perceptual and articulation–graphomotor subtypes remained, and the linguistic subtype no longer existed.

Age-related differences in subtypes have also been reported by Fisk and Rourke (1979). In this study, one subtype was characterized by impaired fingertip perception for children aged 13–14 years, but this subtype did not exist in a group of younger learning-disabled children (aged 9–10 years). Clearly, the deficits of learning-disabled children are related to age. The reasons for these age differences are not clear; however, such differences would be expected with neurological maturation, compensation for early cerebral damage, and/or remedial programming.

CONCLUSIONS

Traditionally, the goal of neuropsychological assessment has been to provide diagnostic information on patients when equivocal evidence of neuropathology exists. The methods and approach to assessment that have evolved are more the results of needs in the medical setting than of theory (see Dean, 1985). This emphasis on diagnosis grew out of the empirical base of neuropsychology, in an age when the neuropsychological examination was relatively benign in comparison to physical diagnostic methods (e.g., Reitan, 1969), which held a clear risk of mortality. However, the past two decades have witnessed geometric growth in the sophistication of noninvasive radiological diagnostic techniques (Luchins, 1982; Raichle, 1979). Indeed, the new generation of computed axial tomography, positron emission tomography, and electromagnetic resonance equipment suggests less reliance upon neuropsychological assessment in the diagnosis of neurological disorders. Although these radiological techniques at present offer means of validating the neuropsychological examination, continued refinement of such imaging devices can only serve to reduce diagnostic dependence on neuropsychological assessment.

Dean (1986a) has argued that the future of neuropsychological assessment will be shaped by reduced reliance on behavioral data for diagnosis and by an increased need to understand the patient's functional deficits in the treatment and rehabilitation of neurological disorders (e.g., Ben-Yishay, Gerstman, Diller, & Haas, 1970). Given a patient's premorbid environment, neuropsychological assessment must seek to define the cognitive, emotional, perceptual, and sensory aspects of the patient's functioning; to establish a baseline in which the rehabilitation can be followed; to predict the return of function in light of damage; to define the treatment priorities for a given patient (given multiple impairments and limited resources); and to define the ways in which the patient's impairments will be expressed as disabilities in his or her premorbid environment (see Diller & Gordon, 1981).

In sum, neuropsychological assessment in the past has focused on acute neurological disorders, and as such has represented a psychometric extension of the neurological workup. It seems clear that increased needs in the rehabilitation setting and more reliance on radiological techniques will be expressed in greater concern for remedial outcomes. The accent in assessment will involve establishing a framework of emotional, cognitive, and physical factors that provide an overview of the patient. Although psychometric findings of cognitive, perceptual, and motor functioning are of growing importance in rehabilitation, few attempts have been made to interface such findings with specific rehabilitation approaches (Ben-Yishay et al., 1970; Golden, 1978).

The questions posed by rehabilitation are quite different from those of diagnosis. Assessment with the objective of rehabilitation planning goes beyond diagnosing dysfunction relative to a normative group. Here, the concern is on defining how these impairments are expressed as disabilities in the patient's premorbid environment (Dean, 1985). Unlike diagnosis, which attempts to segregate a constellation of behaviors into a single disorder, rehabilitation works to define a neurological disorder in terms of the medical, vocational, speech–hearing, and physical aspects in need of treatment (Dean, 1986a). It is apparent that a neurological disorder is seldom expressed as a single dysfunction.

REFERENCES

Anthony, W. Z., Heaton, R. K., & Lehman, R. A. W. (1980). An attempt to cross-validate two actuarial systems for neuropsychological test interpretations. *Journal of Consulting and Clinical Psychology, 48,* 317–326.

Apgar, V., & James, L. S. (1962). Further observations on the newborn scoring system. *American Journal of Diseases of Children, 104,* 419–428.

Barbizet, J. (1970). *Human memory and its pathology.* San Francisco: W. H. Freeman.

Baron, I. S. (1978). Neuropsychological assessment of neurological conditions. In P. R. Magrab (Ed.), *Psychological management of pediatric problems* (Vol. 2, pp. 237–250). Baltimore: University Park Press.

Ben-Yishay, Y., Gerstman, L., Diller, L., & Haas, A. (1970). Prediction of rehabilitation outcomes from psychometric parameters in left hemiplegics. *Journal of Consulting and Clinical Psychology, 34,* 436–441.

Benton, A. L. (1974). Clinical neuropsychology of childhood: An overview. In R. M. Reitan & L. A. Davison (Eds.), *Clinical neuropsychology: Current status and applications* (pp. 186–200). New York: Wiley.

Boll, T. (1972). Right and left cerebral hemisphere damage and tactile perception: Performance of the ipsilateral and contralateral sides of the body. *Neuropsychologia, 12,* 235–238.

Boll, T. J. (1974). Behavioral correlates of cerebral damage in children nine through fourteen. In R. M. Reitan & L. A. Davison (Eds.), *Clinical neuropsychology: Current status and applications.* New York: Wiley.

Boll, T. J. (1981). The Halstead–Reitan Neuropsychology Battery. In S. B. Filskov & T. J. Boll (Eds.),

Handbook of clinical neuropsychology (pp. 577–607). New York: Wiley.

Broca, P. (1960). Remarks on the set of the faculty of articulate language, followed by an observation of aphasia. In G. von Bonin (Trans.), *Some papers on the cerebral cortex.* Springfield, IL: Charles C Thomas. (Original work published 1861)

Chelune, C. J., Heaton, R. K., Lehman, R. A., & Robinson, A. (1979). Level versus pattern of neuropsychological performance among schizophrenic and diffusely brain damaged patients. *Journal of Consulting and Clinical Psychology, 47,* 155–163.

Clements, S. D. (1966). *Minimal brain dysfunction in children* (NINDB Monograph No. 3). Washington, DC: U.S. Department of Health, Education and Welfare.

Crockett, D., Clark, C., & Klonoff, H. (1981). An overview of neuropsychology. In S. B. Filskov & T. J. Boll (Eds.), *Handbook of clinical neuropsychology* (pp. 432–451). New York: Wiley.

Crockett, D., Klonoff, H., & Bjerring, J. (1969). Factor analysis of neuropsychological tests. *Perceptual and Motor Skills, 29,* 791–802.

Crovitz, H. F. (1979). Memory rehabilitation in brain damaged patients: The airplane list. *Cortex, 15,* 131–134.

Das, J. P. (1973). Structure of cognitive abilities: Evidence for simultaneous and successive processing. *Journal of Educational Psychology, 65,* 103–108.

D'Amato, R. C., Gray, J. W., & Dean, R. S. (1988). A comparison between intelligence and neuropsychological functioning. *Journal of School Psychology, 26,* 283–292.

Denckla, M. S. (1972). Clinical syndromes in learning disabilities: The case for "splitting" vs. "lumping." *Journal of Learning Disabilities, 5,* 401–406.

Dean, R. S. (1982). Neuropsychological assessment. In T. Kratochwill (Ed.), *Advances in school psychology* (Vol. 2, pp. 220–241). Hillsdale, NJ: Erlbaum.

Dean, R. S. (1983a, August). *Integrating neuropsychological and emotional variables in the treatment of children's learning disorders.* Paper presented at the annual meeting of the American Psychological Association, Anaheim, CA.

Dean, R. S. (1983b). Neuropsychological assessment. In Staff College (Ed.), *Handbook of diagnostic and epidemiological instruments* (pp. 160–172). Washington, DC: National Institute of Mental Health.

Dean, R. S. (1985). Neuropsychological assessment. In J. D. Cavenar, R. Michels, H. K. H. Brodie, A. M. Cooper, S. B. Guze, L. L. Judd, G. L. Klerman, & A. J. Solnit (Eds.), *Psychiatry* (pp. 1–16). Philadelphia: J. B. Lippincott.

Dean, R. S. (1986a). Perspectives on the future of neuropsychological assessment. In B. S. Plake & J. C. Witt (Eds.), *Buros series on measurement and testing: Future of testing and measurement* (pp. 310–330). Hillsdale, NJ: Erlbaum.

Dean, R. S. (1986b). Lateralization of cerebral functions. In D. Wedding, A. M. Horton, & J. Webster (Eds.), *The neuropsychology handbook: Behavioral and clinical perspectives* (pp. 176–200). New York: Springer.

Dean, R. S. (1986c). Neuropsychological aspects of psychiatric disorders. In G. Hynd & J. Obrzut (Eds.), *Child neuropsychology* (Vol. 2, pp. 54–76). New York: Academic Press.

Dean, R. S., & Rattan, A. I. (1987). Measuring the

effects of failure with learning disabled children. *International Journal of Neuroscience, 37*, 27–30.

Diller, L., & Gordon, W. A. (1981). Rehabilitation and clinical neuropsychology. In S. B. Filskov & T. J. Boll (Eds.), *Handbook of clinical neuropsychology* (pp. 151–169). New York: Wiley.

Doehring, D. G., & Hoshko, I. M. (1977). Classification of reading problems by the Q-technique of factor analysis. *Cortex, 13*, 281–294.

Education for All Handicapped Children Act of 1975, P. L. 94-142, 20 U.S.C. § 1401 (1975).

Ernhart, C. G., Graham, F. K., Eichman, P. L., Marshall, J. M., & Thurston, D. (1963). Brain injury in the preschool child: Some developmental considerations. *Psychological Monographs, General and Applied, 77*(11), 17–33.

Finkelstein, J. H. (1976). BRAIN: A computer program for interpretation of the Halstead–Reitan Neuropsychological Test Battery (Doctoral dissertation, Columbia University). *Dissertation Abstracts International,* 5349B. (University Microfilms No. 77-8864)

Fisk, J. L., & Rourke, B. P. (1979). Identification of subtypes of learning disabled children at three age levels: A neuropsychological, multivariate approach. *Journal of Clinical Neuropsychology, 1*, 289–310.

Fitzhugh, K., & Fitzhugh, L. (1965). Effects of early and late onsets of cerebral dysfunctioning upon psychological test performance. *Perceptual and Motor Skills, 20*, 1099–1100.

Fletcher, J. M., & Satz, P. (1979). Unitary deficit hypotheses of reading disabilities: Has Vellutino led us astray? *Journal of Learning Disabilities, 12*, 22–26.

Freeman, J. M. (Ed.). (1985). *Prenatal and perinatal factors associated with brain disorders* (DHHS Publication No. 85-1149). Washington, DC: U.S. Government Printing Office.

Gibson, W. C. (1962). Pioneers of localization of function in the brain. *Journal of the American Medical Association, 180*, 944–951.

Golden, C. J. (1978). *Diagnosis and rehabilitation in clinical neuropsychology*. Springfield, IL: Charles C Thomas.

Golden, C. J. (1981). A standardized version of Luria's neuropsychological tests: A quantitative and qualitative approach to neuropsychological evaluation. In S. B. Filskov & T. J. Boll (Eds.), *Handbook of clinical neuropsychology* (pp. 231–262). New York: Wiley.

Golden, C. J., Hammeke, T. A., & Purisch, A. D. (1978). Diagnostic validity of a standardized neuropsychological battery derived from Luria's neuropsychological tests. *Journal of Consulting and Clinical Psychology, 46*, 1258–1265.

Goldstein, G. (1979). Methodological and theoretical issues in neuropsychological assessment. *Journal of Behavioral Assessment, 1*, 23–41.

Goldstein, K. H. (1942). *Aftereffects of brain injuries in war*. New York: Grune & Stratton.

Gray, J. W., Dean, R. S., & Rattan, G. (1986). Assessment of perinatal risk factors. *Psychology in the Schools, 24*, 15–21.

Gray, J. W., Dean, R. S., Rattan, G., & Bechtel, B. A. (1988). Mothers' self-reports of perinatal complications. *Journal of Clinical Child Psychology, 17*, 242–274.

Gubbay, S. S., Ellis, E., Walton, J. N., & Court, S. D. (1965). Clumsy children: A study of apraxic and agnostic deficits in 21 children. *Brain, 88*, 295–312.

Halstead, W. C. (1947). *Brain and intelligence*. Chicago: University of Chicago Press.

Hartlage, L. C. (1982). Neuropsychological assessment techniques. In C. R. Reynolds & T. Gutkin (Eds.), *The handbook of school psychology* (pp. 180–195). New York: Wiley.

Heaton, R. K., & Crowley, T. J. (1981). Effects of psychiatric disorders and their somatic treatments on neuropsychological test results. In S. B. Filskov & T. J. Boll (Eds.), *Handbook of clinical neuropsychology* (pp. 86–100). New York: Wiley.

Hebb, D. O. (1949). *The organization of behavior*. New York: Wiley.

Hunt, H. F. (1943). A practical clinical test for organic brain damage. *Journal of Applied Psychology, 27*, 375–386.

Jackson, J. H. (1932). On the duality of the brain. In J. Taylor (Ed.), *Selected writings of John Hughlings Jackson* (Vol. 2, pp. 190–210). London: Hodder & Stoughton. (Original work published 1874)

Kaufman, A. S. (1979). *Intelligent testing with the WISC-R*. New York: Wiley.

Kaufman, A. S., & Kaufman, N. (1983). *Kaufman Assessment Battery for Children*. Circle Pines, MN: American Guidance Service.

Kiernan, R., & Matthews, C. (1979). Impairment Index versus T-score averaging in neuropsychological assessment. *Journal of Consulting and Clinical Psychology, 44*, 951–957.

Klonoff, H., Fibiger, C., & Hutton, G. (1970). Neuropsychological patterns in chronic schizophrenia. *Journal of Nervous and Mental Disease, 150*, 291–300.

Klonoff, H., & Low, M. (1974). Disordered brain function in young children and early adolescents: Neuropsychological and electroencephalographic correlates. In R. M. Reitan & L. A. Davison (Eds.), *Clinical neuropsychology: Current status and applications* (pp. 76–94). New York: Wiley.

Klonoff, H., Low, M., & Clark, C. (1977). Head injuries in children: A prospective 5 year follow-up. *Journal of Neurology, Neurosurgery and Psychiatry, 12*, 1211–1219.

Klonoff, H., & Robinson, G. (1967). Epidemiology of head injuries in children: A pilot study. *Canadian Medical Association Journal, 96*, 1308–1311.

Klonoff, H., & Thompson, G. (1969). Epidemiology of head injuries in adults: A pilot study. *Canadian Medical Association Journal, 100*, 235–241.

Kløve, H. (1974). Validation studies in adult clinical neuropsychology. In R. M. Reitan & L. A. Davison (Eds.), *Clinical neuropsychology: Current status and applications* (pp. 140–162). New York: Wiley.

Knights, R. M. (1973). Problems of criteria in diagnosis: A profile similarity approach. *Annals of the New York Academy of Sciences, 205*, 124–131.

Lezak, M. D. (1976). *Neuropsychological assessment*. New York: Oxford University Press.

Luchins, D. J. (1982). Computed tomography in schizophrenia: Disparities in the prevalence of abnormalities. *Archives of General Psychiatry, 39*, 859–860.

Luria, A. R. (1963). *Restoration of function after brain injury*. New York: Macmillan.

Luria, A. R. (1966). *Higher cortical functions in man*. New York: Basic Books.

Luria, A. R. (1970). The functional organization of the brain. *Scientific American, 3*, 66–78.

Luria, A. R. (1973). *The working brain*. Harmondsworth, England: Penguin.

Luria, A. R., & Majovski, L. V. (1977). Basic approaches used in American and Soviet clinical neuropsychology. *American Psychologist, 32*, 959–968.

Matarazzo, J. D. (1972). *Wechsler's measurement and appraisal of adult intelligence* (5th ed.). Baltimore: Williams & Wilkins.

Matthews, C. G., Shaw, D. J., & Kløve, H. (1966). Psychological test performances in neurologic and "pseudoneurologic" subjects. *Cortex, 2*, 244–253.

Meier, N. R. F. (1963). Selector–integrator mechanisms in behavior. In N. R. F. Meier & T. C. Schneitlar (Eds.), *Principles of animal psychology* (pp. 621–649). New York: Dover Books.

Morris, R., Blashfield, R., & Satz, P. (1981). Neuropsychology and cluster analysis: Potential and problems. *Journal of Clinical Neuropsychology, 3*, 79–99.

Nelson, K. B., & Ellenberg, J. H. (1981). Apgar scores as predictors of chronic neurologic disability. *Pediatrics, 68*, 36–44.

Parsons, O., & Prigatano, G. (1978). Methodological considerations in clinical neuropsychological research. *Journal of Consulting and Clinical Psychology, 46*, 608–619.

Raichle, M. E. (1979). Quantitative in-vivo autoradiography with positron emission tomography. *Brain Research Reviews, 1*, 47–68.

Reed, H. B. C., & Fitzhugh, K. (1966). Patterns of deficits in relation to severity of cerebral dysfunctioning in children and adults. *Journal of Consulting Psychology, 30*, 98–102.

Reed, H. B. C., & Reitan, R. M. (1963). Intelligence test performance of brain damaged subjects with lateralized motor deficits. *Journal of Consulting Psychology, 27*, 102–106.

Reed, H. B. C., & Reitan, R. M. (1969). Verbal and performance differences among brain injured children with lateralized motor deficits. *Perceptual and Motor Skills, 29*, 747–752.

Reed, H. B. C., Reitan, R. M., & Kløve, H. (1965). The influence of cerebral lesions on psychological test performance of older children. *Journal of Consulting Psychology, 29*, 247–251.

Reitan, R. M. (1955). An investigation of the validity of Halstead's measures of biological intelligence. *Archives of Neurology and Psychiatry, 73*, 28–35.

Reitan, R. M. (1958). The validity of the Trail Making Test as an indicator of organic brain damage. *Perceptual and Motor Skills, 8*, 271–276.

Reitan, R. M. (1960). The significance of dysphasia for intelligence and adaptive abilities. *Journal of Psychology, 50*, 355–376.

Reitan, R. M. (1964). *Manual for administering and scoring the Reitan–Indiana Neuropsychological Battery for Children (aged five through eight)*. Indianapolis: University of Indiana Medical Center.

Reitan, R. M. (1966). Problems and prospects in studying the psychological correlates of brain lesions. *Cortex, 2*, 127–154.

Reitan, R. M. (1969). *Manual for administration of neuropsychological test batteries for adults and children*. Indianapolis: Author.

Reitan, R. M. (1971). Sensorimotor functions in brain damaged and normal children of early school age. *Perceptual and Motor Skills, 33*, 655–664.

Reitan, R. M. (1974). Methodological problems in clinical neuropsychology, In R. M. Reitan & L. A. Davison (Eds.), *Child neuropsychology: Current status and applications*. New York: Wiley.

Reitan, R. M. (1976). Neurological and physiological bases of psychopathology. *Annual Review of Psychology, 27*, 189–216.

Reitan, R. M., & Davison, L. A. (Eds.). (1974). *Clinical neuropsychology: Current status and applications*. New York: Wiley.

Reitan, R. M., & Heineman, C. E. (1968). Interactions of neurological deficits and emotional disturbances in children with learning disorders: Methods for their differential assessment. In J. Hellmuth (Ed.), *Learning disorders* (Vol. 3, pp. 112–134). Seattle, WA: Special Child.

Robbins, L. C. (1963). The accuracy of parental recall of aspects of child development and child rearing practices. *Journal of Abnormal and Social Psychology, 66*, 261–270.

Russell, E., Neuringer, C., & Goldstein, G. (1970). *Assessment of brain damage: A neuropsychological key approach*. New York: Wiley.

Rutt, C. N., & Offord, D. R. (1971). Prenatal and perinatal complications in childhood schizophrenics and their siblings. *Journal of Nervous and Mental Disease, 152*, 324–331.

Rutter, M. (1977). Brain damage syndromes in childhood: Concepts and findings. *Journal of Child Psychology and Psychiatry, 18*, 1–21.

Satz, P., Fennell, E., & Reilly, C. (1970). Predictive validity of six neurodiagnostic tests: A decision theory analysis. *Journal of Consulting and Clinical Psychology, 34*, 375–381.

Satz, P., Taylor, G., Friel, J., & Fletcher, J. (1978). Some developmental predictive precursors of reading disabilities: A six-year follow-up. In A. L. Benton & D. Pearl (Eds.), *Dyslexia: An appraisal of current knowledge*. New York: Oxford University Press.

Selz, M., & Reitan, R. M. (1979). Rules for neuropsychological diagnosis: Classification of brain function in older children. *Journal of Consulting and Clinical Psychology, 47*, 258–264.

Seretny, M. L., Dean, R. S., Gray, J. W., & Hartlage, L. C. (1986). The practice of clinical neuropsychology in the United States. *Archives of Clinical Neuropsychology, 1*, 5–12.

Shaffer, D. (1974). Psychiatric aspects of brain injury in childhood: A review. In S. Chess & A. Thomas (Eds.), *Annual progress in child psychiatry and child development* (pp. 87–101). New York: Brunner/Mazel.

Smith, A. (1975). Neuropsychological testing in neurological disorders. In W. J. Friedlander (Ed.), *Advances in neurology* (Vol. 7, pp. 220–222). New York: Raven Press.

Sperry, R. W., Gazzaniga, M. S., & Bogen, J. H. (1969). Interhemispheric relationships: The neocortical commissures; syndromes of hemisphere disconnection. In P. Vinken & G. W. Bruyns (Eds.), *Handbook of clinical neurology* (Vol. 4, pp. 100–114). New York: Wiley.

Spreen, O., & Haaf, R. (1986). Empirically derived learning disability subtypes: A replication attempt and longitudinal patterns over 15 years. *Journal of Learning Disabilities, 19*, 170–180.

Stewart, M. A., Pitts, F. N., Craig, A. G., & Dierof, N. (1966). The hyperactive child syndrome. *American Journal of Orthopsychiatry, 36*, 861–867.

Struss, D. T., & Trites, R. L. (1977). Classification of

neurological status using multiple discriminant function analysis of neuropsychological test scores. *Journal of Consulting and Clinical Psychology, 45,* 145.

Tramontana, M. G., Sherrets, S. D., & Golden, C. J. (1980). Brain dysfunction in youngsters with psychiatric disorders: Application of Selz–Reitan rules for neuropsychological diagnosis. *Clinical Neuropsychology, 2,* 118–123.

Tymchuk, A. (1974). Comparison of Bender error and time scores for groups of epileptic, retarded, and behavior-problem children. *Perceptual and Motor Skills, 38,* 71–74.

Vellutino, F. R., Smith, H., Steger, J. A., & Kaman, M. (1975). Age differences and the perceptual deficit hypothesis. *Child Development, 46,* 493–497.

Vellutino, F. R., Steger, B. M., Moyer, S. C., Harding, C. J., Niles, J. A. (1977). Has the perceptual deficit hypothesis led us astray? *Journal of Learning Disabilities, 10,* 375–385.

Watson, C. G., & Benton, A. L. (1976). Copying and reproduction from memory tasks in differentiation of brain-damaged and control psychiatric patients. *Perceptual and Motor Skills, 42,* 1107–1112.

Wechsler, D. W. (1958). *The measurement and apprais-al of adult intelligence* (4th ed.). Baltimore: Williams & Wilkins.

Wedding, D. (1983). Comparison of statistical and actuarial models for predicting lateralization of brain damage. *Clinical Neuropsychology, 5,* 15–22.

Wehler, R., & Hoffman, H. (1978). Intellectual functioning in lobotomized and non-lobotomized chronic schizophrenic patients. *Journal of Clinical Psychology, 34,* 449–451.

Wernicke, C. (1874). *Der aphasische symptomencomplex.* Breslau, Germany: Cohn & Weigert.

Wheeler, L., Burke, C. J., & Reitan, R. M. (1963). An application of discriminant functions to the problem of predicting brain damage using behavioral variables [Monograph supplement]. *Perceptual and Motor Skills, 16,* 417–440.

Wheeler, L., & Reitan, R. M. (1963). Discriminant functions applied to the problem of predicting cerebral damage from behavior tests: A cross-validation study. *Perceptual and Motor Skills, 16,* 681–701.

Willson, V. L., & Reynolds, C. R. (1982). Methodological and statistical problems in determining membership in clinical populations. *Clinical Neuropsychology, 4,* 134–138.

15

Physiological Approaches to the Assessment of Intelligence

PHILIP A. VERNON
MONICA MORI
University of Western Ontario

A complete theory of the nature of human intelligence and mental abilities must include an understanding of the underlying neurophysiological factors and processes that contribute to variance in these traits. From at least as far back as Alcaeon of Croton, in the 5th century B.C., there has been speculation about possible physiological bases of intelligence (Hynd & Willis, 1985). Such features as the size of the brain; the number of fibers in the corpus callosum; nerve conduction velocity; alpha waves and a variety of parameters of evoked potentials; serum uric acid concentration; neuronal calcium ion concentration; regional cerebral blood flow; and cortical glucose metabolism have been investigated as potential correlates, if not causes, of individual differences in intelligence (Chase et al., 1984; Deary, Hendrickson, & Burns, 1987; Ertl & Schafer, 1969; Eysenck, Barrett, & Frearson, 1987; Haier, Robinson, Braden, & Williams, 1983; Haier et al., 1987; D. E. Hendrickson, 1982; Inouye, Park, & Asaka, 1984; Orowan, 1955; Reed, 1984; Risberg, 1986; Schafer, 1982).

This research notwithstanding, Hynd and Willis (1985) point out that most major theories of intelligence have at best paid only secondary attention to its neurological basis, and with the possible exception of the Kaufman Assessment Battery for Children (K - ABC; Kaufman & Kaufman, 1983), the most commonly used standardized tests of intelligence were developed with minimal (if any) consideration for possible physiological factors that might account for variability in performance on items and subtests. In this chapter, a number of measures that either directly or indirectly provide information about physiological correlates of intelligence are described, and the place of such measures in the assessment of intelligence is discussed. Despite a slow start, rife with inconsistencies, for research in this area, some recent considerable advances have been made that can no longer be ignored by those interested in intelligence and its measurement.

REACTION TIME RESEARCH

A good example of a research paradigm that started slowly—so slowly that it was largely disbanded at one point—but went on to generate considerable interest is that of reaction time (RT) studies, which have investigated relationships between intelligence and measures of speed of information processing. Studied initially by such people as Sir Francis Galton and Charles Spearman, RTs enjoyed only limited early success as correlates of intelligence. Despite the unreliability of his measures and the restricted ability range of his sample, Wissler's (1901) report of a correlation of $-.02$ between RTs amd measures of ability helped to dispel confidence among early researchers (particularly in the United States) that RTs could provide any useful information about the nature of intelligence. Isolated studies continued (e.g., Lemmon, 1927; Peak & Boring, 1926), but few theories of intelligence paid serious attention to RTs until the 1960s (Eysenck, 1967). Since then, a great deal of research on RTs and intelligence has been conducted, much of it summarized and reviewed in Vernon (1987a).

One of the major contributors to this area is Jensen (e.g., 1979, 1980, 1982, 1987), who has conducted extensive research on simple and choice RTs in what he refers to as the "Hick paradigm." In this paradigm, the speed with which subjects respond to visual stimuli under varying conditions of response uncertainty is measured, and their RTs in each condition are subsequently correlated with their scores on one of a number of standard measures of intelligence. Typically, subjects respond under conditions requiring zero, one, two, or three "bits" of decision-making information processing, and a variety of parameters of their performance have been investigated.

Jensen (1987) provides a comprehensive meta-analysis of RT research in the Hick paradigm; he has reviewed, combined, and analyzed the results of 33 studies with a total of 2,317 subjects. He first establishes that the correlation between RTs and intelligence increases as a function of the increasing number of choices to which subjects must attend. Across studies involving 1,129 subjects, Jensen (1987) reports average correlations between RTs and various measures of intelligence of $-.18$, $-.19$, $-.22$, and $-.23$, corresponding to the zero-, one-, two-, and three-bit conditions, respectively. Second, Jensen reports that several other RT parameters—subjects' overall mean RT; their intraindividual variability ($RT\sigma_i$, a measure of the consistency with which subjects can respond at a given speed over a number of trials); the intercept and slope of the regression of RTs on bits; and subjects' movement times or MTs (as distinct from their RTs or decision-making times, MTs measure how quickly subjects can move their hands to ex-

ecute a response)—have also been shown to be correlated with intelligence.

Table 15.1 provides a summary of these Hick paradigm parameters and their correlations with different tests of intelligence, averaged across a number of studies. Both uncorrected zero-order correlations and correlations corrected either for restriction in the range of intelligence of the samples or for attenuation due to unreliability, or both, are reported. Note that the corrected correlation for mean RTs is $-.320$—a not inconsequential value when one considers the radically different nature of the measures being correlated—and that the correlation for subjects' intraindividual variability is even higher ($-.480$ after correction for range and unreliability). Somewhat unexpectedly, perhaps, the slope of the regression of RTs on bits does not correlate any more highly with intelligence than does the intercept, and subjects' mean MTs correlate almost as highly as do their RTs with intelligence. Overall, however, it is clear that the speed and particularly the consistency with which subjects can make relatively simple choices or decisions are significantly related to their performance on complex measures of intelligence.

In a series of studies (Vernon, 1983, 1987b; Vernon & Jensen, 1984; Vernon & Kantor, 1986; Vernon, Nador, & Kantor, 1985a, 1985b), Vernon has regressed subjects' IQ scores on a battery of RT tests, measuring the speed with which the subjects can process a variety of different stimuli of varying complexity and involving short- or long-term memory, or both. Subjects have included university, vocational college, and high school students; adult monozygotic (MZ) and dizygotic (DZ) twins; and a sample of elderly subjects. The measures of intelligence have included the Wechsler Adult Intelligence Scale (WAIS), the Advanced Raven Matrices, and the Multidimensional Aptitude Battery (MAB: Jackson, 1983)—a multiple-choice, group administerable test patterned closely after the WAIS-R, with which it has been reported to be highly correlated (Jackson, 1984). The RT tests have been described in detail elsewhere (Vernon et al., 1985b); briefly, they include measures of speed of scanning alphabetical and numerical stimuli in short-term memory; speed of retrieval of ver-

TABLE 15.1. *n*-Weighted Mean Correlations between Selected Hick Paradigm Parameters and IQ

| | Uncorrected correlations | Corrected correlations | | | Total *n* |
		For range	For unreliability	For range and unreliability	
Mean RT	−.201	−.279	−.309	−.320	1,195
RT intercept	−.117	−.165	−.183	−.250	774
RT slope	−.117	−.165	−.183	−.280	1,558
RTσ_i	−.208	−.288	−.320	−.480	1,397
Mean MT	−.189	−.263	−.292	−.300	1,302

Note. IQ tests include Terman Concept Mastery Test; Raven Matrices (Standard and Advanced); Scholastic Aptitude Test; Wechsler Intelligence Scale for Children (WISC); Wechsler Adult Intelligence Scale (WAIS); School and College Aptitude Test; Armed Services Vocational Aptitude Battery; Lorge–Thorndike Intelligence Test; Comprehensive Tests of Basic Skills; Mill Hill Vocabulary. Adapted from "Individual Differences in the Hick Paradigm" by A. R. Jensen, 1987, in P. A. Vernon (Ed.), *Speed of Information-Processing and Intelligence* (pp. 101–175), Norwood, NJ: Ablex. Copyright 1987 by Ablex. Adapted by permission.

bal information from long-term memory; and the efficiency with which subjects can simultaneously store and process verbal and/or numerical information in short-term memory. Each of these tests is administered by microcomputer.

A summary of the shrunken multiple correlations obtained form the regression of Full Scale IQ scores on some or all of these tests in different studies (not all of the studies included all the RT tests) is presented in Table 15.2. Notice, first, the consistently high magnitude of these correlations, ranging

from .431 to .745. The fluctuations in their relative magnitude are almost certainly largely attributable to differences in the restriction of range of ability of the samples. For example, the correlation of .464, obtained from the regression of WAIS Full Scale IQ scores on mean RTs and intraindividual SDs, was obtained from a sample of high-ability university students whose mean IQ was 122.2 (*SD* = 8.76). Corrected for restriction of range in IQ, this correlation increases to .668 and is now comparable to the other correlations in Table 15.2, obtained from more

TABLE 15.2. Shrunken Multiple *R*'s Obtained from Regressions of IQ Scores on RT Parameters in Different Studies

| Study | Sample | *n* | IQ test | Shrunken multiple *R*'s[a] with: | | |
				Mean RTs	Intraindividual SDs	RTs + SDs
Vernon (1983)	University students	100	WAIS	.434	.431	.464
Vernon, Nador, & Kantor (1985b)	University students	81	MAB (timed)[b]	.605	.625	.687
			MAB (untimed)	.504	.612	.645
Vernon & Kantor (1986)	High school students	113	MAB (timed)[b]	.559	.543	.672
			MAB (untimed)	.662	.653	.743
Vernon (1987b)	MZ twins	100	MAB	.737	.708	.745
	DZ twins	104	MAB	.624	.569	.654
	MZ and DZ twins	204	MAB	.673	.644	.681

[a]*R*'s not corrected for restriction of range.

[b]See text for a description of the timed–untimed distinction.

heterogeneous samples. It still falls short of the correlation of .745, obtained from the sample of 100 MZ twins. This sample's mean IQ was 104.8, and its SD of 13.13 (compared to the population SD of 15) makes it the most heterogeneous of all the samples represented in Table 15.2. Overall, it does not seem unreasonable to conclude that, in the general population, a combination of relatively simple measures of speed and consistency of information processing (such as were used in these studies) would account for approximately 50% of the variance in intelligence test scores.

A second noteworthy feature of the correlations in Table 15.2 relates to those between the RT parameters and the MAB measures designated as timed or untimed. Two studies were conducted to evaluate the extent to which correlations between RTs and IQ test scores could be attributed to the timed nature of many intelligence tests. A number of authors (e.g., Carroll, 1981; Schwartz, Griffin, & Brown, 1983; Sternberg, 1984) have suggested that this feature of speeded intelligence tests, whereby subjects receive bonus points for performing in a given period of time, might account for some part of the relationship between their test scores and their RTs. Although this may be true, the model that Jensen (1982) and Vernon (1983, 1985) proposed to account for this relationship (described below) leads to the seemingly counterintuitive prediction that the IQ scores of subjects who are allowed unlimited time to work on the test might show the highest correlations with RTs.

In the first study to test this, Vernon et al. (1985b) obtained timed and (so-called) untimed MAB scores from a sample of 81 university students. Subjects' timed scores were based on the number of correct answers they were able to give in 5 minutes on each of the 10 subtests of the MAB (the standard administration calls for 7 minutes per subtest). Subjects were aware of the 5-minute limit and were instructed to work as quickly and as accurately as they could during this period. After the 5 minutes elapsed, subjects were told to continue working on each subtest for as long as they required, recording their answers with a different-colored pen. Subsequently, the sum of all their correct answers was designated as their untimed score. As can be seen in Table 15.2, regressions of

subjects' timed scores on RTs, SDs, and RTs + SDs resulted in multiple correlations that were consistently, though only somewhat, higher than those obtained from the regressions of their untimed scores.

As Sternberg (1986) pointed out, a major weakness of this study is the lack of independence, or the overlap, between the scores designated as timed and untimed. To rectify this, Vernon and Kantor (1986) administered the MAB to two independent samples of high school students, one of which was allowed only 5 minutes per subtest and the other of which was allowed unlimited time. As shown in Table 15.2, this procedure resulted in higher correlations between untimed MAB scores and RT parameters than between timed MAB scores and RTs. Closer inspection revealed that this was particularly true for Verbal subtest scores. Zero-order correlations between Performance subtest scores and RTs were more often higher in the timed than in the untimed group.

The model that Jensen (1982) and Vernon (1983, 1985) have developed to account for the strong relationship between RTs and intelligence demonstrated here draws upon three well-established properties of the short-term component of the human information-processing system, or "working memory." First, the working memory has a limited storage capacity: It is well known that it can successfully hold only about seven discrete units (or chunks) of information at any one time. Second, the limited amount of information that the working memory can store is subject to rapid decay or loss in the absence of continued rehearsal. Third, there is a trade-off between the amount of information that can be stored in working memory at one time and the amount of processing of this and other information that can occur at the same time.

Given these properties, even a relatively simple problem-solving task—involving the encoding, chunking, and storage of information; the accessing and retrieval of relevant information from long-term memory; the continued rehearsal of stored information; and the execution of the cognitive processes or components required to actually solve the problem—would have some probability of reaching or exceeding the threshold of the working memory's capacity. Either its limited storage capacity might be reached;

or, depending on the duration of the task, earlier-encoded information might decay or become inaccessible; or the active processing requirements of the task might necessitate the displacement of previously stored information; or any combination of these might occur. More difficult or complex problems, requiring more information to be brought to bear and more processing of this information to be carried out during their solution, would have a higher probability of exceeding the system's capacity.

To overcome these limiting properties of working memory, a fourth property is proposed: speed of information processing. The more quickly the incoming information can be broken down into a small number of chunks, the less likely the system's storage capacity is to be reached. The more quickly the relevant information can be searched for, retrieved, and applied to the problem at hand, the more likely it is that other information will not have been lost because of decay. At each step in solving the problem, the more quickly the processes involved can be executed, the higher the probability that the system will not reach its threshold, and the higher the probability of success.

Not only does this model account for the correlations between intelligence test scores and RT measures of speed of information processing, but it also explains why the correlations are highest when the intelligence tests are administered with unlimited time. In the MAB (and many other IQ tests), items in each subtest are arranged in order of increasing difficulty. When subjects are only allowed 5 minutes to work on a subtest (and it is assumed that they attempt the items in the order that they appear, which most subjects do), they typically run out of time before they have the opportunity to attempt the most difficult items that appear at the end. This can be demonstrated very simply by looking at the mean MAB raw scores of the subjects in Vernon and Kantor's (1986) timed and untimed groups: 181.53 and 251.80, respectively—or a difference of about 70 points. Recall that all of these subjects were high school students, randomly assigned to testing condition, so there is no reason to believe that they actually differed in intelligence. (In addition, there were no significant differences between the groups' mean RTs on any of the speed-of-processing tests.) Thus, the differ-ence between the groups' MAB scores indicates that subjects in the timed condition simply ran out of time before they reached the later, more difficult items, some of which many of them would have been able to solve. Subjects in the untimed group, however, were able to attempt every item, hard or easy, and their total score reflects in part their ability to solve the most difficult items in each subtest. These difficult items, moreover, are the ones that impose the greatest information-processing demands on working memory and whose successful solution depends the most heavily on the speed with which these demands can be met. Thus, untimed test scores include an evaluation of subjects' abilities to process increasingly complex and increasingly large amounts of information, with the result that these scores are highly correlated with the speed with which they can process information as assessed by RT tests. As noted, this was particularly true of untimed Verbal scale scores; the later items of certain Verbal subtests (e.g., Arithmetic) are sufficiently complex to place a high premium on fast speed of processing. It was less true for some Performance scale scores (specifically, Digit Symbol and Spatial), arguably because the later items of these subtests are relatively easy to solve when unlimited time is provided.

Clearly, there is a strong relationship between measures of intelligence and measures of speed of processing, and a cognitive model has been described to account for this relationship. At another level, it may be asked what factors are responsible for individual differences in speed of information processing, and it seems likely that the answer to this question must, at least to some extent, implicate neurophysiological factors. Three recent studies that have investigated the heritability of different speed-of-processing variables have provided evidence in favor of this position. In the first, McGue, Bouchard, Lykken, and Feuer (1984) administered RT tests and a battery of psychometric tests of mental ability to 34 pairs of MZ and 13 pairs of DZ twins, all of whom had been reared apart from a very early point in life. Factor analysis of the RT tests yielded three factors, which the authors labeled Overall Speed of Response, Speed of Information Processing, and Speed of Spatial Processing. The first of these—Overall

Speed of Response—correlated $-.31$ with WAIS IQ scores and showed a moderate and significant heritability of .456. Neither of the other two speed factors proved to be significantly heritable.

In the second study (Vernon, 1987b, 1989), 50 pairs of adult MZ twins and 52 pairs of adult DZ twins were administered the MAB and the battery of RT tests that was employed in other studies referred to above. As mentioned, the RT tests were highly correlated with IQ scores in these samples (see Table 15.2), and all of them proved to be heritable. Using Falconer's formula (two times the difference between the MZ and DZ intraclass correlations), heritabilities ranging between .24 and .90 were computed for mean RTs derived from 11 measures. The median of the heritability coefficents was .51, and the heritability of a general or overall speed-of-response factor extracted from the intercorrelations among the tests was .49. Subjects' intraindividual variability on the RT tests also proved to be heritable. Across the 11 RT measures, heritabilities of intraindividual variability ranged from .41 to .98, with a median of .52. Of particular interest was the finding that the fluctuation in the magnitude of the heritabilities of the mean RTs was not unsystematic, but was positively related to three factors: the degree to which each RT test loaded on the general speed-of-response factor ($r = .391$); the tests' relative complexity ($r = .676$); and the extent to which each RT test was itself correlated with IQ ($r = .603$).

The third study in this area (Ho, Baker, & Decker, 1988) also employed the most sophisticated multivariate data analyses. Sixty pairs of twins (30 MZ, 30 DZ), aged 8–18 years, were administered the WISC-R and two measures of speed of information processing: the Rapid Automatic Naming Test and the Colorado Perceptual Speed Test. These speed-of-processing measures had heritabilities of .52 and .49, respectively, and multivariate biometrical analyses revealed that the correlation between each of the measures and IQ (both r's = approximately .42) was largely attributable to correlated genetic effects. The authors conclude:

These analyses reveal the importance of genetic effects underlying the relationship between general intelligence and speed-of-processing,

lending support to the notion that speed and IQ may share some common biological mechanism(s). That is, genetic influences important to general intelligence appear to be correlated with those genetic influences important to speed-of-processing variables. (p. 258)

In summary, a variety of RT tests that measure the speed with which individuals can process different kinds of information are moderately correlated with standardized measures of intelligence. When combined in multiple-regression analyses, the speed-of-processing variables' correlations with intelligence become quite substantial, accounting for as much as 50% of the variance in IQ scores. The relationship between intelligence and RTs cannot be attributed simply to the fact that some IQ tests are timed. On the contrary, certain measures of intelligence—notably those that place increasing demands on the limited-capacity working memory—correlate most highly with RTs when these tests are administered with no time restrictions. Speed of processing, then, is seen as a mechanism that allows the working memory to overcome its storage and processing limitations when faced with complex problems. Without the ability to execute the cognitive processes required by a problem rapidly, there will be an increased probability that the system will suffer an "information overload" and be unable to solve the problem. More complex items, which typically appear later in each test or subtest than do easier items, and which are more likely to be encountered by subjects in an untimed than in a timed testing condition, will rely the most heavily on speed of information processing for their successful solution. Finally, evidence that RT measures are (albeit indirectly) tapping underlying physiological processes is provided by studies demonstrating their heritability. Of particular interest, moreover, is the finding that the relationship between RTs and intelligence may be largely attributable to shared genetic factors.

ELECTROENCEPHALOGRAPHIC RESEARCH

A more direct index of neurophysiological mechanisms that are related to intelligence is provided by electroencephalographic (EEG) studies of averaged evoked potentials (AEPs). Predating these, some early studies of *spontaneous* EEGs reported high correlations with intelligence (e.g., Giannitrapani, 1969), although the results of different studies were highly inconsistent and do not allow any firm conclusions to be drawn (Gale & Edwards, 1983; Haier et al., 1983). Starting with Ertl and Schafer (1969), however, several parameters of *evoked* potentials (i.e., measures of the electrical activity of the brain in response to or evoked by some external stimulus, such as a light flash or an audible click), including their latency (how quickly the brain reponds to the stimulus) and their amplitude (how much electrocortical activity the stimulus evokes), have been shown fairly consistently to be correlated with intelligence. This section provides an overview of some of the work in this area.

Ertl and Schafer's (1969) study is noteworthy for a number of reasons. To begin with, it was one of the first to investigate the relationship between AEPs and intelligence. Second, it remains one of the very few studies in this area that has employed a large sample (573 primary school children in second, third, fourth, fifth, seventh, and eighth grades) and that has obtained multiple measures of intelligence (WISC, Primary Mental Abilities Test [PMA], and Otis). Not only was the sample large, but it consisted of not markedly dissimilar proportions of males ($n = 317$) and females ($n = 256$), and was quite heterogeneous with respect to IQ (mean WISC IQ = 105.2, SD = 13.1). Latencies of visual AEPs were measured and correlated with IQ scores; the correlations ranged between .10 and −.35. Correlations with late components of the AEPs were consistently higher than were those with early components: Averaged across the three IQ tests, the correlation with early components (E1 and E2) was −.18, and that with late components (E3 and E4) was −.34. This indicated that subjects of higher intelligence responded more rapidly to the stimuli than did subjects of lower intelligence, particularly with respect to those (late) components of the AEPs that are thought to be more closely associated with conscious processing. Ertl and Schafer concluded that AEPs "could be the key to understanding the biological substrate of individual differences in behavioral intelligence" (1969, p. 422).

A number of AEP–intelligence studies appeared at the same time as Ertl and Schafer's or shortly thereafter (e.g., Gucker, 1973; Plum, 1968; Rhodes, Dustman, & Beck, 1969; Shucard & Horn, 1972, 1973; Weinberg, 1969). Each of these reported significant correlations between the latency and/or the amplitude of visual AEPs and measures of intelligence. Some, such as Gucker (1973), reported very high correlations (Spearman's rho = −.75 in a sample of 17 youngsters aged 8–13). Typically, however, correlations were closer in magnitude to those reported by Ertl and Schafer. In Shucard and Horn's (1972) study, one of the more ambitious of the early investigations, 108 adults (60 male, 48 female) were administered 16 tests of intellectual abilities designed to measure fluid and crystallized intelligence (g_F and g_C), and the latency and amplitude of their visual AEPs were measured under three conditions of alertness or arousal. Overall, all but 2 of 300 correlations between AEP latencies and intelligence were in the expected direction (i.e., negative), ranging from .05 to −.32 and averaging approximately −.15. No significant correlations between AEP amplitude and intelligence were observed, and no differences were found in the magnitude of the correlations between AEP latencies and measures of g_C or g_F. Interestingly, the largest correlations were obtained in the low-alertness condition; this finding suggested that more intelligent subjects were better able to regulate their level of alertness, depending upon the demands of the task.

Building upon this, Schafer and Marcus (1973) and Schafer (1979, 1982) proposed the construct of *"neural adaptability"* (NA), whereby subjects of higher intelligence are more likely to show higher-amplitude AEPs to unexpected stimuli and lower-amplitude AEPs to expected stimuli than are subjects of lower intelligence. Both reactions are interpreted as demonstrating a more efficient use of the brain's resources. NA was measured in Schafer's studies by presenting auditory stimuli under three conditions: *"periodic"* (P), in which the stimuli occurred at expected, regular 2-second intervals; "self-stimulation" (S), in which the subjects themselves controlled the rate of stimulus presentation by pressing a hand-held microswitch; and "random" (R), in which the clicks appeared at unexpected intervals. As predicted, Schafer (1982) showed that the AEP amplitudes of high-IQ subjects (mean WAIS IQ = 118) were 25% larger than average ([P + S + R]/3) in the R condition and 24% smaller than average in the S condition. In contrast, the AEP amplitudes of a sample of mentally retarded subjects were only 14% larger than average in the R condition and showed no decrease at all during the S condition. An index of NA, computed as NA = ([R − S]/average), correlated .66 with the WAIS IQs of a subset of 79 of the high-IQ subjects. After correction for restriction in range of IQ, this increased to .82. Even within a very restricted sample of 54 severely retarded adults, Jensen, Schafer, and Crinella (1981) reported a correlation of .31 between NA and g factor scores extracted from a battery of psychometric tests.

Most recently, a series of studies have appeared that were stimulated by the work of the Hendricksons (A. E. Hendrickson, 1982; D. E. Hendrickson, 1982; Hendrickson & Hendrickson, 1980). In their studies, AEP waveforms are interpreted as representations of the amount of "noise" or errors of transmission that occur during information processing. Persons of higher intelligence are hypothesized to have lower probabilities of error and more complex AEPs (i.e., their AEPs should show larger amplitudes for longer periods of time after each stimulus). Two novel parameters of AEP complexity—the "string measure" (essentially, the length of the contour perimeter of the AEP waveform) and a measure of intraindividual variability in waveform complexity—have been derived, and a number of studies have investigated the correlations between these parameters and intelligence.

D. E. Hendrickson (1982), for example, obtained WAIS IQs and auditory AEPs from 219 adolescents. As predicted, the string measure showed a high positive correlation with IQ scores ($r = .72$), and the variance measure showed a high negative correlation ($r = −.72$). That is, the AEPs of higher-IQ subjects were consistently more complex from trial to trial. Eysenck and Barrett (1984) reanalyzed Hendrickson's data and extracted a single general factor from the 11 subtests of the WAIS, as well as a composite AEP measure computed as the difference between the variance and string measures. This composite

AEP measure loaded .77 on the general factor and correlated −.83 with WAIS Full Scale IQ. Blinkhorn and Hendrickson (1982) obtained string and variance measures from a sample of 33 university undergraduates, to whom they also administered the Advanced Raven Matrices, a test of verbal analogies, and a test of divergent thinking. The average correlation between a number of string measures and the Raven was approximately .45, which, corrected for restriction of range, might increase to about .71. However, none of the variance measures correlated with the Raven, nor were there any significant correlations between the AEP measures and the tests of verbal analogies or divergent thinking.

Despite the somewhat equivocal results of Blinkhorn and Hendrickson (1982), other studies employing the string measure have been remarkably consistent in demonstrating a correlation (often quite high) between this parameter and intelligence (Haier et al., 1983; but see also Sandman & Barron, 1986). Haier et al. (1983), however, obtained string measures and measures of N140–P200 amplitude (the amplitude of the major negative–positive deflection) under four conditions of stimulus complexity, and reported that the correlation between the string measure and Advanced Raven Matrices scores increased systematically as a function of increasing stimulus intensity. The highest correlation ($r = .50$) was obtained in the highest-intensity condition. N140–P200 amplitudes were also highly correlated with the Raven (as high as .69) and with the string measure (as high as .80), and when these amplitudes were partialed out, the string–Raven correlations became nonsignificant. Haier et al. (1983) do not claim that the string measure is unimportant, but state that, in their study at least, it is an "epiphenomenon" of N140–P200 amplitudes. They also suggest that differences in stimulus intensity may account for differences in the magnitude of AEP amplitude–intelligence correlations in different studies. Some additional support for this is reported in Robinson, Haier, Braden, and Krengel (1984).

The Hendricksons have advanced a very detailed model of the neurophysiological mechanisms that they believe are responsible for individual differences in AEP parameters and intelligence (A. E. Hendrickson, 1982; see also Vernon, 1985). Briefly, different sensory stimuli, representative of different kinds of information, are held to elicit distinct patterns of electrical pulses (or "pulse trains"), which in turn stimulate the influx of sodium ions from synaptic clefts into the postsynaptic density (PSD) chamber. Within the PSD chamber, the positive-charged sodium ions weaken the hydrogen bonds by which a special form of ribonucleic acid (RNA)—termed "engram RNA" (or eRNA)—is attached to the substrate. As additional pulses arrive at a synapse, more sodium will pass into the PSD chamber, and the original sensory stimulus may be "recognized" when the eRNA becomes completely detached. According to the Hendricksons, this "molecular recognition" is the basis for the retrieval of memory. If for any reason the concentration of sodium in the PSD is either lower or higher than it should be, either a "recognition failure" or a "misrecognition failure," respectively, may occur. Individual differences in the probability of the occurrence of these types of errors are believed by the Hendricksons to form the biological basis of individual differences in intelligence.

A recent paper that provides a new perspective on this theory is that by Deary et al. (1987). These authors focus on a particular feature of the Hendricksons' model: the importance of calcium ions in the assembly of networks of microtubule cross-bridges that interconnect selected regions of the PSD and allow information (i.e., pulse trains) to be transferred from one region to another. In the absence of such a network, information transfer would be disrupted, leading to errors of transmission such as those described above. Such disruption would be manifested in a deterioration of memory, particularly in the learning and recall of new information for which no previous associative networks exist. Deary et al. (1987) note that some individuals with Down syndrome show chronically low levels of calcium, and that many Down syndrome individuals develop Alzheimer-type dementia by their 40s. They also note a high incidence of Parkinson-type dementia in Guam, the Kii Peninsula of Japan, and Southwest New Guinea—all areas where there is a very low concentration of calcium in the drinking water. Finally, Deary

et al. (1987) compared 10 inpatients and 10 outpatients, all of whom had been diagnosed as having Alzheimer-type senile dementia, on the Mini-Mental Health Questionnaire (MMHQ)—which contains sections on orientation, registration, attention, calculation, recall, and language—and on serum calcium level. The outpatient group scored markedly higher than the inpatients on the MMHQ (means of 20.8 and 1.1, respectively), and also showed a significantly higher serum calcium level. When both groups were combined, a correlation of .488 was found between MMHQ scores and calcium level.

In summary, EEG studies have fairly consistently shown a relationship between a number of parameters of AEPs and intelligence. In the absence of any other data, these studies alone provide evidence of the contribution of physiological factors to individual differences in intelligence. Less clear are the precise mechanisms by which differences in AEP latencies, amplitudes, or complexity are related to or bring about differences in mental abilities. Schafer's (1979, 1982) NA model holds that AEPs and test intelligence are both manifestations of the efficiency with which the brain's limited neural energy and resources are used. The Hendricksons have proposed an elaborate neruophysiological theory, some aspects of which have begun to receive empirical support (Deary et al., 1987). Robinson (1982) has proposed an alternative model, based on the mediation of EEG activity by the diffuse thalamo-cortical system (see also Paisey, 1983; Robinson, 1983). Black et al. (1987) have proposed a model of information storage that bears some similarities to, but appears more empirically based than, that of the Hendricksons. Interestingly, a number of early studies demonstrated a positive relationship between certain AEP parameters and RTs (e.g., Donchin & Lindsley, 1966; Dustman, 1965; Morrell & Morrell, 1966); that is, faster RTs were associated with AEPs of larger amplitude and/or shorter latency. These results provide additional information about the physiological basis of RTs and lend support to the notion that faster speed of information processing may itself be conceived as a means of using the brain's limited short-term storage and processing resources efficiently.

REGIONAL CEREBRAL BLOOD FLOW AND CEREBRAL GLUCOSE METABOLISM RESEARCH

Perhaps the most direct currently available evidence of the physiological basis of intelligence is provided by studies of regional cerebral blood flow (RCBF) and by positron emission tomography (PET) studies of cerebral glucose metabolism. Each of these approaches is based on the consumption of energy that accompanies any cortical activity—including, but by no means restricted to, performance on tests of intelligence—and the concomitant need to compensate for this energy consumption by increases in RCBF and/or glucose metabolism. Not only do these studies provide information about brain–behavior correlations (e.g., as do most EEG studies), but they also afford a means of identifying specific regions of the brain that appear to be most involved during the performance of different types of tasks. Thus, as a simple example, they provide a direct means of evaluating the extent to which particular regions of the left hemisphere may be involved during performance on certain verbally loaded tasks, and the extent to which specific parts of the right hemisphere may be involved during performance on certain spatially loaded tasks.

Phelps, Mazziotta, and Huang (1982), for example, review a number of early studies using positron computed tomography (PCT), and conclude "that the deterioration in mentation of dementia patients is reflected accurately by PCT studies of blood flow and metabolism. Both the magnitude of change and the anatomical sites of altered function are measurable by these noninvasive methods" (p. 151). Similarly, Risberg (1986) reviews RCBF research employing ^{133}Xe inhalation and notes that "fairly specific regional flow changes are seen in Alzheimer's disease, dementia with fronto-temporal atrophy (Pick's disease) and in multi-infarct dementia" (p. 139). Thus, specific regions of the brain that are affected by different disorders can be isolated by RCBF studies, as can changes in cortical activity during performance of different tests (e.g., Risberg, Maximilian, & Prohovnik, 1977).

Despite the promise that RCBF research appears to hold, other authors (e.g., Haier et al., 1987) suggest that its usefulness is quite limited compared to that of PET studies of cerebral glucose metabolism. Haier et al. (1987) state that whereas RCBF research "provides low resolution information about cortical function and little information about subcortical structures" (p. 2), PET research "allows detailed, direct, and noninvasive determination of cortical and subcortical glucose metabolic rates" (p. 3). It would appear that if RCBF research is already being criticized for its relatively limited application, then considerable advances indeed must have been made in the methodology for investigating the physiological bases of intelligence!

Early PET studies ("early," in this context, refers to about 1980) were largely comparative in nature, investigating differences in cerebral glucose metabolism between groups suffering from a variety of mental disorders. Because of the considerable expense associated with the purchase and operation of the equipment necessary to conduct PET scans, most studies have also involved relatively few subjects. Alavi et al. (1980), for example, observed that the glucose metabolic rates (GMRs) of six senile dementia subjects were some 20%–30% lower than those of four age-matched normal control subjects, whose GMRs in turn were 50% lower than those of eight young normal subjects. A similar depression of GMR has been found to be exhibited by patients with Alzheimer disease (e.g., Benson, 1982; Benson, Metter, Kuhl, & Phelps, 1982; de Leon et al., 1983). Moreover, Heiss, Herholz, Pawlik, Wagner, and Weinhard (1986) note that the impaired cerebral GMRs of Alzheimer patients can be detected by PET even in the very early stages of the disorder, being particularly noticeable in the parieto-temporal cortex.

More recently, investigations have been made of the relationship between cerebral GMRs and performance on standardized tests of intelligence. Chase et al. (1984), for example, reported correlations between Verbal, Performance, and Full Scale WAIS IQ scores and measures of overall cerebral GMR of .61, .56, and .68, respectively, in a combined sample of 17 Alzheimer patients and 5 normal controls. Of particular interest was the finding that Verbal IQ scores were most highly correlated with the GMR of the left cerebral hemisphere ($r = .68$), particularly the left temporal lobe ($r = .76$), whereas

Performance IQ scores correlated most highly with right-hemisphere GMR ($r = .61$), particularly the right parietal lobe ($r = .70$). As promising as these results seem in terms of identifying particular regions of the left and right hemispheres that are most involved during performance of different tests, it must be pointed out that Chase et al. provide no information about the magnitude of the cross-hemisphere correlations (i.e., Verbal IQ and right-hemisphere GMR or Performance IQ and left-hemisphere GMR).

Typically, PET studies involve the mapping of the concentration of an intravenously administered positron-emitting radionuclide (e.g., fluorodeoxyglucose F18) in different regions of the brain while the subject is at rest. Subsequently, mathematical models are employed to convert the isotope concentrations into estimates of cerebral GMRs. The important feature, however, is that the subject is usually not involved in any task that requires a great deal of cognitive activity. In Chase et al.'s (1984) study, for example, subjects' eyes were patched and their ears plugged during the PET scanning, specifically to eliminate or to minimize the effects of external stimuli. In a novel experiment, Haier et al. (1987) engaged subjects (30 normal males) in either a continuous-performance test (CPT)—a task involving attending to a degraded visual stimulus—or the Advanced Raven Matrices during the 30-minute or so period of the uptake of the isotope into the brain. The purpose was to observe which parts of the brain would show increased GMRs while subjects were actively involved in the performance of the different tasks.

Only 8 of the 30 subjects performed the Raven, but these subjects showed elevated relative GMRs at the left parieto-temporo-occipital junction and in the left occipital lobe, compared to subjects performing the CPT. In fact, the Raven subjects showed greater relative GMRs than the CPT subjects in five regions, all but one of these being in the posterior half of the brain. Haier et al. (1987) note that this finding is consistent with studies of patients with brain lesions, which have found that the posterior half of the brain is particularly important for abstract reasoning.

Within the sample of eight Raven subjects, correlations between cortical absolute GMRs

and Raven scores were high (ranging from $-.44$ to $-.84$), but all were negative. That is, subjects with higher Raven scores tended to show *lower* absolute GMRs than subjects with lower Raven scores. Haier et al. (1987) suggest that this may indicate that more intelligent subjects make more efficient use of their brains and consume less energy. Although this is consistent with Schafer's (1979, 1982) and Vernon's (1985) notions of neural efficiency, it must be pointed out that *no* negative correlations were observed between CPT scores and absolute GMRs. In addition, Haier et al.'s negative Raven–GMR correlations are contrary to the results of Chase et al. (1984) and other studies of cerebral GMRs or RCBF and intelligence (e.g., Butler, Dickinson, Katholi, & Halsey, 1983; Ferris et al., 1980), although these took PET scans while subjects were at rest. Although it almost goes without saying, PET studies such as Haier et al.'s will have to test much larger samples of subjects before any valid conclusions can be drawn from their results. At the same time, it seems likely that larger-scale PET studies will have the potential to provide considerably more information about physiological correlates of intelligence and mental abilities than any other presently available technique.

CONCLUSIONS

Three approaches to studying the physiological bases of intelligence—RT studies, EEG studies, and studies of RCBF and glucose metabolism—have been discussed. These three are by no means the only such approaches that have been taken, nor is the present review an exhaustive account of all of the research that has been conducted within each method. Rather, we have attempted to provide a general overview of what we consider to be some of the more interesting and important findings that each has provided, and to illustrate the potential of each to contribute to a greater understanding of the nature of individual differences in intelligence.

With respect to the *measurement* of intelligence, and/or practical as compared to theoretical implications, each of the approaches discussed in this chapter may also have something to offer. Vernon and Kantor's (1986) study of the correlations between RTs and timed and untimed measures of intelligence, for example, provides a novel perspective on the role of speed versus power tests in the evaluation of different mental abilities. The EEG work of the Hendricksons stimulated Deary et al.'s (1987) identification of low serum calcium levels in Alzheimer patients, and the possible beneficial effects of calcium supplementation on the memory and cognitive abilities of normal older subjects are currently being investigated. PET scans may be particularly useful in enabling Alzheimer disease and other cognitive disorders to be identified earlier than is possible by other presently available means.

As was noted at the beginning of this chapter, few test constructors have given consideration to physiological factors that underlie intelligence and contribute to individual differences in mental abilities. The implication of the physiological research is *not* that standard test batteries should be augmented with apparatus for measuring RTs, detecting AEPs, or making PET scans, nor that these should be used as *alternatives* to standardized tests of intelligence. Rather, the results of these and other similar research paradigms should be given due attention when they provide new information about the nature of intelligence. To disregard such information is to limit our assessments of mental abilities unnecessarily, and to provide us with a less than complete evaluation of a person's intelligence.

REFERENCES

Alavi, A., Ferris, S., Wolf, A., Reivich, M., Farkas, T., Dann, R., Christman, D., MacGregor, R. R., & Fowler, J. (1980). Determination of cerebral metabolism in senile dementia using F-18 deoxyglucose metabolism and positron emission tomography. *Journal of Nuclear Medicine, 21,* 21.

Benson, D. F. (1982). The use of positron emission scanning techniques in the diagnosis of Alzheimer's disease. In S. Corkin, K. L. Davis, J. H. Growdon, E. Vodin, & R. J. Wurtman (Eds.), *Alzheimer's disease: A review of progress in research.* New York: Raven Press.

Benson, D. F., Metter, E. J., Kuhl, D. E., & Phelps, M. E. (1982). Positron computed tomography in neurobehavioral problems. In A. Kertesz (Ed.), *Localization in neuropsychology* (pp. 121–139). New York: Academic Press.

Black, I. B., Adler, J. E., Dreyfus, C. F., Friedman, W. F., LaGamma, E. F., & Roach, A. H. (1987). Biochemistry of information storage in the nervous system. *Science, 236,* 1263–1268.

Blinkhorn, S. F., & Hendrickson, D. E. (1982). Averaged evoked responses and psychometric intelligence. *Nature, 295,* 596–597.

Butler, M. S., Dickinson, W. A., Katholi, C., & Halsey, J. H. (1983). The comparative effects of organic brain disease on cerebral blood flow and measured intelligence. *Annals of Neurology, 13,* 155–159.

Carroll, J. B. (1981). Ability and task difficulty in cognitive psychology. *Educational Researcher, 10,* 11–21.

Chase, T. N., Fedio, P., Foster, N. L., Brooks, R., Di Chiro, G., & Mansi, L. (1984). Wechsler Adult Intelligence Scale performance: Cortical localization by fluorodeoxyglucose F18-positron emission tomography. *Archives of Neurology, 41,* 1244–1247.

Deary, I. J., Hendrickson, A. E., & Burns, A. (1987). Serum calcium levels in Alzheimer's disease: A finding and an aetiological hypotheses. *Personality and Individual Differences, 8,* 75–80.

de Leon, M. J., Ferris, S. H., George, A. E., Christman, D. R., Fowler, J. S., Gentes, C., Reisberg, B., Gee, B., Emmerich, M., Yonekura, Y., Brodie, J., Kricheff, I. I., & Wolf, A. P. (1983). Positron emission tomographic studies of aging and Alzheimer disease. *American Journal of Neuroradiology, 4,* 568–571.

Donchin, E., & Lindsley, D. B. (1966). Average evoked potentials and reaction times to visual stimuli. *Electroencephalography and Clinical Neurophysiology, 20,* 217–223.

Dustman, R. E. (1965). Phase of alpha brain waves, reaction time, and visually evoked potentials. *Electroencephalography and Clinical Neurophysiology, 18,* 433–440.

Ertl, J. P., & Schafer, E. W. P. (1969). Brain response correlates of psychometric intelligence. *Nature, 223,* 421–422.

Eysenck, H. J. (1967). Intelligence assessment: A theoretical and experimental approach. *British Journal of Educational Psychology, 37,* 81–98.

Eysenck, H. J., & Barrett, P. (1984). Psychophysiology and the measurement of intelligence. In C. R. Reynolds & V. Willson (Eds.), *Methodological and statistical advances in the study of individual differences* (pp. 1–49). New York: Plenum Press.

Eysenck, H. J., Barrett, P. T., & Frearson, W. (1987). *The relationships between psychometric test intelligence, personality, timed performance, and electrophysiology of the brain and nerves.* Paper presented at the meeting of the International Society for the Study of Individual Differences, Toronto.

Ferris, S. H., de Leon, M. J., Wolf, A. P., Farkas, T., Christman, D. R., Reisberg, B., Fowler, J. S., MacGregor, R., Goldman, A., George, A. E., & Rampal, S. (1980). Positron emission tomography in the study of aging and senile dementia. *Neurobiology of Aging, 1,* 127–131.

Gale, A., & Edwards, J. A. (1983). Cortical correlates of intelligence. In A. Gale & J. A. Edwards (Eds.), *Physiologial correlates of human behaviour: Vol. 3. Individual differences and psychopathology* (pp. 79–97). London: Academic Press.

Giannitrapani, D. (1969). EEG average frequency and intelligence. *Electroencephalography and Clinical Neurophysiology, 27,* 480–486.

Gucker, D. K. (1973). Correlating visual evoked potentials with psychometric intelligence: Variation in technique. *Perceptual and Motor Skills, 37,* 189–190.

Haier, R. J., Robinson, D. L., Braden, W., & Williams, D. (1983). Electrical potentials of the cerebral cortex and psychometric intelligence. *Personality and Individual Differences, 4,* 591–599.

Haier, R. J., Siegel, B. V., Nuechterlein, K. H., Hazlett, E., Wu, J. C., Paek, J., Browning, H. L., & Buchsbaum, M. S. (1987). *Visuospatial reasoning and attention studied with positron emission tomography.* Paper presented at the meeting of the International Society for the Study of Individual Differences, Toronto.

Heiss, W. D., Herholz, K., Pawlik, G., Wagner, R., & Wienhard, K. (1986). Positron emission tomography in neuropsychology. *Neuropsychologia, 24,* 141–149.

Hendrickson, A. E. (1982). The biological basis of intelligence. Part I: Theory. In H. J. Eysenck (Ed.), *A model for intelligence* (pp. 151–196). Berlin: Springer-Verlag.

Hendrickson, D. E. (1982). The biological basis of intelligence. Part II: Measurement. In H. J. Eysenck (Ed.), *A model for intelligence* (pp. 197–228). Berlin: Springer-Verlag.

Hendrickson, D. E., & Hendrickson, A. E. (1980). The biological basis of individual differences in intelligence. *Personality and Individual Differences, 1,* 3–33.

Ho, H.-Z., Baker, L., & Decker, S. N. (1988). Covariation between intelligence and speed-of-cognitive processing: Genetic and environmental influences. *Behavior Genetics, 18,* 247–261.

Hynd, G. W., & Willis, W. G. (1985). Neurological foundations of intelligence. In B. B. Wolman (Ed.), *Handbook of intelligence: Theories, measurements and applications* (pp. 119–157). New York: Wiley.

Inouye, E., Park, K. S., & Asaka, A. (1984). Blood uric acid level and IQ: A study in twin families. *Acta Genetica et Medica Gemellologica, 33,* 237–242.

Jackson, D. N. (1983). *Multidimensional Aptitude Battery.* Port Huron, MI: Research Psychologists Press.

Jackson, D. N. (1984). *Multidimensional Aptitude Battery manual.* Port Huron, MI: Research Psychologists Press.

Jensen, A. R. (1979). g: Outmoded theory or unconquered frontier? *Creative Science and Technology, 2,* 16–29.

Jensen, A. R. (1980). Chronometric analysis of intelligence. *Journal of Social and Biological Structures, 3,* 103–122.

Jensen, A. R. (1982). Reaction time and psychometric g. In H. J. Eysenck (Ed.), *A model for intelligence* (pp. 93–132). Berlin: Springer-Verlag.

Jensen, A. R. (1987). Individual differences in the Hick paradigm. In P. A. Vernon (Ed.), *Speed of information-processing and intelligence* (pp. 101–175). Norwood, NJ: Ablex.

Jensen, A. R., Schafer, E. W. P., & Crinella, F. M. (1981). Reaction time, evoked brain potentials, and psychometric g in the severely retarded. *Intelligence, 5,* 179–197.

Kaufman, A. S., & Kaufman, N. L. (1983). *Kaufman Assessment Battery for Children (K-ABC).* Circle Pines, MN: American Guidance Service.

Lemmon, V. W. (1927). The relation of reaction time to measures of intelligence, memory, and learning. *Archives of Psychology, 15,* 5–38.

McGue, M., Bouchard, T. J., Jr., Lykken, D. T., &

Feuer, D. (1984). Information processing abilities in twins reared apart. *Intelligence, 8,* 239–258.

Morrell, L. K., & Morrell, F. (1966). Evoked potentials and reaction times: A study of intra-individual variability *Electroencephalography and Clinical Neurophysiology, 20,* 567–575.

Orowan, E. (1955). The origin of man. *Nature, 175,* 683–684.

Paisey, T. J. H. (1983). The diffuse thalamocortical system and Pavlovian theory: Let sleeping dogs lie. *Personality and Individual Differences, 4,* 527–534.

Peak, H., & Boring, E. G. (1926). The factor of speed in intelligence. *Journal of Experimental Psychology, 9,* 71–94.

Phelps, M. E., Mazziotta, J. C., & Huang, S.-C. (1982). Study of cerebral function with positron computed tomography. *Journal of Cerebral Blood Flow and Metabolism, 2,* 113–162.

Plum, A. (1968). *Visual evoked responses: Their relationship to intelligence.* Unpublished doctoral dissertation, University of Florida.

Reed, T. E. (1984). Mechanism for heritability of intelligence. *Nature, 311,* 417.

Rhodes, L. E., Dustman, R. E., & Beck, E. C. (1969). The visual evoked response: A comparison of bright and dull children. *Electroencephalography and Clinical Neurophysiology, 27,* 364–372.

Risberg, J. (1986). Regional cerebral blood flow in neuropsychology. *Neuropsychologia, 24,* 135–140.

Risberg, J., Maximilian, A. V., & Prohovnik, I. (1977). Changes of cortical activity patterns during habituation to a reasoning test. A study with ^{133}Xe inhalation technique for measurement of regional cerebral blood flow. *Neuropsychologia, 15,* 793–798.

Robinson, D. L. (1982). Properties of the diffuse thalamocortical system, human intelligence and differentiated vs. integrated modes of learning. *Personality and Individual Differences, 3,* 393–405.

Robinson, D. L. (1983). The diffuse thalamocortical system and Pavlovian/Eysenckian theory: A response to criticism. *Personality and Individual Differences, 4,* 535–541.

Robinson, D. L., Haier, R. J., Braden, W., & Krengel, M. (1984). Psychometric intelligence and visual evoked potentials: A replication. *Personality and Individual Differences, 5,* 487–489.

Sandman, C. A., & Barron, J. L. (1986). Parameters of the event-related potential are related to functioning in the mentally retarded. *International Journal of Neuroscience, 29,* 37–44.

Schafer, E. W. P. (1979). Cognitive neural adaptability: A biological basis for individual differences in intelligence. *Psychophysiology, 16,* 199.

Schafer, E. W. P. (1982). Neural adaptability: A biological determinant of behavioral intelligence. *International Journal of Neuroscience, 17,* 183–191.

Schafer, E. W. P., & Marcus, M. M. (1973). Self-stimulation alters human sensory brain responses. *Science, 181,* 175–177.

Schwartz, S., Griffin, T. M., & Brown, J. (1983). Power and speed components of individual differences in letter matching. *Intelligence, 7,* 369–378.

Shucard, D. W., & Horn, J. L. (1972). Evoked cortical potentials and measurement of human abilities. *Journal of Comparative and Physiological Psychology, 78,* 59–68.

Shucard, D. W., & Horn, J. L. (1973). Evoked potential amplitude change related to intelligence and arousal. *Psychophysiology*, *10*, 445–452.

Sternberg, R. J. (1984). Toward a triarchic theory of human intelligence. *Behavioral and Brain Sciences*, *7*, 269–315.

Sternberg, R. J. (1986). Haste makes waste versus a stitch in time? A reply to Vernon, Nador, and Kantor. *Intelligence*, *10*, 265–270.

Vernon, P. A. (1983). Speed of information processing and general intelligence. *Intelligence*, *7*, 53–70.

Vernon, P. A. (1985). Individual differences in general cognitive ability. In L. C. Hartlage & C. F. Telzrow (Eds.) *The neuropsychology of individual differences* (pp. 125–150). New York: Plenum.

Vernon, P. A. (Ed.). (1987a). *Speed of information-processing and intelligence*. Norwood, NJ: Ablex.

Vernon, P. A. (1987b). *The heritability of measures of speed of information-processing*. Paper presented at the annual meeting of the Behavior Genetics Association, Minneapolis.

Vernon, P. A. (1989). The heritability of measures of speed of information-processing. *Personality and Individual Differences*, *10*, 573–576.

Vernon, P. A., & Jensen, A. R. (1984). Individual and group differences in intelligence and speed of information processing. *Personality and Individual Differences*, *10*, 573–576.

Vernon, P. A. & Kantor, L. (1986). Reaction time correlations with intelligence test scores obtained under either timed or untimed conditions. *Intelligence*, *10*, 315–330.

Vernon, P. A., Nador, S., & Kantor, L. (1985a). Group differences in intelligence and speed of information-processing. *Intelligence*, *9*, 137–148.

Vernon, P. A., Nador, S., & Kantor, L. (1985b). Reaction times and speed-of-processing: Their relationship to timed and untimed measures of intelligence. *Intelligence*, *9*, 357–374.

Weinberg, H. (1969). Correlation of frequency spectra of averaged visual evoked potentials and verbal intelligence. *Nature*, *224*, 813–815.

Wissler, C. (1901). The correlation of mental and physical tests. *Psychological Review Monographs*, *3*(6, Whole No. 16).

III

ASSESSMENT OF ACADEMIC SKILL

16

Standardized Multilevel Survey Achievement Batteries

ANTHONY J. NITKO
SUZANNE LANE
University of Pittsburgh

This chapter describes traditional group-administered standardized tests, especially as these are administered to children in schools. The particular type of test upon which we focus is the multilevel survey battery. The chapter is organized into three main divisions, corresponding to the past, present, and future of standardized multilevel survey testing.

The first section is a short history of standardized achievement testing, spanning roughly the first 80 years of this century. The second section describes multilevel survey batteries as they exist today—their common features and their differences. Descriptions and examples of specific survey batteries useful for elementary, middle, and high school levels are described in the next two sections. The fifth section discusses uses and misuses of survey batteries in the schools. The sixth section provides guidance on how to evaluate and select a multilevel survey battery for a school testing program. The last section turns to the future, describing how the findings of modern cognitive psychology are beginning to help us understand student competence and proficiency; it also speculates on the impact these findings are likely to have on the design of future achievement tests.

A BRIEF HISTORY OF STANDARDIZED ACHIEVEMENT TESTING

Standardized, norm-referenced tests were unknown in 1880, but by the 1920s and 1930s millions of school children had been tested and classified with them. In 1918, the yearbook of the National Society for the Study of Education listed 84 elementary school and 25 high school standardized tests covering specific school subjects (Monroe, 1918). By 1922, at least 44 group intelligence tests could be listed in the yearbook (Whipple, 1922). This was amazingly rapid growth, considering that the first standardized subject-matter test did not appear until 1908 (Stone, 1908), and that the first commercially published test, the Courtis Standard Research Test in Arithmetic, only appeared in 1914 (Holmen & Doctor, 1972).

Several general conditions contributed to this acceptance and use of tests by schools, including the following:

1. The centralization of school administration; business elites and educators were urging the adoption of the corporate model, with a board of directors and a

conception of school management similar to business management (Tyack, 1974).

2. The acceptance of scientific management, including quantitative analysis, as a proper means to increase educational productivity and efficiency (Callahan, 1962).

3. The development of tests thought to measure innate intellectual ability, the popularization of social Darwinism, and the acceptance of the notion that the pupils, and not the school, were to blame when learning failed to happen (Calhoun, 1973).

The Birth of Modern Survey Testing

It is Joseph Mayer Rice (1857–1934) to whom the fatherhood of modern educational testing and educational research is attributed, although some classify him as an educational muckraker (Tyack, 1974). Rice, a physician, practiced medicine from 1881 to 1888, but then he changed careers, going to Germany to study education and to visit schools.

Upon his return to the United States, a popular magazine, *The Forum* (of which Rice was later the editor at one point), sponsored Rice in a tour of the country's schools. In a series of seven articles between 1897 and 1904, he wrote about the conditions in the schools, their politics, the lack of teacher and administrator competence, and the fact that much of school policy and practice was based on opinion without evidence. (It was precisely these concerns that formed the platform of persons arguing for centralized school administration and for scientific management; see Tyack, 1974.) Rice supported his criticisms by administering standard tests of spelling, arithmetic, handwriting, and composition, and by analyzing the data and publishing them in his articles. The results showed that there were tremendous ranges of achievemnt among pupils and among schools, and that these outcomes were frequently not associated with the amount of classroom time devoted to a subject or with specific teaching practices.

Edward L. Thorndike

Ten years were to pass until published subject-matter tests were available for schools to purchase, although considerable technical development had taken place. It was Edward Lee Thorndike (1874–1949) and his students, however, who (1) consolidated and systematically applied both the technical developments and the "scientific spirit" to educational testing and research in the United States; and (2) convinced educators of the usefulness of educational testing. First, Thorndike established educational psychology as a discipline by conducting learning experiments and disseminating the results in a form accessible to school personnel. Second, he initiated the scientific measurement of educational achievement by publishing, in a form that was easily understood by educational test-developers, the first book on statistical methods for developing mental measurements—*An Introduction to the Theory of Mental and Social Measurements* (Thorndike, 1904). Third, he and his students developed and published the first standardized school achievement tests in arithmetic (Stone, 1908; Courtis, 1910), handwriting (Thorndike, 1910), English composition (Hillegas, 1912), drawing (Thorndike, 1913), and spelling (Buckingham, 1913). In fact, for 5 years after the appearance of Stone's test, the only test published by someone not associated with Thorndike was Leonard P. Ayres's (1912) handwriting scale (Monroe, Odell, Herriott, Englehart, & Hull, 1928). Fourth, through his writings (over 500 publications between 1898 and 1949; see Linden & Linden, 1968) and his participation in professional meetings with educators and psychologists, Thorndike stressed the usefulness and legitimacy of *quantitative* assessment of human ability and achievement.

The School Survey Movement

The school survey movement, stemming from the scientific management posture toward which school boards and administrators were turning, served to foster the widespread acceptance and use of standardized tests of educational achievement. The term "survey" had formerly been used only in connection with land surveys (measuring and mapping parcels of land), but it was linked with a sociological study of Pittsburgh in 1909, which sought to "survey" the sociological characteristics of the city (Kellogg, 1914). Subsequently, the term "survey" came to be used in a study of the Montclair, New Jersey schools by P. H. Hanus (1911) and in a study of the schools of East Orange, by E. C. Moore (1912). Standardized tests, however, were not used. It was in Hanus's survey of the New York City schools in 1911 to 1912 that standardized tests were first used to evaluate the efficiency of a school system (Ayres, 1918): Courtis was called upon to administer his Series A arithmetic tests to some 30,000 students. Although early school surveys frequently did not use tests, by the early 1920s practically all school district surveys used them (Monroe, 1923). By the late 1920s most superintendents welcomed school surveys, with their accompanying tests, as instruments for instituting the progressive administrative reforms they wanted (Tyack, 1974). Thereafter, the school survey movement spread rapidly.

The Call for Objective and Scientific Tests

Early in the movement, there were calls for surveys to be "objective," "scientific," and free from opinion or speculation—to be analogous to the "transits, tables, and chains, used in the land survey" (Ayres, 1915, p. 174). Dissatisfaction with existing tests stimulated the development of better achievement tests (Monroe, 1923; Odell, 1930). Contributing to this demand for tests was the competition for shares of the market among commercial test publishers (Good, 1962).

As superintendents and school boards came to believe in the scientific authority of surveys, research bureaus were established in both school systems and universities. These bureaus developed, published, and disseminated standardized tests, and conducted surveys and other educational research studies. One city research director (Nifenecker, 1918) reported that nearly 900,000 copies of one test were used in 1917.

Although they were not the first to do so (see Kelly, 1914), Daniel Starch and E. C. Elliott (1912, 1913) confirmed a largely known but seldom documented fact—namely, that the marks assigned by teachers to high school students' examination papers in English, geometry, and history varied widely from one teacher to the next. While researchers of this period focused on the unreliability of subjectively determined scores

on essay and short-answer tests, evidence was also uncovered that the scoring of essays could be made more reliable. But as the number of persons to be tested rose, as the demand for scientifically developed tests with standard content increased, and as the success of the Army's large-scale group testing program in World War I became evident, leaders of the measurement movement did not pursue attempts to improve essay testing methods. Rather, they focused their attention on the development and improvement of multiple-choice items.

Development of Multiple-Choice Items

Arthur Sinton Otis, a graduate student of Lewis M. Terman, developed a paper-and-pencil version of Terman's (1916) Stanford Revision of the Binet–Simon Scale that was suitable for use as a group-administered test. In the process, he developed what were probably the first multiple-choice items for intelligence tests[1] (see Robertson, n.d./1972). Otis's paper-and-pencil, multiple-choice format was adopted as the basis for the U.S. Army Alpha Test (Yerkes, 1921; Yoakum & Yerkes, 1920). In 1918, after the war, Otis's own Group Intelligence Scale was published by the World Book Company.

Multilevel survey batteries were developed just prior to 1920. Before that time there were separate subject tests published in separate booklets. Among the early achievement survey batteries were the Educational Survey Test (Pitner & Fitzgerald, 1920), the Illinois Examination (Monroe & Buckingham, 1920; Monroe, 1921), and the Scale of Attainment, Numbers 1–3 (L. C. Pressey, 1920, 1921; S. L. Pressey, 1921). These and other survey batteries did not have the technical quality we have come to expect from such tests today.

Commercial Test Publication

The first commercial test publisher in the United States was the World Book Company, which published the Courtis Standard Re-

---

[1]Multiple-choice items were found in some of the early achievement tests reported in Starch's (1917) testing book—for example, Thorndike's (1914) reading vocabulary scale, Kelly's (1915) reading test, and Starch's (1915) grammar scales.

search Test in Arithmetic in 1914 (Holmen & Doctor, 1972). An important step in achievement testing came when World published the Stanford Achievement Test (Kelley, Rush, & Terman, 1923). This standardized test battery was not the first of its kind (see Monroe et al., 1928); however, it was considered at the time to be the best from the technical standpoint and served as a guide for future commercially prepared achievement batteries. In the 1920s, World became the first commercial publisher to establish a test department, and Otis was named director (Holmen & Doctor, 1972; Robertson, n.d./ 1972).

Houghton Mifflin entered the test publication field with the Stanford Revision of the Binet–Simon Scale (Terman, 1916). The Psychological Corporation, founded by James McKeen Cattell, Edward L. Thorndike, Robert S. Woodworth, and other American Psychological Association (APA) members in 1921, began supplying tests under the direction of Paul Achilles in the late 1920s (Holmen & Doctor, 1972). The California Test Bureau was founded in 1926 by Ethel M. Clark; Lyle Spencer founded Science Research Associates in 1938; and the Educational Testing Service was founded in 1947 through the efforts of the American Council on Education, the Carnegie Foundation for the Advancement of Teaching, and the College Entrance Examination Board (Holmen & Doctor, 1972).

Highlights of Testing to the Present Day

The development of educational and psychological tests proceeded so rapidly that it became exceedingly difficult to keep track of them. By 1939, some 4,200 tests and rating scales had been proposed,[2] ranging from measures of human intelligence to ratings of chimpanzee behavior (Hildreth, 1939). Over the years there have been many bibliographies of tests, but it was the volumes of Oscar Krisen Buros (1905–1978), the *Mental Measurements Yearbooks*, that served professionals and practitioners best.

Oscar Buros was not the only measurement specialist concerned about the quality

of educational tests. Among the concerns of testing critics in the 1930s were these: (1) Specific subject-matter examinations were too narrow in scope; (2) achievement tests focused on factual knowledge; and (3) tests tended to dominate the curriculum and method of teaching in undesirable ways. Of the many measurement specialists responding to these early criticisms, two have been especially notable for their contributions to shaping the direction of standardized educational testing today: Everet Franklin Lindquist and Ralph Winfred Tyler.

The practice of using highly specific objectives to define a curriculum area was widely adopted by scholars between 1918 and 1925 and led to such excesses as listing "nearly three thousand specific objectives for arithmetic, and nearly two thousand for English" (Tyler, 1956/1976, p. 65). Tyler demonstrated that both educational goals and educational testing could be directed toward developing generalized skills and abilities in pupils, rather than toward testing only specific facts. These ideas helped to shift student learning and teaching away from the types of memorization activities that dominated the school curriculum in the 1920s and 1930s and toward broader conceptual levels and transferable skills. These were innovative ideas at the time because the so-called "new tests" (i.e., objective examinations) had been used to test facts only.

Tyler and Lindquist met in 1919 (Tyler, 1973). As contemporaries, their work and influence highlight what has been called the "pupil evaluation movement" (Stanley & Hopkins, 1972). This movement shifted the focus of achievement tests toward assessing higher mental processes (e.g., application of knowledge), interests, and attitudes (Linden & Linden, 1968).

There are many ways to describe the technical development of testing since the 1920s. The way we have chosen here is to illustrate this history with the accomplishments of E. F. Lindquist, whose ideas were frequently so innovative and powerful that what he developed was quickly implemented by others as well.[3] His accomplishments include inno-

---

[2]Most of these tests were not available commercially, nor were they disseminated. The number reported includes many tests that are of historical or research interest.

[3]Our description of Lindquist's accomplishments is based on Feister and Whitney (1968) unless otherwise noted. It should be understood that although Lindquist is cited as a major figure in these developments, many of them were collaborative efforts (see Ebel, 1972; Feister & Whitney, 1968; Lindquist, 1953).

vations and improvements in (1) elementary and high school test development; (2) the type and manner of services offered by test publishers to schools; (3) the use of electronic scoring equipment; (4) the use of the computer as a resource for information about pupils; (5) high school equivalency testing and credit by examination; and (6) the manner in which college admission testing was conducted.

Developed under Lindquist's direction, for example, were the Iowa Tests of Basic Skills (ITBS) for elementary students, and the Iowa Tests of Educational Development (ITED) for high school students. The tests were innovative because instead of emphasizing facts and specific subject-matter learning, they emphasized skills, applications, problem solving, interpretation of materials, and so on. The test manual and other materials provided with the tests stressed the individualization of instruction and, for the elementary school battery, remediation of learning deficits. This trend was soon adopted by other test publishers, and by 1964 nearly all of the major publishers had adopted this "new look" for achievement tests (Linden & Linden, 1968).

For many years publishers had only sold tests to schools, and it was up to the schools to score them, to do any data analysis they wished, and to report the results. Lindquist initiated the practice of having the test publisher (or publisher's agent) provide a complete service—test materials, interpretative materials, and scoring. By 1953 Lindquist had proposed the logical design for, and by 1955 he had supervised the building of, a high-speed, high-volume digital scoring machine that was capable not only of scoring tests, but also of analyzing the data and printing the results on student record forms in a single operation.(Feister & Whitney, 1968; Lindquist, 1953, 1968).[4]

To a considerable extent, the electronic scoring of answer sheets has permitted the expansion of many testing programs at the state and national level. Such programs as the Scholastic Aptitude Tests, the American College Testing (ACT) program, the Graduate Record Examinations, and state testing programs of various kinds depend on high-

speed machines to handle large numbers of examinees' answer documents efficiently and at a reasonable cost. By 1968 Lindquist was describing new developments that permitted examinees to mark responses in several ways and at any place in the test booklet, and recommending ways in which computer-based scoring devices could increase the content validity of achievement tests by allowing for differential weighting of item responses to better reflect curricular emphases.

With World War II came an effort to provide for the education of military personnel and for their easy transition back into civilian life when the war was over. In the 1940s Lindquist make available to the U.S. Armed Forces Institute five tests from the ITED. These were eventually restandardized to become the Tests of General Educational Development (GED), permitting thousands of persons whose formal schooling had been interrupted by the war to demonstrate that their general educational development level was equivalent to 12 years of schooling. Now under the auspices of the American Council on Education, the GED is used widely for high school equivalency certification of adults both in and out of the military, as well as of older adolescents (16–18 years old) who wish to end their formal high school education early.

Lindquist was one of the founders of the ACT program. As Lindquist described it, up through the 1950s the College Board's admissions tests were less than optimal for state colleges and universities, as well as for small denominational and private colleges, especially those in the Midwest (Lindquist, cited in Feister & Whitney, 1968). Such institutions needed a test only to sort out those few very-low-ability students whom they could not handle. Furthermore, Lindquist envisioned not just an aptitude test, but a measure of educational development that could be used for guidance and counseling purposes as well. Because the Measurement Research Center and its data-processing equipment were available, these could be put to use to give a college information that was specific to its own applicant pool, rather than to limit the information to national norms alone (Tyler, 1973). These ideas expanded the nature of college admissions testing and were implemented in the ACT assessment program.

It is possible to continue describing the

[4]The first scoring machine with satisfactory accuracy was produced by IBM in 1935, following the technical suggestions of a Michigan school teacher, Reynold B. Johnson, who later became director of an IBM development laboratory (Ebel, 1972).

many innovations and technical advances made in the measurement field up to the present. This book as a whole reflects many of these, and so describing them further serves no purpose here.

MULTILEVEL SURVEY BATTERIES

The workhorse of standardized achievement testing has been the multilevel survey battery. Although each multilevel survey battery is quite different in content and skill emphasis from others, the organization of all of these batteries is similar. Each battery is group-administered; each contains several subtests; each subtest measures achievement in a specific curricular area; and each subtest is organized so that there is a coordinated series of levels spanning the grades (hence, "multilevel"). For example, a subtest may measure reading comprehension but may be organized into four levels: one level for first and second grades, another for third and fourth grades, one for fifth and sixth grades, and another for seventh and eighth grades. (It is not unusual for two levels to overlap grades—for example, third–fourth–fifth and fifth–sixth–seventh.) A subtest may cover reading, mathematics, listening skills, English usage (mechanics), spelling recognition, vocabulary, knowledge, social studies, general science, work–study skills, or skills in using the library and reference materials. There are usually six to eight curricular areas within a given battery; different publishers have different names for a curricular area.

The subtest is conceptualized as measuring a continuous characteristic (e.g., reading comprehension) that grows or develops over the range of grades for which it is intended to be used. Because the development of a subtest for a given test battery is coordinated over the various levels, it is possible to use empirical data to place the scores of students from every grade on the same numerical scale. The scale quantifies the amount of the characteristic a student possesses. This makes it possible to use a multilevel subtest to measure pupils' growth or year-to-year learning progress.

Because all subtests in a particular survey battery are administered and normed on the same population of pupils, a pupil's relative strengths and weaknesses in each curricular area tested may be compared. Strengths and weaknesses may be ascertained, however, only by comparing a student's percentile rank in one curricular area to that pupil's percentile rank in another. The relative comparison you would obtain is of this type: "Jane is better in reading than in social studies because her score in reading exceeds that of 99% of the students in her grade, whereas her score in social studies exceeds that of only 70% of the students in this grade." Grade equivalent scores cannot be used for such curricular comparisons, although it is common for school personnel to do so erroneously (see, e.g., Nitko, 1983 for an explanation of grade equivalent interpretations).

Common Features of Multilevel Survey Batteries

There are several common features among group-administered survey batteries (Iwanicki, 1980):

1. *Test development features.* Each publisher of a survey battery provides manuals and reports that describe how the test was developed: (a) content and objectives covered; (b) the type of norms developed and how they were developed; (c) type of content or criterion-referencing provided; (d) reliability data; and (e) how the test items were screened for bias and offensiveness.

2. *Test administration features.* Survey batteries generally (a) have two equivalent forms; (b) require 2–3 hours of testing time spread over several school days; (c) provide practice booklets for students; (d) have separate answer sheets for pupils above fourth grade, while permitting lower-grade students to mark directly in the booklet; and (e) permit both in-level and out-of-level testing in regard to a pupil's grade placement. Since a pupil at a given grade placement may be functioning at achievement levels below (or above) the pupil's grade placement, a school may decide to administer that pupil a test level below (or above) the pupil's grade placement. This practice is called "out-of-level testing."

3. *Test norming features.* Survey batteries usually (a) attempt to have norms that represent the national population of students

at each grade level covered; and (b) have fall and spring norms. Sometimes special norms are provided, such as norms for nonpublic schools or norms for school building averages. A school building average is the mean score on a subtest for the students in a particular grade in a particular school building (e.g., the average reading comprehension score for all fourth graders in Lincoln School). A school district may have several school buildings each housing one or more fourth grades. The frequency distribution of all building averages for the fourth grade for all school districts in the national sample constitute the norms for school building averages of fourth graders. These norms should be used rather than norms for individual students' scores when comparing the average performance of fourth graders in a school to fourth graders in the nation (see Nitko, 1983).

4. *Test score features*. In addition to number right scores for each subtest, survey batteries provide the following norm-referenced scores: percentile ranks, normal curve equivalents, stanines, extended normalized scale scores, and/or grade equivalents.

5. *Test score reporting and interpretive features*. Publishers provide manuals for teachers, school administrators, and counselors that give suggestions and examples of how to interpret test scores. Computer-generated reports are available at extra cost, including (a) analyses of the performance of a classroom on clusters of items on each subtest; (b) reports for each subtest of one grade level within a building (e.g., how all fourth-graders at Lincoln School performed in reading comprehension); and (c) a narrative report for each student interpreting the student's score profile. Some batteries have additional material related to how to use the test results to identify a student's strengths and weaknesses. Other batteries provide suggestions for teaching students in a curricular area.

Differences among Survey Batteries

Although survey batteries share common features, they should not be assumed to be interchangeable. Students' scores obtained from different batteries, even on subtests with similar-sounding titles, will be different and cannot be compared directly. Among the features that are different and that seriously affect interpretation of scores are the following:

1. *Emphasis within content areas*. Subtest scores from batteries of different test authors are not interchangeable, even though the subtests have similar-sounding names. For example, a study of the mathematics subtests of four standardized survey batteries for the fourth-grade level indicated that the percentage of items covering a topic such as fractions varied widely from one publisher's test to another—that is, from 5.4% to 14.3% (Freeman, Kuhs, Knappen, & Porter, 1982). This factor would affect pupils' scores significantly. Because each test author chooses to emphasize each subtopic somewhat differently, there may be a serious mismatch between what a given battery calls "reading comprehension" or "social studies" and what a given school and/or teacher emphasizes in class. These mismatches manifest themselves in subtest scores (e.g., grade equivalents in a subject area), which may not represent a student's current level of functioning. The overlap of a test and a school's instructional program is an extremely important consideration in choosing among test batteries.

2. *Quality of developmental scales' articulation between grade levels*. One advantage of a multilevel battery can be its use of a continuous developmental scale on which students are measured. If the scale is contructed properly, it is possible to track students' educational growth over the various grade levels in a broad area such as reading comprehension or mathematical problem solving. But different test developers use different technical methods for creating developmental scales, even when the scales have the same name. For example, different tests use different procedures for creating grade equivalent scales. A chief consideration in the practical use of test results concerns the amount of grade-to-grade overlap in the development scores (Peterson, Kolen, & Hoover, 1989). For example, a fourth-grader may have a grade equivalent of 6.0 on the fourth-grade mathematics and computation subtest, and a grade equivalent of 4.9 on the sixth-grade counterpart of the same subtest. Different techniques for constructing

grade equivalents will create differing amounts of overlap, and hence will result in scores that show a spuriously erratic pattern of growth for youngsters as they progress through the grades.

3. *Quality of services offered to schools.* Test publishers differ in the extent to which they provide technical support and interpretative services to schools using their products. Some publishers sell the product and certain standard services (e.g., computer printouts summarizing test results for a school district), but do not provide knowledgeable consultants who can advise a school on particular nonstandard interpretable problems or even on how to interpret their results in general. A purchaser of a survey battery should explore fully with the publisher's sales representative the nature and cost of technical support services the purchaser will receive with the test battery.

BATTERIES FOR ELEMENTARY AND MIDDLE SCHOOL STUDENTS

Multilevel survey batteries appropriate for elementary and middle school students consist of several subtests associated with separate curricular areas. The survey batteries differ in terms of the number of curricular areas they assess and, to some extent, the knowledge and skills measured in each curricular area. Tables 16.1 and 16.2 present the curricular areas assessed from the preschool level to the end of middle school for a number of widely used survey batteries. For students beyond the third grade, survey batteries typically include subtests in mathematics computation, mathematics concepts, mathematics problem solving, language mechanics, language usage, reading comprehension, spelling, and vocabulary. Additional areas that are assessed by some of the batteries include listening skills, study skills, social studies, and science. For example, the Stanford Achievement Test includes a subtest assessing listening skills for students in kindergarten through ninth grade, whereas the California Achievement Tests afford no direct measure of listening skills at any level. As another example, the ITBS include two subtests measuring study skills—Visual

Materials (interpreting maps, graphs, and tables) and Reference Materials. The Stanford Achievement Test also yields a direct measure of reference skills; however, it yields no direct measure of skills in interpreting maps, graphs, and tables.

Although most, if not all, batteries assess language mechanics and language usage in the form of recognizing examples of correct and incorrect use of written language, they do not provide a direct measure of composition and essay writing. A recent supplement to a few batteries is an optional test assessing writing production. This addition to multilevel survey batteries is a reflection of the growing skepticism regarding the measurement of writing skills with only multiple-choice items. The ITBS, the Metropolitan Achievement Tests and the Stanford Achievement Test are supplemented with optional writing assessment programs. As might be expected with new testing practices, the writing assessment programs are not yet as well standardized as are the objective survey batteries.

Tests appropriate for students in preschool through third grade typically assess mathematics concepts and problem solving, phonetic and structural analysis, listening skills, and knowledge of social studies and natural environments. At the preschool and kindergarten levels, tests also generally measure alphabet knowledge and word reading. Mathematics computations and sentence reading are typically assessed from first through third grades. A few batteries (e.g., the Head Start Measures Battery and CIRCUS) also measure a number of perceptual skills. At this level, a considerable breadth of content is assessed in the social and science/natural environment subtests. For example, the Tests of Basic Experiences 2 (TOBE 2) measure such diverse areas as health, human relations, and geography in the Social Studies subtest, and one score is yielded for this subtest. Because of the diversity within the subtest, it may be difficult to arrive at clear interpretation of this subtest score. This problem is not unique to this instrument; rather, it is common across many of the batteries at this level.

Test items for the preschool and kindergarten level are usually administered with oral teacher-given directions and are generally accompanied by illustrations. Survey batter-

TABLE 16.1. Curriculum Areas Assessed by Survey Batteries Appropriate for Kindergarten through 12th Grade

Area	California Achievement Tests (Forms C and D)	Comprehensive Tests of Basic Skills (Forms U and V)	Iowa Tests of Basic Skills (Forms 7 and 8)/Tests of Achievement and Proficiency	SRA Achievement Tests	Stanford Achievement Test	Sequential Test of Educational Progress—Series III
Reading						
Alphabet knowledge		K–K.9		K–1.5	1.5–7.9	
Word sentence reading		K–K.9				3.5–12.9
Phonetic and structural analysis	K–3.9	K–K.9	K–3.5	K–3.5	1.5–3.9	
Decoding skills	K.6–12.9	K–12.9	K–9	1.5–12.9	1.5–13	3.5–12.9
Vocabulary	K.6–12.9	K–12.9	K–12	1.5–12.9	1.5–13	3.5–12.9
Comprehension				2.5–12.9		
Language						
Punctuation	1.6–12.9	3.6–12.9	1.7–12	1.5–12.9	3.5–13	3.5–12.9
Capitalization	1.6–12.9	3.6–12.9	1.7–12	1.5–12.9	3.5–13	3.5–12.9
Usage	K.6–12.9	1.0–12.9	K–12	2.5–12.9		
Sentence and paragraph organization	3.6–12.9	3.6–12.9	9–12		3.5–13	3.5–12.9
Spelling	1.6–12.9	3.6–12.9	K–12	2.5–12.9		
Mathematics						
Computation	K.6–12.9	1.0–12.9	1.7–12	1.5–12.9	1.5–13	3.5–12.9
Concepts	K–12.9	K–12.9	K–12	K–12.9	1.5–13	3.5–12.9
Problem solving	K–12.9	K–12.9	K–12	K–12.9	1.5–13	3.5–12.9
Study skills						
Maps, graphs, tables	3.6–12.9	3.6–12.9	1.7–12	3.5–12.9	[a]	3.5–12.9
Library and reference	3.6–12		1.7–12	3.5–10.5	3.5–13	3.5–12.9
Science	3.6–12.9	3.6–12.9	3–12	4.5–12.9	1.5–13	3.5–12.9
Social studies	3.6–12.9	3.6–12.9	3–12	4.5–12.9	1.5–13	3.5–12.9
Listening			K–3.5, 3–12[b]	K–2.5	1.5–13	3.5–12.9
Writing production			3–12[b]		3.5–13	

[a] Measured indirectly in the science, social studies, and mathematics domains.
[b] Supplement to the battery.

413

TABLE 16.2. Curriculum Areas Assessed by Survey Batteries Appropriate for Preschool through 3rd Grade

Area	CIRCUS	Head Start Measures Battery	Stanford Early School Achievement Test	Tests of Basic Experiences 2
Reading				
Alphabet knowledge		Pre–K.9		Pre–1.9
Word/sentence reading		Pre–K.9	K–1.9	
Phonetic and structural analysis	Pre–3.5	Pre–K.9	K–1.9	Pre–1.9
Vocabulary comprehension	1.5–3.5			Pre–1.9
Language				
Mechanics	2.5–3.5			
Usage	2.5–3.5			
Production		Pre–3.5		
Mathematics				
Computation	K.5–3.5	Pre–K.9	K–1.9[a]	
Concepts	Pre–3.5	Pre–K.9	K–1.9	Pre–1.9
Problem solving		Pre–K.9	K–1.9	Pre–1.9
Science/natural environment	Pre–3.5	Pre–K.9	K–1.9	Pre–1.9
Perception	Pre–3.5	Pre–K.9		
Social environment	Pre–3.5	Pre–K.9	K–1.9	Pre–1.9
Listening	Pre–3.5		K–1.9	K–1

[a]Optional subtest.

ies at all levels typically use the multiple-choice item format.

The knowledge and skills that are measured by survey batteries range from recall of factual content to understanding of concepts requiring higher cognitive processes. A difference across batteries is their emphasis on measuring general concepts versus more specific factual content. As an example, the intention of the ITBS is to measure general cognitive skills and not factual information. In contrast, the Stanford Achievement Test is oriented toward measuring factual content within the knowledge domains.

Norms and Scores

Most batteries provide separate norms (e.g., for genders, grades, ages, public schools, and private schools) that enable the user to make various comparisons. Batteries typically yield both fall and spring norm scores, which allow for the assessment of individual growth and development. The types and numbers of scores provided differ across batteries, as illustrated in Table 16.3. Test scores are commonly expressed as percentiles, stanines, grade equivalents, standard scores, and normal curve equivalents. With the growing concern regarding the misinterpretation of

grade equivalents, a number of batteries (e.g., the California Achievement Tests) explicitly caution the user against interpreting grade equivalents, whereas other batteries encourage their use (e.g., the ITBS). The Sequential Tests of Educational Progress—Series III (STEP III) provides a score termed the "grade level indicator" to replace grade equivalents. The intent is to provide a measure that does not possess some of the contradictory properties associated with grade equivalents. Grade level indicators relate a student's score to the average performance of other students who actually took the test. Thus, in the development of grade level indicators, there is no extrapolation beyond the norming sample. Although grade level indicators have the range of scores restricted to those attained by the students in the norming sample, they still retain some undesirable features associated with grade equivalents (e.g., students below the median will gain less than one grade level indicator each year).

A common feature among most survey achievement batteries is their concurrent norming with a scholastic aptitude test. "Concurrent norming" means that the norms of both tests include the same students at the same point in time. This permits the direct comparison of the scores on both types of

TABLE 16.3. Scores Provided by Survey Batteries

Battery	Grades	Scores	Publisher
California Achievement Tests (Forms C and D)	K–12.9	Percentiles, NCE, stanines, GE, scaled scores, objectives mastery score	CTB/McGraw-Hill
CIRCUS	K–3.5	Percentiles, NCE, stanines, grade level indicators	ETS, CTB/McGraw-Hill
Comprehensive Tests of Basic Skills (3rd edition)	K–12.9	Percentiles, stanines, GE, NCE, scaled scores (derived from 3-parameter item response model)	CTB/McGraw-Hill
Iowa Tests of Basic Skills (Forms 7 and 8)	K–9	Percentiles, stanines, GE, scaled scores	Houghton Mifflin
SRA Achievement Series (4th edition)	K–12	Percentiles, stanines, GE, NCE, growth scale values (standard scores)	Science Research Associates
Sequential Tests of Educational Progress—Series III (STEP III)	3.5–12.9	Percentiles, NCE, stanines, grade level indicators	ETS, CTB/McGraw-Hill
Stanford Achievement Test (1982 edition)	1.5–13	Percentiles, stanines, GE, scaled scores, NCE	Psychological Corporation
Stanford Early School Achievement Test (1982 edition)	K–1.9	Percentiles, stanines, GE, scaled scores, NCE	Psychological Corporation
Tests of Basic experiences 2 (TOBE 2)	Pre–1.9	Percentiles stanines, scaled scores, NCE	CTB/McGraw-Hill

Note. NCE, normal curve equivalents; GE, grade equivalents; ETS, Educational Testing Service.

tests. Examples of achievement and aptitude tests that were normed in conjunction are (1) STEP III and the School and College Ability Tests; (2) ITBS and the Cognitive Abilities Test; and (3) the Comprehensive Tests of Basic Skills and the Test of Cognitive Skills.

Examples of Published Batteries

Table 16.3 provides a list of some of the available survey batteries, their intended grade levels, scores provided, and their publishers. Three of these survey batteries are discussed in this section: the ITBS, STEP III, and TOBE 2. It should be noted that only aspects of each of the batteries are presented.

Iowa Tests of Basic Skills, Forms 7 and 8

The emphasis of the ITBS is on the measurement of general cognitive skills rather than factual content. It is comprised of three batteries: (1) Early Primary (Levels 5 and 6), (2) Primary (Levels 7 and 8), and (3) Multilevel (Levels 9 through 14). The levels are numbered to correspond roughly to ages. Levels 5 and 6 consist of tests that measure Listening, Word Analysis, Vocabulary, Language Usage, and Mathematics. Level 6 also includes a five-part Reading test that measures decoding and comprehension skills. All of the tests are administered orally except Reading.

Levels 7 and 8 measure six curricular areas: Word Analysis, Vocabulary, Reading (Pictures, Sentences, Comprehension), Language (Spelling, Capitalization, Punctuation, Usage, and Expression), Work–Study (Visual Materials, Reference Materials), and Mathematics (Concepts, Problems, Computations). None of the tests are administered orally.

The Multilevel Battery is intended for the assessment of students in third through ninth grades. It consists of six levels (Levels 9 through 14) on a continuous scale for each test. The battery measures five curricular areas and provides scores for 11 subtests: Vocabulary, Reading, Language (Spelling, Capitalization, Punctuation, Usage, and Expression), Work–Study (Visual Materials, Reference Materials), and Mathematics (Concepts, Problem Solving, Computation). Social Studies and Science tests are available in a separate booklet.

As is the case for most if not all survey batteries, the items in the Language subtest of the ITBS measure recognition of the correct use of written language. However, the ITBS has a supplement available for third through eighth grades that measures a student's writing production. A separate test measuring listening skills is also available for these grades.

In the manual for school administrators, detailed information is provided about each subtest. The ITBS is based on a taxonomy of 248 skill objectives grouped into 69 major categories. On the average, approximately four to five items measure each skill. For example, the Reading Comprehension subtest has 16 skill objectives, which are classified into three major categories: (1) facts—to recognize and understand stated factual details and relationships; (2) inferences—to infer underlying relationships; and (3) generalizations—to develop generalizations from a selection. The Student Criterion-Referenced Skills Analysis reports a student's performance in each of these skill areas. This provides for the test user a rough measure of the skills a student has acquired. The Teacher's Guide states that this report is useful for diagnosing strengths and weaknesses in specific skills, and the information can be used for planning remedial instruction. The user, however, should treat this information as a rough index of a student's acquisition of particular skills. The within-grade Kuder–Richardson 20 (KR_{20}) reliability coefficients range from .788 to .913 for the 13 subtests, but no reliability coefficients are reported for the skill scores. It is reasonable to assume that these coefficients would be lower than subtest reliability coefficients. Thus, without sufficient reliability and validity evidence, making diagnostic judgments on the basis of these skill scores alone is questionable. The publisher's claim that the results provide diagnostic information is not unique to this battery. The manuals accompanying the

majority of the survey batteries imply, to some degree, that some of the results provided are valuable for diagnostic decisions. Concerns regarding this issue are addressed further in the last section of this chapter.

Sequential Tests of Educational Progress—Series III

STEP III consists of six levels (E–J) appropriate for grades levels 3.5 through 12.9, and its emphasis is on the measurement of the application and interpretation of knowledge. It consists of five Basic Assessment Tests: Reading, Vocabulary, Writing Skills, Mathematics Computation, and Mathematics Concepts. Three additional measures— Study Skills and Listening, Social Studies, and Science—are also available. The Writing Skills subtest assesses the student's ability to recognize correct and incorrect examples of written language. Seven of the eight measures are further divided into more specific domains that yield separate scores. The Vocabulary subtest, which measures students' knowledge of synonyms, yields a single score. Locator tests in both the language and mathematics domains are provided to insure that the student is assessed at the appropriate level within these curriculum areas.

STEP III provides a number of computer-generated reports that present student and class scores. The Score Roster reports scores for each student and a summary of the class data. Raw scores, grade level indicators, both national and local percentile ranks and stanines, and optional percentile ranks (i.e., high-socioeconomic-status [SES], low-SES, and large-city) are reported for each test. An Individual Student Report is available that provides a graphic display of the student's percentile bank for each test and the test scores reported on the Score Roster. In addition, this form reports the percentage of items correct in each of the domains for each individual student, as well as the local and national standardized samples. Two additional reports available are the Individual Item Analysis Report and the Group Item Analysis Report, which provide information on student and group performance on each item, respectively. Two reports available for administrators provide graphic displays and tables that present the distribution of scores against the national distribution in terms of percentile ranks and stanines; they also provide a summary of group performance in terms of mean percentile ranks and mean grade level indicators. A Pretest/Posttest Report provides grade level indicators, national percentile ranks, standard scores, and normal curve equivalents for each student, and these are summarized for the group.

The STEP III is a valuable device for surveying characteristics of students and evaluating program effectiveness as the manual states. However, its claims to be a diagnostic tool and a selection device for remedial instruction are not supported. Like those of the ITBS and other achievement batteries, its cluster score reliability coefficients are not satisfactory in terms of justifying decisions concerning individual students.

Tests of Basic Experiences 2

The TOBE 2 battery consists of two overlapping test levels, K and L. Level K is appropriate for students in preschool through the beginning of first grade, and Level L is designed for use at the end of kindergarten to the end of first grade. It claims to measure the differences in students' experiences. TOBE 2 consists of four subtests: Language, Mathematics, Science, and Social Studies. The Mathematics and Language tests are intended to include skills that are a result of instruction, whereas the Science and Social Studies tests are intended to measure a student's daily observations and processing of events. Examples of some of the topics covered in the Social Studies subtest are geography and travel, the environment and use of natural resources, occupations and the world of work, history and chronology, health and safety, and money and consumer behavior. The tests are presented orally, and no reading is required by the examinees.

TOBE 2 can be used to evaluate the effectiveness of instructional programs and to measure students' growth from fall to spring. It also provides materials on instructional activities to facilitate students' progress. The manual states that the scores may be used as a starting point for determining individual instructional needs, but the user should proceed with caution because of the inaccuracy in scores. It further states (appropriately) that

additional information should be obtained for decision-making purposes.

A limited number of reports are available to the user. A Class Evaluation Record, which is provided for each subtest, indicates for each student which individual test items were answered correctly. In addition, for each student it reports raw scores, national percentiles, national stanines, standard scores, and normal curve equivalents for each of the four subtests. The Individual Evaluation Record reports much the same information as the Class Evaluation Record, except that it reports results for an individual student for all subtests. A combined math and language score and a total score are also reported on this record.

BATTERIES FOR HIGH SCHOOL STUDENTS

Multilevel survey batteries for high school students (9th through 12th grades) are organized somewhat differently than are batteries at the elementary level. The fundamental reason for this is the fact that curricula are much more differentiated for high school students, allowing individual students to select courses in most instances. Thus, although nearly all high school students study English, mathematics, science, and social studies, the particular courses and content covered vary widely among students and among school districts. This diversity has made it much more difficult for test publishers to create survey batteries that have a wide appeal.

Survey batteries at the high school level tend to be clustered into three types: minimum-competency tests, tests of basic academic skills, and tests of general educational development. As state legislatures have instituted requirements for passing a test in order for a student to receive a high school diploma, several test publishers have developed tests to measure minimum competencies or "survival" competencies. Generally, these tests cover reading, mathematical computations, and writing skills. The tests are oriented toward the minimum knowledge and skills needed in each of these areas for individuals to survive in low-paying jobs. However, since a high-stakes test such as that required for graduation must be secure, a test sold on the open market generally can-

not be used as a legally mandated requirement. States tend to create their own
"graduation" tests, often by contracting with
commercial publishers.

Tests of basic academic skills tend to be
similar in organization to those described in
the section on elementary-level survey
batteries. Some, in fact, are extensions of
their elementary counterparts (see Table
16.2, for example). Although there is some
variance among test publishers, the high
school survey batteries tend to have subtests
covering two or more areas of reading (vocabulary and reading comprehension are typical), two or more areas of mathematics (computation and problem solving are typical),
English-language usage (mechanics and
forms of expression are typical), use of reference materials, social studies, and general
science. Knowledge and skill in these areas
tend to improve throughout the high school
years for the average student, regardless of
curriculum. However, any one individual's
progression of studies may not "fit" a given
test. For example, some students do not take
general science, but instead may take biology, chemistry, and physics. Thus, all of the
general science concepts may not be learned
until toward the end of those students' high
school experience. Similarly, geometry may
or may not be taken by a non-college-bound
student, so mathematics items using
geometric concepts learned in a typical first
course in geometry may not be appropriate
for some students.

Tests of general educational development
tend to be less closely bound to specific high
school courses, but may be more difficult for
the non-college-bound student than basic
academic skills tests. Such tests tend to have
subtests in vocabulary, reading, English-
language usage, mathematics problem solving, use of reference materials, social science
concepts, and natural science concepts. Tests
of general educational development tend to
contain items that depend less on specific
knowledge of content and facts, and more on
the use of academic skills, general cultural
literacy, verbal reasoning, and "higher-
order" thinking skills (usually the ability to
apply knowledge to new situations).

There are some published tests covering
specific courses, such as algebra, geometry,
physics, world history, and American history. Since each school teaches and/or

emphasizes somewhat different topics in like-
named courses, these specific-course tests
cannot be used as a basis for pupil evaluation
and grading. They may be used, however, to
estimate pupils' general level of knowledge
in an area, to place transfer students, or to
provide local students with norm-referenced
information about their standing relative to
high school students outside their locality.

Norms and Scores

High school survey batteries generally provide separate national norms for students
within grade level. Some publishers provide
separate norms for large city schools, high-
SES communities, private schools, and
Catholic schools. The type of scores provided
include raw scores, national percentile ranks,
special norms percentile ranks, expanded-
scale standard scores, normal curve equivalents, and grade equivalents.

Grade equivalents and expanded-scale
standard scores are provided with such tests
to facilitate the assessment of a student's educational growth over several years. Special
cautions should be taken when interpreting
these scores at the high school level, however. An absolute interpretation of grade equivalents may not be meaningful at the high
school level, because there is such a diversity
of courses taken by students in a given grade
(e.g., 10th grade). Thus, what it means to
have a grade equivalent of 10.4 in mathematics is not at all clear since some students take
geometry, some algebra I, some personal finance, some business mathematics, and so
forth. The expanded-scale standard scores attempt to express a pupil's achievement on a
numerical scale that extends from early
elementary grades through high school. This
is done as a means of tracking pupils' educational growth. However, because elementary
and high school student populations are different, because of curricular differences
within a given subject area, and because the
cognitive processes required to learn in a
subject area change over the grade levels, a
comparison between a score at the
elementary level and at the high school level
may be quite meaningless. Standard scores
for students who are in the same high school
course (e.g., Algebra II), but who may be in
different grades (e.g., 9th, 10th, and 11th
grades), is a more meaningful way to assess

relative achievement in an area (e.g., mathematics).

Examples of Published Tests

Table 16.4 provides a list of survey batteries contained in *The Ninth Mental Measurements Yearbook* (Mitchell, 1985). Two of these batteries are discussed in this section: the ITED and the Tests of Achievement and Proficiency (TAP). As with the discussion of elementary school survey batteries, only aspects of each of these two batteries are presented.

Iowa Tests of Educational Development

The eighth edition of the ITED consists of seven subtests, each organized into two levels: Level I is primarily for 9th- and 10th-graders, and Level II is primarily for 11th- and 12th-graders. Within each subtest, the items are grouped into three "blocks." Students taking Level I are administered Blocks 1 and 2, while students taking Level II are administered Blocks 2 and 3. Since all students are administered Block 2 in common, it is possible to report all scores on the same scale, regardless of which level a student was administered. An advantage of the two-level format is that it permits both within-level and out-of-level testing: 11th- and 12th-grade students whose educational development is somewhat less advanced may take Level I, 9th- and 10th-grade students who are more advanced may take Level II, and students whose grade placement corresponds to their educational development may take the levels appropriate for them. This matching of the test level to a student's level of general educational development is intended to increase the reliability of measurement, while avoiding an overly lengthy test that contains items too difficult for some students and too easy for others.

The ITED emphasizes measuring a student's general educational development, rather than the student's achievement in a specific course. The purpose of the test is to focus on measuring a carefully selected set of cognitive skills that nearly all adults will use in daily life and that are important for continued learning beyond high school (Feldt, Forsyth, & Alnot, 1988):

These skills include understanding the meaning of a wide variety of words, recognizing the essentials of correct and effective writing, solving quantitative problems, critically analyzing discussions of social issues, understanding nontechnical scientific reports and recognizing sound methods of scientific inquiry, perceiving the moods and nonliteral meanings of literacy materials, and using a variety of sources of information. (p. 1)

The ITED contains seven subtests: (1) Test E, Correctness and Appropriateness of Expression; (2) Test Q, Ability to Do Quantitative Thinking; (3) Test SS, Analysis of Social Studies Materials; (4) Test NS, Analysis of Natural Science Materials; (5) Test L, Ability to Interpret Literacy Materials; (6) Test V, Vocabulary; and (7) Test SI, Use of Sources of Information. A student's performances in Tests SS (Part 2), NS (Part 2), and L are combined into a Reading Total score.

Because all of the ITED subtests emphasize higher-order thinking skills (such as interpretation, application, analysis, and evaluation), and because it is a group-administered paper-and-pencil test, a student's performance is affected by his or her reading ability. Students with poor reading ability cannot be expected to learn from their textbooks and other print sources. "The authors . . . advise caution in interpreting the scores of deficient readers" (p. 4). The readability level of the material contained in the ITED, however, is the same (as measured by the Bormuth [1969] formula) as that of typical high school textbooks and general-interest magazine articles in the same areas.

In our view, measuring students' ability to perform higher-order cognitive tasks through a print medium such as a test is appropriate for a number of curricular areas. The dependence of a high school survey battery on students' application of their reading skills to various subject areas, including mathematics and science, is a positive characteristic rather than a negative one. High school achievement tests are unlike some other psychological batteries, such as personality questionnaires and cognitive ability tests, which seek to measure relatively pure "factors." One criterion for selecting an achievement battery is the extent to which it represents important learning outcomes expected of young adults; reading is one such important adult skill. It is estimated, for example, that the average U.S. adult reads approximately 10,000 words

TABLE 16.4. Multilevel Survey Batteries for High School Students

Score/subtest	BSI	CAT	CAP	CTBS	ITED	IOX	LS	MAT	MET	NEDT	STEP III	SRA-Ach	SRA-R	STAS	TAP	GED	Three R's
Reading																	
Structural analysis	X																
Vocabulary	X	X		X							X	X		X			X
Comprehension	X	X	X		X							X		X	X		X
Study skills	X		X								X						X
Total reading	X	X	X	X	X	X	X	X	X	?	X	X	X	X		X	
Language arts																	
Spelling	X	X		X										X			X
Capitalization/ punctuation	X																X
Sentence structure	X																
Verb usage	X																
Language mechanics		X		X	X							X					X
Language expression		X		X			X					X					
English			X											X			
Writing						X			X								
Total language		X	X	X							X	X		X	X	X	
Mathematics																	
Basic operations	X																
Basic operations with decimals	X																
Basic operations with fractions	X																

Applications

Compreh. geo. form

Computation

Concepts applications

Total math

Quantitative thinking

Basic skills

Total

Reference skills

Sources of information

Social studies

Science

Natural science

Algebra

Geometry

Interpreting literary materials

Life skills

Note. BSI, Basic Skills Inventory; CAT, California Achievement Tests; CAP, California Assessment Program: Achievement Series; CTBS, Comprehensive Tests of Basic Skills; ITED, Iowa Tests of Educational Development; IOX, Instructional Objectives Exchange Basic Skills System; LS, Life Skills; MAT, Metropolitan Achievement Tests; MET, Minimum Essentials Test; NEDT, National Educational Development Tests; STEP III, Sequential Tests of Educational Progress—Series III; SRA-Ach, SRA Achievement Series; SRA-R, SRA Survival Skills in Reading; STAS, Stanford Test of Academic Skills; TAP, Tests of Achievement and Proficiency; GED, Tests of General Educational Development; Three R's, The Three R's Test. That data are from Mitchell (1985).

per day (Pool, 1983). Furthermore, the importance of translating practical mathematical problems (which can be expressed rather easily in written form) to symbolic mathematical form, so that they may be amenable to solution, is an important ability for daily living (e.g., Clement, Lochhead, & Monk, 1981).

The ITED subtests scores have internal-consistency reliability coefficients ranging from .86 to .97. Item cluster scores within each subtest may be obtained as an aid to identifying specific strengths and weaknesses of individual students. Cluster scores are based on the items measuring a specific, within-subtest content area (similar to an instructional objective). There are an average of six or seven clusters per subtest, each containing between 3 and 18 items, and each with KR_{20} reliabilities ranging from .23 to .79 (cluster scores are less reliable than subtest scores, as is to be expected). For example, the Form X, Level I, 9th-grade social studies subtest (Test SS) has the following clusters: Literal Comprehension (9 items, KR_{20} = .62); Interpretation of Information (13 items, KR_{20} = .69); Inferences and Relationships (7 items, KR_{20} = .46); Classification of Ideas (5 items, KR_{20} = .71); and Author's Position and Techniques (8 items, KR_{20} = .60). Low item cluster reliabilities indicate that before drawing conclusions about a student's strengths and weaknesses, a teacher must use additional, non-ITED information to supplement the diagnosis. (Every teacher has such additional information available as part of the teaching process.) The ITED item cluster scores taken alone are only a rough measure of the student's acquisition of narrow skills.

Tests of Achievement and Proficiency

The TAP, Form G, is marketed as an extension of the ITBS, emphasizing the measurement of basic skills and knowledge. Like the ITBS, the TAP is organized by level within each subtest: Level 15 (9th grade), Level 16 (10th grade), Level 17 (11th grade), and Level 18 (12th grade). And, like both the ITBS and the ITED, the multilevel edition of TAP permits both within-level and out-of-level testing for each subtest. The TAP is also available in a single-level edition.

The TAP has six subtests, with an additional two supplementary tests: (1) Reading Comprehension, (2) Mathematics, (3) Written Expression, (4) Using Sources of Information, (5) Social Studies, and (6) Science; the supplementary tests are (7) Writing and (8) Listening. Each subtest is separately scored. In addition, two other scores are reported. One score is an Applied Proficiency Skills score, based on 63 items selected from the first four tests that reflect such abilities as reading labels, advertisements, graphs, and maps; recognizing correctly expressed ideas in letters; and correctly computing in purchasing situations. A second "score" is YES, NO, MAYBE with regard to attaining minimum competency in reading and mathematics. A student whose TAP Reading Comprehension score is above the median score for 8th-grade students, for example, receives a YES, indicating minimum competency in reading. An empirical and theoretical derivation of these minimum-competence scores would be useful, but none is provided (Wardrop, 1985).

The TAP manual provides detailed information about the content and skill classification of each item. The test authors recommend that teachers use these classifications to tabulate "error counts," in order to help individualize instruction. The procedure is similar to obtaining an item cluster score on the ITED. Individual classification score reliability coefficients are not reported, but they are expected to be much lower than the subtest scores. The KR_{20} reliabilities of the subtests range from .82 to .98. The authors appropriately warn teachers that scores based on small clusters of items are subject to error and should be used together with classroom assessments and discussions with students.

Like the ITED, the TAP attempts to measure skills that are not linked to specific high school courses or curricula. Futhermore, the TAP also measures students' ability to apply knowledge and skill. The tests differ in their emphasis on the measurement of higher-order or critical thinking skills. The TAP is much more oriented to application of basic skills. For example, in mathematics the ITED is less concerned with computation than is the TAP, and in science the ITED is much more concerned with a student's ability to critically evaluate statements made in a scientific context than is the TAP. One way to characterize (and perhaps to oversimplify) the difference between the two tests is that the TAP focuses on selected generalized basic skills that are essential to functioning in daily life, whereas the ITED focuses on selected aspects of general educational development that are essential both to contribute to society and to continue with more advanced learning.

USES AND MISUSES OF SURVEY BATTERIES

Survey batteries measure whether a student has achieved broad, long-term educational goals as contrasted with specific, short-term learning objectives. A student may require a year's instruction to learn enough mathematics or reading to demonstrate a significant improvement on a standardized survey test. During the year, however, the student would have been taught many specific facts, techniques, and skills, and would have had the opportunity to demonstrate his or her specific learning through classroom participation, homework assignments, and teacher-made tests. One purpose of a survey battery is to confirm that this specific learning has been integrated into the student's knowledge structure.

Since survey batteries tend to measure long-term learning goals best, they are best used for long-term instructional planning. Long-term instructional planning may focus on activities within a particular classroom, but it may also focus on instructional activities that occur outside a particular classroom. Examples of uses for the results from a survey battery within a classroom are (1) adapting instruction to a pupil's general level of educational development; (2) adapting instruction to a pupil's profile of stengths and weaknesses; (3) planning a general instructional strategy using information about a pupil's level of prerequisite knowledge; (4) grouping pupils within a classroom according to their level of educational development in a curricular area; (5) providing pupils with an operational description of the types of performance expected of them; (6) providing pupils with norm-referenced feedback concerning their progress toward the learning of long-term objectives; and (7) corroborating a teacher's judgment about the progress of specific students toward long-term learning objectives (cf. Hieronymus, 1976). Examples of extraclassroom uses for the results of a survey battery are (1) describing the attainment of a group (several classrooms at the same level within a school building or across several buildings within a school district) for purposes of evaluating curricular strengths and weaknesses; (2) providing criterion measures of long-term educational goals for educational research; (3) providing parents with feedback concerning pupils' progress toward long-term learning goals; and (4) providing school board, taxpayers, and their representatives with information of the effectiveness of a local school system (see Hieronymus, 1976).

Abuse or misuse of standardized test results occurs among educators at all levels, including support service personnel. Four broad categories of standardized test misuses are as follows (Airasian, 1979): (1) using the score on the test in a way that does not take into account the fact that it contains measurement error; (2) using only the test score as a criterion or justification for making an important decision about an individual or an educational program; (3) interpreting a pupil's score as if the test were a pure measure of the characteristic that the publisher claims the test measures; and (4) failing to attribute the cause of a test score to a complex set of antecedent conditions (e.g., interpreting a pupil's score as if it were caused solely by the pupil's ability or solely by a teacher's incompetence). To this list we would add (5) failing to express correctly the meaning of a test score (e.g., stating that a particular grade-equivalent score level is a desired standard that all students should attain) (Gardner, 1989).

Although measurement error for empirically documented standardized survey batteries is generally small, the scores contain such error nevertheless. The likely size of the measurement error in an individual's score may be estimated by using the standard error of measurement that the test publisher provides. Some writers recommend adding to and subtracting from each pupil's obtained score a numerical constant equal to the value of the standard error of measurement. The resulting numbers represent the upper and lower boundaries of a band or range of values within which a pupil's true score is likely to fall. The procedure creates a 68% confidence interval for a pupil's true score. This procedure avoids overinterpretation of test scores by expressing each pupil's "score" as possibly being any value within a range of values, rather than a particular, precise, single point on a number line.

A narrower band may be obtained by adding to and subtracting from a pupil's obtained score a constant equal to .67 times the standard error of measurement. This will form a 50% confidence interval for a pupil's true score. A narrower interval is recommended when two pupils' scores are being compared or when one pupil's scores on two different subtests are being compared. Nonoverlapping bands in such comparisons indicate that the true scores are likely to be different, whereas overlapping bands indicate that the true scores may be the same (or very similar), even when the obtained scores are different. Narrower bands avoid errors of *underinterpreting* genuine differences in scores. Errors of *overinterpretation* (i.e., concluding that two different scores represent genuine qualitative differences in ability) are best avoided by corroborating information from test scores with information from other sources (e.g., teacher observation, classroom performance, pupil interview, etc.).

A second category of standardized test misuse involves the failure to formally incorporate into the educational decision-making process information other than the test score. Examples of this include using a readiness test score as the sole basis for deciding to place a pupil in first grade; sectioning a class into reading or mathematics groups solely on the basis of reading or mathematics test scores; placing pupils into special programs solely on the basis of their intelligence test scores (whether these are obtained from individual or group-administered tests); and judging one teacher as better than another only on the basis of the achievement test results of that teacher's class. These kinds of test misuse, which are rather common, are best avoided by being certain that all information relevant to the educational decision at hand is considered before the decision is made. Since educational decisions seriously affect the lives of students, the temptation of unprofessional experience (i.e., using only the scores on standardized tests) should be avoided when making such decisions.

The third category of test misuse involves interpreting a test score as if it were a pure measure of the trait implied by the test title—for example, interpreting a pupil's reading comprehension subtest score as it were a measure only of reading comprehension instead of a measure of a combination of several factors, among which reading comprehension belongs. In sensible professional practice, the person interpreting the test score must take into account that the pupil's test performance is influenced by such factors as motivation (both intrinsic to the student and extrinsically imposed by the mannerisms of the test administrator); idiosyncratic terminology, content, and form of expression in the test question; test-taking skills (e.g., knowing how to make good use of the available testing time); knowledge of test-wiseness strategies (e.g., marking an answer for every item when there is no penalty for wrong answers); and various personality variables such as risk-taking propensity (i.e., willingness to mark an answer when uncertain of the correctness of that answer). A pupil's test score is a measure of all of these traits, as well as of the trait described in the test title.

The fourth category of standardized test misuse includes those instances in which someone interprets a pupil's score as if it were the result of only one cause. A pupil's score cannot be attributed to only one factor intrinsic to the student. Examples of the factors other than a student's ability that may operate to cause a score to rise or fall are (1) the match between the test's questions and what was emphasized in class; (2) the student's levels of general educational development and general scholastic aptitude; (3) the extent to which the student was given an unfair advantage over other students (e.g., taught answers to specific test questions); and (4) home factors that influence a pupil's attitudes toward school and the test. Note that the test score itself provides only a description of the student's performance; it contains absolutely no information regarding the cause of that performance.

The fifth category of test mususe involves perpetuating misinformation about the meaning of scores on a standardized test. Raw scores or percent-correct scores cannot be interpreted unless the content and difficulty level of a test are also described (e.g., 80% takes on a different meaning if a student took an "easy" fourth-grade mathematics test or a "difficult" sixth-grade test). Percentile ranks cannot be interpreted unless the reference group is also described. In other words, the group may be average third graders or gifted fifth graders (e.g., a percentile rank of 30 means that the student's score is higher than 30% of the group at the time the test was administered, but exceeding 30% of an average group of students has a different connotation than exceeding 30% of a gifted group.) Grade-equivalents cannot be interpreted as standards, grade-placements, degrees of mastery, or as units of normal growth (Nitko, 1983) (e.g., if a fourth-grade student attains a grade-equivalent of 6.8 on a fourth-grade standardized mathematics test, it cannot be claimed that the student is able to do sixth-grade mathematics, without further documentation).

SUGGESTIONS FOR EVALUATING AND SELECTING A BATTERY

Although most survey batteries cover educational objectives judged to be common to many schools, potential users should examine and review each test individually in order to decide whether it is appropriate for a particular school. The intended purposes for the testing are of primary concern when selecting a battery. The content of each test should be evaluated, and the technical merit of the test needs to be judged. A number of logistical concerns also require attention.

A number of texts afford a comprehensive overview of the criteria for evaluating a survey battery (see, e.g., Anastasi, 1988; Mehrens & Lehmann, 1984; Nitko, 1983); therefore, only a brief overview is provided in this chapter. Gronlund (1976) also provides a list of general factors that should be considered prior to implementing an elementary or high school survey battery. Because a large degree of variation exists in high school curricula, Gronlund emphasizes different factors that need to be considered

when selecting a survey battery for high school students.

Test Evaluation

Content Evaluation

Prior to the selection of an achievement battery, it is imperative to examine the test's content carefully. Information necessary to evaluate the test content may be obtained by examining copies of the test, reviewing the test manual and interpretative materials, reviewing technical reports supplied by the publisher, reading published reviews of the test, contacting experts in relevant subject matters, and contacting experienced users of the test. Some of the factors that should be considered when reviewing the test's content include the following:

The adequacy with which the test publisher has described the domain(s) that the test claims to measure and the purpose(s) of the test.

The adequacy with which the sample items on the test measure the domain defined by the publisher.

The degree to which the items reflect the current state of the art in the content area, as well as the content taught in the school for which the test is being considered.

The degree to which the test measures the range of knowledge and skills that the publisher intends it to measure.

The degree to which the items are free from sources of irrelevant difficulty and are fair to various groups.

The quality and clarity of the test items.

Technical Evaluation

To evaluate the usefulness of a test, additional information is needed concerning the technical quality of the test and the extent to which the claims for the test can be supported by empirical evidence. Some of the factors that should be examined when evaluating the test's technical merits concern the normative data, reliability, and validity:

The degree to which the norm-referenced scores are adequate for making decisions requiring norm-referenced information, as well as the representativeness of the standardization sample, should be evaluated.

The age of the normative data and when the publisher plans to re-norm the test.

The reliability of the test should be evaluated in relation to the intended uses and decisions.

The validity—that is, the usefulness of the test scores for a particular purpose—needs to be addressed. Three basic aspects of validity that are of concern are content, criterion-related, and construct validity. For achievement test batteries, content validity, as described previously, is essential.

Additional Evaluation Issues

A number of other factors need to be considered prior to selecting a battery. The clarity and completeness of the instructions for administering and score the test battery should be evaluated, as well as the quality of any accompanying instructional and interpretative aids. Practical issues, such as cost, testing time, available scoring procedures (computer vs. hand scoring), and the availability of alternate forms, should also be considered.

Sources for Testing Information and Test Reviews

When selecting and evaluating achievement tests, it is advisable to see what tests are available for a particular purpose. A number of resources are available that list tests and provide basic information about them. These include the following: *Tests in Print III* (Mitchell, 1983; *Tests in Print IV* will be published in 1991); *Tests: A Comprehensive Reference for Assessment in Psychology, Education, and Business* (2nd ed.) (Keyser & Sweetland, 1986); *The Educational Testing Service Test Collection Catalogue, Volume I: Achievement Tests and Measurement Devices* (Educational Testing Service, 1986); *A Guide to Assessment Instruments for Limited English Speaking Students* (Pletcher, Locks, Reynolds, & Sisson, 1977); and various test publishers' catalogues.

Conducting an on-line computer search for tests can be more efficient than searching through printed resources. Bibliographic Retrieval Services (also known as BRS Information Technology) is available in many academic libraries, through which both Educational Testing Service File (ETSF) and Mental Measurements Yearbook Database (MMYD) can be accessed. These databases can be searched using such descriptions as the test title, the subject tested, age level, and so on. In this manner, tests can be identified even when their titles are not initially known.

We recommend that a test evaluation process include reading published reviews of the tests in consideration. When reading them, the reviewers' comments should be judged in relation to the way the test results are intended to be used. The best sources for test reviews are the *Mental Measurements Yearbooks* (MMYs; see Conoley & Kramer, 1989, for the latest of these), *Test Critiques* (see Keyser & Sweetland, 1985–1990), journals (published by various professional associations), publications from educational agencies and clearinghouses, and testing and measurement textbooks.

The MMYs are a series of volumes that present critical reviews of tests, with each test reviewed by one or more expert. The *Tenth Mental Measurements Yearbook* (Conoley & Kramer, 1989), for example, contains over 560 new reviews of approximately 400 tests. The tests included in any MMY must meet the following criteria: a high degree of use and a publication or revision since the preceding MMY was released. Approximately 10% of the tests reviewed are classified as achievement tests. Each test entry contains the following information: test title, intended age (grade level of the subjects), publication date(s), special comments, number/type of scores reported, number of forms available, time limits, costs, author(s), publisher, and bibliography. Beginning in 1989, the MMYs are to be published every other year. In alternate years, a softbound supplement is to be published that reviews recent tests. Along with new reviews, the reviews in the supplement are to be reprinted in the subsequent MMY. The previously mentioned *Tests in Print* (see Mitchell, 1983, for the latest) serves as a cumulative and cross-referenced index to the MMYs. Thus, *Tests in Print* is a convenient way to locate a test review if you do not have access to the on-line MMYD.

Test Critiques (Keyser & Sweetland, 1985–1990) is also a series of volumes specializing in test reviews. The reviews in this volume are presented using a common framework: INTRODUCTION (the test's purpose, format, history), PRACTICAL APPLICATIONS/USES (relevant setting, appropriate/ inappropriate subjects, administration/ scoring/interpretation guidelines), TECHNICAL ASPECTS (reliability/validity studies), and CRITIQUE (strengths/weaknesses). Each volume reviews more than 100 tests. A test is reviewed again if it is revised. Five indexes help you to locate particular reviews: author, publisher, title, subject matter, and cumulative. The latter lists the tests reviewed in the current and previous volumes.

Professional journals in the field of testing and measurement (e.g., the *Journal of Educational Measurement*) may review a recent or revised test. Others (e.g., the *Journal of Educational and Psychological Measurement*) publish validity studies. Test reviews are also presented in journals that emphasize a specific educational or developmental area, such as reading, mathematics, child development, learning disabilities, school psychology, and special education.

Testing and measurement textbooks often describe specific tests for purposes of illustration. Some textbooks evaluate one or more achievement batteries. Textbooks are not comprehensive sources of test reviews, however, because textbook space is limited and the author(s) are selective regarding the tests they decide to include. Textbooks should be used as supplements to the primary review sources described previously.

COGNITIVE PSYCHOLOGY'S IMPACT ON THE DESIGN OF ACHIEVEMENT TESTS

Traditional approaches to test development have largely ignored the measurement of the underlying cognitive processes required for task performance. More recent efforts in achievement testing (e.g., Bergan, 1986; Lane, 1986), ability testing (e.g., Embretson, 1985; Pelligrino, Mumaw, & Shute, 1985), and diagnostic assessment (e.g., Brown & Burton, 1978; Tatsuoka, 1983, 1987; Tat-

suoka & Tatsuoka, 1983) focus on the cognitive processes underlying performance. These efforts draw from advances in cognitive psychology, artificial intelligence, computer technology, and psychometrics. The remainder of this chapter focuses on recent works related to (1) the measurement of achievement and (2) diagnostic assessment. Cognitive psychology's impact on measuring achievement is illustrated through two research efforts. The first research effort, which has implications for test design and instruction, involves an analysis of the types of knowledge required for mathematical problem solving (Mayer, Larkin, & Kadane, 1984). The second effort is an approach to test design that takes into consideration the cognitive processes underlying task performance. This cognitive approach to test design was used in the development of the Head Start Measures Battery (HSMB; Bergan, 1986) at the University of Arizona Center for Educational Evaluation and Measurement. After discussing these two research efforts, a brief overview of the traditional approaches to diagnostic assessment is presented, followed by a discussion of some of the recent developments related to diagnostic testing.

Measuring Achievement

The identification of task demands (Newell & Simon, 1972) that impose various requirements on cognitive processing is at the basis of recent test design procedures (e.g., Bergan, 1986; Embretson, 1985). Because the stimulus content of items can control the cognitive demands that are necessary for successful performance on a task, careful selection and control of the stimulus can provide information regarding the theoretical constructs that underlie task performance (Embretson, 1985).

Mayer et al. (1984) have provided a cognitive approach to the study of mathematical problem solving—in particular, algebra story problems. Algebra story problems were chosen because they are the most common measure of mathematical problem solving found on achievement tests as well as aptitude tests at the intermediate level. Theories of problem solving are based on the assumption that solving a particular problem type requires both domain-specific knowledge and general strategies (Simon, 1980). The research conducted by Mayer and his colleagues focused on the nature of knowledge that is required for solving mathematics problems. Four basic phases in problem solving were identified (translation, understanding, planning, and execution phase), each dependent upon a distinct type of knowledge. Mayer et al. hypothesized that students who answer an algebra story problem incorrectly lack the knowledge required at one (or more) of these phases. Moreover, if two students perform incorrectly on the same problem, the type of knowledge the students lack may differ.

In the translation phase, the algebra story problem needs to be translated from words into an internal representation. This process requires linguistic (e.g., ability to distinguish between operators and numbers) and factual knowledge. Mayer et al.'s results indicated that in the translation phase, students tend to have problems in formulating a correct mental representation of sentences that express relations among variables. During the understanding phase, the internal representation needs to be organized into a coherent structure. Schematic knowledge—in particular, knowledge of problem types (e.g., area = length × width)—is required in this phase. Mayer and his colleagues found that when a problem does not fit into a student's schema of problem types, it is likely to be misinterpreted; thus, an incorrect answer will be produced. The planning phase, which requires strategic knowledge, involves the procedures used to solve a particular problem. Two of Mayer et al.'s findings related to this phase are of particular interest. First, the way the problem is represented influences the strategy used for its solution; second, there are strong individual differences among students in their preferred strategies for solving equations. Lastly, the execution phase requires algorithmic knowledge. A student who has been successful in the first three phases may still produce an incorrect answer if he or she is unable to apply arithmetic and algebraic algorithms.

The preliminary research conducted by Mayer and his colleagues has implications in the areas of testing and instruction. Test items, for example, can be constructed to measure each type of knowledge outlined in their research. A test designed to differentiate between the knowledge types would (1) provide more specific information regarding students' abilities in solving algebra story problems, and (2) provide valuable information for individual instructional planning. This is in contrast to the single score provided by achievement batteries for mathematics problem solving.

Another line of work, which incorporated research advances in cognitive psychology and psychometrics, resulted in the development of the HSMB (Bergan, 1986b). The HSMB enables the user to obtain information on a student's position on skill sequences in six knowledge domains and to plan instruction commensurate with the student's level of knowledge and skills. In general, the development of the HSMB was based on (1) the specification of theoretical models of cognition in the six domains, and (2) the testing of hypotheses associated with task specifications and skill sequences in each domain. The six domains that the HSMB measures are Language, Math, Reading, Perception, Nature/Science, and Social Development.

The empirical validation of the hierarchical skill sequences for the HSMB involved an application of latent-trait theory that reflected a hypothesis-testing approach to test development. Latent-trait models (Bock & Aitkin, 1981; Bock & Lieberman, 1970; Lord, 1980), with the aid of recent technological advances (see Thissen, 1985), were used to test hypotheses related to skill sequences, composed of items reflecting varying cognitive demands. Bergan and Stone (1985) provide a more thorough description of this approach to test design. Lane (1986) also provides a detailed description of the theoretical and empirical development of the HSMB Reading scale utilizing this approach.

Diagnostic Assessment

Test results obtained by survey batteries provide little information concerning the optimal instruction for a student (Bejar, 1984). Diagnostic tests are intended to provide more detailed coverage of specific instructional areas than are multilevel survey batteries, which cover a broader range of curriculum areas in less detail. Two primary purposes of diagnostic assessment are (1) to provide information about specific errors in performance on items measuring a narrowly defined domain, and (2) to identify the probable cause of a student's incorrect performance. The latter provides valuable information for remedial instruction; however, diagnostic tests typically have focused on the former purpose.

Traditional Diagnostic Assessment

Traditionally, diagnostic tests have reflected one of four approaches (Nitko, 1983):

1. The "trait profile difference" approach, which is based on the individual-difference model, uses norm referencing as the primary method of score interpretation. In this approach, a student's performance level is obtained by referencing subtest scores to norms.
2. In the "behavioral objectives" model, the content of the domain is described by fine-grained, specific objectives, and information is provided on whether each objective is mastered.
3. The "prerequisite" approach attempts to identify the prerequisite knowledge and skills that a student may lack.
4. The "erroneous behavior identification" approach attempts to identify and classify the kinds of errors a student produces.

Examples of how different diagnostic approaches can be used to interpret the same student's item responses are given in Table 16.5.

New Developments in Diagnostic Assessment

The cognitive perspective offers an alternative approach to diagnostic assessment, and, moreover, affords a direct link to remediation. The attempt is to provide a representation of (1) the knowledge structure and (2) the cognitive processes required for correct task performance in a domain. A basis is provided for specifying instructional objectives, for identifying a student's present knowledge state, and for detecting a probable cause for a student's inability to acquire an instructional objective (Glaser, 1982). Although the term "diagnostic" should be reserved for tests yielding indices of performance that detect

specific types of errors made by the examinee, as suggested by McArthur and Choppin (1984), these tests should also be able to identify the misconceptions behind these errors. Finally, the cognitive approach to diagnostic assessment has been influenced by the work in artifical intelligence and to a large extent incorporates computer technology. As an example, Brown and Burton (1978) developed an intelligent computerized diagnostic tutor (BUGGY) that identifies students' misconceptions in solving subtraction problems.

A line of research in the area of cognitive psychology that has direct implications for diagnostic testing and instruction was conducted by Siegler (1976, 1978). Siegler investigated the underlying rule structure of students' performance on Inhelder's and Piaget's (1958) balance beam task. His "rule assessment" approach to learning is based on two assumptions: (1) Human reasoning is rule-governed, with rules progressing from lesser to greater sophistication as a function of age and learning; and (2) rule progressions can be assessed by formulating sets of problem types that yield distinct patterns of correct answers and errors as a function of the rules a student knows. This methodology provides a means of studying the relationshop between existing knowledge and learning, which is essential for educational diagnosis and instructional planning. Once a student's knowledge state is assessed, information is provided on the set of rules the student needs to acquire to advance to the next level. Through this methodology, one can determine what rules a student uses in task performance, what rules he or she needs to acquire to progress, and what rules are common to various groups of students.

The use of artificial intelligence in formulating procedures for educational diagnosis is exemplified in the work of Brown and Burton (1978). They developed computer models of students' performance on subtraction problems. Through a procedural network analysis, they decomposed subtraction problems into subskills and identified correct and incorrect ways to apply each subskill. The network analysis attempted to identify all possible incorrect applications of a subskill. A student's knowledge was assessed by matching his or her response pattern to a set of subtraction problems with a similar re-

TABLE 16.5. Examples of How Different Diagnostic Approaches Interpret the Same Student Response Data

Illustrative test items along with possible responses of a student

(1)	(2)	(3)	(4)	(5)	(6)	(7)	(8)	(9)
19	16	33	522	542	31	45	631	452
−11	−15	−11	−111	−430	−27	−36	−427	−361
8	1	22	411	112	$\sqrt{16}$	$\sqrt{11}$	$\sqrt{216}$	$\sqrt{111}$

Total score = 5/9 or 56%. Percentile rank = 20.

Trait profile approach. The total score on the subtraction test is compared to the total scores on other subtests (addition, multiplication, etc.) and a profile of strengths and weakness developed.

Example. Items such as (1) through (9) may constitute the test and the total score and norm-referenced score determined.

Possible interpretation of example. The student is weak in subtraction.

Prerequisite hierarchy approach combined with behavioral objectives approach. The items are associated with behavioral objectives and the objectives are organized into a prerequisite sequence. If a higher-level objective is failed, testing identifies which prerequisite objectives are known and unknown.

Example. The objectives below are in a prerequisite hierarchy and each is measured by the items above as shown in brackets next to each objective. Each objective is scored separately (objectives adapted from Ferguson, 1969).

Objectives	*Score*
(4) . . . subtracts 3-digit numbers, which requires borrowing from either tens' or hundreds' place. [Items (8) and (9)]	0/2 or 0%
(3) . . . subtracts 2-digit numbers, with borrowing from tens' place. [Items (6) and (7)]	1/2 or 50%
(2) . . . subtracts two 2-digit and two 3-digit numbers when borrowing is not required. [Items (3), (4), and (5)]	3/3 or 100%
(1) . . . subtracts two 2-digit numbers when number is less than or equal to 20. [Items (1) and (2)]	2/2 or 100%

Possible interpretation. The student has not mastered Objective (4) and Objective (3). Prerequisite Objectives (1) and (2) have been mastered. Begin instruction with Objective (3).

Error classification approach. Student's erroneous responses are studied and categorized according to type. The report is in terms of the error category.

Example. The responses to Items (6), (7), (8), and (9) are wrong so these are targeted for study and error identification.

Possible interpretation. The student fails to rename (or regroup) from tens' to units' or from hundreds' to tens'.

Erroneous process identification approach, using student's knowledge structure. Student's erroneous and correct responses are studied in order to identify a consistent process a student uses that accounts for the observed responses. Identification of the algorithm used by the student may necessitate knowing how the student conceptualizes the problems. The student's erroneous (or "buggy") algorithms are reported along with an explanation of how the student may have come to use them.

Example. Items (1) through (9) are studied to see if one or more consistent rules (algorithms) have been used by the student to obtain the responses shown.

Possible interpretation. The student appears to be using the following rule consistently: "Subtract the smaller digit from the larger digit." This rule will work for items (1) through (7), but not for (6) through (9). This incorrect rule may have been learned initially for solving single-digit subtraction problems and is now interfering with learning how to solve more complex problems.

Note. From "Designing Tests That Are Integrated with Instruction" by A. J. Nitko. In R. L. Linn (Ed.), *Educational Measurement* (p. 456), 1989, New York: Macmillan. Copyright 1989 by Macmillan. Reprinted by permission.

sponse pattern produced by the application of the incorrect subskills in the model. Incorrect answers were explained by assuming that students use erroneous rules resulting form misconceptions ("bugs") in knowledge. The assumption is that students have "bugs" in the algorithms that they apply, which can systemically generate incorrect answers on certain problems. Brown and Burton's methodology goes beyond error analysis, in that it not only attempts to describe a student's errors, but also attempts to reveal the misconceptions behind them. Erroneous responses are attributed to specific causes, those being faulty algorithms or rules. This initial effort, along with related work (Brown & VanLehn, 1980; VanLehn, 1981), resulted in a program called DEBUGGY, which diagnoses a number of erroneous rules resulting from misconceptions in whole number subtraction problems.

Tatsuoka and Baille (1982) developed another computer program, SIGNBUG, to diagnose students' misconceptions when solving signed-number addition and subtraction problems. SIGNBUG is also based on a logical error analysis of a procedural network. It provides a means for detecting erroneous algorithms resulting from misconceptions students have acquired. Although both of these programs (i.e., SIGNBUG and DEBUGGY) afford valuable diagnostic information that allows for instruction to be tailored to individual needs and for curriculum evaluation, they are designed for very specific content areas in mathematics.

A more general procedure that can be used in various domains for diagnosing students' misconceptions involves using one of several indices that summarize each person's pattern of responses to test items. For the purpose of diagnosis, such person-based indices can be used for identifying aberrant response patterns resulting from the application of erroneous algorithms, and therefore are useful for the initial detection of students who may have acquired misconceptions. They cannot, however, identify sources of misconceptions or provide information for remedial instruction. Examples of indices recommended for detecting aberrant response patterns include the norm conformity index (Tatsuoka & Tatsuoka, 1983), the modified-caution index (Harnisch & Linn, 1981), and the individual-consistency index (Tatsuoka &

Tatsuoka, 1983). Tatsuoka and Tatsuoka (1983) provide a lengthy discussion of the similarities and differences among the various indices. In particular, they point out that all but the individual-consistency index are dependent on the relative difficulties of the items for a given group. In contrast, the individual-consistency index is individually oriented and reflects a student's own procedural skill.

A third method for diagnosing misconceptions by examining erroneous response patterns has been termed "rule space" and is based on latent-trait theory (Tatsuoka, 1983). This method addresses the evidence indicating that many erroneous rules produce correct answers (Birenbaum & Tatsuoka, 1982, 1983). Item responses are decomposed, and a component scoring sytem is applied that enables the detection of specific erroneous rules. As an example, this procedure was applied to item responses from a signed-number subtraction test (Tatsuoka, 1983). A two-component response pattern of signs and absolute values was analyzed, rather than a binary response pattern. This allowed for the diagnosis of the sources of misconceptions and provided information for instruction remediation.

These methods provide valuable contributions to the area of diagnostic assessment and clearly illustrate the integration of the psychology of cognition, artificial intelligence, computer technology, and psychometrics.

In addition to detecting procedural errors, new diagnostic instruments should be capable of identifying flaws in students' conceptual or declarative knowledge and the structure or organization of students' knowledge (Glaser, Lesgold, & Lejoie, 1987; Marshall, 1988). To further facilitate instruction, assessments need to identify both the knowledge that needs to be structured and the knowledge that is ill-structured. Diagnosis should identify, for example, which connections or relationships are missing from or erroneously made in a student's knowledge organization. Hence, future achievement test developers need to understand how knowledge is acquired and structured. This goes beyond the current focus of survey batteries, which generally do a good job of describing what a student can and cannot do with knowledge.

Cognitive psychologists have investigated

a number of methods for assessing students' knowledge structures (see Nitko, 1989, for a brief review). A common thread underlying all of these methods is the belief that as students become more "expert" in a subject their knowledge of concepts becomes interrelated, more structured, and more accessible. Although these methods are still at the research stage, they hold promise for providing valuable diagnostic information useful for instructional purposes. In addition, the use of computer technology to implement knowledge structure assessment is currently being examined (see Ju, 1989, for an example of this).

REFERENCES

Aaronson, M. (1974). *Childhood mental health measurement sources*. Rockville, MD: Early Child Care Research Center for Studies of Child and Family Mental Health, National Institute of Mental Health.

Airasian, P. W. (1979). A perspective on the uses and misuses of standardized achievement tests. *National Council on Measurement in Education, 10*(3), 1–12.

Anastasi, A. (1988). *Psychological Testing* (6th ed.). New York: Macmillan.

Ayres. L. P. (1912). *Scale for measuring quality of handwriting of school children* (Russell Sage Foundation Bulletin No. E-113). New York: Russell Sage Foundation.

Ayres. L. P. (1915). A survey of school surveys. *Indiana University Bulletin, 13*, 172–181.

Ayres. L. P. (1918). History and present status of educational measurements. In G. M. Whipple (Ed.), *The seventeenth yearbook of the National Society for the Study of Education: Part II. The measurement of educational products* (pp. 9–15). Bloomington, IL: Public School.

Backer, T. E. (1977). *A directory of information on tests* (TM Report No. 62). Princeton, NJ: ERIC Clearinghouse on Tests, Measurements, and Evaluation, Educational Testing Service.

Bejar, I. I. (1984). Educational diagnostic assessment. *Journal of Educational Measurement, 21*, 175–189

Bergan, J. R. (1986). *Head Start Measures Battery*. Tucson: University of Arizona, Center for Educational Evaluation and Measurement.

Bergan, J. R., & Stone, C. A. (1985). *Restricted item response models for developmental assessment*. Paper presented at the annual meeting of the American Educational Research Association, Los Angeles.

Birenbaum, M., & Tatsuoka, K. K. (1982). On the dimensionality of achievement test data. *Journal of Educational Measurement, 19*, 259–266.

Birenbaum, M., & Tatsuoka, K. K. (1983). The effect of a scoring system based on the algorithm underlying the students' response patterns on the dimensionality of achievement test data of problem solving type. *Journal of Educational Measurement, 20*, 17–26.

Bock, R. D., & Aitkin, M. (1981). Marginal maximum likelihood estimation of item parameters: Application of an algorithm. *Psychometrika, 46*, 443–459.

Bock, R. D., & Lieberman, M. (1970). Fitting a response model for *n* dichotomously scored items. *Psychometrika, 35*, 179–197.

Bormuth, J. R. (1969). *Development of readability analyses* (Final Report, Project No. 7-0052, Contract No. OEG-3-7-070052-0326). Washington, DC: Office of Education, Bureau of Research, U.S. Department of Health, Education and Welfare.

Brown, J. S., & Burton, R. R. (1978). Diagnostic models for procedural bugs in basic mathematical skills. *Cognitive Science, 2*, 155–198.

Brown, J. S., & VanLehn, K. (1980). Repair theory: A generative theory of bugs in procedural skills. *Cognitive Science, 4*, 379–426.

Buckingham, B. R. (1913). *Spelling ability: Its measurement and distribution* (Contributions to Education No. 59). New York: Bureau of Publications, Teachers College, Columbia University.

Calhoun, D. (1973). *The intelligence of a people*. Princeton, NJ: Princeton University Press.

Callahan, R. E. (1962). *Education and the cult of efficiency*. Chicago: University of Chicago Press.

Clement, J., Lochhead, J., & Monk, G. S. (1981). Translation difficulties in learning mathematics. *American Mathematical Monthly, 88*, 286–290.

Conoley, J. R., & Kramer, J. J. (Eds.). (1989). *Tenth Mental Measurements Yearbook*. Lincoln, NE: Buros Institute of Mental Measurements, University of Nebraska Press.

Courtis, S. A. (1910). *Manual of instructions for giving and scoring the Courtis Standard Tests in the Three R's*. Detroit: Department of Cooperative Research, Detroit Public Schools.

Ebel, R. L. (1972). *Essentials of educational measurement* (2nd ed.). Englewood Cliffs, FJ: Prentice Hall.

Educational Testing Service. (1986). *The Educational Testing Service Test Collection Catalogue, Volume I: Achievement tests and measurement devices*. Phoenix: Oryx Press.

Embretson, S. E. (Ed.). (1985). *Test design: Developments in psychology and psychometrics*. New York: Academic Press.

Feister, W. J., & Whitney, D. R. (1968). An interview with Dr. E. F. Lindquist. *Epsilon Bulletin, 42*, 17–28.

Feldt, L. S., Forsyth, R. A., & Lindquist, E. F. (1981). *Iowa lower tests of educational development* (7th ed.). Chicago: Science Research Associates.

Feldt, L. S., Forsyth, R. A., & Alnot, S. D. (1988). *Teacher, administrator, and counselor manual: Iowa Tests of Educational Development*. Chicago, IL: Riverside.

Freeman, D. J., Kuhs, T. M., Knappen, L. B., & Porter, A. C. (1982). A closer look at standardized tests. *Arithmetic Teacher, 29*(7), 50–54.

Gardner, E. (1989). *Five common misuses of tests*. (Digest No. 108, March). Washington, DC: Eric Clearinghouse on Tests, Measurement, and Evaluation, American Institutes for Research.

Good, H. G. (1962). *A history of American education* (2nd ed.). New York: Macmillan.

Glaser, R. (1982). Instructional psychology: Past, present, and future. *American Psychologist, 37*, 292–305.

Glaser, R., Lesgold, A., & Lajoie, S. (1987). Toward a cognitive theory for the measurement of achievement. In R. R. Running, J. A. Clover, J. S. Conoley, & J. C. Witt (Eds.), *The Influence of Cognitive Psychology on Testing* (Vol. 3, pp. 41–85). N.J.: Erlbaum.

Gronlund, N. E. (1976). *Measurement and evaluation in teaching* (3rd ed.). New York: Macmillan.

Hanus, P. H. (1911). *Report on the program of studies in the public schools of Montclair, New Jersey*. Cambridge, MA: Author.

Harnisch, D. L., & Linn, R. L. (1981). An analysis of item response patterns: Questionable test data and dissimilar curriculum practices. *Journal of Educational Measurement, 18*, 133–146.

Hieronymus, A. N. (1976). *Uses of Iowa Tests of Basic Skills in Evaluation*. Paper presented at the 61st Annual Education Conference, Iowa City.

Hieronymus, A. N., Linquist, E. F., & Hoover, D. (1984). *Iowa Tests of Basic Skills, Forms 7 and 8*. Chicago, IL: Riverside Publishing.

Hildreth, G. H. (1939). *A bibliography of mental tests and rating scales* (2nd ed.). New York: Psychological Corporation.

Hillegas, M. B. (1912). A scale for the measurement of quality in English composition by young people. *Teachers College Record, 13*, 331–384.

Holmen, M.G., & Docter, R. F. (1972). *Educational and psychological testing: A study of the industry and its practices*. New York: Russell Sage Foundation.

Inhelder, B., & Piaget, J. (1958). *The growth of logical thinking from childhood to adolescence*. New York: Basic Books.

Iwanicki, E. F. (1980). A new generation of standardized achievement test batteries: A profile of their major features. *Journal of Educational Measurement, 17*, 155–162.

Ju, T-P. (1989). *The development of a microcomputer-assissted measurement tool to display a person's knowledge structure*. Pittsburgh, PA: Unpublished Ph.D. dissertation.

Kelley, T. L., Rush, G. M., & Terman, L. M. (1923). *The Stanford Achievement Test*. New York: World.

Kelly, F. J. (1914). *Teachers' marks: Their variability and standardization* (Contributions to Education No. 66). New York: Bureau of Publications, Teachers College, Columbia University.

Kelly, F. J. (1915). *The Kansas Silent Reading Test*. Emporia, KS: Bureau of Educational Measurements and Standards, Kansas State Normal School.

Kellogg, P. (1914). *The Pittsburgh district: Civic frontage*. New York: Russell Sage Foundation.

Keyser, D. J., & Sweetland, R. C. (Eds.). (1986). *Tests: A comprehensive reference for assessment in psychology, education, and business* (2nd ed.). Kansas City, MI: Test Corporation of America.

Keyser, D. J., & Sweetland, R. C. (Eds.). (1985–1990). *Test critiques* (Volumes I through VIII). Austin, TX: Pro-Ed.

Lane, S. (1986). *Validation of cognitive skill sequences in the beginning reading domain using latent trait models*. Unpublished doctoral dissertation, University of Arizona.

Linden, K. W., & Linden, J. D. (1968). *Modern mental measurement: A historical perspective*. Boston: Houghton Mifflin.

Lindquist, E. F. (1953). The Iowa electronic test processing equipment. In *Proceedings of the 1953 ETS Invitational Conference on Testing Problems* (pp. 160–168). Princeton, NJ: Educational Testing Service.

Lindquist, E. F. (1968). *The impact of machines on educational measurement* (Phi Delta Kappa Monograph). Bloomington, IN: Phi Delta Kappa International.

Lord, F. M. (1980). *Applications of item response theory to practical testing problems*. Hillsdale, NJ: Erlbaum.

Marshall, S. P. (1988). Assessing problem solving: A short-term remedy and a long-term solution. *Research agenda for mathematics education: The teaching and assessing of mathematical problem solving* (pp. 159–177). Hillsdale, NJ: Erlbaum.

Mayer, R. E., Larkin, J. H., & Kadane, J. B. (1984). A cognitive analysis of mathematical problem-solving ability. In R. J. Sternberg (Ed.), *Advances in the psychology of human intelligence* (Vol. 2, pp. 231–273). Hillsdale, NJ: Erlbaum.

McArthur, D. L., & Choppin, B. (1984). Computerized diagnostic testing. *Journal of Educational Measurement, 21*, 391–397.

Mehrens, W. A., & Lehmann, I. J. (1984). *Measurement and evaluation in education and psychology* (3rd ed.). New York: Holt, Rinehart, & Winston.

Mitchell, J. V., Jr. (Ed.). (1983). *Tests in print III*. Lincoln, NE: Buros Institute of Mental Measurements.

Mitchell, J. (Ed.). (1985). *The ninth mental measurements yearbook*. Lincoln: University of Nebraska Press.

Monroe, W. S. (1918). Existing tests and standards. In G. M. Whipple (Ed.), *The seventeenth yearbook of the National Society for the Study of Education: Part II. The measurement of educational products* (pp. 71–104). Bloomington, IL: Public School.

Monroe, W. S. (1921). The Illinois Examination. University of *Illinois Bulletin*, 19(9), 1–7.

Monroe, W. S. (1923). *An introduction to the theory of educational measurements*. Boston: Houghton Mifflin.

Monroe, W. S., & Buckingham, B. R. (1920). *Illinois examination teacher's handbook*. Urbana, IL: Bureau of Educational Research, University of Illinois.

Monroe, W. S., Odell, C. W., Herriott, M. E., Englehart, M. D., & Hull, M. R. (1928). *Ten years of educational research, 1918–1927* (Bulletin No. 42). Urbana: Bureau of Educational Research, College of Education, University of Illinois.

Moore, E. C. (1912). *Report of the examination of the school system of East Orange, New Jersey*. East Orange, NJ: Board of Education.

Moss, M. H. (1979). *Tests of Basic Experiences 2*, Monterey, CA: CTB/McGraw Hill.

Newell, A., & Simon, H. A. (1972). *Human problem solving*. Englewood Cliffs, NJ: Prentice-Hall.

Nifenecker, E. A. (1918). Bureaus of research in city school systems. In G. M. Whipple (Ed.), *The seventeenth yearbook of the National Society for the Study of Education. Part II: The measurement of educational products* (pp. 52–56). Bloomington, IL: Public School Publishing Company.

Nitko, A. J. (1983). *Educational tests and measurement: An introduction*. New York: Harcourt Brace Jovanovich.

Nitko, A. J. (1989). Designing tests that are integrated with instruction. In R. L. Linn (Ed.), *Educational measurement* (3rd ed., pp. 447–474). New York: Macmillan.

Odell, C. W. (1930). *Educational measurements in high school*. New York: Century.

Otis, A. S. (1918). *Group Intelligence Scale*. Yonkers, NY: World.

Pellegrino, J. W., Mumaw, R. J., & Shute, V. J. (1985). Analyses of spatial aptitude and expertise. In S. E. Embretson (Ed.), *Test design: Developments in psychology and psychometrics*. New York: Academic Press.

Peterson, N. S., Kolen, M. J., & Hoover, H. D. (1989). Scaling, norming, and equating. In R. L. Linn (Ed.), *Educational measurement* (3rd ed., pp. 221–262). New York: Macmillan.

Pitner, R., & Fitzgerald, F. (1920). An educational survey test. *Journal of Educational Psychology, 11*, 207–223.

Pletcher, B. P., Locks, N. A., Reynolds, D. F., & Sisson, B. A. (1977). *Guide to assessment instruments for limited English speaking students*. Alexandria, VA: Eric Document Reproduction Service (TM 011 805).

Pool, I. S. (1983). Tracking the flow of information. *Science, 222*, 609–613.

Pressey, L. C. (1920). Scale of attainment No. 1: An examination of achievement in second grade. *Journal of Educational Research, 2*, 572–581.

Pressey, L. C. (1921). Scale of attainment No. 3: For measuring "essential achievement" in the third grade. *Journal of Educational Research, 4*, 404–412.

Pressey, S. L. (1921). Scale of attainment No. 2: An examination for measurement in history, arithmetic, and English in the eighth grade. *Journal of Educational Research, 3*, 359–369.

Robertson, G. J. (1972). Development of the first group mental ability test. In G. H. Bracht, K. D. Hopkins, & J. C. Stanley (Eds.), *Perspectives in educational and psychological measurement* (pp. 183–190). Englewood Cliffs, NJ: Prentice-Hall. (Original work not dated).

Siegler, R. S. (1976). Three aspects of cognitive development. *Cognitive Psychology, 8*, 481–520.

Siegler, R. S. (1978). The origins of scientific reasoning. In R. S. Siegler (Ed.), *Children's thinking: What develops*. Hillsdale, NJ: Erlbaum.

Simon, H. A. (1980). Problem solving and education. In D. T. Tuma & F. Reif (Eds.), *Problem solving and education: Issues in teaching and research* (pp. 81–96). Hillsdale, NJ: Erlbaum.

Snow, R. E., & Lohman, D. F. (1989). Implications of cognitive psychology for educational measurement. In R. L. Linn (Ed.), *Educational Measurement* (3rd ed., 263–331). New York: Macmillan.

Stanley, J. C., & Hopkins, K. D. (1972). *Educational and psychological measurement and evaluation*. Englewood Cliffs, NJ: Prentice-Hall.

Starch, D. (1915). The measurement of achievement in English grammar. *Journal of Educational Psychology, 6*, 615–626.

Starch, D. (1917). *Educational measurements*. New York: Macmillan.

Starch, D., & Elliott, E. C. (1912). Reliability of grading high school work in English. *School Review, 20*, 442–457.

Starch, D., & Elliott, E. C. (1913). Reliability of grading work in history. *School Review, 21*, 676–681.

Stone, C. W. (1908). *Arithmetic abilities and some factors determining them* (Contributions to Education No. 19). New York: Bureau of Publications, Teachers College, Columbia University.

Tatsuoka, K. K. (1983). Rule space: An approach for dealing with misconceptions based on item response theory. *Journal of Educational Measurement, 20*, 345–354.

Tatsuoka, K. K. (1987). Validation of cognitive sensitivity for item response curves. *Journal of Educational Psychology, 24* (3), 233–245.

Tatsuoka, K. K., & Baille, R. (1982). *SIGNBUG: An error diagnostic computer program for signed-number arithmetic on the PLATO system*. Urbana: University of Illinois, Computer-Based Education Research Laboratory.

Tatsuoka, K. K., & Tatsuoka, M. M. (1983). Spotting erroneous rules of operation by the individual consistency index. *Journal of Educational Measurement, 20*, 221–230.

Terman, L. M. (1916). *The measurement of intelligence*. Boston: Houghton Mifflin.

Thissen, D. (1985). *MULTILOG Version 4.0, user's guide*. Lawrence: University of Kansas.

Thorndike, E. L. (1904). *An introduction to the theory of mental and social measurements*. New York: Teachers College, Columbia University.

Thorndike, E. L. (1910). Handwriting. *Teachers College Record, 11*, 1–93.

Thorndike, E. L. (1913). A scale for measuring achievement in drawing. *Teachers College Record, 14*, 345–382.

Thorndike, E. L. (1914). The measurement of ability in reading. *Teachers College Record, 15*(4), 1–71.

Tyack, D. B. (1974). *The one best system: A history of American urban education*. Cambridge, MA: Harvard University Press.

Tyler, R. W. (1973). E. F. Lindquist, educational pioneer. In W. E. Coffman (Ed.), *Frontiers of educational measurement and information systems—1973* (pp. 5–11). Boston: Houghton Mifflin.

Tyler, R. W. (1976). The curriculum—then and now. In A. Anastasi, *Psychological testing* (4th ed., pp. 63–79). New York: Macmillan. (Original work published 1956)

VanLehn, K. (1981). *Empirical studies of procedural flaws, impasses, and repairs in procedural skills*. (Tech. Rep. No. ONR-8). Palo Alto, CA: Palo Alto Research Center.

Wardrop, J. L. (1985). Review of Test of Achievement and Proficiency, Form T. In J. Mitchell (Ed.), *The ninth mental measurements yearbook* (pp. 1610–1611). Lincoln: University of Nebraska Press.

Whipple, G. M. (1922). An annotated list of group intelligence tests. In G. M. Whipple (Ed.), *The twenty-first yearbook of the National Society for the Study of Education: Intelligence tests and their use* (pp. 93–113). Bloomington, IL: Public School.

Yerkes, R. M. (Ed.). (1921). Psychological examining in the United States Army. In *Memoirs of the National Academy of Sciences* (Vol. 15). Washington, DC: U. S. Government Printing Office.

Yoakum, C. S., & Yerkes, R. M. (Eds.). (1920). *Army mental tests*. New York: Henry Holt.

17

Curriculum-Based Assessment

LYNN S. FUCHS
DOUGLAS FUCHS
George Peabody College, Vanderbilt University

According to Salvia and Ysseldyke (1985), assessment involves collecting data for the purpose of specifying and verifying students' problems and formulating decisions about referral, screening, classification, instructional planning, and program modification. Decisions in the first three assessment phases—referral, screening, and classification—constitute the identification process: Norm-referenced comparisons among pupils are made to judge whether students are sufficiently discrepant from peers to require special interventions.

In the last two phases, decisions are more relevant to instructional content and methods. During instructional planning, instructional deficiencies are identified, a student's learning characteristics and behaviors are described, the educational setting is evaluated, and an instructional plan or hypothesis is generated (Fuchs & Fuchs, 1986a). Program modification involves measuring, the student's progress, evaluating the effectiveness of the instructional hypothesis in light of the student's progress, and then continuing the cycle of postulating and testing instructional hypotheses (Fuchs, 1986).

Traditional assessment formats have addressed the identification phases of assessment almost exclusively. In recent years, however, with an increased focus on improving the effectiveness of programs for poorly achieving students (Glaser, 1981), assessment procedures that facilitate instructional planning and program modification have received more attention. Among these strategies devoted to the instructionally relevant assessment phases is curriculum-based assessment.

"Curriculum-based assessment" is a familiar-sounding term to most professionals in meaurement and education. The term is highly descriptive and may even appear self-explanatory. Nevertheless, the term refers to a range of conceptually and practically different measurement and evaluation procedures, some of which are relatively informal and undeveloped, others of which are technically sophisticated and as prescriptive as many commercial assessment instruments. The purpose of this chapter is to provide a brief overview of alternative curriculum-based assessment procedures, and then to provide more detailed discussion of a particular variant of curriculum-based assessment, known as "curriculum-based measurement."

OVERVIEW OF ALTERNATIVE FORMS OF CURRICULUM-BASED ASSESSMENT

Traditional Forms

As most commonly used, the term "curriculum-based assessment" refers to the evaluation of instructional needs by measuring pupils' performance on materials employed for instruction (Gickling, 1981; Tucker, 1985). The sequence and materials of instruction are reviewed carefully, and a measurement procedure is designed that mirrors the nature of the current instruction and that draws test items from teaching materials. Key assumptions about the utility of this assessment paradigm include the following. First, measurement on instructional content can assist teachers in remediating students' deficiencies on material already covered. Second, it can allow teachers to devise more effective strategies for subsequent instructional units. Third, such assessment is likely to be relatively sensitive to (and therefore reveal) student growth, since it highlights the immediate instructional focus. Finally, such evaluation provides an objective data base for assigning grades to students (Nitko, 1983).

This curriculum-based assessment process sounds very much like day-to-day assessment procedures in regular classrooms, where teachers design tests to conform to instructional content and to sample instructional material. Moreover, for many commercially available instructional materials (such as basal reading series), this type of curriculum-based test, which samples the instructional content, is readily available and frequently employed (Fuchs, Tindal, & Fuchs, 1986).

Two Specialized Strategies

In addition to these conventional procedures, which represent traditional classroom assessment practice, more elaborate, systematic curriculum-based assessment procedures have been developed for use primarily in more specialized settings, such as remedial and special eduation programs. Two examples of these more elaborate approaches are "precision teaching" (e.g., White & Haring, 1980) and "mastery learing" (e.g., Bloom, 1976).

Precision Teaching

Precision teaching is a measurement and evaluation strategy that consists of the following steps. First, the instructional program is broken into a hierarchy of skills, such as say-

ing phonemes in response to graphemes, reading consonant–vowel–consonant word patterns, and reading final-E-patterned words. Next, for each step in the skills hierarchy, the teacher designs a measurement procedure. For example, with respect to saying phonemes, the teacher may prepare a set of flashcards, each one showing a letter of the alphabet; shuffle the deck and expose each card until the student says a grapheme (or for a maximum of 2 seconds until a total of 60 seconds elapses); and score the number of phonemes correct per minute. For reading consonant–vowel–consonant words, the teacher may develop 50 flashcards, each one showing a different consonant–vowel–consonant word; shuffle the deck and expose each one until the child responds (or for a maximum of 3 seconds until a total of 60 seconds elapses); and record the number of correct words per minute. For final-E words, a similar procedure, incorporating final-E word cards, may be employed. Of course, different practitioners will inevitably design alternative measurement procedures, but each should be tailored to assess one step within the instructional hierarchy.

Once these instructional steps and measurement procedures are specified, the teacher begins instruction on the first step and concurrently measures the student's performance on that skill in the sequence. Measurement occurs frequently, even daily, with scores graphed on semilogarithmic paper. The practitioner analyzes the graphed performance in prescribed ways to formulate instructional decisions, primarily in accordance with a behavioral paradigm. Once the student's performance reaches a predesignated criterion, the teacher progresses to the next step in the instructional hierarchy and simultaneously begins to measure performance on that next step. (See White & Haring, 1980, for a more detailed description.)

Mastery Learning

Mastery learning resembles precision teaching in important ways. Material to be learned over a certain time period is divided into smaller units, and a performance criterion for each unit is established. Following instruction on a learning unit, a test representing the instructional material is administered; the results of this test provide feedback to teacher and student regarding mastery of the unit and necessary corrective strategies. The teacher provides corrective feedback and readministers tests until the student achieves mastery of the learning unit. The student then progresses to a more difficult skill in the learning hierarchy. It is hypothesized that through this process of formative testing, combined with systematic correction of individual learning difficulties, each student will receive appropriate amounts of high-quality instructional time and engaged learning time (see Block & Burns, 1976). Bloom (1976) has argued that, under these conditions, virtually all students can achieve mastery of school curriculum.

Mastery learning differs from precision teaching in the following ways. First, with mastery learning, no systematic graphing of pupil performance is incorporated into the assessment process. Second, decision rules about instructional uses of the data base are simpler with mastery learning than with precision teaching. In mastery learning, the decision rule involves reteaching if the assessment score falls below mastery; precision teaching requires that assessment information be used to determine not only when, but how, to alter teaching strategies. Third, assessment is ongoing in precision teaching, with multiple scores across alternate testings aggregated for decision making. In contrast, the teacher using mastery learning determines when the unit has been taught satisfactorily and, at that time, administers a one-shot test. Only when students (1) fail to meet criterion performance and (2) receive additional, corrective instruction is another form of the test readministered.

Nevertheless, mastery learning and precision teaching, as well as the more traditional forms of classroom assessment described above, are all forms of curriculum-based asssessment that share at least three critical features: (1) They all assess progress on short-term objectives; (2) once mastery of one objective is achieved, the measurement focus shifts; and (3) the specific measurement tasks are designed by practitioners. Each of these features represents an important problem for these three curriculum-based assessment approaches.

Critical Problems

Assessment of Short-Term Objectives

Assessment that focuses on progress through a series of short-term objectives is high in instructional validity; that is, the correspondence between tests and instruction is strong. Nevertheless, it appears to suffer from several validity problems. First, assessment of short-term objectives fails to represent the ultimate desired performance accurately. In other words, although assessment of subskills such as phoneme and word category reading mirrors the sequence of instruction, it does not accurately represent the task of decoding and comprehending text—the true goal of reading. Second, and relatedly, correlations between scores on short-term objectives tests and scores on global achievement tests, including reading comprehension measures, are relatively low (Fuchs, 1982). This indicates that use of short-term objectives jeopardizes at least two forms of validity: content validity (or the correspondence between a test and the content of the true domain) and criterion validity (or the relation between a test and important criterion outcomes). (See Yalow & Popham, 1983, for a discussion of curricular, content, and criterion validity.)

Shifting Measurement Focus

A second important problem with traditional curriculum-based assessment, precision teaching, and mastery learning is that evaluation of student progress across the school year is difficult when the measurement focus shifts with each mastered objective. This is because measurement points at different times of the year are not comparable: For example, in September, scores may represent saying phonemes; in April, they may represent reading R-controlled words. So, for example, finding that a student has higher scores in September than in April hardly denotes that the student has regressed over the school year. Alternatively, if one tries to characterize progress by summarizing the rate at which a student masters objectives, critical problems still remain. For example, it is doubtful whether mastery of different objectives, such as saying phonemes and reading R-controlled words, can be considered equally difficult. Without objectives representing equal intervals, it is not possible to interpret an "objectives mastered per time period" metric (see Fuchs, 1982, and Deno & Fuchs, 1987, for additional discussion of this problem).

Practitioner-Designed Tests

A third problem with traditional curriculum-based assessment, precision teaching, and mastery learning stems from the fact that, in implementing such assessment systems, practitioners must design the measurement procedures themselves or rely on commercial criterion-referenced instruments marketed by curriculum publishers. In either case, the psychometric adequacy of these measures is dubious.

With respect to teacher-constructed tests, the reliability and validity is unknown. Given the time-consuming and costly nature of reliability and validity studies, it is not feasible to investigate psychometric characteristics of myriad teacher-constructed measures. On the other hand, research investigating commercial criterion-referenced measures is disappointing. Among 12 commercial criterion-referenced tests, authors of only 4 test manuals addressed reliability or validity at all, and authors of only 2 instruments reported investigation of more than one aspect of test adequacy (Tindal et al., 1985). Independent empirical analyses of commercial basal series criterion-referenced tests reveal varying degrees of reliability and validity, with many estimates falling considerably below acceptable levels (Tindal et al., 1985). Consequently, the technical adequacy of most measures used within traditional classroom curriculum-based assessment, precision teaching, and mastery learning remains largely unknown.

Together, these problems of questionable criterion and content validity, shifting measurement focus, and uncertain psychometric adequacy are serious. The challenge to the measurement field has been to design a curriculum-based assessment procedure that simultaneously (1) reflects the requirements for strong correspondence between assessment and curriculum and for instructional utility (as traditional curriculum-based assessment, precision teaching, and mastery learning do), and (2) addresses the problems inherent in traditional curriculum-based assessment, precision teaching, and mastery learning.

One line of systematic inquiry has focused on development of an alternative curriculum-based assessment paradigm that attempts to maintain the usefulness of assessment for instructional decision making, but also addresses the problems described above. Investigation of this form of curriculum-based assessment, known as "curriculum-based measurement" (Deno, 1985, 1987; Deno & Fuchs, 1987), has been conducted over the past decade. The remainder of this chapter is devoted to description and discussion of curriculum-based measurement.

CURRICULUM-BASED MEASUREMENT

Distinguishing Features

Focus on Long-Term Goals

As a variant of curriculum-based assessment, curriculum-based measurement incorporates important distinguishing features. First, the focus of curriculum-based measurement is the long-term programmatic goal, rather than a series of short-term objectives. With curriculum-based measurement, practitioners specify what they hope students will achieve by year's end. These long-term curricular goals structure the assessment process: Throughout the school year, a student's performance on that same goal is measured.

So, for example, an Individual Educational Program (IEP) team may specify that, at the close of the school year, Wanda will read the Ginn 720 third-grade text fluently and with comprehension. With such a goal, the teacher will assess the student's progress by regularly (at least twice weekly) directing Wanda to read different passages from Ginn 720 and scoring her fluency (e.g., words read correctly per minute) and/or her comprehension (e.g., content words retold from the passage). Each measurement will be conducted in the same way, on a passage representing the same level of difficulty, drawn from the same text. The teacher will graph Wanda's scores on an equal-interval chart and analyze the graph in accordance with prescribed rules to evaluate the adequacy of student progress. Then, the teacher will use the data base of Wanda's responses to determine the nature of instructional modifications.

This focus on a stable long-term goal across the school year addresses the first two problems associated with short-term objective approaches to curriculum-based assessment. The focus on a long-term goal within curriculum-based measurement enhances the criterion and content validity of the assessment. Content validity is improved because the assessed behavior more closely resembles the outcome behavior truly desired (e.g., reading and comprehending text). With respect to criterion validity, research indicates the curriculum-based measurement incorporating long-term goals correlates better with criterion measures of achievement than does measurement across a series of short-term objectives (Fuchs, 1982). Moreover, a meta-analysis contrasting curriculum-based assessment of long- versus short-term objectives corroborates correlational analyses. We (Fuchs & Fuchs, 1986b) coded studies in terms of long-term or short-term goal assessment and in terms of type of dependent measure—probe-like measure (e.g., reading a word list for 1 minute) or global achievement test (e.g., Stanford Diagnostic Reading Test). Results suggested an interaction between these variables. When curriculum-based assessment of long-term goals was used, effect sizes on global achievement tests were larger; when assessment focused on short-term objectives, effect sizes on probe-like measures were greater. Consequently, it appears that curriculum-based measurement's focus on long-term goals improves the content and criterion validity over that of more traditional curriculum-based assessment systems with short-term objectives.

A second problem addressed by curriculum-based measurement's focus on long-term goals is the comparability of measurements across time. Since the student is always measured on alternate forms of the same test (i.e., passages in reading or sets of stimulus items in spelling and math), one can summarize performance across time, and can formulate meaningful evaluative statements about the student's progress across the year and across alternative instructional components.

Prescriptive Measurement and Evaluation Procedures

A second distinguishing feature of curriculum-based measurement is that it specifies the measurement and evaluation procedures to be used, including methods for generating test stimuli, administering and scoring tests, and analyzing the data base. Moreover, the psychometric adequacy of these procedures has been demonstrated in studies of their reliability, validity, and sensitivity to student growth. Consequently, although the test stimuli (e.g., reading passages, spelling lists, math problem types) are derived from the particular curriculum specified in the student's programmatic goal, the assessment methods are highly prescriptive and based on research indicating that certain measurement and evaluation methodologies can insure psychometric adequacy, across most curricula from which test stimuli might be drawn (see Fuchs, Deno, & Marston, 1983, for an example). This feature of curriculum-based measurement solves the third problem inherent in the short-term objectives approaches to curriculum-based assessment, by specifying prescriptive assessment methodologies across curricula. Below, the research program on curriculum-based measurement is reviewed briefly.

Review of Research on Curriculum-Based Measurement in Reading

To specify a useful curriculum-based measurement system that enhances instructional planning, one must answer the following questions: (1) What behavior should be measured? (2) How should that measurement be conducted? and (3) How should the assessment information be used for instructional decision making? (See Deno & Fuchs, 1987.) Criteria for answering each question include the system's technical adequacy, feasibility, and effectiveness in enhancing instructional planning and student achievement. To provide readers with an introduction to the research base on curriculum-based measurement, we review investigations in the area of reading here, using the three broad questions as the organizing framework and employing the three criteria for judging the usefulness of alternative procedures. Readers are referred to Mirkin, Fuchs, and Deno (1982) and to Deno and Fuchs (1987) for additional information in spelling and written expression, and to Fuchs, Fuchs, and Hamlett (1989) for additional information in math.

What Behavior Should Be Measured?

In the area of reading, potentially useful measurement behaviors are question answering, recall production, cloze responses, and oral passage reading.

Question Answering. Question answering is the most common curriculum-based reading assessment strategy (Fuchs, Fuchs, & Maxwell, 1988). Despite its popularity in classrooms, question answering has been criticized for several reasons. First, it appears to tap comprehension of only selected parts of text that others have judged important (Hansen, 1979). Second, an individual's question-answering ability may be related to how well answers can be inferred directly from the questions, without referring to the reading text (Hansen, 1979). Third, even systematic methods for devising questions frequently result in disparate reading placements for a given student (Peterson, Greenlaw, & Tierney, 1978).

Despite these problems, we (Fuchs, Fuchs, & Maxwell, 1988) found that the criterion, construct, and concurrent validity of question answering were all acceptable when questions were derived systematically to represent idea units of high thematic importance. This procedure for formulating reading comprehension questions (see Jenkins, Heliotis, Haynes, & Beck, 1986) involves (1) having proficient adult readers parse passages into pausal units; (2) identifying pausal units for which concurrence exists; (3) having adult readers rate the thematic importance of each pausal unit on a 4-point scale; (4) computing the average rating for each unit; and (5) writing short-answer questions for pausal units with average ratings at the highest or next-to-highest thematic importance level. Unfortunately, the feasibility of practitioners' employing such a time-consuming procedure appears problematic, and evidence to support the validity of less systematic procedures for generating questions from text is lacking.

Recall Measures. Curriculum-based recall measures involve students' reading passages and retelling in their own words what occurred in the passages, without referring back to the text. In terms of initial preparation, recall is a straightforward and feasible curriculum-based measurement strategy; it only requires selection of suitable reading material. However, methods of scoring recalls can be difficult and time-consuming (see Johnston, 1982).

In investigating alternative curriculum-based measurement reading tasks, including different recall administration and scoring procedures, we (Fuchs, Fuchs, & Maxwell, 1988) found that (1) the overall validity of recall methods was high and (2) correlations between criterion outcome measures (the Stanford Achievement Test—Reading Comprehension and Word Study Skills subtests) and total words written during recall were comparable to those for more complicated scoring methods. Moreover, correlations for written recalls were higher than for oral recalls. Therefore, a recall score of total words written may represent a valid and feasible reading measure for curriculum-based measurement. To check the appropriateness of the recall focus, however, content words retold (nouns, adjectives, verbs, and adverbs matching those in the original text) can be scored. Although content words represent a time-consuming index to score, computers can be used efficiently to score student samples (see Fuchs, Hamlett, & Fuchs, 1987).

Cloze Responses. Cloze responses constitute another potentially useful reading behavior in curriculum-based measurement. In a typical cloze procedure, every *n*th word is deleted from a passage and replaced with a blank. The pupil is required to restore deletions meaningfully. A cloze procedure can be difficult to produce; the teacher must prepare and photocopy text passages with blanks. On the other hand, scoring methods vary in ease of implementation, with exact replacements a logistically feasible alternative and with synometrically correct replacements more difficult. We (Fuchs, Fuchs, & Maxwell, 1988) found that written cloze formats demonstrated adequate criterion and concurrent validity. However, in contrast to other types of curriculum-based measurement procedures in reading, the cloze technique failed to correlate better with reading comprehension than with decoding criterion measures. This finding may reflect several potential problems with cloze responses, including that they (1) may measure textual redundancy rather than comprehension (Tuinman, Blanton, & Gray, 1975); (2) may be more dependent on sentence structure than on the larger textual structure (Suhorsky, 1975); and (3) may fail to index inferential comprehension and other higher-order reading skills (Alderson, 1978).

Oral Passage Reading. Oral passage reading, or fluency, requires students to read aloud for a specified amount of time; words read correctly per minute are scored. Oral passage reading tests are easy to prepare, requiring only selection of appropriate passages, and are easy to score. Nevertheless, such tests do require individual administration, which can be time-consuming compared to group-administered cloze, recall, or question-answering measures.

Although oral passage reading is not typically viewed as an index of reading comprehension, evidence supports its validity as a comprehension measure. Correlations between oral passage reading scores and well-accepted criterion measures are consistently strong when (1) both measurements are derived from passages of similar difficulty (Deno, Mirkin, & Chiang, 1982; Fuchs, 1981; Gates, 1921) and (2) readers at the elementary and/or high school level are measured (Sassenrath, 1972). Moreover, when the validities of question answering, recall measures, cloze procedures, and oral passage reading were compared, correlations between each measure and the criterion index of reading comprehension were comparable except for oral passage reading. The oral passage reading index correlated statistically significantly higher with the criterion index than did each of the other measures. Furthermore, growth over time on oral passage reading has been shown to relate to growth on global tests of reading comprehension (Fuchs, Deno, & Mirkin, 1984).

Consequently, in most curriculum-based measurement systems, oral passage reading is employed as the reading behavior. That is, once the IEP team has specified the curriculum series and level it hopes the student will master at the end of the school year, curriculum-based measurement is conducted by having the student read passages orally. Correct words read per minute are scored, graphed, and used for determining instructional decisions. With some experimental curriculum-based measurement systems, recalls produced on computers have been employed. In such systems, the number of content words retold in 4 minutes is scored (Fuchs, Hamlett, & Fuchs, 1987). Research on the computerized curriculum-based measurement application, which incorporates reading recall measurement procedures, is being conducted (see Fuchs, Hamlett, & Fuchs, 1987).(See Fuchs, Hamlett, & Fuchs, 1990, for information on another computerized curriculum-based measurement system.)

How Should Measurement Be Conducted?

Once the behavior to be measured has been determined, a second question concerns how measurement of that behavior will occur. For example, once oral passage reading, with words read correct per minute, has been selected as the curriculum-based measurement reading behavior, one still must determine how measurement passages will be selected, how long each measurement will last, and how frequently measurement will occur. Below, each of these methodological questions is addressed. For discussion of additional measurement methodology issues, such as selection of a mastery unit, a mastery criterion, difficulty level, and size of the measurement domain, the reader is referred to Mirkin, Fuchs, and Deno (1982).

Selecting Measurement Passages. Given a textbook containing numerous passages from which curriculum-based assessments might be drawn, the practitioner of curriculum-based measurement must determine a method for selecting measurement passages. Traditional psychometric theory indicates that random selection, over the long run, should yield equivalent samples (Hays, 1973). Random selection has been subjected to experimentation within curriculum-based measurement (Deno, Mirkin, Chiang, & Lowry, 1980), and research has demonstrated concurrent validity with respect to criterion achievement tests. Despite this strong criterion validity, additional studies reveal that random selection from reading texts produces considerable intraindividual instability in measurements across days (S. L. Deno, personal communication, October 1988; Fuchs, 1988a). Consequently, additional research exploring methods to reduce this instability through alternative passage-selecting procedures is required. Until an alternative procedure is developed, however, passages to be used as stimuli for curriculum-based measurement in reading are drawn from text randomly. Pages with excessive dialogue, poetry, or games are eliminated from the passage pool.

Selecting a Measurement Duration. In selecting a measurement duration, or the length of time each curriculum-based test will last, several technical considerations are relevant, including concurrent validity, sensitivity to student growth, and instability in the data. Fuchs, Tindal, and Deno (1984) examined how the duration of a curriculum-based reading test affected the measure's concurrent validity. Forty-five students were tested on 30- and 60-second curriculum-based reading measures. The median correlation between the 30- and 60-second samples was +.92 (range = .83 to .97). Hence, the 30-second sample appears to relate well to longer, 60-second curriculum-based reading tests.

In terms of sensitivity to student growth, Fuchs, Tindal, and Deno (1984) investigated the effect of sample duration on the level and slope of time-series data. Two second-grade girls, who were seriously below grade level in reading, were tested daily on curriculum-based reading tests. The experimental questions were examined through a multiple-baseline, reversal design (Hersen & Barlow, 1976), consisting of daily 30-second measurement samples and daily 3-minute measurement samples. Analysis of graphed data for both students revealed that the median number of words correct per minute was consistently higher with the 30-second measurements than with the 3-minute tests. Despite this superior level of performing in the 30-second phases, the trends were relatively flat. That is, trends in the 3-minute phases showed greater acceleration. The consistently higher median performances in the 30-second phases appeared to be related to

the initial step down with each introduction of a 3-minute phase. Consequently, analysis of the relationship between performance level and measurement duration yielded conflicting results. It is possible that, given additional days of the 3-minute phases, performance under the longer measurement condition might have surpassed performance under the 30-second tests. So, although measurement duration exhibited a consistent controlling effect, the exact nature of that effect is unclear, and the superiority of one sample duration over another was not established.

Within the context of this same experiment (Fuchs, Tindal, & Deno, 1984), the effect of sample duration on the variability of time-series data also was investigated. The variability of each phase was summarized in terms of total bounce and standard error of estimate. Mann–Whitney tests on these indices revealed that the longer sample duration resulted in greater intraindividual stability.

Given difficulties with intraindividual instability in curriculum-based measurement procedures described under "Selecting Measurement Passages," the salience of reduced instability with longer sample durations should be noted. Nevertheless, longer sample durations are less feasible for implementation of routine curriculum-based measurement. Consequently, in selecting a sample duration, we have incorporated a compromise solution: 60-second durations. Research exploring 1-minute curriculum-based reading samples indicates their acceptability and comparability to samples of other practical durations (Fuchs, 1982).

Determining a Measurement Frequency. In determining a measurement frequency, key technical, practical, and efficacy considerations are relevant. In terms of technical criteria, Fuchs et al. (1983) showed that, for even initially imprecise curriculum-based measures of academic proficiency, aggregating performance across as few as two points resulted in stable estimates of student performance. However, to establish a reliable estimate of a student's growth rate, it appears that more data points are required. For example, White (1971) demonstrated that a minimum of seven data points is necessary to project a reliable performance trend, whereas Deno (personal communication, October 1987) found that as many as 10 assessments were required before the estimate of growth fell within a relatively stable range. These studies indicate that, to insure an adequate data base for decisions concerning the efficacy of student programs and to avoid prolonged use of inappropriate instructional strategies, practitioners should collect data daily.

Although no studies have compared the effects of different measurement schedules on student achievement, a meta-analysis of curriculum-based assessment aggregated studies in terms of daily versus thrice-weekly versus twice-weekly measurement (Fuchs & Fuchs, 1986c) found that average effect sizes associated with these three respective measurement frequencies were .85, .41, and .69. These effect sizes did *not* represent significant difference in achievement outcomes. Nevertheless, given the technical considerations reviewed above, it is possible that a well-controlled experimental study of alternative measurement frequencies, in which more frequent measurement would permit more and better instructional decisions to be formulated, might produce differential achievement outcomes.

Although technical and effectiveness considerations seem to support daily measurement, practical considerations suggest less frequent measurement. Research indicates that practitioners devote more than 2 minutes to preparing for measurement, measuring, scoring performance, recording scores, and putting away materials for one student in one academic area (Fuchs, Fuchs, Hamlett, & Hasselbring, 1987; Wesson, Fuchs, Tindal, Mirkin, & Deno, 1986). Multiplied across a caseload of 15–25 students, each of whom is measured on three curriculum tasks, the time teachers devote to curriculum-based measurements can be considerable.

Nevertheless, recent computer applications appear to improve the feasibility of curriculum-based measurement. Software (Fuchs, Hamlett, & Fuchs, 1987, 1990) automatically performs the following tasks: (1) generates the alternative curriculum-based measurement tests; (2) administers tests as students set at a computer terminal; (3) scores tests; (4) saves scores along with students' responses; (5) graphs scores; (6) an-

alyzes performance trends according to explicit decision rules and recommends the need for instructional and goal changes; and (7) diagnoses patterns of students' response errors and makes recommendations about instructional changes based on these diagnoses. This software substantially decreases the time teachers devote to curriculum-based measurement activities, and thereby increases the feasibility of the assessment system (Fuchs, Hamlett, Fuchs, Stecker, & Ferguson, 1988). Consequently, when students and teachers have ready access to computers, technological developments support frequent (if not daily) curriculum-based measurement.

How Should Assessment Information Be Used for Instructional Decision Making?

Although teachers may collect student performance data according to designated schedules, they often fail to employ the assessment information to develop students' educational programs effectively (Baldwin, 1976; White, 1974). For example, Tindal, Fuchs, Mirkin, Christenson, and Deno (1981) found that teachers often maintained instructional programs for long periods even when performance trends indicated that those programs were not producing student improvement. In addition, although teachers may recognize when interventions are ineffective, they frequently have difficulty in generating important instructional modifications (Fuchs, Deno, & Mirkin, 1982). The questions of when and how to modify student programs have been addressed with data evaluation rules, with some degree of success.

Examples of data evaluation rules are provided in the work of Haring, White, and Liberty (1979). Haring et al. developed guidelines requiring practitioners to assess patterns in successive student scores in relation to a goal line connecting baseline data to the desired goal criterion performance level. These data evaluation rules (see White & Haring, 1980) suggest both when and how to modify programs. Although research indicates that use of the rules developed by White and associates may improve student achievement, it remains unclear whether these rules for specifying both when and how to change programs are superior to rules simply indicating when to change programs (Martin, 1980).

Deno and his colleagues have employed alternative sets of decision rules for assisting teachers in using curriculum-based measurement to develop instructional programs. One category of decision rules, known as "treatment-oriented" rules, is referenced to the level of performance in preceding instructional phases. It focuses on both when and how to develop instructional changes (see Mirkin, Deno, et al., 1982, for additional information). Specifically, with treatment-oriented rules, the practitioner introduces instructional changes every 3–4 weeks, summarizes performance within each instructional phase, compares summary statistics associated with different phases, and borrows instructional principles within relatively effective phases to determine the nature of subsequent instructional alterations. Research indicates that treatment-oriented decision rules may require technical sophistication for effective implementation (Fuchs, 1988c; Fuchs, Wesson, Tindal, Mirkin, & Deno, 1982).

A more simple approach to data evaluation, also developed by Deno and colleagues, is "goal-oriented" (see Mirkin, Deno, et al., 1982). With goal-oriented decision rules, data evaluation is referenced to a goal line connecting baseline and goal performance levels. Every 3–4 weeks, when data for at least 10 measurement points have been collected, a trend line estimating the current student growth rate is calculated. The steepness of this trend line is compared to that of the goal line. If the trend line is flatter than the goal line, an instructional change is introduced; if the trend line is steeper than the goal line, the goal performance criterion is increased. Research indicates that a goal-oriented approach to data evaluation, which requires instructional changes whenever necessary and stipulates goal increases whenever possible, facilitates effective development of instructional programs (Fuchs et al., 1988).

Recently, we (Fuchs, Fuchs, & Hamlett, in press; Fuchs, Fuchs, Hamlett, & Allinder, in press; Fuchs, Fuchs, Hamlett, & Stecker, in press) have developed procedures for assisting teachers in determining not only when, but also how, to change instructional programs. The curriculum-based measure-

ment data base is employed differently for determining *how* to modify instructional programs than for timing *when* to make instructional revisions. For timing instructional changes, the level and growth of performance, reflected in total scores, are employed. For determining the nature of instructional changes, actual student responses generated by the curriculum-based measurement are used. These procedures for determining the nature of instructional interventions are described further within the section below on "Case Studies in Curriculum-Based Measurement." The effectiveness of these procedures for determining the nature of instructional interventions has been demonstrated (Fuchs, Fuchs, & Hamlett, 1989; Fuchs, Fuchs, Hamlett, & Allinder, in press; Fuchs, Fuchs, Hamlett, & Stecker, in press).

Case Studies in Curriculum-Based Measurement

Three case studies in curriculum-based measurement are presented below to provide readers with a concrete understanding of how curriculum-based measurement is conducted. The first case study, that of George, describes a curriculum-based measurement system for reading; the second, that of Charles, a system for spelling; and the third, that of Donald, a system for math.

Case Study in Reading: George

In implementing curriculum-based measurement in reading, the first step is goal selection—that is, the identification of a level within a curriculum that the teacher hopes the student will master by the year's end. In this case study, Mrs. H. selects level 3-1 of the Ginn 720 reading series as the curriculum level she hopes George, a fifth-grade pupil with a learning disability, will master. In November, George enters Mrs. H.'s resource program, where he receives 1 hour of help each day in reading, spelling, and math.

The second step in the process is to measure the student in the corresponding curriculum level according to the requirements of curriculum-based measurement. In this case study (as well as those below), computerized curriculum-based measurement procedures are described. (For curriculum-based measurement case studies that do not employ computer-adapted procedures, see Fuchs, 1989.) Consequently, in reading, a recall measurement procedure is employed. Mrs. H. has George work at the computer doing reading assessments three times, in order to formulate an estimate of his initial level of proficiency on the Ginn 720 level 3-1 material. Each time George completes a reading assessment, the following process occurs:

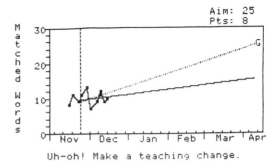

FIGURE 17.1. George's curriculum-based measurement graph in reading.

1. A 400-word passage from Ginn 720 level 3-1 is sampled randomly.
2. After George indicates to the computer that he is ready to begin testing, the computer presents the passage on the screen for a total of 3 minutes, while George uses the <ARROW> keys to "turn" pages.
3. After 3 minutes elapse, the computer removes the passage.
4. When George indicates to the computer that he is ready to begin writing his recall of the passage, a blank screen is presented with a simple word-processing program, on which George writes his recall of the passage within a 4-minute time limit.
5. George's recall is scored in terms of the number of unique words he has written that match words in the original passage (recalled words must include at least 50% of the letter sequences in the original words in order to be scored correct).
6. George sees his score for that day, along with a graph showing his performance record and highlighting his current score with a blinking light.

(Before the first reading assessment, George works with a typing program until increases in his typing speed plateau.)

In George's case, his initial three assessments yield scores of 8, 11, and 9 matched words. Estimating that his current level of performance in the Ginn 720 level 3-1 reading book is a median of 9 matched words, Mrs. H. sets George's April 10 goal as 25 matched words. The initial assessments are shown in Figure 17.1, George's reading graph. The broken vertical line signifies the introduction of a goal; the "G" indicates the goal criterion; and the broken diagonal line is

the "goal line," depicting the anticipated rate of improvement between baseline and goal dates. At this time, Mrs. H. begins to implement her daily instructional program, which includes 5 minutes of oral reading, 15 minutes of silent reading, completion of two workbook pages introduced with modeling and corrected with feedback, and 10 minutes of reading with a partner.

After eight additional assessments, encompassing $3\frac{1}{2}$ weeks of instructional intervention (at least two assessments per week), the computer analyzes George's scores while Mrs. H. inspects George's performance record on the computer. The computer draws a quarter intersect trend line (see White & Haring, 1980) through the eight assessments and extrapolates this line to the goal date. As can be seen in the solid diagonal line in Figure 17.1, this trend line is flatter than the goal line. This indicates that George's rate of progress is inadequate to reach the goal. Therefore, the computer recommends to Mrs. H. that she make a teaching change in order to stimulate a better rate of improvement (see the message at the bottom of Figure 17.1).

In order to assist Mrs. H. in formulating the nature of this instructional change, Mrs. H. reviews George's responses at the computer in the following way. Among George's most recent four assessments, the computer selects the score that is closest to the average score across the four recalls. The computer puts the corresponding passage on the screen; Mrs. H. reads the passage, using the <ARROW> keys to "turn" pages. Then the computer shows George's recall (see Figure 17.2), as well as a series of structured prompts. These prompts help Mrs. H. to

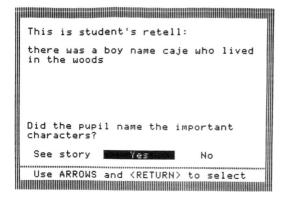

FIGURE 17.2. George's recall with a question about story content.

analyze the extent to which George has included key story elements in his recall. This process of showing passages, corresponding recalls, and structured questions concerning story components is repeated for at least two and up to four passages, depending on the number of recalls the teacher wishes to review. Based on Mrs. H.'s responses to the structured questions, the computer recommends two story elements for George to work on in the next month. The teacher can add this recommendation and review of recalls to other key information she has available in order to structure a modification in George's reading program. At this time, Mrs. H. enters an instructional change onto the computer, and this is shown as a solid vertical line on George's graph. Then she continues to teach, using this instructional modification, and to have George complete assessments at the computer.

In this way, Mrs. H. uses a prescriptive set of curriculum-based measurement procedures to monitor George's progress toward the goal of proficient reading in Ginn 720 level 3-1 material. George's scores on the recall assessments are used as overall indicators of his proficiency on the material; as these scores increase, Mrs. H. infers that his overall reading skills are improving. The data base of scores is used to determine whether George's rate of progress and the corresponding instructional program are adequate for goal attainment. If not, George's instructional program is modified. The data base of actual recall responses is employed to diagnose patterns of responses and errors

George makes during assessment, and to structure the nature of potentially effective instructional modifications. In this way, the curriculum-based measurement data base is used to address the instructional phases of the assessment process—that is, planning and modifying instruction.

Case Study in Spelling: Charles

As with reading, the first step in the curriculum-based measurement spelling process is to specify the goal or the curriculum level on which the teacher hopes the student will be proficient by the year's end. In this case example, the school does not have a specified spelling curriculum series. So Mrs. W. decides that she wants a sixth-grade student, Charles, to spell proficiently in the fourth-grade Zaner–Bloser spelling program by the year's end.

The next step in the process is to formulate an initial estimate of Charles's current performance level in this material. Mrs. W. designates a sixth-grade reader, Laurie, to work with Charles at the computer each time he is assessed in spelling. Mrs. W. has Charles and Laurie work at the computer to estimate Charles's current performance level. Each time they work at the computer, Charles and Laurie take a set of lists of spelling words, which have been printed by the computer. Each list includes 20 words randomly sampled from the level D (fourth-grade) Zaner–Bloser word list, and each list is labeled with a number. A different list is used for each assessment. At the computer, the following process occurs:

1. Laurie tells Charles the list number and password of the list to be used during testing on that day.
2. In response to prompts by the computer, Charles enters that list number and password into the computer so that it can retrieve the corresponding list of words.
3. When Charles is ready to begin testing, he presses <RETURN>.
4. The computer beeps, which is Laurie's prompt to say, "Word 1: _____ " and read the word.
5. Charles checks that the term "Word 1" shows at the top of the screen, and he types the corresponding word onto the screen.

6. When he has finished typing the word, Charles presses RETURN and the next beep and screen, showing Word 2, appears (if Charles takes more than 15 seconds to type a word, the computer automatically beeps and advances him to the next word).

7. Laurie reads "Word 2: _____ ," and Charles checks that "Word 2" shows at the top of the screen and types the word.

8. This process continues until 20 words have been spelled or 3 minutes elapse, whichever occurs sooner.

9. Performance is scored in terms of letter sequences (pairs of letters within words) correct, as well as words correct and incorrect.

10. The computer shows these scores for that assessment to Charles, along with a graph of letter sequences correct, which highlights the most recent score with a flashing light.

Charles's initial assessments yield scores of between 37 and 52 letter sequences correct. Using a median of 43 as the estimate of Charles's current performance level, Mrs. W. sets 80 correct letter sequences as the initial goal criterion for May 15. Figure 17.3 displays Charles's graph, with baseline scores, the first goal introduction line (broken vertical line), goal ("G"), and goal line (diagonal broken line).

Then Mrs. W. specifies her initial daily instructional program, which consists of the following: writing each word on the weekly spelling list 10 times, using each word in a sentence, and spelling each word from memory. Mrs. W. implements this program in November, December, and January, during which time Charles is measured at least twice weekly. When Mrs. W. (1) inspects Charles's performance record at the computer and (2) has plotted at least eight points since the last vertical line, the computer analyzes the data base as it does with reading. A quarter intersect line of best fit is drawn through the scores that are plotted since the last vertical line. When this line of best fit (the solid diagonal line) is less steep than the goal line (the broken diagonal line), this indicates that the current instructional program is not producing an improvement rate that will allow goal attainment. Consequently, the comput-

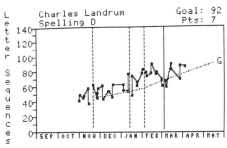

FIGURE 17.3. Charles's curriculum-based measurement graph in spelling.

er recommends to Mrs. W. that she introduce an instructional modification. (See data pattern between February 2 and March 3.)

At that time, Mrs. W. uses information about Charles's responses to assist her structuring an instructional change. The computer provides analysis of the student's responses in the following ways. First, it identifies the pool of 50 words the student has spelled most recently. Second, it calculates for each word the number of letter sequences correct, and rank-orders the 50 words from most (100% correct letter sequences) to least correct. Third, it groups the 50 words into three categories: "corrects" (100% letter sequences correct), "near misses" (30%–99% letter sequences correct), and "far misses" (30% letter sequences correct). Fourth, the computer conducts a skills analysis on the pool of "near misses": For each word, the computer identifies the spelling rule violations it finds. (The potential spelling rule violations are dual consonant, final E, "c/s," "c/ck," "-dge," "-ch/-tch," "-le," "-ss/-ff/-ll/-zz," suffix, "ance," "sure," vowel teams, final vowel, "-ign/-igh," vowel + R, U + L + consonant, "ild," vowel + N, blends, doubling omission, "shun" family, digraphs, crazy combos, irregular words, single consonant, and single vowel.) Fifth, the computer lists the pool of words that fall within each spelling rule violation, and counts the number of words per spelling rule violation. Finally, the computer selects the three most frequent rule violations (or, in the case of a tie, the more "teachable" rule violation). (See Fuchs, Fuchs, Hamlett, & Allinder, in press, for additional information.)

The computer presents the following information to the teacher. First, it shows a screen that (1) lists the numbers of words falling into categories of "corrects," "near misses," and "far misses"; (2) gives the three categories of most frequent errors, with examples of each error type; and (3) provides a frequency count of types of error (see Figure 17.4). Second, the computer shows complete lists of "corrects," "near misses," and "far misses," for the teacher to inspect, with the percentage of correct letter sequences in the left-hand margin and error types the computer finds within the "near misses" category (see Figure 17.5). Third, for any rule violation category the teacher selects, the computer provides a teaching rule as well as examples of words falling into that category (see Figure 17.6).

As shown in Figures 17.4, 17.5, and 17.6,

among Charles's most recently spelled 50 words, 15 words fall in the "corrects" category, 28 in the "near misses" category, and 7 in the "far misses" category. Charles's most frequent error violations are dual consonants, single vowels, and vowel + R. Mrs. W. can use this information to help her structure an effective intervention for Charles.

Consequently, using the scores for correct letter sequences generated during curriculum-based measurement, Mrs. W. can monitor the adequacy of Charles's progress toward the instructional goal (i.e., proficient spelling of the fourth-grade Zaner–Bloser list). She can also evaluate the effectiveness of the instructional program in facilitating Charles's goal mastery. When the rate of improvement and the corresponding program appear inadequate, Mrs. W. can respond to the assess-

```
Charles Landrum--ZB D   (Page 1)

Corrects (100% LS):              15 word(s)
Near Misses (30-99% LS):         28 word(s)
Far Misses (0-29% LS):            7 word(s)

FREQUENT ERRORS

Dual Cons

SAMPLE-SAMBLE
LEARNER-LEANER
MUMBLE-MOBBLE
APART-APEOT
CHART-CHARD
TRACTOR-TRATER

Single Vowel

LISTEN-LESTEN
MUMBLE-MOBBLE
MUMBLE-MOMMBE
SHIPMENT-SHAPMENT
TICKLE-TEAKLE

Vowel + R

CALENDAR-CANDER
APART-APEOT
TRACTOR-TRATER
HERO-HEAROW
```

```
0 FSLZ            4 Vowel Teams      0 Crazy Combos
3 Final E         0 c/s Error        0 ion/ioh Error
2 Blends          1 -le Error        0 Vow+l+cons
1 Doubling        4 Final Vowel      0 'sure' Words
6 Dual Cons       0 'ild' word       0 'ance' Words
4 Vowel + R       1 -doe Error       0 Irregular
2 Vowel + N       0 -ch/tch          0 Apostrophe
1 Suffixes        2 c/ck             5 Single Vowel
1 Digraphs        1 'shun' Words     1 Single Cons
```

FIGURE 17.4.   Charles's diagnostic feedback screen summarizing patterns of responses.

```
Charles Landrum--ZB D  (Page 2)

----------Corrects (100% LS)-------------------------------------------
 100 MARCH-MARCH
 100 DEATH-DEATH
 100 SOMETIMES-SOMETIMES
 100 THANKFUL-THANKFUL
 100 BAKER-BAKER
 100 UNCOVER-UNCOVER
 100 SHY-SHY
 100 WEAKNESS-WEAKNESS
 100 FORGOT-FORGOT
 100 EYES-EYES
 100 KNIFE-KNIFE
 100 ARMY-ARMY
 100 POWERLESS-POWERLESS
 100 WIFE-WIFE
 100 MIX-MIX
----------Near Misses (30-99% LS)-------------------------------------
  80 JULY-JAULY
  77 SHIPMENT-SHAPMENT        Single Vowel
  75 PATCHES-PATCES           Digraphs
  75 QUIETER-QUITER           Vowel Teams
  75 LEARNER-LEANER           Dual Cons
  75 TROUBLE-TRUBBLE          Vowel Teams
  71 SHOWER-SHAWER            Vowel Teams
  71 SAMPLE-SAMBLE            Dual Cons
  71 LISTEN-LESTEN            Single Vowel
  66 BADGE-BAGE               -dge Error
  66 TASTE-TAST               Final Vowel
  66 CHART-CHARD              Dual Cons
  66 ALONE-ALON               Final E
  66 RESTLESS-REASLESS        Suffixes        Blends
  60 HERO-HEAROW              Final Vowel     Vowel + R
  60 RARE-RAR                 Final E
  60 LAZY-LAZZ                Final Vowel
  57 TICKLE-TEAKLE            c/ck            Single Vowel
  57 FRENCH-FANCH             Vowel + N       Blends
  57 MUMBLE-MOBBLE            Dual Cons       Single Vowel
  50 UNLUCKY-UNLUKE           Final Vowel     c/ck
  50 TRACTOR-TRATER           Vowel + R       Dual Cons
  50 CABBAGE-CABATCH          Final E         Doubling
  50 APART-APEOT              Vowel + R       Dual Cons
  44 CALENDAR-CANDER          Vowel + R       Vowel + N       Single Cons
  42 MUMBLE-MOMMBE            -le Error       Single Vowel
  40 RAIL-REAL                Vowel Teams
  37 STATION-STANCH           'shun' Words
----------Far Misses (0-29% LS)---------------------------------------
  28 SAMPLE-SCEMBE
  25 CERTAIN-CHANTEN
  25 RUSSIAN-RUNCH
  25 SQUEEZE-SCEASE
  20 TREATMENT-TEMPEMT
  20 LIMB-LEAM
  14 GIGGLE-GELLY
```

FIGURE 17.5. List of Charles's "corrects," "near misses," and "far misses" among the last 50 words spelled.

ment information by introducing an instructional modification. To help her determine the nature of instructional components that may produce spelling growth for Charles, Mrs. W. relies on the data base of responses generated through the curriculum-based measurement. Analysis of the responses provides Mrs. W. with information about the nature of Charles's spelling errors.

Case Study in Math: Donald

As with reading and spelling, the first step in the curriculum-based measurement process in math is determining the goal (i.e., the material on which the teacher hopes the student will be proficient by the year's end). Using the computerized curriculum-based measurement procedures in math, the

```
        Vowel + R

1. When a vowel precedes r, it has a
blended sound.

2. When a vowel precedes r and a
vowel, the first vowel has a short
sound.

        Grades 1-3        Grades 4-6
        bark              collar
        barrel            peril
        important         monitor

        Press <RETURN> to continue.
```

FIGURE 17.6. Example of a teaching rule screen for spelling.

teacher can select a subset of 85 math computation objectives, which cover the four basic operations, decimals, fractions, and estimation. For the Tennessee statewide curriculum, the teacher can select among six pre-designated sets of objective clusters, each one of which represents a grade level of the Tennessee Basic Skills First Math Program.

For Donald, a fifth-grade student with learning disabilities, the teacher, Mr. T., has selected the fourth-grade Tennessee curriculum as the year-end goal level. This pool of objectives comprises the following:

• Multidigit addition with regrouping.
• Multidigit subtraction with regrouping.
• Multiplication facts.
• Division facts.
• Multiplying two two-digit numbers without regrouping.
• Multiplying one- by two-digit numbers with regrouping.
• Dividing three- by one-digit numbers without remainders.
• Dividing two- or three- by one-digit numbers with remainders.
• Adding and subtracting simple or mixed decimals without regrouping.
• Adding and subtracting mixed decimals to the hundredths.

The next step in the math curriculum-based measurement process is to estimate the initial level of performance on this curriculum level. The teacher has the computer print alternate forms of tests that encompass the set of relevant objectives. So, for Donald, the computer prints 50 alternate forms of a test. Each 25-problem test is one page long (see Figure 17.7 for an example); it consists of the same problem types, but with the position of problems and the numerals included within problems determined randomly. Each problem sheet is labeled with a different number and password. Each time Donald is assessed at the computer, he takes a different alternate form of the test.

To estimate Donald's initial performance level on this fourth-grade math curriculum, Mr. T. has him complete an initial set of assessments. Each time Donald is assessed, the following occurs:

1. The computer prompts Donald to enter the problem sheet number and password, and checks to make sure the number and password match.
2. When Donald is ready to begin working, he presses RETURN, and then the computer allows 3 minutes of work time. (For first grade, a 1-minute time limit is used; for second grade, 1.5 minutes; for third and fourth grades, 3 minutes; for fifth grade, 4 minutes; and for sixth grade, 5 minutes.)
3. At the end of the time limit, the computer rings continuously until Donald indicates he has stopped working by pressing RETURN.
4. A response sheet appears on the screen, formatted with 25 blocks (just like the math test), and Donald enters his responses in an untimed format (the screen incorporates a word processor that allows Donald to edit any response at any time).
5. When Donald finishes entering his responses, the computer scores the performance in terms of numbers of correct problems and digits written.
6. The computer shows Donald his scores, along with a graph that highlights his day's performance with a blinking light.

Donald's initial assessments range between 7 and 21 digits correct. Using a median of 16 digits as the estimate of Donald's current performance level, Mr. T. sets a May 15 goal criterion of 30 digits correct. Figure 17.8 shows Donald's graph, with baseline scores, the goal introduction line (broken vertical line), the goal ("G"), and the goal line (broken diagonal line). Mr. T. then specifies his daily instructional program, which consists of daily worksheet completion (introduced with modeling and corrected with

Sheet #1   MATH 4

Password: ARM

Name: _____   Date: _____

A	B	C	D	E
5.48 - 1.53	14 X 64	4256 7106 + 13	5426 1116 + 97	$6\frac{1}{2} + 2 =$

F	G	H	I	J
$4\frac{1}{3} - 1 =$	1201 - 1052	88804 + 18338	601 X 6	225 X 5

K	L	M	N	O
3)300	7 X 6	4)631	1 X 4	2 X 1

P	Q	R	S	T
$\frac{7}{11} - \frac{4}{11} =$	9)63	8)24	8 X 3	5 X 6

U	V	W	X	Y
18.1 + 27.66	1 X 6	22 X 30	6)36	9)9

FIGURE 17.7.   Example of a fourth-grade curriculum-based measurement math test.

feedback) and two problems completed at the board. Mr. T. implements this program during November and December, during which time additional assessments are completed. When Mr. T. reviews Donald's performance, the computer analyzes these assessments. At this time, the trend line through these assessments is less steep than the goal line, so the computer recommends that Mr. T. introduce a change into his instructional program.

Whenever Mr. T. requests help in determining the nature of an effective instructional revision, the computer analyzes Donald's responses in the following way. Using the assessments that have been collected

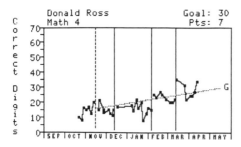

Wait. Not enough scores for decision.

FIGURE 17.8.   Donald's curriculum-based measurement math graph.

within the most recent 2 weeks, the computer groups the problems into the 10 types specified by the curriculum (see Figure 17.9). For each type, the computer provides the ratio of problems attempted to those possible, and the percentage of digits correct within the attempted problems. Then, each

problem type is assigned to one of the following categories: "not attempted"—0% problems attempted; "nonmastered"—0%–74% problems attempted with less than 85% accuracy *or* at least 75% problems attempted with less than 40% accuracy; "partially mastered"—fewer than 75% attempted with greater than 85% accuracy *or* more than 75% attempted with accuracy between 40% and 84%; and "mastered"—at least 75% attempted with at least 85% accuracy.

The computer provides this analysis to Mr. T. in the following way. First, a Mastery Profile screen is shown, which shows the problem types by category (see top part of Figure 17.9). Second, an Objectives History (see bottom part of Figure 17.9) is provided. This Objectives History shows the following: (1) 2-week time intervals in the columns; (2) the objective types in the rows; (3) mastery categories in boxes (black, mastered; checkered, partially mastered; stripes, nonmas-

```
MASTERY PROFILE FOR Donald Ross
APR 1-APR 15 (4 probes)

                                     Attempts   Accuracy

MASTERED

PARTIALLY MASTERED
     A1  + multidigit w/ regrouping    11/12       73%
     M1  X basic facts, factors to 9   13/24       89%
     D1  - basic facts, divisors 6-9    2/16      100%
     F1  +/- simple or mixed no regrouping 10/12   84%
     .1  +/- mixed decimals to hundredths  7/8      83%

NONMASTERED
     S1  - two 4-digits w/ regrouping    3/4       36%
     D2  - 3- by 1-digit no remainder    2/4       17%

NOT ATTEMPTED
     M2  X two 2-digits no regrouping    0/4        0%
     M3  X by 1- or 2-digit w/ regrouping 0/12      0%
     D3  - 2- or 3- by 1-digit w/ remainder 0/4     0%
```

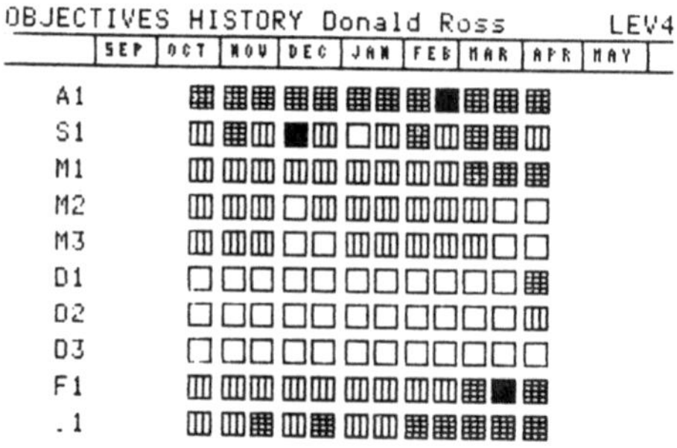

FIGURE 17.9.   Donald's skills analysis.

tered; white, not attempted). As the teacher moves the cursor onto any box, information corresponding to the intersection of that objective and time is displayed. This information includes a description of the objective type, the number of assessments reflected in that box, the ratio of attempted to possible problems, and the percentage of correct digits among the attempted problems. This Mastery Profile and Objectives History can be used to assist the teacher in specifying the content of revised instructional components.

Mr. T. can use the curriculum-based measurement for two basic purposes, as described in the reading and spelling case studies. First, he can employ the graphed assessment scores to evaluate the adequacy of student growth and of the corresponding instructional program. This data base of graphed assessment scores allows Mr. T. to determine when an instructional modification is required. Second, Mr. T. can use the analysis of student responses to diagnose the pattern of errors Donald manifests. This response data base allows Mr. T. to determine the nature of effective interventions. These two types of information derived from the curriculum-based measurement fulfill the functions of instructional assessment.

Issues in Curriculum-Based Measurement

These case studies illustrate how curriculum-based measurement procedures can be used for instructional planning. Using the scores generated through measurement, practitioners can monitor students' progress toward instructional goals. When rates of improvement appear inadequate, practitioners can revise instructional programs in an attempt to enhance students' progress. The curriculum-based measurement response data base can be analyzed to inform practitioners about directions for useful instructional revisions.

The research base on curriculum-based measurement provides the data base for structuring many key elements of this monitoring system. Elements derived from this research base include (1) identification of psychometrically adequate but feasibly implemented behaviors for tracking student growth in reading, spelling, and written expression; (2) delineation of prescriptive methods for conducting measurement that

facilitate reliable estimates of student performance; and (3) specification of procedures for utilizing curriculum-based measurement data bases to enhance teachers' instructional decision making and students' achievement.

Nevertheless, several other elements of the curriculum-based measurement system have been derived from logical analyses of alternative procedures rather than from empirical studies. These elements require additional research. Areas for further investigation include (1) instability in student performance, with a focus on methods for reducing sources of error, such as noncomparability of stimulus materials; (2) various measurement behaviors in math; (3) alternative methods of data analysis, which insure accurate estimates of growth rates even as they do not require unnecessarily long instructional phases; and (4) the effectiveness of diagnostic feedback or error analysis, in which teachers rely on the response data base to help formulate the nature of instructional decisions. To sum up, curriculum-based measurement provides an initial structure for assessment that can facilitate instructional development. However, research exploring additional key elements of the system still is required.

SUMMARY

In this chapter, an overview of alternative forms of curriculum-based assessment procedures has been presented; these include traditional classroom assessment, precision teaching, and mastery learning. Three critical problems with these forms of curriculum-based assessment have been described: questionable criterion and content validity; noncomparability of assessment points across time; and inadequate psychometric features of teacher-constructed and commercially available criterion-referenced tests. Curriculum-based measurement is offered as a variant of curriculum-based assessment that attempts to circumvent these problems. Portions of the research base on curriculum-based measurement have been reviewed; three case studies illustrating the use of the procedures have been presented; and, finally, additional areas of necessary research have been specified.

Acknowledgments. Development of the procedures described in this chapter was funded in part by Grant Nos. G008530198 and G008730087 from the Office of Special Education Programs, U.S. Department of Education, to Vanderbilt University. Points of view or opinions stated in this chapter do not necessarily represent official agency positions.

REFERENCES

Alderson, J. C. (1978). Cloze procedures. In O. K. Buros (Ed.), *The eighth mental measurements yearbook* (pp. 1171–1174). Highland Park, NJ: Gryphon Press.

Baldwin, V. (1976). Curriculum concerns. In M. A. Thomas (Ed.), *Hey, don't forget about me* (pp. 64–73). Reston, VA: Council for Exceptional Children.

Block, J. H., & Burns, R. B. (1976). Mastery learning. In. L. S. Schulman (Ed.), *Review of research in education* (Vol. 4, pp. 3–49). Itasca, IL: F. E. Peacock.

Bloom, B. S. (1976). *Human characteristics and school learning*. New York: McGraw-Hill.

Deno, S. L. (1985). Curriculum-based measurement: The merging alternative. *Exceptional Children, 52,* 219–232.

Deno, S. L. (1987). Curriculum-based measurement. *Teaching Exceptional Children, 20,* 41–42.

Deno, S. L., & Fuchs, L. S. (1987). Developing curriculum-based measurement for special education problem solving. *Focus on Exceptional Children, 19*(8), 1–16.

Deno, S. L., Mirkin, P. K., & Chiang, B. (1982). Identifying valid measures of reading. *Exceptional Children, 49,* 36–45.

Deno, S. L., Mirkin, P. K., Chiang, B., & Lowry, L. (1980). *Relationships among simple measures of reading and performance and standardized achievement tests* (Research Report No. 20). Minneapolis: University of Minnesota, Institute for Research on Learning Disabilities. (ERIC Document Reproduction Service No. ED 197 507)

Fuchs, L. S. (1981). *The concurrent validity of progress measures of basal reading material.* Unpublished doctoral dissertation, University of Minnesota.

Fuchs, L. S. (1982). Reading. In P. K. Mirkin, L. S. Fuchs, & S. L. Deno (Eds.), *Considerations in designing a continuous evaluation system: An integrative review* (Monograph No. 20, pp. 29–73). Minneapolis: University of Minnesota, Institute for Research on Learning Disabilities.

Fuchs, L. S. (1986). Monitoring the performance of mildly handicapped pupils: Review of current research and practice. *Remedial and Special Education, 7*(5), 5–12.

Fuchs, L. S. (1988a). *Intraindividual instability in curriculum-based measurement.* Manuscript in preparation.

Fuchs, L. S. (1988b). *Improving data-based instruction through computer technology: Final report.* Unpublished manuscript.

Fuchs, L. S. (1988c). Effects of computer-managed instruction on teachers' implementation of systematic monitoring programs and student achievement. *Journal of Educational Research, 81,* 294–304.

Fuchs, L. S. (1989). Evaluating solutions. Monitoring and revising intervention programs. In M. R. Shinn (Ed.), *Curriculum-based measurement: Assessing special children* (pp. 153–181). New York: Guilford Press.

Fuchs, L. S., Deno, S. L., & Marston, D. (1983). Improving the reliability of curriculum-based measures of academic achievement for psychoeducational decision making. *Diagnostique, 8,* 135–149.

Fuchs, L. S., Deno, S. L., & Mirkin, P. K. (1982). *The effects of frequent continuous evaluation of student goals on teacher decision* (Research Report No. 97). Minneapolis: University of Minnesota, Institute for Research on Learning Disabilities. (ERIC Document Reproduction Service No. ED 226 043)

Fuchs, L. S., Deno, S. L., & Mirkin, P. K. (1984). Effects of frequent, curriculum-based measurement and evaluation on pedagogy, student achievement, and student awareness of learning. *American Educational Research Journal, 21,* 449–460.

Fuchs, L. S., & Fuchs, D. (1986a). Linking assessment to instructional intervention: An overview. *School Psychology Review, 15,* 318–323.

Fuchs, L. S., & Fuchs, D. (1986b). Curriculum-based assessment of progress toward long- and short-term goals. *Journal of Special Educatin, 20,* 69–82.

Fuchs, L. S., & Fuchs, D. (1986c). Effects of systematic formative evaluation on student achievement: A meta-analysis. *Exceptional Children, 53,* 199–208.

Fuchs, L. S., Fuchs, D., & Hamlett, C. L. (1988). Effects of alternative goal structures within curriculum-based measurement. *Exceptional Children, 55,* 429–438.

Fuchs, L. S., Fuchs, D., & Hamlett, C. L. (1989). Monitoring reading progress using student recalls: Effects of two feedback systems. *Journal of Educational Research, 83,* 103–111.

Fuchs, L. S., Fuchs, D., Hamlett, C. L., & Allinder, R. M. (in press). The importance of skills analysis to curriculum-based measurement in spelling. *Exceptional Children.*

Fuchs, L. S., Fuchs, D., Hamlett, C. L., & Hasselbring, T. S. (1987). Using computers with curriculum-based progress monitoring: Effects on teacher efficiency and satisfaction. *Journal of Special Education Technology, 8*(4), 14–27.

Fuchs, L. S., Fuchs, D., Hamlett, C. L., & Stecker, P. M. (in press). The contribution of skills analysis in curriculum-based measurement in math. *School Psychology Review.*

Fuchs, L. S., Fuchs, D., & Maxwell, L. (1988). The validity of informal measures of reading comprehension. *Remedial and Special Education, 9*(2), 20–29.

Fuchs, L. S., Hamlett, C. L., & Fuchs, D. (1987). *Improving data-based instruction through computer technology: Description of Year 3 software.* Unpublished manuscript.

Fuchs, L. S., Hamlett, C. L., & Fuchs, D. (1990). *Monitoring Basic Skills Progress* [Computer Program]. Austin, TX: PRO-ED.

Fuchs, L. S., Hamlett, C. L., Fuchs, D., Stecker, P. M., & Ferguson, C. (1988). Conducting curriculum-based measurement with computerized data collection: Effects on efficiency and teacher satisfaction. *Journal of Special Education Technology*, 9(2), 73–86.

Fuchs, L. S., Tindal, G., & Deno, S. L. (1984). Methodological issues in curriculum-based reading assessment. *Diagnostique*, 8, 19–26.

Fuchs, L. S., Tindal, G., & Fuchs, D. (1986). Effects of mastery learning procedures on student achievement. *Journal of Educational Research*, 79, 286–291.

Fuchs, L. S., Wesson, C., Tindal, G., Mirkin, P. K., & Deno, S. L. (1982). *Instructional changes, student performance, and teacher preferences: The effects of specific measurement and evaluation procedures* (Research Report No. 64). Minneapolis: University of Minnesota, Institute for Research on Learning Disabilities. (ERIC Document Reproduction Service No. ED 218 849)

Gates, A. I. (1921). An experiment and statistical study of reading and reading tests. *Journal of Educational Psychology*, 12, 303–113, 378–391, 445–464.

Gickling, E. E. (1981). The forgotten learner. *Nevada Public Affairs Review*, 1, 19–22.

Glaser, R. (1981). The future of testing: A research agenda for cognitive psychology and psychometrics. *American Psychologist*, 12, 696–706.

Hansen, C. L. M. (1979). Chicken soup and other forms of comprehension. In J. E. Button, T. Lovitt, & T. D. Rowland (Eds.), *Communications research in learning disabilities and mental retardation*. Baltimore: University Park Press.

Haring, N. G., White, O. R., & Liberty, K. A. (1979). *Field initiated research studies: An investigation of learning and instructional hierarchies in severely and profoundly handicapped children: Annual report*. Seattle: University of Washington, Child Development and Mental Retardation Center, Experimental Education Unit.

Hays, W. (1973). *Statistics for the social sciences* (2nd ed.). New York: Holt, Rinehart & Winston.

Hersen, M., & Barlow, D. H. (1976). *Single case experimental designs: Strategies for studying behavior changes*. New York: Pergamon Press.

Jenkins, J. R., Heliotis, J., Haynes, M., & Beck, K. (1986). Does passive learning account for disabled readers' comprehension deficits in ordinary reading situations? *Learning Disability Quarterly*, 9, 69–76.

Johnston, P. B. (1982). *Implications of basic research for the assessment of reading comprehension* (Technical Report No. 206). Urbana: University of Illinois, Center for the Study of Reading. (ERIC Document Reproduction Service No. ED 201–987)

Martin, M. A. (1980). *A comparison of variations in data utilization procedures on the reading performance of mildly handicapped students*. Unpublished doctoral dissertation, University of Washington.

Mirkin, P. K., Deno, S. L., Fuchs, L. S., Wesson, C., Tindal, G., Marston, D., & Kuehnle, K. (1982). *Procedures to develop and monitor progress on IEP goals*.

Minneapolis: University of Minnesota, Institute for Research on Learning Disabilities.

Mirkin, P. K., Fuchs, L. S., & Deno, S. L. (Eds.). (1982). *Considerations in designing a continuous evaluation system: An integration review* (Monograph No. 20). Minneapolis: University of Minnesota, Institute for Research on Learning Disabilities.

Nitko, A. J. (1983). *Educational tests and measurement: An introduction*. New York: Harcourt Brace Jovanovich.

Peterson, J., Greenlaw, M. J., & Tierney, R. J. (1978). Assessing instructional placement with the IRI: The effectiveness of comprehension questions. *Journal of Educational Research*, 71, 247–250.

Salvia, J., & Ysseldyke, J. E. (1985). *Assessment in special and remedial education* (3rd ed.). Boston: Houghton Mifflin.

Sassenrath, J. M. (1972). Alpha factor analyses of reading measures at the elementary, secondary, and college levels. *Journal of Reading Behavior*, 5, 304–315.

Suhorsky, J. (1975). *An investigation of the relationship between undeleted text preceding a cloze test and cloze test results*. Unpublished doctoral dissertation, University of Maryland.

Tindal, G., Fuchs, L. S., Fuchs, D., Shinn, M. R., Deno, S. L., & Germann, G. (1985). Empirical validation of criterion-referenced tests. *Journal of Educational Research*, 78, 203–209.

Tindal, G., Fuchs, L. S., Mirkin, P. K., Christenson, S., & Deno, S. L. (1981). *The relationship between student achievement and teacher assessment of short- and long-term goals* (Research Report No. 61). Minneapolis: University of Minnesota, Institute for Research on Learning Disabilities. (ERIC Document Reproduction Service No. ED 218 846)

Tucker, J. (1985). Curriculum-based assessment: An introduction. *Exceptional Children*, 52, 199–204.

Tuinman, J. J., Blanton, W. E., & Gray, G. (1975). A note on cloze as a measure of comprehension. *Journal of Psychology*, 90, 159–162.

Wesson, C., Fuchs, L. S., Tindal, G., Mirkin, P. K., & Deno, S. L. (1986). Facilitating the efficiency of ongoing curriculum-based measurement. *Teacher Education and Special Education*, 9, 166–172.

White, O. R. (1971). *A pragmatic approach to the description of progress in the single case*. Unpublished doctoral dissertation, University of Oregon.

White, O. R. (1974). *Evaluating the educational process*. Seattle: University of Washington, Child Development and Mental Retardation Center, Experimental Education Unit.

White, O. R., & Haring, N. G. (1980). *Exceptional teaching* (2nd ed.). Columbus, OH: Charles E. Merrill.

Yalow, E., & Popham, J. (1983). Content validity at the crossroads. *Educational Researcher*, 12(8), 10–14, 21.

18

Criterion-Referenced Assessment of School Achievement

RONALD K. HAMBLETON
CRAIG JURGENSEN
University of Massachusetts at Amherst

Probably the most significant change in educational testing over the last 20 years has been the rise of criterion-referenced testing. Criterion-referenced tests provide a basis for interpreting test scores in terms of well-defined domains of content rather than in terms of relevant norm groups, as is customary with norm-referenced tests. Thus, with the rise of criterion-referenced tests in American education, educators and psychologists have been able to assess students in terms of their knowledge of content, rather than in terms of their performance in relation to other students (see, e.g., Berk, 1984a, 1984b; Hambleton, 1985).

Test score uses such as placement and diagnosis for individuals, and evaluation of school programs, are being well served today by scores from criterion-referenced tests. The purposes of this chapter are (1) to provide an introduction to the field of criterion-referenced testing; (2) to highlight several technical advances; and (3) to address some promising test score uses.

DEFINITIONS

The term "criterion-referenced measurement" appears to have been first used by Glaser and Klaus (1962). In addition, Nitko

(1980) cites the use of criterion-referenced scales by Fisher (see Chadwick, 1864) and Thorndike (1910, 1913). Glaser (1963), however, is generally credited with first defining the distinctions between norm-referenced and criterion-referenced approaches to the measurement of achievement and establishing criterion-referenced tests as a legitimate alternative to norm-referenced tests, though he in turn acknowledged the prior work of Flanagan (1951) and Ebel (1962). Glaser maintained that the primary difference between the two types of measurements could be found in the standard used as a reference. He felt that criterion-referenced tests of achievement depended upon an "absolute standard of quality," whereas norm-referenced tests depended upon a relative standard of quality. Glaser's articulation of the basic differences between norm-referenced and criterion-referenced tests initiated considerable debate over the merits of the two types of tests, as well as over how criterion-referenced tests should be defined—and what they should be called.

Hambleton (1990) has reported that since Glaser's seminal paper in 1963, more than 800 articles on criterion-referenced testing have been written. In current practice, criterion-referenced tests are also referred to as "proficiency tests," "mastery tests," "objective-referenced tests," "competency tests," and "basic skills tests." Gray (1978) cited 57 definitions of criterion-referenced measurement and asserted that, despite Glaser's (1963) straightforward description of criterion-referenced measurement, confusion existed as to what such measurement involved. Using Glaser's (1963) original notion of an "achievement continuum" along which the objectives of interest can be placed, and Popham's (1973) assertion that most criterion-referenced measurement specialists advocated referencing test scores to a "domain" of learner behaviors, as two important perspectives on criterion-referenced testing, Gray conducted an analysis of the definitions of criterion-referenced tests in the literature. This led to two primary classifications of criterion-referenced tests: "continuum" and "domain." Gray reported that about 60% of the definitions did not adhere to Glaser's original requirement that criterion-referenced tests should support measurement of the continuum of specific skills or objectives underlying achievement. Gray's finding is interesting, but the distinction between "continuum" and "domain" definitions of criterion-referenced testing is more artificial than real. Criterion-referenced testing specialists almost certainly recognize (or should) that regardless of the explicit or implicit reference to a continuum of skills or behaviors in their definition, there exists an achievement continuum on which the skills and items can be placed, and that this placement is important for sequencing instruction and interpreting test performance.

The most widely used definition of a criterion-referenced test in the field today was offered by Popham (1978a): "A criterion-referenced test is used to ascertain an individual's status with respect to a well-defined behavioral domain" (p. 93). Several points about Popham's definition require elaboration. First, terms such as "objectives," "competencies," and "skills" can be used interchangeably with the term "behavioral domain." Second, the need for *well-defined* behavioral domains or (equivalently) objectives cannot be overemphasized. Item validity and test score interpretations are improved when the objectives are well defined, because the content or behavioral domains to

which the test scores are referenced can be more clearly identified. Popham (1984) stated that a criterion-referenced test must "unambiguously describe just what it's measuring" (p. 29) if it is to offer any measurement advantages over a norm-referenced test. The breadth and complexity of the behavioral or content domain defining an objective are not limited, however; rather, the intended purpose of the test will influence the breadth, nature, and complexity of the behavioral domains. Diagnostic tests of specific reading or arithmetic skills will typically be organized around more narrowly defined objectives than will year-end assessments designed to measure student achievement within the broader domains of the curriculum. For example, diagnostic tests may provide a basis for assessing reading skills such as identifying the main idea of a passage, or determining the meaning of words from the context in which they are used. On the other hand, year-end reading tests, which are not intended for use in diagnosis, may cover broader objectives such as reading comprehension, vocabulary, and study skills.

Third, a criterion-referenced test can (and often will) measure more than a single objective. When the test assesses student performance on multiple objectives, test items can be (and usually are) organized into nonoverlapping subtests that correspond to the objectives assessed in the test. Student performance on the test can be reported for each objective. Fourth, Popham's definition of a criterion-referenced test does not refer to a cutoff score or standard. Minimum standards of performance, "cutoffs," are commonly established for each objective, but this need not be the case. For example, a student may be said to have "mastered" the skill of single-digit plus single-digit addition when performance exceeds the (say) 90% standard. In this use of the score, a cutoff score is needed. However, the student's performance can be descriptively interpreted by stating that "Student A correctly answered 95% of the single-digit addition problems on the test and therefore can be estimated to handle about 95% of the test items that make up the domain of items measuring the objective." In this latter interpretation, there is no reference to a standard or cutoff score. One interpretation may be more appropriate than the other in a given situation. Clearly, the decision to use a cutoff score or a descriptive interpretation will depend on the purpose of the test. The fact that criterion-referenced tests do not always require a standard may surprise people who have confused the word "criterion" in criterion-referenced test with a "standard" or "cutoff score." Glaser's (1963) definition of a criterion-referenced test used the word "criterion" to refer to the domain of content or behaviors to which test scores are referenced, not to the more traditional psychometric interpretation of "criterion" as a standard or cutoff score.

Two additional points about criterion-referenced tests are also important, according to Hambleton (1985, 1990). First, the number of items measuring each objective and the cutoff score, will, in general, vary from one objective to the next. Second, mastery–nonmastery decisions commonly involve the comparison of a student's percentage (or proportion correct) scores with the corresponding cutoff score for the relevant objective. In the simplest decision-making approach, a student with a percentage score equal to or greater than the cutoff score is assumed to be a "master" of the content or behaviors assessed; otherwise, the student is assumed to be a "nonmaster." More complicated models for decision making, which consider the relative seriousness of different decision errors, are reviewed by van der Linden (1980).

In sum, there is no "rule book" that (1) prescribes the optimal number of test items/objectives, number of objectives in a test, or item format; (2) requires a common cutoff score across objectives; or even (3) describes how mastery–nonmastery decisions are made. These test specifications are set to accommodate the needs of the testing program and its practical constraints (such as limits on the available testing time). What are not optional for valid criterion-referenced testing, however, are the existence of a set of clearly defined objectives and a statement of the intended uses of the test scores. Within the framework provided by these two requirements, tremendous scope exists for the construction and use of tests to assess students' performance in relation to a body of content.

NORM-REFERENCED TESTS VERSUS CRITERION-REFERENCED TESTS

The development of criterion-referenced testing methods and the recognition of their differences from norm-referenced testing took place relatively quickly following the appearance of Glaser's (1963) article. In fact, a well-developed set of technical guidelines for test development, evaluation, and uses was ready for widespread use by the late 1970s, though setting cutoff scores still remains an unsolved problem for measurement specialists (see, e.g., the special issue of *Applied Psychological Measurement*, edited by R. K. Hambleton, in 1980). These developments were aided considerably by the Popham and Husek (1969) paper, which addressed the practical implications of constructing criterion-referenced tests. From a purely practical perspective, criterion-referenced tests, because of their design, are intended to provide information about the specific skills and behaviors a student has or has not mastered (i.e., what he or she can and cannot do). Norm-referenced tests, on the other hand, provide information about a student's behavior in relation to that of other students. Scores are often reported using percentiles, stanines, grade equivalents, or standard scores. Both norm-referenced data and criterion-referenced data are important, but for different purposes, and each is best obtained from a test that has specifically been constructed to provide the desired information.

Norm-referenced measurement and criterion-referenced measurement are not mutually exclusive concepts. A criterion-referenced test provides a basis for making norm-referenced measurements, although the opposite is less likely. This is because many objectives of interest may not be assessed in a norm-referenced test, and those that are can typically be assessed with only an item or two. Because the two types of tests use similar types of directions, draw upon the same item formats, and require the same types of cognitive processing on the part of examinees, it is not usually possible to distinguish one type of test from the other simply by looking at them. The differences between the two tests are significant, however, and they are more than just the way in which their scores are interpreted, as some authors suggest.

There are four substantive differences between norm-referenced tests and criterion-referenced tests. Hambleton (1985) categorizes these as (1) test purpose, (2) content specificity, (3) test development, and (4) test score generalizability. The difference in purpose between norm-referenced and criterion-referenced tests can be characterized as "the basic distinction" (Popham & Husek, 1969). Norm-referenced tests are designed and constructed to provide a basis for making comparisons among students in the content area(s) measured by the test. Test norms are generally used as the standard of comparison. Since the number of items used to assess student performance on specific objectives is small, and therefore of limited practical value, criterion-referenced test score interpretations made from norm-referenced tests generally have limited validity and reliability. Criterion-referenced tests, in contrast, are constructed to facilitate a sharper interpretation of student performance in relation to the set of objectives covered by the test. Scores can be used to (1) describe student performance, (2) make mastery–nonmastery decisions, or (3) evaluate program effectiveness. Just as criterion-referenced interpretations can be made on the basis of norm-referenced tests, norm-referenced interpretations may be made from criterion-referenced tests. However, comparisons of students based on criterion-referenced test scores are unstable (unreliable) when test scores are relatively homogeneous, as they may be before or following instruction on the objectives measured in the test.

The second difference is concerned with test construction. Construction of both norm-referenced and criterion-referenced tests begins with the development of test blueprints or specifications that define the content, characteristics, and intent of the test. Although norm-referenced tests can utilize objectives to define and limit the intended content domain, the use of well-defined objectives is central to the development of a good criterion-referenced test. Popham (1984) has suggested that one way to rigorously define the item domain for each objec-

tive measured in a criterion-referenced test would involve specifying four aspects: (1) description, (2) sample test item, (3) content description, and (4) response description. Stringent adherence to domain or item specifications is essential in constructing criterion-referenced tests, because the resulting scores are referenced back to the item specifications at the interpretation stage. Clear "targets" for test score interpretations are essential with criterion-referenced tests.

The third difference between norm-referenced and criterion-referenced tests is in the area of test development. Norm-referenced tests are designed to "spread students out" so as to increase the stability of the students' rankings. To accomplish this, norm-referenced test score variance must be increased; this is accomplished by selecting items of moderate difficulty (item difficulty levels of .30 to .70) and high discriminating power (point biserial correlations of over .30). In general, the increased score variability of norm-referenced tests will improve test validity and reliability, but can also result in tests' failing to contain the items that "tap" the central concepts of a particular area of achievement (Popham, 1973, 1978a). For a full review of norm-referenced test development methods, readers are referred to Linn (1989). Criterion-referenced test interpretations, on the other hand, do not depend on score comparisons among students. Criterion-referenced test scores are interpreted "directly" by referencing scores to the appropriate domains of content (Hambleton, 1985). Test item pools are formed by preparing items that conform to test specifications and measure the objectives. Items that do not meet content specifications, that are poorly written, or that item statistics suggest are flawed are removed from the item pool at the outset.

The fourth major difference is score generalizability. Norm-referenced performance is interpreted best in relation to a "norm" group. It is of limited value and is rarely appropriate to generalize student performance to a body of content, because of the way in which test items are selected for inclusion in a norm-referenced test. By contrast, test score generalization is a valuable attribute of criterion-referenced measurement. Because student performance on a specific set of test items is rarely of interest, and because items can be matched to domains of content, test score generalizations beyond the specific items on a test can be made to the larger domains of content measuring each objective assessed by a criterion-referenced test. For example, the criterion-referenced performance of a student who can successfully identify the main idea of paragraphs taken from a fourth-grade basal reader can be generalized to the student's ability to identify the main idea in all other material covered by the item specifications that define the item pool for the objective.

It should be kept in mind that methods of developing norm-referenced and criterion-referenced tests are different, and that the tests provide users with different types of information. Each type of test has purposes for which it is more appropriately suited than the other. For further discussion of the differences between norm-referenced and criterion-referenced tests, see Ebel (1978), Popham (1978b), Popham and Husek (1969), or Hambleton (1990); for further discussion of definitions of criterion-referenced tests, see Nitko (1980).

TEST CONSTRUCTION

Criterion-referenced tests are constructed to support valid generalizations about individual students' performance in relation to specified domains of content or behavior (Glaser & Nitko, 1971). The validity of the interpretations and decisions made about student performance is increased when the test embodies a representative sample of domain tasks. To support these particular inferences, significant differences exist between the ways in which norm- and criterion-referenced tests are constructed. The differences are reflected in the information required for the test blueprint, item preparation methods, and item selection procedures. In this section, these differences are explained; 12 steps for preparing criterion-referenced tests are presented; and various item formats are discussed that may be used by test developers.

Item Specifications

Hambleton (1985) cites four purposes for domain specifications, or item specifications, as they are sometimes called. First, domain specifications provide item writers with content and technical guidelines for preparing test items. Item congruence with domain specifications is essential for the preparation of valid test items. Second, they provide content and measurement specialists with a clear description of the content and/or behaviors outlined by the objectives. Third, when the skills and/or behaviors of the objectives are matched with actual test items, the validity of interpretations of student performance is enhanced. Finally, domain specifications clearly specify the breadth and scope of the objectives. Both Hambleton (1985) and Popham (1978a, 1984) have emphasized that behavioral objectives alone are not adequately detailed to serve as item specifications. Although they are easy to write and are familiar elements of many school curricula, behavioral objectives allow too much latitude in item writing and test interpretation to be used without the increased information included in domain or item specifications.

Item specifications can be divided into four parts (Popham, 1984):

1. *Description:* A concise statement about the content and/or behaviors comprising the objective (which often reads like a description of a behavioral objective).

2. *Directions and sample test item:* More or less self-explanatory. This part guides the item-writing process and provides the user with a quick idea about the nature of the items in the domain.

3. *Content limits:* A detailed description of the content and/or behaviors measured by the objective and the item pool. The specificity and clarity of this section should allow item reviewers to separate items that meet domain specifications from those that do not. In some instances, this process may be facilitated by detailing what content or behaviors are *not* included in the description.

4. *Response limits:* A description of the types of incorrect answers that need to be prepared when multiple-choice items are used, or the guidelines for scoring "constructed" responses, or scoring criteria for performance tasks. The structure and content of incorrect answers (distractors) or scoring criteria for constructed or performance tasks should be stated in as much detail as possible.

General description

Examinee will be able to apply Ohm's law in various word problems.

Directions and sample test item

Directions: Read the word problem below and answer it by circling the correct answer. All the answer choices have been rounded to the first decimal place.

Test item: A current of 4.2 amperes flows through a coil whose resistance is 1.4 ohms. What is the potential difference applied at the ends of the coil?

    a. 0.3 volts   b. 3.0 volts   c. 5.6 volts   d. 5.9 volts

Content limits

1. All problems will be similar to but different from the ones presented in classroom instruction.

2. The examinees will not be told in the directions to use Ohm's law, nor should they be given the mathematical formula.

3. The directions will specify how the answers have been rounded off.

4. The examinee can be asked to calculate *any* of the variables in Ohm's law.

5. The variables given in the word problem will always have correct units and contain a decimal form (e.g., 2.5 volts, not $2\frac{1}{2}$).

Response limits

1. Answer choices will be placed in a numerical sequence from smallest to largest number.

2. The incorrect answer choices will be of the correct unit and in a decimal form.

3. The alternatives will include the correct answer and three plausible distractors:

Calculating current

Correct answer: $\dfrac{\text{voltage}}{\text{resistance}}$

Plausible distractors: $\dfrac{\text{resistance}}{\text{voltage}}$, resistance × voltage,

resistance + voltage

Calculating voltage:

Correct answer: current × resistance

Plausible distractors: $\dfrac{\text{current}}{\text{resistance}}$, $\dfrac{\text{resistance}}{\text{current}}$

resistance + current

Calculating resistance:

Correct answer: $\dfrac{\text{voltage}}{\text{current}}$

$\dfrac{\text{current}}{\text{voltage}}$, current × voltage,

current + voltage

FIGURE 18.1. A sample domain specification in the electronics field (prepared by Ronald K. Hambleton and Linda Murray).

Specification of the domain of the content of behaviors defining the objectives covered in a test can proceed using the components and procedures suggested by Hambleton (1985) or Popham (1984). A sample domain specification is given in Figure 18.1. The mechanism through which the objectives are identified, however, will vary from one application to the next. For example, Popham and Rankin (1981) described the development of the Detroit Public Schools' High School Proficiency Program, and Ogle and Fritts (1981) described the development of criterion-referenced reading tests for the Skokie, Illinois public schools. The Detroit project involved teachers, administrators, parents, community representatives, and students in a review of school curricula and the identification of a small set of important broad objectives. The objectives developed for the Skokie reading tests were the result of a cooperative effort between college reading faculty and school district teachers, who divided the reading curriculum into content strands and difficulty levels congruent with the curriculum's scope and sequence. In both cases, the objectives were reviewed and revised before item specifications were written.

Similarly, the goals of a handicapped student's individualized education program (IEP) are usually developed in a meeting between the student's parents and his or her teachers. These goals (and the objectives that help define them) represent the IEP's basis for obtaining criterion-referenced tests of the student's academic and/or behavioral gains.

Twelve Steps for Preparing a Criterion-Referenced Test

Twelve steps for preparing a criterion-referenced test are offered below. The intended purposes of the test and its resulting scores will dictate the degree of attention to detail and thoroughness with which these steps are carried out. A classroom or special education teacher developing a test to assess students' acquisition of multiplication facts may complete only several of the steps. On the other hand, a school district preparing a high school graduation exam, a state department of education preparing minimum-competency tests, or a certifying board preparing an exam will complete *all* of the steps with considerable attention to detail.

The steps are as follows:

1. Preliminary considerations
   a. Specify test purposes and describe objectives.
   b. Specify groups to be measured, special testing requirements resulting from student age, race, sex, socioeconomic status, linguistic differences, handicaps, and so on.
   c. Determine time and financial resources available for test production.
   d. Identify and select qualified staff (note individual strengths and role in test development).
   e. Specify an initial estimate of test length (include number of objectives and items, as well as approximate time requirements).
2. Review of objectives
   a. Review the descriptions of the objectives to determine their acceptability.
   b. Select final group of objectives to be measured by the test.
   c. Prepare item specifications for each objective and review them for completeness, accuracy, clarity, and practicality.
3. Item writing
   a. Draft a sufficient number of items for pilot testing.
   b. Carry out item editing.
4. Assessment of content validity
   a. Identify a sufficient pool of judges and measurement specialists.
   b. Review the test items to determine their match to the objectives, their representativeness, and their freedom from bias and stereotyping.
   c. Review the test items to determine their technical adequacy.
5. Revisions to test items
   a. Based upon data from steps 4b and 4c, revise test items (when possible and necessary) or delete them.
   b. Write additional test items (if needed) and repeat step 4.
6. Field test administration
   a. Organize the test items into forms for pilot testing.
   b. Administer the test forms to appropriately chosen groups of examinees.
   c. Conduct item analyses and item bias studies.
7. Revisions to test items
   a. Revise test items when necessary or delete them, using the results from step 6c.
8. Test assembly
   a. Determine the test length, the number of forms needed, and the number of items per objective.

b. Select test items from available pool of valid test items.

c. Prepare test directions, practice questions, test booklet layout, scoring keys, answer sheets, and so on.

d. Specify modifications to instructions, medium of presentation or student response, and time requirements that may be necessary for students with special needs.

9. Selection of a standard

a. Determine if a standard is needed to accomplish the test purpose.

b. Initiate (and document) a process to determine the standard to separate "masters" and "nonmasters."

c. Specify considerations that may affect the standard when applied to handicapped students (i.e., alternative administration or modification to accommodate students with special needs).

d. Identify "alternative" test score interpretations for students requiring modified administration.

10. Pilot test administration

a. Design the test administration to collect score reliability and validity information.

b. Administer the test form(s) to appropriately chosen groups of examinees.

c. Identify and evaluate administration modifications to meet individual special needs that may affect validity and reliability of tests.

d. Evaluate the test administration procedures, test items, and score reliability and validity.

e. Make final revisions based on the available technical data.

11. Preparation of manuals

a. Prepare a test administrator's manual.

b. Prepare a technical manual.

12. Additional technical data collection

a. Conduct reliability and validity investigations.

A few brief remarks on each of the test development steps follow:

1. Step 1 insures that a test development project is well organized. The early articula-tion of test purpose(s) and factors that might affect test quality will help manage resources. Also, identifying special groups (e.g., handicapped students) insures that when the test is administered, it will measure students' achievement rather than reflecting their special needs.

2. Domain specifications are invaluable to item writers when they are well done. Considerable time and money can be saved later in revising test items if item writers are clear about their tasks.

3. Some training of item writers in the proper use of domain (or item) specifications and in the principles of item writing is often desirable, particularly if novel item formats are to be included in the test.

4. Step 4 is essential. Items are evaluated by reviewers to assess their match to the objectives, their technical quality, and their freedom from bias and stereotyping.

5. Any necessary revisions to test items should be made at step 5; when additional test items are needed, they should be written, and step 4 repeated.

6. The test items are organized into booklets and administered to a sample of examinees like those for whom the test is intended. (The desirable sample size will depend on the importance of the test.) Necessary revisions to test items can be made at this stage. Item statistics are used to identify items that may need revision.

7. Whenever possible, malfunctioning test items should be revised and added to the pools of acceptable test items. When substantial revisions are made to an item, it should be placed again at step 4.

8. Final test booklets are compiled at this step. When parallel forms are required, and especially if the tests are short, item statistics should be used to insure that matched forms are produced.

9. A standard-setting procedure must be selected, implemented, and documented. If a description of student performance is used in place of or as a supplement to a standard, its interpretability and relation to the test's purpose should be explained.

10. Test directions must be evaluated, scoring keys must be checked, and the reliability and validity of scores and decisions must be assessed.

11. For important tests such as those used

for awarding high school diplomas, a test administration manual and a technical manual should be prepared.

12. No matter how carefully a test is constructed or evaluated initially, reliability and validity studies must be carried out on an on-going basis.

Item Generation and Item Format

Perhaps the most critical task in criterion-referenced test construction, following the preparation of domain (or item) specifications, is generating test items that measure the objectives while conforming to the constraints outlined in the domain specifications. Specifying relevant student skills and behaviors in the domain specifications will facilitate the item-writing process. Nevertheless, translating specific tasks into test items that conform to the objectives and allow teachers to make valid diagnostic or mastery interpretations about student performance is a difficult process. The difference of purpose between criterion- and norm-referenced tests renders many traditional psychometric item analysis and item selection measures inappropriate for criterion-referenced test construction. For example, norm-referenced test developers can utilize statistics such as item difficulty and item discrimination indices in order to select effective items (i.e., those that contribute to test score variability). Criterion-referenced test developers, on the other hand, should rely less on these measures and should select items on the basis of their ability to assess student knowledge or instructional effectiveness (see, e.g., Hambleton, 1985). Therefore, construction and selection of criterion-referenced test items rely heavily on domain specifications and the ability of item writers to construct valid items.

The most widely used criterion-referenced test item format is the multiple-choice question. This format is familiar to item writers, and the features required of a "good" multiple-choice question are well known to test developers (e.g., Bloom, Madaus, & Hastings, 1981; Roid & Haladyna, 1982). Gulliksen (1986) and Carlson (1985), however, have offered useful examples of and insights into alternative item formats that, although not necessarily new, are infrequently used.

These alternative formats include the following:

- Matching
- Master list or keylist
- Tabular format or matrix
- Best–worst answer
- Greater–less–same or before–after–same
- Rank order
- Question and short answer
- Statement and comment
- Experiment–results
- Experiment–results–interpretation

Gulliksen (1986) and Carlson (1985) suggest that expanding the array of item formats used in tests may promote more accurate measurement and interpretation of student performance. The variation of item formats is a mechanism for refining the specificity of information about the objectives test items can access. Carlson (1985) has also pointed out that some item formats are more suitable than others for assessing particular areas of achievement and cognitive levels of objectives. For example, a knowledge-level objective may be measured using a matching item, whereas an experiment–results–interpretation item format may produce better inferential information for an objective at the analysis level of Bloom et al.'s (1956) taxonomy of cognitive abilities.

Test developers should select item formats that best assess the skills or behaviors involved in the objectives measured by the test, and should follow the test construction steps provided above. Despite the widespread use of the multiple-choice item format, other formats are often desirable and may be necessary for the valid assessment of some objectives of interest. Appropriate attention to detail and adherence to item specifications during test construction will insure that the test validly samples the test domain and permits meaningful generalizations about student performance. Item validity is, therefore, a critical consideration in test construction, selection of item formats, and determination of the test's overall validity. Item validity requires consideration of three item characteristics: (1) item–objective congruence (the degree to which a particular item specifically measures some facet of the content included in the domain specification); (2) technical quality of the item; and (3) item bias (Hambleton, 1985). Hambleton (1984) has provided an easy-to-use "item content review form" for rating test items on these three points.

PSYCHOMETRIC CHARACTERISTICS OF CRITERION-REFERENCED TEST SCORES

Reliability Issues and Methods

We have noted earlier that criterion-referenced test scores are used principally in two ways: (1) to describe students and/or (2) to make mastery–nonmastery decisions. With the first use, of interest is the precision with which domain scores are estimated. Of interest with the second use is the test–retest decision consistency or parallel-form decision consistency. Decisions are of limited value if it cannot be documented that they remain consistent over parallel-form administrations of a test or over test–retest administrations.

It should be clear that the usual approaches to assessing the reliability of norm-referenced test scores (test–retest reliability, parallel-form reliability, and corrected split-half reliability) do not address directly either of these uses of criterion-referenced test scores; therefore, they are of limited value in the context of criterion-referenced measurement (Hambleton & Novick, 1973). It has been argued that classical reliability indices are not useful with criterion-referenced tests because the scores often are fairly homogeneous, and so classical reliability indices will be low. But this is not the real problem. If low reliability indices were the problem, the difficulty could be resolved by interpreting the indices more cautiously in light of homogeneous test score distributions or by designing reliability studies to insure more heterogeneous score distributions. Actually, norm-referenced test reliability indices are not useful with criterion-referenced test scores because they fail to provide the needed information about score and decision consistency.

The reliability topic has probably received more attention from psychometricians than any other in the criterion-referenced testing field. The interested reader is referred to Berk (1980, 1984a) for reviews. A few of the more practical contributions to the topic are considered next.

Reliability of Domain Score Estimates

The standard error of measurement associated with domain score estimates (proportion-correct scores) can easily be calculated. It is useful in setting up confidence bands for examinees' domain scores. Fortunately, it is not influenced to any considerable extent by the homogeneity of examinees' domain scores (Lord & Novick, 1968). One disadvantage is that a constant level of error is assumed across the full range of test scores.

Another approach to determining the accuracy of domain score estimates was reported by Millman (1974). He suggested that the standard error of estimation derived from the binomial test model given by the expression $\sqrt{\hat{\pi}(1-\hat{\pi})/n}$ could be used to set up confidence bands around domain score estimates. In this expression, n is the number of items measuring the objective and $\hat{\pi}$ is the proportion-correct score for the examinee on the set of items measuring the objective. Variations on the binomial error model have been described by Berk (1980).

Reliability of Mastery Classifications

Hambleton and Novick (1973) suggested that the reliability of mastery classification decisions should be defined in terms of the consistency of decisions from two administrations of the same test or parallel forms of a test. Let us suppose that two examinees are to be classified into mastery states (e.g., "mastery" vs. "nonmastery" or achievement levels, denoted A, B, C, D, and F). Hambleton and Novick suggested the formula below to measure the proportion of examinees who are consistently classified on the two administrations:

$$p_o = \sum_{j=1}^{m} p_{jj}$$

where p_{jj} is the proportion of examinees classified in the jth mastery state on the two administrations and m is the number of mastery states. In practice, m is usually equal to 2. The index p_o is the observed proportion of decisions that are in agreement. Among the factors affecting the value of p_o are test length, quality of test items, choice of cutoff score, group heterogeneity, and the closeness of the group mean performance to the cutoff score. The p_o statistic has considerable appeal and is easy to calculate. For important tests, such as those used for awarding high school diplomas or licenses to practice in a profession, a level of decision consistency over 90% seems desirable. Decision consistency levels between 70% and 90% seem acceptable for teacher-devised or commercially prepared criterion-referenced tests that are used to monitor students on a day-to-day basis (see, e.g., Subkoviak, 1988).

The concept of "decision consistency" is a useful one with criterion-referenced tests, but the approach described above requires the administration of a single test twice, or the administration of parallel forms of a test. In both cases, testing time is doubled. This approach is often difficult to implement in practice because of limited testing time. One way to avoid the need for extra time in assessing reliability with norm-referenced tests involves, first, using the split-half method to determine the reliability of scores from a test half as long as the one of interest. Next, the Spearman–Brown formula is used along with the split-half reliability estimate to predict the reliability of scores with the test of interest. Unfortunately, this approach cannot be applied to the problem of assessing consistency of decisions emanating from a single administration of a criterion-referenced test, because there is no "step-up formula" analogous to the Spearman–Brown formula. A different approach for estimating decision consistency from a single administration was developed by Subkoviak (1976). Although the mathematical development of the formula is not comparable, Subkoviak's formula and a more complicated one by Huynh (1976) are the analogues of the corrected split-half reliability index, which is used with norm-referenced tests to estimate parallel-form reliability from a single test administration.

Validity Issues and Methods

Although many contributions to the criterion-referenced testing literature have been made since the late 1960s (for reviews, see Hambleton, 1984; Hambleton, Swami-

nathan, Algina, & Coulson, 1978; Millman, 1974; Popham, 1978a), the important topic of criterion-referenced test score validity has received only limited attention from researchers. Very often, measurement specialists have assumed the validity of criterion-referenced test scores instead of making a concerted effort to establish the validity of the scores in any formal way. The argument seems to be that, if the appropriate test development steps are carried out, a valid criterion-referenced test will necessarily result. But the validity of the resulting scores will depend on their intended use in addition to the care with which the test was constructed. A review of 12 commercially prepared criterion-referenced tests was conducted by Hambleton and Eignor (1978). Not one of the test manuals reviewed included a discussion of what Hambleton and Eignor felt was a satisfactory test score validity investigation. Evidence that the items matched the objectives was the only evidence publishers reported concerning test score validity. No evidence of the accuracy of the domain scores or of the "mastery" and "nonmastery" classifications was presented.

Fortunately, there are now a number of signs that the situation is changing. First, several publications are now available to describe the nature of the validity questions and how they should be approached (Fitzpatrick, 1983; Hambleton, 1984; Kane, 1982; Linn, 1979, 1980; Madaus, 1983; Messick, 1989). Also, there are several exemplary validity studies in the literature (Kirsch & Guthrie, 1980; Ward, Frederiksen, & Carlson, 1980).

Many developers of criterion-referenced tests have argued that in order to "validate" their tests and test scores, it is sufficient to assess "content validity." Usually judgments are obtained from persons with content expertise concerning the match between test content and the objectives a test is designed to measure. Since these judgments focus on test content, the expression "content validity" is used to describe the nature of the activities carried out by the content specialists; however, it should be clear that content validity refers to certain characteristics of the test content. The content validity of a test does not vary from one sample of examinees to the next, nor does the content validity of a test vary over time. However, any use of a test (whether norm-referenced or criterion-referenced) is ultimately dependent on the scores obtained from a test administration, and the validity of the scores depends upon many factors (particularly the intended use of the scores) in addition to test content. It is possible that examinees' item responses and resulting test scores do not adequately reflect or address the skills of interest, even though the test itself is judged to be content-valid.

Fortunately, a wide assortment of methods can be used to gather validity evidence relevant to the intended uses of a set of test scores:

1. *Intraobjective methods* include item analyses, the evaluation of test content (determination of item and content validity), and score reliability.
2. *Interobjective methods* include what are often called "convergent" and "divergent" validity studies—studies to determine whether test scores correlate with variables they might reasonably be expected to relate to, and studies to determine whether test scores are uncorrelated with variables they should not be related to.
3. *Criterion-related methods* include prediction studies and studies of the relationships between test scores and mastery classifications, on the one hand, and independent measures of performance (such as those that might be obtained from teachers, instructors, or supervisors), on the other.
4. *Experimental methods* include determining the sensitivity of test scores and mastery classifications to the effects of instruction on test content.
5. *Multitrait–multimethod studies* address what it is that a test actually measures.

Accumulating validation evidence is a never-ending process. The amount of time and energy that should be expended on the validation of test scores and mastery classifications must be directly related to the importance of the testing program. Criterion-referenced tests used to monitor student progress in a curriculum on a day-to-day basis demand less attention and fewer resources, obviously, than tests used to determine whether or not students graduate

from high school or tests used to certify or license professionals (e.g., physicians, dentists, insurance salespersons, and environmental health specialists).

In the brief section that follows, several validity investigations that are unique to criterion-referenced tests are described.

Construct Validity Investigations

Construct validation studies have not been common in criterion-referenced measurement. This may be because criterion-referenced test score distributions are often homogeneous (e.g., it often happens that before instruction most individuals do poorly on a test, and after instruction most individuals do well). Correlational methods do not work well with homogeneous score distributions because of problems due to score range restrictions. But, as Messick (1975) has noted, "Construct validation is by no means limited to correlation coefficients, even though it may seem that way from the prevalence of correlation matrices, internal consistency indices, and factor analysis" (p. 958).

Construct validation studies begin with a definite statement of the proposed use of the test scores. A clearly stated use will provide direction for the kind of evidence that is worth collecting. Some of the investigations that can be undertaken to estimate the construct validity of a set of criterion-referenced test scores are described next.

Guttman Scalogram Analysis. It frequently occurs that objectives can be arranged linearly or hierarchically on the basis of a logical analysis. Guttman scaling is a relevant procedure for the construct validation of criterion-referenced test scores in situations where the objectives can be organized into either a linear or a hierarchical sequence. To use Guttman scalogram analysis as a technique in a test score validation methodology, one first needs to specify the hierarchical structure of a set of objectives. To the extent that examinees' mastery–nonmastery status on the objectives in the hierarchy is predictable from a knowledge of the hierarchy, one has evidence to support the construct validity of the objective scores. For example, examinees who fail an objective located in the middle of a learning hierarchy of objectives would be expected (predicted) to fail all objectives located at higher levels in the hierarchy. If they do, support for the validity of the tests used to make the mastery–nonmastery decisions is available. If they do not, then either the test leads to invalid classifications of examinees, or the hierarchy is invalid, or both the test *and* the hierarchy have questionable validity. In sum, in situations where examinees' mastery–nonmastery status is not predictable, one of three situations has occurred: The hierarchy is incorrectly specified, the objective scores are not valid measures of the intended objectives, or a combination of the two explanations is true.

Factor Analysis. Factor analysis is commonly employed for the dimensional analysis of items in a norm-referenced test, or of scores derived from different norm-referenced tests, but it is seldom used in construct validation studies of criterion-referenced test scores. One reason for its lack of use is that the usual input data for factor-analytic studies are correlations, and correlations are often low between items on a criterion-referenced test or between criterion-referenced test scores and other variables because score variability is often not very great. Also, interitem correlations are often low because of the unreliability of item scores. However, the problem of limited score variability can be reduced to some extent by choosing a heterogeneous sample of examinees—for example, a group including both masters and nonmasters.

The research problem becomes a problem of determining whether or not the factor pattern matrix has a prescribed form. The prescribed form is set by the researchers and is based upon a logical analysis of the objectives and other research evidence concerning the structure of the objectives measured by the test. Evidence that the estimated structure among the variables matches the prescribed form will support both the research hypotheses and the validity of the scores as measures of the desired variables.

Experimental Studies. There are many sources of error that reduce the validity of an intended use of a set of criterion-referenced test scores—for example, clarity of test directions, speededness of the test, level of motivation, and so on. Experimental studies of potential sources of error to determine their effects on test scores are an important method of assessing the construct validity of a set of test scores. Logical analysis and observations of testing methods and procedures can also be used to detect sources of invalidity in a set of test scores.

Multitrait–Multimethod Approach. The category of construct validation also includes "multitrait–multimethod" validation of objective scores (Campbell & Fiske, 1959). Multitrait–multimethod validation includes any techniques addressing the question of how much examinees' responses to items reflect the "trait" (objective) of interest, and how much they reflect methodological effects.

Criterion-Related Validity Investigations

Even if scores derived from criterion-referenced tests are descriptive of the objectives they are supposed to reflect, the usefulness of the scores as predictors of, say, "job success" or "success in the next unit of instruction" cannot be insured. Criterion-related validity studies of criterion-referenced test scores do not differ in procedure from studies conducted with norm-referenced tests. Correlational, group separation, and decision accuracy methods are commonly used (Messick, 1989). Also, selection of reasonable and practical criterion measures that do *not* themselves require extensive validation efforts remains as serious a problem for conducting validation studies with criterion-referenced tests as it is for norm-referenced tests. There are, however, two important differences: First, test scores are usually dichotomized (examinees above a cutoff score are described as masters, and those below it are described as nonmasters. Second, and related to the first, readily interpretable validity indices reflecting the agreement between decisions based on the test and an external dichotomous criterion measure are reported, instead of correlational measures (which are commonly reported in criterion-related validity investigations with norm-referenced tests).

Criterion-referenced test scores are commonly used to make decisions. In instructional settings, an examinee is assumed to be a master when his or her test performance exceeds a minimum level of performance. Decision validity, which is simply a particular kind of criterion-related validity, involves (1) setting a standard of test performance, and (2) comparing the test performance of two or more criterion groups in relation to the specified standard.

One advantage of decision validity studies is that the results can be reported in a readily interpretable way (percentage of correct decisions). Alternatively, the correlation between two dichotomous variables (group membership and the mastery decision) can be reported and used as an index of decision validity. Other possible statistics are reported by Hambleton (1984) and Popham (1978a). Finally, the validity of a set of decisions will depend on several important factors: (1) the quality of the test under investigation, (2) the appropriateness and size of the criterion groups, (3) the characteristics of the examinee sample, and (4) the minimum level of performance required for mastery. All four factors will have an impact on decision validity. Clearly, since a number of factors substantially influence the level of decision validity, it must be clearly recognized that what is being described through a summary statistic of interest is *not* the test itself, but the *use* of the test in a particular way with a specified group of examinees. The same point applies equally well to interpreting norm-referenced reliability and validity indices.

APPLICATIONS

Setting of Standards

One of the two primary purposes of criterion-referenced testing is to make decisions about individuals. This requires a standard or cutoff score on the test score scale to separate examinees into (at least) two categories, often labeled "masters" and "nonmasters." Sometimes these decisions have major implications for examinees, such as the awarding or denying of certification or licensure. At other times, the decisions may be made at the classroom level and have implications for students that involve only a day or two of instruction. Obviously, the importance of the pending decisions is a major factor in the amount of effort that is needed to set a standard.

Many of the available standard-setting methods have been described, compared, and critiqued in the literature (see, e.g., Jaeger, 1989; Livingston & Zieky, 1982; Shepard, 1984). The methods can be organized into three categories, labeled "judgmental," "empirical," and "combination." The judgmental methods require data from judges for setting standards, or require judgments to be made about the presence of variables (e.g., guessing) that influence the setting of a standard. The empirical methods require actual test data to aid in the standard-setting process. The combination methods use both judgmental data and empirical data in the standard-setting process. Livingston and Zieky (1982) have developed helpful guidelines for applying several of the methods. A full description of the methods is not possible here; therefore, only a few of the most popular methods are highlighted.

Judgmental Methods

In judgmental methods, individual items are inspected, the level of concern being how a minimally competent person would perform on the test items. Judges are asked to assess how or to what degree an individual who could be described as minimally competent would perform on each item.

With Nedelsky's method, judges are asked to identify distractors in multiple-choice test items that they feel a minimally competent student should be able to eliminate as incorrect. The minimum passing level for that item then becomes the reciprocal of the number of remaining alternatives. It is the "chance score" on the test item for the minimally competent student. The judges proceed with each test item in a similar fashion, and on completion of the judging process, each judge sums the minimum passing levels across the test items to obtain a standard. Individual judges' standards are averaged to obtain a standard for the set of test items.

With Ebel's method, judges rate test items along two dimensions: relevance and difficulty. There are four levels of relevance in Ebel's method: essential, important, acceptable, and questionable. Ebel's method uses three levels of difficulty: easy, medium, and hard. These levels form a 3 x 4 grid. The judges are asked to do two things: (1) to locate each of the test items in the proper cell, based on their relevance and difficulty; and (2) to assign a percentage to each cell (i.e., the percentage of items in the cell that minimally qualified examinees should be able to answer). The number of test items in each cell is multiplied by the appropriate percentage (agreed upon by the judges), and the sum of all the cells, when divided by the total number of test items, yields the standard.

When using Angoff's method, which may be the most popular method in use today, judges are asked to assign a probability to each test item directly, thus circumventing the analysis of a grid or the analysis of answer choices. Each probability is to be an estimate of the likelihood of a minimally competent examinee's answering the test item correctly. Individual judges' test score standards can then be averaged to obtain a standard for the set of test items.

Empirical Methods

Two of the typical methods in this category depend upon the availability of an outside criterion, performance measure, or true ability distribution. The test itself, and the possible cut-off scores, are observed in relation to these criterion scores. An "optimal" cut-off score is then selected. For instance, Livingston's (1975) utility-based approach leads to the selection of a cut-off score that optimizes a particular utility function. Livingston has suggested the use of a set of linear or semilinear utility functions in viewing the effects of decision-making accuracy based upon a particular cut-off score. A cut-off score is selected to maximize the utility function.

On the other hand, a method by van der Linden and Mellenbergh (1977) leads to the selection of a cut-off score that minimizes "expected losses." A test score is used to classify examinees into two categories: masters and non-masters. Also, an external criterion, specified in advance, is used to dichotomize the candidate population into "successes" and "failures." Then the expected loss (the quality to be minimized) is specified, and the cut-off score that minimizes expected losses over the sample of candidates is chosen. Essentially, expected losses occur when candidates who score high on the external criterion ("successes") are failed on the test, or when low-scoring candidates ("failures") on the external criterion are passed on

the test. The goal then is to choose a cut-off score that minimizes the expected losses.

Combination Methods

With combination methods, judgments are made about the mastery status of a sample group of examinees from the population of interest. Choice of method determines the nature of the required judgments. Next, one or more groups for whom mastery determinations have been made are administered the test.

The borderline-group method requires that judges first define what they would envision as minimally acceptable performance on the content area being assessed. The judges are then asked to submit a list of students whose performances would be so close to the borderline that they could not be reliably classified as masters or nonmasters. The test is administered to this group, and the median test score for the group may be taken as the standard. Alternately, it may be decided to pass more or less than 50% of the minimally competent students.

With the contrasting-groups method, once judges have defined minimally acceptable performance for the content domain being assessed, the judges are asked to identify those examinees they are certain are either masters or nonmasters in relation to the specified domain of content or behaviors. The test is administered to these groups; the score distributions for the two groups on an objective-by-objective basis are then plotted, and the point of intersection is taken as the initial standard. The standard can be moved up to reduce the number of false-positive errors (examinees who are identified as masters by the test, but who have not adequately mastered the objectives) or down to reduce the number of false-negative errors (examinees who are identifed as nonmasters by the test, but who have adequately mastered the objectives). The direction in which to move the standard will depend on the relative seriousness of the two types of error. If the score distributions overlap completely, no decisions can be made reliably. The ideal situation would be one in which the two distributions do not overlap at all. The validity of this approach to standard setting depends to a great extent on the appropriateness of the judges' initial classifications of examinees.

In summary, probably the most difficult and controversial problem in criterion-referenced testing concerns setting the cutoff score or, as it is sometimes called, the standard, on the test score scale to separate masters from nonmasters. This problem has no parallel in norm-referenced testing. It is now well recognized by most criterion-referenced test users that there is no magic test score point waiting to be discovered as the standard by psychometricians. Rather, setting standards is ultimately a judgmental process that is best done by well-trained and appropriately-chosen individuals, who (1) are familiar with the test content and knowledgeable about the standard-setting method they will be expected to use; (2) have access to item performance and test score distribution data in the standard-setting process; and (3) understand the social and political context in which the tests are being used. A set of guidelines for designing and implementing a defensible standard-setting process has been prepared by Hambleton and Powell (1983).

Uses (with Emphasis on Special Education)

The usable information available from norm-referenced tests is generally limited to global inferential statements such as this: "Connie did relatively well on the Wide Range Achievement Test. Her performance places her at the 85th percentile in reading; 15% of the children in her grade scored better than she did." Although additional observational and clinical information may be gleaned from an analysis of a student's test performance, the actual test data rely heavily on the comparison made with the norm group.

Criterion-referenced scores (either on the entire test or on individual objectives), by contrast, can be used to make mastery–nonmastery decisions, to describe students' performance in relation to well-defined objectives, and/or to evaluate the effectiveness of instructional programs. Because there is a well-defined connection between the objectives and the domains of content that represent them, the skills and behaviors sampled by a criterion-referenced test allow users to easily identify the relationship between the test's specific tasks and the objectives. That is, the tasks included on a criterion-referenced test comprise a repre-sentative sample of observable behaviors from the test domain (Glaser & Nitko, 1971). This connection allows test users (1) to draw conclusions about a student's performance (e.g., "John has demonstrated mastery of the concept 'noun' by correctly underlining the noun contained in four out of five simple declarative sentences"); (2) to describe student competence (e.g., "Karyn is able to correctly perform 20 single-digit plus single-digit [sums to 18] problems in 1 minute with 95% accuracy"); or (3) to evaluate instructional efficacy (e.g., "Following 1 week of instruction, the percentage of students who were able to describe the primary functions of the human circulatory, digestive, and respiratory systems increased from 15% to 97%").

Decisions about individuals can be made from student performance on either norm- or criterion-referenced tests, though there is usually a contextual difference in which the decisions are made (Popham & Husek, 1969). In situations requiring a degree of selectivity (e.g., selecting one student "over" another for inclusion in a particular program), norm-referenced tests are generally more appropriate. Such selectivity is, for example, often a consideration in determining admission to programs for talented and gifted students or programs for the "learning-disabled." On the other hand, decisions about student performance (ascertaining that a student either has or has not mastered a particular skill) are more accurately made via the use of criterion-referenced tests. For example, a criterion-referenced test will enable a teacher to make more appropriate decisions about his or her students' abilities to differentiate the features of nominal, ordinal, interval, and ratio scales of measurement. A norm-referenced test would inform the teacher about who knew more or less than others about the topic, but would not inform him or her about how much a student knew about the subject. Student performance on the test items included in the test would indicate which students were masters of the features of scales of measurement and which students were candidates for additional instruction. With information about individual students, the teacher can make mastery–nonmastery decisions about the students' competence with the content, or, by aggregating the results, can make inferences about his or her own instructional effectiveness.

Describing students' performance on criterion-referenced tests enhances the communication of information to parents, teachers, administrators, and the students themselves. Putting aside the fact that the psychometric nature of norm-referenced test reporting is difficult for many parents and teachers to interpret meaningfully, norm-referenced performance interpretations provide only limited information about a student's ability. The student's skills are reported in relation to those of other students (i.e., the student's performance can essentially be summarized as "better than," "worse than," or "equal to" that of the norm group), but little is known about the student's "absolute" behavioral proficiency. In contrast, descriptions of proficiency in relation to a set of objectives defining the school curriculum permit users to interpret precisely what the student "can" and "cannot" do. A student who is learning the skill of multiplying fractions gets a clear idea of his or her proficiency and progress through tracking daily performance on a 10-problem criterion-referenced test. The student can compare his or her present competence with that shown in earlier efforts and can say, "Today I multiplied 8 out of 10 fractions correctly. On Monday I only got 5 right." The statement communicates success and progress to the student; indicates content and performance to parents; permits the teacher to diagnose the student's strengths and weaknesses with the skill; and helps provide direction for future instruction. Criterion-referenced tests provide a tool for integrating "testing and instruction so that test results can be used to guide learning rather than simply to identify successful students" (Nitko & Hsu, 1974).

Insuring the effectiveness of instruction is a critical feature of educational systems. Current concern with "excellence" and "accountability" in education provides the motivation—and the need—to evaluate the efficacy of instructional goals, programs, methods, and materials, particularly within special education programs. Criterion-referenced assessment of instructional efficacy allows users to define the desired outcomes of an instructional sequence, to assess students' entry levels, to implement the instructional program, and finally to measure students' proficiency with the outcome skills or behaviors. The important feature of this sequence is the user's ability to define the desired outcomes of the instructional sequence and to match them with the tasks or items included on the "pre" and "post" tests.

Although criterion-referenced tests are generally thought of as tools to collect information for formative rather than summative evaluation, this distinction is not so clearly defined. Bloom et al. (1981) have described the main purpose of formative evaluation as providing information to both the student and the teacher, with the goal of guiding the student to skill mastery. Summative evaluation, on the other hand, they describe as providing more general assessment information about what the student learns over time. Both types of evaluation can effectively employ criterion-referenced measurement when the goals of the process are making decisions about student mastery, describing student performance, or evaluating instructional effectiveness. For example, a teacher in an elementary-level special education resource room, working with children who have diverse individual needs but must for practical purposes be grouped together for skills instruction, can evaluate instructional effectiveness at weekly and semester intervals. To do so, teaching objectives are defined for each instructional group, using the curricular content (and, where appropriate, the IEP goals) of the individual children. From these instructional objectives, the skills to be taught each week are listed and items (questions) written to assess each skill. A test is administered at the beginning of each week, and a parallel form follows the week's instruction. Analysis of students' responses on the criterion-referenced tests provides information for developing and modifying materials or teacher techniques, which can also be communicated to the students' "mainstream" teachers. By evaluating each student's performance on the test items, a teacher is able to evaluate the effects of instruction and plan whether to proceed to the next step in the instructional sequence or to provide additional practice and instruction. This is formative evaluation.

Similarly, a criterion-referenced test covering the semester's instructional objectives can be administered to students at the beginning of the semester and again at the end. The "summative" information collected from this larger test, and the data obtained by comparing pre- and post-test performance, helps the teacher to evaluate long-term learning outcomes. This information can be used to report students' progress to parents, review the adequacy of IEP goals and objectives, and/or evaluate overall instructional efficacy.

The commitment of special educators to individual rather than normative assessments for planning and decision making stems from the recognition that traditional standardized assessments used for diagnosing handicapping conditions provide little useful information for describing students' strengths and weaknesses, for determining their skill mastery levels, or for making effective noncategorical instructional placement decisions. Reschly (1981) cites criterion-referenced testing as an example of changing assessment techniques that are now more widely available, better organized, and more clearly tied to specific educational objectives and materials. These tests can be used by school psychologists and others to specify academic competencies and deficits more clearly, to monitor progress in programs, and to evaluate the effects of programs. If used by school psychologists to follow up cases, especially as part of the mandated re-evaluations of classification/placement decisions, they provide a means to insure that special programs are beneficial, not dead-end and inferior.

Criterion-referenced tests are frequently included in the testing category of "informal" assessments. This misconception is unfortunate, since it carries the connotation that criterion-referenced tests are less rigorously prepared than "formal" norm-referenced tests. The validity of informal measures, such as classroom assignments, tests and quizzes, behavioral checklists and inventories, and writing or language samples, is based on their apparent congruence with classroom instructional programs (Berk, 1984b). A criterion-referenced test that accurately measures the objective(s) of an instructional program, and is constructed from an analysis of the skills or behaviors to be learned (domain specifications), will provide valuable information about individual students' learning and skill proficiency.

The closeness and precision with which criterion-referenced tests can assess student learning in relation to instructional objectives parallel special education's efforts to assess and accommodate the needs of individual learners. Inherent in the methods and techniques of criterion-referenced testing currently being promoted and expanded by special education professionals as "curriculum-based assessment" is the belief that "the essential measure of success in education is the student's progress in the curriculum of the local school" (Tucker, 1985, p. 199). In terms of criterion-referenced testing, we might say that curriculum-based tests are constructed to allow teachers to assess students' performance in relation to the objectives of local curricula (where these objectives may also be called "competencies," "tasks," "outcomes," or "responsibilities").

The assessment of student performance using the objectives and materials of local curricula serves several purposes within both special and regular education. First, when students' skills are assessed in relation to locally adopted educational objectives and curricula, it is not necessary to compare the performance of individual students with frequently inappropriate national norms. This is particularly true for special education students, whose performance on standardized tests generally places them within the unstable lower extremes of score distributions and provides them with limited opportunity to demonstrate their individual skill levels. Information provided by criterion-referenced tests of students' proficiency in local curricula, because it is focused on skills and behaviors necessary for success with the curricular outcomes toward which all district teachers and students are working, enhances the integration of individual special education students into mainstream settings. Second, by measuring and describing what students "can" do as entry levels for planning future instruction, special education takes a significant step away from the constraints of the "deficit model" of student assessment, planning, and evaluation—that is, planning special education services around what students "can't" do and viewing them as deficient learners. The use of local curricula redirects the emphasis from students' disabilities to the common goals of learning. Proficiency is therefore interpreted in relation to standards shared by all district students.

Third, a student's performance on tasks defined by a local curriculum promotes the linkage of assessment data with effective teaching approaches and curricular modifications. The adaptations and modifications required to meet individual students' needs are more easily communicated among district teachers and specialists when there is one curriculum. Together, clear district curricular objectives, criterion-referenced assessment information, and information from a student's IEP greatly enhance the ability of school psychologists and special education teachers to develop instructional recommendations for classroom implementation.

Fourth, criterion-referenced assessment of student achievement in relation to the desired outcomes of local curricula permits direct and frequent measurement of student progress, which is critical for monitoring and evaluating student growth. The administration of norm-referenced tests, which tend to measure poorly specified or overly broad content areas, at the beginning and end of the school year (or prior to IEP review) can frequently be replaced by the administration of criterion-referenced tests measuring actual learning outcomes desired by local curricula. Finally, the use of criterion-referenced tests developed from local curricula promotes the conceptualization of the IEP as a curricular map (Choate et al., 1987). The assessment of students in relation to curricular goals enables their skill proficiencies to be clearly summarized, with direct links to the materials, teaching techniques, and strategies necessary for future instruction.

SUMMARY

In this chapter, the concept underlying criterion-referenced tests has been introduced, along with the necessary steps in test development and the assessment of the psychometric properties of the test scores. Criterion-referenced testing is primarily focused on the problem of assessing individuals in relation to well-defined domains of content. These assessments may take the form of descriptions or decisions. Emphasis has been given in this chapter to the uses of criterion-referenced tests in special education. These uses seem clear and compelling.

At the present time, research is underway on (1) improving methods for setting standards, (2) reporting formats to maximize test score usefulness, and (3) developing new approaches for describing objectives. Other studies in progress that offer potential for improving criterion-referenced testing practices include research with microcomputers for storing, administering, and scoring criterion-referenced tests, and research with item response models for developing continuous growth or developmental scales to which objectives, test items, and examinees can be referenced.

REFERENCES

Berk, R. A. (1980). A consumer's guide to criterion-referenced test reliability. *Journal of Educational Measurement, 17,* 323–349.

Berk, R. A. (Ed.). (1984a). *A guide to criterion-referenced test construction.* Baltimore: Johns Hopkins University Press.

Berk, R. A. (1984b). *Screening and diagnosis of children with learning disabilities.* Springfield, IL: Charles C Thomas.

Bloom, B. S., Engelhart, M. D., Furst, E. J., Hill, W. H., & Krathwohl, D. R. (1956). *Taxonomy of educational objectives: The classification of educational goals. Handbook I: Cognitive domain.* New York: David McKay.

Bloom, B. S. Madaus, G. F., & Hastings, J. T. (1981). *Evaluation to improve learning.* New York: McGraw-Hill.

Campbell, D. T., & Fiske, D. W. (1959). Convergent and discriminant validation by the multitrait–multimethod matrix. *Psychological Bulletin, 56,* 81–105.

Carlson, S. B. (1985). *Creative classroom testing: 10 designs for assessment and instruction.* Princeton, NJ: Educational Testing Service.

Chadwick, E. (1864). Statistics of educational results. *The Museum: A Quarterly Magazine of Education, Literature and Science, 3,* 479–484.

Choate, J., Bennett, T., Enright, B., Miller, L., Poteet, J., & Rakes, T. (1987). *Assessing and programming basic curriculum skills.* Boston: Allyn & Bacon.

Ebel, R. L. (1962). Content standard test scores. *Educational and Psychological Measurement, 22,* 15–25.

Ebel, R. L. (1978). The case for norm-referenced measurements. *Educational Researcher, 7,* 3–5.

Fitzpatrick, A. R. (1983). The meaning of content validity. *Applied Psychological Measurement, 7,* 3–13.

Flanagan, J. C. (1951). Units, scores, and norms. In E. T. Lindquist (Ed.), *Educational measurement* (pp. 695–763). Washington, DC: American Council on Education.

Glaser, R. (1963). Instructional technology and the measurement of learning outcomes: Some questions. *American Psychologist, 18,* 519–521.

Glaser, R., & Klaus, D. J. (1962). Proficiency measurement: Assessing human performance. In R. Gagné (Ed.), *Psychological principles in systems development* (pp. 421–427). New York: Holt, Rinehart & Winston.

Glaser, R., & Nitko, A. J. (1971). Measurement in learning and instruction. In R. L. Thorndike (Ed.), *Educational measurement* (2nd ed., pp. 625–670). Washington, DC: American Council on Education.

Gray, W. M. (1978). A comparison of Piagetian theory and criterion-referenced measurement. *Review of Educational Research, 48*, 223–249.

Gulliksen, H. (1986). Perspective on educational measurement. *Applied Psychological Measurement, 10*, 109–132.

Hambleton, R. K. (Ed.). (1980). Contribution to criterion-referenced testing technology [Special issue]. *Applied Psychological Measurement, 4*(4), 421–581.

Hambleton, R. K. (1984). Validating the test scores. In R. A. Berk (Ed.), *A guide to criterion-referenced test construction* (pp. 199–230). Baltimore: Johns Hopkins University Press.

Hambleton, R. K. (1985). Criterion-referenced assessment of individual differences. In C. R. Reynolds & V. L. Willson (Eds.), *Methodological and statistical advances in the study of individual differences* (pp. 393–424). New York: Plenum Press.

Hambleton, R. K. (1990). *A practical guide to criterion-referenced testing.* Boston: Kluwer.

Hambleton, R. K., & Eignor, D. R. (1978). Guidelines for evaluating criterion-referenced tests and test manuals. *Journal of Educational Measurement, 15*, 321–327.

Hambleton, R. K., & Novick, M. R. (1973). Toward an integration of theory and method for criterion-referenced tests. *Journal of Educational Measurement, 10*, 159–171.

Hambleton, R. K., & Powell, S. (1983). A framework for viewing the process of standard-setting. *Evaluation and the Health Professions, 6*, 3–24.

Hambleton, R. K., Swaminathan, H., Algina, J., & Coulson, D. B. (1978). Criterion-referenced testing and measurement: A review of technical issues and developments. *Review of Educational Research, 48*, 1–47.

Huynh, H. (1976). On the reliability of decisions in domain referenced testing. *Journal of Educational Measurement, 13*, 253–264.

Jaeger, R. M. (1989). Certification of student competence. In R. L. Linn (Ed.), *Educational measurement* (3rd ed., pp. 485–514). New York: Macmillan.

Kane, M. T. (1982). The validity of licensure examinations. *American Psychologist, 37*, 911–918.

Kirsch, I., & Guthrie, J. T. (1980). Construct validity of functional reading tests. *Journal of Educational Measurement, 17*, 81–93.

Linn, R. L. (1979). Issues of validity in measurement for competency-based programs. In M. A. Bunda & J. R. Sanders (Eds.), *Practices and problems in competency-based measurement* (pp. 108–123). Washington, DC: National Council on Measurement in Education.

Linn, R. L. (1980). Issues of validity for criterion-referenced measures. *Applied Psychological Measurement, 4*, 547–561.

Linn, R. L. (Ed.). (1989). *Educational measurement* (3rd ed.). New York: Macmillan.

Livingston, S. A. (1975). *A utility-based approach to the evaluation of pass/fail testing decision procedures* (Report No. COPA-75-01). Princeton, NJ: Educational Testing Service.

Livingston, S. A., & Zieky, M. J. (1982). *Passing scores: A manual for setting standards of performance on educational and occupational tests.* Princeton, NJ: Educational Testing Service.

Lord, F. M., & Novick, M. R. (1968). *Statistical theories of mental test scores.* Reading, MA: Addison-Wesley.

Madaus, G. (Ed.). (1983). *The courts, validity, and minimum competency.* Boston, MA: Kluwer.

Messick, S. (1975). The standard problem: Meaning and values in measurement and evaluation. *American Psychologist, 30*, 955–966.

Messick, S. (1989). Validity. In R. L. Linn (Ed.), *Educational measurement* (3rd ed., pp. 13–114). New York: Macmillan.

Millman, J. (1974). Criterion-referenced measurement. In W. J. Popham (Ed.), *Evaluation in education: Current applications* (pp. 308–398). Berkeley, CA: McCutchan.

Nitko, A. J. (1980). Distinguishing the many varieties of criterion-referenced tests. *Review of Educational Research, 50*, 461–485.

Nitko, A. J., & Hsu, T. C. (1974). Using domain-referenced tests for student placement, diagnosis, and attainment in a system of adaptive, individualized instruction. *Educational Technology, 14*, 48–53.

Ogle, D., & Fritts, J. B. (1981). Criterion-referenced reading assessment valuable for process as well as data. *Phi Delta Kappan, 62*, 640–641.

Popham, W. J. (1973). *Of measurement and mistakes.* Invited testimony before the U.S. House of Representatives, Committee on Education and Labor, General Subcommittee on Education, Washington, DC. (ERIC Document Reproduction Service No. ED 078 020)

Popham, W. J. (1978a). *Criterion-referenced measurement.* Englewood Cliffs, NJ: Prentice-Hall.

Popham, W. J. (1978b). The case for criterion-referenced measurement. *Educational Researcher, 7*, 6–10.

Popham, W. J. (1984). Specifying the domain of content or behaviors. In R. A. Berk (Ed.), *A guide to criterion-referenced test construction* (pp. 29–48). Baltimore: Johns Hopkins University Press.

Popham, W. J., & Husek, T. R. (1969). Implications of criterion-referenced measurement. *Journal of Educational Measurement, 6*, 1–9.

Popham, W. J., & Rankin, S. C. (1981). Minimum competency tests spur instructional improvement. *Phi Delta Kappan, 62*, 637–639.

Reschly, D. J. (1981). Psychological testing in educational classification and placement. *American Psychologist, 36*, 1094–1102.

Roid, G. H., & Haladyna, T. M. (1982). *A technology for test-item writing.* New York: Academic Press.

Shepard, L. A. (1984). Setting performance standards. In R. A. Berk (Ed.), *A guide to criterion-referenced test construction* (pp. 169–198). Baltimore: Johns Hopkins University Press.

Subkoviak, M. J. (1976). Estimating reliability for the single administration of a mastery test. *Journal of Educational Measurement, 13*, 265–176.

Subkoviak, M. J. (1988). A practitioner's guide to computation and interpretation of reliability indices for mastery tests. *Journal of Educational Measurement, 25*, 47–55.

Thorndike, E. L. (1910). Handwriting. *Teachers College Record, 11*, 1–93.

Thorndike, E. L. (1913). A scale for measuring achievement in drawing. *Teachers College Record, 14*, 345–382.

Tucker, J. A. (1985). Curriculum-based assessment: An introduction. *Exceptional Children, 52*, 198–204.

van der Linden, W. J. (1980). Decision models for use with criterion-referenced tests. *Applied Psychological Measurement, 4*, 469–492.

van der Linden, W. J., & Mellenbergh, G. J. (1977). Optimal cutting scores using a linear loss function. *Applied Psychological Measurement, 1*, 593–599.

Ward, W. C., Frederiksen, N., & Carlson, S. B. (1980). Construct validity of free-response and machine-scorable forms of a test. *Journal of Educational Measurement, 17*, 11–29.

19

Implications of Cognitive Psychology for Assessment of Academic Skill

ERNEST T. GOETZ
ROBERT J. HALL
Texas A&M University

THOMAS G. FETSCO
Northern Arizona University

To educate, we must have a clear understanding of what students do and do not know. Furthermore, we must be able to ascertain with some certainty whether or not our instructional efforts have been effective. Academic assessment, then, needs to provide information that will help us evaluate programs of instruction as well as pinpoint problems related to the understanding or application of specific academic skills. In that regard, the sole legitimate function of academic assessment is to serve instruction; yet there are a variety of manners in which this function can be filled. Assessment purportedly can help us identify students who need special instructional assistance, recognize the nature of students' difficulties, plan instruction, and evaluate students' progress and instructional effectiveness.

Assessment can take many forms, but testing is the most visible, familiar, and concrete manifestation of assessment. Indeed, for many, the use of standardized tests has become synonymous with both testing and academic assessment. In part, this is due to the national merchandising and commercial availability of standardized tests and their apparent objectivity and precision. As a result, standardized tests have assumed a position of great importance in educational evaluation and decision making. It is important to remember, however, that standardized testing is but one facet of academic assessment. Nonetheless, the importance of standardized tests should not be underestimated. The trends toward "accountability" for instruction and minimum-competency tests for students (not to mention teachers) have increased the stakes being wagered on standardized tests. The collective gnashing of teeth over the state of the educational system (e.g., National Commission of Excellence in Education, 1983) reflects, in large measure, a reaction to declining achievement test scores. When someone demands to know "why Johnny can't read" (Flesch, 1955), the real underlying question is "Why didn't Johnny score higher on a standardized test of reading?"

A different question is "How well do standardized tests serve instruction?" For the sake of argument, we would like to entertain the notion that, on balance, the needs of assessment and instruction in our schools would be better served without standardized tests. Nevertheless, we do not intend to devote this chapter to debating this point. If we had been able to convince the distinguished editors of this volume of the validity of this conclusion, the volume would have looked quite different. Obviously, the use of standardized tests will not be abandoned in the near future. Therefore, we begin by briefly examining some of the shortcomings of standardized tests, both in terms of their inadequacies for key assessment and evaluation functions, and in terms of their potentially harmful side effects on student motivation. The major focus of the chapter is on alternative approaches to assessment, which draw on recent work in cognitive psychology. After a general discussion of alternative approaches to assessment, we examine, in some detail, assessment of spelling as a means of contrasting standardized testing with a cognitive approach to assessment. Finally, we examine some directions for future development.

PROBLEMS WITH STANDARDIZED TESTS

Dissatisfaction with standardized tests certainly is not new. In 1957, Cronbach decried the separation between the correlational, individual-difference tradition that underlies standardized tests and the experimental tradition that led to the development of current cognitive psychology. In 1967, Anastasi cited the "isolation of psychometrics from other relevant areas of psychology" as "one of the conditions that have led to the prevalent public hostility towards testing" (p. 297). In 1978, Buros lamented the lack of significant progress in testing in the last half century.

Given that we will have nothing original to say here about the shortcomings of standardized tests, why should old arguments once again be rehashed? The answer is that recent cognitive research provides new insight into student information processing and motivation. Underscoring the concerns of many researchers is the notion that "skill and will" form an inseparable package. Motivation, it is argued, provides a context for cognition that is not reducible to simple admonitions or encouragements to "Just do your best," "Good work," or "You're really doing well" (Paris, 1988). Furthermore, mainstream cognitive, developmental, and motivational research has focused as never before on school learning tasks and the development of academic competence. It is now possible both to describe alternative approaches to

academic assessment based on an understanding of the cognitive requirements of schoolwork and to appraise the motivational impact of standardized tests and of other approaches to academic assessment. Thus, we believe that the topic of this chapter is both timely and important.

In our view, there are two major difficulties with current standardized tests and the way they are used. First, standardized tests seem ill suited to some of the functions for which they are currently employed. As presently written and used, standardized tests do not adequately support instruction. Second, standardized tests may reinforce or contribute to views of student ability and achievement that are counterproductive for some students. By stressing competition and social comparison, norm-referenced tests may contribute to the decline in academic motivation and self-concept that many students experience during their school years. As we will see, these motivational side effects, both direct and indirect, can be debilitating.

What Are Standardized Tests Intended to Do, and How Well Do They Do It?

Advocates of standardized testing in the schools list a number of functions for which these tests are appropriate (e.g., Kaufman & Kaufman, 1985; Salvia & Ysseldyke, 1988). We consider five of the functions most often cited to justify the use of standardized tests: (1) identifying students with special needs, (2) discriminating among students with learning problems, (3) providing information for instructional planning, (4) evaluating instruction, and (5) meeting legal requirements (i.e., legislative mandates).

Identifying Students with Special Needs

One reason often cited for administering standardized tests is that they provide a quick and expeditious method for determining who needs special help (Aiken, 1985; Lutey & Copeland, 1982; Sattler, 1988). Although standardized tests used in this capacity may require little time, screening information often is readily available from other sources. For example, in the typical special education referral, the teacher has already screened and identified a learning problem. In fact, teachers appear to be fairly accurate in identifying those who need academic and behavioral programs beyond the scope of the regular classroom (Algozzine, Christenson, & Ysseldyke, 1982). The teacher's decision to refer is the single best predictor of whether a child is placed in special educatuon (Algozzine & Ysseldyke, 1986; Algozzine, Ysseldyke, & Christenson, 1983). The question then becomes "Why administer tests when we have teacher referral information?"

The obvious response to this is that teachers may vary in their ability to identify learning problems accurately. Use of standardized tests by school psychologists trained to administer and interpret them, it is argued, can guard against haphazard and idiosyncratic referrals stemming from regular classroom teachers' "suspicion of disability" for students whose behavior is bothersome (Ysseldyke et al., 1983). There is, for example, always the danger that being classified as "hyperactive" may be much like being branded a "nymphomaniac": It may signify only that one has been more active than someone else thinks one should be.

Given this danger, it would seem to be good policy for professionals outside the classroom, such as school psychologists, to intervene. But the use of standardized tests to refute or to verify teacher referral may not be the best way to approach this problem. The more effective long-term solution might be to work with teachers to improve the accuracy of their referrals. One way to do this is to increase teachers' abilities to work with children who have learning problems. If teachers were to become better equipped to deal with a wider range of learning problems, then presumably fewer children would be referred for special services, and those who were referred would be those in real need of such help. Consequently, there appear to be long-range benefits in working with teachers to improve the accuracy of their referrals and their ability to handle a wider variety of problems independently (Chalfant, Van Dusen, & Moultrie, 1979; Gerber & Semmel, 1984; Harrington & Gibson, 1986). This teacher assistance does not require the use of standardized tests, and could be enhanced by information provided from a cognitive–motivational analysis of children's problems.

Discriminating among Students with Learning Problems

A second reason given for using standardized tests is to assist in determining the nature and severity of learning problems (Adelman & Taylor, 1986; Algozzine & Ysseldyke, 1986; Luria, 1961). Basically, standardized tests have not done well in this regard. For example, the distinction between auditory and visual perceptual skills as causes of reading problems, a cornerstone of special education services over the past 30 years, has received no convincing empirical support (Forness & Kavale, 1987; Kavale & Forness, 1987). In fact, with a shift in emphasis to complex information-processing accounts of performance, there is a decided move away from explanations that feature simplistic dichotomies (i.e., either the defect is auditory or it is visual). As Farnham-Diggory (1986) points out, "Learning disabilities are simply not going to fit into a small, neat set of categories, because human minds don't" (p. 154).

The utility of "learning disability" as a diagnostic category has also been challenged. Ysseldyke, Algozzine, Richey, and Graden (1982) found that learning-disabled and low-achieving regular education students did not differ significantly on several measures of aptitude, achievement, or perceptual processes. Kavale and Forness (1984), reporting on a meta-analysis of Wechsler Intelligence Scale for Children—Revised (WISC-R) subtest pattern analyses, concluded that no regrouping scheme for pattern analysis was successful in differentiating learning-disabled children from their regular education peers. Going one step further, Willson, Stanton, and Olivarez (1989) and Stanton, Willson, and Olivarez (in press) have questioned the validity of profile analysis because of differential subtest reliabilities and standard errors.

From a different but related perspective, Brown and French (1979) and Wozniak (1980) cite findings by Russian psychologists that mildly retarded and learning-disabled children often do not differ significantly in terms of their scores on static tests of ability and achievement. However, when actually asked to learn something, learning-disabled children demonstrated a quicker learning rate or learned to a higher level of competence than the mildly retarded children. Taken together, the implication from these findings is that accurate differential diagnosis is extremely difficult to achieve using current standardized assessment procedures, and that information–processing assessments of learning may be helpful in improving the accuracy of differential diagnoses.

Providing Information for Instructional Planning

A third possible reason for using standardized tests is that they may provide useful information for planning instruction. In reality, however, standardized tests are ill equipped to provide this kind of information (Meyers, Pfeffer, & Erlbaum, 1985). As Bejar (1984, p. 175) has noted, "Standardized test results frequently have little or no impact on instruction because the test results offer little help in designing instruction that is optimal for an individual student." There appear to be at least two reasons for this.

First, standardized tests only provide small samples of performance related to a subset of relevant educational objectives (Linn, 1986). Improvements in standardized testing made possible by the development and generalization of item response theory (Lord, 1980; Mislevy, 1983) have allowed test constructors to increase the number of instructional objectives tested by reducing the number of items necessary to measure a given objective reliably. Broader coverage of objectives allows for more reliable global scores of achievement and finer discriminations between and among individuals. However, because there are so few items per objective, it is difficult for school psychologists or teachers to use the pattern of responses from an individual child or group of children to guide changes in the curriculum.

Advances in the psychometrics underlying testing have resulted in more reliable indicators of general strength or weakness within specific academic domains, but have had little impact on our understanding of the source of a child's problem or what might be done to improve skill acquisition within the academic domains. This difficulty can perhaps be traced to the isolated, atheoretical path by which psychometrics has developed (Anastasi, 1967; Cronbach, 1957; Willson, 1987). As Glaser, Lesgold, and Lajoie (1987, p. 41) observed, "Tests can predict failure

without a theory of what causes success, but intervening to prevent failure and enhance competence requires deeper understanding." How, then, might assessment be used to inform instruction? As Glaser et al. (1987) and others (e.g., Benton & Kiewra, 1987; Willson, 1987) have suggested, cognitive psychology can provide a theory of what causes success and can improve the instructional utility of assessment. Willson, Kulikowich, Alexander, and Farrell (1988) have outlined a causal model of test performance that identifies essential components of such a theory, including prior knowledge, learner processes, task characteristics, response characteristics, instruction, and motivation.

A second reason why standardized tests often have little impact on instruction is that they fail to account for the social nature of learning (Vygotsky, 1978). Individuals not present at the assessment have only limited access to valuable observational information about children's learning (Nolen, 1986). Also, children's functioning within an instructional context and curriculum may bear little resemblance to their performance on standardized tests (Fuchs & Fuchs, 1986; Howell, 1986; Shinn, Tindal, & Stein, 1988). In short, standardized tests are not designed to provide instructional information.

Evaluating Instruction

A fourth reason cited for administering standardized tests is that they may be used to evaluate the effectiveness of educational programs. Implied in this use of standardized tests is the evaluation of student and teacher competence. The importance of this function of standardized tests has been noted in several of the educational reform documents produced in the 1980s (Madaus, 1985). For example, the authors of *A Nation at Risk* (National Commission on Excellence in Education, 1983) advocated that standardized tests of achievement by administered at major transition points in students' schooling. These tests would be used to certify students' credentials before moving them from one academic level to the next, and would be used to identify students in need of both remedial and enrichment activities. Such plans are now in place in many states.

Although appealing on the surface, this use

of standardized tests also has its problems. Current standardized tests do not adequately measure some desired educational outcomes. For example, many of the reform reports of the 1980s have stressed that schools need to teach thinking and problem-solving skills (Anderson, Hiebert, Scott, & Wilkinson, 1985). Although achievement tests may assess knowledge accumulation, they do not adequately assess thinking or problem-solving skills. This places teachers in an awkward position. Given the emphasis placed on test results, they are forced to teach to a test in order to be fair to themselves and to their students. Thus, if the test stresses only knowledge accumulation (product), valuable thinking and problem-solving skills (process) may be neglected in the classroom. In contrast, because of the emphasis on thinking and problem solving, cognitive information-processing theories should be useful in designing assessments that would encourage teachers to focus instruction on higher-order thinking and problem-solving skills.

Meeting Legal Requirements

Finally, many believe that there is an overriding legislative mandate for the use of standardized tests. That is, state and federal governments require the use of these tests to determine special education eligibility. Interestingly, this argument is often the last line of defense for advocates of standardized tests. The logic goes something like this: "Sure there are problems, but in order to satisfy the eligibility requirements of P.L. 94-142, we have to use standardized tests." However, those who invoke this logic often overlook some important considerations. Federal and state legislatures did not create standardized testing and then thrust it upon the public. A more reasonable interpretation is that federal and state legislatures simply availed themselves of existing technology. In fact, the legal system has often been more of an adversary of than an advocate for standardized testing, ruling in more than one instance that standardized tests may contribute to unequal educational opportunity (e.g., *Larry P. v. Riles*, 1979). This suggests that rather than using legal mandates as support for existing testing technologies, psychologists could better spend their time investigating alternatives.

Summary

In this brief review, we have attempted to remind readers that although general improvements in the area of psychometrics (i.e., more sophisticated item analysis and sampling techniques) have resulted in tests that are of superior technical quality, they have yet to provide educators with the type of information that can be used to guide effective instruction. Highly reliable and valid standardized tests may result in clear-cut categorical decisions about who does or does not qualify for special education services (Boodoo, 1984; Willson & Reynolds, 1984). By referring a child, however, a teacher is asking not only for verification that the child has a problem, but also for help in understanding the nature of the problem as it relates to the questions of where to begin and what to do. A problem exists whether or not the child qualifies for services. In sum, we would argue that standardized testing has been much less than perfect in meeting the assessment needs of the educational community. Before we consider alternatives, however, our discussion turns to possible side effects of standardized testing. In particular, for some students, there may be motivational consequences that can be linked to standardized testing, thus furthering the argument against their use as currently practiced.

How and How Much Do Standardized Tests Influence Motivation?

Successful instruction requires attention, effort, and commitment from the student. That is, "Motivation is relevant to learning because learning is an active process requiring conscious and deliberate effort" (Stipek, 1988, p. ix). As Stipek and others point out, motivation influences cognitive performance in a number of subtle and not-so-subtle ways. Student motivation can lead to the development of productive and nonproductive response patterns for a specific type of problem within a knowledge domain, for all problems within a knowledge domain, or for problems occurring across many different knowledge domains. It is worth considering, then, how standardized tests contribute to or detract from student motivation for academic achievement. In reflecting on this issue, we would like to examine possible direct effects (when students take standardized tests and are informed of the outcome) and indirect effects (when teachers and school psychologists prepare students for tests, administer tests, and interpret test results). In our view, tests and their motivational consequences have both short-term and long-term effects that can influence students' test performance and their learning in school.

What Happens as a Student Takes a Standardized Test?

Typically, the student who takes a standardized test is confronted with a situation where the teacher's or other test giver's instructions and responses to questions are formalized, scripted, and restricted. For group-administered and certain subtests of individually administered tests, there is often time pressure to complete subtests. This time pressure may be in the form of explicit statements, such as "You will have 20 minutes to complete this test. Ready, begin," or it may be implicit (i.e., gentle reminders to respond or forlorn looks on the part of the examiner indicating that the student is to produce a response). In the former case, time constraints are part of the standardization procedure; in the latter, the examiner is aware that the current response is but one of many that will be required, and thus communicates a need to the child to move on to the next item. Many students, therefore, may be unable to complete the test or may complete it only by responding hurriedly and/or haphazardly.

Finally, to avoid floor and ceiling effects that would detract from the test's ability to discriminate among low-ability students on the one hand and high-ability students on the other, tests begin with easy questions and graduate to increasingly difficult ones. Because of limited test time and the need to reliably tap essential skill or knowledge for a particular grade with the fewest possible questions or problems, items on individually administered standardized tests are steeply graded. Hence, after some initial successes, most students are likely to experience problems that they are unable to solve. Under these circumstances, testing virtually insures that every student will finish each subtest with a string of failures, no matter how hard he or she tries.

What Motivational Effects Are Testing Practices Likely to Have?

For some students, simply telling them that they are going to take an ability test and that it is important for them to follow instructions and do their best may keep them from doing their best. It is interesting to note that early experiments on achievement motivation and text anxiety often varied instructions. The same test was represented either as a valid and significant test of academic ability or as something less portentous (e.g., Sarason, 1972). Ability test instructions improved the performance of students with high achievement motivation and low test anxiety, and lowered the performance of students with high test anxiety and low achievement motivation. We would assume that stressing the importance of tests as measures of achievement rather than ability would produce the same deleterious effects for students with high test anxiety.

In a similar fashion, time pressure appears to work against students with high test anxiety and low achievement motivation, prompting them to perform at levels well below those they exhibit when time pressure is removed. For highly anxious students, the time pressure that makes it impossible to complete all problems leads to poorer performance in both accuracy and rate (Hill & Eaton, 1977). Paradoxically, then, the need to go fast can actually lead highly anxious students to go slower.

How Is Maladaptive Test Behavior to Be Understood?

Test anxiety theory originally characterized achievement behavior as an approach–avoidance conflict. Achievement motivation was defined as the tendency to approach success, whereas test anxiety was defined as the tendency to avoid failure (Atkinson, 1964). Test anxiety and achievement motivation were thought to be the results of associative or classical conditioning (see Dweck & Elliot, 1983, for a review). A more recent information-processing analysis (Sarason, 1975; Wine, 1971) suggests a cognitive explanation for the deleterious effects of test anxiety. The basic idea is that students who are highly anxious about tests worry about how well they are doing and about the consequences of failure. They also are more likely to have doubts about their own ability. From an information-processing perspective, the major difficulty with such thoughts is that they compete for the limited attentional resources associated with working memory. The girl who is busy worrying about what her parents will think if she scores poorly on an exam will not be able to concentrate sufficiently to do well on the test. The boy who is overly concerned with the need to work quickly and with the amount of time left on a timed test may actually be slowed down by his worries. Several investigations have supported the conclusion that it is the cognitive activity of worrying, rather than the emotional or physiological features of anxiety, that leads to depressed test performance by highly anxious students (Doctor & Altman, 1969; Morris & Liebert, 1970). More recently, Hembree (1988) has found a stronger relationship between worry and test performance than between emotionality and test performance.

Plass (1979) has offered a different analysis of how anxiety depresses performance that is in line with the emphasis on strategies that characterizes much recent work in cognitive psychology (e.g., Weinstein, Goetz, & Alexander, 1988). Plass identifies four major strategies employed by highly test-anxious students that result in poor performance: (1) task refusal or quitting; (2) slow pace with off-task behavior; (3) slow, cautious work; and (4) fast, inaccurate answering.

Why Should Students Who Are Worried about Failure Adopt Strategies That Doom Them to Failure?

One possible view of self-defeating strategies is that they serve as a means of minimizing the psychological damage done by poor test performance. When failure seems inevitable, people employ defensive strategies to protect self-esteem (Covington, 1983). The critical common feature of the strategies identified by Plass is that each can be used to explain poor performance on the test without having to resort to low ability as the cause. Thus, the student who employs task refusal or quitting is free to think, "I didn't even try," or "I quit after the third question." The slow, off-task student can rationalize, "I didn't try very hard," or "My mind just wasn't on it." The slow, cautious student might think, "I did

real well on the problems I finished, but I just didn't get very far." Finally, the fast, inaccurate student can take pride in having finished all or most of the test while thinking, "I had to rush, so I made some mistakes I wouldn't ordinarily make." Each of these lines of reasoning is an example of Kelly's (1967, 1973) "discounting principle": A given cause of failure is discounted if a more plausible cause is available. Thus, by providing plausible alternative explanations for failure, the apparently maladaptive strategies serve to protect the students' self-esteem by discounting low ability as an explanation of failure.

No matter how test anxiety works, it is worth noting that it may not be equitably distributed. Hill (1980) has argued, on the basis of empirical review, that debilitating test anxiety is especially prevalent among low-income and minority students. Consequently, conditions that heighten the effects of test anxiety (e.g., time pressure, instructions that emphasize the importance of the test as a measure of ability or achievement) work to produce a powerful source of test bias.

> Such motivational test bias will cause many students to perform well below their optimal level of functioning in the test situation, thereby invalidating their results if one is interested in what the children have learned, as opposed to whether they can demonstrate that learning under heavy testing pressure. (Hill, 1980, p. 37)

Whereas most of the work on test anxiety rests on the assumption that test anxiety is a *cause* of poor test performance, some researchers have argued that test anxiety is an *effect* of poor test performance, or of the factors that cause it. For example, Tobias (1985) asserts that test anxiety is the result of poor study habits and test-taking abilities—skills that tests accurately reflect. Hill and others have conducted research on testing conditions that is germane to this issue. They found that students with high test anxiety often performed as well as those with low anxiety when conditions that exacerbated test anxiety were minimized or removed; test anxiety was thereby implicated as a cause of poor test performance (see Hill, 1980, for a review). Finally, Hembree's (1988) recent meta-analysis, integrating the results of 562 studies, revealed that improved test performance and grade point average consistently accompanied reductions in test anxiety, once again supporting a causal role for test anxiety.

As mentioned previously, standardized tests are typically constructed in a manner that makes it extremely unlikely that students will go out winners. Time constraints often make it difficult or impossible to complete group-administered tests. Even when a student can complete the test, it is a near-certainty that his or her final experiences with test items will not be successful. The need to avoid ceiling effects and the presentation of items in order of increasing difficulty make the final items unsolvable for nearly all students, no matter how hard they try. On an individually administered test, the use of stopping rules along with items of steeply graduated difficulty guarantees that, despite a student's best efforts, the student will not finish the test before encountering a number of problems that he or she simply cannot solve.

What Effects Might These Little Defeats Have on Student Motivation?

Seligman's (e.g., 1975) work on learned helplessness may be illustrative here. Seligman's original research with animals demonstrated that repeated uncontrollable shocks, prior to a learning task in which shocks could be escaped or avoided, caused many dogs to fail to learn to escape or avoid the shocks. Although the task was simple for dogs not previously exposed to uncontrollable shocks (a dog only had to learn to jump over a barrier to avoid a shock), dogs that had experienced uncontrollable shocks never learned to master the controllable shocks of the escape avoidance task. In Seligman's view, they had acquired the belief that the shocks were uncontrollable; they had learned to be helpless.

In humans, helplessness in the form of depressed performance on problem-solving tasks has been induced simply by presenting children with unsolvable problems or tasks designed to be impossible to complete in the time permitted (e.g., Dweck, 1975; Dweck & Reppucci, 1973). These, of course, are exactly the conditions many students encounter at the end of most standardized tests. Thus,

for students susceptible to helplessness (i.e., those who have not experienced much control over academic outcomes or who are unfamiliar with academic success), standardized tests may be an effective means of inducing learned helplessness. On a test (or, for that matter, any instructional task), learned helplessness would correspond to the belief that failure is inevitable. Thus, it is not surprising that at least two of the strategies identified by Plass (1979)—namely, task refusal or quitting and slow pace with off-task behavior—are readily interpretable as manifestations of learned helplessness.

Learned helplessness, once induced, might easily persist from one subtest to the next. Given the number of standardized tests that students encounter during their schooling, helplessness induced by standardized tests might prove very persistent and might generalize from standardized tests to teacher-made classroom tests or homework assignments. Indeed, many of the potential liabilities of standardized tests would apply as well to teacher-made tests. The dreary image of helplessness-oriented students (Dweck & Elliot, 1983) who appear to have simply given up, resigning themselves to putting in their time in school with no hope of success, is sadly consistent with Seligman's (1975) animal research and clinical observations of humans and with the observations of many teachers and critics of our schools (e.g., Holt, 1964; Silberman, 1970).

What About the Indirect Effects of Standardized Testing?

Unfortunately, in terms of student motivation, the indirect effects of standardized testing may be no better than the postulated direct effects (test anxiety and learned helplessness). Norm-referenced standardized tests are likely to contribute to an atmosphere in school that focuses students' attention on social comparison. Standardized ability measures, given the assumptions from which they were developed and are typically interpreted, are likely to foster the belief that ability is a stable characteristic of the individual that is unlikely to change. Recent research on academic motivation suggests that both of these outcomes may be damaging to the motivation and achievement of some students.

In norm-referenced tests, a student's score is interpreted by seeing where it places that student in comparison to other students in the same grade in a norming sample. A student whose score places him or her at the 93rd percentile has done very well; a student at the 48th percentile has done about average; but a student who scores at the 17th percentile is well below average. Depending on a student's expectations (or those of a parent or teacher), any of these students might consider his or her performance a failure or success, but there is a strong tendency to view half of the students who take standardized tests as losers. Scoring below average or below grade level is frequently the cause of concern or despair. But it is important to remember that if the test's norms are valid, half of the students *must* score below the median. As Stipek (1984, p. 165) observed, "All children can surpass their own past performance levels, but not all children can surpass the performance level of their peers."

The emphasis on social comparison promoted by standardized tests takes on added significance in light of the work of Nicholls (1979, 1983) and Eccles, Midgley, and Parsons (1984). These researchers have argued that different classroom environments can focus students' attention on different questions. Classrooms that stress mastery of skills and improvement of personal competence prompt the child to ask, "How can I solve this problem?" or "How can I understand this concept?" Focus on such questions has been labeled "task involvement" and identified as optimal for the development of academic potential. Learning is an end in itself, and students select tasks that are of reasonable difficulty and maximal instructional value to them. Competition and social comparison, on the other hand, are likely to focus attention on questions of the form, "How smart am I?" In terms of developing academic potential, such ego involvement is nonoptimal.

Eccles et al. (1984) reviewed a number of studies that examined the effects of classroom practices highlighting competition and social comparison. Such practices were found to produce lower motivation to learn; lower levels of aspiration and of perceived ability; less favorable attitudes toward school, teachers, and other students; and lower self-esteem than classroom practices that focused attention on mastery of skills and improvement of competence.

A related effect of emphasizing students' performance on standardized tests is that it may influence student's beliefs about abilities. Ability tests have been developed on the assumption that intellectual or academic ability is a stable individual trait that can be accurately measured, and teachers' and parents' interpretation of test scores often reflects these assumptions. Dweck and her colleagues (e.g., Dweck, 1986; Dweck & Bempechat, 1983; Dweck & Elliot, 1983), however, have argued that different views of academic ability (i.e., intelligence) are possible, and that students' views of ability have important motivational consequences. Some students view intelligence as a fairly stable global trait, of which each individual has a certain fixed amount. Intelligence, then, is an attribute "that can be judged as adequate or inadequate, and that is both limited and limiting" (Dweck & Bempechat, 1983, p. 244). This is the "entity" view of intelligence. Other students view intelligence as a collection of knowledge and skills that can be learned or acquired. They view intelligence as "something they produce—something with great potential to be increased through their efforts" (Dweck & Bempechat, 1983, p. 244). This view of intelligence as "unstable," or changeable, and controllable is called the "incremental" or "instrumental" view.

The student's view of intelligence is said to determine the type of achievement-related motive that predominates. Thus, it profoundly influences a variety of achievement-related behaviors and attitudes. Students with the entity view of intelligence will strive to "look smart." Given a choice of tasks, they will tend to select tasks at which they can excel, or tasks where failure is inevitable but easily discountable (Covington, 1983). They are likely to think of teachers as judges and to regard errors as failures. Faced with failure, they are likely to become helpless. On the other hand, students with the incremental view of intelligence will strive to "get smarter." They will tend to choose tasks that are challenging and instructional. They are likely to think of teachers as resources or guides, and to view errors as natural and informative. Faced with failure, they are likely to persist and to increase their efforts, perceiving and responding to a challenge.

To summarize, in terms of their motivational impact, the indirect, long-term effects of testing, for many students may be very harmful. As Stipek (1984) has observed:

> There is a sad paradox in the development of children's achievement related cognitions. Most children learn to value high performance based on a normative standard. But a normative standard, by definition, precludes all children reaching the relatively high level of performance to which they learn to aspire. Moreover, by sixth grade, children have developed a concept of stable ability which limits the effectiveness of effort. Thus, by the time children enter junior high school, high achievement relative to peers may be perceived by many as hopeless. (p. 168)

Nicholls (1979) summed up his assessment of the situation by asserting:

> It is unfortunate that educational psychologists have been so energetic in providing means of identifying individual differences in ability in terms of norms, thus focusing teacher attention on normative comparison of children (Hunt, 1975). While doing this, they have done little to help teachers identify behavior indicative of optimum motivation or to provide them with strategies for instigating and maintaining it. This looks like a consequence of our preoccupation with "fair" competition and the associated interest in determining individual differences in capacity or ability. Ironically, this very preoccupation with comparison of individuals in terms of intellectual potential seems bound to make equal attainment of potential impossible. (p. 1079)

Although the abolition of standardized tests may not be the best solution to the problem of student motivation, and is probably impossible in any case, it is best to take the problem very seriously. Eccles et al. (1984; see also Stipek, 1984, 1988) summarized the results of 25 studies published between 1964 and 1983 that examined developmental changes in motivational variables, such as attitudes toward school in general, attitudes toward specific subjects (e.g., English, math), self-concept, locus of control, helplessness, and text anxiety. Eccles et al. concluded that there is a general decline in these variables through the school years. Children tend to become more pessimistic and negative about themselves

and school as they get older. Their general self-concept and their perceptions of their academic abilities decline; they become less likely to expect success; they become more vulnerable to negative feedback and susceptible to helplessness; and they become less favorably disposed toward academic subjects, teachers, and school generally. In view of these problems, the high dropout rates that plague our schools, particularly in urban centers, are readily understandable.

ALTERNATIVES TO STANDARDIZED TESTING: COGNITIVE APPROACHES TO ASSESSMENT

In our view, standardized tests as currently employed have little instructional utility, and may have serious motivational side effects for some students. Difficulties stem from the atheoretical tradition of psychometric methods used in the development of standardized tests. Focus has been on normative measurement of individual-difference traits; thus, psychometric concerns for enhancing reliability and validity have taken precedence over the need to understand the nature of learning and academic tasks or to guide instruction. As Willson (1987) notes, however, conventional reliability and validity may have little to do with instructional utility. To paraphrase Mark Antony (with apologies to William Shakespeare), the trouble with standardized tests is that they have come not to vary students, but to appraise them.

In this section, we examine some alternative approaches to assessment that have come from work in cognitive psychology. As outlined here, cognitive approaches to assessment focus on task analysis, error analysis, and the development of skill. Dynamic and process assessment techniques are also included.

Task Analysis

As applied to academic tasks, the purpose of task analysis is to provide a detailed description of what a student must know and do in order to complete a task successfully. Thus, task analysis guides instruction by specifying, in some detail, the knowledge and skills that must be taught and learned. The impetus for the development of task analysis originated with industry and with the military. Although its origins can be traced back to when the behavioristic perspective was predominant, task analysis has adapted very comfortably to current cognitive psychology (see Lachman, Lachman, & Butterfield, 1979, for a discussion). In fact, task analysis is a key component of Belmont and Butterfield's (1977) "instructional approach" in cognitive psychology and is refined into two separate but related approaches in Gagne's (1985) landmark text, *The Cognitive Psychology of School Learning*. We refer to these approaches as "prerequisite skills analysis" and "procedural analysis."

Prerequisite skills analysis (e.g., Gagne & Paradise, 1961) represents a hierarchy of knowledge and skills that must be acquired before a person can perform a certain task. At the top of the hierarchy is the most advanced skill, the one that is the focus of the analysis. As one moves down through the hierarchy, one finds successively simpler skills. The idea is that to perform at any given level in the hierarchy, a person must have acquired all the required skills at the lower levels. Thus, the emphasis is on the mastery of increasingly complex and sophisticated skills, culminating in the ability to perform a given academic task. The prerequisite or required skills for a given task are those that appear at lower levels of the hierarchy and are linked to it.

Prerequisite skills analysis proceeds by repeatedly addressing the question, "What would the student need to know how to do in order to perform this task independently?" For example, in order to add fractions, students must be able to identify a common denominator, multiply the numerator and denominator for each fraction by the same number, and add the fractions. Each of these skills, however, is complex and assumes mastery of simpler skills. Therefore, the question is repeated for each of the prerequisite skills identified, and the process is repeated until one reaches a level of basic skill for which further reduction is unnecessary.

Procedural analysis specifies what a student must do while actually performing a task. This specification is often given in the form of underlying component processes. For example, Sternberg's (e.g., 1977) semi-nal work on the componential analysis of analogical reasoning specified that in order to solve an analogy problem (A:B::C:?), a student must *encode* the terms of the problem, *infer* the relationship between the A and B terms, *map* the relationship between the A and C terms, and *apply* the relationships identified through inferring and mapping to generate (or recognize) an appropriate answer. Procedural analysis can also be couched in more general, functional terms. For example, Flower and Hayes's (e.g., 1981) analysis of the task of writing includes the major functions of *planning* what is to be written (i.e., establishing a goal for writing, generating and organizing one's thoughts); *translating* one's thoughts into words, sentences, and text; and *reviewing* (i.e., evaluating and revising) what has been written.

Procedural task analysis often specifies the order in which the processes or operations occur during task performance. This specification can take a variety of forms. The familiar flowchart representations of cognitive processes were borrowed from computer programming and reflect the influence of the computer model in the information-processing approach. Procedural networks (e.g., Brown & Burton, 1978) are another example of computer modeling of human cognitive processes. Anderson (e.g., 1982, 1983) has chosen to represent cognitive procedures in terms of the rule structures of procedural knowledge that govern their operation. Procedural knowledge is embodied in production systems that are sets of "if–then" rules (Newell & Simon, 1972). The "if" portion of a production specifies the conditions that must be met before the rule will be applied, and the "then" portion specifies the action (or cognitive operation) that will be taken when it is applied. The order of application of the productions in a production system is determined by the logic of their conditional interrelationships. When the action of one production produces the conditions of another, the sequence of application is determined (e.g., *if* the fractions do not have a common denominator, *then* find the common denominator; *if* the fractions have a common denominator, *then* add the numerators).

As we have said, a common feature of these various approaches to cognitive task analysis is that they can guide instruction by specifying what students are to be taught. They also share the ability to increase the strength of symbiosis between assessment and instruction by providing a means for understanding the nature and cause of students' difficulties on academic tasks, as we shall see in the section that follows. An advantage of the production system representation, however, is that Anderson (1982) has provided a theory of the acquisition of procedural knowledge or the development of skill that seems to be a potentially significant contiribution to academic assessment, as we shall examine later.

Error Analysis

The cognitive approach to error analysis can best be understood in the context of other views of diagnosis. Three major approaches characterize diagnostic assessment (Bejar, 1984). The most common of these approaches is often referred to as "deficit measurement." Here assessment focuses on the measurement of discrete or single symptoms; the question to be answered is "Does the observed score differ enough from the expected score to indicate a weakness in the domain being measured?" For example, the Kaufman Assessment Battery for Children (K-ABC; Kaufman & Kaufman, 1983) set out to identify children's strengths and weaknesses in simultaneous and sequential processing (see Goetz & Hall, 1984; Hall, Goetz, & Fetsco, 1989; and Sternberg, 1984, for critiques of this test from the information-processing perspective). Discrepancy score definitions of learning disabilities (e.g., Willson & Reynolds, 1984) also represent the deficit approach.

There are two major limitations to this approach. First, the standard against which a student's score is interpreted is another score (predicted or from another test or subscale) from the same student. Thus, since scores are not perfectly reliable, differences between scores cannot be interpreted at face value. Second, since student errors are used only to test for deficits, much potentially useful information on the nature of students' problems is lost or ignored.

Recent work by Willson and his colleagues (Stanton, et al., 1988; Willson, Stanton, & Olivarez, 1988) illustrates problems with profile analysis. Theoretically derived discrep-

ancy score distributions revealed difficulties that were then confirmed by reanalysis of original standardization data from the WISC-R. Their research uncovered two major problems with Kaufman's (1979) score profile analysis as currently used. First, Willson, Stanton, and Olivarez (1989) revealed that application of Kaufman's (1979) 3-point difference rule for identifying discrepant subtest scores resulted in classification of as much as 24% of the standardization sample as exhibiting an atypical pattern of performance for some subtests (e.g., Coding and Digit Span). Second, Stanton et al. (in press) showed that Kaufman's null hypothesis approach resulted in four subtests' (Information, Vocabulary, Picture Completion, and Object Assembly) accounting for over 64% of the variance in all discrepancy scores. A study by Olivarez, Willson, and Stanton (1988) revealed similar problems with Kamphaus and Reynolds's (1987) extension of Kaufman's profile analysis to the K-ABC. It would appear, therefore, that profile analysis is of little diagnostic value.

Another major approach to diagnostic assessment is "conventional error analysis." Using this approach, practitioners sort student errors into diagnostic categories and then tally the number of errors in each category. The recently developed Kaufman Test of Educational Achievement (K-TEA; Kaufman & Kaufman, 1985) is an example of this approach. Although conventional error analysis certainly provides more detailed information about what a child does or does not know than does deficit measurement, those left to interpret conventional error analyses often find that the enumeration and classification of errors do not necessarily advance our understanding of children's behaviors. Knowing how many errors a student has made may tell us little about why he or she made those errors. Even if a student avoids excessive errors, he or she may not possess sufficient flexibility or fluency at the skill to be considered fully competent. What is lacking in conventional error analysis is a theory of competent performance that permits the practitioner to place errors in a context.

The third approach to diagnostic assessment represents an integration and extention of the other two approaches. Bejar (1984) refers to this approach as the "cognitive approach." Characteristic of the cognitive approach to error analysis is the integration of representations for both the student and the task. Thus, errors are not simply categorized and counted, but are attributed to specific causes and linked more directly to remediation. One important example of this approach is the work of Brown and Burton (1978), who have constructed a procedural network to diagnose performance on subtraction problems. An information-processing task analysis guides their error analysis. With their "buggy" model, they attempt to identify incorrect or inadequate operations, analogous to "bugs" in a computer program. Brown and Burton's effort is geared toward explaining the misconceptions that lead to student errors, rather than just establishing that certain errors are present.

Siegler's (1976) rule assessment is another example of the cognitive approach to error assessment. The rule-assessment approach is based on the assumptions that: (1) children's problem-solving attempts are based on rules that become increasingly sophisticated with development, and (2) the rule that governs a child's problem-solving attempts can be discerned through analysis of the pattern of correct responses and errors on carefully constructed problem sets. Recently, this approach has been successfully applied to the study of analogical reasoning in children (Alexander, Willson, White, & Fugua, 1987).

Development of Skill

The elimination of errors, however, is not sufficient to characterize the development of skill. Skilled performance is also characterized by the seemingly effortless application of just the right technique. Anderson (1982) has proposed a theory of the acquisition of cognitive skill in which he describes three general stages of knowledge representation. The first stage, in which knowledge is "declarative," is characterized by verbal mediation. Individuals, noting that certain new facts or pieces of information are important to learning a skill, engage in self-monitoring activities that serve to keep unlearned or unfamiliar information active in short-term or working memory. This information is then organized for use in interpretive procedures that form the rudiments of developing skilled behaviors. In the second stage, knowledge

compilation, knowledge begins to move from the declarative to the "procedural." This stage is generally characterized by practice and reduction in the use of verbal mediators to guide performance. As noted by Fitts (1964), this is a "smoothing-out" stage. Finally, information in the form of a skilled response passes to a procedural stage where the skill is gradually speeded up and fine-tuned. In its final form, skilled performance is characterized by the development of automaticity (e.g., LaBerge & Samuels, 1974; Schneider & Schiffrin, 1977), which speeds up processing and frees up cognitive or attentional resources.

Admittedly, this brief synopsis oversimplifies Anderson's seminal work. Nonetheless, it serves to point out that evaluators must go beyond attempts to determine the relative presence or absence of some skilled behavior. We must seek to assess the skill in terms of its progress toward automatic, fine-tuned performance. The appropriate instructional support will differ, depending on the student's stage of skill acquisition (Glaser et al., 1987). In assessing skill development, it is essential to attend to the speed with which the task and/or its component processes is performed, as well as to the accuracy of performance.

If instructional assessment were to focus on cognitive error analysis or the development of skill, there might be motivational benefits for students experiencing academic problems. A diagnostic, cognitive error analysis would appear to foster a focus on the task rather than on social comparison as in norm-referenced testing, and might be expected to encourage task involvement over ego involvement from the student. One of the profound implications of Brown and Burton's (1978) approach is that student's performance, even when strewn with errors, may often be interpreted as the predictable output of the application of procedures that are logical and systematic, but incomplete or flawed in some detail (cf. Case, 1978). Emphasis on assessing the development of skill and directing instruction toward the development of ever more automated and fine-tuned performance may also foster task involvement and establish a standard for measuring success (i.e., improvement over the student's own skill level) against which all students can succeed.

Dynamic and Process Assessment

Several authors have concluded that the best way of dealing with the inadequacies of standardized tests is to supplement or replace them with direct measures of learning (Budoff & Corman, 1976; Feuerstein, Rand, & Hoffman, 1979; Howell, 1986; Swanson, 1984; Vygotsky, 1978). These learning-based assessment procedures have been labeled "dynamic assessment procedures" by some (Brown & Ferrara, 1985; Carlson & Wiedl, 1980) and "process assessment procedures" by others (Haywood, Fuller, Shifman, & Chatelanet, 1975; Kratochwill, 1977; Meyers et al., 1985). Traditionally included as dynamic or process assessment models are the work of Budoff and his associates (Budoff & Corman, 1976); Vygotsky's work with the zone of proximal development (Vygotsky, 1978); Haywood's work with the learning efficiency of children with cultural–familial retardation (Gordon & Haywood, 1969; Haywood & Switzky, 1974); and Feuerstein's work with mediated learning (Feuerstein, et al., 1979; Feuerstein, Rand, Hoffman, & Miller, 1980). Other recently developed process assessment models are Meyers et al.'s (1985) process assessment model; Swanson's (1984) multidimensional assessment model; and the direct assessment or curriculum-based assessment model (Fuchs & Fuchs, 1986; Howell, 1986; Shinn, Rosenfield, & Knutson, 1989).

Although "dynamic assessment" and "process assessment" have been used interchangeably, it may be more helpful to view them as two different research trends within the area of learning-based assessment. From this viewpoint, "dynamic assessment" refers to learning-based assessments that are intended to supplement standardized tests in the process of differential diagnosis. "Process assessment," on the other hand, refers to a set of assessment procedures aimed more directly at identifying and remediating learning problems. Both have implications for how we currently assess children.

Dynamic Assessment

The purpose of dynamic assessment has been to supplement information provided by standardized ability and achievement tests. Research in this area has centered on establishing the relationship among measures of static ability, achievement, and dynamic learning (Brown & Ferrara, 1985; Ferrara, Brown, & Campione, 1986; Fetsco, 1987), and on using learning measures to assist in differential diagnosis (Brown & French, 1979; Luria, 1961; Wozniak, 1980).

Three major findings have emerged from the research on dynamic assessment. First, dynamic assessments of learning efficiency provide information about children that goes beyond information provided by static measures of achievement or ability (Bryant, Brown, & Campione, 1983; Campione, Brown, Ferrara, & Bryant, 1984; Fetsco, 1987). A second major finding is that dynamic assessments can reveal learning efficiency in culturally different or economically deprived children that may be undetected or underestimated by static measures of ability or achievement. When these children are involved in actual learning, their efficiency is higher than would be predicted by static measures (Babad & Budoff, 1974; Budoff & Corman, 1976; Green & Rohwer, 1971; Rohwer, Lynch, Levin, & Suzuki, 1968). In a recent study, Hernandez (1987) reported that learning-disabled Hispanic children may actually demonstrate better learning efficiency than learning-disabled Anglo children. One interpretation of these findings is that current screening procedures, including the use of standardized achievement and ability tests, result in a disproportionate number of Hispanic students' being misclassified as learning disabled. Thus, dynamic assessment's apparent increased sensitivity to individual skill differences may be particularly important in the evaluation of performance for culturally different children.

A third finding is that dynamic assessments are useful in detecting within-group variation for children who perform poorly on static measures of ability and achievement. In general, the finding has been that children who appear similar on the basis of static test results may differ greatly in their learning efficiency when called upon to learn something new. Static test scores may conceal some important sources of variation (Budoff, 1967; Budoff & Friedman, 1964; Budoff, Meskin, & Harrison, 1971; Carlson & Wiedl, 1978). As mentioned previously, this finding is particularly relevant to the use of standardized tests in differentiating between children who are mildly retarded and those who are learning-disabled (Brown & French, 1979; Wozniak, 1980).

Process Assessment

Process assessment of learning problems involves a fairly substantial departure from the typical norm-referenced approach to assessing learning problems. Process assessment differs from the typical use of standardized tests in terms of focus and goals, assessment content, and assessment procedures.

The focus and goals of process assessment differ from typical assessment procedures in the following ways:

1. Process assessment focuses more on the learning processes children use in solving academic problems and acquiring academic content and skills than it does on the products of learning (Howell, 1986).

2. Standardized tests tend to focus on nomothetic or interindividual variance, whereas process assessment focuses on idiographic or intraindividual variance (Fuchs & Fuchs, 1986). This is because intraindividual differences are important in planning instructional interventions (Newland, 1973).

3. Process assessment can employ the student's own curriculum materials (Howell, 1986), and may require the child to actually learn something (Rohwer, Ammon, Suzuki, & Levin, 1971).

4. Process assessment typically involves multiple samplings of children's learning, as opposed to standard psychoeducational assessments, in which testing is done in one or two sessions. Taking more samples of learning means that a more reliable estimate of children's performance can be established.

5. Process assessment procedures are more likely to be what Fuchs and Fuchs (1986) call "ecologically sensitive." That is, assessment situations can be created that mimic the instructional environment.

6. Finally, process assessment has as its purpose the improvement of instruction rather than the prediction of academic performance (Brown & French, 1979).

If the focus and goals of process and standardized assessment differ, then their content and procedures may also differ. This is

indeed the case. For process assessment, the content of the assessment has been broadened to include material from the information-processing analysis of learning in particular, and from instructional psychology in general. For example, Meyers et al. (1985) suggest that assessment should include measures of how the child, the task, and the learning environment interact. Swanson (1984), in his multidimensional assessment model, suggests that assessment should include measures of the child's knowledge base, strategy abstraction and planning, metacognitive abilities, and executive control. Collections of direct assessment papers appear in two recent issues of *School Psychology Review*. Featured in these special issues are discussions of assessment and evaluation for curriculum (Howell, 1986; Shinn, Rosenfield, & Knutson, 1989), attentional and metacognitive behaviors (Lloyd & Loper, 1986), academic environments (Lentz & Shapiro, 1986), academic programs (Deno, 1986), computers as a technological addition to curriculum-based methodology (Fuchs & Fuchs, 1989), and research on the use of curriculum-based assessment and measurement with secondary school students (Gickling, Shane, & Croskery, 1989; Tindal & Parker, 1989). As can be seen from these examples, process assessment models address a larger variety of factors than may be present in typical standardized assessments of learning problems.

The assessment procedures used in process assessment vary, depending on the nature of the problem, the learning task, and the instructional environment (Meyers et al., 1985). The emphasis is not on the administration of tests, but on the application of procedures that are likely to produce meaningful instructional interventions for a given context. In general, however, process assessment has drawn heavily from experimental psychology, and from procedures typically included in or used as educational interventions. For example, cognitive task analysis and cognitive error analysis, as discussed earlier, have prominent places in the process assessment arsenal.

Dynamic and process assessment procedures may also help to alleviate the difficulties of students with motivational problems. By placing assessment in a supportive instructional social context, they may work to lessen rather than increase the difficulties of students who exhibit delilitating test anxiety in traditional assessment contexts. By adopting the idiographic approach to assessment and seeking to improve performance, these assessment techniques seem better suited to promoting task involvement than do the nomothetic, evaluative conventions of norm-referenced standardized testing procedures.

COGNITIVE ASSESSMENT VERSUS STANDARDIZED TESTING: AN ILLUSTRATIVE EXAMPLE

To illustrate differences between the cognitive approach to assessment and that represented by standardized testing, we examine, in depth, the academic task of spelling. Both general and specific considerations guided our selection of spelling. First, despite the high regard historically expressed for good spellers (Madsen & Gould, 1979), spelling is not one of the best-understood, best-developed, or most successful parts of the school curriculum. Simply stated, spelling is challenging because it is driven by one's understanding and application of rules and exceptions to rules. Second, there is clear and consistent evidence that failure to learn to spell accurately and rapidly is one of the most common and persistent characteristics of children labeled as learning-disabled (Gerber, 1984; Poplin, Gray, Larsen, Banikowski, & Mehring, 1980), as reading-retarded (Rutter & Yule, 1973), or as dyslexic (Boder, 1973; Farnham-Diggory, 1986; Nelson, 1980; Nelson & Warrington, 1974; Sweeney & Rourke, 1978). Finally, spelling represents a unique academic problem-solving task, in that phonemic or morphemic elements are self-contained units, yet directly related to surrounding elements. Skilled spellers may recognize errors only when the spelling attempt is complete and "it just doesn't look right" or when contextual information is present (i.e., the case of homophones).

How does spelling compare to other academic skills, such as reading, mathematics, and writing? Consider the following. Like reading, spelling provides the problem solver with numerous decision points. At each decision point, the speller must resolve uncertainty before the problem is judged complete. Unlike reading tasks, however, spelling problems have clearer, better-demarcated beginnings and endings; hence, completion of spelling tasks is less formidable and more likely to occur.

Spelling, although not the converse of reading, overlaps with processes important to reading (e.g., phonological awareness, phonological recoding in lexical access, and phonetic recoding in work memory) and serves as a highly visible tool-skill for writing. Uncertainty or lack of confidence about a particular spelling may cause the writer to choose a known word of less impact or precision. This may detract from the intended content or meaning of the author and lead readers to form negative attributions about the writer's ability. To the extent, then, that spelling interferes with the developing process of writing, individuals (especially those with a history of academic difficulty) may be less inclined to write. This, we would argue, is unfortunate. Writing can foster the development of cohesive and coherent thinking about difficult-to-understand topics; in addition, like spelling and mathematics, it can provide permanent products that can be analyzed by teachers.

Similar to mathematics, spelling offers many opportunities for "debugging" (Brown & Burton, 1978), or getting a feel for where in the process a child's misapplication of a rule, misinterpretation, or incomplete knowledge base results in an error in the final product. Because algorithms underpin operational mathematics (i.e., adding, subtracting, multiplying, and dividing), problems often can be readily identified and precisely remediated. Factual errors or systematic departures from appropriate, recursive computational procedures can lead teachers to specific interventions that will result in errorless solutions. Although spelling is not nearly so precise as mathematics, many words are totally rule-driven, and most if not all words contain some regular morphemic units. Thus, spellers often try to generate additional spelling variants to resolve their uncertainty about which variant "looks right." These additional variants make up a rich informational base of logical and "legal" spelling attempts that can be analyzed for the amount and type of processing that has occurred. What is important here is that, like mathematics, spelling offers the teacher or psychologist a chance to view portions of the process by which a child arrives at an answer, and thus can lead to a more precise match between what a teacher should be teaching and what a child needs to be learning.

In contrast to mathematics and reading, spelling products are generated by the speller in the absence of constraining information. Skilled spellers may use words already written on the page to key the production of a new spelling, but generally there is little information to constrain initial attempts at problem solving. Spelling problems, therefore, provide excellent opportunities for teachers or psychologists to trace the thinking processes of students.

Theoretical Issues in Spelling

Much of the contemporary theoretical work in spelling is based on a two-channel (i.e., auditory or visual) processing model (Franham-Diggory & Nelson, 1984; Frith, 1980). Errors are viewed as static, simple functions of a global failure in the visual or auditory processing "channels." Researchers and clinicians operating from this theoretical perspective, such as Boder (1973), Fox and Rough (1983), Seymour and Porpodas (1980), and Sweeney and Rourke (1978), accord enormous importance to the readability rather than the logic of students' errors when judging whether a child's processing problems are primarily auditory (i.e., phonetic or nonlexical) or visual (i.e., lexical).

Recently, there has been movement away from the notion that spelling errors are static functions of visual or auditory processing problems, and toward a view that spelling errors are dynamic indicators of a child's ability to represent orthographic information. Read's (1975) monograph on how children categorize speech sounds in English provided the impetus for this change in perspective. Research efforts in this decade have been interpreted to show that errors produced by both normally achieving and learning-disabled students follow a developmental course and are logical products of problem solving, given spellers' imperfect levels of knowledge (e.g., see Bookman, 1984; Englert, Hiebert, & Stewart, 1985; Gentry, 1984; Gerber, 1984, 1985, 1987; Gerber & Hall, 1982; Henderson & Beers, 1980; Nulman & Gerber, 1984; Read, 1986).

Novice spellers, including those labeled learning-disabled, progress with growing speed and precision over a course that includes the development of component processing mechanisms such as phonemic segmentation analysis, grapheme–phoneme translation, and pattern recognition. By viewing spelling skill acquisition only from the perspective of static, categorical error analyses, concept-driven components of processing tend to be overshadowed or ignored in favor of building-block or bottom-up processing components. From work by Gerber and Hall (1982) indicating contingent use of general word knowledge, purposeful invention and application of rule systems to govern choices, and overt error monitoring, it is clear that spelling performance is not solely a function of intact, well-developed data-driven processes. Thus, as Gerber and Hall (1987) point out, "extant information-processing models of spelling performance fail to capture the dynamic nature by which factual and procedural spelling knowledge is accrued" (p. 40).

Kaufman Test of Educational Achievement: Comprehensive Form

We restrict our examination of standardized achievement tests to the K-TEA. We have chosen the K-TEA because it is new, comprehensive, well documented, and competently developed from a psychometric perspective. The K-TEA (Kaufman & Kaufman, 1985) is an individually administered measure of school achievement for children and adolescents in 1st through 12th grades. The test offers age- and grade-based norms for fall and spring semesters; global norm-referenced scoring for the domains of Reading Decoding, Reading Comprehension, Mathematics Application, Mathematics Computation, and Spelling; and "criterion-referenced assessment in the analysis of students' errors in the various content areas" (Kaufman & Kaufman, 1985, p. 1). The error analysis, a feature unique to the K-Tea, is of particular interest to us in this chapter. It allows practitioners to aggregate students' incorrect responses into predetermined error categories and then to compare the total number of errors within categories to norms derived by ceiling item within grade. With this method, a given student's strong, average, and weak skills within the larger acedemic domain can be pinpointed.

Question development within academic domains, subject selection for the standardization sample, item selection, norming, and empirical demonstration of the test's technical adequacy all reflect state-of-the-art psychometric development. To establish procedures and categories for the clinical analysis of errors for each subtest, "curriculum experts" in the relevant academic fields were charged with "(1) defining the specific skills making up each subtest and (2) examining the types of errors students are likely to make on subtest items" (McCloskey, Kaufman, Kaufman, & McCloskey, 1985, p. 86). The final error analysis method for the K-TEA was based on "the recommendations of these experts, a review of the current literature on instructional theory and practice, discussions with many practicing school psychologists and educational diagnosticians, and the actual errors made by students participating in the standardization programs" (McCloskey et al., 1985, p. 86).

In summary, the authors of the K-TEA have been careful in developing this assessment package. It is intended to help practitioners with the task of providing more detailed information about children's skill development. For each subtest, the theoretical and pedagogical basis for developing the error analysis is presented, accompanied by tables summarizing (through definitions and examples) key concepts and distinctions. Although we view this as a step forward for educational and diagnostic assessment, we see flaws in this approach that may lead to incomplete or misleading representations of children's skill development. To illustrate our concerns, we analyze the K-TEA Spelling subtest from an information-processing perspective. First, however, we briefly describe the K-TEA Spelling subtest and error analysis, followed by a cognitive assessment of spelling.

K-TEA Spelling Subtest

The K-TEA Spelling subtest contains 50 words that are administered to children in a standard dictation format. Children write their responses on a separate spelling sheet that is part of the individual test record. Spelling attempts are analyzed for errors by the examiner after the testing session. Given the ceiling rule (five consecutive misses within a block) and the steeply graded word list, children are likely to produce between five and nine incorrect spellings. Thus, for most children, the pool of possible errors to be analyzed is small. The error analysis categories for spelling include Prefixes and Word Beginnings, Suffixes and Word Endings, Closed-Syllable (short) Vowels, Open-Syllable (long) and Final-E Pattern Vowels, Vowel Digraphs and Diphthongs, R-Controlled Patterns, Consonant Clusters and Digraphs, Single and Double Consonants, and Whole-word Error Type. The Whole-Word Error Type category is used to "indicate that the error is most accurately described as one that involves more than word part errors" (McCloskey et al., 1985, p. 104). The authors present a documented rationale for including a behavioral error analysis and suggest that diagnosticians can use error analysis information

> to identify skill areas in which intervention should be planned or further diagnostic testing should be carried out, to prepare interim instructional objectives for classroom intervention or short-term Individualized Education Program objectives for special education students, and to help identify teaching techniques that effectively increase skill mastery levels. (McCloskey et al., 1985, p. 87)

Cognitive Assessement of Spelling

As good as the K-TEA appears to be, we are concerned that this test, like any other measure using a similar error analysis technique, may not be good enough. As the field of school psychology moves more toward academic consultation (Stewart, 1987), psychologists, in collaborating with teachers on curriculum and educational programming decisions, will need to extract more information from the assessment process. For assessment to be instructionally useful, it must specify the kind and amount of skill already present in the learner. Furthermore, the rate at which a child typically takes in new information and a child's reaction to corrective feedback will both influence the quality of performance. Thus, instruction should become an extension of assessment driven by theoretical models of cognition and motivation. Initial testing should be designed to determine where to begin instruction in terms of the particular skill to be taught and the context in which to maximize the probability of learning that skill. Ongoing assessment should be designed to evaluate child progress and to determine whether and when the context and pace of instruction need to be altered to promote continued success.

Cognitive Analysis of the K-TEA Spelling Subtest

The discussion to this point has provided a general context for understanding what might be important considerations for data collection and analysis. In this section, we focus specifically on the Spelling subtest of the K-TEA in order to illustrate how an information-processing analysis of performance might differ from the built-in K-TEA error analysis.

To illustrate the error analysis and information-processing procedures, we review only one of the eight error analysis categories used for Reading Decoding and Spelling, Vowel Diphthongs and Digraphs. In general, the word part classification system used in the K-TEA Reading Decoding and Spelling subtests divides words into their predictable or unpredictable vowel and consonant parts. For multisyllabic words containing roots and affixes, however, affixes are considered to be single word parts. The authors argue that affixes are taught as single decodable units and thus should be analyzed at the unit level rather than at the phonemic level. Although this position is pragmatically defensible, it highlights the product–process problem endemic to error classification systems.

Academic problem solving typically is evaluated in terms of its final products, but those products are produced via a process that, over time, becomes more differentiated and sophisticated. Failure to consider the effects of the developing process on the quality of the final product leads to gaps in our understanding of skill acquisition. For example, consider interpretation of performance in the K-TEA category Suffixes and Word Endings. Gerber and Hall (1987) have pointed out that "immature spelling behavior reminds us that phonemic boundaries in words have psychological, not physical, reality" (p. 39). For example, when the nasalized consonant (i.e., N) is dropped from "-ing"

endings, it may reflect a speller's need to rapidly produce the most salient acoustic markers in the word and not his or her confusion about "-ing" endings. Moreover, at a time when young children are mastering phoneme–grapheme relationships, they also are learning to manage cognitive resources and to deal with limitations of working memory. Gerber and Hall (1982) have demonstrated, with samples of learning-disabled children, that learners may be able to recognize and articulate why certain spelling variants are correct much earlier than they are able to use the same rule-based knowledge to inform their spelling attempts. Lack of convergence in reading and spelling development for young children, then, may make it difficult to use information from the Reading Decoding error analysis categories to corroborate findings obtained on the Spelling subtest, as suggested in K-TEA case study analyses (e.g., the Howard H. case in Kaufman & Kaufman, 1985, pp. 133–144).

Kaufman and Kaufman (1985) contend that the error classification system chosen for the Spelling and Reading Decoding subtests is the one that most closely relates to teaching in these academic areas; hence, diagnostic error analyses can be translated into instructionally viable intervention strategies. Given that the authors present no empirical justification to support their contentions about diagnostic and prescriptive utility, we would caution readers that predetermined error types may constrain interpretations of performance by aggregating nonidentical processing errors into crude categories. Simply stated, error types may not capture processing differences across unique orthographic environments. The problem is that the error types identified are constrained by the items included on the test, and item development and selection was driven by the norm-referenced need to discriminate consistently high- from low-scoring students across the grade range. Sensitivity to differences between high- and low-scoring students does not insure sensitivity to students' knowledge, strategies, or skills.

For spellers, the most difficult graphemic representations to master involve the production of correct letter sequences to represent unstressed vowels (Read, 1975, 1986). Skill development in this area has a long developmental course that is too lengthy and complex to deal with in this chapter. Tense- or long-vowel sound representation, however, develops early, is relatively predictable, and is generally rule-based. Thus, young children encounter many opportunities in writing and spelling to generate regular words with long-vowel sounds. For these reasons, we have chosen for analysis the K-TEA category Vowel Digraphs and Diphthongs. A "digraph" is a pair of letters that represent a single speech sound. For vowel digraphs "ai," "ea," "oa," "ee," and "ay" occurring in a single syllable, the general rule is that the vowel pair will assume the long vowel sound of the first vowel (e.g., as in "deep" or "reach"). For vowel digraphs "ie," and "ei," the most common, hence predictable, sound is the tense /e/ as in "believe" or "receive." Since the usual spelling for the tense /e/ is "ie," the speller must note that this digraph departs from the general rule but represents a regular spelling. In contrast, "diphthongs," or glided vowels, are two vowels in a syllable that assume a blended sound (e.g., "oi" and "oy" correspond to the /oi/ sound as in "oil" and "boy," and "ou" and "ow" correspond to the /ow/ sound as in "out" and "cow").

Of the 50 words in the K-TEA Spelling subtest, 15 words contain vowel digraphs or diphthongs. "Reach," "afraid," "increase," "praise," and "grievance" are listed as words that contain predictable vowel digraphs. Note, however, that the digraph in the word "grievance" is predictable only if one knows that the "I before E" rule alters the general application of the vowel-pairing rule. The words "said," "friend," and "ocean" all contain digraphs that are unpredictable. Predictable diphthongs are found in the words "blue," "school," "understood," "employed," and "loyalty," whereas the words "does" and "because" contain unpredictable diphthong patterns. Of the 15 words, only the word "ocean" contains more than one unpredictable word part (i.e., the "c" is sounded as /sh/). However, the letter C can lawfully represent the /sh/ sound when followed by an E, as in the word "oceanic"; an H, as in the word "chandelier"; or an I, as in the words "facial" or "special." In the case of the word "oceanic," simply adding an affix to the word "ocean" changes the syllabic pattern to produce predictable letter sequences. Thus, the E and A appear to perform according to the

vowel-pairing rule, even though their pronunciation is a predictable function of the separate syllables in which they appear. The E, as part of a consonant–vowel cluster at the end of the first syllable, takes the predictable long-vowel sound of an "open" syllable; the A, as part of a vowel–consonant cluster at the beginning of the second syllable, assumes the predictable short-vowel sound of a "closed" syllable. "Ocean" occurs early enough in the word list (#19) to be administered to many first-graders. Although we would not expect 6- and 7-year-olds to use word variants like "oceanic" to help them spell the word "ocean," a more carefully chosen word to illustrate unpredictable letter sequences would have avoided this problem altogether. The point to be made is that from an information-processing perspective, each word must be subjected to this type of content analysis to protect against potential confusion. Hypotheses about what underlies incorrect performance should be formulated in terms of specific misunderstandings or misconceptions about the rule structure governing the mapping of graphemes to phonemes. Rather than focusing on specific words, however, let us look more closely at the general parameters regulating how information is collected within this category.

Development of skill involving representation of vowel digraphs and diphthongs occurs relatively early; thus, it should be the case that young children are afforded many opportunities to spell words containing these phonemic elements. On the K-TEA, 9 of 15 (60%) words containing vowel digraphs or diphthongs occur in the first 20 words, and 12 of 15 (80%) within the first 25 words. Given the nature of the stopping rule for the K-TEA (testing stops when all words in a block of five are misspelled), a raw score of 15 insures that at least 20 words will be attempted. From the standard scores by grade tables in the K-TEA manual, this would mean that an average second-grader (standard score of 100) in the spring semester or a below-average (standard score of 85) fourth-grader in the fall semester will be exposed to at least 20 items on the Spelling subtest. Moreover, by the spring semester of the second grade, 7 of 10 children will correctly spell the first word in the third block ("bring"). Practically speaking, then, most second-graders demonstrate enough ability to attempt at least nine words with digraphs or diphthongs. We would judge this category, therefore, to be consistent with developmental theory, in that opportunities to observe performance coincide with the approximate age at which skill in this area is being acquired. What, then, if anything, is problematic about this category?

An information-processing analysis of skill in this area would seek to establish the level of skill development systematically and separately for vowel digraphs and vowel diphthongs. Moreover, care would be taken to demonstrate whether digraph or diphthong problems are specific to certain exemplars; whether there is a relationship between the level of representation and the length or complexity of the word to be spelled; and whether the time taken to produce correct letter sequences indicates pauses or hestiations that can be interpreted to reflect uncertainty. In the last-mentioned case, interletter latencies can inform the investigator about "automaticity" (Gerber, 1987) (Anderson's "procedural" level of skill development) or about how information is being clustered, without having to ask students what they were thinking about during problem solving. Given Skinner's (1987) recent admonitions to the field of cognitive psychology for asking about rather than observing behavior, it is timely to remind school psychologists that one key to interpretable observation is the systematic presentation of problems designed to accumulate information about what has been achieved.

In sum, we would argue that the Spelling subtest of the K-TEA offers too few opportunities to observe how children respond to different phonemic elements within varied orthographic environments. Too much emphasis has been placed on evaluating performance that is tied to idiosyncratic understanding of unpredictable letter sequences, and not enough emphasis has been given to generating corroborative evidence useful for informing instructional programs. Where to begin and how to implement instruction are questions that teachers want answered. Substantive responses to these questions will come from systematic data collection informed by theory and clear understanding of the cognitive requirements necessary for competent performance on a given task.

Teachers who refer children for testing are generally not ignorant of what those children typically can produce. What they lack are the time and expertise for systematic collection of data that can be interpreted against a developmental theory of performance or integrated with other data to provide information about how generalized problem-solving algorithms are defined and accessed by individual children. The case study analysis presented by Gerber and Hall (1989) illustrates how school psychologists can use information-processing markers to guide their interpretation of student performance and to inform their recommendations for instructional programming.

We are not arguing here for the introduction or addition of complexity for complexity's sake. It is understood that because of constraints of time and training, many practitioners are reluctant to engage in post hoc applications of relatively well-defined but time-consuming systems for interpreting performance. By our willingness to acknowledge and to try to represent the inherent complexity of an academic skill, however, we come closer to understanding the process. Thus, efficient, specifically targeted instructional programs can be developed that take into account the effects of individual differences interacting with task demands.

CONCLUSIONS AND IMPLICATIONS

Many of the ideas and suggestions contained in this chapter are certainly not revolutionary. The emphasis we have placed on ideas such as error analysis and the importance of linking assessment more directly to instruction are clearly consistent with how many psychologists would define effective assessment. The problem, therefore, is not one of ideas, but one of practice. Although we believe that many psychologists agree in theory on what is effective assessment, we are equally convinced that these ideas are not put into practice to the fullest extent possible. Assessment, as practiced in many schools, is really just testing for the purposes of making normative judgments about students and controlling entry into special programs. Consequently, it seems fitting to speculate on exactly what changes need to occur before effective assessment becomes the rule and not the exception. In this regard, we make recommendations for test selection and development, training, and institutional changes.

Test Selection and Development

The obvious place to start is with currently available standardized tests. If we are to continue to use these tests as the mainstay of the assessment procedure, then what changes must occur to make them more relevant to instruction?

Users of standardized tests must be better consumers of the tests they use. Judging the adequacy of a standardized test for instructional planning may require different emphases than are necessary for evaluating the technical adequacy of tests for normative judgments. In judging the adequacy of a test for instructional planning, three criteria need to be addressed. First, the test should allow for systematic error analysis. Error analysis is the cornerstone of the cognitive approach, because it translates directly into instructional recommendations. In order for an error analysis to be effectively conducted, the items must assess critical skills and knowledge. Also, there must be a sufficient number of items to insure a thorough investigation of the limits of performance. Although relatively few items are sufficient to establish a student's normative standing with respect to some skill or content area, more items are necessary to develop a detailed and accurate model of the student's knowledge, strategies, and cognitive processes.

The second criteria is that the test should allow for the systematic assessment of learning within a domain. The test should allow the examiner to instruct the student and to systematically assess the value of instruction for that child. Once again, this requires a large number of items, as assessments of acquisition and transfer require separate but parallel item banks.

Finally, the test should have been developed from a theoretical perspective. That is, the test should reflect someone's notion of how learning progresses in a given area. Items should be included that assess key constructs within that theory.

If these criteria are applied to currently available tests, it becomes very clear that no standardized test can meet these criteria without major modifications. In fact, the tests' developers may reasonably argue that they were never intended to meet these criteria. This suggests that test manufacturers may have to re-evaluate their priorities, or at least to attend to their priorities in different ways.

For example, validity will still be an important test development issue. However, from a cognitive perspective, criterion-related validity will have little or no value at least in the case in which one standardized test serves as the criterion for another. On the other hand, content and construct validity will have enormous importance. Obviously, item selection is essential to effective assessment from the perspective we advocate. Items need to be selected that assess learning or performance in a systematic fashion, and that somehow reflect information from a theory of learning. It will no longer be defensible to select items purely on the basis of their psychometric properties, with little or no attenton to their theoretical utility (Willson, 1987).

Training

Training of assessment personnel needs to be critically evaluated. Professional programs that emphasize assessment over testing need to be the norm. How do we identify these programs? Leaders of these programs should clearly demonstrate their understanding of the difference between assessment and testing in the instruction and training provided for future educational professionals. The emphasis should be on the development of skilled and knowledgable problem solvers, rather than technicians. In-depth, working understanding of students' cognitive and motivational processes and of the demands of academic skills and tasks should supplant technical adequacy in the administration of standardized tests as the goal of professional training. Tests should be portrayed as but one source of data, not the only source. Professionals trained today need the skills necessary to adapt current assessment devices until adequate testing instruments become available.

Institutional Changes

Changing how psychologists are trained, however, may have little impact on how assessment is conducted. Many practicing psychologists may legitimately claim that they have already tried to be more than "gatekeepers," but that legal and institutional requirements within the educational system have beaten them down. We acknowledge this as a major stumbling block to the improvement of assessment procedures. Nontheless, it is not insurmountable.

Psychologists and teachers are often at odds with each other because each group believes that the other lacks essential information for educating special children. The remedy for this appears to be promoting situations in which each can learn from the other. In this regard, we applaud attempts within school districts to form child study or preassessment teams where psychologists and teachers can learn together. We suggest that teacher training programs and professional programs in psychology can profit from this example.

In terms of legal requirements that impede progress in assessment, the obvious answer would appear to be working to change legislative philosophies. It is time that we stop viewing legislation as something that is imposed on us, and instead see it as something we have in part created. Current pieces of legislation such as P.L. 94-142 did not invent assessment procedures; they simply reflected modal practices. Also, many attempts to improve P.L. 94-142 have simply attempted to fine-tune ideas that are fundamentally flawed. For example, the attempts to develop statistically more appropriate achievement–ability discrepancy formulas (Willson & Reynolds, 1984) may be attempts to fine-tune a diagnostic category that would best be abandoned.

The future of our educational system is inextricably tied to the future of academic assessment. In these times of increasing concern about the adequacy of the education currently provided to our students, and uncertainty about the future of our schools, it is heartening to note that the cognitive approach to assessment holds promise for the improvement of academic instruction. We must remember, however, that "better learning through cognitive assessment" is at present only a promise—a promise of which many educators are as yet unaware, far removed from the present reality of most students and schools. To transform this promise into a new reality in our schools will require a great deal of effort as well as increased communication and collaboration among educational researchers, psychological and assessment professionals, and teachers. Until these things come to pass, many students will continue to fail needlessly.

REFERENCES

Adelman, H., & Taylor, L. (1986). *An introduction to learning disabilities*. Glenview, IL: Scott, Foresman.

Aiken, L. R. (1985). *Psychological testing and assessment* (5th ed.). Boston: Allyn & Bacon.

Alexander, P. A., Willson, V. L., White, C. S., & Fuqua, J. D. (1987). Analogical reasoning in young children. *Journal of Educational Psychology, 79*, 401–408.

Algozzine, B., Christensen, S., & Ysseldyke, J. E. (1982). Probabilities associated with the referral to placement process. *Teacher Education and Special Education, 5*, 19–23.

Algozzine, B., & Ysseldyke, J. (1986). The future of the LD field: Screening and diagnosis. *Journal of Learning Disabilities, 19*, 394–398.

Algozzine, B., Ysseldyke, J., & Christianson, S. (1983). An analysis of the incidence of special class placement: The masses are burgeoning. *Journal of Special Education, 17*, 141–147.

Anastasi, A. (1967). Psychology, psychologists, and psychological testing. *American Psychologist, 22*, 297–306.

Anderson, J. R. (1982). Acquisition of cognitive skill. *Psychological Review, 89*, 369–406.

Anderson, J. R. (1983). *The architecture of cognition*. Cambridge, MA: Harvard University Press.

Anderson, R. C., Hiebert, E. H., Scott, J. A., & Wilkinson, I. A. G. (1985). *Becoming a nation of readers: The report of the Commission on Reading*. Washington, DC: Department of Education, National Institute of Education.

Atkinson, J. W. (1964). *An introduction to motivation*. Princeton, NJ: Van Nostrand.

Babad, E. Y., & Budoff, M. (1974). Sensitivity and validity of learning potential measurement in three levels of ability. *Journal of Educational Psychology, 66*, 439–447.

Bejar, I. I. (1984). Educational diagnostic assessment. *Journal of Educational Measurement, 21*, 175–189.

Belmont, J. M., & Butterfield, E. C. (1977). The instructional approach to developmental cognitive research. In R. V. Kail, Jr., & J. W. Hagen (Eds.), *Perspectives on the development of memory and cognition* (pp. 437–481) Hillsdale, NJ: Erlbaum.

Benton, S. L., & Kiewra, K. A. (1987). The assessment of cognitive factors in academic abilities. In R. R.

Ronning, J. A. Glover, J. C. Conoley, & J. C. Witt (Eds.), *The influence of cognitive psychology on testing* (pp. 145–189). Hillsdale, NJ: Erlbaum.

Boder, E. (1973). Developmental dyslexia: A diagnostic approach based on three atypical reading–spelling patterns. *Developmental Medicine and Child Neurology, 15*, 663–687.

Boodoo, G. M. (1984). A multivariate perspective for aptitude–achievement discrepancy in learning disability assessment. *Journal of Special Education, 18*, 489–494.

Bookman, M. O. (1984). Spelling as a cognitive-developmental linguistic process. *Academic Therapy, 20*, 21–32.

Brown, A. L., & Ferrara, R. A. (1985). Diagnosing zones of proximal development. In J. V. Wertsch (Ed.), *Culture, communication, and cognition: Vygotskian perspectives* (pp. 275–304). England: Cambridge University Press.

Brown, A. L., & French, L. A. (1979). The zone of potential development: Implications for intelligence testing in the year 2000. *Intelligence, 3*, 255–277.

Brown, J. S., & Burton, R. R. (1978). Diagnostic models for procedural bugs in basic mathematical skills. *Cognitive Science, 2*, 155–192.

Bryant, N., Brown, A. L., & Campione, J. C. (1983). *Preschool children's learning and transfer of matrices problems: A study of proximal development*. Unpublished manuscript, University of Illinois.

Budoff, M. (1967). Learning potential among institutionalized young adult retardates. *American Journal of Mental Deficiency, 72*, 404–411.

Budoff, M., & Corman, L. (1976). Effectiveness of a learning potential procedure in improving problem-solving skills of retarded and nonretarded children. *American Journal of Mental Deficiency, 81*, 260–264.

Budoff, M., & Friedman, M. (1964). "Learning potential" as an assessment approach to the adolescent mentally retarded. *Journal of Consulting Psychology, 28*, 433–439.

Budoff, M., Meskin, J., & Harrison, R. H. (1971). Educational test of the learning potential hypothesis. *American Journal of Mental Deficiency, 76*, 159–169.

Buros, O. K. (Ed.). (1978). *The eighth mental measurements yearbook*. Highland Park, NJ: Gryphon Press.

Campione, J. C., Brown, A. L., Ferrara, R. A., & Bryant, N. R. (1984). The zone of proximal development: Implications for individual differences and learning. In B. Rogoff & J. V. Wertsch (Eds.), *Children's learning in the zone of proximal development* (pp. 77–91). San Francisco: Jossey-Bass.

Carlson, J. S., & Wiedl, K. H. (1978). Use of testing-the-limits procedures in the assessment of intellectual capabilities in children with learning disabilities. *American Journal of Mental Deficiency, 82*, 559–564.

Carlson, J. S., & Wiedl, K. H. (1980). *Dynamic assessment: An approach toward reducing test bias*. Paper presented at the annual meeting of the Western Psychological Association. (ERIC Document Reproduction Service No. ED 191 884)

Case, R. (1978). Intellectual development from birth to adulthood: A neo-Piagetian interpretation. In R. S. Siegler (Ed.), *Children's thinking: What develops?* (pp. 37–71). Hillsdale, NJ: Erlbaum.

Chalfant, J. C., Van Dusen, P. M., & Moultrie, P. (1979). Teacher assistance teams: A model for within

building problem solving. *Learning Disability Quarterly, 2*, 85–96.

Covington, M. V. (1983). Strategic thinking and the fear of failure. In J. Segal, S. F. Chipman, & R. Glaser (Eds.), *Thinking and learning skills: Current research and open questions* (Vol. 1, pp. 389–416). Hillsdale, NJ: Erlbaum.

Cronbach, L. J. (1957). The two disciplines of scientific psychology. *American Psychologist, 12*, 671–684.

Deno, S. L. (1986). Formative evaluation of individual student programs: A new role for school psychologists. *School Psychology Review, 15*, 358–374.

Doctor, R. M., & Altman, F. (1969). Worry and emotionality as components of test anxiety: Replication and further data. *Psychological Reports, 24*, 563–568.

Dweck, C. S. (1975). The role of expectations and attributions in the alleviation of learned helplessness. *Journal of Personality and Social Psychology, 31*, 674–685.

Dweck, C. S. (1986). Motivational processes affecting learning. *American Psychologist, 41*, 1040–1048.

Dweck, C. S., & Bempechat, J. (1983). Children's theories of intelligence: Consequences for learning. In S. G. Paris, G. M. Olson, & H. W. Stevenson (Eds.), *Learning and motivation in the classroom.* (pp. 239–256). Hillsdale, NJ: Erlbaum.

Dweck, C. S., & Elliot, E. S. (1983). Achievement motivation. In E. M. Hetherington (Ed.), *Handbook of child psychology* (4th ed.): *Vol. 4. Socialization, personality, and social development* (pp. 643–691). New York: Wiley.

Dweck, C. S., & Reppucci, N. D. (1973). Learned helplessness and reinforcement responsibility in children. *Journal of Personality and Social Psychology, 25*, 109–116.

Eccles, J. P., Midgley, C., & Parsons, T. F. (1984). Grade-related changes in the school environment: Effects on achievement motiuvation. In J. G. Nicholls (Ed.), *Advances in motivation and achievement: Vol. 3. The development of achievement motivation.* (pp. 283–351). Greenwich, CT: JAI Press.

Englert, C. S., Hiebert, E. H., & Stewart, S. R. (1985). Spelling unfamiliar words by analogy strategy. *Journal of Special Education, 19*, 291–306.

Farnham-Diggory, S. (1986). Commentary: Time, now, for a little serious complexity. In S. J. Ceci (Ed.), *Handbook of cognitive, social, and neuropsychological aspects of learning disabilities* (Vol. 1, pp. 123–158). Hillsdale, NJ: Erlbaum.

Farnham-Diggory, S., & Nelson, B. (1984). Cognitive analyses of basic school tasks. *Applied Developmental Psychology, 1*, 21–74.

Ferrara, R. A., Brown, A. L., & Campione, J. C. (1986). Children's learning and transfer of inductive reasoning rules: Studies of proximal development. *Child Development, 57*, 1087–1099.

Fetsco, T. G. (1987). *Assessing the zone of proximal development for spelling*. Unpublished doctoral dissertation. Texas A&M University.

Feuerstein, R., Rand, Y., & Hoffman, M. B. (1979). *The dynamic assessment of retarded performers: The Learning Potential Assessment Device, theory, instruments, and techniques*. Baltimore: University Park Press.

Feuerstein, R., Rand, Y., Hoffman, M. B., & Miller, R.

(1980). *Instrumental enrichment*. Baltimore: University Park Press.

Fitts, P. M. (1964). Perceptual–motor skill learning. In A. W. Melton (Ed.), *Categories of human learning* (pp. 243–285). New York: Academic Press.

Flesch, R. P. (1955). *Why Johnny can't read*. New York: Harper.

Flower, L., & Hayes, J. R. (1981). A cognitive process theory of writing. *College Composition and Communication, 32*, 365–387.

Forness, S. R., & Kavale, K. A. (1987). Holistic inquiry and the scientific challenge in special education: A reply to Iano. *Remedial and Special Education, 8*, 47–51.

Fox, B., & Routh, D. K. (1983). Reading disability, phonemic analysis, dysphonetic spelling: A follow-up study. *Journal of Clinical Child Psychology, 12*, 28–32.

Frith, U. (Ed.). (1980). *Cognitive processes in spelling*. London: Academic Press.

Fuchs, L. S., & Fuchs, D. (1986). Linking assessment to instructional interventions: An overview. *School Psychology Review, 15*, 318–323.

Fuchs, L. S., & Fuchs, D. (1989). Enhancing curriculum-based assessment through computer applications: Review of research and practice. *School Psychology Review, 18*, 317–327

Gagne, E. D. (1985). *The cognitive psychology of school learning*. Boston: Little, Brown.

Gagne, R. M., & Paradise, N. E. (1961). Abilities and learning sets in knowledge acquisition. *Psychological Monographs: General and Applied, 75* (Whole no. 518).

Gentry, J. R. (1984). Developmental aspects of learning to spell. *Academic Press, 20*, 11–19.

Gerber, M. M. (1984). Orthographic problem-solving ability of learning disabled and normally achieving students. *Learning Disability Quarterly, 7*, 157–164.

Gerber, M. M. (1985). Spelling as concept-governed problem solving: Learning disabled and normally achieving students. In B. Hutson (Ed.), *Advances in reading/language research* (Vol. 3, pp. 39–75). Greenwich, CT: JAI Press.

Gerber, M. M. (1987, April 22). *Acquisition and automaticity of spelling in learning-handicapped students*. Paper presented at the annual meeting of the American Educational Research Association, Washington, DC.

Gerber, M. M., & Hall, R. J. (1982). *Development of spelling in learning disabled and normally achieving children*. Unpublished manuscript, University of California at Santa Barbara.

Gerber, M. M., & Hall, R. J. (1987). Information processing approaches to studying spelling deficiencies. *Journal of Learning Disabilities, 20*, 34–42.

Gerber, M. M., & Hall, R. J. (1989). Cognitive-behavioral training in spelling for learning handicapped students. *Learning Disability Quarterly, 12*, 159–171.

Gerber, M. M., & Semmel, M. I. (1984). Teacher as imperfect test: Reconceptualizing the referral process. *Educational Psychologist, 19*, 137–148.

Gickling, E. E., Shane, R. L., & Croskerg, K. M. (1989). Developing math skills in low achieving high school students through curriculum-based assessment. *School Psychology Review, 18*, 344–355.

Glaser, R., Lesgold, A., & Lajoie, S. (1987). Toward a cognitive theory for the measurement of achievement. In R. R. Ronning, J. A. Glover, J. C. Conoley, & J. C. Witt (Eds.), *The influence of cognitive psychology on testing* (pp. 41–85). Hillsdale, NJ: Erlbaum.

Goetz, E. T., & Hall, R. J. (1984). Evaluation of the Kaufman Assessment Battery for Children from an information-processing perspective. *Journal of Special Education, 18*, 281–296.

Gordon, J. E., & Haywood, H. C. (1969). Input deficit in cultural–familial retardation: Effects of stimulus enrichment. *American Journal of Mental Deficiency, 73*, 604–610.

Green, R. B., & Rohwer, W. D., Jr. (1971). SES differences on learning and ability tests in black children. *American Educational Research Journal, 8*, 601–609.

Hall, R. J., Goetz, E. T., & Fetsco, T. G. (1989). Information processing and cognitive assessment: II. Assessment in the schools. In J. N. Hughes & R. J. Hall (Eds.), *Cognitive–behavioral psychology in the schools: A comprehensive handbook* (pp. 87–115). New York: Guilford Press.

Harrington, R. G., & Gibson, E. (1986). Preassessment procedures for learning disabled children: Are they effective? *Journal of Learning Disabilities, 19*, 538–541.

Haywood, H. C., Fuller, J. W., Jr., Shifman, M. A., & Chatelanet, G. (1975). Behavioral assessment in mental retardation. In P. McReynolds (Ed.), *Advances in psychological assessment* (Vol. 3, pp. 96–136). San Francisco: Jossey-Bass.

Haywood, H. C., & Switzky, H. N. (1974). Children's verbal abstracting: Effects of enriched input, age, and IQ. *American Journal of Mental Deficiency, 78*, 556–565.

Hembree, R. (1988). Correlates, causes, effects, and treatments of test anxiety. *Review of Educational Research, 58*, 47–77.

Henderson, E. H., & Beers, J. W. (Eds.). (1980). *Developmental and cognitive aspects of learning to spell: A reflection of word knowledge*. Newark, DE: International Reading Association.

Hernandez, A. (1987). *A comparison of the zone of proximal development in Anglo and Hispanic learning disabled elementary pupils*. Unpublished doctoral dissertation, Texas A&M University.

Hill, K. T. (1980). Motivation, evaluation, and educational testing policy. In L. J. Fyans (Ed.), *Achievement motivation: Recent trends in theory and research* (pp. 34–95). New York: Plenum.

Hill, K. T., & Eaton, W. O. (1977). The interaction of test anxiety and success/failure experiences in determining children's arithmetic performance. *Developmental Psychology, 13*, 205–211.

Holt, J. (1964). *How children fail*. New York: Pitman.

Howell, K. W. (1986). Direct assessment of academic performance. *School Psychology Review, 15*, 324–335.

Hunt, J. McV. (1975). Psychological development and the educational enterprise. *Educational Theory, 25*, 333–353.

Kamphaus, R. W., & Reynolds, C. R. (1987). *Clinical and research applications of the K-ABC*. Circle Pines, MN: American Guidance Service.

Kaufman, A. S. (1979). *Intelligent testing with the WISC-R*. New York: Wiley.

Kaufman, A. S., & Kaufman, N. L. (1983). *Kaufman Assessment Battery for Children: Interpretive manual*. Circle Pines, MN: American Guidance Service.

Kaufman, A. S., & Kaufman, N. L. (1985). *Kaufman Test*

of Educational Achievement: Comprehensive form manual. Circle Pines, MN: American Guidance Service.

Kavale, K. A., & Forness, S. R. (1984). A meta-analysis of the validity of Wechsler scale profiles as recategorizations: Patterns or parodies. *Learning Disability Quarterly, 7*, 136–156.

Kavale, K. A., & Forness, S. R. (1987). Substance over style: Assessing the efficacy of modality testing and teaching. *Exceptional Children, 54*, 228–234.

Kelly, H. H. (1967). Attribution theory in social psychology. In D. Levine (Ed.), *Nebraska Symposium on Motivation* (Vol. 15, pp. 192–240). Lincoln: University of Nebraska Press.

Kelly, H. H. (1973). The process of causal attribution. *American Psychologist, 28*, 107–128.

Kratochwill, T. (1977). The movement of psychological extras into ability assessment. *Journal of Special Education, 11*, 299–311.

LaBerge, D., & Samuels, S. J. (1974). Toward a theory of automatic information processing in reading. *Cognitive Psychology, 6*, 293–323.

Lachman, R., Lachman, J. L., & Butterfield, E. C. (1979). *Cognitive psychology and information processing: An introduction*. Hillsdale, NJ: Erlbaum.

Larry P. v. Riles, 495 F. Supp. 926 (N.D. Cal. 1979), *appeal docketed*, No. 80-4027 (9th Cir. Jan. 17, 1980).

Lentz, Jr., F. E., & Shapiro, E. S. (1986). Functional assessment of the acacemic environment. *School Psychology Review, 15*, 346–357.

Linn, R. L. (1986). Educational testing and assessment: Research needs and policy issues. *American Psychologist, 41*, 1153–1160.

Lloyd, J. W., & Loper, A. B. (1986). Measurement and evaluation of task related learning behaviors: Attention to task and metacognition. *School Psychology Review, 15*, 336–345.

Lord, F. M. (1980). *Applications of item response theory to practical testing problems*. Hillsdale, NJ: Erlbaum.

Luria, A. R. (1961). Study of the abnormal child. *American Journal of Orthopsychiatry, 31*, 1–16.

Lutey, C., & Copeland, E. (1982). Cognitive assessments of the school-age child. In C. R. Reynolds & T. B. Gutkin (Eds). *The handbook of school psychology* (pp. 121–155). New York: Wiley.

Madaus, G. F. (1985). Testing as an administrative mechanism in educational policy: What does the future hold? *Educational Horizons, 65*, 34–39.

Madsen, S., & Gould, B. (1979). *The teacher's book of lists*. Glenview, IL: Scott, Foresman.

McCloskey, G. M., Kaufman, A. S., Kaufman, N. L., & McCloskey, L. K. (1985). Clinical analysis of errors. In A. S. Kaufman & N. L. Kaufman, *The Kaufman Test of Educational Achievement: Comprehensive Form manual* (pp. 85–162). Circle Pines, MN: American Guidance Service.

Meyers, J., Pfeffer, J., & Erlbaum, E. (1985). Process assessment: A model for broadening assessment. *Journal of Special Education, 19*, 73–89.

Mislevy, R. J. (1983). Item response models for grouped data. *Journal of Educational Statistics, 8*, 271–288.

Morris, L. W., & Liebert, R. M. (1970). Relationship of cognitive and emotional components of test anxiety to physiological arousal and academic performance. *Journal of Counseling and Clinical Psychology, 35*, 332–337.

National Commission on Excellence in Education.

(1983). *A nation at risk: The imperative for educational reform*. Washington, DC: U.S. Government Printing Office.

Nelson, H. E. (1980). Analysis of spelling errors in normal and dyslexic children. In U. Frith (Ed.), *Cognitive processes in spelling* (pp. 475–493). London: Academic Press.

Nelson, H. E., & Warrington, E. K. (1974). Development of spelling retardation and its relation to other cognitive abilities. *British Journal of Psychology, 65*, 265–274.

Newell, A., & Simon, H. (1972). *Human problem solving*. Englewood, NJ: Prentice-Hall.

Newland, T. E. (1973). Assumptions underlying psychological testing. *Journal of School Psychology, 11*, 316–322.

Nicholls, J. G. (1979). Quality and equality in intellectual development. *American Psychologist, 34*, 1071–1084.

Nicholls, J. G. (1983). Conceptions of ability and achievement motivation: A theory and its implications for education. In S. G. Paris, G. M. Olson, & H. W. Stevenson (Eds.), *Learning and motivation in the classroom* (pp. 211–238). Hillsdale, NJ: Erlbaum.

Nolen, P. A. (1986). Assessment: Projections of its decline and fall with suggestions for its resurrection. *Journal of Learning Disabilities, 19*, 203–205.

Nulman, J. H., & Gerber, M. M. (1984). Improving spelling performance by imitating a child's errors. *Journal of Learning Disabilities, 17*, 328–333.

Olivarez, A., Jr., Willson, V. L., & Stanton, H. C., Jr. (1988, April). *Empirical examination of the null hypothesis approach to K-ABC profile interpretation*. Paper presented at the annual meeting of the American Educational Research Association, New Orleans.

Paris, S. G. (1988, April). *Fusing skill and will: The integration of cognitive and motivational psychology*. Paper presented at the annual meeting of the American Educational Research Association, New Orleans.

Plass, J. A. (1979). *Optimizing children's achievement test strategies and performance: The role of time pressure, emotional anxiety, and sex*. Unpublished master's thesis. University of Illinois.

Poplin, M., Gray, R., Larsen, S., Banikowski, A., & Mehring, T. (1980). A comparison of components of written expression abilities in learning and non-learning disabled children at three grade levels. *Learning Disability Quarterly, 3*, 46–53.

Read, C. (1975). *Children's categorization of speech sounds in English*. Urbana, IL: National Council of Teachers of English.

Read, C. (1986). *Children's creative spelling*. London: Routledge & Kegan Paul.

Rohwer, W. D., Jr., Ammon, M. S., Suzuki, N., & Levin, J. R. (1971). Population differences and learning proficiency. *Journal of Educational Psychology, 62*, 1–14.

Rohwer, W. D., Jr., Lynch, S., Levin, J. R., & Suzuki, N. (1968). Grade level, social strata, and learning efficiency. *Journal of Educational Psychology, 59*, 26–31.

Rutter, M., & Yule, W. (1973). Specific reading retardation. In L. Mann & D. Sabatino (Eds.), *The first review of special education* (pp. 1–50). Philadelphia: Buttonwood Farms.

Salvia, J., & Ysseldyke, J. E. (1988). *Assessment in*

special and remedial education (4th ed.). Boston: Houghton Mifflin.

Sarason, I. G. (1972). Experimental approaches to test anxiety: Attention and the uses of information. In C. D. Spielberger (Ed.), *Anxiety: Current trends in theory and research* (Vol. 2, pp. 381–403). New York: Academic Press.

Sarason, I. G. (1975). Test anxiety, attention, and the general problem of anxiety. In C. D. Spielberger & I. G. Sarason (Eds.), *Stress and anxiety* (Vol. 1, pp. 165–187). Washington, DC: Hemisphere.

Sattler, J. M. (1988). *Assessment of children* (3rd ed.). San Diego, CA: Author.

Schneider, W., & Shiffrin, R. M. (1977). Controlled and automatic human information processing: I. Detection, search, and attention. *Psychological Review, 84*, 1–66.

Seligman, M. E. P. (1975). *Learned helplessness: On depression, development, and death*. San Francisco: W. H. Freeman.

Seymour, P. H. K., & Porpodas, C. D. (1980). Lexical and non-lexical processing of spelling in dyslexia. In U. Frith (Ed.), *Cognitive processes in spelling* (pp. 443–473). London: Academic Press.

Shinn, M. R., Rosenfield, S. & Knutson, N. (1989). Curriculum-based assessment: A comparison of models. *School Psychology Review, 18*, 299–316.

Shinn, M. R., Tindal, G. A., & Stein, S. (1988). Curriculum-based measurement and the identification of mildly handicapped students: A research review. *Professional School Psychology, 3*, 69–85.

Siegler, R. S. (1976). Three aspects of cognitive development. *Cognitive Psychology, 8*, 481–520.

Silberman, C. E. (1970). *Crisis in the classroom: The remaking of American education*. New York: Random House.

Skinner, B. F. (1987). Whatever happended to psychology as the science of behavior? *American Psychologist, 42*, 780–786.

Stanton, H. C., Jr., Willson, V. L., & Olivarez, A., Jr. (in press). Empirical validation of the null hypothesis approach to WISC-R profile interpretation. *Journal of School Psychology*.

Sternberg, R. J. (1977). *Intelligence, information processing, and analogical reasoning: The componential analysis of human abilities*. Hillsdale, NJ: Erlbaum.

Sternberg, R. J. (1984). What should intelligence tests test? Implications of a triarchic theory of intelligence for intelligence testing. *Educational Researcher, 13*, 5–15.

Stewart, K. J. (1987). *Academic consultation: Differences in doctoral and non-doctoral training and practice*. (ERIC Document Reproduction Service No. ED 268 453)

Stipek, D. J. (1984). The development of achievement motivation. In R. Ames & C. Ames (Eds.), *Research on motivation in education: Vol. 1, Student motivation* (pp. 145–174). New York: Academic press.

Stipek, D. J. (1988). *Motivation to learn: From theory to practice*. Englewood Cliffs, NJ: Prentice-Hall.

Swanson, H. L. (1984). Process assessment of intelligence in learning disabled and mentally retarded children: A multidirectional model. *Educational Psychologist, 19*, 149–162.

Sweeney, J. E., & Rourke, B. P. (1978). Neuropsychological significance of phonetically accurate and phonetically inaccurate spelling errors in younger and older retarded spellers. *Brain and Language, 6*, 212–225.

Tindal, G., & Parker, R. (1989). Development of written retell as a curriculum-based measurement in secondary programs. *School Psychology Review, 18*, 328–343.

Tobias, S. (1985). Test anxiety: Interference, defective skills, and cognitive capacity. *Educational Psychologist, 20*, 135–142.

Vygotsky, L. S. (1978). *Mind in society: The development of higher psychological processes*. Cambridge, MA: Harvard University Press.

Weinstein, C. E., Goetz, E. T., & Alexander, P. A. (Eds.). (1988). *Learning and study strategies*. New York: Academic Press.

Willson, V. L. (1987, August). *Cognitive psychology and test development: Out with the old*. Invited address to Division 5 at the annual meeting of the American Psychological Association, New York.

Willson, V. L., Kulikowich, J. M., Alexander, P. A., & Farrell, D. (1988, April). *A cognitive theory for test design: Implications for assessing domain-specific and strategic knowledge*. Paper presented at the annual meeting of the American Educational Research Association, New Orleans.

Willson, V. L., & Reynolds, C. R. (1984). Another look at evaluating aptitude–achievement discrepancies in the diagnosis of learning disabilities. *Journal of Special Education, 18*, 477–488.

Willson, V. L., Stanton, H. C., Jr., & Olivarez, A., Jr. (1989). Psychometric issues in "Intelligent Testing" using the null hypothesis approach. *Learning and Individual Differences, 1*, 247–254.

Wine, J. (1971). Test anxiety and the direction of attention. *Psychological Bulletin, 76*, 92–104.

Wozniak, R. H. (1980). Theory, practice, and the "zone of proximal development" in Soviet psychoeducational research. *Contemporary Educational Psychology, 5*, 175–183.

Ysseldyke, J. E., Algozzine, B., Richey, L., & Graden, J. (1982). Declaring students eligible for learning disability services: Why bother with the data? *Learning Disability Quarterly, 5*, 37–43.

Ysseldyke, J. E., Thurlow, M. L., Graden, J. L., Wesson, C., Deno, S. L., & Algozzine, B. (1983). Generalizations from five years of research on assessment and decision making. *Exceptional Educational Quarterly, 4*, 75–93.

20

Assessment of Mathematics Ability

WARREN D. CROWN

Rutgers, The State University of New Jersey

B elow are reproductions of some work done by school-age youngsters on various types of mathematics tests. What kinds of generalizations can we make about the individual children? What can we tell about the children whose work is represented? Does Maria have a problem with multidigit subtraction? If so, what is it? What exactly is Sam doing? Does Adam understand multiplication of monomials? What evidence is there?

These are some of the kinds of questions that teachers and clinicians responsible for the assessment of individual children's mathematics ability must ask themselves. The answers are usually to be found in the children's responses to questions posed on a mathematics test. But these are not the only kinds of questions that can be answered with the data available from the administration of such tests. "How does the achievement of my third-grade class compare to that of the other third grades in the school?", "Is the math program in the district achieving satisfactory results?", and "How does Martin's achievement in math compare with that of other students his age?" are questions of a marked-ly different type from the first set, and yet they still must be answered by an analysis of actual student work. A tremendous number and variety of questions rely on measures of student performance for their answers. As a result, many different types of mathematics assessments have been developed and are currently used in schools. Each one gives evidence of a unique sort about the ability of an individual or group of individuals. This chapter is intended to help the reader sort out the differences among the available instruments and to identify the situations in which any given test might be profitably used.

The chapter begins, however, with a description of the mathematics curriculum as it is currently taught in schools in the United States, followed by a short discussion of changes that are likely to be seen in that curriculum in coming years. To understand the nature of mathematics assessment, one must first have an overview of the content being tested. The chapter then proceeds to an analysis of student performance in the standard mathematics program and the kinds of difficulties most frequently encountered.

Maria	*Sam*	*Daniel*	*Adam*	*Allison*
304	63	$4 \times 6 = 26$	$(x^2)\,(x) =$	60% of 50 =
-173	$+24$		a. $2x^2$	a. 110
271	15		$\sqrt{}$ b. x^3	b. 30
			c. $x^2 + x$	$\sqrt{}$ c. 3
			d. x	d. 300

Much research has been done to ascertain the degree to which American children master the mathematics that they have been taught, and to identify the sorts of conceptual misunderstandings and faulty algorithms exhibited by students who have difficulty. This knowledge, too, is important, because it defines the skills of the norming population against which our test-taking students are being measured. Finally, the chapter concludes with a more targeted discussion of testing issues and choices in mathematics.

THE SCHOOL MATHEMATICS CURRICULUM OF TODAY

Elementary Content

The major elementary mathematics textbook series in this country are very similar in scope and sequence. They cover arithmetic of whole numbers, decimals, and fractions; measurement; geometry; descriptive statistics; and applications of these topics. Occasionally, a topic that is presented at a given grade level in one textbook series may appear at the following grade level in another series, but the difference is rarely greater than a single level. The placement of topics is affected as much by state curriculum guidelines and by "what the competition is doing" as by thoughtful analyses of the average skills of a particular age group or by reviews of the research findings in the area. So, in effect, the United States can be said to have a reasonably well-defined national elementary mathematics curriculum.

In mathematics, the elementary textbooks define the actual as well as the official curriculum. More than in any other area, teachers of elementary mathematics see their textbooks as their programs. They deviate from them rarely and feel ill prepared to change their focus. Time and again, surveys of elementary teachers show that they feel mathematics is the subject they are least competent to teach and the one they least enjoy teaching. As a result, most teachers spend little time or effort designing creative and challenging mathematics instruction beyond the suggestions of their textbooks. The typical elementary teacher works through the text with his or her students page by

page, planning to reach the end of the book at the end of the year. Even so-called "individualized" programs frequently provide nothing more than the opportunity for the student to go through the book at his or her own pace.

This standard curriculum is embodied in a series of nine single-grade-level textbooks that cover kindergarten through eighth grade. The overwhelming emphasis in these books is on computation, with the dominant instructional sequence being a focus on algorithmic skill followed by plenty of practice. In a recent popular third-grade textbook, for example, 51% of the pages are devoted to the teaching and practice of computational algorithms. Another 20% of the pages focus on problem solving; these are comprised predominantly of one-step story problems, giving rise to more whole-number computation. The remaining 29% of the text covers numeration (12%); measurement (10%); geometry (5%); and probability, descriptive statistics, and graphing (2%).

Secondary Content

Secondary school mathematics students in the United States frequently fall into one of two tracks: the "academic math" track or the "general math" track. Academic students will take courses in algebra, geometry, trigonometry, precalculus, and calculus. General math students will take courses primarily concerned with applications of their elementary mathematics skills—courses with titles such as "Consumer Mathematics," "Mathematics for Life," "Survival Mathematics," or just plain "General Math." With the current trend toward state testing for high school proficiency in the content areas, more and more schools are using the general math courses to prepare students to pass the tests.

Compared to the elementary curriculum, there is more diversity among the mathematics courses offered and textbooks used in secondary mathematics, and the teachers certainly feel more comfortable with the content, but there is still a focus on algorithmic procedures. Memorized procedures to solve simultaneous equations in Algebra I, to solve "work" word problems in Algebra II, or to find the length of the hypotenuse of a right triangle in Geometry are the secondary equivalent of memorizing the steps for doing a long-division problem in fifth grade.

Traditionally Tested Categories

In an effort to manage this large body of knowledge and skills that represents the school mathematics curriculum for kindergarten through 12th grade, test authors have broken it up into three testable components: Concepts, Computation, and Applications (sometimes called Problem Solving). Most standardized tests have mathematics subtests with titles very similar to these three terms. Concepts tests usually measure the pure mathematical knowledge that forms the basis for mathematical operations: the meaning of "four"; the relationship between tens and hundreds; the definition of a square; the difference between prime and composite numbers; the relationship of given measurement units; and so on.

Computation tests measure ability to perform the standard algorithms for mathematical operations. An "algorithm" is simply a set of rules or procedures to be followed in a given order to accomplish some task. So, for instance, an algorithm for two-digit multiplication that is mastered by most schoolchildren instructs a child to do the following: (1) Multiply the ones digit of the multiplier by the ones digit of the multiplicand; (2) record the ones digit of the product; (3) record the tens digit of the product, if any, over the tens digit of the multiplicand (to be "carried"); (4) multiply the ones digit of the multiplier by the tens digit of the multiplicand; (5) add to this product the "carried digit," if any; and so on. Algorithms that are typically tested in arithmetic Computation subtests include all of the four basic arithmetic operations (addition, subtraction, multiplication, and division) with whole numbers, decimals, integers, and fractions, as well as operations with percent and exponentiation.

The Applications subtests are, in many ways, the most interesting of the three types of tests. These are the tests that purport to measure the extent to which a given student can *use* his or her mathematical knowledge and skills to solve problems. They include verbal problems as well as graphically presented situations, in an attempt to put pure mathematics in a real-world context.

TRENDS IN SCHOOL MATHEMATICS FOR THE 1990s AND BEYOND

Problem-Solving Ability as an Instructional Goal

Change has been a prominent characteristic of the school mathematics curriculum since the "new math" curricula of the late 1960s gave way to the "back to basics" movement of the 1970s. One of the major forces for change in the future will be a document published in 1989 by the National Council of Teachers of Mathematics (NCTM). In *Curriculum and Evaluation Standards for School Mathematics*, the NCTM identifies five goals for mathematics learners and establishes standards by which progress toward those goals can be measured. The five goals include: learning to value mathematics; gaining confidence in one's own ability; becoming a mathematical problem solver; learning to communicate mathematically; and learning to reason mathematically. The very first standard in the document addresses the issue of mathematical problem solving, and much of the rest of the document revolves around student attainment of problem-solving skills and a spirit of mathematical inquiry.

By addressing problem solving as the first curriculum standard in the *Standards*, NCTM reinforces a position that it took in 1980 with a much shorter publication, *An Agenda for Action*. The first recommendation in the *Agenda* is that problem solving be *the* focus of school mathematics instruction. Recognizing that "performance in problem solving will measure the effectiveness of our personal and national possession of mathematical competence," the document recommends that "the development of problem-solving ability should direct the efforts of mathematics educators" (p. 2). In a further elaboration of that recommendation, the organization made clear what it considers to be the relationship between problem-solving ability and the other components of the mathematics program:

> The current organization of the curriculum emphasizes component computational skills apart from their application. These skills are necessary tools but should not determine the scope and sequence of the curriculum. The

need of the student to deal with personal, professional, and daily experiences of life requires a curriculum that emphasizes the selection and use of these skills in unexpected, unplanned settings. (NCTM, 1980, p. 2)

The increased emphasis on problem solving and related skills was evident in the first generation of textbooks to be written after the publication of *An Agenda for Action*, and recent texts offer students even more such experience. The emphasis is also evident in the most recently published standardized test batteries. The administration manual that accompanies Forms E and F of the California Achievement Tests (CAT) suggests that these latest forms of the Mathematics subtests "have increased emphasis on problem solving in the context of practical situations. Logical thinking and reasoning receive particular attention" (California Test Bureau/ McGraw-Hill, 1985). Indeed, at the upper levels of the test battery, the number of problem-solving items was increased over that in the previous version by as much as 40%.

Even though authors, teachers, and testing companies have been willing to increase the amount of time spent with problem-solving activities, educational and testing issues with respect to problem-solving skills still abound. There is certainly no consensus on effective ways to increase students' abilities to solve novel mathematical problems, and research in the area is just beginning to shed some light on appropriate rudimentary instructional strategies. Similarly, assessment of problem-solving abilities will only improve slowly as we begin to understand the cognitive processes involved. Effective assessment instruments will ultimately need to go far beyond simple one-step word problems in multiple-choice format.

"Meaning" in School Mathematics

Another, not unrelated, development in school mathematics instruction that will affect the curriculum of the 1990s is an increased attention to "meaning" in mathematics. Many mathematics educators believe that problem-solving skills would improve dramatically if students "understood" better the mathematics that they spend so long

learning simply how to "do." As noted in *The Framework for Mathematics Instruction* (California State Board of Education, 1985),

"Teaching for understanding emphasizes the relationships among mathematical skills and concepts and leads students to approach mathematics with a commonsense attitude, understanding not only how but also why skills are applied. Mathematical rules, formulas, and procedures are not powerful tools in isolation, and students who are taught them out of any context are burdened by a growing list of separate items that have narrow application. Students who are taught to understand the structure and logic of mathematics have more flexibility and are able to recall, adapt, or even recreate rules because they see the larger pattern. (p. 12)

One of the instructional approaches most commonly employed to foster this mathematical understanding is the use of concrete manipulative materials to model important concepts and operations. Bruner (1963) was one of the first to discuss the "concrete–pictorial–abstract" mastery sequence that learners of mathematical concepts exhibit. When young children are first capable of dealing meaningfully with the notion of addition, they rely on the use of some objects with which to model the two sets being added and then the addition itself by combining the sets. The most common objects used for this purpose are fingers; almost everyone has seen small children counting out the answers to arithmetic problems on their fingers. But Bruner and others make the case that all learners profit from such concrete manipulations as their introduction to mathematical operations. Bruner (1963) calls this level the "enactive" stage. The next level of mastery is called the "iconic" or "pictorial" stage, at which point the learner is able to deal with either actual pictorial representations of those concrete objects or mental representations. The physical, manipulative engagement with the objects is no longer needed. The final and most sophisticated level of mastery is the "abstract" or "symbolic" stage, at which time the learner can deal simply with the symbols that represent the mathematical quantities in the problem.

Proponents of the movement to inject more meaning into mathematics instruction suggest that appropriate concrete models be used to introduce important concepts to learners of any age. Materials sometimes used in the elementary grades include place-value blocks (sometimes called "Dienes blocks" after their developer), Cuisinaire Rods, bundles of Popsicle sticks, and fraction wheels. Such materials are also available for secondary instruction, although they are much less frequently used. They include geoboards, algebra tiles, manipulative line segments and polygons, and three-dimensional geometric figures.

An important consequence of the stress on concrete materials in instruction is the potential diagnostic benefit to be derived. A first-grade girl who says, "Seven," when an examiner asks, "How much is four plus three?" may be saying that for either of two reasons. An optimistic, but possibly naive, explanation would be that she has been through the appropriate concrete–pictorial–abstract developmental sequence and that now she is dealing with the task in a very sophisticated manner. A more depressing scenario would suggest that she may simply have memorized the answer after hearing her teacher and classmates say it repeatedly. It may even be just a lucky guess. How is the examiner to know which of the explanations is accurate? He or she can just ask, "*Why* is four plus three seven?" A child who has a command of the content will be able to show the process concretely or draw a picture of it. A child who has memorized the fact will simply say something like "I just know it is." These kinds of data, collected all the time by teachers who insist that their students "understand" the mathematics that they learn, are invaluable in diagnostic situations. More examples of this type of questioning are presented in later sections of this chapter.

Revision of Tests and Test Interpretations

The mathematics education community is becoming increasingly concerned about the kind of testing that is done in schools and some resultant changes in testing programs are already becoming evident. The two major concerns are (1) that tests currently in use do not adequately measure those goals of mathematics instruction that mathematics teachers hold most dear (e.g., the problem-solving skills and "understandings" described

earlier), and (2) that tests, especially state-mandated tests, are increasingly being used to drive curriculum decisions.

Assessment is considered to play such a crucial role in the determination of the design of curriculum that the 1989 NCTM *Curriculum and Evaluation Standards for School Mathematics* devotes a full quarter of its length to a discussion of the topic. The document goes on to echo a recommendation in NCTM's *An Agenda for Action.* Recommendation 5 states, "The success of mathematics programs and student learning must be evaluated by a wider range of measures than conventional testing" (1980, p. 13). The discussion following this recommendation elaborates on this topic:

> Today, many people use test scores as the sole index of the quality of mathematics programs or of the success of student achievement. Test scores alone should not be considered synonymous with achievement or program quality. A serious danger to the education of our youth is the increasing tendency on the part of the public to assume that the sole objective of schooling is a high test score. This is often assumed without the critical knowledge of what is being tested or whether test items fit desired goals. . . . It is imperative that the goals of the mathematics program dictate the nature of the evaluations needed to assess program effectiveness, student learning, teacher performance, or the quality of materials. Too often the reverse is true: the tests dictate the programs, or assumptions of the evaluation plan are inconsistent with the program's goals. (1980, pp. 13–14)

In a recent editorial, Leinwand (1986) discussed what he considered to be a strong motivational factor with regard to teachers' behavior:

> In most schools standardized test results are the single most important measure of educational success in the eyes of the administration, the parents, the community, and the media. This being the case, most teachers make every reasonable effort to prepare their students for this content. (p. 3)

In the coming years, mathematics tests will need to measure some of the higher-order outcomes of mathematics instruction more accurately and reliably. In order to enable them to do so, mathematics educators will need to do a better job of specifying, in a measurable way, what those outcomes are.

STUDENT PERFORMANCE IN THE STANDARD SCHOOL MATHEMATICS PROGRAM

The National Assessment of Educational Progress

To understand what it means to be "performing at the third-grade level" or to be doing "average work for a sixth-grader," one must have a sense of which skills are taught and which are mastered at those levels. Probably the most reliable source of such data in recent years has been the federally funded National Assessment of Educational Progress (NAEP). The NAEP has been in operation since 1969, gathering data about the educational achievement of students in the United States in many different content areas. Specifically, national mathematics assessments were done on populations of 9-, 13-, and 17-year-olds in 1973, 1978, and 1982. In 1985–86, responsibility for national assessment shifted to the Educational Testing Service, with some slight changes in methodology. The 1985–1986 assessment was done on populations of 3rd-, 7th-, and 11th-graders.

This most recent NAEP used test items that spanned seven different content areas (Fundamental Mathematical Methods; Discrete Mathematics; Data Organization and Interpretation; Measurement; Geometry; Relations, Functions, and Algebraic Expressions; and Numbers and Operations) spread over five different cognitive processes (Problem Solving and Reason, Routine Application; Understanding and Comprehension, Skill, and Knowledge) (Carpenter, 1989). About half of the items in the first three assessments were free-response; in the fourth, all were multiple-choice.

When the tests are completed, they are administered to a population of 50,000–70,000 students in the three age groups. Results are reported only in terms of the national percentage of students of a given age who get a particular item correct. Frequently, in the NAEP reports, these item results are supplemented by an analysis done by a group of mathematics educators.

The results presented below are a sample of those from the reports of the 1978, 1982, and 1985 assessments (Education Commission of the States, 1979, 1983; National Council of Teachers of Mathematics, 1989) and will serve to give the reader an overview of the levels of mathematics achievement exhibited by students in the United States. Those readers desiring a more detailed picture of typical performance should consult the NAEP reports themselves.

Knowledge and Skills

Computation skills among students are generally well developed. Performance on the basic fact and algorithm problems presented to the NAEP subjects over the years show mastery by a large percentage of students at roughly the expected ages, about a year or two after the content had been covered in their school curriculum. One particularly troublesome skill, multidigit subtraction with regrouping (borrowing), is an exception. In the 1982 assessment, 48% of the 9-year-olds successfully subtracted 237 from 504 when the problem was presented to them vertically. Only 17% of the same students obtained the correct answer to the instruction "Subtract 237 from 504" (ECS, 1983). The large difference between these two figures suggests that many students are performing adequately in the simpler task by having memorized a procedure for its completion. The harder task involves, in addition to being able to complete the symbolic algorithm, recognizing that 504 is the minuend and 237 the subtrahend and understanding the place-value importance of keeping the numbers properly aligned.

In the 1985 assessment, 7th-graders' performances in whole-number computation showed roughly 80%–90% mastery in whole-number addition, subtraction, and multiplication exercises (Kouba, Carpenter, & Swafford, 1989, p. 70). Although there were no division exercises in the 1985 test, the 1982 assessment (ECS, 1983) showed a rate of about 75% for easier division exercises and sometimes lower than 60% for difficult whole-number division problems. Only 57% of the thirteen-year-olds could correctly solve this problem (p. 11):

12 $\overline{)2496}$

Fraction and decimal competence has, understandably, always lagged behind whole-number performance. Also more evident in these areas, however, is the gap between conceptual understanding and rote algorithmic performance. In the 1985 assessment, almost 80% of the 7th-grade students could change a mixed fraction to an improper fraction (a procedure often taught by rote), but fewer than half of the 7th- *or 11th*-grade students recognized that 5 1/4 was the same as 5 + 1/4 (a question requiring some degree of understanding of the notation) (Kouba et al., 1989, p. 80).

Decimal performance is slightly better than that for fractions, possibly because of the close relationship between decimal operations and whole-number operations, but the conceptual versus procedural gap is still present. In the 1985 assessment (Kouba et al., 1989, p. 83), 62% of the 7th graders were able to multiply 7.2 × 2.5, but only 47% were able to identify correctly the largest number in this list: 0.36, 0.058, 0.375, 0.4

Problem Solving

Results from all of the recent mathematics assessments show that students in this country are relatively adept at solving one-step verbal problems (those that require the use of just one mathematical operation for their solution), especially those that involve just whole numbers. The following problem appeared in the 1985 assessment:

Jake has 32 toy trucks. He buys 45 more. How many does he have in all? (Kouba et al., 1989, p. 74)

Eighty-eight percent of the 3rd graders and 95% of the 7th graders tested were able to solve the problem correctly.

A somewhat more difficult multiplication problem on the 1978 assessment asked:

Kate averages 10 miles per hour on her bike. At this rate how far will she travel in 5 hours? (ECS, 1979, p. 3)

Only 54% of the 9-year-olds answered that one correctly, but 88% of the 13-year-olds

and 94% of the 17-year-olds did so. The low score for the younger children was due almost certainly to the fact that multiplication is a relatively new skill in the third and fourth grades.

One-step problems involving fractions and decimals and especially those involving percent cause more difficulty for the older students. One of the percent problems on the 1982 assessment was:

A store is offering a discount of 15 percent on fishing rods. What is the amount a customer will save on a rod regularly priced at $25.00? (ECS 1983, p. 24)

Only 14% of the 13-year-olds and 44% of the 17-year-olds answered that item correctly. Again, the performance of the younger students can be excused on the basis that they are just beginning to study percent concepts, but the performance of the seventeen-year-olds is not amenable to the same explanation.

Students also have trouble with multi-step problems, those requiring more than one arithmetic operation for their solution. One such problem on the 1985 assessment asked:

Chris buys a pencil for 35 cents and a soda for 59 cents. How much change does she get back from $1.00? (Kouba et al., 1989, p. 76)

Only 29% of the 3rd graders and 77% of the 7th graders were able to choose the correct answer to that question from among four choices.

Students of all ages did less well on nonroutine problems than on the standard verbal problems. Nonroutine problems are those that require some additional reasoning or some original solution strategy. One such problem asked of 9-year-olds in the 1982 assessment was:

Jason bought 3 boxes of pencils. What else do you need to know to find out how many pencils he bought? (ECS, 1983, p. 25).

Among the 9-year-olds tested, only 35% could successfully answer that question.

Another nonroutine problem, this time from the 1978 assessment, was:

Right now Bob has $12 in the bank and Carol has $26 in the bank. From now on, each will save $1 every week. How much money will Bob have saved when he has half as much as Carol? (ECS, 1979, p. 24)

The percentages of each population that answered this item correctly were: 9-year-olds—12%; 13-year-olds—20%; and 17-year-olds—32%.

To summarize these results, it seems that the majority of students in schools in the United States are mastering computational skills with whole numbers and decimals approximately 1 to 2 years after the skills are introduced in the curriculum; that they are somewhat less successful with fractions; and that they frequently have difficulties with simple percent computations. One-step word problems present little difficulty when the underlying computational facility is present, but two-step problems and nonroutine problems prove exceptionally challenging.

Results such as these are important and useful to people who assess the mathematical ability of individual students or who must interpret the assessments made by others. At least three relevant generalizations about school mathematics learning can be made from the NAEP data presented above. First, it is not necessarily "the norm" to master the curriculum of a given grade level before that grade is completed. Over and over again, results of the NAEP show that the majority of students take as much as 2 years before mastering some curriculum topics. With some students, growth in those areas occurs even after that amount of time. So, to the extent that a phrase such as "performing at the third-grade level" means performing like an average third-grader, most students "performing at the third-grade level" have *mastered* only some of the first- and second-grade curriculum and very little of the third-grade curriculum.

The second important generalization to be made from the NAEP data is that test items requiring students simply to apply a computational algorithm that they may have memorized step-by-step measures only their ability to remember that algorithm, not necessarily their understanding of the process. The difference in 9-year-olds' performances on the two three-digit subtraction items discussed earlier is evidence that students' performances are frequently much

better when such exercises are seen in their "traditional" form than when they are presented in such a way as to require a little understanding of the concepts involved.

Third, students' knowledge of concepts and ability to perform computations, even when present, do not automatically translate into the ability to apply that knowledge and those processes in problem-solving situations. Problem solving requires additional thought and reasoning ability that can be measured only by asking the students to solve problems.

ERROR PATTERNS IN STUDENT WORK

One of the most frequently recurring themes in the analysis of standardized test data or survey test data such as those from the NAEP is the regularity with which identifiable error patterns appear in student work. Let us look again at Maria's subtraction work, which was reproduced at the beginning of this chapter.

$$\begin{array}{r} 304 \\ -173 \\ \hline 271 \end{array}$$

Readers can certainly see that the answer Maria provided is incorrect; they can probably locate the spot in the problem where Maria ran into difficulty; and they may even have an idea as to why she made the mistake that she did. Many children make such mistakes, not only in subtraction but in every area of their mathematics work. The discovery and identification of those errors are critical aspects of diagnosis in mathematics, but unfortunately they are often ignored.

Robert Ashlock (1986) writes about making teachers more sensitive to the types of errors made by students and to the potential use of these errors as diagnostic data. He suggests that a significant weakness of most testing programs is the failure of the scoring procedures to distinguish among the various processes used to get a correct answer. Frequently, they fail even to distinguish between students who use a faulty process to arrive at an incorrect answer and students who have no idea at all how to proceed.

Indeed, the emphasis in these programs is on the answer itself—on its correctness or incorrectness—and not on the processes used to arrive at it. Such being the case, a great many potentially available diagnostic data are lost to those analyzing the test performance.

It is not just the authors and publishers of commercially available tests who are guilty of ignoring mathematical processes. Classroom teachers often make the same mistake. When a teacher takes home a set of test papers and "grades" them by marking some items correct and some incorrect, and fails to take the opportunity to analyze the students' work samples to identify error patterns that may indicate widespread misunderstandings, that teacher is likewise focusing too much on answers and not enough on process.

Research on Error Patterns in Mathematics

How important are these error patterns? How long do they last? What role does their discovery play in the further education of the child? These are some of the questions that researchers in mathematics education try to answer. Some answers are already available.

Cox (1975) has stated that "When children make errors in computation, teachers should assume that the error is neither careless nor random. . . . Without instructional intervention, systematic errors will continue for long periods of time" (p. 152). She studied systematic errors in the addition and subtraction work of elementary school children and reported that 23% of the children who made systematic errors in one testing were making the same error, or another very similar error, in another testing 1 year later.

Errors in children's computation are not simply the result of carelessness or lack of knowledge of basic arithmetic facts. They are very frequently indicative of well-developed but faulty procedures for the solution of a given type of problem. Readers may have guessed that Maria's "faulty algorithm" in the subtraction problem shown above was that she subtracted the smaller digit from the larger digit in each of the three columns of the exercise, leaving her with an incorrect answer for the middle column. This is one of the most frequently seen faulty algorithms in children's work; children who use this method of subtraction will make predictable errors in any subtraction problem they encounter that requires regrouping (borrowing).

Faulty algorithms are true algorithms in the sense that they are sets of rules or steps to follow to accomplish some task, but they are "faulty" in that, for at least some of the problems in which they are applied, the final result is a wrong answer. Children who use them have a high degree of confidence in them, believing frequently that when they get some problems wrong they have just been careless in the application of the algorithm, rather than that the algorithm itself is faulty. This confidence explains the longevity of the error patterns seen in longitudinal studies like the one done by Cox (1975). It is for this reason that the identification of such faulty algorithms is so important: Identification must precede any effective instructional intervention.

Roberts (1968), in another analysis of children's computation, noted four error categories or "failure strategies," as he called them: (1) wrong operation; (2) obvious computational error (usually a basic fact recall error); (3) defective algorithm; and (4) random response (a response with no discernible relation to the given problem). He found more random responses and wrong operations at the lower ability levels than at the upper ability levels, but in every ability group except the very lowest quartile, the greatest number of errors resulted from defective algorithms. In fact, 39% of all of the errors made by the students in the top quartile were attributable to this cause.

Kilian, Cahill, Ryan, Sutherland, and Taccetta (1980) analyzed the whole-number multiplication work of 121 upper elementary students—3,294 multidigit problems in all. Their report shows that 56% of the errors were procedural, including some 24% that were attributable to "carrying" mistakes. And the development of faulty algorithms is not just limited to arithmetic students. Any Algebra I teacher can attest to the number of students who really believe that x plus x^2 is x^3. It is clear that faulty algorithms are responsible for a large percentage of student errors in mathematics and that a better understanding of where they come from, how to detect them, and then how to remediate them would considerably improve our ability to deliver effective mathematics instruction.

The Genesis of Faulty Algorithms

Error patterns are frequently clues to important underlying misunderstandings. An analysis of the patterns of individual students often leads to the discovery of missing fundamental concepts that are prerequisite to the procedures in question. Ashlock (1986) offers an interpretation of the origin of the faulty notions:

> Children's mathematical ideas and computational procedures may be correct or erroneous, but the *process* of abstracting those ideas and procedures is basically the same. From a set of experiences with a concept or process, a child pulls out or abstracts those things which the experiences have in common. The intersection of the experiences defines the idea or process for the child. (p. 5)

If the original set of experiences with any given concept or process to which a student is exposed is not rich enough to allow the appropriate abstraction of ideas, the actual abstraction may well be faulty.

Consider, as an example, the process of regrouping in multidigit whole-number addition. Many popular elementary math programs present first-grade students exclusively with exercises that involve no regrouping (carrying), such as these:

$$\begin{array}{r} 34 \\ +23 \\ \hline \end{array} \qquad \begin{array}{r} 54 \\ +15 \\ \hline \end{array} \qquad \begin{array}{r} 27 \\ +62 \\ \hline \end{array}$$

The process that students internalize for completing such problems is one whereby they consider each column as a separate one-digit addition problem and solve both problems independently:

$$\begin{array}{r} 34 \\ + 27 \\ \hline 511 \end{array} \qquad \begin{array}{r} 54 \\ + 18 \\ \hline 612 \end{array} \qquad \begin{array}{r} 27 \\ + 63 \\ \hline 810 \end{array}$$

This process works just fine, as long as none of the exercises assigned requires regrouping, and so the students get many right answers, receive a good deal of positive reinforcement, and develop a sense of confidence with respect to the procedure.

In second grade, the curriculum moves on to present multidigit problems that do require regrouping. In spite of what may be

some very good symbolic teaching at that point, the old procedure proves very resistant to change. Using the old process, considering a two-digit problem nothing more than two one-digit problems shoved close together, students arrive at answers like these:

$$\begin{array}{r} 34 \\ + 27 \\ \hline 511 \end{array} \qquad \begin{array}{r} 54 \\ + 18 \\ \hline 612 \end{array} \qquad \begin{array}{r} 27 \\ + 63 \\ \hline 810 \end{array}$$

This faulty addition algorithm, which is very frequently seen, comes about as a direct result of the instructional sequence that is used to present the content to students. Using Ashlock's (1986) terminology, the student has been allowed to "abstract" certain ideas from his or her initial experiences with two-digit addition. Because the initial experiences were so limited and narrow, however, the abstracted ideas are not adequate to deal with the full range of two-digit addition problems, and the student is now making very predictable errors.

Complicating the situation even more is the fact that most faulty algorithms produce at least some correct answers. If the student in the example above is presented with a mixed set of two-digit addition problems, some requiring regrouping and some not, the result will be a paper on which about half of the answers are correct. The student, unaware of the basic fault with the algorithm, will be confused and frustrated with the quality of the work, and it becomes the teacher's job to diagnose and correct the problem.

For obvious reasons, faulty algorithms occur most frequently when the educational experiences to which the student has been exposed have failed to emphasize the underlying concepts and meanings in the mathematics, and have relied instead on rote memorization of procedures. Students attempting to mimic the processes demonstrated by their teachers have difficulty doing so when those processes make little sense to them. A good example of such difficulty is the confusion that a great many students exhibit between fraction multiplication and addition. Students who have learned a rule for the multiplication of fractions that says "Just multiply the numerators together and the denominators together" have no trouble finding correct answers:

$$\frac{2}{3} \times \frac{5}{7} = \frac{10}{21}$$

But, since addition of fractions is a much more complex procedure and the "rules" are much harder to memorize without some underlying meaning, interference between the two processes is very common, frequently giving rise to addition like this:

$$\frac{2}{3} + \frac{5}{7} = \frac{7}{10}$$

Diagnosis and Error Patterns

Diagnosis is characteristic of all good teaching and should be done regularly by anyone responsible for the instruction of mathematics students. Most of this diagnosis can be done informally by carefully observing the students as they work and by asking probing questions as the opportunities to do so present themselves. Frequently, however, the need arises to do more formal diagnosis. The vehicle used by many clinicians in the field to do this diagnosis is the structured interview. Although many of the advantages of the process are discussed in the next section of this chapter, some preliminary observations are offered here because of their relevance to the detection of error patterns.

One of the approaches to the identification of error patterns is the careful analysis of student's written work. This approach would certainly have led to the successful identification of all of the sample error patterns already discussed. But frequently the patterns are more complex. Even in cases where the patterns may be obvious, the underlying misconceptions may be a mystery. In such cases, discussions with the students in question can often be profitable. Schoen (1979) allows us a look at the diary of a math tutor having such a discussion with a student who had a familiar problem:

I asked Jeff to multiply some pairs of fractions, exercises he could do with ease. Satisfied that he at least knew the mechanics of multiplication of fractions, I next asked him to add 1/4 + 2/4. His answer was 3/8. Next, what is 1/4 + 1/2? The response was 2/6.

"But doesn't 1/2 = 2/4? Why are the answers different?"

Jeff didn't know but the contradiction was no problem for him. I next considered a pie divided into thirds and asked, "Two of the pieces are how much of the pie?"

Jeff's immediate answer was, "2/3."

So, I queried hopefully, "Shouldn't 1/3 + 1/3 = 2/3?"

"Yes," was the confident response. But when I wrote 1/3 + 1/3 and asked Jeff to write the sum, he wrote 2/6. When pressed on the different sums and whether both could be right, Jeff hesitantly agreed that one must be wrong. (Schoen, 1979, p. 34)

Jeff was using the faulty algorithm described previously for finding the sum of two fractions, and this fact could easily have been determined from an analysis of his written work. But the evidence from the interview would give the diagnostician other very valuable information. Jeff was apparently not bothered by two different answers for the same addition problem; he did not use his understanding of equivalent fractions to assist in the solution of the problem; and he was unable to make the transfer from an understanding of the physical representation of the problem to its symbolic notation. These findings are insights into Jeff's mathematical reasoning that would be critical in attempting to remediate his problem. It should have been clear to the tutor that Jeff needed more help than just a repetition of the "rules" for adding fractions.

Another example of the usefulness of the interview technique can be seen with Sam's work. One of Sam's addition problems was displayed at the very beginning of this chapter:

$$\begin{array}{r} 63 \\ +24 \\ \hline 15 \end{array}$$

Sam's answer may appear to be a completely random response having no relation to the problem given. It certainly appeared that way to the interviewer who asked Sam to explain what he had done. Sam's response was "I added the 6 and the 3. That gave me 9. Then I added the 2 and the 4. That gave me another 6. 9 and 6 is 15." Sam certainly did not show any understanding of two-digit addition, or even of two-digit numeration, but his response was also far from random. His explanation clearly demonstrated several misconceptions about numeration and notation that would have to be addressed before he could go any farther with two-digit addition.

Frequently, students' explanations about correctly answered questions can be illustrative as well. Ginsburg (1977, pp. 85–86) describes the discussion that took place between a second-grader named Chris ("C" in the dialogue below) and an interviewer ("I"). Chris had just written $9 + 5 = 14$:

I: Now I'm going to ask you something about 14. How come you wrote 14 with a 1 and then a 4?

C: Cause that's how I write 14.

I: I notice that when you write 14 you have a 1, and on the right of that is a 4. What does that 4 stand for?

C: 'Cause it's 14.

I: All right. What does the 1 stand for?

C: That's how you write 14.

I: Why don't you write it like this [41]?

C: That's 41.

I: All right. Why do you write 41 like that?

C: Because there's a 4 there and a 1 there.

I: Why did they invent that way of doing it? What could it possibly mean? What does that 1 stand for?

C: 1.

I: What does that 4 stand for?

C: 4.

Chris had correctly written the answer to a basic addition fact, but when the interviewer probed for his interpretation of the meaning of the number he wrote (14), it became clear that Chris had no idea about its meaning. He seemed to be operating as many young children do—mimicking the notation and operations that they have seen used by their teachers.

The findings from these three examples are illustrative of the kind of information that can be obtained by discussing mathematics with children. Often such discussion can uncover faulty algorithms and their underlying misconceptions that would remain hidden if the diagnostician had to depend only on the written work of the students.

ISSUES AND CHOICES IN MATHEMATICS ASSESSMENT

Many different types of professionals are, at times, put in the position of assessing (or interpreting the assessment of) the mathematics ability and performance of an individual child. Classroom teachers, mathematics supervisors, resource room teachers, school counselors, school psychologists, professional diagnosticians, and mathematics education researchers all must engage in this task regularly. The variety of assessment instruments and procedures that are available and could be helpful to them is staggering, and choices among the options must be intelligently made. Each type of instrument gives evidence of a unique sort about the ability of an individual or group of individuals. This section of the chapter deals with some of the differences among available instruments and the purposes for which it would be appropriate to choose one type over another.

Content Coverage and Its Relationship to the Curriculum

One of the most important issues in the selection of an assessment instrument is the match between the content tested and the content taught. At any given time, good assessment is characterized by what is locally considered to be valuable in mathematics learning (Underhill, Uprichard, & Heddens, 1980). The likely changes ahead in the mathematics curriculum taught in the United States have already been discussed. There are also differences in what is considered valuable by different school districts and different teachers.

Freeman, Kuhs, Knappen, and Porter (1982) have suggested that the use of different textbook series, the variety of district-mandated objectives, and the sense that teachers are sensitive to the differences in rate of learning among students all contribute to the differences among classrooms in what mathematics content is actually taught. They also found striking differences in the content tested by some of the most popular standardized achievement tests. They concluded that "because of the profound variety in content taught in schools and content tested, significant mismatches between the content of classroom instruction and the content of a standardized test are likely" (Freeman et al., 1982, p. 50). When teachers spend time teaching content that is not tested, there are two negative consequences: First, the students' knowledge and skills in those areas taught are not reflected in their scores on the tests; and second, because time must be taken to teach the untested content, time spent teaching tested content is diminished, and achievement is likely to suffer. Overall, the test is likely to underestimate a student's ability to the extent of the mismatch between content taught and content tested.

How great is the potential mismatch? Alford (1986) reviewed two research studies that attempted to answer that question for the upper elementary grades. Her conclusion was that all textbooks at those grade levels emphasized computational skills far more than did any of the tests reviewed. Typically, 70%–80% of the exercises in the texts were computational in nature, whereas the test items were much more evenly divided among computation, concepts, and applications. In the very best of matched pairs, a sampling of only two-thirds of the material in the text appeared on the test. In the worst of the matched pairs, the percentage of congruence between material tested and that taught in the texts was as low as 20%.

The administration manual for one widely used standardized achievement test battery (the California Achievement Tests, Forms E and F) suggests that the content selection was based on a comprehensive review of popular instructional materials, including basal texts in mathematics, curriculum guides, other tests, state objectives lists, and other resource and reference materials. And yet, of the 24 addition and subtraction computation items in the test recommended for students finishing the second grade, there is not one item that requires the student to subtract a two-digit number from another two-digit number—arguably the most important computational skill taught in second grade. Similarly, among the 50 computation items in the test recommended for students finishing fourth grade, there is not a single multidigit multiplication problem—again a critical skill for students in that grade (see California Test Bureau/McGraw-Hill, 1985).

How could such omissions have occurred? A clue to the answer is provided in the section of the administration manual that deals with the statistical characteristics of the tests. It says there that only those items with the best overall statistical quality that also met the established content criteria were selected

for the tests. When the authors speak of the "overall statistical quality" of an item, they refer to its ability to differentiate well among students—the primary purpose of an achievement test. When a given item fails to distinguish clearly among students of differing ability levels, regardless of the relationship of its content characteristics to the content taught at the given grade level, it is most often rejected for use in the test. The authors of a widely used individually administered achievement test (Peabody Individual Achievement Test), in discussing the final stages of the item selection process, state:

> Clearly, by this stage, any initial balance in measuring systematically all of the mathematical processes was lost. Items were not retained in the battery because they were measuring a particular concept, but rather because of their difficulty level and their qualities as a good screening test item [sic]. (Dunn & Markwardt, 1970, p. 18)

Testing is the systematic observation or sampling of behavior (Anastasi, 1982). Because any test must only *sample* behavior and cannot look exhaustively at all possible behaviors in a given content area, choices must be made about the types of behaviors that will be included in the tested sample. These choices are typically dictated by the main purposes of the testing program. As has been seen in this discussion, the main purposes of some testing programs lead to choices of behaviors to test that do not necessarily correspond to those taught in the curriculum. It is therefore essential that the users of assessment instruments establish the degree of compatibility between the content tested in those instruments and the content locally taught.

Achievement and Diagnostic Testing

There is great confusion in the educational community about the differences between achievement testing and diagnostic testing; as a consequence, results from one type of test or the other are often misused. Aiken (1985) suggests that achievement tests inform students and parents and teachers about students' scholastic accomplishments and deficiencies. They measure the extent to which examinees have achieved the cognitive objectives of instruction. The most reliable reports of these accomplishments and deficiencies, however, specify the very broad areas of content in which the student is either accomplished or deficient, not the actual skills that have been mastered or are in need of remediation. Ashlock (1986) suggests:

> For diagnostic purposes, standardized achievement tests have some value but it is limited. They usually sample such a broad range of content that you do not learn what you need to know about specific concept and skill categories. Diagnostic tests sample a narrower range of content, often in a way that permits you to identify areas of strength and weakness. (p. 11)

Notwithstanding these differences, test publishers and authors will frequently cite the diagnostic uses of their achievement tests. The manual that accompanies the Peabody Individual Achievement Test (PIAT) states, "Hopefully, the PIAT will aid in individualizing instruction. The results should help the teacher to adjust her curriculum and methods, especially if the test is given near the first of the school year" (Dunn & Markwardt, 1970, p. 56). This claim is similar to claims made by almost every publisher of standardized achievement tests, but they are almost always unsubstantiated. Because these tests have been designed primarily to provide normative data about the performance of groups of students in broadly defined content areas (such as "Computation" or even "Mathematics"), the number of items measuring skills in more narrowly defined areas (such as "Two-Digit Multiplication") is simply too small to offer reliable measures of ability. Data concerning precisely those small, narrowly defined skills are what the teacher needs to be able to make instructional decisions for individual students; knowing that a given student is at the 35th percentile in "Computation" is, at best, of limited diagnostic value to that teacher.

There is another troubling aspect of the claims made by the publishers of both achievement and diagnostic tests. Many such claims imply that the knowledge of a given student's test results, in and of itself, will make the teacher a better teacher—that this knowledge will "help the teacher to adjust . . . curriculum and methods" to the student's benefit. Many school administrators perpetuate this belief by returning to teachers very detailed item analyses of students' recent test performance, expecting that this information will somehow enable the teachers to become better teachers of mathematics. Even the best diagnostic instruments, however, only point out those areas in which students are experiencing success or difficulty. They give very little information about *why* a student has not mastered a given skill, about what went wrong in his or her attempt to learn a particular concept, or about what might be an appropriate technique to use in remedial instruction. These are all questions for which a teacher's training and experience must provide the answers. To be sure, the identification of areas of weakness is a critical part of the diagnostic process, but to think that this information suggests more than it does is to delude ourselves.

Norm-Referenced and Criterion-Referenced Testing

The differences discussed above between achievement and diagnostic tests can be generalized here to those between norm-referenced and criterion-referenced tests. Achievement tests are nearly always norm-referenced, although some publishers argue that they may have a criterion-referenced component; most good diagnostic tests are criterion-referenced, even though some of them offer some norm-referenced data on student performance. Lidz (1981) describes the design and purposes of norm-referenced tests:

> Norm-referenced tests are designed to give information about an individual's standing in relation to a population of other people with whom he shares some important characteristics. Norm-referenced test items are selected to maximize individual differences and variability. The score on the test indicates that an individual knows more or less or the same as his peers but doesn't necessarily reveal in detail what he knows or his error patterns (p. 58)

On the other hand, criterion-referenced tests are designed specifically to give a detailed analysis of the skills of the particular examinee—not necessarily in relation to what skills others have, but with respect to a predetermined set or hierarchy of skills that comprise the content area in question.

A norm-referenced test should be used when what is desired is a group measure to be used for differentiation among students or other comparative purposes. A criterion-referenced test should be used when the need is for a measure of the achievement of each of a set of specific content objectives. Norm-referenced tests are typically broader in focus and frequently contain more complex tasks than do criterion-referenced tests, since there is less need to specify completely the skills needed to perform adequately on each item.

Increasingly, publishers of standardized achievement tests are suggesting that the results of their tests can be used in a criterion-referenced mode. The test coordinator's handbook for the CAT (California Test Bureau/McGraw-Hill, 1985) states, "Because the tests combine the most useful characteristics of norm-referenced and criterion-referenced tests, they provide information about the relative ranking of students against a norm-group as well as specific information about the instructional needs of students" (p. 1). This statement is elaborated upon, and considerably weakened, much later in the handbook:

> The CAT E and F objectives, called category objectives, represent categories of skills, each comprising two or more specific skills or instructional goals. An objective is measured by four or more items and is scored separately to yield mastery information. Since the items associated with a category objective can only sample related skills, the objective mastery scores indicate general strengths or weaknesses in the area defined by the category objective. A mastery score does not necessarily mean that all related skills have been mastered. (California Test Bureau/McGraw-Hill, 1985, p. 83)

Examples of the CAT's "category objectives" are Addition of Whole Numbers ("The student will add whole numbers"), Measurement ("The student will demonstrate an understanding of measurement"), and Geometry ("The student will demonstrate an understanding of geometry"). Needless to say, a report that Sarah Hopkins got five out of eight items correct for the category objective Geometry tells the teacher very little about what kind of instruction Sarah needs in geometry.

Criterion-referenced tests that are designed for just that purpose have item-level objectives that sound more like this: "The student will add two two-digit numbers with regrouping from the ones place to the tens"; "The student will measure to the nearest inch the length of an object that is less than 6 inches long"; or "The student will find the length of the hypotenuse, given the lengths of the other two sides of a right triangle." The number of items per objective varies with the different tests, but most researchers recommend between three and five items to test each objective (Cox, 1975; Grossnickle & Reckzeh, 1973; Underhill et al., 1980). Evidence that Sarah was able or unable to complete a certain percentage of items with such objectives is clearly of more diagnostic value to the classroom teacher or diagnostician than that she got five out of eight problems correct in the Geometry category.

The movement toward the provision of more criterion-referenced data and scores to schools after the administration of standardized achievement tests has come about as a result of the understandable desire on the part of school personnel to minimize the time students spend in test taking. If reliable data about students' specific strengths and weaknesses were available to teachers at the same time that the needed norm-referenced data were available to administrators, then teachers could get on with the task of teaching without needing further testing time. Unfortunately, these instruments are far better norm-referenced instruments than they are criterion-referenced instruments, and such reliable data are simply not available in any great quantity. The provision of the data that are available simply points the knowledgeable teacher in the proper direction for further, better-designed, criterion-referenced diagnostic testing.

Teacher-Made and Standardized Tests

One decision that needs to be made very early in the diagnostic or achievement testing cycle is whether to use a commercially available standardized test or a locally constructed test, usually designed by the classroom teacher alone.

The advantage of standardization is the assurance that the testing conditions are "standard" for all of the examinees; that is, that the instructions are the same, the time allowed the same, the materials used the same, and the methods of scoring the same for everyone taking the test. These standardizing conditions are obviously necessary when one hopes to gain any useful norm-referenced data from the administration of a test. But it should not be assumed that the same conditions are equally important for all testing situations.

Teacher-made tests and other locally constructed tests are certainly easier to keep up to date and easier to target to specific instructional goals or objectives. As described earlier, commercially available tests use, as their basis, a core of general educational objectives that are common to large numbers of school districts. It is in this attempt to make such tests as widely popular as possible that test authors frequently fail to meet the specific needs of a particular school or community. When the faculty of a school decide to make a curricular change, such as de-emphasizing arithmetic operations on fractions in favor of giving more attention to processes of problem solving in mathematics, it is relatively easy to modify local tests quickly to accommodate the change. A nationally normed standardized test will only be modified if that particular curricular change is perceived to be a national trend; even if they are modified, the earliest the changes will appear is in the next version of the test— some 2–8 years after the curricular changes have been made.

There are obvious reasons to use a combination of standardized and teacher-made tests in any local school situation. Each type of test has its own advantages and disadvantages, however, and these should be understood and considered when one is selecting a test to meet a particular objective.

Free-Response and Multiple-Choice Testing

Another issue of great concern to mathematics educators is the almost universal use of multiple-choice items in nationally normed standardized tests. The manual of one of the few tests that until its most recent versions was still free-response, the Stanford Diagnostic Mathematics Test, gives its authors' reason for switching formats very succinctly: "The test's multiple choice format allows for efficiency of scoring by machine and by hand; and students' test results can be examined both in reference to national norms and in terms of test questions measuring specific behaviors" (Beatty, Madden, Gardner, & Karlsen, 1984, p. 5). The need to be able to grade test papers quickly; to be able to produce a great variety of both norm-referenced and criterion-referenced scores based on a single sample of student behavior; and to be able to use sophisticated item response theory models for the assessment of student performance have made the use of computer scanning techniques for scoring absolutely essential. Given the relatively limited state of the art in the field of artificial intelligence, computer technology can only be relied upon to accurately determine which of a number of answer options have been selected by a student, not to "understand" a free response to an item written by the student.

The reliance on the multiple-choice format, however, subtly changes what is being measured in several ways. Reisman (1982) suggest that most multiple-choice tests are not direct measures of mathematics the way teachers teach it or the way textbooks present it. Although much can be learned from a collection of multiple-choice responses, the format itself detracts from the usefulness of, or information carried by, each individual response. The opportunity to guess at an answer from among a choice of four or five possible responses makes those individual responses suspect; it can mask existing deficits and can artificially enhance students' scores.

The free-response format requires students to produce an answer rather than select it. This process offers the advantage of extracting student responses that carry a great deal of information in addition to that required to answer the test item. In free-response answers, the skilled diagnostician can discover faulty algorithms and other error patterns, place-value misconceptions, problems with spatial orientation, and many other indicators of mathematics learning difficulties that are not evident in multiple-choice responses. When the test results are to be used for other than norm-referenced purposes, these kinds of findings are critical.

Pure, unadulterated guessing is only one of the ways in which students respond to multiple-choice items when they do not know the answers. Multiple-choice mathematics tests, especially, lend themselves to a variety of test-taking strategies that tend to mask the presence or absence of the skills being measured. Wilson (1973) and Vande-Walle (1983, p. 40–59) discuss some of the most popular ones.

Checking the answer choices given to find one that works is a process that, for complicated mathematical procedures, frequently works more efficiently than working the problems from beginning to end. Using this strategy, students can select the correct answer choice with great confidence, although they may be unable to solve the same problem in a free-response format. As an example, how would most adults "solve" this Algebra I item?

Find the (x,y) pair that satisfies both of these equations:

$$x + 3y = 7$$
$$x - 5y = -1$$

a. $(1,4)$ b. $(-1,4)$ c. $(4,1)$ d. $(4,-1)$

Another often-suggested strategy is that of estimation. Students who have developed a good sense of number size and number relationships can often choose the correct answer to a multiple-choice test item by simply estimating the size of the probable answer and matching it against the answer options. In this case, the student must have some idea of the necessary procedure for solving the problem, but need not necessarily be able to accomplish all of the steps. This process works nicely for problems like this:

$$\tfrac{4}{5} + \tfrac{5}{6} =$$

a. $\tfrac{9}{11}$ b. $\tfrac{19}{30}$ c. $\tfrac{9}{30}$ d. $\tfrac{20}{30}$

Yet another strategy that good test-takers use is the elimination of answer choices that make no sense, either in the context of the problem or numerically. Such elimination reduces number of possible options and increases the chance of choosing the correct one from among them, even if the "proper"

mathematical solution technique is unknown to the student. This process can be used in conjunction with estimation skill to tackle the fraction addition problem just shown.

The likelihood that most students use strategies like those described above when completing a multiple-choice mathematics test makes the interpretation of the scores for individual students on individual subtests of the test problematical. Attempts to assess any student's specific abilities on even smaller collections of multiple-choice items are bound to lead to misjudgments.

Individual and Group Testing

The vast majority of achievement and diagnostic tests used in this country are group-administered, but there are tests of both types that are constructed exclusively for individual administration. The obvious disadvantage of individual testing is the amount of time that a trained clinician must spend with each examinee. The advantages of such testing, however, are frequently well worth the additional time and effort.

In an individually administered wide-range survey test, it is possible to quickly locate that section of the test that is correctly targeted for the student's ability level and to administer only those items in the critical range. Most individual test manuals give guidelines for the establishment of a basal (lower) level and a ceiling (higher) level for each examinee to help define the critical range. Asking students to complete only those test items that are appropriate keeps bright students from getting bored with a large number of items that are too easy, and keeps slower students from getting frustrated by items that are too difficult. In either case, student attention and therefore performance are likely to be enhanced.

But, from a diagnostic point of view, possibly the chief advantage of an individually administered test is the opportunity it affords the well-trained examiner to monitor student performance and make clinical observations and judgments. The misconceptions and faulty algorithms that students often develop have already been extensively discussed in this chapter. They are much more likely to be identified, and their origins are much more likely to be uncovered, in a situation where a clinician and student are interacting about a particular piece of mathematical content than in a group testing setting. A clinician who is sensitive to the existence of such error patterns is able to probe for the rationale and reasoning behind a student's answers, both correct and incorrect, and so to develop a much more complete profile of the examinee's mathematical understanding.

Schoen (1979) suggests that for most purposes, the convenience, objectivity, and reliability of group-administered standardized tests make them preferable to either standardized or teacher-constructed individual clinical interviews, but that the interview technique is a valuable supplement to any good testing program. The intelligent observation of students' attempts to solve mathematics problems allows one to learn a great deal about how those students think.

SUMMARY

Mathematics is frequently considered to be the easiest of the traditional school subjects in which to assess student ability and performance. Most teachers and students take an approach to the content that suggests, "There is just one right answer, and you can either do it or you can't." As a result, they feel very comfortable with tests that feature multiple-choice or short-numerical-answer formats. This chapter begins with a discussion of the school mathematics curriculum and the direction in which it is heading: an increased emphasis on problem-solving ability and on "meaning" in the mathematical processes. The following sections, which describe typical student performance and frequent error patterns seen in the current curriculum, illustrate the importance of the new curricular movements.

The last section focuses on issues and concerns in mathematics testing. If the goals of the new mathematics programs are to be realized, better use must be made of existing measurement instruments, and new instruments must be developed. Educators must come to realize that although the ubiquitous, group-administered, multiple-choice, standardized achievement test serves some needs exceedingly well, it serves others not at all. Successful teachers and clinicians will be the ones who can correctly identify the objectives of their testing programs and then select or construct assessment instruments that can meet those objectives.

REFERENCES

Aiken, L. R. (1985). Psychological testing and assessment (5th ed.). Boston: Allyn & Bacon (1985).

Alford, L. E. (1986). Research report: Alignment of textbook and test content. Arithmetic Teacher, 34(3), 25.

Anastasi, A. (1982). Psychological testing (5th ed.). New York: Macmillan.

Ashlock, R. B. (1986). Error patterns in computation. Columbus, OH: Charles E. Merrill.

Beatty, L. S., Madden, R., Gardner, E. F., & Karlsen, B. (1984). The Stanford Diagnostic Mathematics Test, Forms G & H. New York: Psychological Corporation.

Bruner, J. S. (1963). Toward a theory of instruction. Cambridge, MA: Harvard University Press.

California State Board of Education. (1985). The framework for mathematics instruction. Sacramento: Author.

California Test Bureau/McGraw-Hill. (1985). California Achievement Tests, Forms E and F. Monterey, CA: Author.

Carpenter, T. P. (1989). Introduction. In M. M. Lindquist (Ed.), Results from the Fourth Mathematics Assessment of the National Assessment of Educational Progress (pp. 1–9). Reston, VA: National Council of Teachers of Mathematics.

Cox, L. S. (1975). Using research in teaching. Arithmetic Teacher, 22(2), 151–157.

Dunn, L. M., & Markwardt, F. C., Jr. (1970). Peabody Individual Achievement Test and manual. Circle Pines, MN: American Guidance Service.

Education Commission of the States. (1979). The National Assessment of Educational Progress: Mathematical Applications. Denver: Author.

Educational Testing Service. (1983). The Third National Mathematics Assessment: Results, trends, and issues. Princeton, NJ: Author.

Freeman, D. J., Kuhs, T. M., Knappen, L. B., & Porter, A. C. (1982). A closer look at standardized tests. Arithmetic Teacher, 29(7), 50–54.

Ginsburg, H. (1977). Children's arithmetic: The learning process. New York: Van Nostrand Reinhold.

Grossnickle, F. E., & Reckzeh, J. (1973). Discovering meanings in elementary school mathematics. New York: Holt, Rinehart & Winston.

Kilian, L., Cahill, E., Ryan, C., Sutherland, D., & Taccetta, D. (1980). Errors that are common in multiplication. Arithmetic Teacher, 27(5), 22–25.

Kouba, V. L., Carpenter, T. P., & Swafford, J. O (1989). Number and operations. In M. M. Lindquist (Ed.), Results from the Fourth Mathematics Assessment of the National Assessment of Educational Progress (pp. 64–93). Reston, VA: National Council of Teachers of Mathematics.

Leinwand, S. (1986). Curricular improvement versus standardized testing. Arithmetic Teacher, 33(8), 3.

Lidz, C. D. (1981). Improving assessment of schoolchildren. San Francisco: Jossey-Bass.

Education Commission of the States. (1979). National Assessment of Educational Progress. In Mathematical applications: Selected results from the Second Assessment of Mathematics. Denver: Author.

Education Commission of the States. (1983). National Assessment of Educational Progress. *The Third National Mathematics Assessment: Results, trends and issues*. Denver: Author.

National Council of Teachers of Mathematics (NCTM). (1980). An agenda for action: Recommendations for school mathematics of the 1980's. Reston, VA: Author.

National Council of Teachers of Mathematics (NCTM). (1989). *Curriculum and evaluation standards for school mathematics*. Reston, VA: Author.

Reisman, F. K. (1982). *A guide to the diagnostic teaching of arithmetic* (3rd ed.). Columbus, OH: Charles E. Merrill.

Reisman, F. K., & Hutchinson, T. A. (1985). *The Sequential Assessment of Mathematics Inventory: Individual Assessment Battery*. Columbus, OH: Charles E. Merrill.

Roberts, G. H. (1968). The failure strategies of third grade arithmetic pupils. *Arithmetic Teacher, 15*, 442–446.

Schoen, H. (1979). Using the individual interview to assess mathematics learning. *Arithmetic Teacher, 27*(3), 34–37.

Underhill, R. G., Uprichard, A. E., & Heddens, J. W. (1980). *Diagnosing mathematical difficulties*. Columbus, OH: Charles E. Merrill.

VandeWalle, J., & Mick, H. (1983). Classroom assessment of conceptual understanding. In *Mathematics assessment for the classroom teacher*. Charlottesville, VA: Virginia Council of Teachers of Mathematics.

Wilson, J. W. (1973). Standardized tests very often measure the wrong things. *Mathematics Teacher, 66*, 369.

21

Diagnostic Assessment of Reading

BEVERLY D. STRATTON
MARTHA CROUTHERS GRINDLER
Georgia Southern College

T esting is an important component of education today. Performing well on tests is just as important. Students' scores on tests determine placement in ability groups as well as promotion or retention decisions. The lives of students are in part determined by their test performance.

Because we live in a highly test-conscious society, we need to use assessment instruments that are valid and reliable in making major decisions on the basis of student performance. Another important consideration is that time spent in testing is time taken away from instruction. However, if teachers use results as a basis for instruction, time is not wasted. The preponderance of testing today means that we need to utilize results effectively.

DEFINITION OF DIAGNOSIS

"Diagnosis" is technically defined as "the act or result of identifying disorders from their symptoms" (Harris & Hodges, 1981, p. 86). When the term "diagnosis" is used in education, it often includes the planning of instruction based on evaluation of the problem and consideration of causal factors.

Diagnosis is a form of evaluation based on multiple assessment of reading and/or reading-related behaviors. Diagnosis entails making judgments about the adequacy of performance and the factors that impinge on this performance.

PRINCIPLES OF DIAGNOSIS

The diagnosis of reading problems is a complex process, and should be guided by principles that help insure the validity of the data collected and the tentative decisions made. This summary of the diagnostic principles reflects the major points emphasized in the current literature.

1. Diagnosis should be continuous. Spache (1976) cautions that all the information needed to achieve a full understanding of any disabled reader's problems cannot be obtained in one testing session. Since learners' reading abilities grow in different ways and at different rates, ongoing diagnosis is critical to make instructional decisions that will afford optimal benefit to students (Alexander & Heathington, 1988). Diagnosis involves gathering data, looking for patterns of achievement, proposing hypotheses, and testing them with the implementation of various teaching strategies.

2. A thorough diagnosis needs to be a blueprint for instruction (Heilman, 1972). Testing in many American schools has become an end in itself. When test results are not used for instructional purposes, the educational objectives of the testing program are defeated. Intelligent instruction must be based on accurate information regarding a student's strengths and weaknesses. Testing instruments need to be selected in view of the kind of information most useful to the

instructional program. The diagnosis should be as thorough as necessary, but should not extend beyond what is required. So much time should not be spent on testing that little time is left for remediation.

3. Diagnostic methods and instruments should be varied. Conventional assessment (i.e., standardized tests, informal inventories, screening inventories) is only one aspect of the diagnostic process. Analysis of performance samples (i.e., tapes of the student's reading and writing, as well as systematic teacher observation of everyday performance) needs to be an integral part of the diagnostic program.

4. Diagnostic evaluation needs to provide a holistic picture of the learner. Reading is interwoven into the entire language process, and each part of this process influences the others. Because of the interrelationships among the language arts (i.e., reading, speaking, listening, and writing), growth in one area can enhance growth in other language areas as well.

5. Language skills need to be assessed in a variety of contexts. According to Glazer and Searfoss (1988), the "continuous assessment of language model" (C-A-L-M) suggests that the observation and collection of data must occur over time and in many reading environments. These environments occur when people, materials, space, and language come together to communicate. Reading environments include instructional settings (large and small groups when the teacher provides instructional intervention), individual settings (one-on-one work focusing on literacy activities), formal settings (assessment procedures, including both standardized and informal assessment instruments), interactive settings (small-group work with an academic goal), and recreational settings (reading in noninstructional settings).

CURRENT DIAGNOSTIC PRACTICES

Reading is probably the most frequently assessed subject in schools today. Almost all states' minimum-competency tests include a reading component.

A recent survey (Carey, 1984) of test usage in one state reported that the average student in that state can expect to take between 12 and 15 major standardized achievement test batteries during a normal public school experience (kindergarten through 12th grade). In the state of Georgia, by the end of the fourth grade, students will have taken three standardized tests (the California Achievement Tests in kindergarten and the Iowa Tests of Basic Skills in second and fourth grades).

Testing represents a considerable expenditure of time and money; yet many teachers and administrators have questioned the value of testing programs. An in-depth study of one school system was unable to discover a single teacher who used the test results for any curricular or instructional purpose (Carey, 1985). The only person in favor of the test and the testing program in the school district was the superintendent, who had a functional need to report test scores to the local school board and, in the case of certain groups of students, to the state.

Standardized testing has had limited impact in the classroom. Teachers consider standardized tests to be of little value (Stiggins, Conklin, & Bridgeford, 1986). Test results do not lead to higher achievement, nor do they influence subsequent teacher practices (Kellaghan, Madaus, & Airasian, 1982). Standardized tests clearly have their greatest influence outside the classroom and are primarily useful for administrative and public relations purposes (Stiggins, 1985). This is regrettable, because standardized tests in the reading classroom have potential for diagnosis, are generally reliable, and provide estimates of student performance. We discuss three types of standardized tests below, and also make brief mention of two less formal methods of reading assessment (informal reading inventories and basal reading tests).

Standardized Reading Tests

Evaluation should be an important part of the teaching process, because it determines important aspects of planning as content is selected, objectives are written, and remediation/enrichment activities are selected. Standardized reading tests are used extensively in most elementary schools. Three common types of standardized tests are achievement tests, diagnostic reading tests, and criterion-referenced tests. Each type of test provides different information and serves different purposes.

Achievement Tests

Achievement tests in reading are norm-referenced and compare a student's performance on the test with that of a representative group of students. They generally measure a broad range of reading skills and abilities. These tests typically yield grade equivalents, percentile rankings, and/or stanine scores in word recognition (or vocabulary) and comprehension, and a total score (combining word recognition and comprehension scores). These survey tests are more meaningful for group comparisons than for diagnosing individuals, since they generally do not yield enough information about specific skills to permit an adequate diagnosis.

Examples of general achievement tests are as follows:

California Achievement Tests, Forms E and F (California Test Bureau/McGraw-Hill, 1985). Eleven levels, ranging from K.0 to 12.9.

Iowa Tests of Basic Skills (Hieronymus, Hoover, & Linquist, 1982). Ten levels, for kindergarten through ninth grade.

Metropolitan Achievement Tests, sixth edition (Prescott, Balow, & Hogan, 1985). Norm-referenced and criterion-referenced. Two forms with eight levels, ranging from K.0 to 12.9.

Stanford Achievement Test Series (Gardner, Rudman, Karlsen, & Merwin, 1984). Ten levels, ranging from K.0 to 13; alternate forms available for levels from 2.5 to 13.

Diagnostic Tests

Diagnostic tests are also norm-referenced and provide specific information about an individual's reading strengths and weaknesses in content-oriented skills. Diagnostic tests may permit comparison among subabilities of the same individual, and sometimes comparisons of strong and weak points of a group or class (Harris & Hodges, 1981).

Diagnostic tests are generally administered after some instruction has occurred. They can be administered to a group, but are usually given individually. The purpose of such testing is to identify a student's reading strengths and weaknesses in more detail.

An ideal situation would be to administer an achievement test to a group to identify students who demonstrate inadequacies. A standardized diagnostic test could then be used for individual students, to identify specific areas for further instruction or perhaps remediation. From this information, the teacher would design a prescriptive reading plan for his or her students.

Hayward (1968) suggests three questions that need to be asked when selecting a diagnostic reading test:

1. Does the test measure the necessary component skills, and do the subscores represent meaningful areas for providing remedial instruction?
2. Are the subscore reliabilities sufficiently high (above .90) for individual application?
3. Are the intercorrelations among the subscores sufficiently low (below .65) to warrant differential diagnosis?

An example of a group-administered diagnostic test is the Stanford Diagnostic Reading Test (SDRT), third edition (Karlsen, Madden, & Gardner, 1984). Forms G and H, with four levels (Red, Green, Brown, and Blue), are available. The primary purpose of the SDRT is to diagnose pupils' strengths and weaknesses in reading.

The Red level is intended for use at the end of first grade, in second grade, and with low-achieving students in third grade and above. It measures auditory discrimination, basic phonics, auditory vocabulary, word recognition, and comprehension of short sentences and paragraphs.

The Green level is intended for use in third and fourth grades and with low-achieving students in fifth grade. It assesses auditory discrimination, phonetic and structural analysis, auditory vocabulary, and literal and inferential comprehension.

The Brown level is used for students in fifth through eighth grades and low-achieving high school students. This level provides information related to phonetic and structural analysis; auditory vocabulary; literal and inferential comprehension of textual, functional, and recreational material; and rate of reading.

The Blue level is appropriate for students in eighth grade through community college and provides diagnostic information regarding phonetic and structural analysis; knowledge of word meaning and word parts; reading rate, including skimming and scanning; and literal and inferential comprehension of textual, functional, and recreational materials.

Individually administered diagnostic reading tests have standardized procedures for administration and scoring and may provide some normative information. The most widely used instruments in this category include the Diagnostic Reading Scales (Spache, 1981b), the Durrell Analysis of Reading Difficulty (Durrell & Catterson, 1980), and the Woodcock Reading Mastery Tests (Woodcock, 1973). Each test provides instructions for estimating instructional reading levels and may be helpful when making placement decisions. However, administration, scoring, and interpretation procedures differ for each instrument. These instruments are considered useful primarily in aiding the reading teacher in making diagnostic decisions about students' reading performance.

The Woodcock Reading Mastery Tests (Woodcock, 1973) are a diagnostic battery of five individually administered reading tests; these include Letter Identification, Word Identification, Word Attack, Word Comprehension, and Passage Comprehension. These tests are designed to assess specific reading skills for students from kindergarten through 12th grade. Forms A and B of the test are available.

The data obtained from general achievement tests and diagnostic tests must be interpreted carefully. General achievement tests allow the teacher to compare a disabled reader with the average learner. Diagnostic tests enable the reading teacher to isolate the content areas in which students may have trouble adapting his or her reading to the specific content fields.

Criterion-Referenced Tests

A criterion-referenced test measures a student's reading performance in specific skills against criteria identified as required for mastery. Usually these criteria are stated as performance objectives.

Scores on criterion-referenced tests are reported in two ways. A scaled score shows how the pupil scored in relation to the total number of questions on the test. A minimum scaled score is given; any score below this is considered to be failing and definitely suggests a weakness. Of more use in diagnosing a student's strengths and weaknesses are the lists of skills needing instruction and/or remediation, both as part of objectives not achieved and as weak areas of achieved objectives.

The use of norm-referenced reading tests in American schools has become a controversial issue (Rupley & Blair, 1988). Some educators feel that such tests serve no meaningful purpose in education. Rupley and Blair (1988) cite two major criticisms: (1) Norm-referenced tests are biased against bilingual and culturally different students, and (2) they provide little information for planning an instructional program.

Rudman et al. (1980) found that teachers prefer norm-referenced tests over criterion-referenced tests. However, Lazer-Morris, Polin, May, and Burry (1980) reported that most experts consider norm-referenced tests to be narrow of focus, biased, and unreliable. Rupley and Blair (1979) state that achievement tests are extremely limited in identifying reading strengths and weaknesses. Wilson (1981) considers them nearly useless for classroom diagnosis. The preferred alternative is the criterion-referenced test because of its diagnostic, placement, and remediation uses, as well as its ease of interpretation. Several differences between criterion-referenced and norm-referenced measures are briefly summarized in Table 21.1.

Regardless of the standardized test measure used, the teacher is the most important part of the reading instruction program. No test is more important than the teacher; testing is merely a diagnostic tool to be used by the teacher. Reading diagnosis enables the teacher to gain insights into students' strengths and weaknesses in such areas as word recognition, comprehension, study skills, and content area reading.

It is impossible in one chapter to list all standardized tests that are available to reading teachers and specialists. More information may be found in the following sources: (1) the various *Mental Measurements Yearbooks;* (2) *Tests in Print;* (3) test manuals; and (4) reference books on testing.

TABLE 21.1. Comparison of Criterion- and Norm-Referenced Tests

Dimension	Criterion-referenced measures	Norm-referenced measures
1. Intent	Information on degree to which absolute external performance standards have been met	Information for relative internal comparisons
	Description of maximum performance by individuals, groups, and treatment	Comparisons of individuals, particularly when high degree of selectivity is required
2. Directness of measurement	Great emphasis	Less emphasis
3. Variability among scores	Relatively low	Realtively low
4. Difficulty of items	Items tend to be easy, but with some range	Item difficulty localized around 50 percent
5. Item type	Great variety, but less reliance on selection items	Variety, but emphasis on selection items
6. Discrimination of items	Not emphasized	Greatly emphasized
7. Methods of establishing validity	Reliance on content validity	Emphasis on criterion-related validity
8. Emphasis on reliability	Focus on reliability of domain sampling; therefore internal consistency of some interest	Greater concern with parallel form and test–retest estimates of performance stability
9. Influence of guessing	Can be of consequence	Generally not a problem
10. Importance of which items are missed	High	Emphasis on number of missed items
11. Necessity for maintaining security of test items	Relatively low	Relatively high
12. Area of education best served	Instruction	Guidance, selection, grading

Note. From *Elementary Education: A Basic Text,* by F. Reisman and B. Payne, 1987, Columbus, OH: Charles E. Merrill. Copyright 1987 by Charles E. Merrill Publishing Company. Reprinted by permission.

Informal Reading Inventories

A number of commercially produced, generic informal reading inventories (IRIs) have been developed and published. These inventories are not bound to a particular basal reading program or set of instructional materials. Typically, these IRIs contain graded word lists; graded oral paragraphs with accompanying comprehension questions; and, in some inventories, supplemental language arts tests. Reviews of commercial IRIs have been published by Cramer (1980), Harris and Niles (1982), Jongsma and Jongsma (1981), and Pikulski (1974).

IRIs assess the student's specific word recognition and comprehension skills, and enables the teacher to estimate independent, instructional, and frustration reading levels as well as listening comprehension. Baumann (1988) reports that the primary disadvantage of commercially developed IRIs is their weakened content validity, since the passages used in the assessment are not selected from instructional materials. Several studies, however, have indicated that students' performance on commercial IRIs is generally quite consistent with their performance on other estimates of instructional reading level (Blanchard, Borthwick, & Hall, 1983; Bristow, Pikulski, & Pelosi, 1983; Coleman & Hormer, 1982).

Although IRIs supply valuable information for student placement, they take a great deal of time to administer, primarily because they must be administered orally to individual students. Recently, software packages have been developed to aid in the assessment process. IRIs are not yet capable of replacing more comprehensive assessment tools in print, but they have the potential for yielding information on various aspects of students' reading skills (Strickland, Feeley, & Wepner, 1987).

Basal Reading Tests

A form of reading assessment that falls between formal standardized tests and informal tests made by the teacher consists of the basal reading tests that accompany all the basal reader programs in schools today. Typically, these tests are given at the end of a unit or level in the book. These basal reading tests are probably the most powerful determinant of reading instruction (Rupley & Blair, 1988).

DIAGNOSTIC CONSIDERATIONS

Reading is a complex process, and the causes of reading disability are numerous. Rarely will a single factor be found to cause a student to be disabled in reading (Robinson, 1946). Various factors, operating singly or more often together, can block the student's further progress in reading until they are discovered or eliminated, or until instructional procedures can implemented to enable the student to adjust to or circumvent their effects (Bond, Tinker, Wasson, & Wasson, 1984, p. 51).

When one is diagnosing a student's reading strengths and weaknesses, it is imperative to make use of any pertinent information that may already be available. This makes the diagnosis efficient and avoids the replication of diagnostic data. Cumulative school records may contain information related to the student's school history, such as previous grades/schools attended, attendance records, teachers' observations/comments, and health history. Health problems, poor attendance, and/or long periods of absences can leave gaps in the sequential development of reading skills and may be partly responsible for the student's lack of reading success.

Research has proven a connection between socioeconomic status and reading performance (Downing & Leong, 1982). There is a consistent connection between low socioeconomic status and poor achievement in read-ing (Downing & Leong, 1982). Research also indicates that such factors as parents' education, occupation, and economic level have important influences on reading achievement (Ekwall, 1977). Consideration of socioeconomic status and the educational level of the parents may indicate the availability of books, positive reading role models, parental ability to provide help, and a general idea of the environment in which a child lives.

When test scores of low-socioeconomic-status children compare unfavorably with children of a higher socioeconomic background, limited experiences and background development may be reflected. Hence the content of some reading material has limited comprehensibility for disadvantaged students unless provisions for background and concept development are included in instruction.

Language is one type of difference among social classes and other subcultures that seems to influence progress in acquiring reading skill (Downing & Leong, 1982). Language differences may reduce a student's inclination to take risks (Wilson, 1981). Children at the lower end of the continuum in language development—those with very limited vocabularies, poor articulation, and poor ability to communicate—will obviously have difficulty with reading (Spache & Spache, 1977). Language and subsequent vocabulary development are crucial factors in learning to read and in improving reading comprehension. The relationship between vocabulary development and reading achievement is among the best documented in reading (Beck, Perfetti, & McKeown, 1982; Duffelmeyer, 1980; Johnson & Pearson, 1984).

Information concerning the native language of the parents, their fluency in English, and the student's language facility is valuable. Walter Loban's (1976) 12-year study provided evidence that reading, writing, and speaking were all positively related. Students who were slow in oral language also tended to be low in reading achievement. Rupley and Blair (1979) point out that bilingual children are often labeled as retarded readers, with only minimal progress in reading expected—an illogical assumption, since such students can become successful readers. The language abilities students bring to school, no matter how variant, can provide a rich foundation for learning and developing reading proficiency.

The role of intelligence is critical in reading diagnosis (Wilson, 1981). A measure of mental ability assists the teacher in setting realistic, attainable goals of potential reading achievement. Wilson (1981), however, points out several problems in using the results of group IQ tests. A group test generally requires that students be able to read in order to take the test. Obviously, poor reading will be reflected in depressed general intellectual functioning scores. Therefore, the preferred assessment of intellectual performance should be obtained from measures that are individually administered and do not involve reading.

In spite of IQ tests' questionable cultural bias and lack of reliability, individually administered IQ tests appear to assess similar aptitudes that are needed for success in learning to read (Smith & Johnson, 1976). Many studies of the relationships between mental test results and reading achievement seem to support the belief in the predictive value of intelligence measures (Spache & Spache, 1977).

Research concerning cognitive style, or preferred manner of intellectual functioning, and reading difficulties had been conducted by Dunn, Price, Dunn, and Saunders (1979). Marie Carbo (1982) has developed the Reading Style Inventory, which is based on the model of learning styles described by Rita and Kenneth Dunn. This 52-item computerized questionnaire can generate a printout for a group or an individual that includes (1) "perceptual strengths/preferences," "preferred reading environment," and "emotional profile," as well as the student's sociological, physical, and instructional preferences; (2) recommended methods; and (3) recommended materials (Mason, 1986). Carbo (1987) reports that research conducted over a 4-year period indicates that when instructional approaches are matched to students' reading styles, students make better-than-average gains in reading, enjoy learning to read, and develop better self-concepts "even though those youngsters . . . had previously been labeled 'emotionally disturbed,' 'learning disabled,' or 'poor readers'" (p. 433).

The importance of the students as a source of data is often overlooked. Wilson (1981) suggests getting the students thinking about how reading is working for them. Questions might include the following:

Do you think you read better than, worse than, or about the same as other students in your class?
What do you do best when reading?
What causes you most difficulty in reading?
Are you reading a book for fun? (If yes, ask for the title.)
If you were to describe reading to a kindergarten child, what would you say?
Why do you read books of your choice (for information, for fun, have to, other)?

Paratore and Indrisano (1987) suggest examining students' awareness of the reading process through interviews with questions such as these:

When you come to a word you can't read, what do you do?
When you have a question you can't answer, what do you do?
What do you do to help yourself remember what you've read?
How do you check your reading?
If a young child asked you how to read, what would you tell him or her to do?

Diagnostic teaching or "minilessons" can add to the data accumulated from a variety of diagnostic measures. Harris and Sipay (1975) note that the use of "miniature sample lessons" is one way to determine appropriate instructional strategies for students who are experiencing reading difficulties. Diagnostic information should be used to modify instructional procedures and to help determine the "appropriate" approach for the individual student. Diagnostic teaching centers on the continuous diagnosis of skill development of the student and the implementation of modified instructional strategies to meet the specific needs of the individual.

Once the test information is obtained, it should be accurately communicated. Spache (1976) reports that despite refinements in diagnosis and remediation, there is still a widespread lack of integration between these two processes. In many instances, part of the difficulty seems to be "that these two processes are carried on by different persons between whom there is a distinct lack of communication" (p. 436). It is critically important, therefore, to relay the diagnostic information accurately to the person who will play the primary role in the planning, implementation, and evaluation of instruction.

It is also necessary to communicate the diagnostic information to the student. Time should be spent in explaining the diagnosis and its implications for future instructional needs, so that the reader can begin to take responsibility for his or her own learning. This feedback should be included in a student interview to serve three purposes: (1) to delegate responsibility, (2) to establish purpose, and (3) to offer direction.

Selection and use of specific reading activities should come directly from an accurate and ongoing diagnosis of the student's needs. Effective instruction can come only after diagnosis of the needs of the learner, and this is based on the extent to which the teacher knows each child within the classroom.

Alexander and Heathington (1988) consider the parents as a valuable resource in the planning process. Although some parents "simply will not make themselves available," other parents "are interested in doing all they can to help their child overcome his problem in reading" (p. 392).

A diagnostic sequence (see Appendix 21.1) summarizes the procedures important in the diagnostic assessment of reading. This chart illustrates the implementation of the basic concepts presented in this chapter. A diagnostic summary sheet (see Appendix 21.2) is also provided.

In summary, effective diagnosis of language skills can never be accomplished with a single instrument. Administrators, curriculum coordinators, reading specialists, and teachers together need to develop diagnostic batteries that make use of available data, as well as different assessment techniques that include systematic observation and interview methods. Diagnostic teaching or minilessons can provide direction for instruction that is independent of and can validate other assessment instruments. Evaluation of all facets of language, utilizing a variety of the student's samples from various contexts in which reading occurs, is necessary in order to make informed instructional decisions.

THE STATUS OF READING TESTS

Farr and Carey (1986) suggest that reading tests have not changed significantly in the past 50 years. Advances have typically been in statistical procedures and scoring machines that relay information to the teacher much more quickly. The tests themselves look much like those developed in the 1920s.

A test procedure generally requires reading a paragraph or short passage and answering questions that check for comprehension. Assessment of word recognition has typically remained the same on both norm- and criterion-referenced tests: Words are printed in isolation, and the test taker is asked to select a synonym. What is preferable is that reading skills be assessed in much the same way as they are used in the classroom. The vocabulary words should be embedded in reading passages rather than presented in isolation.

New assessment procedures are needed that are consistent with contemporary understanding of reading. In pilot studies with 15,000 students in 3rd, 6th, 8th, and 10th grades in Illinois, Valencia and Pearson (1987) are developing many novel assessment formats:

1. *Summary writing.* Students are asked to pick the best summary from three or four summaries written by other students.

2. *Multiple acceptable responses.* During discussion, groups are asked to consider alternative acceptable responses to inferential or evaluative questions. Another option is for students to consider given responses as "really complete," "on the right track," or "totally off base."

3. *Question selection.* From a list of 20 questions, students pick 10 questions that they feel would help a peer to best understand the important ideas of a selection.

4. *Prior knowledge.* Two machine-scorable formats for assessing prior knowledge are used. One asks for "yes–no–maybe" predictions about whether certain ideas are likely to be included in a selection on a given topic. Another asks readers to rate the relatedness on vocabulary words to a central concept.

However, when these alternatives are considered, it is essential that validity, reliability, and usable strategies be addressed.

SUMMARY

Diagnostic assessment is an important component of education today. The purpose of diagnosis is to relate a pattern of test results directly to instructional strategies. The diagnosis of reading problems is a complex process, and the results of data obtained from testing must be interpreted carefully.

This chapter has identified specific tests available to the diagnostician for obtaining information concerning student's reading strengths and weaknesses. It has also discussed the utilization of pertinent information that may already be available, such as information related to the physical environmental, language, cognitive, affective, and educational correlates of reading.

Finally, the current status of reading tests has been addressed. Emphasis has been placed on holistic evaluation procedures as a means of accurately collecting as much information as possible to better understand the strategies students use when reading.

APPENDIX 21.1. DIAGNOSTIC PROCEDURE

Diagnostic steps	Problems to explore	Assessment techniques	Diagnostic procedure
1. Identify the problem reader	Low reading achievement on group tests; declining achievement; lack of interest and motivation; behavior problem; poor reading performance in class	Cumulative school records; group standardized achievement scores; systematic observation; interviews	Evaluate standardized reading achievement scores; compare reading achievement with achievement in nonreading subjects
2. Determine the student's optimal reading performance	Level of mental ability; listening comprehension level; oral language skills	Cumulative school records; nonreading group intelligence tests; individual intelligence test; systematic observation; interviews	Convert mental age score to grade equivalent; estimate optimal level
3. Identify possible correlates that may be contributing to the reading problem	Physical factors; cognitive and language factors; emotional factors; environmental factors; educational factors	Cumulative school records; systematic observation; interviews; screening tests in vision and hearing; informal interest and attitude inventories; behavior inventories	Administer screening tests and informal inventories; identify related problems needing further study by other professionals
4. Determine nature of the reading problem	Reading levels: independent, instructional, frustration; interest in reading; reading skills: sight, vocabulary, word analysis, meaning vocabulary comprehension, study skills, rate of reading; diagnostic teaching	Systematic observation; interviews; diagnostic reading tests; informal reading inventory	Collate existing data; identify specific reading strengths and weaknesses from pattern of reading-related behaviors over time and variety of contexts; administer appropriate assessment instruments

(continued)

APPENDIX 21.1. (*continued*)

Diagnostic steps	Problems to explore	Assessment techniques	Diagnostic procedure
5. Record and summarize data	Identify reading strengths and weaknesses	Diagnostic summary (see Appendix 21.2)	Diagnostic summary
6. Interpret data and communicate to teacher (tutor), student, parents	Determine reading strengths and weaknesses; determine possible factors contributing to problem; determine appropriate instructional strategies and materials	Diagnostic summary	Develop instructional plan; monitor and evaluate student progress

APPENDIX 21.2. DIAGNOSTIC SUMMARY SHEET

Student's name _____

Grade in school _____

Examiner _____

Date _____

Word Analysis Skills

__ Adequate in all areas

__ Use of context clues adequate

__ Aware of context clues but needs improvement

__ Guesses at words by first letter only

__ Attempts to sound out word letter-by-letter

__ Lacks knowledge of consonants

__ Lacks knowledge of consonant clusters

__ Lacks knowledge of vowel sounds

__ Lacks knowledge of common phonograms (word families)

__ Unable to blend sounds adequately

__ Appears unaware of common syllable division

__ Appears unaware of common vowel rules (vowel–consonant–final E, consonant–vowel, consonant–vowel–consonant)

__ Excessive locational errors

__ Initial

__ Medial

__ Final

__ Calls word without association of any word attack skills (context, configuration, morphology, phonics, structural analysis)

__ Appears to have no strategy to decode words not known at sight

__ Overdependent on phonic analysis

__ Inadequate sight words for grade level

Comprehension

__ Above grade level

__ Adequate for grade level

__ Below grade level

__ Difficulty with word meaning

__ Difficulty with literal questions

__ Difficulty with inference questions

__ Difficulty with facts

__ Difficulty with sequence

__ Difficulty with critical thinking

__ Utilizes metacognitive strategies

__ Employs appropriate self-talk

Oral versus Silent Reading

__ Comprehends better in oral reading

__ Comprehends better in silent reading

__ Comprehends approximately the same in oral and silent reading

Sight Vocabulary

Basic Sight Words (Words of High Utility)

__ No difficulty with basic sight words

__ Some basic sight words not known

__ Many basic sight words not known

__ Few or no basic sight words known

Sight Words in General

__ No difficulty with sight words at or below grade level

__ Some sight words not known

__ Many sight words not known

__ Few or no sight words not known

Oral Reading Errors

__ Omissions

__ Insertions

__ Substitutions

__ Repetitions

__ Mispronunciations

__ Self-corrected errors

__ Hesitations

Rate of Reading

__ Silent rate adequate

__ Silent rate slow for grade level

__ Oral rate adequate

__ Oral rate slow for grade level

__ High rate at expense of accuracy

__ Practices flexible reading rate dependent on type of material and purpose for reading

Semantic–Syntactic Abilities

__ Makes meaningful substitutions

__ Makes nonmeaningful substitutions

__ Meaningful substitutions reflect student's dialect

Listening Comprehension

__ Understanding of material heard is below grade level

__ Understanding of material heard is at or above grade level

__ Understanding level not determined

Characteristics of the Reader

__ Head movement

__ Finger pointing

__ Disregard for punctuation

__ Loss of place

__ Does not read in natural voice tones

__ Word-by-word reading

__ Poor phrasing

__ Lack of expression

__ Pauses

__ Voicing or lip movement

Note. Adapted from *Ekwall Reading Inventory* (2nd ed.) by E. Ekwall, 1986, Boston: Allyn & Bacon. Adapted by permission.

REFERENCES

Alexander, J. E., & Heathington, B. S. (1988). *Assessing and correcting classroom reading problems*. Glenview, IL: Scot, Foresman/Little, Brown College Division.

Baumann, J. F. (1988). *Reading assessment: An instructional decision-making perspective*. Columbus, OH: Charles E. Merrill.

Beck, I. L., Perfetti, C. A., & McKeown, M. G. (1982). Effects of long-term vocabulary instruction on lexical access and reading comprehension. *Journal of Educational Psychology, 74*, 35–40.

Blanchard, J. S., Borthwick, P., & Hall, A. (1983). Determining instructional reading level: Standardized multiple choice versus IRI probed recall questions. *Journal of Reading, 26*, 684–689.

Bond, G. L., Tinker, M. A., Wasson, B. B., & Wasson, J. B. (1984). *Reading difficulties: Their diagnosis and correction* (5th ed.). Englewood Cliffs, NJ: Prentice-Hall.

Bristow, P. S., Pikulski, J. J., & Pelosi, P. S. (1983). A comparison of five estimates of reading instructional level. *The Reading Teacher, 37*, 273–279.

California Test Bureau/McGraw-Hill. (1985). *California Achievement Tests, Forms E and F*. Monterey, CA: Author.

Carbo, M. (1982). *Reading Style Inventory*. Roslyn Heights, NY: Learning Research Associates.

Carbo, M. (1987). Reading styles research: What works isn't always phonics. *Phi Delta Kappan, 68*, 431–435.

Carey, R. F. (1984). *Selecting a test for the state testing program*. Providence: Rhode Island Department of Education. (Mimeo)

Carey, R. F. (1985). *Program evaluation as ethnographic research*. Providence: Rhode Island Department of Education.

Coleman, M., & Harmer, W. R. (1982). A comparison of

standardized reading tests and informal placement procedures. *Journal of Learning Disabilities, 15*, 369–398.

Cramer, E. H. (1980). Informal reading inventories go commercial. *Curriculum Review, 19*, 424–429.

Downing, J., & Leong, C. K. (1982). *Psychology of reading*. New York: Macmillan.

Duffelmeyer, F. A. (1980). The influence of experience-based vocabulary instruction on learning word meanings. *Journal of Reading, 24*, 35–40.

Dunn, R., Price, G. E., Dunn, K., & Saunders, W. (1979). Relationship of learning style to self concept. *The Clearing House, 53*, 155–158.

Durrell, D. D., & Catterson, J. H. (1980). *Durrell Analysis of Reading Difficulty (3rd ed.)*. New York: Psychological Corporation.

Ekwall, E. (1977). *Diagnosis and remediation of the disabled reader*. Boston: Allyn & Bacon.

Ekwall, E. (1986). *Ekwall Reading Inventory*. (2nd ed.). Boston: Allyn & Bacon.

Farr, R., & Carey, R. F. (1986). *Reading: What can be measured?* (2nd ed.). Newark, DE: International Reading Association.

Gardner, E. F., Rudman, H. C., Karlsen, B., & Merwin, J. C. (1984). *The Stanford Achievement Test Series*. New York: Psychological Corporation.

Glazer, S. M., & Searfoss, L. W. (1988). *Reading diagnosis and instruction: A C-A-L-M approach*. Englewood Cliffs, NJ: Prentice-Hall.

Harris, A. J., & Sipay, E. R. (1975). *How to increase reading ability* (6th ed.). New York: David McKay.

Harris, L. A., & Niles, J. A. (1982). An analysis of published informal reading inventories. *Reading Horizons, 22*, 159–172.

Harris, T. J., & Hodges, R. E. (Eds.) (1981). *A dictionary of reading and related terms*. Newark, DE: International Reading Association.

Hayward, P. (1968). Evaluating diagnostic reading tests. *The Reading Teacher, 21*, 353–371.

Heilman, A. W. (1972). *Principles and practices of teaching reading* (3rd ed.). Columbus, OH: Charles E. Merrill.

Hieronymus, A. N., Hoover, H. D., & Linquist, E. F. (1982). *Iowa Tests of Basic Skills*. Chicago: Riverside.

Johnson, D. D., & Pearson, P. D. (1984). *Teaching reading vocabulary* (2nd ed.). New York: Holt, Rinehart & Winston.

Jongsma, K. S., & Jongsma, E. A. (1981). Test review: Commercial informal reading inventories. *The Reading Teacher, 34*, 697–705.

Karlsen, B., Madden, R., & Gardner, E. F. (1984). *Stanford Diagnostic Reading Test* (3rd ed.). New York: Psychological Corporation.

Kellaghan, T., Madaus, G., & Airasian, P. (1982). *The effects of standardized testing*. Boston: Kluwer-Nijhoff.

Lazer-Morris, C., Polin, L., May, R., & Burry, J. (1980). *A review of the literature in test use* (Report No. 144). Berkeley: University of California, Center for the Study of Evaluation.

Loban, W. (1976). *Language development: Kindergarten through grade twelve*. Urbana, IL: National Council of Teachers of English.

Mason, G. (1986). New software: What'll they think of next? *The Reading Teacher, 39*, 746.

Paratore, J. R., & Indrisano, R. (1987). Intervention assessment of reading comprehension. *The Reading Teacher, 40*, 778–783.

Pikulski, J. J. (1974). A critical review: Informal reading inventories. *The Reading Teacher, 28*, 141–151.

Prescott, G. A., Balow, I. H., & Hogan, T. P. (1985). *Metropolitan Achievement Tests*. New York: Psychological Corporation.

Reisman, F., & Payne, B. (1987). *Elementary education: A basic text*. Columbus, OH: Charles E. Merrill.

Robinson, H. M. (1946). *Why pupils fail in reading*. Chicago: University of Chicago Press.

Rudman, H. C., Kelly, J. L., Wanous, D. S., Mehrens, W. A., Clark, C. M., & Porter, A. C. (1980). *Integrating assessment with instruction* (Research Series No. 75). Lansing: Michigan State University, Institute for Research on Teaching.

Rupley, W. H., & Blair, T. R. (1979). *Reading diagnosis and remediation: A primer for classroom and clinic*. Chicago: Rand McNally.

Rupley, W. H., & Blair, T. R. (1988). *Teaching reading: Diagnosis, direct instruction, and practice* (2nd ed.) Columbus, OH: Charles E. Merrill.

Smith, R. J., & Johnson, D. D. (1976). *Teaching children to read*. Reading, MA: Addison-Wesley.

Spache, G. D. (1976). *Investigating the issues of reading disabilities* (4th ed.). Boston: Allyn & Bacon.

Spache, G. D. (1981a). *Diagnosing and correcting reading difficulties* (2nd ed.). Boston: Allyn & Bacon.

Spache, G. D. (1981b). *Diagnostic Reading Scales*. Monterey, CA: CTB/McGraw-Hill.

Spache, G. D., & Spache, E. B. (1977). *Reading in the elementary school*. Boston: Allyn & Bacon.

Stiggins, R. J. (1985). Improving assessment where it means the most: In the classroom. *Educational Leadership, 43*, 69–74.

Stiggins, R. J., Conklin, N. F., & Bridgeford, N. J. (1986). Classroom assessment: A key to effective education. *Educational Measurement: Issues and Practice, 5*, 5–17.

Strickland, D. S., Feeley, J. T., & Wepner, S. B. (1987). *Using computers in the teaching of reading*. New York: Teachers College Press.

Valencia, S., & Pearson, P. D. (1987). Reading assessment: Time for a change. *The Reading Teacher. 40*, 726–732.

Wilson, R. M. (1981). *Diagnostic and remedial reading for classroom and clinic* (4th ed.). Columbus, OH: Charles E. Merrill.

Woodcock, R. W. (1973). *Woodcock Reading Mastery Tests*. Circle Pines, MN: American Guidance Service.

22

Diagnostic Achievement Testing in Reading

JEANNE S. CHALL
MARY E. CURTIS
Harvard University

O ur purpose in this chapter is twofold: to describe the process of diagnostic testing in reading, and to illustrate how it is used to design instructional programs for students. We begin by discussing some general characteristics of this kind of testing and the procedures involved. We then describe the particular approach to diagnosis that we use in the Harvard Reading Laboratory, focusing on the theory underlying that approach and on the ways in which theory is translated into practice. Finally, we present examples of how results from diagnostic testing can be used to guide the design and evaluation of programs of instruction.

AN OVERVIEW OF DIAGNOSTIC TESTING IN READING

Diagnostic achievement testing involves identifying the relationships among a student's strengths and needs in reading, so that steps toward improvement can be taken. As such, it differs from survey achievement testing of a more general nature done in classrooms, as well as from diagnostic testing done in hospital settings (Chall & Curtis, 1987).

Whereas survey achievement testing is designed to provide information about how well students read, diagnostic achievement test-

ing is used to discover areas of strengths and needs in students who have already been identified as not reading as well as they could. Because of this, diagnostic testing tends to be more extensive than survey testing, consisting of several different tasks at different levels of difficulty.

Diagnostic testing in hospital settings is designed to provide information about the underlying causes of a reading difficulty, whether they be perceptual, cognitive, linguistic, neurological, and/or emotional. In contrast, diagnostic achievement testing is designed to focus on the educational aspects of the difficulty, the goal being to establish instructional solutions rather than to describe underlying causes. In both kinds of diagnostic testing, however, special training and expertise are required.

Components Assessed in Diagnostic Achievement Testing

To identify the relationships among a student's strengths and needs in reading, the examiner (whether a reading specialist or a teacher) must assess the student's knowledge and skill in different areas, or components, of reading. In this section, we describe some of the components that an examiner will assess, focusing on norm-referenced and criterion-referenced tests. Later, we discuss how more informal testing plays an essential role as well.

Word Recognition and Word Analysis

Tests of reading vary in the extent to which they make apparent students' skill in word recognition and their knowledge of the principles of word analysis. Although some tests designed for group administration may require identification of words in context (e.g., the Metropolitan Achievement Tests), or in isolation (e.g., the Gates–MacGinitie Reading Tests), a student's performance on tests like these will always be affected by other factors such as knowledge of word meanings.

Other group tests assess students' skills in word identification more directly. For example, on the Comprehensive Tests of Basic Skills, students are asked to select from among a set of words the one read aloud by the examiner. And, on the Stanford Diagnostic Reading Test, students are asked to match up the sound made by letters in one word (e.g., the "ie" in "tie") with a word that contains the same sound ("fly").

The most direct measure of word identification, however, is provided by tests in which students read aloud a list of words of increasing difficulty (e.g., the Wide Range Achievement Test or the Slosson Oral Reading Test). Students may be asked to read aloud lists composed of high-frequency "sight words" (i.e., words that must be recognized as wholes, such as "one" and "work") as well as words that can be identified through word analysis. Testing continues until students reach the point in the list where the words are too difficult for them to continue.

Often an examiner will choose a test that assesses word analysis and word recognition skills separately. The Roswell–Chall Diagnostic Reading Test of Word Analysis Skills is an example. Knowledge of the sounds of single consonants, consonant blends, short- and long-vowel sounds, the rule of "silent E," and so on is assessed, in addition to a student's performance on a graded list of sight words.

Although most tests use actual words to assess word analysis, nonsense words are sometimes used as well. The Woodcock Reading Mastery Tests is an example of a test battery that does this. Nonsense words can help to identify students who rely on whole-word recognition strategies because of a lack in their knowledge about symbol–sound correspondences (Johnson, 1973). However, nonsense words can also confuse students who expect that a string of letters will correspond to a meaningful unit. For instance, "brake" will be said in response to "brate," simply because the former is a word while the latter is not. Moreover, with use of nonsense words, great care must be taken to insure that the test is a test of letter patterns that occur frequently in the language. Otherwise, students' performances will have little or no generalizability to their skill in dealing with real words.

Spelling is another way in which students' skills in word identification can be examined (e.g., the Wide Range Achievement Test). Correct and incorrect spellings reveal much about facility with particular letter–sound relationships, as well as the overall approach that students take when dealing with print (i.e., visual vs. phonetic).

Oral Reading

Since reading requires identification of words in context, examiners obtain information about strengths and needs in this area with tests that require students to read passages aloud. Such tests usually contain a series of passages that increase in level of difficulty, from about a first-grade level or below to the high school level and beyond. The examiner records the errors that a student makes while reading, and testing continues until the passages become too difficult for the student. The Gray Oral Reading Tests and the Gilmore Oral Reading Tests are examples.

With an oral reading test, an examiner gets information about the level of text difficulty that students can read, along with the frequency and kinds of oral reading errors they make (e.g., mispronunciations, omissions, substitutions, etc.). A student's failure to pause at phrases or sentence boundaries, or difficulty in identifying "signal words" such as "when," "then," or "although," signifies areas of need in reading as well. The reading specialist will also compare a student's performance on words in context with his or her performance on words in isolation. Often it will be the case that when a student's word identification in context is better than in isolation, the student is using context to compensate for poor word analysis and/or word recognition skills (e.g., see Perfetti, 1985; Stanovich, 1986).

Oral reading tests usually include a set of comprehension questions to be asked after the student has completed reading each passage. Performance on these questions may even be included in the computation of the oral reading score. The rationale for this is that students' accuracy or fluency in reading affects their understanding of the meaning of a text. However, for some students, the constraint of reading words aloud imposed by an oral reading test makes comprehension more difficult for them than it would have been if they had been allowed to read silently. For other students, the constraint of answering questions makes their oral reading less accurate or fluent than it would have been if the questions had not been asked. In either case, testing comprehension after oral reading results in less information than would have been gained from assessing each component separately.

Assessing comprehension after each passage also increases testing time—an important consideration when testing is being done for the purpose of teaching and time is limited. Later, we describe a procedure for estimating a score on an oral reading test that can be used when comprehension questions are not asked.

Knowledge of Word Meanings

Because reading is a major avenue for acquiring meaning vocabulary, students who are not reading as well as they should will often have needs related to knowledge of word meanings. Teachers and reading specialists may choose among a variety of tests to obtain information about these needs. Some tests, although they do not test vocabulary separately, require that students use the context in a passage to select among possible meanings of a word (e.g., the Metropolitan Achievement Tests). On tests like this, more than one answer option will usually be correct, in a context-free sense, and students must consider the word as it occurs in context to determine the correct answer.

Performance on vocabulary tests that require the use of context can suggest a number of different things about students' reading. If students know multiple meanings for a word, their answer will reflect how able they are to use context to decide which meaning applies. But, when students are not familiar with a word, their answer indicates their ability to use context to derive its meaning. Hence, for diagnostic and instructional purposes, a student's performance on vocabulary in context items often leads to more questions than answers, requiring the examiner to do additional formal and informal testing to establish strengths and needs.

Another way to gain information about vocabulary knowledge is through tests that require recognition of word meanings presented in isolation (e.g., the Iowa Tests of Basic Skills and the Gates–MacGinitie Reading Tests). By assessing students' ability to recognize synonyms for a sample of words, teachers and reading specialists can make inferences about the breadth of students' vocabulary knowledge (e.g., see Curtis, 1987). Because such tests require reading, however, they measure word identification as well as word meaning. When a student's word recognition and analysis are inadequate, such tests may not show the true strength of the student's meaning vocabulary, since misreading a test item or answer alternative can cause the student to mark the wrong meaning.

For a truer measure of the student's vocabulary knowledge, one that requires no reading is preferable. The Diagnostic Assessment of Reading and Teaching Strategies includes a Word Meaning subtest in which words of increasing difficulty are read to the student, who is asked to define them. Similar to the Vocabulary subtests on the Stanford–Binet and the Wechsler intelligence scales, this orally administered test can be used as an approximation of a student's verbal ability, irrespective of reading. Thus, it can be used as a measure of reading potential.

The Vocabulary subtests of the Stanford Diagnostic Reading Test and the Stanford Achievement Tests for the lower grades can also serve as "truer" measures of word meaning, since they also are administered orally. The student is asked to circle the right alternative out of several printed words and is helped to identify them by the examiner's reading aloud of the items and the choices.

Analogies, classification tasks, and cloze procedures are still other ways in which vocabulary knowledge is assessed by standardized tests. In general, students who know the meanings of many words usually have deep knowledge about the words they know and are able to use context to derive meanings they do not know. Therefore, performances on various item types are highly interrelated (e.g., see Davis, 1944). However, for purposes of making instructional decisions about those students who do not know many word meanings, use of different kinds of vocabulary formats can provide valuable information.

Comprehension

Standardized tests of reading have sometimes been criticized for including items that require little or no understanding of what has been read (e.g., see Anderson, 1972). For the most part, however, items on standardized tests do require students to do more than make a match between words or phrases in a passage and an alternative on a multiple-choice test.

At the lowest grade levels, students may be asked to select from among a set of pictures the one that is best described by a sentence. At higher grade levels, students are asked to determine the main idea of a passage, to identify an author's purpose in writing a selection, to recognize particular kinds of text (e.g., a fable or a legend), and so on. As grade level increases, reading passages become more difficult (conceptually and structurally), and the responses required from the reader become more varied and complex.

In assessing strengths and needs in reading comprehension, an examiner will often compare a student's reading performance with what he or she is able to understand from a listening task. From research on the relationship between reading and listening (e.g., see Sticht & James, 1984), we know that listening comprehension ability is generally better than reading throughout the elementary grades. During high school, reading and listening comprehension are about equal. By comparing comprehension performances on reading and listening tasks, therefore, an examiner is better able to distinguish between a reading comprehension problem that stems from a reading difficulty (i.e., the problem does not arise during listening) and more

general, language-based comprehension needs.

At all levels and kinds of comprehension assessment, performance can be influenced by a student's knowledge about the content of a passage as well. Presently, we know of no comprehension test designed to measure directly the extent of students' content knowledge or the ways in which content knowledge affects their comprehension. Furthermore, whether such a test can or should be designed is a sensitive and unresolved issue (e.g., see Farr & Tone, 1983).

Teachers and reading specialists can use information from existing standardized tests in ways that inform them about content knowledge as a possible source of comprehension difficulty, however. When a student misses many or all of the test questions that accompany a particular passage, insufficient content knowledge is often the source of difficulty. Furthermore, word meanings are also a kind of content knowledge. Students who experience a comprehension problem because of a mismatch between what they know and what a passage requires them to know will often perform poorly on a test of word knowledge as well.

Summary

Up to this point, we have discussed diagnostic testing of several different components of reading, emphasizing the options available to teachers and reading specialists for assessing each. Decisions about which tests to use, as well as which components are the most essential to assess, depend on characteristics of the student being tested, particularly the student's level of reading development. Moreover, these decisions depend on who is doing the testing. An examiner's theoretical approach to reading (e.g., the extent to which skills, content knowledge, or strategies are emphasized), and the way in which that theory gets translated into practice, determine the diagnostic testing process she or he uses.

Independent of decisions about which components to assess and which tests to use, however, are some general procedures associated with diagnostic testing. We discuss these in the next section.

Procedures in Diagnostic Testing

General procedures in diagnostic achievement testing include test administration; conversion of test scores; and establishing a pattern of strengths and needs.

Test Administration

Choosing the correct level of difficulty of a test is of vital importance in achieving a valid measure of a student's strengths and needs. In the case of more general, survey-type achievement testing, the appropriate level of difficulty of a test is determined by the student's grade level in school. However, for students known to be experiencing difficulty, such a practice can often yield very little information. Students miss the majority of items, and inferences about their strengths and needs are not possible. Because of this, in diagnostic achievement testing, an examiner will choose a level of test difficulty that reflects a student's reading ability rather than his or her grade placement. When the student is known to the examiner, the student's current reading level is used as a guide. When the student's current functioning level is not known, the specialist can use the score from a word recognition or oral reading test to select the correct level for testing additional components.

During testing, examiners note evidence of interest, strain, "carelessness," the ways in which problems are attacked, students' reactions when items become too difficult (e.g., erasing, talking), and so on. Often, spontaneous verbalizations can give interesting insights. In addition, between tests, the examiner will usually engage the student in an informal discussion of his or her interests in and out of school, school subjects that are liked best and least, subjects that are easy and difficult, books that have been read recently, and so on. It can also be helpful to ask students about their perceived strengths and needs in reading. Specifically, what is hard? Where does the student think the difficulty lies? Why? What kind of assistance has the student had with this difficulty? All of this takes little time and is done casually.

For some students, the standard time limits are not sufficient for them to complete the test. When a student is still getting most of the items correct at the point when time is up, examiners will often make a note of where the student is, and suggest that he or she continue working until the items become too difficult. At the end of the test, the examiner notes the additional time that was taken and calculates a score based on the untimed performance, as well as one based on the last item completed within the standard time limit. Conversely, when students reach a point of difficulty where it is obvious that answers are being marked randomly, the examiner will generally stop the test, even if the full time allowed in the manual has not been reached.

Conversion of Test Scores

Following the selection and administration of tests, a student's scores on the various tests must be converted into comparable units so that the scores can be interpreted. Most published norm-referenced reading tests offer several types of conversions—grade equivalents, percentile ranks, and stanines. Information from criterion-referenced tests varies with the test and the way in which it calibrates its findings into age, grade levels, or mastery of specific skills or abilities tested.

The grade equivalent score converts the raw score into the school grade (year and month) typical of students who achieve it. Thus, a comparison can be made between the student's grade placement and the grade equivalent of the standardization group at the particular time of the test (e.g., 3.9 for a third-grader tested in May would be "on grade"). Since most reading materials tested by readability formulas also use grade level scores, converting test scores to grade equivalents facilitates making a match between a student's ability, as reflected by a test, and the materials that will be used for instruction. Grade equivalent scores are also useful in showing progress over time—a need in all remedial and regular instructional programs.

Percentiles, which use a scale of 100, indicate the relative rank of students, with high percentiles reflecting above-average rank and those below 50 reflecting a below-average placing. Percentiles, like grade equivalents, are useful for comparing students with others of the same age or grade. However, percentiles do not indicate progress over time as meaningfully as do grade equivalents. Although a gain in a percentile indicates improved achievement, it does not tell as clearly how the gain is reflected in reading behaviors and skills. Furthermore, percentiles do not translate as easily into levels of difficulty of reading materials.

Stanines are similar to percentiles. They are conversion scores on a scale of 9, with 5 the norm and 9 the highest rank. Since they are based on the same principle as percentiles, they share the same characteristics.

Until quite recently, grade equivalents were perhaps the most widely used of these conversions. This was because of their many values—estimation of students' achievement in relation to norms, of discrepancies between achievement and potential, of gains over time, and of materials appropriate for instruction. The usefulness of grade equivalent scores has been questioned, however. The International Reading Association (IRA) has suggested that the use of grade equivalents can lead to the mistaken assumption that "a grade equivalent of 5.0 on a reading test means that the test taker will be able to read fifth grade material" (IRA, 1982, p. 464).

Overall, however, we have found that grade equivalent scores are quite helpful. Results from work in our reading laboratory indicate that grade equivalent scores on tests of silent reading comprehension reflect the grade level at which students benefit from instruction (Chall, Curtis, & Fletcher, 1988). Even in cases where a difference exists between students' grade equivalents and the actual difficulty level of the material from which they are able to learn, the very robust correlations that exist between grade equivalents and instructional levels (from .80 to .90) convince us of the value of using this kind of score conversion in diagnosis.

Establishing a Pattern of Strengths and Needs

Once a student's scores on the various components of reading have been converted into comparable units, the specialist then examines them in order to identify a "pattern," or more complete picture of the student's strengths and needs in reading. Patterns emerge from the different ways in which the components tested seem to be affecting one another. Even when two students receive

TABLE 22.1. A Comparison of Two Diagnostic Profiles

Component	Student A	Student B
Chronological age	13	13
School grade placement	7	8
Total reading score	6.2	7.0
Component reading scores		
Word identification	3.0	7.8
Oral reading	4.8	8.4
Word meaning	4.6	9.8
Comprehension	7.1	4.9

Note. Test scores have been converted to grade equivalents.

the same score on a more general, survey-type test of reading, different patterns among the various components of reading may underlie that single overall score.

To illustrate, Table 22.1 contains two profiles of test scores (shown in grade equivalents) for two 13-year-olds scoring about a grade level below their grade placement in school on an overall reading achievement test. Student A, a seventh-grader, has a total grade equivalent in reading of 6.2. Student B, an eighth grader, has a total grade equivalent of 7.0. Hence, both students are about a grade level in reading below their grade placement in school. Different patterns among the components of reading underlie their total reading scores, however. Student A appears to be experiencing difficulty in all aspects of reading, although comprehension seems to be a relative strength. On the other hand, Student B's difficulties seem to be largely confined to the comprehension component. Word identification, oral reading, and word meaning are all strengths.

The process of identifying and interpreting a pattern is guided by the specialist's knowledge about what reading involves and how it develops. Along with the decision about what aspects of reading to assess, interpretation of the relationship among test scores also determines what steps the specialist will recommend for remediating a student's reading difficulty. Because of the importance of this process and its dependence on the view of reading and reading development to which a specialist adheres, we turn next to a description of the particular approach to diagnostic achievement testing that we use in the Harvard Reading Laboratory. In doing so, our goal is to provide more detail about the way in which reading specialists identify patterns and how patterns are used to guide the design and the evaluation of instruction.

AN APPROACH TO DIAGNOSTIC TESTING AND INTERPRETATION

The Harvard Reading Laboratory was established in 1966 as an integral part of the graduate programs in reading, language, and learning disabilities. From its inception, the laboratory has served three purposes: the training of reading specialists and researchers; the collection of data for ongoing research efforts; and the provision of services to the community.

Throughout the academic year, graduate students enrolled in courses work individually with children and adults referred to the laboratory for reading problems. The work consists of testing and identifying a student's reading problem; developing a plan for remediation based on the diagnosis; teaching twice weekly for 1-hour sessions; assessing students' progress at the end of each semester; and preparing reports for the laboratory, students' schools, and their parents. All of the laboratory work is closely supervised by the laboratory directors and teaching assistants.

The laboratory serves about 30 teacher–student pairs each semester. Students range in age from 7 years to adult, reading one or more grade levels below grade placement and/or intellectual potential. Referrals are made by school personnel, parents, or (in the case of college students and adults) the students themselves. Students are invited to return for as many semesters as they need in order to reach a level of reading that will enable them to read effectively in school or at work, and to continue to progress without the special help provided by the laboratory. Typically, this is achieved in two to four semesters, although some students attend only one semester and others attend as many as six semesters.

Two diagnostic assessments are held during the year, one at the beginning of each semester. End-of-year testing is used to assess progress.

The theory guiding the assessment and interpretation of test scores for each student is based on two assumptions: (1) that reading is best conceived of as a set of interrelated components, consisting of processes, content knowledge, as well as strategies (e.g., see Perfetti & Curtis, 1987); and (2) that the relationship among these components changes as reading ability develops (Chall, 1983). Thus, the age, the grade placement, and the reading level of the student all suggest the components of reading that will be assessed.

Lower Reading Levels (First through Third Grades)

Reading at the lower grade levels consists of two different stages: first, learning to associate combinations of letters with their spoken equivalents; and then learning to use knowledge about letter–sound correspondences, along with language redundancies, to gain accuracy and fluency in reading (Chall, 1983). As a consequence, at the lower reading levels, the most essential components to assess are word analysis, word recognition, and oral reading of connected text.

Formal Testing

For assessment of word analysis and word recognition, tests such as the Roswell–Chall Diagnostic Reading Test of Word Analysis Skills (Roswell & Chall, 1978), the Reading subtest of the Wide Range Achievement Test (Jastak & Jastak, 1984), and others are used. For word recognition, in addition to obtaining grade level information, we look closely at the students' correct and incorrect responses. How proficient are students on the most common, high-frequency words? When they make errors, are the errors real words or nonwords? For word analysis, questions such as the following are considered: Which letter–sound correspondences have students mastered? Which are they experiencing difficulty with?

A spelling test, such as the Spelling subtest of the Wide Range Achievement Test (Jastak & Jastak, 1984), is also used at these lowest levels to further assess students' abilities in word analysis and their knowledge of high-frequency words. Comparison between reading and spelling grade levels, as well as reading and spelling errors, provide important supplementary information about how well students are able to deal with the way words look and sound.

Oral reading tests (such as the Gray Oral Reading Tests [Gray, 1967]) are also administered. Oral reading of connected text provides all sorts of useful information, such as the level of difficulty of text a student can read accurately; the difficulty level that can be read fluently; the kinds of errors students make and their sensitivity to context; and so on.

When we administer oral reading tests, if students make gross errors in reading (e.g., saying "duck" for "dog"), we tell them the correct word after making note of the error. We find that when this is not done, students will often "misread" other words in a text in order to make sense out of the original error.

Oral reading time and categories of reading errors are types of information we look at from the oral reading test. In addition, we compute a "criterion" grade level score, developed by Chall; this is less formal than the standardized grade equivalent scores provided by the test, and it is more useful for selecting materials at the appropriate difficulty level for instruction. This score is based on the number of "real errors" (errors that would interfere with students' understanding of what they have read) made on passages at varying levels of readability. Real errors include such things as nonrecognitions, mispronunciations, insertions, and so on. Not included as real errors are those that seem to be temporary or careless and not detrimental to students' understanding (such as repetitions, substitutions of "the" for "a," addition or omission of plural S, or pronunciations due to dialects or speech impediments).

The "criterion" oral score is estimated by the readability level of the most difficult passage on which the student makes 3%–5% real errors. So, for example, if a student makes two real errors on a 50-word passage at the first-grade level, three on a 67-word passage at the second-grade level, and seven on a 67-word passage at the third-grade level, the student's "criterion" oral level would be estimated to be at the second-grade level.

Oral reading grade levels and test performance are also compared to grade levels on word analysis, word recognition, and spelling. Questions such as the following are considered: Is there a difference between a student's reading of words in context and out?

Do more word substitutions occur with context than without? Do students seem more or less fluent when reading in context than they do when reading words in isolation?

At these lower reading grade levels, tests of reading vocabulary and reading comprehension are often less essential to diagnosis than at higher grade levels. This is because, at this level, the content of what students are being asked to read is often familiar to them and contains words that they themselves already use in their speech. However, results from vocabulary and comprehension tests can help to identify those students who do lack experience with frequently occurring concepts and linguistic and text structures. Thus, when time and circumstances permit, we administer vocabulary and comprehension tests for those reading at about first- to third-grade level as well. Such tests also can provide us with an estimate of students' ability to work independently.

Informal Testing

After the more formal testing, we undertake a trial teaching session in an informal atmosphere, to obtain further information on the methods and materials that are suitable and acceptable to the student. These trial teaching sessions serve a further function: They confirm for the student that he or she *can* learn. According to Roswell and Natchez (1989),

> Not only is enlisting the pupil's participation therapeutic in and of itself, but it serves as powerful motivation for future learning in remedial sessions and in school. Therefore, trial procedures are recommended as an integral part of the diagnostic examination to guide the teacher to the most effective approaches and to demonstrate to the pupil the methods most suited to his or her learning. (p. 68)

For nonreaders and students on a first-grade reading level who have difficulties with sight word recognition and word analysis, we use the Trial Lessons of Word Study suggested by Roswell and Natchez (1989). The method indicated is viewed as an initial approach that will change as the student progresses and as other approaches are needed to assure further reading development.

Thus, an initial method is not considered a permanent judgment.

Three major word recognition approaches are tried—visual, phonic, and visual–motor. If none of these is effective, a kinesthetic approach may be used.

The visual approach to word recognition involves learning words by picture clues. Several words are used with a picture illustrating a well-known object. The teacher selects unknown words for teaching and points to the picture and the word, pronouncing it. The student repeats this several times, and is then tested on the word without the picture.

For a phonic approach, we first see whether the student is able to do auditory blending (e.g., the teacher produces slowly and distinctly the sounds of a word, such as "C-A-T," and the student is asked to tell the word). For students who cannot yet do this, we try a phonic approach through "spelling patterns" or "word families" (e.g., teaching, "at," "bat," "sat," then adding other words by changing the initial consonants).

If the student is able to do auditory blending, the examiner teaches or reviews several consonant sounds and one vowel. The student sounds and blends these. Then the consonant is changed. This approach to phonics is more difficult than the word family approach, but it has more value in learning to read.

A visual–motor approach is particularly useful for learning words not spelled regularly and for learning to spell. The teacher selects three words that the student does not know, prints each on a separate card, and tells what each word is. The student closes his or her eyes and tries to visualize it, names it (the student may open his or her eyes to take another look), and then writes it from memory.

For students at first- to third-grade reading levels, the examiner also tries out story materials for oral reading at levels suggested by the standard test results (word recognition and oral reading of connected text). Materials on lower and higher levels are also tried. Students are asked about which level they find "just right," "easy," "hard," and so on, and which content they find interesting thereby helping the examiner to determine which materials seem most effective and congenial to the student.

Intermediate Reading Levels (Fourth through Eighth Grades)

At the lower reading levels, the student's task is to master the medium (i.e., the printed words and sounds); at the intermediate levels, the task begins to become one of mastering new vocabulary, information, and ideas (Chall, 1983). As a result, the most essential components to assess at these levels are word meaning and comprehension.

Formal Testing

For assessment of students' knowledge of word meanings, we begin with a test assessing recognition of synonyms (such as that provided by the Gates–MacGinitie Reading Tests [MacGinitie, 1978]). Such a score provides us with a general estimate of students' breadth of vocabulary knowledge; this, when compared to their scores on other reading components, helps us to establish whether knowledge of word meanings is a strength or need.

For assessment of comprehension, we begin with a reading achievement test at the student's reading level, such as the Comprehension subtest of the Gates–MacGinitie or the Metropolitan Achievement Tests (Prescott, Balow, Hogan, & Farr, 1978). As with knowledge of word meanings, this provides an overall estimate of students' strength on this component when compared to their other test scores. In addition, timed versus untimed administration is used when appropriate (i.e., untimed administration is used if students are still getting items correct when the time limit is up). Comparison of timed and untimed scores helps to establish whether reading rate is the source of difficulty.

An assessment of writing, given to all students in the laboratory who are at or above a third-grade level of reading, can also be informative about the nature of comprehension difficulties. In the writing assessment, students are asked to respond to two tasks, one narrative and one expository in nature (e.g., see Chall & Jacobs, 1983). Students choice of content and vocabulary, sentence structure and sentence length, text organization, and ease of text production can all provide important clues about their sensitivity to print.

Although less critical at this stage of reading than earlier, word identification will often be assessed both in isolation and in context. Of particular interest are the strategies that students have available for dealing with less frequent words, and their fluency in identifying these.

Informal Testing

Informal, trial lessons at the intermediate reading levels have essentially the same goals as for the lower grades: to try out various methods and materials. However, greater attention is paid at fourth- through eighth-grade levels to methods for teaching word meanings, silent reading comprehension, and study skills.

Informal measures of meaning vocabulary will be used if it seems that vocabulary is a need. For example, we use an oral format to determine whether students are able to define more difficult words than they are able to do when the testing format required reading. If this is the case, word recognition may be a greater source of difficulty than knowledge of word meanings (see Chall, 1987). We also consider the precision of students' definitions. When students tie their definitions to specific contexts in which words can occur, they can experience difficulties when encountering these words in new contexts, even contexts that differ only slightly from more familiar ones (e.g., see Curtis, 1987). We look also at what students do when they encounter words whose meanings are unfamiliar to them. Do they skip them? Do they try to use context to figure them out? If they try to use context, how successful are they?

In establishing both the breadth and depth of students' reading and listening vocabularies, graded word lists can be invaluable. Sources that we consult include the following:

Dale and O'Rourke (1981), *The Living Word Vocabulary*, which lists the grade levels at which students know word meanings, including the levels for different meanings of multiple-meaning words (up to 12th grade).

Dale and Chall (1948), which contains the Dale list of 3,000 words whose meanings are familiar to fourth-graders.

Dale and Chall (in press), which contains an updated list of 3,000 words known to fourth-graders.

Johnson and Moe (1983), *The Ginn Word Book for Teachers*, which lists the frequency with which words appear in print, according to various sources, and in the oral language of first-graders; grade level recommendations are included.

For students who test low on meaning vocabulary, trial lessons can help to establish the way by which the meanings of new words will be learned. Methods we try include the following: (1) a direct method, in which definitions of unknown words are given, sentence contexts are provided, and learning is tested by recall and production in the same and in new contexts; (2) an indirect method, in which unknown words are tested in context and the students are asked to derive the meanings from context; (3) a structural method, in which the meanings of unknown words are discussed in terms of word parts (such as prefixes, suffixes, root words, and morphemes), and the student is asked to give definitions for different combinations of word parts. A student may find one method easier to learn than another, or several may be effective. Generally, we find it helpful to use all three. Therefore, we try the others later, even if a student has difficulty with them at the time of the initial testing.

To define the source of a comprehension problem further, students are given different content area materials at various levels of difficulty to read. Through brief and informal discussions after the reading, we look to see whether a student's difficulties lie primarily in (1) lack of knowledge about basic vocabulary, concepts, and ideas in particular subject areas; (2) limited understanding of the organizational aspects of text (e.g., topic sentences, examples, details, etc.); (3) difficulty in summarizing, drawing inferences, or predicting what will come next, and so on; or (4) dealing with the demands of print (i.e., word recognition and analysis) while comprehending. Listening comprehension skills may also be assessed informally as well.

Trial lessons for students with difficulties in comprehension determine the teaching strategies and materials that will be most appropriate, such as wide and varied reading;

identification of main ideas, facts, and conclusions; or techniques such as reciprocal teaching (Palinscar & Brown, 1984).

For a student experiencing difficulty in oral reading, trial lessons at these levels consist of "trying materials on" for fit to determine their difficulty for the student and to get the student's reactions to the content and style. At fourth- through eighth-grade reading levels, it is particularly important to determine the level that is appropriate with teacher assistance (i.e., a challenging level), as well as a more comfortable, independent level (see Vygotsky, 1978).

LINKS BETWEEN DIAGNOSIS AND REMEDIATION

To illustrate the links between diagnosis and remediation, we begin by presenting diagnostic and remedial information for two students who sought help for their reading. They were diagnosed by one of us and received remediation under her direction. One was retested twice following the original diagnosis. Following the presentation of these cases, we conclude with a more general discussion of how patterns in diagnostic information are used to design a program of instruction.

George

George's reading and related skills were assessed three times using the procedures suggested above. He was first diagnosed at 7 years, 3 months of age, in the middle of first grade. George spent two years in kindergarten because his teacher and parents felt that he was developing slowly and needed the extra time "to catch up."

He was referred for a reading diagnosis by a well-known speech therapist, who found George to be delayed in language development and to have a serious speech difficulty. He had also been diagnosed by a neurologist as having delayed neurological development. Both thought that his language and neurological difficulties would put him at high risk for a reading difficulty, and therefore recommended an early reading diagnosis.

George was having great difficulty in learning to read in first grade, which was a great concern, since it was the impression of all that he was at least of average or higher ability. Furthermore, the average achievement of first-graders in his class in the middle of the year in a private school was considerably above grade level—and he seemed to be falling ever farther behind the others.

The reading diagnosis had several objectives, among which was to obtain an estimate of George's intellectual potential and of his reading achievement. More specifically, how did his reading compare with his cognitive abilities? Should he have been achieving more in reading?

To obtain an estimate of George's intellectual abilities (his reading potential), the Wechsler Intelligence Scale for Children—Revised (WISC-R; Wechsler, 1974) was used. If this test had not been given, the word meaning score of a test that does not rely on reading the words could have been used instead.

To obtain measures of his reading achievement, George was tested on the components suggested above for students reading at a first-grade level. For each component, the information sought included his achievement level, the kinds of errors he made, and the patterns of his strengths and weaknesses. The following subtests from an experimental version of the Diagnostic Assessment of Reading and Teaching Strategies (Roswell & Chall, in press) were used: Word Recognition, Phonemic Awareness, Word meaning (administered orally), Oral reading, Silent Reading Comprehension, and Spelling.

The first column of Table 22.2 presents George's scores on the initial diagnosis. His overall achievement in reading placed him on about a first-grade level, with his greatest weakness in reading connected text. He hesitated at almost every word, reflecting extreme difficulty with fluency. He was better at recognizing single words, and his knowledge of phonic elements was better still. He knew most consonant sounds, some blends, and short-vowel sounds in consonant–vowel–consonant (CVC) words.

These test scores indicated a serious problem with reading—not so much in terms of his placement in first grade, but in terms of his age (he should have been in second grade). His problem was most severe when his achievement in reading and spelling was

TABLE 22.2. Reading Development over a
2-Year, 4-Month Period for George

Components	First testing	Second testing	Third testing
Chronological age	7-3	8-7	9-7
School grade placement	1.6	2.9	3.9
Diagnostic Assessment of Reading and Teaching Strategies			
Word Recognition	1	3	4
Oral Reading	1	3	4
Phonemic Awareness	2	3	4
Word Meaning	4	4	4
Silent Reading Comprehension			5 to 6
Spelling	1	1	1
Gates–MacGinitie Reading Tests			
Vocabulary		2.5	
Comprehension		2.8	
Total		2.6	

compared to his meaning vocabulary and to his WISC-R scores. George could define words on a fourth-grade level when the words were presented orally. And, as Table 22.3 reveals, on the individually administered intelligence test, George tested in the superior range. His score on the WISC Vocabulary subtest, also administered orally, confirmed the high Word Meaning score on the Reading Test. Thus, George was found to have high potential for learning to read and, judging from the WISC Vocabulary and other subtest scores, superior cognitive abilities.

His difficulties with reading were considered to stem from his language and neurological difficulties (based on independent evaluations by the speech therapist and the neurologist). His father had also had difficulty with speech, reading, and spelling when he was a boy, and was still a slow reader. Further evidence for George's neurological difficulties was his very labored and immature writing. He also performed below age norms on the Bender Visual–Motor Gestalt Test (Bender, 1946).

On the basis of the initial assessment, it was recommended that George receive re-

medial instruction for two 1-hour sessions per week after school. The prognosis for his improvement was considered good, for he had many strengths, particularly his high ability, motivation, and good cheer. The pattern of his scores indicated that he needed a great deal of help in reading connected text. Indeed, his oral reading was so poor and labored that it was thought best not to administer a silent reading test. Informal tests and trial lessons were used to determine how he could best learn to recognize words and which kinds of materials he liked, and also to help him realize that he could learn. The informal tests revealed that he could learn by phonic blending and also by a sight method. He was able to read from a primer, but he needed help with it.

The remedial plan, based on the pattern of scores from the formal and informal tests, was designed to help George further develop his strengths (phonics and word recognition), as well as to work on his weakness—oral

TABLE 22.3. Scores on the Wechsler Intelligence Scale for Children (WISC-R) for George

Test or scale	Scaled score
Verbal subtests	
Information	12
Similarities	12
Arithmetic	13
Vocabulary	13
Comprehension	14
(Digit Span)	(11)
Performance subtests	
Picture Completion	9
Picture Arrangement	12
Block Design	16
Object Assembly	15
Coding	12
Overall scales	
Verbal	64 (IQ = 117)
Performance	64 (IQ = 120)
Full Scale	128 (IQ = 121)

Note. A scaled score of 10 on the Verbal and Performance subtests indicates average performance for chronological age.

reading for accuracy and fluency. Oral reading was done collaboratively on story material with his teacher, each taking turns reading a paragraph at a time. The teacher was urged to read at a natural pace, not to slow down, in order to provide a model for George's unnaturally slow reading. It was also suggested that the teacher supply words not easily recognized by George in order to build up his fluency. As he became more fluent, he could be encouraged to try words spelled regularly and composed of phonic elements he had already learned.

George was tested a second time, about a year and a half after the initial diagnosis, when he was aged 8 years, 7 months and was completing third grade. The second column of Table 22.2 presents these test scores. During the second testing he worked quickly and with much interest. He did extremely well, compared to his scores on tests given nearly a year and a half earlier. He had made gains of up to 2 years or more in reading skills, and was achieving overall on a third-grade level. Excellent gains were made in Word Recognition (words in isolation) and in (connected) Oral Reading; he progressed from a first-grade level to a third-grade level. On Silent Reading Comprehension, he scored on a third-grade level, but when difficult words were supplied by the examiner, he was able to read and understand selections at fourth- and fifth-grade levels. When offered the choice of reading or not reading these more difficult selections, he chose to do so, seeming to enjoy the challenge. The lower Gates–MacGinitie scores for Vocabulary and Comprehension were due to the timed nature of the test; with no time limits, he could score higher. Overall, his comprehension was excellent, and any difficulties he had on these tests were primarily with word recognition, not with word meanings or with understanding of the ideas.

George's spelling, however, did not improve. His achievement remained on a first-grade level, and his handwriting was still very immature. His skills in phonics continued to progress, and he was now able to benefit from instruction in the more advanced word analysis skills—vowel diphthongs and more advanced structural analysis.

His Word Meaning score was still at fourth-grade level, not changing from the first assessment, but remaining above his age and grade placement. Although his word recognition and analysis scores improved considerably, the pattern of his scores indicated greater strength in word meaning and comprehension. Indeed, during the Gates–MacGinitie and during trial teaching, he was still having difficulty with word recognition and fluency, and these difficulties seemed to hold him back on his comprehension. They caused him to pause, to misread, and to slow down. As the paragraphs became difficult, he asked the examiner to tell him what the words were.

The program of instruction and tutoring that George had been receiving was most successful. It seemed that he had made the transition from beginning reading to at least the beginning of fluent reading. He was now able to read connected text at a third-grade level with some degree of fluency and automaticity. It was recommended that the tutoring continue in order to take him to a more advanced level, in preparation for using reading as a tool for learning in the intermediate grades.

The remedial plan now needed to include some materials on a challenging level, to be read collaboratively with the teacher—for instance, stories or selections on a fourth- or fifth-grade readability level, with the teacher supplying the difficult words or helping him sound them out if he did not recognize them. Since he found greater interest in more mature literature and ideas, there was a further benefit in using more difficult materials. For silent reading, third- or fourth-grade materials were considered more appropriate. Here, too, it was suggested that he be helped with words that he could not identify easily.

To enhance his fluency and rate of reading, it was recommended that George continue to read, independently, interesting materials at a third-grade level or even somewhat below, particularly when he read without a teacher's help. It was also recommended that he receive instruction in sounding out longer words, and in spelling and handwriting.

George's third testing, a year later when he was completing the third grade at age 9 years, 7 months, revealed a different pattern of scores (see Table 22.2, third column). His recognition of single words and of connected texts was now accurate at a fourth-grade level; phonics was also at an equivalent of fourth grade; and Silent Reading now his highest score. He was able to read and comprehend a selection at a fifth- to sixth-grade level. His superior intelligence, curiosity, and motivation were now able to come forth as his word recognition and analysis improved sufficiently for him to read the words and ideas he could understand but could not previously identify.

George's spelling and handwriting had not progressed since first grade, revealing his early difficulty with print, especially when the order of letters had to be reproduced accurately.

Another interesting aspect of George's reading was the relatively stable level of his knowledge of word meanings when he was tested orally. It had not improved since the first testing, $2\frac{1}{2}$ years earlier. This may be explained by the fact that he had done little reading of difficult text during the 2 years past, and thus had not encountered words that were above a fourth-grade level—specialized and abstract words.

Remedial instruction was still needed and was recommended. This time emphasis was to be put on spelling, on handwriting and composing, and on word meanings. Much of the needed improvement in word meanings would result from wider reading of more challenging text, but direct teaching of words, and of the meanings of prefixes and suffixes, was also recommended as a supplement. George also would continue to benefit from practice in oral reading for accuracy and fluency.

Robert

Robert was aged 12 years, 4 months, entering the seventh grade, when he was referred for an evaluation of his reading and related reading skills by a psychiatrist who was treating him for behavior disorders. His mother reported that Robert had a hard time with his reading. He did not stop for punctuation, had a short attention span, and was impatient.

When Robert entered kindergarten, he had had great difficulty in separating from his mother. In kindergarten the teacher said he was very bright, and he was put into an advanced first grade. But then he did very little. He had an above-average IQ, but because of emotional difficulties he did not do well. He was in public school during first

TABLE 22.4. Scores on Reading and Related Tests for Robert

Component	Findings at assessment
Chronological age (years, months)	12.4
School grade placement	7.0
Diagnostic Assessment of Reading and Teaching Strategies	
Word Recognition Phonic Screening	7 to 8 Mastered the fundamentals, although he read some common one-syllable (CVC) words inaccurately
Oral Reading	6
Silent Reading Comprehension	8
Spelling	5 to 6
Word Meaning	9 to 10
Gates–MacGinitie, Level D, Silent Reading Comprehension	7.3 timed 8.5 untimed

through third grades and was taken out for reading help. He was in a Montessori school during fourth and fifth grades. He was happier there, although it did not seem to help him academically. His last reading score, as reported by his school, was a 49th percentile.

Robert was a likable boy who was alert and interested in the various tests and activities. He seemed to enjoy the activities. An experimental form of the Diagnostic Assessment of Reading and Teaching Strategies (Roswell & Chall, in press) was administered. The results are presented in Table 22.4.

Overall, Robert was found to read on about grade level. He did best on the Word Meaning subtest (presented orally), scoring on a 9th- to 10th-grade level. His next strongest area was silent reading comprehension. He scored at the eighth-grade level on the individual silent reading comprehension test and on the Gates–MacGinitie when it was given untimed. Since he read somewhat slowly, his level was about a grade lower when the test was given with time limits.

The two Roswell–Chall subtests on which Robert had the lowest scores were related more to accuracy of word recognition and production—Oral Reading (sixth-grade level) and Spelling (fifth- to sixth-grade level)—than to comprehension. His oral reading was particularly inaccurate and lacked fluency. Even when reading a fourth-grade-level passage, he read haltingly and was not fluent.

Robert's writing samples revealed great difficulty with handwriting, and he wrote a paragraph without any punctuation or capitalization. His ideas, however, were adequate for the task.

The WISC-R was administered, and the scaled scores for each of the subtests are presented in Table 22.5.

Robert's WISC scores indicated that overall he tested within the normal range, with higher scores on the Verbal tests than on the Performance. This is quite common among students who have the particular difficulties with literacy that he exhibited—weaknesses in word recognition, spelling, and handwriting, and strengths in word meaning and reading comprehension. His below-average scores in the Arithmetic (auditory processing of complex material) and Digit Span (sequencing) subtests of the WISC are also quite common among students with overall good intelligence who have reading disability. Furthermore, his relatively good score on Similarities, which measures abstract verbal reasoning, and on Vocabulary pointed to good overall verbal abilities and high potential (if given proper instruction) for better reading achievement in later grades. The performance subtest on which he scored below average (Coding) also can be explained by his great difficulty with visual–motor integration. On the Beery–Buktenica Developmental Test of Visual–Motor Integration, he showed great difficulty in copying geometric forms. He turned the forms around, a mark of immaturity and great difficulty. His score was characteristic of children much younger.

Since Robert had difficulty with some aspects of reading, spelling, and writing, he needed special help in these areas. His intellectual abilities suggested that he could achieve higher on all aspects of reading, and because of the greater demands that would be made on him in junior high school, it was important that he be given special instruction. Good remedial attention would make it possible for him to function on a higher level in school, which in turn would enhance his self-confidence and his productivity.

Robert's score patterns indicated greatest strengths in language and cognition, and greatest weaknesses in the recognition and reproduction aspects of reading, spelling, and writing. It was recommended that remedial instruction include work on accuracy and fluency in oral reading, spelling, writing, and reading comprehension.

The Design of Remediation

From the diagnostic information presented for George and Robert, one sees differences in the patterns of strengths and weaknesses between the two students and for the same student at different times. These patterns, along with information from observations during the testing and the results from informal tests, were used to plan successful instructional programs. We find it useful to think in terms of three broad categories of these patterns:

1. Skills and abilities that are unique to reading and measured by tests of word recognition of single words, phonics (or word analysis, decoding), spelling, and accuracy and fluency in oral reading of connected text (without reference to comprehension). Read-

TABLE 22.5. WISC Scores for Robert

Test or scale	Scaled score
Verbal subtests	
Information	13
Similarities	13
Arithmetic	8
Vocabulary	13
Comprehension	14
(Digit Span)	(9)
Performance subtests	
Picture Completion	14
Picture Arrangement	11
Block Design	10
Object Assembly	12
Coding	5
Overall scales	
Verbal	61 (IQ = 113)
Performance	52 (IQ = 102)
Full Scale	113 (IQ = 109)

ing rate is also important here, and although it is not always tested directly, it can be inferred from other test scores.

2. Factors such as language, cognition, and background knowledge, which are not reading-specific but ultimately determine the extent of an individual's literacy development. These are used to estimate reading potential at any point, irrespective of reading skills, and are measured by such tests as the WISC, the Stanford–Binet, tests of listening comprehension, and oral tests of word meaning. They can even be measured by giving orally an alternate form of a standardized test, to be compared with the scores from one given in the standard manner.

3. Aspects that reflect the interaction of the language/cognitive factors with reading skills. These are measured by standardized reading achievement tests of vocabulary and reading comprehension, which require word recognition and word analysis even when they claim to be measuring word meanings and comprehension.

George's initial test results showed that he was stronger on language and cognition than on reading skills. Indeed, most children who fall behind in first through third grades, if English is their native language, will be lower in reading skills than in language and cognition. Although George made progress in reading skills by the end of the third grade, he still had difficulty in using them effectively for reading and meaning. Moreover, it is important to note that, although his lowest score at the end of the second grade was in reading for meaning, his overall pattern of scores (along with information from informal tests) indicated greater need for word recognition and fluency.

Robert's patterns of scores also indicated greater strengths in language and cognition than in the reading skills of word recognition, spelling, and mechanics of writing.

Other patterns occur, particularly in the intermediate and upper grades: Greater strengths are found in word recognition and word analysis, and greater weaknesses in word meanings, cognition, and background knowledge. In such cases, more careful observations and trial teaching sessions are needed to determine the level and kind of instruction needed for developing meaning vocabularies and reading comprehension.

Once patterns of strengths and needs have been identified, recommendations for instruction can be made. Care must be taken to insure that a well-rounded instructional plan is suggested—one that will develop the full range of a student's reading ability (i.e., one that builds on strengths as well as needs). Attention must also be given to the student's interests and preferences, in an effort to maximize the pleasure that he or she will gain from reading.

Although instructional recommendations vary according to the student's level of reading development and pattern of test scores, we have found that the following guidelines help in the design of a successful program (Chall & Curtis, 1987):

1. *Each session is divided into a number of different activities that address different components.* Even when a student needs a great deal of help with a particular component (e.g., phonics), that component is not the focus of the entire session. Instead, only a part of the lesson is devoted to it, and sometimes a game later in the session is used to reinforce and review.

2. *Teachers participate in activities with students.* For example, when oral reading is an area of need, the teacher takes turns with his or her student in reading portions of the text. Collaboration not only helps to provide a model and shares the burden with the student; it also creates a relaxed and friendly environment that is more conducive to learning.

3. *In general, the lower the reading level and the younger the student, the more direct the instruction should be.* Students reading at higher levels are more able to learn on their own, but they too require a program that provides guidance and instructional activities tailored for their needs.

4. *The level of difficulty of instructional materials should be above what students are able to achieve on their own.* With encouragement and support from their teachers, we find that students make the most progress when they are challenged.

In summary, we have presented a view of diagnostic achievement testing in reading that is based on assessing various reading components and on viewing reading as a developmental process. The procedures discussed are those that we use at the Harvard Reading Laboratory, and they involve assessing students' strengths and needs in reading and related areas for the purpose of designing instruction that will bring students' reading achievement up to their potential.

REFERENCES

Anderson, J. R. (1972). How to construct achievement tests to assess comprehension. *Review of Educational Research, 42,* 145–170.

Bender, L. (1946). *Bender Visual–Motor Gestalt Test.* San Antonio, TX: The Psychological Corporation.

Chall, J. S. (1983). *Stages of reading development.* New York: McGraw-Hill.

Chall, J. S. (1987). Two vocabularies for reading: Recognition and meaning. In M. G. McKeown & M. E. Curtis (Eds.), *The nature of vocabulary acquisition* (pp. 7–17). Hillsdale, NJ: Erlbaum.

Chall, J. S., & Curtis, M. E. (1987). What clinical diagnosis tells us about children's reading. *The Reading Teacher, 40,* 784–788.

Chall, J. S., Curtis, M. E., & Fletcher, M. B. (1988). *Grade equivalent scores: Do they have instructional value?* Unpublished manuscript.

Chall, J. S., & Jacobs, V. A. (1983). Writing and reading in the elementary grades: Developmental trends among low SES children. *Language Arts, 60,* 617–626.

Curtis, M. E. (1987). Vocabulary testing and vocabulary instruction. In M. G. McKeown & M. E. Curtis (Eds.), *The nature of vocabulary acquisition* (pp. 37–51). Hillsdale, NJ: Erlbaum.

Dale, E., & Chall, J. S. (1948). A formula for predicting readability. *Educational Research Bulletin, 27,* 11–20, 37–54.

Dale, E., & Chall, J. S. (in press). *Readability revisited and the new Dale–Chall readability formula.* Unpublished manuscript.

Dale, E., & O'Rourke, J. (1981). *The living word vocabulary.* Chicago: World.

Davis, F. B. (1984). Fundamental factors of comprehension in reading. *Psychometrika, 9,* 185–197.

Farr, R., & Tone, B. (1983). Text analysis and validated modeling of the reading process (1973–1981). In R. J. DeSanti (Ed.), *Teachers' needs and concerns regarding reading instruction* (pp. 21–68). New York: University Press of America.

Gray, W. S. (1967). *Gray Oral Reading Tests.* New York: Bobbs-Merrill.

International Reading Association (IRA). (1982). Misuse of grade equivalents. *The Reading Teacher, 35,* 464.

Jastak, J. F., & Jastak, S. (1984). *The Wide Range Achievement Test.* Wilmington, DE: Author.

Johnson, D. D. (1973). Guidelines for evaluating word attack skills in the primary grades. In W. H. MacGinitie (Ed.), *Assessment problems in reading* (pp. 21–26). Newark, DE: International Reading Association.

Johnson, D. D., & Moe, A. J. (1983). *The Ginn word book for teachers.* Lexington, MA: Ginn.

MacGinitie, W. H. (1978). *Gates–MacGinitie Reading Tests.* Chicago, IL: Riverside.

Palinscar, A. S., & Brown, A. L. (1984). Reciprocal teaching of comprehension-fostering and comprehension-monitoring activities. *Cognition and Instruction, 1,* 117–175.

Perfetti, C. A. (1985). *Reading ability.* New York: Oxford University Press.

Perfetti, C. A., & Curtis, M. E. (1987). Reading. In R. F. Dillon & R. J. Sternberg (Eds.), *Cognition and instruction* (pp. 13–57). New York: Academic Press.

Prescott, G. A., Balow, I. H., Hogan, T. P., & Farr, R. C. (1978). *Metropolitan Achievement Tests.* San Antonio, TX: The Psychological Corporation.

Roswell, F. G., & Chall, J. S. (1978). *Roswell-Chall Diagnostic Reading Test of Word Analysis Skills* (Revised and Extended). LaJolla, CA: Essay.

Roswell, F. G., & Chall, J. S. (in press). *Diagnostic Assessment of Reading and Teaching Strategies.* Chicago: Riverside.

Roswell, F. G., & Natchez, G. (1989). *Reading disability: A human approach to evaluation and treatment of reading and writing difficulties.* New York: Basic Books.

Stanovich, K. E. (1986). Matthew effects in reading: Some consequences of individual differences in the acquisition of literacy. *Reading Research Quarterly, 21,* 360–407.

Sticht, T. G., & James, J. H. (1984). Listening and reading. In P. D. Pearson (Ed.), *Handbook of reading research* (pp. 293–317). New York: Longman.

Vygotsky, L. S. (1978). *Mind in society.* Cambridge, MA: Harvard University Press.

Weschler, D. (1974). *Weschler Intelligence Scale for Children—Revised.* San Antonio, TX: The Psychological Corporation.

23

Clinical Assessment of Children's Academic Achievement

RANDY W. KAMPHAUS
JERRY SLOTKIN
CATHERINE DeVINCENTIS
University of Georgia

An integral component of the typical psychoeducational assessment battery is an individually administered test of academic achievement that assesses multiple achievement domains, generally including reading and mathematics. The popularity of such "clinical" or individually administered tests of achievement has blossomed since the passage of P.L. 94-142. One of the specific reasons that these measures are popular is that they are crucial for the diagnosis of a specific learning disability in one of the academic achievement areas outlined by P.L. 94-142.

It is important for diagnosticians to have a thorough working knowledge of clinical measures of achievement for the purpose of diagnosing learning disabilities, because of the measurement problems associated with this diagnostic group (Reynolds, 1984). One striking aspect of clinical measures of achievement is the lack of attention they receive from researchers. Chapters of this nature that assess the current and relative status of these measures are nonexistent, whereas chapters comparing measures of adaptive behavior or intelligence are relatively commonplace. Information on these clinical achievement measures can be found in the series of *Mental Measurement Yearbooks* and a few textbooks (e.g., see Salvia & Ysseldyke,

1985). This chapter attempts to fill a void in the literature by evaluating the relative strengths and weaknesses of a number of clinical achievement measures, and by addressing more global issues affecting the field.

In this chapter, we try to summarize the "state of the art" in the individual assessment of academic achievement. We first define the types of tests that we are evaluating. Then, each of the popular tests of achievement is reviewed in turn, and strengths and weaknesses of each are noted. Finally, some global issues affecting this type of assessment are discussed; the current status of these instruments is summarized; and implications for practice and test development are discussed.

SCREENING VERSUS DIAGNOSTIC MEASURES

This chapter focuses exclusively on individually administered, norm-referenced tests of academic achievement that are used primarily for making eligibility decisions for special education. Hence, although informal reading inventories and other non-norm-referenced measures are sometimes used by clinicians, they are not discussed here because of the lack of a normative base. Similarly, tests of reading or mathematics only are not included in this chapter; these tests are also used in making placement decisions, but they are discussed in great detail in other chapters in this volume. Similarly, several other chapters in this volume are devoted to other aspects of achievement testing.

The measures evaluated in this chapter are sometimes difficult to label as primarily screening or primarily diagnostic measures of academic achievement, although our intent is to focus on screening measures. They are screeners in the sense that they typically only provide norm-referenced information for global achievement areas, making them less useful for designing specific curricular interventions. On the other hand, these measures are typically used for diagnostic purposes at a more global level; specifically, they are used to identify broad areas of strength or weakness (e.g., reading comprehension) for the purposes of diagnosing learning disabilities. If a diagnostician is interested in determining the specific areas or types of reading comprehension skills that a child is lacking, then a more appropriate measure would be something like the Woodcock Reading Mastery Tests—Revised. These individually administered tests of achievement have come to be called "screeners" because, although they do contribute to the diagnosis of strong or weak content domains, they do not give diagnostic information regarding strengths or weaknesses within a particular content domain.

EVALUATIONS OF POPULAR SCALES

The following are descriptions and evaluations of some of the most widely used clinical measures of academic achievement. The descriptions of each scale highlight its major benefits and liabilities. These text descriptions are supplemented by three appendices to the chapter: Appendix 23.1 describes subtests, age and grade ranges, and administration times; Appendix 23.2 presents the derived scores available for each measure; and Appendix 23.3 presents technical information (standardization, reliability, and validity).

One caveat is necessary before proceeding with this section. These tests are frequently revised and the adulation or criticism leveled at each test applies only to the version reviewed. In addition, new tests are constantly being published. Tests were only reviewed if they were formally published; "beta" versions could not be reviewed.

Basic Achievement Skills Individual Screener

The Basic Achievement Skills Individual Screener (BASIS; Psychological Corporation, 1983) is a screening measure designed for relatively quick assessment of fundamental academic skills. It assesses an individual's skills in the areas of Reading, Mathematics, and Spelling; there is also an optional Writing exercise that provides the examiner additional latitude in assessment. The BASIS is intended for use with individuals aged 6 through 18.

Although reviewers have commented on the ease of administration of the BASIS (Huebner, 1984; Ysseldyke, 1985) and on the clear instructions for administration provided by the manual (Huebner, 1984; Radencich, 1985), some have described administration procedures as complicated (Conley, 1986), and the manual as repetitious (Radencich, 1985), wordy, and not well organized (Hambleton & deVries, 1985). The BASIS yields a variety of scores, including standard scores (mean = 100, $SD = 15$), percentile ranks, stanines, normal curve equivalents, age and grade equivalents, and Rasch scaled scores. The authors are to be commended for their incorporation of Rasch scaled scores, which allow the examiner to assess individual developmental changes within a specified domain. However, the inclusion of age and grade equivalents without appropriate caveats for their use is unfortunate. For example, the concept of grade equivalence is often confused with that of grade placement (Floden, 1985).

One strong asset of the BASIS is the inclusion of both norm-referenced and criterion-referenced scores (Huebner, 1984). The criterion-referenced scores are based on grade-referenced clusters that reflect the subject matter appropriate to individual grade levels. These scores are designed to reflect the student's grade placement or textbook level. Unfortunately, empirical research conducted in developing these grade-referenced clusters utilized students from first through eighth only.

The BASIS was standardized in 1982 with a nationally representative sample. Standardization was based on the 1970 census data, resulting in somewhat outdated norms. Another weakness regarding the norming of the BASIS is the small number of subjects ($n = 30$) in the 18-year-old age group (Huebner, 1984). Similarly, although the authors' attempt to include an adult sample is commendable, this sample of 232 "post-high school" adults is extremely inadequate for diagnostic purposes. Among other reasons, the adult sample is inadequate because it is not thoroughly described.

In general, the psychometeric properties of the BASIS are adequate at certain age and grade levels. Internal-consistency and stability coefficients as reported in the manual were quite high, ranging from .84 to .97 and from .82 to .96, respectively. Unfortunately, the test–retest procedure involved only students in the second, fifth, and eighth grades.

The BASIS demonstrates strong content validity. Items were initially selected through reviews of textbooks and achievement tests. Subsequent item analysis yielded support for the items used in the final version of the test. It should be noted that the content sampled by each domain is restricted; this should be considered when using this test. Specifically, the Mathematics subtest, which is purported to include both computation and problem solving, appears to be a test of computation only. Also, the Reading subtest emphasizes comprehension (Floden, 1985).

Although the authors indicate that the BASIS can be used with children aged 6 through 18, the data presented in the manual do not support this notion. Specifically, the BASIS only demonstrates good age and grade differentiation validity through age 14 and ninth grade. In fact, mean raw scores for the "post-high school" sample decline below those of younger age groups.

The concurrent validity of the BASIS has not been well established. Correlation coefficients ranging from .25 to .61 between the BASIS and students' report cards were reported. In addition, correlation coefficients

were calculated between the BASIS and various group-adminstered achievement tests, using raw scores and stanines; studies were not conducted with other individually administered achievement tests. The concurrent validity coefficients reported were not strong, mostly ranging from .50 to .60.

In summary, the BASIS is a quick and easy screening measure that provides useful information concerning an individual's basic academic skills. Overall, the BASIS demonstrates strong content validity and reliability. Given the lack of demonstrated age and grade differentiation validity beyond age 14 and ninth grade, it would seem most appropriate to use the BASIS with children aged 6 through 14. Finally, further research investigating the concurrent validity of the BASIS is necessary.

Diagnostic Achievement Battery

The Diagnostic Achievement Battery (DAB; Newcomer & Curtis, 1984) is designed to assess the academic functioning of children aged 6 through 14 in three general areas: Spoken Language, Written Language, and Mathematics. It is organized according to an elaborate hierarchical model. Each of the three general areas is comprised of more specific "components," which are further divided into 12 subtests.

One asset of the DAB is the ease with which it can be administered. Unfortunately, no information regarding length of administration is reported in the manual. The DAB yields subtest standard scores, quotients (standard scores derived for composites), percentile ranks, normal curve equivalents, T-scores, z-scores, and stanines. The authors are to be commended for their exclusion of age and grade equivalents.

Although administration of the DAB is relatively easy, comprehension of its manual is not. Specifically, it appears that the composite scores (quotients) follow from the hierarchical model presented by the authors, but the interpretations of these scores are not well explained. In fact, the reader is inundated with a number of quotients, terms, and jargon, which may cause more confusion than enlightenment. Another shortcoming of the manual involves the presentation of an incomplete table of percentile ranks for quotients. That is, percentile ranks are given only for those quotients divisible by 5 (e.g., 85, 90, 95).

The DAB was standardized on 1,534 individuals who were representative of the U.S. population. The year of standardization was not reported in the manual. The sample was stratified with respect to gender, residence, race, geographic area, and parental occupation. Based on the information presented in the manual, it appears that the DAB standardization sample deviated somewhat from the U.S. population on several of these variables (e.g., race; Lewandowski, 1985). Although parental occupation is an acceptable measure of socioeconomic status, the classification system used (white-collar, blue-collar, other) is too general.

The psychometric properties of the DAB in general are inadequate. Although fairly high stability coefficients are reported, the small sample ($n = 34$), consisting of only children aged 9 through 13, makes these results less convincing. Internal-consistency coefficients ranged from .58 to .98. The low coefficients were primarily found in the 13-year-old age range; the authors suggest that these low coefficients may be a result of sampling error. Such an explanation seems plausible, given that only 360 subjects from the standardization sample and 220 children from the first item analysis were used for the calculation of internal-consistency coefficients. Unfortunately, the representativeness of these subsamples is not known. Furthermore, this type of sampling error may have affected other age groups, and therefore raises serious questions about the results in general. It should be noted that the reliability and validity tables presented in the manual do not consistently report coefficients for all DAB composites.

In an attempt to establish content validity, item analysis was performed using item difficulty and discrimination. Although the authors define an acceptable range of item difficulty as .15 to .85, coefficients for individual items ranging from 0.00 to 1.00 are reported. Adequate item discrimination is reported. Items for the DAB were selected primarily through curricular review. However, more detailed information concerning item development would be helpful. As Lesiak (1984) notes, the rationale for item selection on several subtests is not provided.

The authors attempted to demonstrate concurrent validity of the DAB by correlating it with a wide range of well-known achievement tests. These correlation coefficients ranged from "NS" (not significant) to .81. However, this range is misleading, in that only one coefficient is greater than .66. Moreover, there is necessarily a loss of information concerning the magnitude of the correlation coefficient when it is simply reported as "NS."

Of concern is the procedure used in evaluating construct validity. Subtest mean raw scores were correlated with individuals' ages and grade levels. Although correlational analyses provide information concerning the strength and direction of the relationship between mean raw scores and age or grade, they give no indication of the magnitude of the difference of mean raw scores between two age or grade levels. In fact, the method used by the authors in the norming procedures indicates that this magnitude, in many instances, is very small. The authors combined consecutive age groups, originally of 6-month intervals, whose mean scores differed by 1 point or less. Thus, the norm tables contain age intervals ranging from six months to 24 months. This collapsing of age groups clearly demonstrates a lack of age differentiation among the original 6-month intervals.

The authors should be commended for designing an achievement test with an underlying theoretical basis. However, adequate support for their hierarchical model is not provided. The authors report significant intercorrelations among subtests that comprise given composites, but there are two difficulties with the results reported. First, many of the correlations are of moderate size. Second, several subtests that are subsumed under different composites show high intercorrelations. A more appropriate method of investigating the validity of such an elaborate model is factor analysis. Such a method statistically extracts the components of an instrument, which may then be compared to the authors' hypothetical model.

Overall, the DAB is easy to administer and assesses a wide range of academic areas. However, the DAB manual could be significantly improved by providing information of greater clarity and breadth. For example, such information as administration time, year of standardization, and a complete percentile rank table would be most helpful. Furthermore, the rationale and implications for any derived scores presented in the manual should be clearly enumerated. Psychometrically, the DAB is relatively inadequate and would profit from more extensive, methodologically sound research.

Diagnostic Achievement Test for Adolescents

The Diagnostic Achievement Test for Adolescents (DATA; Newcomer & Bryant, 1986) is an instrument designed to assess academic achievement levels of adolescents aged 12 through 18. It assesses students' skills in the general areas of Mathematics, Reading, and Writing, each of which is comprised of two subtests. In addition, the DATA contains Science, Social Studies, and Reference Skills subtests, for a total of nine subtests. The authors also provide an achievement screener that is made up of the Word Identification, Math Calculation, and Spelling subtests (representing the three general areas). Administration time for the entire battery is 1–2 hours; the screener takes "considerably less" time.

Administration and scoring of the DATA are fairly easy (Schumm 1987). However, one potential pitfall for the inexperienced examiner is that different basal and ceiling rules exist for the DATA subtests, although these rules are clearly explained. The DATA yields standard scores, percentile ranks, normal curve equivalents, T-scores, z-scores, and stanines. The authors should be commended for not including grade and age equivalent scores. Like the DAB, the DATA presents an incomplete table of percentile ranks for the composite standard scores (referred to as "quotients" in the manual).

The DATA was standardized on a national sample of 1,135 individuals from September 1985 through February 1986. The sample was stratified on gender, residence, race, geographic region, and ethnicity. Unfortunately, socioeconomic status was not included among the stratification variables. As a result, the representativeness of this sample is highly questionable with respect to this most important variable. Furthermore, there are significantly fewer 12- and 18-year-old subjects than subjects of other ages in the sample.

Overall, the psychometric properties of the DATA are fair. The internal-consistency and stability coefficients reported in the manual are good (ranging from .88 to .98 and from .71 to .95, respectively). However, the credibility of these coefficients is weakened by the samples on which they were calculated. For example, the internal-consistency data were calculated using a sample of 50 subjects from each 1-year interval, randomly selected from the standardization sample. Unfortunately, random selection does not insure that the subsample will still be representative of the U.S. population. It is unclear why only a portion of the standardization sample was used. A similar problem exists with the sample selected for test–retest reliability. A total of 58 subjects from Cedar Park, Texas, ranging in age from 12 to 18, were used. Such a sample is inadequate with respect to both its size and its representativeness of the U.S. population.

The content validity of the DATA appears good. Textbooks were consulted for the initial item selection, after which content experts evaluated the items for relevance to the curriculum and wording. Item analysis techniques were then employed, including item discrimination and difficulty. The results of this item analysis were acceptable.

In an attempt to establish concurrent validity, the DATA was correlated with a number of group-administered achievement tests. Relevant correlations ranged from "NS" (not significant) to .85. Although many of these coefficients are quite acceptable, several are not. Furthermore, some of these relationships cannot be fully evaluated, given the authors' use of the vague "NS." Finally, the correlation of the DATA with other individually administered achievement tests would have been more informative and desirable (Schumm, 1987).

One of the most popular ways of establishing an instrument's construct validity is age differentiation. The DATA shows inconsistency in this regard. The groups for which the problems are most apparent are ages 17 and 18. The mean raw scores for each of the subtests show little change at these age levels. Although there is a lack of differentiation at other ages for different subtests, no other pattern exists. This lack of age differentiation is evident in the norm tables. The authors combined age groups, originally of

6-month intervals, whose mean raw scores differed by less than 1 point. Consequently, the norm tables contain age intervals ranging from 6 to 24 months (e.g., 17 years, 0 months to 18 years, 11 months).

In summary, the DATA is fairly easy to administer and score. It assesses a broad range of academic skills and includes a useful writing exercise. However, the DATA standardization sample is inadequate in both size and representativeness; hence, its psychometric properties necessarily suffer. The utility of the DATA could be improved by the inclusion of a larger sample with some measure of socioeconomic status used as a stratification variable.

Wide Range Achievement Test—Revised

The Wide Range Achievement Test—Revised (WRAT-R; Jastak & Wilkinson, 1984) is an individually administered achievement test designed to measure a subject's basic skills in the areas of Reading, Spelling, and Arithmetic. This test is intended to remove the effects of comprehension, so that the examiner can determine whether the problem in question is due to an inability to learn the codes that are prerequisites to learning the basic skills in these three areas. There are two record formats: Level One and Level Two. Level One is for use with children aged 5 through 11; Level Two is for use with individuals aged 12 through 74. Administration time ranges from 20 to 30 minutes.

The WRAT-R is a fairly easy test to administer and score. However, administration procedures do vary within each level and across subtests. Scores yielded include standard scores, percentile ranks, grade equivalents, stanines, T-scores, and normal curve equivalents.

The WRAT-R was standardized in 1984 on a national sample of 5,600 individuals. The authors are to be commended for the use of such a large sample size, which allowed for the inclusion of 200 subjects in each age group (Witt, 1986). Stratification variables included geographic region, gender, and race. Unfortunately, statistical techniques were employed to attempt to compensate for the nonrandom selection of the adult sample. Moreover, the omission of soioeconomic sta-

tus as a stratification variable greatly weakens the credibility of the sample.

Overall, the psychometric properties of the WRAT-R are inadequate (Witt, 1986). The manual reports high internal-consistency coefficients (.82 to .96) and stability coefficients (.79 to .95). Information concerning the sample and time interval used, which is not presented in the manual, would aid in the evaluation of the stability coefficients provided.

The methods employed to establish the content validity of the WRAT-R are poor (Witt, 1986). The authors contend that content validity is "apparent." Reviews of achievement tests or related textbooks would aid in validating the selection of the item pool. Although the authors performed Rasch analyses, which determined item difficulty, this single procedure is not sufficient to establish content validity.

One common method of determining construct validity is age differentiation. In general, the WRAT-R demonstrates adequate age differentiation through adulthood. Finally, the technical manual does not report evidence of concurrent validity—a great inconvenience for the user. The authors state that such information is contained in a second manual, which had not been released at the time this chapter was written.

Although the WRAT-R exhibits much improvement over the original WRAT, more work is definitely needed. For instance, information not yet provided concerning concurrent validity detracts from the credibility of the instrument. The omission of socioeconomic status as a stratification variable and the failure of the authors to establish adequate content validity should also be caveats for the examiner.

Peabody Individual Achievement Test—Revised

The Peabody Individual Achievement Test—Revised (PIAT-R; Markwardt, 1989) is a power test designed to assess an individual's academic functioning in six general areas: Mathematics, Reading Recognition, Reading Comprehension, Spelling, Written Expression, and General Information. It is intended for use with children aged 5 years, 0 months through 18 years, 11 months. The entire PIAT-R takes approximately 40–60 minutes to administer.

The PIAT–R is very easy to administer and score. Starting points are provided based on the child's age for the General Information subtest. Starting points on subsequent subtests are determined by the previous subtest's raw score (a routing method). Basal and ceiling rules are easy to follow and are identical for each subtest except that of Written Expression. The use of an easel format generally allows for simpler administration. The starting point for the Written Expression subtest is determined differently. Examiners either administer Level I, which assesses prewriting skills such as writing the child's name, words, and dictated sentences, or Level II, which asks the child to write a story in response to one of two stimulus pictures provided. As a rule of thumb, the author suggests that Level I is more appropriate for children below the second grade and Level II for children at or above the second-grade level.

The PIAT-R yields standard scores ($M = 100$, $SD = 15$), normal curve equivalents, and stanines for each subtest (again excepting the Written Expression) and for Total Reading and Total Test scores. The Written Expression subtest yields a "developmental scaled score" that ranges between 1 and 15. This yields slightly more range than the stanine score offered for this test, rendering it a rather "gross" screening measure of written expression skill.

The PIAT-R was standardized on a national sample of 1,563 subjects. Stratification variables included geographic location, parental education, gender, and race. The stratification was based on 1985 census figures, making the norms current.

The PIAT-R reliability data are very impressive. Test–retest coefficients for the total test composite ranged from .92 to .99, and the coefficients for individual subtests ranged from .78 to .97.

In an attempt to establish the content validity of the PIAT-R, subject-matter experts were employed to select items and develop content blueprints. These content validity efforts do give PIAT-R users a good sense for the types of skills they are assessing in each domain. The breadth of the General Information domain is particularly impressive (Fodness, 1989).

Attempts to establish concurrent and construct validity were fairly weak. Basically, the validity of the PIAT-R rests on the validity of the original PIAT (Dunn & Markwardt, 1970). This is hardly satisfactory as there is only a 35% item overlap between these two measures. The PIAT-R validity is likely to be supportive, but it should be tested.

Overall, the PIAT is an easily administered and scored test of achievement. Its reasonably good content validity makes it a useful screener. Although the Written Expression subtest does not yield very useful scores, we expect that it will be a welcome addition. The PIAT-R is clearly an improvement over its predecessor.

Quick-Score Achievement Test

The Quick-Score Achievement Test (Q-SAT; Hammill, Ammer, Cronin, Mandlebaum, & Quinby, 1987) was designed to be a brief but accurate measure of a student's level of academic functioning. Specifically, the Q-SAT is comprised of four subtests (Writing, Arithmetic, Reading, Facts) and has two equivalent forms. It is for use with children aged 7 years, 0 months through 17 years, 11 months, and takes approximately 30 minutes to 1 hour to administer.

The Q-SAT is easy to administer and fairly easy to score. All responses are scored as either 1 or 0, and basal and ceiling rules are clearly explained. Although the examiner must be aware that varied entry points exist for the Arithmetic and Reading subtests, these entry points (arranged by grade level rather than age) are noted at the top of the record form. Some difficulties may arise in scoring the Facts subtest. The authors' claim that "no qualitative scoring judgments are required of the examiner, as responses are obviously either correct or incorrect" (Hamill et al., 1987, p. 7) is a point of contention. Often, only simple or vague one-word answers are provided in the key for questions that may have a number of correct responses. For example, the answer given in the manual to the question "What is tuberculosis?" is "a disease." Clearly, a myriad of potentially correct responses that do not include the word "disease" are possible. Furthermore, no specific instructions are provided in the manual to allow the examiner to query responses; thus, qualitative scoring judgments are necessary. It would be helpful if, for each question, the authors had provided several correct as well as incorrect responses from which to choose, similar to the format found in the Woodcock–Johnson Tests of Achievement.

The Q-SAT yields a variety of scores, including standard scores for subtests and composite, percentile ranks, normal curve equivalents, stanines, T-scores, and z-scores. The authors are to be commended for their omission of grade and age equivalents. Like the DAB and the DATA, the Q-SAT manual provides an incomplete table of percentile ranks for the composite standard score.

The Q-SAT was nationally standardized on 1,495 individuals in the spring of 1986. Stratification variables included gender, residence (urban vs. rural), race, geographic region, and ethnicity. Unfortunately, the composition of the sample with regard to socioeconomic status is not known.

Although the reliability coefficients reported in the Q-SAT manual are good, there are some problems with the procedures employed. For instance, internal-consistency coefficients ranged from .80 to .95, but only 550 students from the standardization sample were used for these calculations. The reasons for the exclusion of the remaining 945 subjects from the standardization sample are not apparent.

The two forms of the Q-SAT were found to be roughly equivalent, with coefficients ranging from .85 to .96. Test–retest reliability was then measured using the equivalent forms, which were administered within a 2-day interval and appropriately counterbalanced. Reliability coefficients ranged from .77 to .96.

In selecting items for the Q-SAT, relevant achievement tests and textbooks were consulted. Item analysis revealed acceptable point-biserial coefficients for both forms. However, with respect to difficulty level, the authors comment that only 65% of the median coefficients range between .15 and .85. Although the authors believe that such a figure is acceptable, it would seem that at many age levels the difficulty level of the items is inappropriate. For example, all median coefficients of difficulty for ages 7 through 8 do not exceed .02 for three of the four subtests on both forms. Similar problems exist for ages 9 through 10 on two of the four subtests.

The Q-SAT demonstrates fair concurrent validity. The correlation coefficients between the Q-SAT and other related achievement tests ranged from .24 to .78.

The method used in evaluating age and grade differentiation validity of the Q-SAT is not adequate. Subtest mean raw scores were correlated with subjects' ages and grades to test these types of validity. Correlational analyses provide information with regard to the strength and direction of the relationship between two variables. However, the authors give no information concerning the magnitude of the difference of the subtest mean raw scores between two consecutive age groups or grade levels. Moreover, the authors indicate that this magnitude in many circumstances is quite small. In the norming procedures, consecutive age groups, originally of 6-month intervals, whose mean scores differed by 1 point or less were combined. Resulting age intervals range from 6 to 36 months.

In summary, although the Q-SAT is easy to administer, its scoring procedures may be complicated with respect to the Facts subtest. As discussed earlier, a more comprehensive list of correct and incorrect responses for each item would insure simpler and more accurate scoring. The failure to include socioeconomic status as a stratification variable raises doubts concerning the representativeness of the sample. Other areas that should receive attention include the incomplete table of percentile ranks and the statistical procedures used in investigating the psychometric properties of the Q-SAT. In general, the Q-SAT may be a useful screener, but it would benefit from more sound and extensive research.

Kaufman Test of Educational Achievement

The Kaufman Test of Educational Achievement (K-TEA) Comprehensive Form (Kaufman & Kaufman, 1985a) was designed to assess a student's level of academic achievement in five areas: Reading Decoding, Reading Comprehension, Mathematics Application, Mathematics Computation, and Spelling. Furthermore, it allows the examiner to evaluate subjects' performances on specific areas within these subtests. It takes 60–75 minutes to administer and is for use with individuals in 1st through 12th grades or aged 6 years, 0 months through 18 years, 11 months. The authors of the K-TEA also provide the K-TEA Brief Form (Kaufman & Kaufman, 1985b), a shortened version of the K-TEA Comprehensive Form.

The easel format makes the K-TEA simple to use. Scoring procedures are also clear and straightforward. It yields a variety of scores, including standard scores for subtests and composites, percentile ranks, stanines, normal curve equivalents, and age and grade equivalents. In addition, the tables presented in the manual enable the examiner to determine individual strengths and weaknesses. Because the K-TEA was normed in both the fall and the spring, more accurate evaluations of subjects' performances are possible. Unfortunately, the K-TEA does not appear to accurately evaluate students with very high achievement scores (e.g., gifted children), because the highest standard score one can obtain is 120. Furthermore, accurate assessment of children aged 6–9 is difficult if the students are well below their grade or age level.

The K-TEA was normed in the fall and the spring of 1983. The fall standardization sample consisted of 1,067 subjects, and the spring sample employed 1,409 subjects. Both samples were stratified with respect to grade, geographic region, race, socioeconimic status, and gender. The inclusion of students in special education, a procedure not commonly used, gives additional strength to the representativeness of the standardization sample.

In general, the psychometric properties of the K-TEA are very good. Internal-consistency coefficients range from .90 to .98 for all subtests across grades and from .92 to .98 with respect to age. Test–retest coefficients reported for 1st through 6th grades and for 7th through 12th grades ranged from .90 to .96 and from .90 to .97, respectively.

In selecting items for use on the K-TEA, content blueprints were employed. Specifically, experts in each area of interest specified the skills to be assessed by each subtest; from these specifications, an item pool was generated. In addition to conventional item analysis procedures, the Rasch–Wright latent-trait model (Rasch, 1960; Wright, 1977) was used in item selection. Finally, the Angoff method (Angoff & Ford, 1973) of detecting item bias was employed. The utilization

of these procedures gives the K-TEA strong content validity.

The K-TEA demonstrates adequate concurrent validity. Correlation coefficients ranged from .37 to .90 with several related achievement tests.

Finally, evidence indicates that the K-TEA possesses strong construct validity. Acceptable age and grade differentiation exists for both the fall and the spring samples. Internal-consistency validity coefficients ranged from .77 to .85 for subjects by grade and from .72 to .88 with respect to age.

In general, the K-TEA Comprehensive Form demonstrates excellent psychometric properties. The inclusion of fall and spring norms aids in accurate evaluation of an individual's performance throughout the academic year. Moreover, the K-TEA provides the examiner with detailed information concerning an individual's specific skills. However, it appears that the K-TEA may lack adequate difficulty for gifted children, or adequate floor for younger children with severe delays.

The K-TEA Brief Form provides a general assessment of an individual's performance in the areas of Reading, Mathematics, and Spelling, and takes approximately 30 minutes to administer. Like the K-TEA Comprehensive Form, it is for use with children in 1st through 12th grades or aged 6 through 18. Administration and scoring procedures are similar to those of the K-TEA Comprehensive Form. Intercorrelation coefficients between the Comprehensive and the Brief Forms range from .80 to .92 across grades and from .83 to .93 across ages.

The manual for the K-TEA Brief Form also provides fall and spring norms. The fall standardization sample consisted of 589 subjects and was stratified with respect to gender, grade, geographic region, race and socioeconomic status. The spring norms, however, were obtained through an equipercentile equating procedure. Because the resulting fall norms, in general, were equivalent to those of the K-TEA Comprehensive Form, it was expected that the spring norms of the K-TEA Comprehensive Form would correspond to those of the Brief Form. Thus, the spring norms presented in the manual of the K-TEA Brief Form are based on the spring norms of the Comprehensive form, not on a separate spring standardization sample.

Like the Comprehensive Form, the Brief form exhibits very good internal consistency (r's = .85 to .93 across grades and .89 to .95 across ages) and stability (r's = .84 to .94 across grades). Similar methods (i.e., content blueprints and item analysis) were employed and indicate that the K-TEA Brief Form demonstrates good content validity. The concurrent validity coefficients with other individually administered achievement tests range from .42 to .95. Finally, the manual presents good evidence of age and grade differentiation validity. Internal-consistency validity coefficients ranged from .76 to .81 across grades and from .79 to .81 across age.

Like the Comprehensive Form, the K-TEA Brief Form does not seem to be suited for older children with high achievement scores or for younger children with extreme difficulties. In general, though, the K-TEA Brief Form appears to be a useful and acceptable alternative to the Comprehensive Form for the assessment of overall reading, mathematics, and spelling skills when the examiner is constrained by time.

Woodcock–Johnson Psycho-Educational Battery, Tests of Achievement

The Woodcock–Johnson Tests of Achievement consist of 10 subtests designed to assess academic skill levels in four areas: Reading, Mathematics, Written Language, and Knowledge. These areas, or "clusters," subsume the various subtests. The Tests of Achievement, for use with individuals aged 3 to 80, are but one part of the Woodcock–Johnson Psycho-Educational Battery (Woodcock, 1978); the battery also contains the Tests of Cognitive Ability and the Tests of Interest Level. Although the Woodcock–Johnson Battery was designed to be used as a cohesive unit, the Tests of Achievement are frequently administered separately and concurrently with other intelligence tests. For the purposes of this chapter, only the Tests of Achievement (hereafter referred to as the W-J) are discussed.

Administration of the W-J is relatively easy. The test utilizes an easel format, has easy-to-follow basal and ceiling rules, and takes approximately 45 minutes to administer. Scoring, conversely, is much more difficult and often takes as long as administration. All items are scored either 1 or 0, and the scoring criteria given in the easel are generally explicit. However, nothing in any of the manuals addresses the procedure to follow when multiple basal and/or ceiling levels are obtained, making accurate and consistent scoring more difficult. Moreover, as Kaufman (1985) has noted, there are many cases in which clerical errors may result from unnecessarily complex scoring procedures. For example, calculating derived scores from raw scores can be quite confusing. One must go through numerous machinations involving several tables (which have many columns) in order to obtain the standard scores and percentiles for both the subtests and clusters. Although the steps one must follow are clearly delineated by the authors, an examiner may easily become bewildered by the sheer quantity of numbers he or she must sift through; this makes the likelihood of a scoring error rather high (Kaufman, 1985).

In addition to standard scores and percentiles for both individual subtests and clusters, the W-J yields a number of other scores, some of which may be unfamiliar to examiners. These include age and grade equivalent scores, instructional ranges, normal curve equivalents, relative performance indices, and functioning levels. The uniqueness of some of these scores makes the W-J more difficult to interpret.

On a more positive note, the recent publication of a microcomputer scoring package, COMPUSCORE (Hauger, 1984), circumvents many of the potential scoring problems an examiner may encounter. One need only input a subject's personal data as well as raw scores; the program outputs the various scores for each cluster. This program reduces scoring time for the W-J to approximately 30 minutes.

The W-J was standardized on a national sample of 4,732 individuals (3,935 of whom were of school age) between 1976 and 1977. The sample was stratified with respect to gender, race, occupational status, geographic region, and type of community (urban–nonurban). An individual subject weighting procedure was performed in order to obtain a distribution of data that mirrored the U.S.

population. It is clear that the author's standardization efforts were carefully and well conducted. One problem, however, is that the data are based on 1970 U.S. census figures, making the norms somewhat outdated. Also, because some cells in the preschool and 65+ norming samples were small and not representative of the population (thus requiring large weights), the adequacy of those samples must be questioned (Cummings, 1985). As such, the W-J would seem most appropriate for school-age children.

Overall, the psychometric properties of the W-J are quite impressive. The reliability coefficients of both the subtests and clusters are excellent, with median split-half reliabilities ranging from .83 to .95 for subtests and .92 to .96 for achievement clusters (coefficients are across grade where applicable and across age where not).

Items for the W-J were originally generated through contributions from outside experts, including experienced teachers and curriculum consultants. The final pool of items was selected by applying the Rasch–Wright latent-trait model of item analysis. Another asset of the W-J is the use of meaningful clusters (Kaufman, 1985). A concomitant weakness, however, is that the Written Language cluster does not involve a writing sample, and is thus somewhat of a misnomer. Generally, though, the W-J's content validity is more than adequate.

The W-J demonstrates very good concurrent validity. Scores for each of the clusters were correlated with those on several other popular acheivement tests. The coefficients ranged from .46 to .92, with all but three of the coefficients above .70.

Construct validity of the W-J was evaluated primarily by cluster analysis. As Kaufman (1985) notes, this statistical approach offers moderate support for the choice and composition of clusters. Although this is not emphasized in the technical manual, the W-J also seems to show adequate grade differentiation for school-age subjects and age differentiation for preschool subjects with respect to both subtests and clusters. Subjects age 20 and older were put in three groups (20–39, 40–64, 65+) and showed a consistent pattern of decreasing scores. The meaning of this is not readily apparent.

Overall, the W-J is well constructed and exhibits strong psychometric properties. It is most useful as a diagnostic tool as part of a comprehensive assessment battery, rather than just as a screener. Unfortunately, the W-J possesses an elaborate and confusing scoring system. Although the COMPU-SCORE program makes scoring the battery much simpler, the probability of clerical errors remains too high. As previously discussed, the W-J seems best suited for school-age children.

At the time of final editing of this chapter, a revision of the W-J was being shipped. This new instrument is unknown, but it can be said that the revised W-J has a strong foundation from which to build. This is likely to make the revision of great interest to test users.

PSYCHOMETRIC ISSUES

Content Validity

It is truly remarkable how few of the tests discussed above include strong evidence of content validity. In stark contrast, the developers of many group-administered tests of achievement have taken great pains to hire curriculum consultants to define appropriate content, and to conduct various statistical analyses of content validity. A notable exception to this observation is the BASIS, whose developers devote virtually an entire manual chapter to an explanation of the procedures used for item selection. One gets the impression from this chapter that the BASIS development team sincerely tried to select item content that reflected typical school curricula. The content validation approach used by the BASIS, and to a lesser extent the K-TEA (the developers of the K-TEA did have some content domain experts develop content blueprints), depended heavily on the review of curriculum materials and the abilities of content domain experts. As a contrasting example, the manual for the WRAT-R gives little evidence of a match between test items and school curricula.

It seems eminently clear that the item content of clinical measures of achievement can be selected so as to be reasonably congruent with popular school textbooks and other curriculum materials. At the very least, the developers of new achievement measures, and those wishing to revise existing measures, should involve a board of consulting editors for various content areas in the test development process. This would increase the likelihood that the item development for every subtest would be guided by at least one content domain expert. Presumably, good content validity also enhances the accuracy of interpretation of obtained scores such as grade equivalents or latent-trait scaled scores. Developmental norms such as these are likely to be of more value to teachers if they are based on appropriate sampling of the relevant content domain.

Norming

There has been a vast improvement in the quality of the national standardization samples for measures of the type considered in this chapter, although there is considerable room for improvement. Some tests, such as the DAB and DATA, do not yet show clear evidence of having controlled for socioeconomic status in the selection of their norming samples. This makes the accuracy of their obtained scores somewhat suspect.

In direct contrast is the K-TEA Comprehensive Form, which provides not only separate norms for the spring and the fall of the academic year, but also separate norms by age and grade of the child. The K-TEA Comprehensive Form provides a laudable norming standard for other tests of achievement, in that its norming procedures are state-of-the-art, and the variety of norms available allow the test user considerable interpretive flexibility. The inclusion of at least spring and fall grade-referenced norms for other clinical tests of achievement would be of great use to diagnosticians.

Derived Scores

The W-J provides a wide array of derived scores that is likely to please some test users and befuddle others. Included in the W-J menagerie are many latent-trait-based scores. Latent-trait derived scores are likely to become the developmental norm of choice for the future, since they possess one important characteristic that grade equivalents do not possess: They are on an interval scale, with equal units along the scale, as opposed to grade equivalents, which are on an ordinal scale with unequal units. These developmental norms (Rasch scores) are fea-

tured on the BASIS. This is a popular metric (usually referred to as "scaled scores") used by a variety of major group achievement tests. These scaled scores will be a welcome addition to the clinical assessment arena for researchers and administrators, because they provide a more sophisticated way of evaluating achievement gains over time.

If tests of the future do depend more on latent-trait scores, we recommend that test manuals include more information on the interpretation of these scores. We have found that most clinicians are unaware of the properties of these scores. For example, many of our colleagues are unaware that the Rasch scaled scores of the BASIS cannot be compared across content domains (curriculum areas). Other new scores that are introduced should also be discussed in detail in the tests' manuals.

CONCLUSIONS

There has been a dramatic improvement in the quantity and quality of individually administered screening tests of academic achievement in the past decade. Whereas psychologists and other clinicians used to have only a few options for screeners of achievement (namely, the WRAT and PIAT), they now have a vast array of tests from which to choose, each with features that improve upon older technology. The BASIS, for example, has set a new standard for content validity that enhances administration and interperetation. The K-TEA and PIAT-R set a new standard of technical quality by offering a variety of norm-referenced comparisons. Other tests in the works will also probably bring improvements to this field. The exciting aspect of all of these new tests is that clinicians now have numerous choices that allow them to tailor assessment to the needs of each child undergoing evaluation.

Hence, it is onward and upward for the development of screening measures of academic achievement. The current scales challenge would-be test developers to provide further innovations; there are still many unmet needs. One of the most pressing needs is for better measures of written and oral expression.

Although there are currently a number of fine tests available, some tests lack impressive psychometric properties. The DATA, for example, fits this category. Clinicians have to be savvy enough to choose an achievement test that is psychometrically adequate and practically useful. More chapters of this variety may assist practitioners in making these test selection decisions. We also advise that clinicians consult a number of "experts" before making decisions regarding test use.

APPENDIX 23.1. TEST DESCRIPTIONS

Test	Subtests	Age range	Grade range	Administration time
BASIS	Reading, Mathematics, Spelling, Writing (optional)	6 years, 0 months to 18 years, 11 months	K–8	1 hour
DAB	Story Comprehension, Characteristics, Synonyms, Grammatic Completion, Alphabet/Word Knowledge, Reading Comprehension, Capitalization, Punctuation, Spelling, Written Vocabulary, Math Reasoning, Math Calculation	6 years, 0 months to 14 years, 11 months	N/A	Not reported
DATA	Word Identification, Reading Comprehension, Spelling, Writing Comprehension, Math Calculation, Math Problem Solving, Social Studies, Reference Skills	12 years, 0 months to 18 years, 11 months	N/A	1–2 hours
K-TEA Brief Form	Reading, Mathematics, Spelling	6 years, 0 months to 18 years, 11 months	1–12	30 minutes
K-TEA Comprehensive Form	Reading Decoding, Reading Comprehension, Mathematics Applications, Mathematics Computation, Spelling	6 years, 0 months to 18 years, 11 months	1–12	60–75 minutes
PIAT-R	Mathematics, Reading Recognition, Reading Comprehension, Spelling, General Information	5 years, 3 months to 18 years, 11 months	K–12	30–40 minutes
Q-SAT	Reading, Writing, Arithmetic, Facts	7 years, 0 months to 17 years, 11 months	N/A	30–60 minutes
WRAT-R	Reading, Spelling, Arithmetic	5 years, 0 months to 74 years, 11 months	N/A	20–30 minutes
W-J	Letter–Word Identification, Word Attack, Passage Comprehension, Calculation, Applied Problems, Dictation, Proofing, Science, Social Studies, Humanities	3 years, 0 months to 80+ years	K–12	30–45 minutes

Note. N/A, not available.

APPENDIX 23.2. DERIVED SCORES AVAILABLE

Test	Standard scores	Grade equivalents	Age equivalents	Normal curve equivalents	Latent-trait standard scores	Stanines	Percentile ranks	Others
BASIS	Yes	Yes	Yes	Yes	Yes	Yes	Yes	—
DAB	Yes	No	No	Yes	No	Yes	Yes	T-scores, z scores
DATA	Yes	No	No	Yes	No	Yes	Yes	T-scores, z scores
K-TEA, Brief and Comprehensive forms	Yes	Yes	Yes	Yes	No	Yes	Yes	—
PIAT-R	Yes	Yes	Yes	Yes	No	Yes	Yes	—
Q-SAT	Yes	No	No	Yes	No	Yes	Yes	T-scores, z-scores
WRAT-R	Yes	Yes	No	Yes	No	Yes	Yes	T-scores
W-J	Yes	Yes	Yes	Yes	No	No	Yes	Relative performance index (RPI), instructional ranges, relative mastery

APPENDIX 23.3. TECHNICAL INFORMATION

Tests	Standardization information				Reliability[a]		Validity (methods employed)[a]		
	Sample size	Date	Location/ no. of states	Stratification variables	Internal consistency	Stability	Content	Concurrent	Construct
BASIS	3,296	Fall 1982	National/23 states	Geographic region, sex, SES, school systems enrollment, ethnicity, public vs. nonpublic schools	By grade, KR20 = .84–.86; by age, KR20 = .87–.97	Test–retest = .74–.95	Textbook reviews, achievement test reviews, item difficulty, item discrimination	BASIS vs. report cards, .25–.61; vs. achievement tests, .50–.60	Grade differentiation, age differentiation
DAB	1,534	Not reported	National/13 states	Sex, residence, race, geographic region, occupation of parents	By age, coefficient α = .58–.98	Test–retest = .80–.99	Item difficulty, item discrimination	DAB vs. Durrell, .47; TOLD, NS–.53; WRMT, .41; WRAT, .56; TOWL, .37–.81; KeyMath, .58–.66	Grade differentiation, age differentiation, differential validity
DATA	1,135	1985–1986	National/15 states	Sex, residence, race, geographic region, age, ethnicity	By age, coefficient α = .88–.98	Test–retest = .71–.95	Textbook reviews, panel of experts, item discrimination, item difficulty	DATA vs. SDRT, .34–.51; SDMT, NS–.70; ITBS, NS–.85; ITED, .26–.83	Age differentiation, differential validity
K-TEA Brief Form	589[c]	Fall 1983	National/15 states	Sex, grade, geographic region, SES, race	By age, split-half = .87–.95; by grade, split-half = .85–.93	Test–retest = .84–.94	Blueprint by panel of experts, Rasch model item analysis, textbook reviews, achievement test reviews	K-TEA Brief vs. WRAT, .42–.87; PIAT, .59–.84; K-ABC (achievement), .45–.95	Age differentiation, grade differentiation, internal consistency

Test	N	Date	Sample	Standardization variables	Reliability (split-half/internal)	Test-retest/Alternate forms	Content validity	Construct/Concurrent validity	Other analyses
K-TEA Comprehensive Form	1,067 1,409	Fall 1983 Spring 1983	National/15 states	Sex, grade, geographic region, SES, race	By age, split-half = .83–.99; by grade, split-half = .90–.98	Test-retest = .83–.97	Blueprint by panel of experts, achievement test reviews, Rasch model item analysis textbook reviews	K-TEA Comprehensive vs. K-TEA Brief, .80–.93; WRAT, .37–.90; PIAT, .63–.86; K-ABC (achievement), .49–.92; SAT, .65–.85; MAT, .64–.80; CTBS, .51–90	Age differentiation, grade differentiation, internal consistency
PIAT-R	1,563	Fall 1986	National/20 states	Geographic region, sex, race, parental education level	By age, split-half = .83–.99; by grade, split-half = .84–.99	By age, test-retest = .65–.99; by grade, test-retest = .83–.99	Content blue prints, panel of experts, item discrimination, item difficulty, Rasch model item analysis	PIAT-R vs. PPVT-R, .62–.81	Age differentiation, grade differentiation
Q-SAT	1,495	Spring 1986	National/15 states	Sex, residence, race, geographic region, ethnicity	By age, coefficient α = .80–.95	Alternate forms = .77–.96	Textbook reviews, achievement test reviews, item difficulty, item discrimination	Q-SAT vs. SRA, .57–.66; CAT, .37–.64; ITBS, .24–.60	Age differentiation, grade differentiation, differential validity
WRAT-R	5,600	1984	National/17 states	Geographic region, sex, race	N/A	Test-retest = .79–.97	Item difficulty (Rasch model)	Not reported	Age differentiation
W-J	4,732	1976–1977	National/18 states	Sex, race, geographic region, urbanization, occupation	By age, split-half = .83–.95	Not reported	Panel of experts, Rasch model item analysis	W-J vs. ITBS, .62–.84; PIAT, .68–.91; WRAT, .46–.90; Keymath, .80–.82	Cluster analysis

Note. SES, socioeconomic status; KR$_{20}$, Kuder–Richardson 20; TOLD, Test of Language Development; NS, not significant; WRMT, Woodcock Reading Mastery Test; TOWL, Test of Written Language; SDRT, Stanford Diagnostic Reading Test; SDMT, Stanford Diagnostic Mathematics Test; ITBS, Iowa Tests of Basic Skills; ITED, Iowa Tests of Educational Development; K-ABC, Kaufman Assessment Battery for Children; SAT, Stanford Achievement Tests; MAT, Metropolitan Achievement Tests; CTBS, Comprehensive Tests of Basic Skills; N/A, not available; SRA, Science Research Associates Achievement Series; CAT, California Achievement Tests.

[a] As reported in test manual.

[b] Separate analyses were not performed for individual achievement tests.

[c] Equated to fall sample of the K-TEA Comprehensive Form.

REFERENCES

Angoff, W. H., & Ford, S. F. (1973). Item-face interaction on a test of scholastic aptitude. *Journal of Educational Measurement, 10*, 95–106.

Brown, L., & Bryant, B. R. (1984). Critical reviews of three individually administered achievement tests: Peabody Individual Achievement Test, Wide Range Achievement Test, and Diagnostic Achievement Battery. *Remedial and Special Education, 5*, 53–60.

Conley, M. W. (1986). [Review of Basic Achievement Skills Individual Screener]. *Reading Teacher, 39*, 418–420.

Cummings, J. A. (1985). [Review of Woodcock–Johnson Psycho-Educational Battery]. In J. V. Mitchell (Ed.), *The ninth mental measurements yearbook* (pp. 1759–1762). Lincoln, NE: Buros Institute of Mental Measurements.

Dunn, L. M., & Markwardt, F. C. (1970). *Peabody Individual Achievement Test manual*. Circle Pines, MN: American Guidance Service.

Floden, R. E. (1985). [Review of Basic Achievement Skills Individual Screener]. In J. V. Mitchell (Ed.), *The ninth mental measurements yearbook* (pp. 134–135). Lincoln, NE: Buros Institute of Mental Measurements.

Fodness, R. (1989, September). [Review of Peabody Individual Acheivement Test—Revised]. *Communique*.

Hambleton, R. K., & deVries, D. K. (1985). [Review of Basic Achievement Skills Individual Screener]. *Journal of Counseling and Development, 63*, 383–384.

Hammill, D. O., Ammer, J. J., Cronin, M. E., Mandlebaum, L. H., & Quinby, S. S. (1987). *Quick-Score Achievement Test: Q-SAT*. Austin, TX: Pro-Ed.

Hauger, J. (1984). *COMPUSCORE for the Woodcock–Johnson Psycho-Educational Battery*. Allen, TX: DLM Teaching Resources.

Huebner, E. S. (1984). [Review of Basic Achievement Skills Individual Screener (BASIS)]. *Journal of Psychoeducational Assessment, 2*, 173–176.

Jastak, S., & Wilkinson, G. S. (1984). *The Wide Range Achievement Test—Revised administration manual*. Wilmington, DE: Jastak Associates.

Kaufman, A. S. (1985). [Review of Woodcock–Johnson Psycho-Educational Battery]. In J. V. Mithcell (Ed.), *The ninth mental measuremants yearbook* (pp. 1762–1765). Lincoln, NE: Buros Institute of Mental Measurements.

Kaufman, A. S., & Kaufman, N. L. (1985a). *Kaufman Test of Educational Achievement Comprehensive Form manual*. Circle Pines, MN: American Guidance Service.

Kaufman, A. S., & Kaufman, N. L. (1985b). *Kaufman Test of Educational Achievement Brief Form manual*. Circle Pines, MN: American Guidance Service.

Lesiak, J. (1984). [Review of Diagnostic Achievement Battery]. *Journal of Psychoeducational Assessment, 2*, 353–358.

Lewandowski, L. J. (1985). [Review of Diagnostic Achievement Battery]. *Reading Teacher, 39*, 306–309.

Markwardt, F. C. (1989). *Peabody Individual Achievement Test—Revised*. Circle Pines, MN: American Guidance Service.

Newcomer, P. L., & Bryant, B. R. (1986). *Diagnostic Achievement Test for Adolescents*. Austin, TX: Pro-Ed.

Newcomer, P. L., & Curtis, D. (1984). *Diagnostic Achievement Battery examiner's manual*. Austin, TX: Pro-Ed.

Psychological Corporation. (1983). *Basic Achievement Skills Individual Screener manual*. New York: Author.

Radencich, M. C. (1985). BASIS: Basic Achievement Skills Individual Screener. *Academic Therapy, 20*, 377–382.

Rasch, G. (1960). Probabilistic models for some intelligence and attainment tests. Copenhagen: Danish Institute for Educational Research.

Reynolds, C. R. (1984). Critical measurement issues in learning disabilities. *Journal of Special Education, 18*, 451–476.

Salvia, J. & Ysseldyke, J. E. (1985). *Assessment in special remedial education*. Boston: Houghton-Mifflin.

Schumm, J. S. (1987, November). [Review of Diagnostic Achievement Test for Adolescents (DATA)]. *Journal of Reading*, pp. 188–189.

Witt, J. C. (1986). Review of the Wide Range Achievement Test—Revised. *Journal of Psychoeducational Assessment, 4*, 87–90.

Woodcock, R. W. (1987). *Development and standardization of the Woodcock–Johnson Psycho-Educational Battery*. Allen, TX: DLM Teaching Resources.

Wright, B. D. (1977). Solving measurement problems with the Rasch model. *Journal of Educational Measurement, 14*, 97–116.

Ysseldyke, J. E. (1985). [Review of Basic Achievement Skills Individual Screener]. *Journal of Counseling and Development, 64*, 90–91.

IV

SPECIAL TOPICS IN MENTAL TESTING

24

Conceptual and Technical Problems in Learning Disability Diagnosis

CECIL R. REYNOLDS
Texas A&M University

For many years, the diagnosis and evaluation of learning disability (LD) have been the subjects of almost constant debate in the professional, scholarly, and lay literature, but this has been expecially true since the passage of Public Law 94-142. The lack of consensus regarding the definition of LD is reflected in the day-to-day implementation of P.L. 94-142; in the absence of a readily operationalized definition, many clinicians and administrative agencies, particularly school districts, experience difficulty in deciding who is eligible for services. Both under- and overidentification of LD children create significant problems. Undercounting deprives LD children of special services to which they are entitled; overcounting results in the inappropriate placement of students who are not handicapped, loss of valuable staff time, and increased expense of operating programs (Chalfant, 1984). Overcounting thus drains resources from other programs and students; if it continues to be rampant, it could result in the demise of LD programs altogether. Errors in LD diagnosis will never be completely eliminated, but the amount of error must be reduced as much as possible, while still insuring that as many LD children as possible receive the special services to which they are entitled.

FEDERAL AND STATE CRITERIA: THE "SEVERE DISCREPANCY" COMPONENT

Two broad factors seem to determine who is LD: (1) the prevailing definition of LD, and (2) how that definition is applied on a day-to-day basis in practice. The rules and regulations implementing P.L. 94-142 provide a definition of LD for use by all states receiving federal funds for special education program. According to this definition, the diagnosis

is made based on (1) whether a child does not achieve commensurate with his or her age and ability when provided with appropriate educational experience and (2) whether the child has a severe discrepancy between achievement and intellectual ability in one or more of seven areas relating to communication skills and mathematical abilities.

These concepts are to be interpreted in a case by case basis by the qualified evaluation team members. The team must decide that the discrepancy is not primarily the result of (1) visual, hearing, or motor handicaps; (2) mental retardation; (3) emotional disturbance; or (4) environmental, cultural, or economic disadvantage. (Rules and Regulations Implementing Education for All Handicapped Children Act of 1975, 1977, p. 655082)

Although this definition gives some guidance, the field has generally regarded it as vague, subjective, and resulting in diagnosis by exclusion in many cases. Operationalization of the federal definition has varied tremendously across states, resulting in great confusion and disagreement over who should be served as LD. In fact, the probability of LD diagnosis in the schools varies by a factor of nearly 5, purely as a function of a child's state of residence.

This definition is mandated by federal law only for use by public schools and related agencies that accept federal funding for handicapped children, including LD children. Apparently because schools are where children are served in the vast majority of cases, because schools often pay for outside evaluations, and because other agencies tend to look toward federal directives as a safe haven in the current litigious era, this definition or a close variant is the most often encountered in practice as well as in clinical texts (e.g., Hynd & Willis, 1988). Interpretations of the definition abound in private and clinic practices, just as in the schools, with greater disparities even than in educational settings.

A review by Chalfant (1984) of state education agency (SEA) definitions across the United States identifies five major components that appear to be reasonably consistent across states. Such a review of private clinical settings and mental health agencies is improbable and would seem to offer little in the way of clarification. In addressing problems of LD diagnosis, Chalfant's major components offer a sound beginning.

1. "Failure to achieve," or perhaps more aptly, "school failure," represents a lack of academic attainment in one of the principal areas of school learning; this lack is sometimes seen as relative to grade placement and sometimes as compared to intellectual potential for achievement.
2. "Psychological process disorders" are disorders in one or more of the basic psychological processes that are believed to underlie school learning. Though never listed or defined in their entirety, such processes include attention and concentration, understanding and using written and spoken language, conceptualization, and information processing of all types.
3. "Exclusionary criteria" require that the observed symptoms *not* be due to other factors, such as sensory incapacity; mental retardation; emotional disturbances; or educational, economic, or related disadvantages.
4. "Etiology," probably the most ill defined of all factors, typically reflects a student's medical and developmental histories, which must be evaluated in order to locate factors believed to be causative in LD. These include a history of brain injury or substantive neurological problems, motor coordination, hyperactivity, delayed speech and language development, and pre- or perinatal difficulties.
5. The federal regulations specify that a child's failure to achieve communsurate with age and ability must result in a "severe discrepancy between achievement and intellectual ability" in one or more of the seven areas listed in the federal regulations. It is important to note that many states seem to ignore the "and intellectual ability" component of this definition, focusing only on the mean achievement level of all children of the same age, regardless of ability.

All five components are important, and each should be addressed in the diagnosis of LD, case by case. Each is hindered by problems of operational and technical clarity. Often no etiological factors are present. Rigid use of exclusionary criteria prohibit a finding of "multiply handicapped." Just what is to be considered a "psychological process," and are there any other "processes"? How is a "severe discrepancy" to be determined? Endless questions remain before objective diagnosis of LD will occur, yet much can be done at present.

As Chalfant (1984) has argued, I agree that the "psychological process" and "severe discrepancy" components of the definition are the most salient and the most promising areas to pursue. This chapter focuses on the problems of the "severe discrepancy" criterion, examining conceptual and technical problems of the past and present, as well as reviewing a proposed solution (Reynolds, 1984).

The "severe discrepancy" component is featured here not only because it is the most pervasive of Chalfant's (1984) components, but for the same reason it was included in the federal definition initially. When the rules and regulations for P.L. 94-142 were being developed, many experts in the field testified before Office of Education hearings, submitted numerous papers and related documentation, and were brought together for discussion and debate at open meetings. When the results of these hearings and debates are examined, the reason for the particular emphasis of the P.L. 94-142 definition becomes clear. The only consensus regarding definition or characteristics of this thing called LD was that it resulted in a major discrepancy between what one would expect academically of LD children and the level at which they were actually achieving.

The importance of the "severe discrepancy" statement in the federal definition quoted above was immediately obvious, just as was the potentially subjective nature of the term, especially as it may be applied to individual cases. In an effort to provide guidance in determining a "severe discrepancy" between expected and obtained academic levels, several formulas were proposed by the Bureau of Education for the Handicapped (now the Office of Special Education and Rehabilitation). Some of the formulas defined an expected grade equivalent (EGE), and others went further to provide cutoffs for a severe discrepancy. Some of the formulas considered included the following (CA stands for chronological age, MA for mental age):

Formula 5 is the formula for determining a severe discrepancy that was proposed by the bureau in 1976 in the process of setting up rules and regulations for implementation of P.L. 94-142. This formula was published in the *Federal Register*, and considerable commentary was gathered.

Much of the commentary has been reviewed (Danielson & Bauer, 1978). All of these various formulas were ultimately rejected for a host of interrelated reasons, though most centered around their mathematical inadequacy (see Berk, 1984, Ch. 4). Though more is said on this subject later, these formulas attempted mathematical operations that are not considered appropriate to the level of measurement being employed. The various formulas proffered used age and grade equivalents (which as scaling metrics are only ordinal-level data), and treated them as interval-scale and sometimes even ratio-scale data in some formulas (e.g., Formula 5). Thus, the various additions, subtractions, divisions, and ratios proposed in these formulas were essentially meaningless and in all cases misleading. In the final rules and regulations, no criteria for "severe discrepancy" were offered, and agencies were left to develop their own individual criteria for implementing the federal definition.

The present chapter continues addressing the need for objective diagnosis in more detail, and then looks at the reasons why there are such tremendous disparities in the numbers of children identified as LD from one locale to another; examines the forms of bias (including over- and underidentification) taken by different models of severe dis-

$$EGE = \text{no. years in school} \times \frac{IQ}{100} + 1.0 \qquad \text{(Formula 1)}$$

$$EGE = \frac{IQ \times CA}{100} - 5 \qquad \text{(Formula 2)}$$

$$EGE = (MA + CA + \text{grade age})/3 - 5 \qquad \text{(Formula 3)}$$

$$EGE = (2MA + CA)/3 - 5 \qquad \text{(Formula 4)}$$

$$\text{Severe discrepancy} = CA\left(\frac{IQ}{300} + 0.17\right) = 2.5 \qquad \text{(Formula 5)}$$

crepancy; and proposes a specific approach that seems to solve most problems occurring in other models of determining a severe discrepancy. Finally, setting cutoff scores and choosing appropriate tests are addressed along with the issue of who should be diagnosing LD.

OBJECTIVE DETERMINATION OF A SEVERE DISCREPANCY

Clinical judgment has a revered and appropriate place in all diagnostic decision making. Even though it has been amply demonstrated that statistical or actuarial approaches are always as good as—and often better than—clinical judgment (Meehl, 1954; Wiggins, 1981), people should play the central role in making decisions about people. Clinical judgment, however, must be guided by statistical criteria whenever possible. A uniform approach to determining severe discrepancy seems an opportune point of departure for giving empirical guidance in LD diagnosis, particularly because the profession generally accepts the salience of the criterion (Reynolds, 1984) and because of its reason for inclusion in LD definition in the first place. Most states, in fact, require the demonstration of a severe discrepancy for diagnosis of LD. It is important to note, however, that determining a severe discrepancy does not constitute the diagnosis of LD; it only establishes that the primary symptom of LD exists. A severe discrepancy is a necessary but insufficient condition for a diagnosis of LD; the remaining four factors discussed by Chalfant (1984) demand serious consideration. Determining a severe discrepancy requires considerable statistical sophistication, but computers and easily used programs for calculating severe discrepancies are now so widely available (e.g., Reynolds & Stanton, 1988) that previously cumbersome and lengthy computational demands are no longer a problem.

DIFFERENCES IN PREVALENCE RATES ACROSS AND WITHIN STATES

The various models for determining a severe discrepancy in use among SEAs, private agencies, and individual clinicians are countless. They range from application of previously rejected federal formulas to the use of constant grade equivalent discrepancies (e.g., performance 2 years below grade level for age) to regulations requiring an achievement deficit *and* a processing strength (i.e., a processing skill that exceeds general intellectual functioning) to attempts at application of several different regression models of aptitude–achievement differences. Many variations of these "models" are evident in written guidelines, though some agencies provide no guidelines beyond those given in the federal definition. Each of these procedures, whether intentional or not, sets a mathematical limit on the number of children who can be identified as LD. Although other factors such as referral rates will affect the actual number of children identified, the range of incidence of figures easily can vary from less than 2% to more than 35% of a random sample of the population, depending upon which agency's criteria are being applied. These percentages assume a 100% referral rate and the use of a single aptitude or intelligence measure and a single achievement measure. As more tests (or multiple scores from only two tests) are employed, these percentages increase dramatically.

In the context of a 2-hour psychoeducational evaluation, it is not uncommon for various models to allow an astute diagnostician to diagnose (conservatively estimated) between 50% and 80% of a random sample of the population as LD. Much of this problem is due to a psychometric naiveté that permeates much of the rule making for diagnosis at the SEA level, as well as in other federal and state agencies; it is also due in part to certain myths harbored by many clinicians about how test scores behave.

As an example, consider that some states have adopted a model of the "severe discrepancy" criterion whereby children who exhibit a difference of one standard deviation (1 SD) between aptitude and achievement (when both tests' scores are expressed on a common scale) are eligible for a diagnosis of LD by a multidisciplinary team. Since 1 SD below the mean of a normal distribution (assuming that we are only interested in cases where achievement is below aptitude) falls at about the 16th percentile, many believe this to create a pool of eligibility of 16% of the population, Other states use 1.5 SDs as a criterion, hoping to generate a pool of about 6% eligibility in the population (obviously, setting different cutting scores will create disparities in the number of children identified). Such inferences are faulty for several reasons.

The concept of *SD* refers to a *distribution* of scores. If two scores are positively correlated, the distribution of scores created by subtracting the scores of a set of students on both tests from one another will not be the same as the two univariate distributions; the *SD* of this newly created distribution will be significantly smaller than that of the two original distributions. The Wechsler Intelligence Scale for Children—Revised (WISC-R) Verbal and Performance IQs (VIQ and PIQ) are normed on the same sample of children, are scaled to the same mean (100) and SD (15), and are correlated about .60 to .65. A difference of "1 SD" between these two scores (15 points) occurs in 25% of the population, independent of the direction of the difference. In a truly random sample of the population (allowing IQ to range from about 45 to 155), the 1-*SD* criterion, with the direction of the difference specified, would declare only 12.5% of the population eligible. Most criteria, however, have an exclusionary clause and do not allow children with IQs in the lower ranges to be considered (e.g., IQ < 85). This will further reduce the number of children eligible, usually quite unbeknownst to the individual writing such a rule. Such criteria also fail to consider the regression of IQ on achievement or the joint distributions of multiple-difference score distributions when more than one aptitude or achievement score is being considered. Such factors will also wreak havoc with the anticipated results of the measurement models promulgated under various state guidelines.

This discussion could be carried further, but need not be here. The tremendous disparities in measurement models adopted by various agencies within their written LD guidelines; the varying levels of expertise with which the models have been implemented; and the variance of individual clinicians in their daily practice are obvious, major contributing factors to the differences in the relative proportions of children diagnosed as LD from agency to agency and among the states. Lack of specific definition; improper application or lack of application of the "severe discrepancy" criterion; and the failure to develop appropriate mathematical models with references to the criterion are the primary, and certainly interrelated, difficulties in this regard.

FALSE POSITIVES AND FALSE NEGATIVES IN CURRENT PRACTICE

Given current practices, what types of children are being served as LD who may not actually have LD? Who is being missed? The response to these two questions is a direct function of the measurement model being addressed; in other words, the answer is a resounding "It depends." Given the diversity of models of "severe discrepancy," no specific reply may be given, but it is possible to evaluate the types of systematic errors likely to be made under various models that may be applied. A general comparison of some of the various models to be considered may be found in Table 24.1. Ultimately, each of these models is evaluated in detail, particularly as it deals with the IQ–achievement relationship.

Grade Level Discrepancy Models

"Grade level discrepancy models" are models such as "2 years below grade level for age" or even models prescribing performance levels that may change over grades. An example of the latter might be 1 year below grade level for age in first through sixth grades; 1½ years for seventh through ninth grades; and 2 years for 10th through 12th grades. Note that the specific discrepancy required here is not under examination, but rather the general model expressed in such a position. These models frequently may have attached to them additional exclusionary criteria, such as no IQs below 85 or perhaps below 70. These models, which are still prevalent (though not to the extent they were some years ago), overidentify children who fall into the "slow learner" range of intellectual skill (i.e., 70 < IQ < 90) as LD. Although these children certainly have problems with academic

TABLE 24.1. Responsiveness of Certain General Models of Severe Discrepancy to Critical Variables

	Deviation from grade level	Expectancy formulas	Simple-difference, standard-score comparisons	Regression discrepancy analysis
Ease of implementation	Yes	Questionable	Yes, if values are tabled	Yes, if values are tabled
Years in school	No	Some	No	No
Increasing range and variability of scores at upper grades	Yes, if a graduated procedure	Questionable	Yes	Yes
Systematic and consistent treatment of IQ–achievement interrelationship	No	Questionable	No	Yes
Error of measurement	No	No	Yes	Yes
Regression toward mean	No	No	No	Yes
A priori approximation of incidence[a]	No	No	No	No
Comparability of norms[b]	N/A	No	Yes, certain group tests; possible certain individual tests	Yes, certain group tests; possibly certain individual tests

Note. N/A, not applicable. Adapted from "Quantifying a Severe Discrepancy: A Critical Analysis" by T. Cone and L. Wilson, 1981, Learning Disability Quarterly, 4, 359–371. Copyright 1981 by Council on Learning Disabilities. Adapted by permission.
[a]All discrepancy criteria ultimately set an incidence figure, though this figure will be particularly difficult to estimate under some models. Criteria usually are not adopted on this basis, however.
[b]This variable is treated in greater detail in a later section of this chapter.

attainment, and some are certainly LD, most of these children are functioning academically at a level quite consistent with their age and overall level of intellectual ability. As such, no severe discrepancy between expected and obtained achievement levels is present. These children do exhibit mild intellectual handicaps and are problems for teachers in regular classrooms; thus there exists much pressure to place these children in special education programs. Nevertheless, the intent of P.L. 94-142 was not to provide services in special education for these children. Rather, they should be served in the regular education program, with appropriate assistance made available to their classroom teachers.

On the other hand, the use of grade level discrepancy criteria will deny LD services to children with above-average IQs who should be served in special education. Whereas a sixth-grader with an IQ of 85 who is reading 2 years below grade level for age (equivalent to an achievement score of about 80–85 on an IQ scale) is eligible for services under these models (though the student's achievement is

commensurate with his or her IQ level), a sixth-grader with an IQ of 160 who is reading at or just below grade level (say, with a reading score of 90–100 on an IQ scale) is not eligible. Although the multidisciplinary team will certainly want to consider other information prior to making a determination, it seems inconsistent with the concept of LD that the former child should be eligible and the latter not eligible for services. The use of grade level discrepancy models will result in systematic overidentification of children with IQs below 100 as LD, and systematic underidentification of children with IQs of more than 100. Only for children with IQs of precisely 100 is there no bias in diagnosis with these models.

Standard-Score Comparison Models

Standard-score comparison models are generally more appropriate than models employing grade level discrepancy, but can also result in bias in eligibility. Many standard-score models currently in effect do not take into account the regression of IQ on achievement. Such models will systematically include as LD more children with IQs over 100 than should be otherwise justifiable. Conversely, children with IQs below 100 will be excluded in unacceptable numbers. This is exactly the opposite of what happens with grade level discrepancy models; as noted, it occurs because of the well-known regression between IQ and achievement. Common clinical methodology leads one to believe that children with a mean IQ of 130 will have a mean equivalent achievement score of 130. However, given the magnitude of most concurrent validity coefficients (assuming values in the low .70s), the mean achievement level of children with obtained IQ of 130 will be in the range of 121–123. Thus, the "expected" achievement level of a child with an IQ of 130 is not 130 at all, but 121–123. For the low-IQ child, the reverse happens: The expected achievement level of a child with an IQ of 85 will be about 88–89. This produces the over- and underidentification phenomenon as a function of IQ, noted above.

In addition, standard-score models that attempt to define a "severe discrepancy" on the basis of the frequency of occurrence of a discrepancy between an obtained aptitude and an obtained achievement score, on the basis of the *SD* of the two univariate distributions (i.e., the intelligence and the achievement score distributions taken independently), will miss the desired frequency significantly. This problem has been discussed earlier. It will also bias diagnosis systematically as a function of IQ, in addition to identifying far fewer children than its progenitors believe. This problem may be amplified when the reliabilities of the two scales are dissimilar.

Grade Level Exclusionary Models

Some school districts and clinicians exclude children who do not score below grade level, regardless of any discrepancy among IQ, expected achievement level, and obtained achievement level, and regardless of the type of mathematical model applied. Any such exclusionary model will result in the systematic denial of services to children with IQs above 100; the higher the IQ, the more likely the denial of services. Yet these are likely to be just the children who stand to benefit most from services for the LD.

Failure to Consider Multiple Comparisons

Typically, the determination of a "severe discrepancy" under any of the models presented above is based on a comparison between two scores, one a measure of aptitude and the other a measure of achievement. Rarely are only two scores compared, however. More typical is the case where, for example, all three WISC-R IQs are compared to a series of achievement scores, resulting in from 9 to 15 actual comparisons. Unless the multivariate or joint distributions are considered, the number of children found to have a "severe discrepancy" will be substantially greater than anticipated, resulting in significant overidentification in each segment of the population. In the case of multiple comparisons, the likelihood of chance occurrences of severe discrepancies is large.

Summary

The question of who is served as LD who is not actually LD is a complex one; the answer depends upon the particular model of severe discrepancy being employed and its precise method of implementation. Given the most prevalent LD criteria, the prominence of grade level exclusionary criteria, and biases in the referral process favoring low-IQ, low-achieving children, it appears that the largest group of children being served as LD who may not in fact be LD consists of intellectually borderline and low-average children. These children are difficult to instruct in regular education classrooms, but may not be severely impaired educationally. Such children are indeed mildly handicapped; however, they should be served, under current legislation, in the regular education program with support services (e.g., consultation from professional school psychologists) available to their classroom teachers.

DETERMINING A SEVERE DISCREPANCY: STANDARD-SCORE APPROACHES

At best, determining a severe discrepancy is at once crucial, complex, controversial, and hotly debated. In order to avoid biasing diagnosis as a function of IQ, a regression model of some type must be adopted. To avoid measurement error, the simple difference score must be reliable; the difference must be relatively infrequent in the normal population if it is to indicate an abnormal state (being LD decidedly is *not* normal, but is a pathological state).

Formulas such as the five given earlier, and variations of these formulas that in any way involve the use of grade equivalent or age equivalent scores, are rejected as grossly inadequate and misleading. Although the reasons for this are many, age and grade equivalents do not possess the necessary mathematical properties for use in any kind of discrepancy analysis. (These problems are discussed at length in a variety of sources. The interested reader will find most relevant information in Angoff, 1971; Birk, 1984; Reynolds, 1981a; and Thorndike & Hagen, 1977.) In addition to these problems, grade equivalents have other features that make them undesirable, including their ease of misinterpretation, their lack of relation to curriculum markers (though they appear directly related), and their more general imprecision.

Only standard-score models have any real potential for solution to the question of severe discrepancy. The following presentations thus employ only standard or scaled scores, typically of the age-corrected deviation score genre, such as those employed by the current Wechsler scales, the Kaufman Assessment Battery for Children (K-ABC), and related scales. Other means of determining a severe discrepancy will probably result in a biasing of the diagnostic process, producing misclassification of an inordinate number of children.

Reliability of a Discrepancy

As noted above, the difference between a child's scores on the aptitude and achievement measures should be large enough to indicate, with a high degree of confidence (i.e., $p < .05$), that it is not due to chance or to errors of measurement (see also Reynolds, 1981a). This requires an inferential statistical test of the hypothesis that the aptitude and achievement scores for the child in question are the same. Payne and Jones (1957) first introduced such a test to interpret individual

variation in scores within tests of intelligence. More complex calculations involving the reliabilities of the respective scales and the correlation between the two measures have been proffered (e.g., Salvia & Ysseldyke, 1981), but the simpler computational formula shown below is the algebraic equivalent of the more complex formulas (Reynolds & Willson, 1984; Willson & Reynolds, 1984; Zimmerman & Williams, 1982). The test for significance of the difference of two obtained scores $(X_i - Y_i)$ when the scores are expressed as z-scores is as follows:

$$z = \frac{X_i - Y_i}{\sqrt{2 - r_{xx} - r_{yy}}} \qquad \text{(Formula 6)}$$

In Formula 6, X_i and Y_i represent the individual child's score on an aptitude measure X and an achievement measure Y, and r_{xx} and r_{yy} represent the respective internal-consistency reliability estimates for the two scales. These reliability estimates should be based on the responses of the standardization sample of each test and should be age-appropriate for the child being evaluated; they are most often reported in test manuals. Several factors can spuriously inflate reliability estimates. For example, reliability estimates based on item scores across an age range of more than 1 year will be spuriously inflated (see Stanley, 1971). The test statistic is a z-score that is referred to as the normal curve. For a one-tailed test with $p = .05$, the critical value of $z = 1.65$. If $z > 1.65$, one can be sufficiently confident that the difference is not due to errors inherent in the two tests. Although a one-tailed test at the .05 level is probably justifiable for evaluating children referred for the possibility of LD, a two-tailed test or a higher level of confidence (e.g., $p = .01$) would provide a more conservative measure of observed differences. For a two-tailed test, the critical value of z at $p = .05$ is 1.96. All other critical values can be determined from any table of values of the normal curve.

After reliability has been established, the frequency of occurrence of a difference score must be evaluated.

Frequency of a Discrepancy

In evaluating the frequency of a discrepancy score, one must first decide what type of discrepancy score to assess (e.g., a residualized difference between predicted and obtained achievement scores, differences between estimated true scores and residualized true scores, true difference scores, etc.). In part, this decision depends upon how one interprets the P.L. 94-142 definition of LD.

To establish that a discrepancy is severe, one must decide which of the following two questions to address:

1. Is there a severe discrepancy between this child's score on the achievement measure and the average achievement score of all other children with the same IQ as this child?
2. Is there a severe discrepancy between this child's measured achievement level and this child's measured level of intellectual functioning?

Both of these questions involve intraindividual variations in test performance (as opposed to purely interindividual norm-referenced comparisons). Although this is obvious in the case of the second question, it may not be so evident for the first, which involves an intraindividual comparison because the determination of the "average achievement score of all other children with the same IQ" is based upon the IQ obtained by the individual child in question. Though both of these are clearly intraindividual-difference models, the mathematical models for answering these two questions differ considerably.

The former appears to be the more pressing question for evaluating children with learning problems and is the more consistent with the intent of P.L. 94-142, because the aptitude or ability one wants to define is the aptitude or ability to achieve in academic areas (Reynolds, 1984, 1985b). Evaluating the second question is easier in terms of calculation; one can follow Kaufman's (1979) or our (Reynolds & Gutkin, 1981) recommended methodology for assessing VIQ–PIQ differences on the Wechsler scales. Several approaches to the first question have been proffered.

The Simple-Difference-Score Model

The simple-difference-score distribution approach defines as the appropriate discrepancy score the simple differences between the obtained aptitude score and the obtained achievement score when both measures are expressed on a common scale $(X_i - Y_i)$, where X_i is the individual child's score on an aptitude measure and Y_i is the same child's score on an achievement measure. This model was one of the first attempts to use standard scores to assess the frequency of a discrepancy, and is appealing in its ease of use and its superficial elegance. It has an intuitive appeal, much as does the use of grade equivalents. In this model, the frequency of occurrence of a discrepancy $(X_i - Y_i)$ of a given magnitude is calculated, and the precise percentage of children showing such a discrepancy is readily apparent. In the absence of detailed information on the joint distribution of the two measures, the frequency of occurrence of any given discrepancy can be determined by the following formula, which also estimates a "severe discrepancy":

$$\text{severe discrepancy} = SD \; z_a \sqrt{2 - 2 \; r_{xy}} \quad (7)$$

In Formula 7, SD represents the standard deviation of the two scales (scaled to a common metric), and z_a is the z-score corresponding to the point on the normal curve that designates the frequency of occurrence of a "severe discrepancy." The r_{xy} term is simply the correlation between the two measures. The formula estimates, assuming that the distribution of difference scores is perfectly normal, the percentage of the population showing a simple difference of the specific magnitude of interest (independent of the direction of the difference), since the SD of the difference-score distribution will be equal to $SD \sqrt{2 - 2r_{xy}}$. A guideline for determining a value of z_a to indicate that a discrepancy is severe is described in a later section.

The use of this model is common in certain aspects of clinical assessment and diagnosis, most prominently in the evaluation of the meaning of VIQs and PIQs on the Wechsler scales (Kaufman, 1979; Reynolds & Gutkin, 1981). In this context, the simple-difference-score distribution is of considerable value, and discussions of its application can be found in the references above. In the evaluation of aptitude versus achievement or expected versus obtained levels of academic function, however, the simple-difference-score model is inadequate, primarily because it fails to account for regression effects in the relation between IQ and achievement. And, in diagnosing and evaluating LD, we are always interested in the regression of IQ on achievement. The results of failure to account for regression effects have been discussed previously and need not be reiterated here. However, the simple-difference-score model fails on this criterion. It will systematically overestimate the frequency of LD among those with above-average ability and systematically underestimate the frequency of LDs among those with below-average ability (when both are expressed in z-score form). This is not theory; it is an unavoidable factual consequence of the positive correlation between aptitude and achievement. Thus with the simple-difference-score model, the number of children identified as LD will be much greater among those of above-average ability. There is no theoretical or logical reason to believe that this reflects the state of nature. Though recommended by Hanna, Dyck, and Holen (1979), this model, despite its simplicity and ease of application, must be rejected on mathematical as well as theoretical grounds. Its use in the assessment of aptitude–achievement differences seems unsound.

Several similar models have been proposed, including one by McLeod (1979) that attempts to account for regression and for measurement error in the process of diagnosis. Elsewhere (Reynolds, 1984), I have critiqued these various models; all fall far short of their promise, typically on technical grounds, but some on conceptual grounds as well.

Regression Modeling of Severe Discrepancy

To assess the first question above, a regression model (i.e., a mathematical model that accounts for the imperfect relationship between IQ and achievement) is required. Once regression effects have been assessed, the frequency of occurrence of the difference between the academic performance of the child in question and all other children having the same IQ can be determined. The correct model specifies that a severe discrepancy between aptitude (X) and achievement

(Y) exists when, assuming the two tests are scaled to a common metric,

$$\hat{Y} - Y_i > SD_y \, z_a \sqrt{1 - r_{xy}^2} \qquad \text{(Formula 8)}$$

where

Y_i is the child's achievement score
X_i is the child's aptitude score
$\hat{Y}$ is the mean achievement score for all children with IQ = X_i
SD_y is the standard deviation of Y
z_a is the point on the normal curve corresponding to the relative frequency needed to denote "severity"
r_{xy}^2 is the square of the correlation between the aptitude and achievement measures

It is necessary to use $\hat{Y} - Y_i$ as the discrepancy score, because IQ and achievement are not perfectly correlated. For example, if the IQ and achievement tests have the same mean and standard deviation (mean = 100, SD = 15) and if they correlate at .60, then the average achievement score for all children with IQs of 80 is 88 and for all children with IQs of 120 is 112. Therein lies the need to compare the achievement level of all other children with the same IQ. The term $\hat{Y}$ is calculated through use of a standard regression equation. When all scores are expressed in z-score form (mean = 0, SD = 1), the simplest form to use for all mathematical calculations, Y is easily determined to be

$$Y_z = r_{xy} \, X_z \qquad \text{(Formula 9)}$$

where

Y_z is the mean score on Y, in z-score form, of all children with IQ = X
r_{xy} is the correlation between X and Y
X_z is the child's score on X (the IQ or aptitude measure) in z-score form

Since few test manuals provide z-scores and most do not like to make the conversion for this purpose, a formula for use on a calculator is given below:

$$\hat{Y} = \left[r_{xy} \left(\frac{X - \bar{X}}{SD_x} \right) \right] SD_x + \bar{X} \qquad \text{(Formula 10)}$$

These terms should all be familiar; the previously undefined values are $\bar{X}$ (the mean of X; e.g., on the WISC-R, 100) and SD_x (the standard deviation of X; e.g., on the WISC-R, 15). The only piece of information required to calculate Formula 8 that is not given in all test manuals, besides the child's own score on the tests, is the correlation between the aptitude and the achievement measure. This must usually be obtained from a literature review or estimated, although for some tests (most notably the K-ABC), many aptitude–achievement correlations are given in test manuals (e.g., see Kamphaus & Reynolds, 1987).

The correlation r_{xy} can also be estimated. Using data from national standardizations of several major intelligence and achievement tests, we (Reynolds & Stanton, 1988) have developed Formula 11 to estimate r_{xy} when it is unknown, although the equation's accuracy is far from the degree desired.

$$r_{xy} = \sqrt{0.5}\ \sqrt{r_{xx}\ r_{yy}} \qquad \text{(Formula 11)}$$

The values r_{xx} and r_{yy} are the internal-consistency reliability coefficients for the aptitude and the achievement measures in question.

Now that $\hat{Y}$ can always be calculated exactly or estimated reasonably when r_{xy} is unknown, we can return to Formula 8. In this equation, the term $SD_y \sqrt{1 - r_{xy}}$ is the standard deviation for the distribution $\hat{Y} - Y_i$. Since this distribution is normal, we can estimate the frequency of occurrence of any given difference $(\hat{Y} - Y_i)$ with great accuracy. Thus z_a is the number of standard deviations between the two scores $(\hat{Y} - Y_i)$ that corresponds to the point of "severity" on the normal curve. Next, we must establish a value of z_a, a controversial matter in itself.

Establishing a Value for z_a in Discrepancy Models

There are no strictly empirical criteria or research methods for establishing a value for z_a for any of the above models. This is true because there is no consensus regarding the definition of LD generally, and specifically none that would allow the generation of a *true and globally accepted* estimate of the prevalence of the group of disorders subsumed under the term "LD." To complicate

this issue further, there is no professional consensus in the LD community regarding whether it is better to risk identifying some children as LD who are not in fact LD, in hopes that nearly all true LD children will receive services, or to risk identifying as non-LD a significant number of children who are in fact LD, in order to identify as few non-LD children as LD as possible. However, under the latter scenario, as well as with the assumption of an equal-risk model (associated equal risks with both types of diagnostic errors, false positives and false negatives), the proper procedure would be not to identify *any* children as LD, since the proportion of the population who exhibit this disorder is so small (e.g., see Schmidt's [1974] discussion of probability and utility assumptions). Such a consensus, coupled with valid estimates of prevalence, would provide considerable guidance in establishing a recommended value of z_a. In the absence of such guidance, one may relay only upon rational, statistical, and traditional criteria for guidance.

It has been argued previously that for a discrepancy to be considered severe, it should occur relatively infrequently in the normal population of individuals under consideration (see also Kamphaus & Reynolds, 1987; Reynolds, 1984). Of course, "relatively infrequently" is open to the same problems of interpretation as is "severe discrepancy." Strong tradition and rational arguments exist in psychology, particularly in the field of mental retardation, that "severity" should be defined as 2 SDs from the mean of the distribution under consideration. With regard to a diagnosis of mental retardation, we define a score 2 SDs below the mean of an intelligence scale as a severe intellectual problem, making an individual eligible (provided that other criteria are met) for a diagnosis of mental retardation. Qualitative descriptions such as "mentally or cognitively deficient" or "lower extreme" are common designations below this point in the distribution. At the opposite end of the curve, most definitions of intellectual giftedness refer to IQs falling 2 SDs or more above the mean, with descriptions such as "very superior" and "upper extreme" being common. These practices are widely accepted.

In the field of inferential statistics, confidence levels of .05 in an inference or judgment that a hypothesis is to be rejected are the accepted standard in the field. The .05 figure corresponds, roughly, to two standard errors (2 SEs; for a two-tailed test) of the difference being evaluated or to 2 SDs from the mean of the distribution of the test statistic employed (e.g., z, t, F, etc.). There is thus considerable precedent in the social as well as physical sciences for implementation of 2 SDs as the criterion for characterizing a discrepancy as "severe." (For a .05 level of confidence, the actual value of z is 1.96 rather than 2.00, but is certainly close enough to the 2.00 value to support its use.) Thus a value of $z_a = 2.00$ is recommended for determining whether a difference score is severe. This value needs further qualification, however.

Since a difference score, whether defined as $\hat{Y} - Y_i$ or some other value, will be less than perfectly reliable, we must somehow consider this unreliability in defining a severe discrepancy. If we consider it a greater risk to fail to identify as LD a child who is LD than to identify by mistake a child as LD who may not be LD, then we can propose a reasonable solution. Note that without this assumption, we would minimize total errors by not identifying *any* children as LD. Although several methods of accounting for potential unreliability in a discrepancy score are possible, the concept of the confidence interval is both popular and applicable. Adopting the traditional .05 confidence level for a one-tailed test, we can define the value of z_a corrected for unreliability as 2 and reduce the final cutoff score by $1.65\ SE_{\hat{Y} - Y_i}$, thus giving protection corresponding to the one-tailed .05 confidence level times the standard error of the relevant difference score. (A one-tailed value is clearly appropriate here, since we must decide in advance which side to protect; both sides cannot be protected.)

The final model, then, specifies that a severe discrepancy exists between a child's current level of achievement (Y_i) and the mean level of achievement of all other children with the same IQ ($\hat{Y}$; see Formula 10) equals or exceeds the value given in Formula 12 below.

$$\hat{Y} - Y_i \geqslant 2\ SD_y\ \sqrt{1 - r_{xy}^2} - 1.65 SE_{\hat{Y} - Y_i} \quad (12)$$

The calculation of the standard error of $\hat{Y} - Y_i$ ($SE_{\hat{Y} - Y_i}$) is explained in detail elsewhere

(Reynolds, 1984) and need not be repeated. Its use is clearly optional, although it does seem advisable to account for error in the process. It is important to note here that this is not the type of measurement error assessed by Formula 6.

The number of children eligible for a diagnosis of LD under these two formulas will vary as a function of the standard error of the difference scores. If $r_{xy} = .60$ and $r_{xx} = r_{yy} = .90$ (a quite realistic set of assumptions), the new cutoff for $z = 1.393$ instead of 2.00. This new value corresponds to 8.2% of the total population for consideration as LD. A one-tailed confidence interval is appropriate here, because we are only interested in preventing false negatives in diagnosis of LD children, so only one side needs protection. As noted previously, to guard against over-identification (false positives), the best procedure would be not to identify any children as LD, since the prevalence is so low. Once can make an argument for serving only the most severely handicapped LD children as a compromise in reducing false positives, but still providing services to some children and consequently increasing the number of false negatives (see Figure 24.1). Under these circumstances, the expressions in Formula 12 would be changed to "$+ 1.65\ SE_{\hat{Y} - Y_i}$." This protects the opposite side of the region of severity. The region of "severe discrepancy" under each consideration is depicted in Figure 24.2. One should be cautioned that such a restrictive application of a criterion of severity would result in significantly less than 1% of the population of school-age children being eligible for an LD diagnosis.

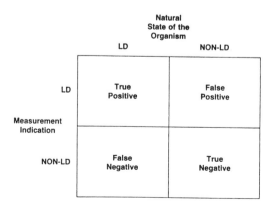

FIGURE 24.1. Possible outcomes when considering a diagnosis of LD.

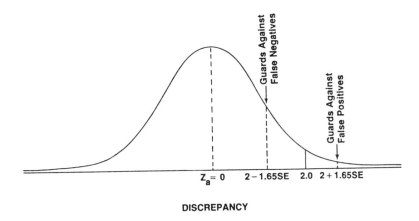

FIGURE 24.2. Illustration of confidence intervals designed to guard against the false-positive or false-negative diagnoses depicted in Figure 24.1.

This calculation (Formula 12) allows us to identify more children than are likely to be truly LD children; on the other hand, it accounts for many possible inaccuracies in the process that might inhibit identification of a truly LD child, with the exception of the problem of multiple comparisons (i.e., when one compares multiple IQs with many achievement scores; see Reynolds, 1984, for discussion). The other four components of the most prevalent LD definitions, as previously presented, may then be evaluated to make the final judgment regarding whether or not a child is entitled to and in need of services for the LD.

The procedures outlined above can certainly objectify determination of severe discrepancy in LD diagnosis. However, it bears repeating here that not all children who have a severe discrepancy between aptitude and achievement are in fact LD. Even a quick reading of the statutory definition shows that many other factors may cause such a discrepancy, and the reasoned use of clinical judgment is clearly appropriate. However, clinical judgment is wrong at least as often and typically more often than empirical, actuarial judgments. We may think that with regard to LD diagnosis we "know one when we see one," but if there is no "severe discrepancy," chances are we are wrong.

The procedure outlined above provided guidance for the objective determination of a severe discrepancy. It is crucial to bear in mind, however, that mathematical manipulations cannot transform the quality of the initial data. The next section reviews the requi-

site characteristics of the test and assessment data to be included in evaluating a severe discrepancy.

QUALITY OF INPUT DATA

The quality of the input or test data used is crucial in assessing a discrepancy. Tests with poor psychometric characteristics (especially with low internal-consistency reliability estimates) can be misleading or can fail to detect a severe discrepancy (see also Reynolds, 1986). This section provides standards for tests to be used in the assessment of a potentially severe discrepancy. Though one will not always be able to choose tests that meet all of these standards, the more that can be met, the better. Of course, the characteristics of the examiner(s)—that is, the person(s) gathering the data—are of equal or possibly even greater importance. More is said on this topic in the next section.

1. *A test should meet all requirements stated for assessment devices in the rules and regulations for implementing P.L. 94-142.* This not only is a requirement of law, but is consistent with good professional practice. For example, administering a test in accordance with the instructions provided by the test maker is prerequisite to interpretation of a test's scores. If a standardized test is not given precisely according to the instructions provided, inestimable amounts of error are introduced, and norm-referenced scores are no longer interpretable. Thus, all personnel

evaluating children with educational problems must be conversant with the requirements of P.L. 94-142 and adhere closely to these standards.

2. *Normative data should meet contemporary standards of practice and should be provided for a sufficiently large, nationally stratified random sample of children.* In practice, this standard is nearly impossible to meet in all respects. Yet it is important to approximate it as closely as possible, because standardization samples are crucial to establishing levels of performance for comparison purposes. To know that an individual answered 60 out of 100 questions correctly on an achievement test and 75 out of 100 questions correctly on an intelligence test conveys very little information. On which test did this individual earn the better score? Without knowledge of how a specified reference group has performed on these tests, one cannot answer this question.

Raw scores on a test, such as the number or percentage of correct responses, take on meaning only when they are evaluated against the performance of a normative or reference group. For convenience, raw scores are typically converted to standard or scaled scores of some type. The reference group from which the norms are derived is defined prior to the standardization of the test. Once the appropriate reference population has been defined, a random sample of this group is tested under procedures as nearly identical as possible, with the same administration, scoring, timing rules, and the like for all. This group is known as the "standardization sample."

Ebel (1972) and Angoff (1971) have discussed a number of conditions necessary for the appropriate development and use of normative reference group data. The following are taken, with some elaboration, principally from these two sources. Some of these conditions place requirements on the test being normed, some on the psychological trait being measured, and others on the test user. All affect test score interpretation.

a. *The psychological trait being assessed must be amenable to at least ordinal scaling.* If a nominal scale were employed, only the presence or absence of the trait would be of interest, and relative amounts of the trait could not be determined; under this unusual condition, norms would be superfluous if not distracting or misleading. Intelligence and achievement tests typically meet this criterion.

b. *The test must provide an adequate operational definition of the trait under consideration.* With a proper operational definition, other tests can be constructed to measure the same trait and should yield comparable scores for individuals taking both tests.

c. *The test should assess the same psychological construct throughout the entire range of performance.* Some achievement tests obviously fail this criterion. Various versions of the Wide Range Achievement Test, for example, measure only what can generously be construed as prereading and prespelling skills at lower ranges of performance on these subtests. Continuous norms and scaling across different variables is confusing at best.

d. *The normative reference group should consist of a large random sample that is representative of the population to whom the test will be administered or performance compared.* Of course, truly random samples for test standardization are not even remotely possible, since individuals must agree to participate. As soon as one parent refuses to allow a child to be tested, the sample is no longer random. To help with this problem, most test publishing companies stratify their samples according to demographic characteristics of the population, and then compare the outcome to actual population characteristics to see how closely the elusive perfect sample has been approximated. Despite some quite unrealistic opinions to the contrary (e.g., Hopkins & Hodge, 1984), this is an excellent strategy for developing standardization samples, as is exemplified in such standardization projects as those for the WISC-R and the K-ABC.

e. *The sample of examinees from the population should* "have been tested under standard conditions, and . . . take the tests as seriously, but no more so, than other students to be tested later for whom the norms are needed" (Ebel, 1972, p. 488).

f. *The population sampled must be relevant to the test and to the purpose for which the test is to be employed.* Because the point about purpose is so often misinterpreted (especially with regard to the evaluation of exceptional children—the children we most often assess), many adequately normed psychological tests are maligned for failure to include enough handicapped children in their normative samples. The major intelligence scales designed for use with children (i.e., the various Wechsler scales, the K-ABC, and the McCarthy Scales of Children's Abilities) have been normed on stratified random samples of children representative of children in the United States at large. With these as the reference groups, scores from these scales may be correctly interpreted as providing an indication of a child's current intellectual standing with regard to other children in the United States. Some authors (e.g., Salvia & Ysseldyke, 1981) criticize tests such as the McCarthy Scales as inappropriate for measuring the intellectual levels of various categories of exceptional children, because large numbers of these children were not included in the test's standardization sample. Whether this is a valid criticism depends upon the purpose to which the test is applied. If knowledge of an LD child's level of intellectual functioning relative to age-mates in the United States is desired, comparing the child's performance on an IQ test to that of other LD children is inappropriate. However, if we are interested in learning how the child compares intellectually to other LD children, then a reference group of LD children is appropriate (although the latter information is not frequently sought, and it has not been shown to be more useful in developing appropriate intervention strategies).

Salvia and Ysseldyke (1981) contend that it is inappropriate to base predictions of future intellectual or academic performance on test scores for an exceptional child that have been derived through comparison with the performance of the larger, normal population. To make predictions, they would require that the reference group have similar sociocultural background, experience, and handicapping conditions. Although this may be an appropriate—indeed, a noble—hypothesis for research study, implementation must await empirical verification, especially since the idea runs counter to traditional practice and considerable evidence. All interpretations of test scores should be guided principally by empirical evidence. Once norms have been established for a specific reference group, the generalizability of the norms becomes a matter of actuarial research. Just as norms based on one group may be inappropriate, *a priori* acceptance of either hypothesis would be incorrect

(Reynolds & Brown, 1984). Current evidence demonstrates rather clearly that test scores predict most accurately (and equally well for a variety of subgroups) when based on a large, representative random sample of the population (e.g., Hunter, Schmidt, & Rauschenberger, 1984; Jensen, 1980; Reynolds, 1982). Exceptions will be found, however. The System of Multicultural Pluralistic Assessment (SOMPA; Mercer & Lewis, 1979), for example, was normed on a large sample of children from California. However, despite the size and representative nature of this sample of children in California, these norms have not withstood empirical evaluation for children in other states, such as Arizona, Texas, and Florida.

g. *Normative data should be provided for as many different groups as may be useful for comparisons of an individual*. Although this may at first glance seem contradictory to the foregoing conclusions, there are instances when it is useful to know how a child compares to members of other specific subgroups; whenever possible, such data should be made available. The more good reference groups available for evaluating a child's performance on a test, the more useful the test may become.

Once the reference group has been obtained and tested, tables of standardization or scaled scores are developed. These tables are based on the responses of the standardization sample and are called "norms tables."

3. *Standardization samples for tests whose scores are being compared must be the same or highly comparable*. Under the best of all conditions, the aptitude, achievement, or other tests on which children are being compared to themselves or to others should be conormed; that is, their standardization samples should consist of precisely the same children. When this is not possible, the norms for each test should be based on comparable samplings of the same population that meet all of the requirements stated under point 2 above. Standardization of the scales should have been undertaken in the same general time period, or else equating studies should be done. Scales normed on different samples and at different times are not likely to have the same means and *SD*s across samples, even though they may be scaled to a common metric within their re-

spective samples. This gives the two tests the appearance of actually having the same mean and the same *SD*, even though this may not at all be true. Ample evidence demonstrates that general levels of performance on aptitude and achievement measures vary in the population across time. As just one example, the population mean level of performance on the 1949 WISC is now very close to 110, and the 1974 revision (the WISC-R) now has a mean of nearly 104, though both are scaled within their respective normative samples to a mean of 100. Use of an achievement test normed in 1984 and an intelligence test normed in 1970 would add approximately 3 points to the size of the intelligence–achievement score difference for children with achievement levels below their IQ, purely as an artifact of the times when the two tests were standardized. In the face of the paucity of conormed scales, using highly similar samples tested at a similar time (or with equating studies completed) is acceptable, but conorming will always be superior, provided that the sample meets the conditions of point 2.

4. *For diagnostic purposes, individually administered tests should be used.* For purely screening purposes (e.g., referral for comprehensive evaluation), group-administered tests may be appropriate, though for young children individual screening is preferable (Reynolds & Clark, 1983). For all children, but especially for handicapped children, too many uncontrolled and unnoticed factors can affect test performance in an adverse manner. The test administrator is more likely to detect these factors under the conditions of individual assessment, where close observation of the child is possible. Furthermore, individual assessment is more conducive to the use of special adaptations and testing procedures that may be required. Finally, individual assessment allows for careful clinical observation of the child during performance of a variety of academic and intellectual tasks, which is central to the proper assessment of learning problems for children of all ages (Kaufman, 1979; Reynolds & Clark, 1983). Generally, individual assessment affords a better opportunity to maximize the child's performance and provides higher-quality data from which to devise interventions.

5. *In the measurement of aptitude, an individually administered test of general intellectual ability should be used.* Such a test should sample a variety of intellectual skills; basically, it should be a good measure of what psychologists refer to as "*g*," the general intellectual ability that permeates performance on all cognitive tasks. If ability tests are too specific, a single strength or weakness in the child's ability spectrum may inordinately influence the overall estimation of aptitude. It is also important to assess multiple abilities in deriving a remedial or instructional plan for a handicapped student and in preventing ethnic bias (Reynolds, 1982). Highly specific ability measures (e.g., the Bender–Gestalt, the Columbia Mental Maturity Scale, the Peabody Picture Vocabulary Test—Revised) are necessary complements to a good assessment, but are inadequate for estimating the general ability level of handicapped children. In the assessment of learning disabilities, it is important that the chosen measure of aptitude not be influenced adversely by the child's area of specific disability. For example, a measure of intelligence that relies heavily upon expressive vocabulary and assessment of general funds of information for a reading-disabled child may be inappropriate. Since acquisition of general information and vocabulary development occur largely as a function of reading, such an intelligence measure is likely to underestimate the ability level of such a child.

6. *Age-based standard scores should be used for all measures, and all should be scaled to a common metric.* The formulas presented earlier for deriving severe discrepancies require the use of at least interval data. Scoring systems such as age or grade equivalents, which are essentially ordinal scales, should be avoided whenever score comparisons are to be made. Such scores may be helpful for purely descriptive purposes, but they are unacceptable for comparing scores of individuals or groups except under special, infrequent circumstances. Scores that are ratios of age and/or grade equivalents, such as IQs derived from the traditional formula of $(MA/CA) \times 100$, are also inappropriate. Grade-based standard scores are inappropriate as well. In setting forth the "severe discrepancy" criterion, P.L. 94-142 specifically notes that a child's achievement should not be commensurate with his or her age *and* ability; thus, age is properly considered in age-based standard scores. The scores should be corrected at appropriate intervals. Age groupings for the

derivation of standard scores may cover from 2 to 6 months, but in no case should groups extend more than 6 months for children below age 6 years or more than 12 months for children above 6 years.

Age and grade equivalents remain immensely popular, despite their serious psychometric deficiencies and misleading nature. In most instances relevant to diagnosis, grade equivalents are abused because they are assumed to have scaled-score properties when they in fact represent only an ordinal scale of measurement. Grade equivalents ignore the dispersion of scores about the mean when the dispersion is constantly changing from grade to grade. Under no circumstances do grade equivalents qualify as standard scores. The calculation of a grade equivalent is quite simple. When a test is administered to a group of children, the mean raw score is calculated at each grade level, and this mean raw score then is called the "grade equivalent" for a raw score of that magnitude. If the mean raw score for beginning fourth grade (grade 4.0) on a reading test is 37, then any person earning a score of 37 on the test is assigned a grade equivalent of 4.0. If the mean raw score for beginning fifth grade (5.0) is 38, then a score of 38 would receive a grade equivalent of 5.0. However, a raw score of 37 could represent a grade equivalent of 3.8; 38 could be 4.0; and 39 could be 5.0. Thus, differences of 1 raw-score point can cause dramatic differences in the grade equivalents received, and the differences will be inconsistent in magnitude across grades.

Table 24.2 illustrates the problems associated with the use of grade equivalents in evaluating a child's academic standing relative to his or her peers. Frequently in research, as well as in clinical practice, children of normal intellectual capacity are diagnosed as LD through the use of grade equivalents when they perform "2 years below grade level for age" (or some variant of this, such as $1\frac{1}{2}$ years below) on a test of academic attainment. The use of this criterion for the diagnosis of LD or other academic disorders is clearly inappropriate (Reynolds, 1981a). As shown in Table 24.2, a child with a grade equivalent reading score 2 years below the appropriate grade placement for his or her age may or may not have a reading problem. At some ages, this score would be well within the average range; at others, it may indicate a severe reading problem. If math, spelling, or science were to be added to this table, the percentile ranks in each column would be quite different, adding to the difficulties of interpretation.

Grade equivalents are also used as stan-

TABLE 24.2. Standard Scores and Percentile Ranks Corresponding to Performance "Two Years below Grade Level for Age" on Four Major Reading Tests

Grade placement	Two years below placement	Wide Range Achievement Test		Peabody Individual Achievement Test[a]		Woodcock Reading Mastery Test[b]		Stanford Diagnostic Reading Test[b]	
		SS[c]	%R[d]	SS	%R	SS	%R	SS	%R
1.5	Pk.5	65	1	—		—		—	
2.5	K.5	72	3	—		—		—	
3.5	1.5	69	2	—		64	1	64	1
4.5	2.5	73	4	75	5	77	6	64	1
5.5	3.5	84	14	85	16	85	16	77	6
6.5	4.5	88	21	88	21	91	27	91	27
7.5	5.5	86	18	89	23	94	34	92	30
8.5	6.5	87	19	91	27	94	34	93	32
9.5	7.5	90	25	93	32	96	39	95	37
10.5	8.5	85	16	93	32	95	37	95	37
11.5	9.5	85	16	93	32	95	37	92	30
12.5	10.5	85	16	95	37	95	37	92	30

[a]Reading Comprehension subtest only.

[b]Total test.

[c]All standard scores in this table have been converted for ease of comparison to a common scale having a mean of 100 and a standard deviation of 15.

[d]Percentile rank.

dards of performance, which they clearly are not. Contrary to popular belief, grade equivalent scores do not indicate what level of reading text a child should be using. Grade equivalent scores on tests simply do not have a one-to-one correspondence with reading series placement or the various formulas for determining readability levels.

Grade equivalents are also inappropriate for use in any sort of discrepancy analysis of an individual's test performance or for use in many statistical procedures (Reynolds, 1981a). First, the growth curve between age and achievement in basic academic subjects flattens out at upper grade levels. In Table 24.2, for instance, there is very little change in standard-score values corresponding to 2 years below grade level for age after about seventh or eighth grade. In fact, grade equivalents have almost no meaning in reading at this level, since reading instruction typically stops by high school. Thus, grade equivalents really only represent extrapolations from earlier grades. Since the average reading level in the population changes very little after junior high school, grade equivalents at these ages become virtually nonsensical, with large fluctuations resulting from a raw-score difference of 2 or 3 points on a 100-item test. In math and other areas where instruction specifically continues, this is not the case, but it only adds to our overall problem.

Second, grade equivalents assume that the rate of learning is constant throughout the school year and that there is no gain or loss during summer vacation. Third, grade equivalents involve an excess of extrapolation. Since tests are not administered during every month of the school year, scores between the testing intervals (often a full year) must be extrapolated on the assumption of constant growth rates. Interpretation of frequently extrapolated values based on an assumption of constant growth rates is fundamentally just silly. Fourth, different academic subjects are acquired at different rates, and performance varies across content areas. Thus "2 years below grade level for age" may indicate much more serious deficiency in math, for example, than in reading comprehension.

Finally, grade equivalents exaggerate small differences in performance between individuals and for a single individual across tests. Some test authors even caution users on test record forms that standard scores only, and not grade equivalents, should be used for comparison purposes. The Wide Range Achievement Test (WRAT; Jastak & Jastak, 1978) includes a caution at the bottom of the child's test record form stating that standard scores only and not grade equivalents should be used for interpretive purposes. Despite this caution, many school psychologists and educational diagnosticians persist in reporting grade equivalents for the WRAT as well as for other achievement tests. The popularity of these scores is based primarily on misconceptions regarding their psychometric properties.

The principal advantage of using standardized or scaled scores with children lies in the comparability of score interpretation across age. By "standard scores," of course, are meant scores that are scaled to a constant mean and SD, such as the Wechsler deviation IQ, rather than the ratio IQ scores employed by the early Binet and the Slosson Intelligence Test, which give the false appearance of being scaled scores. Ratio IQs or other types of quotients have many of the same problems as grade equivalents and should be avoided for many of these same reasons. The SD of the Slosson Intelligence Test varies from approximately 11 to as much as 32, depending upon the age group under consideration; this causes major problems in interpretation and explanation of performance to teachers and parents. Standard scores of the deviation IQ type have the same percentile rank across age, since they are based not only on the mean but on the variability in scores about the mean at each age level. Grade and age equivalents do not consider the dispersion of scores about the mean.

Standard scores are more accurate and precise. Extrapolation of scores to arrive at an exact score point is typically not necessary, whereas the opposite is true of grade equivalents. Extrapolation is also typically not necessary for scores within 3 SDs of the mean, which accounts for more than 99% of all scores encountered.

Scaled scores can be set to any desired mean and SD (the fancy of the test author is not infrequently the principal determinant). Fortunately, a few scales can account for the vast majority of standardized tests. Table 24.3 depicts the relationship among various scaled-score systems. If the standardization

TABLE 24.3. Conversion of Standard Scores Based on Several Scales to a Commonly Expressed Metric

				Scales					
$\bar{X} = 0$ $SD = 1$	$\bar{X} = 0$ $SD = 3$	$\bar{X} = 36$ $SD = 6$	$\bar{X} = 50$ $SD = 10$	$\bar{X} = 50$ $SD = 15$	$\bar{X} = 100$ $SD = 15$	$\bar{X} = 100$ $SD = 16$	$\bar{X} = 100$ $SD = 20$	$\bar{X} = 500$ $SD = 100$	Percentile rank
2.6	.8	52	76	89	139	142	152	760	99
2.4	17	51	74	86	136	138	148	740	99
2.2	17	49	72	83	133	135	144	720	99
2.0	16	48	70	80	130	132	140	700	98
1.8	15	47	68	77	127	129	136	680	96
1.6	15	46	66	74	124	126	132	660	95
1.4	14	44	64	71	121	122	128	640	92
1.2	14	43	62	68	118	119	124	620	88
1.0	13	42	60	65	115	116	120	600	84
0.8	12	41	58	62	112	113	116	580	79
0.6	12	40	56	59	109	110	112	560	73
0.4	11	38	54	56	106	106	108	540	66
0.2	11	37	52	53	103	103	104	520	56
0.0	10	36	50	50	100	100	100	500	50
−0.2	9	35	48	47	97	97	96	480	42
−0.4	9	34	46	44	94	94	92	460	34
−0.6	8	33	44	41	91	90	88	440	27
−0.8	8	31	42	38	88	87	84	420	21
−1.0	7	30	40	35	85	84	80	400	16
−1.2	6	29	38	32	82	81	76	380	12
−1.4	6	28	36	29	79	78	72	360	8
−1.6	5	26	34	26	76	74	68	340	5
−1.8	5	25	32	23	73	71	64	320	4
−2.0	4	24	30	20	70	68	60	300	2
−2.2	3	23	28	17	67	65	56	280	1
−2.4	3	21	26	14	64	62	52	260	1
−2.6	2	20	24	11	61	58	48	240	1

samples of the two tests are the same or are highly comparable, and the reliability coefficients for the two scales are reasonably similar, then Table 24.3 can also be used to equate scales to a common metric for ease of comparison. To use Table 24.3 for this purpose, one should enter the column corresponding to the mean and *SD* for the test in question and locate the child's score; read to the far left column (headed $\bar{X} = 0$, $SD = 1$); and repeat this procedure for other tests one wishes to place on the same scale.

7. *The measures employed should demonstrate a high level of reliability, which should be documented in the technical manual accompanying the test.* The specific scores employed in the various discrepancy formulas should have associated internal-consistency reliability estimates (where possible) of no less than .80 and preferably of .90 or higher. Coefficient alpha is the recommended procedure for estimating reliability, and should be reported routinely for each age

level in the standardization sample of the test at not more than 1-year intervals. It is recognized that alpha will not be appropriate for all measures. Test authors and publishers should routinely use alpha where appropriate and should provide other reliability estimates as may be appropriate to the nature of the test. When alpha is not reported, an explanation should be given. Authors and publishers should be careful not to inflate reliability estimates spuriously through inappropriate sampling or other computational methods (Stanley, 1971). Internal-consistency reliability (e.g., alpha) will almost always be the most appropriate reliability estimate for intelligence and achievement tests. Internal-consistency estimates are the most appropriate of all reliability estimates for these tests because they best determine the accuracy of test scores.

8. *The validity coefficient* r_{xy}, *which represents the relationship between the measures of aptitude and achievement, should be*

based on an appropriate sample. This sample should consist of a large, stratified random sample of normally functioning children. A large sample is necessary to reduce the sampling error in r_{xy} to an absolute minimum, since variations in r_{xy} will affect the calculation of a severe discrepancy and affect the distribution of difference scores, which is the area of greater concern. Normally functioning children are preferred for the samples, because the definition of "severe discrepancy" is based in part on the frequency of occurrence of the discrepancy in the normal population. When conorming of aptitude and achievement measures is conducted, this problem is simplified greatly, since r_{xy} can be based on the standardization sample of the two measures (which should meet the standards in point 2 above) without any handicapped children included. Some states (notably California) use validity coefficients based in estimates derived from research using handicapped children. This practice is not recommended, because the IQ and achievement score distributions of handicapped children are not normal; thus, they restrict the range of scores and lower the correlation between IQ and achievement, making it appear artificially smaller than it is in reality.

9. *The validity of test score interpretations should be clearly established.* Though clearly stated in the rules and regulations for P.L. 94-142, this requirement should receive special emphasis, particularly with regard to Cronbach's (1971) discussion of test validation. Validation with normal samples is insufficient for application to diagnosis of handicapping conditions; validity should be demonstrated for exceptional populations. This requirement is an urgent one, especially in certain areas of achievement where few adequate scales exist. To determine deviations from normality, validation with normal samples should typically be regarded as sufficient. This requirement does not require separate normative data for each handicapping condition. The generalizability of norms and of validity data is in part a function of the question one seeks to answer with the test data and is ultimately an empirical question (Reynolds, Gutkin, Elliot, & Witt, 1984).

10. *Special technical considerations should be addressed when one uses performance-based measures of achievement (e.g., writing skill).* Some measures, such as

written expression, involve special problems of reliability and validity. This is also true of such tasks as the Wechsler Vocabulary and Comprehension measures, in which examiners are frequently called upon to make fine distinctions regarding the quality of a response. Interrater reliability of scoring on any measure calling for judgments by the examiner should be reported and should be .85 to .90 or higher. Highly speeded and primarily memory-based tasks will also pose special technical problems that must be addressed.

11. *Bias studies on the instruments in use should be reported.* Criterion-related validity should receive emphasis in this regard, but not to the exclusion of other studies of bias. Bias should be addressed with respect to appropriate demographic variables that may moderate the test's validity. At a minimum, these should include race, sex, and socioeconomic status (though not necessarily simultaneously). In the assessment and diagnosis of LD in particular, sex bias needs to be investigated, since boys outnumber girls in classes for the LD by about 3.5 to 1. The procedures for evaluating bias in all aspects of a test are presented in a comprehensive form in Berk (1982) and in Jensen (1980). Although measures that exhibit little or no statistical bias are the measures of choice, other measures can be used with appropriate correction.

All of the points made above should be considered in the evaluation of test data used for determining a severe discrepancy. It bears repeating that the discrepancy formulas presented here yield results that are only as reliable as the test data used in them. Integrally related to the quality of test data are the characteristics of the examiner; the next section explores this issue.

WHO SHOULD BE DIAGNOSING LEARNING DISABILITIES?

In the public schools, in one sense, the question of who should be diagnosing LD has been resolved by P.L. 94-142. According to the 1977 rules and regulations implementing this law, only a multidisciplinary team is empowered to diagnose handicapping conditions of any type in the schools. It remains legitimate to ask, however, who should be doing the primary assessment of the discrepancy criterion (as well as the psychological process criterion) and interpreting these results to the team. It would be convenient to proffer a job title and move on; however, the educational and certification requirements for any given job in the schools vary greatly from state to state. This variation is troublesome, because the quality of the personnel conducting the diagnosis or interpreting it to the team and to the parents is as important to the diagnosis of LD as the quality of the data and the objectivity of the definition.

The task of LD diagnosis is the most difficult of all psychoeducational diagnostic tasks; thus the most highly trained personnel available should be reserved for assignment to evaluating potential LD children. This is clearly not what has been happening in practice. Although accurate diagnosis of LD in school-age children is considered the most difficult type of diagnosis mandated by P.L. 94-142, it is precisely the area of evaluation and diagnosis most often relegated to the least qualified, most poorly trained diagnostic personnel in the schools. Arguments and data (Bennett, 1981; Bennett & Shepherd, 1982) clearly show that the specialists and diagnosticians commonly assigned the task of LD diagnosis do not possess the requisite knowledge of tests and measurements to allow them to interpret test scores adequately. On a test of beginning-level measurement concepts, Bennett and Shepherd's (1982) LD specialists answered barely 50% of the questions correctly. A group of first-year graduate students in an introductory measurement class answered more than 70% of the same questions correctly. Using the best-trained staff will not solve the problems involved in diagnosis and evaluation of LD children, but it would be a step in the right direction. Who precisely are the best-trained staff members will vary from state to state; the point is that this subject desperately needs attention.

Personnel such as psychiatrists and social workers are often legally acceptable diagnosticians for LD, but have no training in psychological or educational assessment. Without the assistance of a qualified psychologist, it is doubtful that accurate diagnoses will occur. Psychologists who diagnose LD need specialized training as well—not only in psychopathology, but in psychometrics and special education (areas poorly treated in many clinical programs).

CONCLUSION

This chapter reviews the state of the art in determining a "severe discrepancy" between a child's achievement and his or her age and ability. Other factors to be considered in this determination are found in P.L. 94-142 and in Chalfant (1984), but are also dictated by the theoretical approach adopted. The state of the art in determining a severe discrepancy is known, but now needs to be implemented. As implementation moves forward, we need to turn our attention toward objectification of the remaining four key aspects of LD diagnosis reviewed in Chalfant (1984). Next, given the relative importance of these five factors, we should tackle the "psychological process" criterion. This criterion is absolutely crucial, but must of necessity be theory-driven. However controversial and complex the issues may be, we must move forward on all fronts.

It is inappropriate at this stage to recommend a single, specific theoretical model from which to assess LD. What is imperative, however, is that *a clear theoretical rationale is necessary for a coherent diagnosis and evaluation of LD children*. Consequently, at least at the local education agency level if not at the SEA level, the theoretical and conceptual basis for any given criteria for designating a child as LD should be clearly stated and understood by district diagnostic personnel, and its supporting body of literature should be cited (Reynolds, 1985a). Clinicians need to adopt a theoretical model and to strive earnestly for internal consistency in their own case-by-case work. It is less important at this stage of inquiry in the discipline just which theoretical or conceptual model is adopted than it is that a theoretical model be clearly stated and implemented at a state-of-the-art level. To do less is to cheat the children we seek to serve.

REFERENCES

Angoff, W. H. (1971). Scales, norms, and equivalent scores. In R. L. Thorndike (Ed.), *Educational measurement* (2nd ed.). Washington, DC: American Council on Education.

Bennett, R. E. (1981). Professional competence and the assessment of exceptional children. *Journal of Special Education, 15,* 437–446.

Bennett, R. E., & Shepherd, M. J. (1982). Basic measurement proficiency of learning disability specialists. *Learning Disability Quarterly, 5,* 177–184.

Berk, R. A. (Ed.). (1982). *Handbook of methods for detecting test bias*. Baltimore: Johns Hopkins University Press.

Berk, R. A. (1984). *Screening and diagnosis of children with learning disabilities*. Springfield, IL: Charles C. Thomas.

Chalfant, J. C. (1984). *Identifying learning disabled students: Guidelines for decision making*. Burlington, VT: Northeast Regional Resource Center.

Cone, T., & Wilson, L. (1981). Quantifying a severe discrepancy: A critical analysis. *Learning Disability Quarterly, 4*, 359–371.

Cronbach, L. J. (1971). Test validation. In R. L. Thorndike (Ed.), *Educational measurement* (2nd ed.). Washington, DC: American Council on Education.

Danielson, L. C., & Bauer, J. W. (1978). A formula-based classification of learning disabled children: An examination of the issues. *Journal of Learning Disabilities, 11*, 163–176.

Ebel, R. (1972). *Essentials of educational measurement*. Englewood Cliffs, NJ: Prentice-Hall.

Hanna, G., Dyck, N., & Holen, M. (1979). Objective analysis of aptitude-achievement discrepancies in LD classification. *Learning Disability Quarterly, 2*, 32–38.

Hopkins, H., & Hodge, S. (1984). Review of the Kaufman Assessment Battery (K-ABC) for Children. *Journal of Counseling and Human Development, 63*, 105–107.

Hunter, J. E., Schmidt, F. L., & Rauschenberger, J. (1984). Methodological, statistical, and ethical issues in the study of bias in psychological tests. In C. R. Reynolds & R. T. Brown (Eds.), *Perspectives on bias in mental testing*. New York: Plenum.

Hynd, G., & Willis, W. (1988). *Pediatric neuropsychology*. New York: Grune & Stratton.

Jastak, J. E., & Jastak, S. (1978). *Wide range achievement test*. Wilmington, DE: Jastak Associates.

Jensen, A. R. (1980). *Bias in mental testing*. New York: Free Press.

Kamphaus, R. W., & Reynolds, C. R. (1987). *Clinical and research applications of the K-ABC*. Circle Pines, MN: American Guidance Service.

Kaufman, A. S. (1979). *Intelligent testing with the WISC-R*. New York: Wiley-Interscience.

McLeod, J. (1979). Educational underachievement: Toward a defensible psychometric definition. *Journal of Learning Disabilities, 12*, 42–50.

Meehl, P. E. (1954). *Clinical versus statistical prediction*. Minneapolis: University of Minnesota Press.

Mercer, J., & Lewis, J. (1979). *System of Multicultural Pluralistic Assessment: Technical manual*. New York: Psychological Corporation.

Payne, R. W., & Jones, H. G. (1957). Statistics for the investigation of individual cases. *Journal of Clinical Psychology, 13*, 115–121.

Reynolds, C. R. (1981a). The fallacy of "two years below grade level for age" as a diagnostic criterion for reading disorders. *Journal of School Psychology, 19*, 350–358.

Reynolds, C. R. (1982). The problem of bias in psychological assessment. In C. R. Reynolds & T. B. Gutkin (Eds.), *The handbook of school psychology*. New York: Wiley.

Reynolds, C. R. (1984). Critical measurement issues in learning disabilities. *Journal of Special Education, 18*, 451–476.

Reynolds, C. R. (1985a). Measuring the aptitude–achievement discrepancy in learning disability diagnosis. *Remedial and Special Education, 6*, 37–55.

Reynolds, C. R. (1985b). Toward objective diagnosis of learning disabilities. *Special Services in the Schools, 1*, 161–176.

Reynolds, C. R. (1986). Assessment of exceptional children. In R. T. Brown & C. R. Reynolds (Eds.), *Psychological perspectives on childhood exceptionality*. New York: Wiley-Interscience.

Reynolds, C. R., & Brown, R. T. (1984). An introduction to the issues. In C. R. Reynolds & R. T. Brown (Eds.), *Perspectives on bias in mental testing*. New York: Plenum.

Reynolds, C. R., & Clark, J. A. (1983). Cognitive assessment of the preschool child. In B. Bracken & K. Paget (Eds.), *Psychoeducational assessment of the preschool child*. New York: Grune & Stratton.

Reynolds, C. R., & Gutkin, T. B. (1981). Test scatter on the WPPSI: Normative analyses of the standardization sample. *Journal of Learning Disabilities, 14*, 460–464.

Reynolds, C. R., Gutkin, T. B., Elliot, S. N., & Witt, J. C. (1984). *School psychology: Essentials of theory and practice*. New York: Wiley.

Reynolds, C. R., & Stanton, H. C. (1988). *Discrepancy determinator I*. Bensalem, PA: TRAIN.

Reynolds, C. R., & Willson, V. L. (1984, April). *Another look at aptitude–achievement discrepancies in the evaluation of learning disabilities*. Paper presented at the annual meeting of the National Council on Measurement in Education, New Orleans.

Rules and Regulations Implementing Education for All Handicapped Children Act of 1975, P.L. 94-142, 42 Fed. Reg. 42474 (1977).

Salvia, J., & Ysseldyke, J. (1981). *Assessment in special and remedial education* (2nd ed.). Boston: Houghton Mifflin.

Schmidt, F. L. (1974). Probability and utility assumptions underlying use of the Strong Vocational Interest Blank. *Journal of Applied Psychology, 4*, 456–464.

Silverstein, A. B. (1981). Pattern analysis as simultaneous statistical inference. *Journal of Consulting and Clinical Psychology, 50*, 234–240.

Stanley, J. C. (1971). Reliability. In R. L. Thorndike (Ed.), *Educational measurement* (2nd ed.). Washington, DC: American Council on Education.

Thorndike, R. L., & Hagen, E. (1977). *Measurement and evaluation in education and psychology*. New York: Wiley.

Wiggins, J. S. (1981). Clinical and statistical prediction: Where are we and where do we go from here? *Clinical Psychology Review, 1*, 3–18.

Willson, V. L., & Reynolds, C. R. (1984). Another look at evaluating aptitude–achievement discrepancies in the diagnosis of learning disabilities. *Journal of Special Education, 18*, 477–487.

Zimmerman, D. W., & Williams, R. H. (1982). The relative error magnitude in three measures of change. *Psychometrika, 47*, 141–147.

25

Visual–Motor Assessment

JACK A. CUMMINGS
MARC LAQUERRE
Indiana University

A critical dimension of psychoeducational assessment is the framework from which the examiner operates. There are a variety of orientations that the examiner may assume, and to a great extent the examiner's frame of reference dictates the data gathered within the context of the psychoeducational evaluation. The nomothetic approach is an orientation that commonly characterizes psychological examiners and their reports. Within the nomothetic approach, there is a reliance on objective, standardized tests. Comparisons are made between the performance of an individual and the normative performance derived from a representative standardization sample.

Criticism of the nomothetic approach to assessment is often directed at the assumptions that form its foundation. For example, Hutt (1977) questions three of these assumptions. The examiner using the nomothetic approach assumes that individuals arrive at their standard score by an "accumulation of the same or similar elements of the test" (Hutt, 1974, p. 3). Second, the nomothetic approach also assumes the equivalence of motivational factors that may either enhance or hinder a person's performance on the measure. Third, the nomothetic approach assumes that all subjects have had the same or similar experiences (social, educational, etc.). These assumptions limit the inferences that the clinician can make regarding the individual's score. Perhaps the greatest prob-

lem with the nomothetic approach is that the scores overpower the clinician's report of motivational and background factors. The most salient information yielded by the nomothetically oriented report is a deviance score, or what is essentially an index of difference.

In contrast to the nomothetic orientation is the hypothesis-testing approach (Kaufman, 1979). Within this approach, the role of the examiner is to develop hypotheses about the child from various sources (behavioral observations, background data, interviews with significant others, test results, and profiles of strengths and weaknesses generated from tests). In the psychoeducational assessment, the purpose is to "test" the various hypotheses generated, and to pay specific attention to those hypotheses that relate to the referral question(s). As noted by Cummings (1986), it is crucial that the examiner not adopt an attitude of trying to validate or confirm hypotheses. Evidence must be considered that would either support *or* negate a given hypothesis. Confirmatory assessment is a dangerous practice that often results in a search for pathology, rather than an appropriate and fair evaluation of an individual. This is not a minor semantic difference, but rather an important aspect of an examiner's philosophy toward assessment.

Hutt (1977) uses the terms "process diagnosis" and "inferential diagnosis" to highlight the importance of attending to the examinee as the various testing tasks are attempted and completed. While the examinee is proceeding through the aspects of the test, the psychologist attends to process variables—that is, what the examinee has difficulty with, what strategies the examinee uses to cope with those sections, and which aspects of the test the examinee is able to complete successfully. As the evaluation is proceeding, the psychologist makes inferences as to the conditions under which the examinee succeeds and fails. These inferences are treated as experimental hypotheses, with subsequent evidence being considered within a hypothesis-testing framework.

Although the relative strengths and weaknesses of the formal, nomothetic approach versus process and inferential diagnosis may be debated, it is important to acknowledge that the latter may subsume the former. We recommend a data-based, eclectic approach to psychoeducational assessment. It is imperative that professionals use assessment measures that are of adequate technical quality. Results should be interpreted within the context of behavioral observations, data gathered via interviews, and the referral question(s). It should be emphasized that the hallmark of high-quality assessment is that it is responsive to the referral question.

The remainder of this chapter is divided into four main sections. The first section begins with a simplistic model of visual–motor functioning; this is followed by an examination of two underlying assumptions for visual–motor assessment. The second section includes reviews of common measures of visual–motor functioning. Among the measures reviewed are the Bender–Gestalt Test and several of its scoring systems: the Developmental Test of Visual–Motor Integration; the McCarthy Scales of Children's Abilities; the Minnesota Percepto-Diagnostic Test—Revised; the Motor-Free Visual Perception Test; the Slingerland Screening Tests for Identifying Children with Specific Language Disability—Revised; and the Southern California Sensory Integration Tests—Revised. The third section of the chapter focuses on the distinction between a product-oriented and a process-oriented view of observation; in this section, the role of keen observation is stressed. The last major section of the chapter is devoted to an examina-

tion of the relationship between visual–motor functioning and academic achievement.

A MODEL OF VISUAL–MOTOR FUNCTIONING AND ASSUMPTIONS FOR VISUAL–MOTOR ASSESSMENT

Williams (1983) provides a useful paradigm for understanding a child's visual–motor performance. Her basic model of the interaction of perceptual and motor functioning is presented in Figure 25.1. Stimulus reception and processing represent the first step of the process that occurs in a motor act. External information must be taken in via the child's senses. For instance, if the task is to copy a triangle, the child will need to look at the stimulus triangle. The second step is sensory integration. Sensory synthesis is the process by which data currently being taken in are compared to sensory data previously stored in long-term memory. In the case of a child being asked to copy a triangle, sensory synthesis is illustrated by the child's interpretation of the visual input and recognition of the stimulus as a triangle. The third phase is effector activity. After the stimulus is recognized, the individual makes a decision to act and then implements the act. It is at this point that drawing behavior begins. The fourth step is information feedback. The motor movement triggers a host of stimuli that may guide future motor activity. Let us assume that the child has begun to draw the first side of the triangle. Feedback will come from (1) proprioceptive (movement) and kinesthetic receptors (position in space); (2) visual receptors in the movement, which will result in a line drawn on the paper; (3) touch or pressure receptors in the hand, which will inform the child as to the adequacy of his or her grip on the pencil; and possibly (4) auditory receptors in the form of verbal feedback.

It can be argued that two assumptions have guided the emergence of visual–motor assessment with preschool and elementary school children. One assumption posits that visual–motor skills are prerequisites for successful school performance. For instance, the work of Frostig and her colleagues (Frostig, Maslow, Lefever, & Whittlesey, 1964) has attempted to illuminate the relationship between delayed visual–motor development

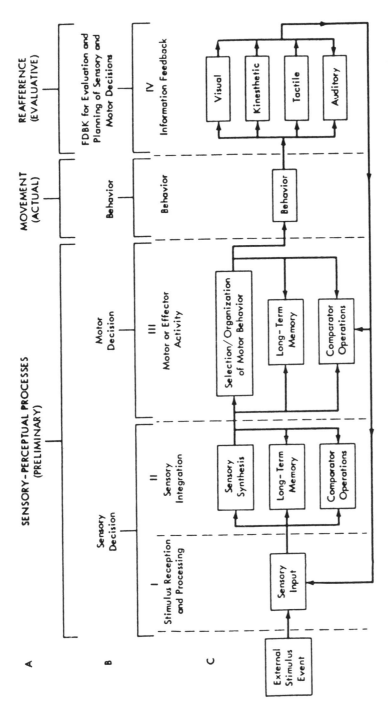

FIGURE 25.1. A simplified schema of perceptual–motor functioning. From *Perceptual and Motor Development* (p. 4) by H. J. Williams, 1983, Englewood Cliffs, NJ: Prentice-Hall. Copyright 1983 by Prentice-Hall. Reprinted by permission.

and poor school achievement. Her work in this area has led Frostig to conclude that visual–motor screening should be undertaken to determine a child's school readiness.

A second assumption is that learning disabilities are a manifestation of visual–motor deficits. This has had a large impact on the assessment of visual–motor skills. Theorists in the field of learning disabilities, such as Frostig and Maslow (1973), and Getman (1965), have advanced the notion that learning disabilities are based in perceptual pathology. Others have proposed methods of identifying and remediating visual–motor deficits in young children. The popularity of these theories has led to subsequent development and use of visual–motor assessment measures as means of identifying children with potential learning disabilities. However, in recent years the nature of the relationship between visual–motor skills and learning disabilities has been questioned. The link between the two is anything but certain. Research on the nature of the link between visual–motor skills and academic achievement is reviewed in a subsequent section of this chapter.

COMMON MEASURES OF VISUAL–MOTOR FUNCTIONING

Most of the measures reviewed in this section of the chapter are of the paper-and-pencil genre (e.g., the Bender–Gestalt Test, the Developmental Test of Visual–Motor Integration, and the Minnesota Percepto-Diagnostic Test—Revised). These tests typically require the examinee to draw or copy various geometric designs onto a sheet of paper. The reproductions are scored for errors or various types of deviations (e.g., failure to integrate parts, rotations, expansion, etc.). The Motor-Free Visual Perception Test and portions of the Slingerland Screening Tests adopt a multiple-choice format that eliminates the motor component; the child's task is to visually recognize and match designs. The McCarthy Scales of Children's Abilities are included as an example of a more multifaceted battery of measures encompassing the assessment of visual–motor skills.

Bender–Gestalt Test

The Bender–Gestalt Test is perhaps the best known of the paper-and-pencil visual–motor assessment measures. The test is used in the assessment of visual–motor skills as well as the assessment of personality. In a survey of school psychologists, Goh, Teslow, and Fuller (1981) found the Bender–Gestalt Test to be the instrument most frequently used test to assess perceptual–motor functioning; their results revealed that 93% of the psychologists surveyed indicated that they used the Bender–Gestalt Test for this purpose.

The Visual Motor Gestalt Test, more commonly referred to as the Bender–Gestalt Test, was developed in 1938 by Lauretta Bender. Bender was working at Bellevue Hospital when she became interested in Gestalt psychologists' study of visual perception in humans. Wertheimer (1923) had developed approximately 30 Gestalt designs. Bender adapted nine of these figures and began using them with her patients. The Bender Visual Motor Gestalt Test evolved from her work with these nine designs. Although Bender never proposed a standardized scoring system for the test, she did provide, in the original monograph, some guidelines for identifying patterns of errors that could be used to assist the diagnosis of schizophrenia and other neuroses (Bender, 1938). Later, Bender (1946) published a second manual of instructions for the Bender–Gestalt Test.

Description of Stimuli and Administration

The Bender–Gestalt Test is composed of nine designs. A reproduction of these designs is presented in Figure 25.2. The examiner presents each card, starting with A and then proceeding in numerical order from 1 through 8. The examinee is asked to copy the designs onto an unlined sheet of $8\frac{1}{2} \times 11$ paper. Koppitz (1964, p. 15) suggests the following instructions: "I have nine cards here with designs on them for you to copy. Here is the first one. Now, go ahead and make one just like it." The designs are presented one at a time. There is no time limit, and the test usually requires about 6 minutes to administer.

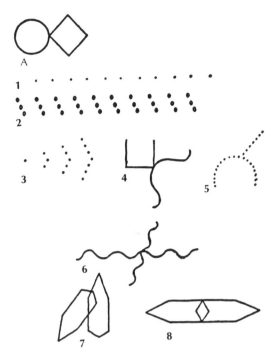

FIGURE 25.2. The nine designs of the Bender–Gestalt Test, adapted from Wertheimer (1923). From *A Visual Motor Gestalt Test and Its Clinical Uses* (Research Monograph No. 3) by L. Bender, 1938, New York: American Orthopsychiatric Association. Copyright 1938 by the American Orthopsychiatric Association. Reprinted by permission.

Early Scoring Systems

Billingslea (1948) was the first to attempt to provide an objective scoring system for the Bender–Gestalt Test. His system initially consisted of 38 "factors" and 137 "indices," many of which required precise measurement. His procedure proved extremely time-consuming; in fact, Billingslea reported a scoring time of 15 hours per protocol. Subsequently, he reduced the number of factors to 25 and the number of indices to 63. However, after the scoring system was used with a sample of 100 psychoneurotic patients and 50 normal individuals, few of the factors were found to be sufficient in differentiating the two groups. Billingslea concluded that, in general, the system was unreliable and lacked validity. Consequently, the Billingslea scoring system failed to achieve widespread use.

The Pascal and Suttell (1951) and the Hain (1964) scoring systems are frequently mentioned in the research literature. Pascal and Suttell (1951) attempted to provide a system capable of distinguishing persons with psychogenic disorders from normal individuals. The system was standardized on a sample of psychiatric patients and a matched group of normal individuals. The sample included 474 persons from the ages of 15 to 50 and was stratified by age and education. The scoring system involves the identification of 105 possible errors in the reproduction of the designs. Each error is weighted from 2 to 8; these weighted error scores are summed and converted to a standard score, based on education. The authors reported an interrater reliability of .90. The test–retest stability coefficient, for a time interval of 24 hours, was reported as .71. Summarizing two studies, Pascal and Suttell (1951) cited diagnostic accuracy figures ranging from .76 to .83. The popularity of the Pascal–Suttell system has waned in recent years; some have pointed to the complexity and time-consuming nature of the scoring system as factors that have limited its use (Lacks, 1984).

The Hain (1964) scoring system is similar to the Hutt and Briskin (1960) system (see the description of the Lacks system, below), in that it proposes the use of "signs" that are scored only once per protocol. Hain presents 15 signs that are scored; each sign has a specific weight assigned to it. Hain suggests a cutoff score of 9 or greater. Hain's system has numerous limitations. For instance, the sample was composed of only 83 individuals. Furthermore, Hain failed to provide any information regarding the representativeness of the sample. Factors such as intelligence and age were not controlled, and the author admitted that differences across groups might be attributable in part to those factors. In addition, Hain did not provide information about the reliability of the scoring system.

Koppitz Developmental Bender Test Scoring System

The Koppitz Developmental Bender Test Scoring System (Koppitz, 1964) has emerged as one of the most commonly used systems with children in both school and clinical settings (Neale & McKay, 1985). As suggested in the title of her scoring system, Koppitz emphasizes that the Bender–Gestalt Test, when used with children, must be seen as a developmental test. Her scoring system entails the identification of 30 mutually exclusive errors that are scored as either present or absent. Four major types of errors are scored: rotations, distortions, errors of integration, and errors of perseveration. Koppitz (1975) provides numerous clear examples of these errors and when they should be scored. The errors are summed to produce a Total Bender Developmental Score, which is a raw score. The highest possible score attainable on the test is 30, though, according to Koppitz, scores above 20 are rare. Koppitz (1975) provides information that enables the transformation of the Total Developmental Score to age equivalent scores and to percentile ranks, based on the 1975 restandardization data. In addition, Furr (1970) has published a table of standard scores ($M = 100$, $SD = 15$) for the Bender, based on Koppitz's (1964) original normative information.

The Koppitz Developmental Bender Test Scoring System was restandardized in 1974 (Koppitz, 1975). This most recent standardization included a sample of 975 elementary school pupils ranging in age from 5 years, 0 months to 10 years, 11 months. Children from the following geographic regions were included: 15% from the West, 2% from the South, and 83% from the Northeast. In terms of racial composition, 86% of the sample was white, 8.5% black, 4.5% Mexican-American and Puerto Rican, and 1% Oriental. Seven percent of the students were from rural areas, 31% from small towns, 36% from the suburbs, and 26% from large metropolitan areas. Koppitz does not provide information regarding the gender or socioeconomic status of the subjects in the sample. In addition, there are obvious problems with the geographic representativeness of the sample: The Northeast was highly overrepresented, while the South, Midwest, and West were underrepresented.

Koppitz (1975) presents the results from 31 studies, which produced a range of interjudge reliabilities from .79 to .99. More recent studies of the interjudge reliability of the Koppitz scoring system reveal figures that cluster around .90. Neale and McKay (1985) reported an interjudge reliability of .92. Aylward and Schmidt (1986) found interjudge reliabilities of .93, .86, and .87. These results were derived from comparisons of total Koppitz scores. Aylward and Schmidt's (1986) study, however, revealed lower interjudge reliabilities when individual error items were analyzed. These reliabilities ranged from .71 to .94.

An important dimension of any test score is its stability. Nine studies of the test–retest stability of Bender scores are presented by Koppitz (1975). These studies examined the test–retest stability of scores obtained from children of varying grade levels and at various testing intervals. Test–retest stability coefficients ranging from .50 to .90 were reported. Although there appears to be no identifiable pattern of stability variation based on grade level, the length of the interval between initial testing and retesting is critical to the stability of the scores. The pattern indicates that the scores decrease as the length of the interval between the initial testing and the retesting increases. This pattern is not surprising, given the developmental nature of the test. Normally, a child's visual–motor integration skills will improve as the child develops; therefore, the greater the interval between the initial testing and retesting, the greater the opportunity for the child's visual–motor skills to have improved. This improvement will influence the child's performance on the test.

The emergence of the Koppitz Developmental Bender Test Scoring System as one of the most commonly used scoring systems coincided with the increased usage of the Bender–Gestalt Test with children (Lacks, 1984). Although the Koppitz scoring system is designed for the assessment of children, some researchers have used it with adults. This is not advisable, since the norms that Koppitz provides were established with a sample of children. The Lacks scoring system, described next, is more appropriate for use with adults.

Lacks Adaptation of the Hutt–Briskin Scoring System

The Lacks scoring system is an adaptation of Hutt and Briskin's (1960) system. The Hutt–

Briskin scoring system proposed the use of 12 factors to detect psychopathology. Errors such as rotation, overlapping difficulty, fragmentation, and retrogression are examples of these discriminators. Hutt (1977) has since revised his scoring system, as his interest in the Bender–Gestalt Test has focused increasingly on its utility as a projective measure. Hutt (1977) did not provide extensive standardization information for the original Hutt–Briskin scoring system or for any of the subsequent revisions. In 1984, however, Lacks adapted the original Hutt–Briskin system. She has provided standardization data and a detailed scoring manual.

The Lacks adaptation of the Hutt–Briskin scoring system entails examining each protocol for the presence or absence of the 12 discriminators. Each error is scored only once per protocol. The presence of five or more errors on a protocol signifies some organic dysfunction.

The standardization sample for the Lacks adaptation of the Hutt–Briskin, by Lacks's own admission, was only "broadly representative" of the population. The sample consisted of 495 nonpatient adults, the majority of whom were drawn from the St. Louis metropolitan area. Relative to ethnicity, Lacks distinguished only between blacks and whites. She makes no mention of such ethnic groups as Hispanic, Oriental, or Native American, and one must assume that they were excluded from the sample. The range of age and education categories were chosen to correspond with those used by the U.S. Bureau of the Census.

Lacks (1984) reports four studies examining the diagnostic accuracy of her adaptation of the Hutt–Briskin scoring system. Each of the studies utilized a cutoff error score of 5 as an indication of brain dysfunction. The studies revealed that the Lacks scoring system correctly distinguished known organic psychiatric patients from nonorganic patients at levels of accuracy ranging from .82 to .86. The test–retest stability of the scoring system was examined in a study summarized by Lacks. In this study, 40 patients of mixed diagnoses were retested at intervals varying from 5 to 21 days. The mean interval was reported to be 10 days. The study revealed a test–retest stability coefficient of .79. Two studies of interrater reliability revealed coefficients ranging from .87 to .95.

Developmental Test of Visual–Motor Integration

The Developmental Test of Visual–Motor Integration (VMI; Beery, 1982) was designed to serve as a screening instrument that would assist in the prevention of learning and behavior problems through early detection. Though the test can be used with children and adults, it was designed for use with preschool children. The VMI consists of 24 figures that are arranged sequentially, from simple to complex; 2 of these figures are from the Bender–Gestalt Test. Unlike the Bender–Gestalt Test, the VMI presents the designs in a protocol. Each page is divided into six blocks. The three blocks on the upper portion of the page contain designs; the child is instructed to copy the design into the empty block below the stimulus design. In comparison to the Bender–Gestalt Test, the VMI is more structured, in that the design is printed on the page and there are boundaries within which the design is to be copied.

The child's reproductions are scored as either "pass" or "fail." The manual provides numerous scoring examples that facilitate making such determinations. In addition to scoring examples, developmental comments are included to assist in the interpretation of a child's performance. A total raw score is computed by adding the number of figures passed. The manual provides a table that allows for the conversion of raw scores to developmental age equivalents. Additional tables are provided that allow raw scores to be converted into either percentile ranks or standard scores. The standard scores are based on a mean of 10 and standard deviation of 3 points.

The VMI was standardized in 1981 on a sample of 3,090 children ranging in age from 2 years, 9 months to 19 years, 8 months (Beery, 1982). Within the normative sample, the representation of gender was approximately equal: 51.3% were boys and 48.7% were girls. The sample was 64.9% white, 15.7% black, 7.3% Hispanic, and 12.1% other. Children from low-income families (those earning a total net income of $12,500 or less) represented 27.2% of the sample.

The remaining 72.8% of the children were from high-income families. Regarding residence, 70.8% of the children in the sample were from suburban settings, 21.9% from urban settings, and 7.3% from rural settings. The geographic representation of the sample was not specified in the manual. As such, one cannot determine whether all those in the sample were drawn from a single district in one state or whether the sample is representative of the nation as a whole.

The interjudge reliability for 120 VMI protocols was established as part of the 1981 norming effort (Beery, 1982). Between school psychologists and resource teachers, the coefficient was .90. The reliability coefficients were .95 when the scoring of resource teachers was compared to that of classroom teachers, and .93 when the scoring of psychologists was compared to that of classroom teachers.

Beery (1982) reviewed the results of nine other studies that have addressed the issue of interrater reliability of the VMI. The reliability coefficients from these studies ranged from .58 to .99, with a median correlation of .93. Berry also reports the results of five studies regarding the test–retest stability of the VMI; these stability figures ranged from .63 (7-month interval) to .92 (2-week interval). The median correlation of these studies was .81. It should be noted that these studies did *not* involve remediation between the first and second time each child was assessed.

Based on the similarities between the task dimensions of the Bender–Gestalt and the VMI, one would assume a large degree of shared variance between the two measures. However, Wright and DeMers (1982) note that the two are not necessarily equivalent. With a sample of 86 children referred for learning and adjustment difficulties, Wright and DeMers (1982) found a correlation of .67 between the two measures. The ability estimate provided by the VMI was two standard deviations higher than the Bender–Gestalt Test scored by Koppitz's system. Likewise, in a separate study, DeMers, Wright, and Dappen (1981) found that VMI provided a higher ability estimate than the Bender–Gestalt Test. DeMers et al. (1981) also used a referral sample. Two other investigations (Brown, 1977; Lehman & Breen, 1982) employed samples drawn from regular

classes (nonreferral samples) and found the opposite of the results reported above: Instead of the VMI providing a higher estimate, the Koppitz scoring of the Bender–Gestalt Test was significantly higher in both studies. DeMers et al. (1981) speculate that the difference could be associated with the nature of the samples (i.e., referred students may score higher on the VMI than on the Bender–Gestalt).

The preceding studies were completed using the 1967 norms for the VMI. The relationship or relative equivalence between the 1967 and 1981 norms is not addressed in the technical manual (Beery, 1982). Thus it is difficult to determine whether the findings from the mean score comparisons cited above would have changed if the 1981 norms had been used. Comparison studies completed after the 1981 norms were released were not located in our computer search.

When the Bender–Gestalt and VMI are correlated, the coefficients tend to be in the moderate range. The coefficients have ranged from .43 (Brown, 1977) to .71 (Lehman & Breen, 1982). Wright and DeMers (1982) and Spirito (1980) both reported coefficients of .67 between the Bender–Gestalt and VMI. Squaring the .67 coefficient to obtain an estimate of shared variance indicates that 45% is the degree of overlap between the two measures. As such, it appears that Wright and DeMers were correct when they stated that the two measures were not equivalent. The caveat here, again, is that these investigations were done with the 1967 norms for the VMI.

McCarthy Scales of Children's Abilities

In a chapter addressing the assessment of visual–motor functioning, one might not expect to see coverage of the McCarthy Scales of Children's Abilities. The McCarthy Scales (McCarthy, 1972) were designed to assess the general intelligence level of young children and to provide information regarding their strengths and weaknesses in various ability areas. Among the abilities assessed are those that would be traditionally labeled as visual–motor. The scales are appropriate for use with children from the ages of $2\frac{1}{2}$ to $8\frac{1}{2}$.

Eighteen subtests grouped into six scales compose the McCarthy Scales of Children's

Abilities. Three of the scales (Verbal, Perceptual–Performance, and Quantitative) are combined to produce a fourth scale, the General Cognitive. The Memory and Motor scales do not contribute to the General Cognitive scale. Of particular importance to the purpose of this chapter are the Perceptual–Performance and the Motor scales.

The Perceptual–Performance scale consists of seven subtests: Block Building, Puzzle Solving, Tapping Sequence, Right–Left Orientation, Draw-A-Design, Draw-A-Child, and Conceptual Grouping. These subtests are thought to tap such abilities as visual–motor coordination; nonverbal reasoning through the manipulation of concrete materials; and visual organization in a variety of spatial, visual–perceptual, and conceptual tasks. The Motor scale is thought to evaluate a child's gross and fine motor coordination. Subtests that compose the Motor scale are Leg Coordination, Arm Coordination, Imitative Action, Draw-A-Design, and Draw-A-Child.

All subtest raw scores are converted to scaled scores, which are in turn summed up and converted to standard scores. The general Cognitive scale yields a General Cognitive Index (GCI), which has a mean of 100 and a standard deviation of 15. The other scales provide what are essentially T-scores.

In stark contrast to the visual–motor measures described previously, the standardization of the McCarthy Scales is excellent. McCarthy employed the following stratification variables: sex, race (white–nonwhite), geographic region (North, Northeast, Central, South, and West), and father's occupation. The representation of these variables were based on 1970 U.S. census data. The sample totaled 1,032, with 100–106 children in each of the 10 age groups.

Two studies were conducted to ascertain the reliability of the McCarthy Scales of Children's Abilities. One such effort determined the stability coefficients of each of the scales for three age groups. The manual reports reliabilities that range from .69 to .91. The internal consistency of the scales was also assessed using the split-half procedure. The following reliabilities were reported: Verbal, .88; Perceptual–Performance, .84; Quantitative, .81; General Cognitive, .93; Memory, .79; and Motor, .79.

The concurrent validity and predictive va-

lidity of the test were evaluated. Concurrent validity was addressed with a group of 35 first-graders. Correlations between the General Cognitive Index and other measures of intelligence were reported: Wechsler Preschool and Primary Scale of Intelligence (WPPSI) Verbal, .63; WPPSI Performance, .62; WPPSI Full Scale, .71; Stanford–Binet, .81. Additional correlations between the GCI and future achievement were provided to support the predictive validity of the McCarthy Scales. With a group of first-graders, the correlation between the GCI and performance on the Metropolitan Achievement Tests was reported as .49.

Minnesota Percepto-Diagnostic Test—Revised

The Minnesota Percepto-Diagnostic Test was first published in 1963 by Fuller and Laird. Since then the test has been revised twice; the most recent revision, The Minnesota Percepto-Diagnostic Test—Revised (MPDT-R), occurred in 1982 (Fuller, 1982). The MPDT-R was developed as a measure of visual perception and visual–motor skills. Fuller (1982) recommends the use of multiple-discriminant analysis formulas that account for such variables as IQ, total rotation score, and separation and distortion scores. The use of these formulas yield discriminant scores that, according to the author, can be used to classify subjects as brain-damaged and non-brain-damaged. Fuller contends that the various scores yielded by the MPDT-R can be used separately and jointly for differential diagnosis of the following:

- Learning disabilities as visual, auditory, or mixed.
- Children as normal, emotionally disturbed, schizophrenic, and organically brain-damaged.
- Adults as normal, brain-damaged, and having personality disturbances.

The MPDT-R utilizes two geometric designs, both of which are found on the Bender–Gestalt Test (designs A and 3). The two designs are reproduced in three distinct orientations apiece on six white cards.

As with the Bender–Gestalt Test, the administration of the MPDT-R involves instructing the examinee to copy each of the designs. The examinee's designs are then scored for rotations and errors of separation and distortion. The rotation scores across six cards are summed to produce a total rotation score. This total rotation score then may be converted into a T-score. The three circle–diamond designs are scored for errors of separation and distortion, whereas the three dot designs are scored only for distortion. These separation and distortion scores are summed to yield total scores.

Fuller (1982) reports that a sample of 4,000 children and adolescents was used in the development of the revised 1982 norms. The children ranged in age from 5 to 20. Fuller states that 480 children in the sample had intelligence test scores that fell below 87. Black children represented less than 4% of the sample. The sample was drawn from the following states: Georgia, Indiana, Illinois, Iowa, Michigan, Minnesota, New York, and Texas. Obviously, it was largely a Midwest sample, with blacks underrepresented. Information regarding the representation of gender and such demographic variables as socioeconomic status and community size is not included in the manual. Likewise, data are not included on the degree to which Hispanics were represented in the sample.

Interrater reliability of the MPDT-R is not reported by Fuller (1982), but Vance, Lester, and Thatcher (1983) investigated it. In their study, they calculated the interrater reliability between scores of professionals and novices. Reliabilities for four error scores were as follows: separation of circle–diamond, .93; total rotation, .90; distortion of dot design, .79; and distortion of circle–diamond, .37. In accounting for the low reliability of scoring of the distortion of the circle–diamond design, Vance et al. (1983) suggest that the scoring criteria for this figure are subjective, allowing for flexibility of clinical judgment.

Fuller (1982) reports stability coefficients obtained from a sample of 165 children (aged 7–12). With a test–retest interval of 1 year, the stability coefficients ranged from .37 to .60. In a separate sample of 177 children (aged 9–12), with a test–retest interval of 3 months, the stability coefficients ranged from .53 to .70. In addition to these stability coefficients, Fuller includes a table of stability coefficients for the MPDT-R rotation raw scores for different diagnostic categories (emotionally disturbed, brain-damaged, nor-

mal, and schizophrenic). These coefficients ranged from .74 to .85. The test–retest interval, however, was not reported for these diagnostic categories.

In support of the validity of the MPDT-R, Fuller and his colleagues have reported a series of studies (Fuller, 1964, 1965, 1973; Fuller & Friedrich, 1973, 1974, 1975, 1976; Fuller & Hawkins, 1969; Fuller & Shaw, 1963; Holland, Fuller, & Barth, 1982; Wallbrown, Wallbrown, & Engin, 1977) exploring the accuracy of the MPDT-R in diagnosing known groups. The study by Holland et al. (1982) illustrates this general program of research. They used the 1969 version in attempting to differentiate brain-damaged from non-brain-damaged children. There were 31 children in the brain-damaged group and 33 in the non-brain-damaged group. The children were classified into groups on the basis of their medical histories, electroencephalogram (EEG) results, and neurological examinations. Holland et al. (1982) found that a two-step procedure including the rotation T-score and the actuarial table correctly identified 75% of the children. When age and Full Scale, Verbal, and Performance IQs from the Wechsler Intelligence Scale for Children—Revised (WISC-R; Wechsler, 1974) were added to the Minnesota Percepto-Diagnostic Test scores, a discriminant analysis increased the accuracy of the prediction by 9%, thus correctly categorizing 83% of the children. A comprehensive review of the use of the MPDT-R as a measure for differential diagnosis is beyond the scope of the present chapter. However, the reader is encouraged to scrutinize the research studies done by Fuller and his colleagues, as well as to use the MPDT-R technical manual (Fuller, 1982) as a guide to locating other pertinent references.

Motor-Free Visual Perceptual Test

The Motor-Free Visual Perception Test (MVPT; Colarusso & Hammill, 1972) was developed to assess visual perception without the confounding motor component that typifies measures such as the Bender–Gestalt Test or the VMI. The selection of items was intended to represent five facets of visual perception: spatial relations, visual discrimination, figure–ground, visual closure, and visual memory. The 36-item test uses a multiple-choice format; the examinee is required to pick the correct response from four options. A total of 881 children aged 4–8 comprised the standardization sample. Children classified as needing special education were excluded from the sample. Colarusso and Hammill (1972) state that the sample included children from all races, economic levels, residential areas (rural, suburban, urban), and 22 states. No data are presented on the residential representativeness of the sample: For instance, were rural children represented in the standardization sample in the same proportions as in the general population, according to current U.S. census data? Likewise, no data are given on the gender composition of the sample (i.e., were boys underrepresented, overrepresented, or adequately represented?). The authors do mention that the children came from 22 states, but one is left to wonder which states. In short, insufficient data are presented on the standardization procedures to permit the determination of the sample's adequacy. Thus, one should exercise caution when attempting to interpret normative scores from the MVPT.

The reliability estimates were generally in the borderline–adequate range. With the exception of a Kuder–Richardson 20 coefficient of .71 for 4-year-olds, the coefficients ranged from .78 to .82 for the other age levels. The test–retest stability was also borderline–adequate; the stability coefficients ranged from .77 to .83.

Validation efforts included a content analysis and "three types of construct validity . . . age differentiations, correlations with similar tests, and internal consistency" (Colarusso & Hammill, 1972, p. 9). Like the authors' coverage of details regarding the standardization, the discussion of the content analysis is inadequate. It is merely stated that the items were developed and retained relative to the five facets of visual perception listed above. However, supporting evidence is presented for age differentiation. The concurrent validation efforts revealed significant overlap with the Frostig Developmental Test of Visual Perception (Frostig et al. 1964). Modest correlations of the MVPT (.32 and .31, respectively) were reported with the Pinter–Cunningham Primary Test (Pinter & Cunningham, 1965) and with the Slosson Intelligence Test (Slosson, 1963).

The correlations of the MVPT with measures of academic achievement also were modest. The median correlation was .38. Colarusso and Hammill (1972) acknowledged the limited degree of overlap, stating that "no claims are made regarding the relationship of the ability tapped to reading or to any other school skills: actually our findings suggest that little commonality exists between the MVPT and measures of school achievement or intelligences" (p. 14).

In a review, Rosen (1985) raised a significant question about the use of the test. "If the MVPT is a measure of 'motor-free' visual perception, we need to know how important it is to measure such an ability and what useful or critical outcomes do motor-free visual perception abilities contribute to" (p. 1418).

Slingerland Screening Tests for Identifying Children with Specific Language Disability—Revised

The Slingerland Screening Tests for Identifying with Specific Language Disability—Revised (Slingerland, 1974; Slingerland & Ansara, 1974) have four forms for different educational levels (Form A, first and second grades; Form B, second and third grades; Form C, third and fourth grades; Form D, fifth and sixth grades). The Slingerland may be administered in either an individual or a group format. For Forms A, B, and C, there are eight subtests. Form D includes additional subtests designed to assess personal orientation. Among the tasks required of the examinee are copying words and letters from a page and poster board; visual discrimination (matching letters when the item distractors are rotated or reversed); writing orally dictated words; and determining initial and final sounds.

Although the measure's full title would imply that it assesses verbal comprehension/expression, this is not the case. Fujuki (1985, p. 1398) notes that the Slingerland is not a "language" measure, but instead should be viewed as an indicator of "various auditory, visual and motor skills related to specific academic areas." Herein lies the rationale for covering this measure in a chapter on visual–motor assessment.

A significant problem with the Slingerland is its lack of normative data. This is a large oversight on the part of the authors.

Although they recommend that users of the test develop local norms, the absence of national norms is not defensible. Very few test users are capable of devoting the time and energy to the development of adequate local norms.

Another problem with the Slingerland is its reliability. Wiig (1985) notes that the subtest stability coefficients (with the exception of Auditory Recall) ranged from .23 to .59 (Form A), .35 to .59 (Form B), and .20 to .62 (Form C). The interrater coefficients were below .80 for Forms A and B and .91 for Form C. Ironically, the internal consistency was calculated to be psychometrically acceptable (i.e., .94 and above for Forms A, B, and C). However, these internal-consistency coefficients indicate that the entire collection of subtests is measuring the same construct; that is, there appears to be little subtest specificity.

Much caution should be observed if the Slingerland is going to be included in the clinician's psychoeducational battery. The measure may have value as a means for observing a child's visual–motor skills that relate directly to the school tasks of copying and writing. However, even for this use, a more acceptable approach with greater ecological validity would be to observe the child in the natural setting when these academic skills are required. This, in conjunction with the examination of permanent products (e.g., writing samples from workbooks, homework, seatwork, etc.), would provide a better picture of the child's potential difficulties.

Southern California Sensory Integration Tests—Revised

The Southern California Sensory Integration Tests—Revised (SCSIT-R; Ayres, 1980) are a battery of tests designed to assess the sensory integration development of children. Ayres (1980) asserts that the tests seek to evaluate the nature of sensory integration dysfunction. The battery includes 17 subtests, which are thought to assist in the differentiation of four types of sensory integration disorder: form and space perception; praxis (ability to plan motor activity); postural and bilateral integration (integration of the motor functioning of the two sides of the body); and tactile defensiveness.

There are 14 subtests that appear relevant to perceptual–motor assessment. These subtests are as follows: Kinesthesia, Manual Form Manipulation, Finger Identification, Graphesthesia, Localization of Tactile Stimuli, Double Tactile Stimuli Perception, Motor Accuracy—Revised, Imitation of Postures, Crossing Midline of Body, Bilateral Motor Coordination, Right–Left Discrimination, Standing Balance with Eyes Open, Standing Balance with Eyes Closed, and Design Copying. A child's performance on each of the tests is scored according to specified criteria. These raw scores are then converted to standard scores (z-scores) that are based upon the age of the examinee. It is suggested that these scores be plotted on a graph to provide a comprehensive profile of the child's sensory integration development. A child's performance on each subtest can then be compared with his or her performance on other subtests.

The manual provides only limited information concerning the standardization of the tests included within the battery. It is reported that the normative data were collected on four separate occasions; therefore, much of the information is presented for four different groups of tests. Ayres (1980) states in general terms that the normative sample represented the geographic and socioeconomic levels of metropolitan Los Angeles and the surrounding areas. However, specific data are not provided. The standardization of the Motor Accuracy—Revised subtest is the most complete, with data relative to distribution of variables such as age, sex, and race. The standardization of the remaining subtests is less complete; the representation of such demographic variables as race and socioeconomic status is not indicated. The age range of the sample for all but three visual perception tests, Design Copying, and Motor Accuracy—Revised was from 4 to 8. For the other tests, the norm sample included children from the ages of 4 to 10. The total number of children included in the norm sample is not indicated.

The reliability of the tests included in the battery, except for Motor Accuracy—Revised, was assessed by test–retest coefficients of stability. Internal consistency was used to evaluate the reliability of the Motor Accuracy—Revised subtest. These reliability coefficients ranged from .73 to .83. The stability coefficients for the other subtests were reported for varying age levels. Tables provided in the manual reveal a wide range of stability coefficients (.01 to .89). Nearly half of the coefficients reported fall below .50. Ayres (1980) attempts to explain such low stability by hypothesizing that neurophysiological processes, by nature, are unstable when compared to other psychological constructs. Regardless of such a hypothesis, these low stability coefficients limit the examiner's ability to interpret subtest scores in a meaningful and reliable fashion. The manual does not provide any discussion regarding the validity of the battery.

Although the SCSIT-R is a unique attempt at assessing the development of a variety of sensory integration functions in children, the battery in its present state has serious limitations. The standardization fails to meet traditional psychometric standards; numerous subtests yield scores that are unreliable at certain age levels, and treatment of the validity of the battery is nonexistent. In a review of the SCSIT-R, Westman (1978) states, "A disadvantage is that the tester must become an expert on all behaviors measured and on the battery itself in order to use it safely" (p. 1409). These weaknesses hamper the usefulness of the battery.

PRODUCT VERSUS BEHAVIOR

An important point that is often overlooked by less experienced clinicians is the difference between product and behavior. The scoring systems for the common paper-and-pencil visual–motor measures (e.g., the Bender–Gestalt Test and the VMI) focus on product: That which is drawn is scored in a quantitative fashion. In contrast, the more experienced practitioner attends to the process, observing the client's behavior while the client is producing the drawing. It is the observation of the act of drawing that leads to greater insight and understanding of the child's difficulties. This point is not intended to diminish the importance of a careful analysis of the product, but rather to highlight an often overlooked aspect of visual–motor assessment with the Bender and similar tests.

Developing a sense of "norms" for process behaviors requires keen observation of both normal and atypical children. The former are an important group to watch; too often, clinicians assume normal, age-appropriate behavior patterns to be atypical, because they are rarely confronted with the task of carefully observing normal children. A good illustration of this point is provided in the literature on the WISC-R. Kaufman (1976) asked experienced clinicians to estimate the Verbal–Performance discrepancies of normal children. The clinicians grossly underestimated the magnitude of these discrepancies. They assumed that since so many of the children referred for learning problems were exhibiting discrepancies of 10 to 15 points or more, normal children would exhibit 3- or 4-point discrepancies. Analysis of the standardization data collected on normal children proved that discrepancies of 12 points and greater occurred in large numbers of children who had not been referred for special education services. The important implication is that without a good foundation in normal behavior patterns, a clinician will arrive at erroneous conclusions. Since clinicians have the most contact with children who have been referred because they are experiencing difficulties in a setting, it is incumbent on the practitioners to observe normal children. The problem of developing internal norms based on an atypical sample may be avoided by vigilant observation of normal children.

Haywood (1986) makes an excellent point when she suggests that the most efficient way to refine one's observational skills is to focus on specific body movements. She uses walking to illustrate the way to break down a behavior. One can scrutinize the heel strike pattern, trunk rotation, synchronous–asynchronous arm swing, elbow flexion, or knee flexion. Alternatively, one may watch children engaged in writing. Again, the initial focus is on specific body parts and their contribution to the act. After scrutinizing the parts, the entire Gestalt of the act should be sought.

An additional aid to developing appropriate internal norms is video production equipment. Videotaping motor acts takes considerable effort, but may well be worth the time and expense. The camera should have zoom capabilities; a wide-angle shot is usually not sufficient because of inadequate focus. A child in a natural setting, moving about, makes sharp focus an elusive goal except for the skilled camera operator. Another problem is that the behavior is limited to one view unless there are two or more cameras. Despite these technical problems, videotape is very advantageous. The videotape may be replayed, and a sequence may be viewed as many times as necessary. The sequence can also be viewed in slow motion, or frame by frame. Herein lies the rationale for overcoming difficulties of video production to capture behaviors. Without the aid of video equipment, even the keenest observer has to rely on memory for a "replay" or "freeze frame."

Familiarity with symptoms associated with various eye difficulties is another way for clinicians to enhance their observation skills. Knowledge of children's behaviors when they are experiencing eye problems will reduce the possibility of overlooking a potential visual acuity problem. Most of the symptoms may be observed in the context of the individual psychological evaluation or the classroom. In some cases, the child's teacher will report the presence of a symptom; the psychologist should follow up such a report with questions on the presence of other visual acuity symptoms. When a visual problem is suspected, a referral should be made for a comprehensive eye examination. It should not be assumed that because a child has passed a Snellen eye screening, there is no possibility of a visual acuity problem.

THE RELATIONSHIP OF VISUAL–MOTOR SKILLS TO ACADEMIC ACHIEVEMENT

Numerous researchers have reported statistically significant correlations between visual–motor test performance and performance on measures of academic achievement. Koppitz and her colleagues (Koppitz, 1975; Koppitz, Mardis, & Stephens, 1961; Koppitz, Sullivan, Blyth, & Shelton, 1959) did a series of investigations examining the relationship of her developmental scoring system to first- and second-grade achievement. Likewise, other researchers have examined the magnitude of the variance shared by the Bender–Gestalt and various measures of academic achievement (Carter, Spero, & Walsh, 1978; Henderson, Butler, & Goffeney, 1969; Keogh, 1965; Norfleet, 1973; Obrzut, Hansen, & Heath, 1982; Obrzut, Taylor, & Thweatt, 1972). Generally, the findings of these in-

vestigations indicate that children who reproduce the Bender–Gestalt designs with numerous errors are also those who have difficulty in attaining basic academic skills. Tolor and Brannigan (1980) point out that although these correlations are statistically significant (usually ranging from .30 to .50), the Bender–Gestalt provides little additional predictive power when one controls for the effect of intelligence. When the Bender–Gestalt has been observed to increase the power of the prediction in regression studies, it has usually been in studies focusing on reading achievement in the early elementary grades (Tolor & Brannigan, 1980).

Lesiak (1984) reviewed 32 empirical investigations pertaining to the use of the Bender–Gestalt as a predictor of reading achievement. These investigations were divided into two categories: studies in which the Bender–Gestalt was administered concurrently with measures of reading achievement, and studies in which the Bender–Gestalt was used to differentiate good and poor readers. Lesiak (1984) drew two conclusions from her review. The first was that the Bender–Gestalt is inferior to broad-based reading readiness tests as a predictor of reading skills. She stated that the Bender–Gestalt "adds little or nothing to the predictive utility of most standardized reading readiness tests" (Lesiak, 1984, p. 402). Lesiak's (1984) second conclusion was that the Bender is not *consistent* in differentiating good and poor readers. Lesiak ended her article by questioning the utility of the Bender–Gestalt as a measure to be included in a diagnostic reading battery.

In a comprehensive meta-analysis, Kavale (1982) reported findings that both agree with and challenge Lesiak's (1984) and Tolor and Brannigan's (1980) conclusions. Kavale (1982) integrated the findings of 161 studies and 1,571 correlations in an attempt to clarify the relationship between visual perception skills and reading achievement. The analysis represented an aggregation of results from 32,500 subjects whose mean age was 7.88 years. Kavale (1982) reported that the mean correlation between visual perception and reading ability was .375, which is consistent with Lesiak's conclusion. Likewise, when he used traditional factor-analytic procedures with the composite correlation matrix (principal components with varimax rotation), he found that visual perception did not break out as unitary skill, but rather loaded across reading, cognitive, and visual differentiation factors. In order to clarify the relationship further, he used a canonical correlation analysis, a procedure that is sensitive to the contributions of the respective variables. From his review of the canonical correlation and additional multiple-regression analyses, Kavale concluded that visual perception accounted for "moderate proportions of the total shared variance in reading ability" (1982, p. 51).

A concern linked to the ability of visual–motor assessment to predict achievement of school-age children is the relationship of visual–motor skills to the attainment of basic academic skills (learning to read or solve arithmetic problems). Kephart (1967), Delacato (1966), and Ayres (1980) are representative of those who consider basic visual–motor learning to be a prerequisite to the attainment of academic skills. Along a similar vein, the Getman (1965) and Frostig et al. (1964) approaches emphasize the role of visual–motor processes. Lerner (1986) points out that early Western philosophers acknowledged a relationship between motor development and learning. She states that Plato's first level of education was gymnastics, and that Spinoza recommended teaching the body so the mind could reach an intellectual level of thought.

Kephart, Delacato, Ayres, Getman, and Frostig agree that if an individual is evaluated and subsequently judged to be deficient in a motor, perceptual–motor, or perceptual skill, a training program should be aimed at developing the specific skill or a constellation of abilities. For instance, within Kephart's (1967) perspective, if an individual is judged deficient in ocular control, a five-stage ocular training procedure should provide the basis for developing the skill. First, the child is taught to follow an object with his or her eyes. In essence, the eyes are taught to move in different directions—laterally, vertically, diagonally, and in circles. In the second stage, the target to be followed is switched to a small flashlight. The third stage increases the demands on the child's motor skill by having the child follow the light source with eyes and with a finger. The child must move eyes and finger in concert to follow the movements of the light. In the fourth stage, a tactile/kinesthetic element is added by hav-

ing the child touch the light while it is moved in various directions. In the final stage of ocular training, the child is given a ball to hold, and the teacher moves the ball in different directions. The child holds the ball with both hands and is instructed to watch the movements of the ball.

A more recent conceptualization emphasizing the role of visual–motor functioning is Ayres's (1980) sensory–motor integration approach. The emphasis within this approach is not on teaching specific and discrete skills, but rather on enhancing the brain's ability to learn. It is assumed that normal neural development proceeds along an orderly sequence; thus, therapy is designed to enhance and facilitate this neural sequence of development. Among the training activities are various balancing tasks, tactile stimulation, and swinging a child who is neither sitting or lying in a hammock (vestibular stimulation).

Lerner (1986) concludes that research investigations have failed to yield conclusive evidence that motor training exercises improve academic learning skills. She bases this conclusion on reviews done by Goodman and Hammill (1973) and Hammill, Goodman, and Wiederholt (1974). Others, such as Reynolds (1981), have come to a similar conclusion. Reynolds notes that the problem rests within a deficit model of remediation. The focus of the assessment is on the weakness that the child exhibits, and the training is aimed at the weakness. Taking a neurological perspective, Reynolds states that when "viewed from contemporary neuropsychological models, the deficit approach to remediation is doomed to failure since it takes damaged or dysfunctional areas of the brain and focuses training specially of these areas" (1981, p. 343).

Kamphaus and Reynolds (1987), Kaufman (1979), and Reynolds (1981) all suggest that remediation should be designed within the context of the child's strengths. Rather than attempting to remediate the child's weaknesses, the clinician should locate strengths and use these to accomplish the same objectives; the notion is that a child's strengths are used to circumvent weaknesses. Reynolds (1981) frames this within Luria's neuropsychological model of intelligence; that is, an intact complex functional system is used to take over and accomplish what would have normally been done by the dysfunctional system.

CONCLUDING COMMENTS

An inescapable conclusion from a review of the psychometric characteristics of the visual–motor measures is that much caution is required in their use. When the *Standards for Educational and Psychological Testing* (American Psychological Association, 1985) are used to judge the adequacy of their standardization samples, all except the McCarthy Scales must be judged as inadequate, or at the very least as limited in generalizability. Even the McCarthy standardization could be criticized, despite its well-described, nationally representative sample, because the norms are almost 20 years old. These problems with the quality of the measures' standardization samples mean that the observational skills of the psychological examiner assume greater importance. The child's behaviors exhibited during the process of drawing are what yield insight into the nature of the child's difficulties. Less emphasis should be placed on the product and its comparison to the average performance of the normative group, whereas greater emphasis should be placed on careful observation of the child's visual–motor act.

REFERENCES

American Psychological Association. (1985). *Standards for educational and psychological testing*. Washington, DC: 1985.

Aylward, E. H. & Schmidt, S. (1986). An examination of three tests of visual–motor integration. *Journal of Learning Disabilities, 19*, 328–330.

Ayres, A. J. (1980). *Southern California Sensory Integration Tests—Revised*. Los Angeles: Western Psychological Services.

Beery, K. E. (1982). *Revised administration, scoring teaching manual for the Developmental Test of Visual–Motor Integration*. Cleveland, OH: Modern Curriculum Press.

Bender, L. (1938). *A Visual Motor Gestalt Test and its clinical use* (Research Monograph No. 3). New York: American Orthopsychiatric Association.

Bender, L. (1946). *Instructions for the use of the Visual Motor Gestalt Test*. New York: American Orthopsychiatric Association.

Billingslea, F. (1948). The Bender–Gestalt: An objective scoring method and validating data. *Journal of Clinical Psychology, 4*, 1–27.

Brown, M. J. (1977). Comparison of the Developmental Test of Visual–Motor Integration and the Bender–Gestalt. *Perceptual and Motor Skills, 45*, 981–982.

Carter, D., Spero, A., & Walsh, J. (1978). A comparison of the Visual Aural Digit Span and the Bender–Gestalt as discriminators of low achievement in the primary grades. *Psychology in the Schools, 15*, 194–198.

Colarusso, R. P., & Hammill, D. D. (1972). *MVPT—Motor-Free Visual Perception Test manual*. Novato, CA: Academic Therapy.

Cummings, J. A. (1986). Projective drawings. In H. M. Knoff (Ed.), *The assessment of child and adolescent personality* (pp. 199–244). New York: Guilford Press.

Delacato, C. (1966). *Neurological organization and reading*. Springfield, IL: Charles C Thomas.

DeMers, S. T., Wright, D., & Dappen, L. (1981). Comparison of scores on two visual–motor tests for children referred for learning or adjustment difficulties. *Perceptual and Motor Skills, 53*, 863–867.

Frostig, M., & Maslow, P. (1973). *Learning problems in the classroom: Prevention and remediation*. New York: Grune & Stratton.

Frostig, M., Maslow, P., Lefever, D. W., & Whittlesey, J. R. B. (1964). The Marianne Frostig Developmental Test of Visual Perception. *Perceptual and Motor Skills, 19*, 463–499.

Fujuki, M. (1985). Review of Slingerland Screening Tests for Identifying Children with Specific Language Disability. In J. V. Mitchell (Ed.), *The ninth mental measurements yearbook* (Vol. 2, pp. 1398–1399). Lincoln: University of Nebraska Press.

Fuller, G. B. (1964). Peceptual consideration in children with a reading disability. *Psychology in the Schools, 1*, 314–317.

Fuller, G. B. (1965). The objective measurement of perception in determining personality disorganization among children. *Journal of Clinical Psychology, 21*, 305–307.

Fuller, G. B. (1973). Three categories of visual–motor performance of children with a reading disability and their theoretical implications. *Psychology in the Schools, 10*, 19–23.

Fuller, G. B. (1982). *The Minnesota Percepto-Diagnostic Test* (1982 revision). Brandon, VT: Clinical Psychology.

Fuller, G. B., & Friedrich, D. (1973). Predicting potential school problems. *Perceptual and Motor Skills, 37*, 453–454.

Fuller, G. B., & Friedrich, D. (1974). A diagnostic approach to differentiate brain damaged from non-brain damaged adolescents. *Journal of Clinical Psychology, 30*, 361–363.

Fuller, G. B., & Friedrich, D. (1975). Three diagnostic patterns for children with reading disabilities. *Academic Therapy, 10*, 219–231.

Fuller, G. B., & Friedrich, D. (1976). Differential diagnosis of psychiatric patients with the MPDT. *Journal of Clinical Psychology, 32*, 336.

Fuller, G. B., & Hawkins, W. F. (1969). Differentiation of organic from non-organic retarded children. *American Journal of Mental Deficiency, 74*, 104–110.

Fuller, G. B., & Laird, J. (1963). The Minnesota Percepto-Diagnostic Test [Monograph Supple.]. *Journal of Clinical Psychology, 16*, 1–33.

Fuller, G. B., & Shaw, C. (1963). Visual orientation in reading disability: Diagnostic considerations. *Journal of Child Psychiatry, 2*, 484–494.

Furr, K. D. (1970). Standard scores for the Koppitz

Developmental Scoring System. *Journal of Clinical Psychology, 26,* 78–79.

Getman, G. (1965). The visual–motor complex in the acquisition of learning skills. In J. Hellmuth (Ed.), *Learning disabilities* (Vol. 1, pp. 47–76). Seattle, WA: Special Child.

Goh, D. S., Teslow, C. J., & Fuller, G. B. (1981). The practice of psychological assessment among school psychologists. *Professional Psychology, 12,* 696–706.

Goodman, L., & Hammill, D. (1973). The effectiveness of the Kephart–Getman activities in developing perceptual–motor and cognitive skills. *Focus on Exceptional Children, 9,* 1–9.

Hain, J. D. (1964). The Bender Gestalt Test: A scoring method of identifying brain damage. *Journal of Clinical Psychology, 25,* 268–271.

Hammill, D., Goodman, L., & Wiederholt, J. (1974). Visual–motor processes: Can we train them? *The Reading Teacher, 28,* 467–478.

Haywood, K. M. (1986). *Life span motor development.* Champaign, IL: Human Kinetics.

Henderson, N. B., Butler, B. V., & Goffeney, B. (1969). Effectiveness of the WISC and Bender–Gestalt test in predicting arithmetic and reading achievement for white and non-white children. *Journal of Clinical Psychology, 25,* 268–271.

Holland, J. M., Fuller, G. B., & Barth, C. E. (1982). Performance of brain-damaged and non-brain-damaged institutionalized children on the Minnesota Percepto-Diagnostic Test. *Journal of Clinical Psychology, 38,* 159–163.

Hutt, M. L. (1977). *The Hutt adaptation of the Bender–Gestalt Test.* New York: Grune & Stratton.

Hutt, M. L., & Briskin, G. J. (1960). *The clinical use of the revised Bender Gestalt Test.* New York: Grune & Stratton.

Kamphaus, R. E., & Reynolds, C. R. (1987). *Clinical and research applications of the K-ABC.* Circle Pines, MN: American Guidance Service.

Kaufman, A. S. (1976). A new approach to the interpretation of test scatter on the WISC-R. *Journal of Learning Disabilities, 9,* 160–168.

Kaufman, A. S. (1979). *Intelligent testing with the WISC-R.* New York: Wiley.

Kavale, K. A. (1982). Meta-analysis of the relationship between visual perceptual skills and reading achievement. *Journal of Learning Disabilities, 15,* 42–51.

Keogh, B. K. (1965). The Bender–Gestalt as a predictive and diagnostic test of reading performance. *Journal of Consulting Psychology, 29,* 83–84.

Kephart, N. (1967). Perceptual–motor aspects of learning disabilities. In E. C. Frierson & W. B. Barbe (Eds.), *Educating children with learning disabilities* (pp. 405–413). New York: Appleton-Century-Crofts.

Koppitz, E. M. (1964). *The Bender Gestalt Test with young children.* New York: Grune & Stratton.

Koppitz, E. M. (1975). *The Bender Gestalt Test with young children: Vol. 2. Research and application, 1963–1973.* New York: Grune & Stratton.

Koppitz, E. M., Mardis, V., & Stephens, T. (1961). A note on screening school beginners with the Bender Gestalt Test. *Journal of Educational Psychology, 52,* 80–81.

Koppitz, E. M., Sullivan, J., Blyth, D., & Shelton, J. (1959). Prediction of first grade school achievement with the Bender Gestalt Test and Human Figure Drawings. *Journal of Clinical Psychology, 15,* 432–435.

Lacks, P. (1984). *Bender Gestalt screening for brain dysfunction.* New York: Wiley.

Lehman, J., & Breen, M. (1982). A comparison analysis of the Bender–Gestalt and Beery/Buktenica Tests of Visual–Motor Integration as a function of grade level for regular education students. *Psychology in the Schools, 19,* 52–54.

Lerner, J. (1986). *Learning disabilities.* Boston: Houghton Mifflin.

Lesiak, J. (1984). The Bender Visual Motor Gestalt Test: Implications for the diagnosis and prediction of reading achievement. *Journal of School Psychology, 22,* 391–405.

McCarthy, D. (1972). *The McCarthy Scales of Children's Abilities.* New York: Psychological Corporation.

Neale, M. D. & McKay, M. F. (1985). Scoring the Bender–Gestalt Test using the Koppitz Developmental System: Interrater reliability, item difficulty and scoring implications. *Perceptual and Motor Skills, 60,* 627–636.

Norfleet, M. (1973). The Bender Gestalt as a group screening instrument for first grade potential. *Journal of Learning Disabilities, 6,* 383–388.

Obrzut, J. E., Hansen, R. L., & Heath, C. P. (1982). The effectiveness of visual information processing training with Hispanic children. *Journal of General Psychology, 107,* 165–174.

Obrzut, J. E., Taylor, H. D., & Thweatt, R. C. (1972). Re-examination of Koppitz' Developmental Scoring System. *Perceptual and Motor Skills, 34,* 279–282.

Pascal, G., & Suttell, B. (1951). *The Bender Gestalt Test.* New York: Grune & Stratton.

Pinter, R., & Cunningham, B. V. (1963). *Pinter–Cunningham Primary Test* (rev. ed.). New York: Harcourt, Brace & World.

Reynolds, C. R. (1981). Neuropsychological assessment and the habilitation of learning: Considerations in the search for the aptitude X treatment interaction. *School Psychology Review, 10,* 343–349.

Rosen, C. L. (1985). Review of the Motor-Free Visual Perception Test. In J. V. Mitchell (Ed.), *The ninth mental measurements yearbook* (Vol. 2, pp. 1398–1399). Lincoln: University of Nebraska Press.

Slingerland, B. H. (1974). *Teacher's manual to accompany Slingerland Screening Tests for Identifying Children with Specific Language Disability—Revised Edition* (Form D). Cambridge, MA: Educators.

Slingerland, B. H., & Ansara, A. S. (1974). *Teacher's manual to accompany Slingerland Screening Tests for Identifying Children with Specific Language Disability—Revised Edition* (Forms A, B, and C). Cambridge, MA: Educators.

Slosson, R. L. (1963). *Slosson Intelligence Test.* East Aurora, NY: Slosson Educational.

Spirito, A. (1980). Scores on Bender–Gestalt and Developmental Test of Visual–Motor Integration of learning disabled children. *Perceptual and Motor Skills, 50,* 1214.

Tolor, A., & Brannigan, G. C. (1980). *Research and clinical applications of the Bender–Gestalt Test.* Springfield, IL: Charles C Thomas.

Vance, H. B., Lester, M. L., & Thatcher, R. W. (1983). Interscorer reliability of the Minnesota Percepto-Diagnostic Test—Revised. *Psychology in the Schools, 20*, 420–423.

Wallbrown, J. D., Wallbrown, F. H., & Engin, A. W. (1977). The validity of two clinical tests of visual motor perception. *Journal of Clinical Psychology, 33*, 491–495.

Wechsler, D. (1974). *Manual of the Wechsler Intelligence Scale for Children—Revised.* New York: Psychological Corporation.

Wertheimer, M. (1923). Studies in the theory of Gestalt psychology. *Psychologische Forschung, 4*, 301–350.

Westman, A. S. (1978). Review of Southern California Sensory Integration Test—Revised. In O. K. Buros (Ed.), *The eighth mental measuremnts yearbook* (Vol. 2, pp. 1408–1409). Highland Park, NJ: Gryphon Press.

Wiig, E. H. (1985). Review of the Slingerland Screening Tests for Identifying Children with Specific Language Disability. In J. V. Mitchell (Ed.). *The ninth mental measurements yearbook* (Vol. 2). Lincoln: University of Nebraska Press.

Williams, H. J. (1983). *Perceptual and motor development.* Englewood Cliffs, NJ: Prentice-Hall.

Wright, D., & DeMers, S. T. (1982). Comparison of the relationship between two measures of visual–motor coordination and academic achievement. *Psychology in the Schools, 19*, 473–477.

26

Bias in Assessment of Aptitude

CECIL R. REYNOLDS
Texas A&M University

STEVEN M. KAISER
Utica Public Schools

The issue of bias in testing has been a source of intense and recurring social controversy throughout the history of mental measurement. Discussions pertaining to test bias are frequently accompanied by emotionally laden polemics decrying the use of mental tests with any minority group member, since ethnic minorities have not been exposed to the cultural and environmental circumstances and values of the white middle class. Intertwined within the general issue of bias in tests has been the more specific question of whether intelligence tests should be used for educational purposes. Although scientific and societal discussion pertaining to differences among groups on measures of cognitive or intellectual functioning in no way fully encompasses the broader topic of bias in mental measurement, there is little doubt that the so-called "IQ controversy" has received the lion's share of public scrutiny over the years. It has been the subject of numerous publications in the more popular press (see Gould, 1981, or Jensen, 1980, Ch. 1), and court actions and legislation have addressed the use of IQ tests within schools and industry (e.g., *Diana v. State Board of Education*, 1970; *Griggs v. Duke Power Co.*, 1971; *Hobson v. Hansen*, 1967; *Larry P. v. Riles*, 1979).

The controversy has been fueled by actions taken by organizations such as the Associa-tion of Black Psychologists (ABP). In 1969, ABP adopted a policy statement supporting parents who refused achievement, aptitude, performance, and intellectual testing of their children for purposes related in any way to "labeling," to placement in "special" classes, to "tracking," and/or to the perpetuation of inferior educational opportunities for blacks. However, as it turned out, ABP defined all applications of psychological tests as falling within these boundaries. Positions taken by groups such as the ABP (and by individuals) have served psychology's purposes well by raising professional and societal awareness regarding the use of testing with minority populations. However, the early denuncia-tions of probable bias in mental measure-ments with any groups other than the white middle class often lacked sound empirical backing, and political posturing with rather strong language concerning discrimination, racism, and the "genocide" of minorities (e.g., Jackson, 1975; Williams, 1970, 1974) was common.

This chapter focuses on the empirical evaluation of test bias, with particular emphasis placed upon statistical criteria and methods for investigating possible biases in mental measurements. Brief discussions of the major historical developments leading up to the present subspecialty of bias research in testing, as well as of examiner effects, label-

611

ing, and litigation pertaining to testing between and among populations, are also presented. Contrary to the state of bias research 20 years ago, when the concerns described here reached a state of crisis, a considerable body of research and rather sophisticated techniques to detect bias have been generated within the field. There is little doubt but that empirical investigations and methods will continue to grow in the decades to come.

GENERAL CONSIDERATIONS IN BIAS RESEARCH

A Brief Historical Review

The issue of bias in mental testing has been important to the study of individual differences and to social policy since Binet first offered a series of graduated intellectual tasks for purposes of placing a child and tracking his or her growth in terms of level of cognitive development. The work of Galton has been noted over the years to be the most important precursor to the modern mental testing movement. He is perhaps best known for establishing the first anthropometric laboratory, where, for a small fee, persons could perform sensory and motor tasks and be provided with their relative standing in regard to group data gathered during the course of Galton's research. Galton's views were a strong contributing factor to the *Zeitgeist* of his era concerning individual differences. He felt that human intelligence was built upon elementary sensations because sensations were the gateway to the mind, and that intelligence could be assessed through the measurement of such simple functions. Galton also believed that level of intellectual functioning was largely genetically determined and that it was a highly heritable trait.

By the turn of the century, attempts to validate a link between sensation and intellect had proved discouraging. Independent estimates of intellectual ability (e.g., teachers' ratings, academic standing, occupational achievement, etc.) did not correlate with acuity data (Heidbreder, 1933), and researchers such as Cattell (an American disciple of Galton and the first to coin the term "mental measurement") gradually abandoned attempts to analyze in-

telligence via the senses in favor of tasks that presumably demanded reasoning, problem solving, the acquisition of knowledge— "thinking," if you will—for successful execution. However, despite the general abandonment of his theory, Galton had a profound impact upon the fields of differential psychology and mental measurement. He developed and implemented twin studies, questionnaire studies, and correlational studies in his investigations of human intellect. As Fancher (1979) has noted, "Among his important contributions was the very idea that tests could be employed to measure psychological differences between people. . . . He thus elevated the scientific study of individual differences to the level of a major psychological specialty with important social implications" (p. 254). Galton's heriditarian views were influential as well and were retained long past the demise of his original theories of intellect.

Binet and Simon tackled the problem of developing a reliable measure of intellectual ability near the turn of the century, in response to a social concern and in direct competition with Galtonian wisdom. The French Ministry of Education was interested in formulating a means by which intellectually retarded children could be selected for special educational attention. This historical note seems an odd juxtaposition, considering that one reason why intelligence testing has been more recently condemned is that the practice is thought to relegate children with low scores to inferior, "dead-end" educational programming as opposed to providing a means of selection for treatment. Binet concluded that the measurement of intellectual functioning necessitated the use of tasks that would tap complex mental processes. He found particularly enticing the notion of systematically evaluating an individual's relative ability in the (then-presumed) intellectual faculty of judgment. Binet rejected the premise that lower-order sensory acuity measures could adequately reflect human thought processes, and argued that individual differences in human intellect were more readily apparent in functions such as memory, verbal comprehension, reasoning, and judgment.

The Binet–Simon scales (Binet & Simon, 1905) were quickly translated and embellished throughout the world. The scales had a strong advocate in the United States in Goddard, who translated the scales into English; in 1909, Goddard recommended to the American Association for the Study of the Feeble-Minded that scores from the scales be used to classify the mentally deficient (Pintner, 1923). The apparent accuracy of the Binet–Simon system served to kindle interest in the application of intelligence testing for a wide variety of social purposes within the United States. Inspection of early psychological texts and journals before and after World War I shows that research, social policy, and theory related to mental measurement were ubiquitous. There is also clear evidence of concern surrounding the differential impact of mental testing across groups.

Pintner and Keller (1922) collected voluminous data on national and racial groups and reported a wide variation in median IQ. Further analyses separated those children whose parents did and did not speak English in the home; results of testing with the Binet placed children from non-English-speaking homes an average of 8 points below children whose families spoke English in the home. Nonverbal intellectual testing, however, served to increase the scores of the non-English home environment group. Pintner and Keller concluded that "those children who hear a foreign language in their homes may suffer a serious handicap when tested only by revisions of the Binet Test" (1922, p. 222). Although many regard the issue of test bias as a product of relatively recent social concerns, the educational and psychological literature from this earlier era (e.g. Kohs, 1923; Pintner, 1923; Pressey & Pressey, 1922) readily attests to the fact that scholars were concerned about factors other than innate intelligence affecting (and presumably biasing) mental measurement test performance. Freeman's (1926) text provides a fairly representative example of what psychologists and educators read then, and still read to a certain extent today. The position statement also illustrates the long-standing and rocky relationship between the practical uses of mental measurement and the theoretical exploration of environmental and genetic factors on intellectual development. Freeman summarized:

> The detailed examination of the scientific evidence which is at hand indicated the correctness of the moderate view as contrasted with ethnic extreme. . . . [O]ne may regard intelligence tests as an entirely new and perfect instrument for detecting native capacity. At the other extreme [one] may discount them and regard them as merely somewhat improved instruments for measuring the results of teaching. The consideration of the historical development of tests, in common with an analysis of their results, shows that neither of these views is correct. Intelligence tests have made a marked advance toward the measurement of native capacity, but these scores are still influenced to a considerable degree by the effects of training, and in their interpretation this influence must always be taken into account. (pp. 474–475)

The Nature–Nurture Issue

Bond (1981) observes that there has been a strong tendency by both professionals and the lay public alike to draw conclusions regarding the relative impact of genetic and environmental factors on test performance if mean performance levels among groups are disparate and those tests in use are shown not to be biased in a statistical sense. Bond goes on to point out that the discussion pertaining to race differences in intelligence is a major reason why bias research and intelligence testing have remained such volatile social issues. He asks the reader to consider this statement: "Test results indicate that white students, on the average, achieve higher levels of competence in most academic subjects than black students, on the average" (p. 56). The statement, viewed objectively, merely addresses a presumed result of past academic achievement and does not provide an etiology for the observed difference. However, consider this statement: "Test results indicate that white students as a group possess greater aptitude for academic work than black students" (p. 56). The seemingly minor change in language quickly elevates the statement into the realm of "genetic" or "innate" superiority of one group over another, and understandably triggers a decidedly emotional response.

The investigation of test bias can proceed unabated without attention to the "nature–nurture" question. This is not to say that the relative impact of endowment and experience on human intellectual development is not a viable issue in the scientific arena. It is, but our methodology is inadequate at present to permit convincing conclusions to be drawn. The "nature–nurture" question has been a part of the human quest for self-comprehension since the time humans were able to formulate the question. Jensen (1980) has clearly stated that research on test bias ought not to be confused with polemic discussion pertaining to genetic and environmental contributions to individual differences. He notes that data obtained from all test scores are measures of phenotypic and not genotypic expression. A "phenotype," in scientific usage, is the detectable expression of the interaction of a genotype with the environment. Consequently, investigation of test bias is, by its very nature, investigation of possible bias in the measurement of phenotypes. If bias is not found in a statistical sense within a test, conclusions drawn concerning genetic differences between/among groups using the "nonbiased" measure are simply another set of assertions requiring further investigation. Such a finding only means that we can research genetic and environmental contributions to individual differences without the contamination of nominally induced score aberrations.

Although Jensen (1980) takes the stand that advancement in psychometric knowledge is a vital component to a better understanding of the reasons underlying individual and group differences, he concludes:

> The answers to questions about test bias surely need not await a scientific consensus on the so-called nature–nurture question. A proper assessment of test bias, on the other hand, is an essential step towards a scientific understanding of the observed differences in all the important educational, occupational, and social correlates of test scores. Test scores themselves are merely correlates, predictors, and indicators of other socially important variables, which would not be altered in the least if tests did not exist. The problem of individual differences and group differences would not be made to disappear by abolishing tests. One cannot treat a fever by throwing away the thermometer. (p. xi)

Jensen's oft-cited comments in the *Harvard Educational Review* concerning the possible role of genetics as a causative factor for the consistent disparity reported (see Shuey, 1966) in mean IQs between blacks and whites seems an odd twist in comparison to the passage quoted above. And yet the two

positions are not discordant if one is able to separate systematic *investigation* of bias in tests and measures from *estimation* of the relative impact of constitution and environment upon test scores. It is interesting to note that both environmental proponents and genetic proponents in the nature–nurture issue have defended their positions using essentially the same data. Loehlin, Lindzey, and Spuhler (1975, Ch. 10) conclude that because data seem to favor both camps, resolution of the issue is in no way imminent. Rosenthal (1975) has analyzed the available evidence concerning heredity and behavior, including three commonly applied research strategies: family studies, twin studies, and adoption studies. Although research using these methodologies has reaffirmed the significance of genetic factors in the formation of a variety of human traits (Cancro, 1971; Loehlin et al., 1975; Minton & Schneider, 1980; Rosenthal, 1975; Tyler, 1965), it is now generally agreed that heredity and environment operate *interactively* in determining traits, with the influence of each depending upon the action of the other (Minton & Schneider, 1980).

Tyler (1965) has suggested that the most important information to be gleaned from this domain of research is not the proportional contribution of nature and nurture (i.e., what "percentage" each is responsible for) in the making of traits or abilities, but the amenability of traits or abilities to change and the ways in which change can be effectively carried out. Minton and Schneider (1980) have endorsed Tyler's position, stressing that "genetic" does not automatically imply a low level of modifiability, nor does "environmental" signal that a trait or ability is easily changeable. The authors point out that certain genetically based disorders such as phenylketonuria can be readily prevented by the environmental adjustment of diet, whereas social workers, psychologists, and other social service providers frequently find it impossible to modify deviant behaviors generally assumed to be a direct function of environmental circumstances. Finally, Sternberg (1985)—in response to Jensen's (1985) summary statements concerning the large role played by the factor of general intelligence (or "*g*") in group differences seen with intelligence tests—provides a perspective clearly intended to engender further thought on testing and the nature–nurture issue. Although Sternberg accepts the g data as scientifically viable at present, he adds that research along this line continues to "answer none of the more interesting and timely questions, such as why the score difference holds, what can be done to remedy it, or why the difference matters in the first place" (p. 244).

Mean Score Differences as Test Bias

A popular lay view has been that differences in mean levels of performance on cognitive or ability tasks among groups constitute bias in tests; however, such differences alone clearly are not evidence of test bias. A number of writers in the professional literature have mistakenly taken this position (Alley & Foster, 1978; Chinn, 1979; Hilliard, 1979; Jackson, 1975; Mercer, 1976; Williams, 1974; Wright & Isenstein, 1977). Those who support this definition of test bias correctly state that there is no valid a priori scientific reason to believe that intellectual or other cognitive performance levels should differ across race. It is the inference that tests demonstrating such differences are inherently biased because there can in reality be no differences that is fallacious. Just as there is no a priori basis for deciding that differences exist, there is no a priori basis for deciding that differences do not exist. From the standpoint of the objective methods of science, a priori or premature acceptance of either hypothesis ("differences exist" vs. "differences do not exist") is untenable. As stated by Thorndike (1971), "The presence (or absence) of differences in mean score between groups, or of differences in variability, tells us nothing directly about fairness" (p. 64). Likewise, Jensen (1976) notes, "Score differences per se, whether between individuals, social classes, or racial groups, obviously cannot be a criterion of bias" (p. 341). Some adherents to the "mean score differences as bias" viewpoint also require that the distribution of test scores in each population or subgroup be identical before one can assume that the test is fair: "Regardless of the purpose of a test or its validity for that purpose, a test should result in distributions that are statistically equivalent across the groups tested in order for it to be considered nondiscriminatory for those groups" (Alley & Foster, 1978, p. 2).

Portraying a test as biased regardless of its purpose or validity is psychometrically naive. Mean score differences and unequivalent distributions have been the most uniformly rejected of all criteria examined by sophisticated psychometricians involved in investigating the problems of bias in assessment. Ethnic group differences in mental test scores are among the best-documented phenomena in psychology, and they have persisted over time at relatively constant levels (Reynolds & Gutkin, 1980a).

Jensen (1980) has discussed the "mean score differences as bias" position in terms of the egalitarian fallacy. The egalitarian fallacy contends that all human populations are in fact identical on all mental traits or abilities. Any differences with regard to any aspect of the distribution of mental test scores indicates that something is wrong with the test itself. Such an assumption is totally scientifically unwarranted. There are simply too many examples of specific abilities and even sensory capacities that have been shown to differ unmistakably across human populations. The result of the egalitarian assumption, then, is to remove the investigation of population differences in ability from the realm of scientific inquiry. Logically followed, this fallacy leads to other untenable conclusions as well. Torrance (1980), an adherent of the cultural bias hypothesis, pointed out that disadvantaged black children occasionally earn higher scores on creativity tests—and therefore, have more creative ability—than many white children because their environment has forced them to learn to "make do" with less and with simpler objects. The egalitarian assumption would hold that this is not true, but rather that the content of the test is biased against white or high-socioeconomic-status (high-SES) children.

The attachment of minorities to the "mean score differences as bias" definition is probably related to the nature–nurture controversy at some level. Certainly data reflecting racial differences on various aptitude measures have been interpreted to indicate support for a hypothesis of genetic differences in intelligence and to imply that one race is superior to another. However, as discussed previously, the so-called nature–nurture issue is not an inextricable component of bias investigation. Assertions as to the relative impact of genetic factors on group ability levels step into a new arena of scientific inquiry, with differing bodies of knowledge and methods of research. Suffice it to say that in the arena of bias investigation, mean differences on aptitude or achievement measures among selected groups are not evidence per se that the measures are biased.

Culture-Free Tests, Culture Loading, and Culture Bias

A third area of bias investigation that has been confusing in both the professional (e.g., Alley & Foster, 1978; Chinn, 1979) and the lay literature has been the interpretation of culture loading and culture bias. A test can be culture-loaded without being culturally biased. "Culture loading" refers to the degree of cultural specificity present in the test or individual items of the test. Certainly, the greater the cultural specificity of a test item, the greater the likelihood of the item's being biased when it is used with individuals from other cultures. The test item "Who was the first president of the United States?" is a culture-loaded item. However, the item is general enough to be considered useful with children in the United States. The cultural specificity of the item is too great, however, to allow the item to be used on an aptitude measure of 10-year-old children from other countries. Virtually all tests in current use are bound in some way by their cultural specificity. Culture loading must be viewed on a continuum from general (defining the culture in a broad, liberal sense) to specific (defining the culture in narrow, highly distinctive terms).

A variety of attempts have been made to develop a "culture-free" (sometimes referred to as "culture-fair") intelligence test (Cattell, 1979). However, the reliablity and validity of these tests are uniformly inadequate from a psychometric perspective (Anastasi, 1986; Ebel, 1979). The difficulty in developing a culture-free measure of intelligence lies in the test's being irrelevant to intellectual behavior within the culture under study. Intelligent behavior is defined within human society in large part on the basis of behavior judged to be of value to the survival and improvement of the culture and the individuals within the culture. A test that is "culture-blind," then, cannot be expected to predict intelligent behavior within a variety of cultural settings. Once a test has been developed within a culture (a culture-loaded test), its generalizability to other cultures or subcultures within the dominant societal framework becomes a matter for empirical investigation.

Jensen (1980) admonishes that when one is investigating the psychometric properties of culture-loaded tests across differing societies or cultures, one cannot assume that simple inspection of the content will determine which tests or items are biased against those cultures or societies not represented in the tests or item content. Tests or items that exhibit characteristics of being culturally loaded cannot be determined to be biased with any degree of certainty unless objective statistical inspection is completed. Jensen refers to the mistaken notion that anyone can judge tests and/or items as being "culturally unfair" on superficial inspection as the "culture-bound fallacy."

The Question of Labeling Effects

The relative impact of placing a label on a child's behavior or developmental status has also been a hotly discussed issue within the field of psychometrics in general, and bias investigation in particular. The issue has undoubtedly been a by-product of the practice of using intellectual measures for the determination of mental retardation. Although the question of labeling effects is a viable and important one, it requires consideration in bias research only in much the same way as does the ongoing debate surrounding the nature–nurture question. However, there are some important considerations regarding bias in referral for services, diagnosis, and labeling, which no interested student of the diagnostic process in psychology can afford to ignore.

Rosenthal is the researcher most closely associated with the influence of labeling upon teachers' and parents' perceptions of a child's ability and potential. Even though his early studies had many methodological and statistical difficulties, labeling effects have been shown in some subsequent experimental studies (e.g., Critchley, 1979; Foster & Ysseldyke, 1976; Jacobs, 1978), but not in others (e.g., MacMillan, Jones, & Aloia,

1974; McCoy, 1976). However, these studies have generally been of a short-term nature, and have usually been conducted under quite artificial circumstances. Typically, participants are asked to rate the behavior or degree of pathology of a child seen on videotape. Categorical labels for the child are systematically varied while the observed behaviors remain constant. The demand characteristics of such a design are substantial. Long-term effects of labeling and special education placement in real-life situations have been examined less vigorously. Comparisons of the effects of formal diagnostic labels with the informal, often cursory, personal labeling process that occurs between teachers and children over the course of a school year, and that is subsequently passed on to the next grade via the teachers' lounge (Dworkin & Dworkin, 1979), need to be made. The strict behaviorist position (Ross, 1974, 1976) also contends that formal diagnostic procedures are unnecessary and potentially harmful because of labeling effects. However, whether or not the application of formal labels has detrimental effects on children remains an open question now, much as it did at the conclusion of a monumental effort to address these important questions well over a decade ago (Hobbs, 1975).

Even without the application of formal, codified labels by psychologists or psychiatrists, the mental labeling, classification, and appraisal of individuals by people with whom they come into contact are common, constant occurrences (Reynolds, 1979a). Auerbach (1971) found that adults often interpret early learning difficulties as primarily emotional disturbances, unrelated to learning problems. According to Bower (1974), children who start the first grade below the mean age of their classmates and are below average in the development of school readiness skills or have behavior problems are more likely to be regarded as emotionally disturbed by school staff and are more likely to be referred to residential placement than their peers. The American Psychological Association (1970) acknowledges that such constant appraisal of individuals occurs at the informal level, and in an official position statement takes the stance that specialized, standardized psychological techniques have been developed to supersede our informal,

often casual approach to the appraisal of others. The specialized psychological techniques available to the trained examiner add validity and utility to the results of such appraisals. The quantification of behavior permits systematic comparisons of individuals' characteristics with those of a selected reference or norm group. It is not unreasonable to anticipate that the informal labeling of children so often indulged in by teachers and parents is substantially more harmful than accurate psychoeducational diagnostics intended to accrue beneficial activity toward the child. Should noncategorical funding for services to exceptional children become a reality (Gutkin & Tieger, 1979), or should the use of normative assessment ultimately be banned, the informal labeling process will continue and in all likelihood will exacerbate children's problems.

From the standpoint of *test* bias issues, the question of labeling children or not labeling children is moot. Test bias is concerned with the accuracy of such labels across some nominal grouping system (typically, race, sex, and SES have been the variables of interest). It is a question of whether race, sex, or any other demographic variable of interest influences the diagnostic process or the placement of a child in special programs, independent of the child's cognitive, emotional, and behavioral status. Several well-designed studies have investigated the influences of race and SES on the class placement recommendations of school psychologists (i.e., bias in test interpretation). One of the studies investigated teacher bias as well.

Frame (1979) investigated the accuracy of school psychologists' diagnoses and consistency of treatment plans, with regard to bias effects associated specifically with race and SES. In Frame's study, 24 school psychologists from a number of school districts diagnostically rated and provided treatment plans for hypothetical cases in which all information except race, SES, and the achievement level of the child's school was held constant. No differences in the accuracy of diagnosis (as defined by interrater reliability) occurred as a function of race or SES. Differences did occur with regard to treatment recommendations, however. With all other data held constant, lower-SES black children were less likely to be recommended for special education placement than their white counterparts or higher-SES black children. A more general trend was for higher-SES children to be recommended for special class placement more often than children of lower SES.

In a similar vein, Matuszek and Oakland (1979) asked whether SES and race influenced teacher or psychologist placement recommendations, independent of other characteristics such as adaptive behavior, IQ, and classroom achievement levels. This study included 76 teachers, 53 psychologists, and 106 child studies. Matuszek and Oakland concluded that "The data from this study clearly indicate that they [psychologists] did not make different recommendations on the basis of race" (1979). Consistent with the results of Frame (1979), psychologists were more likely to recommend special class placement for high-SES status children than for low-SES children when other variables were held constant. Teachers showed no bias in regard to special education placement recommendations on the basis of race or SES. Upon investigating special education placement recommendations as a function of minority group status (black, Native American, or Oriental), Tomlinson, Acker, Canter, and Lindborg (1977) reported that psychologists recommended special education resource services more frequently for minority than for white children. Placement in a special education class, however, was recommended more frequently for white than minority children. A rather extensive study of placement in classes for the educable mentally retarded (EMR) in California also failed to find any racist intent in the placement of minority children in special classes (Meyers, MacMillan, & Yoshida, 1978). In fact, the tendency was *not* to place black children in special education classes, even though they might be failing in the regular classroom. An even earlier study by Mercer (1971), one of the major critics of IQ testing with minorities, reached the same conclusion.

The general tendency not to label black children also extends to community mental health settings. Lewis, Balla, and Shanok (1979) reported that when black adolescents were seen in mental health settings, behaviors symptomatic of schizophrenia, paranoia, and a variety of psychoneurotic disorders were frequently dismissed as only "cultural aberrations" appropriate to coping with the frustrations created by the antagonistic white culture. Lewis et al. further noted that white adolescents exhibiting similar behaviors were given psychiatric diagnoses and referred for therapy and/or residential placement. Lewis et al. contended that this failure to diagnose mental illness in the black population acts as bias in the denial of appropriate services. A tendency for psychologists to regard depressed performance on cognitive tasks by blacks and low-SES groups as a "cultural aberration" has also been shown. An early empirical study by Nalven, Hofmann, and Bierbryer (1969) demonstrated that psychologists generally rated the "true intelligence" of black and low-SES children higher than that of white and middle-class children with the same Wechsler Intelligence Scale for Children (WISC) IQ. This tendency to "overrate" the intellectual potential of black and low-SES children probably accounts, at least in part, for psychologists' reluctance to recommend special education placement for these children; it could also be viewed as a discriminatory denial of services, depending on whether the provision of services is considered beneficial or harmful to the individual.

These studies clearly indicate that the demographic variables of race and SES do not, independent of other pupil characteristics, influence or bias psychologists' diagnostic or placement behavior in a manner that would cause blacks or lower-SES children to be labeled inaccurately or placed inappropriately or in disproportionate numbers in special education programs. The empirical evidence, rather, argues in the opposite direction: Black and low-SES children are *less* likely to be recommended for special education class placement than their white or high-SES peers with similar cognitive, behavioral, and emotional characteristics. The data simply do not support Williams's (1970) charge that black children are placed in special education programs on the basis of race or test bias against blacks. When referrals for placement in gifted programs are considered separately from "referrals" generally, the disproportionate representation of minorities in special education programs can be accounted for by the disproportionately higher incidence of referral among minority student populations (Tomlinson et al., 1977; Waits & Richmond, 1978).

Early Bias Research

Jensen (1980) reports that the first attempts to investigate bias in mental tests were restricted to the exploration of certain internal characteristics of items within any given measure. More specifically, emphasis was placed on the relative impact of SES differences on item performance. Earlier thinking in the mental test movement followed the logic that if mental tests did in fact measure some general trait presumed to be "within" the individual, then items ought not to discriminate strongly between or among social classes. Items most discriminating in this regard were considered suspect and, in essence, biased. Jensen further notes that this genre of research (the investigation of group × item interactions, in modern statistical parlance) proved faulty and consequently inconclusive, because the influence of chronological age on the type of task under inspection requires control and because content inspection of items reveals little information about an item's underlying structure. Concerning the latter, there is little or no scientific rationale behind the contention that highly discriminatory items are, by default, biased if it can be demonstrated that those items are tapping different aspects of intellectual ability (e.g., if those items load more highly on g) than items presumably less biased as determined by minimal differences across levels of SES. In effect, it can be argued that those high-discrimination items under inspection are adequately measuring a unique aspect of intellectual functioning and not differing levels of SES per se, if the high-discrimination items can be shown to exhibit unique psychometric properties.

Two doctoral dissertations completed at midcentury served to propel bias research into a new arena of sophistication. Both dissertations deserve special notice because they attempted to address directly the issue of cultural fairness of commonly used tests of the period; were ambitious in their scope; and served to demonstrate that an awkward, seemingly unruly research topic was amenable to systematic investigation.

Eells (see Eells, Davis, Havighurst, Herrick, & Typer, 1951) tested the hypothesis that the SES of a child's environment was, on the average, related to mean IQ differences, because children were exposed to qualitatively different experiences in such factors as vocabulary spoken at home and discussion of topics that would seem to expand a youngster's general knowledge and reasoning skills. Eells postulated that the intellectual demands of various mental tests were more closely aligned to the environment of high-SES than to that of low-SES groups, and consequently reflected in mean score differences the extent to which any given youngster experienced a more "stimulating" environment. Eells proceeded with an ambitious project, including thousands of children, a lengthy battery of commonly used tests of the time, and demographic data related to family SES. High-, middle-, and low-SES groups were created from family economic/social data; for the low-SES group, further divisions were made along ethnic lines. Children were either 9, 10, 13, or 14 years of age.

Briefly, Eells translated the percentage of children passing each item (there were 658 items in all) with respect to age and economic groupings into a normalized index, and thus transformed item difficulty level into an interval scale. It should be noted here that the percentage of children passing any given item cannot realistically be considered as a product of a flat distribution; consequently, comparisons based on these percentages are misleading. For example, although intervals may appear to be equal (say, .50 and .55, and .90 and .95—both representing a .05 percentage difference), they fail to take into account the distribution of item performance on mental tasks, generally assumed to be normal because of the normal distribution within the population of intellectual ability.

Jensen (1980) notes that Eells's data revealed sizable variation in terms of item difficulties across low- and high-SES groups and across the age ranges tested. Although virtually all items investigated reflected superiority of the high-SES group over the low-SES group, magnitudes fluctuated, as seen by discordant percentages of items that reached statistically significant levels among the differing age groupings. Eells also found that ethnic groupings did not appreciably influence test item performance, as groups (Eells divided subjects into an "ethnic" group and an "old American" group) fared about as well on most items. Furthermore, the largest status differences were found to be greater on easier test items, defined as those items with less verbal and less general informational content. This finding ran contrary to Eells's anticipated results, although he did not find that status differences were, in general, greater with items that demanded stronger verbal skills and information presumably more accessible to high-SES youngsters of the time. Finally, Eells examined patterns in the choice of multiple-choice distractors between high-SES and low-SES groups. He found that high-SES students tended to select with greater frequency more plausible distractors—ones closer to the correct answers—than did low-SES students. Low-SES students appeared to guess more, as their overall patterns across items were random in comparison.

Although Eells conceded that his data were less than consistent, he nonetheless became the first to advocate clearly and strongly the development and use of culture-fair tests. His research effort undoubtedly served to accelerate interest in the empirical aspects of bias investigation, as well as to heighten sensitivity to those aspects of test items that might have a differential impact between/among groups. Yet his main desire—to design culture-fair tests that would eliminate bias—failed in rather short order. A second dissertation from this period yielded more consistent data with regard to the issue of culture fairness and the culture-bound fallacy, and also remains as a hallmark in bias research.

McGurk (1951) addressed the question of whether items from commonly used intelligence tests could be determined, through inspection by qualified persons, to be culturally biased. He enlisted 78 judges with presumed sensitivity (e.g., professors of psychology and sociology, teachers, counselors, etc.) to the cultural content within tasks, and asked each to rate selected items as being low, neutral, or high in cultural content. McGurk's aim was to find those items from intellectual tests that the judges consistently rated as being most and least culturally loaded. Definition was left up to the individual opinion, and ultimately high or low cultural content was decided upon when a significant proportion of the judges made the same classification of individual items. What "fell out" from the first stage of the project were 103 items felt to be highly culturally loaded and 81 items considered generally culture-free by the experts.

McGurk made comparisons of performances by black and by white high school seniors on the 184 items. He then selected 37 pairs of items from these data, matched on the basis of difficulty levels (determined by percentage passing). Each pair included a least and a most culturally loaded item, as determined by the judges, that black and white students had subsequently passed in similar numbers. The 37 pairs were then administered to a large sample of white students and a smaller sample of blacks in both Pennsylvania and New Jersey. Because McGurk had such a surplus of white students, he was able to create black–white pairs who had similar curriculum exposure and who had attended the same school district, including present placement at the time of testing. Pairings were also made to match social and economic factors.

McGurk's carefully planned study yielded some interesting results. First, mean differences on items characterized as least and most culturally loaded ran contrary to what one might expect if one assumed that whites would do better on more culturally bound tasks. In fact, black–white mean differences on the items judged least culturally loaded were twice as great as differences on the items judged most culturally loaded. McGurk determined that blacks performed, relatively speaking, better on those items classified as most culturally loaded, even when item difficulty was held constant. Second, correlations between item difficulties showed similar magnitude between the least and most loaded questions, providing strong evidence that blacks and whites showed similar patterns on the relative difficulties of items. Third, further analysis of selected low-SES and high-SES groups revealed that whites showed greater differences between low- and high-SES groups on the most culturally loaded items. However, blacks evidenced a pattern opposite to the white group: Black differences between the low- and high-SES students were found to be greater within the least culturally loaded items and weaker with those items judged high in culture content.

Where Can Research Go?

Harrington (1975, 1984) has taken a quite different, experimentally oriented approach to the issue of test bias. Whereas Eells's and McGurk's work shows where bias investigation has come from, Harrington perhaps shows the myriad of avenues of investigation for the future. In earlier research, Harrington (1968a, 1968b) suggested that the existence of genetic × environmental interactions in intelligence could affect item selection in the construction of intelligence tests, in a manner resulting in bias (mean differences in total test scores) against minorities. Harrington has thus raised the issue of representation in the test development sample, but from a slightly different perspective than that of other researchers. Many have argued that the small numbers of minority children in standardization samples are unable to exert any significant impact on the item analysis data, and that the content of the test subsequently becomes biased against groups with less than majority representation. Harrington's (1975, 1976) approach to researching this question is both innovative and interesting. Harrington first began by creating experimental populations of rats with varying proportions of "minority" composition (group membership was defined on a genetic basis). For his experimental populations, Harrington used six species of rats from genetically homogeneous groups. Harrington then set out to develop six intelligence tests, using standard psychometric procedures. Six test development populations were developed with varying degrees of minority group representation. Items for use in test development for each population were the same and consisted of a large number of performance measures on black and/or white Hebb–Williams-type mazes (Hebb–Williams mazes are accepted standard tasks for the measurement of rat intelligence).

After the administration of all items to each of the six populations, a test was constructed separately for each population. Following traditional psychometric practice, internal-consistency analyses were undertaken, and items showing the greatest item–total correlations within each population were retained for the "IQ test" for that population. A total of 50 items were retained within each of the six populations. Harrington then hypothesized that if minority group representation in the population did not affect item selection, the six measures would be essentially equivalent forms (i.e., group performance would be independent of the test form employed). To test this hypothesis, Harrington randomly sampled each of the six test development populations and administered all six of the newly developed tests to the new grouping of subjects.

There were significant positive correlations between the group mean on any individual test and the degree of group representation in the population used to develop the test. For example, for Test A, Group A had the greatest representation in the test development sample and the highest mean score on the instrument subsequently developed; for Test B, Group c had the greatest proportionate representation and the highest score on that instrument. Harrington (1984) concluded that the greater the proportional representation of a homogeneous group in the test base population [the test development sample] the higher the mean score of the group on the test derived on that population.

From some further analyses of this data set, Harrington concluded that it is not possible for tests developed and normed on a white majority to have equivalent predictive validity with blacks or any other minority group. Harrington also contends that the generalization of his results with animals to humans is direct and not analogical, since his experiments are a direct empirical test of common psychometric assumptions and practice. Harrington's comments on predictive validity are particularly crucial, since, as will be seen, most definitions of test bias rely heavily on the differential prediction of some specified criterion (Anastasi, 1986; Bartlett & O'Leary, 1969; Cleary, 1968; Cleary, Humphreys, Kendricks, & Wesman, 1975; Cronbach, 1970; Darlington, 1971; Einhorn & Bass, 1971; Hunter & Schmidt, 1976; Hunter, Schmidt, & Hunter, 1979; Kallingal, 1971; Kennedy, 1978; Linn & Werts, 1971; Potthoff, 1966; Reynolds, 1978, 1980b, 1980c; Reynolds, Bossard, & Gutkin, 1980; Reynolds & Gutkin, 1980b).

Although Harrington's (1975, 1976) results

are impressive and seem to call into question certain of the basic psychometric assumptions underlying test construction (particularly as they apply to the development of intelligence tests), his generalizations fail on three major points. First, as will be seen later in this chapter, intelligence and other aptitude tests have repeatedly been shown to have equivalent predictive validity across racial groupings in a variety of circumstances with a fairly diverse set of criterion measures.

Second, well-documented findings that Japanese-Americans, Chinese-Americans, and Jewish-Americans typically score as well as or better than whites on traditional intelligence tests and tests of some specific aptitudes (Gross, 1967; Marjoribanks, 1972; Tyler, 1965; Willerman, 1979) are entirely contradictory to Harrington's (1975, 1976) results, given these groups' proportionately small representation in the test development population of such instruments. Neither can Harrington's theory explain why African infants, with zero representation in the standardization samples of such instruments as the Bayley Scales of Infant Development (Bayley, 1969), consistently score at higher levels than do American infants (Gerber & Dean, 1957; Leiderman, Babu, Kagia, Kraemer, & Leiderman, 1973; Warren, 1972). In addition, Harrington's theory cannot explain why Canadian children of French descent and American children earn approximately equivalent scores on the Wechsler Intelligence Scale for Children—Revised (WISC-R) Information subtest (Beauchamp, Samuels, & Griffore, 1979), or why native Eskimos and white Canadian children earn equivalent scores on Raven's Progressive Matrices (MacArthur, 1968). Again, such findings are in direct contradiction to predictions drawn from Harrington's results.

Third, Harrington's theory of minority–majority group score differences cannot account for different *patterns* of cognitive performance between minority groups (Bogen, DeZure, Tenhouten, & Marsh, 1972; Dean, 1979a; Dershowitz & Frankel, 1975; Reynolds, McBride, & Gibson, 1979; Vance, Hankins, & McGee, 1979; Willerman, 1979). Different patterns of performance under Harrington's model imply differential bias in item selection, depending on the type of test involved. The degree of differential bias would also have to remain

relatively constant across a number of different test batteries and test development samples with varying degrees of minority representation. This is at present an untenable assumption. Furthermore, there is evidence that SES is most strongly related to *level* of performance and race to *pattern* of performance (Jensen & Reynolds, 1982; Willerman, 1979). How this type of differential effect of test scores by minority category could occur under the Harrington model is not clear.

Hickman and Reynolds (1986) attempted to replicate Harrington's work, using large samples of black and white children taken from a stratified random sampling of children throughout the United States. Using item data collected during the national standardization of the Kaufman Assessment Battery for Children, (K-ABC), the investigators selected items for three intelligence scales separately under two conditions: A set of "black" tests was created using only responses of the black children, and a set of "white" tests was created using only the responses of the white children. The item data used to create the "black" IQ tests were taken from a test development sample where the proportionate representation of blacks was 100% and whites was 0%. For the "white" IQ test, the test development sample used to select items was 100% white. This set of circumstances created the most extreme of conditions conducive to finding the Harrington effect. However, the pattern of race differences on the tests so created was contrary to Harrington's predictions: The pattern was totally unaffected by use of the Harrington procedure to select items for each of the tests. Whether items were selected from an analysis of the all-black sample or the all-white sample, the resulting pattern of mean differences was the same as when population proportionate sampling was used —the method Harrington contends is responsible for biasing item selection against minorities.

The Harrington effect has not been demonstrated with human subjects, despite attempts to do so under rather favorable conditions. Why it does not is uncertain; further research seems necessary to clarify this effect so amply demonstrated with Harrington's animal studies, yet failing to materialize with humans.

AREAS OF GENERAL CONCERN

Many potentially legitimate objections to the use of educational and psychological tests with minorities have been raised by black and other minority psychologists. Too frequently, the objections of these groups are viewed as facts without a review of any empirical evidence (e.g., Council for Exceptional Children, 1978; Hilliard, 1979). The problems most often cited in the use of tests with minorities typically fall into the following categories:

1. *Inappropriate content*. Black or other minority children have not been exposed to the material involved in the test questions of other stimulus materials. The tests are felt to be geared primarily toward white, middle-class homes and values.

2. *Inappropriate standardization samples*. Ethnic minorities are underrepresented in the collection of normative reference group data. Williams (cited in Wright & Isenstein, 1977) criticized the WISC-R (Wechsler, 1974) standardization sample for including blacks only in proportion to the U.S. total population. Out of 2,200 children in the WISC-R standardization sample, 330 were members of minority groups. Williams contends that such small actual representation has no impact on the test. In earlier years, it was not unusual for standardization samples to be all white (e.g., the original WISC; Wechsler, 1949).

3. *Examiner and language bias*. Since most psychologists are white and primarily speak only standard English, it is thought that they intimidate black and other ethnic minorities. They are also unable to communicate accurately with minority children. Lower test scores for minorities, then, are said to reflect only this intimidation and difficulty in the communication process, not lower ability levels.

4. *Inequitable social consequences*. It is argued that as a result of bias in educational and psychological tests, minority group members, who are already at a disadvantage in the educational and vocational markets because of past discrimination, are disproportionately relegated to dead-end educational tracks and thought to be unable to learn. Labeling effects also fall under this category.

5. *Measurement of different constructs*. Related to point 1 above, this position asserts that the tests are measuring significantly different attributes when used with minority children than when used with children from the white middle-class culture. Mercer (1979), for example, has contended that when IQ tests are used with minorities, they are measuring only the degree of "Anglocentrism" (adherence to white middle-class values) of the home.

6. *Differential predictive validity*. Although tests may accurately predict a variety of outcomes for white middle-class children, it is argued that they fail to predict any relevant criteria at an acceptable level for minority group members. Corollaries to this objection are a number of competing positions regarding the selection of an appropriate common criterion against which to validate tests across cultural groupings. Many black psychologists consider scholastic or academic attainment levels to be biased as criteria.

THE PROBLEM OF DEFINITION

The definition of test bias has produced considerable, and as yet unresolved, debate among measurement and assessment experts (Angoff, 1976; Bass, 1976; Bernal, 1975; Cleary et al., 1975; Cronbach, 1976; Darlington, 1971, 1976, 1978; Einhorn & Bass, 1971; Flaugher, 1978; Gordon, 1984; Gross & Su, 1975; Humphreys, 1973; Hunter & Schmidt, 1976, 1978; Linn, 1976; McNemar, 1975; Novick & Petersen, 1976; Petersen & Novick, 1976; Reschly, 1980; Reynolds, 1978; Reynolds & Brown, 1984; Sawyer, Cole, & Cole, 1976; Schmidt & Hunter, 1974; Thorndike, 1971). Although the resulting debate has generated a number of selection models with which to examine bias, selection models focus on the decision-making system and not on the test itself. The various selection models are discussed at some length in Hunter and Schmidt (1974), Hunter, Schmidt, and Rauschenberger (1984), Jensen (1980), Petersen and Novick (1976), and Ramsay (1979). The choice of a decision-making system (especially a system for educational decision making) must ultimately be a societal one; as such, it will depend to a large extent on the value system and goals of the society. Thus, before a model for test use in selection can be chosen, it must be decided whether the ultimate goal is equality of opportunity, equality of outcome, or representative equality (these concepts are discussed in more detail in Nichols, 1978).

"Equality of opportunity" is a competitive model wherein selection is based on ability. As more eloquently stated by Lewontin (1970), under equality of opportunity "true merit . . . will be the criterion of men's earthly reward" (p. 92). "Equality of outcome" is a selection model based on ability deficits. Compensatory and remedial education programs are typically constructed on the basis of the equality-of-outcome model. Children of low ability or children believed to be at high risk for academic failure are selected for remedial, compensatory, or other special educational programs. In a strictly predictive sense, tests are used in a similar manner under both of these models. However, under equality or opportunity, selection is based on the prediction of a high level of criterion performance; under equality of outcome, selection is determined by the prediction of "failure" or a preselected low level of criterion performance. Interestingly, it is the failure of compensatory and remedial education programs to bring the disadvantaged learner to "average" levels of performance that has resulted in the charges of test bias now in vogue.

The model of "representative equality" also relies on selection, but selection that is proportionate to numerical representation of subgroups in the population under consideration. Representative equality is typically thought to be independent of the level of ability within each group; however, models can be constructed that select from each subgroup the desired proportion of individuals (1) according to relative ability level of the group, (2) independent of group ability, or (3) according to some decision rule between these two positions. Even under the conditions of representative equality, it is imperative to employ a selection device (test) that will rank-order individuals within groups in a reliable and valid manner. The best way to insure fair selection under any of these models is to employ tests that are equally reliable and equally valid for all groups concerned. The tests employed should also be

the most reliable and most valid for all groups under consideration. The question of test bias per se then becomes a question of test validity. Test use (i.e., fairness) may be defined as biased or nonbiased only by the societal value system; at present, this value system is leaning strongly toward some variant of the representative-equality selection model. As noted above, all models are facilitated by the use of a nonbiased test. That is, the use of a test with equivalent cross-group validities makes for the most parsimonious selection model, greatly simplifying the creation and application of the selection model that has been chosen.

This leads to the essential definitional component of test bias. "Test bias" refers in a global sense to *systematic* error in the estimation of some "true" value for a group of individuals. The key word here is "systematic"; all measures contain error, but this error is assumed to be random unless shown to be otherwise. Bias investigation is a statistical inquiry that does not concern itself with culture loading, labeling effects, or test use/test fairness. Concerning the last of these, Jensen (1980) comments,

> [U]nbiased tests can be used unfairly and biased tests can be used fairly. Therefore, the concepts of bias and unfairness should be kept distinct. . . . [A] number of different, and often mutually contradictory, criteria for fairness have been proposed, and no amount of statistical or psychometric reasoning per se can possibly settle any arguments as to which is best. (pp. 375–376)

There are three types of validity as traditionally conceived: content, construct, and predictive (or criterion-related). Test bias may exist under any or all of these categories of validity. Though no category of validity is completely independent of any other category, each is discussed separately here for the purpose of clarity and convenience. (All true evidence of validity is as likely as not to be construct validity, and the other, more detailed divisions are for convenience of discussion.) Frequently encountered in bias research are the terms "single-group validity" and "differential validity." "Single-group validity" refers to the phenomenon of a test's being valid for one group but not another. "Differential validity" refers to a condition where a test is valid for all groups concerned, but the degree of validity varies as a function of group membership. Although these terms have been most often applied to predictive or criterion-related validity (validity coefficients are then examined for significance and compared across groups), the concepts of single-group and differential validity are equally applicable to content and construct validity.

RESEARCH STRATEGIES AND RESULTS

The methodologies available for research into bias in mental tests have grown rapidly in number and sophistication over the last two decades. Extensive reviews of the questions to be addressed in such research and their corresponding methodologies are available in Jensen (1980), Reynolds (1982), and Reynolds and Brown (1984). The most popular methods are reviewed below, along with a summary of findings from each area of inquiry. The sections are organized primarily by methodology within each content area of research (i.e., research into content, construct, and predictive validity).

Bias in Content Validity

Bias in the item content of intelligence tests is one of the favorite topics of those who decry the use of standardized tests with minorities (e.g., Hilliard, 1979; Jackson, 1975; Williams, 1972; Wright & Isenstein, 1977). As previously noted, the earliest work in bias centered around content. Typically, critics review the items of a test and single out specific items as being biased because (1) the items ask for information that minority or disadvantaged children have not had equal opportunity to learn; and/or (2) the scoring of the items is improper, since the test author has arbitrarily decided on the only correct answer and minority children are inappropriately penalized for giving answers that would be correct in their own culture but not that of the test maker; and/or (3) the wording of the questions is unfamiliar, and a minority child who may "know" the correct answer may not be able to respond because he or she does not understand the question. Each of these three criticisms, when accurate, has the same basic empirical result: The item becomes relatively more difficult for

minority group members than for the majority population. This leads directly to a definition of content bias for aptitude tests that allows empirical assessment of the phenomenon.

An item or subscale of a test is considered to be biased in content when it is demonstrated to be relatively more difficult for members of one group than for members of another in a situation where the general ability level of the groups being compared is held constant and no reasonable theoretical rationale exists to explain group differences on the item (or subscale) in question.

With regard to achievement tests, the issue of content bias is considerably more complex. Exposure to instruction, general ability level of the group, and the accuracy and specificity of the sampling of the domain of items are all important variables in determining whether the content of an achievement test is biased (see Schmidt, 1983). Research into item (or content) bias with achievement tests has typically, and perhaps mistakenly, relied on methodology appropriate for determining item bias in aptitude tests. Nevertheless, research examining both types of instruments for content bias has yielded quite comparable results.

One method of locating "suspicious" test items requires that item difficulties be determined separately for each group under consideration. If any individual item or series of items appears to be exceptionally difficult for the members of any group, relative to other items on the test, the item is considered potentially biased and removed from the test. A more exacting and widespread approach to identifying biased items involves analysis of variance (ANOVA) and several closely related procedures wherein the group × item interaction term is of interest (e.g., Angoff & Ford, 1973; Cardall & Coffman, 1964; Cleary & Hilton, 1968; Plake & Hoover, 1979; Potthoff, 1966; Stanley, 1969).

The definition of content bias set forth above actually requires that the differences between groups be the same for every item on the test. Thus, in the ANOVA procedure, the group × item interaction should not yield a significant result. Whenever the differences in items are not uniform (a significant group × item interaction does exist), one may contend that biased items exist. Earlier in this area of research, it was hoped that the empirical analysis of tests at the item level would result in the identification of a category of items having similar content as biased, and that such items could then be avoided in future test development (Flaugher, 1978). Very little similarity among items determined to be biased has been found. No one has been able to identify those characteristics of an item that cause the item to be biased. It does seem that poorly written, sloppy, and ambiguous items tend to be identified as biased with greater frequency than those items typically encountered in a well-constructed standardized instrument. The variable at issue then may be the item reliability. Item reliabilities are typically not large, and poorly written or ambiguous test items can easily have reliabilities approaching zero. Decreases in reliability are known to increase the probability of the occurrence of bias (Linn & Werts, 1971). Informal inventories and locally derived tests are much more likely to be biased than professionally written standardized tests that have been scrutinized for bias in the items and whose item characteristics are known.

Once items have been identified as biased under the procedures described above, attempts have been made to eliminate "test bias" by eliminating the offending items and rescoring the tests. As pointed out by Flaugher (1978) and Flaugher and Schrader (1978), however, little is gained by this tactic. Mean differences in performance between groups are affected only slightly, and the test becomes more difficult for everyone involved, since the eliminated items typically have moderate to low difficulty. When race × item interactions have been found, the interaction typically accounts for a very small proportion of variance. For example, in analyzing items on the WISC-R, Jensen (1976), Sandoval (1979), and Mille (1979) found the groups × item interaction to account for only 2%–5% of the variance in performance. Using a similar technique with the Wonderlic Personnel Test, Jensen (1977) found the race × item interaction to account for only about 5% of the test score variance. Thus, the elimination of the offending items can be expected to have little, if any, significant effect. These analyses have been of a post hoc nature (i.e., after the tests have been standardized), however, and the use of empirical methods for determining item bias during the test development phase (as with the K-ABC) is to be encouraged.

With multiple-choice tests, another level of complexity is added to the examination of content bias. With a multiple-choice question, three or four distractors are typically given in addition to the correct response. Distractors may be examined for their attractiveness (the relative frequency with which they are chosen) across groups. When distractors are found to be disproportionately attractive for members of any particular group, the item may be defined as biased. When items are constructed to have an equal distribution of responses to each distractor for the total test population, then chi-square can be used to examine the distribution of choices for each distractor for each group (Burrill, 1975).

Jensen (1976) investigated the distribution of wrong responses for two multiple-choice intelligence tests, the Peabody Picture Vocabulary Test (PPVT) and Raven's Progressive Matrices (the Raven). Each of these two tests was individually administered to 600 white and 400 black children between the ages of 6 and 12. The analysis of incorrect responses for the PPVT indicated that the errors were distributed in a nonrandom fashion over the distractors for a large number of items. However, no racial bias in response patterns occurred, since the disproportionate choice of distractors followed the same pattern for blacks and whites. On the Raven, blacks made different types of errors than whites, but only on a small number of items. Jensen followed up these items and compared the black response pattern to the response pattern of white children at a variety of age levels. For every item showing differences in black–white response patterns, the black response could be duplicated by the response patterns of whites approximately 2 years younger than blacks.

Veale and Foreman (1983) have advocated inspecting multiple-choice tests for bias in distractor or "foil" response distribution as a means of refining tests *before* they are finalized for the marketplace. They note that there are many instances whereby unbiased external criteria (such as achievement or ability) or culturally valid tests are not readily accessible for detecting bias in the measure under study. Veale and Foreman add that inspection of incorrect responses to distractor items can often lead to greater insight concerning cultural bias in any given question than would inspection of percentage of correct responses across groups. Veale and Foreman (1983) provide the statistical analyses for their "overpull probability model" along with the procedures for measuring cultural variation and diagramming the source of bias within any given item.

Consider the following example provided by the authors:

Pick out the correct sentence below:
(A) Janie takes her work seriously.
(B) Janie work take too much time.
(C) Working with books are my favorite thing.
(D) Things people like to do is their business.
(Veale & Foreman, 1983)

In this example, blacks are strongly attracted to distractor D, while other groups are more inclined to pick C, as seen by Veale and Foreman's "overpull" computations. The D distractor, at face value, may be having a differential impact on black performance because of the "street" language presumed to be more common in the black culture. There is also the question upon further inspection as to whether the stem of this particular item provides clear direction (i.e., "correct *standard* English") to the testee. Knowledge of the differential response patterns across groups allows for item refinement, and subsequent statistical inspection can insure that distractors are not overly attractive or distracting to one group or another in revised format.

Investigation of item bias during test development is certainly not restricted to multiple-choice items and methods such as those outlined by Veale and Foreman. The possibilities are numerous (see Jensen, 1980, Ch. 9). For example, Scheuneman (1987) has used the results of linear methodology on Graduate Record Examination (GRE) item data to show some interesting influences on black–white performance when item characteristics (e.g., vocabulary content, one true or one false answer to be selected, diagrams to be used or not used, use of antonym items, etc.) are uniformly investigated. Although Scheuneman indicates that future research of this type should reduce the number of vari-

ables to address (there are 16 hypotheses), the results nonetheless suggest that bias or content research across groups is a viable way in which to determine whether differential effects can "be demonstrated through the manipulation of relatively stable characteristics of test items" (p. 116). Scheuneman presented pairs of items, with the designated characteristic of a question format under study present in one item and absent or modified in the other. Paired experimental items were administered in the experimental section of the GRE General Test, given in December 1982. Results indicated that certain "item elements"—common in general form to a variety of questions—appeared to have a differential impact on black and white performance. For example, significant group × version interactions were seen for one correct true versus one correct false response and for adding/modifying prefixes/suffixes to the stimulus word in antonym items. The question is thus raised as to whether the items showing differential impact are measuring the content domain (e.g., verbal, quantitative, or analytical thinking) as opposed to an aspect of "element" within the presentation to some degree. Scheuneman concludes that more research is needed to establish ways in which more systematic rules and procedures of test construction can be developed.

Another approach to the identification of biased items has been pursued by Jensen (1976). According to Jensen, if a test contains items that are disproportionately difficult for one group of examinees as compared to another, the correlation of P decrements between adjacent items will be low for the two groups. ("P decrement" refers to the difference in the difficulty index, P, from one item of a test to the next item. Typically, ability test items are arranged in ascending order of difficulty.) Jensen (1974, 1976) also contends that if a test contains biased items, the correlation between the rank order of item difficulties for one race with another will also be low. Jensen (1974, 1976, 1977) calculated cross-racial correlation of item difficulties for large samples of black and white children on five major intelligence tests: the PPVT, the Raven, the Revised Stanford–Binet Intelligence Scale Form L-M, the WISC-R, and the Wonderlic Personnel Test. Cross-racial correlations of P decrements were re-

TABLE 26.1. Cross-Racial Analysis of Content Bias for Five Major Intelligence Scales

| Scale | Cross-racial correlation of rank order of item difficulties[a] | |
	Black–White correlations[b]	White–Mexican American correlations[b]
Peabody Picture Vocabulary Test (Jensen, 1974b)	.99 (.79), .98 (.65)	.98 (.78), .98 (.66)
Raven's Progressive Matrices (Jensen, 1974b)	.99 (.98), .99 (.96)	.99 (.99), .99 (.97)
Stanford–Binet Intelligence Scale (Jensen, 1976)	.96	
Wechsler Intelligence Scale for Children—Revised (Jensen, 1976)	.95	
(Sandoval, 1979)[c]	.98 (.87)	.99 (.91)
(Mille, 1979)(1949 WISC)	.96, .95	
Wonderlic Personnel Test (Jensen, 1977)	.94 (.81)	

[a]Correlation of P decrements across race is included in parentheses if reported.

[b]Where two sets of correlations are presented, data were reported separately for males and females and are listed males first. The presence of a single correlation indicates that data were pooled across gender.

[c]Median values for the 10 WISC-R subtests excluding Digit Span and Coding.

ported for several of the scales. Jensen's results are summarized in Table 26.1, along with the results of several other investigators also employing Jensen's methodology.

As is readily apparent in Table 26.1, little evidence to support any consistent content bias within any of the scales investigated was found. The consistently large magnitude of the cross-racial correlations of P decrements is impressive and indicates a general lack of content bias in the instruments as a whole. As previously noted, however, some individual items were identified as biased; yet they collectively accounted for only 2%–5% of the variance in performance differences and showed no detectable pattern in item content.

Another approach to this question is to use the partial correlation between a demographic or other nominal variable and item score, where the correlation between total test score and the variable of interest has been removed from the relationship. If a significant partial correlation exists, say, between race and an item score after the race–total test score relationship has been partialed out, then the item is performing differentially across race within ability level. Bias has been demonstrated at this point under the definition offered above. The use of the partial correlation (typically a partial point-biserial r) is the simplest and perhaps the most powerful of the item bias detection approaches, but

its development is relatively recent and its use not yet common. An example of its application may be found in Reynolds, Willson, and Chatman (1984).

A common practice in recent times has been a return to including expert judgment by professionals and members of minority groups in the item selection for new psychological and educational tests. This approach was used in development of the K-ABC, the revision of the Wechsler Preschool and Primary Scale of Intelligence (WPPSI-R), the PPVT-R, and a number of other contemporary tests. The practice typically asks for an "armchair" inspection of individual items as a means of locating and expurgating biased components to the measure under development. Since, as previously noted, no detectable pattern or common characteristic of individual items statistically shown to be biased has been observed (given reasonable care in the item-writing stage), it seems reasonable to question the "armchair" approach to determining biased items. The bulk of scientific data since the pioneering work of McGurk (1951) has not supported the position that anyone can—upon surface inspection—detect the degree to which any given item will function differentially across groups (Shepard, 1982). Several researchers since McGurk's time have identified items as being disproportionately more difficult for minority group members than for members of the majority culture and have subsequently compared their results with a panel of expert judges. The data have provided some interesting results.

Although examples of the failure of judges to identify biased items now abound, two studies demonstrate this failure most clearly. After identifying the eight most racially discriminating and eight least racially discriminating items on the Wonderlic Personnel Test, Jensen (1976) asked panels of five black psychologists and five white psychologists to sort out the eight most and eight least discriminating items when only these 16 items were presented to them. The judges sorted the items at a level no better than chance. Sandoval and Mille (1979) conducted a somewhat more extensive analysis, using items from the WISC-R. These two researchers had 38 black, 22 Mexican-American, and 40 white university students from Spanish, history, and education classes identify items from the WISC-R that would be more difficult for a minority child than a white child and items that would be equally difficult for each group. A total of 45 WISC-R items were presented to each judge; these items included the 15 most difficult items for blacks as compared to whites, the 15 most difficult items for Mexican-Americans as compared to whites, and the 15 items showing the most nearly identical difficulty indices for minority and white children. The judges were asked to read each question and determine whether they thought the item was (1) easier for minority than for white children, (2) easier for white than for minority children, or (3) of equal difficulty for white and minority children. Sandoval and Mille's (1979) results indicated that the judges were not able to differentiate accurately between items that were more difficult for minorities and items that were of equal difficulty across groups. The effects of the judges' ethnic background on the accuracy of item bias judgments were also considered. Minority and nonminority judges did not differ in their ability to identify accurately biased items, nor did they differ with regard to the type of incorrect identification they tended to make. Sandoval and Mille's (1979) two major conclusions were that "(1) judges are not able to detect items which are more difficult for a minority child than an Anglo child, and (2) the ethnic background of the judge makes no difference

in accuracy of item selection for minority children" (p. 6). In each of these studies, the most extreme items were used, which should have given the judges an advantage.

Anecdotal evidence is also available to refute the assumption that "armchair" analyses of test bias in item content are accurate. Far and away, the most widely cited example of a biased intelligence test item is item 6 of the WISC-R Comprehension subtest: "What is the thing to do if a boy (girl) much smaller than yourself starts to fight with you?" This item is generally considered to be biased against black children in particular, because of the scoring criteria. According to the item's critics, the most logical response for a black child is to "fight back," yet this is a 0-point response. The correct (2-point) response is to walk away and avoid fighting with the child—a response that critics claim invites disaster in the black culture, where children are taught to fight back and would not "know" the "correct white response." Black responses to this item have been empirically investigated in several studies, with the same basic results: The item is relatively easier for black children than for white children. When all items on the WISC-R are ranked separately according to the difficulty level for blacks and whites, this item is the 42nd least difficult item (where 1 represents the easiest item) for black children and the 47th least difficult for white children (Jensen, 1976). Mille (1979), in a large-n study of bias, reached a similar conclusion, stating that this item "is relatively easier for blacks than it is for whites" (p. 163). The results of these empirical studies with large samples of black and white children are unequivocal: When matched for overall general intellectual skill, more black than white children will get this item correct—the very item most often singled out as a blatant example of the inherent bias of intelligence tests against blacks (see also Reynolds & Brown, 1984).

Even without empirical support for its accuracy, a number of prestigious writers support the continued use of the "face validity" approach of using a panel of minority judges to identify "biased" test items (Anastasi, 1986; Kaufman, 1979; Sandoval & Mille, 1979). Those who support the continued use of this technique see it as a method of gaining greater rapport with the public. As pointed out by Sandoval and Mille (1979),

"Public opinion, whether it is supported by empirical findings, or based on emotion, can serve as an obstacle to the use of a measurement instrument" (p. 7). The elimination of items that are offensive or otherwise objectionable to any substantive segment of the population for whom the test is intended seems an appropriate action that may aid in the public's acceptance of new and better psychological assessment tools. However, the subjective-judgment approach should not be allowed to supplant the use of more sophisticated analyses in the determination of biased items. The subjective approach should serve as a supplemental procedure, and items identified through this method (provided that some interrater agreement can be obtained—an aspect of the subjective method yet to be demonstrated) as objectionable can be eliminated when a psychometrically equivalent (or better) item can be obtained as a replacement and the intent of the item is kept intact (e.g., with a criterion-referenced measure, the new item must be designed to measure the same objective). The reliability, construct validity, and predictive validity of measures should not suffer any substantial losses for the purposes of increasing face validity.

Researchers such as Tittle (1982) have stressed that the possibility of and need for cooperation between those advocating statistical validity and those advocating face validity in nonbiased test construction are greater than one might think, given the above-cited research. Judgmental analysis allows for the *perception* of fairness in items, tests, and evaluations, and this perception should not be taken lightly. Tittle (1982) argues that "judgmental methods arise from a different, nonstatistical ground. In examining fairness or bias primarily on statistical grounds, we may again be witnessing a technical solution to a problem that is broader than the technical issues" (p. 34). Tests under construction should include definitive information concerning the nonbiased nature of the measure from a statistical standpoint, in addition to support by minority groups or other interested parties who have had the opportunity to inspect the test for the perception of fairness. Tittle notes that Cronbach (1980) does not find the issue of fairness as determined by subjective judgment to be outside the realm of test validation. Cronbach

states, "The politicalization of testing ought not [to] be surprising. Test data influence the fortunes of individuals and the support given to human service programs" (p. 100). Tittle (1975, 1982) argues that the general field of test development requires greater consensus regarding specific, multidimensional steps taken in formulating "fair" measures, because "fairness" in testing will never be realistically viewed by the public from a unidimensional statistical standpoint. She concludes:

In the test development setting there needs to be a closer examination [of] and agreement on the test development process, the judgmental and statistical data that are used as the basis to identify the final set of test items. Such agreement would permit both users and developers to reach a conclusion as to whether a test is "fair" for a particular subgroup, e.g., minorities and women. (p. 33)

Berk (1982) has proposed a three-step process for test development that responds to many of the issues outlined by Tittle. Berk's conceptualization includes (1) judgmental review to explore for content that is, for example, stereotypic, culture-specific, or offensive in language; (2) statistical analyses to detect performance discrepancies between/ among groups; and (3) *a posteriori* analysis of statistical data to determine whether item or test bias is present and, if so, to make appropriate adjustments. He argues that the way in which bias is perceived by society and the empirical methodologies used to detect bias require unification of the statistical and judgmental viewpoints if an equitable and lasting solution to "fair" test development is to be realized.

Thus far, this section has focused on the identification of biased items. Several studies evaluating other hypotheses have provided data that are relevant to the issue of content bias of intelligence tests, specifically the WISC-R.

Jensen and Figueroa (1975) investigated black–white differences in mental test scores as a function of differences in Level I (rote learning and memory) and Level II (complex cognitive processing) abilities. These researchers tested a large number of blacks and whites on the WISC-R Digit Span subtest and then analyzed the data separately for digits forward and digits backward. The content of the digits-forward and digits-backward procedures is the same. Thus, if score differences are due only to bias in content validity, score differences across race should remain constant for the two tasks. On the other hand, since the information-processing demands of the two tasks are quite different, the relative level of performance on the two tasks should not be the same if blacks and whites differ in their ability to process information according to the demands of the two tasks. Jensen and Figueroa (1975) found the latter to be the case. The black–white score difference on digits backward was more than twice the magnitude of the difference for digits forward. Granted, this methodology can provide only indirect evidence regarding the content validity of an instrument; however, its importance is in providing a different view of the issues and an alternative research strategy. Since the Jensen and Figueroa results do not indicate any content bias in the Digit Span subtest, they add to a growing body of literature that strongly suggests the lack of cultural bias in well-constructed, standardized tests.

Another study (Reynolds & Jensen, 1983) examined each of the 12 WISC-R subtests for cultural bias against blacks using a variation of the group × item ANOVA methodology

discussed earlier. Reynolds and Jensen matched 270 black children with 270 white children from the WISC-R standardization sample on the basis of gender and WISC-R Full Scale IQ. IQs were required to match within one standard error of measurement (about 3 points). When multiple matching cases were encountered, children were matched on the basis of SES. Matching the two groups of children on the basis of the Full Scale IQ essentially equated the two groups for g. Therefore, examining black–white differences in performance on each subtest of the WISC-R made it possible to determine which, if any, of the subtests were disproportionately difficult for blacks or whites. A significant F ratio in the multivariate analysis of variance (MANOVA) for the 12 WISC-R subtests was followed with univariate F tests between black and white means on each of the 12 WISC-R subtests. A summary of the Reynolds and Jensen (1983) results is presented in Table 26.2. Blacks exceeded whites in performance on two subtests: Digit Span and Coding. Whites exceeded blacks in performance on three subtests: Comprehension, Object Assembly, and Mazes. A trend was apparent for blacks to perform at a higher level on the Arithmetic subtest, while whites tended to exceed blacks on the Picture Arrangement subtest.

TABLE 26.2. Means, Standard Deviations, and Univariate F's for Comparison of Performance on Specific WISC-R Subtests by Groups of Blacks and Whites Matched for WISC-R Full Scale IQ

WISC-R variable	Blacks $\bar{X}$	SD	Whites $\bar{X}$	SD	D^a	F^b	p
Information	8.40	2.53	8.24	2.62	−.16	0.54	NS
Similarities	8.24	2.78	8.13	2.78	−.11	0.22	NS
Arithmetic	8.98	2.62	8.62	2.58	−.36	2.52	.10
Vocabulary	8.21	2.61	8.27	2.58	+.06	0.06	NS
Comprehension	8.14	2.40	8.58	2.47	+.44	4.27	.05
Digit Span	9.51	3.09	8.89	2.83	+.62	6.03	.01
Picture Completion	8.49	2.88	8.60	2.58	+.11	0.18	NS
Picture Arrangement	8.45	2.92	8.79	2.89	+.34	1.78	.10
Block Design	8.06	2.54	8.33	2.76	+.27	1.36	NS
Object Assembly	8.17	2.90	8.68	2.70	+.51	4.41	.05
Coding	9.14	2.81	8.65	2.80	−.49	4.30	.05
Mazes	8.69	3.14	9.19	2.98	+.50	3.60	.05
Verbal IQ	89.63	12.13	89.61	12.07	−.02	0.04	NS
Performance IQ	89.29	12.22	90.16	11.67	+.87	0.72	NS
Full Scale IQ	88.61	11.48	88.96	11.35	+.35	0.13	NS

Note. NS, not significant.
[a]White $\bar{X}$−black $\bar{X}$ difference.
[b]Degrees of freedom = 1, 538.

Although these results can be interpreted to indicate bias in several of the WISC-R subtests, the actual differences were very small (typically on the order of 0.10–0.15 standard deviation), and the amount of variance in performance associated with ethnic group membership was less than 5% in each case. The results are also reasonably consistent with Jensen's theory of mental test score differences and their relationship to Level I and Level II abilities. The Digit Span and Coding subtests are clearly the best measures of Level I abilities on the WISC-R, while Comprehension, Object Assembly, and Mazes are more closely associated with Level II abilities.

From a large number of studies employing a wide range of methodology, a relatively clear picture emerges: Content bias in well-prepared standardized tests is irregular in its occurrence, and no common characteristics of items that are found to be biased can be ascertained by expert judges (minority or nonminority). The variance in group score differences on mental tests associated with ethnic group membership when content bias has been found is relatively small (typically ranging from 2% to 5%). Even this small amount of bias has been seriously questioned, as Hunter (1975) describes such findings basically as methodological artifacts. Although the search for common "biased" item characteristics will continue, and psychologists must pursue the public relations issues of face validity, "armchair" claims of cultural bias in aptitude tests have found no empirical support in a large number of actuarial studies contrasting the performance of a variety of racial groups on items and subscales of the most widely employed intelligence scales in the United States; neither differential nor single-group validity has been demonstrated.

Bias in Construct Validity

There is no single method for the accurate determination of the construct validity of educational and psychological tests. Defining bias in construct validity thus requires a general statement that can be researched from a variety of viewpoints with a broad range of methodology. The following rather parsimonious definition is proferred:

Bias exists in regard to construct validity when a test is shown to measure different hypothetical traits (psychological constructs) for one group than for another, or to measure the same trait but with differing degrees of accuracy.

As befits the concept of construct validity, many different methods have been employed to examine existing tests for potential bias in construct validity. One of the most popular and necessary empirical approaches to investigating construct validity is factor analysis (Anastasi, 1986; Cronbach, 1970). Factor analysis, as a procedure, identifies clusters of test items or clusters of subtests of psychological or educational tests that correlate highly with one another, and less so or not at all with other subtests or items. It thus allows one to determine patterns of interrelationships of performance among groups of individuals. For example, if several subtests of an intelligence scale load highly on (are members of) the same factor, then if a group of individuals score high on one of these subtests, they would be expected to score at a high level on other subtests that load highly on that factor. Psychologists attempt to determine, through a review of the test content and correlates of performance on the factor in question, what psychological trait underlies performance; or, in a more hypothesis-testing approach, they will make predictions concerning the pattern of factor loadings. Hilliard (1979), one of the more vocal critics of IQ tests on the basis of cultural bias, has pointed out one of the potential areas of bias in comparisons of the factor-analytic results of tests across races:

If the IQ test is a valid and reliable test of "innate" ability or abilities, then the factors which emerge on a given test should be the same from one population to another, since "intelligence" is asserted to be a set of mental processes. Therefore, while the configuration of scores of a particular group on the factor profile would be expected to differ, logic would dictate that the factors themselves would remain the same. (p. 53)

Although researchers do not necessarily agree that identical factor analyses of an instrument speak to the innateness of the abilities being measured, consistent factor-analytic results across populations do provide strong evidence that whatever is being measured by the instrument is being measured in the same manner and is, in fact, the same construct within each group. The information derived from comparative factor analysis across populations is directly relevant to the use of educational and psychological tests in diagnosis and other decision-making functions. Psychologists, in order to make consistent interpretations of test score data, must be certain that a test measures the same variable across populations.

Two basic approaches, each with a number of variations, have been employed to compare factor-analytic results across populations. The first and more popular approach asks how similar the results are for each group; the second and less popular approach asks whether the results show a statistically significant difference between groups. The most sophisticated approach to the latter question has been the work of Jöreskog (1969, 1971) in simultaneous factor analysis in several populations. However, little has been done with the latter approach within the context of test bias research, and Jöreskog's methods can be quite abstruse.

Mille (1979) has demonstrated the use of a simpler method (actually developed by Jensen and presented in detail in Jensen, 1980) for testing the significance of the difference between factors for two populations. In Mille's method, all factor loadings are converted to Fisher's z-scores. The z-scores for corresponding factors are paired by variable and then subtracted. The differences in factor loadings, now expressed as differences in z-scores, are squared. The squared scores are summed and the mean derived. The mean of the squared differences is then divided by the following quantity:

$$\frac{1}{n_1 - 3} + \frac{1}{n_2 - 3}$$

where

n_1 = number of subjects in Group 1
n_2 = number of subjects in Group 2

This division yields a test statistic that is distributed as a chi-square with 1 degree of freedom. Mille's methodology has also received little use in the bias in assessment literature. As one part of a comprehensive internal analysis of test bias on the 1949 WISC, Mille (1979) compared the first principal-component factor across race for blacks and whites at the preschool, first-grade, third-grade, and fifth-grade levels. This factor, often thought of as a measure of g, did not differ significantly across race at any age level. Mille's results with the WISC indicate that factor loadings on g are essentially equivalent and that when score differences occur between groups, the differences reflect whatever is common to all variables that make up the test, rather than some personological or moderator variable that is specific to one group.

A number of techniques have been developed to measure the similarity of factors across groups. Katzenmeyer and Stenner (1977) described a technique based essentially on factor score comparisons. A "factor score" is a composite score derived by summing an individual's *weighted* scores on all variables that appear on a factor. Weights are derived from factor analysis and are directly related to the factor loadings of the variables. According to Katzenmeyer and Stenner's procedure, factor scores are first derived based on the combined groups of interest (e.g., the scores of blacks and whites as a single, homogeneous group are factor-analyzed). Then the scores of each group are factor-analyzed separately and factor scores are again determined. The correlation between the factor scores from the total-group analysis and the factor scores from the single-group analysis is then used as an estimate of the factorial similarity of the test battery across groups. The method is actually somewhat more complex, as described by Katzenmeyer and Stenner (1977), and has not been widely employed in the test bias literature; however, it is a practical technique with many utilitarian implications and should receive more attention in future literature.

The two most common methods of determining factorial similarity or factorial invariance involve the direct comparison of factor loadings across groups. The two primary techniques for this comparison are (1) the calculation of a coefficient of congruence (Harman, 1976) between the loadings of corresponding factors for two groups; and (2) the simple calculation of a Pearson product–

moment coefficient of correlation between the factor loadings of the corresponding factors. The latter technique, though used with some frequency, is less satisfactory than the use of the coefficient of congruence, since in the comparison of factor loadings certain of the assumptions underlying the Pearson r may be violated. When one is determining the degree of similarity of factors, a value of .90 or greater is typically, though arbitrarily, taken to indicate equivalent factors (factorial invariance). However, the most popular methods of calculating factorial similarity produce quite similar results (Reynolds & Harding, 1983), at least in large-n studies.

In contrast to Hilliard's (1979) strong statement that studies of factorial similarity across race have not been reported in the technical literature, a number of such studies have appeared over the last decade, dealing with a number of different tests. The focus here is primarily on studies comparing factor-analytic results across races for aptitude tests.

Because the WISC (Wechsler, 1949) and its successor, the WISC-R (Wechsler, 1974), have been the most widely employed individual intelligence tests with school-age children, it is appropriate that the cross-race structure of these two instruments has received extensive investigation for both normal and referral populations of children. Using a large, random sample, Reschly (1978) compared the factor structure of the WISC-R across four racially identifiable groups: whites, blacks, Mexican-Americans, and Native American Papagos, all from the southwestern United States. Consistent with the findings of previous researchers with the 1949 WISC (Lindsey, 1967; Silverstein, 1973), Reschly (1978) reported substantial congruency of factors across races when the two-factor solutions were compared (the two-factor solution typically reiterated Wechsler's *a priori* grouping of the subtests into a Verbal and a Performance, or nonverbal, scale). The 12 coefficients of congruence for comparisons of the two-factor solution across all combinations of racial groupings ranged only from .97 to .99, denoting factorial equivalence of this solution across groups. Reschly also compared three-factor solutions (three-factor solutions typically include Verbal Comprehension, Perceptual Organization, and Freedom from Distractibility factors), finding congruence only between whites and

Mexican-Americans. These findings are also consistent with previous research with the WISC (Semler & Iscoe, 1966). The g factor present in the WISC-R was shown to be congruent across race, as was also demonstrated by Mille (1979) for the WISC. Reschly (1978) concluded that the usual interpretation of the WISC-R Full Scale IQ as a measure of overall intellectual ability appears to be equally appropriate for whites, blacks, Mexican-Americans, and Native American Papagos. Jensen (1985) has presented compelling data indicating that the black–white discrepancy seen in major tests of aptitude reflects primarily the g factor. Reschly also concluded that the Verbal–Performance scale distinction on the WISC-R is equally appropriate across race and that there is strong evidence for the integrity of the WISC-R's construct validity for a variety of populations.

Support for Reschly's (1978) conclusions is available from a variety of other studies of the WISC and WISC-R. Applying a hierarchical factor-analytic method developed by Wherry and Wherry (1969), Vance and Wallbrown (1978) factor-analyzed the intercorrelation matrix of the WISC-R subtests for 150 referred blacks from the Appalachian region of the United States. The two-factor hierarchical solution determined for Vance and Wallbrown's (1978) blacks was highly similar to hierarchical factor solutions determined for the standardization samples of the Wechsler scales generally (Blaha, Wallbrown, & Wherry, 1975; Wallbrown, Blaha, & Wherry, 1973). Vance and Wallbrown's (1978) results with the WISC-R are also consistent with a previous hierarchical factor analysis with the 1949 WISC for a group of disadvantaged blacks and whites (Vance, Huelsman, & Wherry, 1976).

Several more recent studies comparing the WISC-R factor structure across races for normal and referral populations of children have also provided increased support for the generality of Reschly's (1978) conclusions and the results of the other investigators cited above. Oakland and Feigenbaum (1979) factor-analyzed the 12 WISC-R subtests' intercorrelations separately for stratified (race, age, sex, SES) random samples of normal white, black, and Mexican-American children from an urban school district of the northwestern United States. Pearson r's were calculated between corresponding factors for each group. For the g factor, the black–white correlation between factor loadings was .95, the Mexican-American–white correlation was .97, and the black–Mexican-American correlation was .96. Similar comparisons across all WISC-R variables produced correlations ranging only from .94 to .99. Oakland and Feigenbaum concluded that the results of their factor analyses "do not reflect bias with respect to construct validity for these three racial–ethnic . . . groups" (1979, p. 973).

Gutkin and Reynolds (1981) determined the factorial similarity of the WISC-R for groups of black and white children from the WISC–R standardization sample. This study is particularly important to examine in determining the construct validity of the WISC-R across races, because of the sample employed in the investigation. The sample included 1,868 white and 305 black children obtained in a stratified random sampling procedure designed to mimic the 1970 U.S. census data on the basis of age, sex, race, SES, geographic region of residence, and community size. Similarity of the WISC-R factor structure across race was investigated by comparing the black and white groups for the two- and three-factor solutions on (1) the magnitude of unique variances, (2) the pattern of subtest loadings on each factor, (3) the portion of total variance accounted for by common factor variance, and (4) the percentage of common factor variance accounted for by each factor. Coefficients of congruence comparing the unique variances, the g factor, the two-factor solutions, and the three-factor solutions across races all achieved a value of .99. The portion of total variance accounted for by each factor was the same in both the two- and three-factor racial groups. Gutkin and Reynolds (1981) concluded that for white and black children the WISC-R factor structure was essentially invariant, and that no evidence of single-group or differential construct validity could be found.

Subsequent studies comparing the WISC-R factor structure for referral populations of white and Mexican-American children have also strongly supported the construct validity of the WISC-R across races. Dean (1979b) compared three-factor WISC-R solutions across races for whites and Mexican-Americans referred because of learning problems in the regular classroom. Analyzing the 10 regular WISC-R subtests, Dean reported coefficients of congruence between corresponding factors of .84 for Factor 1 (Verbal Comprehension), .89 for Factor 2 (Perceptual Organization), and .88 for Factor 3 (Freedom from Distractibility). Although not quite reaching the typical value of .90 required to indicate equivalent factors, Dean's results do indicate a high degree of similarity. The relative strength of the various factors was also highly consistent across races.

Gutkin and Reynolds (1980) also compared two- and three-factor principal-factor solutions to the WISC-R across race for referral populations of white and Mexican-American children. Gutkin and Reynolds (1980) made additional comparisons of the factor solutions derived from their referral sample to solutions derived by Reschly (1978; personal communication, 1979), and also to solutions from the WISC-R standardization sample. Coefficients of congruence for the Gutkin and Reynolds two-factor solutions for whites and Mexican-Americans were .98 and .91, respectively. The g factor showed a coefficient of congruence value of .99 across races. When Gutkin and Reynolds (1980) compared their solutions with those derived by Reschly (1978) for normal white, black, Mexican-American, and Papago children, and with results based on the WISC-R standardization sample, the coefficients of congruence all exceeded .90. When three-factor solutions were compared, the results were more varied, but also supported the consistent similarity of WISC-R factor-analytic results across race.

DeFries et al. (1974) administered 15 mental tests to large samples of Americans of Japanese ancestry and Americans of Chinese ancestry. After examining the pattern of intercorrelations among the 15 tests for each of these two ethnic groups, DeFries et al. concluded that the cognitive organization of the two groups was virtually identical. In reviewing this study, Willerman (1979) concluded that "The similarity in factorial structure [between the two groups] suggests that the manner in which the tests are constructed by the subjects is similar regardless of ethnicity and that the tests are measuring the same mental abilities in the two groups" (p. 468).

At the adult level, Kaiser (1986) and Scholwinski (1985) have analyzed the Wechsler Adult Intelligence Scale—Revised (WAIS-

R); Wechsler, 1981) and reported substantial similarity between factor structures for black and white samples obtained from the WAIS-R standardization data. Kaiser completed separate hierarchical analyses for all black subjects ($n = 192$) and white subjects ($n = 1,664$) in the WAIS-R standardization sample and calculated coefficients of congruence of .99 for the g factor, .98 for the Verbal factor, and .97 for the Performance or nonverbal factor. Scholwinski selected 177 black and 177 white subjects from the standardization sample, closely matched on the basis of age, sex, and Full Scale IQ. Separate factor analyses again showed that structures generated from the Wechsler format showed strong similarity across black–white groups beyond childhood and adolescent levels of development.

At the preschool level, factor-analytic results also tend to show consistency of construct validity across races, though the results are less clear-cut. In a comparison of separate factor analyses of the McCarthy Scales of Children's Abilities (McCarthy, 1972) for groups of black and white children, Kaufman and DiCuio (1975) concluded that the McCarthy Scales showed a high degree of factorial similarity between the two races. The conclusion was not straightforward, however. Four factors were found for the blacks and three for the whites. Kaufman and DiCuio based their conclusion of factorial similarity on the finding that each "white" factor had a coefficient of congruence of .85–.93 with one "black" factor. One black factor on the McCarthy Scales had no white counterpart with a coefficient of congruence beyond .74 (the Memory factor), and the black and white Motor factors showed a coefficient of congruence of only .85.

When investigating the factor structure of the WPPSI across race, Kaufman and Hollenbeck (1974) found much "cleaner" factors for blacks and whites than with the McCarthy Scales. The two factors, essentially mirroring Wechsler's Verbal and Performance scales, were virtually identical between the races. Both factors also appear closely related to the hierarchical factor solution presented by Wallbrown et al. (1973) for blacks and whites on the WPPSI. When comparing factor analyses of the Goodenough–Harris Human Figure Drawing Test scoring item, Merz (1970) found highly similar factor structures for

blacks, whites, Mexican-Americans, and Native Americans.

Other investigators have found differences across races in the factor structures of several tests designed for preschool and primary-grade children. Goolsby and Frary (1970) factor-analyzed the Metropolitan Readiness Test (MRT) together for separate groups of blacks and whites, finding differences in the factor structure of this grouping of tests across races. When evaluating the experimental edition of the Illinois Test of Psycholinguistic Abilities, Leventhal and Stedman (1970) noted differences in the factor structure of this battery for blacks and whites. Two more recent studies have clarified somewhat the issue of differential construct validity of preschool tests across race.

The MRT (Hildreth, Griffith, & McGauvran, 1969) is one of the most widely employed of all preschool screening measures, and its 1969 version is composed of six subtests: Word Meaning, Listening, Matching, Letter Naming, Numbers, and Copying. Reynolds (1979b) had previously shown this to be essentially a one-factor (General Readiness) instrument. In a subsequent study, Reynolds (1979c) compared the general factor making up the MRT across races (blacks and whites) and genders. Substantial congruency was noted: Coefficients of congruence across each pair of race–sex groupings ranged only from .92 to .99, with the lowest coefficient derived from the intraracial comparison for white females and white males. Eigenvalues, and subsequently the proportion of variance accounted for by the factor, were also highly similar for the race–sex groupings. Reynolds (1979c) concluded that these findings supported the presence of a single General Readiness factor and the construct validity of the MRT across race and sex; that is, the results indicated that the MRT measures the same abilities in the same manner for blacks, whites, males, and females. The lack of differential or single-group construct validity across sex has also been demonstrated with aptitude tests for school-age children (Reynolds & Gutkin, 1980c).

In a more comprehensive study employing seven major preschool tests (the McCarthy Draw-A-Design and Draw-A-Child subtests, the Lee–Clark Reading Readiness Tests, the Tests of Basic Experiences Language and

Mathematics subtests, the Preschool Inventory—Revised Edition, and the MRT), Reynolds (1980a) reached a similar conclusion. A two-factor solution was determined with this battery for each of the four race–sex groups as above. Coefficients of congruence ranged only from .95 to .99 for the two factors, and the average degree of intercorrelation was essentially the same for all groups, as were eigenvalues and the percentage of variance accounted for by the factors. Reynolds (1980a) again concluded that the abilities being measured were invariant across race and that there was no evidence of differential or single-group construct validity of preschool tests across races or genders. The clear trend in studies of preschool tests' construct validity across race (and sex) is to uphold validity across groups. Such findings add support to the use of existing preschool screening measures with black and white children of both sexes in the very necessary process of early identification (Reynolds, 1979a) of potential learning and behavior problems.

As is appropriate for studies of construct validity, comparative factor analysis has not been the only method of determining whether single-group or differential validity exists. Another method of investigation involves comparing internal-consistency reliability estimates across groups. Internal-consistency reliability is determined by the degree to which the items are all measuring a similar construct. To be unbiased with regard to construct validity, internal-consistency estimates should be approximately equal across races. This characteristic of tests has been investigated with blacks, whites, and Mexican-Americans for a number of popular aptitude tests.

With groups of black and white adults, Jensen (1977) calculated internal-consistency estimates (using the Kuder–Richardson 21 formula) for the Wonderlic Personnel Test (a frequently used employment/aptitude test). Kuder–Richardson 21 values of .86 and .88 were found, respectively, for blacks and whites. Using Hoyt's formula, Jensen (1974) determined internal-consistency estimates of .96 on the PPVT for each of three groups of children: blacks, whites, and Mexican-Americans. When children were categorized by gender within each racial grouping, the values ranged only from .95 to .97. On

Raven's Progressive Matrices (colored), internal-consistency estimates were also quite similar across race and sex, ranging only from .86 to .91 for the six race–sex groupings. Thus, Jensen's (1974, 1977) research with three popular aptitude tests shows no signs of differential or single-group validity with regard to homogeneity of test content or consistency of measurement across groups.

Sandoval (1979) and Oakland and Feigenbaum (1979) have extensively investigated internal consistency of the various WISC-R subtests (excluding Digit Span and Coding, for which internal-consistency analysis is inappropriate) for whites, blacks, and Mexican-Americans. Both of these studies included large samples of children, with Sandoval's (1979) including over 1,000. Sandoval found internal-consistency estimates to be within .04 of one another for all subtests except Object Assembly. This subtest was most reliable for blacks (.95), while being about equally reliable for whites (.79) and Mexican-Americans (.75). Oakland and Feigenbaum (1979) reported internal-consistency estimates that never differed by more than .06 among the three groups, again with the exception of Object Assembly. In this instance, Object Assembly was most reliable for whites (.76), with about equal reliabilities for blacks (.64) and Mexican-Americans (.67). Oakland and Feigenbaum also compared reliabilities across sex, finding highly similar values for males and females. Dean (1977) examined the internal consistency of the WISC-R for Mexican-American children tested by white examiners. He reported internal-consistency reliability estimates consistent with, although slightly exceeding, values reported by Wechsler (1974) for the predominantly white standardization sample. The Bender–Gestalt Test has also been reported to have similar internal-consistency estimates for whites (.84), blacks (.81), and Mexican-Americans (.72), and for males (.81) and females (.80) (Oakland & Feigenbaum, 1979).

Several other methods have also been used to determine the construct validity of popular psychometric instruments across races. Since intelligence is considered a developmental phenomenon, the correlation of raw scores with age has been viewed as one measure of construct validity for intelligence tests. Jensen (1976) reported that the correlations between raw scores on the PPVT and age were

.79 for whites, .73 for blacks, and .67 for Mexican-Americans. For Raven's Progressive Matrices (colored), correlations for raw scores with age were .72 for whites, .66 for blacks, and .70 for Mexican-Americans. Similar results are apparent for the K-ABC (Kamphous & Reynolds, 1987). Thus, in regard to increase in scores with age, the tests behave in a highly similar manner for whites, blacks, and Mexican-Americans.

Construct validity of a large number of popular psychometric assessment instruments has been investigated across races and genders with a variety of populations of minority and white children and with a divergent set of methodologies (see Reynolds, 1982, for a review of methodologies). All roads have led to Rome: No consistent evidence of bias in construct validity has been found with any of the many tests investigated. This leads to the conclusion that psychological tests (especially aptitude tests) function in essentially the same manner, that test materials are perceived and reacted to in a similar manner, and that tests measure the same construct with equivalent accuracy for blacks, whites, Mexican-Americans, and other American minorities of both sexes and at all levels of SES. Single-group validity and differential validity have not been found and probably do not exist with regard to well-constructed and well-standardized psychological and educational tests. This means that test score differences across race are real and not an artifact of test bias; that is, the tests are measuring the same constructs across these variables. These differences cannot be ignored. As Mille (1979) has succinctly stated, "If this . . . difference [in test scores] is the result of genetic factors, acceptance of the cultural bias hypothesis would be unfortunate. If the difference is the result of environmental factors, such acceptance would be tragic" (p. 162).

Bias in Predictive or Criterion-Related Validity

Evaluating bias in predictive validity of educational and psychological tests is less closely related to the evaluation of group mental test score differences than to the evaluation of individual test scores in a more absolute sense. This is especially true for aptitude (as opposed to diagnostic) tests, where the primary purpose of administration is the prediction of some specific future outcome or behavior. Internal analyses of bias (such as in content and construct validity) are less confounded than analyses of bias in predictive validity, however, because of the potential problems of bias in the criterion measure. Predictive validity is also strongly influenced by the reliability of criterion measures, which frequently is poor. The degree of relationship between a predictor and a criterion is restricted as a function of the square root of the product of the reliabilities of the two variables.

Arriving at a consensual definition of bias in predictive validity is also a difficult task, as has already been discussed. Yet, from the standpoint of the practical applications of aptitude and intelligence tests, predictive validity is the most crucial form of validity in relation to test bias. Much of the discussion in professional journals concerning bias in predictive validity has centered around models of selection. These issues have been discussed previously in this chapter and are not reiterated here. Since this section is concerned with bias in respect to the test itself and not the social or political justifications of any one particular selection model, the Cleary et al. (1975) definition, slightly rephrased here, provides a clear and direct statement of test bias with regard to predictive validity.

A test is considered biased with respect to predictive validity if the inference drawn from the test score is not made with the smallest feasible random error or if there is constant error in an inference or prediction as a function of membership in a particular group.

This definition is a restatement of previous definitions by Cardall and Coffman (1964), Cleary (1968), and Potthoff (1966), and has been widely accepted (though certainly not without criticism; e.g., Bernal, 1975; Linn & Werts, 1971; Schmidt & Hunter, 1974; Thorndike, 1971).

Oakland and Matuszek (1977) examined procedures for placement in special education classes under a variety of models of bias in prediction, and demonstrated that the smallest number of children are misplaced when the Cleary et al. (1975) conditions of fairness are met. (However, under legislative "quota" requirements, Oakland and Matuszek favor the Thorndike [1971] conditions of selection.) The Cleary et al. definition is also apparently the definition espoused in government guidelines on testing and has been held in at least one recent court decision (*Cortez v. Rosen*, 1975) to be the only historically, legally, and logically required condition of test fairness (Ramsay, 1979), although apparently the judge in the *Larry P. v. Riles* (1979) decision adopted the "mean score differences as bias" approach. A variety of educational and psychological personnel have adopted the Cleary et al. (1975) regression approach to bias, including (1) noted psychological authorities on testing (Anastasi, 1986; Cronbach, 1970; Humphreys, 1973); (2) educational and psychological researchers (Bossard, Reynolds & Gutkin, 1980; Kallingal, 1971; Pfeifer & Sedlacek, 1971; Reynolds & Hartlage, 1978, 1979; Stanley & Porter, 1967; Wilson, (1969); (3) industrial/organizational psychologists (Bartlett & O'Leary, 1969; Einhorn & Bass, 1971; Gael & Grant, 1972; Grant & Bray, 1970; Ramsay, 1979; Tenopyr, 1967); and (4) even critics of educational and psychological testing (Goldman & Hartig, 1976; Kirkpatrick, 1970; Kirkpatrick, Ewen, Barrett, & Katzell, 1968).

The evaluation of bias in prediction under the Cleary et al. (1975) definition (the regression definition) is quite straightforward. With simple regression, predictions take the form of $Y_i = aX_i + b$, where a is the regression coefficient and b is a constant. When this equation is graphed (forming a regression line), a represents the slope of the regression line and b the Y intercept. Since our definition of fairness in predictive validity requires errors in prediction to be independent of group membership, the regression line formed for any pair of variables must be the same for each group for whom predictions are to be made. Whenever the slope or the intercept differs significantly across groups, there is bias in prediction if one attempts to use a regression equation based on the combined groups. When the regression equations for two (or more) groups are equivalent, prediction is the same for all groups. This condition is referred to variously as "homogeneity of regression across groups," "simultaneous regression," or "fairness in prediction." Homogeneity of regression across groups in illustrated in Figure 26.1. In this case, the single regression equation is

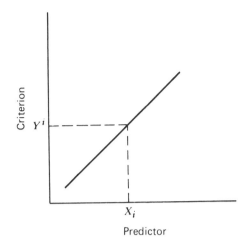

FIGURE 26.1. Equal slopes and intercepts result in homogeneity of regression that causes the regression lines for group a, and b, and the combined group c to be identical.

appropriate with all groups, any errors in prediction being random with respect to group membership (i.e., residuals uncorrelated with group membership). When homogeneity of regression does not occur, for "fairness in prediction" to occur, separate regression equations must be used for each group.

In actual clinical practice, regression equations are seldom generated for the prediction of future performance. Instead, some arbitrary or perhaps statistically derived cutoff score is determined, below which "failure" is predicted. For school performance, IQs two or more standard deviations below the test mean are used to infer a high probability of failure in the regular classroom if special assistance is not provided for the student in question. Essentially, then, clinicians are establishing mental prediction equations that are assumed to be equivalent across races, genders, and so on. Although these mental equations cannot be readily tested across groups, the actual form of criterion prediction can be compared across groups in several ways. Errors in prediction must be independent of group membership. If regression equations are equal, this confition is met. To test the hypothesis of simultaneous regression, slopes and intercepts must both be compared. An alternative method is the direct examination of residuals

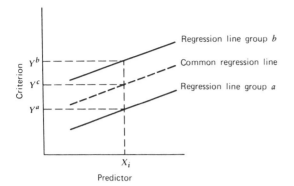

FIGURE 26.2. Equal slopes with differing intercepts result in parallel regression lines and a constant bias in prediction.

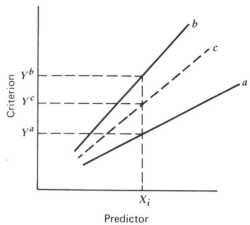

FIGURE 26.3. Equal intercepts and differing slopes result in nonparallel regression lines, with the degree of bias dependent on the distance of the individual's score (X_i) from the origin.

through ANOVA or a similar design (Reynolds, 1980b).

In the evaluation of slope and intercept values, two basic techniques have been most often employed in the research literature. Gulliksen and Wilks (1965) and Kerlinger (1973) describe methods for separately testing regression coefficients and intercepts for significant differences across groups. Using separate, independent tests for these two values considerably increases the probability of a decision error and unnecessarily complicates the decision-making process. Potthoff (1966) has described a useful technique that allows one to test simultaneously the equivalence of regression coneficients and intercepts across K independent groups with a single F ratio. If a significant F results, the researcher may then test the slopes and intercepts separately if information concerning which value differs is desired. When homogeneity of regression does not occur, there are three basic conditions that can result: (1) Intercept constants differ, (2) regression coefficients (slopes) differ, or (3) slopes and intercepts differ. These conditions are depicted pictorially in Figures 26.2, 26.3, and 26.4, respectively.

The regression coefficient is related to the correlation coefficient between the two variables and is one measure of the strength of the relationship between two variables. When intercepts differ and regression coefficients do not, a situation such as that shown in Figure 26.2 results. Relative accuracy of prediction is the same for the two groups (a and b); yet the use of a regression equation

derived by combining the two groups results in bias that works against the group with the higher mean criterion score. Since the slope of the regression line is the same for all groups, the degree of error in prediction remains constant and does not fluctuate as a function of an individual's score on the independent variable. That is, regardless of group member b's score on the predictor, the degree of underprediction in performance on the criterion is the same. As illustrated in Figure 26.2, the use of the common score of Y_c for a score of X overestimates how well members of group a will perform and underestimates the criterion performance of members of group b.

In Figure 26.3, nonparallel regression lines illustrate the case where intercepts are constant across groups but the slope of the line is different for each group. Here, too, the performance of the group with the higher mean criterion score is typically underpredicted when a common regression equation is applied. The amount of bias in prediction that results from using the common regression line is the distance of the score from the mean. The most difficult, complex case of bias is represented in Figure 26.4. Here we see the result of significant differences in slopes and intercepts. Not only does the amount of bias in prediction accruing from the use of a common equation vary in this instance; the actual direction of bias

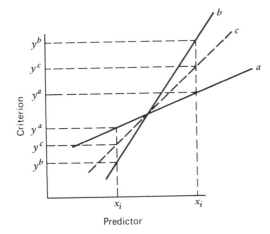

FIGURE 26.4. Differing slopes *and* intercepts result in the complex condition where the amount and the direction of the bias are functions of the distance of an individual's score from the origin.

can reverse, depending on the location of the individual's score in the distribution of the independent variable. Only in the case of Figure 26.4 do members of the group with the lower mean criterion score run the risk of having their performance on the criterion variable underpredicted by the application of a common regression equation.

A considerable body of literature has developed in recent years regarding the differential predictive validity of tests across races for employment selection and college admissions. In a recent review of 866 black–white test validity comparisons from 39 studies of test bias in personnel selection, Hunter et al. (1979) concluded that there was no evidence to substantiate hypotheses of differential or single-group validity with regard to the prediction of job performance across races for blacks and whites. A similar conclusion was reached by O'Conner, Wexley, and Alexander (1975). A number of studies have also focused on differential validity of the Scholastic Aptitude Test (SAT) in the prediction of college performance (typically measured by grade point average of GPA). In general, these studies have found either no differences in the prediction of criterion performance for blacks and whites or a bias (underprediction of the criterion) against whites (Cleary, 1968; Cleary et al., 1975; Goldman & Hewitt, 1976; Kallingal, 1971; Pfeifer & Sedlacek, 1971; Stanley, 1971; Stanley &

Porter, 1967; Temp, 1971). When bias against whites has been found, the differences between actual and predicted criterion scores, although statistically significant, have been quite small.

Reschly and Sabers (1979) evaluated the validity of WISC-R IQs in the prediction of Metropolitan Achievement Tests (MAT) performance (Reading and Math subtests) for whites, blacks, Mexican-Americans, and Native American Papagos. The choice of the MAT as a criterion measure in studies of predictive bias in particularly appropriate, since item analysis procedures were employed (as described earlier) to eliminate racial bias in item content during the test construction phase. Anastasi (1986) has described the MAT as an excellent model of an achievement test designed to reduce or eliminate cultural bias. Reschly and Sabers's (1979) comparison of regression systems indicated bias in the prediction of the various achievement scores. Again, however, the bias produced generally significant underprediction of white performance when a common regression equation was applied. Achievement test performance of the Native American Papago group showed the greatest amount of overprediction of all nonwhite groups. Though some slope bias was evident, Reschly and Sabers typically found intercept bias resulting in parallel regression lines. Using similar techniques, but including teacher ratings, Reschly and Reschly (1979) also investigated the predictive validity of WISC-R factor scores with the samples of white, black, Mexican-American, and Native American Papago children. A significant relationship occurred between the three WISC-R factors first delineated by Kaufman (1975) and measures of achievement for the white and nonwhite groups, with the exception of the Papagos. Significant correlations occurred between the WISC-R Freedom from Distractibility factor (Kaufman, 1975) and teacher ratings of attention for all four groups. Reschly and Reschly concluded that "These data also again confirm the relatively strong relationship of WISC-R scores to achievement for most non-Anglo as well as Anglo groups" (1979, p. 239).

Reynolds and Hartlage (1979) investigated the differential validity of Full Scale IQs from the WISC-R and its 1949 predecessor, the WISC, in predicting reading and arithmetic achievement for black and white children who had been referred by their teachers for psychological services in a rural Southern school district. Comparisons of correlations and a Potthoff (1966) analysis to test for identity of regression lines revealed no significant differences in the ability or function of the WISC and WISC-R to predict achievement for these two groups. Reynolds and Gutkin (1980b) replicated this study for the WISC-R with large groups of white and Mexican-American children from the Southwest. Reynolds and Gutkin contrasted regression systems between WISC-R Verbal, Performance, and Full Scale IQs and the "academic basics" of reading, spelling, and arithmetic. Only the regression equation between the WISC-R Performance IQ and arithmetic achievement differed for the two groups. The difference in the two equations was due to an intercept bias that resulted in the overprediction of achievement for the Mexican-American children. Reynolds, Gutkin, Dappen, and Wright (1979) also failed to find differential validity in the prediction of achievement for males and females with the WISC-R.

In a related study, Hartlage, Lucas, and Godwin (1976) compared the predictive validity of what they considered to be a relatively culture-free test (Raven's Progressive Matrices) with a more culture-loaded test (the 1949 WISC) for a group of low-SES, disadvantaged rural children. Harlage et al. found that the WISC had consistently larger correlations with measures of reading, spelling, and arithmetic than did Raven's Matrices. Although it did not make the comparison with other groups that is necessary for the drawing of firm conclusions, the study does support the validity of the WISC, which has been the target of many of the claims of bias in the prediction of achievement for low-SES, disadvantaged rural children. Henderson, Butler, and Goffeney (1969) also reported that the WISC and the Bender–Gestalt Test were equally effective in the prediction of reading and arithmetic achievement for white and nonwhite groups, though their study had a number of methodological difficulties, including heterogeneity of the nonwhite comparison group. Reynolds, Willson, and Chatman (1985) evaluated the predictive validity of the K-ABC for blacks and for whites. Occasional evidence of bias was found in each direction, but mostly of the direction of overprediction of the academic attainment levels of blacks. However, for most of the 56 Potthoff comparisons of regression lines, no evidence of bias was revealed.

A study by Goldman and Hartig (1976) produced quite different results with the 1949 WISC. These researchers reported that when validities were calculated for the prediction of achievement separately for whites, blacks, and Mexican-Americans, the predictive validity of the WISC was good for white children but near zero for the nonwhite groups. A closer examination of the methodology of the study gives considerable insight into this unusual finding. The criterion measure, academic GPA, showed considerable restriction of range for the black and Mexican-American groups. In addition, calculation of the academic GPA inexplicably included, in addition to traditional academic subjects, grades from music, health, art, instrumental music, and physical education, where very high grades approaching zero variance were common. It is clearly inappropriate to include inflated grades from such school activities in the calculation of "academic GPA."

The use of academic GPA, especially in presecondary settings, is fraught with other problems, including unreliability, questionable validity, and the lack of constant scaling. Teachers may be grading on some absolute scale of achievement; relative to other children in the classroom; relative to how well teachers believe children should be performing; or on the basis of effort, motivation, or even attractiveness. Some parents will even demand stricter or more lenient grading standards for their children than for others. To confound the problems of academic GPA as a criterion, grading practices vary not only among classrooms and schools, but within classrooms as well (the Goldman and Hartig children came from 14 different schools). When groups are to be combined across schools, and homogeneity of the new group is then to be assumed, the equivalence of the schools regarding environments, academic standards, and grading practices must first be demonstrated empirically (Jensen, 1980). Reading the Goldman and Hartig (1976) paper leads one to question whether the researchers had not decided on the outcome *a priori* and then set out to prove it! The predictive validities reported for white children in this study are also considerably lower than are typically reported for the WISC. Thus the contradictory nature of this study, as compared to a large number of other studies, must certainly be called into question. Studies with a number of other aptitude tests also contradict Goldman and Hartig (1976).

Bossard et al. (1980) published a regression analysis of test bias on the 1972 Stanford–Binet Intelligence Scale for separate groups of black and white children. Neither progression system nor correlations differed at $p < .05$ for the prediction of the basic academic skills of reading, spelling, and arithmetic achievement for these two groups of referred children. An earlier study by Sewell (1979), a black opponent of testing, did not compare regression systems, but also found no significant differences in validity coefficients for Stanford–Binet IQs predicting California Achievement Test (CAT) scores for black and white first-grade children.

A series of studies comparing the predictive validity of group IQ measures across races has been reviewed by Jensen (1980) and Sattler (1974). Typically, regression systems have not been compared in these studies; instead, researchers have compared only the validity coefficients across races—a practice that tells only whether the magnitude of the relationships is similar, not whether the test is actually nonbiased. The comparison of validity coefficients is nevertheless relevant, since equivalence in predictive validities is a first step in evaluating differential validity. That is, if predictive validities differ, then regression systems must differ; the reverse is not necessarily true, however, since the correlation between two variables is a measure of the strength or magnitude of a relationship and does not dictate the form of a relationship. Although the number of studies evaluating group IQ tests across races is small, they have typically employed extremely large samples. The Lorge–Thorndike verbal and nonverbal IQs have been most often investigated. Jensen (1980) and Sattler (1974) concluded that the few available studies suggest that standard IQ tests in current use have comparable validities for black and white children at the elementary school level.

Guterman (1979) reported on an extensive analysis of the predictive validity of the Ammons and Ammons Quick Test (QT; a measure of verbal IQ) for adolescents of different social classes. Social class was determined by a weighted combination of Duncan's SES index and the number of years of education of each parent. Three basic measures of scholastic attainment were employed as criterion measures: (1) the Vocabulary subtest of the General Aptitude Test Battery (GATB); (2) the test of Reading Comprehension from the Gates Reading Survey; and (3) the Arithmetic subtest of the GATB. School grades in academic subjects for 9th, 10th and 12th grades were also used to examine for bias in prediction. Guterman reached similar conclusions with regard to all criterion measures across all social classes: Slopes and intercepts of regression lines did not differ across social class for the prediction of any of the criterion measures by the IQ derived from the QT. Several other social knowledge criterion measures were also examined. Again, slopes were constant across social class, and, with the exception of sexual knowledge, intercepts were also constant. Guterman concluded that his data provide strong support for equivalent validity of IQ measures across social class. In reanalyzing the Guerman (1979) study, Gordon and Rudert (1979) reached even stronger conclusions. By analyzing the Guterman data by race within the various SES categories through a method of path analysis, Gordon and Rudert (1979) demonstrated that the QT was also not biased across race in the prediction of academic attainment and that IQ (as determined by the QT) plays the same role in status attainment models for blacks and whites and has stronger direct effects on later status attainment than does SES. Certainly with school-age children and adults, there is compelling evidence that differential and single-group predictive validity hypotheses must be rejected.

As with construct validity, at the preschool level the evidence is less clear and convincing but points toward a lack of bias against minorities. Because of doubts expressed about the usefulness of customary readiness tests with students of certain racial and ethnic backgrounds and with low-SES children, Mitchell (1967) investigated the predictive validity of two preschool readiness tests used in the U.S. Office of Education Cooperative First-Grade Reading Study of 1964–1965. Chosen for study were the MRT, Form A (1964–1965 revision) and the Murphy–Durrell Reading Readiness Analysis (1964 revision). Mitchell's sample included 7,310 whites, 518 blacks, and 39 Mexican-Americans. Criterion measures chosen were the Stanford Achievement Test (1963 revision) and the Primary I Reading and Spelling subtests. Mitchell's results do not support a hypothesis of lower predictive validity for nonwhites than for whites on either readiness scale. Although some significant differences occurred in the obtained correlations with achievement for blacks and whites, 26 correlations were higher for blacks. Mitchell concluded that the two readiness tests performed their functions as well with black as with white children and that the general level of predictive validity was similar. This overstates the case somewhat, since only validity coefficients and not regression systems were compared, but Mitchell's (1967) study does support the predictive validity of these readiness tests across race.

Oakland (1978) assessed the differential predictive validity of four readiness tests (the MRT, the Tests of Basic Experiences battery, the Slosson Intelligence Test and the Slosson Oral Reading Test) across races (black, white, and Mexican-American) for middle- and lower-SES children. The MAT, the CAT, and the California Test of Mental Maturity (CTMM) served as criterion variables. Since the CTMM is an IQ test, prediction of CTMM scores by the various readiness tests is excluded from the following discussion. Although Oakland (1978) did not use any test of statistical significance to compare the correlations between the independent and dependent variable pairs across races and SES, a clear pattern was found, showing higher levels of prediction for white as opposed to nonwhite groups. Oakland also did not compare regression systems, limiting his study to the report of the various validity coefficients for each race–SES grouping. Oakland's (1978) results clearly indicate potential bias in the prediction of early school achievement by individual readiness or screening tests. The lower correlations for nonwhite groups, however, given their lower mean criterion scores, lead to anticipation of bias favoring

nonwhites in the prediction of early school achievement.

To investigate this possibility, Reynolds (1978) conducted an extensive analysis of predictive bias for seven major preschool tests (the Draw-A-Design and Draw-A-Child subtests of the McCarthy Scales; the Mathematics and Language subtests of the Tests of Basic Experiences; the MRT; the preschool Inventory—Revised Edition; and the Lee–Clark Reading Readiness Test) across races and genders for large groups of blacks and whites. For each preschool test, validity coefficients, slopes, and intercepts were compared, with prediction of performance on four subtests of the MAT (Word Knowledge, Word Discrimination, Reading, and Arithmetic) as the criterion measure. The general advantage of the MAT as a criterion in external studies of bias has previously been pointed out. In the Reynolds (1978) study, the MAT had the added advantage of being chosen by the teachers in the district: Data were gathered on a large number of early achievement tests, and the teachers selected the MAT as the battery most closely measuring what was taught in their classrooms. Regression systems and validity coefficients were compared for each independent–dependent variable pair for white females (WF) versus white males (WM), black females (BF) versus black males (BM), WF versus BF, and WM versus BM,, resulting in 112 comparisons of validity coefficients and 112 comparisons of regression systems. Mean performance on all criterion measures was in the following rank order: WF > WM > BF > BM. The mean validity coefficients (by Fisher z-transformation) between the independent and dependent variables across the 12-month period from pre- to posttest were .59 for WF, .50 for WM, .43 for BF, and .30 for BM. Although the mean correlations were lower for blacks, the 112 comparisons of pairs of correlations revealed only three significant differences, a less-than-chance occurrence with this number of comparisons (Sakoda, Cohen, & Beall, 1954). Using the Potthoff (1966) technique for comparing regression lines produced quite different results. Of the 112 comparisons of regression lines, 43 (38.4%) showed differences. For comparisons with race as the major variable (and sex controlled), 31 (55.2%) of the 56 comparisons showed significantly different regression lines. Clearly, racial bias was significantly more prevalent than sex bias ($p < .01$) in prediction. In comparing the various pretests, bias occurred most often with the Preschool Inventory and the Lee–Clark, whereas none of the comparisons involving the MRT showed bias. Though race clearly influenced homogeneity of regression across groups, the bias in each case acted to overpredict performance of lower-scoring groups; thus the bias acted against whites and females and in favor of blacks and males. A follow-up study (Reynolds, 1980b) has indicated one potential method for avoiding bias in the prediction of early school achievement with readiness or screening measures.

Brief screening measures, especially at the preschool level, typically do not have the high level of reliability obtained by such instruments as the WISC-R or the Stanford–Binet. As previously discussed, Linn and Werts (1971) have convincingly demonstrated that poor reliability can lead to bias in prediction. Early screening measures, as a rule, also assess a very limited area of functioning, rather than allowing the child to demonstrate his or her skills in a variety of areas of cognitive functioning. the one well-researched, reliable, broad-based readiness test, the MRT, has failed to show bias with regard to internal or external criteria. Comprehensive and reliable individual preschool instruments such as the WPPSI and the McCarthy Scales, while showing no internal evidence of test bias, have not been researched with regard to predictive bias across race. Reynolds (1980b) examined the predictive validity of the seven preschool measures described previously when these were combined into a larger battery, thus increasing the scope and reliability of the assessment.

Since our definition of predictive bias requires that errors in prediction be independent of group membership, Reynolds (1980b) directly examined residuals (a "residual term" is the remainder when the predicted score for an individual is subtracted from the individual's obtained score) across races and genders when the seven-test battery was used to predict MAT scores in a multiple-regression formula. Subtests of the seven-test battery were also examined. Results of a race × sex ANOVA of residuals for each of the MAT subtests when the seven-test battery was employed revealed no significant differences in residuals across races and genders, and no significant interactions occurred. When a subset of the larger battery was submitted to the same analysis, racial bias in prediction did not occur; however, a significant F resulted for sex effects in the prediction of two of the four MAT subscores (Word Discrimination and Word Knowledge). Examination of the residuals for each group showed that the bias in prediction was again against the group with the higher mean criterion scores: There was a consistent underprediction of performance for females. The magnitude of the effect was small, however, being on the order of 0.13 to 0.16 standard deviation. Thus, at the preschool level, the only convincing evidence of bias in predictive validity is a sex effect, not a race effect. Although females tend to be slightly overidentified through early screening, it is intersting to note that, while special education classes are more blatantly sexist than racist in composition, it is boys who outnumber girls at a ratio of about 3.5:1 to 4:1. Few, if any, would argue that this disproportionate representation of males in special education is inappropriate or due to "test bias."

Kamphaus and Reynolds (1987) reviewed the available literature on predictive bias with the K-ABC and concluded that overprediction of black children's performance in school is more common with the K-ABC, particularly the K-ABC Sequential Processing scale, than with other tests. The effects are small, however, and are mitigated in large part by using the K-ABC Mental Processing Composite. Some bias also occurs against blacks, but when the extensive nature of the bias research with the K-ABC is considered, results with the K-ABC are not substantially different from the results with the WISC-R (with the exception of overprediction of black academic performance by the K-ABC Sequential Processing scale).

With regard to bias in predictive validity, the empirical evidence suggests conclusions similar to those regarding bias in content and construct validity. There is no strong evidence to support contentions of differential of single-group validity. Bias occurs infrequently and with no apparently observable pattern, except when instruments of poor reliability and high specificity of test content are examined. When bias occurs, it is most often in the direction of favoring low-SES, disadvantaged ethnic minority children, or other low-scoring groups. Clearly, bias in predictive validity cannot account for the disproportionate number of minority group children diagnosed and placed in EMR and emotionally disturbed (EMH) settings.

CONCLUSION

There is little question that the issue of bias in mental testing is an important one with strong historical precedence in the social sciences and, ultimately, formidable social consequences. Because the history of mental measurement has been closely wed from the outset to societal needs and expectations, testing in all forms has remained in the limelight, subjected to the crucible of social inspection, review, and (at times) condemnation. However, the fact that tests and measures of human aptitude and achievement continue to be employed in most modern cultures indicates strongly that the practice has value, despite the recurring storms of criticism over the years. The ongoing controversy related to test bias and the "fair" use of measures will undoubtedly remain with the social sciences for at least as long as we intertwine the nature–nurture question with these issues and affirm differences between/among groups in mean performance on standardized tests. Numerous scholars in the field of psychometrics have been attempting to separate the nature–nurture issue and data on mean score differences from the more orderly, empirically driven specialty of bias investigation, but the separation will undoubtedly not be a clean one. A sharp distinction has developed between the popular press and scientific literature with regard to the interpretation of mental measurement research. The former all too often engenders beliefs that biased measures are put into use for socially pernicious purposes (e.g., Gould, 1981); the latter has attempted to maintain balanced scientific analysis and inquiry in fields (i.e., psychology and education) often accused of courting political, social, and professional ideologies. The former appears to have created confusion in public opinion concerning the possibility of "fair" testing, to say the least. The latter—reported in this chapter—has been demonstrating through a rather sizable body of data that the hypothesis of cultural bias on tests is not a particularly strong one at present. In any event, societal scrutiny and ongoing sentiment about testing have without question served to force the psychometric community to refine its definition of bias further, to inspect practices in the construction on nonbiased measures, and to develop statistical procedures to detect bias when it is occurring. We can argue whether the social sciences have from the outset overstepped their bounds in implementing testing for social purposes before adequate data and methods were developed, but the resulting advancements made in bias technology in response to ongoing public inspection are undeniable.

Data from the empirical end of bias investigation do suggest several guidelines to follow in order to insure equitable assessment. Points to consider include (1) investigation of possible referral source bias, as there is evidence that persons are not always referred for services on the basis of impartial, objective rationales; (2) inspection of test developers' data for evidence that sound statistical analyses for bias across groups to be evaluated with the measure have been completed; (3) assessment with the most reliable measure available; and (4) assessment of multiple abilities with multiple methods. In other words, psychologists need to view multiple sources of accurately derived data prior to making decisions concerning children. We may hope that this is not too far afield from what has actually been occurring in the practice of psychological assessment, though one continues to hear isolated stories of grossly incompetent placement decisions being made (e.g., Mason, 1979). This does not mean that psychologists should be blind to a child's environmental background. Information concerning the home, community, and school environment must all be evaluated in the individualized decision-making process. Exactly how this may be done is addressed in other chapters of this volume. Neither, however, can the psychologist ignore the fact that low-IQ, disadvantaged children from ethnic minority groups are just as likely to fail academically as are white, middle-class low-IQ children, provided that their environmental circumstances remain constant. Indeed, it is the purpose of the assessment process to beat the prediction—to provide insight into hypotheses for environmental interventions that will prevent the predicted failure.

A philosophical perspective is emerging in the bias literature that is requiring test developers not only to demonstrate whether their measures demonstrate differential content, construct, and predictive validity across groups *prior* to publication, but also to incorporate in some form content analyses by interested groups to insure that offensive materials are omitted. Although there are no sound empirical data to suggest that persons can determine bias upon surface inspection, the synergistic relatonship between test use and pure psychometrics must be acknowledged and accommodated in orderly fashion before tests gain greater acceptance within society. Ideally, a clear consensus on "fairness" (and steps taken to reach this end) is needed between those persons with more subjective concerns and those interested in gathering objective bias data during the after test construction. Accommodation along this line will ultimately insure that all parties interested in any given test believe that the measure in question is nonbiased and that the steps taken to achieve "fairmess" can be held up to public scrutiny without reservation. Given the significant and reliable methods developed over the last several decades in bias research, it is untenable at this point to abandon statistical analyses in favor of "armchair" determinations of bias. Test authors and publishers need to demonstrate factorial invariance across all groups for whom the test is designed in order to make the instrument more readily interpretable. Comparisons of predictive validity across races and genders during the test development phase are also needed. With the exception of some recent achievement tests, this has not been common practice, yet it is at this stage that tests can be altered through a variety of item analysis procedurres to eliminate any apparent racial and sexual bias.

A variety of criteria must be explored further before the question of bias is empirically resolved. Many different achievement tests and teacher-made, classroom-specific tests need to be employed in future studies of predictive bias. The issues of differential validity of tests in the affective domain and the limited data available are reviewed in Volume 2 of this work by Moran (Chapter 22). This is an important area for examination as more objective determinations of emotional disturbance are required. It will also be important to stay abreast of metholodological advances that may make it possible to resolve some of the current issues and to identify common characteristics among the (now seen by irregular or random and infrequent) findings of bias.

REFERENCES

Alley, G., & Foster, C. (1978). Nondiscriminatory testing of minority and exceptional children. *Focus on Exceptional Children*, 9, 1–14.

Anastasi, A. (1986). *Psychological testing* (4th ed.). New York: Macmillan.

American Psychological Association. (1970). Psychological assessment and public policy. *American Psychologist*, 31, 264–266.

Angoff, W. H. (1976). Group membership as a predictor variable: A comment on McNemar. *American Psychologist*, 31, 612.

Angoff, W. H., & Ford, S. R. 91973). Item–race interaction on a test of scholastic aptitude. *Journal of Educational Measurement*, 10, 95–106.

Auerbach, A. G. 91971). The social control of learning disabilities. *Journal of Learning Disabilities*, 4, 25–34.

Bartlett, C. J., & O'Leary, B. S. (1969). A differential prediction model to moderate the effect of heterogeneous groups in personnel selection. *Personnel Psychology*, 22, 1–18.

Bass, A. R. 91976). The "equal risk" model: A comment on McMemar. *American Psychologist*, 31, 611–612.

Bayley, N. (1969). *Bayley Scales of Infant Development*. New York: Psychological Corporation.

Beauchamp, D. P., Samuels, D. D., & Griffore, R. J. (1979). WISC-R Information and Digit Span scores of American and Canadian children. *Applied Psychological Measurement*, 3, 231–236.

Berk, R. A. (Ed.). (1982). *Handbook of methods for detecting test bias*. Baltimore: Johns Hopkins University Press.

Bernal, E. M. (1975). A response to "Educational uses of tests with disadvantaged students." *American Psychologist*, 30, 93–95.

Binet, A., & Simon, T. (1905). Methodes nouvelles pour le diagnostic du niveau intellectuel des anormaux. *L'Année Psychologique*, 11, 191–244.

Blaha, J., Wallbrown, F., & Wherry, R. J. (1975). The hierarchial factor structure of the Wechsler Intelligence Scale for Children. *Psychological Reports*, 35, 771–778.

Bogen, J. E., DeZure, R. Tenhouten, N., & Marsh, J. (1972). The other side o the brain: IV. The A/P ratio. *Bulletin of the Los Angeles Neurological Society*, 37, 49–61.

Bond, L. (1981). Bias in mental tests. In B. F. Green (Ed.), *Issues in testing: Coaching, disclosure, and ethnic bias*. San Francisco: Jossey-Bass.

Bossard, M. D., Reynolds, C. R., & Gutkin, T. B. (1980). A regression analysis of test bias on the Stanford–Binet Intelligence Scale. *Journal of Clinical Child Psychology,*

Bower, E. M. (1974). The three-pipe problem: Promotion of competent human beings through a pre-school, kindergarten, program and other sundry elementary matters. In G. J. Williams & S. Gordon (Eds.), *Clinical child psychology: Current practices and future perspectives.* New York: Behavioral.

Burrill, L. (1975). *Statistical evidence of potential bias in items and tests assessing current educational status.* Paper presented at the annual meeting of the Southeastern Conference on Measurement in Education, New Orleans.

Cancro, R. (1971). Genetic contributions to individual differences in intelligence: An introduction. In R. Camcro (Ed.), *Intelligence: Genetic and environmental influences.* New York: Grune & Stratton.

Cardall, C., & Coffman, W. E. (1964). *A method of comparing the performance of different groups on the items in a test* (Research Bulletin No. 64-61). Princeton, NJ: Educational Testing Service.

Cattell, R. B. (1979). Are culture fair intelligence tests possible and necessary? *Journal of Research and Development in Education, 12,* 3–13.

Chinn, P. C. (1979). The exceptional minority child: Issues and some answers. *Exceptional Children, 46,* 532–536.

Cleary, T. A. (1968). Test bias: Prediction of grades of Negro and white students in integrated colleges. *Journal of Educational Measurement, 5,* 118–124.

Cleary, T. A., & Hilton, T. L. (1968). An investigation of item bias. *Educational and Psychological Measurement, 28,* 61–75.

Cleary, T. A., Humphreys, L. G., Kendrick, S. A., & Wesman, A. (1975). Educational uses of test with disadvantaged students. *American Psychologist, 30,* 15–41.

Cortez v. Rosen. (1975). United States District Court of Northern District of California (not reported in FEP)

Council for Exceptional Children. (1978). Minorities position policy statements. *Exceptional Children, 45,* 57–64.

Critchley, D. L. (1979). The adverse influence of psychiatric diagnostic labels on the observation of child behavior. *American Journal of Orthopsychiatry, 49,* 157–160.

Cronbach, L. J. (1970). *Essentials of psychological testing.* New York: Harper & Row.

Cronbach, L. J. (1976). Equity in selection—where psychometrics and political philosophy meet. *Journal of Educational Measurement, 13,* 31–42.

Cronbach, L. J. (1980). Validity on parole: How can we go straight? In W. B. Schraeder (Ed.), *New directions for testing and measurement: Vol. 5. Measuring achievement: Progress over a decade.* San Francisco: Jossey-Bass.

Darlington, R. B. (1971). Another look at "cultural fairness." *Journal of Educational Measurement, 8,* 71–82.

Darlington, R. B. (1976). A defense of rational personnel selection, and two new methods. *Journal of Educational Measurement, 13,* 43–52.

Darlington, R. B. (1978). Cultural test bias: Comments on Hunter and Schmidt. *Psychological Bulletin, 85,* 673–674.

Dean, R. S. (1977). Reliability of the WISC-R with

Mexican-American children. *Journal of School Psychology, 15,* 267–268.

Dean, R. S. (1979a). Distinguished patterns for Mexican-American children on the WISC-R. *Journal of Clinical Psychology, 35,* 790–794.

Dean, R. S. (1979b, September). *WISC-R factor structure for Anglo and Hispanic children.* Paper presented at the annual meeting of the American Psychological Assocation, New York.

DeFries, J. C., Vandenberg, S. G., McClearn, G. E., Kuse, A. R., Wilson, J. R., Ashton, G. C., & Johnson, R. C. (1974). Near identity of cognitive structure in two ethnic groups. *Science, 183,* 338–339.

Dershowitz, Z., & Frankel, Y. (1975). Jewish culture and the "WISC and WAIS test patterns. *Journal of Consulting and Clinical Psychology, 43,* 126–134.

Diana v. State Board of Education, C.A. No. C-70-37 (N.D. Cal. 1970).

Dworkin, N., & Dworkin, Y. (1979). The legacy of Pygmalion in the classroom. *Phi Delta Kappan, 61,* 712–715.

Ebel, R. L. 91979). Intelligence: A skeptical view. *Journal of Research and Development in Education, 12,* 14–21.

Eells, K., Davis, A., Havighurst, R. J., Herrick, V. E., & Typer, R. W. (1951). *Intelligence and culture differences.* Chicago: University of Chicago Press.

Einhorn, H. J., & Bass, A. R. (1971). Methodological considerations relevant to discrimination in employment testing. *Psychological Bulletin, 75,* 261–269.

Fancher, R. E. 91979). *Pioneers of psychology.* New York: Norton.

Flaugher, R. L. (1978). The many definitions of test bias. *American Psychologist, 33,* 671–679.

Flaugher, R. L., & Schrader, W. B. (1978). *Eliminating differentially difficult itmes as an approach to test bias* (Research Bulletin No. 78-4). Princeton, NJ: Educational Testing Service.

Foster, G., & Ysseldyke, J. (1976). Expectancy and halo effects as a result of artificially induced teacher bias. *Contemporary Educational Psychology, 1,* 37–45.

Frame, R. (1979, September). *Diagnoses related to school achievement, client's race, and socioeconomic status.* Paper presented at the annual meeting of the American Psychological Association, New York.

Freeman, F. N. (1926). *Mental tests: Their history, principles and applications.* Boston: Houghton Mifflin.

Gael, S., & Grant, D. L. (1972). Employment test validation for minority and non-minority telephone company service representatives. *Journal of Applied Psychology, 56,* 135–139.

Gerber, M., & Dean, R. F. (1957). Gesell tests on African children. *Pediatrics, 20,* 1055–1065.

Goldman, R. D., & Hartig, (1976). The WISC may not be a valid predictor of school performance for primary-grade minority children. *American Journal of Mental Deficiency, 80,* 583–587.

Goldman, R. D., & Hewitt, B. N. (1976). Predicting the success of black, Chicano, Oriental, and white college students. *Journal of Educational Measurement, 13,* 107–117.

Goolsby, T. M., & Frary, R. B. (1970). Validity of the Metropolitan Readiness Test for white and Negro students in a Southern city. *Educational and Psychological Measurement, 30,* 443–450.

Gordon, R. A. (1984). Digits backward and the Mercer–Kamin law: An empirical response to Mercer's treatment of internal validity of IQ tests. In C. R. Reynolds & R. T. Brown (Eds.), *Perspectives on Bias in Mental Testing*, NY: Plenum.

Gordon, R. A., & Rudert, E. E. (1979). Bad news concerning IQ tests. *Sociology of Education, 52*, 174–190.

Gould, S. J. (1981). *The mismeasure of man*. New York: Norton.

Grant, D. L., & Bray, D. W. (1970). Validation of employment tests for telephone company installation and repair occupations. *Journal of Applied Psychology, 54*, 7–14.

Griggs v. Duke Power Co., 401 U.S. 424 (1971).

Gross, A. L., & Su, W. (1975). Defining a "fair" or "unbiased" selection model. *Journal of Applied Psychology, 60*, 345–351.

Gross, M. (1967). *Learning readiness in two Jewish groups*. New York: Center for Urban Education.

Gulliksen, H., & Wilks, S. S. (1965). Regression tests for several samples. *Psychometrika, 15*, 91–114.

Guterman, S. S. (1979). IQ tests in research on social stratification: The cross-class validity of the tests as measures of scholastic aptitude. *Sociology of Education, 52*, 163–173.

Gutkin, T. B., & Reynolds, C. R. (1980). Factorial similarity of the WISC-R for Anglos and Chicanos referred for psychological services. *Journal of School Psychology, 18*, 34–39.

Gutkin, T. B., & Reynolds, C. R. (1981). Factorial similarity of the WISC-R for white and black children from the standardization sample. *Journal of Educational Psychology. 73*, 227–231.

Gutkin, T. B., & Tieger, A. G. (1979). Funding patterns for exceptional children: Current approaches and suggested alternatives. *Professional Psychology, 10*, 670–680.

Harman, H. (1976). *Modern factor analysis* (2nd ed.). Chicago: University of Chicago Press.

Harrington, G. M. (1968a). Genetic–environmental interaction in "intelligence": I. Biometric genetic analysis of maze performance of *Rattus Norvegicus*. *Developmental Psychobiology, 1*, 211–218.

Harrington, G. M. (1968b). Genetic–environmental interaction in "intelligence": II. Models of behavior, components of variance, and research strategy. *Developmental Psychobiology, 1*, 245–253.

Harrington, G. M. (1975). Intelligence tests may favour the majority groups in a population. *Nature, 258*, 708–709.

Harrington, G. M. (1976, September). *Minority test bias as a psychometric artifact: The experimental evidence*. Paper presented at the annual meeting of the American Psychological Association, Washington, DC.

Harrington, G. M. (1984). An experimental model of bias in mental testing, In C. R. Reynolds & R. T. Brown (Eds.), *Perspectives on bias in mental testing*. New York: Plenum.

Hartlage, L. C., Lucas, T., & Godwin, A. (1976). Culturally biased and culture fair tests correlated with school performance in culturally disadvantaged children. *Journal of Clinical Psychology, 32*, 235–237.

Heidbreder, E. (1933). *Seven psychologies*. Englewood Cliffs, NJ: Prentice-Hall.

Henderson, N. B., Butler, B. B., & Goffeney, B. (1969). Effectiveness of the WISC and Bender–Gestalt test in predicting arithmetic and reading achievement for white and non-white children. *Journal of Clinical Psychology, 25*, 268–271.

Hickman, J. A., & Reynolds, C. R. (1986). Race differences on mental tests: A test of Harrington's experimental model. *Journal of Special Education, 20*, 409–430.

Hildreth, G. H., Griffiths, N. L., & McGauvran, M. E. (1969). *Metropolitan Readiness Tests*. New York: Harcourt Brace Jovanovich.

Hilliard, A. G. (1979). Standardization and cultural bias as impediments to the scientific study and validation of "intelligence." *Journal of Research and Development in Education, 12*, 47–58.

Hobbs, N. R. (1975). *The future of children*. San Francisco: Jossey-Bass.

Hobson v. Hansen, 269 F. Supp. 401 (D.C. 1967).

Humphreys, L. G. (1973). Statistical definitions of test validity for minoriity groups. *Journal of Applied Psychology, 58*, 1–4.

Hunter, J. E. (1975, December). *A critical analysis of the use of item means and item–test correlations to determine the presence or absence of content bias in achievement test items*. Paper presented at the National Institute of Education Conference on Test Bias, Annapolis, MD.

Hunter, J. E., & Schmidt, F. L. (1976). Critical analysis of the statistical and ethical implications of various definitions of test bias. *Psychological Bulletin, 83*, 1053–1071.

Hunter, J. E., & Schmidt, F. L. (1978). Bias in defining test bias: Reply to Darlington. *Psychological Bulletin, 85*, 675–676.

Hunter, J. E., Schmidt, F. L., & Hunter, R. (1979). Differential validity of employment tests by race: A comprehensive review and analysis. *Psychological Bulletin, 86*, 721–735.

Hunter, J. E., Schmidt, F. L., & Rauschenberger, J. (1984). Methodological, statistical, and ethical issues in the study of bias in psychological tests. In C. R. Reynolds & R. T. Braun (Eds.), *Perspectives on bias in mental testing*, New York: Plenum.

Jackson, G. D. (1975). Another psychological view from the Association of Black Psychologists. *American Psychologist, 30*, 88–93.

Jacobs, W. R. (1978). The effect of the learning disability label on classroom teachers' ability objectively to observe and interpret child behaviors. *Learning Disability Quarterly, 1*, 50–55.

Jensen, A.R. (1969). How much can we boost IQ and scholastic achievement? *Harvard Educational Review, 39*, 1–123.

Jensen, A. R. (1974). How biased are culture-loaded tests? *Genetic Psychology Monographs, 90*, 185–224.

Jensen, A. R. (1976). Test bias and construct validity. *Phi Delta Kappan, 58*, 340–346.

Jensen, A. R. (1977). An examination of culture bias in the Wonderlic Personnel Test. *Intelligence, 1*, 51–64.

Jensen, A. R. (1980). *Bias in mental testing*. New York: Free Press.

Jensen, A. R. (1985). The nature of the black–white difference on various tests: Spearman's hypothesis. *Behavioral and Brain Sciences, 8*, 193–263.

Jenson, A. R., & Figueroa, R. A. (1975). Forward and backward Digit Span interaction with race and IQ. *Journal of Educatiooal Psychology, 67*, 882–893.

Jensen, A. R., & Reynolds, C. R. (1982). Race, social class, and ability patterns of the WISC-R. *Personality and Individual Differences, 3*, 423–438.

Jöreskog, K. G. (1969). A general approach to confirmatory maximum likelihood factor analysis. *Psychometrika, 34,* 183.

Jöreskog, K. G. (1971). Simultaneous factor analysis in several populations. *Psychometrika, 36,* 409–426.

Kaiser, S. M. (1986). *Ability patterns of black and white adults on the Wechsler Adult Intelligence Scale— Revised independent of general intelligence and as a function of socioeconomic status.* Unpublished doctoral dissertation, Texas A&M University.

Kallingal, A. (1971). The prediction of grades for black and white students at Michigan State University. *Journal of Educational Measurement, 8,* 263–265.

Kamphaus, R. W., & Reynolds, C. R. (1987). *Clinical and research application of the K-ABC.* Circle Pines, MN: American Guidance Service.

Katzenmeyer, W. G., & Stenner, A. J. (1977). Estimation of the invariance of factor structures across sex and race with implications for hypothesis testing. *Educational and Psychological Measurement, 37,* 111–119.

Kaufman, A. S. (1975). Factor analysis of the WISC-R at 11 age levels between 6½ and 16½ years. *Journal of Consulting and Clinical Psychology, 43,* 135–147.

Kaufman, A. S. (1979, October). *The future of psychological assessment and its relationship to school psychology.* Invited address to the Fourth Annual Midwestern Conference on Psychology in the Schools, Boys Town, NE.

Kaufman, A. S., & DiCuio, R. (1975). Separate factor analyses of the McCarthy Scales for groups of black and white children. *Journal of School Psychology, 13,* 10–18.

Kaufman, A. S., & Hollenbeck, G. P. (1974). Comparative structure of the WPPSI for blacks and whites. *Journal of Clinical Psychology, 30,* 316–319.

Kennedy, D. A. (1978). Rationality, emotionality, and testing. *Journal of School Psychology, 16,* 16–24.

Kerlinger, F. N. (1973). *Foundations of behavioral research.* New York: Holt, Rinehart & Winston.

Kirkpatrick, J. J. (1970, September). *The psychological testing establishment: Vested interest versus responsibility.* Paper presented at the annual meeting of the American Psychological Association, Miami Beach, FL.

Kirkpatrick, J. J., Ewen, R. G., Barrett, R. S., & Katzell, R. A. (1968). *Testing and fair employment.* New York: New York University Press.

Kohs, S. C. (1923). *Intelligence measurement.* New York: Macmillan.

Larry P. v. Riles, 495 F. Supp. 926 (N.D. Cal. 1979).

Leiderman, P. H., Babu, B., Kagia, J., Kraemer, H. C., & Leiderman, F. G. (1973). African infant precocity and some social influences during the first year. *Nature, 242,* 247–249.

Leventhal, D. S., & Stedman, D. J. (1970). A factor analytic study of the Illinois Test of Psycholinguistic Abilities. *Journal of Clinical Psychology, 26,* 473–477.

Lewis, D. O., Balla, D. A., & Shanok, S. S. 9179). Some evidence of race bias in the diagnosis and treatment of the juvenile offender. *American Journal of Orthopsychiatry, 49,* 53–61.

Lewontin, R. C. (1970). Race and intelligence. *Bulletin of the Atomic Scientists, 26,* 2–8.

Lindsey, J. (1967). *The factorial organization of intelligence in children as related to the variables of age,* sex, and subculture. Unpublished doctoral dissertation, University of Georgia.

Linn, R. L. (1976). In search of fair selection procedures. *Journal of Educational Measurement, 13,* 53–58.

Linn, R. L., & Werts, C. E. (1971). Considerations for studies of test bias. *Journal of Educational Measurement, 8,* 1–4.

Loehlin, J., Lindzey, G., & Spuhler, J. N. (1975). *Race differences in intelligence.* San Francisco: W. H. Freeman.

Lord, F. M. (1977). A study of item bias, using item characteristic curve theory. In Y. H. Poortinga (Ed.), *Basic problems in cross-cultural psychology.* Amsterdam: Swets & Zeitlinger.

MacArthur, R. S. (1968). Some differential abilities of northern Canadian youth. *International Journal of Psychology, 3,* 43–51.

MacMillan, D. L., Jones, R. L., & Aloia, G. F. (1974). The mentally retarded label: A theoretical analysis and review of research. *American Journal of Mental Deficiency, 79,* 241–261.

Marjoribanks, K. (1972). Ethnic and environmental influences on mental abilities. *American Journal of Sociology, 78,* 323–337.

Mason, E. J. (1979). A blessing dressed up like the plague? *The School Psychologist, 35,* 6.

Matuszek, P., & Oakland, T. (1979). Factors influencing teachers' and psychologists' recommendations regarding special class placement. *Journal of School Psychology, 17,* 116–125.

McCarthy, D. (1972). *McCarthy Scales of Children's Abilities.* New York: Psychological Corporation.

McCoy, S. A. (1976). Clinical judgements of normal childhood behaviors. *Journal of Consulting and Clinical Psychology, 44,* 710–714.

McGurk, F. V. J. (1951). *Comparison of the performance of Negro and white high school seniors on cultural and noncultural psychological test questions.* Washington, DC: Catholic University Press.

McNemar, Q. (1975). On so-called test bias. *American Psychologist, 30,* 848–851.

Mercer, J. R. (1971). The meaning of mental retardation. In R. Koch & J. Dobson (Eds.), *The mentally retarded child and his family: A multidisciplinary handbook.* New York: Brunner/Mazel.

Mercer, J. R. (1976, August). *Cultural diversity, mental retardation, and assessment: The case for nonlabeling.* Paper presented at the Fourth International Congress of the International Association for the Scientific Study of Mental Retardation, Washington, DC.

Mercer, J. R. (1979). In defense of racially and culturally nondiscriminatory assessment. *School Psychology Digest, 8,* 89–115.

Merz, W. A. (1970). *Factor analysis of the Goodenough-Harris drawing test items across four ethnic groups.* Ann Arbor, MI: University Microfilms. (No. 10–19, 714)

Meyers, C. E., MacMillan, D. L., & Yoshida, R. K. (1978). Validity of psychologists' identification of EMR students in the perspective of the California decertification experience. *Journal of School Psychology, 16,* 3–15.

Mille, F. (1979). Cultural bias in the WISC. *Intelligence, 3,* 149–164.

Minton, H. L., & Schneider, F. W. (1980). *Differential psychology.* Monterey, CA: Brooks/Cole.

Mitchell, B. C. (1967). Predictive validity of the Metropolitan Readiness Tests and the Murphy–Durrell Reading Analysis for white and for Negro pupils. *Educational and Psychological Measurement, 27,* 1047–1054.

Nalven, F. B., Hoffman, L. J., & Bierbryer, B. (1969). The effects of subject's age, sex, race, and socioeconomic status on psychologists' estimates of "true IQ" from WISC scores. *Journal of Clinical Psychology, 25,* 271–274.

Nichols, R. C. (1978). Policy implications of the IQ controversy. In L. S. Schulman (Ed.), *Review of research in education* (Vol. 6). Itasca, IL: F. E. Peacock.

Novick, M. R., & Petersen, N. S. (1976). Towards equalizing educational and employment opportunity. *Journal of Educational Measurement, 13,* 77–88.

Oakland, T. (1978). Predictive validity of readiness tests for middle and lower socioeconomic status Anglo, black and Mexican American children. *Journal of Educational Psychology, 70,* 574–582.

Oakland, T., & Feigenbaum, D. (1979). Multiple sources of test bias on the WISC-R and the Bender–Gestalt Test. *Journal of Consulting and Clinical Psychology, 47,* 968–974.

Oakland, T., & Matuszek, P. (1977). Using tests of nondiscriminatory assessment. In T. Oakland (Ed.), *Psychological and educational assessment of minority group children.* New York: Brunner/Mazel.

O'Conner, E. J., Wexley, K. N., & Alexander, R. A. 91975). Single group validity: Fact or fallacy? *Journal of Applied Psychology, 60,* 352–355.

Petersen, N. S., & Novick, M. R. (1976). An evaluation of some models for culture fair selection. *Journal of Educational Measurement, 13,* 3–29.

Pfeifer, C. M., & Sedlacek, W. E. (1971). The validity of academic predictors for black and white students at a predominately white university. *Journal of Educational Measurement, 8,* 253–261.

Pintner, R. (1923). *Intelligence testing.* New York: Henry Holt.

Pintner, R., & Keller, R. (1922). Intelligence tests of foreign children. *Journal of Educational Psychology, 13,* 214–222.

Plake, B., & Hoover, H. (1979, September). *A methodology for identifying biased achievement test items that removes the confounding in a items by groups interaction due to possible group differences in instructional level.* Paper presented at the annual meeting of the American Educational Research Association, Toronto.

Potthoff, R. F. (1966). *Statistical aspects of the problem of biases in psychological tests.* (Institute of statistics Mimeo Series No. 479). Chapel Hill: University of North Carolina, Department of Statistics.

Pressey, S. L., & Pressey. L. L. (1922). *Introduction to the use of standardized tests.* Yonkers, NY: World.

Ramsey, R. T. (1979). *The testing manual: A guide to test administration and use.* Pittsburgh: Author.

Reschly, D. J. (1978). WISC-R factor structures among Anglos, blacks, Chicanos, and Native American Papagos. *Journal of Consulting and Clinical Psychology, 46,* 417–422.

Reschly, D. J. (1980). Concepts of bias in assessment and WISC-R research with minorities. In H. Vance & F. Wallborwn (Eds.), *WISC-R: Research and interpretation.* Washington, DC: National Association of School Psychologists.

Reschly, D. J., & Reschly, J. E. (1979). Validity of WISC-R factor scores in predicting achievement and attention for four sociocultural groups. *Journal of School Psychology, 17,* 355–361.

Reschly, D. J., & Sabers, D. (1979). Analysis of test bias in four groups with the regression definition. *Journal of Educational Measurement, 16,* 1–9.

Reynolds, C. R. (1978). *Differntial validity of several preschool assessment instruments for blacks, whites, males, and females.* Unpublished doctoral dissertation, University of Georgia.

Reynolds, C. R. (1979a). Should we screen preschoolers? *Contemporary Educational Psychology, 4,* 175–181.

Reynolds, C. R. (1979b). A factor analytic study of the Metropolitan Readiness Test. *Contemporary Educational Psychology, 4,* 315–317.

Reynolds, C. R. (1979c). The invariance of the factorial validity of the Metropolitan Readiness Tests for blacks, whites, males and females. *Educational and Psychological Measurement, 39,* 1047–1052.

Reynolds, C. R. (1980a). Differential construct validity of a preschool battery for blacks, whites, males and females. *Journal of School Psychology, 18,* 112–125.

Reynolds, C. R. (1980b). A examination for test bias in a preschool battery across race and sex. *Journal of Educational Measurement, 17,* 137–146.

Reynolds, C. R. (1980c, April). *Differential predictive validity of a preschool battery across race and sex.* Paper presented at the annual meeting of the American Educational Research Association, Boston.

Reynolds, C. R. (1982). Methods for the detecting construct and predictive bias. In R. A. Berk (Ed.), *Handbook of methods of detecting test.* Baltimore: John Hopkins University Press.

Reynolds, C. R., Bossard, M. D., & Gutkin, T. B. (1980, April). *A regression analysis of test bias on the Stanford–Binet Intelligence Scale.* Paper presented at the annual meeting of the American Educational Research Assocation, Boston.

Reynolds, C. R., & Brown, R. T. (Eds.). (1984). *Perspectives on bias in mental testing.* New York: Plenum.

Reynolds, C. R., & Clark, J. H. (1986). Profile analysis of standardized intelligence test performance on very high functioning individuals. *Psychology in the Schools, 23,* 5–12.

Reynolds, C. R., & Gutkin, T. B. (1979). Predicting the premorbid intellectual status of children using demographic data. *Clinical Neuropsychology, 1,* 36–38.

Reynolds, C. R., & Gutkin, T. B. (1980a, September). *WISC-R performance of blacks and whites matched on four demogtaphic variables.* Paper presented at the annual meeting of the American Psychological Association, Montreal.

Reynolds, C. R., & Gutkin, T. B. (1980b). A regression analysis of test bias on the WISC-R for Anglos and Chicanos referred to psychological services. *Journal of Abnormal Child Psychology, 8,* 237–243.

Reynolds, C. R., & Gutkin, T. B. (1980c). Stability of the WISC-R factor structure across sex at two age levels. *Journal of Clinical Psychology, 36,* 775–777.

Reynolds, C. R., Gutkin, T. B., Dappen, L., & Wright, D. (1979). Differential validity of the WISC-R for boys and girls referred for psychological services. *Perceptual and Motor Skills, 48,* 868–879.

Reynolds, C. R., & Harding, R. E. (1983). Outcome in two large sample studies of factorial similarity under six methods of comparison. *Educational and Psychological Measurement, 43,* 723–728.

Reynolds, C. R., & Hartlage, L. C. (1978, March). *Comparison of WISC and WISC-R racial regression lines.* Paper presented at the annual meeting of the Southeastern Psychological Association, Atlanta.

Reynolds, C. R., & Hartlage, L. C. (1979). Comparison of WISC and WISC-R regression lines for academic prediction with black and with white referred children. *Journal of Consulting and Clinical Psychology, 47,* 589–591.

Reynolds, C. R., & Jansen, A. R. (1983). WISC-R subscale patterns of abilities of Blacks and Whites matched on Full Scale IQ. *Journal of Educational Psychology, 75,* 207–214.

Reynolds, C. R., McBride, R. D., & Gibson, L. J. (1979, March). *Black–white IQ discrepancies may be related to differences in hemisphericity.* Paper presented at the annual meeting of the National Association of School Psychologists, San Diego.

Reynolds, C. R., Willson, V. L., & Chatman, S. P. (1984). Item bias on the 1981 revision of the Peabody Picture Vocabulary Test using a new technique for detecting bias. *Journal of Psychoeducational Assessment, 2,* 219–227.

Reynolds, C. R., Willson, V. L., & Chatman, S. P. (1985). regression analyses of bias on the Kaufman Assessment Battery for Children. *Journal of School Psychology, 23,* 195–204.

Rosenthal, D. (1975). Heredity in criminality. *Criminal Justice and Behavior, 2,* 3–21.

Ross, A. O. (1974). A clinical child psychologist "examines" retarded children. In G. J. Williams & S. Gordon (Eds.), *Clinical child psychology: Current trends and future perspectives.* New York: Behavioral.

Ross, A. O. (1976). *Psychological aspects of learning disabilities and reading disorders.* New York: McGraw-Hill.

Sakoda, J. M., Cohen, B. H., & Beall, G. (1954). Test of significance for a series of statistical tests. *Psychological Bulletin, 51,* 172–175.

Sandoval, J. (1979). The WISC-R and internal evidence of test bias with minority groups. *Journal of Consulting and Clinical Psychology, 47,* 919–927.

Sandoval, J., & Mille, M. (1979, September). *Accuracy judgements of WISC-R item difficulty for minority groups.* Paper presented at the annual meeting of the American Psychological Association, New York.

Sattler, J. M. (1974). *Assessment of children's intelligence.* Philadelphia: W. B. Saunders.

Sawyer, R. L., Cole, N. S., & Cole, J. W. (1976). Utilities and the issue of fairness in a decision theoretic model for selection. *Journal of Educational Measurement, 13,* 59–76.

Scheuneman, J. D. (1987). An experimental, exploratory study of causes of bias in test items. *Journal of Educational Measurement, 29,* 97–118.

Schmidt, F. L., & Hunter, J. E. (1974). Racial and ethnic bias in psychological tests: Divergent implications of two definition of test bias. *American Psychologist, 29,* 1–8.

Schmidt, W. H. (1983). Content biases in achievement tests. *Journal of Educational Measurement, 20,* 165–178.

Scholwinski, E. J. 91985). *Ability patterns of white and black adults as determined by the subscales on the Wechsler Adult Intelligence Scale—Revised.* Unpublished doctoral dissertation, Texas A&M University, 1985.

Semler, I., & Iscoe, I. (1966). Structure of intelligence in Negro and white children. *Journal of Educational Psychology, 57,* 326–336.

Sewell, T. E. (1979). Intelligence and learning tasks as predictors of scholastic achievement in black and white first-grade children. *Journal of School Psychology, 17,* 325–332.

Shepard, L. A. (1982). Definitions of bias. In R. A. Berk (Ed.), *Handbook of methods for detecting test bias.* Baltimore: Johns Hopkins University Press.

Shuey, A. M. (1966). *The testing of Negro intelligence* (2nd ed.). New York: Social Science Press.

Silverstein, A. B. (1973). Factor structure of the Wechsler Intelligence Scale for Children for three ethnic groups. *Journal of Educational Psychology, 65,* 408–410.

Stanley, J. C. (1969). Plotting ANOVA interactions for ease of visual interpretation. *Educational and Psychological Measurement, 29,* 793–797.

Stanley, J. C. (1971). Predicting college success of the educationally disadvantaged. *Science, 171,* 640–647.

Stanley, J. C., & Porter, A. C. (1967). Correlation of scholastic aptitude test scores with college grades for Negroes vs. whites. *Journal of Educational Measurement, 4,* 199–218.

Sternberg, R. J. (1985). The black–white differences and Spearman's g: Old wine in new bottles that still doesn't taste good. *Behavioral and Brain Sciences, 8,* 244.

Temp, G. (1971). Validity of the SAT for blacks and whites in thirteen integrated institutions. *Journal of Educational Measurements, 8,* 245–251.

Tenopyr, M. L. (1967, September). *Race and socioeconomic status as moderators in predicting machine-shop training success.* Paper presented at the annual meeting of the American Psychological Association, Washington, DC.

Thorndike, R. L. (1968). [Review of *Pygmalion in the classroom* by R. Rosenthal and L. Jacobsen]. *American Educational Research Journal, 5,* 708–711.

Thorndike, R. L. (1971). Concepts of culture-fairness. *Journal of Educational Measurement, 8,* 63–70.

Tittle, C. K. (1975). Fairness in educational achievement testing. *Education and Urban Society, 8,* 86–103.

Tittle, C. K. (1982). Use of judgemental methods in item bias studies. In R. A. Berk (Ed.), *Handbook of methods for detecting test bias.* Baltimore: John Hopkins University Press.

Tomlinson, J. R., Acker, N., Canter, A., & Lindborg, S. (1977). Minority status, sex, and school psychological services. *Psychology in the Schools, 14,* 456–460.

Torrance, E. P. (1980). Psychology of gifted children and youth. In W. M. Cruickshank (Ed.), *Psychology of exceptional children and youth.* Englewood Cliffs, NJ: Prentice-Hall.

Tyler, L. E. (1965). *The psychology of human differences.* (2nd ed.). New York: Appleton-Century-Crofts.

Vance, H. B., Hankins, N., & McGee, H. (1979). A preliminary study of black and white differences on the Revised Wechsler Intelligence Scale for Children. *Journal of Clinical Psychology, 35,* 815–819.

Vance, H. B., Huelsman, C. B., & Wherry, R. J. (1976). The hierarchical factor structure of the Wechsler Intelligence Scale for Children as it relates to disadvantaged white and black children. *Journal of General Psychology, 95,* 287–293.

Vance, H. B., & Wallbrown, F. H. (1978). The structure of intelligence for black children: A hierarchical approach. *Psychological Record, 28,* 31–39.

Veale, J. R., & Foreman, D. I. (1983). Assessing cultural bias using foil response data: Cultural variation. *Journal of Educational Measurement, 20,* 249–258.

Waits, C., & Richmond, B. O. (1978). Special education—who needs it? *Exceptional Children, 44,* 279–280.

Wallbrown, F. H., Blaha, J., Wallbrown, J., & Engin, A. (1974). The hierarchical factor structure of the Wechsler Adult Intelligence Scale. *British Journal of Educational Psychology, 44,* 47–65.

Wallbrown, F. H., Blaha, J., & Wherry, R. J. (1973). The hierarchical factor structure of the Wechsler Preschool and Primary Scale of Intelligence. *Journal of Counsulting and Clinical Psychology, 41,* 356–362.

Warren, N. (1972). African infant precocity. *Psychological Bulletin, 78,* 535–367.

Wechsler, D. (1949). *Wechsler Intelligence Scale for Children.* New York: Psychological Corporation.

Wechsler, D. (1974). *Wechsler Intelligence Scale for Children—Revised.* New York: Psychological Corporation.

Wechsler, D. (1981). *Wechsler Adult Intelligence Scale—Revised.* New York: Psychological Corporation.

Wherry, R. J., & Wherry, R. J., Jr. (1969). WHEWH program. In R. J. Wherry (Ed.), *Psychology department computer programs.* Columbus: Ohio State University, Department of Psychology.

Willerman, L. (1979). *The psychology of individual and group differences.* San Francisco. W. H. Freeman.

Williams, R. L. (1970). Danger: Testing and dehumanizing black children. *Clinical Child Psychology Newsletter, 9,* 5–6.

Williams, R. L. (1972, September). *The BITCH-100: A culture specific test.* Paper presented at the annual meeting of the American Psychological Association, Honolulu.

Williams, R. L. (1974). From dehumanization to black intellectual genocide: A rejoinder. In G. J. Williams & S. Gordon (Eds.) *Clinical child psychology: Current practices and future perspectives.* New York: Behavioral.

Wilson, K. M. (1969). *Black students entering CRC colleges: Their characteristics and their first year academic performance* (Research memo No. 69-1). Poughkeepsie, NY: College Research Center.

Wright, B. J., & Isenstein, V. R. (1977). *Psychological tests and minorities* (DHEW Publication No. ADM 78-482). Washington, DC: U.S. Government Printing Office.

27

Assessment of Children's Knowledge of Basic Concepts

ANN E. BOEHM
Teachers College, Columbia University

This chapter focuses on efforts to understand the role of basic relational concepts for young children in school, to highlight aspects of children's development of these concepts, and to present methods of assessing this development. A multiple-step assessment approach is proposed that combines observation, standardized testing procedures, and interview techniques (strategy probes) to reveal the strategies and styles young children use to answer questions focused on basic relational concepts. The strategy probes can be used to expand upon the results gained from traditional tests (both norm-referenced and criterion-referenced) and to suggest instructional interventions. This same multiple-step assessment approach can be used as well with assessment devices in other areas.

IMPORTANCE OF CONCEPTS TO LEARNING

The importance of concepts to learning has been well documented in both the developmental and educational literature. Indeed, concepts are widely viewed as an essential component of thinking. Concepts are used across cultures to describe or explain objects and events, to communicate with others, and to organize experiences. The concepts that a child acquires are influenced by

his or her culture and environmental experiences, as well as by each child's unique ways of perceiving that experience. It follows that concepts are also an important part of a child's preschool and primary school experience. A parent uses concepts when speaking to a child ("You can watch television after you pick up your toys"). A teacher uses concepts when giving directions ("Come to the front of the room") and when presenting instruction ("Which box has the fewest apples?"). The clarity and completeness of a child's concepts have been cited by Russell (1956) as constituting the best measure of a child's probable success in school. It is not surprising, then, that educators are concerned about assessing children's concept understanding.

Although there is consensus that concepts are an essential component of mental life, there is no universally agreed-upon definition of a concept. Flavell (1970) attributes this problem to the fact that concepts vary in their inclusiveness (e.g., "tools" vs. "colors"), position in the generalizability hierarchy (e.g., "vegetables" vs. "liberty"), preciseness (e.g., "big" vs. "narrow"), and importance. There is greater agreement, however, regarding some functions served by concepts and some features of their development, including the following:

They are symbolic in nature (Vinacke, 1951). They help individuals organize their experience and thinking (Ausubel, 1968; Klaus-meier, 1976; Sigel, 1964).

Their acquisition is facilitated through language and relies on the comprehension of language (Bruner, 1964; Gagné, 1985; Klausmeier, 1971; Lichtenstein & Ireton, 1984; Vygotsky, 1962).

Concepts, in turn, facilitate communication (Ausubel, 1968).

Levels of concept attainment change with development from early childhood through adolescence (Gagné, 1985; Klausmeier, 1971; Piaget, 1970).

Their acquisition is related to conditions in the learner and in the environment (Klausmeier, 1971; Vinacke, 1951).

They are building blocks for problem solving and thinking (Boehm, 1976; Kagan, 1966; Klausmeier, 1976).

They are the basic units of learning and instruction (Carroll, 1964).

The range of concepts that children are likely to encounter during early schooling is broad and includes objects, colors, sizes, shapes, numbers, qualities of objects and events, relationships between objects and events, and sequences in space or time. Emotional and affective expressions and personal relationships all involve concepts as well. Gagné (1985) specifies the following five categories of abilities: (1) verbal formation, (2) intellectual skills, (3) cognitive strategies, (4) attitudes, and (5) motor skills. Among the subcategories of intellectual skills, Gagné includes the notion of "concrete concepts," which take the form of simple relational concepts, of concepts of attributes, and of common objects such as "cat" and "tree."

Carroll (1964) has noted that many concepts used in school are relational in nature. The focus of this chapter is on relational concepts, referred to hereafter as "basic concepts." Basic concepts include such concepts as "top" and "bottom," "more" and "less," and "first" and "last," which are important both to language and to reasoning or thinking. All involve a child's ability to make relational decisions about persons, things, and events (Boehm, 1971, 1976, 1982, 1986a, 1986b). They help children describe objects, quantities, and experiences; order events; give directions; and express ideas and feelings. Basic concepts are also essential for making

comparisons and classifying; they serve as building blocks for more complex concepts; and they are essential for problem solving. However, basic relational concepts are difficult for many children, since they have no constant referent or imagery set (Boehm, 1976, 1982; deVilliers & deVilliers, 1978). The group with the "most" people in one situation may have the "fewest" in another; the "tallest" animal in one group may be the "shortest" in another. Many basic concepts describe positions that are reversible: For instance, the object "on top" of one pile may be placed at the "bottom" of a different pile; the "first" car in one line may be the "last" in another. Children with early learning problems, such as delay in language development or in understanding basic concepts such as these, are at risk for experiencing school problems (Lichtenstein & Ireton, 1984; Wiig & Semel, 1976).

Role in Instruction

As noted earlier, both teachers and parents use basic concepts in their verbal interchanges with children. It is difficult to describe objects and events or to present directions or instructions without using concepts in general, and relational concepts in particular. Kaplan (1979) and Kaplan and White (1980), for example, reviewed a sample of 1,417 oral directions given by teachers from kindergarten to third grade. These directions were analyzed for (1) the number of behaviors needed to follow (execute) the direction, and (2) the number of qualifiers that set conditions on the response. Of these directions, 71% were found to have no more than one behavior and one qualifier. But the other 29% contained two or more behaviors and/or qualifiers. Of the terms defined by Kaplan and White as qualifiers, 41% were also identified (Boehm, 1971) as basic relational concepts.

In a second study, Kaplan (1979) developed a task called "The Directions Game," which systematically varied the number of behaviors and qualifiers in directions. This task was administered to 36 children at each grade level from kindergarten to fifth grade, along with the Boehm Test of Basic Concepts (BTBC) to children in kindergarten, first grade, and second grade. Lorge–Thorndike Cognitive Abilities scores were obtained for children in third through fifth grades. The results indicated that with increasing age, children were able to execute increasingly complex directions. Young children in particular had much difficulty following directions containing more than one or two behavior (procedural) steps and one qualifier. There was a strong relationship ($r = .71$) between concept mastery as measured by the BTBC and following directions. "Adding a qualifier to a direction appears to reduce the number of behaviors that can be executed correctly" (Kaplan, 1979, p. 47).

In a reanalysis of Kaplan's transcripts, we (Boehm, Kaplan, & Preddy, 1980) found that teachers in kindergarten, first grade, and second grade used 33 of 50 terms assessed by the BTBC directly in their oral directions as well as antonyms, synonyms, and comparative forms of these terms. One out of every two of these teacher directions contained at least one BTBC term plus many "easier" concepts such as "under," "across," and "down," now included on the BTBC— Preschool Version (Boehm, 1986b).

The use of basic relational concepts by preschool teachers in their spoken exchanges with 3- and 4-year-old children was studied (Boehm, Classon, & Kelly, 1986). A wide range ($n = 62$) of relational concept terms was used by two teachers of 3-year-olds and four teachers of 4-year-olds in two classroom settings (nursery and urban day care). Teachers, who were unaware of the specific purpose of the study, recorded these samples of their spoken interactions with children over a 1-hour period.

Curricular materials presented to young children also are likely to include a large number of relational concepts. We (Preddy, Kaplan, & Boehm, 1980) found that 44 of the 50 basic concept words included on the BTBC appeared among the first 1,000 words of the Thorndike and Lorge (1944) *The Teachers Wordbook of 30,000 Words*, and that all 50 of the BTBC concepts appeared in reading and mathematics workbooks. These findings were based on a 20-page random sample from five publishers in each area at three levels (kindergarten, first grade, and second grade), along with synonyms, antonyms, and related terms (Preddy, et al., 1980). These same terms also appeared among the words likely to be encountered in reading materials. In order to establish a core

vocabulary for the Educational Developmental Laboratories, Taylor, Franckenpohl, and White (1979) studied the basal reading series of nine publishers and reviewed important vocabulary studies. All of the BTBC terms and related terms appeared in these reading materials for kindergarten through third grade except "medium-sized," "separated," and "backward." Thus, basic concepts are necessary for children's early reading as well as for understanding them when presented orally.

It is reasonable to expect that relational concepts should occur frequently in other Latin-based language curricular texts as well. Nason (1981), for example, reviewed the occurrence of basic relational concepts in textbooks and workbooks used in the lower elementary grades in Puerto Rico. She found that all 50 concepts included on the Spanish translation of the Boehm (the Prueba Boehm de Conceptos Básicos, or PBCB; Boehm, 1970, 1973) appeared in readers and workbooks used in first and second grade. Furthermore, 42 were among the first 1,000 words in *Recuento del Vocabulario Español, Vol. 1* (Rodriguez Bou, 1952), a compendium of words that serves as a major source for developing curricular materials in Puerto Rican schools.

Relationship to Achievement, Testing, and Children with Special Needs

Since basic concepts are an integral part of teachers' oral directions and appear frequently in curricular materials across subject matter areas, it is not surprising that basic concept knowledge contributes to school achievement. This relationship has been supported across studies both in the mainland United States (Beech, 1981; Brown, 1976; Estes, Harris, Moers, & Woodrich, 1976; Levin, Henderson, Levin, & Hoffer, 1975; Moers & Harris, 1978; Piersel & McAndrews, 1982; Steinbauer & Heller, 1978; Steinert, 1979) and in Puerto Rico (Nason, 1986; Preddy, Boehm, & Shepherd, 1984).

The importance of basic relational concepts has been demonstrated in a number of other ways, including (1) their inclusion in the procedural directions of intelligence tests (Bracken, 1986; Kaufman, 1978) and achievement tests (Cummings & Nelson, 1980); and (2) their difficulty for populations with special needs, such as Native Americans (Mickelson & Galloway, 1973); the hearing-impaired (Brown, 1976; Davis, 1974; Dickie, 1980), the blind (Caton, 1976, 1977), the learning-disabled (DiNapoli, Kagedan-Kage, & Boehm, 1980; Kavale, 1982), the educable mentally retarded (Chin, 1976; Nelson & Cummings, 1981), and children with deviant development of syntax (Spector, 1977, 1979). In sum, the importance of basic relational concepts to early learning and early curricula and to children with special learning needs has been well documented from diverse perspectives.

Basic Concepts and Thinking Skills

Basic concepts are also important to the development of thinking skills (Boehm, 1976, 1984). As children progress through the early grades, concepts often are used in combination with other concepts, such as the direction "Mark all the words that begin with the letter T." Transcriptions of first-grade teachers' oral directions (Kaplan, 1979) revealed that they often used more than one relational concept in a direction. Thirty-four percent of their directions contained two or more BTBC concepts, their antonyms or synonyms, or simpler relational concepts.

In order to encode and follow directions such as these containing several relational concepts, many proceses are involved. Children need to do the following:

- Listen to the direction and process spoken elements.
- Remember critical components.
- Select the relevant elements and information.
- Be familiar with object or situations presented.
- Know each basic concept individually and retrieve it from memory.
- Coordinate and act upon multiple components of information.
- Be able to identify multiple members of a class as triggered by the terms "all" or "every."

Furthermore, increasing levels of abstraction may apply to the same concept, from simple to complex. For example, a box may be the same color, size, or shape as another box, or it may be the same in respect to all of these attributes. Children need to learn how to combine concepts and to use them for comparing and classifying things. For example, a child who is able to point to the "widest" block in a picture may not be able to point to the block that is "wider than one," but not the "widest."

Thus, in addition to assessing children's understanding of individual concepts, teachers need to understand how children handle these as tools of thinking when using them in these ways:

- In combination.
- To make intermediate-position comparisons (e.g., "Find the ball that is bigger than one but not the biggest").
- To make a comparison to a standard (e.g., "Find the basket with more apples than the first basket").
- To classify.
- To order.
- To follow multiple-step directions.

To help teachers determine how children use concepts at more complex levels, an *Applications* booklet was introduced with the BTBC—Revised (BTBC-R; Boehm, 1986a) as a first step in assessing basic concepts as tools of thinking.

The kinds of problems children encounter and errors they make are as important as their successes in planning for instruction. Why do children respond in a particular way? What strategies are they using? Each of these questions needs to be considered when assessing basic concepts.

This lengthy introduction has been presented to highlight both the complexity of concept learning and the importance of basic concepts to learning and problem solving. The difficulty that children with learning problems have with basic concepts is relevant to the topic of this book. If basic concepts are also basic building blocks of learning, their assessment needs to occur early, during a child's preschool and primary school experience. It can be expected that normally progressing children will be familiar in some context with most basic concepts by the time they enter second grade.

A MULTIPLE-STEP MODEL FOR ASSESSING BASIC CONCEPTS

Given the importance and complexity of relational concepts, I believe we need to engage in a multiple-step concept assessment procedure that includes the following:

1. Standardized tests that target a broad array of relational concepts.
2. Review of errors made during testing to identify patterns.
3. Observation over time of a child's spontaneous use of the target concepts and/or correct use of these concepts in response to a teacher's or parent's direction.
4. Interviews that focus on the strategies and styles a young child uses to arrive at answers and that tap the child's linguistic repertoire.
5. Mini-teaching experiences to help determine how ready the child is to acquire a concept.

The multiple-step assessment procedure proposed incorporates the positive features of testing, error analysis, observation, and clinical interviewing. At the same time, this approach involves converging measures and has increased ecological validity, which has been cited by Ysseldyke and Thurlow (1984) as an essential concern for assessors.

French and Nelson (1985) studied young children's productive use of temporal and causal terms by requesting children to respond to queries concerning six familiar events that had a clear organized structure, with a specific goal ("e.g., buying food, making cookies"; p. 6). Children aged 2 years, 11 months to 5 years, 6 months were asked to tell what happened when they engaged in particular activities such as "going to a restaurant or when getting dressed" (p. 6). Contrasting with the majority of the available research data, French and Nelson's findings indicated that very young children do understand and produce temporal logical relationships. Based on these findings, the authors noted the limitations of production tasks for the assessment of children's understanding of the "range of application of a term" (p. 7). However, because a term may have been acquired for a particular context, it may be context-bound. With development,

children's use of concepts will become decontextualized. Therefore, children's understanding of a term cannot be generalized to the full adult meaning of the term and must be considered in relation to the context of its use. According to French and Nelson, the context of an item is more likely to have a negative effect on measures of comprehension than on measures of production. This same limitation relating to context applies to any receptive test and points to the need for converging methods, including both comprehension and production measures.

Formal Testing of Basic Concepts

Testing of young children's repertoire of basic concepts is a challenge for most early childhood educators. The challenge arises from the fact that it is not possible to explore the range and depth of a child's understanding from a single test or task. As discussed above, the forms of basic concept assessment can range from informal observation to standardized tests. Standardized tests, in turn, can range in comprehensiveness from brief screening devices that include a small number of basic concepts to longer tests covering a large number of concepts. The results from tests for which norms have been collected can provide information to the assessor regarding a child's performance relative to that of other children of the same age and socioeconomic background. The overall performance of a particular child can also be compared to that of other children from the same geographic area and community, if local norms are established. Ideally, the test will be used as part of a battery to predict readiness for instruction or to identify children "at risk." Criterion-referenced use of results can be made as well by considering a child's understanding of a specific concept or content area in addition to the total score. Although the results from criterion-referenced interpretations of tests can lead to behavioral objectives and recommendations for classroom instruction, they do not address a number of critical issues. Lidz (1982) has pointed out that criterion-referenced tests do not yield information regarding (1) how a child solves a problem, (2) how the child is best taught, and (3) what accounts for a child's failures. By analyzing a child's errors (Boehm, 1982, 1986a), the assessor can begin to formulate hypotheses that can be shared with the teacher and parent.

Many screening tests used with young children include a small sample of basic concepts. These are not described in detail here. Other tests, such as CIRCUS (Anderson et al., 1976) and the Sequential Assessment of Mathematics Inventories (SAMI; Reisman & Hutchinson, 1985), include subtests that assess related basic concepts. As one example, the SAMI Mathematical Language subtest, which is intended for children in kindergarten and first grade, includes the basic concepts "like," "above," "top," "bottom," "middle," "in back," "right," "same," and "faster." A few standardized tests, however, assess a large number of basic relational concepts. These include the BTBC-R (Boehm, 1986a) the BTBC—Preschool Version (Boehm, 1986b), the Bracken Basic Concept Scale (Bracken, 1984), and the Tests of Basic Experiences 2 (TOBE 2; Moss, 1978). An overview of each of these tests follows.

1. The BTBC-R is a group-administered test for children in kindergarten through second grade that surveys understanding of 50 relational concepts of spatial position, size, direction, quantity, sequence, and time, for the purpose of instructional planning. Two forms, C and D, and a Spanish translation are available. A total score can be obtained along with item scores, which serve as the major basis of interpretation. Norms are presented by grade, socioeconomic status, and time of year. An *Applications* booklet consisting of 25 items assesses children's ability to use basic concepts in combination and in sequences, and to make comparisons.

2. The BTBC—Preschool Version represents a downward extension of the BTBC-R and assesses understanding of 26 basic concepts among children 3–5 years of age, or older children with special educational needs. Picture cards are presented, and children, who are individually tested, point to their response. Two items are included per concept, allowing assessors to identify concepts that children know, that they do not know, or that are emerging.

3. The Bracken Basic Concept Scale is an individually administered scale testing 258 concepts among children 2–7 years of age in 11 categorical areas, including color, letter identification, numbers/counting, compari-

son, shapes, direct/position, size, quantity, social/emotional, textural material, and time/sequence. One form and a Spanish translation of the full diagnostic test are available. The scale is divided into two instruments: the full diagnostic test, and a screening test (for which two forms are available) consisting of 30 items that can be administered to small groups. Items are arranged hierarchically by difficulty levels within a category, so that concepts need not be assessed below a basal level or above a ceiling level. Total, category, and item scores are yielded.

4. The purpose of the TOBE 2 is to help schools evaluate the richness of a child's concepts in order to plan appropriate instruction. TOBE 2 is a battery of four subtests (Mathematics, Language, Science, and Social Studies), which are included at each of two overlapping levels (preschool–kindergarten and kindergarten–first grade). Some basic concepts are included in each of these areas, along with other concepts.

Each of these tests has its own strengths and limitations, depending on the purposes of the user, which may include (1) determining a child's school readiness, (2) planning language instruction, or (3) identifying concepts children know or have not yet mastered. Whatever the purpose of the user, it is important to realize that within the 10, 15, or 20 minutes normally alloted for testing basic concepts, no one test can ever measure the extent of a child's concept understanding; test results must be considered only as a starting point for interpretation. It should not be surprising to teachers and assessors that different tasks and different representations of objects tap different aspects of a child's understanding, and that learning concepts such as "more" and "less" is not an all-or-none affair. Spector (1979), for example, has pointed to a number of possible reasons for difficulty on the BTBC items—concerns that apply to other tests as well. These include the following:

- Inability to focus on key words in the directions.
- The length and complexity of the direction.
- Deficits in spatial perception.
- Lack of knowledge or confusion regarding the concept label.

• Relatively high level of abstraction required.
• Difficulty with polar concepts.
• Poor auditory memory for sentences.

Another concern centers on the small sample of items on most tests used with young children. Since many concepts or areas need to be covered, often only a few basic concepts are sampled, or only one item is included to cover a concept area. This difficulty is further compounded when tests employ basal and ceiling limits, restricting the number of concepts assessed.

Whether they are norm-referenced or criterion-referenced, the scores from standardized tests in general, and specifically from tests of basic concepts, can serve only as a starting point for interpretation. Assessors need to play a key role in this process. Fewell (1984) notes that far more is required of examiners than in the traditional use of assessment methods. Fewell urges process-oriented assessment in which "examiners must individualize assessment, being more sensitive to nuances of the environment that might be critical for differences in outcome. They must read the clues, make decisions, act, and evaluate" (1984, p. 177).

A modified norm-referenced model of assessment has been proposed by Ysseldyke and Thurlow (1984). This model represents a blend of norm-referenced and continuous-monitoring approaches. The key aspects include instructional diagnosis and prereferral interventions. A major outcome of assessment, according to Ysseldyke and Thurlow, must be improved instruction, including appropriate sequences, materials, grouping, and interactions with teachers.

In considering the results of standardized tests, a first step is to review a child's responses. For example, did the child choose the opposite of the target concept, over-include additional objects, or respond only to part of the instruction? In order to establish a basis for reviewing errors, it is necessary to explore the developmental literature in language and concept acquisition. This review may help identify typical stumbling blocks children encounter or errors that they make, which in turn contributes to the error analysis step of test interpretation.

Reviewing How Relational Concepts Develop as a Basis for Error Analysis

An extensive and growing literature documents the stages of acquisition of relational concepts. Studies such as those by Blewitt (1982), Clark (1983), Coker (1978), French and Nelson (1985), Johnston and Slobin (1979), Richards (1982), and Richards and Haupe (1981), which trace the development of children's understanding of relational concepts, indicate or suggest that most children's errors are not random, but are related to their past experiences and level of concept development. A review of errors can be an important component of child assessment, providing the teacher or assessor with the opportunity to raise important questions or hypotheses about the learner. Between the ages of 2 and 6, children demonstrate significant growth in their ability to use relational terms in their day-to-day interactions in language and to respond to questions and requests. Studies of concept attainment in general indicate that the child moves from being able to apply concepts generally in concrete situations to being able to apply them precisely at increasing levels of abstraction. According to Clark (1983), as early as age $2\frac{1}{2}$ to 3, children can understand some relational terms in the same way as adults do. Brown (1976) found that children as young as 3 can accurately express temporal order. By the time children are 6, most have extensive knowledge of most relational terms, at least at their simpler levels of application (Boehm, 1966, 1982). But a child's ability to apply a concept is dependent on the context in which it is used and the ability of the child to access that concept. The caution of Flavell and Wohlwill (1969, p. 95) in particular is relevant for assessors: "The child's responses may be expected to oscillate from one occasion to the next, to be maximally susceptible to the effects of task-related variables."

An extensive literature traces the acquisition of individual relational concepts in children aged 2–6 (see, e.g., Brown, 1976; Carey, 1978; Clark, 1983; French & Nelson, 1985; Harris & Strommen, 1971; Kuczaj & Maratos, 1975; Johnston & Slobin, 1979; Richards, 1982). The results of studies such as these indicate the following:

Errors decrease in type and frequency with age.

Concept terms vary in their linguistic complexity and therefore in difficulty.

Task requirements, such as the number of objects in a display or whether the child needs to point to something, demonstrate a concept relationship, tell stories about pictures, or describe named events, all affect the difficulty of a concept.

The familiarity of events used to represent a concept affects the difficulty of that concept.

The context of a concept (spatial or temporal) affects its difficulty.

Thus, children who may understand the basic meaning of a concept term may not be able to apply it across appropriate contexts.

A number of relevant issues are addressed by French and Nelson (1985) in their book *Young Children's Knowledge of Relational Terms*. These researchers present an analysis of temporal and causal structure of a small set of relational terms (including "before," "after," and "first") used by preschool children in the course of describing familiar events such as "making cookies." Forty-three children, aged 2 years, 11 months through 5 years, 6 months, were included in their study. French and Nelson found that young children used relational terms in the course of describing familiar events and that they used these terms correctly. A number of their conclusions have implications for assessors, including the following:

Results of investigations differ, depending on the *particular* relational term studied and how the term is assessed.

Children as young as 3 do use relational terms to describe events about which they are familiar and they do so correctly.

Comprehension of some terms may appear to lag behind production, since the *context of comprehension measures is more likely to be unfamiliar* to the child.

Thus, the seeming disparity between comprehension and production may be accounted for by context. Extralinguistic knowledge (children's event knowledge) and general event representations (those for which children already have mental representations) are important to the learning of relational terms. Assessment therefore needs to incorporate information gained from both production and comprehension tasks; it also needs to take into account a child's event knowledge, as well as his or her ability to apply concepts to both familiar and unfamiliar events.

An error analysis, based on a review of the literature on basic concept development, can serve as a starting point for program planning by targeting concepts for instruction and by suggesting possible reasons for difficulty. But an error analysis alone does not yield the *reason* for a child's misunderstanding. Assessors need both to observe and to interview children in order to gain this information. By analyzing the kinds of errors children make, assessors can begin to trace the stages of concept development. Elsewhere (Boehm, 1976; 1982, p. 153), I have suggested a basic concept development checklist. Developmental stages can be incorporated into an observation checklist, which assessors and teachers can use as they observe children across situations and as they try to make meaning out of test responses for purposes of instructional planning.

Observations over Time of Basic Concept Usage

Systematic observation of basic concept usage across situations is a necessary next step. Although early childhood specialists have long focused on the importance of observation in early childhood assessment (Almy, 1975; Cohen, Stern, & Balaban, 1983; Cazden, 1971), researchers have not necessarily focused on the strategies children use to solve problems. Viewing the child across settings certainly does provide important insight into his or her behavior; it does not, however, necessarily indicate why a child responds in a particular way.

Elsewhere (Boehm and Weinberg, 1987), we present detailed procedures for collecting systematic observation information with young children. Although observation is an important component of comprehensive assessment, it must be carried out over time in order to take into account the different en-

Basic concept(s) of interest (list here): _____   Name of child: _____

Observations over time

Level of concept use		Fill-in dates and examples			
Responsive	1. In response to teacher directions in: • familiar situations • new situations				
	2. Across contexts: • Spatial • Temporal				
Productive	3. To describe everyday events				
	4. To answer questions				
Higher levels	5. In combination with other concepts.				
	6. To make comparisons: • To a standard • Intermediate position				
	7. To classify and/or to order				

FIGURE 27.1. Pupil Checklist of Concept Mastery.

vironmental contexts in which the concept might be applied. Such observation needs to extend well beyond one testing session and one classroom visit; rather, teachers need to observe and record children's use of concepts across activities and throughout the school year. A sample Pupil Checklist of Concept Mastery is presented in Figure 27.1.

Strategy Interviews

Lidz (1983) advocates process-oriented assessment, which is aided by observing methods children use to solve problems. Piaget's (1929) technique focused on such observation, and the research of Piaget and others (Flavell, 1970; Ginsburg, 1986) has furthered our understanding of how children think and develop. Through presenting novel tasks, Piaget was able to identify important developmental stages of critical thinking. The clinical interview was an essential part of his procedure. According to Ginsburg (1986, p. 246), the clinical interview serves three distinguishable purposes: It "aims at discovering cognitive activities; specifying them with precision; and evaluating levels of competence." Although Piagetian research did not generally focus on the learning areas children are likely to encounter in school, Piaget's clinical interview procedure has important implications for strategy assessment.

Recent research findings in cognitive psychology are closely related to school tasks and have important implications for the assessment of young children. As all caretakers will attest, young children are active participants in the learning process. They explore, pretend, and question endlessly. Each of these activities can provide a window to the processes, strategies, and tactics children use to solve problems. Cognitive psychologists "seek to understand how the individual processes information in learning situations—processing which occurs following the input stimulus and prior to the individual's response" (Myers & Lytle, 1986, p. 138). As children develop, they also develop knowledge about their own strategies to solve problems. Myers and Lytle, for example, focus on "think-aloud" procedure as a means of assessing the learning processes used in reading comprehension. The think-aloud procedure typically involves asking individuals to read a passage, one sentence at a time, and verbalize all of his or her thoughts (i.e., "think aloud") about each sentence. Earlier studies using this procedure focused on secondary, college, and adult students; however, Myers and Lytle (1986) have expanded the methodology to elementary-age students and have used it as part of an assessment battery for children with reading problems. They point to process assessment as a model for assessing children with learning and adjustment problems, and note that the think-aloud procedure is an example of one promising technique needing further research. Ginsburg, Kossan, Schwartz, and Swanson (1983) point out that the think-aloud procedure has had a long history.

Lidz (1983) recommends that preschool assessors consider process as well as product variables. She cautions against an over-emphasis on performance as opposed to process or style. She urges process-oriented assessment that is aided by observing methods children use to solve problems, including a child's response to efforts directed at eliciting responses.

A workable next step following testing, then, is that of interviewing the child. One should keep in mind Lidz's caution (1983, p. 23): "The young child especially has limited ability to provide reasons or elaboration regarding behavior" in comparison with an older child, and the assessor needs to find a means of eliciting responses. "Strategy interviewing," based on Piaget's clinical interview, is a productive step toward eliciting reasons from young children. What this term refers to is a set of activities that probe children's responses without suggesting answers, in order to eliminate some of the interpretive leaps often called for when one relies on test results alone or a review of error patterns. This step requires only an additional 10–15 minutes of time and can yield invaluable information that allows assessors to refine their hypotheses (such as questions regarding attention, memory, language, the testing situation, lack of exposure, and the child's cognitive processes) and to plan more appropriate interventions. The strategy interview may also be viewed as a form of convergent measure of basic concept understanding. The strategy interview can take place after a short break, later in the day, or on a successive day. An example follows to illustrate the approach.

A boy who was 3 years, 5 months years old and attended an urban day care center was administered the BTBC—Preschool Version, which assesses a child's understanding of relational concepts such as "over," "under," "both," "longest," and "shortest"; as noted earlier, this instrument includes a card booklet and is individually administered. The child appeared to enjoy the task, but performed at the 10th percentile. His attention was good, and the child spontaneously named and counted objects included on the picture cards. He demonstrated the inconsistency typical of many 3-year-olds by answering correctly only one of the two items per concept measuring the relational term "tallest." The interview helped establish that his correct response was not a guess and that he was not able to access the concept on the corresponding item.

Some of the boy's verbalizations, though, were illustrative of important strategies. For example, he correctly selected the "tallest" of three animals and then volunteered that it was the "biggest"—he had refined the concept of "biggest." On other items he talked about each item choice. On an item requesting that he point to the clown bending "backwards," he responded correctly and then noted the other two clown choices as being "bendwards" and "upwards." This child had a clear concept of "backwards" in this context, but not on the second test item for "backwards" (a dog looking straight ahead, up in the air, and with its head turned to look backwards).

Later in the morning, the child and his assessor worked together again so as to understand *how* he had arrived at his answers. A strategy interview was conducted with some of the items he had answered correctly and a number of items he had responded to incorrectly, with a dialogue such as the following, which began by repeating the question:

Q: How did you know your answer was right?
A: Because this is right (*pointing*) and this isn't (*pointing*).
Q: Why wasn't this one right (*pointing*)?
A: Because it's the biggest and this is the mommy and this is the baby.
Q: And how did you know it was the shortest?
A: I told you already, it's little.

With other items, assessors might use probes such as these:

"How did you know it wasn't _____ ?"
"Where is the [target object]?"
"Tell me about the picture."
"How would you tell a little kid to figure out the answer?"

The strategy probe then continues, with each question contingent on the child's previous response until the assessor has a picture of how the child arrived at his or her answer. Although some children first respond to some questions with answers such as "I guessed" or "Because I'm smart," further probing generally reveals a good deal more.

My colleagues and I have been collecting videotapes of this type of exchange in day care centers serving children from low-income families, and have used these tapes in meetings with the teachers and parents. If videotaping is not feasible, audiotaping is a possible alternative. The 10–15 extra minutes involved are well worth the effort. The children are easily engaged and have demonstrated a considerable range of concept language and important problem-solving strategies. A number of points for use by teachers in developing instruction become clear, such as (1) a child's use of related concepts that may be appropriate synonyms, or related but less precise terms; (2) use of other number, size, and object concept terms; (3) useful strategies for eliminating inappropriate choices; (4) consistent errors; (5) the robustness of a response (does the child want to change immediately with a probe?); and (6) the wealth of language and understanding the child possesses. It becomes much clearer when a child does know a concept, when he or she confuses a concept with its antonym, when the concept is just emerging and unstable, and when the child is ready to learn the concept then and there.

The following are illustrative examples of strategy interviewing. The first example is from an interview carried out with a 4-year-old student who had been assessed with the BTBC—Preschool Version earlier in the school day. The assessor selected a number of items on which to focus with the following exchange:

Q: Point to the wagon with blocks around it [item 41].
A: (*Child points*)
Q: How did you know that one was the answer? How did you know that?
A: (*No answer*)
Q: What makes this (*points*) have blocks around it?
A: (*No answer*)
Q: You know, someone else told me that this one had the blocks around it. Was that person right?
A: No.

Q: Why? Why not? How come?

A: *(No answer)*

Q: Can you tell me? What is different about this *(points)* and this *(points)?*

A: *(No answer)*

Q: Is something different about these two *(points)?*

A: No.

Q: How about this one? Is this one different from this one *(points)?*

A: No.

Q: Are these blocks around the wagon *(points)?*

A: No.

Q: Where are they?

A: Inside.

Q: Where are these blocks *(points)?*

A: Next to it.

Q: Are these next to the wagon? What makes these be around the wagon?

Q: Because they make a circle.

This example demonstrates that strategy interviewing takes considerable patience, but also shows how the examiner learned that the student knew related synonyms, such as "circle" for "around." In addition, the examiner learned that the student not only knew, but could use accurately, the concepts of "inside" and "next to it."

The second example is from a later portion of the interview with the same student, also using the content from the BTBC—Preschool Version:

Q: Point to the lowest airplane [item 42].

A: *(Points incorrectly to the airplane in the middle)*

Q: Why did you pick that answer?

A: *(No answer)*

Q: Tell me about these pictures. Tell me about these airplanes.

A: *(No answer)*

Q: Where is the airplane *(points to the airplane on the bottom)?*

A: Down.

Q: How about this one *(points to the airplane in the middle)?*

A: In the circle.

Q: In the circle? Is there a circle?

A: No.

Q: In the middle, maybe?

A: In the middle.

Q: So which one is the lowest? Is the one on the top *(points)*, or the middle, or the bottom the lowest?

A: The top.

This example illustrates how an examiner can probe enough to clarify the extent of a student's concept knowledge. Although this student knew related concepts, such as "down," he still did not know which airplane was the "lowest." His answers were consistently wrong. In addition, the examiner learned that the student had some understanding of the related concept dimension "top–bottom," since he did not select the distractor in the middle.

The third example is from an interview carried out with a 5-year-old student, to whom the BTBC-R was administered:

Q: Show me the third car from the boy [item 47].

A: *(Points incorrectly to the third train car starting from right to left; misses the referent boy and does not count from it)*

Q: Why did you pick that one? How did you figure that one out?

A: Because I know if it is like this: one *(points)*, two *(points)*, three *(points)*.

Q: But what if we start from the boy and said: *third* from the boy?

A: That one would be the third from the boy *(points incorrectly to the third from right to left)*.

Q: That one would be the third from the boy? Well, let's count: one *(points)*.

A: Two, three *(laughs)*.

Q: What happened? Which one is the third car from the boy?

A: One, two, three *(points incorrectly)*.

This example shows how with the interviewing, an examiner can establish that a student does have a concept. In this case, it was clear that the student knew the ordinal number "third." He missed the item, though, because of his difficulty in counting for a given referent.

Another example with the same student follows.

Q: Point to the fish that is medium-sized [item 41].

A: *(Points incorrectly to the smallest fish)*

Q: Why did you pick this one? How did you figure that out?

A: Because I think that one is big *(points to the big one)* and *(eyes opening widely)* this one got to be the medium *(points to the medium-sized fish)*.

Q: Tell me how you figured that out.

A: Because if this one was big *(points)*, that one *had* to be little *(points)*, and this one *had* to be medium *(points)*.

This interview shows how an examiner, through probing, can encourage a student to reflect upon his or her answers. This student implemented useful strategies for eliminating inappropriate choices. By comparing the big and the little fish, the student gained insight into his error and made an accurate choice.

Children can self-correct, refocus attention, gain insight, or hold steadfastly to their original response. With some children, we need to reassure them that we are not trying to trick them, but are just trying to understand how they figured out their answers. Changes in development over the ages of 3, 4, and 5 also are clearly demonstrated.

Strategy assessment is related to, but not identical to, dynamic assessment procedures or the assessment of learning potential. In the Learning Potential Assessment Device (LPAD; Feuerstein, 1979), assessors use trial teaching in order to identify effective strategies that can result in instructional modification. A "test–teach–test" format is used to assess a child's zone of potential development through gains the child makes when optimal teaching strategies are used. Dynamic assessment procedures provide extensive information regarding the conditions that facilitate learning; they also require a considerable investment of time. The purpose of the strategy assessment proposed here is not to assess a child's zone of potential development, but to provide assessors with a wealth of information based on a small investment of time.

Mini-Teaching Experiences

If time permits, the assessor may wish to teach one or two basic concepts that the child has missed, using concrete objects (colorful blocks, cars, trucks, miniature furniture, etc.). Here the child is encouraged to manipulate the objects. The examiner breaks

the task apart and presents tasks in a step-by-step manner. For example, for the concept "middle," the examiner may have the child name the colors and then move the three blocks or cars used into different orders. Then the assessor identifies the color of the block in the middle and asks the child to move and name other blocks in the middle position. Finally, the assessor can represent the test item to see whether there is any transfer. The idea here is to see whether the child can respond to the concept with minimal teaching. Some children pick up the concept immediately; others comprehend one aspect of a concept, such as being able to move cars "near" and "far" from each other, but are not yet able to catch on to the comparative position "nearest." The skill of the assessor in presenting tasks systematically to identify what a child knows is crucial here. Therefore, the results of mini-teaching experiences need to be interpreted cautiously until more research evidence is available. This interchange, however, often reveals alternate concept terms understood by the child, good attention, ability to follow simple directions, and understanding of easier concepts.

The outcome of the multiple-step assessment procedure described in this part of the chapter can be used for instructional planning, for increasing one's understanding of a child's unique response styles, and as the basis for parent and teacher workshops. In this context, a child's test score or percentile does not need to assume undue importance. The strategy component of the assessment process needs to be the major focus of attention, to be followed by brief teaching interventions. Swanson (1984, p. 150) indicates that "A process model of assessment assumes that learning disabled and mentally retarded children can produce a strategic series of thought that is (directly or indirectly) related to their intelligent task performance." As suggested earlier, these activities need to be followed by observation over time, to determine a child's ability to use concepts in the context of the classroom at increasing levels of complexity. The steps involved in comprehensive assessment of basic concepts are summarized in Table 27.1.

The early identification of children's basic concept understanding can result in instructional programs with positive immediate and long-term outcomes. It is effective in-

TABLE 27.1. Steps in Comprehensive Assessment of Basic Concepts

Step	Assessor role
1. Formal test administered using standardized procedure (Session 1)	Observe/record child's: • Response pattern • Attention to task • Spontaneous verbalizations
2. Review of responses	Review child's errors; compare with developmental information regarding concepts
3. Strategy interview (Session 2)	Interview to determine: • Child's knowledge of related concepts • How child eliminates options • Concept words used by child
4. Mini-teaching experience (Session 2)	Present brief examples: • Does child catch on immediately to concept? • Does child learn a component of the idea taught? • Can child generalize to a second example?
5. Ongoing observation (over time)	Observe and record examples. Does child use concept: • Across situations? • In both spatial and temporal contexts? • In combination with other concepts? • As a tool of thinking?

struction that needs to be the major outcome of assessment.

MOVING FROM ASSESSMENT TO INSTRUCTION

A number of studies document the effects of basic concept instruction at the preschool (Armour-Thomas, 1984; Blai, 1973; Levin et al. 1975) and primary school levels (Moers & Harris, 1978; Nason, 1986). Overall, the findings indicate that children who have had special instruction in basic concepts during prekindergarten, kindergarten, or first grade have made gains both in their concept understanding and on standardized tests of achievement.

As one example, Nason (1986) studied the effects of systematic instruction in basic concepts on basic concept attainment, and on achievement in language and mathematics, among first-grade children from low-income backgrounds in Puerto Rico. First, Nason (1981) established that all 50 concepts used on the Spanish translation of the BTBC, the PBCB (Boehm, 1970, 1973) appeared in readers and workbooks used in Puerto Rico in first and second grades. Forty-two of the concepts assessed were among the first 1,000 words in *Recuento del Vocabulario Español*,

Vol. 1 (Rodriguez Bou, 1952), a compendium of frequently used words in Puerto Rico and a major source for developing instructional materials. Nason also established that basic concepts appear in directions to achievement tests used in Puerto Rico.

Subjects were 150 first-grade children (mean age = 6 years, 1 month) from schools located in low-income public housing communities in San Juan. Basic concept understanding was assessed using the PBCB (island-wide norms only; Preddy et al., 1984). An instructional program was developed to teach concepts to 75 of these children. The program involved trained teachers using lessons based on translated materials from the *Boehm Resource Guide for Basic Concept Teaching* (Boehm, 1976). A structured, sequential presentation of concepts was followed.

• Concrete objects and pictorial representations.
• Productive use in the child's own speech.
• Application at more abstract levels.

The interventions lasted for 40 minutes each and occurred four times a week for 8 weeks. Teachers of the "traditional" (*n* = 50) group were provided with test results and allowed to use results in the traditional way. Finally, there was a control group ($n = 25$) that received the posttest only.

The group receiving systematic concept instruction demonstrated a significant increase in understanding of instructed concepts as compared to the traditional and control groups—a finding that held over time. Of significance was the finding of generalized benefit to the instructed group on measures of achievement in language and mathematics. This finding did not result with the other two groups. Finally, at posttest, the mean PBCB scores for the instructed group were similar to those for the middle-socioeconomic-status Puerto Rican norming group at the end of first grade.

An extensive research literature has been devoted to identifying successful strategies for grouping, presenting, and teaching concepts. Reviews by Clark (1971), Tennyson and Cocchiarella (1986), and Tennyson and Park (1980) are particularly relevant, as is the work of Gagné (1985) and Klausmeier (1976). Strategies particularly relevant to teaching basic relational concepts have been presented elsewhere (Boehm, 1976, 1986a).

SUMMARY

This chapter has highlighted both the complexity of concept acquisition and the importance of basic relational concepts to learning and to complying with teachers' oral directions. If basic concepts are important building blocks of learning and thinking, they need to be assessed early, during a child's preschool and primary school experience. Basic concept assessment can play an important role in adjusting instruction to meet a child's needs. Assessment can help one to (1) gain an understanding of a child's overall repertoire of basic concepts; (2) pinpoint concepts that are understood, that are partially understood, or that need to be developed; (3) identify strategies a child uses to approach a problem and the kinds of errors made; (4) predict a child's readiness for instruction; and (5) obtain results that can be translated into instruction.

A comprehensive assessment model of basic concepts is proposed, which involves a number of steps and which needs to be continued throughout the school year. These steps include (1) standardized testing, (2) review of errors based on findings in the research literature, (3) strategy interviews, (4) mini-teaching opportunities, and (5) systematic observation over time.

REFERENCES

Almy, A. (1975). *The early childhood educator at work*. New York: McGraw-Hill.

Anderson, S. B., Bogatz, G. A., Draper, T. W., Jungeblut, A. Sidwell, G., Ward, W. C., & Yates, A. (1976). *Teachers edition of the manual and technical report: CIRCUS, Levels, A and B*. Menlo Park, CA: Addison-Wesley.

Armour-Thomas, E. (1984). *Microcomputer teaching concepts: Types of computer feedback in learning of relational concepts at kindergarten level*. Unpublished doctoral dissertation, Teachers College, Columbia University.

Ausubel, D. P. (1968) *Educational psychology: A cognitive view*. New York: Holt, Rinehart & Winston.

Beech, M. A. (1981). Concurrent validity of the Boehm Test of Basic Concepts. *Learning Disability Quarterly, 4*, 53–60.

Blai, B. (1973). Concept learning-mastery in Harcum Junior College Laboratory Nursery School/Kindergarten. *Psychology, 10*(2), 35–36.

Blewitt, P. (1982). Word meaning acquisition in young children: A review of theory and research. In H. W. Reese & L. P. Lipsitt (Eds.), *Advances in child development and behavior* (Vol. 17, pp. 139–195). New York: Academic Press.

Boehm, A. E. (1966). *The development of comparative concepts in primary school children*. Unpublished doctoral dissertation, Columbia University.

Boehm, A. E. (1971). *Boehm Test of Basic Concepts*. New York: Psychological Corporation.

Boehm, A. E. (1970). *Prueba Boehm de Conceptos Básicos*. New York: Psychological Corporation.

Boehm, A. E. (1973). *Prueba Boehm de conceptos básicos*. New York: Psychological Corporation.

Boehm, A. E. (1976). *Boehm resource guide for basic concept teaching*. New York: Psychological Corporation.

Boehm, A. E. (1982). Assessment of basic concepts. In D. Paget & B. A. Bracken (Eds.), *The psychoeducational assessment of preschool children* (pp. 145–161). New York: Grune & Stratton.

Boehm, A. E. (1984). *Assessing and teaching basic concepts and thinking skills*. Paper presented at the Conference on Early Childhood Education, New York.

Boehm, A. E. (1986a). *Boehm Test of Basic Concepts—Revised*. San Antonio, TX: Psychological Corporation.

Boehm, A. E. (1986b). *Boehm Test of Basic Concepts—Preschool Version*. San Antonio, TX: Psychological Corporation.

Boehm, A. E., Classon, B., & Kelly, M. (1986). *Preschool teachers' spoken use of basic concepts*. Unpublished manuscript, Teachers College, Columbia University.

Boehm, A. E., & Weinberg, R. A. (1987). *The classroom observer* (2nd ed.). New York: Teachers College Press.

Bracken, B. A. (1984). *Bracken Basic Concept Scale*. San Antonio, TX: Psychological Corporation.

Bracken, B. A. (1986). Incidence of basic concepts in the directions of five commonly used American tests of intelligence. *School Psychology International, 7,* 1–10.

Brown, D. (1976). Validation of the Boehm Test of Basic Concepts (Doctoral dissertation, University of Wisconsin). *Dissertation Abstracts International, 36,* 4338A.

Bruner, J. S. (1964). The course of cognitive growth. *American Psychologist, 19,* 1–15.

Carey, S. (1978). The child as word learner. In M. Halle, J. Bresnan, & G. Miller (Eds.), *Linguistic theory and psychological reality* (pp. 264–291). Cambridge, MA: MIT Press.

Carroll, J. B. (1964). Words, meanings, and concepts. *Harvard Educational Review, 34,* 178–202.

Caton, H. (1976). *The tactile test of basic concepts.* Louisville, KY: American Printing House for the Blind.

Caton, H. (1977). The development and evaluation of a tactile analogue to the Boehm Test of Basic Concepts, Form A. *Journal of Visual Impairment and Blindness, 71,* 382–386.

Cazden, C. (1971). Evaluation of learning in preschool education: Early language development. In B. Bloom, J. Hastings, & G. Madaus (Eds.), *Handbook on formative and summative evaluation of student learning* (pp. 345–398). New York: McGraw-Hill.

Chin, J. (1976). The development of basic relational concepts in educable mentally retarded children (Doctoral dissertation, Teachers College, Columbia University). *Dissertation Abstracts International, 36,* 4338A.

Clark, D. C. (1971). Teaching concepts in the classroom: a set of teaching prescriptions derived from experimental research [Monograph]. *Journal of Educational Psychology, 62,* 253–278.

Clark, E. (1983). Meanings and concepts. In P. H. Flavell & E. M. Markman (Eds.), *Handbook of child psychology* (4th ed.): *Vol. 3. Cognitive development* (pp. 787–840). New York: Wiley.

Cohen, D. H., Stern, V., & Balaban, N. (1983). *Observing and recording the behavior of young children* (3rd ed.). New York: Teachers College Press.

Coker, P. L. (1978). Syntactic and semantic factors in the acquisition of *before* and *after. Journal of Child Language, 5,* 261–277.

Cummings, J. A., & Nelson, R. B. (1980). Basic concepts in oral directions of group achievement tests. *Journal of Educational Research, 73,* 259–261.

Davis, J. (1974). Performance of young learning-impaired children on a test of basic concepts. *Journal of Speech and Hearing Research, 17,* 342–351.

deVilliers, J. G., & deVilliers, P. A. (1978). *Language acquisition.* Cambridge, MA: Harvard University Press.

Dickie, D. C. (1980). Performance of severely and profoundly hearing impaired children on aural/oral and total communication presentations of the Boehm Test of Basic Concepts (Doctoral dissertation, Michigan State University). *Dissertation Abstracts International, 40,* 6227A–6228A.

DiNapoli, N., Kagedan-Kage, S. M., & Boehm, A. E. (1980). *Basic concept acquisition in learning-disabled children.* (ERIC Document Reproduction Service No.

ED 240 718.) Unpublished manuscript, Teachers' College, Columbia University, New York.

Estes, G., Harris, J., Moers, F., & Woodrich, D. (1976). Predictive validity of the Boehm Test of Basic Concepts for achievement in first grade. *Educational and Psychological Measurement, 36,* 1031–1035.

Feuerstein, R. (1979). *The dynamic assessment of retarded performers: The Learning Potential Assessment Device, theory, instruments, and techniques.* Baltimore: University Park Press.

Fewell, R. R. (1984). Assessment of preschool handicapped children. *Educational Psychologist, 19,* 172–179.

Flavell, J. H. (1970). Concept development. In P. H. Mussen (Ed.), *Carmichael's manual of child psychology* (3rd ed. pp. 983–1059). New York: Wiley.

Flavell, J. H., & Wohlwill, J. F. (1969). Formal and functional aspects of cognitive development. In D. Elkind & J. H. Flavell (Eds.), *Studies in cognitive development: Essays in honor of Jean Piaget* (pp. 67–120). New York: Oxford University Press.

French, L. A., & Nelson, K. (1985). *Young children's knowledge of relational terms: Some ifs, ors, or buts.* New York: Springer-Verlag.

Gagné, R. M. (1985). *The conditions of learning* (4th ed.). New York: Holt, Rinehart & Winston.

Ginsburg, H. P. (1986). Academic diagnosis. In J. Valsiner (Ed.), *The individual subject and scientific psychology* (pp. 235–260). New York: Plenum Press.

Ginsburg, H. P., Kossan, N. E., Schwartz, R., & Swanson, D. (1983). Protocol methods in research on mathematical thinking. In H. P. Ginsburg (Ed.), *The development of mathematical thinking* (pp. 7–47). New York: Academic Press.

Harris, L., & Strommen, E. (1971). The role of front-back features in children's "front, back, and beside" placement of objects. *Merrill Palmer Quarterly, 18,* 259–271.

Johnston, J. R., & Slobin, D. I. (1979). The development of locative expressions in English, Italian, Serbo-Croation and Turkish. *Journal of Child Language, 6,* 529–545.

Kagan, J. A. (1966). A developmental approach to cognitive growth. In H. J. Klausmeier & C. W. Harris (Eds.), *Analysis of concept learning* (pp. 97–116). New York: Academic Press.

Kaplan, C. H. (1979). *A developmental analysis of children's direction following behavior in grades K–5.* Unpublished doctoral dissertation, Columbia University.

Kaplan, C. H., & White, M. A. (1980). Children's direction-following behavior in grades K–5. *Journal of Educational Research, 74,* 43–48.

Kaufman, A. (1978). The importance of basic concepts in individual assessment of preschool children. *Journal of School Psychology, 16,* 207–211.

Kavale, K. A. (1982). A comparison of learning disabled and normal children on the Boehm Test of Basic Concepts. *Journal of Learning Disabilities, 15,* 160–161.

Klausmeier, H. J. (1971). Cognitive operations in concept learning. *Educational Psychologist, 9,* 1–8.

Klausmeier, H. J. (1976). Conceptual development during the school years. In J. R. Levin & K. K. Allen (Eds.), *Cognitive learning in children* (pp. 5–29). New York: Academic Press.

Kuczaj, S., & Maratos, M. (1975). On the acquisition of

front, back, and side. *Child Development, 46,* 202–210.

Levin, J. R., Henderson, B., Levin, A. M., & Hoffer, G. L. (1975). Measuring knowledge of basic concepts by disadvantaged preschoolers. *Psychology in the Schools, 12,* 132–139.

Lichtenstein, R., & Ireton, H. (1984). *Preschool screening.* New York: Grune & Stratton.

Lidz, C. S. (1982). *Improving assessment of school children.* San Francisco: Jossey-Bass.

Lidz, C. S. (1983). Issues in assessing preschool children. In K. D. Paget & B. A. Bracken (Eds.), *The psychoeducational assessment of preschool children* (pp. 17–27). New York: Grune & Stratton.

Mickelson, N. I., & Galloway, C. G. (1973). Verbal concepts of Indian and non-Indian school beginners. *Journal of Educational Research, 67,* 55–56.

Moers, F., & Harris, J. (1978). Instruction in basic concepts and first grade achievement. *Psychology in the Schools, 15,* 84–86.

Moss, M. (1978). *Tests of Basic Experiences 2.* Monterey, CA: California Test Bureau/McGraw-Hill.

Myers, J., & Lytle, S. (1986). Assessment of the learning process. *Exceptional Children, 53,* 138–144.

Nason, F. O. (1981). *The frequency of appearance of the fifty concepts of the Prueba Boehm de Conceptos Basicos in the curricular materials for grades K–2 of the public schools in Puerto Rico.* Unpublished manuscript, Teachers College, Columbia University.

Nason, F. O. (1986). *Systematic instruction of basic relational concepts: Effects on the acquisition of concept knowledge and of language and mathematics achievement of Puerto Rican first graders from low income families.* Unpublished doctoral dissertation, Teachers College, Columbia University.

Nelson, R. B., & Cummings, J. A. (1981). Basic concept attainment of educably mentally handicapped children: Implications for teaching concepts. *Education and Training of the Mentally Retarded, 16,* 303–306.

Piaget, J. (1929). *The child's conception of the world.* New York: Harcourt, Brace.

Piaget, J. (1970). Piaget's theory. In P. H. Mussen (Ed.), *Carmichael's manual of child psychology* (3rd ed., pp. 703–732). New York: Wiley.

Piersel, N. C., & McAndrews, T. (1982). Concept acquisition and school progress: An examination of the Boehm Test of Basic Concepts. *Psychological Reports, 50,* 783–786.

Preddy, D., Boehm, A. E., & Shepherd, M. J. (1984). PBCB: A norming of the Spanish translation of the Boehm Test of Basic Concepts. *Journal of School Psychology, 22,* 407–413.

Preddy, D., Kaplan, C., & Boehm, A. E. (1980). *How important are basic concepts to instruction? Validation of Boehm Test of Basic Concepts.* Unpublished manuscript, Teachers College, Columbia University, New York.

Reisman, F. K., & Hutchinson, T. A. (1985). *Sequential Assessment of Mathematics Inventories.* Columbus, OH: Charles E. Merrill.

Richards, M. M. (1982). Empiricism and learning to mean. In S. Kuczaj (Ed.), *Language development:*

Vol. 1. Syntax and semantics (pp. 365–396). Hillside, NJ: Erlbaum.

Richards, M. M., & Haupe, L. S. (1981). Contrasting patterns in the acquisition of spatial/temporal terms. *Journal of Experimental Child Psychology, 32,* 485–512.

Rodriguez Bou, I. (1952). *Recuento del vocabulario Español* (Vol. 1). San Juan, Puerto Rico: Imprenta Universitaria.

Russell, D. H. (1956). *Children's thinking.* Boston: Ginn.

Sigel, I. E. (1964). The attainment of concepts. In M. L. Hoffman & L. W. Hoffman (Eds.), *Review of child development research* (pp. 209–248). New York: Russell Sage Foundation.

Spector, C. C. (1977). *Concept comprehension of normal kindergarten children with deviant syntactic development.* Unpublished doctoral dissertation, New York University.

Spector, C. C. (1979). The Boehm Test of Basic Concepts: Exploring the test results for cognitive deficits. *Journal of Learning Disabilities, 12,* 564–567.

Steinbauer, E., & Heller, M. S. (1978). The Boehm Test of Basic Concepts as a predictor of academic achievement in grades 2 and 3. *Psychology in the Schools, 15,* 357–360.

Steinert, M. C. (1979). Construct and criterion-related validity of the Boehm Test of Basic Concepts (Doctoral dissertation, Kent State University, 1978). *Dissertation Abstracts International, 39,* 7147A.

Swanson, H. L. (1984). Process assessment of intelligence in learning disabled and mentally retarded children: A multidirectional model. *Educational Psychologist, 19,* 149–162.

Taylor, S. F., Franckenpohl, H., & White, C. E. (1979). A revised core vocabulary. In S. E., Taylor, H. Franckenpohl, C. E. White, B. W. Nieroroda, C. L. Browning, & E. P. Bisner (Eds.), *EDL core vocabularies in reading, mathematics, sciences, and social studies* (pp. 3–67). New York: Educational Development Laboratories/McGraw-Hill.

Tennyson, R. D., & Cocchiarella, M. J. (1986). An empirically based instructional design theory for teaching concepts. *Review of Educational Research, 86,* 40–71.

Tennyson, R. D., & Park, O. (1980). The teaching of concepts: A review of instructional design research literature. *Review of Educational Research, 50,* 55–70.

Thorndike, E. L., & Lorge, I. (1944). *The teachers wordbook of 30,000 words.* New York: Bureau of Publications, Teachers College, Columbia University.

Vinacke, E. W. (1951). The investigation of concept formation. *Psychological Bulletin, 48,* 1–31.

Vygotsky, L. S. (1962). *Thought and language.* Cambridge, MA: MIT Press.

Wiig, E., & Semel, E. (1976). *Learning disabilities in children and adolescents.* Columbus, OH: Charles E. Merrill.

Ysseldyke, J. E., & Thurlow, M. L. (1984). Assessment practices in special education: Adequacy and appropriateness. *Educational Psychologist, 19,* 123–136.

28

Assessment of Linguistic Minority Group Children

RICHARD A. FIGUEROA
University of California at Davis

Linguistic diversity has always been the norm in the United States. In the 1930s, for example, Pintner and Arsenian's (1937) analysis of the 15th U.S. census estimated that "25 percent of the school population of this country was bilingual in 1930." Contemporary linguistic minorities are part of a national tradition, which includes the expectation that after a few generations, children of non-English-speaking groups will speak only (or predominantly) English.

A DEFINITION

"Linguistic minority" is a broad term that can encompass people from non-English-language ancestry irrespective of English-language proficiency, all the way to minimum levels of English-language proficiency irrespective of ancestry. By and large, children are designated as members of a "linguistic minority" when they score below various cutoff levels on English-language proficiency tests.

In this chapter, the following definition is used to describe "linguistic minority group" children: those who come from non-English-language background (NELB) homes (i.e., where a language other than English is spoken, be it continuously or intermittently), and where communicative demands in that language constitute a genre (Heath, 1986)

among the linguistic experiences of the child. This definition goes beyond an individual's English-language proficiency. It includes English-proficient children from bilingual or monolingual NELB homes. Though an NELB definition is not a novel one (Oxford-Carpenter et al., 1984), the reason for using it in this chapter is that psychometric tests have always shown a hypersensitivity to non-English-language home environments (as well as non-English-language proficiency) on several key test parameters (American Psychological Association, 1985, Ch. 13). The definition excludes children from racial–ethnic homes (e.g., Asian-American, Hispanic-American, etc.) where there is no experience with a language other than English. Again, this exclusion stems from the test score traits of such children (Figueroa, 1987).

The preponderance of the data presented in this chapter are from the empirical literature on testing Hispanic, Asian, and American Indian children. These groups constitute the present majority of the linguistic minority group population in the United States. Admittedly, this excludes many other language groups—a necessity forced by limitations of space and limitations of scientific testing literature on such groups. However, the findings on Hispanic, Asian, and American Indian children should provide generalizable applications to other groups.

TABLE 28.1. U.S. Census Estimates of Ancestry Groups Usually Designated as "Linguistic Minorities"

Group	Population	Percentage of total U.S. population (226,545,805)
Hispanics	14,608,673[a]	6.5
Mexican	8,679,000	(3.8)
Puerto Ricans	2,005,000	(0.9)
Cubans	806,000	(0.4)
Central Americans, South Americans, and others	3,113,000	(1.4)
Asians	3,466,421[b]	1.5
Chinese	812,178	(0.4)
Filipinos	781,894	(0.4)
Japanese	716,331	(0.3)
Indians (from India)	387,223	(0.2)
Koreans	357,393	(0.2)
Vietnamese	245,025	(0.1)
Other Asians	166,377	(0.1)
Pacific Islanders	259,566[b]	0.1
American Indians	806,590[c]	0.4
Total		8.5

[a] The data are from U.S. Bureau of the Census (1985b).
[b] The data are from U.S. Bureau of the Census (1983a).
[c] The data are from U.S. Bureau of the Census (1985a).

THE DEMOGRAPHIC PROFILE

Population estimates on "linguistic minorities" are difficult to establish because of the unknown numbers of illegal immigrants and the rapid demographic impact that political events can have (e.g., El Salvador and Vietnam). More often than not, census estimates and projections are either quickly outdated or proven wrong. With these caveats in mind, Table 28.1 presents the 1980 U.S. Bureau of the Census estimates of ancestry groups usually designated as "linguistic minorities."

The two main categories of "linguistic minorities" presented in Table 28.1 (Hispanic and Asian) vary substantially in median family income. In many ways, these differences act as markers distinguishing "successful" from "nonsuccessful" linguistic minorities in terms of political influence, school outcomes, and psychometric test data. When the total U.S. median family income is used as a guide ($26,433), linguistic minorities align themselves along the following continuum: Japanese ($27,354), Indians (from the country of India) ($24,993), Filipinos ($23,687), "other Asians" ($23,470), Cuban-Americans ($22,587), Chinese ($22,559), Ko-

reans ($20,459), Central/South Americans ($19,785), Hawaiians ($19,196), Mexican-Americans/Mexicans ($19,184), Pacific islanders ($14,242–$18,218), Vietnamese ($12,840), Puerto Ricans ($12,371), and American Indian (on reservations) ($9,924). It appears, in fact, that $20,000 is a critical boundary that seems to differentiate linguistic minorities with small, middle-class, well-educated families from those with large, often disadvantaged, undereducated families (U.S. Bureau of the Census, 1983b, 1985a, 1985b). Interestingly, the largest group in this latter category (Hispanics) is projected to grow from 7% of the total U.S. population in 1985 to 9.4% in the year 2000, and 19% by the year 2080 (U.S. Bureau of the Census, 1987). It should be noted, however that the upper ranges of these estimates are much higher (e.g., 36.5% by the year 2020; U.S. Bureau of the Census, 1986), and that the school-age populations of some of these groups are quite large (presently 15% for Hispanics; Arias, 1986).

Table 28.2 presents the numerical profile of "foreign-born persons" in the United States. Tables 28.1 and 28.2 encompass the NELB population of interest in this chapter, but essentially fail to describe its actual size within linguistic ancestry groups and foreign-born groups. Fortunately, a comprehensive study of NELB and of limited-English-proficient (LEP) persons is available (Oxford-Carpenter et al., 1984). These authors, using a variety of data from U.S. Bureau of the Census studies and the 1976 Children's English and Services Study (Dubois, 1980), have calculated estimates and projections of Hispanic (Mexican, Puerto Rican, Latin-American, and European Spanish), Asian (Chinese, Filipino, Japanese, Vietnamese, and Korean), and "non-Spanish/non-Asian" (including other Asian-language background) NELB and child LEP populations. They have estimated that between 1985 and the year 2000, the Hispanic NELB population will increase by 38% (from 13,191,300 to 18,145,200); the Asian NELB population by 12% (from 2,023,000 to 2,262,000); and the "non-Spanish/non-Asian" NELB population by 12% (from 17,066,300 to 19,085,900).

This same study (Oxford-Carpenter et al., 1984) also notes that 16 states have or will have over half a million NELB persons: Arizona, California, Colorado, Connecticut, Florida, Illinois, Louisiana, Massachusetts, Michigan, New Jersey, New Mexico, New York, Ohio, Pennsylvania, Texas, and Wisconsin.

As far as the estimates for the child (5–14) LEP population are concerned, they have calculated that between 1985 and the year 2000, the Hispanic child LEP population will increase by 47% (from 1,794,300 to 2,630,000); while the Asian and "non-Spanish/non-Asian" child LEP populations will increase by 19% (from 111,200 to 132,600) and 18% (from 539,000 to 637,400), respectively.

The states most heavily affected by this elementary-school-age group will be California, Texas, and New York, each with over half a million elementary-school-age LEP pupils. Concentrations of various LEP groups, however, are manifest in various locations throughout the United States: Chinese in California and New York; Filipinos in California; Japanese in California and Hawaii; Portuguese in California and Massachusetts; Native American Navajos in New Mexico and Arizona; Yiddish, Greeks, and Italians in New York; and French in Louisiana.

In this demographic scenario, several

TABLE 28.2. 1980 U.S. Census Estimates of "Foreign-Born Persons" in the United States

Place of birth	Population
Europe	4,743,550
Mexico, Central America, and West Indies	4,664,903
Asia	2,539,777
Canada	842,859
South America	561,011
Africa	199,723
Other	78,896

Note. The data are from U.S. Bureau of the Census (1980).

points need to be underscored. First, the largest NELB group, Hispanics, is also the youngest and hence the one that will most dramatically affect schools and testing. Second, this group has progressively become more and more segregated in U.S. schools (Arias, 1986), thereby receiving less and less of the most effective method for acquiring English-language skills (i.e., interaction with English-speaking peers). Third, there is a strong likelihood that the projections described will seriously underestimate the actual numbers, if and when sociopolitical disintegration speeds up in Latin America. And fourth, unlike every other NELB group in the history of the U.S., Hispanics may successfully establish bilingual territories, institutions, and schools (e.g., as Cubans are presently doing in Miami). The educational implications of all this are considerable. So are the technical and political implications for the measurement of intelligence and achievement.

THE HISTORICAL CONTEXT: INTELLIGENCE TESTING

Concomitant with the importation, translation, and norming of the French Binet scales, the early half of this century saw a pronounced interest in the mental capacity of racial and language groups in the United States. This research program, often referred to as "race psychology" (Garth, 1931), has received its share of condemnations because of its faith in the psychometric measurement of innate ability (e.g., Gould, 1981). Notwithstanding the hereditarian naiveté in this literature, there is value in reviewing these efforts because of their findings and interpretations about linguistic minorities. What happened with bilingual populations in the early days of testing psychology continues to the present; in effect, therefore, this history is contemporary and relevant. For this reason, an extended review of the historical literature is presented.

Four points are worth noting about the pre-1950s literature on the intelligence test scores of linguistic minorities:

1. *Nonverbal test scores were consistently higher than verbal test scores for virtually all language groups.* This ubiquitous dichotomy between verbal and nonverbal test scores was consistently attributed to the "language handicap" of linguistic minorities, even though caution sometimes was called for in interpreting the verbal IQs of these groups (Brown, 1922; Darsie, 1926; Koch & Simmons, 1926). Occasionally, verbal tests such as the Binet were modified to remove some of the English verbal loading (Darsie, 1926; Fukuda, 1923; Louttit, 1931; Yeung, 1921). Mitchell (1937) went so far as to suggest adding a "corrective factor" to the intelligence test of Spanish-speaking children. All too often, however, once acknowledgment of the "language handicap" had been made, attributions to mental capacity were nevertheless drawn (Brown, 1922; Garretson, 1928; Garth, 1923, 1928), or linguistic factors were then tortuously discounted (Brigham, 1923; Brill, 1936; Garretson, 1928; Garth, 1927; Haught, 1931; Paschal & Sullivan, 1925; Sheldon, 1924). Brigham (1923), for example, clearly noted how the Army's Alpha Test (similar in many verbal subtests to the Wechsler Intelligence Scale for Children–Revised [WISC-R]) produced appreciably lower IQs for Southern European and Hispanic Army recruits. Commenting on how these means increased with length of U.S. residency, he attributed these results to "a gradual deterioration in the class of immigrants examined in the army, who came to this country in each succeeding five year period since 1902" (Brigham, 1923, p. 111), rather than to increased exposure to English. Brigham is actually unique in that he underwent a radical conversion. By 1930, he wrote:

For purposes of comparing individuals or groups, it is apparent that tests in the vernacular must be used only with individuals having equal opportunities to acquire the vernacular of the test. This requirement precludes the use of such tests in making comparative studies of individuals brought up in homes in which the vernacular of the test is not used, or in which two vernaculars are used. The last condition is frequently violated here in studies of children born in this country whose parents speak another tongue. It is important, as the effects of bilingualism are not entirely known. (1930, p. 165)

In some instances, it was argued that the inability to acquire English was in itself an index of genetic ability; length or quality of English-language exposure was not specified (Darsie, 1926; Goodenough, 1926). Similarly, nonverbal IQs came to be perceived as measures of innate ability (Darsie, 1926, p. 11) and as being truly free of linguistic contamination (Goodenough, 1926). On this last point, some data and some cautious researchers (Darcy, 1946; Koch & Simmons, 1926; Lester, 1929; Paschal & Sullivan, 1925) indicated otherwise. Koch and Simmons for example, noted this and cautioned:

While the Pantomime test reduces to a minimum the language handicaps of the foreign groups, it is not to be assumed that the test permits all of our subjects to operate under equally favorable conditions. It is questionable, for instance, whether our groups have had an equal opportunity to familiarize themselves with many of the concepts included in its content. Then, too, those foreign children who in the practice test [similar to the Kaufman Assessment Battery for Children (K-ABC) "practice" items] do not understand what is desired are not easily set aright. Although an interpreter was used in such cases, the very fact of this attention tended to confuse or embarrass the pupil. Lastly, the foreign groups are likely to be handicapped because of certain habits or attitudes which they carry over from a language situation involving English to a nonverbal, though language, situation. The Mexican who has built up the habit of pondering over commands given in English before proceeding to the execution of them may react in the same way to an American's gesture commands and, hence, attack the test with little confidence or dispatch. A hesitating manner, whether for this or other reasons, was very evident, especially among the rural and less advanced city Mexican groups. (1926, p. 35)

The pre-1950 testing data also established that verbal and nonverbal IQs could not be substituted for each other; concurrent validity was not sufficiently high (Darcy, 1946). Also, predictive validities (to academic achievement) were all too often lower for nonverbal scores (a fact that applies to English-speaking children as well). In effect, the measures of intelligence yielding the highest scores for linguistic minorities (and what many then considered the most appropriate) failed by not predicting to a critical external index of validity—that is, academic achievement (Darsie, 1926; Feingold, 1924; Garth, 1928).

2. *Most studies ignored the effects of a second language on test scores*. The broad recognition that immigrant groups showed a "language handicap" in English verbal test scores failed to compel researchers to account for the impact of this "handicap" on psychometric test scores. Neither proficiency in English nor controls for the mediating factors in the acquisition of English (e.g., time in the United States, home language use) became recognized as important correlates with depressed verbal scores, though the issues were raised by several researchers who conducted some of the major reviews of this literature (Brill, 1936; Darcy, 1946; Feingold, 1924; Hung-Hsia, 1929; Sanchez, 1932a, 1934a) or who deliberately addressed this matter (Koch & Simmons, 1926; Pintner & Keller, 1922).

Even when the data pointed to a strong relationship between length of exposure to English and verbal test scores (Brigham, 1930; Goodenough, 1926; Manuel, 1935; Paschal & Sullivan, 1925), studies generally ignored this fact (e.g., Garth, 1925a) or proclaimed that if subjects were born in the United States, the impact of another language was eliminated or effectively attenuated (e.g., Darsie, 1926).

There are two plausible reasons for this linguistic naiveté in the research literature. First, applied psychology was not very interested in the phenomena of bilingualism. Second, xenophobia was part of a larger national attitude about the genetic and political threat posed by immigrant groups. The testing literature generally depicted bilingualism in negative terms. It was seen as retarding intellectual development (Smith, 1931), producing mental confusion (Saer,

1923), and handicapping the acquisition of English (Portenier, 1947). Yet, interesting if not anomalous data also unwittingly began to document some novel characteristics about "bilinguals." Older bilinguals from nondisadvantaged backgrounds performed as well as if not better than controls (Darcy, 1946; Feingold, 1924; Manuel, 1935; Pintner & Arsenian, 1937). The primary language often diminished with the acquisition of English (Johnson, 1938; Manuel, 1935), progressively precluding its use with translations of English tests. The influence or impact of the primary language on English-language scores was manifested over long periods of time (Saer, 1923; Wang, 1926). Two languages without adequate educational development were worse than a single non-English language with educational development (Altus, 1949; Arsenian, 1945; Smith, 1949, 1957). Also, bilinguals' digit recall scores were often anomalous (Darsie, 1926; Hung-Hsia, 1929; Luh & Wy, 1931; Manuel, 1935), in that digits-forward tasks were harder to execute than digits-backward tasks—a phenomenon noted by Jensen and Inouye (1980), but never really explained in terms of the processing/cognitive operations involved.

Just as interesting are the data on the technical properties of test scores of immigrant groups. These data tentatively support the following hypotheses: (a) The internal properties of test scores, archetypically represented by the reliability coefficient, appeared insensitive to "bilingualism" (Brigham, 1930; Herr, 1946; Sanchez, 1934a); and (b) the external properties of test scores, most notably represented by indices of predictive validity, did seem sensitive to "bilingualism" (Altus, 1945; Davenport, 1932; Feingold, 1924; Garth, 1928; Paschal & Sullivan, 1925; Pintner & Keller, 1922; Wheeler, 1932; Wood, 1929; Yoder, 1928).

3. *The design of most studies was typically inadequate*. "Italians," "Jews," "Indians," "Mexicans," and so on were usually compared to U.S. natives as if the former were as linguisitically homogeneous as the latter. It has already been noted that language factors were ignored, but so were differences in socioeconomic status (SES; Garretson, 1928) and differences in the quality of schooling offered immigrant children (Darsie, 1926; Garretson, 1928; Haught, 1934; Koch & Simmons, 1926; Paschal & Sullivan, 1925). Even

the representativeness of the samples used (Koch & Simmons, 1926) was all too often suspect. Ironically, these issues were acknowledged (Arlitt, 1921; Brill, 1936; Darsie, 1926; Paschal & Sullivan 1925; Sanchez, 1932a, 1932b, 1934a, 1934b).

The measurement problems presented by "bilinguals" typically elicited four responses: Tests were administered in English, or nonverbal tests were used, or tests were directly translated into another language (using U.S. norms), or tests were normed in the other language. The first two problems have already been addressed. Of the last two, translating tests was by far the more widely used procedure (Lester, 1929; Mahakian, 1939; Manuel, 1935; Mitchell, 1937; Paschal & Sullivan, 1925; Saer, 1923). Norming tests within language groups was done, but usually produced less-than-adequate measures (Ammons & Aguero, 1950; Luh & Wy, 1931).

Translating tests, to this day, remains a favorite measurement "solution" for testing non-English-speaking and LEP subjects. However, it was recognized very early (Manuel, 1935; Sanchez, 1934a) that this procedure assumes equivalent difficulty values of words used across languages. Manuel's (1935) translation of the Binet attempted to control for this by actually using Spanish lexical items with difficulty levels known to be approximately similar to those that were empirically derived in the Binet norming. The study is severely flawed because of its use of the English-derived norms and its inability to control for the subjects' English-language proficiency as well as their years in school. However, it is of considerable importance insofar as it clearly illustrates that translations, no matter how carefully constructed, ultimately fail. Manuel's Spanish-version IQs were no different from the English-version IQs (82.5 vs. 80.5). The difficulty levels of the 56 Binet subtests used (ages 6–18) varied substantially across languages, with more success manifested in the Spanish version of the subtests at younger ages (6–8) and more success in the English version at the older ages (9–12). Also, prediction of academic achievement was not equivalent across language versions of the Binet. Finally, some of the conclusions that Manuel lists are poignant and relevant beyond the issue of translating tests:

(4) The peculiar language experiences of these bilingual children result in a handicap which persists for an undetermined period and is difficult to evaluate in individual cases. It is probable that, in the first few grades at least, the handicap is a dual one, in the sense that these children have no adequate language tool in either Spanish or English.

(5) Without some allowance for language difficulty, the English edition of the *Stanford–Binet* should not be used with average Spanish-speaking children before the third grade or before they have reading ability about equal to that of the low third grade.

(6) Success with certain tests in English because of school experience with the vocabulary or situation used in the test may cause the examiner to overestimate the pupil's general ability to use English.

(7) Tests presenting special language difficulties should either be omitted or given in the language with which the child has the greater promise of success. . . .

(10) There is every reason to believe that the removal of language and environmental handicaps would be accompanied by a significant rise in the scores of both intelligence and achievement tests. (1935, pp. 37–38)

Exemplary studies are rare during this period. A notable example is Darcy's (1946) investigation of Italian and American students. Working with preschoolers, Darcy set out to determine what the impact of bilingualism on measured intelligence was and whether a nonverbal test could be validly substituted for the Binet. Subjects were matched by age, sex, gender, and SES. Half were bilinguals, the other half monolinguals. A home language survey was used to distinguish subjects from single- and dual-language homes. On the Binet, monolinguals' average IQ was statistically higher than bilinguals' (99 vs. 91). On the nonverbal test (Atkins Object-Fitting Test), the opposite appeared (89 vs. 98). Darcy's results provide the most unambiguous documentation of bilinguals' "language handicap" on verbal tests of intelligence. She also established that verbal tests could not be substituted for nonverbal tests.

4. *National chauvinism and "genetic" attributions about mental ability permeated the studies on "race psychology."* Beyond the problems already examined in testing various linguistic groups, the pre-1950s literature

almost seemed motivated to demean those speaking a foreign language. Italians, Jews, Mexicans, Chinese, Indians, Japanese, and virtually all non-American, non-Northern Europeans suffered at the hands of researchers who questioned their innate ability (Brigham, 1930; Garth, 1925; Goodenough, 1926; Haught, 1934; Pintner, 1924) and who advocated national policies against immigration because of the threat these groups supposedly posed (Brown, 1922; Brigham, 1930; Goodenough, 1926; Saer, 1923; Symonds, 1924). Goodenough's (1926) study, for example, illustrates the worst of this type of research. She attributed the "squalor" and poor "hygienic conditions" of Italian and black neighborhoods as much to inferior genetic ability as to "social pressure" or "race prejudice." The "language handicap" was discounted, since "The Italian continues to rank low even on non-verbal tests" (1926, p. 391). Even when she presented data clearly showing that when degree of English exposure was compared to achieved IQ, the rank-order correlation was .754, her interpretation was this: "A more probable explanation is that those nationality-groups whose average intellectual ability is inferior do not readily learn the new language" (1926, p. 393). Armenian, Italian, "Spanish-Mexican," "Negro," "Hoopa Valley Indian," Portuguese, French, Swiss, Assyrian, Slavonian, and Servian children, given their low nonverbal IQs (which were said to be "completely independent of language" and "entirely fair"), "rank very much below the American children and those of North European stock" (p. 395).

Even when the data themselves proved ambiguous about the intelligence of Asians (Darsie, 1926; Luh & Wy, 1931; Sandiford & Kerr, 1926), Mexicans (Lamb, 1930), Italians (Darcy, 1946; Pintner, 1924), or Jews (Brill, 1936; Feingold, 1924) and whether it was equal to or higher than that of Americans, the policy and social implications drawn were negative. Chauvinism, xenophobia, and the temptation toward genetic attributions plagued these early studies. Even researchers who were cautious and warned against the complexities potentially attenuating research findings with linguistic groups seemed gripped by this climate (Darsie, 1926; Garth, 1925a; Koch & Simmons, 1926):

These studies taken all together seem to indicate the mental superiority of the white race. There may be some question, however, about the indicated intellectual inferiority of the yellow races. Altogether, it may be said that the investigators recognize that these experimental results are crude and so they must be taken tentatively. Nevertheless, they and all similar studies have real value, since they are the beginnings of the application of scientific method to the problem of racial psychology. (Garth, 1925a, p. 359)

THE HISTORICAL CONTEXT: ACHIEVEMENT TESTING

Pre-1950 studies on the academic achievement levels of virtually all linguistic minorities concluded that they significantly underachieved in comparison to their Anglo peers at every grade level (Caldwell & Mowry, 1933; Garretson, 1928; Garth, 1925a; Garth, Smith, & Abell, 1928; Johnson, 1938; Livesay, 1936; Manuel, 1935; McElwee, 1935; Pratt, 1929; Reynolds, 1933/1973; Smith, 1942; Yeung, 1921). The academic retardation extended anywhere from 6 months to 4 years.

But an interesting set of trends emerged from these studies. In achievement tests or subtests wherein complex English-language skills were engaged (vocabulary, reading comprehension, sentence completion, analogies, opposites, word and paragraph meaning, essay and composition), language minority pupils routinely did poorly (Johnson, 1938; Livesay, 1936; Manuel, 1935; McElwee, 1935; Pratt, 1929). In arithmetic, mathematics, history, or spelling, academic deficits were either not as pronounced or nonexistent, especially with Chinese and Japanese pupils (it is interesting to note the similarity of this to the verbal–nonverbal dichotomy found in language minority IQs). Another trend marked by some of these studies was the tendency for linguistic minorities, particularly Chinese and Japanese, to perform better on school grades than on achievement test scores (Bell, 1935; Smith, 1942). Also, some studies documented that bilingualism affected standardized achievement scores but not academic grades (Smith, 1942).

Unlike the early research literature on intelligence, the early achievement studies on linguistic minority pupils gave more attention to the complex background variables possibly affecting academic achievement: SES, language proficiency, and schooling.

Socioeconomic Status

The immigrant/refugee experience in the United States usually begins with poverty. Societal responses to linguistic, cultural, and economic differences, particularly during economic recessions, have all to often been repressive and brutal (Asian American Studies, 1983; Bell, 1935; DeWitt, 1976; Phelan, 1901). The early days of the testing movement were times of extremely negative perceptions about Asians, Italians, Jews, and Mexican-Americans. Those of Northern European descent who were Americanized and of middle-class status did not suffer from the same discrimination (Haven, 1931). The early testing literature on the academic achievement of linguistic minorities routinely reported the low, low SES of Native Americans (Garth, 1925b), Mexicans (Garretson, 1928), Japanese (Darsie, 1926), Chinese (Yeung, 1921), and Italians (Goodenough, 1926). But it was essentially a missed opportunity, insofar as these data were not controlled for (e.g., Garretson, 1928) in the studies on academic achievement.

Language Proficiency

As with IQ testing, English-language proficiency or "bilinguality" constituted a "handicap" (Caldwell & Mowry, 1933), insofar as achievement test scores were routinely lower for pupils from NELB homes. Like the early literature on intelligence, the early achievement testing literature failed to use its own documentation of linguistic groups' tenacity in their primary-language maintenance (Darsie, 1926; Garretson, 1928; Johnson, 1938; Portenier, 1947; Pratt, 1929; Smith, 1942; Yeung, 1921) and the possible variation in test score effects stemming from the first-language (L_1), first-/second-language (L_1/L_2), and second-language (L_2) statuses of immigrant students.

Smith's (1942) study investigating the impact of "bilingualism" on academic achievement is exceptional in this regard. The study used an empirical, albeit indirect, measure of bilinguality, the Hoffman Bilingual Schedule (Hoffman, 1934); subjects were Japanese, Korean, Chinese, Hawaiian, and Caucasian college students with varying levels of "bilingualism" (where 0 = English only, the Japanese scored 21, Koreans 18, Chinese 12, Hawaiians 5, and Caucasians 2). Smith found that bilingualism and college aptitude test score *were* negatively correlated. However, the correlations were very small for all the subjects studied (−.150 for those completing one semester and −.116 for those completing three semesters). The same magnitude in the correlations was found between bilingualism and college grade point averages (GPAs), except that these were in the opposite direction (.156 and .159). Smith's (1942) summary of these findings is interesting, in that it more accurately reflects the common beliefs about bilingualism than the actual findings in her study: "The negative correlation . . . between bilingual and college aptitude scores suggests that our students are still handicapped by bilingualism at the time of college entrance" (p. 361).

Like the early literature on intelligence testing, the early research on the academic achievement of linguistic minorities, while recognizing the existence and importance of the "language handicap" variable, essentially left it alone. What is particularly poignant, in retrospect, is the accuracy with which so many of the *parameters* related to "bilingualism" were described and studied (Arsenian, 1937, 1945; Manuel, 1935; Manuel & Wright, 1929; Saer, 1923; Sanchez, 1934a, 1934b; Smith, 1939), yet essentially unaccounted for in most of the testing literature. Manuel and Wright (1929), for example, cogently describe some of these parameters:

> The first handicap is that of having more to learn. In addition to this, [the student] has for a considerable time much less ability to respond to the language of the school as an instrument of instruction. We still have a long way to go before we shall know the rate at which this handicap diminishes, the point at which it becomes practically negligible, and the best methods of adjusting to it. It is not so easy to estimate the amount of the difficulty after 3, 4, 5, or more years in the public schools. Opinion seems to be divided. (quoted in Reynolds, 1933/1973, p. 31)

Schooling

Inherently, achievement tests evaluate not only what a student has learned, but also what a school system provides. Early studies of linguistic minority pupils, while investigating their academic performance in comparison to Anglo students and while attributing much of the academic retardation to the "language handicap," sketched a fairly bleak picture of their schooling. They attended the poorest schools (Darsie, 1926; Manuel, 1935; Reynolds, 1933/1973). They were segregated (Bell, 1935; Garth, 1920; Haught, 1934; Koch & Simmons, 1926), were older, were retained in grade more often, had higher rates of irregular attendance, and dropped out in greater proportions (Darsie, 1926; Garretson, 1928; Garth, 1920, 1925a, 1925b; Haught, 1934; Koch & Simmons, 1926; Reynolds, 1933/1973; Yeung, 1921). Rural schools were particularly inadequate (Bell, 1935; Darsie, 1926; Reynolds, 1933/1973), and migrant pupils were exceptionally mistreated:

[I]n certain instances, in order to receive this [migratory pupils] financial aid, districts have undertaken to educate migratory children without employing the additional teachers necessary. Cases have occurred in which they have crowded 125 or more migratory pupils into one classroom. In other cases the schools for migratory pupils are open from 7:00 A.M. to 12:00 noon. In the afternoon the children may be found working in the fields with their parents . . . (Reynolds, 1933/1973, p. 49)

Teachers perceived these students in negative ways, undoubtedly responding to their socioeconomic and linguistic characteristics as well as to societal prejudices about foreign laborers (Bell, 1935). Darsie (1926), for example, collected teacher perceptions about Japanese pupils in the 1920s that were typically maintained about second-language learners in American public schools: "On the other hand, with regard to more purely intellectual traits, the Japanese are judged as inferior. This is shown in the ratings of general intelligence, desire to know and originality" (p. 76.).

One historical aspect of linguistic minority education and achievement that is usually overlooked is bilingual education. Virtually every language group in the United States over the last 200 years has set up its own "foreign-language school" wherein literacy and language skills in the primary language are taught concurrently with the curriculum of the public schools. In the first half of this century, the Japanese and Chinese language schools were the most successful versions of these; large numbers of these pupils routinely attended these schools in the 1920s, 1930s, and 1940s. The majority of the studies reviewed on these schools (Bell, 1935; Darsie, 1926; Smith, 1942; Symonds, 1924; Yoshioka, 1929) and their influence on the academic and English-language achievement of Japanese and Chinese students found that attendance at these schools did not adversely affect academic achievement or English-language competency (in some, there was a slight indication to the contrary). The best-controlled study reviewed (Bell, 1935) found that on the Stanford Achievement Test, Japanese achievement scores were not affected by attendance in these language schools, whereas segregation of Japanese students in the public schools very significantly accounted for underachievment. The importance of these academic experiences in the primary language lies in their possible impact on contemporary Asian-American achievement, as well as the relevance of primary-language instruction (and testing) to present-day underachieving minorities.

A final word on schooling: With large numbers of linguistic minority students failing in the regular education programs, the early 1900s saw the beginning of a trend toward more extensive testing of these students and their placement in classes for the handicapped (Miller, 1916; Reynolds, 1933/1973).

MEASURING THE INTELLIGENCE OF LINGUISTIC MINORITIES

Segue to the Present

If 1950 is used as an arbitrary boundary from "then" to "now," several developments mark the discussion on testing linguistic minorities. First, the term "linguistic minority" has retained its historical connotation of "underprivileged and undereducated." Though there are many groups that technically qualify as linguistic minorities, the research and applied concerns about testing these students presently tend to focus on the larger populations designated as linguistic minorities: Hispanics, Native Americans, and Southeast Asians. Japanese and Chinese children, designated as "whiz kids" by *Time* magazine (Brand, 1987), are stereotypically perceived as so mainstreamed and successful that the only controversies surrounding their test scores have to do with their overrepresentation in gifted programs and university enrollments, even though this perception is often misleading (Kitano, 1962; Lan, 1976; Stevenson et al., 1985; Yee, 1976).

Second, intelligence tests have become pivotal in the quasi-medical practice of diagnosing mental handicaps and giftedness in the public schools (Berk, Bridges, & Shih, 1981; Knoff, 1983; Mehan, Hertweck, & Meihls, 1986; Smith & Knoff, 1981). The greatest use of intelligence tests occurs in schools. School psychologists have come to be the principal users of IQ tests.

Third, intelligence testing and achievement testing have come under the scrutiny of the judiciary because of their pivotal role in decisions regarding tracking and special education, particularly as these affect black and language minority pupils; correspondingly, this scrutiny has produced a heated response from testing psychology about bias and fairness (Heller, Holtzman, & Messick, 1982; Jensen, 1982).

Fourth, for the Hispanic populations, testing issues have taken on a new dimension. Psychometric Spanish-language tests are now available and are widely used. For these children, bilingual assessments and psychometrics appear to be as inevitable as they are controversial (Brady, Manni, & Winikur, 1983a; Martinez, 1985; Wilen & Van Maanen Sweeting, 1986).

Fifth, contemporary tests of intelligence continue to show the classic linguistic minority profile: high nonverbal IQ, low verbal IQ (Clarizio, 1982; Vernon, 1982). However, the latter is no longer attributed to a "language handicap." Nominally, at least, "bilingualism" is now associated with depressed verbal IQs (Kaufman, 1979). Information and vocabulary tests and subtests of intelligence are particularly affected by the bilingual factor

(Cummins, 1984; Figueroa, Delgado, & Ruiz, 1984).

Sixth, "bilingualism" is no longer considered detrimental to intelligence and learning. Many data suggest quite the opposite (Dolson, 1985), though this conclusion is far from being well established.

Seventh, nonverbal IQs are the recommended means for measuring the intelligence of linguistic minority children and youths (Clarizio, 1982; Sattler, 1982), even though in school psychology there is no consistent practice in this regard (Cummins, 1984; Figueroa, 1986; Rueda, Cardoza, Mercer & Carpenter, 1984; Twomey, Gallegos, Andersen, Williamson, & Williamson, 1980). Nonverbal IQ is considered free of linguistic contamination (Macnamara, 1966); however, not enough data are available to substantiate this assertion reliably, and some evidence to the contrary exists (Anastasi & Cordova, 1953; Figueroa, Delgado, & Ruiz, 1984; Lewis, 1959; Yee & LaForge, 1974).

In spite of widespread protest and litigation surrounding the use of IQ to measure the intelligence of linguistic minorities, the prevalent attitude among IQ test users is cryptically captured by the executive director of the California Association of School Psychologists, Richard Rosso: "I don't think there's anything on the horizon to replace the IQ test" (quoted in Levine, 1987, p. 54).

The Regulatory Context

Since the 1960s, researchers have documented that Hispanic pupils in many school districts throughout the United States are overrepresented in classes for the mentally handicapped (Brady, Manni, & Winikur, 1983b; Heller et al., 1982; Mercer, 1973; Ortiz, 1986; Tucker, 1980). In 1970, this type of overrepresentation led to the first of many lawsuits against state education agencies.

In *Diana v. State Board of Education* (1970), nine Mexican-American elementary school pupils brought a class action suit against the state of California before Federal Judge Robert Peckham of the U.S. District Court of Northern California. Their suit alleged that they had been misdiagnosed as mentally retarded on the basis of biased and invalid tests of intelligence (the Stanford–Binet and the Wechsler Intelligence Scale for

Children [WISC]) and that this had subjected them to stigma and irreparable educational harm. The allegation of bias rested on two principles: (1) The tests were administered in the wrong language, since the children were predominantly Spanish-speaking; and (2) the tests failed to take into account the children's Mexican, rural, and migrant cultural background. Perhaps because of the documented history of these issues, and most certainly because of the acknowledged fact that in the 1960s and 1970s classes for the mildly retarded were overpopulated with black and Hispanic pupils by as much as 200% (Mercer, 1973), California agreed to settle *Diana* out of court. The following are the six provisions in that settlement:

A) Children must be tested in their own language and in English;
B) They may be tested on non-verbal sections of intelligence tests;
C) Mexican American children in EMR [educable mentally retarded] classes should be re-tested and re-evaluated using non-verbal test sections;
D) School districts throughout the state must submit summaries of the retesting efforts and their plans for transitional programs for children no longer eligible for EMR programs;
E) A test of IQ that reflects Mexican American culture would be developed and normed on Mexican American children; and
F) If there is a disparity between the racial–ethnic representation of the district and the EMR classes, to a significant degree as determined by a value beyond a standard deviation of the Hispanic, school district population proportion, the districts so involved should submit an explanation. (*quoted in* Figueroa, 1986, p. 2)

In California, the *Diana* settlement has not fared well (Figueroa, 1986; Rueda, Figueroa, Mercado, & Cardoza, 1984). Most of its provisions are either not followed (A), or they have been extensively compromised (B, C, D, F), or they have been dropped (E). But *Diana*'s impact on other testing cases has been extensive: *Arreola v. Santa Ana Board of Education* (1968); *Guadalupe Organization Inc. v. Tempe Elementary School District No. 3* (1978); *Ruiz v. State Board of Education* (1971); *Covarrubias v. San Diego Unified School District* (1972); *Jose P. v.*

Ambach (1979); and *Dyrcia S. v. Board of Education* (1979).

When the Education for All Handicapped Children Act was being considered in the early 1970s, the *Diana* issues received sufficient attention to have a direct effect on subsequent federal provisions in Public Law 94-142 requiring that testing and evaluation materials be racially and culturally nondiscriminatory, and that these be "administered in the child's native language or mode of communication, unless it is clearly not feasible to do so" (§ 612(5)(c)).

What was singularly poignant in the mid-1970s subsequent to P.L. 94-142 was that intelligence tests in a non-English language, normed for U.S. bilinguals, did not exist (nor do they exist now). Many school psychologists who routinely administer intelligence tests to linguistic minorities comply with P.L. 94-142 by translating the tests, more often than not extemporaneously with the help of a bilingual secretary (Figueroa, 1986; Twomey et al., 1980).

In 1985, a new edition of the *Standards for Educational and Psychological Testing* (American Psychological Association, 1985) recognized the unique challenges posed by bilinguals. Chapter 13 is titled "Testing Linguistic Minorities." In many ways, the narrative introduction of Chapter 13 is more important than the seven standards promulgated. The introductory section acknowledges the following:

1. Verbal tests for a non-native speaker can become tests of English-language proficiency.
2. "Bilingualism" includes a wide array of speech, literacy, and comprehension skills.
3. Information-processing speed may be slowed down and impede problem-solving accuracy on tests given in the weaker language.
4. Validity may be attenuated if the linguistic characteristics of language minority test takers are not given "due consideration."
5. Translating tests does not correspondingly translate psychometric properties.
6. Language proficiency tests in L_1 and L_2 are important for educational placement decisions, and these should encompass such skills as "communicative competence, literacy, grammar, pronunciation, and comprehension" (p. 74).
7. Social language skills, though useful, may not suffice for making judgments about instructional placements (in L_2, it is implied).

8. Multiple testing "may be desirable" for linguistic minorities.
9. Children's verbal elaboration with adults (as often required in intelligence tests) may be mediated by cultural norms.

Three (13.4, 13.6, 13.7) of the seven standards flow directly from the introduction. Two (13.2, 13.3) ask test publishers to describe "in detail" any "linguistic modifications" that they recommend (a standard badly in need of detail itself); and to give directions and information on the appropriate use and interpretation of tests that will be used with linguistic minorities (for those linguistic groups for whom it is feasible to provide this information). Standard 13.5 recommends that the level of English in employment and professional tests be commensurate with the occupation under consideration. Finally, there is Standard 13.1. Potentially the most important one, it is also among the most vague. It recommends that "threats to test reliability and validity" should be minimized by the *testers*, and recommends that the "professional judgement" of the tester determine when a test may be linguistically inappropriate for a bilingual person. It vaguely seems to suggest that bilingual, cross-culturally trained testers may best be able to carry out this standard. In a separate section of the *Standards* volume, Standard 6.10 seems to make this point in a slightly more forceful manner when it recommends that test users "should not attempt to evaluate test takers whose special characteristics—ages, handicapping conditions, or linguistic, generational, or cultural backgrounds—are outside the range of their academic training or supervised experience" (p. 43). However, this does not mean that such testing is proscribed. If a tester is confronted by a language minority child, Standard 6.10 recommends "consultation" about modification, selection, and interpretation of tests from "a professional who has had relevant experience."

In terms of testing a Hmong child who speaks very little English, for example, it is difficult to see how Standards 13.1 and 6.10 will effectively bridge the linguistic (and cultural) distance between the child on the one hand and the test and tester on the other. In fact, data rather unequivocally suggest that for language minority children,

the extant regulatory corpus has made a marginal impact on how testing (particularly intelligence testing) is being done (Cummins, 1980; Figueroa, 1986; Ortiz, 1986; Rueda, Figueroa, Mercado, & Cardoza, 1984; Twomey et al., 1980). This inertia may well be explained by the present lack of knowledge of the professions involved in intelligence testing with respect to culture, language, bias, and bilingual testing.

Culture

In the psychometric literature on intelligence, culture is insignificant (Sandoval, 1979; Sandoval, Zimmerman & Woo, 1980; Sattler, 1982). There is no cultural impact detected in reliabilities, validities, or factorial structures in virtually all of the scientific literature on IQ tests in the United States. This is an exceptionally interesting fact. Cultural differences between linguistic minority children and Anglo-American children not only constitute the focus of scientific branches of psychology (Ascher, 1985; Kagan & Klein, 1973; Laosa, Swartz, & Diaz-Guerrero, 1974; Mordkowitz & Ginsburg, 1987) and education (Stevenson, Azoma, & Hakuta, 1986), not to mention anthropology and sociology; they also account for a considerable amount of literature relevant to testing. For over a decade, Kagan (1986) has documented the cooperative motivational styles of Mexican and Mexican-American children in contrast to the competitive styles of Anglo-American children. Culturally mediated learning preferences have been documented for Asian-American and Mexican-American children (Heath, 1986). Even the medical effects of protein-calorie malnutrition peculiar to young rural Third World children and conducive to specific learning disabilities (Cravioto & Arrieta, 1985, 1986) have been documented. Yet the literature on IQ tests finds that non-U.S. cultural variance in test scores is negligible. "Cultural bias" in IQ tests from an empirical, psychometric perspective has yet to be proven.

Two reasons are tentatively offered as explanations for this anomaly. First, the psychometric literature has not developed or attended to any measures that are culturally specific to any linguistic minority. Mercer's (1979) Sociocultural Scales give the impression of providing such a measure, but in fact they are essentially culture-specific to the United States. The sociologically grounded items in the Sociocultural Scales derive their meaning and importance only in relation to their covariation with U.S. IQs. Second, the model within which cultural factors have been explored relative to intelligence tests has essentially been one wherein non-U.S. cultures would disordinally interact with the U.S. culture inherent in U.S. intelligence tests, especially verbally loaded intelligence tests. Different cultures may not interact in such a way as to disrupt item sequences or indices of prediction (Figueroa, 1983). Cultures, like languages, may affect each other, but it need not be in such a disruptive manner as to reorder the sequence of knowledge acquisition or the relationship between incidental learning (IQ) and academic learning in the United States.

The school psychologist who administers intelligence tests to linguistic minority children is confronted with the dilemma of either ignoring culture (because its effects on test scores remain negligible or unknown), or incorporating other scientific data on cross-cultural differences in an idiosyncratic, thoroughly heuristic manner.

Language

In 1974, the U.S. Supreme Court in *Lau v. Nichols* unanimously and significantly departed from previous "equal education opportunity" decisions based on the *Brown v. Board of Education* (1954) principle of "the same for all." Some 1,800 Chinese-speaking children in the San Francisco School District were not receiving any help in L_2 acquisition. In the words of Justice Douglas: "Under . . . State-imposed standards there is no equality of treatment merely by providing students with the same facilities, text books, teachers, and curriculum; for students who do not understand English are effectively foreclosed from any meaningful education" (p. 3). Though the Court did not recommend any specific remedy, *Lau v. Nichols* does establish that where significant numbers of pupils have unique linguistic needs, the regular program is not enough and something different ("Teaching English . . ., instruction in Chinese", and "other" choices [p. 2]) must be done. This

decision helped the bilingual education movement. Most critically, however, *Lau* instigated an unparalleled research interest in bilingualism and second-language acquisition, and their relationship to learning and instruction in the United States. The scientific evidence on these topics is compelling, relatively unequivocal, and exceptionally germane to psychometric measurement of intelligence with linguistic minorities.

As already noted, the pre-1950s literature generally concluded that bilingualism was a "language handicap" on intelligence tests. Bilingualism was generally perceived as a negative experience directly linked to low intelligence and low academic achievement. The preponderance of this literature has been faulted on technical grounds (Darcy, 1953). Subsequently, a growing body of research has asserted that bilingualism may be associated with enhanced cognitive abilities and academic achievement (Bain & Yu, 1980; Cummins, 1984; Hakuta, 1986; Lambert & Tucker, 1972; Peal & Lambert, 1962; Swain & Lapkin, 1982). But caveats apply. As described by a California state agency (Office of Bilingual, Bicultural Education, 1982), five principles intervene. Four of these are relevant to testing.

1. "The Linguistic Threshold: For bilingual students, the degree to which proficiencies in both L_1 and L_2 are developed is positively associated with academic achievement" (Office of Bilingual, Bicultural Education, 1982 p. 7). When students do not develop either language to near-native proficiency, this condition leads to underachievement (Skutnabb-Kangas & Toukomaa, 1976) and limited access to verbally mediated cognitive functions (e.g., analogy, definition, categorization, contrast, etc.). Low proficiency in both languages is usually described as "semilingualism." It is associated with "subtractive bilingualism" (Cummins, 1984)—that is, bilingualism in which the child's native language is held in low esteem by the larger society; in which no effort is made to use or maintain the primary language in schooling; and in which the home language neither engages nor promotes literacy. Primary-language loss occurs, and second-language acquisition (particularly in abstract functions) is impaired, since schooling for several years remains marginally com-

prehensible. On the other hand, when students develop both L_1 and L_2, scholastic achievement is enhanced (Dolson, 1985; Fernandez & Nielsen, 1986).

2. "The Dimensions of Language Proficiency . . .: Language proficiency is the ability to use language for both academic purposes and basic communicative tasks" (Office of Bilingual, Bicultural Education, 1982, p. 9). Second-language learners acquire "basic interpersonal communicative skills" (BICS) in their second language (Cummins, 1981) within 2 years, given sufficient contact with L_2 speakers. BICS involve concrete language. It is cognitively easy and typically used in social contexts wherein meaning is attained through multiple, contextualized cues. Second-language learners take longer to attain *"cognitive academic language proficiency"* (CALP; Cummins, 1981)— approximately 5 or 6 years. CALP involves more abstract, decontextualized uses of language. School language and verbal IQ test language are excellent examples of CALP. To the degree that CALP is either precluded in the primary language (no schooling in the primary language while under conditions of "subtractive bilingualism") and pre-empted or delayed in the secondary language (as BICS in L_2 are being acquired), academic achievement and verbal IQ may be chronically depressed (Bachman & Palmer, 1982; Cummins, 1981, 1984; Rivera, 1984a, 1984b; Saville-Troike, 1984).

3. "Common Underlying Proficiency . . .: For language minority students, the development of the primary language skills necessary to complete academic tasks forms the basis for similar proficiency in English" (Office of Bilingual, Bicultural Education, 1982, p. 11). It does not matter in which language CALP is developed, since, once acquired, L_2 academic functioning supposedly covaries with L_1 academic ability without the person's having to learn new CALP (Cummins, 1979; Lapkia & Swain, 1977). The critical focus is CALP, not L_1 or L_2. Accordingly, the efficient and effective acquisition of CALP, particularly under conditions of subtractive bilingualism, should override considerations of quick immersion into a second language. With CALP in place, L_2, academic achievement, and verbal intelligence become possible (Hakuta, 1986).

4. "Second Language Acquisition: . . .

Acquisition of basic communicative competence in a second language is a function of comprehensible second language input" (Office of Bilingual, Bicultural Education, p. 13), as well as a host of other factors. Competent, adult second-language learners can become "bilingual" in a fairly deliberate process of memorizing the vocabulary, syntax, and grammar of the second language, while attempting to speak correct, often formulaic utterances. Children can be taught in a similar fashion. Research suggests, however, that the more natural process by which the first language was learned may be the more efficacious (Krashen, 1980). Under conditions of "comprehensible input" (Krashen, 1980)—that is, when generalization from L_1 content and linguistic structures is possible— L_2 acquisition mirrors L_1 acquisition (Clement, Gardner, & Smythe, 1980). Additive factors in this process include the following: opportunity for peer interactions in L_2; intelligence; an outgoing personality (one willing to risk errors and to seek contact in L_2; Wong-Fillmore, 1979); individual strategic behaviors (e.g., many children opt for a period of silence, often to the point of appearing language-impaired); motivation (Gardner & Lambert, 1972); anomie; and anxiety (Stevick, 1976). The complexity of this process has clear and direct implications for schools in terms of integration, individual differences, situational variables, and "supportive affective environments" (Office of Bilingual, Bicultural Education, 1982, p. 13).

For tests and testing, the complexity presented by the research on "bilingualism" is compelling for norming and research designs. How these factors can be measured and effectively used or controlled poses a serious problem in measurement. Tests of language proficiency (L_1 and L_2) exist and proliferate on a yearly basis. But their quality tends to be marginal, and they do not approach the complexity delineated by the available research. Most, in fact, are measures of CALP. But even with the available language proficiency instruments (Merino & Spencer, 1983), the psychometric literature on intelligence has yet to empirically examine the impact of the complex *language* variable on test scores—a condition essentially unchanged since the days of "the language handicap" (see Argulewicz & Abel, 1984;

Connelly, 1983; Dean, 1980; Gutkin & Reynolds, 1980; Meyers, MacMillan, & Yoshida, 1978; Mishra, 1980, 1981a, 1982; and Valencia, 1984, 1985a, 1985b for examples of research that typically ignore linguistic differences in the language minority subjects).

Bias

With children who are clearly not proficient in English, there are no research data on bias in intelligence tests. In spite of the fact that many such children are routinely referred and tested for possible special education placements (Rueda, Cardoza, Mercer, & Carpenter, 1984), nothing is essentially known about the validity of the two most prevalent methods of determining their intelligence: using nonverbal tests of intelligence (either tests with translated instructions or commercially available translations of the tests themselves, such as the Spanish version of the K-ABC), or using an interpreter who translates test items and instructions extemporaneously during the testing sessions. The latter procedure has very few data on its impact, and most of these are either uninformative (Swanson & DeBlassie, 1971, 1979) or anecdotal (Langdon, 1986). Ironically, researchers and journals have not hesitated to publish studies based on translations of tests or test instructions (Lynn & Hampson, 1986; Sattler & Altes, 1984; Valencia, 1979, 1983, 1984; Valencia, Henderson, & Rankin, 1981; Valencia & Rankin, 1983).

With linguistic minority children who are not perceived to be obviously limited in their English proficiency, the research on bias is extensive and unequivocal. When "Mexican-Americans," "Hispanics," "Asian-Americans," or "American Indians" are studied, there is generally no evidence of bias in test item characteristics (Argulewicz & Abel, 1984; Jensen, 1974, 1982; Mishra, 1982; Sandoval, 1979; Sandoval et al., 1980); reliabilities (Arnold, 1969; Dean, 1977; Henderson & Rankin, 1973; Jensen, 1974; Karabinus & Hurt, 1969; Mishra & Hurt, 1970; Sandoval, 1979; Scruggs, Mastropieri, & Argulewicz, 1983; Valencia, 1985b); factor structures (Corman & Budoff, 1974; Dean, 1980; Gutkin & Reynolds, 1980; Mishra, 1981a; Reschly, 1978); and concurrent/predictive validi-

ties (Dean, 1979; Henderson & Rankin, 1973; Karabinus & Hurt, 1969; Oakland, 1980; Reschly & Reschly, 1979; Reschly & Sabers, 1979; Schroeder & Bemis, 1969; Valencia, 1984, 1985b).

Yet a strong argument can be made that these data are flawed. As was the case in the pre-1950s literature, contemporary studies on test bias with linguistic minority children ignore the possible effect of a second language on test scores. The findings of the scientific literature on bilingualism, second-language acquisition, BICS and CALP, bilingual education, and the measurement of language proficiency are generally overlooked or omitted from considerations of bias in intelligence tests. The fact that this omission seems not to have attenuated validities or reliabilities may appear to dispel any need for designing studies that examine or control the language factor. But data exist to argue the contrary.

Some researchers have explained anomalous results on the basis of the "bilingual factor" (Figueroa, 1987; Jensen, 1973, 1974) even when the "bilingualism" of the sampled populations was not considered an issue. Jensen has even concluded that data on the concurrence between Raven's Progressive Matrices and the Peabody Picture Vocabulary Test (PPVT) show that "there is evidence that a vocabulary test in English may be a biased test of intelligence for Mexican Americans" (1976, p. 342). Elsewhere, (Figueroa, 1987), in studying the representative sample ($n = 520$) of Hispanic children in the System of Multicultural Pluralistic Assessment (SOMPA; Mercer, 1979) norming study, I found that approximately one-third of them came from homes where Spanish was spoken, one-third where English and Spanish were both spoken, and one-third where English was spoken, even though *all* the children were judged English-competent by their teachers and the school psychologists who tested them. Furthermore, when 60% of them were retested ten years later, their 1972 WISC-R IQs proved to be consistently sensitive to language background in predicting 1982 reading and math scores on the Standard Test of Academic Skills (Gardner, Callis, Merwin, & Madden, 1972; Figueroa & Sassenrath, 1989), as well as academic GPAs (grades for reading, math, science, and social studies). Table 28.3 presents these

TABLE 28.3. Longitudinal Predictive Correlations between WISC-R IQs (1972) and Reading, Mathematics, and Academic GPAs (1982) for Three Language-Background Groups in the SOMPA Hispanic Sample

	English (n = ±153	English/Spanish (n = ±95	Spanish (n = ±99
1972 VIQ			
1982 Reading	.60	.50	.45
1982 Math	.55	.50	.42
1982 GPA	.28	.11	.23
1972 PIQ			
1982 Reading	.52	.40	.39
1982 Math	.54	.44*	.23***
1982 GPA	.33	.22*	−.06***
1972 FSIQ			
1982 Reading	.61	.53	.47
1982 Math	.60	.55	.37**
1982 GPA	.33	.19	.13

Note. The data are from Figueroa (1987). VIQ, Verbal IQ; PIQ, Performance IQ; FSIQ, Full Scale IQ.

*$p < .05$ for comparison of English/Spanish group to Spanish group.

**$p < .01$ for comparison of Spanish group to English group.

***$p < .005$ for comparison of Spanish group to English group.

data. The predictive validity coefficients of the Performance IQs (PIQs) are particularly interesting. The correlations of math and GPA with PIQ were significantly different between the English-only and Spanish-only groups and the English/Spanish and Spanish-only groups (see table). Clearly, the rank ordering of potentially bilingual children (Spanish-only backgrounds) on the WISC-R PIQ does not correspond to the rank ordering of their academic achievement—a problematic fact for intelligence tests and schooling, should these data be corroborated (as in Mishra, 1983).

The literature on bias, quite like the pre-1950s literature suggests that on internal indices psychometric tests are insensitive to cultural and linguistic differences. But on external indices a different conclusion seems possible (Dean, 1977; Oakland, 1978; Valencia, 1982). Still, such data are meager, compared with the amount of research asserting that there is no bias. Until more comprehensive studies of linguistic minority children are undertaken, the question of test bias may not be answerable. Many possible intervening variables explored and documented in other empirical fields of research need to be incorporated in the study of intelligence test bias. Among these are language, acculturation (Padilla, 1980), processing speed (Dornic, 1979), short-term memory

(Figueroa, 1987; Jensen & Inouye, 1980), motivational styles (Kagan, 1986), culture (Holtzman, Diaz-Guerrero, & Swartz, 1975), learning styles (Heath, 1986; Wong-Fillmore & Valadez, 1986), and bilingual schooling.

In 1975, Cleary, Humphreys, Kendrick, and Wesman (1975) published a report commissioned by the American Psychological Association, "Educational Uses of Tests with Disadvantaged Students." It is a pivotal document because its main conclusions about the predictive fairness of tests with minorities have held up, and because the assumptions behind research on bias have seldom been made so explicit. As Cleary et al. (1975) noted, in using tests it is assumed that there is a single society, that "curriculum content" and teaching in the country are generally uniform, and that testing and its purposes are important. Under the first two assumptions, it may seem appropriate to test 500 LEP pupils who have been in the United States for 6 months on a verbal IQ test. The test will be reliable. It may predict English-only academic achievement and grades moderately well. But it may say very little about intelligence and bias (see also Naglieri, 1982).

Bilingual Testing

Intelligence tests that are adequately normed and standardized in another language are available (Figueroa, Delgado, & Ruiz, 1984; Vernon, 1982). However, the norming samples are usually from another country. The most widely used tests of intelligence in the United States that have been normed abroad are for Hispanic populations. These include the following: the Escala de Inteligencia para Nivel Escolar Wechsler (Gomez-Palacio, Padilla, & Roll, 1983), a Mexican-normed version of the WISC-R (Wechsler, 1974), which is hereafter referred to as the WISC-RM; the Kaufman Bateria de Evaluacion Intelectual (Gomez-Palacio, Rangel, & Padilla, 1985), a Mexican-normed version of the K-ABC (Kaufman & Kaufman, 1983), which is hereafter referred to as the K-ABCM; the Test de Vocabulario en Imagenes Peabody (Dunn, Padilla, Lugo, & Dunn, 1986), a Mexican-normed version of the PPVT (Dunn & Dunn, 1981), which is hereafter referred to as the PPVTM; and the Prueba de Habilidad Cognoscitiva of the Bateria Woodcock Psico-Educativa en Español (Woodcock, 1982) a version of the Woodcock–Johnson Psycho-Educational Battery (Woodcock & Johnson, 1977), which is hereafter referred to as the Bateria Woodcock.

These are widely used tests that present a host of challenges. They inherently require bilingual skills from the testers—a trend acknowledged by bilingual school psychology programs and models (Figueroa, Sandoval, & Merino, 1984), but potentially litigious for nonbilinguals, given Standard 6.10 of the *Standards for Educational and Psychological Testing* (American Psychological Association, 1985, cited above). Also, though they constitute an improvement over straight translations of English intelligence tests, they have severe limitations. Their predictive validity to schooling in the United States, even bilingual schooling, is unknown. Their norming samples are either limited or unknown. The Mexico City-normed tests (WISC-RM, K-ABCM, and PPVTM), for example, are normed on *public school* pupils. These children are almost exclusively from low-middle-SES to low-SES families. In the WISC-RM and the K-ABCM, the raw-score points needed for every scaled score tend to be fewer than those in the U.S. norms. The Mexico City tests are essentially normed on what would be characterized as a socioeconomically disadvantaged population. The fact that many Hispanic immigrant and native

children are from similar backgrounds is relevant but vitiated, insofar as they usually have not attended the public school system in Mexico City. Another complicating factor is that once a child has been in the United States for more than 3 months, L_1 generally begins to decline while BICS in L_2 develop. For most Hispanic children, a foreign test of intelligence can produce depressed profiles in the same manner and for the same reasons as the U.S. WISC-R (e.g., Rueda, Cardoza, Mercer, & Carpenter, 1984).

The Bateria Woodcock has a more serious problem. Its norming sample is not adequately described, and it assumes that children from Costa Rica, Mexico, Peru, Puerto Rico, and Spain can all be used as a single entity to generate norms for use in the United States and Latin America. The assumptions about cultural, linguistic, and scholastic similarity are gratuitous and unsupported.

Two other "types" of intelligence tests are usually available to bilingual pupils. There are commercial or homemade translations of tests. As the *Standards* volume (American Psychological Association, 1985) has noted, translations must demonstrate psychometric equivalence. There are also "adjusted IQs," a procedure with an extensive history and presently formalized in Mercer's (1979) concept of "estimated learning potential" (ELP). However, data show that ELP IQs are just as sensitive to language background as regular IQs (Figueroa, 1987).

Currently, bilingual testing is essentially an art form. The tester must infer and estimate the impact of language, culture, and schooling in the English versions of intelligence tests, and then do the same with even more marginal tests in anoter language. Very little scientific progress has been made over the last 70 years in this endeavor, even though the problems and complexities in bilingual testing have been acknowledged (Clarizio, 1982; Duran, 1988; Gerken, 1978; Mowder, 1979; Olmedo, 1981; Zirkel, 1972).

MEASURING THE ACADEMIC ACHIEVEMENT OF LINGUISTIC MINORITIES

The national concern for educational excellence in the 1980s has had a major impact on the amount of achievement testing undertaken in schools. Either in state-mandated minimum-standards testing or in standardized achievement testing programs based on nationally derived norms of academic achievement, linguistic minority pupils uniformly tend to show a verbal–quantitative discrepancy (Lucero, 1985; Sue & Kirk, 1972). Also, two distinct patterns of achievement emerge: high-achieving Asian-American students, and underachieving Hispanic, Native American, and some recently arrived Southeast Asian students (Lucero, 1985; as already noted, this dichotomy is also manifested in SES). Reasons proposed for this difference are multivariate and run the usual gamut from genetics to environment (DeBlassie, 1980; Trueba, 1987; Vernon, 1982). Among the assumptions inherent in educational measurement, as underscored by Cleary et al. (1975), the assumption of a relatively uniform curriculum across the country is particularly suspect with respect to underachieving linguistic minorities.

These pupils tend to be educated in more segregated schools (Arias, 1986; National Commission on Secondary Education for Hispanics, 1984). Their educational programs all to often are carried out in nonacademic tracks (Oakes, 1985). Their teachers treat them differently (Buriel, 1983; U.S. Commission on Civil Rights, 1973). They tend to be older, to drop out earlier (Knox & Innan, 1984), to experience environments that place them more at risk (Henggeler & Tavormina, 1978), and to overpopulate special education classes (Brown, Rosen, & Hill, 1980). The most controversial program for linguistic minority students is bilingual education. As previously described, this is not a new phenomenon in the United States; however, attention has been more sharply focused on bilingual education since the *Lau v. Nichols* (1974) decision. Questions about the effectiveness of bilingual programs have either been marred because of inadequate evaluation studies (Hakuta, 1986) or have been politicized to the point of misrepresentation in the popular media by the federal government (U.S. General Accounting Office, 1987). The research literature when held to scientific standards (McLaughlin, 1985; Willig, 1985; Yates, 1982) supports the practice of primary-language schooling, in concurrence with other international studies (Hakuta, 1986) as well as with the historical literature on the foreign-language schools in the United States. Regrettably, the impact of bilingual programs on the achievment levels of Hispanic and recently arrived Asian linguistic minorities has been marginal. Only a small proportion of language minority children attend these programs (Valdivieso, 1986). Also, few of these programs have been properly funded in order for longitudinal effects to be studied. As the most controlled study in this area indicates, the longer children stay in these programs, the higher their academic achievement *in English* (Ramirez, Wolfson, Talmadge, & Merino, 1986).

Achievement Tests

For many language minority pupils in regular programs or in poorly administered bilingual or remedial programs, academic achievement occurs under conditions of subtractive bilingualism and inadequate bilingual proficiency. Achievement tests measure the conditions of their education, their linguistic proficiencies, and what they have learned (Ulibarri, 1985). However, like tests of intelligence, achievement tests demonstrate good internal psychometric properties (Mishra, 1981b; Powers & Jones, 1984), while at the same time manifesting some deficiencies in their external characteristics, particularly in prediction (Asian American Task Force on University Admissions, 1985; Duran, 1983; Gandara, Keogh, & Yoshioka-Maxwell, 1980; Goldman & Hewitt, 1975; Powers, Escamilla, & Haussler, 1986).

As Ulibarri (1985) has noted, questions of bias relative to achievement measures must address the questions of predictive validity and linguistic contamination. Achievement tests can become measures of English-language proficiency, especially when an analysis of their instructions, content, and format clearly shows that these rest on linguistic skills commensurate with those of monolingual pupils (idioms, facts, CALP, etc.). Even for high-achieving Asian-American pupils, this factor emerges (Lucero, 1985; Vernon, 1982). For example, it is argued that the University of California has artificially embarked on an admissions policy designed to lower the number of eligible high school graduates entering higher education by taking advantage of this contaminating factor (Asian American Task Force on University Admissions, 1985). The verbal Scholastic Aptitude Test (SAT) scores for Asian-American pupils are lower than their quantitative SAT scores. If it is required that both be above 400, many Asian-American pupils will be excluded from the university.

The use of achievement tests to track or exclude linguistic minority students, given all the mediating factors associated with linguistic backgrounds, constitutes a serious national and scientific problem that has been extant for nearly a century. In the face of political opposition to bilingual education and the concomitant impact of this on the efficacy of such programs, achievement testing in the primary language seems futile. Furthermore, the available domestic technology in this regard (see Center for Bilingual Education, 1978; Watson, Grovell, Heller, & Omark, 1980) suffers from regional norming and lack of controls for bilingualism. Foreign tests of achievement, particularly the Bateria Woodcock and the K-ABCM, assume equivalence of curricula across countries—a fact not supported by other available data (Organizacion de los Estados Americanos, 1972).

As with intelligence tests, much of the literature on achievement tests ignores the language variable in linguistic minorities, even when subjects are identified by it. Mishra, for example, chose his subjects in the following manner: "All of the sample subjects came from families of low socioeconomic background, and their ethnicity was determined by using criteria of Spanish surname and the conventional use of the Spanish language at home and with Mexican American peers at school" (Mishra, 1981b, p. 155). Yet this language difference played no part in his results or conclusions. He found the Wide Range Achievement Test "reliable," "valid," "nondiscriminatory," and "useful" with "biculture minorities" (Mishra, 1981b, p. 157). Much of the achievement testing literature since the 1920s concurs; yet, clearly, these conclusions are incomplete in not addressing the language, schooling, and cultural factors identified in the current empirical literature.

CONCLUSION

The main conclusion of this chapter is that very little progress has been made in the accurate measurement of intelligence and achievement with linguistic minorities. There is ample and compelling evidence that the language variable has left a clear and distinct imprint on virtually every study over the last 70 years that has used linguistic minority subjects. In view of the present demographic profile and projections with respect to children who come from NELB homes, there is a great need to expand the presently available psychometric technology and psychological research so that we can measure, control, and explain the interactions among language, education, acculturation, and tests.

With respect to intelligence, a psychometric solution may be too expensive. Hispanic, Asian, and Native American children are too diverse and heterogeneous in terms of primary languages, English-language proficiencies, acculturation, and schooling factors. The n for just a Hispanic national sample would have to be in the thousands. If intelligence is as important as it has been perceived to be over the last century, its measurement with linguistic minorities may have to rely on nonverbal psychometric measures with stronger correlations to academic learning or on theoretical and experimental methods (Campione, Brown, & Ferrara, 1982; Case, 1972, 1981, 1984; Cronbach, 1957, 1975; Feuerstein, Rand, & Hoffman, 1979; Sternberg, 1982). Likewise, those who measure intelligence may have to upgrade their technical skills to a more professional level while at the same time mastering a new knowledge base—one that might include a different language and skills in areas as diverse as ethnographic research (Spindler, 1982), L_2 acquisition, bilingualism, and bilingual schooling.

With respect to achievement tests, research is needed to investigate the parameters associated with the depressed test scores in verbally loaded subjects of virtually all linguistic minorities, as well as the relationship of this phenomenon to nonverbal intelligence and GPA levels, which are often higher than those measured or predicted by achievement tests. If adequate schooling programs in the primary language come to be recognized as being efficient and productive, achievement batteries with national norms in these languages will be necessary and useful.

REFERENCES

Altus, W. D. (1945). Racial and bi-lingual group differences in predictability and in mean aptitude test scores in an Army special training center. *Psychological Bulletin, 42,* 310–320.

American Psychological Association. (1985). *Standards for educational and psychological testing.* Washington, DC: Author.

Ammons, R. B., & Aguero, A. (1950). The Full-Range Picture Vocabulary Test: VII. Results for a Spanish-American school-age population. *Journal of Social Psychology, 32,* 3–10.

Anastasi, A., & Cordova, F. (1953). Some effects of bilingualism upon the intelligence test performance of Puerto Rican children in New York. *Journal of Educational Psychology, 44,* 1–19.

Argulewicz, E. N., & Abel, R. R. (1984). Internal evidence of bias in the PPVT-R for Anglo-American and Mexican-American children. *Journal of School Psychology, 22,* 299–303.

Arias, B. (Ed.). (1986). The education of Hispanic Americans: A challenge for the future [Special issue]. *American Journal of Education, 95*(1).

Arlitt, A. H. (1921). On the need for caution in established race norms. *Journal of Applied Psychology, 5,* 179–183.

Arnold, R. D. (1969). Reliability of test scores for the young bilingual disadvantaged. *Reading Teacher, 22,* 341–345.

Arreola v. Santa Ana Board of Education, No. 160-577 (Orange County Ct., Cal. 1968).

Arsenian, S. (1937). *Bilingualism and mental development.* New York: Bureau of Publications, Teachers College, Columbia University.

Arsenian, S. (1945). Bilingualism in the post-war world. *Psychological Bulletin, 42,* 65–86.

Ascher, C. (1985). The social and psychological adjustment of Southeast Asian refugees. *Urban Review, 17,* 147–152.

Asian American Studies. (1983). *Asians in America: A selected annotated bibliography.* Davis: University of California at Davis.

Asian American Task Force on University Admissions. (1985). *Task Force report.* Davis: University of California at Davis.

Bachman, L. F., & Palmer, A. S. (1982). The construct validation of some components of communicative proficiency. *Tesol Quarterly, 16,* 449–464.

Bain, B. C., & Yu, A. (1980). Cognitive consequences of raising children bilingually: "One parent, one language." *Canadian Journal of Psychology, 34,* 304–313.

Bell, R. (1935). *Public school education of second-generation Japanese in California.* Stanford, CA: Stanford University Press.

Berk, R. A., Bridges, W. P., & Shih, A. (1981). Does IQ really matter? A study of the use of IQ scores for the tracking of the mentally retarded. *American Sociological Review, 46,* 58–71.

Brady, P. M., Manni, J. L., & Winikur, D. W. (1983a). A three-tiered model for the assessment of culturally and linguistically different children. *Psychology in the Schools, 20,* 52–57.

Brady, P. M., Manni, J. L., & Winikur, D. W. (1983b). Implications of ethnic disproportion in programs for the educable mentally retarded. *Journal of Special Education, 17.*

Brand, D. (1987, August, 31). The new whiz kids. *Time,* pp. 42–49.

Brigham, C. C. (1923). *A study of American intelligence.* Princeton, NJ: Princeton University Press.

Brigham, C. C. (1930). Intelligence tests of immigrant groups. *Psychological Review, 37,* 158–165.

Brill, M. (1936). Studies of Jewish and non-Jewish intelligence. *Journal of Educational Psychology, 27,* 331–352.

Brown v. Board of Education, 347 U.S. 483 (1954).

Brown, G. H., Rosen, N. L., & Hill, T. S. (1980). *The condition of education for Hispanic Americans.* Washington, DC: U.S. Government Printing Office.

Brown, G. L. (1922). Intelligence as related to nationality. *Journal of Educational Research, 5,* 324–327.

Buriel, R. (1983). Teacher–student interactions and their relationship to student achievement: A comparison of Mexican American and Anglo American children. *Journal of Educational Psychology, 75,* 889–897.

Caldwell, F. F., & Mowry, M. D. (1933). The essay versus the objective examination as measures of the achievement of bilingual children. *Journal of Educational Psychology, 24,* 696–702.

Campione, J. C., Brown, A. L., & Ferrara, R. A. (1982). Mental retardation and intelligence. In R. J. Sternberg (Ed.), *Handbook of human intelligence* (pp. 392–490). New York: Cambridge University Press.

Case, R. (1972). Learning and development: A neo-Piagetian interpretation. *Human Development, 15,* 339–358.

Case, R. (1981). Intellectual development: A systematic reinterpretation. In F. H. Farley & N. J. Gordon (Eds.), *Psychology and education: The state of the union* (pp. 142–177). Berkeley, CA: McCutchan.

Case, R. (1984). The process of state acquisition: A neo-Piagetian view. In R. J. Sternberg (Ed.), *Mechanisms of cognitive development* (pp. 19–44). New York: W. H. Freeman.

Center for Bilingual Education. (1978). *Assessment instruments in bilingual education.* Los Angeles: California State University, National Dissemination and Assessment Center.

Clarizio, H. F. (1982). Intellectual assessment of Hispanic children. *Psychology in the Schools, 19,* 61–71.

Cleary, T. A., Humphreys, L. G., Kendrick, S. A., & Wesman, A. (1975). Educational uses of tests with disadvantaged students. *American Psychologist, 15,* 15–40.

Clement, R., Gardner, R. C., & Smythe, P. C. (1980). Social and individual factors in second language acquisition. *Canadian Journal of Behavioral Science, 12,* 293–302.

Connelly, J. B. (1983). Recategorized WISC-R score patterns of older and younger referred Tlingit Indian children. *Psychology in the Schools, 20,* 271–275.

Corman, L., & Budoff, M. (1974). Factor structures of Spanish-speaking and non-Spanish-speaking children on Raven's Progressive Matrices. *Educational and Psychological Measurement, 34,* 977–981.

Covarrubias v. San Diego Unified School District, Civ. No. 70-394-S (S.D. Cal. 1972).

Cravioto, J., & Arrieta, R. (1985). *Nutricion, desarrollo mental, conducta y aprendizaje*. Mexico City: Impresiones Modernas.

Cravioto, J., & Arrieta, R. (1986). Nutrition, mental development, and learning. *Human Growth, 3*, 501–536.

Cronbach, L. J. (1957). The two disciplines of scientific psychology. *American Psychologist, 12*, 671–684.

Cronbach, L. J. (1975). Five decades of public controversy over mental testing. *American Psychologist, 30*, 1–14.

Cummins, J. (1979). Linguistic interdependence and the educational development of bilingual children. *Review of Educational Research, 49*, 222–251.

Cummins, J. (1980). Psychological assessment of immigrant children: Logic or intuition? *Journal of Multilingual and Multicultural Development, 1*, 97–111.

Cummins, J. (1981). The role of primary language development in promoting educational success for language minority students. In Office of Bilingual and Bicultural Education, California State Department of Education (Ed.), *Schooling and language minority students: A theoretical framework* (pp. 3–50). Los Angeles: California State University, Evaluation, Dissemination and Assessment Center.

Cummins, J. (1984). *Bilingual special education: Issues in assessment and pedagogy*. San Diego, CA: College Hill.

Darsie, M. L. (1926). The mental capacity of American-born Japanese children. *Comparative Psychology Monographs, 3*, 1–89.

Darcy, N. T. (1946). The effect of bilingualism upon the measurement of the intelligence of children of preschool age. *Journal of Educational Psychology, 38*, 21–44.

Darcy, N. T. (1953). A review of the literature on the effects of bilingualism upon the measurement of intelligence. *Journal of Genetic Psychology, 82*, 21–57.

Davenport, E. L. (1932). The intelligence quotients of Mexican and nonMexican siblings. *School and Society, 36*, 304–306.

Dean, R. S. (1977). Analysis of the PIAT with Anglo and Mexican American children. *Journal of School Psychology, 15*, 329–333.

Dean, R. S. (1979). Predictive validity of the WISC-R with Mexican-American children. *Journal of School Psychology, 17*, 55–58.

Dean, R. S. (1980). Factor structure of the WISC-R with Anglos and Mexican-Americans. *Journal of School Psychology, 18*, 234–239.

DeBlassie, R. R. (1980). *Testing Mexican American youth*. Hingham, MA: Teaching Resources.

DeWitt, H. A. (1976). *Anti-Filipino movements in California: A history, bibliography and study guide*. San Francisco: R & E Research Associates.

Diana v. State Board of Education, C.A. No. C-70-37 (N.D. Cal. 1970).

Dolson, D. P. (1985). Bilingualism and scholastic performance: The literature revisited. *NABE Journal, 10*, 1–35.

Dornic, S. (1979). Information processing in bilinguals: Some selected issues. *Psychological Research, 40*, 329–348.

Dubois, D. D. (1980). *The Children's English and Services Study: A methodological review*. Washington,

DC: U.S. Department of Education, National Center for Education Statistics.

Dunn, L. M., & Dunn, L. M. (1981). *Peabody Picture Vocabulary Test—Revised*. Circle Pines, MN: American Guidance Service.

Dunn, L. M., Padilla, E. R., Lugo, D. E., & Dunn, L. M. (1986). *Test de Vocabulario en Imagenes Peabody: Adaptacion Hispanoamericana*. Circle Pines, MN: American Guidance Service.

Duran, R. P. (1983). *Hispanics' education and background: Predictors of college achievement*. New York: College Entrance Examination Board.

Duran, R. P. (1988). Testing of linguistic minorities. In R. Linn (Ed.), *Education measurement* (3rd ed., pp. 573–587). New York: Macmillan.

Dyrcia S. v. Board of Education, No. C-2562 (E.D.N.Y. 1979).

Education for All Handicapped Children Act of 1975, P.L. 94-142, Washington, D.C.: 94th Congress (1975).

Feingold, G. A. (1924). Intelligence of the first generation of immigrant groups. *Journal of Educational Psychology, 15*, 65–82.

Fernandez, R. M., & Nielsen, F. (1986). Bilingualism and Hispanic scholastic achievement: Some baseline results. *Social Science Research, 15*, 43–70.

Feuerstein, R., Rand, Y., & Hoffman, M. B. (1979). *The dynamic assessment of retarded performers: The Learning Potential Assessment Device, theory, instruments, and techniques*. Baltimore: University Park Press.

Figueroa, R. A. (1983). Test bias and Hispanic children. *Journal of Special Education, 17*, 431–440.

Figueroa, R. A. (1986). Diana revisited. Los Angeles: California State University, Evaluation, Dissemination and Assessment Center.

Figueroa, R. A. (1987). *Special education assessment of Hispanic pupils in California: Looking ahead to the 1990's*. Sacramento: California State Department of Education, Office of Special Education.

Figueroa, R. A., Delgado, G. L., & Ruiz, N. T. (1984). Assessment of Hispanic children: Implications for Hispanic hearing-impaired children. In G. L. Delgado (Ed.), *The Hispanic deaf: Issues and challenges for bilingual special education* (pp. 124–153). Washington, DC: Gallaudet College Press.

Figueroa, R. A., Sandoval, J., & Merino, B. (1984). School psychology and limited-English-proficient children: New competencies. *Journal of School Psychology, 22*, 131–144.

Figueroa, R. A., & Sassenrath, J. M. (1989). A longitudinal study of the predictive validity of the System of Multicultural Pluralistic Assessment (SOMPA). *Psychology in the Schools, 26*, 5–19.

Fukuda, T. (1923). Some data on the intelligence of Japanese children. *American Journal of Psychology, 34*, 599–602.

Gandara, P., Keogh, B. K., & Yoshioka-Maxwell, B. (1980). Predicting academic performance of Anglo and Mexican-American kindergarten children. *Psychology in the Schools, 17*, 174–177.

Gardner, E. F., Callis, R., Merwin, J. C., & Madden, R. (1972). *Stanford Test of Academic Skills*. New York: Psychological Corporation.

Gardner, R. C., & Lambert, W. E. (1972). *Attitudes and motivation in second language learning*. Rowley, MA: Newbury House.

Garretson, O. K. (1928). A study of causes of retardation among Mexican children in a small public school system in Arizona. *Journal of Educational Psychology, 19*, 31–40.

Garth, T. R. (1920). Racial differences in mental fatigue. *Journal of Applied Psychology, 4*, 235–244.

Garth, T. R. (1923). A comparison of the intelligence of Mexican and mixed and full blood Indian children. *Psychological Review, 30*, 388–401.

Garth, T. R. (1925a). A review of racial psychology. *Psychological Bulletin, 22*, 343–364.

Garth, T. R. (1925b). The intelligence of full blood Indians. *Journal of Applied Psychology, 9*, 382–389.

Garth, T. R. (1927). The intelligence of mixed blood Indians. *Journal of Applied Psychology, 11*, 268–275.

Garth, T. R. (1928). A study of the intelligence and achievement of full-blooded Indians. *Journal of Applied Psychology, 12*, 511–516.

Garth, T. R. (1931). *Race psychology: A study of racial mental differences.* New York: McGraw-Hill.

Garth, T. R., Smith, H. W., & Abell, W. (1928). A study of the intelligence and achievement of full-blooded Indians. *Journal of Applied Psychology, 12*, 511–516.

Gerken, K. C. (1978). Performance of Mexican American children on intelligence tests. *Exceptional Children, 44*, 438–443.

Goldman, R. D., & Hewitt, B. N. (1975). An investigation of test bias for Mexican American college students. *Journal of Educational Measurement, 12*, 187–196.

Gomez-Palacio, M. M., Padilla, E. R., & Roll, S. (1983). *Escala de Inteligencia Para Nivel Escolar Wechsler.* Mexico City: El Manual Moderna.

Gomez-Palacio, M., Rangel, E., & Padilla, E. (1985). *Kaufman Bateria de Evaluacion Intelectual: Manual de aplicacion y calificacion.* Mexico City: Direccion General de Educacion Especial.

Goodenough, F. L. (1926). Racial differences in the intelligence of school children. *Journal of Experimental Psychology, 9*, 388–397.

Gould, S. J. (1981). *The mismeasure of man.* New York: Norton.

Guadalupe Organization Inc. v. Tempe Elementary School District No. 3, 587 F.2d 1022 (9th Cir. 1978).

Gutkin, T. B., & Reynolds, C. R. (1980). Factorial similarity of the WISC-R for Anglos and Chicanos referred for psychological services. *Journal of School Psychology, 18*, 34–39.

Hakuta, K. (1986). *Mirror of language: The debate on bilingualism.* New York: Basic Books.

Haught, B. F. (1931). The language difficulty of Spanish-American children. *Journal of Applied Psychology, 15*, 92–95.

Haught, B. F. (1934). Mental growth of the Southwestern Indian. *Journal of Applied Psychology, 18*, 137–142.

Haven, S. E. (1931). The relative effort of children of native vs. foreign born parents. *Journal of Educational Psychology, 22*, 523–535.

Heath, S. B. (1986). Sociocultural contexts of language development. In Bilingual and Bicultural Education Office, California State Department of Education (Ed.), *Beyond language: Social and cultural factors in schooling language minority students* (pp. 143–186). Los Angeles: California State University, Evaluation, Dissemination and Assessment Center.

Heller, K. A., Holtzman, W. H., & Messick, S. (1982). *Placing children in special education: A strategy for equity.* Washington, DC: National Academy Press.

Henderson, R. W., & Rankin, R. J. (1973). WPPSI reliability and predictive validity with disadvantaged Mexican-American children. *Journal of School Psychology, 11*, 16–20.

Henggeler, S. W., & Tavormina, J. B. (1978). The children of Mexican-American migrant workers: A population at risk. *Journal of Abnormal Child Psychology, 6*, 97–106.

Herr, S. E. (1946). The effect of pre-first-grade training upon reading readiness and reading achievement among Spanish American children. *Journal of Educational Psychology, 37*, 87–102.

Hoffman, M. N. H. (1934). *The measurement of bilingual background.* New York: Bureau of Publications, Teachers College, Columbia University.

Holtzman, W. H., Diaz-Guerrero, R., & Swartz, J. D. (1975). *Personality development in two cultures.* Austin: University of Texas Press.

Hung-Hsia, H. (1929). The mentality of the Chinese and Japanese. *Journal of Applied Psychology, 13*, 9–31.

Jensen, A. R. (1973). *Educability and group differences.* New York: Harper & Row.

Jensen, A. R. (1974). How biased are culture-loaded tests? *Genetic Psychology Monographs, 90*, 185–244.

Jensen, A. R. (1976). Construct validity and test bias. *Phi Delta Kappan, 58*, 340–346.

Jensen, A. R. (1982). Reaction time and psychometric g. In H. J. Eysenck (Ed.), *A model for intelligence* (pp. 93–132). Berlin: Springer-Verlag.

Jensen, A. R., & Inouye, A. R. (1980). Level I and Level II abilities in Asian, white, and black children. *Intelligence, 4*, 41–49.

Johnson, L. W. (1938). A comparison of the vocabularies of Anglo-American and Spanish-American high-school pupils. *Journal of Educational Psychology, 29*, 135–144.

Jose P. v. Ambach, No. C-270 (E.D.N.Y. 1979).

Kagan, J., & Klein, R. E. (1973). Cross-cultural perspectives on early development. *American Psychologist, 947*–964.

Kagan, S. (1986). Cooperative learning and sociocultural factors in schooling. In *Beyond language: Social & cultural in schooling language minority students* (pp. 231–285). Los Angeles: California State University, Evaluation, Dissemination and Assessment Center.

Karabinus, R. A., & Hurt, M., Jr. (1969). The Van Alstyne Picture Vocabulary Test used with six-year-old Mexican-American children. *Educational and Psychological Measurement, 29*, 935–939.

Kaufman, A. S. (1979). *Intelligent testing with the WISC-R.* New York: Wiley-Interscience.

Kaufman, A. S., & Kaufman, N. L. (1983). *K-ABC: Kaufman Assessment Battery for Children.* Circle Pines, MN: American Guidance Service.

Kitano, H. L. (1962). Changing achievement patterns of the Japanese in the United States. *Journal of Social Psychology, 58*, 257–264.

Knoff, H. M. (1983). Effect of diagnostic information on special education placement decisions. *Exceptional Children, 49*, 440–444.

Knox, D. R., & Innan, R. B. (1984). *The American Indian educational dropout.* Rosslyn, VA: Inter America Research Associates.

Koch, H. L., & Simmons, R. (1926). A study of the test performance of American, Mexican and Negro children. *Psychological Monographs*, 35, 1–116.

Krashen, S. (1980). The theoretical and practical relevance of simple codes in second language acquisition. In R. C. Scarcella & S. S. Krashen (Eds.), *Research in second language acquisition* (pp. 7–18). Rowley, MA: Newbury House.

Lamb, E. O. (1930). Racial differences in bi-manual dexterity of Latin and American children. *Child Development*, 1, 204–231.

Lambert, W. E., & Tucker, G. R. (1972). *Bilingual education of children: The St. Lambert experiment*. Rowley, MA: Newbury House.

Lan, D. (1976). *Prestige with limitations: Realities of the Chinese American elite*. San Francisco: R & E Research Associates.

Langdon, H. W. (1986). *The interpreter/translator in a school setting*. Sacramento: California State Department of Education, Office of Special Education.

Laosa, L. M., Swartz, J. D., & Diaz-Guerrero, R. (1984). Perceptual–cognitive and personality development of Mexican and Anglo-American children as measured by human figure drawings. *Developmental Psychology*, 10, 131–139.

Lapkin, S., & Swain, M. (1977). The use of English and French cloze tests in a bilingual education program evaluation: Validity and error analysis. *Language Learning*, 27, 279–314.

Lau v. Nichols, 414 U.S. 563 (1974).

Lester, O. D. (1929). Performance tests and foreign children. *Journal of Educational Psychology*, 20, 303–309.

Levine, A. (1987, November 23). Getting smart about IQ. *U.S. News and World Report*, pp. 53–55.

Lewis, D. G. (1959). Bilingualism and non-verbal intelligence: A further study of test results. *British Journal of Educational Psychology*, 29, 17–22.

Livesay, T. M. (1936). Racial comparisons in performance on the American Council Psychological Examination. *Journal of Educational Psychology*, 28, 631–634.

Louttit, C. M. (1931). Test performance of a selected group of part-Hawaiians. *Journal of Applied Psychology*, 15, 43–52.

Lucero, R. O. (1985, March). *ATP racial/ethnic data report: Comparative data 1981–1982–1983–1984*. New York: College Entrance Examination Board.

Luh, C. W., & Wy, T. M. (1931). A comparative study of the intelligence of Chinese children on the Pintner performance and the Binet tests. *Journal of Social Psychology*, 2, 402–408.

Lynn, R., & Hampson, S. (1986). Intellectual abilities of Japanese children: An assessment of $2\frac{1}{2}$–$8\frac{1}{2}$ year-olds derived from the McCarthy Scales of Children's Abilities. *Intelligence*, 10, 41–58.

Macnamara, J. (1966). *Bilingualism and primary education: A study of the Irish experience*. Edinburgh: Edinburgh University Press.

Mahakian, C. (1939). Measuring the intelligence and reading capacity of Spanish-speaking children. *Elementary School Journal*, 39, 760–768.

Manuel, H. T. (1935). *Spanish and English editions of the Stanford–Binet in relation to the abilities of Mexican children* (University of Texas Bulletin No. 3532). Austin: University of Texas.

Manuel, H. T., & Wright, C. E. (1929). The language difficulty of Mexican children. *Journal of Genetic Psychology*, 36, 458–468.

Martinez, M. A. (1985). Toward a bilingual school psychology model. *Educational Psychologist*, 20, 143–152.

McElwee, E. W. (1935). Differences in reading attainment of Italian and Jewish children. *Journal of Applied Psychology*, 19, 730–732.

McLaughlin, B. (1935). *Second language acquisition in childhood* (2nd ed., Vol. 2). Hillsdale, NJ: Erlbaum.

Mehan, H., Hertweck, H., & Meihls, J. L. (1986). *Handicapping the handicapped*. Stanford, CA: Stanford University Press.

Mercer, J. R. (1973). *Labeling the mentally retarded*. Berkeley: University of California Press.

Mercer, J. R. (1979). *The System of Multicultural Pluralistic Assessment*. New York: Psychological Corporation.

Merino, B. J., & Spencer, M. (1983). The comparability of English and Spanish versions of oral language proficiency instruments. *NABE Journal*, 7, 1–31.

Meyers, C. E., MacMillan, D. L., & Yoshida, R. K. (1978). Validity of psychologists' identification of EMR students in the perspective of the California decertification experience. *Journal of School Psychology*, 16, 3–15.

Miller, H. (1916). *The school and the immigrant*. Cleveland, OH: Survey Committee of the Cleveland Foundation.

Mishra, S. P. (1980). The influence of examiners' ethnic attributes of intelligence test scores. *Psychology in the Schools*, 17, 117–127.

Mishra, S. P. (1981a). Factor analysis of the McCarthy Scales for groups of white and Mexican-American children. *Journal of School Psychology*, 19, 178–182.

Mishra, S. P. (1981b). Reliability and validity of the WRAT with Mexican-American children. *Psychology in the Schools*, 18, 154–158.

Mishra, S. P. (1982). The WISC-R and evidence of item bias for Native-American Navajos. *Psychology in the Schools*, 19, 458–464.

Mishra, S. P. (1983). Validity of WISC-R IQ's and factor scores in predicting achievement for Mexican American children. *Psychology in the Schools*, 20, 442–444.

Mishra, S. P., & Hurt, M. J. (1970). The use of Metropolitan Readiness Tests with Mexican-American children. *California Journal of Educational Research*, 21, 182–187.

Mitchell, A. J. (1937). The effect of bilingualism on the measurement of intelligence. *Elementary School Journal*, 38, 29–37.

Mordkowitz, E. R., & Ginsburg, H. P. (1987). Early academic socialization of successful Asian-American college students. *Quarterly Newsletter of the Laboratory of Comparative Human Cognition*, 9, 85–91.

Mowder, B. (1979). Assessing the bilingual handicapped student. *Psychology in the Schools*, 16, 43–50.

Naglieri, J. A. (1982). Does the WISC-R measure verbal intelligence for non English-speaking children? *Psychology in the Schools*, 19, 478–479.

National Commission on Secondary Education for Hispanics. (1984). *"Make something happen": Hispanic and urban high school reform*. Washington, DC: Hispanic Policy Development Project.

Oakes, J. (1985). *Keeping track*. New Haven, CT: Yale University Press.

Oakland, T. (1978). Predictive validity of readiness tests for middle and lower socioeconomic status Anglo, black, and Mexican American children. *Journal of Educational Psychology, 70*, 574–582.

Oakland, T. (1980, September). *Predictive validity of the WISC-R IQ's and Estimated Learning Potential*. Paper presented at the annual meeting of the American Psychological Association, Montreal.

Office of Bilingual, Bicultural Education. (1982). *Basic principles for the education of language-minority students: An overview*. Sacramento: California State Department of Education.

Olmedo, E. L. (1981). Testing linguistic minorities. *American Psychologist, 36*, 1078–1085.

Organizacion de los Estados Americanos. (1973). *America en cifras, 1972*. Washington, DC: Author.

Ortiz, A. (1986). Characteristics of limited English proficient Hispanic students served in programs for the learning disabled: Implications for policy and practice (Part II). *Bilingual Special Educational Newsletter, 4*, 1–5.

Oxford-Carpenter, R., Pol, L., Lopez, D., Strupp, P., Gendell, M., & Peng, S. (1984). *Demographic projections: Non-English-language-background and limited-English-proficient persons*. Rosslyn, VA: National Clearing House for Bilingual Education.

Padilla, A. M. (1980). *Acculturation: Theory, models and some new findings*. Boulder, CO: Westview Press.

Paschal, F. C., & Sullivan, L. R. (1925). Racial influences in the mental and physical development of Mexican children. *Comparative Psychology Monographs, 3*, 1–76.

Peal, E., & Lambert, W. E. (1962). The relation of bilingualism to intelligence. *Psychological Monographs: General and Applied, 76*, 1–23.

Phelan, J. D. (1901). Why the Chinese should be excluded. *North American Review, 173*, 663–676.

Pintner, R. (1924). Results obtained with the non-language group test. *Journal of Educational Psychology, 15*, 473–483.

Pintner, R., & Arsenian, S. (1937). The relation of bilingualism to verbal intelligence and school adjustment. *Journal of Educational Research, 31*, 255–263.

Pintner, R., & Keller, R. (1922). Intelligence tests of foreign children. *Journal of Educational Psychology, 13*, 214–222.

Portenier, L. G. (1947). Abilities and interests of Japanese-American high school seniors. *Journal of Social Psychology, 25*, 53–61.

Powers, S., Escamilla, K., & Haussler, M. M. (1986). The California Achievement Test as a predictor of reading ability across race and sex. *Educational and Psychological Measurement, 46*, 1067–1070.

Powers, S., & Jones, P. B. (1984). Factorial invariance of the California Achievement Test across race and sex. *Educational and Psychological Measurement, 44*, 967–970.

Pratt, H. G. (1929). Some conclusions from a comparison of school achievement of certain racial groups. *Journal of Educational Psychology, 20*, 661–668.

Ramirez, J. D., Wolfson, R., Talmadge, G. K., & Merino, B. (1986). *First year report: Longitudinal study of immersion programs for language minority children* (Submitted to U.S. Department of Education, Wash-

ington, DC). Mountain View, CA: Science Research Associates.

Reschly, D. J. (1978). WISC-R factor structures among Anglos, Blacks, Chicanos, and Native American Papagos. *Journal of Consulting and Clinical Psychology, 46*, 417–422.

Reschly, D. J., & Reschly, J. E. (1979). Validity of WISC-R factor scores in predicting achievement and attention for four sociocultural groups. *Journal of School Psychology, 17*, 355–361.

Reschly, D. J., & Saber, D. L. (1979). Analysis of test bias in four groups, with the regression definition. *Journal of Educational Measurement, 16*, 1–9.

Reynolds, A. (1973). *The education of Spanish-speaking children in five Southwestern states* (Bulletin No. 11). Washington, DC: U.S. Department of the Interior. (Original work published 1933)

Rivera, C. (Ed.). (1984a). *Communicative competence approaches to language proficiency assessment: Research and application*. Clevedon, England: Multilingual Matters.

Rivera, C. (Ed.). (1984b). *Language proficiency and academic achievement*. Clevedon, England: Multilingual Matters.

Rueda, R., Cardoza, D., Mercer, J. R., & Carpenter, L. (1984). *An examination of special education decision making with Hispanic first-time referrals in large urban school districts* (Final Report—Longitudinal Study I). Los Alamitos, CA: Southwest Regional Laboratory for Educational Research and Development.

Rueda, R., Figueroa, R., Mercado, P., & Cardoza, D. (1984). *Performance of Hispanic educable mentally retarded, learning disabled, and nonclassified students on the WISC-RM, SOMPA, and S-KABC* (Final Report—Short-Term Study I). Los Alamitos, CA: Southwest Regional Laboratory for Educational Research and Development.

Ruiz v. State Board of Education, C.A. No. 218394 (Super. Ct. Cal., Sacramento County 1971).

Saer, D. J. (1923). The effect of bilingualism on intelligence. *British Journal of Psychology, 14*, 25–38.

Sanchez, G. (1932a). Group differences and Spanish-speaking children—critical review. *Journal of Applied Psychology, 16*, 549–558.

Sanchez, G. I. (1932b). Scores of Spanish-speaking children on repeated tests. *Journal of Genetic Psychology, 40*, 223–231.

Sanchez, G. I. (1934a). Bilingualism and mental measures: A word of caution. *Journal of Applied Psychology, 18*, 756–772.

Sanchez, G. I. (1934b). The implications of a basal vocabulary to the measurement of the abilities of bilingual children. *Journal of Social Psychology, 5*, 395–402.

Sandiford, P., & Kerr, R. (1926). Intelligence of Chinese and Japanese children. *Journal of Educational Psychology, 17*, 361–367.

Sandoval, J. (1979). The WISC-R and internal evidence of test bias with minority groups. *Journal of Consulting and Clinical Psychology, 47*, 919–927.

Sandoval, J., Zimmerman, I. L., & Woo, J. M. (1980, September). *Cultural differences on WISC-R verbal items*. Paper presented at the annual convention of the American Psychological Association, Montreal.

Sattler, J. M. (1982). *Assessment of children's intelligence and special abilities*. Boston: Allyn & Bacon.

Sattler, J. M., & Altes, L. M. (1984). Performance of

bilingual and monolingual Hispanic children on the Peabody Picture Vocabulary Test—Revised and the McCarthy Perceptual Performance scale. *Psychology in the Schools, 21,* 313–316.

Saville-Troike, M. (1984). What really matters in second language for academic achievement? *Tesol Quarterly, 18,* 199–217.

Schroeder, G. B., & Bemis, K. A. (1969). *The use of the Goodenough Draw-A-Man Test as a predictor of academic achievement.* Albuquerque, NM: Southwestern Cooperative Educational Laboratory.

Scruggs, T. E., Mastropieri, M. A., & Argulewicz, E. N. (1983). Stability of performance on the PPVT-R for three ethnic groups attending a bilingual kindergarten. *Psychology in the Schools, 20,* 433–435.

Sheldon, W. (1924). The intelligence of Mexican children. *School and Society, 19,* 139–142.

Skutnabb-Kangas, T., & Toukomaa, P. (1976). *Teaching migrant children's mother tongue and learning the language of the host country in the context of the socio-cultural situation of the migrant family.* Helsinki: Finnish National Commission for UNESCO.

Smith, C. R., & Knoff, H. M. (1981). School psychology and special education students' placement decisions: IQ still tips the scale. *Journal of Special Education, 15,* 55–64.

Smith, M. E. (1931). A study of five bilingual children from the same family. *Child Development, 2,* 184–187.

Smith, M. E. (1939). Some light on the problem of bilingualism as found from a study of the progress in mastery of English among preschool children of non-American ancestry in Hawaii. *Genetic Psychology Monographs, 21,* 119–284.

Smith, M. E. (1942). The effect of bilingual background on college aptitude scores and grade point ratios earned by students at the University of Hawaii. *Journal of Educational Psychology, 33,* 356–364.

Smith, M. E. (1949). Measurement of vocabularies of young bilingual children in both of the languages used. *Journal of Genetic Psychology, 74,* 305–310.

Smith, M. E. (1957). Word variety as a measure of bilingualism in preschool children. *Journal of Genetic Psychology, 90,* 143–150.

Spindler, G. (1982). *Doing the ethnography of schooling.* New York: Holt, Rinehart & Winston.

Sternberg, R. J. (Ed.). (1982). *Handbook of human intelligence.* New York: Cambridge University Press.

Stevenson, H. W., Azoma, H., & Hakuta, K. (1986). Family influences on school readiness and achievement in Japan and the United States: An overview of a longitudinal study. In H. W. Stevenson, H. Azoma, & K. Hakuta (Eds.), *Child development and education in Japan.* New York: W. H. Freeman.

Stevenson, H. W., Stigler, J. W., Lee, S., Lucker, W., Kitamura, S., & Hsu, C. (1985). Cognitive performance and academic achievement of Japanese, Chinese, and American children. *Child Development, 56,* 718–734.

Stevick, E. (1976). *Memory, meaning and method.* Rowley, MA: Newbury House.

Sue, D. W., & Kirk, B. A. (1972). Psychological characteristics of Chinese-American students. *Journal of Counseling Psychology, 19,* 471–478.

Swain, M., & Lapkin, S. (1982). *Evaluating bilingual education: A Canadian case study.* Clevedon, England: Multilingual Matters.

Swanson, E. N., & DeBlassie, R. (1971). Interpreter effects on the WISC performance of first grade Mexican-American children. *Measurements and Evaluation in Guidance, 4,* 172–175.

Swanson, E. N., & DeBlassie, R. (1979). Interpreter and Spanish administration effects on the WISC performance of Mexican American children. *Journal of School Psychology,* 231–236.

Symonds, P. M. (1924). The intelligence of the Chinese in Hawaii. *School and Society, 19,* 442.

Trueba, H. T. (1987). *Success or failure? Learning and the language minority student.* New York: Newbury.

Tucker, J. A. (1980). Ethnic proportions in classes for the learning disabled: Issues in nonbiased assessment. *Journal of Special Education, 14,* 93–105.

Twomey, S. C., Gallegos, C., Andersen, L., Williamson, B., & Williamson, J. (1980). *A study of the effectiveness of various nondiscriminatory and linguistically and culturally appropriate assessment criteria for placement of minority students in special education programs.* Merced, CA: Planning Associates.

Ulibarri, D. M. (1985). *Standardized achievement testing of non-native English-speaking students in elementary and secondary schools.* Rosslyn, VA: National Clearinghouse for Bilingual Education.

U.S. Bureau of the Census. (1980). *General social and economic characteristics, United States summary.* Washington, DC: U.S. Government Printing Office.

U.S. Bureau of the Census. (1983a). *Asian and Pacific islander population by state* (PC 80-51-12). Washington, DC: U.S. Government Printing Office.

U.S. Bureau of the Census. (1983b). *1980 census of population: Vol 1. Characteristics of population. Chapter C. General social and economic characteristics. Part I. U.S. summary* (PC 80-1-C1). Washington, DC: U.S. Government Printing Office.

U.S. Bureau of the Census. (1985a). *American Indians, Eskimos, and Aleuts on identified reservations and in the historic areas of Oklahoma* (PC 80-2-1D, Part 1). Washington, DC: U.S. Government Printing Office.

U.S. Bureau of the Census. (1985b). *Persons of Spanish origin in the United States, March 1985: Advance report* (Current Population Reports, Series P-20, No. 403). Washington, DC: U.S. Government Printing Office.

U.S. Bureau of the Census. (1986). *Projections of the Hispanic population: 1983 to 2080* (Current Population Reports, Series P-25, No. 995). Washington, DC: U.S. Government Printing Office.

U.S. Bureau of the Census. (1987). *Population profile of the United States: 1984/85* (Current Population Reports, Series P-23, No. 150). Washington, DC: U.S. Government Printing Office.

U.S. Commission on Civil Rights. (1973). *Teachers and students: Differences in teacher interaction with Mexican-American and Anglo students. Report V: Mexican American educational study.* Washington, DC: U.S. Government Printing Office.

U.S. General Accounting Office. (1987). *Bilingual education: A new look at the research evidence* (Briefing report to the Chairman, Committee on Education and Labor, House of Representatives). Washington, DC: U.S. Government Printing Office.

Valdivieso, R. (1986). Hispanics and schools: A new perspective. *Educational Horizons, 64,* 190–196.

Valencia, R. R. (1979). Comparison of intellectual performance of Chicano and Anglo third-grade boys on the Raven's Coloured Progressive Matrices. *Psychology in the Schools, 16*, 448–453.

Valencia, R. R. (1982). Predicting academic achievement of Mexican-American children: Preliminary analysis of the McCarthy Scales. *Educational and Psychological Measurement, 42*, 1269–1278.

Valencia, R. R. (1983). Stability of the McCarthy Scales of Children's Abilities over a one-year period for Mexican-American children. *Psychology in the Schools, 20*, 29–34.

Valencia, R. R. (1984). Reliability of the Raven Coloured Progressive Matrices for Anglo and for Mexican American children. *Psychology in the Schools, 21*, 49–52.

Valencia, R. R. (1985a). Predicting academic achievement in Mexican-American children using the Kaufman Assessment Battery for Children. *Educational and Psychological Research, 5*, 11–17.

Valencia, R. R. (1985b). Stability of the Kaufman Assessment Battery for Children for a sample of Mexican-American children. *Journal of School Psychology, 23*, 189–193.

Valencia, R. R., Henderson, R. W., & Rankin, R. J. (1981). Relationship of family constellation and schooling to intellectual performance of Mexican American children. *Journal of Educational Psychology, 73*, 524–532.

Valencia, R. R., & Rankin, R. J. (1983). Concurrent validity and reliability of the Kaufman version of the McCarthy Scales Short Form for a sample of Mexican-American children. *Educational and Psychological Measurement, 43*, 915–925.

Vernon, P. E. (1982). *The abilities and achievements of Orientals in North America*. New York: Academic Press.

Wang, S. L. (1926). A demonstration of the language difficulty involved in comparing racial groups by means of verbal intelligence tests. *Journal of Applied Psychology, 10*, 102–106.

Watson, D. L., Grovell, S., Heller, B., & Omark, D. (1980). *Nondiscriminatroy assessment: Test matrix, V2*. San Diego, CA: Superintendent of Schools, Department of Education, San Diego County.

Wechsler, D. (1974). *Wechsler Intelligence Scale for Children—Revised*. New York: Psychological Corporation.

Wheeler, L. R. (1932). The mental growth of dull Italian children. *Journal of Applied Psychology, 16*, 650–667.

Wilen, D. K., & Van Maanen Sweeting, C. (1986). Assessment of limited English proficient Hispanic students. *School Psychology Review, 15*, 59–75.

Willig, A. C. (1985). A meta-analysis of selected studies on the effectiveness of bilingual education. *Review of Educational Research, 55*, 269–317.

Wong-Fillmore, L. (1979). Individual differences in second language acquisition. In C. J. Fillmore, W. S. Wang, & D. K. Kempler (Eds.), *Individual differences in language ability and language behavior*. New York: Academic Press.

Wong-Fillmore, L., & Valadez, C. (1986). Research on bilingual instruction. In M. C. Wittrock (Ed.), *Handbook of research on teaching*. New York: Macmillan.

Wood, M. M. (1929). Mental test findings with Armenian, Turkish, Greek and Bulgarian subjects. *Journal of Applied Psychology, 13*, 266–273.

Woodcock, W. R. (1982). *Bateria Woodcock Psicoeducativa en Español*. Hingham, Massachusetts: Teaching Resources Corporation.

Woodcock, W. R., & Johnson, M. B. (1977). *Woodcock–Johnson Psycho-educational Battery*. Hingham, MA: Teaching Resources Corporation.

Yates, J. (1982). *Baker de Kanter review: Inappropriate conclusions on the effectiveness of bilingual education*. Unpublished manuscript, University of Texas at Austin.

Yee, A. H. (1976, Febuary). Asian Americans in educational research. *Educational Researcher*, pp. 5–8.

Yee, L. Y., & LaForge, R. (1974). Relationship between mental abilities, social class, and exposure to English in Chinese fourth graders. *Journal of Educational Psychology, 66*, 826–834.

Yeung, K. T. (1921). The intelligence of Chinese children in San Francisco and vicinity. *Journal of Applied Psychology, 5*, 267–274.

Yoder, D. (1928). Present status of the question of racial differences. *Journal of Educational Psychology, 19*, 463–470.

Yoshioka, J. G. (1929). A study of bilingualism. *Journal of Genetic Psychology, 36*, 473–429.

Zirkel, P. A. (1972). Spanish-speaking students and standardized tests. *Urban Review, 5*(6), 32–40.

29

Assessment of Creativity in Children and Adolescents

PATRICIA A. HAENSLY
Texas A&M University

E. PAUL TORRANCE
University of Georgia

Those who attempt to analyze and describe the mental process by which particular geniuses have arrived at their creative contributions often find this a difficult if not impossible task. Professor George Andrews, who rediscovered the last treatise of the mathematical genius Ramanujan in dusty Cambridge University files, has tried to verbalize the kind of thinking exhibited by Ramanujan in his development of a new theory of discrete intervals in mathematics. On an episode of the PBS television series *NOVA* (Sykes, 1988), Andrews expressed his dilemma after examining in great detail the endless pages of Ramanujan's formulas and calculations and trying to trace the mental process Ramanujan used to arrive at endpoints previously unknown to mathematicians. Andrews, though himself an accomplished mathematician and highly articulate translator of mathematical process, was unable to analyze the elements of Ramanujan's thinking process or define its specific attributes, other than to say that it was a brilliant, orderly assembly of ideas not previously available in the mathematical world.

Although some of the process could be described as a logical sequence of ideas, there seems no apparent logical explanation for the origin or source of the numerous leaps of insight made by Ramanujan. Ramanujan claimed he received his numerous insights mystically from the Hindu goddess Namagiri. Ramanujan's mathematical thinking processes and the source of his creativity are so elusive as to suggest an explanation other than rational, reflecting our current limitations on capturing this elusive phenomenon semantically. Rational or otherwise, the validity of Ramanujan's ideas is now being supported by other mathematicians as they painstakingly tease out the theorems and principles that he saw so clearly. Creativity is indeed a complex phenomenon.

Today, many of the leading creativity scholars and practitioners believe that the essential source of creativity is the irrational, suprarational, preconscious—something other than the rational, logical mind. Alex F. Osborn (1963), who originated one of the most widely taught of the disciplined, systematic procedures of creative problem solving, used the terms "critical intelligence" and "creative intelligence." He argued that these two kinds of intelligence could not function optimally at the same time, and he pioneered training methods for calling into play whichever kind of intelligence or information processing was needed. He invented a variety of kinds of technology for facilitating the shift from one kind of "intelligence" to the other. What Osborn described as "critical intelligence" appears to be essentially what has been described as the specialized functioning of the left hemisphere, and what he labeled as "creative intelligence" seems to fit what is now described as the specialized functioning of the right hemisphere. For example, Osborn's rules for brainstorming were designed to aid in suspending left-hemisphere functioning and in activating right-hemisphere functioning. After the brainstorming has been done, there is an evaluation phase in which criteria are formulated and applied in judging the alternatives produced through brainstorming. This phase is designed to activate the left-hemisphere functions. The entire process (Parnes, Noller, & Biondi, 1971) may be described as one of the alternating shifts from right- to left- and back to right-hemisphere functioning.

Other creativity theorists and developers of creative problem-solving models and training technology have considered these two different kinds of information processing, although they have not used the right- and left-hemisphere labels in describing them. Edward de Bono (1970) uses the terms "lateral" and "vertical" thinking. Essentially, his lateral thinking seems to involve left-hemisphere functions. Rollo May (1975) uses the terms "rational" and "suprarational." His rational thinking would seem to involve the specialized cerebral functions of the left hemisphere, and suprarational thinking seems to call for the specialized cerebral functions of the left and right hemispheres, respectively. Gordon's (1961) position has been that in creative thinking the irrational, emotional aspects of mental functioning are more important than the intellectual. Once creative ideas have been produced, they must be subjected to the tests of logic, but such ideas do not occur as the result of logical processes.

Though we recognize the complexity of creativity and the elusiveness, as yet, of its essential constituency, we should not be deterred from trying to identify individuals with outstanding creative potential by using whatever information is currently available to us. Despite conceptual limitations regarding what is to be measured in creativity assessment, and an inadequate data base for

reliability and validity studies (Brown, 1989), evidence of a relationship between test behavior and real-life creative achievement has been accumulating. Longitudinal studies, spanning several decades, of high school students and elementary school pupils who had earlier been administered the Torrance Tests of Creative Thinking (TTCT; Torrance, 1966, 1972a, 1972b, 1981, 1982) indicate a moderate capability of these tests to predict quantity and quality of public and personal creative achievements. These studies have also produced information on environments that are more likely to be associated with highly creative productivity and those more likely to be associated with little or no productive endeavor. It is this kind of information that will permit educators and psychologists to extend creative potential and increase life satisfaction by constructing personal and material environments to facilitate creative expression and reduce inhibitive factors.

It is especially critical that we recognize during the early years of schooling the capability of the very young child to express or produce creative work. Delaying attempts at assessment, incomplete though it may be, may jeopardize the chances of these children for receiving instruction in the creativity-relevant skills that will permit their creative potential to flourish (e.g., Amabile, 1983a; Bloom, 1985; Brown, 1989; Feldman, 1986).

We begin this chapter by examining briefly the current views on creativity as a concept appropriate for assessment; we delineate the role of creativity in human performance and the importance ascribed to it by investigators from various philosophical foundations. An overview of the definitions of creativity that have evolved as investigators have attempted to extract measurable elements follows, along with special emphasis on the implications of these definitions for assessment. The overview includes a general description of (1) characteristics of creativity; (2) its complex origin (i.e., wherein does creativity reside—the process, person, product, or environment?) and the implications its origin has for investigation and assessment; and (3) the notion of levels of creative endeavor—an idea that is especially critical to our assessment of creative ability in children and adolescents, where less advanced levels of creative product and performance are more likely to be found. The purpose of such an extended introduction to assessment of creativity is to insure that those who use the instruments to be described later understand the framework within which assessment results must be interpreted. Creativity assessment data used superficially, carelessly, or with incorrect assumptions can only hinder progress toward freeing potential and creating receptive environments.

The second section of this chapter focuses on how and when creativity should be assessed, with reference to instruments most commonly used, their source, and their technical quality. This section is organized according to the categories of process, person, and product mentioned above. Considerations regarding interpretation, or "making sense of assessment," and appropriate application of assessment conclude the chapter.

CREATIVITY AS A PHENOMENON FOR ASSESSMENT

Current Views

Guilford, in his frequently cited presidential address to the American Psychological Association (Guilford, 1950), admonished psychologists for their lack of attention to college graduates' inability to solve problems in which old information was nonproductive and new solutions had to be found. Guilford's interest in this area of endeavor originated in his earlier work as a graduate student engaged in the administration of IQ tests to children, where he experienced great frustration with the inability of intelligence tests to assign worth to children's "ingenuity, inventiveness and originality of thinking" (Guilford, 1976, p. 8). Guilford (1950) introduced his American Psychological Association audience to the complexity of the task of assessment of the phenomenon with this circular and not very specific definition:

> In its narrow sense, creativity refers to the abilities that are most characteristic of creative people. Creative abilities determine whether the individual has the power to exhibit creative behavior to a noteworthy degree. Whether or not the individual who has the requisite abilities will actually produce results of a creative nature will depend upon his motivational and temperamental traits. (1950, p. 444)

Guilford went on to elaborate on the problem of defining creative traits and the creative personality. The questions he posed at that time remain with us today and have definite implications for assessment and the application of assessment results: "(1) How can we discover creative promise in our children and our youth? And (2) How can we promote the development of creative personalities?" (Guilford, 1976, p. 3).

In an attempt to organize the definitions of creativity that subsequently proliferated, Taylor (1960; reported in Taylor, 1988) used the main themes of the approximately 60 definitions he had encountered to establish six classes of definitions. These classes include "aesthetic or expressive" (i.e., focusing on the individual's expression of ideas or work, unique to self); "psychoanalytic or dynamic" (focusing on the preconscious or unconscious); "Gestalt or perception" (focusing on any recombination of ideas); and "Varia" (focusing on somewhat nebulous newknowledge production). Although the foregoing definitions do not lend themselves well to assessment, Taylor's other two definitions focus on ideas and objects useful or applicable to some group at some point in time, and "solution thinking," or any of the many specific processes that contribute to solving problems in new ways.

Discussants over the past 40 years have debated, at length, the existence of creativity as a legitimate ability. In particular, investigators have been unable to agree on the source of creativity, whether it is in the process, product, person, or environment. Investigators have alternately dwelled on creativity as a *specific mental process* (differentiated from intelligence and other mental processes), a definable cluster of *personality characteristics* that results in creative behavior, and a unique kind of *product;* they have also differed on the type of particular environments needed for creative expression. Concurrently, investigators have also grappled with the task of identifying who and what is creative and where and when we may unequivocally designate some performance or product of performance as creative.

Although continuing to disagree on the exact nature of creative ability, and therefore on the components to measure and use as valid and reliable predictors, current researchers recognize not only the legitimacy of creativity as a phenonemon but also as a mental process uniquely related to that other elusive phenomenon, intelligence. Investigators (e.g., Albert, 1983; Amabile, 1983a, 1983b; Barron & Harrington, 1981; Bloomberg, 1973; Brown, 1989; Glover, Ronning, & Reynolds, 1989; Haensly & Reynolds, 1989; MacKinnon, 1962; Simonton, 1984; Sternberg, 1988) again differ as to whether creativity (1) merely complements intelligence; (2) depends on a moderate degree of intelligence (the threshold idea); or (3) is inextricably bound with intelligence, extending human mental capabilities to yet another dimension or level. Included in this last view is the idea that expression of creative ability is governed by a matrix of factors, such as having the right kind of experiences in a field or domain, opportunity to train and to perform, cultural and domain readiness to understand and appreciate the contribution, and chance occurrence or coincidence. These added dimensions, while increasing our understanding of the phenomenon, have also increased the complexity of the task of assessment.

For example, Sternberg (1988) postulates that whether or not creativity is expressed by individuals depends, just as intelligence does, upon the individual's internal world (i.e., the execution and manner of management of various mental abilities); the type, quality, and quantity of the individual's intellectual and personal experiences; and context (i.e., the environment within which the individual functions). The idea that giftedness or outstanding creative ability results from a unique coalescence of multiple abilities coming together in a response, correctly fitted to a contextual need or deficiency, stimulated by personal conflict experienced with current solutions in the context, and extended with a commitment to sufficient quality and intensity over sufficient time (Haensly, Reynolds, & Nash, 1986) emphasizes the personal variables in such a matrix of factors. Feldman (1986) adds an element of chance to such matrices, labeling this coming together of facilitative elements as "fortuitous coincidence." Amabile (1983b) proposes a model in which creative performance is dependent upon the *coexistence* of domain-related skills, creativity-relevant skills, and motivation for the task of application, with individual personality characteristics affect-

ing both the creativity-relevant skills and motivation components. The systems view of creativity proposed by Csikszentimihalyi (1988) further emphasizes the potency of the field in which the individual must function, in stimulating, allowing, and reinforcing particular creative performances or productivity; he again alludes to coincidence and the readiness of a domain to recognize and transmit new ideas or forms as an important factor in whether or not specific creative contributions can be made and recognized.

Defining the Concept

The fact that we cannot precisely define creativity should not overly disturb us. It should, in fact, remind us that by the very nature of this phenomenon, creativity involves more than the semantic world. It encompasses all of our senses and is expressed through and for all modalities. Examples of the richness of imagery in expressing the attributes of creativity, along with numerous visual analogies (Torrance, 1988, pp. 49–57), demonstrate the value of accessing symbol systems other than semantic to enlarge our understanding of creativity. It quite possibly may be beyond our powers to analyze through logic or delimit with semantic boundaries, as well as beyond our own finite capability to understand, a phenomenon that is produced and realized in every conceivable modality through processes that transcend our conscious world. This inability on our part to concretize creativity will perhaps keep us honest and humble enough to remind us that assessment of creative ability and prediction of creative potential, as of other human characteristics, can never be absolute.

In order to extricate variables we might validly use in the assessment of creativity, as well as to appreciate the limitations that any one type of variable may place on accurate assessment, we believe it helpful to examine how creativity has been perceived by investigators in the field.

Characteristics of Creativity

Definitions focused on the primary characteristics of creativity, whether ability, product, or process, have consistently referred to newness. "Every-person" definitions see the novelty that results from sudden closure in a solution to a problem as available to the thinker in any domain (Thurstone, 1952), even if the idea was produced by someone else earlier (Stewart, 1950). Guilford's (1956, 1959, 1960, 1976, 1986) conceptualization of creativity limits this every-person category, to the extent that sensitivity to problems and the ability to redefine and transform meanings, uses, or functions of an object must precede or accompany the operation of divergent production. This sensitivity in itself may constitute a special ability. Guilford also states that the prerequisite for fluent transformation is freedom from functional fixedness, a condition that seems related to nonconformity. Nonconformity versus conformity likewise could reasonably be construed as novelty available to all, and includes new ways of looking at problems (Bartlett, 1958; Crutchfield, 1962; de Bono, 1967; Wilson, 1956), as well as the freedom to conform or not to conform to produce something individually pleasing (Starkweather, 1976). Perceptions that creativity demands absolute novelty to the culture (e.g., Stein, 1953) would severely limit its appearance to a few individuals throughout history.

Additional attributes of creative contributions that have been proposed are that they be true or verifiable and generalizable, surprising in light of what is known at the time (Selye, 1962), although Anderson (1959) allowed that the truth may be as the *individual* understands it. Jackson and Messick (1967) described the requisite characteristics of creative responses as unusualness versus commonality; appropriateness or goodness of fit with the problem; transformation in form; and condensation. This last criterion refers to the bringing together of a set of ideas in such a simple way as to produce a sense of "Why didn't I ever think of that before? It is so clearly fortuitous"—complexity conveyed with such simplicity as to generate new understanding. The personal impact on others produced by each of these characteristics helps clarify their meaning: surprise to the criterion of unusualness; satisfaction to appropriateness; stimulation of ideas to transformation; and savoring or pondering to condensation. Mathematicians responding to Ramanujan's material have communicated such a "savoring" response.

Creativity's Origin: The Process?

The complexity of precisely what we might measure in our assessment of creative ability is compounded not only by the fact that there is disagreement about valid criteria for creative product and performance, but also by the fact that each of the many theoretical approaches to creativity assumes different origins, factors, and processes as critical to development of a creative product (Brown, 1989). Assessment thus might center either on what the individual does to produce creatively, or on the typical traits and personality characteristics of the person, or on the evaluation of the products of that process; or it might identify elements of the environments in which the individual functions to determine why creativity has or has not occurred.

Definitions focusing on process range from the very amorphous to the highly specific. Representative of the many possible such definitions are the following: Ghiselin (1952) speaks of the emergence of insight to produce a new configuration; Kubie (1958) of scanning the preconscious at higher speeds than possible in conscious thought in order to find relationships; Barchillon (1961) of shaking up one's information storage and throwing things together in new ways; Sternberg (1988) of flashes of insight; Guilford (1956) of being sensitive to problems; Spearman (1930) of recognizing and generating relationsips; Ribot (1906) of generating relationships by emphasizing analogy formation; Wittrock (1974) of generative processing through adding new pieces to stored mental schemes and thus constructing new schemes; and Simonton (1988) of chance permutation of elements.

The process definitions that have been used to the greatest extent in assessment to date have focused on "divergent production"—a concept formally introduced through Guilford's (1956) structure-of-intellect model. In Guilford's hypothesizing about what creative ability might include, as a prerequisite to conducting a research program on creativity (Guilford, 1959), he determined that, first of all, the ability to sense problems that call for solution would result in increased opportunities to work on such problems and increased probability of coming up with solutions. He also concluded that the higher the frequency or rate of producing (1) words, (2) ideas, (3) associations, or (4) ways of expressing oneself (i.e., one's fluency), the more likely one would be to arrive at an original and workable solution. The greater the variety of ideas produced (flexibility), the greater also the likelihood of arriving at a clever or less commonplace solution. Guilford (1959) further proposed that the greater one's ability to analyze and synthesize, redefine and transform ideas, objects, and functions of objects, the greater one's likelihood of arriving at an unusual and useful solution.

Critical to our understanding of the limitations of assessment, our construction of valid plans for assessment, and our interpretation of the results of assessment is the realization that divergent production in itself is insufficient for creative endeavor. Although Guilford specified that creative performance in life cannot be accounted for solely by these abilities, he felt sure that they are essential and contribute extensively to the creative performance. In addition, Guilford viewed the ability to sense problems that call for solution, a prerequisite for creativity (as stated above), as reflecting the evaluation operation, not the operation of divergent production. Thus, Guilford did not limit creative performance solely to divergent production, but extended it to the application, as it were, of divergent production.

Brown (1989) and others have expressed concern that tests of divergent thinking measure only a very specific area of creative behavior. Brown suggests that in all likelihood, high divergent-thinking response frequency may be supported as much by training and preparation in a domain, specific ability in that area, and experiences, as it is by the creativity-associated traits of tolerance of ambiguity and resistance to premature closure. Thus, divergent thinking is only one small part of the complex predictive equation for creative productivity.

In fact, recognition of this limitation is evident in the TTCT (Torrance, 1966, 1974), which have also operationalized creativity through fluency and flexibility counts, and added originality and elaboration counts. However, a critical extension to this operationalized definition has been a process definition of creativity developed for research purposes (Torrance, 1967) and for the eventual construction of the creativity tests.

It conveys an idea somewhat similar to Guilford's constructive responses to existing or new situations, as follows;

> . . . the process of becoming sensitive to problems, deficiencies, gaps in knowledge, missing elements, disharmonies, and so on; identifying the difficult; searching for solutions, making guesses, or formulating hypotheses and possibly modifying them and retesting them; and finally communicating the results. (Torrance, 1967, pp. 73–74)

Construction of the TTCT wove the already described and defined processes into a test battery made up of situations for demonstrating the ability to exhibit these processes, with responses to the situations representing a component ability assessed by quantity (fluency) and quality (flexibility, originality, and elaboration) of particular responses. The contrivance of artificial situations to elicit creative responses parallels the approach used by most if not all those who have constructed tests for the assessment of intelligence, as well as of other specific abilities. Personalizing the tests and gathering of information on the person and environment variables that affect responses on these tests are described elsewhere (Torrance, 1988).

The Torrance "survival" definition of creativity (Torrance, 1988) reflects the realization that greater reality in the situations used for assessment brings us closer to representing the true creative ability or potential of individuals, adding validity and reliability to our assessment. The survival definition arose out of research on U.S. Air Force survival training (Torrance, 1955, 1957). Thus, in air crew survival situations, creative solutions required imaginatively gifted recombination of old elements (information about how Native Americans and pioneers lived off the land, how the early explorers survived under Arctic conditions, etc.) into new configurations to fit the current situation and need for survival. A parallel with Sternberg's position on the difference between practical intelligence and the "intelligence" measured on IQ tests (Sternberg & Wagner, 1986) should be evident. But the usefulness of using particulate abilities to assist in the assessment of creative potential, even though they give us only a partial picture of potential, should also be evident.

A view of process involving four particular steps—preparation through information gathering, incubation of ideas, illumination, and verification, all preceded by a sense of need or deficiency in the problem area (Wallas, 1926)—has been explicated as creative problem solving by numerous contemporary investigators (e.g., Parnes, 1962; Parnes et al., 1971). Although some of the assessment of creativity in children and adolescents, especially with regard to responsiveness in the classroom, has involved the evaluation of responses in creative problem solving, much of this level of assessment has depended upon the quite specific measurement of divergent production through responses quantified for their fluency, flexibility, and originality (Guilford, 1976).

Creativity's Origin: The Person?

The Torrance research agenda on creativity has proceeded from a focus on process to the identification of what kind of person one must be to engage in the process successfully, what kinds of environments will facilitate it, and what kind of products will result from successful operation of the process (Torrance, 1965). After a lifetime of studies carrying out this agenda, the conclusion that has been reached and repeatedly supported, especially with data from the 22-year study of elementary school children first tested with the TTCT in 1958 (Torrance, 1981, 1982), is that the salient characteristic of the creative person is "being in love with what one is doing" (see Torrance, in press). This characteristic appears to make possible all the other personality characteristics associated with creative persons: independence of thought and judgment, perseverance, curiosity, willingness to take risks, courage to be different, and willingness to tackle difficult tasks. Assessment of creativity through personality inventories, rating scales, and the like may be a psychological anachronism, although the information provided to the individual may be self-revealing and in this way may assist the individual to improve personal attitudes, thus enhancing creative potential. An example of this application is the finding that an important part of Air Force survival training was practicing means of self-discovery and self-discipline to complement the acquisition

of specific information about survival situations (Torrance, 1955, 1957).

Many investigators have focused consistently over the years on a search for the characteristics of "creative persons," compiling lists that, in turn, might be used to identify individuals with creative potential (e.g., Barron, 1969, 1978; Davis, 1975; MacKinnon, 1976, 1978; Roe, 1951, 1953). Taken singly, identified characteristics cannot add significantly to the power of a creativity prediction equation. However, the importance of characteristics appears to lie in the interaction between the set that refers in some way to creative process (such as tolerance of ambiguity and resistance to premature closure) and the set that refers in some way to motivation for creative endeavor (such as independence of thought, persistence, courage). Nevertheless, biographical inventories may provide valuable information for assessment of creative potential. Whiting (1976) gives validity information on their use with adults in several research-and-development fields, linking biographical data with creative job performance. The Torrance longitudinal studies (Torrance, 1972a, 1972b, 1981, 1982) have identified particular characteristics in children and adolescents that persisted into adulthood and were consistently related to school and postschool creative achievements.

Creativity's Origin: The Product?

Assessment of the creativity of the products of individuals is logically limited to some type of consensual process by judges who are particularly qualified in the domain and specific field of productivity. That is, scientists can hardly be expected to assess the originality and transformation characteristics or quality of a musical composition, any more than most artists would be qualified judges of creative contributions in biochemistry. Once again, the Torrance longitudinal studies (Torrance, 1972a, 1972b, 1981, 1982) provide moderately strong predictive validity data on the relationship between high school creative achievements and achievements after high school. This type of information on the quantity and quality of products and performances during childhood years may in this way be useful in the prediction of future performance, as well as in concurrent assessment of creative ability in children and adolescents. The notion of levels of creativity in products and performances is relevant here and is discussed in the next section.

Levels of Creativity

It seems appropriate in any discussion of assessment of creativity to consider the question of differences in levels of creativity exhibited or expressed. I. A. Taylor (1959) suggested the following five levels: expressive (spontaneous, as in the drawings of children); productive (where free play is somewhat contained by restrictions of the field); inventive (technical contributions to solve practical problems); innovative (based on conceptualization); and emergentative, the highest level (involving an entirely new principle or assumption, such as the Ramanujan work). Ghiselin (1963) differentiated between secondary-level creativity, which extends a concept into a new application, and higher- or primary-level creativity, which radically alters what has gone before. Tourangeau and Sternberg (1981) have proposed a theory regarding the creative level of an analogy, using distance of semantic field utilized in the analogical comparison.

Jackson and Messick (1967) imply the notion of levels through four increasingly complex criteria for creative products, relating these criteria to characteristics of creators and to the responses of audiences toward the products. However, one might also reason that without all of these four criteria— novelty, appropriateness, transformation, and condensation—the product is not truly creative. These criteria may be used to judge effectively the quality of contribution in all domains, but may also appropriately be applied at any level of expertise within a domain. Expanding on this idea, one may propose that judgment of level of creativity must also recognize level of intelligence of the contributor and the contributor's training and expertise within the particular domain (Haensly & Reynolds, 1989).

One last point about definitions and assessment needs to be made here. As in all psychological assessment, we may observe and measure responses that reflect the component abilities of creative process, evaluate products of creative ability, and link abilities with products, thus documenting the potential to produce; however, we cannot prove the absence of potential. Thus, to a degree, we may reliably predict the recurrence of this kind of response *given the appropriate conditions*, supporting our hypotheses about facilitation and/or obstruction of this ability. Information gained from assessment and the conditions under which measurements were made can then inform us regarding the environments within which individuals act creatively. Acting on this information, we are more likely to insure that creative potential will surface at some level for all individuals. Such a purposeful and dynamic agenda is what makes assessment of creative ability stand apart from the more static relationship between assessment and use of assessment data that may exist for many other abilities. In terms of medical models, we may in this way be able to assume a problem-preventative stance for healthful self-actualization early in life through creative expression, rather than a pathological treatment approach for individuals who have become isolated or nonproductively deviant in order to express their creative potential.

ASSESSMENT OF CREATIVITY: HOW AND WHEN

Procedural Considerations

General Psychometric Concerns

Defensible procedure in psychological assessment demands concern for the specificity of procedures in testing, and the assessment of creativity is no exception. Questions of validity and reliability of the instruments; establishment of personal rapport and a material environment that will elicit the behaviors under study; and procedures that are sufficiently standardized to insure that data can be compared among individuals and test administrators are all legitimate concerns. The nature of the phenomenon we are addressing often seems to encourage greater laxness than is defensible, perhaps because those who are more likely to use creativity tests may be those who view restrictions as inhibiting creative expression. Misunderstandings and questionable procedures are common in practice as well as in the research literature. Keeping a clear purpose in mind for the particular test administration will facilitate sound decision making. If the purpose is to make judgments about relative ability in comparison to a defined normative group, one must follow the standardized procedures rigorously. However, experimentation with procedure may be desirable when one wishes to learn more about factors that inhibit or facilitate creative expression, or when creativity tests are being used to stimulate growth in the component abilites of creativity.

In applied settings, the purpose of creativity testing is frequently identification of students to be considered for special programs—for example, gifted programs in schools, special talent development instruction, or specific endeavors especially requiring creative thinking. Another purpose may be the evaluation of instructional treatments or programs. In either case, the ability to generate accurate comparisons will be essential. By contrast, in order to test hypotheses about effective, reasonable (or valid), and reliable assessment of creative functioning, experimentation with different testing conditions and procedures will be necessary, just as it has been in the study of abilities other than creativity.

A third use of creativity tests, training or facilitation of creative functioning, sometimes requires additional justification to critics who would categorize this with "teaching to tests." Yet, as a critical component of educational goals and of life outside the classroom, creative functioning must be taught in as many ways as possible. When test performances have analogues in classroom performance, and/or analogues in performance in the everyday world of work, play, human interaction, and service, it makes great sense to use them in this manner. This use of creativity tests actually falls outside the realm of assessment, but must be mentioned so that the novice user of creativity tests and the expert psychologist alike will respect the line of demarcation between standardized procedure and "creative" use. However, one assessment extension of a nonstandardized procedure with creativity tests must be mentioned. Testing the limits, as described by Sattler (1974) and Kaufman (1979), parallels the procedure used with intelligence tests. That is, children or students might be encouraged strongly and persistently to continue with the production of ideas, in order to test a hypothesis that the test takers are more

capable than they are allowing themselves to demonstrate or than some external variable is allowing.

Specific Creativity Test Guidelines

Practical guidelines for the training of creativity test administrators and scorers, reprinted from the *Journal of Creative Behavior*, have been compiled in a manual published by Scholastic Testing Service, Inc. (Torrance, 1987a). Variations in administration of creativity tests, with documented results from the use of these variations, are also included in this manual. These guidelines would seem just as applicable to any assessment of creativity, although they are particularly relevant to the TTCT.

Admonitions to test administrators include those that are similar for the use of other psychological instruments, such as (1) close adherence to the printed directions, with accurate description and recording of deviations that occur; (2) strict adherence to time limits where recommended; and (3) use of clearly marked booklets with clear directions by test administrators. Directions for motivating the performance of students are specified and include allowance of oral administration of the tests with dialect, colloquial, or conversational language, as well as a lengthy list of examples of positive verbal reinforcement that may be used with the verbal form of the TTCT.

In the above-mentioned manual (Torrance, 1987a), scorers are also provided with standard procedures that include training, establishment of intra- and interscorer reliability, establishment of decision rules for special cases, and ways of keeping students from working so long at the task that fatigue and carelessness occur.

What has been demonstrated clearly is that test administration and testing conditions influence performance on creativity tests. The TTCT have perhaps been subjected to more experiments on ways to administer them than any other tests in the history of educational and psychological testing. We know from the results of extensive experimentation many of the factors that enhance, facilitate, or hinder creative thinking. These factors, tabulated from 36 different experiments on both the TTCT and Wallach–Kogan measures and published between

1968 and 1972 (see Torrance, 1987a, 1987b, 1988) include such things as type, quality, and length of warm-up provided prior to the test administration; timing; stimuli in the testing setting; reinforcement; evaluation; and group versus individual administration. The clear trends indicate that psychological warm-up for the tasks results in small but consistent and statistically significant gains; however, warm-up that lasts too long or is given too far in advance is ineffective in increasing creative responding.

Which Tests for Which Origin?

Psychologists and educators have been developing measures of creativity for probably as long as they have been trying to identify intelligence. Lists of published and unpublished creativity tests may be found in the Torrance Creativity Test Collection, established by Torrance in 1986 at the libraries of the University of Georgia (Athens, Georgia) and the State University College at Buffalo (New York). Between 1971 and 1980, the *Journal of Creative Behavior* published four different lists of specific categories of instruments: commercially available instruments (Kaltsounis, 1971), noncommercially available instruments (Davis, 1971; Kaltsounis, 1972), and an update of noncommercially available instruments (Kaltsounis & Honeywell, 1980). Davis has compiled another list (Davis, 1973) and an overview of the small number of commercially published tests (Davis, 1986). If open-ended tests of analogy production are to be included, many more instruments in specific fields or discipline should be added to the list. An example of this type is the Test der Zahlenreihen und Analogien Gruppenform (Test of Numerical Progressions and Numerical Analogies) (Dr. Cornelia Facaoaru, Ludwig-Maximilians-Unversitat München, München, Federal Republic of Germany).

In the construction of creativity tests, investigators have focused on a number of different aspects for measurement. Categorization of the focus of the 225 creativity tests found in the collection assembled by Torrance indicates the distribution of attention, with personality or attitude measures, verbal tests, and ratings or observation scales constituting the majority of tests (see Table 29.1). Although three-fourths of the tests

TABLE 29.1. The Distribution of the Types of Creativity Tests Developed and the Aspects of Creativity Measured in the Torrance Collection

Type and focus of instrument	No. located	Percentage of total
Verbal	50	22
Figural	21	9
General	28	12
Mathematical/science	6	3
Movement/dance	5	2
Dramatics	2	1
Artistic	1	0.5
Musical	1	0.5
Personality/attitude	62	28
Ratings/observations	42	19
Questionnaires	5	2
Combinations (ratings/ observations and personality/attitude)	2	1
Total	225	100

have been published, only 38% are indicated as in print in the Buros references (Mitchell, 1983, 1985; see Table 29.2). The majority of the tests (88%) have originated since 1950, although a few (6.5%) were developed between 1900 and 1950 (see Table 29.3). Sustained research has taken place with only 16% of the 225 listed tests; 65% of the tests have been the subject of no known research studies (see Table 29.4).

Despite the existence of the considerable number of creativity tests listed in the Torrance Collection, few tests suitable for general use in schools or even in daily psychological assessment situations have been developed to date. The first published battery of creativity tests suitable for general use in the schools was the TTCT (Torrance, 1966), followed by a battery of creativity tests by Guilford (1971), suitable for use in schools

TABLE 29.2. The Availability of Creativity Tests for General Use in the Torrance Collection

Published		In print (Mitchell, 1983, 1985)	Available for general use
Yes	165 (73%)	85 (38%)	22 (10%)
No	60 (27%)	140 (62%)	203 (90%)

TABLE 29.3. Period of Origin of Creativity Tests in the Torrance Collection

Period	No. of tests	Percentage of total
Before 1900	0	0
1900–1930	5	2.0%
1931–1950	10	4.5%
1951–1969	103	46.0%
1970–present	95	42.0%
No date available	12	5.0%

and originating from his tests for adults (see Guilford, 1956, 1977, 1986). Other tests of divergent thinking, available to the reader, have sometimes appeared in the published works of their authors (e.g., Getzels & Jackson, 1962; Wallach & Kogan, 1965). For the purposes of this chapter, we focus within each of the origin-of-creativity categories (i.e., process, person, and product) on the tests that are most representative of the category, suitable for assessment with children and adolescents, readily available, and possessing reasonable psychometric or informative qualities.

Process: Fluency and So Forth

Fluency, flexibility, and originality of idea production are the primary concern of the Torrance batteries of creativity tests, although these processes are also addressed in the nonformalized tests described by Getzels and Jackson (1962) and Wallach and Kogan (1965) in their respective publications and in Williams's (1980) test of divergent

TABLE 29.4. Number of Studies Conducted on Creativity Tests in the Torrance Collection

Number of studies	No. of tests	Percentage of total
No research/unknown	146	65.0%
Few (1–10)	26	11.5%
11–25	11	5.0%
26–50	5	2.0%
Over 51	36	16.0%
Unclear	1	0.5%

thinking. The TTCT, which were 10 years in development and have standardized administration and scoring as well as two forms, are the instruments most widely used by researchers and educators who use creative process tests.

The Torrance Creativity Tests include three batteries or groups of tests and are available through Scholastic Testing Service. The first of these is a general all-purpose battery, known as the TTCT; it contains a verbal test (Thinking Creatively with Words) with seven subtests and a figural test (Thinking Creatively with Pictures) with three subtests, all of which represent the elements of the Torrance research/process definition of creativity described earlier, and are timed for either 5- or 10-minute limits. The verbal subtests include Asking (which requires the respondent to list all of the questions that can be thought of about nonobvious events in a provided picture), Guessing Causes of the events in the picture, and Guessing Consequences of the events. These are followed by Product Improvement, in which the respondent lists all the improvements that could be made on a stuffed toy monkey or elephant pictured in the booklet to make it more fun to play with; Unusual Uses, in which uses for cardboard boxes or tin cans are listed; Unusual Questions, in which questions about the boxes or cans are listed as fluently as possible; and Just Suppose, in which the test taker poses as many ideas as possible about what would happen if an unlikely event (as pictured) occurred. For each of the three subtests of Thinking Creatively with Pictures, and respondent is asked to complete a drawing, having been presented with (1) a kidney-shaped form (a teardrop shape in the alternate form) to be used as the basis for an entire picture; (2) 10 incomplete figures to complete and label; and (3) two pages of circles or parallel lines to be completed and/or joined into a meaningful drawing.

Two forms of the entire battery of subtests are available, contributing to their usefulness for pre- and posttests. The subtests are scored for fluency, flexibility, and originality (based upon statistical-unfrequency norms); the figural subtests are also scored for elaboration (based on the number of details added to the figure or boundary or surrounding space). Scoring is time-consuming, or expensive if returned to trained scorers at Scholastic Testing Service, and sometimes difficult when decisions about the originality of ambiguous responses must be made. The technical–norms manual (Torrance, 1974) provides reliability and validity data, derived from over 1,500 studies using the TTCT. The interscorer reliability coefficients range from about .90 to .99 (as do the fluency scores). The majority of test–retest reliability coefficients are in the .60 to .80 range. Validity data have been derived from correlation studies of "person" characteristics, such as preferences for open-structure activities or aesthetic-related careers, originality in the classroom, humor, wild ideas produced, and lack of rigidity, as rated by both peers and teachers. Product-related validity data have been derived from longitudinal studies of elementary and high school students over periods as long as 22 years (Torrance, 1972a, 1972b, 1981, 1982; Torrance & Wu, 1981). Creative achievements, higher quality of creative achievements, and a higher level of creative aspirations as young adults have been shown to characterize the high-creativity scorers as opposed to the low-creativity scorers; these characteristics appear to increase over time for the high scorers, but remain the same for low scorers.

Over the last 20 years, Torrance has been developing and validating a method for the "streamlined" scoring of the TTCT. Manuals (Torrance & Ball, 1984) for the figural forms have now been published, and some of the validity studies have been completed for the verbal forms but not published. Torrance tells how the 5 norm-referenced and 13 criterion-referenced variables have been developed in the following words:

> I initially sought clues in the biographies and other accounts of history's greatest inventors, scientific discoverers, and artists. All along, I was also searching for clues in the everyday creative behaviors and achievements of children, youth, and adults. I also looked at the variables that other investigators had assessed (e.g., Whipple, 1915/1973; O'Connor, 1945; Broadley, 1943; Guilford, 1967). Recently, I (Torrance, 1979a) have sought clues in the leading technologies for teaching creative problem-solving skills, inventing and similar activities. In each of these systems, I have tried to determine what creative skills are activated and practiced. I have included the leading technologies in the United States, England, and Japan: the Osborn–Parnes Creative Problem Solving Process (Osborn, 1963; Parnes, 1981); Synectics (Gordon, 1961; Prince 1970); Lateral Thinking (de Bono, 1970); Sociodrama (Torrance, 1975); the widely used Japanese procedures known as the "KJ Method" (Kawakita, 1977), and a Japanese method known as the "NM Method" (Nakayama, 1977). In *The Search for Satori and Creativity,* I tried to show how each of these technologies attempts to activate and make use of each test variable used in the present scoring system of the Torrance Tests of Creative Thinking (TTCT) (Torrance, 1979a).
>
> In summary, I tried to be certain that each of the test variables selected: had been important in the great creative achievements in history; was observable and important in the everyday creativity of children, youth, and adults; had been identified as important in the creativity research of the past; and had been found to be teachable through the major technologies used in the United States, England, and Japan. I also required that each test indicator I selected meet the following criteria: clear manifestation in test performances; adequate frequency of occurrence; developmental characteristics; amenability to improvement through instruction, training, and practice; and satisfactory connection between test performances in elementary, high school, and adult creative achiements as demonstrated through longitudinal studies of predictive validity (Torrance & Ball, 1984). (Torrance, 1987a, p. 3)

Thus, the figural batteries are scored for each of the following variables, which are defined and discussed elsewhere (Torrance, 1979a, 1987b):

- Finding the problem
- Producing alternatives (fluency)
- Originality
- Abstracting (highlighting the essence)
- Elaborating
- Telling a story articulately
- Keeping open
- Being aware of and using emotions
- Putting ideas in context
- Combining and synthesizing
- Visualizing richly and colorfully
- Fantasizing
- Using movement and sound
- Looking at things from a different perspective
- Visualizing things internally
- Extending boundaries
- Humor
- Respect for infinity

The TTCT are appropriate for kindergarten children through graduate school and have been translated for use in a wide variety of cultures around the world. The Torrance tests have been translated into more than 32 languages. Children who cannot yet read or for whom writing would be difficult may be given the test orally, with administrators recording their responses. High school students are as likely to find the test a fascinating and enjoyable experience as are younger students. Test administrators are expected to provide a climate for creative responsiveness within the standardized format by encouraging playfulness, production of as many ideas as possible, and so forth.

The second Torrance battery, Thinking Creatively in Action and Movement, was developed for use with preschool children and others with limited verbal and drawing skills, including handicapped students (e.g., emotionally disturbed or deaf students) (Torrance, 1987b). Responses to the four subtests may be given in action and movement or in words; are scored for fluency, originality, and imagination; and are untimed. The test usually takes between 10 and 30 minutes. The subtests are How Many Ways? (to walk or run), scored for fluency and originality; Can You Move Like? (six situations, such as a tree in the wind and different animals), scored for imagination; and What Other Ways? (to put a paper cup in a wastebasket) and What Can You Do With a Paper Cup?, both scored for fluency and originality.

Interscorer reliabilities are about .99 for fluency and .96 for originality. Test–retest reliability coefficients of .84 for the total test and subtest reliabilities of .58 to .79 have been documented. Validity criteria at this time are limited to teacher-observed creative behavior and children's joke humor.

The third battery, Thinking Creatively with Sounds and Words, jointly developed (Torrance, Khatena, & Cunningham, 1973), uses a quite different stimulus for response, in that two long-playing records are used to present four abstract sounds (Sounds and Images) and five onomatopoetic words (Onomatopoeia and Images). The respondent describes the mental images stimulated by the sounds and by the words; each of the sets of stimuli is presented three times to generate more and more original associations. The responses are scored for originality based on statistical infrequency of responses; from 0 to 4 points are assigned to each of the 12 responses. The battery is available in two forms, one for adults and one for children.

Interscorer reliabilities range from .88 to .99 (Torrance, 1982). Alternate-forms reliabilities range from .36 to .92. The test's predictive validity varies greatly (.13 to .45) as derived from over 80 research studies, although it has not as yet been used widely enough to arrive at more stable validity coefficients or appropriate criteria. This battery may be used with children and youths from 3rd to 12th grades; with college students, graduate school, and professional schools; and with adults. It has been found to be especially useful with blind subjects.

One subtest of the Williams Creativity Assessment Packet (CAP; Williams, 1980), available from DOK Publishers, is the Exercise in Divergent Thinking—a test similar to the Torrance figural subtest Picture Completion, but in which responses are scored for both their figural component and their verbal component as represented by the title given to the picture. Respondents are encouraged to draw a picture that no one else would think of and to give a clever title in response to 12 incomplete drawings. Students in 3rd through 5th grades are allowed 25 minutes to complete the drawings, and those in 6th through 12th grades are allowed 20 minutes. The drawings are scored for fluency, flexibility, originality and elaboration; the 0 to 3 points for title are awarded on the basis of length, complexity, creativeness, and humor. Young children may have their titles written in by a teacher or aide.

Ten-month test–retest reliabilities were reported as "in the sixties" (Williams, 1980); these were based on responses of 256 students from 3rd through 12th grades. The specifics regarding validity of the entire CAP instrument are unclear.

Both Wallach and Kogan (1965) and Getzels and Jackson (1962) have provided in their respective publications extensive description of tests for creativity that they have used with students, along with details on administration and scoring for fluency, uniqueness, and other dimensions. These are mentioned here because they may be useful to teachers as either stimuli for creativity enhancement or measures of abilities in their students that might contribute to their creative development. Psychometric data on these instruments are not available; thus their use for serious assessment purposes is limited, even though predictive validity is supported (Bartlett & Davis, 1974).

Process: Divergent Thinking

In 1971, Guilford published a battery of creativity tests suitable for use in schools and based on his structure-of-intellect model. The activity of the divergent-production operation, assumed to represent the creative component of cognitive ability, became the basis of the Guilford creativity tests, measuring 24 different divergent productive abilities (6 products × 4 contents). A battery of these tests, Creativity Tests for Children (CTC), was published by the Sheridan Psychological Services in 1971 (Guilford, 1971). All of these tests of divergent production are described by Guilford (1967, 1977) and include such items as asking the respondent to list as many words as possible that are similar to a given word (associational fluency—i.e., relations between words), or to find a way to remove four matchsticks from a six-square rectangle and leave only three squares (figural transformation). The problem of relating divergent production measured in this way to real-world creative productivity has not been resolved. Meeker, Meeker and Roid (1985) have continued, however, to develop new tests and norms.

The Monitor Test of Creative Potential (TCP; Hoepfner & Hemenway, 1973) has built on the Guilford work and is available from Monitor Publishers in two forms for use in 2nd through 12th grades. The TCP consists of three subtests: Writing Words, Picture Decorations, and License Plate Words, respectively measuring divergent production of semantic units and classes, figural units and implications, and symbolic units and transformations. Writing Words requires word responses that are similar to a given word and is scored for associational fluency and spontaneous flexibility; Picture Decorations requires decorations of three different pictures, yielding a design element score and a pictorial element score; License Plate Words requires creation of words form sets of three letters and is scored for word fluency and originality. The TCP has a standardized administration and scoring guide, and each of

the parts of the subtests is timed. The test may be used with children as young as age 7 and is also appropriate for adolescents and adults. Interscorer reliabilities range from .94 to .99. When children aged 7–9 retook the test 3 months later using the alternate form (a mixed form of reliability), two reliability coefficients obtained were .62 and .67. Validity data were not available.

The Ingenuity Test, developed by Flanagan and published by Science Research Associates, is part of Flanagan's Aptitude Classification Tests (see Flanagan, 1963), used in the nationwide PROJECT TALENT. This test is suitable for use with high school students and has a multiple-choice format in which the options are incomplete—that is, only the first and last letters are provided. The items in which problems are presented are said to test "the ability to invent or discover a solution which represents an unusually neat, clever, or surprising way of solving an existing problem" (Flanagan, 1976, p. 118). Although it appears to offer opportunities for divergent production, a limited number of possibilities are already in place in the options, and arrayed in "guess what falls between these letters" choices. Students tested in the project are being followed after completion of high school, but no validity data are currently available, with the exception that the 1-year follow-ups indicate that high scorers are typically found in art, architecture, and science careers.

A somewhat different view of divergent thinking forms the basis of the Starkweather creativity instruments for preschool children. Starkweather's goal in the construction of tests for identification of creative potential in the very young child was the "development of a game which the child would want to play" (Starkweather, 1976, p. 81). Using the child's response to the game, the researcher would be able to ascertain compulsive conformity *or* nonconformity versus choices made freely to suit one's own preference, willingness to try difficult tasks, and originality. In the Starkweather Form Boards Test, the administrator uses four colored form boards in which the colored picture pieces depict a tree, house, playground, and barnyard, to be inserted against a background of black-and-white line drawings on the form board. Measures of conformity require two sessions with the child. For example, using the tree form board, the child chooses between a rabbit and flowers, although the line drawing model depicts a rabbit; in the second session the child again chooses between a rabbit and flowers, but the line drawing model depicts flowers. Starkweather determined that either conforming over the two sessions by choosing the pictures corresponding to the line drawing provided, or nonconforming by *not* using the model each time, reflects rigidity. The child who is free or willing to be different will choose a personally preferred picture, which will correspond to the drawing provided 50% of the time (Starkweather & Cowling, 1963).

A second test of conformity, the Starkweather Social Conformity Test, is based on the same principle of rigidity versus the freedom to conform or not to conform; the child is provided with an opportunity to select colored place cards for a table setting for his or her mother, father and self, after what colors the child like and dislikes are determined.

The Starkweather Target Game consists of a box with a target, which, when the bull's eye is hit, releases a lid and discloses a surprise picture. Difficulty of the game is adjusted through a pretest to a 50% chance of success for each child by assessing the child's accuracy at rolling the ball from different target distances. The measured variable consists of choices made during the game between an easy distance and a hard distance. For preschool children, the game contains an element of a surprise picture as a motivating force to continue the game. For first- and second-grade children, success in hitting the target retains the children's attention and effort. This game cannot be used for older children because of the difficulty of adjusting for an individual child's skill level.

The Starkweather Originality Test consists of 40 plastic foam pieces of four different shapes, each shape in four different colors. In a warm-up pretest, the administrator encourages the child to think of as many different things a piece from a smaller subset of pieces may be. For the test itself, the administrator puts out a box of 20 pieces and directs the child to take one piece at a time and tell what the piece might be; the same procedure is followed for the second box of 20 pieces. Thus, each of the four shapes generates four responses scored in order, with credit given for each response that is different from previ-

ous responses. Validity for this test was determined by comparing teachers' judgments of the children's originality with the children's test scores; validity was also demonstrated by comparing the children's test scores with their freedom of expression when playing alone with simple toys. Correlations with scores on the Peabody Picture Vocabulary Test (PPVT) were not significant, indicating independence of the type of verbal ability demonstrated through the correct labeling responses required in the PPVT. Interrater reliability in scoring was determined by comparing the scoring of judges familiar with the test to that of a judge naive to the test. The materials for this test must be constructed by the user. Although Starkweather's death has slowed this work temporarily, it is now being accelerated by James Moran at Oklahoma State University.

Process: Association

The ability to produce many verbal responses or ideas to a given stimulus word and to associate diverse elements in relevant ways has been viewed as still another measure of creative process. The Remote Associates Test (RAT; Mednick & Mednick, 1967) is published by Houghton Mifflin. This objective-type measure is comprised of items in which three words are given and the respondent must find a fourth word that links the three or could be associated with all of them. The combination must meet the experimenter-imposed criteria—that is, only "correct" answers add to one's score. There is a .40 to .60 correlation between RAT scores and verbal intelligence scores. Mednick and Mednick (1967) report Spearman–Brown reliabilities of .91 and .92 on samples of 215 and 289 college students. The RAT is suitable for use with senior high school students and college students. It would appear that the RAT may require more convergency in responses than divergency.

The Person: Personality, Attitude, and Interest Inventories

As stated earlier, determining what kind of person one must be to engage successfully in the creative process was one objective of the Torrance (1963) creativity research agenda. Much information in this regard was obtained from the 22-year study of elementary school children first tested with the TTCT in 1958 (Torrance, 1981, 1982). Biographical inventories, often based on the work of individuals such as Barron (1969, 1978), MacKinnon (1976, 1978), and Roe (1951, 1953), have added much to our knowledge about the personality characteristics most frequently associated with the creative process. However, even if it could be assumed that such lists define who might become creative if given the opportunity and reinforcement (creative potential), it would not be feasible to reference all of the inventories and checklists that resulted from these searches. Nevertheless, many trait characteristics seem common enough among creative individuals that the lists may be useful for identifying characteristics of individuals that ought to be recognized and reinforced in order to facilitate creative growth, if not for identifying creativity outright. This may be particularly relevant to our concern in this handbook on assessment of children and adolescents, especially if we can locate instruments with good validity and high reliability. The instruments described here have respectable psychometric qualities, are designed particularly for pupils in preschool through senior high school (sometimes on into the college years), and are both readily available and usable.

A series of inventories spanning this entire age group has been developed by Gary Davis and Sylvia Rimm and is available through Educational Assessment Service. Each is somewhat different in the trait characteristics for which scores are available—apparently an attempt to identify characteristics particularly relevant at the specifically targeted age group. The Group Inventory for Finding Talent (GIFT; Rimm, 1976; Rimm & Davis, 1976, 1980) is a self-report instrument that assesses the traits of independence, flexibility, curiosity, perseverance, and breadth of interests, and identifies past creative activities and hobbies. GIFT is available in three forms—Primary for first and second grades, Elementary for third and fourth grades, and Upper Elementary for fifth and sixth grades—which differ in the size of print and in about one-fourth of the items. All forms are brief, containing 25 yes–no items common to all grade levels, and 7, 9, and 8 items respectively that are specific to each grade

level. In addition to a total score, subscale scores for Imagination, Independence, and Many Interests are obtained. Validity coefficients using teacher ratings plus ratings of stories produced by the children as a criterion range from about .25 to .45 (Davis, 1986). Internal-consistency reliabilities of .80, .86, and .88 are reported for the Primary, Elementary, and Upper Elementary forms. The items are sufficiently broad to be useful with many different groups of children: white, black, and Hispanic-surnamed groups of children; high and low socioeconomic status (SES); urban, suburban, and rural; Israeli, French, and Australian. Sample items include "I ask a lot of questions," "I like things that are hard to do," and "I like to make up my own songs."

Group Inventory for Finding Interests I (GIFFI I; Davis & Rimm, 1982; Rimm & Davis, 1979, 1983) is similarly a self-report instrument, but requires rating 60 items on a 5-point scale from "no" to "definitely." It is designed for students from sixth through ninth grades, and produces a total creativity score with subscale scores for Confidence, Challenge–Inventiveness, Imagination, Creative Arts and Writing, and Many Interests. Internal-consistency reliability coefficients are above .90 and validity coeffients, again determined according to a combined criterion of teacher ratings of creativeness and a creativity rating for a produced story, range from low-moderate to high-moderate (see Davis, 1986, Table 8.2, p. 182). Group Inventory for Finding Interests II (GIFFI II; Davis & Rimm, 1980, 1982; Rimm & Davis, 1983) is similar to GIFFI I, but was developed for 9th through 12th grades. The items are designed to measure independence, self-confidence, risk taking, energy, adventurousness, curiosity, reflectiveness, sense of humor, and artistic interests, as well as to identify creative activities and hobbies. Internal-consistency reliabilities range from .91 to .96, reflecting that the items are measuring a single characteristic. The instrument has been validated with many ethnic groups and all SES levels, as well as in urban, suburban, and rural areas. As in the remainder of the series, the criterion used for validity studies is a combination of teacher ratings of individual creativity with creativity ratings for a produced story, producing a median coefficient of .45 (see Davis,

1986, p. 182 for the range of coefficients obtained).

An alternative that is less psychometrically sound than the Davis and Rimm instruments, but that considers some highly different interests is the Creativity Attitude Survey (CAS; Schaefer, 1971), for children from fourth to sixth grades. The CAS is a self-report, 32-item yes–no instrument designed to measure such things as imagination, humor, interest in art and writing, appreciation of fantasy and wild ideas, and attraction to the magical. Internal-consistency reliabilities of .75 and .81 and a 5-week test–retest reliability of .61 have been reported. The primary criterion used in validity studies has been the test itself, given after creativity training, although one study of 35 fifth-grade students reported teacher evaluation of "concrete evidence of creativity" related to CAS score.

Davis (1976) has developed another inventory for assessing attitudes, motivations, interests, values, beliefs, and other creativity-relevant concerns, the How Do You Think (HDYT). Although this inventory was constructed with college students in mind, there seems no reason why the items (Davis, 1976, p. 252–254) would not prove equally valid for senior high school students as well, even though much more attention is given to creative accomplishments than in the GIFFI instruments. Form B of the HDYT is a 102-item, 5-point rating scale with responses ranging from "agree" to "disagree." Its high internal consistency (a reliability coefficient of .93), and its strong validity in predicting the creativeness of an assigned writing project, an art or handicraft project, ideas for two inventions, and ideas for a creative teaching project (a correlation of .42 between the HDYT and the creative projects), warrant additional study. The test is available from the author.

The Williams CAP (Williams, 1980), in addition to the Exercise in Divergent Thinking subtest described under "Process: Fluency, and So Forth" above, includes an inventory on creative personality traits for students in 3rd through 12th grades, Exercise in Divergent Feeling. The 50-item, 4-point rating scale produces four subscale scores—Curiosity, Imagination, Complexity, and Risk Taking—to complement the total creativity score. The psychometric limita-

tions of the process test, described earlier, apply to this test as well.

Rating Scales

Although both self-report instruments and scales rated by those individuals purporting to know the respondent's characteristics may be confounded by bias and lack of objectivity, checklists and inventories to be completed by individuals who should know a great deal about the respondent abound. A parent rating scale, produced on the same theoretical assumptions about the characteristics of creative individuals as the GIFT and GIFFI inventories, but constructed for preschool and kindergarten children aged 3–6, is the Preschool and Kindergarten Interest Descriptor (PRIDE; Rimm, 1983). This questionnaire, available through Educational Assessment Service, consists of 50 items rated on a 5-point scale and purports to measure the same kinds of traits addressed in the GIFT and GIFFI instruments. The PRIDE requires about 20–35 minutes to complete; it produces a total creativity score and subscale scores for Many Interests, Independence–Perseverance, Imagination–Playfulness, and Originality, and shows an internal-consistency reliability of .92. Validity coefficients of .38, .50, and .32 have been obtained, again using the criterion of combined teacher ratings of creativeness with experimenter ratings of the creativeness of children's pictures and short stories (both determined from a 5-point rating scale).

The Williams Scale, one of the three tests in the CAP (Williams, 1980) described previously, contains 48 items to be rated on a 3-point scale ("often," "sometimes," and "seldom") by a parent or a teacher to assess both the child's process (fluency, flexibility, originality, elaboration) and characteristics (curiosity, imagination, complexity, and risk taking). This information yields a total creativity score. Additional qualitative information is obtained from the rater through four open-ended qualitative questions at the end of the scale items. Again validity is ill defined, although reported to be between .59 and .76.

A rating scale that is perhaps the most widely known and widely used among teachers in gifted programs throughout schools for all age levels is the Renzulli–Hartman Scale for Rating the Behavioral Characteristics of Superior Students (SRBCSS; Renzulli, 1983; Renzulli & Hartman, 1971). The Creativity subscale is only one of five subscales, is composed of 10 items rated on a scale of 1–4, and assesses such characteristics as curiosity, fluency of idea production, risk taking, humor and intellectual playfulness, emotional and aesthetic sensitivity, nonconformity, and critical evaluation. Its validity is thought to be in its ability to identify creative students who should be included in programs for gifted children. Psychometric data are not available for this scale, but the scale is available in the Renzulli publications or from Creative Learning Press.

Products

The use of products to assess creative potential and current creativity among children is widespread and is one means of identifying candidates for qualitatively sound gifted programs in schools. School district personnel concerned with gifted programs most often develop their own rating scales for such products or portfolios of accomplishments in a variety of fields. Some states, such as Louisiana, have focused extensively on the development of statewide rating scales for the many different areas of artistic endeavor and performance, and have implemented statewide guidelines for the evaluation of products and performances (Dial, 1975). Assumed with most such rating scales is that experts in the field of the product or performance will do the rating, and that a consensus approach with multiple judges will be used.

Based on a model for analyzing a product's creativity by Besemer and Treffinger (1981), Besemer and O'Quin (1986) developed a bipolar semantic scale to be used as a judging instrument. The 80-item Creative Product Semantic Scale has three subscales: Novelty, characterizing originality, surprise effect, and germinal quality; Resolution, characterizing the value, logic, and usefulness of the product; and Elaboration and Synthesis, characterizing the product's organicity, elegance, complexity, capability to be understood, and degree of crafting. At this time, this instrument is still in the process of development.

Another example of an instrument current-

ly in the process of development is the Creative Processes Rating Scale (Kulp & Tarter, 1986) for measuring the creative process of children in the visual arts. Uniqueness, rearrangements, magnification and variation, and generation of ideas in transformation of basic shapes in response to five given basic shapes are the elements assessed on a 5-point rating scale by an art expert. Its authors believe that the scale provides a visible alternative for measurement of the child's creative process, thus allowing early recognition of the potentially highly creative child: "The existence of an objective instrument to measure the complex and abstract concepts of visual creativity should provide assistance to both researchers and practitioners in the identification and instruction of visual art practices" (Kulp & Tarter, 1986, p. 170).

A third example of an instrument for evaluating creative products—one that is still in the process of development—is the Test for Creative Thinking–Drawing Production (TCT-DP; Jellen & Urban, 1986). This paper-and-pencil instrument designed for most age and ability groups focuses on drawing products resulting when respondents are presented with a given group of figural stimuli. Thus, it is not a direct measure of product creativity. However, it allows respondents to interpret what they consider to be significant in the development of a creative product and to complete this interpretation through their own creative drawing production. The assumption by the instrument developers is that this interpretation of what would be creative in the test-drawing situation should generalize to naturally produced drawings and should thus serve as a valid predictor of creativity in an individual's drawings.

The test drawings are evaluated according to a specific point list for each of 11 criteria. The authors describe the 11 criteria or "key elements" as linked with the six components of creative thought—that is, with fluency, flexibility, originality, elaboration, risk taking, and composition, all applied to characteristics of the drawing product. The 11 criteria are completion, additions, new elements, connections made with a line, connections made to produce a theme, boundary breaking that is fragment-dependent, boundary breaking that is fragment-independent, perspective (any breaking away from two-dimensionality), humor, unconventionality, and speed. In the TCT-DP, six figural fragments are irregularly placed within a square frame presented on a sheet of paper. Respondents are allowed 15 minutes for the testing procedure. Evaluation of each case requires approximately 3–5 minutes. In addition to belief in the TCT-DP's conceptual soundness for linkage between creative abilities and a visible product, the authors claim as advantages of this intrument the low cost for test material, minimal time required for administration and evaluation, and ease of training for use of the test (Jellen & Urban, 1986). Interrater reliability is reported as ranging between .89 and .97, based on approximately 100 cases. The authors suggest that the criteria of the TCT-DP could be applicable with minor modification to creative acts in music, dance, writing, and dramatics. They also suggest its possibilities as a psychiatrically relevant clinical instrument for interpretation of schizophrenic or primitive thinking.

MAKING SENSE OF OBSERVATIONS AND MEASUREMENTS

A major problem in the assessment of creativity has been deciding what creative abilities/skills are most worth assessing and what sense can be made of the assessment data. In the operational situations of schools, colleges, businesses, and the like, it would not be practical to assess all of these abilities and skills; nor would it necessarily be useful. The abilities and skills assessed through tests must have their analogues in classroom performances, and, in turn, in real-life creative achievements. That linkage or lack of it, as the case may be, is at the heart of controversies over whether creative functioning should be a core concern in education and eventually in society at large, or an after-the-fact concern, nice but not essential.

As elaborated throughout the preceding text, we continue to be dependent on assessing only the elements of performance that might lead to full-blown creative contributions, rather than creativity as a "Gestalt." We need, then, to ask where information may be obtained to substantiate the priority we give to particular elements in verifying creative acts and in increasing our ability to predict productive outcome. Biographies and other accounts of history's greatest inventors, scientific discoverers, and artists have provided such information. Clues have also been located in the everyday creative behaviors and achievements of children, youths, and adults who were at early ages displaying creative performance in their familiar contexts and at levels reflecting their experience and training. Longitudinal studies of children in the process of development (Albert, 1983; Feldman, 1986) provide additional clues about the elements involved in their precocious performance. As stated earlier, the approaches used by leading technologies in the United States, England, and Japan to teach creative problem-solving skills, inventing, and other similar activities have provided further valuable information on the relative necessity of various abilities (Torrance, 1979a). And, throughout each of these searches, it has become obvious that creativity test *indicators* must meet reasonable criteria of clear and frequent manifestation in test performance; must possess the potential for development and improvement through instruction and training; and must demonstrate linkage to creative performance later in life.

Although accurate forecasting of future behavior is considered a desirable goal of psychological assessment, and valid predictions of later behavior can verify the theoretical construct from which a particular assessment instrument evolved, we are reminded of an additional value of such assessment (Heist, 1968). Psychological assessment has often been much more successful at enhancing current knowledge about individuals than at specifying what they will achieve or accomplish in the future. When such information is interpreted wisely and used appropriately, it serves educators and students alike in the attempts to individualize the teaching–learning process. Heist focused on the postadolescent and college levels in the consideration of identification of creative potential, but his ideas are applicable in the earlier years of schooling as well. Furthermore, he limits this identification to the assessment of traits that appear to be part of the complex of creative behavior, rather than to tests that might reflect creative products or process. Thus, the inventories he describes assess values (The Study of Values; Allport, Vernon, &

Lindzey, 1960), personal preferences (the Edwards Personal Preference Schedule; Edwards, 1957), academic motivation and intellectual concerns (the California Psychological Inventory; Gough, 1957), the behavioral syndromes associated with creative individuals (the Omnibus Personality Inventory; Heist, McConnell, Webster, & Yonge, 1968), and attitudes toward one's cognitive and perceptual environment (the Myers–Briggs Type Indicator; Myers & Briggs, 1957). In Amabile's (1983b) and Brown's (1989) componential models for creative behavior, these inventories address both the creativity-relevant skills component and the task motivation component, both of which are believed to originate from traits, training, experience, and perceptions of that experience. In the Amabile and Brown models, creative behavior is expressed as a coalescence of these two components with domain-relevant skills (knowledge, skills, and talent), which are dependent upon inherent ability and education, focused through interest in the domain.

Various researchers have sharply criticized the use of creativity tests that assess the processes of fluency, flexibility, originality, and elaboration; the implication is that these latter are not creative abilities. The relationship of these abilities to creativity and the supporting rationale for identifying and teaching them have been elaborated elsewhere, but they must be reaffirmed here. Possession of these abilities will not guarantee creative behavior, just as a high degree of measured intelligence does not guarantee intelligent behavior. Although these somewhat unitary abilities do not make up the *entire* constellation of abilities needed to perform creatively, assessment should not be avoided. And, subsequently, we should not be deterred from fostering specific creativity-relevant skills in children and adolescents in order to increase the probability of creative performance by these individuals, given the opportune situation and time.

APPROPRIATE APPLICATION OF ASSESSMENT RESULTS

It probably goes without saying that all psychometric and clinical assessment devices and procedures should help teachers, counselors, psychologists, and others who use assessment data do a better job. If test performances are to have their analogues in classroom performances and, in turn, in life outside the classroom, the most obvious and direct application of the results of assessment of creativity in children and adolescents may be in planning lessons and other curricular and extracurricular experiences that support creative responses, and in evaluating outcomes of instruction without bias against creative strengths.

The assessment of creativity in children and adolescents will be pointless, however, if it serves to exclude them from opportunity—that is, to keep them out of special programs where they might begin to learn how to express their ideas and feelings creatively. Assessment data must be more appropriately used to plan instruction that takes advantage of identified creative potential already bubbling forth, and works to release that potential when it has been inhibited and obstructed in its natural development.

Assessment data should have as a primary goal to accomplish the following specific outcomes if they are to help teachers do a better job:

- Awareness among teachers, psychologists, students, and parents of the creative abilities and skills that should be developed and practiced, as well as the personality characteristics, attitudes, and values that support creative responsiveness.
- Awareness of the individual student's strengths for creative learning and problem solving.
- Awareness of gaps or deficits in the student's repertoire of creative abilities and skills.
- Provision of a basis for generating appropriate learning activities and planning instruction.
- Provision of a basis for generating evaluation procedures that assess not only the traditionally tested types of outcomes, but also some of the more elusive objectives of education.

Assessment data as discussed above can be useful in designing individual educational programs (IEPs) or in working with an entire class or group of classes. Though assessment will demonstrate considerable variability among students on any of the creativity indicators, it will quite often be possible to identify common strengths and weaknesses in a class or even in a school population. Cultural homogeneity will often result in an unusually high level of a specific creativity indicator, or sometimes an unusually low level of a specific indicator. For example, in one school system (kindergarten through 12th grade) of Native American children, imagery and boundary extension were strengths, appearing much more frequently than among the larger norm sample. On the other hand, fantasy, expression of feeling and emotion, humor, and putting things in context were significantly less frequent. Direct teaching or encouragement of these skills may be necessary in such cases before creative abilities can be adequately expressed.

An instructional model for integrating the teaching of creative thinking skills into the teaching of reading and social studies, described and illustrated in *Encouraging Creativity in the Classroom* (Torrance, 1970b; see also Torrance, 1979b), focuses on the things that can be done before, during, and after a lesson to enhance incubation and creative thinking and action. Anticipatory and participatory learning are emphasized, calling into play creative thinking skills. Heightening anticipation and expectations creates a desire to know or to find out, again fostering curiosity and making room for creative responses (Botkin, Elmandjra, & Malitza, 1979). Other creativity-relevant skills may be fostered during and after the lesson, again using current levels of functioning via assessment data to guide the extent to which skills must be introduced through direct instruction, nurtured through gentle encouragement, or simply allowed to be practiced and to soar when already at a high level. Bogner (1981) has used psychometric data from the TTCT not only to write IEPs for her gifted students, but to encourage them to write their own IEPs. Some of her students used the checklist of creativity indicators to evaluate their own creative productions, much as in the TCT-DP instrument developed by Jellen and Urban (1986), described earlier.

Perhaps one of the most significant uses of creativity assessment data has been to identify areas of strength among children from racial groups and SES levels who have previously been denied access to special or even ordinary educational opportunities on the basis of weaknesses identified through intelligence tests and/or school achievement data. Results of 16 different studies in different parts of the United States (Torrance, 1971, 1975) indicated no racial or economic differences on either the verbal or figural TTCT. In some cases, black children excelled over white children on certain tasks; since children may respond to tests such as these in terms of their own life experiences, and tasks are open-ended, children are not penalized for lack of academically intellectual experiences.

Through focusing on strengths in creative thinking abilities, Carlson (1975) was able to demonstrate gains on the part of a learning-disabled child in specific behaviors related to academic and social performance. This child's strengths were dependable fluency of ideas and elaboration, as well as original or unique behavior; however, her ability to shift categories and classifications was not a strength. Although gains were achieved by Carlson in a one-to-one setting, others have achieved gains in a similar fashion with an entire class of underachieving children at about the fifth- or sixth-grade level (Carlson, 1975). Using creativity assessment data and the model of creative strengths in a fashion similar to Carlson's approach, a teacher in another district not only demonstrated increased academic achievement in reading, arithmetic, and other areas over that in comparable classes, but also found improvement in health (or attitude) as measured in significantly decreased visits to the school nurse (Torrance, 1987b).

Creativity tests themselves may be used creatively, as demonstrated by one teacher who used them to reduce test-taking phobia (Torrance, 1987b). Children who had been exhibiting anger, frustration, and helplessness about regular achievement tests were given the opportunity to take the TTCT several times, to take it at home, to correspond with the test author, and generally to defuse their anxiety about the test-taking process. Subsequent exposure 3 months later to the standardized achievement testing situation revealed an increased functional attitude by these students, culminating in academic performance growth of about 2 years—much more than might have been expected through academic instruction alone.

Finally, it must be pointed out that even though teachers, educational planners and decision makers, psychologists and clinicians, and sometimes parents seek objective data to assure themselves that particular children have creative ability and the potential for creative productivity, this kind of ability will always be evident to attentive educators at all levels. The assessment instrument through which this ability becomes evident is sensitive observation of children at work and play. Some facets of this complex phenomenon may be more readily apparent than others. The 4-year-old in a program for gifted preschoolers who, oblivious of others, has figuratively transformed his body into the fluid movements of the aquarium fish he is observing intently; the 3-year-old who states that the ants are guests at her picnic; and the child who with great facility transforms the blob of paint that has emerged on his paper into a crab with six "legs," one of which is explained by him to be "detached but the crab will grow it again," are all reflecting creative potential. Their fluid responses to the reality of facts, information, and materials they have encountered are spontaneous indicators of productivity yet to come if such responses are allowed, nurtured, and reinforced. Nontest indicators may be found in regular classroom activities, as well as in classroom situations that have been especially designed to evoke creative behavior. The third-grader who consistently suggests an alternative ending for stories in reading; the eighth-grader who insists that the Yalta agreements have been misconstrued because of facts A, B, and C; and the trigonometry student who selects to arrive at problem solutions through nonclassical procedure variants are all demonstrating their creative potential in what should be highly acceptable ways in the classroom.

However, the effects of suppressive versus facilitative environments on creative expression will also have to be acknowledged if one is to observe creative potential. The misplaced construction of humor inappropriately applied by an adolescent in a rigid class setting may reflect creative potential struggling to express itself. Graffiti, often assumed to be the work of illiterate and uneducated individuals who have a crude sense of societal propriety, speaks for people who seek an audience, legitimate or otherwise. On occas-

ions, graffiti has come to be viewed as a form of creative expression for the social conscience and an art form in its own right, with a recognized audience; it has even found its way into art museums.

Although entrance into programs or recognition for appropriate eductional services will continue to be dependent upon the documented data from proven assessment instruments, the day-to-day response of parents, teachers, and other types of educators to the creativity their children or students spontaneously emit will continue to be critical to the transformation of creative potential into creative productivity. Such levels of assessment in no way deny the contribution of specific domain-related abilities, creativity-relevant abilities (inherent or trained) and the domain-specific acquisition of foundation knowledge that will affect the eventual direction and substance of creative production.

SUMMARY

In summary, we have presented in this chapter an overview of current views of the creativity phenomenon as we believe they apply to assessment, specifically to the assessment of creativity in children and adolescents. Thus, we have not addressed the vast amount of work concerned with understanding, evaluating, and predicting creative productivity that emerges in adulthood, in industrial and corporate settings, in the various scientific fields, or in the aesthetic domains. However, in order to establish an overarching perspective, we have examined an array of definitions and suggested an integrated dimension that takes into account the contribution of processes, personal characteristics and attributes, and types of products that are involved in creative endeavor. A description of instruments currently available to assess creativity as it is present in process, person, and product provides readers with a wide variety of ways to sensibly conduct assessments of creativity with children and adolescents—assessments that will find meaningful application. Furthermore, we have recommended applications of assessment results that we consider to have been fruitful in the past and that seem most closely attuned to the most advanced current understanding of creativity. We particularly advocate the use of such data to structure (or modify when necessary) instruction and the environment in our schools and society, to facilitate the emergence and maximization of creative potential for all the children and adolescents who are our concern in this handbook.

REFERENCES

Albert, R. S. (Ed.). (1983). *Genius and eminence*. New York: Pergamon Press.

Allport, G. W., Vernon, P. E., & Lindzey, G. (1960). *Study of values* (3rd ed.). Boston: Houghton Mifflin.

Amabile, T. M. (1983a). *The social psychology of creativity*. New York: Springer.

Amabile, T. M. (1983b). The social psychology of creativity: A componential conceptualization. *Journal of Personality and Social Psychology, 45*, 357–376.

Anderson, H. H. (Ed.). (1959). *Creativity and its cultivation*. New York: Harper & Row.

Barchillon, J. (1961). Creativity and its inhibition in child prodigies. In *Personality dimensions of creativity*. New York: Lincoln Institute of Psychotherapy.

Barron, F. (1969). *Creative person and creative process*. New York: Holt, Rinehart & Winston.

Barron, F. (1978). An eye more fantastical. In G. A. Davis & J. A. Scott (Eds.), *Training creative thinking* (pp. 181–193). Melbourne, FL: Krieger.

Barron, F., & Harrington, D. M. (1981). Creativity, intelligence, and personality. *Annual Review of Psychology, 32*, 439–476.

Bartlett, F. (1958). *Thinking*. New York: Basic Books.

Bartlett, M. M., & Davis, G. A. (1974). Do the Wallach and Kogan tests predict real creative behavior? *Perceptual and Motor Skills, 39*, 730.

Besemer, S. P., & O'Quin, K. (1986). Analyzing creative products: Refinement and test of a judging instrument. *Journal of Creative Behavior, 20*, 115–126.

Besemer, S. P., & Treffinger, D. J. (1981). Analysis of creative products: Review and synthesis. *Journal of Creative Behavior, 15*, 158–178.

Bloom, B. (1985). *Developing talent in young children*. New York: Ballantyne.

Bloomberg, M. (Ed.). (1973). *Creativity: Theory and research*. New Haven, CT: College and University Press.

Bogner, D. (1981). Creative individual education programs (IEP's) from creativity tests. *Creative Child and Adult Quarterly, 6*, 160–162.

Botkin, J. W., Elmandjra, M., & Malitza, M. (1979). *No limits to learning*. New York: Pergamon Press.

Broadley, M. E. (1943). *Square pegs in square holes*. Garden City, NY: Doubleday.

Brown, R. T. (1989). Creativity: What are we to measure? In J. A. Glover, R. Ronning, & C. R. Reynolds (Eds.), *Handbook of creativity*. New York: Plenum.

Carlson, N. A. (1975). Using the creative strengths of a learning disabled child to increase evaluative effort and academic achievement (Doctoral dissertation, Michigan State University, 1974). *Dissertation Abstracts International, 35*, 5962A. (University Microfilms No. 75-07135)

Crutchfield, R. S. (1962). Conformity and creative thinking. In H. E. Gruber, G. Terrell, & M. Wertheimer (Eds.), *Contemporary approaches to creative thinking* (pp. 120–140). New York: Atherton Press.

Csikszentmihalyi, M. (1988). Society, culture, and person: A systems view of creativity. In R. J. Sternberg (Ed.), *The nature of creativity* (pp. 325–339). Cambridge, England: Cambridge University Press.

Davis, G. A. (1971). Instruments useful in studying creative behavior and creative talent, Part II: Noncommercially available instruments. *Journal of Creative Behavior, 5*, 162–165.

Davis, G. A. (1973). *Psychology of problem solving*. New York: Basic Books.

Davis, G. A. (1975). In frumious pursuit of the creative person. *Journal of Creative Behavior, 9*, 75–87.

Davis, G. A. (1976). In frumious pursuit of the creative person. In A. M. Biondi & S. J. Parnes (Eds.), *Assessing creative growth: The tests and measured changes* (pp. 243–257). Buffalo, NY: Bearly.

Davis, G. A. (1986). *Creativity is forever* (2nd ed.). Dubuque, IA: Kendall/Hunt.

Davis, G. A., & Rimm, S. (1980). *Group Inventory for Finding Interests II*. Watertown, WI: Educational Assessment Service.

Davis, G. A., & Rimm, S. (1982). Group Inventory for Finding Interests (GIFFI) I and II: Instruments for identifying creative potential in the junior and senior high school. *Journal of Creative Behavior, 16*, 50–57.

de Bono, E. (1967). *New think: The use of lateral thinking in the generation of new ideas*. New York: Basic Books.

de Bono, E. (1970). *Lateral thinking: Creativity step by step*. New York: Harper & Row.

Dial, P. C. (1975). *Identifying and serving the talented student in Louisiana schools*. Baton Rouge: Louisiana Department of Education, Gifted and Talented Programs.

Edwards, A. L. (1957). *Edwards Personal Preference Schedule*. New York: Psychological Corporation.

Flanagan, J. C. (1963). The definition and measurement of ingenuity. In C. W. Taylor & F. Barron (Eds.), *Scientific creativity: Its recognition and development* (pp. 89–98). New York: Wiley.

Flanagan, J. C. (1976). Ingenuity test. In A. M. Biondi & S. J. Parnes (Eds.), *Assessing creative growth: The tests and measured changes* (pp. 117–119). Buffalo, NY: Bearly.

Feldman, D. H. (1986). *Nature's gambit*. New York: Basic Books.

Getzels, J. W., & Jackson, D. W. (1962). *Creativity and intelligence*. New York: Wiley.

Ghiselin, B. (Ed.). (1952). *The creative process*. New York: Mentor.

Ghiselin, B. (1963). Ultimate criteria for two levels of creativity. In C. W. Taylor & F. Barron (Eds.), *Scientific creativity: Its recognition and development* (pp. 30–43). New York: Wiley.

Glover, J. A., Ronning, R., & Reynolds, C. R. (Eds.). (1989). *Handbook of creativity*. New York: Plenum.

Gordon, W. J. J. (1961). *Synectics*. New York: Harper & Row.

Gough, H. G. (1957). *The California Psychological Inventory*. Palo Alto, CA: Consulting Psychologists Press.

Guilford, J. P. (1950). Creativity. *American Psychologist, 5*, 444–454.

Guilford, J. P. (1956). Structure of intellect. *Psychological Bulletin, 53*, 267–293.

Guilford, J. P. (1959). *Personality*. New York: McGraw-Hill.

Guilford, J. P. (1960). Basic conceptual problems of the psychology of thinking. *Annals of the New York Academy of Sciences, 91*, 6–21.

Guilford, J. P. (1967). *The nature of human intelligence*. New York: McGraw-Hill.

Guilford, J. P. (1971). *Creativity Tests for Children (CTC)*. Orange, CA: Sheridan Psychological Services.

Guilford, J. P. (1976). Creativity: Its measurement and development. In A. Biondi & S. J. Parnes (Eds.), *Assessing creative growth: The tests and measured changes* (pp. 2–26). Buffalo, NY: Bearly.

Guilford, J. P. (1977). *Way beyond the IQ*. Buffalo, NY: Bearly.

Guilford, J. P. (1986). *Creative talents: Their nature, uses and development*. Buffalo, NY: Bearly.

Haensly, P. A., & Reynolds, C. R. (1989). Creativity and intelligence. In J. A. Glover, R. R. Ronning, & C. R. Reynolds (Eds.), *A handbook of creativity: Assessment, research, and theory*. New York: Plenum.

Haensly, P. A., Reynolds, C. R., & Nash, W. R. (1986). Giftedness: Coalescence, context, conflict, and commitment. In R. J. Sternberg & J. E. Davidson (Eds.), *Conceptions of giftedness* (pp. 128–148). Cambridge, England: Cambridge University Press.

Heist, P. (1968). Considerations in the assessment of creativity. In P. Heist (Ed.), *The creative college student: An unmet challenge* (pp. 208–223). San Francisco: Jossey-Bass.

Heist, P., McConnell, T. R., Webster, H., & Yonge, G. (1968). *The Omnibus Personality Inventory* (rev. version). Berkeley: University of California, Center for Research and Development in Higher Education.

Hoepfner, R., & Hemenway, J. (1973). *Test of Creative Potential (TCP)*. Hollywood, CA: Monitor.

Jackson, P. W., & Messick, S. (1967). The person, the product, and the response: Conceptual problems in the assessment of creativity. In J. Kagan (Ed.), *Creativity and learning* (pp. 1–19). Boston: Houghton Mifflin.

Jellen, H. G., & Urban, K. K. (1986). The TCT-DP (Test for Creative Thinking–Drawing Production): An instrument that can be applied to most age and ability groups. *Creative Child and Adult Quarterly, 11*, 138–155.

Kaltsounis, B. (1971). Instruments useful in studying creative behavior and creative talent, Part I: Commerically available instruments. *Journal of Creative Behavior, 5*, 117–126.

Kaltsounis, B. (1972). Additional instruments useful in studying creative behavior and creative talent, Part III: Noncommercially available instruments. *Journal of Creative Behavior, 16*, 268–274.

Kaltsounis, B., & Honeywell, L. (1980). Additional instruments useful in studying creative behavior and creative talent, Part IV: Noncommercially available instruments. *Journal of Creative Behavior, 14*, 56–67.

Kaufman, A. S. (1979). *Intelligent testing with the WISC-R*. New York: Wiley.

Kawakita, J. (1977). *A study of intellectual exploration*. Tokyo: Kodansha.

Kubie, L. S. (1958). *The neurotic distortion of the creative process*. Lawrence: University of Kansas Press.

Kulp, M., & Tarter, B. J. (1986). The Creative Processes Rating Scale. *Creative Child and Adult Quarterly, 11*, 163–173, 176.

MacKinnon, D. W. (1962). The nature and nurture of creative talent. *American Psychologist, 17*, 484–495.

MacKinnon, D. W. (1976). Architects, personality types, and creativity. In A. Rothenberg and C. R. Hausman (Eds.), *The creativity question* (pp. 175–179). Durham, NC: Duke University Press.

MacKinnon, D. W. (1978). Educating for creativity: A modern myth? In G. A. Davis & J. A. Scott (Eds.), *Training creative thinking* (pp. 194–207). Melbourne, FL: Krieger.

May, R. (1975). *The courage to create*. New York: Norton.

Mednick, S. A., & Mednick, M. T. (1967). *Remote Associates Test*. Boston: Houghton Mifflin.

Meeker, M., Meeker, R., & Roid, G. H. (1985). *Structure of Intellect Learning Abilities Tests (SOI-LAT) manual*. Los Angeles: Western Psychological Services.

Mitchell, J. V. (Ed.). (1983). *Tests in print III*. Lincoln: University of Nebraska Press.

Mitchell, J. V. (Ed.). (1985). *The ninth mental measurements yearbook*. Lincoln: University of Nebraska Press.

Myers, I. B., & Briggs, K. C. (1957). *The Myers–Briggs Type Indicator*. Princeton, NJ: Educational Testing Service.

Nakayama, M. (1977). *NM method*. Tokyo: Sanno College Press.

O'Connor, J. (1945). *Square pegs in square holes*. Garden City, NY: Doubleday.

Osborn, A. F. (1963). *Applied imagination* (3rd ed.). New York: Scribner's.

Parnes, S. J. (1962). Can creativity be increased? In S. J. Parnes & H. F. Harding (Eds.), *A source book for creative thinking* (pp. 185–191). New York: Scribner's.

Parnes, S. J. (1981). *The magic of your mind*. Buffalo, NJ: Bearly.

Parnes, S. J., Noller, R. B., & Biondi, A. M. (1971). *Guide to creative action*. New York: Scribner's.

Prince, G. (1970). *The practice of creativity*. New York: Harper & Row.

Renzulli, J. S. (1983, September–October). Rating the behavioral characteristics of superior students. *G/C/T*, pp. 30–35.

Renzulli, J. S., & Hartman, R. K. (1971). Scale for Rating Behavioral Characteristics of Superior Students. *Exceptional Children, 38*, 243–248.

Ribot, T. (1906). *Essays on the creative imagination*. London: Routledge & Kegan Paul.

Rimm, S. (1976). *GIFT: Group Inventory for Finding Talent*. Watertown, WI: Educational Assessment Service.

Rimm, S. (1983). *Preschool and Kindergarten Interest Descriptor*. Watertown, WI: Educational Assessment Service.

Rimm, S., & Davis, G. A. (1976). GIFT: An instrument for the identification of creativity. *Journal of Creative Behavior, 10*, 178–182.

Rimm, S., & Davis, G. A. (1979). *Group Inventory for Finding Interests I*. Watertown, WI: Educational Assessment Service.

Rimm, S., & Davis, G. A. (1980). Five years of international research with GIFT: An instrument for the identification of creativity. *Journal of Creative Behavior, 14*, 35–46.

Rimm, S., & Davis, G. A. (1983, September–October). Identifying creativity, Part II. *G/C/T*, pp. 19–23.

Roe, A. (1951). A psychological study of physical scientists. *Genetic Psychology Monographs, 43*, 121–235.

Roe, A. (1953). A psychological study of eminent psychologists and anthropologists and a comparison with biological and physical scientists. *Psychological Monographs, 67*(2, Whole No. 352).

Sattler, J. M. (1974). *Assessment of children's intelligence* (rev. ed.). Philadelphia: W. B. Saunders.

Schaefer, C. E. (1971). *Creativity attitude survey*. Jacksonville, IL: Psychologists and Educators.

Selye, H. (1962). The gift for basic research. In G. Z. F. Bereday & J. A. Lauwerys (Eds.), *The gifted child: The yearbook of education* (pp. 339–408). New York: Harcourt, Brace & World.

Simonton, D. K. (1984). *Genius, creativity, and leadership: Historiometric inquiries*. Cambridge, MA: Harvard University Press.

Simonton, D. K. (1988). Creativity, leadership and chance. In R. Sternberg (Ed.), *The nature of creativity* (pp. 386–426). Cambridge, England: Cambridge University Press.

Spearman, C. E. (1930). *Creative mind*. Cambridge, England: Cambridge University Press.

Starkweather, E. K. (1976). Creativity research instruments designed for use with preschool children. In A. M. Biondi & S. J. Parnes (Eds.), *Assessing creative growth: The tests and measured changes* (pp. 79–90). Buffalo, NY: Bearly.

Starkweather, E. K., & Cowling, F. G. (1963). The measurement of conforming and nonconforming behavior in presschool children. *Proceedings of the Oklahoma Academy of Science, 44*, 168–180.

Stein, M. I. (1953). Creativity and culture. *Journal of Psychology, 36*, 311–322.

Sternberg, R. J. (1988). A three-facet model of creativity. In R. Sternberg (Ed.), *The nature of creativity* (pp. 125–147). Cambridge, England: Cambridge University Press.

Sternberg, R. J., & Wagner, R. K. (1986). *Practical intelligence. Nature and origins of competence in the everyday world*. Cambridge, England: Cambridge University Press.

Stewart, G. W. (1950). Can productive thinking be taught? *Journal of Higher Education, 21*, 411–414.

Sykes, Christopher (1988, March 22). *The man who loved numbers* (NOVA Program No. 1508). (Transcript available from Journal Graphics, 267 Broadway, New York, NY 10007)

Taylor, I. A. (1959). The nature of the creative process. In P. Smith (Ed.), *Creativity* (pp. 51–82). New York: Hastings House.

Taylor, C. W. (1988). Various approaches to the definitions of creativity. In R. J. Sternberg (Ed.), *The nature of creativity* (pp. 99–121). Cambridge, England: Cambridge University Press.

Thurstone, L. L. (1952). Creative talent. In L. L. Thurstone (Ed.), *Applications of psychology* (pp. 18–37). New York: Harper & Row.

Torrance, E. P. (1955). Techniques for studying individual and group adaptation in emergencies and extreme conditions. In *Air Force human engineering personnel and training research* (pp. 286–297). Washington, DC: National Academy of Sciences/National Research Council.

Torrance, E. P. (1957). *Psychology of survival*. Unpublished manuscript, Air Force Personnel Research Center, Lackland Air Force Base, TX.

Torrance, E. P. (1963). *Education and the creative potential*. Minneapolis: University of Minnesota Press.

Torrance, E. P. (1965). *Rewarding creative behavior*. Englewood Cliffs, NJ: Prentice-Hall.

Torrance, E. P. (1966). *The Torrance Tests of Creative Thinking: Technical–norms manual* (research ed.). Princeton, NJ: Personnel Press.

Torrance, E. P. (1967). Scientific views of creativity and factors affecting its growth. In J. Kagan (Ed.), *Creativity and learning* (pp. 73–91). Boston: Houghton Mifflin.

Torrance, E. P. (1970b). *Encouraging creativity in the classroom*. Dubuque, IA: William C. Brown.

Torranmce, E. P. (1971). Are the Torrance Tests of Creative Thinking biased against or in favor of disadvantaged groups? *Gifted Child Quarterly, 15*, 75–80.

Torrance, E. P. (1972a). Career patterns and peak creative experiences of creative high school students 12 years later. *Gifted Child Quarterly, 16*, 75–88.

Torrance, E. P. (1972b). Predictive validity of the Torrance Tests of Creative Thinking. *Journal of Creative Behavior, 6*, 236–252.

Torrance, E. P. (1974). *The Torrance Tests of Creative Thinking: Technical–norms manual*. Bensenville, IL: Scholastic Testing Service.

Torrance, E. P. (1975). Sociodrama as a creative problem solving approach to studying the future. *Journal of Creative Behavior, 9*, 182–195.

Torrance, E. P. (1979a). *The search for satori and creativity*. Buffalo, NY: Bearly.

Torrance, E. P. (1979b). An instructional model for enhancing incubation. *Journal of Creative Behavior, 13*, 23–35.

Torrance, E. P. (1981). Predicting the creativity of elementary school children (1958–1980)—and the teacher who made a "difference." *Gifted Child Quarterly, 25*, 55–62.

Torrance, E. P. (1982). Sounds and images productions of elementary school pupils as predictors of the creative achievement of young adults. *Creative Child and Adult Quarterly, 7*, 8–14.

Torrance, E. P. (1987a). *Guidelines for administration and scoring/comments on using the Torrance Tests of Creative Thinking*. Bensenville, IL: Scholastic Testing Service.

Torrance, E. P. (1987b). *Survey of the uses of the Torrance Tests of Creative Thinking*. Bensenville, IL: Scholastic Testing Service.

Torrance, E. P. (1988). The nature of creativity as manifest in its testing. In R. J. Sternberg (Ed.), *The nature of creativity* (pp. 43–75). Cambridge, England: Cambridge University Press.

Torrance, E. P. (in press). *The blazing drive: The creative personality*. Buffalo, NY: Bearly.

Torrance, E. P., & Ball, O. E. (1984). *Torrance Tests of Creative Thinking: Streamlined (revised) manual, figural forms A and B*. Bensenville, IL: Scholastic Testing Service.

Torrance, E. P., Khatena, J., & Cunningham, B. F. (1973). *Thinking Creatively with Sounds and Words*. Bensenville, IL: Scholastic Testing Service.

Torrance, E. P., & Wu, T. H. (1981). A comparative longitudinal study of the adult creative achievements of elementary school children identified as highly intelligent and highly creative. *Creative Child and Adult Quarterly, 6,* 71–76.

Tourangeau, R., & Sternberg, R. J. (1981). Aptness in metaphor. *Cognitive Psychology, 13,* 27–55.

Wallach, M. A., & Kogan, N. (1965). *Modes of thinking in young children.* New York: Holt.

Wallas, G. (1926). *The art of thought.* New York: Harcourt, Brace & World.

Whipple, G. M. (1973). *Manual for mental and physical tests.* New York: Arno Press. (Original work published 1915)

Whiting, B. (1976). How to predict creativity from biographical data. In A. M. Biondi & S. J. Parnes (Eds.), *Assessing creative growth: The tests and measured changes* (pp. 233–241). Buffalo, NY: Bearly.

Williams, F. (1980). *Creativity assessment packet.* Buffalo: NY: DOK.

Wilson, R. C. (1956). The program for gifted children in the Portland, Oregon, schools. In C. W. Taylor (Ed.), *The 1955 University of Utah research conference on the identification of creative scientific talent* (pp. 14–22). Salt Lake City: University of Utah Press.

Wittrock, M. C. (1974). Learning as a generative process. *Educational Psychologist, 11,* 87–95.

30

Computerized Assessment

C. SUE McCULLOUGH
Texas Woman's University

Widespread availability of personal computers has increased the use of computerized assessment procedures in psychological assessment. "Computerized assessment," as defined by this chapter, includes all those procedures that incorporate computer assistance to assess the progress of children in meeting educational or behavioral goals. This includes computer-adapted testing (CAT); traditional tests, questionnaires, or interviews directly administered on the computer; automated data recording of directly observed behavior; test scoring, analysis, and interpretation; and use of computer simulations (or other procedures possible only on the computer) to assess skills related to educational progress.

The focus of this chapter is on reviewing computerized assessment procedures and addressing issues raised by computer users and published research. The chapter is organized into four sections. The introductory section contains a brief history of computerized assessment. The second section defines each application and presents general background information and research findings. The third section reviews issues related to computerized assessment, and the last section discusses future trends.

A BRIEF HISTORY OF COMPUTERIZED ASSESSMENT

The potential for computer utilization in traditional assessment practices has long been recognized. In 1968, Green predicted "the inevitable computer conquest of testing" (Green, 1970, p. 194). The predicted revolution has been slow but deliberate, as psychological and educational measurement has changed under the influence of the computer. The availability of computers during the 1960s permitted the processing of large amounts of data and the analysis of psychometric data in ways never possible before. Latent-trait theory, computer-adapted testing, and computerized assessment, hypothesized years earlier (Cowden, 1946) but not possible prior to the existence of computers, became practical (Weiss, 1983). The advent of minicomputers, and later of microcomputers, made the power of interactive computing practical in research laboratories and finally in applied settings in the 1970s. The major support for the development of basic and applied research in computerized testing applications came from the U.S. military, and, later, the federal government's Office of Personnel Management (formerly the Civil Service Commission). Today, in addition to military and governmental support, private organizations such as the Educational Testing Service and numerous test publishers actively develop and promote computerized testing.

Professional organizations such as the American Psychological Association (APA) and the National Association of School Psychologists (NASP) have recently (APA, 1985) incorporated ethical guidelines on computer utilization into their general ethical guidelines. APA (1986) has also published a guide for developers of computerized personality assessment programs. Practitioners trained in the "old ways" of paper-and-pencil tests have resisted the new technology, apparently because of a lack of appropriate equipment in the educational or clinical setting, a lack of qualified trainers, a lack of high-quality software, a lack of administrative support, and professional caution regarding research support for radical changes in professional functions (McCullough, 1985a). However, there is evidence of growing interest in computer applications in psychology. Special-interest groups have formed within professional organizations; for instance, the Computer and Technological Applications in School Psychology Committee (CTASP) of NASP was formed in 1982. These special-interest groups produce newsletters, software reviews, in-service workshops, and information exchanges for their members, and they have served to nudge their larger parent organizations into the computer age.

In the absence of leadership from the professional organizations or publishers, much of the development and research in computerized assessment began at the "grass-roots" level. Individual psychologists with access to personal computers developed numerous applications to meet their own professional needs (McCullough, 1985b; Roid, 1986). These have included test-scoring and interpretation programs; report-writing programs; statistical programs to assist in determining cutoff scores for learning disability discrepancy rules; creative applications of generic software, such as word processors and spreadsheets; and self-programmed simulations. Basic and applied research has focused on computer-adapted or computer-assisted testing and direct assessment on the computer, usually following traditional paper-and-pencil models. Since about 1982, publishers have begun to produce computerized assessment products such as test-scoring and interpretation programs; computer courseware that includes computer-managed or computer-assisted testing; and CAT programs in reading and mathematics. In general, research on the implications of these developments on children has lagged behind product development and distribution. A review of these computer applications and the published research on them follows.

DEFINITIONS AND BACKGROUND INFORMATION

There are few educational or clinical settings without computers. Virtually all U.S. school districts use computers for management purposes, and over 85% use microcomputers for instructional purposes (Anderson, Welch, & Harris, 1984). Current computer assessment applications in psychology focus predominantly on using the computer as a tool for routine, clerical tasks such as test scoring and analysis, report writing, and data management (McCullough, 1985a).

Utilization of the computer for traditional assessment purposes usually emerges from the need for continuous or periodic assessment of a child's progress toward reaching academic or behavior goals. CAT, computer-managed instruction (CMI), computer-assisted instruction (CAI), computerized interviews, direct computer-assisted observation and recording of behavior, and computer simulations that record and track learning style or other cognitive and behavioral processes are means through which computerized assessment can occur. In addition, computerized scoring and interpretation of test results are a means of uniting empirical research on test score pattern analysis with verifiable behaviors or characteristics of the examinees. Each of these computerized assessment procedures provides a tool for reaching evaluation goals. Each is defined below.

Computer-Adapted Testing

CAT starts with a data base or large collection of facts, skills, and concepts from an array of subject areas placed into the memory banks or secondary storage devices of a computer. For any given area, the computer selects and tests a subset of skills, facts, and concepts, and the individual's basal and ceiling levels are then determined for each area. The adapted or "tailored" part of the test program comes from the branching capabilities used to determine which questions should be asked of which persons. For example, questions about marriage would not be asked of a child. Sophisticated mathematical approaches (based on latent-trait theory) are used to determine item presentation based on previous responses. For example, in a test of mathematical ability, a simple addition problem would not be presented to a person who had already correctly solved a complex algebraic equation. When testing is completed, the computer can then generate and sometimes monitor individualized educational plans or worksheets. In essence, CAT is the ultimate criterion-referenced test.

"Latent-trait theory," which underlies CAT, encompasses several mathematical models that express functional relationships between observable variables and the underlying hypothetical trait constructs that produce the observable variables. When latent-trait theories are applied to tests of ability or achievement, they have become known as "item characteristic curve theory" or "item response theory" (IRT)—terms that are used interchangeably in the research literature. The item characteristic curve is the curve that portrays the probability of a correct response to a test item as a function of trait levels that produce those probabilities. IRT emphasizes both the role of the test item and the response of the examinees (Weiss, 1983).

Latent-trait theory consists of three elements:

1. A set of stimulus variables that is presented to individuals, such as test items on an ability test or achievement test, personality questionnaire items, or items on an attitude scale.
2. The responses of the individual when presented with these stimulus variables (the computer automatically records the response when a key is pressed).
3. Mathematical equations that describe the functional relationship between the observed response to the stimulus variables and the hypothesized underlying trait. These complex formulas allow inference of the individual's performance on the hypothesized trait as a function of the characteristics of the stimulus variables.

When the characteristics of the stimulus variables or test items are known, then latent-trait theory can estimate the unobserv-able trait levels for individuals based on their observed responses to the test items. Although adaptive testing is not dependent on IRT (Weiss, 1983), IRT is useful in the efficient implementation of adaptive testing.

Alfred Binet actually developed the first adaptive test, though his strategy was simplistic in comparison to CATs based on IRT. The Binet test (Form LM) uses a variable entry point estimated by the examiner at the beginning of testing. Test items are scored as they are administered, and the correctness of the responses determine which items to administer next, branching up or down the levels of the test. The Binet test also has a variable termination criterion, meaning that different individuals are given tests of varying lengths, depending upon when they reach their "ceiling level."

Similar to Binet's application of adaptive testing, CAT has been developed to measure traits for individuals with a wide range of possible trait levels, but it has also been used for evaluating mastery. (For more detailed discussion of latent-trait theory, see Weiss, 1983, or Lord & Novick, 1968.)

Computer-Managed/Computer-Assisted Instruction

CMI is found as part of CAI software packages, or as independent programs. CMI uses, and maintains records of, frequent tests of mastery to select what to present next in the instructional program. A concept may be repeated, divided into smaller or easier tasks, or expanded upon, depending upon the individual's test performance. CMI does not rely solely on computer instruction, as CAI does, but rather serves an overseer function. The computer may direct the student to read certain books, listen to certain tapes, see certain films, or the like. When the assignments are completed, the student returns to the computer for testing and further assignments based on his or her test results. Since each student is managed individually, each can proceed at his or her own pace. The computer will summarize each student's progress and keep records for the teacher as well, including conducting an item analysis of its true–false and multiple-choice tests and printing out reports on the group as a whole or on a selected individual.

CAI typically has consisted of tutorial and drill-and-practice exercises with highly structured lessons that involve frequent testing to assess progress and determine which branch of the program to use next. Instruction has usually followed a programmed instruction model, shaping the learning behavior by breaking instruction down into small sequential steps, with frequent reviews and tests for mastery. Studies that have evaluated CAI as a replacement for traditional classroom instruction have found little or no significant difference in student achievement between CAI lessons and classroom learning, though there was some reduction in students' learning time shown with CAI (Lieberman, 1985). In studies that examined CAI as a supplement to, rather than a replacement for, traditional classroom instruction, significant positive effects on learning (as measured in standardized achievement test scores) were found, especially for low-achieving or slower students (Lieberman, 1985). Meta-analyses of this large body of research have summarized some evident trends, such as that found in studying 48 secondary school math and science CAI evaluations. Average test scores rose 0.32 of a standard deviation, which is equivalent of an increase from the 50th to the 63rd percentile (Kulik, Bangert, & Williams, 1983). Learning-disabled, educable mentally retarded, and emotionally disturbed children have also shown significant gains in reading, language, and math achievement when spending as little as 30 minutes per week using CAI lessons and tests (Chiang, 1978).

More recent developments in CAI programs include artificial intelligence procedures designed to simulate skills and strategies of human thinking. These sophisticated programs, now known as "intelligent CAI" (ICAI), have become diagnostic tools that can identify patterns of error, select appropriate instructional content, adjust the level of difficulty, set the rate of progress through the lesson, and deliver the material in a format best suited to the student's learning style (Lieberman, 1985). Teachers and psychologists can gain valuable information for instructional programming from these ICAI programs.

Computer-Administered Interviews

Computerized interviews or questionnaires help to identify problem behavior areas and etiological factors. They are found most often in university counseling centers, child guidance centers, and outpatient mental health centers.

Computerized interviews usually involve an interactive program in which questions or stimuli are presented by a computer to an individual seated in front of the machine. The individual responds to the stimuli on a keyboard (usually with a yes/no or multiple-choice format), and subsequent stimuli are presented as a function of each individual's responses (Clavelle & Butcher, 1977). The computer system involves an interactive decision tree with paths selected according to the responses of the individual. For example, an initial presentation on the screen might be a listing of several different problem areas. If the individual selects "anxiety in the presence of other people" as one problem area, the next stimulus might be a list of social situations in which the subject might experience anxiety. If the subject indicates feeling anxious "around strangers," then the next presentation might inquire whether anxiety occurs with males and/or females or with large or small groups. This process continues for each problem area. Following the completion of intake, the computer furnishes the psychologist with a summary of problem areas, hypothesized causative factors, potential treatment strategies, hypothesized diagnostic categories, and other information of interest (Haynes & Wilson, 1979).

Several benefits of computerized interviews have been identified (Haynes & Wilson, 1979). These include the following:

1. Producing substantial savings in professional time, if intake interviews are an integral part of the assessment process.
2. Providing a massive amount of information on a broad range of topics useful in planning treatment design and implementation, and in identifying additional areas that need attention.
3. Reducing error variance associated with clinical interviews, since the method of presentation is constant across individuals and variance attributed to interviewer fatigue, nonverbal cues, reactions to individuals' responses, or interviewer bias is reduced.
4. Summarizing the findings through computer analysis.

It is important to check the validity of data collected from computerized interviews. This can be accomplished with internal reliability checks during assessment, as well as by comparing derived data with data from other measurement instruments.

Computerized interview programs do have some potential limitations. These include the following:

1. The system may have to be abbreviated or bypassed in crisis situations; the determination of a crisis situation will most likely have to be made by an intake interviewer.

2. System use is usually limited to individuals with "normal" cognitive functioning, since individuals with lower levels of cognitive functioning (e.g., young children, mentally retarded individuals, or long-term psychiatric residents) will experience difficulty reading the questions and/or responding according to directions.

3. Resource limitations must be determined, since tremendous programming efforts, extensive financial commitments, complex interactive designs, and extensive time commitments on the part of subjects are needed to make computer assessment sufficiently flexible to handle most of the intake problems of psychiatric or psychological assessment facilities.

4. Developer/programmer conceptual bias must be determined through studying the types of elicited responses that are constrained by the stimuli presented. Bias in the system may be difficult to detect and overcome.

5. Systems must be constructed that are sufficiently flexible to detect the myriad of concerns held by individuals seeking psychological assistance. Rare but important target behaviors, such as bizarre ideations, delusions, fetishes, or phobias, would be difficult to detect without making the system unmanageably cumbersome (Haynes & Wilson, 1979).

Automated Data-Recording Systems

Psychologists in the schools spend much consultation and observation time recording and directly measuring observable behavior. Usually this is accomplished with paper, pencil, and some favorite recording form upon which appropriate marks are placed to indicate the frequency, duration, setting, and consequences of the target behavior(s). This information is then translated into frequency percentages, duration estimates, and so on (with the help of a hand calculator) and used to plan behavioral interventions. Sometimes more sophisticated observation forms are used that record verbal behaviors and multiple interactions. These, too, must then, be analyzed to obtain meaning from the encoded information. Computerized data-recording systems, sometimes used in conjunction with computer software for analysis of the information, are available. Several small, pocket-sized, computer-type storage devices are marketed to automate the storage, retrieval, and analysis of observation data (Fitzpatrick, 1977a, 1977b).

These automated data-recording systems have two basic modes of operation: parallel and serial input. Each emphasizes different aspects of the observation process and results in a different classification of data. In parallel systems, more than one event can be recorded at a time. For instance, an event key is depressed at the onset of an event and released upon termination. These data are stored in real time to facilitate the retrieval of duration data, and multiple events can be recorded easily, especially if videotaping is available. For example, the videotape may be viewed several times in order to obtain multiple pieces of information. In serial systems, only one character can be recorded at a time. This system is particularly useful in the natural environment when the observer wishes to record the sequential occurrence of a large number of events.

Another automated data-recording system under development (Bourdage, 1989) times and records all responses made while taking a test on a computer. Any test content can be entered into the HyperExaminer program which is HyperCard-based on the Macintosh computer. The program provides feedback on test-taking skills, including the amount of time spent on each item, the exact sequence of responses made while taking the test, and on which questions a right response was changed to a wrong response, a wrong response to a right response, or a wrong response to a different wrong response. The program provides corrective feedback on test content as well as individual and group item analysis information for the examiner. Analysis of the data yields information about behaviors affecting performance during the testing such as pacing, impulsive responding, or changing right answers to wrong answers when going back to review previously answered questions. The program provides direct data on the problem-solving process utilized as the subject took the test on the computer. The program can import video and audio images from CD ROM disks, utilize animation, and is easy to use since it incorporates the Macintosh interface and point-and-click technology.

Automated data systems need to be judged on several criteria, including ability to provide complete information; type and size of memory or storage capabilities; ease of obtaining a printout; portability; ability to synchronize separate data records; the means used to transmit data; adaptability to various environments; and speed of transmission (Fitzpatrick, 1977a).

There are also statistical packages designed to analyze the behavioral data collected and transmitted to computers through automated data collection systems. The software provides: (1) a sorting function that combines and selects events and portions of records; (2) a counting and summing function that tabulates frequencies of selected events, durations, or rates, and constructs histograms; and (3) an organizational description function that computes temporal relationships and histograms (computer data printouts) between pairs of selected events and detects nonrandom occurrences of selected events (Fitzpatrick, 1977b). It is possible to construct a simple program for a microcomputer that will record elapsed time and frequency data (Romanczyk, 1986), so that data can be entered directly into the computer without having to be transferred from another device. For example, the data can be entered easily on a portable or stationary computer located conveniently in the classroom, with a teacher or aide pressing certain keys to indicate beginning or ending behaviors.

Some automated data-recording systems use very complex codes that require long training periods to learn to use, and may require additional hours of careful editing to obtain useful information from the extensive data collected. An alternative to these complex and sometimes expensive systems is a hand-held calculator, especially one with a paper printout that can provide a permanent record, is easily transportable, can record up to 10 figures per line, and is very flexible. There are also clipboard-mounted devices that can be used to monitor duration of behavioral events (Haynes & Wilson, 1979). Another alternative is the use of a small portable computer, such as the Epson HX-20, which has a full-sized keyboard that reduces entry errors found on the small hand-held calculators. The Epson has a built-in clock, a microcassette drive for storing information on miniature cassettes, and a built-in printer. Thus, it is completely self-contained and portable, about the size of a loose-leaf notebook. Romanczyk (1986) has developed software for this unit that will collect up to 26 individual behaviors or events, and does so in either the interval or frequency mode of data collection. New laptop computers have built-in disk drives or mega-memory hard drives that store large amounts of data that can be easily down-loaded to other systems for analyses.

Recording errors are possible with automated systems, and automated systems are limited in the manner in which data can be classified. It may be difficult to code subject groupings, subject characteristics, several concomitant behaviors, or the behavior of more than one subject. More research is needed into sources of error in, and the potentialities of, these systems.

Computerized Scoring and Analysis

Test scoring involves identifying responses as correct or incorrect, computing raw scores for each subtest of a battery, and then converting the raw scores to standard scores using norm tables prepared by the publisher/researcher. No other computerized assessment task has been embraced by psychologists so quickly as computerized scoring of tests. In national surveys, it is clearly a priority usage of school psychologists (Jacob & Brantley, 1987; McCullough & Wenck, 1984). Computerized test scoring varies with the nature of the test being scored. Group tests have long been computer-scored, with literally millions of answer sheets processed each year, producing percentiles, stanines, normal curve equivalents, grade equivalents, and normalized standard scores. Computerized scoring of individually administered psychological tests allows the derivation of complex scores such as factor scores; Bayesian-derived probability scores for low-base-rate behaviors such as suicide (Vanderplas & Vanderplas, 1979); item-option weighted scores (Roid, 1986); weighted scores from tailored, adapted, or multilevel tests calibrated with the three-parameter model (Weiss, 1979); and sociometric ratings from entire classrooms contrasted with self and teacher ratings from individual students (Barclay, 1983). For psychological and vocational tests having complex and numerous scores, such as the Minnesota Multiphasic Personality Inventory (MMPI), the Strong–Campbell Interest Inventory, the Tennessee Self-Concept Scale, or the 16 Personality Factor Questionnaire (16PF), computer scoring provides a richness of interpretive data that could not otherwise be obtained without enormous effort (Roid, 1986).

Some test batteries may be scored easily by computer because each response is clearly right or wrong, or is clearly part of one category or another. For example, arithmetic answers or answers on a rating scale have distinct and limited responses. These responses may be entered into the computer either directly by the examinee (on tests adapted to computer presentation, such as the MMPI and computer-adapted reading and math tests) or later by the examiner, clerk, or a computerized scanning device. The computer tabulates the score and converts it to the appropriate standard score. Other subtests require subjective scoring by the examiner, who must decide whether the response is acceptable, given certain parameters. For instance, a young child's language should not penalize him or her, and judgment is frequently necessary to determine correct responses. Gestures may have accompanied the response to make it more correct than incorrect, for example. The response may also receive a varying amount of credit, depending upon the nature of the response (concrete or abstract). Examples of these kinds of tests include achievement batteries and intelligence tests that involve verbal responses. For these tests, the examiner must compute the raw score for each subtest manually. Then the raw scores are entered into the computer, which converts them into standard scores and may provide other statistical information as well, such as standard

deviations, stanines, percentage of the population obtaining such scores, and so forth. Standardized tests with available computerized scoring programs include the adult, child, and preschool versions of the Wechsler intelligence tests; the Woodcock–Johnson Psycho-educational Battery—Revised (WJ-R); the Kaufman Assessment Battery for Children (K-ABC); the McCarthy Scales of Children's Abilities; the Peabody Picture Vocabulary Test—Revised (PPVT-R); the Peabody Individual Achievement Test—Revised (PIAT-R); the Basic Achievement Skills Individual Screener (BASIS); the Woodcock Reading Mastery Tests; the Key-Math Diagnostic Arithmetic Test—Revised; the Achenbach Child Behavior Checklist; the Vineland Adaptive Behavior Scales; and a growing list of others.

Most test-scoring programs depend on the examiner or clerk to type in raw data. Thus, individual subtests have to be scored in the traditional manner. The computer then displays the standardized scores accurately and in seconds. In some cases, the standard scores are accompanied by a written analysis of the scores; in other cases, a description of what the test measures is accompanied by a discussion of the subject's performance compared to the norm group and/or compared to himself or herself. Some programs can score multiple protocols at one time, while others can do only one at a time. Some programs allow data to be saved in a data bank for future reference and comparisons.

Some programs score more than one type of test—for instance, the Wechsler Intelligence Scale for Children—Revised (WISC-R), the Wide Range Achievement Test—Revised (WRAT-R), and the Vineland Adaptive Behavior Scales. There may be a choice of tests to use in any combination, or it may be impossible to use the program without using all of the specific tests in the scoring program. Some scoring programs also require that all subtests be given in order to complete the scoring. Scoring programs that score multiple types of tests may also offer cross-test analysis and comparison, using a variety of statistical or clinical models. For example, the McDermott Multidimensional Assessment of Children (M-MAC) program (McDermott & Watkins, 1985) follows an actuarial model that considers probability, sources of errors, empirical research, and accepted psychological theory in analyzing 22 different tests.

Computerized Interpretation

Psychologists have long accepted computerized aggregate results for groups, such as national, district, or school norms or classroom summaries. However, applying computerized interpretation to individuals has raised concern for the bounds of acceptable clinical use. Ethical concerns have been raised (Jacob & Brantley, 1987; Zachary & Pope, 1984) and supported. Sixty-five percent of the school psychologists surveyed in 1986 anticipated problems associated with computerized test scoring and interpretation (Jacob & Brantley, 1987).

Test-scoring and interpretation programs include publisher-authorized, privately produced, and public domain versions, and vary in quality and ease of use. The best test interpretation programs are designed on the basis of empirically validated decision rules and are intended for the use of trained professionals experienced with the test instrument and its supportive research. The worst of available programs include private and subjective narratives of individuals who developed the programs with limited reference to empirical studies.

Debate regarding computerized interpretation (Brantley, 1984; Jacob & Brantley, 1987; Matarazzo, 1983; McCullough & Wenck, 1984, 1985; Roid, 1986) has included the following concerns:

Advantages and disadvantages of computerized interpretation of tests as compared to a clinician working without a computer

Legal and ethical concerns regarding responsibility for test interpretation and the effects of computerized interpretive reports in the hands of inexperienced or unqualified individuals, who may respond to the aura of objectivity and authority projected by a computerized report

Proprietary concerns of publishers or developers who may not openly reveal their decision rules for professional review

Insufficient validation of computerized reports, especially those that cannot be evaluated closely

Identification and acceptance of "expert opinion" status with professional review of

software at a level equal to that found with traditional research in professional journals

Scoring-only versus descriptive versus clinician-modeled versus clinical-actuarial interpretations

Each of these concerns merits further discussion.

Advantages and Disadvantages of Computerized Interpretation

Advantages of computerized scoring and interpretation programs are as follows:

1. Scoring is much more consistent and accurate, and retrieval of norms from complex norm tables is greatly facilitated. Scoring errors may result from data entry error, or, more infrequently, from program defects (CTASP, 1987), but overall errors are greatly decreased with computer scoring programs. Psychologists should check to be sure that data entry is accurate and that the resulting standard scores and profiles accurately describe the observed behavior.

2. Consistency as it relates to nonbiased assessment can be enhanced with the use of computerized interpretive programs. School psychologists have been shown to be influenced in their diagnostic decision making by positive or negative referral information about a child's intellectual, academic, and social abilities, (Hersh, 1971); socioeconomic status (Matuszek & Oakland, 1979); and perhaps ethnicity or race (Frame, Clarizio, Porter, & Vinsonhaler, 1982; Matuszek & Oakland, 1979). McDermott (1980) found that diagnostic disagreement increased with higher levels of training and experience. Computerized interpretion programs offer conclusions that are neutral with respect to these biasing factors, and may even produce statistically adjusted data or cautions based on research with minorities. Again, the program merely offers suggestions for the psychologist to consider, but it may serve as a reminder to consider diagnostic conclusions that might not otherwise have been considered.

3. Scoring time is reduced significantly, saving the psychologist routine clerical work and opening up time for other, more rewarding professional pursuits. For example, scoring the Woodcock–Johnson Psycho-Educational Battery-Revised by hand takes approx-

imately 45–60 minutes, with a high probability of error, since many norms tables must be entered and some arithmetic calculations performed. The computer scoring program scores a protocol in less than a minute. A clerk can enter the raw scores and then provide a printout to the psychologist.

4. Interpreting multiscale tests is complex and involves numerous decision rules and reference to a constantly growing body of research. The computer can act as a memory aid and offer a variety of suggestions for possible interpretations of the material, perhaps helping the psychologist recall some possibilities that would not have been considered otherwise. The program may also offer some possible interpretations that make no sense at all, considering all the circumstances of the client. It becomes the psychologist's responsibility to maintain final authority over interpretation of the information collected. (This issue is addressed in more detail later.)

5. Research showing moderator effects (i.e., the fact that certain age groups or ethnic groups have different ranges or patterns of scores) can be included in the computerized interpretation; again, this serves as a reminder for the psychologist to use caution in interpreting the data.

6. Numerous technical advances in profile analysis and statistical processing of scores are impractical to implement with a hand-scoring method, since they require complex calculations by each clinician, with a high probability of calculation errors. The majority of clinicians do not have the time or motivation to do these calculations. Computerized scoring programs do the calculations and present the results for interpretation.

Disadvantages of computerized scoring and interpretation programs include the following:

1. Equipment or trained personnel may be difficult if not impossible to obtain, or training time for psychologists and/or data entry clerks may strain already limited resources. The psychologist in the office who is the "computer buff" may find himself or herself with additional uncompensated duties related to training, troubleshooting, and supervision of the programs' use. Priorities for equipment usage may need to be established.

2. Although the programs reflect current research and theory when purchased, they will require updating over time to remain current with the growing body of psychological research. Few programs make allowances for this fact. Without updating or attention to the need for updating, interpretations given today will still be the same 10 or 20 years from now. An example of this problem is that several major tests have been revised, including the WPPSI, the Woodcock–Johnson Psychoeducational Battery, the Key Math and the Wide Range Achievement Test. Many computer scoring programs remain on the market with the old, outdated norms intact (Krug, 1988).

3. Test-scoring and interpretation programs use advanced technology to introduce efficiency, greater accuracy, and greater consistency into current testing practices—testing practices that had their basis in an earlier period of technological and theoretical development. Computer scoring and interpretation programs may serve to preserve practices that are outdated and no longer serve a rational function within a highly technical and computerized society. The cost of change and the widespread use of individual standardized tests may be used as arguments to resist change to a more efficient and practical mode of assessment. However, these are circular arguments and do not address the fact that there are technologically advanced alternatives to obtaining assessment information that will provide us with better diagnostic information, such as computer-adapted testing and computer simulations that record and track thinking processes. Using a computer to preserve practices that have only a historical basis to justify their existence requires careful examination and debate.

Unauthorized Use

Concern about unqualified users appears to be related to issues of (1) controlling access to computerized programs or reports; (2) the ethical responsibilities of developers, distributors, and psychologist users; and (3) the concern that computer-generated reports have an air of objectivity and authority about them that might give them more weight than they should have in the hands of a client, a teacher, an administrator, or some other unqualified user.

Most large publishing companies maintain strict procedures for individuals purchasing assessment products, including computerized scoring and interpretation programs. However, an institutional order is usually honored and may result in placement of materials in locations accessible to unqualified users.

Another concern is that a psychologist may give a client a computer report as the final psychological report without review or editing of its contents. National organizations such as APA and NASP have emphasized the responsibility of the *individual users* of computerized interpretive reports to be familiar with the research base of such reports, to refer to test manuals as needed, and to use appropriate caution in making decisions from these reports. A computerized interpretive report that is based on data only and is not reviewed for accuracy by the psychologist leaves the psychologist in jeopardy of an ethical violation. The legal standing of such a report may also be questioned, as the programmer may not be licensed to practice in the state in which the report is produced and/or used. This problem is addressed in more detail in the "Issues in Computerized Assessment" section of this chapter.

Documentation of Decision Rules

Validity studies should be performed and documented by the developers of computer scoring and interpretive software. The APA's (1985) standards volume encourages developers to share adequate information with researchers in order for validation studies to proceed, but recognizes the proprietary rights of developers to withhold certain information that might endanger their copyright. Roid (1986) argues that documentation of the validity of decision rules is not incompatible with securing the rights to a program. Some central element of scoring or interpretive program logic could be withheld, but the validity of the program could be ascertained through studying the research base (including all references to published articles) and the numerical decision rules revealed in the documentation of the program, without one's having to know the entire operating specifications of a scoring and interpretive program.

Campbell (1976) argued that research funding to expand and improve a computerized product—that is, to update the product in accord with new research findings—is not usually supported by public or nonprofit foundation grants. Thus, if a commercial product is to be improved over time, revenues must be protected from erosion created by illegal copyright infringement or competing publishers. Experience has shown that an effective control is to withhold keys, norms, or portions of the interpretive decision rules.

One means by which to judge computer scoring and interpretive programs is the quality and extent of the documentation. The documentation should clearly state the theoretical and research base of the program, and should provide examples of the logic and decision rules applied to the data. Limitations in the use of the program should also be clearly enunciated.

Insufficient Validation

Interpretive programs have been produced by large and small publishers and by psychologists for their own personal use; the latter often become public domain programs. Each program usually has a particular theoretical orientation that is used to analyze data from a specific test or tests. For example, WISC-R analyses are available using the Sattler (1982), Kaufman (1980), or other clinical interpretations, or the McDermott (1982) statistical or actuarial methods of interpretation. These analyses vary in the approach used to interpret the data, with each approach supported to some extent by research. One author may emphasize subtest-by-subtest interpretation, while another may emphasize groupings of subtests based on statistical correlations. Yet another may focus solely on Full Scale, Verbal, and Performance standard scores, ignoring individual subtest performance, or may emphasize standard errors of measurement and discrepancy formulas. Which of these analyses is valid? In actual practice, a variety of interpretive approaches may be used, depending upon the nature of the data and the training of the psychologist (Matuszek & Oakland, 1979). We have little research to tell us about the decision-making procedures followed by school psychologists in interpreting the complex array of data with which they work each day (de Mesquita, 1987; McDermott, 1980).

There are also few published data on the validity of the diagnoses produced by these programs. The M-MAC program, a sophisticated multitest scoring and interpretive program, has had some validity studies supported by its publisher (Hale & McDermott, 1984; Glutting, 1986). The classification system employed by the M-MAC program agreed 90% with a school psychologist's classifications for 200 referred school-age children (Hale & McDermott, 1984). Of the 200 children, 199 fit into six primary classifications, roughly equivalent to those used to identify children who do or do not qualify for special education. One problem with this study was the limited choice of tests used for classification. Not every referred child is administered the same four tests as these 200 children.

Although the M-MAC offers 22 instruments from which to choose, some are not widely used instruments. The validity of this program remains to be tested when a number of different tests from a variety of psychologists are entered and compared to the psychologists' classifications and diagnosis.

One study judged the validity of the M-MAC classification system by correlating program output variables with another commonly used evaluation system that purports to make the same kind of judgment, the multidisdiplinary evaluation team. Miller (1987) compared the M-MAC's judgments on significant differences between achievement and ability with judgments made using the same data by a multi-disciplinary team. There was a 52% agreement between the M-MAC and the multidisciplinary evaluation team decisions on whether learning disability special education services were needed. The average percent of agreement in judging reading, math, and spelling abilities was 71%. However, reading achievement was the only area in which team decisions and M-MAC decisions reached significant classification agreement beyond chance.

It should be noted that not every permutation of scores can be programmed into the computer. The programmer makes decisions about what are likely to be the most common patterns of scores and the most common interpretations of these patterns; he or she is guided by a particular theory and body of research in making the choices. It is the psychologist's responsibility in using these programs to be sure that his or her own professional judgment is always the key to appropriate interpretation of scores. The small number of validity studies makes it imperative for the psychologist to be alert to the kinds of diagnoses and interpretations being produced by the program. If the diagnoses start sounding alike, or do not discriminate fine differences in the data, there may be limits to using the program. The important point to remember is that these programs should only offer *hypotheses* to consider as potential interpretations of the data. Nothing in the program or printout should lead one to believe that the program is the final word on the individual's performance.

Attaining "Expert" Status

A generic name for computer-based test interpretion (CBTI) programs is "expert systems software." These programs have developed because of the research into artificial intelligence and complex computer languages that allow simulation of human thinking and decision processes. Expert systems software is used in the medical profession to diagnose illnesses and prescribe appropriate tests and treatment. It is used in the military to simulate "war games" and to make projections given certain scenarios. It guides missiles, tracks satellites, and does environmental and weather studies and projections. In short, its growth in the psychology profession was to be expected. However, one of the issues associated with expert systems CBTI software is the issue of "Who is the expert?"

A CBTI program is usually produced by a developer/programmer who represents a particular point of view or a particular publishing house or test. A tremendous amount of research-and-development time is required to produce an expert systems program that will interpret psychological data, and its developers and producers expect some return on the investment of their time and money. Marketing strategies and advertisements attempt to generate as big a return as possible. This is in keeping with the capitalist bent of our economy. Frequently, advertisements for the program appear in mailboxes and journals long before research on the program has been published. Psychological journals have been a reluctant to recognize psychological computer programs as worthy of the same attention they give to traditional research. That is, validity or descriptive studies may be published, but seldom is the program itself sent out for review by peers, as is the case with traditional research. Descriptions of various programs may appear—at this writing, only one school psychology journal has a "computer" review section—but they are treated as book reviews: simply one person's opinion.

Disagreement exists in the measurement field on the means to determine validity in psychological applications such as CBTI and on the persons responsible for determining validity: publishers/developers or users (Cronbach, 1980; Mitchell, 1986). Moreover, the literature on evaluating the validity of CBTI programs has primarily focused on CBTI programs that interpret the MMPI (Faust & Ziskin, 1989; Moreland, 1985). Even the American Psychological Association *Guidelines for computer-based tests and interpretations* (1986) focuses on CBTI personality assessment programs. CBTI programs now encompass much broader assessment areas than personality assessment, and the more complex programs interrelate and interpret more than one type of test (Sicoly, 1989). The M-MAC is a good example of this latter type of CBTI program. Moreland (1985) established guidelines for evaluating the validity of CBTI programs that have been challenged and expanded to incorporate issues raised by the more complex multidimensional CBTI programs (McCullough, 1989). Many authors have sounded the alarm over the premature use of CBTI programs that have not been rigorously validated (Fowler and Butcher, 1986; Krug, 1989; Lanyon, 1984; Matarazzo, 1986a, 1986b; McCullough, 1985a, 1989; Skinner and Pakula, 1986).

Computer newsletters have attempted to fill the void by publishing edited and summarized software reviews that have been done by several practitioners (CTASP, 1982–1989). Frequently feedback is given through these reviews that results in improvement of the program (CTASP, 1987). However, the payoff to the developer through status and recognition by peers, and perhaps credit toward tenure, is not the same as if the review were carried out by a recognized journal. Thus, by default, the developer and publisher can claim "expert" status in their advertising, with few to challenge them. There are specialized journals in educational, psychological, and computer technology that serve to publish information about new programs. However, the majority of practitioners do not read these very technical journals regularly. There is a need for the "mainline" journals to recognize the contribution to psychology made by research and development in computerized assessment, and to accord computer program development the same status as that given to new test development or other research within the profession. Peer review of computer products would do much to encourage the development of superior products and to eliminate or warn practitioners of poor ones. The "expert" status would thus be earned through stringent peer review, and not self-accorded.

Types of Scoring and Interpretive Programs

Roid and Gorsuch (1984) have proposed a four-category typology useful in labeling and distinguishing among the various commercially available programs: (1) scoring-only, (2) descriptive, (3) clinician-modeled, and (4) clinical actuarial. Such descriptors aid in increasing user knowledge and expectations for the program, and each is discussed here.

Scoring-Only Programs. Quality and scoring features vary across programs. Some programs can score multiple protocols at one time, while others can do only one at a time. As noted earlier, time is saved with a multi-score program if more than one user scores tests with the program or if there is frequently more than one protocol to score at one time.

Some programs score more than one type of test, such as intelligence, achievement, and adaptive behavior scales, and then integrate test results. The user may have multiple tests of each type from which to choose, or may be limited to the few that the program is designed to score. It is important to ascertain the minimum amount of information that must be entered to obtain results. For instance, some programs require that all subtest raw scores be entered in a particular domain in order to calculate the standard score and make the comparisons. The program may not accept a "short-form" version of a test. At the same time, if a zero is entered for a nonadministered subtest, the resulting statistics may not be accurate. Appropriate statistics should accompany partial administrations. That is, if it is not possible to obtain a full-scale score with only a partial administration of the test, then a full-scale score should not be reported. The user should check the documentation to learn the limits and appropriate uses of the program (and the documentation should clearly state these limits). Research and statistical bases for cross-test analyses and comparisons should also be clearly explained and referenced.

Scoring and cross-test comparisons must follow psychometrically correct procedures. That is, grade equivalents should not be compared with standard scores, and grade or age equivalents should not be reported when it is inappropriate to do so (i.e., not substantiated by the test construction and standardization procedures). Printouts should be easy to read and contain all relevant information. There should be a reminder printed that the test data must be interpreted by a professional trained to do so and that the printout does *not* constitute a psychological report. It should also be possible to send the scoring report to either the screen or the printer.

A desirable feature is the ability to transfer the data to permanent storage, preferably with the ability to then transfer it to a graphing, data management, or statistical program for further study (such as a pre–post examination, a compilation of group data, or a graphic representation for parent–teacher conferences).

The program itself should be technically sound. There should be error correction capability, ability to go both backward and forward through screen presentations, visually well-planned screen presentations, clear data entry procedures, and screen notification during data computations (not just a blank screen).

Descriptive Programs. When quantitative data are presented in descriptive programs, they are accompanied by descriptive words or sentences (such as "average," "significant-

ly below average," or "indicates mastery of . . ."), along with a printed profile or other graphic representation, and a list of score comparisons. Some programs with less sophisticated programming use a redundant format to report multiple-scale scores, using the same descriptors over and over. Research studies on the scaling properties of words, modifiers, adverbs, and verb phrases have empirically matched equivalent words and phrases (Hakel, 1968; Lichtenstein & Newman, 1967; Pohl, 1981). With a computer's capability of storing literally thousands of quantitative criteria and descriptive words to give the criteria meaning, sophisticated descriptive computer programs can be expected to produce a comprehensive report summarizing multiple indicators, incorporating a selection of descriptive words based on empirical studies of language, written in narrative paragraph composition, and describing statistical description of differences among subtest scores (Roid, 1986). An example from the Barclay Classroom Assessment System (Barclay, 1983) demonstrates the sophistication of such a program:

> This student is seen as having an outstanding thrust for achievement and is viewed as superior in persistence. She demonstrates impulsive, unpredictable and inconsistent behavior. She appears to be generally open and verbally expressive. In physical activities or working with her hands, she is seen as having an above average level of effort and perseverance. (Roid, 1986, p. 144)

The profile or graph printed of the results can display in one picture an accurate representation of sophisticated statistical operations. The graphics can help to avoid over-interpretation of small differences between profile scales. Graphs can also display confidence intervals based on the standard error for each scale, percentile ranges, distributions of scores as they compare with the normal curve, and differences between each scale value and the mean of all the profile scale values as evidence of test scatter, while indicating which comparisons represent significant differences.

Clinician-Modeled Programs. Clinician-modeled CBTI programs may be programmed to reflect the interpretive process used by a renowned clinician, perhaps the person who designed the test that is being scored and interpreted. In essence, the computer attempts to simulate the thinking and decision-making logic of that particular person. A second type of clinician-modeled interpretive program is constructed from statistically analyzing groups of "expert" clinicians' opinions and building a computer model to simulate their thinking and decision making.

Clinician-modeled CBTI programs offer a consistent interpretive model—one whose theoretical and research base may be well known. For example, Dr. Lovick Miller, developer of the Louisville Behavior Checklist (Miller, 1981), participated in the development of an interpretive program by tape-recording his actual case interpretations. These were studied (Roid, 1986) to identify decision rules. A heuristic simulation was then designed on the computer. Through several cycles of development, results were entered into trial versions of the program and resubmitted to Dr. Miller for reinterpretation (under blind conditions). Examination of the fit between the objectively programmed rules and those actually used by Dr. Miller determined validation of the model. In addition, empirical research findings related to childhood rating scales such as the Louisville validated his interpretations. This same procedure has been shown to be highly accurate in personnel screening (Smith, 1968).

Clinical Actuarial Programs. Clinical actuarial programs developed for educational tests (McDermott, 1980, 1982) and psychological tests (Lachar, 1974) include extensive narrative descriptions and clinical hypotheses based on the clinical research findings for particular score patterns. Numerous multivariate statistical procedures that incorporate test and nontest information in the decision-making algorithms are recent additions to these programs (Barclay, 1983; McDermott & Watkins, 1985). The M-MAC (McDermott & Watkins, 1985) and the Barclay Classroom Assessment System (Barclay, 1983) are examples of this most recent sophisticated technology.

M-MAC examines intelligence, achievement, and adaptive behavior scores of individual students in order to make quantitative judgments about diagnoses such as learning disability or other special education

status. As noted earlier, 22 tests may be used to input raw scores for analysis. However, usually scores from an intelligence measure, such as the WISC-R; and achievement measure, such as the Woodcock–Johnson Psycho-Educational Battery; and an adaptive behavior measure, such as the Vineland Adaptive Behavior Scales, or a socioemotional behavior checklist, such as the Louisville Behavior Checklist, will be entered for analysis. The program uses its stored information on the reliability, standard error of measurement, and intercorrelation of these tests, and calculates the statistical significance of the discrepancy between the scores—for instance, between the WISC-R and Woodcock–Johnson scores. The numerical estimates and clinical descriptions are then printed. The M-MAC also uses the data to prepare an individual education plan, listing educational or behavioral objectives based on the input. As noted earlier, published validity studies are few (Hale & McDermott, 1984; McDermott & Hale, 1982), but the program holds promise of increasing the consistency of the diagnosis of educational disabilities if it is kept updated as the tests it includes are revised.

One disadvantage of the program is the choice of tests included. The intelligence, achievement, and adaptive behavior choices represent commonly used tests in the school setting, but the socioemotional adjustment behavior checklists are less well known and used. How the validity of the program outcomes will be affected, in comparison to a psychologist's interpretations, by the inability to enter all the data collected because the test is not represented in the program has yet to be shown. The program does allow entry of professional judgment in the areas of adaptive behavior and socioemotional adjustment, or the use of other instrument results if the standard error of measurement and correlations with the other instruments are also entered. Some psychologists may find looking up that information not worth the time and effort, or the required information may not be in the test manuals. The computer program is supposed to save psychologists time, not create new tasks for them to do.

Barclay (1983) incorporated 25 years of multivariate statistical studies of self, peer, and teacher ratings of elementary students into a computerized interpretive program that provides a narrative, diagnostic, and prescriptive report on a given classroom. The computer analyzes and integrates a volume of information that would be clearly impractical to attempt by hand. For instance, sociometric choices by each class member are integrated with self and teacher ratings and with achievement scores. The resulting report can be up to 100 pages in length for a particular classroom. The narrative produced is one of high quality, as noted earlier.

Some of the most widely used clinical actuarial programs are those for the MMPI. Validity studies have found rates of accuracy of 79%–90%, as rated by practitioners (Roid, 1986). However, in a study of computerized reports using adult norms to rate adolescent responses as opposed to using the adolescent norms, greater inaccuracy was found with the adult norms (20%) than the adolescent ones (10%) (Lachar, Klinge, & Grisell, 1976).

The accuracy of the computerized descriptions can be assessed by a method of "replicated correlates" (Lachar & Alexander, 1978; Lachar & Gdowski, 1979; Wirt, Lachar, Klinedinst, & Seat, 1977). Practitioners interview each client, then provide detailed ratings on a behavioral and symptom checklist. The clients complete the computer-scored inventory, such as the MMPI or the Personality Inventory for Children, and the scales are plotted onto a standard T-score profile. Each profile scale is divided into "elevations" or segments, such as $80T+$, $70T–79T$, $60T–69T$, $41T–59T$, and $40T$ and below (Roid, 1986). The frequency of each checklist description completed by the practitioner is then calculated for each elevation on the scale. The high-frequency checklist items then become correlates of a given scale. Findings are replicated on a new set of subjects, and only replicated checklist descriptors are used in the computerized report to describe the potential behavior or symptoms of the client.

One means of increasing the validity and accuracy of computerized clinical actuarial reports is to tailor reports to a specific population, such as has been done with the 16PF in law enforcement (Dee-Burnett, Johns, & Krug, 1982) and marriage counseling (Krug, 1983) settings.

Computerized clinical actuarial programs produce detailed, objective, and authoritative-looking reports. Certainly they offer many of the advantages discussed above. The best of these programs come with extensive documentation, including detailed descriptions of the empirical bases for decision rules and narratives, and should have validity studies reported in the research literature. It remains the practitioner's responsibility, however, to validate each computerized report for the individual client, and to make whatever changes or additions are necessary to ensure accuracy. No CBTI program has been found to be 100% accurate. The practitioner must take into account all variables affecting the client, some of which may not be quantifiable for the computer, such as opportunities to succeed, environmental influences in the home or school, and individual responses to these factors.

ISSUES IN COMPUTERIZED ASSESSMENT

As computerized assessment procedures become more prevalent, some issues regarding microcomputer administration of psychological tests and future trends need to be addressed (Duthie, 1984; McCullough, 1985a). Computerized test administration issues include the individual's response set to computers and resulting contamination of test results; cognitive processing differences between paper-and-pencil and computerized assessment; screen format and equipment variability; control of testing materials and procedures; and the practicality of computerized assessment.

Response Set to Computers and Contamination of Test Results

There appears to be a mystique association with computers, a projection of awe and power. Such characters as HAL in *2001—A Space Odyssey*, R2D2 in *Star Wars*, and TWIKKI in *Flash Gordon* are examples of emerging cultural computer archetypes for both children and adults (Duthie, 1984). In addition, some individuals may have had bad experiences with computers, such as being billed incorrectly, displaced from a job, or being told quite often and forcefully not to touch computer equipment available in a classroom or lab without permission and supervision. Some individuals may view the computer as an impersonal, powerful, inhuman beast, to the point where they fear it. Mello (1982) estimates that 30% of office workers dread using computers. He classifies the 5% of this group who show severe, clinically significant phobic behaviors as "cyberphobes."

There are also powerful and subtle cultural and gender biases that may influence performance on a computerized test.

Cultural and regional differences are reflected in the greater prevalence and integration of computers into the curricula in wealthier, larger, urban school districts in the central, northern, and western parts of the United States (Anderson et al., 1984). The children in these districts have more experience with computers, as would children who have computers at home. One study found that past computer experience accounted for a significant amount of variance on an arithmetic reasoning test administered both as a paper-and-pencil test and as a computerized test (Lee, 1986). Gender bias is documented by the fact that boys outnumber girls nearly 2 to 1 in enrollment in computer education classes (Anderson et al., 1984) Male self-selection and female default in using computers have led to the computer center's becoming "male turf"—as socially inappropriate to girls as the boys' locker room (Lockheed & Frakt, 1984). Equity is a major issue in computer education (Anderson et al., 1984; Lipkin, 1984; Lockheed & Frakt, 1984; Miura & Hess, 1984; Schubert & Bakke, 1984) and should be considered as an influence on performance on computerized tests.

Computer-assisted instruction research has provided information on children's attitudes toward computers, an important variable in computerized assessment. Generally, children have shown quite positive attitudes toward computers and computer activities, usually expressing no fear and much enthusiasm about the technology (Lockheed & Frakt, 1984). However, attitudes may be less positive among girls and younger children, especially on the dimensions of ease of use and quality of the computer ("smart–stupid," "special–ordinary") (Williams, Coulombe, & Lievrouw, 1983). Gender differences tend to be strongest among adolescents in computer activity preferences. Girls prefer word processing, data bases, and graphics, while boys

express more interest in further training in computer programming (Lockheed & Frakt, 1984). Most studies also have found increases in favorable attitudes toward computers after use (Lieberman, 1985; Romanczyk, 1986); this provides a strong argument for allowing adjustment and instruction time on the computer before using it as an assessment device. Locating microcomputers in computer labs and learning to program apparently contribute to increases in enthusiasm and positive attitudes toward computers (Lieberman, 1985).

Positive response sets in computerized assessment may enhance information collection. For instance, patients interviewed by a computer program reported a significantly larger amount of alcohol consumption (50% more) than they did when interviewed by a psychiatrist (Lucas, 1977). Another study found that patients visiting psychosexual clinics talked more freely about sexual problems to a computer than to the highly trained professional (Evans, 1979). This suggests that individuals may respond more honestly to a computer, or at least with less inhibition or embarrassment than when interviewed by a professional.

To determine whether taking a test on a computer alters performance, research has compared computer-administered with paper-and-pencil versions of the same test. MMPI research has led the way. At least five companies market computer-administered versions of the MMPI. Research indicates that results are equivalent to those of paper-and-pencil versions on all scales except two (Biskin & Kolotkin, 1977). Significant differences existed between paper-and-pencil and computer administrations of the MMPI on the Cannot Say (?) scale and the Paranoia scale; there appeared to be no set of items that accounted for these scale differences. Different methods were used to omit items on the Cannot Say (?) scale in each condition, which may have contributed to the differences found. Also, since the scores on the Cannot Say (?) scale on the computer were lower than those on the paper-and-pencil version, these results may be explained as representing an increased willingness to make a response commitment in the computer environment. The clinical significance of the differences on the Paranoia scale needs further investigation.

Computer administration of the PPVT produced test–retest correlation coefficients in the ranges of .54 to .74 and were not significantly different from those obtained with manual administration in the standardization sample. Practice effects and IQ differences between the two forms of the test were nonsignificant (Elwood & Clark, 1978). It was concluded that unsupervised administration of the PPVT was possible for normal subjects.

Other studies (Cory, 1977; Cory, Rimland, & Bryson, 1977) have compared biographical variables, operational cognitive tests, and paper-and-pencil tests measuring visual processing of information with computerized tests measuring the same trait. Computerized tests substantially enhanced the predictive accuracy of the operational battery for sonar technicians in the Navy. The computerized Graphic and Interactive Processing (GRIP) tests were developed to measure five "real-world" personal attributes that had proven difficult to measure with paper-and-pencil tests. The GRIP test was more useful than paper-and-pencil tests for identifying personnel skilled in short-term memory, sequential reasoning, interpreting visual displays, adjusting equipment, and working under distractions.

Research into the differences between paper-and-pencil and computerized versions of assessment procedures shows lack of agreement on the comparability of performance between the two methods of assessment, though most studies found nonsignificant differences (Roid, 1986). The type of information being assessed, the manner in which it is assessed, and the relevance to the predictor variable appear to be important factors. The extent to which the response set and computer experience of the individual affect outcomes appears to be a significant factor as well (Lee, 1986; Schwartz, 1984a), but one that needs further research. In any case, it should not be assumed that norms developed on a paper-and-pencil test will be adequate or valid to judge performance on a computerized version of that test.

Cognitive Processing Differences

Three differences between paper-and-pencil administrations and computer administrations suggest that they may be separate cognitive tasks: (1) response time, (2) fatigue,

and (3) presentation mode. It takes longer to take a paper-and-pencil test and requires some thought and writing skill to record the answer on the answer sheet. However, this task requirement may also allow some time for reflection upon the answer chosen. The computer requires only the pressing of a key—a response that can occur so quickly it appears as a reflex response. Taking a test on a computer becomes a less complex task than a paper-and-pencil test. The response given so quickly may not represent the client's "best" response, merely the first one. Given this fact, it is possible that answers may be less thought out and more reflexive in nature. It is possible that different parts of the brain are involved in responding to the processing questions presented on a computer monitor.

Since tests administered on a computer can take less time (e.g., 30 minutes for an MMPI as compared with more than an hour for the paper-and-pencil version), mental fatigue or the lack thereof may affect test results to an unknown degree. Some of the variance in paper-and-pencil versus computerized results may be due to the computerized version's taking less time and effort to complete, leading to less mental fatigue, or due to the outcome's reflecting more impulsive "first-response" answers because of the increased ease of responding. Some degree of the variance may also be due to different cognitive organization of the information presented under computerized conditions.

Depending upon the mode of presentation, the evaluation may be processed by the right or left hemisphere, or may require integration of both (Torrance, 1981). The visual and verbal content of computerized assessment may include more emphasis on one or the other hemisphere's functions. The outcomes of the computerized assessment thus may be influenced by how the individual's learning style accommodates the presentation mode. Computerized assessment can take advantage of the graphics capabilities of the computer. Verbal information can be presented in a variety of formats, either imitating text on a book page, or (more likely) presenting it in a visually more pleasing manner using graphics, color, or screen placement in various ways. The text may scroll out of sight. The individual may or may not have control over timing—that is, determining how long the text remains on the screen. These are variables that may also affect the cognitive processing of information.

Screen Format and Equipment Differences

Standardized formats are the rule with paper-and-pencil tests, but computerized tests often lack a standard presentation format. Some computers have 40, 64, or 80 characters printed on the video screen in a variety of type sizes, fonts, and presentation modes. Some are more readable than others. Some feature color displays with varying color backgrounds and type. Some are black and white, some green and black, some amber. Contrast varies with color and monitor settings. Research has shown color to be a powerful manipulator of attention, memory, and understanding of individuals (Durrett & Trezona, 1982). Thus, screen format or color may influence performance.

The presentation effect of the hardware (equipment) may be intimidating (large and businesslike), or nonstandard (a keyboard with large numbers only, with "stop" and "go" buttons in red and green), or confusing (a keyboard with 92 keys, including multiple-function keys). The monitor may have a 12-inch screen or a 5-inch one. The monitor may reflect a glare from open windows, may be poorly lighted, or may be impossible to see at certain angles. There is a lack of standardization across and within computer systems, leading to a lack of standardization in presentation of the tests across individuals, and thus to serious reliability and validity problems.

Control of Testing Materials

Marketing strategies employed by many publishers employ a metered disk or chip that allows the administration of a certain number of tests or analyses (the number paid for). This is a form of copy protection intended to ensure that the test copyright holder gets a royalty just as if an answer sheet were paid for and used up. The cost per computer-administered test is usually considerably more than that for its paper-and-pencil alternative—from $2 to $10 per administration, more if an analysis is provided. These high costs may provide the motivation for unscrupulous individuals to break the copy protection and have unlimited use of the software. Once the copy protection is broken, the program can be disseminated to unauthorized or untrained individuals, placing it totally out of the control of the psychology profession.

Christopher Evans (1979) addresses this issue in *The Micro Millenium:* "The vulnerability of the professions is tied up with their special strength—the fact that they act as exclusive repositories and disseminators of specialist knowledge" (p. 111). He expects the erosion of power of the established professions to be a striking feature of the "computer revolution." Professionals guard their secrets closely, Evans asserts,

> insisting on careful scrutiny and rigorous training of individuals who wish to enter their ranks. But this state of privilege can only persist as long as the special data and the rules for its administration remain inaccessible to the general public. Once the barriers which stand between the average person and this knowledge dissolve, the significance of the profession dwindles and the power and status of its members shrink. Characteristically, the services which the profession originally offered then become available at a very low cost. . . . In the final analysis, the raw material of a modern profession is nothing more than information, and the professional expertise lies simply in knowing the rules for handling or processing it. (1979, p. 112)

An excellent example to illustrate this issue of professional control is the computer intake interview, now commonly used in hospitals, psychiatric clinics, and doctors' offices. To the layperson, the questions a psychologist asks come from accumulated knowledge and insight, and give the impression that the psychologist is proceeding toward a goal with an understanding of the client's needs. On the basis of the interview, the psychologist may decide to gather more information through tests (computerized or otherwise), or may offer a preliminary hypothesis or diagnosis—a decision that will then lead to recommendations for interventions or remediation strategies. Although this may appear impressive to the layperson, especially if the hypothesis and recommendations "make sense," in most cases the interview questions have become more or less formalized, the hypotheses generated fall into a relatively limited field of choices, and the recommendations follow automatically from the choice of hypotheses. As noted earlier, research has shown that people are more willing to confide in a computer than in a professional.

The point is that utilization of computers may change the locus of control of some of the functions psychologists have been trained to perform. A computer may be able to carry out the routine and time-consuming clerical and record-keeping tasks. Its doing so would free psychologists to have more meaningful contact with clients—to focus on decision making and interactions that require a human touch. Depending upon the nature of the individual psychologists' practice, this change in control of information processing may or may not be threatening, and may have as yet unknown effects upon the client–psychologist relationship. It would remove the psychologist one step from the data-gathering process. It is unclear what effect this would have on work performance and the kind of decisions, interactions, and relationships formed with clients. Some psychologists have sounded warnings and encouraged fellow professionals to consciously consider the positive and negative ramifications of this change (Maddux, 1986; McCullough, 1985a).

Practicality of Computer-Administered Psychological Tests

In a high-volume clinic, a centralized assessment center in a school district, or an environment with a readily accessible multiple-terminal, time-shared, dedicated psychological assessment computer system, computer-administered psychological tests may be practical—that is, if the number and type of computerized tests available are adequate to meet the evaluation needs of the setting. Currently, the majority of computerized tests available are designed for adults, not children. Given that the tests available meet assessment needs, and that several computer terminals are available to give several tests at once, then the cost of test administration and computer hardware may be justified by the savings in administration time. In a setting with limited numbers of multipurpose computers (i.e., the computers are used for word processing, data management and record

keeping, test scoring and analysis, statistics, and financial management), the use of this equipment for test administration may not be a high-priority use.

Furthermore, for psychologists who traditionally go into the child's environment—the school building—to administer assessment batteries, computer equipment may vary from building to building. Availability and location may vary from no computers to a computer in every classroom to a computer lab that is never empty. Finding a computer in a private location with ideal testing conditions (the principal's office does not qualify) enters the realm of the impossible. Just finding a private place to administer the traditional battery sometimes enters that same realm. Portable computers offer a possible solution, but technically these "laptops" suffer from small and poor screen presentation and often from a lack of compatibility with available software. Maintaining a constant power supply, either through careful attention to battery power or through finding a space with electrical outlets conveniently nearby, would be important. Computerized assessment software choices would probably be dictated by the kind of equipment available, not necessarily by what was needed or desired.

Obviously, the use of computerized testing software in the same manner in which we have traditionally used paper-and-pencil tests presents some major problems. Perhaps it is time to consider different ways of meeting evaluation objectives. Instead of trying to figure out how to hook the jet up to the oxcart to reach evaluation goals, perhaps it is time to re-evaluate whether we need the oxcart at all to get where we are going (to paraphrase Papert, 1980). Perhaps the question to ask regarding the practicality of computerized tests is this: Which or what kinds of computerized tests are practical and meet needs not now adquately served by paper-and-pencil tests? Do computerized tests add dimensions to assessment information that cannot be obtained from paper-and-pencil tests? Can this unique information be obtained under the conditions in which computers are found in schools and clinic settings?

Perhaps a practicality issue that really nees to be addressed before a tremendous amount of money and time is spent in developing computerized assessment programs that imitate paper-and-pencil tests is whether practices are being preserved that have no rational basis beyond their historical roots in an earlier period of technological and theoretical development. What is the need for IQ or achievement tests if records of the child's progress are being updated regularly by a computer as part of a CMI or CAT program? What does the evaluation process add to this base of information, whether it is administered via computer or via paper-and-pencil?

To answer these questions, it is necessary to explore in more detail some of the options and research regarding computerized testing. There are some tasks that a computer appears better able to assess than a paper-and-pencil task. These include skills required to use computer equipment, such as sonar technicians must use as they make decisions based on radar and computer-provided information (Cory, 1977). As noted earlier, Cory found that short-term memory, sequential reasoning, interpreting visual displays, and working under distractions were measured with significantly more predictive validity on a computerized test than on a paper-and-pencil test. These were computerized tests developed specifically to measure the skills required in this specialized profession.

Computerized tests may also assess reading skills from a different perspective (Freebody & Cooksey, 1985; Lally, 1981). In a preliminary study of three children, Freebody and Cooksey studied simple timed responses to sets of words and wordlike nonsense items, then accurately estimated vocabulary knowledge through word frequency and response time. Other studies have shown that individuals with larger amounts of domain-specific knowledge are able to access and organize that information faster in appropriate situations (Anderson, 1982; Feltovich, 1981; Neves & Anderson, 1981). The ability of the computer to track, time, and record responses opens up a means of assessment that focuses on the cognitive processes, not the outcome product. For example, in a simulation of a typical school psychology decision-making situation (a referral of a third-grade male who doesn't complete his assignments), experienced practitioners responded more quickly and with fewer, more relevant pieces of information than did inexperienced students (de Mesquita, 1987). Analysis of the thinking process

is possible immediately with the computer record. Training in hypothesis generation and selection of relevant assessment questions and information can follow, and can be evaluated again and again with other simulations.

The implications of this research are that computerized assessment may be practical in evaluating factors related to the learning *process*, instead of focusing on outcome data as traditional paper-and-pencil tests must. Focusing on outcome data alone may not provide the insight necessary to detect inefficient thinking patterns or illogical choice of options. Individuals may arrive at the same outcome by following quite different cognitive and decision processes. The computer can record and represent the process underlying the created product. It can make explicit the series of steps and missteps that has led to the creation of a particular object or result. The user leaves an audit trail of historical information that can be used to communicate, analyze, imitate, train, and clarify how an outcome occurred. It communicates *how* a result was achieved. Computerized assessment is the only vehicle that allows study of the cognitive decision processes directly. The practicality of this information is only beginning to be recognized by researchers (Brown, 1985).

FUTURE TRENDS IN COMPUTERIZED ASSESSMENT

Test Administration

Several innovations have been mentioned previously in this chapter, including using the computer to assess skills in ways not possible with paper-and-pencil tests. To elaborate further, computer technology is changing rapidly, becoming more powerful and sophisticated, and incorporating other technologies that expand its capabilities still further. This includes videodisk–computer interactive programs. Research with this combination of technologies has produced programs that administer a picture preference test (Morf, Alexander, & Fuerth, 1981) or assess and teach communication skills to the deaf (Thorkildsen, 1982). An innovative instructional method that has assessment implications involves presenting a typical social interaction scene, then interacting with the computer to stop the video action to have the student decide what happens next. Depending upon the selection, the videodisk presents the consequences of that choice nearly instantaneously. Social skills training modules utilizing this technology have been developed (Thorkildson, Lubke, Myette, & Parry, 1985–1986). Instead of asking children questions about socioemotional development, it would be possible to assess their skills directly with this type of simulation.

Computer simulations offer school psychologists an opportunity to assess skill levels more directly in a variety of areas. The computer keeps track of the child's responses, leaving the psychologist free to observe, question, and interact with the child without having to write everything down, which can get in the way of free-flowing interaction.

Attempts have been made to automate the Wechsler scales (Elwood & Griffin, 1972; Ray, 1982). Elwood and Griffin used tape decks and complex electronic equipment to administer the full-battery Wechsler Adult Intelligence Scale (WAIS). Ray experimented with a computerized WISC-R protocol that allowed the psychologist to enter and score responses into a portable computer, to be prompted for the next question, and to be informed when a ceiling was reached. With more sophisticated and affordable videodisk–computer interactive systems available, experiments such as these may lead to radical changes in intelligence test administration.

Despite standardization problems with equipment, computerized test administration will probably continue to expand to include a wide variety of tests. Innovative test makers are likely to make use of such technological devices as touch screens, light pens, voice synthesizers and recorders, toggle levers, biofeedback physiological recorders, and voice pattern recogizers. For instance, a voice-operated version of the MMPI allows the client to respond "True" or "False" vocally to items presented on the screen (Richards, Fine, Wilson, & Rogers, 1983).

CAT has been stalled by technical problems, including: (1) the need for large amounts of memory, available initially only in minicomputers or main-frame computers; (2) complex programming and mathematical demands; (3) difficulties in determining start-

ing places; (4) wary psychologists trained in traditional normative comparisons resisting change to IRT; and (5) questions regarding appropriate interpretation of the obtained scores. CAT may be more widely used now that microcomputer versions are being published for the Apple and IBM equipment, allowing psychologists to acquire some practical experience. Interpretation of results requires an understanding of IRT in which the total scores are estimates of the trait, ability, or achievement continuum assessed by the item pool. Roid (1986) explains that an "IRT-based test score can be made interpretable by defining various points along the latent continuum" (p. 55). This is similar to curriculum referencing, which, if done, would result in a scale that could provide both normative and criterion-referenced interpretations.

> The interpretation is normative if all items have been calibrated on representative samples in which all users have confidence and studies have been conducted to determine the relative number of students expected to score at successive points on the continuum (from which some new type of percentile can be derived). Total scores can be given criterion-referenced interpretations by the anchoring of specific items, skills, or meaningful trait levels along the continuum (e.g., as in the Woodcock–Johnson or KeyMath tests . . .). (p. 56)

To illustrate one recent application of IRT theory and CAT, Carroll (1987) described the report of the National Assessment of Educational Progress on national assessments in reading. Standard deviation points from –2 to +2 on the 0–500 scale were described in relation to reading levels—for instance, Rudimentary (150), Basic (200), Intermediate (250), Adept (300), and Advanced (350).

Test Scoring

Computers may assume an increasing role in test scoring as more complex scoring systems for educational and psychological tests are implemented. These include (1) continuous norming (Zachary & Gorsuch, 1985); (2) answer-until-correct scoring for achievement or ability tests (Wilcox, 1981); (3) problem-solving error analysis scoring for achievement tests (Birenbaum & Tatsuoka, 1982, 1983); and (4) item-option weighting (Downey, 1979). This has been an area in which

psychologists have readily accepted computer technology, because it has allowed greater consistency and accuracy of scoring, and
has improved efficiency while eliminating a
routinized chore. When test scoring becomes
even more complex, the assistance of the
computer should be welcomed.

Test Interpretation

Technology advances will allow more sophisticated CBTI programs. Future interpretations of computer manipulated data may include: (1) matching test profiles with criterion group profiles and using multivariate
statistics to determine how they fit (Roid,
1986); (2) establishing predictive links between two or more tests (Zachary, Crumpton, & Speigel, 1985); (3) linking test score
patterns with verifiable behaviors or characteristics of examinees (Roid, 1986); (4) linking
data on aptitude–treatment interactions or
traits with behavior intervention data to predict what instruction will be beneficial to
what children under what conditions
(McCullough, Hopkins, & Bowser, 1982); (5)
linking developmental factors with universal
crises (such as rejection by a best friend or
death and separation) to predict and establish
preventative measures (McCullough, Hopkins, & Bowser, 1982); or (6) producing intervention effectiveness data to increase
accuracy of recommended educational
changes (McCullough, Hopkins, & Bowser,
1982). For example, the psychologist could
input data showing impulsive responding.
The computer would draw upon its data base
to describe possible intervention strategies,
with the additional information that Plan A (a
cognitive–behavioral strategy) has an 80%
chance of success, that Plan B (a token economy) has a 40% chance, and that Plan C (a
computer simulation) has not been tried before. Psychoeducational recommendations
would be supported with research-based information.

SUMMARY AND CONCLUSIONS

Computerized assessment offers psychologists a sophisticated tool, but it is a tool with
limits. A computer does only what it is programmed to do. Since humans are not perfect yet, neither are our tools. The limits on
the system are human limits, mistakes, mis-

interpretation, misuse, and children who do
not fit the system—for example, the 1 out of
200 who could not be classified with the M-
MAC (Hale & McDermott, 1984). Psychologists must always regard computerized tests
and interpretations with caution, in order to
avoid falling victim to their objective and
authoritative air.

"High-tech/high-touch" has been shown to
be important in instructional computer research (Metzger, Ouellette, & Thormann,
1984), where children highly motivated to
use the computers still demanded the teacher's attention and touch. There is too much
information to be gained from the personal
human interaction for us ever to turn assessment over completely to computers. Yet,
used as a creative tool, the computer may be
able to give us insights into behavior and
allow us to observe learning processes directly rather than just outcomes.

As the benefits of incorporating this tool
into our repertoire of professional behaviors
accumulate, we can choose to adapt computers to help us do what we do now more
efficiently, or we can choose to use the technology creatively and change and improve
what we do now. We can hitch the jet to the
oxcart, or we can choose to soar.

REFERENCES

American Psychological Association (APA). (1985) *Stan-
  dards for educational and psychological testing*.
  Washington, DC: Author.
American Psychological Association (APA) Committee
  on Professional Standards and Committee on Psycho-
  logical Tests and Assessment. (1986). *Guidelines for
  computer-based tests and interpretations*. Washington, DC: Author.
Anderson, J. R. (1982). Acquisition of cognitive skill.
  Psychological Review, 89, 369–406.
Anderson, R. E., Welch, W. W., & Harris, L. J. (1984).
  Inequities in opportunities for computer literacy. *The
  Computing Teacher*, 11(8), 10–12.
Barclay, J. R. (1983). A meta-analysis of temperament–
  treatment interactions with alternative learning and
  counseling treatments. *Developmental Review*, 3(4),
  410–443.
Birenbaum, M., & Tatsuoka, K. (1982). The effect of a
  scoring system based on the algorithm underlying the
  students' response patterns on the dimensionality of
  achievement test data of the problem solving type.
  Journal of Educational Measurement, 20, 17–26.
Biskin, B. H., & Kolotkin, R. L. (1977). Effects of computerized administration on scores on the MMPI. *Applied Psychological Measurement*, 1, 543–549.
Bourdage, R. L. (1989). *HyperExaminer* (computer software). Fort Worth, Texas: Texas College of
  Osteopathic Medicine.

Brantley, J. (1984). *Review of computerized Wechsler analysis programs*. Paper presented at the annual convention of the National Association of School Psychologists, Philadelphia.

Brown, J. S. (1985). Process versus product: A perspective on tools for communal and informal electronic learning. In M. Chen & W. Paisley (Eds.), *Children and microcomputers, Research on the newest medium*. Beverly Hills, CA: Sage.

Campbell, D. P. (1976). Author's reaction to Johnson's review. *Measurement and Evaluation in Guidance, 9*, 45–56.

Carroll, J. B. (1987). The national assessments in reading: Are we misreading the findings? *Phi Delta Kappan, 68*, 424–430.

Chiang, A. (1978). *Demonstration of the use of computer-assisted instruction with handicapped children*. Arlington, VA: RMC Research Corporation.

Clavelle, P. R., & Butcher, J. N. (1977). An adaptive typological approach to psychiatric screening. *Journal of Consulting and Clinical Psychology, 45*, 851–859.

Computer and Technological Applications in School Psychology Committee (CTASP). (1982–1989). *CTASP Newsletter*. Washington, DC: National Association of School Psychologists.

Cory, C. H. (1977). Relative utility of computerized versus paper–pencil tests for predicting job performance. *Applied Psychological Measurement, 1*, 551–564.

Cory, C. H., Rimland, B., & Bryson, R. A. (1977). Using computerized tests to measure new dimensions of abilities: An exploratory study. *Applied Psychological Measurement, 1*, 101–110.

Cowden, D. J. (1946). An application of sequential analysis to testing students. *Journal of the American Statistical Association, 41*, 547–556.

Cronbach, L. J. (1980). Validity on parole: How can we go straight? In W. B. Schrader (Ed.), *Measuring achievement: Progress over a decade: Proceedings of the 1979 ETS Invitational Conference*, (pp. 99–108). San Francisco: Jossey-Bass.

Dee-Burnett, R., Jones, E. F., & Krug, S. (1982). *Law enforcement assessment and development report manual*. Champaign, IL: Institute for Personality and Ability Testing.

de Mesquita, P. (1987, March). *The information processing and diagnostic decision making of school psychologists while solving a computer-simulated diagnostic referral problem*. Paper presented at the annual convention of the National Association of School Psychologists, New Orleans.

Downey, R. G. (1979). Item-option weighting of achievement tests: Comparative study of methods. *Applied Psychological Measurement, 3*, 453–461.

Durrett, J., & Trezona, J. (1982). How to use color displays effectively: The elements of color vision and their implications for programmers. *Pipeline, 7*(2), 13–16.

Duthie, B. (1984). A critical examination of computer-administered psychological tests. In M. D. Schwartz (Ed.), *Using computers in clinical practice: Psychotherapy and mental health applications*. New York: Haworth Press.

Elwood, D. L., & Clark, C. L. (1978). Computer administration of the PPVT to young children. *Behavior Research Methods and Instrumentation, 10*, 43–46.

Elwood, D. L., & Griffin, H. R. (1972). Individual intelligence testing without the examiner: Reliability of an automated method. *Journal of Consulting and Clinical Psychology, 38*, 9–14.

Evans, C. (1979). *The micro millennium*. New York: Viking Press.

Faust, D., & Ziskin, J. (1989). Computer-assisted psychological evaluation as legal evidence: Some day my prints will come. *Computers in Human Behavior, 5*(1), 23–36.

Feltovich, P. J. (1981). *Knowledge based components of expertise in medical diagnosis* (Technical Report No. PDS-2). Pittsburgh: University of Pittsburgh Learning Research and Development Center.

Fitzpatrick, L. J. (1977a). Automated data collection for observed events. *Behavior Research Methods and Instrumentation, 9*, 447–451.

Fitzpatrick, L. J. (1977b). BEHAVE—an automated data analysis system for observed events. *Behavior Research Methods and Instrumentation, 15*, 452–455.

Fowler, R. D., and Butcher, J. N. (1986). Critique of Matarazzo's views on computerized testing: All sigma and no meaning. *American Psychologist, 41*, 94–96.

Frame, R., Clarizio, H. F., Porter, A. C., & Vinsonhaler, J. R. (1982). Interclinician agreement and bias in school psychologists' diagnostic and treatment recommendations for a learning disabled child. *Psychology in the Schools, 19*, 319–327.

Freebody, P., & Cooksey, R. W. (1985). Computer assessment of reading vocabulary: A preliminary study of the relationship between knowledge, word frequency and response time. *Reading Psychology, 6*, 157–168.

Glutting, J. J. (1986). The McDermott Multidimensional Assessment of Children: Applications to the classification of childhood exceptionality. *Journal of Learning Disabilities, 19*(6), 321–384.

Green, B. F., Jr. (1970). Comments on tailored testing. In W. H. Holtzman (Ed.), *Computer-assisted instruction, testing, and guidance*. New York: Harper & Row.

Hakel, M. D. (1968). How often is often? *American Psychologist, 23*, 533–534.

Hale, R. L., & McDermott, P. A. (1984). Pattern analysis of an actuarial strategy for computerized diagnosis of childhood exceptionality. *Journal of Learning Disabilities, 17*, 30–37.

Haynes, S. N., & Wilson, C. C. (1979). *Behavioral assessment: Recent advances in methods, concepts, and applications*. San Francisco: Jossey-Bass.

Hersh, J. B. (1971). Effects of referral information on testers. *Journal of Consulting and Clinical Psychology, 37*(1), 116–122.

Jacob, S., & Brantley, J. C. (1987). Ethical–legal problems with computer use and suggestions for best practices: A national survey. *School Psychology Review, 16*, 69–77.

Kaufman, A. S. (1980). *Intelligent Testing with the WISC-R*. New York: Wiley.

Krug, S. E. (1983). *Marriage counseling report manual*. Champaign, IL: Institute for Personality and Ability Testing.

Krug, S. E. (Ed.) (1988). *Psychware Sourcebook 1988–89*. Kansas City, MO: Test Corporation of America.

Krug, S. (1989). *Solid state psychology: The impact of computerized assessment on the science and practice of psychology*. Paper presented at national convention of the American Psychological Association, New Orleans, LA.

Kulik, J. A., Bangert, R. L., & Williams, G. W. (1983). Effects of computer-based teaching on secondary school students. *Journal of Educational Psychology, 75*, 19–26.

Lachar, D. (1974). Accuracy and generalizability of an automated MMPI interpretation system. *Journal of Clinical and Consulting Psychology, 42*, 267–273.

Lachar, D., & Alexander, R. S. (1978). Veridicality of self report: Replicated correlates of the Wiggins MMPI content scales. *Journal of Consulting and Clinical Psychology, 46*, 1349–1356.

Lachar, D., & Gdowski, C. L. (1979). *Actuarial assessment of child and adolescent personality: An interpretive guide for the Personality Inventory for Children profile*. Los Angeles: Western Psychological Services.

Lachar, D., Klinge, V., & Grisell, J. L. (1976). Relative accuracy of automated MMPI narratives generated from adult norm and adolescent norm profiles. *Journal of Consulting and Clinical Psychology, 44*, 20–24.

Lally, M. (1981). Computer-assisted teaching of sight-word recognition for mentally retarded school children. *American Journal of Mental Deficiency, 85*, 383–388.

Lanyon, R. I. (1984). Personality assessment. *Annual Review of Psychology, 35*, 667–701.

Lee, J. A. (1986). Effects of past computer experience on computerized aptitude test performance. *Educational and Psychological Measurement, 46*, 727–733.

Lichtenstein, S., & Newman, J. R. (1967). Empirical scaling of common verbal phrases associated with numerical probabilities. *Psychonomic Science, 9*, 563–564.

Lieberman, D. (1985). Research on children and microcomputers, a review of utilization and effects studies. In M. Chen & W. Paisley (Eds.), *Children and microcomputers: Research on the newest medium*. Beverly Hills, CA: Sage.

Lipkin, J. (1984). Computer equity and computer educators (you). *The Computing Teacher, 11*(8), 19–21.

Lockheed, M. E., & Frakt, S. B. (1984). Sex equity: Increasing girls' use of computers. *The Computing Teacher, 11*(8), 16–18.

Lord, F. M., & Novick, M. R. (1968), *Statistical theories of mental test scores*. Reading, MA: Addison-Wesley.

Lucas, R. W. (1977). Psychiatrists and a computer as interrogators of patients with alcohol-related illnesses: A comparison. *British Journal of Psychiatry, 131*, 160–167.

Maddux, C. D. (1986). Microcomputers in education and counseling: Problems and cautions. *Techniques, 2*(1), 9–14.

Matarazzo, J. D. (1983). Computerized psychological testing [Editorial comment]. *Science, 221*,

Matarazzo, J. M. (1986a). Computerized clinical psychological test interpretation: Unvalidated plus all mean and no sigma. *American Psychologist, 41*, 14–24.

Matarazzo, J. M. (1986b). Response to Fowler and Butcher on Matarazzo. *American Psychologist, 41*, 96.

Matuszek, P. A., & Oakland, T. (1979). Facts influencing teachers and psychologists recommendations regarding special class placement. *Journal of School Psychology, 17*, 116–125.

McCullough, C. S. (1985a). Best practices in computer applications. In A. Thomas & J. Grimes (Eds.), *Best practices in school psychology*. Kent, OH: National Association of School Psychologists.

McCullough, C. S. (1985b). *Computers in school psychology: An overview*. Eugene, OR: International Council for Computers in Education.

McCullough, C. S. (1989). *Evaluating the validity of computer-based test interpretation programs*. Paper presented at the annual convention of the National Association of School Psychologists, Boston, MA.

McCullough, C. S., Hopkins, S., & Bowser, P. (1982). *Measuring potential: Uses and abuses of computers in school psychology* (Monograph prepared for the Iowa Department of Public Instruction). Des Moines: Iowa Department of Public Instruction.

McCullough, C. S., & Wenck, S. (1984). Current microcomputer applications in school psychology. *School Psychology Review, 13*, 429–439.

McDermott, P. A. (1980). Congruence and typology of diagnoses in school psychology: An empirical study. *Psychology in the Schools, 17*, 12–24.

McDermott, P. A. (1982). Actuarial assessment systems for the grouping and classification of schoolchildren. In C. R. Reynolds & T. B. Gutkin (Eds.), *The handbook of school psychology*. New York: Wiley.

McDermott, P. A., & Hale, R. L. (1982). Validation of a systems-actuarial computer process for multidimensional classification of child psychopathology. *Journal of Clinical Psychology, 38*, 477–486.

McDermott, P. A., & Watkins, M. W. (1985). *The McDermott Multidimensional Assessment of Children* [Computer program]. Cleveland, OH: Psychological Corporation.

Mello, J. P., Jr. (1982). Deep in your heart it creeps. *80 Micro, 33*, 373–374.

Metzger, M., Ouellette, D., & Thormann, J. (1984). *Learning disabled students and computers: A teacher's guidebook*. Eugene, OR: International Council for Computers in Education.

Miller, L. C. (1981). *Louisville Behavior Checklist manual*. Los Angeles: Western Psychological Services.

Mitchell, Jr., J. V. (1986). Measurement in the larger context: Critical current issues. *Professional Psychology: Research and Practice, 17*(6), 544–550.

Miura, I. T., & Hess, R. D. (1984). Enrollment differences in computer camps and summer classes. *The Computing Teacher, 11*(8), 22–23.

Moreland, K. L. (1985). Validation of computer-based test interpretations: Problems and prospects. *Journal of Consulting and Clinical Psychology, 53*(6), 816–825.

Morf, M., Alexander, P., & Fuerth, T. (1981). Fully automated psychiatric diagnosis: Some new possibilities. *Behavior Research Methods and Instrumentation, 13*, 413–416.

Neves, D. M., & Anderson, J. R. (1981). Knowledge compilation: Mechanisms for automatization of cognitive skills. In J. R. Anderson (Ed.), *Cognitive skills and Their Acquisition*. Hillsdale, NJ: Erlbaum.

Papert, S. (1980). *Mindstorms, children, computers, and powerful Ideas*. New York: Basic Books.

Pohl, N. F. (1981). Scale considerations in using vague quantifiers. *Journal of Experimental Education, 49*, 235–240.

Ray, S. (1982, March). *Computerized protocol for the WISC-R*. Paper presented at the annual convention of the National Association of School Psychologists, Toronto.

Richards, J. S., Fine, P. R., Wilson, T. L., & Rogers, J. T. (1983). A voice-operated method for administering the MMPI. *Journal of Personality Assessment, 47*, 167–170.

Roid, G. H. (1986). Computer technology in testing. In B. S. Plake, J. C. Witt, & J. V. Mitchell, Jr. (Eds.), *The future of testing: Buros–Nebraska Symposium on Measurement and Testing*. Hillsdale, NJ: Erlbaum.

Roid, G. H., & Gorsuch, R. L. (1984). Development and clinical use of test interpretive programs on microcomputers. In M. D. Schwartz (Ed.), *Using Computers in clinical practice: Psychotherapy and mental health applications*. New York: Haworth Press.

Romanczyk, R. G. (1986). *Clinical utilization of microcomputer technology*. New York: Pergamon Press.

Sattler, J. M. (1982). Assessment of Children's Intelligence and Special Abilities (2nd ed.). Boston: Allyn & Bacon.

Schubert, J. G., & Bakke, T. (1984). Practical solutions to overcoming equity in computer use. *The Computing Teacher, 11*(8), 28–30.

Schwartz, M. D. (1984a). People in the organization: The effects of computer-mediated work on individuals and organizations (a review). In M. D. Schwartz (Ed.), *Using computers in clinical Practice: Psychotherapy and mental health applications*. New York: Haworth Press.

Sicoly, F. (1989). Computer-aided decisions in human services: Expert systems and multivariate models. *Computers in Human Behavior, 5*(1), 47–60.

Skinner, H. A. and Pakula, A. (1986). Challenge of computers in psychological assessment. *Professional Psychology: Research and Practice, 17*(1), 44–50.

Smith, R. D. (1968). Heuristic simulation of psychological decision processes. *Journal of Applied Psychology, 52*, 325–330.

Thorkildsen, R. J. (1982, August). *Review of the use of computer technology in special education settings*. Unpublished manuscript, University of Oregon.

Thorkildsen, R. J., Lubke, M. M., Myette, B. M., &

Parry, J. D. (1985–1986). Artificial intelligence: Applications in education. *Education Research Quarterly, 10*(1), 2–9.

Torrance, E. P. (1981). Implications of whole-brained theories of learning and thinking for computer-based instruction. *Journal of Computer Based Instruction, 7*(4), 99–105.

Vanderplas, J. M., & Vanderplas, J. H. (1979). Multiple versus single-index predictors of dangerousness, suicide, and other rare behaviors. *Psychological Reports, 45*, 343–349.

Weiss, D. J. (1979). Computerized adaptive achievement testing. In H. F. O'Neil, Jr. (Ed.), *Procedures for instructional systems development*. New York: Academic Press.

Weiss, D. J. (1983). *New horizons in testing: Latent trait test theory and computerized adaptive testing*. New York: Academic Press.

Wilcox, R. R. (1981). Solving measurement problems with an answer-until-correct scoring procedure. *Applied Psychological Measurement, 5*, 399–414.

Williams, F., Coulombe, J., & Lievrouw, L. (1983). Children's attitudes toward small computers: A preliminary study. *Educational Communication and Technology Journal, 31*(1), 3–7.

Wirt, R. D., Lachar, D., Klinedinst, J. K., & Seat, P. D. (1977). *Multidimensional description of child personality: A manual for the Personality Inventory for Children*. Los Angeles: Western Psychological Services.

Zachary, R. A., Crumpton, E., & Spiegel, D. F. (1985). Estimating WAIS-R IQ from the Shipley Institute of Living Scale. *Journal of Clinical Psychology, 41*, 78–85.

Zachary, R. A., & Gorsuch, R. L. (1985). Continuous norming: Implications for the WAIS-R. *Journal of Clinical Psychology, 41*, 86–94.

Zachary, R. A., & Pope, K. S. (1984). Legal and ethical issues in the clinical use of computerized testing. In M. D. Schwartz (Ed.), *Using computers in clinical practice: Psychotherapy and mental health applications*. New York: Haworth Press.

V

ASSESSMENT OF SPECIAL POPULATIONS

31

Assessment of Intellectual Competence in Preschool-Age Children: Conceptual Issues and Challenges

KATHLEEN D. PAGET
University of South Carolina

T he issues and challenges associated with the assessment of intelligence in young children have had a long-standing history of discussion in the literature. The stigma of labeling, the limitations of prediction, and the validity of test results with young children are well-known topics to professionals involved in service delivery to preschool-age children and their families. With the passage of the Education of the Handicapped Act Amendments of 1986 (P.L. 99-457), and the resultant increases in services to young children, salient issues are resurfacing and require discussion in the context of current realities.

The purpose of this chapter is to discuss relevant issues and challenges associated with the assessment of intellectual functioning in children 3 through 5 years of age, from the vantage point of recent research, discourse, and policy initiatives. Bandura's (1978) reciprocal-influence model has been proposed elsewhere as an appropriate framework to guide assessment practices for young children (Paget, 1985, in press; Paget & Nagle, 1986; Reynolds, Gutkin, Elliott, & Witt, 1984) and is adopted for use in this chapter. Essentially, the model emphasizes the reciprocal interplay among adult and child characteristics, behavior, and environmental phenomena and the situational speci-

ficity of young children's behavior and skill development. Such a model is imperative as a guide for assessing preschool-age children because of temporal and setting variability in their behavior as well as the emergent nature and inconsistent manifestation of their skills.

Assessment is conceptualized in this chapter as a *process* of ongoing insight into how children think, interact, and behave developmentally (Almy & Genishi, 1979). The term "assessment" is used synonymously with "intervention planning" to reflect the ongoing, reciprocal, and mutable nature of the process. The topic of focus is intelligence in young children, which is aptly termed "intellectual competence" (Scarr, 1981) to reflect the interplay among emerging social, behavioral, and language skills in young children. To quote Scarr (1981), "Whenever one measures a child's cognitive functioning, one is also measuring cooperation, attention, persistence, ability to sit still, and social responsiveness to an assessment situation" (p. 1161). This statement is especially appropriate to the assessment of preschool-age chil-

Portions of this chapter also appear in "Best Practices in the Assessment of Competence in Preschool-Age Children" by K. D. Paget. In A. Thomas and J. Grimes (Eds.), *Best Practices in School Psychology* (rev. ed.), Washington, DC: National Association of School Psychologists.

dren, who display wide variability in experiences and behavior.

With an ecological reciprocal-influence framework as a backdrop, the chapter is divided into three main sections. The first section is focused on the individualized assessment setting—the issues and challenges relative to instrumentation, young children's development and behavior, and examiner-child interactions. The second section is focused on assessment in naturally occurring contexts in a child's life (i.e., the preschool classroom and family). In the third section, the use of play as an assessment medium is discussed.

THE INDIVIDUAL ASSESSMENT SETTING

It goes without saying within an ecological framework that the individualized assessment setting is one of several contexts in which assessment should take place. By definition, the situation is limited by demand characteristics of a particular room or rooms, the individualized nature of interactions, developmental characteristics of the child, and demands from the particular tasks presented. Opportunities abound for gathering useful information about the child's functioning in this context, though the conclusions drawn must take the limitations of the situation into account. The following is a discussion of issues relative to instrumentation, developmental characteristics of young children, and interactive strategies in an individualized assessment situation.

Instrumentation

Recent discourse and research have established formal testing as one of multiple strategies necessary to the assessment process (Anastasi, 1988; Neisworth & Bagnato, 1986, 1988; Paget & Nagle, 1986). Norm-, criterion-, and curriculum-referenced instruments represent the most frequently used instrumentation. With an emphasis on functional assessment tied to intervention planning, curriculum-referenced instruments are increasing in popularity (Bagnato & Neisworth, 1981; Neisworth & Bagnato, 1986, 1988) as important supplements to more traditional norm-referenced instruments.

Bracken (1987) analyzed the technical adequacy of selected preschool instruments and concluded that, for children below the age of 4 years (or functioning developmentally below that age), many tests lack sample practice items and are "limited in floor, item gradient, and reliability" (p. 325). Bandura's (1978) reciprocal-influence model tempers these concerns to a certain extent by emphasizing how the behavioral and personal characteristics brought by young children to an assessment situation affect quantified outcomes and traditional interpretations of psychometric adequacy (Paget & Nagle, 1986).

An important issue relative to instrumentation for preschool-age children is the somewhat artificial separation of some instruments, especially those that are criterion- and curriculum-referenced, into separate areas of functioning. Many popular preschool instruments are described as "multiple-domain" tests, measuring skills in the areas of adaptive–social behavior, cognition, and language. The assumption that each domain represents a separate factor is contradicted by the principle that development is integrated and organized, with considerable overlap existing among areas of functioning (Kagan, 1986; MacMann & Barnett, 1984; Poth & Barnett, 1988). Thus, high reliability coefficients and factorial validity of a preschool instrument may not reflect in a meaningful way the realities of young children's development and functioning.

Interpretation of test data for preschool-age children must account for differences in learning opportunities and experiences with test items. The distinction between functional and specific deficits is of vital importance, because developmental delays on tests may result from inexperience and are interpreted more appropriately as functional rather than specific deficits (Ulrey & Rogers. 1982). In contrast, when two children have had similar experiences, delayed developmental skills may suggest different rates of growth and, in some cases, specific deficits. Moreover, Dunst and McWilliam (1988) suggest that certain types and forms of behavior may not be manifested when attempts are specifically made to elicit them during testing, because there may be no *adaptive* reason for the child to manifest the behavior.

The potential for misuse of tests for preschool children is substantial because of potential variability across settings and time, the potential for longer-term negative consequences of labeling, and the overdiagnosing of children with mild handicaps (Hobbs, 1975). Because of limitations in the instrumentation available, I appeal for their cautious and careful use when the identification of a young child's handicapping condition is essential for obtaining services and insuring his or her chances for optimal development.

Developmental Principles

Assessment of preschool-age children must take into consideration the important psychological differences in thinking, motivation, and experiences between preschool children and those who are of school age. Testing procedures and knowledge of school-age children cannot necessarily be extrapolated downward to preschoolers, because cognitive and emotional factors influence test administration and interpretation (Paget & Nagle, 1986). Thus, though behaviors occurring during the preschool period may indicate a learning deficit or psychopathology if observed in a school-age child, the same behaviors may be normal and expected for the younger child. Piagetian theory and recent studies of preschool cognition provide a framework for understanding these cognitive and behavioral differences between preschoolers and school-age children.

Preoperational Thinking

Piaget (1951) and Piaget and Inhelder (1969) have described the preschool child's thinking as "preoperational" because of the child's restricted, one-dimensional point of view, with a limited focus on a single action or direction. When compared with the thinking of older children, preoperational thought can give the impression of loosely associated thinking and distorted logic. Because of this, we must be aware of the age-appropriateness of a child's reasoning. Thus, a challenge for the examiner is to determine *why* the child failed the task and at what level it was understood.

Behavioral Controls

A child's nonverbal behavior also indicates the limited dimension of preoperational thinking. Young children may "test" behavioral limits, refuse items, or be easily distracted by items of more intrinsic interest. Although resistance and struggle make a reliable cognitive assessment difficult, these behaviors provide important information about the child's level of emotional functioning. For example, a 5- or 6-year old who requires frequent limit setting and attempts to avoid the test procedures may indicate the emotional maturity of a 2- to 3-year-old child. With increased language and extensive imitative behaviors, the child may use "manipulation" or appeal to adults to gain some control (Ulrey & Rogers, 1982). During testing, this growth may be seen in the form of various social behaviors, such as more eye contact, smiling, physical closeness, or verbal responsivity.

Although manipulative behaviors of 3- to 6-year-olds may be viewed as emotionally appropriate, a major problem for the examiner is that these behaviors may not be contingent on task performance behaviors. Thus, the examiner often will have to structure and restructure tasks to elicit optimal attention from a young child. For example, the child may not state an obvious verbal answer or complete a task because he or she may not value that response. This lack of responsiveness may result from not having "learned the rules" for test and school behavior (Ulrey & Rogers, 1982). In these situations, flexibility and creativity are required to distill what the child knows, and the clinician cannot assume that the child values answering specific test items correctly simply because a correct answer is expected. Thus, the application of developmental principles related to socially conditioned behavior controls is crucial for understanding the interplay between behavior and performance during an assessment of intellectual competence.

Language Development

Because most major language or communication skills emerge during the preschool period and can influence the expression of cognitive skills, knowledge of normal language development is important for the professional who evaluates young children. There are several language behaviors that may be mistaken for a language disability.

Two developmental considerations offered by Ulrey and Rogers (1982) involve articulation omissions and dysfluency as a young child learns new words or is constructing more complex sentences. Although dysfluency is normal at 2–3 years of age, it may also occur normally when previously undeveloped speech is emerging at 4–5 years, and therefore is not indicative of a stuttering deficit.

In addition to knowledge of dysfluencies and articulation, we should be aware of differences between spontaneous speech and the child's conceptual understanding. A child may appear to have age-appropriate social speech (e.g., "Hello, how are you today?"), but may still have below-age-level conceptual understanding of words (i.e., defining words or explaining events). Thus, to avoid misinterpretation of test observations and data, a young child's verbal behaviors must be understood in terms of normal language and the child's own development. The use of a language sample from a spontaneous play situation is useful for comparing formal test responses with informal speech.

The professional must also appreciate the level of difficulty of verbal commands used during testing. Many items that attempt to measure concepts such as "alike" or "similar" may be failed because of complex verbal instructions. Failure of a number concept may be the result of complex verbal instructions consisting of two or three steps in a sequence. In short, knowledge of language-level acquisition is invaluable for interpretation of performance on tasks that require verbal receptive and/or expressive skills.

Rapid Growth and Transitions

The rapid developmental changes that characterize a preschool-age child correspond to the transitions, in Piagetian terms, from sensory–motor to preoperational skills to concrete operations (Ulrey & Rogers, 1982). Transitions occur in many areas, including perception, language, social skills, and so on. Professionals must be aware of the important differences in each individual child and must attempt to determine what stage or transition an individual child is demonstrating. In addition, we cannot assume a child is functioning at the preoperational level simply because he or she is between 3 and 6 years of age. A child may demonstrate some behaviors reflecting one level, while other behaviors indicate a higher or lower level. The task for the professional is to determine the child's skills in relation to his or her previous experiences and level of maturation.

The situational variability of the preschool child's behavior and the individual rate of rapid, uneven growth make it difficult to make an accurate appraisal of what the child "generally" does. Murphy (1956) described the young child as changing significantly by the hour. Silverman (1971) found significant differences in preschoolers' dysfluency, depending on whether the children were seen in the home, school, or clinical setting. The range of opportunities available to preschoolers who may or may not have attended programs is a significant variable in understanding situational variability, because test items require various drawing, language, and perceptual–motor skills that are greatly influenced by experiences. Thus, professionals must consider the prior exposure of a child to tasks presented while attempting to discover (1) how the child responds to novel test items, (2) whether the child learns tasks quickly or slowly, and (3) what degree of structure is required. In asking these questions, it soon becomes clear how essential the examiner's flexibility and ingenuity are to the usefulness of testing procedures.

Interactive Strategies

The individual assessment situation with a preschool child affords the examiner an opportunity to use interpersonal interactions as a medium to link assessment and intervention. By doing so, the examiner becomes an important part of the child's environment. This approach is variously termed "testing the limits," "adaptive-process assessment" (Bagnato & Neisworth, 1981), "dynamic assessment" (Lidz, 1983), and the "test–teach–test approach" (Ysseldyke & Mirkin, 1982); its goals are to identify instructional strategies that maximize success and are relevant to classroom teaching. As a supplement rather than a substitute for norm- and criterion-referenced instruments, it is an interventionist approach that begins where the child fails, in an attempt to uncover the problem-solving strategies or styles of response accounting for those failures (Lidz, 1983). The examiner may also alter his or her interactive style to assess the child's social responses to frustration, playfulness, humor, and so forth.

Whereas several practical proposals in this respect are being advanced (Bagnato & Neisworth, 1981), other ideas are at the theoretical stage of formulation. Barnett (1984) suggests adapting Vygotsky's (1978) zone of proximal or potential development where "what children can do with the assistance of others might be . . . more indicative of their mental development than what they can do alone" (p. 85). Lidz (1983) suggests adapting Feuerstein, Rand, and Hoffman's (1979) Learning Potential Assessment Device, in which the direct cause of cognitive deficiencies in children is seen as faulty adult-child mediated learning experiences. Whether formulated at functional or theoretical levels, interventionist assessment strategies have potential for assisting in the direct translation of assessment results into mechanisms that optimize preschool children's learning experiences.

In addition to interactions between the examiner and the child, interactive patterns between the child and caregiver(s) should be observed, and the caregiver(s) should be involved actively in the assessment process. The examiner may wish to observe (1) spontaneous, interactive play with a variety of materials; (2) instruction of a task the child is able to do; (3) instruction of a task the child has been unable to do; and (4) interactions between caregivers when interacting with the child, if more than one caregiver is present. Questions that may be of interest include how each caregiver structures the activity and responds to the successes and failures of the child. In addition, much can be learned from watching interactions between the child and his or her siblings.

ASSESSMENT IN NATURAL CONTEXTS

Because of the developmental and behavioral characteristics of young children discussed earlier and the limitations inherent in any individualized assessment situation, information gathered from observing a young child interact with the social and nonsocial features of his or her home and classroom environments is very important. Although the effects of physical and environmental differences between settings have been part of educational lore for some time, in recent years the systematic study of these variables has increased, particularly in the fields of ecological and environmental psychology (Gump, 1975; Smith & Connolly, 1980). Consequently, we are coming to view each setting as a unique ecosystem in which variables such as arrangement of space and materials, group size and composition, competencies of adults and children, and activities all interact reciprocally with young children's behavior (Rogers-Warren, 1982). Dunst and McWilliam (1988) argue cogently for assessment in natural contexts by stating that "if context plays an important role in affecting behavior[,] then the assessment of given types and forms of interactive behaviors is best performed within the particular context in which the probability of evoking behavior is the highest" (p. 168).

The Preschool Classroom Setting

The assessment of preschool-age children's behavior in their classrooms is the focus of much current research interest and activity (Carta, Sainato, & Greenwood, 1988; Dunst, McWilliam, & Holbert, 1986). Because these classrooms are the site of intervention activities, thorough knowledge of them contributes to a functional link between assessment results and intervention planning. Evidence demonstrates that preschool classroom environments and the manner in which they are managed can have significant effects on the behavior and cognitive development of both handicapped and nonhandicapped children (Bailey, Harms, & Clifford, 1983; Twardosz, 1984).

Several assessment instruments have been developed to quantify children's behaviors in the classroom context and the various components of preschool environments. Among these, several focus on a child's engagement behaviors. These are the Planned Activity Check (PLA-Check; Risley & Cataldo, 1974), Caregiver Assessment of Child Engagement (CACE; McWilliam & Galant, 1984), and the Daily Engagement Rating Scale (DERS; McWilliam, Galant, & Dunst, 1984). PLA-Check determines, for the number of persons present for a given activity, the percentage of children who are engaged and which materials, activities, people, or schedules generate the greatest amount of interest and participation. In contrast to the PLA-Check, which measures group levels of engagement, the CACE and DERS measure engagement levels for individual children. Both are rating scales that permit an assessment of different degrees of engagement. Two types (attentional and active) and three categories (adults, peers, and materials) of engagement are measured on each scale. The CACE measures engagement levels for specific classroom activities, and the DERS provides a daily measure of engagement for all classroom activities taken together.

The Early Childhood Environment Rating Scale (Harms & Clifford, 1980) is designed to provide an overall picture of preschool settings, including the manner in which materials, space, child-level activities, scheduling, and adult supervision are organized and used. The Classroom Observation Instrument (Stallings, 1975), the Infant/Toddler Learning Project Observation System (Rogers-Warren, Santos-Colond, Warren, & Hasselbring, 1984), and the Preschool Assessment of the Classroom Environment Scale (Dunst et al., 1986) all measure dimensions of classroom environments that contribute to learning (e.g., organization, instructional methods, child–caregiver interactions).

In addition to the instruments listed above, Charlesworth (1979) described the importance of focusing on intelligent behavior, not in a test setting, but rather as it is observed in everyday situations. He developed a method called Problem Behavior Analysis, by which problem-solving behavior can be observed in the ongoing activities of children. Essentially, the procedure reveals "a) features of everyday living that are problematic; b) who or what was responsible for these features; and c) how the individual responded to them" (p. 215). This instrument exemplifies the application of functional analysis of behavior in the assessment of cognitively mediated behaviors.

Carta, Greenwood, and Atwater (1985) developed the Ecobehavioral System for Complex Assessment of Preschool Environments (ESCAPE). The ESCAPE combines ecobehavioral assessment strategies and research on teacher effectiveness (1) to quantify teacher and student behaviors and relate

them to academic gain, and (2) to measure simultaneously with behavioral occurrences the situational factors surrounding those behaviors.

With the proliferation of instruments such as those mentioned above, the need arises to determine their psychometric adequacy. Lacking are standardized norms as guidelines for making judgments about the influence of environmental factors on the cognitive growth of young children, although work in this respect is progressing (Carta et al., 1988).

The Family Context

Despite the extensive evidence that the family is the primary influence on a preschool child's development (Bronfenbrenner, 1979), thorough assessment of families as systems has often been overlooked or done "on the run" (Karpel & Strauss, 1983, p. 2). This situation is changing with the increased emphasis on parent and family involvement mandated by P.L. 99-457, although a comprehensive evaluation is a large undertaking for any one professional and points to the need for multidisciplinary interactions when conducting an assessment. Instruments are being developed to assist in the conduct of interviews with family members and of naturalistic observations within and outside the home environment (see Carlson, Chapter 23 of Volume 2 of this handbook; Carlson & Grotevant, 1986; Dunst, Trivette, & Deal, 1988; Paget, 1987).

At the center of this discussion is the message that professionals working in preschool programs, especially psychologists and social workers, need to be versed in family systems theory and the growing literature on family strengths and needs (Bailey & Simeonsson, 1988; Dunst et al., 1988; Turnbull & Turnbull, 1986). Knowledge of the "normal" family life cycle (Karpel & Strauss, 1983), and of the interruptions of these processes by events such as death, divorce, and the birth of a child with special needs (Gallagher, Scharfman, & Bristol, 1984), is important to a comprehensive family assessment. Further consideration should be given to whether severity of a child's handicapping condition, minority status and/or low socioeconomic status, or restructuring after divorce may be causing some families to move through life cycles that are different from those life cycles experienced by intact families. Thus, careful evaluation of "where a family is" in its own developmental life cycle and its adaptation to a special-needs child can have significant implications for determining the goals of later parental involvement.

CHILDREN'S PLAY AS AN ASSESSMENT STRATEGY

Because play follows a regular developmental sequence from infancy through childhood and pervades young children's behavioral patterns across contexts, it is logical to use play behavior as a medium for assessing intellectual competence. Observations of play behaviors and classification of these behaviors according to levels described in the literature can yield important information regarding a child's level of cognitive functioning. These observations can be done in an individualized assessment situation, in a classroom, or in the family context.

Theories of play behavior are being operationalized, and play assessment scales are being developed for use with preschool-age children with various types of handicapping conditions. The instruments themselves are at various stages in their own development, with some used solely for research purposes and others available for practical use. Belsky and Most (1981) describe 12 sequences of behavior, beginning with infant explorations and concluding with pretend substitutions and double substitutions. Nicolich (1977) describes levels of symbolic maturity through the analysis of pretend play and its correspondence to Piagetian stages of development. *A Manual for Analyzing Free Play* (McCune-Nicolich, 1980) helps to explain a procedure for assessment of free play with specified toys, scoring criteria, and videotape analysis. Gowen and Schoen (1984) have prepared a method for evaluating play in an unstructured free-play situation, and for categorizing and evaluating play using content, signifiers, and modes of representational analysis. Lunzer (1958) developed a scale that measures the complexity of play and emphasizes adaptiveness, the use of materials, and integration of materials.

In addition to the instruments mentioned above, Jeffree and McConkey (1976) have described an observation scheme for recording children's imaginative doll play. This scheme assesses the frequency, duration, and diversity of imaginative play. A specified toy set is required, and the procedure takes about 15 minutes. Another structured observation format is provided by Chappell and Johnson (1976), wherein the child is presented with 12 objects and the observer records both unprompted and verbally cued responses.

Largo and Howard (1979) provide a list of play assessment procedures and toys that can be used to help psychologists and educators learn about the developmental progress of play behavior in children. Howes (1980) describes the Peer Play Scale, which is a rating scale of five levels of peer play (parallel, parallel with mutual regard, simple social play, reciprocal and complementary action, and reciprocal social play), and Westby (1980) incorporates structured observation and parent or teacher reporting into the Symbolic Play Scale Checklist. In addition, Lowe and Costello (1976) provide an administrative manual along with a complete description of their instrument, entitled the Symbolic Play Test.

Two additional tests used with children who have handicapping conditions are available only in experimental editions from the authors. Bromwich, Fust, Khokha, and Walden (1981) developed the Play Assessment Checklist for Infants to supplement widely used infant development scales. The test requires a specific set of toys, and the infant (or preschooler who is functioning at a low level) is videotaped interacting with them. Fewell (1984) developed the Play Assessment Scale, which is built around a sequence of play behaviors and produces a play age. Children are given opportunities to interact with various sets of toys, and their interactions are scored using the scale. This scale also includes procedures for eliciting and scoring play at higher levels than the spontaneous play used in the measurement of play age.

The description of instruments mentioned above attests to the recognition that play behaviors of young children comprise an important focus of our assessment activities. A state-of-the-art analysis of the instruments would suggest that they vary greatly along dimensions such as functionality, reliability, and theoretical soundness. Nevertheless, they hold much promise. In addition, curricula and instructional materials that use play as a vehicle for intervention programming are being developed. The interested reader is referred to Fewell and Kaminski (1988) for additional information about these materials.

SUMMARY AND CONCLUSIONS

The assessment of intellectual competence in preschool-age children requires special attention to issues and challenges unique to this age group. Among these issues are the variability in young children's exposure to structured learning situations and experience with assessment measures; rapid developmental changes; and the potential for wide behavioral variability across settings. The competent administration and interpretation of tests constitute just one phase of a multiphase process involving additional assessment of intellectual competence as it is manifested in the natural contexts in which the child functions. The application of developmental principles, testing-the-limits procedures, observation of play behaviors, and family involvement are essential to accurate understanding of a preschool-age child's functioning. Professionals in education and psychology who understand the importance of these issues will find the next decade an exciting one with respect to the expansion of assessment activities with young children.

REFERENCES

Almy, M., & Genishi, C. (1979). *Ways of studying children* (rev. ed.). New York: Teachers College Press.

Anastasi, A. (1988). *Psychological testing* (6th ed.). New York: Macmillan.

Bagnato, S., & Neisworth, J. (1981). *Linking developmental assessment and curricula*. Rockville, MD: Aspen Systems Corporation.

Bailey, D. B., Harms, T., & Clifford, R. M. (1983). Matching changes in preschool environments to desired changes in child behavior. *Journal of the Division for Early Childhood, 1*, 61–68.

Bailey, D. B., & Simeonsson, R. (1988). Home-based early interventions. In S. L. Odom & M. B. Karnes (Ed.), *Early intervention for infants and children with handicaps* (pp. 199–216). Baltimore: Paul H. Brookes.

Bandura, A. (1978). The self system in reciprocal determinism. *American Psychologist, 33*, 344–358.

Barnett, D. W. (1984). An organizational approach to preschool services: Psychological screening, assessment, and intervention. In C. Maher, R. Illback, & J. Zins (Eds.), *Organizational psychology in the schools: A handbook for practitioners* (pp. 53–82). Springfield, IL: Charles C Thomas.

Belsky, J., & Most, R. R. (1981). From exploration to play: A cross-sectional study of infant free play behavior. *Developmental Psychology, 17*, 630–639.

Bracken, B. A. (1987). Limitations of preschool instruments and standards for minimal levels of technical adequacy. *Journal of Psychoeducational Assessment, 4*, 313–326.

Bromwich, R. M., Fust, S., Khokha, E., & Walden, M. (1981). *Play Assessment Checklist for Infants manual*. Unpublished manuscript, California State University, Northridge.

Bronfenbrenner, T. (1979). *The ecology of human development: Experiments by nature and design*. Cambridge, MA: Harvard University Press.

Carlson, C. I., & Grotevant, H. (1986). A comparative review of family rating scales: Guidelines for clinicians and researchers. *Journal of Family Psychology, 1*, 23–47.

Carta, J. J., Greenwood, C. R., & Atwater, J. B. (1985). *ESCAPE: Ecobehavioral System for Complex Assessment of Preschool Environments*. Kansas City: Juniper Gardens Children's Project, Bureau of Child Research, University of Kansas.

Carta, J. J., Sainato, D. M., & Greenwood, C. R. (1988). Advances in the ecological assessment of classroom instruction for young children with handicaps. In S. L. Odom & M. B. Karnes (Eds.), *Early intervention for infants and children with handicaps* (pp. 217–240). Baltimore: Paul H. Brookes.

Chappell, G. E., & Johnson, G. A. (1976). Evaluation of cognitive behavior in the young nonverbal child. *Language, Speech, and Hearing Services in Schools, 7*, 17–27.

Charlesworth, W. R. (1979). An ethological approach to studying intelligence. *Human Development, 22*, 212–216.

99th Congress (1986). *Education of the Handicapped Act Amendments of 1986* (Report No. 99-860). Washington, DC: U.S. Government Printing Office.

Dunst, C. J., & McWilliam, R. A. (1988). Cognitive assessment of multiply handicapped young children. In T. Wachs & R. Sheehan (Eds.), *Assessment of young developmentally disabled children* (pp. 213–240). New York: Plenum.

Dunst, C. J., McWilliam, R. A., & Holbert, K. (1986). Assessment of preschool classroom environments. *Diagnostique, 11*, 212–232.

Dunst, C. J., Trivette, C. M., & Deal, A. (1988). *Enabling and empowering families*. Cambridge, MA: Brookline Books.

Feuerstein, R., Rand, Y., & Hoffman, M. B. (1979). *The dynamic assessment of retarded performers: The Learning Potential Assessment Device, theory, instruments, and techniques*. Baltimore: University Park Press.

Fewell, R. R. (1984). Assessment of preschool handicapped children. *Educational Psychologist, 19*, 172–179.

Fewell, R. R., & Kaminski, R. (1988). Play skills development and instruction for young children with handicaps. In S. L. Odom & M. B. Karnes (Eds.), *Early intervention for infants and children with handicaps* (pp. 145–158). Baltimore: Paul H. Brookes.

Gallagher, J., Scharfman, W., & Bristol, M. (1984). The division of responsibilities in families with preschool handicapped and nonhandicapped children. *Journal of the Division of Early Childhood, 8,* 3–11.

Gowen, J., & Schoen, D. (1984). *Levels of child object play.* Unpublished manuscript, Carolina Institute of Research on Early Education of the Handicapped, Frank Porter Graham Child Development Center, Chapel Hill, NC.

Gump, P. (1975). Ecological psychology and children. In E. M. Hetherington (Ed.), *Review of research in child development* (Vol. 5). Chicago: University of Chicago Press.

Harms, T., & Clifford, R. (1980). *Early Childhood Environment Rating Scale.* New York: Teachers College Press.

Hobbs, N. (1975). *The classification of children.* San Francisco: Jossey-Bass.

Howes, C. (1980). Peer Play Scale as an index of complexity of peer interaction. *Developmental Psychology, 16,* 371–372.

Jeffree, D. M., & McConkey, R. (1976). An observation scheme for recording children's imaginative doll play. *Journal of Child Psychology and Psychiatry, 17,* 189–197.

Kagan, J. (1986). *The nature of the child.* New York: Basic Books.

Karpel, M., & Strauss, E. (1983). *Family evaluation.* New York: Gardner Press.

Largo, R. H., & Howard, J. A. (1979). Developmental progression in play behavior of children between nine and thirty months: Spontaneous play and initiation. *Developmental Medicine and Child Neurology, 21,* 299–310.

Lidz, C. S. (1983). Dynamic assessment and the preschool child. *Journal of Psychoeducational Assessment, 1,* 59–72.

Lowe, M., & Costello, A. J. (1976). *The Symbolic Play Test.* Windsor, England: National Foundation for Educational Research–Nelson.

Lunzer, E. A. (1958). A scale of the organization of behavior for use in the study of play. *Educational Review, 11,* 205–217.

MacMann, G. M., & Barnett, D. W. (1984). An analysis of the construct validity of two measures of adaptive behavior. *Journal of Psychoeducational Assessment, 2,* 239–248.

McCune-Nicolich, L. (1980). *A manual for analyzing free play.* Unpublished manuscript, Douglas College, Rutgers University.

McWilliam, R., & Galant, K. (1984). *Caregiver Assessment of Child Engagement.* Unpublished manuscript, Family, Infant, and Preschool Program, Western Carolina Center, Morganton, NC.

McWilliam, R., Galant, K., & Dunst, C. J. (1984). *Daily Engagement Rating Scale.* Unpublished, Family, Infant, and Preschool Program, Western Carolina Center, Morganton, NC.

Murphy, L. (1956). *Personality in young children.* New York: Basic Books.

Neisworth, J. T., & Bagnato, S. J. (1986). Curriculum-based developmental assessment: Congruence of test-

ing and teaching. *School Psychology Review, 15,* 180–199.

Neisworth, J. T., & Bagnato, S. J. (1988). Assessment in early childhood special education. In S. L. Odom & M. B. Karnes (Eds.), *Early intervention for infants and children with handicaps* (pp. 23–50). Baltimore: Paul H. Brooks.

Nicolich, L. (1977). Beyond sensorimotor intelligence: Assessment of symbolic maturity through analysis of pretend play. *Merrill–Palmer Quarterly, 23,* 89–101.

Paget, K. D. (1985). Preschool services in the schools: Issues and implications. *Special Services in the Schools, 2,* 3–25.

Paget, K. D. (1987). Systemic family assessment: Concepts and strategies for school psychologists. *School Psychology Review, 16,* 429–442.

Paget, K. D. (in press). The individual assessment situation: Basic considerations for preschool-age children. In B. A. Bracken (Ed.), *The psychoeducational assessment of preschool children* (rev. ed.). Newton, MA: Allyn & Bacon.

Paget, K. D., & Nagle, R. J. (1986). A conceptual model of preschool assessment. *School Psychology Review, 15,* 154–165.

Piaget, J. (1951). *Judgment and reasoning in the child.* London: Routledge & Kegan Paul.

Piaget, J., & Inhelder, B. (1969). *The psychology of the child.* New York: Basic Books.

Poth, R., & Barnett, D. W. (1988). Establishing the limits of interpretive confidence: A validity study of two preschool developmental scales. *School Psychology Review, 17,* 322–330.

Reynolds, C. R., Gutkin, T. B., Elliott, S. N., & Witt, J. C. (1984). *School psychology: Essentials of theory and practice.* New York: Wiley.

Risley, T. H., & Cataldo, M. F. (1974). *Evaluation of planned activities: The PLA/Check measure of classroom participation.* Unpublished manuscript, Center for Applied Behavior Analysis, Lawrence, KS.

Rogers-Warren, A. K. (1982). Behavior ecology in classrooms for young, handicapped children. *Topics in Early Childhood Special Education, 2,* 21–32.

Rogers-Warren, A. K., Santos-Colond, J., Warren, S. F., & Hasselbring, T. S. (1984, December). *Strategies and issues in quantifying early intervention.* Paper presented at the National Center for Clinical Infant Programs Conference, Washington, D.C.

Scarr, S. (1981). Testing for children: Assessment and the many determinants of intellectual competence. *American Psychologist, 36,* 1159–1168.

Silverman, E. (1971). Situational variability of preschooler's dysfluency. *Perceptual and Motor Skills, 33,* 4021–4022.

Smith, P. K., & Connolly, K. J. (1980). *The ecology of preschool behavior.* Cambridge, England: Cambridge University Press.

Stallings, J. A. (1975). Implementation and child effects of teaching practices in follow through classrooms. *Monographs of the Society for Research in Child Development, 40*(7–8, Serial No. 163).

Turnbull, A. P., & Turnbull, H. R. (1986). *Families, professionals, and exceptionality: A special partnership.* Columbus, OH: Charles E. Merrill.

Twardosz, S. (1984). Environmental organization: The physical, social, and programmatic context of behavior. In M. Hersen, R. Eisler, & P. Miller (Eds.),

Progress in behavior modification (Vol. 18, pp. 123–
161). New York: Academic Press.

Ulrey, G., & Rogers, S. J. (1982). *Psychological assessment of handicapped infants and young children*.
New York: Thieme & Stratton.

Vygotsky, L. S. (1978). *Mind in society: The development of higher psychological processes*. Cambridge,
MA: Harvard University Press.

Westby, C. E. (1980). Assessment of cognitive and language abilities through play. *Language, Speech and
Hearing Services in Schools, 11,* 154–168.

Ysseldyke, J. E., & Mirkin, P. K. (1982). The use of
assessment information to plan instructional interventions: A review of the research. In C. R.
Reynolds, & T. B. Gutkin (Eds.), *The handbook of
school psychology* (pp. 395–409). New York: Wiley.

32

Mental Testing of the Hearing-Impaired Child

PATRICIA M. SULLIVAN
SUZANNE K. BURLEY
Boys Town National Research Hospital

Children with hearing impairments present a unique challenge to professionals in psychology and education. Helen Keller once said that blindness cut her off from the world of things and deafness from the world of people (Bartlett, 1980). Hearing impairment, irrespective of degree, causes a communication problem involving both speech and language. Speech and language difficulties may affect an individual's performance on psychological tests, academic achievement, communication abilities, and interpersonal relationships. Our society places heavy emphasis on standard English and oral-communication-related skills. Indeed, judgments regarding an individual's intelligence and social status are often made on the basis of his or her speech and language fluency. Consequently, hearing-impaired individuals are sometimes stigmatized and misdiagnosed because of a basic human difference—speech and language difficulties that set them apart from the hearing population.

The intellectual evaluation of hearing-impaired children is both a science and an art (Sullivan, 1986a). It is a science because it entails the assessment of a hearing-impaired child's intellectual behavior in a standardized situation with specialized tests and/or testing procedures. It is an art because the examiner must use these scientific procedures in a skillful manner that does not penalize the child for his or her handicap, and must interpret the results creatively to generate appropriate clinical hypotheses. Science and art are combined in scoring the tests and making viable recommendations to benefit the hearing-impaired child.

The intellectual evaluation process does not focus exclusively on a test score or number. The focus is on a range of competencies that are assessed both qualitatively and quantitatively. Test results with hearing-impaired children are often affected by rapport and ability to communicate with the examiner, as well as by fatigue, anxiety, and stress. Test results are always interpreted in relation to other deafness-specific variables. These include, but are not limited to, etiology of hearing loss, mode of communication, type and degree of hearing impairment, age of onset, educational placement, and additional handicapping conditions.

Ideally, tests should have norms for deaf children, but in reality few such tests are available. In their absence, the psychological examiner must use tests normed on hearing youngsters and apply the results to deaf children. We may hope that in the future more tests of intellectual abilities will develop deaf norms. Until this occurs, existing tests must be interpreted cautiously with deaf children.

This chapter is designed to assist psychologists, special educators, and professionals in

allied fields in providing adequate intellectual assessment of hearing-impaired
children and in interpreting testing results.
To this end, the parameters of hearing impairment and pertinent demographic variables are thoroughly defined. The existing
literature on the intellectual assessment of
hearing-impaired children is reviewed.
General testing considerations that may impinge on a given hearing-impaired child's
performance are presented, and available
tests are reviewed. Finally, some mental
testing issues with hearing-impaired children
in the future are projected.

HEARING IMPAIRMENT
DEFINED

Evaluations of hearing-impaired children require an understanding of what hearing
losses entail. Specifically, one needs a sound
understanding of three areas: type, degree,
and age at onset of the auditory impairment.
All three factors may have a significant impact on speech and language development to
varying extents. They can be related to educational placement, academic achievement,
rehabilitation, and overall psychosocial
adjustment. Therefore, any psychological
evaluation of a hearing-impaired individual
should contain pertinent audiological information regarding the child.

"Hearing-impaired" is a generic term
encompassing the entire range of auditory
impairments. Conflicting definitions of terms
exist. In this chapter, "hearing-impaired" refers to all degrees of auditory impairment on
a continuum from mild to profound. The
term "hard-of-hearing" should not be used
synonymously with the term "deaf." A hard-
of-hearing person is one whose hearing is
disabled to an extent that makes hearing difficult, but does not preclude the understanding of speech through the ear alone, without
or with a hearing aid (Frisina, 1974). The
term "deaf" is used to describe an individual
whose hearing is disabled to an extent that
precludes the understanding of speech
through the ear alone, without or with a
hearing aid (Frisina, 1974). It must be
emphasized that some hearing-impaired individuals describe themselves as deaf, irrespective of their degree of hearing impairment. This is an issue of personal choice and

indicates the person's desire to be associated
with the deaf cultural community.

Type of Hearing Loss

There are three commonly recognized types
of hearing impairments: "conductive," "sensory–neural," and "mixed." A conductive
hearing loss results from a defect in the external or middle ear that impedes the
transmission of sound. Conductive hearing
losses are the most common types of hearing
impairments in school-age children (Salvia &
Ysseldyke, 1981). One common cause of conductive hearing loss is otitis media, an in-
flammation of the middle ear, which is medically treatable. Other causes of conductive
losses are dysfunctions or perforations of the
ear drum, wax obstruction of the outer ear
canal, and infections of the eustachian tube.
An individual with a conductive loss has little
difficulty with speech discrimination if
sounds are presented at adequate intensity
levels (Lloyd & Kaplan, 1978). For most
types of conductive hearing losses, medical
treatment can restore hearing.

Sensory–neural hearing impairments are
uncorrectable by medical intervention. Sensory–neural impairments involve abnormalities within the inner ear structure. These
may consist of damage to the bony structures
within the inner ear, to the auditory nerve
carrying sound messages to the brain, or to
the hearing center of the brain itself. Difficulties with sound and speech discrimination
are evident. The discrimination difficulty
tends to become more severe as the degree
of loss increases (Lloyd & Kaplan, 1978).
Even hearing aids do not correct discrimination difficulties.

The third common type of hearing impairment is a mixed hearing loss. Mixed hearing
losses result from a combination of conductive and sensory–neural factors. Some conductive problems in mixed hearing losses are
medically correctable, but sensory–neural
problems are not.

Degree of Hearing Loss

Hearing impairments are classified according
to various categories as measured by an au-
diometer. Table 32.1 presents a classification
scheme that suggests the relationship among
hearing threshold level, probable extent of

TABLE 32.1. A Classification Scheme for Hearing Impairments

Hearing level (dB)	Description	Communication implications and needs
20–26	Normal limits	Generally not a significant handicap, but child may benefit from a hearing aid.
27–40	Mildly impaired	Slight handicap for some children; difficulty hearing faint speech and speech at a distance. Child needs hearing aid and preferential seating; may benefit from hearing aids and lip reading. Mild language and speech difficulties.
41–55	Moderately impaired	A significant handicap. Child understands speech at a distance of 3–5 feet; needs hearing aids, auditory training, lip reading, speech therapy, and preferential seating. Some speech and language problems.
56–70	Moderately to severely impaired	Marked handicap; conversation must be loud to be understood. Child will have difficulty in groups and classroom discussions even with amplification; has same needs as child with moderate loss, may need self-contained support services while mainstreamed. Speech and language development may be delayed.
71–90	Severely impaired	Severe handicap. Child may hear a loud voice a foot from the ear; may be able to identify environmental noises; has same needs as child with significant hearing impairment. Severe language and speech difficulties. Child routinely requires special assistance from resource programs, but may be integrated at a later time.
90 or over	Profoundly impaired	Extreme handicap. Child may be able to hear loud sounds; routinely requires special class or school placement, in addition to special auditory, speech, lip reading, and language intervention.

Note. The data are from Downs (1976), Gellis & Kagan (1976), and Moores (1987).

handicap, and needs of the individual. It is emphasized that the information provided is offered only as a guideline and that some individuals with given degrees of impairment may differ from the descriptions provided.

Age at Onset of Hearing Loss

The psychological report should also contain information regarding the age at onset of deafness. This information is critical in deriving conclusions or expectations in terms of academic achievement and of language and speech acquisition. Two commonly used terms are "prelingual" and "postlingual" hearing impairments.

Prelingual hearing impairments are present at birth or occur at an age prior to the development of speech and language. Individuals with such impairments typically have pronounced speech and language difficulties.

Postlingual losses occur at ages following the normal acquisition of speech and language. Depending upon the exact age at onset, such individuals tend to have fewer speech and language difficulties than those with prelingual impairments.

Impact on Speech and Language Development

For the examiner who lacks experience in assessing hearing-impaired children, the communication barrier presents a significant challenge in terms of providing valid psychological services. This is because the hearing handicap causes severe impairment of the normal acquisition of receptive and expressive language skills (Sullivan & Vernon, 1979). In order to understand the difficulty a hearing-impaired child has in acquiring speech and language, a brief review of normal linguistic development is essential.

For hearing children, language is acquired and learned through prelinguistic and linguistic stages within an auditory environment. Psycholinguists generally agree that a critical period from birth to approximately 3 years of age exists for normal language acquisition and that the mode is primarily auditory (Lenneberg, 1967; Schlesinger, 1974). Accordingly, hearing children learn the rules of their respective cultural language by being active participants through an oral

medium: speech. "Speech" and "language" are not synonymous. Speech is the acoustic–articulatory code by which oral language is represented, and language is a code for representing ideas, which may take many forms (Easterbrooks, 1987). Speech is just one vehicle or mode of conveying language. Speech ability generally depends upon auditory ability; language, as noted, can take many forms, including oral and sign language.

Hearing children learn the language of their culture by interaction, not by direct teaching. They have generally mastered the basic elements of language and have acquired a vocabulary of approximately 5,000 words by kindergarten age. In comparison, the prelingually deaf child usually begins school with a dearth of vocabulary and English syntax skills. In addition, most prelingually hearing-impaired children have lifelong syntactical deficiencies in the use of the English language. In spite of educational attempts, hearing-impaired children rarely overcome their language deficiencies. One explanation is that hearing children are bombarded with language throughout their waking hours, whereas deaf children receive language input for an hour or so a day in school (Vernon, 1970a). In addition, whatever language deaf children receive, it is usually inadequate and expressed in an incompatible modality—that is, speech (Moores, 1987).

Given that approximately 90% of deaf children have hearing parents, their linguistic environment is less than ideal. Further complicating the environment of a deaf child are the often late diagnosis of deafness and the tendency of school environments to provide hearing teachers. Generally speaking, adults have difficulty in learning a new language, such as sign language, fluently. Therefore, one could infer that profoundly deaf children do not interact in a fully accessible communicative environment in the most viable mode. The theory of a critical period of language acquisition has important implications for both hearing-impaired children and significant adults within their environment, in that both often learn language outside this critical period.

In contrast to deaf children of hearing parents, deaf children of deaf parents are experienced communicators well before preschool age (Levine, 1981). They are linguistically proficient in the syntax, morphology, and semantics of sign language. This is their "native" tongue, which they naturally acquire (Klima & Bellugi, 1972; Moores, 1987; Stokoe, 1972a, 1972b). A number of studies have compared deaf children of deaf parents who were exposed to early manual communication with deaf children of hearing parents. These studies found that deaf children of deaf parents did better academically, socially, and linguistically than deaf children of hearing parents. This suggests that early exposure to language in the most viable modality is advantageous (Brasel & Quigley, 1975; Meadow, 1968; Quigley & Frisina, 1961; Schlesinger & Meadow, 1972; Stevenson, 1964; Stuckless & Birch, 1966; Vernon & Koh, 1970).

To summarize, hearing children learn language through the auditory modality. In traditional deaf education, prelingually deafened children generally learn language through memorization, which is unnatural in terms of language development. In addition, speech attainment is difficult for these children because of their impaired auditory mechanism. Intelligible speech does occur in some deaf individuals, but appears to be the exception rather than the rule (Levine, 1981). Even if speech is intelligible, the deaf youngster may continue to experience difficulty in communicating because of limited syntax, morphology, and vocabulary. Overall, the acquisition of standard English does pose significant implications for academic achievement in language-based curricula. Deaf students aged 20 or above have an average reading level of fourth grade, and only 10% of hearing-impaired 18-year-olds read at or above the eighth-grade level (Trybus & Karchmer, 1977).

Etiology

The etiology or causes of hearing impairments are varied, and some increase the probability that the hearing-impaired child will present with secondary handicaps. The major causes of deafness consistently identified over the last two decades are heredity, maternal rubella, prematurity, Rh incompatibility, and meningitis (Hudgins, 1973; Moores, Weiss, & Goodwin, 1978; Ries, 1973; Vernon, 1968a, 1969a). With the exception of heredity, these conditions are known to be associated with brain damage, learning difficulties, aphasia, mental illness, and mental retardation (Vernon, 1969a). Another leading cause of deafness is cytomegalovirus (CMV), which has only recently been identified. Some studies suggest that this viral infection may cause serious neurological manifestations, including mental retardation (Eichhorn, 1982; Strauss, 1985).

Heredity

Estimates from retrospective studies suggest that individuals with hereditary deafness comprise from 5.6% (Vernon, 1969a) to 50% (Sank & Kallman, 1963) of the hearing-impaired population. It is generally accepted that some 50% of early childhood deafness in the United States is hereditary (Moores, 1987). Hereditary hearing impairments can be prelingual as well as postlingual and can affect different systems of the auditory apparatus. Hereditary deafness may be transmitted by dominant genes, recessive genes, sex-linked genes, and mutations. Konigsmark (1972) has identified over 60 different types of hereditary hearing impairments, and there are known genetic syndromes associated with hearing losses. A detailed, descriptive explanation of the primary genetic transmissions in early childhood deafness, as well as genetic syndromes, is beyond the scope of this chapter. The reader is referred to Konigsmark (1972).

Genetically deafened children are the least likely of all major etiological groups to be multiply handicapped (Karchmer, 1985; Vernon, 1976). As a group, genetically deafened children have far better psychological adjustment, writing skills, academic achievement, and intelligence than children deafened from nongenetic causes (Vernon, 1969a, 1970a). Given that a large proportion of hearing individuals are carriers of genes that may cause deafness, heredity will continue to be a major etiology of deafness (Moores, 1987).

Maternal Rubella

Maternal rubella is a devastating viral disease that attacks the developing fetus. Pregnant women usually are asymptomatic, making detection difficult. The first trimester of pregnancy appears to be most critical, as the virus attacks and damages developing tissues and organs. Not only does the infection attack developing fetal cells, but it can remain active for 6 to 18 months following birth, continuing to affect the developing infant.

Maternal rubella is sporadic in nature and produces occasional epidemics. Since the advent of the rubella vaccine, there has been a steady decline in the incidence of rubella. The physical sequelae include hearing, vision, urogenital, and endocrine disorders (Vernon & Hicks, 1980) and possibly diabetes (Shaver, Boughman, & Nance, 1985). Late-appearing neuropsychological disorders, including mental retardation, autism, impulsivity, hyperactivity, rigidity, and learning disabilities, have also been reported (Vernon & Hicks, 1980). In these cases, Vernon and Hicks (1980) found that a significant percentage of children who were diagnosed as retarded later were found not to be, and vice versa. This was attributed to two possibilities: The virus may have continued to be active, or the inactivity of the virus may have caused differential effects on the central nervous system, which were manifested in behavior. These phenomena, strange as they may be, are often seen in rubella children, and psychologists need to be aware of them. Children with rubella etiologies need to have periodic re-evaluations.

Prematurity

Attributing deafness to prematurity is problematic. At times, it may be due to indirect causes, such as anoxia or complications resulting from premature birth. For example, 45% of the rubella subjects and 14% of the Rh-factor subjects in Vernon's (1969a) classic study of multihandicapped deaf children were also premature.

Prematurity appears to be more common among the deaf population than the hearing. Because of advances in medicine, it is predicted that there will be an increase in the number of deaf children born prematurely, especially deaf children with multiple handicaps. Increasingly sophisticated medical technology will be able to save more premature infants than ever before. In Vernon's (1969a) study, two-thirds of the hearing-impaired subjects had multiple handicaps, with aphasia, cerebral palsy, and emotional disturbance being the most common combinations. The lower the birth weight of an infant, the higher the probabilities of mental retardation, cerebral palsy, and emotional disturbance.

Rh Factor

"Rh factor," also known as "mother–child blood incompatibility," is another common etiology of deafness. Complications during pregnancy occur if an Rh-negative mother carries an Rh-positive fetus. The mother builds up antibodies that are passed on to the fetus, destroying the Rh-positive cells of the fetus. Children affected by Rh-factor complications tend to demonstrate handicapping conditions such as deafness, cerebral palsy, aphasia, and retardation (Vernon, 1967c). Over 70% of children deafened from Rh incompatibility present with multiple handicaps (Moores, 1987). However, medicine has made strides in eliminating complications resulting from Rh factor.

Meningitis

Meningitis continues to be a common cause of postnatal deafness in the school-age population (Karchmer, 1985; Moores, 1987), as well as a leading cause of brain damage (Degraff & Creger, 1963) that may manifest itself behaviorally. Ford (1960) has reported that half of meningitis victims are under the age of 5 years, and that the majority of these are under $2\frac{1}{2}$ years of age. Since the advent of antibiotic therapy, many of those infected with meningitis in early childhood have survived. Because of this higher survival rate, the neurophysiological sequelae tend to be far more severe (Haggerty & Ziai, 1964; Mindel & Vernon, 1971; Swartz & Dodge, 1965), because the disease attacks the brain in the life of the child when important developmental changes are taking place (Vernon, 1967a). Karchmer (1985) found that 8.3% of children deafened by meningitis had one or more physical disabilities, that 12.9% had one or more cognitive disabilities, and that 4.8% presented with both physical and cognitive disabilities. Vernon's (1967a) study indicated a high incidence (38%) of multiple handicaps, such as aphasia, mental retardation, hemiplegias, and emotional disorders. Although the incidence of meningitic deafness has decreased over time, those who are deafened from this disease may suffer severe neurological sequelae.

Cytomegalovirus

Because CMV has just begun to receive attention from the medical community, its full ramifications are not clearly known. However, it is recognized as a common cause of congenital deafness (Strauss, 1985). Approximately 2,000 out of 33,000 children infected will be born with a significant sensory–neural hearing impairment (Hanshaw, 1982). One out of 100 infants born with CMV are asymptomatic, whereas 10%–15% will develop central nervous system damage, including hearing loss, developmental delays, low IQ, psychomotor retardation, and learning problems that may go undetected until a later age (Gehrz, 1984; Stagno, Pass, & Dworsky, 1982). Those born with symptomatic CMV (1 out of 1,000 of all infants with the virus) usually present with observable and severe neurological defects at birth. These include prematurity, low birth weight, microcephaly, psychomotor retardation, seizure disorders, mental retardation, and hearing loss (Gehrz, 1984; MacDonald & Tobin, 1978; Strauss, 1985).

CMV is a member of the herpes group of viruses, for which there is no cure at the present time. It is known to be transmitted through the placenta, during the birth process, and through breast milk (Moores, 1987; Strauss, 1985). Although some studies have been done, more longitudinal research needs to be conducted to determine the full range of manifestations of this disease, especially for asymptomatic cases that produce delayed abnormalities.

MULTIPLE HANDICAPS

The major etiologies of deafness just presented, except for heredity, increase the probability that hearing-impaired children will present with multiple handicaps. Because hearing-impaired children are often labeled "multihandicapped," psychologists and professionals must be familiar with this categorization. An "additional handicapping condition" is defined as any physical, mental, emotional, or behavioral disorder that significantly adds to the complexity of educating a hearing-impaired student (Gentile & McCarthy, 1973). Examples include mental retardation, visual impairment, learning disabilities, behavioral/emotional disorders, cerebral palsy, and early infantile autism.

Incidence of Multiple Handicaps

Determining the prevalence of the multihandicapped hearing-impaired child population is problematic for several reasons. Evaluation techniques have not been well formulated (Mindel & Vernon, 1971). Opinions as to what constitutes additional handicapping conditions vary, and misdiagnoses frequently complicate the clinical picture. Some multihandicapped children have not been identified and served, in spite of the mandates of P.L. 94-142 (Rules and Regulations for Implementing Education for All Handicapped Children Act of 1975, 1977). Furthermore, some multihandicapped children may be placed in facilities other than educational settings and may not even be identified as having hearing impairments.

Accordingly, it is difficult to gather precise prevalence data on multiple handicapping conditions among the hearing impaired population. Nevertheless, the Office of Demographic Studies (ODS) at Gallaudet University has attempted to gather annual data on a national basis since 1968. Karchmer (1985) cautions that the 1981–1982 annual survey, which covered 54,775 hearing-impaired students in more than 6,000 schools, excluded individuals with severe disabilities who were placed in institutions other than educational facilities, as well as those in programs for deaf–blind children. In spite of these limitations, the survey indicated that approximately one-third (30.6%) of the children surveyed presented with an additional educationally significant handicap, and that 9.6% of the sample had two or more additional handicapping conditions. Jensema and Mullins (1974) estimated that one-third of hearing-impaired youngsters enrolled in special educational programs throughout the United States are multiply handicapped. Thus, the incidence of multiple handicapping conditions appears to be relatively stable and is generally accepted to comprise one-third of the hearing-impaired school-age population.

Impact on Psychological Services

The assessment of deaf individuals—particularly those with additional handicaps—presents a challenge to the examiner, who must adhere to the requirements of non-discriminatory assessment procedures.

In assessing multihandicapped hearing-impaired children, the evaluation should focus upon more than an IQ score alone. A range of competencies, including social–emotional status, independent living skills, communication abilities, and cognitive functioning, should be assessed both quantitatively and qualitatively. Qualitative information can be gleened through observations, interviews, and diagnostic teaching (Sattler, 1982). Until appropriate instruments are developed, the following modifications are suggested in assessing multihandicapped hearing-impaired children:

- Simplifying verbal format
- Using measures of adaptive behavior
- Selecting items from test batteries that are suitable to extrapolate level of functioning
- Modifying response format to accommodate the handicaps
- Testing of limits to estimate rate of learning
- Reproducing test materials in large print
- Waiving time limitations

Deafness and Mental Retardation

The number of mentally retarded students enrolled in educational programs for the deaf is higher than in the general population. Estimates are that 8% (Karchmer, 1985; Rawlings & Gentile, 1970) or 6% (Craig & Craig, 1975) of the students enrolled in such programs are also mentally retarded. These rates suggest that the incidence of mental retardation among the deaf has decreased since the late 1960s, when the rates ranged from 11% to 19% (Moores, 1987). A change in the cutoff IQ score from 85 to 70 may be a factor here. Also, one reason for the higher incidence rates in earlier years may have been that professionals lacked understanding of the communication difficulties inherent in deafness and mistakenly assumed that language and speech deficits were symptoms of mental retardation. In addition, today some professionals may be more reluctant to label a deaf child as retarded. Thus, it is imperative that any assessment resulting in low scores be viewed with caution unless the examiner is proficient in communicating with the deaf child. American Association on Mental Deficiency (AAMD) diagnostic criteria for mental retardation include both subaverage intellectual functioning and impairments in adaptive behavior. The assessment of a child, deaf or not, should include adaptive behavior assessments before the diagnosis of mental retardation is rendered.

Deafness and Blindness

The ODS annual survey indicates that approximately 2% of hearing-impaired school-age children are legally blind and that 4% have uncorrected visual problems. Stein, Palmer, and Weinberg (1982) assessed the characteristics of the deaf–blind population over a 7-year period. Neurological conditions were often evident, and three-fourths of the children were functioning at levels significantly below what would be expected of children who were either blind or deaf. Vernon, Bair, and Lotz (1979) reported that adequate assessment instruments do not exist for this population. Tests that have been developed primarily for the deaf or blind are not appropriate for those who lack both hearing and vision. Tests developed for blind children emphasize language and depend on the ability to hear (Bauman, 1968). They are inappropriate for prelingually deafened children. For those who are postlingually deafened and have a good command of the English language, verbal tests may be administered in Braille, sign language, or sight-saving print. Although the Callier–Azusa Scale (Stillman, 1975) was designed for the deaf–blind, it is limited to low-functioning children up to age 9. Assessing deaf–blind children is very difficult and is best left to psychologists who possess both sign language/Braille skills and experience with deaf–blind populations.

Usher syndrome is a genetic condition resulting in congenital deafness and progressive blindness (retinitis pigmentosa). Although it is a rare disease within the general population, its incidence rate of 5%–10% among the deaf population is high (Vernon, 1969b). Standard ophthalmoscopic examinations and testing of visual fields are unable to detect this genetic condition in its early stages, and more sophisticated ophthalmological techniques such as electroretinography are required. Most deaf–blind individuals with Usher syndrome begin to manifest visual problems, beginning with night blindness and progressive constriction of the visual fields, in early adolescence. Aphasia, memory deficits, psychosis, mental retardation, and loss of olfactory sensitivity can be present in Usher syndrome (Vernon, 1969b). All hearing-impaired children should receive routine screening for this genetic disorder.

Deafness and Learning Disabilities

Technically, hearing-impaired children are excluded by definition from categorization as learning-disabled. However, clinical experience suggests that learning disabilities do occur among hearing-impaired children, and that such children are frequently misdiagnosed and underserved. Prevalence rates range from 6.7% (Power, Elliott, & Funderburg, 1987) to 7.5% (Karchmer, 1985). As in hearing children with learning disabilities, discrepancies between academic achievement and ability are cardinal characteristics. Other characteristics are behavior and attention problems, differences in learning styles, language problems, memory difficulties, inconsistent performance, and poor organizational skills. These learning difficulties are not attributable to hearing loss alone (Sullivan & Vernon, 1979).

Given that hearing-impaired children exhibit language difficulties, assessment and identification are difficult. Another complication in diagnosis is that what may appear to be learning problems may actually be the result of poor education/teaching methods and/or inappropriate language-instructional modalities. Differentiating between the two factors is difficult at best. Generally, the average prelingually deafened youngster is about 4 years behind hearing youngsters of similar age in academic achievement. Academic retardation of 6 years or more may suggest emotional disturbance, mental incapacity, inadequate instructional practices, learning disabilities, or language-learning disorders (Levine, 1981).

Deafness and Emotional/Behavioral Disorders

A greater percentage of deaf children have behavioral and emotional problems than do their hearing peers (Sullivan, 1985a). Incidence rates of psychiatric disturbance or emotional/behavioral problems range from 9% to 22% (Meadow, 1981; Meadow & Trybus, 1979). These problems may be due to a number of complex, interacting variables, including parental reactions to the hearing-impaired child, lack of fluency in parent–child communication, inability to communicate with others in the environment, high-risk etiologies, or some form of maltreatment. Available data suggest that from 11% to 50% of the hearing-impaired population may be abused or neglected (Sullivan, Vernon, & Scanlan, 1987). Because abused children frequently exhibit emotional or behavioral problems that are secondary to the maltreatment, hearing-impaired children who exhibit emotional/behavioral problems should have a clinical interview to rule out abuse as a causative agent.

Deaf children have been frequently diagnosed as mentally ill or mentally retarded by poorly trained psychologists and psychiatrists who misinterpret their language difficulties as indicating psychosis. Compared to hearing children, deaf children are more likely to be labeled as immature, hyperactive, and aggressive. Like mental tests, measures of emotional/behavioral disturbance for the deaf should be nonverbal in nature. Behavioral rating scales completed by individuals who are very familiar with the child are excellent for this purpose.

Deafness and Cerebral Palsy

Approximately 3% of deaf school-age children have some form of cerebral palsy. About half of this multihandicapped population have average or better intelligence, but language problems are common (Vernon, 1970b). A deaf child with cerebral palsy presents a particular testing challenge, because most nonverbal tests contain timed subtests that require fine motor dexterity. Due to the nature of such a child's handicaps, it is difficult to differentiate between physical and cognitive deficits in testing situations. An additional handicap for such youngsters is that sign language may be difficult or impossible because of pronounced motoric involvement. Any assessment procedure should be selected and administered so as not to penalize the children for their motor disabilities. It is often helpful to use a child's language board for communication purposes, to allow pointing responses, and to make sure that emitted responses are repeatable (Levine, 1986).

Deafness and Autism

Over the course of time, the concept of autism has changed. What previously was thought to be a psychogenic emotional disorder is now being conceptualized as a biogenic developmental disorder in which cognitive dysfunction plays a central role (Morgan, 1986). Although autism occurs at all levels of intelligence, it usually co-occurs with mental retardation. Severely and profoundly mentally retarded children do present with some autistic-like behavior. Differential diagnosis depends upon social responsiveness and pretend/imitative play that is commensurate with mental age (Wing & Attwood, 1987). Another major differentiating characteristic is that autistic children often demonstrate strengths in motor and spatial abilities. These islands of ability are typically seen in psychotic but not mentally retarded children (Goldman, Stein, & Guerry, 1983).

Because young autistic children do not appear to respond to auditory stimuli, suspicion of deafness often occurs. In addition, some very young deaf children may present with repetitious behaviors, as well as delayed speech and language skills suggestive of autism (Wing & Attwood, 1987). In general, most autistic children are not deaf. However, a diagnosis of autism should not be excluded because a child is found to be deaf. The incidence of autism is higher in the deaf population (7%–11%) than in the hearing (0.07%) (Chess, 1977). Autism is often present in neuropathological conditions that can be associated with deafness, including congenital rubella, tuberous sclerosis, congenital syphilis, and fragile-X syndrome (Darby, 1976; Piggott, 1979; Rutter, 1979). The diagnostic criteria set forth in the *Diagnostic and Statistical Manual of Mental Disorders*, third edition (DSM-III; American Psychiatric

Association, 1980) for Autism may be applied to deaf children.

Deaf autistic children often exhibit pronounced language deficits over and above what may be attributed to the hearing impairment. Specifically, they demonstrate pronounced difficulties in verbal and nonverbal communication, in comparison to average hearing-impaired youngsters. It has been frequently observed in clinical practice that such youngsters often show deficits in gestures for very basic needs, facial expression, imitation, and spontaneous communication. Even the very young average hearing-impaired youngster without language initiates communication of very basic needs through gestures. However, even though some hearing-impaired autistic youngsters may display rudimentary gestures and imitative sign language skills, these are rather egocentric means of self-gratification. They may also represent echolalia or a mechanical form of abnormal language usage. Although many young impulsive hearing-impaired children do demonstrate brief eye contact, an autistic hearing-impaired child will demonstrate marked deficits in eye contact or eye gazing.

Educational Placement

Since the advent of P.L. 94-142 (Rules and Regulations . . ., 1977), there has been an emphasis on placement of handicapped children in the least restrictive environment. Placements may occur in regular classrooms, resource rooms, or residential schools. The concept of "least restrictive environment" has often been misinterpreted as meaning "mainstreaming." Mainstreaming as opposed to institutionalization has some advantages. Mainstreaming into regular classrooms is less isolating for handicapped children; they benefit academically and socially if integrated and are more likely to become socially accepted, as stigmatizing diminishes with exposure to normal children (Linton & Juul, 1980).

However, mainstreaming the deaf child in some cases can be the "*most* restrictive environment." Handicapped children can still be isolated and unaccepted by other children within the mainstream. Being unaccepted and subjected to repeated failure while placed in unrealistic educational programs can be devastating to a child's self-esteem. Studies have shown that placement in regular classes does not improve the social status of educable mentally retarded children (Sattler, 1982). Therefore, they may be less handicapped academically and emotionally if placed in special classes with peers of similar ability levels. Another issue is that when one insists on mainstreaming in a situation where the handicap and its effect on learning are overlooked, the child may be denied his or her right to be different. Mainstreaming is often referred to as "normalization" and can be maladaptive. Attempts to create normality can be a disservice to the child and his or her parents. Being able to accommodate to limitations and view them realistically is adaptive, as it allows the handicapped child to discover means to compensate for his or her difficulties.

Self-contained local day programs for the hearing-impaired were established on the grounds that they were more financially feasible and that it was beneficial for children to be reared at home. This is true for some but not all hearing-impaired children. Since deafness is a low-incidence handicapping condition, enrollments of hearing-impaired children are small in some programs. Children may be lumped together into one classroom, regardless of age, abilities, grades, and interests. These children are lacking in peers of similar age and abilities with whom to develop social skills and the opportunity to become acculturated into the deaf community.

In resource rooms, hearing-impaired children are usually mainstreamed and the resource room provides specialized classes, such as English/language instruction. The teacher of the hearing-impaired in the resource room may also provide special assistance to the child in his or her mainstream classes.

Itinerant services may be provided by the local school district to hearing-impaired children who are mainstreamed full-time. The itinerant teacher may have a caseload consisting of hearing-impaired children placed in a number of different schools. Special assistance pertaining to the child's academic courses is provided on a schedule that may vary from daily to weekly.

Residential schools may be either private or state-funded. Usually each state has one state-supported residential school for the deaf. The residential program contains supervised living facilities to house students who reside too far away to commute on a daily basis. The student population tends to consist of those with profound, prelingual hearing impairments. Advocates of self-contained day programs feel that residential placements deprive deaf children of the opportunity of living within a family environment. However, residential schools play an important role in socializing deaf students into the deaf community that is maintained by a common language, American Sign Language (ASL). Deaf people have established and maintained a community similar to those of ethnic minority groups (Moores, 1987). Disadvantages of residential schools are isolation, prolonged absence from family, and the possibility of maltreatment (Sullivan et al., 1987).

In summary, several options are available for educating hearing-impaired children. Placement decisions must be determined on the basis of each child's individual needs. Needless to say, the educational options reviewed have positive and negative attributes that must be considered for each individual child.

Social/Cultural Aspects

An understanding of issues regarding the culture of the deaf is important for professionals serving hearing-impaired children. Ethnocentrism is a particular characteristic of life in America, and bilingualism has historically not been well received. Early immigrants to America encountered much prejudice; as a result, cohesion occurred among ethnic groups. Children of immigrants enrolled in schools found emotional support in their ethnic community and families through their native language. The deaf community, like many ethnic groups, has a hierarchical social structure within its own culture and language (Meadow, 1972). However, the deaf minority group is significantly different from hearing ethnic groups. Since approximately 90% of deaf children are born of hearing parents, their enculturation does not take place within their immediate families. They often feel alienated from their immediate families because of language and communication barriers; sadly, most hearing parents of deaf children do not become fluent in sign language (Moores, 1987).

For deaf children of hearing parents, enculturation and socialization into the deaf community depend upon where they attend school. Approximately one-half of these children attend residential schools, which are important transmitters of cultural norms and ASL. These children are enculturated into the deaf community by older deaf children and deaf peers who have deaf parents (Meadow, 1972). Thus, deaf culture is passed from child to child in many cases; this distinguishes it sociologically from the hearing culture, which is passed from adult to child. Others attend local school programs and attempt to identify with the hearing majority group, in which they function with varying degrees of success (Woodward & Markowicz, 1982). These children do not normally socialize with members of the deaf community and usually do not have contact with deaf adults. Adolescents and young adults who have attended schools other than residential schools often attempt later to become enculturated into the deaf community. This is often accomplished via meeting another person who is hearing-impaired, through the various organizational functions of the deaf community, and through postsecondary educational programs for the hearing impaired.

Membership into the deaf community is defined by language rather than hearing impairment (Erting, 1978). The language of the deaf community is ASL, which recent linguistic studies have shown to be a language in its own right. ASL is not a major communication mode in most classrooms. Traditionally and currently, most education programs are administered by hearing people. Thus, ASL has not been seen as a viable language, but one that constitutes "broken English." The main emphasis in most educational programs for the deaf is on acquiring standard English. If sign language is used in classrooms, it is usually presented in grammatical English form, such as in total communication (to be discussed below). As membership into the deaf community is defined by ASL, deaf adults who have been educated in schools other than residential ones may have difficulty becoming completely accepted members of the deaf community (Padden & Markowicz, 1976). The

10% of hearing-impaired children with deaf parents become members of the deaf community by birth, language, and experience. They are enculturated by their parents and enculturate peers with hearing parents.

Communication Mode

Since the beginning of education for the deaf, much controversy, which is still unresolved, exists among educators as to the most appropriate communication modality to use in teaching language skills to deaf children. There are two basic methods of communication in school systems today, and each school of thought clings to its communication philosophy with a zeal akin to religious fervor.

Oral/Aural Method

The oral/aural method emphasizes the use of speech, hearing aids, lipreading, and residual auditory skills. The use of sign language and finger spelling is discouraged, because it is felt that reliance on manual communication will interfere with the development of oral skills. Those who benefit from the oral/aural approach are usually children with considerable residual hearing. By junior or senior high school, those who are labeled "oral failures" are frequently sent to residential schools, where they are permitted to utilize manual communication. This occurs after the critical period of language acquisition and creates a period of resentment, disappointment, and anger in parents, who may well feel betrayed (Meadow, 1980).

To parents of newly identified hearing-impaired children, the oral/aural approach has high appeal. This is because it offers oral speech skills as an end product. Lipreading is a misunderstood ability. It is a learned skill, and some deaf individuals have a poor aptitude for it. In addition, only 30% of English words can be clearly distinguished on the lips, and much of lipreading is guesswork (Hardy, 1970). If parents have communication expectations that the child cannot meet, pronounced psychological difficulties ensue. The book *How You Gonna Get to Heaven If You Can't Talk with Jesus* (Woodward, 1982), both in title and in content, thoroughly discusses these issues.

Total Communication

"Total communication" is a philosophy incorporating the oral method, signs, and finger spelling. Students are taught through the use of speech reading, signs, finger spelling, and aural means; they express themselves via speech, signs, and finger spelling. Overall, the combined method of speech and manual signs parallels English word order for the purpose of instruction. However, the fact that a program advocates or utilizes total communication does not mean in and of itself that staff personnel are efficient signers.

Using any form of manual communication with hearing-impaired children has often been stigmatized. Traditionally, these were the "children of a lesser god," to quote Medoff's (1980) play title. This attitude has changed, and today manual systems of communication are frequently included in educational programs. These take varying forms and include Signed English, Signing Exact English, and ASL. The oral versus manual controversy still exists to some extent, but the question of which form of sign language to implement has been added to it in some locales.

LITERATURE REVIEW

Any literature review of mental testing with hearing-impaired children must be presented within the context of the time at which it was undertaken and how the results were interpreted. Three distinct stages or viewpoints have been identified (Vernon, 1967b, 1968b; Moores, 1987): the deaf as intellectually inferior, as concrete, and as essentially normal. Other germane issues are the use of administration modifications and the relationship between IQ and academic achievement with deaf children.

The Deaf as Intellectually Inferior

Historically, the mental testing movement in America developed from the study of individual differences (Sattler, 1982). Early research compared the performance of hearing and deaf children to analyze the effects of language upon cognitive development (Pintner & Patterson, 1915, 1917). The criterion measures employed in this research were primarily verbal in nature; they included the Binet Scale and various visual memory tasks that were heavily dependent upon verbal mediation. Results of these and other studies invariably indicated lower scores for deaf than for hearing children (Pintner, Eisenson, & Stanton, 1941). These findings were interpreted to indicate that deaf children were inferior to hearing children in intelligence, and, in effect, equated intelligence with verbal language proficiency. Unfortunately, these studies widely influenced perceptions of the intellectual abilities of deaf children. Many were erroneously labeled as mentally retarded and/or were institutionalized on the basis of primarily verbal assessment instruments (Donoghue, 1968; Rosen, 1967; Vernon, 1976). Even in the 1970s and 1980s, deaf victims of such misdiagnoses have been identified (Vernon & Sullivan, 1982).

The Deaf as Intellectually Concrete

Subsequent research (Graham & Shapiro, 1953; Myklebust, 1964; Myklebust & Burchard, 1945; Schick, 1934; Streng & Kirk, 1938) indicated that deaf children functioned within the average range of intelligence when performance or nonverbal tests were used to assess cognitive abilities. Myklebust emerged as the dominant expert in the field of psychology of deafness. Although Myklebust believed that deaf children were not inferior to hearing ones in intelligence, he theorized that qualitative differences in cognitive processes existed between the two groups, despite quantitatively similar scores on nonverbal tests of intelligence (Myklebust & Brutton, 1953). This qualitative inferiority was attributed to deaf children's being more concrete and less abstract than hearing children in their approach to cognitive tasks. As Myklebust saw it, deafness pervaded the entire being of a deaf child to make him or her qualitatively different from a hearing child in the perceptive, cognitive, affective, personality, social, and behavioral domains. This mode of thought was certainly an improvement over that of Pintner and his colleagues; however, it continued to stigmatize the intellectual abilities of deaf children by purporting that they were less abstract than those of hearing children.

The Deaf as Intellectually Normal

In the 1960s, research began to address the age-old question of the relationship of language to the thinking process (Vernon, 1967b, 1968b). In an extensive review of 33 research studies employing nonverbal tests of intelligence with over 8,000 deaf individuals, Vernon concluded that the distribution of nonverbal intelligence within the deaf population is essentially normal. Rosenstein (1961) also reviewed several studies and reported that when linguistic factors in tasks presented were within the language experience of the deaf subjects, no differences were found between deaf and hearing children in conceptual performance. Furth (1964) reviewed the literature on language and cognition and concluded that the problems deaf children have on some tasks may be explained by a lack of cognitive problem-solving strategies (a problem that dissipates with age) or by the fact that some tasks require language-based strategies for successful completion.

Subsequent studies found differential performance on subtests of the Wechsler Performance scales. On the Wechsler Intelligence Scale for Children (WISC; Wechsler, 1949), deaf children were found to earn relatively high scores on Block Design (Clarke & Leslie, 1971) and Object Assembly (Clarke & Leslie, 1971; Lavos, 1962) and to have difficulty with Coding (Clarke & Leslie, 1971; Evans, 1966). On the WISC—Revised (WISC-R; Wechsler, 1974), younger deaf children were found to earn significantly lower scaled scores on Picture Arrangement and Coding than hearing children (Anderson & Sisco, 1977). When etiology of deafness and mode of test administration were controlled, lower Coding and higher Object Assembly scores were found only for deaf children with multiple handicaps, and no significant differences were found for Picture Arrangement (Sullivan, 1982a). This suggests that differential patterns of subtest performance found in previous research may have been a function of comprehension of subtest directions. Interestingly, a majority of the previously discussed research did not control for etiology of deafness and did not report or control the communication mode of test administration with deaf children.

Variance in deaf children's performance on intelligence tests has been reported in relation to etiology and communication mode of subtest administration (Sullivan, 1982a; Vernon, 1969a). Children with genetic etiologies and deaf children of deaf parents have been found to have above-average nonverbal IQs (Brill, 1972; Kusche, Greenberg, & Garfield, 1983; Sisco & Anderson, 1980; Sullivan, 1982a; Vernon, 1969a). Children with high-risk etiologies for additional handicapping conditions (i.e., maternal rubella, meningitis, complications of Rh factor, and prematurity) generally have average to low-average nonverbal IQs (Sullivan, 1982a; Vernon, 1969a). As noted earlier, children with multiple handicaps comprise approximately one-third of the deaf school-age population (Jensema & Mullins, 1974; Moores, 1987).

Further and perhaps definitive support for the deaf as intellectually normal has come from factor-analytic studies. Braden (1985) factor-analyzed the WISC and WISC-R Performance scales and the Hiskey–Nebraska Test of Learning Aptitude with hearing and deaf subjects. Only one principal factor with an eigenvalue greater than 1.0 was extracted and found to be identical for the hearing and deaf samples. This factor was labeled "$g + P$" to represent its composite loadings on a general factor (g) and a Performance factor (P). Thus, deaf and hearing children exhibit essentially identical nonverbal intellectual structure.

Use of Administration Modifications

The Performance scales of the various Wechsler tests are the nonverbal intelligence tests used most frequently with hearing-impaired children (Levine, 1974). Although nonverbal in format, these tests contain spoken language instructions that tell the child what he or she is expected to do. A speech-only administration has been recognized as inappropriate for severely and profoundly deaf children with poor speech-reading skills. Indeed, such children earn significantly lower IQs on the WISC-R Performance scale when the standardized directions are presented in a speech-only format (Sullivan, 1982a).

To obviate this difficulty, administration modifications have been suggested. These include pantomime (Graham & Shapiro, 1953; Murphy, 1957; Sullivan, 1982b) and visual aids (Murphy, 1957; Neuhaus, 1967; Ray, 1979; Reed, 1970; Sullivan, 1982b). The effect of these modifications on the reliability and validity of test results with hearing-impaired subjects has been questioned (Gerweck & Ysseldyke, 1974; Sattler, 1982).

Sullivan (1982a) addressed the issue of administration modification by comparing profoundly deaf children's IQ scores on the WISC-R Performance scale across a variety of administration modes: speech-only, pantomime (Sullivan, 1982b), visual aids (Sullivan, 1982b), and total communication (the simultaneous use of speech and sign language). The pantomime and visual-aid modifications were adapted from previously recommended administration formats (Graham & Shapiro, 1953; Murphy, 1957; Neuhaus, 1967; Reed, 1970); they are reprinted in Sattler (1988).

Profoundly deaf children earned significantly higher Performance IQs when the WISC-R was given in total communication than when subtests were administered in a speech-only mode. A difference of 18 IQ points (total communication = 98, speech-only = 80) was found in a sample of children whose primary communication mode was total communication; this suggests that such children should be administered tests of intelligence in their native language. Furthermore, deaf children obtained higher subtest scores and Performance IQs when the test was administered in total communication (104) than when pantomime (88) or visual-aid modifications (90) were employed. It was calculated that an average Performance IQ of 93 would result in deaf children if a combination of administration modes (i.e., pantomime, visual aids, and total communication) were to be used.

This research provided empirical support for the use of sign language in the administration of the standardized subtests of the WISC-R Performance scale to hearing-impaired children in residential and public schools who are instructed in total communication. This administration mode resulted in significantly higher IQs than did pantomime, visual-aid modifications, or spoken subtest directions. Accordingly, examiners assessing the nonverbal intelligence of deaf children who communicate in sign language should be skilled in a manual system of communication. Furthermore, pantomime and visual-aid modifications should be used cautiously with hearing-impaired children and identified as administration modes in psychological reports. They should be used only when the examiner cannot communicate in sign language; although preferable to a speech-only administration, they result in lower IQs than does a sign language administration.

The Performance scale of the WISC-R was standardized with a sample of 1,228 deaf children between the ages of 6 and 16 (Anderson & Sisco, 1977). This was accomplished by requesting protocols from psychologists who had already completed testing with the children. The sample was selected and stratified according to race, parental occupation, rural versus urban status, and geographical region in a manner representative of the national population according to the 1970 U.S. census. Etiology of hearing impairment was not reported in the standardization process. Several different communication modes were employed with the subjects, although the majority received subtest instructions using a combination of sign language and speech. This standardization included the following administration modes and sample percentages: total communication (77.2), speech (2.2), finger spelling with speech (4.4), gestures (1.3), pantomime (7.3), other (6.6), and not reported (1.0).

This standardization indicated that deaf children performed similarly to hearing children on all performance subtests, with the exception of Picture Arrangement and Coding. Younger deaf subjects were found to earn significantly lower scaled scores on these subtests than the hearing population. Furthermore, significant differences between mean Performance IQs and standard deviations were obtained for deaf and hearing children (deaf IQ = 95.70, SD = 17.55, vs. hearing IQ = 100, SD = 15). However, some evidence indicates that the lower mean Performance IQ obtained in this standardization may have been due to the variety of administration modes employed; these may have resulted in lower scores because of difficulties in children's comprehension of subtest directions (Sullivan, 1982a). Some 22% of the Anderson and Sisco (1977) standardization sample received the test via administration modes that research has indicated result in significantly lower IQ scores than when sign language is used (Sullivan, 1982a).

Ray (1979, 1982) has developed administration adaptations for the WISC-R Performance scale. These are based for the most part on previously published suggestions. In essence, they are composed of additional sample items for each subtest and are not scored. These have been marketed and touted as appropriate for use with deaf children, without sufficient validation to support such use (Sullivan, 1985b). The standardization was inadequate, no reliability or validity data are reported, and the statistical techniques given in the manual are inappropriate for the data and fallaciously interpreted (Genshaft, 1985; Sullivan, 1985b). When Ray's adaptations are used, the resulting scores are similar to those of prelingually deafened children, without additional handicapping conditions, who receive the test in sign language. If the examiner is fluent in sign language, Ray's adaptations are unnecessary. Data are needed to support the efficacy of these adaptations with deaf children, as well as validity and reliability evidence.

A final administration modification that must be considered is the use of an interpreter to translate the examiner's directions into sign language. We (Sullivan & Burley, 1988) addressed this issue using the WISC-R with a sample of 150 deaf youngsters, half of whom were tested by psychologists fluent in sign language and the other half by psychologists who used interpreters. Both the Verbal and Performance scales of the WISC-R were given to the children who ranged in age from 6 to 16. Significantly lower Verbal IQs were found for the sample when the test was administered through an interpreter (mean = 65) than when the examiners were able to sign the questions themselves (mean = 80). Significantly lower Performance IQs were also found when an interpreter was used to give sign language instructions (mean = 99) than when the examiner used sign language (mean = 110). A total of 15% of children in the sample earned Performance IQs of 130 or higher; the majority of these had genetic etiologies and/or deaf parents.

In summary, administration modifications, in whatever form, must be used cautiously with deaf children on tests of intelligence. The administration mode of choice with a given hearing-impaired child is that child's normal communication mode. This may be oral/aural, some form of sign language, or via an interpreter. In this set of circumstances, the regular WISC-R norms should be employed. When administration modifications (i.e., pantomime, visual aids, the Ray adaptations) are used, the WISC-R deaf norms should be employed. Furthermore, the psychological report should specifically identify the modifications implemented; should indicate that the child's score is relative to a mean IQ of 95 and a standard deviation of 18; and should indicate that the score may underestimate the child's potential given that the test was not administered in the child's "native" language.

The Relationship between IQ and Academic Achievement

The relationship between performance on intelligence tests and academic achievement has been consistently documented in hearing children (Matarazzo, 1972). This relationship has not been as well documented in the literature on hearing-impaired children, and conflicting results have been reported. Performance IQs on the WISC-R were found to correlate significantly with academic achievement in a sample of 59 prelingually deaf children (Hirshoren, Kavale, Hurley, & Hunt, 1977). Both WISC-R Performance IQs and Deaf Learning Quotients on the Hiskey–Nebraska Test of Learning Aptitude (Hiskey, 1966) correlated significantly with academic achievement for 23 black but not for 36 white deaf children (Hurley, Hirshoren, Kavale, & Hunt, 1978). The predictive and practical validity of the WISC-R Performance scale and the Hiskey–Nebraska with deaf children for placement decisions has subsequently been questioned (Hirshoren, Hurley, & Hunt, 1977; Hurley et al., 1978).

The reasons for this failure to find a consistent significant correlation between nonverbal intelligence and academic achievement in deaf children are not readily apparent. It may be that nonverbal intelligence is not highly correlated with academic achievement. The relationship between language ability and academic achievement is well established in hearing children (Johnson & Myklebust, 1967). Indeed, higher median correlations between Verbal IQ (.55) than

Performance IQ (.33) and academic achievement have been reported with the WISC in hearing children (Zimmerman & Woo-Sam, 1972).

Watson, Sullivan, Moeller, and Jensen (1982) examined the relationship between nonverbal intelligence and English-language ability in deaf children. An average multiple correlation of .68 was obtained between subtests of the WISC-R Performance scale, the Hiskey–Nebraska Test of Learning Aptitude, the Test of Language Development (Newcomer & Hammill, 1977), and the Reynell Developmental Language Scales (Reynell, 1977). The best predictors of English-language performance were subtests requiring visual memory skills. English-language proficiency is a prerequisite for reading achievement.

We (Sullivan, Brookhouser, & Burley, in press) investigated the relationship between verbal and nonverbal IQ and reading and arithmetic achievement in a sample of 109 gifted deaf children across the United States. The WISC-R was the intelligence measure, and several subtests of the Stanford Achievement Test—Special Edition for Hearing Impaired Children (SAT-HI; 1982) were employed to test academic achievement. All children were tested in sign language. Verbal IQ correlated more highly with academic achievement (i.e., Reading, .38; Math Computation, .44; Math Applications, .45) on the SAT-HI than did Performance IQ (i.e., Reading, .29; Math Computation, .36; Math Applications, .36). These correlations are consistent with those found between the WISC-R Verbal scale and the regular Stanford Achievement Test in hearing children (Reschly & Reschly, 1979). This suggests that, in both hearing and deaf children, verbal IQ is a better predictor of academic achievement than nonverbal IQ.

However, the fact remains that verbal intelligence tests are inappropriate as the sole measure of mental abilities in a hearing-impaired child. They should be administered only by psychologists who are fluent in the child's native language and should be interpreted with caution. Most hearing-impaired children have significant Verbal–Performance discrepancies, with the Performance IQ being invariably higher. Our research suggests that, as in hearing children, verbal IQ is a better predictor of aca-

demic achievement than nonverbal IQ in deaf children. This is not surprising, given that most academic subjects require language-based reasoning abilities.

GENERAL TESTING CONSIDERATIONS

Certain crucial considerations are fundamental to the mental testing of the hearing-impaired child (Sullivan & Vernon, 1979). Failure to be aware of them can result in diagnostic errors. A variety of factors and circumstances can lead hearing-impaired children to function below capacity on tests. These include poor attending behaviors, impulsive response patterns, inappropriate assessment instruments, inexperienced examiners, and a lack of understanding of the task expected because of poor examiner–child communication. Accordingly, there is far more danger that a low IQ is inaccurate than that a high one is invalid (Sullivan & Vernon, 1979; Vernon, 1976). The tests given to hearing-impaired children by inexperienced psychologists are more often in error than tests given by psychologists familiar with the dynamics of hearing impairment (Sullivan & Vernon, 1979; Vernon, 1976).

Examiner's Skill

A major assumption underlying the mental assessment of any individual is that the examiner possesses the clinical competence to administer, score, and interpret the test used in the assessment. With deaf children, the clinical competence of the examiner ideally includes graduate-level coursework and a supervised internship in the psychology of deafness, as well as fluent expressive and receptive sign language skills in ASL, Signed English, and/or Signing Exact English (Sullivan, 1986a; Turkington, 1982). The number of psychologists in the United States with this level of competence is steadily increasing; however, the demand for them far exceeds their supply. In an attempt to secure and define adequate mental health services for the hearing-impaired population, Sussman has delineated criteria for competence (cited in Turkington, 1982).

A less preferred level of clinical competence is that of an examiner who has had no specific coursework or training in deafness, but who has acquired sign language skills and some on-the-job experience with deaf children. The least preferred level of clinical competence is that of an examiner with no specific coursework or training in deafness and no sign language skills. Such an individual must either rely on an interpreter to communicate with a deaf child or use pantomime, gestures, or speech to administer tests. Intellectual assessments completed by examiners with these two levels of competence are generally less reliable than those obtained by examiners with deafness-specific training and sign language skills (Sullivan, 1986a; Vernon & Sullivan, 1979).

Verbal Tests

Tests of intellectual abilities that depend upon the use of verbal language measure the hearing-impaired child's language difficulties more validly than his or her intelligence (Sullivan & Vernon, 1979; Vernon, 1976). The language proficiency of a deaf child is usually unrelated to his or her intellectual abilities. Hard-of-hearing children may give the impression of being able to understand verbally administered tests, but this is often a false positive. Even mild and moderate hearing impairments can have a significant affect on language ability (Sullivan & Vernon, 1979). The most valid measure of intelligence on a child with any degree of hearing impairment is a performance or nonverbal test of abilities.

However, most generalizations have exceptions. Sometimes it is necessary to use a verbal test to measure a psychological attribute in a hearing-impaired child. This can occur when the deaf child has the sufficient English-language proficiency in reading skills to complete a verbal test. The intent here is to measure achievement and not potential. Examples include educational and linguistic tests used to measure reading and language skills. Verbal intelligence tests can be very useful in making placement decisions regarding a deaf child's abilities to handle language-based academic subjects in mainstreamed or college settings, as well as to predict academic achievement. However, it is emphasized that results of verbal intelligence tests should never be interpreted as an intelligence quotient or used as the sole measure of in-

telligence with a deaf individual. Furthermore, they should only be administered when fluent communication exists between the examiner and examinee (Sullivan, 1986a).

Mode of Communication

Mental tests used in the evaluation of hearing-impaired children should be administered in that child's native language (Rules and Regulations . . ., 1977). "Native language" is the normal mode of communication used by the deaf child—namely, oral/auditory communication, sign language, or total communication. Accordingly, deaf children who communicate in an oral/auditory mode should be tested in a communication mode that emphasizes speech, speech reading, natural gestures, and/or mime. Deaf children who communicate in sign language should be evaluated in ASL, Signed English, Signing Exact English, or the particular sign language system that is used for communication.

If oral/auditory communication is used, several considerations apply (Sullivan & Vernon, 1979). The examiner should make sure the child is watching his or her face. A failure to insure full visual attention is the most common mistake made by those not trained in working with hearing-impaired children. If the examiner gets the child's attention and maintains eye contact, the child will know to attend to the examiner's lips. A pleasant face is easiest to lipread, and it does not help to make exaggerated lip movements. One should speak clearly and distinctly. Mustaches, beards, gum or other objects in the mouth, and hand movements near the mouth make speech reading impossible. The examiner also needs to make sure there are no obstructions that block the child's view of the lips, or lights that may cause a glare on the examiner's face or in the child's eyes. The optimal distance between tester and testee for lipreading purposes is from 2 to 3 feet.

With most hearing-impaired children, it is imperative to speak or sign in short, simple sentences. It will often be necessary to repeat instructions or directions if the child does not respond initially as directed. Care must be taken to insure that the child understands what he or she is being directed to do. Hearing-impaired children have been conditioned to nod their heads and smile in agreement when they have no idea what is being communicated to them. When a child does not respond to a test direction, it is difficult to ascertain whether the child is incapable of completing the task or does not understand the task expected. In such situations, it is recommended that the examiner repeat the questions or directions to rule out lack of comprehension as a reason for the inaction of the child. If the examiner does not understand what the child is saying, it is best to be honest and tell him or her so, instead of being misleading and nodding affirmatively when the examiner has no idea what the child is saying. The child will soon realize that the examiner does not understand him or her, and this situation can have an adverse effect on rapport with the child, as well as on the reliability of testing results.

It is helpful if the child wears his or her hearing aid or auditory training unit (if he or she uses one) during the evaluation. However, hearing aids amplify all sounds in the environment, so care should be taken in scrambling blocks or in handling other testing materials not to make excessive noise. This can be both distracting and painful to the child. The usefulness of a hearing aid for a given child depends on the idiosyncratic interaction of a variety of variables; these include type and degree of hearing loss, age of onset, previous auditory training, and the ability to perceive acoustic signals from an impaired inner-ear mechanism. It is important to realize that, unlike glasses for a visual impairment, hearing aids do not *correct* a hearing impairment.

An interpreter is a person skilled in some form of sign language or in auditory/verbal communication and in English. This individual translates the examiner's spoken instructions into sign language and the child's sign language into speech. In the case of an oral interpreter, the individual restates the speech of the examiner; this individual may also interpret the child's speech for the examiner. A major disadvantage of using interpreters is a loss of rapport between the examiner and the child. This is because the child attends primarily to the interpreter rather than to the examiner. Care should be taken to insure that interpreters hired for the express purpose of mental testing of a hearing-impaired child are certified. Varying certifications are available, and it is worthwhile

for examiners employing these individuals to make sure interpreters are qualified in this regard. It must be remembered that the results of such an evaluation are not likely to meet high standards of validity (Sullivan & Burley, 1988; Sullivan & Vernon, 1979; Vernon & Brown, 1964).

Time Factors

Complete and valid intellectual assessments of hearing-impaired children often require more time than is needed with hearing children (Sullivan & Vernon, 1979; Vernon, 1976). Several introductory trials and examples of the test should be given to the child before actual testing begins. Tests that emphasize timed responses are often not as valid as those that do not (Vernon & Brown, 1964). Hearing-impaired children often react to being timed by trying to finish the task as quickly as possible, rather than concentrating on doing correct work. When an interpreter is employed, a longer time frame for the evaluation is to be expected.

Testing Young Hearing-Impaired Children

Test scores on preschool-age and primary-school-age hearing-impaired children tend to be extremely variable and unreliable (Sullivan & Vernon, 1979; Vernon, 1976). For this reason, low scores in particular should be viewed as questionable in the absence of other supporting data, such as a comparable performance on a measure of adaptive behavior and additional performance-type intelligence tests. Preschool-age hearing-impaired children should be re-evaluated periodically to insure appropriate placement.

Review of Available Tests

At the end of this chapter, Appendix 32.1 provides an update of previous recommendations regarding intelligence tests for use with the hearing-impaired (Vernon, 1976; Vernon & Brown, 1964; Sullivan & Vernon, 1979), as well as a review of tests not previously evaluated. Parts of Appendix 32.1 are adapted with permission from Sullivan and Vernon (1979).

TESTING IN THE FUTURE

Cronbach, a well-known leader in the field of tests and measurement, has asserted that IQ testing has run its course and that professionals and consumers are waiting for something new (quoted in Trotter, 1986). Future intelligence tests will probably measure distinct aptitudes and abilities in children (Hale, 1983). However, prediction of school achievement will continue to be the major function of mental tests.

Historically, research on the intelligence of deaf children has lagged behind that done with hearing children. It was not until the late 1960s and early 1970s that the distribution of nonverbal intelligence within the deaf population was accepted as being essentially normal. The factor structure of nonverbal intelligence in deaf children was not identified until the 1980s.

Issues involved in mental testing with hearing-impaired children in the future are most likely to include prediction issues, the incorporation of neuropsychology into evaluation, the use of computers, and new conceptions on the construct of intelligence.

Prediction Issues

A hearing-impaired child usually has a substantial history of language or school failure before he or she is given an intellectual evaluation. Often, those who select educational programs and modes of communication instruction either do not take a given child's intellectual functioning level into consideration or overgeneralize test results to predict success in a given setting. Ideally, program failure should be predicted before its occurrence. Administering predictors after the criterion of academic or instructional mode failure occurs is a misuse of intellectual assessment. More research is needed addressing the predictive validity of existing intelligence tests with hearing-impaired children in regard to academic achievement, type of school placement (i.e., residential vs. mainstreamed), and communication mode (i.e., oral/aural or some form of sign language).

Incorporating Neuropsychology into Evaluation

The heterogeneity of the hearing-impaired school-age population, with one-third possessing additional handicapping conditions, necessitates a more thorough understanding of a given child's cognitive and educational strengths and weaknesses. We know that the structure of nonverbal intelligence is essentially identical for hearing and deaf children (Braden, 1985). We do not know whether the same is true for verbal intelligence. The verbal intelligence of deaf children is likely to differ from that of normally hearing children, as the myelination of the auditory association cortex is probably not similar. Verbal intelligence is a better predictor of academic achievement in both hearing children (Zimmerman & Woo-Sam, 1972) and hearing-impaired children (Sullivan & Burley, 1988) than is nonverbal intelligence.

We need to identify varying patterns of cognitive abilities among the hearing-impaired population. To this end, evaluations of neuropsychological functioning with existing tests and the incorporation of such evaluations in the development of new mental tests are indicated. Thus, new tests will need to be normed on hearing-impaired children. This will allow us to predict learning success and possibly to link test results directly to remediation strategies.

Computer Usage

As with hearing children, more computer-based assessment may be expected in mental testing with hearing-impaired children. To this end, computer programs will need to be developed that do not unfairly penalize deaf children for poor English/reading skills in the assessment of intelligence. Computer graphics and the presentation of many sample items, with immediate feedback on the correctness of the response, may be heuristic methods to explore.

New Concepts of Intelligence

Sternberg (1985, 1986) has developed a new theory of intelligence, with "componential" (analytic), "experiential" (creative), and "contextual" (environmental manipulation) components. His studies on giftedness have indicated that gifted people have keen insight as a common denominator and that insight can be taught (Sternberg, 1985). Feuerstein, Rand, and Hoffman (1979) have demonstrated enhanced performance on IQ tests in borderline-functioning hearing children by teaching them how to employ the cognitive strategies of stimulus discrimination and verbal mediation.

These new concepts on the construct on intelligence have exciting possibilities for application with deaf children. As tests are developed that are based upon these theories, norms will be needed on hearing-impaired samples. Perhaps the most stimulating possibility is that the hearing-impaired child, or any child for that matter, will be viewed in terms of what he or she can do cognitively rather than what he or she cannot do. Such tests could be used for diagnosing intellectual strengths and weaknesses and identifying optimal instructional strategies.

CONCLUSIONS

It is essential to recognize that existing tests of mental abilities do not measure innate intelligence in hearing-impaired children. These tests sample only a small portion of a child's intellectual abilities. Thus, IQ scores are only estimates of ability, and they can and do change over time and experience. Perhaps most importantly, the results of an IQ test cannot tell us everything we need to know in making judgments about a hearing-impaired child's competence. Information from many sources that have been presented in this chapter needs to be integrated with information from intelligence tests in order to arrive at an accurate psychodiagnostic picture of a hearing-impaired child.

In the early 20th century, Theodore Roosevelt supported research in the emerging mental testing movement because he wanted to put an end to "hyphenated Americans" (Bartlett, 1980). Hyphenated descriptions of children have remained. Perhaps in the next century we will develop a more thorough understanding of cognitive competence and performance, as well as more accurate measurements of these functions. After all, we are all better at some things than we are at others.

APPENDIX 32.1. INTELLIGENCE TESTS AS USED WITH THE HEARING-IMPAIRED

Test: Bayley Scales of Infant Development (Bayley, 1969)

Age range: 2–30 months

Evaluation: The Bayley Mental Scale, Motor Scale, and Infant Behavior Record are well standardized developmental measures for hearing children and meet satisfactory reliability standards. Although not valid for predicting later functioning or achievement, the three scales provide valuable estimates of current developmental status that may be used with hearing-impaired infants. Approximately 36 of the 163 items on the Mental Scale require auditory and/or language skills. These items should be corrected in final scoring, according to the procedure employed on the Merrill–Palmer Scale of Mental Tests (Stutsman, 1931). The items should be attempted, in order for the examiner to gain data on language skills using the child's communication mode. However, many hearing-impaired children may be expected to fail most auditory/language-related items. All items are arranged developmentally. If the child passes a performance item at a higher level than a language item, the language item(s) should be credited that precede the successfully completed performance item.

Test: Developmental Activities Screening Inventory (DASI; DuBose & Langley, 1977)

Age range: 6 months–5 years

Evaluation: The DAIS is a valuable performance screening measure of cognitive development. Test items tap a variety of skills, including fine motor coordination, cause–effect and means–end relationships, number concepts, size discrimination, and association and seriation abilities. Limitations include an inadequate description of normative data and procedures in the manual; in addition, the composite developmental quotient is a psychometrically weak quantification of test performance. Concurrent validity appears to be adequate, but reliability data are not reported. Items are untimed, are easily administered, and do not penalize children with auditory impairments or language disorders. Administration adaptations are also available for visually impaired youngsters. The test appears to be appropriate for use with multihandicapped hearing-impaired children. Instructional suggestions for the concepts assessed are included.

Test: Goodenough–Harris Human Figure Drawing Test (Harris, 1963)

Age range: 3–15 years

Evaluation: The Goodenough–Harris Test is not recommended for assessing hearing-impaired children. Norms are outdated; hearing-impaired subjects were not included in the standardization; and only one aspect of intelligence (detail recognition) is measured.

Test: Hiskey–Nebraska Test of Learning Aptitude (Hiskey, 1966)

Age range: 3–17 years

Evaluation: The Hiskey is one of the best tests available for use with hearing-impaired children. Both hearing-impaired and hearing norms are provided, and comparisons, when appropriate, can be made of a given child's performance. Deaf norms are to be used, regardless of the child's degree of hearing loss, when pantomime administration directions are employed. Hearing norms should be used when the spoken subtest directions or total communication is employed. The discrepancy between scores using hearing and deaf norms is most probably due to the use of pantomime instructions. Although it is useful at younger age levels, the Hiskey should be supplemented with another of the measures described here when it is used with children 3 and 4 years of age. Pantomime subtest directions are easy to master; however, the test should only be administered by skilled examiners familiar with its administration procedures. Although normative data are inadequately described, reliability and concurrent validity data are adequate.

Test: Kaufman Assessment Battery for Children (K-ABC; Kaufman & Kaufman, 1983)

Age range: $2\frac{1}{2}$–$12\frac{1}{2}$ years

Evaluation: The K-ABC was developed to assess intelligence and achievement. The battery includes a Nonverbal scale recommended for use with youngsters aged 4–$12\frac{1}{2}$ who are demonstrating hearing and language disorders. The K-ABC appears appropriate for use with the hearing-impaired. Hearing-impaired children have exceptional difficulties with the subtests comprising the Sequential Processing scale, but their performance is comparable to that of the norming sample on all other scales (Gibbins, Ulissi, & Brice, in press). The Nonverbal scale may be the most appropriate to administer to hearing-impaired children. Performance on the K-ABC is highly correlated with academic achievement, particularly reading with the exception of the Sequential Processing scale (Gibbins et al., in press). Additional research is needed to demonstrate the validity of this test with hearing-impaired children. Until this is forthcoming, it is recommended that the K-ABC be supplemented with an additional nonverbal measure of intelligence.

Test: Merrill–Palmer Scale of Mental Tests (Stutsman, 1931)

Age range: 2–5 years

Evaluation: In spite of limited standardization and outdated norms, the variety of items presented within the Merrill–Palmer Scale are interesting to children and require a minimum of spoken instructions. A wide range of items that do not require verbal responses are included. Adjustments in scoring can be made for the items that are refused, omitted, or failed because of language difficulties. A composite score can be calculated by prorating methods. A weakness identified in the use of this test with hearing-impaired children is the time factor involved. Although the test can be administered nonverbally, it requires a skilled examiner with a thorough knowledge of the psychology of hearing impairment. As this is one of the few tests available with an adequate number of 2- and 3-year-olds in the standardization sample, it is a useful screening measure to ascertain developmental functioning. The test may also be used as a supplement to other performance measures.

Test: Smith–Johnson Nonverbal Performance Scale (Smith & Johnson, 1977)

Age range: 2–4 years

Evaluation: The Smith–Johnson is a fair test for use with young hearing-impaired children (Sullivan, 1985c). Norms for both sexes and for the hearing and hearing-impaired are provided. However, the hearing norms are somewhat dated (1960), and the hearing-impaired normative sample included 36% with profound hearing losses and 64% with mild and moderate losses. The majority of hearing-impaired subjects were hard-of-hearing rather than severely and profoundly deafened. The test may be more appropriate for use with the hard-of-hearing. Subtest directions are presented in pantomime, and many repetitions may be given. Although not recommended by the authors, total communication is suggested in the administration of this test to children who use this communication mode. Fourteen categories of subtests are presented, and the child's performance level is categorized as below average, average, or above average in comparison to peers of the same sex and chronological age. As may be expected in preschool measures, test–retest reliabilities are low. Both reliability and validity data with hearing-impaired children are inadequately described in the manual. This test may also be used with hearing children who exhibit language difficulties.

Test: Snijders–Oomen Non-Verbal Intelligence Scale for Young Children (SON; Snijders & Snijders-Oomen, 1975)

Age range: 2½–7 years

Evaluation: The SON contains separate norms for hearing and deaf children. The deaf standardization sample included all Dutch children enrolled in educational institutions, with the younger age groups underrepresented. The test is appealing because test directions can be administered either orally or in pantomime. The manual also provides a translation from Dutch to English. Reliability appears adequate, although little information regarding validity is provided in the manual. The test's major weakness is that norms were based upon deaf children in the Netherlands. However, this test is better normed than the Leiter with preschool-age children and is a good supplement to the Hiskey with younger hearing-impaired children. American norms need to be developed.

Test: Stanford–Binet Intelligence Scale: Fourth Edition (Thorndike, Hagen & Sattler, 1986)

Age range: 2–adulthood

Evaluation: Because of its heavy emphasis on language proficiency, the Stanford–Binet is totally inappropriate for use with hearing-impaired preschoolers and school-age children. However, the probability of its use with young children is quite high, given the mandate of P.L. 94-142 to identify handicapped children at the preschool level. Any

youngster who scores low on the Binet should be given an audiological examination routinely, as many children who present with mild to moderate hearing losses are frequently unidentified in the early years (Sullivan & Vernon, 1979).

Test: Test of Nonverbal Intelligence (TONI; Brown, Sherbenow, & Dollar, 1982)

Age range: 5 years, 0 months to 85 years, 11 months

Evaluation: The TONI was designed for use with language- and/or hearing-impaired individuals. Administration requires no verbal directions or verbal responses from the examinee. An ideal aspect of this test is the set of training items, which familarizes the examinee with the test format. Reliability and validity appear adequate; however, the sequencing of test items is uneven. The TONI should be supplemented with another instrument. It is very useful with multihandicapped children.

Test: Wachs Analysis of Cognitive Structures (Wachs & Vaughn, 1978)

Age range: 3–6 years

Evaluation: The Wachs Analysis of Cognitive Structures is based upon Piagetian theories of cognitive development and is primarily nonverbal in format. It appears to have promise for use with the hearing-impaired, although they were not included in the normative sample. This test may be used to supplement another measure on this table.

Test: Wechsler Preschool and Primary Scale of Intelligence (WPPSI), Performance subtests (Wechsler, 1967)

Age range: 3 years, 11 months to 6 years, 8 months

Evaluation: As most subtest directions are difficult to explain either in oral/aural communication, pantomime, or total communication, the WPPSI is not recommended for use with young hearing-impaired children.

Test: Arthur Adaptation of the Leiter International Performance Scale (Arthur, 1950)

Age range: 2–18 years

Evaluation: The Leiter is not appropriate for use with very young and preschool hearing-impaired children, because norms for these age ranges are extrapolated from those for older children. In general, the test is psychometrically inadequate, inappropriately standardized, and lacking in reliability and validity for use with all hearing impaired children. These limitations offset the ease of pantomime administration. See Ratcliffe and Ratcliffe (1979) for a review of these issues.

Test: Raven's Progressive Matrices (Raven, 1948)

Age range: 9 years–adulthood

Evaluation: Although the hearing-impaired were not included in the norming sample, Raven's Progressive Matrices may be appropriate for use as a second test to supplement another performance measure. The matrices are appealing because of their ease of administration and are simple to score. With hearing-impaired children, care should be taken to insure that they are not responding impulsively.

Test: Wechsler Intelligence Scale for Children—Revised (WISC-R), Performance scale (Wechsler, 1974)

Age range: 6–16 years

Evaluation: The WISC-R Performance scale is an excellent test for use with school-age hearing-impaired children. It is ideally used with the Hiskey–Nebraska Test of Learning Aptitude as a supplementary performance test. The Performance scale has been standardized with a hearing-impaired sample (Anderson & Sisco, 1977). However, research is needed to demonstrate the efficacy of these norms. A number of different sign systems and administrations were used in the standardization procedure, which may account for the population's mean Performance IQ of 95 and standard deviation of 18. These parameters must be considered in interpreting scores. Previously recommended administration modifications, such as pantomime and visual aids, should not be employed if the child is instructed in total communication. All six subtests should be administered. If the child has undue difficulty with Picture Arrangement and Coding only, which is frequently the case with the hearing-impaired, the Performance IQ may be prorated from the other four subtests. If the child has difficulty with Coding only, Mazes may be substituted and the Performance IQ may be computed from five subtests. However, these procedures affect test reliability

and underscore the importance of administering more than one performance intelligence measure. The Ray (1979) adaptations are not recommended because of norming, validation, and reliability inadequacies.

Note. Portions of this appendix are adapted from "Psychological Assessment of Hearing Impaired Children" by P. M. Sullivan and M. Vernon, 1979, *School Psychology Digest, 8,* 271–29. Copyright 1979 by P. M. Sullivan. Adapted by permission.

REFERENCES

American Psychiatric Association. (1980). *Diagnostic and statistical manual of mental disorders* (3rd ed.). Washington, DC: Author.

Anderson, R. J., & Sisco, F. H. (1977). *Standardization of the WISC-R Performance scale for deaf children.* Washington, DC: Gallaudet University, Office of Demographic Studies.

Arthur, G. (1950). *The Arthur Adaptation of the Leiter International Performance Scale.* Chicago: Stoelting.

Bartlett, J. (1980). *Bartlett's familiar quotations: 125th anniversary edition.* Boston: Little, Brown.

Bauman, M. (1968). *A report and a reprint: Tests used in the psychological evaluation of blind and visually handicapped persons and a manual of norms for tests used in counseling blind persons.* Washington, DC: American Association of Workers for the Blind.

Bayley, N. (1969). *Bayley Scales of Infant Development.* New York: Psychological Corporation.

Braden, J. P. (1985). The structure of nonverbal intelligence in deaf and hearing subjects. *American Annals of the Deaf, 130,* 496–501.

Brasel, K., & Quigley, S. (1975). *The influence of early language and communication environments in the development of language in deaf children.* Champaign: University of Illinois, Institute for Research on Exceptional Children.

Brill, R. G. (1972). The relationship of Wechsler IQ's to academic achievement among deaf students. *Exceptional Children, 28,* 315–321.

Brown, L., Sherbenow, R. J., & Dollar, S. J. (1982). *Test of Nonverbal Intelligence.* Austin, TX: Pro-Ed.

Chess, S. (1977). Follow-up report on autism in congenital rubella. *Journal of Autism and Childhood Schizophrenia, 7,* 69–81.

Clarke, B. R., & Leslie, P. T. (1971). Visual–motor skills and reading ability of deaf children. *Perceptual and Motor Skills, 33,* 263–268.

Craig, W., & Craig, H. (1975). Directory of services for the deaf. *American Annals of the Deaf, 120.*

Darby, J. D. (1976). Neuropathologic aspect of psychosis in children. *Journal of Autism and Childhood Schizophrenia, 6,* 339–352.

Degraff, A. C., & Creger, W. P. (Eds.). (1963). *Annual review of medicine.* Palo Alto, CA: George Banta.

Donoghue, R. (1968). The deaf personality: A study in contrasts. *Journal of Rehabilitation of the Deaf, 2*(1), 35–51.

Downs, M. P. (1976). The handicap of deafness. In J. L. Northern (Ed.), *Hearing disorders* (pp. 195–206). Boston: Little, Brown.

Du Bose, R., & Langley, D. B. (1977). *Developmental Activities Screening Inventory*. New York: New York Times Teaching Resources.

Easterbrooks, S. R. (1987). Speech/language assessment and intervention with school age hearing impaired children. In J. G. Alpiner & P. A. McCarthy (Eds.), *Rehabilitative audiology: Children and adults* (pp. 188–195). Baltimore: Williams & Wilkins.

Eichhorn, S. K. (1982). Congenital cytomegalovirus infection: A significant cause of deafness and mental deficiency. *American Annals of the Deaf, 127*, 838–843.

Erting, C. (1978). Language policy and deaf ethnicity in the United States. *Sign Language Studies, 19*, 139–152.

Evans, L. (1966). A comparative study of the WISC Performance Scale and Raven's Progressive Matrices with deaf children. *Teacher of the Deaf, 64*, 76–82.

Feuerstein, R., Rand, Y., & Hoffman, M. B. (1979). *The dynamic assessment of retarded performers: The Learning Potential Assessment Device, theory, instruments, and techniques*. Baltimore: University Park Press.

Ford, F. R. (1960). *Diseases of the nervous system in infancy, childhood and adolescence* (4th ed.). Springfield, IL: Charles C Thomas.

Frisina, R. (1974). *Report of the Committee to Redefine Deaf and Hard of Hearing for Educational Purposes*. Paper presented at the Conference of Executives of American Schools for the Deaf, Washington, DC.

Furth, H. (1964). Research with the deaf: Implications for language and cognition. *Psychological Bulletin, 62*, 145–162.

Gehrz, R. C. (1984). *CMV: Diagnosis, prevention and treatment*. (Available from Children's Hospital of St. Paul, St. Paul, Minnesota 55102).

Gellis, S., & Kagan, B. (1976). *Current pediatric therapy*. Philadelphia: W. B. Saunders.

Genshaft, J. L. (1985). Review of Wechsler Intelligence Scale for Children—Revised: For the Deaf. In J. V. Mitchell (Ed.), *The ninth mental measurements yearbook* (pp. 1720–1721). Lincoln, NE: Buros Institute of Mental Measurements.

Gentile, A., & McCarthy, B. (1973). *Additional handicapping conditions among hearing impaired students, United States: 1971–1972*. Washington, DC: Gallaudet University, Office of Demographic Studies.

Gerweck, S., & Ysseldyke, J. (1974). Limitations of current psychological practices for the intellectual assessment of the hearing impaired: A response to the Levine study. *Volta Review, 77*, 243–258.

Gibbins, S., Ulissi, S. M., & Brice, P. (in press). The use of the Kaufman Assessment Battery for Children with the hearing impaired. *American Annals of the Deaf*.

Goldman, J., Stein, C. L., & Guerry, S. (1983). *Psychological methods of child assessment*. New York: Brunner/Mazel.

Graham, E. E., & Shapiro, E. (1953). Use of the Performance scale of the Wechsler Intelligence Scale for Children with the deaf child. *Journal of Consulting Psychology, 17*, 396–398.

Haggerty, R., & Ziai, M. (1964). Acute bacterial meningitis. *Advances in Pediatrics, 13*, 129–181.

Hales, R. L. (1983). Intellectual assessment. In M. Hersen, A. Kazdin, & A. Bellack (Eds.), *The clinical psychology handbook* (pp. 345–376). New York: Pergamon Press.

Hanshaw, J. B. (1982). On deafness, cytomegalovirus and neonatal screening. *American Journal of Diseases of Children, 136*, 886–887.

Hardy, M. P. (1970). Speechreading. In H. Davis & A. S. Silverman (Eds.), *Hearing and deafness* (pp. 335–345). New York: Holt, Rinehart & Winston.

Harris, D. (1963). *Children's drawings as measures of intellectual maturity*. New York: Harcourt Brace Jovanovich.

Hirshoren, A., Hurley, O. L., & Hunt, J. T. (1977). The WISC-R and the Hiskey–Nebraska Test with deaf children. *American Annals of the Deaf, 122*, 392–394.

Hirshoren, A., Kavale, K., Hurley, O. L., & Hunt, J. T. (1977). The reliability of the WISC-R Performance scale with deaf children. *Psychology in the Schools, 14*, 412–415.

Hiskey, M. S. (1966). *Hiskey–Nebraska Test of Learning Aptitude*. Lincoln, NE: Union College Press.

Hudgins, R. (1973). *Causes of deafness among students of the Clarke School for the Deaf* (106th annual report). Northampton, MA: Clarke School for the Deaf.

Hurley, O. L., Hirshoren, A., Kavale, K., & Hunt, J. T. (1978). Intercorrelations among tests of general mental ability and achievement for black and white deaf children. *Perceptual and Motor Skills, 46*, 1107–1113.

Jensema, C., & Mullins, J. (1974). Onset, cause, and additional handicaps in hearing impaired children. *American Annals of the Deaf, 119*, 701–705.

Johnson, D. J., & Myklebust, H. (1967). *Learning disabilities: Educational principles and practices*. New York: Grune & Stratton.

Karchmer, M. A. (1985). A demographic perspective. In E. Cherow (Ed.), *Hearing impaired children and youth with developmental disabilities: An interdisciplinary foundation for service* (pp. 36–56). Washington, DC: Gallaudet University Press.

Kaufman, A. S., & Kaufman, N. L. (1983). *Kaufman Assessment Battery for Children (K-ABC)*. Circle Pines, MN: American Guidance Service.

Klima, E. S., & Bellugi, U. (1972). The signs of language in child and chimpanzee. In T. Alloway (Ed.), *Communication and effect* (pp. 67–96). New York: Academic Press.

Konigsmark, B. (1972). Genetic hearing loss with no associated abnormalities: A review. *Journal of Speech and Hearing Disorders, 37*, 89–99.

Kusche, C. A., Greenberg, M. T., & Garfield, T. S. (1983). Nonverbal intelligence and verbal achievement in deaf adolescents: An examination of heredity and environment. *American Annals of the Deaf, 128*, 458–466.

Lavos, G. (1962). WISC psychometric patterns among deaf children. *Volta Review, 64*, 547–552.

Lenneberg, E. H. (1967). *Biological foundations of language*. New York: Wiley.

Levine, E. S. (1974). Psychological tests and practices with the deaf: A survey of the state of the art. *Volta Review, 76*, 298–319.

Levine, E. S. (1981). *The ecology of early deafness: Guides to fashioning environments and psychological assessments*. New York: Columbia University Press.

Levine, M. N. (1986). Psychoeducational evaluation of children and adolescents with cerebral palsy. In P. J. Lazarus & S. S. Strichart (Eds.), *Psychoeducational evaluation of children and adolescents with low-incidence handicaps* (pp. 267–284). New York: Grune & Stratton.

Linton, T., & Juul, K. (1980). Mainstreaming: Time for reassessment. *Educational Leadership*, 37(5), 433–437.

Lloyd, L., & Kaplan, H. (1978). *Audiometric interpretation: A manual of basic audiometry*. Baltimore: University Park Press.

MacDonald, H., & Tobin, J. (1978). Congenital cytomegalovirus infection: A collaborative study on epidemiological, clinical and laboratory findings. *Developmental Medicine and Child Neurology, 20*, 471–482.

Matarazzo, J. D. (1972). *Wechsler's measurement and appraisal of adult intelligence*. Baltimore: Williams & Wilkins.

Meadow, K. P. (1968). Early manual communication in relation to the deaf child's intellectual, social, and communicative functioning. *American Annals of the Deaf, 113*, 29–41.

Meadow, K. P. (1972). Sociolinguistics, sign language, and the deaf subculture. In T. J. O'Rourke (Ed.), *Psycholinguistics and total communication: The state of the art* (pp. 19–33). Silver Springs, MD: T. J. Publishers.

Meadow, K. P. (1980). *Deafness and child development*. Berkeley: University of California Press.

Meadow, K. P. (1981). Studies of behavior problems of deaf children. In L. Stein, E. Mindel, T. Jabaley (Eds.), *Deafness and mental health* (pp. 3–22). New York: Grune & Stratton.

Meadow, K. P., & Trybus, R. (1979). Behavioral and emotional problems of deaf children: A review. In L. J. Bradford & W. G. Hardy (Eds.), *Hearing and hearing impairment* (pp. 395–403). New York: Grune & Stratton.

Medoff, M. (1980). *Children of a lesser god*. Clifton, NJ: James T. White.

Mindel, E., & Vernon, M. (1971). *They grow in silence*. Silver Springs, MD: National Association of the Deaf.

Moores, D. F. (1987). *Educating the deaf: Psychology, principles, and practices* (3rd ed.). Boston: Houghton Mifflin.

Moores, D. F., Weiss, K. L., & Goodwin, M. W. (1978). Early education programs for hearing impaired children: Major findings. *American Annals of the Deaf, 123*, 925–936.

Morgan, S. B. (1986). Early childhood autism: Changing perspectives. *Journal of Child and Adolescent Psychotherapy, 3*, 3–9.

Murphy, K. P. (1957). Test of abilities and attainments. In A. W. G. Ewing (Ed.), *Educational guidance and the deaf child* (pp. 213–251). Manchester, England: Manchester University Press.

Myklebust, H. R. (1964). *The psychology of deafness*. New York: Grune & Stratton.

Myklebust, H., & Brutton, M. (1953). A study of visual perception in deaf children. *Acta Otolaryngologica, 105*, 1–126.

Myklebust, H. R., & Burchard, E. M. (1945). A study of the effects of congenital and adventitious deafness on the intelligence, personality and social maturity of school children. *Journal of Educational Psychology, 34*, 321–332.

Neuhaus, M. (1967). Modifications in the administration of the WISC Performance subtests for children with profound hearing losses. *Exceptional Children, 33*, 573–574.

Newcomer, P. L., & Hammill, D. D. (1977). *The Test of Language Development*. Austin, TX: Empiric Press.

Padden, C., & Markowicz, H. (1976). Cultural conflicts between hearing and deaf communities. In F. B. & A. B. Crammatte (Eds.), *Proceedings of the VII World Congress of the World Federation of the Deaf*. Washington, DC: National Association of the Deaf.

Piggott, L. R. (1979). Overview of selected basic research in autism. *Journal of Autism and Developmental Disorders, 9*, 199–218.

Pintner, R., Eisenson, J., & Stanton, M. (1941). *The psychology of the physically handicapped*. New York: Crofts.

Pintner, R., & Patterson, D. G. (1915). The Binet Scale and the deaf child. *Journal of Educational Psychology, 6*, 201–210.

Pintner, R., & Patterson, D. (1917). A comparison of deaf and hearing children in visual memory span for digits. *Journal of Experimental Psychology, 2*, 76–88.

Power, A., Elliott, R., & Funderburg, R. (1987). Learning disabled hearing-impaired students: Are they being identified? *Volta Review, 89*, 99–105.

Quigley, S., & Frisina, D. (1961). *Institutionalization and psycho-educational development of deaf children*. Washington, DC: Council for Exceptional Children.

Ratcliffe, K. J., & Ratcliffe, M. W. (1979). The Leiter Scales: A review of validity findings. *American Annals of the Deaf, 124*, 38–45.

Raven, J. (1948). *Progressive Matrices*. New York: Psychological Corporation.

Rawlings, B., & Gentile, A. (1970). *Additional handicapping conditions, age of onset of hearing loss, and other characteristics of hearing impaired students, United States, 1968–1969*. Washington, DC: Gallaudet University, Office of Demographic Studies.

Ray, S. (1979). *Wechsler Intelligence Scales for Children—Revised: For the Deaf*. Northwestern State University, Natchitoches, LA: Author.

Ray, S. (1982). Adapting the WISC-R for deaf children. *Diagnostique, 7*, 147–157.

Reed, M. (1970). Deaf and partially hearing children. In P. Mittler (Ed.), *The psychological assessment of mental and physical handicaps* (pp. 403–441). London: Methuen.

Reschly, D., & Reschly, J. E. (1979). Validity of WISC-R factor scores in predicting achievement and attention for four sociocultural groups. *Journal of School Psychology, 17*, 355–361.

Reynell, J. (1977). *Reynell Developmental Language Scales—Revised*. Windsor, England: National Foundation for Educational Research.

Ries, P. (1973). *Reported causes of hearing loss for hearing impaired students: 1970–1971* (Annual Survey of Hearing Impaired Children and Youth, Series D, No. 11). Washington, DC: Gallaudet College, Office of Demographic Studies.

Rosen, A. (1967). Limitations of personality inventories for assessment of deaf children and adults as illustrated by research with the MMPI. *Journal of Rehabilitation of the Deaf, 1*, 47–52.

Rosenstein, J. (1961). Perception, cognition and language in deaf children. *Exceptional Children, 27*, 276–284.

Rules and Regulations for Implementing Education for All Handicapped Children Act of 1975, P.L. 94-142, 42 Fed. Reg. 42474 (1977).

Rutter, M. (1979). Definition of childhood autism. In L. A. Lockman, K. F. Swaiman, J. S. Drage, K. B. Nelson, & H. M. Marsden (Eds.), *Workshop on the neurobiological basis of autism* (NINCDS Monograph No. 23, DHEW Publication No. 79-1855, pp. 3–29). Washington, DC: U.S. Government Printing Office.

Salvia, J., & Ysseldyke, J. E. (1981). *Assessment in special and remedial education* (2nd ed.). Boston: Houghton Mifflin.

Sank, D., & Kallman, F. (1963). The role of heredity in early total deafness. *Volta Review, 65,* 461–476.

Sattler, J. M. (1988). *Assessment of children's intelligence and special abilities* (3rd ed.). Boston: Allyn & Bacon.

Schick, H. F. (1934). A performance test for deaf children of school age. *Volta Review, 34,* 657–663.

Schlesinger, H. S., & Meadow, K. (1972). *Sound and sign: Childhood deafness and mental health.* Berkeley: University of California Press.

Schlesinger, I. M. (1974). Relational concepts underlying language. In R. L. Schiefelbusch & L. L. Lloyd (Eds.), *Language perspectives: Acquisition, retardation and intervention* (pp. 129–151). Baltimore: University Park Press.

Shaver, K. A., Boughman, J. A., & Nance, W. E. (1985). Congenital rubella syndrome and diabetes: A review of epidemiologic, genetic and immunologic factors. *American Annals of the Deaf, 130,* 526–532.

Sisco, F. H., & Anderson, R. J. (1980). Deaf children's performance on the WISC-R relative to hearing status of parents and child-rearing experiences. *American Annals of the Deaf, 125,* 923–930.

Smith, A. J., & Johnson, R. E. (1977). *Smith–Johnson Nonverbal Performance Scale.* Los Angeles: Western Psychological Services.

Snijders, J. T., & Snijders-Oomen, N. (1975). *Snijders-Oomen Non-Verbal Intelligence Scale for Young Children.* Amsterdam: Swets Test Services.

Stagno, S., Pass, R. F., & Dworsky, M. E. (1982). Maternal cytomegalovirus infection and perinatal transmission. *Clinical Obstetrics and Gynecology, 25,* 563–576.

Stanford Achievement Tests, Special Edition for Hearing Impaired (1982). New York: Harcourt, Brace, Jovanovich.

Stein, L., Palmer, P., & Weinberg, B. (1982). Characteristics of a young deaf–blind population. *American Annals of the Deaf, 127,* 828–837.

Sternberg, R. J. (1985). *Beyond IQ.* Cambridge, England: Cambridge University Press.

Sternberg, R. J. (1986). *Intelligence applied.* New York: Harcourt Brace Jovanovich.

Stevenson, E. A. (1964). A study of the educational achievement of deaf children of deaf parents. *California News, 80,* 1–3.

Stillman, R. D. (1975). *Assessment of deaf–blind children: The Callier–Azusa Scale.* Dallas, TX: Callier Hearing and Speech Center.

Stokoe, W. (1972a). *Semiotics and human sign languages.* The Hague: Mouton.

Stokoe, W. (1972b). *The study of sign language.* Silver Spring, MD: National Association of the Deaf.

Strauss, M. (1985). A clinical pathologic study of hearing loss in congenital cytomegalovirus infections. *Laryngoscope, 95,* 951–962.

Streng, A., & Kirk, S. A. (1938). The social competence of deaf and hard-of-hearing children in a public day school. *American Annals of the Deaf, 83,* 244–249.

Stuckless, E., & Birch, J. (1966). The influence of early manual communication on the linguistic development of deaf children. *American Annals of the Deaf, 111,* 499–504.

Stutsman, R. (1931). *Merrill–Palmer Scale of Mental Tests.* Chicago: Stoelting.

Sullivan, P. M. (1982a). Administration modifications on the WISC-R Performance scale with different categories of deaf children. *American Annals of the Deaf, 127,* 780–788.

Sullivan, P. M. (1982b). Modified instructions for administering the WISC-R Performance scale subtests to deaf children. In J. M. Sattler, *Assessment of children's intelligence and special abilities* (2nd ed., pp. 548–551). Boston: Allyn & Bacon.

Sullivan, P. M. (1985a). Socially and emotionally impaired deaf youth: Assessment and intervention models. In G. B. Anderson, & D. Watson (Eds.), *The habilitation and rehabilitation of deaf adolescents* (pp. 81–108). Washington, DC: National Academy of Gallaudet University.

Sullivan, P. M. (1985b). Review of Wechsler Intelligence Scales for Children—Revised: For the Deaf. In J. V. Mitchell (Ed.), *The ninth mental measurements yearbook* (Vol. 2, pp. 1721–1723). Lincoln, NE: Buros Institute of Mental Measurements.

Sullivan, P. M. (1985c). Review of Smith–Johnson Nonverbal Performance Scale. In J. V. Mitchell (Ed.), *The ninth mental measurements yearbook* (Vol. 2, pp. 1404–1405). Lincoln, NE: Buros Institute of Mental Measurements.

Sullivan, P. M. (1986a). Psychological evaluation. In J. VanCleve (Ed.), *Encyclopedia of deaf people and deafness* (Vol. 2, pp. 332–336). New York: McGraw-Hill.

Sullivan, P. M. (1986b). Intelligence. In J. Van Cleve (Ed.), *Encyclopedia of deaf people and deafness* (Vol. 2, pp. 83–86. New York: McGraw-Hill.

Sullivan, P. M., Brookhouser, P. E., & Burley, S. K. (in press). Intellectually gifted deaf adolescents: Etiologic, academic and behavioral correlates. *International Journal of Pediatric Otorhinolaryngology.*

Sullivan, P. M., & Burley, S. K. (1988). *The relationship between IQ and academic achievement in a residential deaf school population.* Unpublished manuscript.

Sullivan, P. M., & Vernon, M. (1979). Psychological assessment of hearing impaired children. *School Psychology Digest, 8,* 271–290.

Sullivan, P. M., Vernon, M., & Scanlan, J. (1987). Sexual abuse of deaf youth. *American Annals of the Deaf, 132,* 256–262.

Swartz, M. N., & Dodge, P. R. (1965). Bacterial meningitis—a review of selected aspects: II. Special neurological problems, postmeningitic complications and clinicopathological correlations (concluded). *New England Journal of Medicine, 272,* 954–926.

Thorndike, R. L., Hagen, E. P., & Sattler, J. M. (1986). *Stanford–Binet Intelligence Scale: Fourth Edition.* Chicago: Riverside.

Trotter, R. J. (1986, August). Three heads are better than one. *Psychology Today,* pp. 56–62.

Trybus, R. J., & Karchmer, M. A. (1977). School achievement scores of hearing impaired children: National data on achievement status and growth patterns. *American Annals of the Deaf, 122,* 62–69.

Turkington, C. (1982, June). Mental health services for the deaf. *APA Monitor*, pp. 24–25.

Vernon, M. (1967a). Meningitis and deafness. *Laryngoscope, 10*, 1856–1874.

Vernon, M. (1967b). Relationship of language to the thinking process. *Archives of General Psychiatry, 16*, 325–333.

Vernon, M. (1967c). Rh factor and deafness. *Exceptional Children, 34*, 5–12.

Vernon, M. (1968a). Current etiological factors in deafness. *American Annals of the Deaf, 113*, 106–115.

Vernon, M. (1968b). Fifty years of research on the intelligence of the deaf and hard of hearing. *Journal Rehabilitation of the Deaf, 1*, 1–12.

Vernon, M. (1969a). *Multiply handicapped deaf children: Medical, educational and psychological considerations* (Research monograph, Grant No. RD-2407-S). Washington, DC: Council for Exceptional Children.

Vernon, M. (1969b). Usher's syndrome: Deafness and progressive blindness. *Journal of Chronic Diseases, 22*, 133–151.

Vernon, M. (1970a). Psychological evaluation and interviewing the hearing impaired. *Rehabilitation Research and Practice Review, 1*,(2), 45–52.

Vernon, M. (1970b). Clinical phenomenon of cerebral palsy and deafness. *Exceptional Children, 36*, 743–751.

Vernon, M. (1976). Psychological evaluation of hearing impaired children. In L. Lloyd (Ed.), *Communication assessment and intervention strategies* (pp. 195–224). Baltimore: University Park Press.

Vernon, M., Bair, R., & Lotz, S. (1979). Psychological evaluation and testing of children who are deaf–blind. *School Psychology Digest, 8*, 291–295.

Vernon, M., & Brown, D. W. (1964). A guide to psychological tests and testing procedures in the evaluation of deaf and hard of hearing children. *Journal of Speech and Hearing Disorders, 29*, 414–423.

Vernon, M., & Hicks, D. (1980). Relationship of rubella, herpes simplex, cytomegalovirus and certain other viral disabilities. *American Annals of the Deaf, 125*, 529–534.

Vernon, M., & Koh, S. (1970). Effects of manual communication on deaf children's educational achievement, linguistic competence, oral skills, and psychological development. *American Annals of the Deaf, 115*, 527–536.

Vernon, M., & Sullivan, P. M. (Advisors). (1982). *Deaf not dumb: A look at the psychological evaluation of the deaf* [Film]. Boys Town, NE: Father Flanagan's Boys' Home.

Wachs, O. D., & Vaughn, M. A. (1978). *Wachs Analysis of Cognitive Structures*. Los Angeles: Western Psychological Services.

Watson, B., Sullivan, P., Moeller, M. P., & Jensen, J. (1982). The relationship of performance on nonverbal intelligence tests and English language ability in prelingually deaf children. *Journal of Speech and Hearing Disorders, 47*, 199–203.

Wechsler, D. (1949). *Wechsler Intelligence Scale for Children*. New York: Psychological Corporation.

Wechsler, D. (1967). *Wechsler Preschool and Primary Scale of Intelligence*. New York: Psychological Corporation.

Wechsler, D. (1974). *Wechsler Intelligence Scale for Children—Revised*. New York: Psychological Corporation.

Wing, L., & Attwood, A. (1987). Syndromes of autism and atypical development. In D. Cohen & A. Donnellan (Eds.), *A handbook of autism and pervasive developmental disorders* (pp. 3–19). New York: Wiley.

Woodward, J. (Ed.). (1982). *How you gonna get to heaven if you can't talk with Jesus*. Silver Spring, MD: T. J. Publishers.

Woodward, J., & Markowicz, H. (1982). Language and the maintenance of ethnic boundaries in the deaf community. In J. Woodward (Ed.), *How you gonna get to heaven if you can't talk with Jesus* (pp. 3–9). Silver Spring, MD: T. J. Publishers.

Zimmerman, I. L., & Woo-Sam, J. (1972). Research with the Wechsler Intelligence Scale for Children: 1960–1970. *Psychology in the Schools, 9*, 232–271.

33

Assessing the Psychological and Educational Needs of the Moderately and Severely Mentally Retarded

CHRISTINE W. BURNS
University of Northern Colorado

An important distinction must be made between "assessment" and the narrower term "testing." Assessment is a process that enables one to analyze critically and evaluate the nature of children's characteristics. Assessment may involve tests, interviewing, observation of behavior in natural or structured settings, and recording of physiological functions. Tests represent a specific aspect of the assessment process. Anastasi (1968) defines a test as "an objective and standardized measure of a sample of behavior" (p. 21). This chapter focuses on the assessment of the moderately and severely mentally retarded.

GOALS AND LIMITATIONS OF ASSESSMENT

The psychological and educational assessment of the moderately and severely retarded may be defined in terms of three goals: (1) diagnosis, (2) documentation of status or progress, and (3) planning or prescribing intervention. A diagnostic goal is appropriate when it is necessary to determine whether a child's performance reflects established criteria for the diagnosis of mental retardation. Normative instruments are typically used to yield information to confirm or disconfirm the diagnosis. When there is a

need to verify a child's current status or change in status from one occasion to another, the goal of assessment is that of documentation of status or progress. The goal of planning or prescribing interventions involves assessment to obtain a profile of a child's unique strengths and deficits from which an intervention program can be developed.

Underlying these goals is the basic assumption of psychological assessment: that the instruments used are valid for the purpose selected and will document accurately the skills, traits, attributes, or behaviors of interest. A number of factors exist that limit this assumption with the moderately and severely mentally retarded. These limitations may affect the formulation of referral questions, the selection of instruments and/or techniques, and the degree of confidence with which inferences can be drawn about assessment results. Limitations are imposed by definitional issues, child characteristics, examiner characteristics, and measurement issues.

Definitional Issues

There is a lack of consensus on the definitions of basic terms. Labels such as "severely disabled," "moderately impaired," "moderately

TABLE 33.1. Classification System for Mental Retardation

Level of functioning, based on IQ	Classification
50–70	Mild retardation
35–49	Moderate retardation
20–34	Severe retardation
Below 20	Profound retardation

retarded," or "multiply handicapped" have frequently been used to describe a child who is handicapped in some way. The variability of labels applied to "special children" (Simeonsson, 1986) has contributed to the confusion and to the difficulties in generalization of assessment and treatment results.

The most widely endorsed definition for "mental retardation" has been set forth by the American Association on Mental Deficiency (AAMD): "Mental retardation refers to significantly subaverage general intellectual functioning resulting in or associated with impairments in adaptive behavior and manifested during the developmental period" (Grossman, 1983, p. 1). The heterogeneous nature of the population of mentally retarded individuals requires some classification system that will allow subgroupings. The most common system subdivides the mentally retarded into four levels, as presented in Table 33.1.

Child Limitations

Mentally retarded children are very likely to have impaired functioning in more than one area. Limitations that affect the psychological assessment of these children can be grouped into two categories: internal and external limitations. Limitations of an internal nature are those that affect the child's level of responsiveness and reactivity. Levels of arousal, or state, may vary widely from extended periods of sleep and drowsiness to a state of agitation and excessive activity for the severely handicapped. Such variability may be reflective of neurological insults (Touwen & Kalverboer, 1973). It may also be an expression of the effects of medications administered to manage seizures or other medical conditions. The variability of state in mentally retarded children may contribute to differ-

ent performances from one observation to the next (Simeonsson, 1986).

Limitations of an external nature include aspects of the child's sensory and/or motor functioning. For example, impairments of vision, kinesthesis, or hearing may limit the child's performance and expression in the assessment process. Repetitive, rhythmic habit patterns such as rocking, head banging, and head rolling, which are found to varying degrees in these children, constitute another limitation of an external nature (Kravitz & Boehm, 1971). These behaviors severely limit a child's ability to attend to the stimuli presented by the examiner, and therefore interfere with accurate assessment of the child's abilities.

Examiner Limitations

Examiners frequently lack the special knowledge or skills to carry out the psychological assessment of the moderately and severely mentally retarded. Graduate training programs, in their clinical assessment classes and practicum experiences, emphasize assessment of those individuals with mild mental handicaps; little exposure is provided to the moderately and severely retarded populations. An examiner's personal orientation may also limit adequate assessment of this population. Such personal bias may result in misidentification of the problems and in inappropriate domains' being selected for assessment. Although complete objectivity may be difficult to achieve, awareness of one's personal orientation as a source of bias in assessment may help to reduce this aspect of examiner limitations.

Measurement Limitations

There is a paucity of practical instruments for assessing the severely mentally retarded population. In addition, normative tables generally do not permit the estimation of functioning levels for this population. For example, the Wechsler Intelligence Scale For Children—Revised (WISC-R; Wechsler, 1974) does not permit calculation of an IQ below 40. The Stanford–Binet Intelligence Scale—both Form L-M (Terman & Merrill, 1973) and the recent Fourth Edition (Thorndike, Hagen, & Sattler, 1986)—does permit calculations of IQs below 40; however, it is important to note that these values are extrapolated data. There were no children in the standardization sample functioning at this low level. Extrapolated test scores are not appropriate for individual diagnosis, because their reliability is unknown. Reynolds and Clark (1985) have developed a method that allows for the interpretation of low-functioning individuals' performance in cases where variability in performance might otherwise be obscured by the lack of sufficient floor in tests appropriately normed for the individuals' chronological age.

Current psychological assessment procedures can be grouped into three major strategies on the basis of the approach to assessment. The three approaches are psychometric, behavioral, and qualitative–developmental. With any particular strategy, the focus of the assessment may be categorized within one of four domains: cognitive, communicative, personal/social, and behavioral functioning.

PSYCHOMETRIC ASSESSMENT

Psychometric assessment enables one to quantify a child's characteristics and compare these devised quantitative values against a norm or standard. The interpretation of the variability in mental abilities through profile analysis can provide valuable information for educational and therapeutic programming.

However, when one attempts to conduct a profile analysis with very low-functioning individuals, little variability in scores is observed. Whether this is due to an actually "flat" profile or to an artifact of the test (i.e., insufficient floor) is not always apparent (Reynolds & Clark, 1985). Depending on the age of the individual being assessed and the particular scale used, a large range of raw-score points may be compressed into a single scaled-score point at the lower end of the distribution. This is a problem with tests such as the Wechsler scales and the Kaufman Assessment Battery for Children (K-ABC; Kaufman & Kaufman, 1983a, 1983b), where subtests of the intelligence scales are set to a scaled-score mean of 10 and a standard deviation of 3. For example, on the K-ABC, when a 12½-year-old is being tested, raw scores from 0 to 7 all earn scaled scores of 1 on Gestalt Closure and on Spatial Memory. At

least one scaled score above 4 is required before a strength or weakness in any area can identified; more than 13 raw-score points are necessary with some students to achieve a scaled score of 4. The same problem exists on the WISC-R: At the upper age limit, as many as 31 raw-score points may only earn a scaled score of 1 or 2 on several subtests. Therefore, even though considerable variability may exist in an individual's abilities, this variability may be obscured by the test if the individual's overall level of intellectual functioning is in the IQ range below 55.

A Method of Intraindividual Analysis

Some examiners, in an attempt to overcome the problem described above, will use age or grade equivalents for the purposes of intraindividual comparisons. However, score comparisons based on age and grade equivalent score systems are inaccurate and misleading (Reynolds, 1981). Reynolds and Clark (1985) have proffered a method that enables one to conduct comparative or intraindividual analysis for the moderately to severely intellectually impaired. The method essentially requires within-individual "rescaling" or "restandardization" of the test scores. The method can be applied to any test on which age equivalents and age-corrected scaled scores are both provided. This method is only successful with individuals with a mental age of 2½ years or higher; it works best with very low-functioning adolescents. The profile analysis can be conducted by following the steps listed below, as first developed by Reynolds and Clark (1985):

1. Select an appropriate test of intellectual abilities that contains multiple scales or subtests. The test should be normed for the age level that approximates the best estimate of the individual's mental age. Age equivalents and age-corrected scaled scores must be available for each subtest of the intelligence scale.

2. Administer *all* subtests of the intelligence scale to the individual and record the raw scores.

3. Determine the age equivalent that most closely corresponds to the individual's raw score for each subtest. If subtests other than those of the intelligence portion of a scale (e.g., K-ABC Achievement subtests)

were given, they should not be included in this step.

4. Calculate the *median* age equivalent for performance on the intelligence subtests. For most analyses, the mean is a more precise and stable measure of central tendency; however, the mean cannot be used and age equivalents cannot be averaged across subtests, because the standard deviation will vary across subtests. Therefore, the median is the best determination of mental tendency in this instance.

5. The median age equivalent on the intelligence subtests is to be treated as the chronological age for the purpose of calculating scaled scores for each subtest. Eliminate any subtests that would not have been administered, since, on some tests, not all subtests are given at every age. Transform the individual's raw scores into scaled scores by entering the appropriate tables based upon the individual's median age equivalent.

6. Calculate the remaining scores (e.g., Verbal, Performance, and Full Scale IQs on a Wechsler scale). Verify that the overall summary score (Wechsler Full Scale IQ or K-ABC Mental Processing Composite) approximates 100. The summary score will not be exactly 100, because of the rounding and interpolation error inherent to age equivalents. However, if the overall score deviates from the range of 94 to 106, recheck calculations.

7. The interpretation of the profile of scores is conducted in a manner consistent with Kaufman's (1979) model for the WISC-R, the McCarthy Scales, and the K-ABC. The steps just given have essentially renormed the test within the individual and have enhanced ipsative comparisons.

It is important to note that one major assumption underlies the application of this model—namely, that the internal-consistency reliabilities and internal structure of the test are the same for the individual being evaluated as for individuals with the chronological age corresponding to this individual's median age equivalent. If these assumptions do not hold, measurement error will be introduced into the profile analysis to an unknown extent. The following is an illustration, using the WISC-R with a low-functioning adolescent.

Kay, aged 16 years, was enrolled in a self-contained classroom for the severely intellec-

tually handicapped. As part of her 3-year reevaluation, she achieved a WISC-R Verbal IQ of 46, a Performance IQ of 49, and a Full Scale IQ of 43. All of her scaled scores ranged from 1 to 5; detection of any intraindividual weaknesses or strengths was impossible because of the collapse of so many raw-score points into the first scaled-score point.

In accordance with the steps listed above, age equivalent scores were determined for the raw score of each subtest. The median age equivalent on all intelligence subtests was determined to be 6 years, 6 months. Kay's complete performance is described in Table 33.2.

This method of analysis revealed areas of strength for Kay on two subtests, Information and Picture Completion. The Information subtest uniquely assesses general factual knowledge that has been stored in long-term memory. It appears that once Kay was able to transfer learning successfully from her short-term memory system to long-term memory, she could retain that information. Educators

TABLE 33.2. Kay's Scores on the WISC-R

WISC-R subtest	Raw score	Age equivalent	Scaled score
Information	10	8 years, 2 months	14
Similarities	6	6 years, 2 months	9
Arithmetic	6	6 years, 6 months	10
Vocabulary	15	6 years, 6 months	10
Comprehension	10	6 years, 10 months	11
Digit Span	6	6 years, 2 months	9
Picture Completion	17	9 years, 6 months	14
Picture Arrangement	11	6 years, 6 months	10
Block Design	9	6 years, 6 months	10
Object Assembly	14	7 years, 2 months	11
Coding	30	8 years, 2 months	9

Note. Kay's chronological age was 16 years, 0 months. Her WISC-R IQs were as follows: Verbal, 46; Performance, 49; Full Scale, 43.

could facilitate Kay's learning by teaching her specific strategies to organize information for transfer to the long-term memory system. In general, intellectually handicapped seem to lack even the simplest strategies of being able to rehearse material long enough for it to be transferred to long-term memory.

Selected Measures

The number of psychometric measures available is vast. No attempt is made here to provide a comprehensive review of all such instruments; however, this section reviews a sampling of psychometric measures of intellectual functioning and adaptive behavior that are appropriate for different developmental ages. The Wechsler scales, the Stanford–Binet, and the K-ABC are all well established and are specifically described elsewhere in this volume.

Intellectual Functioning

Infancy. The Bayley Scales of Infant Development (Baley, 1969) constitute a measure of infant development for children from 2 months to 2½ years of age. Two standard scores are provided: a Mental Developmental Index, obtained from the Mental Scale, and a Psychomotor Developmental Index, obtained from the Motor Scale. An Infant Behavior Record rating scale is also available. The Mental Scale contains 163 items arranged by tenths of months. The items involve shape discrimination, sustained attention, purposeful manipulation of objects, imitation and comprehension, vocalization, memory, problem solving, and naming objects. The 81 items on the Motor Scale cover gross and fine motor abilities. The Infant Behavior Record allows one to systematically assess and record the observations of the child's behavior during the examination.

The Bayley was standardized on a representative national sample of 1,262 normal infants and children in 14 age groups, from 2 months to 30 months of age. Split-half reliability coefficients for the 14 age groups range from .81 (median $r_{xx} = .88$) on the Mental Scale and from .68 to .92 (median $r_{xx} = .84$) on the Motor Scale (Sattler, 1988). Validity of the Bayley Scale was established by correlating the Mental Scale and the Stanford–Binet: Form L-M for a sample of 120

children aged 24 to 30 months, yielding a correlation of .57.

The Bayley Scales have been used widely with handicapped infants and young children, as well as with older individuals whose severity of handicapped places them in the functional range of the scales. However, it is important to indicate the qualifications that apply to the use of infant scales with older children and adults.

Early Childhood. The Miller Assessment for Preschoolers (MAP; Miller, 1982) is a brief yet comprehensive preschool screening instrument that identifies children who exhibit mild to moderate developmental delays. Developmental domains assessed include neural foundations, coordination, verbal tasks, nonverbal tasks, and complex tasks. The MAP may be used in cases of more severe developmental deviations to provide a developmental overview and to delineate patterns of strengths and needs.

The MAP was designed for children 2 years, 9 months to 5 years , 8 months of age. The test is individually administered in about 20–30 minutes. The standardization was conducted on 1,200 preschoolers in nine U.S. census regions; the sample was stratified by age, race, sex, size of residence community, and socioeconomic factors. Percentiles for six age groups for overall performance and for five performance indices are provided.

Middle Childhood/Adolescence. The Wechsler scales and the Stanford–Binet are the instruments most frequently used with this age group.

Adaptive Behavior

Many definitions of adaptive behavior have been proposed; perhaps the most widely accepted is the definition proffered by the AAMD: "the effectiveness with which the individual meets the standards of personal independence and social responsibility" (Grossman, 1983, p. 1). Witt and Martens (1984), in a review of the various definitions and interpretations of adaptive behavior, noted that most definitions consider adaptive behavior to be age- and culture-specific and include areas such as independent functioning, social responsibility, and cognitive development.

The AAMD provides general categories of adaptive behavior skills for preschoolers, children and early adolescents, and late adolescents and adults (Grossman, 1983). Preschool skills include sensory–motor, communication, and self-help skills. Childhood and adolescent skills are aimed primarily at practical application of academic skills and appropriate interpersonal functioning. Late adolescent and adult skills focus largely on community, vocational, and economic responsibilities.

Adaptive behavior instruments are generally used for two purposes (Cone & Hawkins, 1977; Taylor, 1985). The first purpose is to identify those individuals who vary significantly from "normal" expectations in areas such as independent functioning and socialization. These tests or instruments, sometimes referred to as "descriptive" (Cone & Hawkins, 1977), are used to make classification/placement decisions as well as to identify general strengths and weaknesses. The majority of the descriptive instruments for assessing adaptive behavior are standardized on nonhandicapped individuals.

Another set of instruments yields much more specific information related to the identification of educational/instructional objectives. Cone and Hawkins (1977) refer to these instruments as "prescriptive"; they are often developed for and standardized on more severely handicapped children. In comparison to descriptive tests, prescriptive tests usually include more specific and sequential items related to a smaller number of areas. Instruments do exist that include both descriptive and prescriptive items. For a comprehensive coverage of the issues involved in assessing adaptive behavior, the reader should consult a recent special edition of the *Journal of Special Education* (edited by Kamphaus, 1987).

The AAMD Adaptive Behavior Scale— School Edition (ABS-SE; Lambert, Windmiller, Tharinger, & Cole, 1981) is the most recent in a series of revisions of the original AAMD scale. The ABS-SE consists of two parts. Part One is organized developmentally and designed to evaluate a person's skills and habits in nine behavior domains: Independent Functioning, Physical Development, Economic Activity, Language Development, Numbers and Time, Prevocational Activity, Self-Direction, Responsi-

bility, and Socialization. These domains are important to the understanding of the development of personal independence in daily living. The behaviors are rated within a dependence–independence continuum. Part Two is comprised of 12 domains that provide measures of adaptive behavior related to personality and behavior disorders: Aggressiveness, Antisocial versus Social Behavior, Rebelliousness, Trustworthiness, Withdrawal versus Involvement, Mannerisms, Appropriateness of Interpersonal Manners, Acceptability of Vocal Habits, Acceptability of Habits, Activity Level, Symptomatic Behavior, and Use of Medications. The informant must indicate whether the examiner exhibits each behavior occasionally, frequently, or not at all. The informant is usually someone who is very familiar with the behavioral repertoire of the child (e.g., teacher, parent).

The ABS-SE was standardized on a sample of 6,500 children aged 3 years, 3 months to 17 years, 2 months. Five empirically derived factor scores—Personal Self-Sufficiency, Community Self-Sufficiency, Personal–Social Responsibility, Social Adjustment, and Personal Adjustment—and a comparison score based on a combination of the first three factor scores are provided. Raw scores are converted into scaled scores ($M = 100$, $SD = 3$). Percentile ranks are provided for the 21 domains and the comparison score. Separate tables are provided for regular, educable mentally retarded (EMR), and trainable mentally retarded (TMR) students. Reliability coefficients are variable, depending upon age level, classification group, and factor. Median reliabilities are as follows: Personal Self-Sufficiency, $r_{xx} = .81$; Community Self-Sufficiency, $r_{xx} = .89$; Personal–Social Responsibility, $r_{xx} = .88$; Social Adjustment, $r_{xx} = .94$; and Personal Adjustment, $r_{xx} = .65$. Criterion-related validity was established by correlating factor scores and IQ for a sample of 3,737 regular, EMR, and TMR children between 3 and 12 years of age. Median correlations were reported as follows: Personal Self-Sufficiency, $r_{xy} = .33$; Community Self-Sufficiency, $r_{xy} = .67$; Personal–Social Responsibility, $r_{xy} = .34$;, Social Adjustment, $r_{xy} = .10$; and Personal Adjustment, $r_{xy} = .18$.

The Comprehensive Test of Adaptive Behavior (CTAB; Adams, 1984) evaluates how well students with physical and mental handicaps function independently in their environments. It was designed as both a descriptive and a prescriptive test of adaptive behavior. The CTAB includes 500 empirically sequenced items that measure adaptive behavior across six areas: (1) Self-Help Skills, (2) Home Living Skills, (3) Independent Living Skills, (4) Social Skills, (5) Sensory and Motor Skills, and (6) Language Concepts and Academic Skills. The CTAB uses a combination of an examiner test form and a parent/guardian survey to build a profile of an individual's adaptive behavior across all the settings in which he or she lives, works, and learns. The CTAB is designed to be used with individuals aged 5 to 60. The entire CTAB standardization form was administered to over 6,000 retarded individuals. The standardization sample included children, adolescents, and adults in schools, community-based programs, and institutions. Norms are reported as standard scores, percentile ranks, and age equivalents. The CTAB is inappropriate for normally developing individuals, because skills are not sequenced in normal developmental order.

Validity studies revealed that the CTAB total score correlates .55 and .38 with the WISC-R (Wechsler, 1974) and Form L-M of the Stanford–Binet Intelligence Scale (Terman & Merrill, 1973), respectively, and .68 with the Vineland Social Maturity Scale (Doll, 1965). Interrater reliability coefficients for all CTAB categories, subcategories, and total test range from .89 to .99, with a median value of .98. Test–retest reliability coefficients range from .81 to .99, with a median value of .95. Internal-consistency correlations (coefficient alpha), provided separately for males and females at seven age levels for each CTAB category, are all uniformly high; they range from .78 to .995, with a median correlation of .98. Standard errors of measurement ($SEMs$) for each CTAB category are reported separately for males and females for each of seven different age levels (range 5–6 to 19–22) of retarded individuals enrolled in school, and for each of seven different age levels (range 10–14 years to 60+ years) of nonschool retarded individuals. The $SEMs$ are generally low, ranging from 1.7 to 5.2 for the school sample and 1.9 to 4.8 for the nonschool sample.

The Normative Adaptive Behavior Checklist (NABC; Adams, 1984b) is a brief descriptive test that quickly identifies individuals with adaptive behavior deficits. The NABC contains 120 items that measure adaptive behaviors across the same six skill areas as the CTAB. It was normed on 6,130 individuals from infancy through age 21; all items were also administered to an additional 6,000 individuals with mental and physical handicaps. The norms are reported as standard scores, percentile ranks, and age equivalents. Validity data reported in the test manual are limited to data collected on the CTAB. Interrater reliability estimates for individual domains and the total test score are high, ranging from .96 to .99. Test–retest reliability coefficients range from .79 to .99 (.79 for the Independent Living Skills domain and .99 for Self-Help Skills, Language Concepts and Academic Skills, and the total score). Internal-consistency correlations (coefficient alpha) are uniformly high, with a median correlation of .985. $SEMs$ are generally quite low (2.1 or less for the subcategories, 4.9 or less for the total domain scores).

The Scales of Independent Behavior (SIB; Bruinink, Woodcock, Weatherman, & Hill, 1985) constitute an individually administered measure of skills needed to function independently in home, social, and community settings. The SIB can be used from infant to adult levels (40 years of age and older). The instrument is organized into four adaptive behavior skill clusters (Motor, Social Interaction and Communication, Personal Living, and Community Living) and three maladaptive behavior clusters (Internalized, Asocial, and Externalized). A Broad Independence (Full Scale) cluster score is obtained from the adaptive skill clusters, and a Maladaptive Behavior Index can be derived from the maladaptive behavior clusters. A 32-item short form is available for individuals at any developmental level, and an Early Development scale of adaptive behavior is available for children $2\frac{1}{2}$ years of age and younger or for severely and profoundly handicapped individuals who function developmentally at below the $2\frac{1}{2}$ year level. The norm sample consisted of 1,764 individuals. The norms are given as age equivalents, percentile ranks, standard scores ($M = 100$, $SD = 15$), and stanines.

Split-half, test–retest, and interrater reliabilities are reported in the manual. Split-half reliabilities range from .83 to .96 for the four cluster and Full Scale scores. Test–retest reliabilities over a 4-week interval ranged from .71 to .96 for the adaptive behavior clusters and from .69 to .90 for the maladaptive behavior indices. Interrater reliabilities are reported to be in the .90s. Both construct and criterion-related validity data are reported. Construct validity was established by correlating adaptive behavior scores and chronological age in groups of handicapped and nonhandicapped individuals (r's = .68 to .82). The authors attempted to provide further evidence for construct validity by indicating that adaptive and maladaptive behavior scores of handicapped samples were lower than those of normal samples. Criterion-related validity was established by correlating the SIB and the ABS-SE (r's = .66 to .81). Correlations between the SIB and the Woodcock–Johnson Broad Cognitive Ability Score ranged from .66 to .82. The SIB Maladaptive Behavior Indices and the Quay–Peterson Revised Behavior Problem Checklist Scales showed correlations ranging from −.66 to .12.

The Vineland Adaptive Behavior Scales (VABS; Sparrow, Balla, & Cicchetti, 1984), which constitute a revision of the *Vineland Social Maturity Scale* (Doll, 1935, 1965), assess personal and social sufficiency of individuals from birth to adulthood. There are three versions of the revised VABS: the Interview Edition, Survey Form; the Interview Edition, Expanded Form; and the Classroom Edition. Each version measures adaptive behavior in four domains: Communication, Daily Living Skills, Socialization, and Motor Skills. In addition, the Survey Form and Expanded Form include a Maladaptive Behavior domain. Each Form of the VABS requires a respondent familiar with the behavior of the individual to answer behavior-oriented questions posed by a trained interviewer or to complete a questionnaire. The Survey Form contains 297 items administered over a 20- to 60-minute period. The Expanded Form, which takes approximately 60–90 minutes to administer, contains 577 items, including the 297 items of the Survey Form. The Classroom Edition contains 244 items, designed for children from 3 years, 0 months to 12 years, 11 months of age. It provides an assessment of adaptive behavior in the classroom. The form is to be completed by the classroom teacher in approximately 20 minutes.

The Survey Form and Expanded Form provide norm-referenced information based on the performance of a representative national standardization sample of about 4,800 handicapped and nonhandicapped individuals. Separate norms are provided for mentally retarded, emotionally disturbed, and physically handicapped children and adults. The Classroom Edition was also standardized on a representative sample of about 3,000 students, aged 3 years, 0 months to 12 years, 11 months. The norms are represented as standard scores (M = 100 and SD = 15) for the four domain scores and for the Adaptive Behavior Composite. National percentile ranks, stanines, and age equivalents are also reported.

Split-half, test–retest, and interrater reliabilities are reported in the manual. Median split-half reliabilities for the Survey Form are as follows: Communication domain, r_{xx} = .89; Daily Living Skills domain, r_{xx} = .90; Socialization domain, r_{xx} = .86; Motor Skills domain, r_{xx} = .83; Adaptive Behavior Composite, r_{xx} = .94; and Maladaptive Behavior domain, r_{xx} = .86. Test–retest reliabilities after a 2- to 4-week interval are reported to be in the .80s and .90s for the Survey Form. Interrater reliability coefficients for the Survey Form and Expanded Form range from .62 to .75. *SEM*s range from 3.4 to 8.2 over the four domains on the Survey Form and from 2.2 to 4.9 for the Adaptive Behavior Composite. On the Expanded Form, standard errors of measurement range from 2.4 to 6.2 over the four domains and from 1.5 to 3.6 for the Adaptive Behavior Composite.

Concurrent validity was established by correlating the VABS with a variety of tests. A correlation of .55 was reported with the original Vineland. Correlations between the Vineland Adaptive Behavior Composite and the K-ABC Mental Processing Composite and Achievement scale were .32 and .37, respectively. Correlations with the WISC or WISC-R were .52 for emotionally disturbed children, .70 for visually handicapped children, and .47 for hearing-impaired children.

BEHAVIORAL/ECOLOGICAL ASSESSMENT

Elements of Behavioral Assessment

Behavioral assessment provides valuable assessment methods for evaluating the educational and psychological needs of the moderately and severely mentally impaired. Behavioral assessment is an approach to gathering data about an individual that emphasizes environmental and/or organism control over behavior, a reliance on direct observation of behavior, the use of multiple assessment methods, and consideration of the temporal and contextual basis within which the target behavior is embedded (Mash, 1979). The methods of behavioral assessment include observation in the natural environment (using event recording, interval recording, duration recording, etc.) the use of permanent products (e.g., accident reports, videotapes of client behavior for future behavior analysis), behavioral checklists of client behavioral excesses and deficits, and the use of enactment analogues (e.g., role playing) (Powers, 1985; Powers & Handleman, 1984).

Behavioral assessment is idiographic in application. Controlling variables, response covariations, and treatment strategies are understood to be specific to the individual (Powers, 1985). This is in contrast to the previously discussed nomothetic assessment (psychometric assessment), which leads to generalizations about an individual's performance in comparison to a normative group.

Behavioral assessment has multiple functions, including (1) allowing predictions of future behavior under particular circumstances; (2) facilitating evaluation of specific behavioral excesses, deficits, or skills; (3) transforming vague problems into specific questions; (4) providing information on the individual's resources for change; and (5) serving as a pretreatment measure for the rate of responding (Kanfer & Nay, 1982).

With the use of Kanfer and Saslow's (1969) "stimulus–organism–response–contingencies of reinforcement–consequence" (S-O-R-K-C) analysis, the assessment of the moderately and severely mentally retarded takes on a multidimensional, multisituational focus. Powers (1985) has noted that this model is an improvement over the antecedent–behavior– consequence (A-B-C) paradigm for this population because of the importance of the contingencies and schedules of reinforcement (K) and the organism (O). Attention to organismic variables emphasizes that the individual's physiological conditions and prior learning histories are to be considered in the assessment and treatment planning (Powers & Handleman, 1984).

Behavioral assessment should take on an ecological/systems perspective. First, when assessing the target behavior (the molecular level of assessment), attention should be given to stimulus (S) and consequence (C) variables. Relevant stimulus conditions include time, place, and setting. The next level of analysis is a molar analysis (i.e., an analysis of the molar contexts within which the behavior is embedded is conducted) (Powers, 1985). Within these different environments, there may be resources that facilitate or hinder the production or nonproduction of the behavior.

Moderately and severely mentally retarded children exhibit disturbances in developmental rate or sequence of language, motor, cognitive, perceptual, and adaptive functioning; therefore, when one is conducting a behavioral assessment with such a child, attention to both normal and atypical developmental sequences is critical.

Objectives of Behavioral Assessment

The four objectives of behavioral assessment noted by Nelson and Hayes (1981) can provide a framework for the behavioral assessment of moderately and severely retarded children. The four steps are (1) identification of target behaviors; (2) determination of controlling variables, both environmental and organismic; (3) development of the intervention plan; and (4) evaluation of the effects of intervention. Both molecular and molar levels of behavior analysis are integrated into the assessment.

Identification of the Target Behavior

When one is identifying a target behavior, several criteria should be met in the definition of the behavior. The definition should be objective, clear, and complete (Hawkins & Dores, 1975).

Determination of Controlling Variables

The second step is accomplished by applying the S-O-R-K-C analysis (Kanfer & Saslow, 1969). Three major classes of controlling variables exist: current environmental variables (stimuli and consequences), organismic variables, and contingencies of reinforcement (Nelson & Hayes, 1979). In addition, when one is assessing the moderately and severely mentally retarded, schedules of reinforcement and responses are important.

Stimuli. Stimulus (S) antecedents are those environmental conditions that precede the target behavior and that are presumed to exert some control over emission of the target behavior. These variables can be identified by initially informally recording all events and interactions immediately preceding the target behavior.

Organismic Variables. Organismic (O) variables include biological states, such as hunger, fatigue, health, and sensory acuity (Nelson & Hayes, 1979); genetic, biochemical, or neurological variables (Mash & Terdal, 1981); and prior learning histories (Powers & Handleman, 1984). These variables should be included in the assessment so that the resultant intervention reflects the specific behavioral excesses or deficits under the control of biological or genetic factors (Powers, 1985).

Responses. The assessment of the child's responses (R) to antecedent or consequent stimuli includes specification of at least five dimensions: frequency, duration, topography, pervasiveness, and magnitude (Powers, 1985).

Contingencies of Reinforcement. Schedules of reinforcement (Ferster & Skinner, 1957) and the contingencies of reinforcement (K; Kanfer & Saslow, 1969) influence the rate, correctness, durability, topography, or potency of a child's response. Several contingencies of reinforcement are relevant for this population, including variation of reinforcement (Egel, 1981), stimulus-specific reinforcement (Litt & Schreibman, 1981), variation of intertrial interval (Koegel, Dun-

lap, & Dyer, 1980), and stimulus variation during the task (Dunlap & Koegel, 1980).

Consequences. Consequences (C) are defined functionally: Reinforcing consequences increase the likelihood that behavior will increase or maintain over time; aversive consequences increase the likelihood that behavior will decrease over time.

A variety of methods can be used to collect data for the S-O-R-K-C analysis, including direct observation, behavioral checklists, archival data, and third-party interviews (Kazdin, 1980; Ollendick & Hersen, 1984; Powers & Handleman, 1984).

Development of an Intervention Plan

The purpose of the third step is to collect information on the various situational contexts within which the target behavior occurs. Several objectives have been identified for this ecological analysis (Kanfer & Saslow, 1969; Powers & Handleman, 1984). These include (1) clarifying the problem situation by determining who supports and objects to the behavior; (2) assessing reinforcers and punishers that are salient for the child, and determining which individuals have been effective in reinforcing or punishing behavior in the past; (3) assessing the child's developmental status for biological and physical changes that might limit functioning, and the child's social status for affiliations and community resources that might contribute to the acquisition and maintenance of more adaptive behavior; (4) assessing the extent of self-control, conditions necessary for self-control, and situations (persons, places, events) that cause a breakdown in self-control; (5) assessing social relationships for significant others who elicit appropriate (and inappropriate) behavior, and determining which reinforcers are operative in social situations; and (6) assessing sociocultural and environmental correlates to the target behavior, including prevailing cultural norms and physical environments that elicit appropriate or inappropriate behavior. Failure to account for the ecological resources and constraints may increase the likelihood that interventions will not generalize across persons or settings or maintain over time (Powers, 1985).

Evaluation of the Effects of Intervention

The evaluation occurs both during and after the intervention. The evaluation should include two elements: selection of practical dependent measures, and the choice of an appropriate design (Nelson & Hayes, 1979).

QUALITATIVE–DEVELOPMENTAL ASSESSMENT

Defining Qualitative Assessment

Qualitative assessment differs from psychometric assessment in its non-normative focus; the focus is on analyzing the nature and state of development, not on comparing a child's performance with that of a standardization group. Qualitative and behavioral assessment differ in their focus in that behavioral assessment focuses on functional rather than structural or developmental aspects (Simeonsson, 1986).

Three objectives define those assessment implications unique to the qualitative approach: (1) analysis of cognitive structures, (2) documentation of developmental competence, and (3) identification of stage of functioning.

In qualitative assessment, one analyzes the cognitive structures or processes the child demonstrates to solve problems that are encountered, whether through sensory–motor means or through mental operations. For example, the focus of assessment is not on the child's level of arithmetic achievement, but rather on the operations the child uses to solve problems. In qualitative–developmental assessment, the focus is on the documentation of competence—on describing characteristics demonstrated by a child, regardless of impairment or disability. Designation of the stages of development is another common feature of theories of qualitative development. Identification of children in terms of stages of functioning is useful descriptively in order to plan treatments that are developmentally sequenced (Simeonsson, 1986). The usefulness of this approach may be seen with a group of severely mentally retarded children who have a homogenous label, but may in fact be heterogeneous in regard to level of qualitative function.

Selected Measures and Procedures

The number of measures based on qualitative–developmental theories that have been developed into formal instruments is quite limited; however, a plethora of informal measures and procedures have been described in the literature (Simeonsson, 1986).

Cognition

The goal of qualitative assessment of cognition is to identify the nature and level of the child's learning. The domains assessed differ from stage to stage as they reflect the changing developmental structures of cognition in the child.

The most widely used measure of sensory–motor development is the Infant Psychological Development Scale (Uzgiris & Hunt, 1975). The scale covers development in the areas of Object Permanence, Object Means, Limitation, Causality, Objects in Space, and Schemes. Functional levels are defined for each of the areas in terms of one of the six substages of the sensory–motor period. Another instrument that has been applied with this population is the Albert Einstein Scales of Sensori Motor Intelligence (Corman & Escalona, 1969). These subscales are included: Prehension, Object Permanence, and Spatial Relationships.

Assessment of preoperational development focuses on the emergence of representational competence and its expression, in common as well as unique domains of thought (Simeonsson, 1986). Preoperational reasoning is characterized by intuitive and egocentric thinking, expressed in artificialism, animism, and syncretism. Measures in this area are drawn from the clinical and empirical literature. Piaget's original writings on the child's conception of time (1927/1971), reality (1937/1971), the world (1926/1975), and movement (1946/1971) provide illustrations of clinical interviews and procedures.

Assessment of cognition at the concrete operational level has centered around the conservation task developed by Piaget. The conservation task assesses the child's ability to demonstrate the reversibility of thought, inherent in mental operations. In the basic conservation assessment paradigm, equivalence of mass, number, or length, for example, is established for two sets of objects by a child. A perceptual transformation is then made of the objects. The child's task is to determine whether the essential quality (mass, number, length) is conserved in spite of the perceptual transformation.

Inhelder (1968) addresses the diagnosis of reasoning in mentally retarded children. Persons who only reach the stage of concrete operations are defined as mildly mentally retarded. Those who only reach the preoperational stage at maturity are defined as moderately or severely retarded; those who do not develop beyond the sensory–motor stage at maturity are defined as profoundly retarded. Mentally retarded persons fail to achieve formal operations at maturity; therefore, no description of the assessment of formal operations is provided within this chapter.

Personal–Social Functioning

The assessment of personal and social characteristics from a qualitative–developmental perspective focuses primarily on the way in which the child constructs social reality (Simeonsson, 1986). At the sensory–motor level, emerging self–other differentiation can be assessed through observation of the child's use of toys (Lowe, 1975). Assessment of personal and social skills at the preoperational and later stages has been conducted with perspective-taking tasks—for example, Urberg and Docherty's (1976) five role-taking tasks, or Secord and Peevers's (1973) person perception interview.

Behavior

The Carolina Record of Individual Behavior (CRIB; Simeonsson, Huntington, Short, & Ware, 1982) was designed to encompass the sensory–motor level of functioning and therefore is suitable for young handicapped children or for those functioning at a very low developmental level. It consists of three sections (A, B, and C); A addresses developmental characteristics, and B and C document behavioral characteristics. The CRIB was derived in part from items on the Infant Behavior Record (Bayley, 1969). The CRIB is an observational measure and can be completed either on the basis of observing the administration of a developmental measure such as the Bayley Scales of Infant Development (Bayley, 1969), or on the basis of a period of systematic interaction with the child.

A qualitative measure of behavior that includes the sensory–motor stage as well as the preoperational stage is that of peer play development. The child–peer interaction is scored along physical dimensions such as proximity and use of objects, and along social dimensions such as reciprocity and communication (Parten, 1932).

For those individuals functioning at or above the preoperational stage, problem solving is an applicable assessment domain. Shure and Spivack (1972) have developed a measure of probelm-solving skills that consists of a series of problem situations described or illustrated to a child, who is then asked to list the steps he or she would take to solve the problem.

Measures such as the Imaginary Audience Scale (IAS; Elkind & Bowen, 1979) may be valuable in the assessment of handicapped adolescents and young adults whose impairments and limited social experiences may contribute to unrealistic perceptions of themselves and their peers. The IAS presents common social situations requiring the respondent to indicate a preferred way of resolving a personal dilemma (e.g., unaffected, accepting, self-conscious). A feature of potential significance for the mentally handicapped is that half of the items measure "abiding self" (permanent traits) and half measure "transient self" (situational factors (Simeonsson, 1986). Analyses across these dimensions may be useful in identifying the extent to which self-appraisal of handicapped adolescents is a function of factors seen as permanent and unchangeable (e.g., impairment) and those seen as situational and changeable (e.g., social experiences).

SUMMARY

The present chapter has described psychometric, behavioral/ecological, and qualitative–developmental approaches to the assessment of the moderately and severely mentally retarded. All approaches can be used to assess this population within a variety of domains, including cognition and social–emotional functioning.

The task of assessing the moderately and severely mentally handicapped is a challenging one. The assessment process should be guided by flexibility—that is, matching strategies and domains to achieve specific assessment objectives for a particular child. Flexible methodology is necessary to assess the complex individual differences of this population. The future of assessment with the moderately and severely retarded is likely to be significantly affected by advances in technology (e.g., computers), which offer hope for assessing those previously believed to be "untestable."

REFERENCES

Adams, G. L. (1984a). *Comprehensive Test of Adaptive Behavior*. San Antonio, TX: Psychological Corporation.

Adams, G. L. (1984b). *Normative Adaptive Behavior Checklist*. San Antonio, TX: Psychological Corporation.

Anastasi, A. (1968). *Psychological testing* (3rd ed.). New York: Macmillan.

Bayley, N. (1969). *Bayley Scales of Infant Development*. New York: Psychological Corporation.

Bruinink, R. H., Woodcock, R. W., Weatherman, R. F., & Hill, B. K. (1985). *The Scales of Independent Behavior*. Allen, TX: DLM Teaching Resources.

Cone, J., & Hawkins, R. (1977). *Behavioral assessment: New directions in clinical psychology*. New York: Brunner/Mazel.

Corman, H. H., & Escalona, S. K. (1969). Stages of sensorimotor development: A replication study. *Merrill–Palmer Quarterly, 15*, 351–361.

Doll, E. A. (1935). A genetic scale of social maturity. *American Journal of Orthopsychiatry, 5*, 180–188.

Doll, E. A. (1965). *Vineland Social Maturity Scale*. Circle Pines, MN: American Guidance Service.

Dunlap, G., & Koegel, R. L. (1980). Motivating autistic children through stimulus variation. *Journal of Applied Behavior Analysis, 13*, 619–627

Egel, A. L. (1981). Reinforcer variation: Implications for motivating developmentally disabled children. *Journal of Applied Behavior Analysis, 14*, 345–350.

Elkind, D., & Bowen, R. (1979). Imaginery audience behavior in children and adolescents. *Developmental Psychology, 15*, 36–44.

Ferster, C. B., & Skinner, B. F. (1957). *Schedules of reinforcement*. New York: Appleton-Century-Crofts.

Grossman, H. (Ed.). (1983). *Classification in mental retardation*. Washington, DC: American Association on Mental Deficiency.

Hawkins, R. P., & Dobes, R. W. (1977). Behavioral definitions in applied behavior analysis: Explicit or implicit. In B. C. Etzel, J. M. Le Blanc, & D. M. Baer (Eds.), *New developments in behavioral research: Theory, methods, and applications* (pp. 167–188). New York: Wiley.

Inhelder, B. (1968). *The diagnosis of reasoning in the mentally retarded*. New York: John Day.

Kamphaus, R. W. (1987). Adaptive behavior [Special Issue]. *Journal of Special Education, 21*(1).

Kanfer, F. H., & Nay, W. R. (1982). Behavioral assessment. In G. T. Wilson & C. M. Franks (Eds.), *Contemporary behavior therapy: Conceptual and empirical foundations* (pp. 367–402). New York: Guilford Press.

Kanfer, F. H., & Saslow, G. (1969). Behavioral diagnosis. In C. M. Franks (Ed.), *Behavior therapy: Appraisal and status* (pp. 417–444). New York: McGraw-Hill.

Kaufman, A. S. (1979). *Intelligent Testing with the WISC-R*. New York: Wiley

Kaufman, A. S., & Kaufman, N. L. (1983a). *Kaufman Assessment Battery for Children: Administration and scoring manual*. Circle Pines, MN: American Guidance Service.

Kaufman, A. S., & Kaufman, N. L. (1983b). *Kaufman Assessment Battery for Children: Interpretive manual*. Circle Pines, MN: American Guidance Service.

Kazdin, A. E. (1980). *Behavior modification in applied settings*. Homewood, IL: Dorsey Press.

Koegel, R. L., Dunlap, G., & Dyer, K. (1980). Interatrial interval duration and learning in autistic children. *Journal of Applied Behavior Analysis, 13*, 91–96.

Kravitz, H., & Boehm, J. J. (1971). Rhythmic habit patterns in infancy: Their sequence, age of onset and frequency. *Child Development, 42*, 399–413.

Lambert, N., Windmiller, M., Tharinger, D., & Cole, L. (1981). *AAMD Adaptive Behavior Scale—School Edition*. Washington, DC: American Association on Mental Deficiency.

Litt, M. D., & Schreibman, L. (1981). Stimulus-specific reinforcement in the acquistion of receptive labels by autistic children. *Analysis and Intervention in Developmental Disabilities, 1*, 171–186.

Lowe, M. (1975). Trends in the development of representative play. *Journal of child Psychology and Psychiatry, 16*, 35–47.

Mash, E. J. (1979). What is behavioral assessment? *Behavioral Assessment, 1*, 23–29.

Mash, E. J., & Terdal, L. G. (Eds.). (1981). *Behavioral assessment of childhood disorders*. New York: Guildford Press.

Nelson, R. O., & Hayes, S. C. (1979). Some current dimensions of behavioral assessment. *Behavioral Assessment, 1*, 1–16.

Nelson, R. O., & Hayes, S. C. (1981). Nature of behavioral assessment. In M. Hersen & A. Bellack (Eds.), *Behavioral assessment: A practical handbook* (2nd ed., pp. 3–37). New York: Pergamon Press.

Ollendick, T. H., & Hersen, M. (1984). An overview of child behavioral assessment. In T. H. Ollendick & M. Hersen (Eds.), *Child behavioral assessment: Principles and procedures* (pp. 3–19). New York: Pergamon Press.

Powers, M. D. (1985). Behavioral assessment and the planning and evaluation of intervention for developmentally disabled children. *School Psychology Review, 14*, 155–161.

Powers, M. D., & Handleman, J. S. (1984). *Behavioral assessment of severe developmental disabilities*. Rockville, MD: Aspen.

Parten, M. B. (1932). Social participation among pre-school children. *Journal of Abnormal and Social Psychology, 27,* 243–269.

Piaget, J. (1971). *The child's conception of movement and speed.* New York: Ballantine Books. (Original work published 1946).

Piaget, J. (1971). *The child's conception of time.* New York: Ballantine Books. (Original work published 1927).

Piaget, J. (1971). *The construction of reality in the child.* New York: Ballantine Books. (Original work published 1937).

Piaget, J. (1975). *The child's conception of the world.* Totowa, NJ: Littlefield, Adams. (Original work published 1926).

Reynolds, C. R. (1981). The fallacy of "two years below grade level for age" as a diagnostic criterion for reading disorders. *Journal of School Psychology, 19,* 350–358.

Reynolds, C. R., & Clark, J. (1985). Profile analysis of standardized intelligence test performance of very low functioning individuals. *Journal of School Psychology, 23,* 277–283.

Sattler, J. M. (1988). *Assessment of children* (3rd ed.). San Diego: J. M. Sattler.

Secord, B. H., & Peevers, P. F. (1973). Developmental changes in attributions of descriptive concepts to persons. *Journal of Personality and Social Psychology, 27,* 120–128.

Shure, M., & Spivack, G. (1972). Means–ends thinking, adjustment, and social class among elementary school-aged children. *Journal of Consulting and Clinical Psychology, 38,* 348–353.

Simeonsson, R. J. (1986). *Psychological and de-velopmental assessment of special children.* Boston: Allyn & Bacon.

Simeonsson, R. J., Huntington, G. S., Short, R. J., & Ware, W. (1982). The Carolina Record of Individual Behavior: Characteristics of handicapped infants and children. *Topics in Early Childhood Special Education, 2,* 43–55.

Sparrow, S., Balla, D., & Cicchetti, D. (1984). *Vineland Adaptive Behavior Scales.* Circle Pines, MN: American Guidance Service.

Taylor, R. L. (1985). Measuring adaptive behavior: Issues and instruments. *Focus on Exceptional Children, 18*(2), 1–8.

Terman, L. M., & Merrill, M. A. (1973). *Stanford–Binet Intelligence Scale: 1972 norms edition.* Boston: Houghton Mifflin.

Thorndike, R. L., Hagen, E. P., & Sattler, J. M. (1986). *Stanford–Binet Intelligence Scale: Fourth Edition.* Chicago: Riverside.

Touwen, B. C. L., & Kalverboer, A. F. (1973). Neurological and behavioral assessment of children with minimal brain dysfunction. *Seminars in Psychiatry, 5,* 79–94.

Urberg, K. A., & Docherty, E. M. (1976). Development of role-taking skills in young children. *Developmental Psychology, 12,* 198–204.

Uzgiris, I. C., & Hunt, J. (1975). *Ordinal scales of intellectual development.* Urbana: University of Illinois Press.

Wechsler, D. (1974). *Wechsler Intelligence Scale for Children—Revised.* New York: The Psychological Corporation.

Witt, J., & Martens, B. (1984). Adaptive behavior: Tests and assessment issues. *School Psychology Review, 13,* 478–484.

Index